CW01083391

ANCIENT GREEK GRAMMAR

ANCIENT GREEK GRAMMAR

for the Study of the New Testament

Heinrich von Siebenthal

Peter Lang
Oxford · Bern · Berlin · Bruxelles · New York · Wien

Bibliographic information published by Die Deutsche Nationalbibliothek
Die Deutsche Nationalbibliothek lists this publication in the Deutsche Nationalbibliografie; detailed bibliographic data is available on the Internet at http://dnb.d-nb.de.

A catalogue record for this book is available from the British Library.

A CIP catalog record for this book has been applied for at the Library of Congress.

Cover design by Peter Lang

ISBN 978-1-78997-586-4 (print) • ISBN 978-1-78997-587-1 (ePDF)
ISBN 978-1-78997-588-8 (ePub) • ISBN 978-1-78997-589-5 (mobi)

Published by Peter Lang Ltd, International Academic Publishers,
52 St Giles, Oxford, OX1 3LU, United Kingdom
oxford@peterlang.com, www.peterlang.com

This publication has been peer reviewed.

Printed in Germany

Contents

Preface

The *Ancient Greek Grammar for the Study of the New Testament* ("AGGSNT" or "AGG") is meant to serve as a tool for theologians and others interested in interpreting the Greek New Testament. It is a reference grammar that systematically covers all areas relevant to well-founded text interpretation including textgrammar. Combining accuracy with accessibility was one of the main objectives in producing the AGG. The information it provides is based on the best of traditional and more recent research in the study of Ancient Greek and linguistic communication. The mode of presentation is largely shaped by the needs of prospective users, typically non-specialists: (1) Every Greek, Latin or other non-English expression is translated into English. (2) Knowledge of Classical Greek is not presupposed (as it is in the standard grammar of Blass-Debrunner-Funk); differences between classical and non-classical usage, however, are regularly indicated. (3) While the AGG primarily describes the grammatical phenomena of Ancient Greek, great care has been taken to point out what linguistic phenomena of English correspond to them functionally and what may be considered an adequate translational equivalent. Aiming at both professional quality of content and user-friendly presentation a tool was produced that would hopefully be of service to beginning students and more experienced exegetes alike.

This is a grammar of Ancient Greek; it is not limited to a description of the grammatical phenomena of Koine Greek attested in the Greek New Testament. Since the New Testament is a comparatively small corpus, it cannot be expected to show all the regularities governing its language. And if grammarians had to rely solely on the data provided by the New Testament, they would come up with a rather incomplete picture of what determined the use of this language grammatically. This might be considered sufficient for reading the New Testament itself. It would, however, certainly be insufficient when extra-biblical Koine and non-Koine sources have to be taken into account (as is imperative to well-founded text interpretation). For this reason, the paradigms and principal parts, e.g., were completed on the basis of extra-biblical sources. In particular, forms and uses of Classical Greek are regularly indicated (mostly in a smaller type) whenever these differ from New Testament or Koine usage; an overview of such differences is also given in Appendix 1. Furthermore fairly frequently peculiarities of Septuagint Greek are mentioned as well (though not in any systematic way). So, the AGG is intended as a companion to the interpretation of the Greek New Testament, also offering whatever is essential grammatically for the reading of other Ancient Greek authors including Classical ones such as Plato or Xenophon as well as later ones (many of them striving to meet Atticist standards) like Polybius, Plutarch, and especially Josephus and Philo. Due to its contrastive approach and the overview in Appendix 1 people who, used to the Classical (Attic) idiom, turn to the Greek New Testament may find the AGG a helpful resource informing them about the distinctive features of the New Testament variety, which will inter alia keep them from looking at New Testament texts through purely Classical spectacles and thus lessen the danger of over-interpretation.

Beginning students of New Testament Greek will welcome the AGG as a useful supplement to their textbook. Its systematic presentation helps them gain a better understanding of the elements of Ancient Greek and their use. And a wide range of tables, overviews, translated examples, and indexes such as the one keyed to the principal parts may facilitate the learning process.

More particularly, the AGG is expected to become a valued reference tool of more advanced learners and especially of people serious about interpreting the Greek New Testament along linguistically well-founded lines. It offers them a clear presentation of the essentials of the lower levels of Ancient Greek text structures (the first two parts): the writing system and phonology and, in more detail, inflectional morphology. Its major focus, however, is on the higher levels: the bulk of the AGG (Part 3) is actually devoted to a detailed treatment of syntax (including an overview of "figures of speech"), while Part 4 contains an introduction to some essentials of the highest level of text structures (textgrammar). To help users deal with problems of lexical semantics there is also an outline of the rules of Ancient Greek word-formation that are most relevant when dealing with the Greek New Testament (in Appendix 2). Those who wish to look more carefully into the various topics treated in the AGG or to keep track of relevant scholarly discussions may turn to the systematic bibliographical guide (integrated into the bibliography) and to the bibliographical references appearing beside or beneath most headings. These will point them to the relevant sections of the most important secondary sources, particularly to those of Blass-Debrunner-Funk/Blass-Debrunner-Rehkopf with its unsurpassed abundance of details on problematic passages.

Unless otherwise stated, New Testament quotations are taken from the 28th edition of Nestle-Aland, Septuagint ones mostly from Rahlfs-Hanhart (on the format used for these ↑p.xix[1]) and Hebrew/Aramaic Old Testament quotations from the *Biblica Hebraica Stuttgartensia* (Targum quotations from the Targum Databases of BibleWorks 10, mainly based on the editions of *Mikraot Gedolot HaKeter*, Bar Ilan University Press, 1992–). For the remaining texts various electronic editions have been used, in most cases those of the Thesaurus Linguae Graecae or of the Perseus Project, for Josephus, Philo, and the "Apostolic Fathers" also those of BibleWorks 10. It should also be noted that the translation given for any of these quotations is not meant to suggest that this is the only possible or even the best interpretation or rendering of the text in question; its primary function is to help users understand the grammatical points being made.

The AGG is based on the author's German publication *Griechische Grammatik zum Neuen Testament* (Giessen/Basel: Brunnen/Immanuel, 2011), which is a revised and expanded edition of the *Griechische Grammatik zum Neuen Testament*, originally authored by Ernst G. Hoffmann and Heinrich von Siebenthal (1st ed. in 1985, 2nd ed. in 1990). After the first edition of the grammar appeared it quickly became a standard tool for New Testament studies in German speaking Europe.

Particularly since the publication of the 2011 edition a number of scholars from different parts of the world suggested that the work should be translated into English. It was clear to me from the outset that a straightforward translation would be of limited value only. A fairly thoroughgoing revision was definitely called for. Above all it would have to do justice to the special background from which typical English-speaking users will approach Ancient Greek, a language whose structure is so radically different from Modern English particularly regarding the nominal and the verbal systems. So, although the AGG in its substance is the same as the German original, its explanations are quite different due to the many adjustments to the needs of the prospective users (including bibliographical ones).

The most important secondary sources used in preparing the AGG are as follows: Bornemann-Risch, a standard grammar of Classical Greek, was the organizational starting point and a key source of information. Among the many other scholarly titles consulted are Blass-Debrunner-Funk/Blass-Debrunner-Rehkopf and Zerwick, moreover Meier-Brügger 1992, Duhoux, Adrados 1992, Horrocks, and Reiser 1986/2001, also Kühner-Blass, Kühner-Gerth, Schwyzer, Smyth, Lejeune, as well as Moulton-Howard and Turner, on questions of verbal aspect especially the relevant chapters of Runge-Fresch. The section on the "figures of speech" is largely based on Bühlmann-Scherer. Part 4 dealing with textgrammar draws on findings made accessible through a variety of specialist studies published in German and in English (for details ↑p.569).

In the preparation of the German original of the present grammar a number of scholars have been involved more or less extensively, most of them in the final stages before the actual publication.

Before the first edition was published in 1985 my former professor Ernst Risch (1911–1988) at the university of Zurich, an Indo-European specialist of international renown (one focus being on the Ancient Greek language), carefully read the manuscript. His feedback led to a whole series of improvements, especially with regard to phonology, morphology and core parts of syntax.

In the final stages of the 2011 revision and expansion the whole book or parts of it were critically examined by the following scholars: Walter Burkert, Emeritus Professor of Classical Philology, University of Zurich; Yves Duhoux, Professor of Classical Philology, Catholic University of Leuven; Christina Gansel, Professor of German Linguistics (textlinguistics expert), University of Greifswald; Thomas A. Fritz, Professor of German Linguistics (textlinguistics expert), Catholic University of Eichstätt-Ingolstadt; Armin Baum, Professor of New Testament, Giessen School of Theology; David A. Black, Professor of New Testament and Greek, Southeastern Baptist Theological Seminary, Wake Forest/USA; Friedrich Damrath, Greek and Hebrew Tutor, Laubach-Kolleg; Carsten Ziegert, at the time SIL Linguist in Chad (since 2015 Lecturer in Biblical Languages, Giessen School of Theology).

A few words on the earlier history of this grammar seem to be in order at this point: The Swiss theologian and Classical philologist Ernst G. Hoffmann (1903–1985), a student of A. Schlatter and A. Debrunner, had been planning for quite some time to publish a scholarly based Greek Grammar of the New Testament as a reference tool for theologians. Over many years he collected a wealth of material from relevant primary and secondary sources, until in 1979 a first provisional version was completed. He invited me to critically review the work and to take part in the preparation of the final version. I thoroughly revised Hoffmann's work and expanded it considerably, which he welcomed whole-heartedly. The changes I proposed mainly affected the syntax part, which I eventually rewrote almost completely. In collaboration with assistants and students of the Freie Evangelisch-Theologische Akademie (now Staatsunabhängige Theologische Hochschule) Basel, I finally prepared a camera-ready copy for the publication of the *Griechische Grammatik zum Neuen Testament* Hoffmann-von Siebenthal, a first edition of which appeared in 1985 and a second (bibliographically updated) one in 1990, followed by the revision and expansion of 2011 which the AGG is based on.

As to the AGG itself I am greatly indebted to three scholars: (1) Dr. Eckhard J. Schnabel, Mary French Rockefeller Distinguished Professor of New Testament, Gordon-Conwell Theological Seminary in South Hamilton/Massachusetts (USA), who was the first to suggest that an English version of the *Griechische Grammatik zum Neuen Testament* should be made available and who kept on encouraging me over the years to bring the work to completion; (2) James Clark, MA MSc. MTh. MEd., New Testament Lecturer, FCC Seminary, Inverness (Scotland), who, too, expressed the need for an English version of the grammar to be prepared and kindly agreed to read the manuscript as it was being produced; his comments have proved very valuable indeed; (3) Dr. des. Christoph Heilig, MLitt, presently coordinator of the programme for doctoral studies at the department of theology at the University of Zurich, whose thorough critique of the 2011 German edition has led to a variety of enhancements, mainly affecting Part 4 on textgrammar.

At this point I would also like to express my profound gratitude to the publishers Peter Lang, Oxford, for accepting the work for publication.

Now, may as many people as possible be helped by the *Ancient Greek Grammar for the Study of the New Testament* deal with the text of the Greek New Testament in a well-founded manner, and may they at same time be encouraged to take seriously in an increasing way the Lord it is all about!

Basel, Summer 2019 Heinrich von Siebenthal

Abbreviations

New Testament
Mt, Mk, Lk, Jn, Ac, Ro, 1Cor, 2Cor, Ga, Eph, Php, Col, 1Th, 2Th, 1Tm, 2Tm, Tt, Phm, He, Jas 1Pe, 2Pe, 1Jn, 2Jn, 3Jn, Jd, Re

Old Testament[1]
Gn, Ex, Lv, Nu, Dt, Jos, Jdg, Ru, 1Sm, 2Sm, 1Kgs, 2Kgs, 1Chr, 2Chr, Ezr, Ne, Est, Job, Ps, Pr, Ec, Sol, Is, Jr, Lm, Eze, Dn, Ho, Jl, Am, Ob, Jon, Mic, Na, Hab, Zph, Hg, Zch, Mal

Apocrypha
Bar, EpJer, 1Esd, 2Esd, Jdth, 1Macc, 2Macc, 3Macc, 4Macc, Ps Sol, Sir, Sus, Tob, Wsd

Symbols

*	reconstructed or unattested	//	enclose sound elements
↑	see/cf.	=	largely the same as
¯	macron (indicates long vowel)	≠	unlike
˘	micron (indicates short vowel)	≈	similar to
´	indicates stressed syllable	→	is replaced by
>	leads to	↔	mutually replaceable; contrasts
<	goes back to	°	↑185a and 252a

Hebrew and Aramaic Transliteration

א	בּ	ב	גּ	ג	דּ	ד	ה	ו	ז	ח	ט	י	כּ	כ	ל	מ	נ	ס	ע	פּ	פ	צ	ק	ר	שׂ	שׁ	תּ	ת
ʾ	b	ḇ	g	ḡ	d	ḏ	h	w	z	ḥ	ṭ	y	k	ḵ	l	m	n	s	ʿ	p	p̄	ṣ	q	r	ś	š	t	ṯ

ָ	ַ	ֲ	ֵי	ֶי	ֵ	ֶ	ֱ	ְ	ִי	ִ	וֹ	ֹ	ָ	ֳ	וּ	ֻ
ā	$a/^{a}$ (1)	ă	ê	ệ	ē	e	ĕ	ə (2)	î	ī	ô	ō	o (3)	ŏ	û	u

(1) The raised variety stands for the “furtive pataḥ”.
(2) Unless the silent variety is intended.
(3) In an unstressed closed syllable.

1/2/3 sg./pl.	first/second/third person singular/plural	ACP	accusative with participle
/2nd (degree)	second degree (object)	act.	active
a.	accusative	ad loc.	ad locum (on the passage under consideration)
abs.	absolute	add.	additive
acc.	accusative	adj.	adjective
ACI	accusative with infinitive	AdjP	adjective phrase
ACI-S	subject of ACI	adv.	adverb

1 Note that references to the LXX (for practical reasons) usually have the same format (book, chapter, verse) as do references to the English versions currently in use. Only for references to LXX Psalm (and Jeremiah) passages the numbering of the Rahlfs-Hanhart edition is followed.

advers.	adversative
Advl	adverbial
AdvlA	adverbial adjunct
AdvlC	adverbial complement
AdvP	adverb phrase
AGG(SNT)	referring to the present grammar
alt.	alternative
ant.	anterior
aor.	aorist
App	apposition
Aram.	Aramaic
art.	article
Att.	Attic Greek
Attr	attributive modifier
attr.	attributive
aug.	augment
AV	Authorized Version
BD	Blass-Debrunner
BDAG	Bauer-Danker-Arndt-Gingrich
BDF	Blass-Debrunner-Funk
BDR	Blass-Debrunner-Rehkopf
Bibl.	Biblical
BNP	Brill's New Pauly
BR	Bornemann-Risch
Byz.	Byzantine Majority Text
CAGL	Bakker, Companion
caus.	causal
CausA	causal adjunct
CausC	causal complement
c/conj.	coordinating conjunction
CG	Classical Greek
cl.	clause
COED	Concise Oxford English Dictionary
comp.	comparative
compl.	complement
conc.	concessive
ConcA	concessive adjunct
ConcC	concessive complement
cond.	conditional
CondA	conditional adjunct
CondC	conditional complement
conj.	conjunction
conjug.	conjugation
conseq.	consequential
d.	dative
dat.	dative
DCI	dative with infinitive
DCP	dative with participle
decl.	declension
declar.	declarative
dem.	demonstrative
dep.	dependent
DuG	Duden. Grammatik
dur.	durative
EAGLL	Giannakis, Encyclopedia
ECM	Editio Critica Maior
Engl.	English
ESV	English Standard Version
et pass.	et passim (= and quite often)
EvalA	evaluative adjunct
EVV	English versions/translations
explan.	explanatory
f.	feminine
fem.	feminine
Fr.	French
fut.	future
g.	genitive
GaJü	Gansel/Jürgens
GCI	genitive with infinitive
GCP	genitive with participle
gen.	genitive
gen.abs.	genitive absolute
Givón	Givón 2001, Syntax
GKC	Gesenius-Kautzsch-Cowley
HALOT	Koehler-Baumgartner, Lexicon
Hebr.	Hebrew; Hebraism
HN	head noun/phrase
imp.	imperative
ind.	indicative
indef.	indefinite
inf.	infinitive
InfP	infinitive phrase
imp.	imperative
instr.	instrumental
InstrA	instrumental adjunct
InstrC	instrumental complement
inter.	interrogative (pronoun/adverb)
IntA	adjunct of interest
IntC	complement of interest
interrog.	interrogative
intr.	intransitive
Ion.	Ionic Greek

ipf.	imperfect
iter.	iterative
i.t.s.	in the sense (of/that)
KG	Koine Greek
KJV	King James Version
LAW	Lexikon der Alten Welt
Lat.	Latin
lit.	(more) literally
LN	Louw-Nida, Lexicon
loc.	local
LocA	local adjunct
LocC	local complement
LSJ	Liddell-Scott-Jones
LXX	Septuagint
m.	masculine
ManA	manner/modal adjunct
ManC	manner/modal complement
masc.	masculine
MB	Meier-Brügger 1992
MH	Moulton-Howard
mid.	middle
mod.	modal
MT	Masoretic Text
n.	nominative
NA	Nestle-Aland
neg.	negative particle/pronoun, negation
NETS	New English Translation of the Septuagint
NCI	nominative with infinitive
NCP	nominative with participle
NIV	New International Version
nom.	nominative
NP	noun phrase
NT	New Testament
ntr.	neuter
O	object
OA	object adjunct
OA^{id}	object adjunct with an identifying function
OA^{prop}	object adjunct specifying properties
OC	object complement
OC^{id}	object complement with an identifying function
OC^{prop}	object complement specifying properties
OCD	Hornblower, Oxford Classical Dictionary
Od	direct object
O^{dat}	dative object
Og	genitive object
Oi	indirect object
Op	prepositional object
opt.	optative
o.s.	oneself
OT	Old Testament
P	predicator (predicate verb)
Par.	parallel
parad.	paradigm
pass.	passive; also ↑"et pass."
p.c.	participle conjunct
periphr.	periphrastic
pers.	person, personal
pf.	perfect
pl.	plural
pleon.	pleonastic
plpf.	pluperfect
poss.	possessive
post.	posterior
p.p.	principal parts
Pp.	proposition
PpP	preposition phrase
prep.	preposition
pres.	present
pron.	pronoun
ptc.	participle
PtcP	participle phrase
purp.	purpose-oriented
PurpA	adjunct of purpose
PurpC	complement of purpose
redup.	reduplication
refl.	reflexive
rel.	relative (pronoun/adverb)
ResA	adjunct of result
ResC	complement of result
restr.	restrictive
S	subject; Appendix 1 margin also: Semitism (↑p. 637)
SA	subject adjunct

SA^{id}	subject adjunct with an identifying function
SA^{prop}	subject adjunct specifying properties
sc.	scilicet ("one may understand" → "supply in thought")
SC	subject complement
SC^{id}	subject complement with an identifying function
s/conj.	subordinating conjunction
SC^{prop}	subject complement specifying properties
sg.	singular
simul.	simultaneous
s.o.	someone
st.	stem
sth.	something
sts.	sometimes
subj.	subjunctive
subo.	subordinate
sup.	referring to the superordinate construction
superl.	superlative
s.v.	sub verbo (under the headword)
s.vv.	sub verbis (under the headwords)
temp.	temporal
TempA	temporal adjunct
TempC	temporal complement
TextA	text adjunct
THGNT	Greek New Testament produced at Tyndale House Cambridge
TOB	Traduction Œcuménique de la Bible
trans./tr.	transitive
UBSGNT	Greek New Testament produced by the United Bible Societies
v.	vocative, vowel
V	verb
Var.	textual variant
voc.	vocative
Z	Zerwick

0 Introduction

0.1 The language family of Greek (↑Meier-Brügger 2003 E402ff; CAGL: 171ff)

Greek is a member of the Indo-European language family, which includes the majority of European and several Asian languages. The ancestor of these languages is called "Proto-Indo-European" or "Indo-European" (spoken ca. 4000–3500 B.C.).

The major branches of the Indo-European language family are (in roughly east to west order):

1. Indian subcontinent and Chinese Turkestan:
Indo-Iranian with Indic and Iranian; **Tocharian**.

2. Asia Minor, Greece, and Balkans:
From the 2nd millennium B.C.: **Anatolian** (best known: Hittite) in the east.
Greek in the west.
From the 1st millennium B.C.: **Phrygian** in Asia Minor.
From the early centuries A.D.: **Armenian** in the east and **Albanian** in the Balkans.

3. Italian peninsula: **Italic**, best known (and by far best attested):
Latin, ancestor of modern Romance languages (that developed from varieties spoken in the former Roman provinces): Romanian, Romansh, Sardinian, French, Dalmatian, Italian, Provençal, Spanish, Catalan, and Portuguese.

4. Other parts of Europe (particularly areas north of the Alps):
Celtic: Continental Celtic and Insular Celtic (British Isles and, as a result of migrations from there, Brittany).
Germanic: East Germanic (Gothic, Vandalic, Burgundian), North Germanic (Scandinavian), and Northwest Germanic (ancestor inter alia of German, Dutch, and English).
Balto-Slavic:
Baltic: inter alia Lithuanian, Latvian, Old Prussian;
Slavic: South Slavic (Bulgarian, Macedonian, Serbian, Croatian, Slovene), East Slavic (Russian, Belarusian, Ukrainian; the earliest attested [East] Slavic variety is Old Church Slavonic, used in Bible translations from the 9th century A.D.), West Slavic (inter alia Polish, Sorbian, Czech, and Slovac).

0.2 Overview of the history of Greek

(↑MB: E 304–318; Meier-Brügger 2003 E 417–421; BR: XIV-XV; Nesselrath: 135ff; Adrados 2005; Horrocks [detailed and up-to-date]; CAGL: 169ff, 527ff; BDF §1ff; Debrunner-Scherer; Reiser 2001)

Greek as a distinct language is probably the result of an evolutionary process that began ca. 2000 B.C., when a major wave of immigration set in from the Balkans into the region of modern-day Greece (or Ἑλλάς "Hellas") where the immigrants eventually merged with the local population. The Greeks (or Ἕλληνες "Hellenes", as they called themselves from the 8th century B.C.) spread in stages on the Aegean islands and (before the end of the 2nd millennium B.C.) on the west coast of Asia Minor, also in the east as far as the coast of the Black Sea, and (after 800 B.C.) in the west, especially in Southern Italy and Sicily ("Magna Graecia"). As a result of Alexander's campaigns (334–323 B.C.) they temporarily gained control of most of the Levant and Middle Eastern countries reaching as far as India; so, for centuries the whole of the ancient world was thoroughly Hellenized. Hellenism, alongside Christianity, in fact became the principle driving force of Western civilization.

The spread of Hellenism included the spread of the Greek language, so much so that Greek was prominent at all levels even in Rome as in all the larger cities of the West well into the 3rd century A.D.[1]

After the division of the Roman Empire at the end of the 4th century, in the West Greek was superseded by Latin. In the East it came under increasing pressure as well until the Greek speaking area eventually shrunk to the size of what is modern-day Greece. There, however, the Greek language has held its ground until the present day against every kind of political and cultural threat.

During the Middle Ages the West was largely without the knowledge of Greek. In the 15th/16th century only it was rediscovered and restored to favour with Renaissance humanism calling for a return to the primary sources of Classical Antiquity (↑Latin slogan "ad fontes" *[back] to the sources*).

The earliest Greek texts available come from a period between ca. 1400 and 1200 B.C. They are written in a syllabic script ("Linear-B") on clay tablets that were discovered by archaeologists in palaces excavated on the island of Crete (at Knossos) and on the Greek mainland (especially at Mycenae, Pylos, Tiryns, and Thebes). The language of these texts is called "**Mycenaean Greek**" (or "Mycenaean"). The Mycenaean Greeks had intense trading relations with the Phoenicians (Northwest Semites), which is shown inter alia by the fact that Semitic loanwords are attested already in their variety of Greek, e.g. *ku-ru-so* = *kʰrūsos* χρῡσός *gold*.[2] After the fall of the Cretan-Mycenaean civilization ca. 1200 B.C. the Greeks appear to have lost their knowledge of writing almost completely (only in Cyprus a variety of the ancient syllabic script continued to be used for a time).

Later the contacts with the Phoenicians led to an innovation that turned out to be of revolutionary significance: before the end of the 8th century B.C. the Greeks adopted the Phoenician **alphabet** that had been developed by West Semites in the early 2nd millennium B.C.; it comprised twenty-two letters that primarily represented only consonants (the intended vowels had to be inferred from the context). Since the Greek sound system differs significantly from the West Semitic one, the alphabet needed adjusting. Not only were changes introduced in the way letters represented consonants, letters also began to be used to express vowels, which was a step forward that is not to be underestimated in the history of writing (↑1e,3).[3] Due inter alia to differences between the various Greek dialects the Phoenician alphabet was altered differently in different places, until in the 4th century B.C. the Ionic Alphabet (developed in Miletus) with its twenty-four letters was generally accepted as the standard alphabet for writing Greek (↑1).[4]

Ever since the alphabet was adopted in the 8th century B.C. to this day an ever-increasing number of texts written in Greek have been produced, at first mainly inscriptions, as time went by texts of every type, soon including literary and philosophical-scientific works as well. Many of these texts,

---

1 For details ↑Reiser 2001: 4ff, and especially Horrocks: 124ff.

2 ↑inter alia Ugaritic *ḫrṣ*, Phoenician *ḥrṣ* or Biblical Hebrew חָרוּץ *ḥārûṣ* (↑HALOT s.v.). Also ↑MB: E 201–206; 309f.

3 Most of the alphabetic scripts used in the world today originated here (↑Haarmann chapter 6), hence inter alia the fact that sounds such as /a/, /e/, /i/, /o/, and /u/ are widely expressed by letters that originally stood for West Semitic (including Hebrew) consonants: ʾ (𐤀 ʾā́lep̄) > A, *h* (𐤄 hēʾ) > E, *y* (𐤉 yôḏ) > I, ʿ (𐤏 ʿáyin) > O, and *w* (𐤅 wāw) > U.

4 For details ↑MB: E208 and Horrocks: viii–xx.

a considerable number of them ancient ones, are available to us (either directly or in handed down form). These are the primary sources that are so vital to a solid study of the Greek language. Based on these the following varieties may be distinguished within the history of the Greek language:[5]

1. **Mycenaean Greek**, ca. 1400 to 1200 B.C. (↑above).

2. **Ancient Greek**, ca. 800 B.C. to A.D. 550, which may be subdivided as follows:

a) ***Pre-classical and Classical Greek***, ca. 800 to 300 B.C.
A number of dialects have been identified that are marked by more or less extensive differences of sounds, word-forms, syntax, or vocabulary. One usually distinguishes four major dialects that are peculiar to a specific geographical area (termed "epichoric"):

(1) Ionic-Attic:
Ionic (in the middle part of the west coast of Asia Minor and on most of the Aegean islands as well as in the Greek colonies by the Black Sea and in Southern Italy);
Attic (in the district of Attica with Athens as its capital).

(2) Arcado-Cyprian:
Arcadian (various ancient dialects used in the district of Arcadia);
Cypriot (in Cyprus written in a native syllabic script ["Cypriot syllabary"]).

(3) Aeolic (on Lesbos and its environs as well as in the districts of Thessaly and Boeotia).

(4) West Greek (Doric in the wider sense):
Doric (from the town of Megara and the island of Aegina southwards, in most of the Greek colonies in Southern Italy and Sicily; with many local dialects inter alia in Corinth, Argos, Laconia, and on the islands of Rhodes and Crete);
North-West Greek (inter alia in the districts of Locris, Phocis, and Elis);
Pamphylian (in the Southern part of Asia Minor).

Alongside these epichoric dialects there were also literary dialects (originating in certain epichoric ones). These were used across dialect boundaries for composing works of particular literary genres, thus the Ionic dialect for writing the earliest known scientific prose (from the 6th century B.C. on early historians ["logographers"], in the 5th century Herodotus ["Father of History"], in the 5th/4th century Hippocrates ["Father of Medicine"]). The highest rank among the literary dialects, however, was held by the language of the "Homeric" epic poems, the Iliad and the Odyssey, (put to writing from the 8th century B.C. on). This language appears to be an artificial variety developed by ancient Ionians on the basis of Aeolic; it had a sustained impact on the language of poetry (e.g. on Hesiod ca. 700 B.C.) as on Greek literary style in general.

In the second half of the 5th century B.C. Athens enjoyed a period of political and cultural prosperity ("Classical" period). **Attic** increased in importance among the Ancient Greek dialects, so much so that it rose to the rank of a standard language in which most of the literary works were written: the tragedies of Aeschylus, Sophocles, and Euripides (6th/5th century), as well as the writings of the philosophers Plato (5th/4th century) and Aristotle (4th century), of the historians Thucydides (5th century), and Xenophon (5th/4th century), also of the orators Lysias (5th/4th century), Isocrates (5th/4th century), and Demosthenes (4th century). In view of the quality of these and other works, deemed classical, Attic is also called "**Classical Greek**". And it is this variety that Greek courses at schools and universities are usually centred on.[6]

5 For details on the dialects ↑MB: E314–316, Nesselrath: 142–155, and Horrocks: 9–66 (with helpful examples). For a brief grammar of the Homeric language ↑BR §309–315.

6 Often works in other dialects supplementing it: Homer (archaic Ionic), Herodotus (Ionic), the lyric works of Sappho and Alcaeus (both ca. 600 B.C.; Aeolic), choral lyric (e.g. Pindar [6th/5th century], also remainders in the choral parts of Attic tragedies; Doric), the biographies of Plutarch (1st/2nd century A.D.; Koine replete with Atticisms), the NT (Koine). – More on Attic ↑Horrocks: 67–78.

In later times Attic continued to play an outstanding role: in the movement known as Atticism emerging in the 2nd century B.C., becoming particularly influential in the time of Augustus (1st century B.C./A.D.), and culminating in the 2nd century A.D. This movement declared Attic Greek to be the standard of correct language use; changes of sounds, vocabulary or grammar caused by a natural development of the language were branded as something to avoid. As a result the language split up into two main varieties: a) scholarly Greek, based on ancient usage, and b) popular Greek, subject to a continual natural development, spoken by the general public. This, essentially, is the origin of the rivalry that existed until recently between Katharévusa (Καθαρεύουσα "pure [language]") and Dhimotikí (Δημοτική "[language] of the people").[7]

b) ***Koine*** (also "Hellenistic Greek"), ca. 300 B.C. to A.D. 550

Attic was the official language of Alexander's empire and of those of his successors (the "Diadochi"). During this period (336–30 B.C.), the so-called "Hellenistic" period, on the basis of Attic a supra-regional vernacular evolved as the lingua franca of the entire Hellenistic world, usually called "**Koine**" (ἡ κοινὴ διάλεκτος "the common language"). It gradually became the unrivalled standard with the ancient Greek dialects almost completely disappearing. Various sounds and forms characteristic of Attic Greek were replaced by ones more generally used (e.g. -ττ- by -σσ- [↑355a] or ξύν by σύν *with* [↑184q]); moreover there was an overall tendency towards greater clarity as well as simplicity of expression (something typical of any standard language; ↑p. 637).

Apart from this vernacular there was a **literary Koine**. It was not used for poetry and literature in the narrow sense; for these, authors kept striving after an elevated style of Greek (based on Attic norms). It was, however, the medium on the one hand of technical prose as it is found e.g. in the works of the historian Polybius (2nd century B.C.), of medical writers such as Dioscorides (1st century A.D.), or of astrologers such as Vettius Valens (2nd/3rd century A.D.), on the other hand attested in romance novels such as those of Chariton and Xenophon Ephesius (1st/2nd century A.D.). Other works written in literary Koine are e.g. the "Letter of Aristeas" ("LXX" legend; 2nd century B.C.), the "Tablet of Cebes" (a popularizing philosophical dialogue; 1st century A.D.), and the writings of the Corpus Hermeticum (2nd/3rd century A.D.). A work to be placed at a lower level of style is the "Romance of Alexander" of Pseudo-Callisthenes (available form ca. A.D. 300); it is, however, of considerable interest to New Testament scholars involved in comparative studies, since its narrative style is particularly close to that of many parts of the New Testament. The most important testimony of a more elevated style of the Hellenistic vernacular is found in the philosophical "sermons" (διατριβαί) of Epictetus (1st century A.D.).[8]

Koine Greek is also the language of the Septuagint ("LXX"; translation of the Old Testament into Ancient Greek, with a variety of linguistic styles; most of it originating in the 3rd/2nd century B.C.),[9] of the New Testament and of the "Apostolic Fathers".[10]

3. **Byzantine Greek** (also "Medieval Greek") is the language of the Byzantine (Eastern Roman) Empire, in use from the reign of Emperor Justinian (527–565) till the Fall of Constantinople to Ottoman Turks (1453), divided into the two inherited varieties, the Atticizing Greek of the Church and the scholars on the one hand, and popular Koine Greek on the other.[11]

4. **Modern Greek** is the language used by the Greeks under Ottoman (Turkish) rule (1453–1830), above all, however, since the founding of the modern Greek state (1830). The rivalry already men-

7 Also ↑Debrunner-Scherer §154–159, Adrados: 198ff, and Horrocks: 133–141.

8 ↑Reiser 2001: 21–24, in more detail also Horrocks: 78–123 and 141ff.

9 For details on the language of the LXX ↑Reiser 2001: 23f, and Horrocks: 106–108.

10 For details ↑Reiser 2001: 6–28, Debrunner-Scherer §5f/114ff, and Horrocks: 147ff.

11 For details ↑Nesselrath: 162–167, especially Adrados: 226ff, and Horrocks: 189–369.

tioned between the traditionalist "pure language" (Katharévusa) and the "language of the people" (Dhimotikí) was officially ended in the nineteen seventies in favour of the "language of the people".[12]

Examples illustrating differences between historically distinguishable varieties of Greek:[13]

	"they carry into the house":	"four":	"when":
Mycenaean Greek:	woikonde pheronsi	(qetro-)	hote
Ancient Greek:			
a) Pre-classical and Classical Greek:			
• East-Ionic:	ἐς τὴν οἰκίην φέρουσι(ν)	τέσσερες	ὅτε
• **Attic** (Classical Greek):	εἰς τὴν οἰκίαν φέρουσι(ν)	τέτταρες	ὅτε
• Arcadian:	ἰν ταν ϝοικιαν φερονσι	(τζετρα-)	ὅτε
• Aeolic (Boeotian):	ἐν τᾶν ϝυκιᾶν φερονθι	πετταρες	ὅκα
• Doric (dialect of Argos):	ἐνς τὰν ϝοικίᾱν φέροντι	τέτορες	ὅκα
b) **Koine** (inter alia NT Greek):	εἰς τὴν οἰκίαν φέρουσι(ν)	τέσσαρες	ὅτε
Modern Greek:			
• *Katharévusa*:	στὴν οἰκίαν φέρουσι (*stin ikían férussi*)	τέσσαρες	ὅτε
• *Dhimotikí*:	στό σπίτι φέρνουν	τέσσερις	σάν

0.3 New Testament Greek (↑Reiser 2001:29–90; BDF §1–7; Horrocks: 147–152)

The variety of Ancient Greek used in the New Testament is basically the vernacular of the Hellenistic period, Koine Greek. Philologically or linguistically, it is a variety that in most respects may be regarded as literary Koine. The **style of language** (i.e. the characteristic use of the language) encountered in the New Testament writings is to a large extent comparable to that of technical (particularly including romance) prose (↑p.4).[14] Apart from Hebrews[15] and parts of Luke and Acts it is, however, at a lower literary level; in some places it clearly approaches the style of the contemporary spoken language (as we know it from literary sources, most particularly from non-literary papyri of the Hellenistic period). In any case, no attempts to meet classical (Atticist) stylistic standards are in evidence within the New Testament.[16]

12 For details ↑Nesselrath: 167f, especially Adrados: 291–311, and Horrocks: 371–470.

13 Based on Risch: 2.

14 According to Horrocks: 147, it is "a reasonably close reflection of the everyday Greek of the majority of the literate population in the early centuries AD, subject, as always, to the influence of the ordinary written language of business and administration learned in school."

15 Schwyzer I: 126, calls it "the first monument of Christian artistic prose" (original: "das erste Denkmal christlicher Kunstprosa").

16 In contrast to what we find in several works of the higher type of literary Koine, including those of the Jewish authors Philo (philosopher, active in Alexandria; 1st century B.C./1st century A.D.) and Josephus (historian, active in Palestine and Rome; 1st century A.D.).

Because of this disregard of classical standards, the authors of the New Testament have been the object of ridicule to educated people ever since their time, which was dominated by Atticism (↑p.4). The New Testament style of language has often been classified as "vulgar" or as "ordinary street language". According to Reiser such judgments are unjustified even with regard to the Gospel of Mark and the Book of Revelation. He adds: "The authors of the New Testament consistently demonstrate considerable literary skills and use their Greek with absolute confidence, even though that Greek did not meet the requirements of the educated upper class. [...] The Church Fathers, therefore, spoke of the sermo humilis, of the 'simple', 'lowly' style of the New Testament, at the same time understanding humilis in the sense of 'humble'."[17]

One striking feature characterizing the New Testament variety of Koine Greek are the so-called **Semitisms**. This term refers to linguistic phenomena that cannot be explained in terms of normal Greek usage, but are thought to go back to Hebrew or Aramaic uses.[18] Which of such unconventional phenomena exactly are to be regarded as Semitisms and what factors may have caused their appearance in New Testament Greek, is an issue that has been the subject of scholarly debate for centuries; none of the solutions proposed so far seems to stand up to rigorous philological scrutiny.

In the 17th and 18th centuries the deviations from the Classical Greek within the New Testament idiom were interpreted in different ways. The "Hebraists" explained them as being influenced by Hebrew usage, the "Purists", apologetically motivated, regarded them as particularly "pure" Greek. Eventually the Hebraist view prevailed in that period.

Towards the end of the 19th century/the beginning of the 20th century there was a "paradigm shift": A. Deissmann, J. H. Moulton, A. Thumb and others demonstrated by means of non-literary papyri discovered in Egypt and freshly studied Hellenistic inscriptions that most of the peculiarities of New Testament Greek are to be classified as Koine phenomena. In the light of subsequent philological studies the list of "Semitisms" has kept getting shorter and shorter.

There was, however, a counterreaction in the second half of the 20th century, which culminated in a second flowering of a rather extreme version of the "Hebraist" view, defended by several specialists.[19] These (as many in the 19th century) thought that the peculiarities of New Testament Greek are best explained by positing the existence of a special "Jewish Greek", a variety clearly distinguishable from the remainder of Koine Greek. The existence of such a distinct Koine dialect, however, was neither proven nor is it probable.[20] The parts of the New Testament with a "Jewish" touch are on the whole, as Reiser convincingly shows, rather influenced by the language of the Septuagint, not unlike many protestant sermons of our time are by the language of the Authorized/King James Version or some other leading Bible translation (Reiser, of course, referring to Luther's German translation).

---

17 Original (Reiser 2001: 29f): "Die Autoren des Neuen Testaments zeigen durchweg beachtliche literarische Fähigkeiten und sind sich ihres Griechisch vollkommen sicher, auch wenn dieses Griechisch den Ansprüchen eines Gebildeten der Oberschicht nicht genügte. [...] Die Kirchenväter sprachen deshalb vom sermo humilis, dem 'schlichten', 'niedrigen' Stil des Neuen Testaments; dabei verstanden sie humilis zugleich im Sinn von 'demütig'." For more on this topic also ↑Reiser 2001: 31–33, as well as Horrocks: 147–152.

18 One speaks of "Hebraism" or "Aramaism" depending on what specific language the phenomenon in question is thought to go back to, "Semitism" being used as a generic term.

19 Reiser 2001: 35, on details of the Semitism topic 33–49; ↑also Horrocks: 148– 152.

20 ↑Reiser 2001: 35.

The linguistic phenomena that are usually classified as "Semitisms" are probably to be connected above all with the special content communicated by the New Testament; and this naturally impacted the utilized linguistic form in various ways. A major influence was no doubt exerted by the texts that had a foundational significance, especially by the **Septuagint**, the standard translation of the Old Testament into Greek (for their many Old Testament quotations the authors of the New Testament usually make use of this version).[21] It is particularly the **vocabulary** that was affected[22] by this (though less extensively than is sometimes assumed), almost exclusively a number of religious and theological expressions whose specific meanings arose through semantic borrowing, e.g.:[23]

δόξα	profane:	*opinion*;	*honour, glory*;	–
	LXX/NT:	–;	*honour, glory*;	concrete *glory/splendour* (≈ Hebrew כָּבוֹד *kāḇôḏ*)
διαθήκη	profane:	*last will/testament*;		–
	LXX/NT:	*last will/testament*;		mostly *agreement/covenant* (≈ Hebrew בְּרִית *bərîṯ*)
ῥῆμα	profane:	*word, saying*;		–
	LXX/NT:	*word, saying*;		also *matter, thing* (≈ Hebrew דָּבָר *dāḇār*)

Certain Septuagint **idioms**, however, are well-attested (e.g. in the language of Luke, inter alia in Lk 1 and 2) being regarded as especially solemn and dignified, e.g.:[24]

καὶ ἐγένετο …(↑217e)	*And it came about …*
ἀποκριθεὶς εἶπεν … or the like (↑239)	*he answered (and said) …*
πᾶσα σάρξ	*all flesh* (= every living/human being)
τὰ πετεινὰ τοῦ οὐρανοῦ	*the birds of the sky* (= the birds)

Latinisms occur in the New Testament as well, but these are less significant than the Semitisms. A number of direct Latinisms are found inter alia in the following semantic domains: military (e.g. κεντυρίων centurio *centurion/captain*; outside the Gospel of Mark: ἑκατόνταρχος/ἑκατοντάρχης),

21 Uses that directly go back to the Septuagint, a version mostly translating "literally", and uses that imitate its style of language, are termed **Septuagintisms**. These should not be confused with the (few genuine) **Hebraisms** in a narrow sense ("Hebraizing" uses that are not attested in the Septuagint) or with the (comparatively rare) **Aramaisms** ("Semitisms" that cannot be explained as Hebraisms). ↑Reiser 2001: 35.
Thus the transliterated foreign word κορβᾶν (Hebrew קָרְבָּן *qorbān*; a cultic expression) in Mk 7:11 is a Hebraism in a narrow sense (interestingly, it is immediately followed by a translation into Greek: ὅ ἐστι δῶρον *that is a gift [for God]*). πάσχα *passover* (Aramaic פַּסְחָא *pasḥā'* / פִּסְחָא *pisḥā'*; Hebrew פֶּסַח *pésaḥ*) e.g. may be classified as an Aramaism (used also in the Septuagint).

22 Textgrammatical or textpragmatic regularities (↑297ff) no doubt were extensively affected, too (research into to these, however, is not sufficiently advanced to permit solid comparative studies). Also ↑Reiser 2001: 38.

23 ↑Reiser 2001: 38ff, where further examples are listed.

24 ↑Reiser 2001: 44ff, where further examples are listed.

administration (e.g. κῆνσος census *capitation/poll tax*), and commerce (e.g. δηνάριον denarius *denarius*). Furthermore several Latin suffixes are used as well, in the New Testament, however, only in names and comparable words (e.g. πρὸς Φιλιππησίους [< *-enses*] instead of Φιλιππεῖς or -έας *to the Philippians*; also ↑358h). There are also various expressions translated from Latin, e.g. terms designating certain offices such as ἀνθύπατος *proconsul*. Finally, we also find a handful of Latinizing idioms such as συμβούλιον λαμβάνειν consilium capere *to come to a decision*.[25]

For a summary of major differences between the Classical and the Koine/New Testament varieties of Ancient Greek ↑355–356.

0.4 On the history of Ancient Greek grammar

↑Schwyzer I: 4–11; LAW: 1129–1133; MB: E101; Nesselrath: 87–132; CAGL: 483ff; Pfeiffer: 1ff.

The earliest grammatical observations known to us were made in the **pre-classical** period (↑p.3) by people involved in reciting and handing down cultic hymns and the “Homeric” epic poems: they took note of strange looking letters, sounds, forms, words and phrases and tried to explain them.[26] As early as the 6th century B.C. one was acquainted with the series of grammatical cases. Towards the end of the 5th century the Sophists (educational elite of the 5th/4th century) came to observe ways in which letters, syllables, rhythms, word-forms, word meanings, and style operate.

Such topics were explored also by **Aristotle** (384–322) and by **Stoic philosophers** (from ca. 300 B.C.). And it is these philosophers, essentially, that the grammatical terminology in use today goes back to (it has reached us by way of the Latin tradition). Stoic philosophers also developed sophisticated accounts of inflection and tense.

Scholars at **Alexandria**, the leading centre of learning of the Hellenistic period (↑p.4), started from these findings further refining them (here was the cradle of the combined study of the classical literature and language, classical scholarship).

Among the Alexandrian grammarians of the Hellenistic period the following are particularly significant: **Zenodotus of Ephesus** (born ca. 325 B.C.), **Aristophanes of Byzantium** (ca. 257–180) and, probably the most influential of the three, **Aristarchus of Samothrace** (ca. 216–144). They described inflection (declension and conjugation including irregularities; ↑23ff and 64ff) in its definitive form regarded as authoritative to this day. A pupil of Aristarchus, **Dionysius Thrax** (second part of the 2nd century B.C.) wrote down the new findings in a systematic manner in his Τέχνη γραμματική “Grammar”; this work served as a basis for teaching Greek until the 13th century A.D.

---

25 Also ↑BDF §5, on occasional Coptic and Persian expressions also §6.

26 In the Classical period to such endeavours were joined in by discussions about issues regarding the philosophy of language, e.g. regarding the relationship between a word and the reality it refers to (↑Plato “Cratylus”): is it intrinsic (determined *by nature* φύσει) or arbitrary (*by convention/institution* νόμῳ/θέσει)? – To modern linguistics “arbitrariness” is axiomatic (↑e.g. Bussmann: 32).

In the period of the **Roman Empire** (from 27 B.C.) the two most significant ancient grammarians were active: a) **Apollonius Dyscolus** (first part of the 2nd century A.D.), who wrote numerous, mostly lost, works on the accents, prosody (measuring syllables based on length and pitch), morphology, and (extant in its entirety) syntax; b) his son **Herodian** (Aelius Herodianus; active in Rome; 2nd century A.D.), who wrote primarily about the accents and morphology; his studies are very accessible and mostly comprehensive and count as the principle source of grammarians' writings from Late Antiquity.

The main emphasis of grammarians of the **Byzantine** (Medieval) **period** (↑p. 4), the "National Grammar", was on preserving and passing on examples of classical usage they considered normative, especially regarding vocabulary and word-forms (↑p. 4). The writings that survive from that period do not provide us with additional insights into the grammar of Ancient Greek; still, they enable us to reconstruct a great deal from antiquity that we no longer have any direct access to.[27]

In the West, where Latin was predominant from the 4th century A.D., knowledge of Greek was lost almost completely (↑p. 2). In the age of **Renaissance humanism** (15th/16th century) with its rediscovery of Classical Antiquity and its interest in studying the sources, a turnaround occurred.[28] Guided by scholarly Greeks (many of them had fled their homeland at the fall of the Byzantine empire), a growing number of people learned Ancient Greek, at first in Italy, later, starting from there, north of the Alps as well. In fact, everywhere in the Christian West people began to study the Ancient Greek language and Ancient Greek literature again, and new text editions of ancient authors were produced. This movement was spurred on especially by the advent of movable type printing towards the end of the 15th century. Thus, as early as 1471 the first printed Greek grammar appeared in Venice, the so-called Ἐρωτήματα ("questions") of Manuel Chrysoloras, which was soon followed by a large number of printed editions of writings in Ancient Greek.

Of the numerous humanists active in that age the following two must not be left unmentioned:

a) Desiderius **Erasmus** of Rotterdam (1469?–1536), a leading European authority on Latin and Greek, who was active mainly in England, Germany, and Switzerland. With great intensity and exemplary methodology, he devoted himself to studying Ancient Greek writings, inter alia the classical authors, the New Testament, and the "Apostolic Fathers", which led to a steady flow of publications. His most significant publication was, no doubt, the first printed Greek New Testament to be published (1516 by Froben in Basel); this edition (in a later, slightly revised form) became the authoritative basic text used by theologians and Bible translators for their work on the Greek New Testament until the end of the 19th century. Of special interest to grammarians is Erasmus' rejection[29] of the itacistic (Modern Greek)

27 ↑Nesselrath: 104–116, for more details on this period including bibliography.

28 ↑Nesselrath: 118–121, for more details on this period.

29 In: De recta Latini Graecique sermonis pronuntiatione (1528). ↑Nesselrath: 120.

pronunciation of Ancient Greek, as it was taught by Reuchlin and Melanchthon, and his preference for the etacistic one, hence often called "Erasmian" pronunciation (though it was favoured by others before him; ↑1a).

b) Martin Luther's friend Philipp **Melanchthon** (1497–1560), who along with others (including his great-uncle Johannes Reuchlin [1455–1522]) contributed substantially to the spread of Greek in German-speaking Europe during that period. Inter alia he published a Greek grammar,[30] which was the standard Greek grammar of German-speaking people till the first half of the 19th century.

Well into the 19th century Greek grammars served mainly as tools for language teaching, textual criticism, and text interpretation. Meanwhile scholars had also begun to explore Greek as well as other languages regarding their family relationships and historical development (↑p. 1ff). So, until the beginning of the 20th century there were two rival approaches to the study of Greek: a) the historical-comparative (clearly diachronic) approach, and b) the descriptive (more clearly synchronic) approach, specifically geared to the needs of the study of classical authors (classical philology). Already in the 19th century leading specialists such as G. Curtius (1820–1885) and K. Brugmann (1849–1919) realized the two approaches had a complementary role, a view that is regarded as axiomatic by **modern** representatives of **Greek linguistics**.[31]

The four-volume descriptive grammar Kühner-Blass (1890/92) and Kühner-Gerth (1898/1904) with its unsurpassed abundance of examples was produced in that era, likewise the first edition of the comprehensive school grammar of Smyth (1920), where the descriptive approach is predominant.

The historical-comparative approach, on the other hand, determines the large grammar of Brugmann-Thumb[31] and its successor Schwyzer (1939/1950; with A. Debrunner as its final editor), which is still the standard historical grammar of Greek (though in the meantime parts of it are in need of revision), as well as the overviews of Greek linguistics of Hoffmann-Scherer (1969) and Debrunner-Scherer (1969) respectively, as well as (the most recent one) of Meier-Brügger (1992).

During the past one and a half centuries there have been a sizable number of further scholars contributing significantly at least to certain domains of Ancient Greek grammar, such as[32] J. Wackernagel (1853–1938),[33] F. Sommer (1874–1962), P. Chantraine (1899–1974), J. Humbert (1901–1980), E. Risch (1911–1988),[34] M. Lejeune (1907–2000), more recently also Y. Duhoux. The following specialists inter alia have contributed towards fruitfully combining previous findings with insights of modern linguistics: F. R. Adrados (*Sintaxis*, 1992), R. M. Vázquez et al.

30 *Institutiones Linguae Graecae* (1st ed. 1518), later also *Grammatica Graeca* (↑Hummel: 746).

31 Brugmann-Thumb: VI and 2f; MB: E101.

32 For particularly important titles ↑bibliography of the present grammar.

33 Wackernagel's classic on syntax has recently been made available in English by David Langslow who updated the work by adding notes and bibliography.

34 Inter alia the co-author (responsible for the linguistic approach) of the grammar Bornemann-Risch ("BR"), which in many respects served as the basis of the present grammar (↑preface).

(*Gramática* I, 1999), G. Horrocks (*Greek*, 1997/2010), A. Rijksbaron (inter al. in Boas-Rijksbaron, *Grammar*, 2019).

In most of the works mentioned so far, the primary focus was on Classical (Attic) Greek (↑p. 3f). Since the first half of the 19th century Greek scholarship turned its attention specifically to the grammar of **New Testament Greek** as well. A variety of comprehensive treatments and studies on specific subjects began to appear.[35]

The most important comprehensive grammars of New Testament Greek[36] include those of Winer,[37] Buttmann,[38] Blass,[39] Robertson,[40] Moulton-Howard, Radermacher,[41] Springhetti[42] as well as Blass-Debrunner ("BD"; English version of the 1959 edition: "BDF" [Blass-Debrunner-Funk]) and (its most recent revision) Blass-Debrunner-Rehkopf ("BDR"), today's standard grammar for detailed exegesis (though parts of it are in need of revision, especially the syntax of the verb).[43]

Further important titles are referred to throughout the present grammar. Among the most relevant ones are those on syntax (as a whole or on certain parts considered particularly relevant):[44] Zerwick (1963), Brooks/Winbery (1979), and Wallace (1995; comprehensive syntax); on discourse grammar: Levinsohn (1992/2000), and Runge (2010); on subjects going beyond these: Porter (1992: mainly on important areas of syntax; e.g. 2015: includes a wide range of subjects relevant to exegesis drawing on recent findings of a variety of linguistic and non-linguistic fields).

---

35 Note that the first grammar of New Testament Greek appeared much earlier (↑Lee: 62); it is the (785 page) volume of Georg Pasor (1655) *Grammatica graeca sacra Novi Testamenti Dom. Nostri Jesu Christi in tres Libros tributa* (Groningen: Coellen).

36 Many of these assume that users are familiar with Classical Greek (↑preface).

37 Georg B. Winer (1822) *Grammatik des neutestamentlichen Sprachidioms* (8th ed., revised by Paul W. Schmiedel; Göttingen: Vandenhoeck & Ruprecht: 1897–1898); variously translated into English, e.g.: W. F. Moulton (1882) *A Treatise on the Grammar of the New Testament Greek.* (3rd ed. revised; Edinburgh: T. & T. Clark).

38 Alexander Buttmann (1859) *Grammatik des neutestamentlichen Sprachgebrauchs.* Berlin; translated into English by J. H. Thayer (1873) *A grammar of the New Testament Greek.* Andover: Draper.

39 Friedrich Blass (1896) *Grammatik des neutestamentlichen Griechisch* (Göttingen: Vandenhoeck & Ruprecht).

40 ↑Bibliography of the present grammar (1st ed. 1914); Robertson's grammar on pages 3ff contains a well-documented overview of the history of Ancient Greek grammar, with a special focus on the history of New Testament Greek grammar.

41 Ludwig Radermacher (1925) *Neutestamentliche Grammatik: Das Griechisch des Neuen Testaments im Zusammenhang mit der Volkssprache* (2nd ed. Tübingen: Mohr).

42 Aemilius Springhetti (1966) *Introductio historica-grammatica in Graecitatem Novi Testamenti* (Rome: Pontificia Universitas Gregoriana).

43 From the 4th edition (1913) Albert Debrunner (1884–1958) was responsible for this work, from the 14th to the 18th edition (1975–2001) Friedrich Rehkopf.

44 For the most important works on verbal aspect ↑192; especially noteworthy (in each case with comprehensive bibliographies) are the ones of Campbell (2007/2008a/b) and most particularly the volume of Runge/Fresch (2016) with its ground-breaking contributions.

0.5 Levels of text structures and the present grammar (↑inter alia Givón I: 7ff)

The present grammar, as already indicated in the preface, is meant to serve as a tool for theologians and others interested in interpreting the Greek New Testament. It is to help them explain in a reasoned way what the texts or parts of texts of the Greek New Testament (to some extent also of other relevant Ancient Greek writings) communicate linguistically.

Linguistic **communication**, i.e. the conveying or exchanging of informational content (by persons) for a particular purpose, is the main function of language. This applies to every (natural) language including Ancient Greek. Linguistic communication operates by means of texts[45] of diverse types (invitations, requests, inquiries, offers, complaints, protests, appeals, birth and marriage announcements, death notices, anecdotes etc.).[46] For a linguistic utterance to count as text (as defined by modern linguists) it needs not only to convey a certain content, it must also have a recognizable (communicative) function. This only makes it a (meaningfully) coherent text.[47]

The coherence of a text is closely connected with its linguistic structure. Text interpretation is about studying such structures and the elements they are made up of in order to understand as accurately as possible the intended content and objectives.[48] And for a correct interpretation of the elements and combination rules of text structures we need to turn to lexicons and grammars, of course.

While lexicons tell us primarily about how words are typically related to content (the lexical meaning of words), grammars mainly deal with the forms, functions, and combination rules found at the various **levels of text structures**. In the present **grammar** (as in most other grammars) these levels are treated in separate parts, appearing hierarchically from the lowest to the highest (in most other grammars, the highest level, the textgrammatical one, is not taken into account as yet):[49]

1 Writing System and Phonology (↑1–20);
2 Structure of Words – Morphology (↑21–125);
3 Syntax (↑126–290; deviations from "norms": 291–296);
4 Textgrammar (↑297–353; also ↑p.569).

In the appendices there are further matters to help text interpreters:

---

45 In the case of living languages by means of written and spoken texts, in the case of "dead" languages (i.e. languages that are no longer spoken) such as Ancient Greek exclusively by means of written texts or (spoken) texts handed down in written form (↑297[2]).

46 For an overview of text types attested in the NT ↑305 (based on Reiser 2001: 92–194).

47 ↑297–302.

48 ↑308–314 for an overview of factors relevant to text comprehension and text interpretation.

49 Letters of the alphabet/sounds, words/word-forms and (normally) clauses/sentences, in themselves, do not amount to a text. Texts, however, are typically made up of adequately chosen and combined clauses/sentences, the clauses/sentences are (typically) made up of adequately chosen and combined words/word-forms, and the words/word-forms are (always) made up of adequately chosen and combined letters/sounds.

Appendix 1: Classical and NT Greek: differences (↑355–356);
Appendix 2: Word-formation (↑357–371).

In the remainder of this introduction we will illustrate briefly the roles the various parts of the grammar may play in text interpretation; our example is the narrative text Mt 13:45f, a parable uttered by Jesus (as reported by Matthew) to point out the outstanding value of the "kingdom of heaven" he proclaimed (text function; main point):

Πάλιν ὁμοία ἐστὶν ἡ βασιλεία τῶν οὐρανῶν ἀνθρώπῳ ἐμπόρῳ ζητοῦντι καλοὺς μαργαρίτας· εὑρὼν δὲ ἕνα πολύτιμον μαργαρίτην ἀπελθὼν πέπρακεν πάντα ὅσα εἶχεν καὶ ἠγόρασεν αὐτόν.	*Again the kingdom of heaven is like a merchant, searching for fine pearls. When he found one pearl of great value, he went away and sold everything that he had and bought it.*

Part 1 **Writing System and Phonology** (↑1–20) introduces us mainly
a) to the elements of the lowest level of text structure, to the letters of the alphabet, the sounds and syllables they represent, as well as to the diacritical and punctuation marks in use, a level without which the text structure is unlikely to either enter our minds or to make sense to us in any way at all, and
b) to the rules ("sound laws") that help us to deal with grammatical peculiarities such as ζητοῦντι (< *ζητέοντι) *searching* (dat. sg.).

Part 2 **Structure of Words – Morphology** (↑21–125) is about the second level of text structure which is of crucial importance to text interpretation, the level of words (i.e. sound combinations indicating either [lexical] content or [grammatical] functions);[50] most importantly it presents us with the various inflectional patterns ("paradigms") enabling us to identify the specific word-forms of a text and to connect them with the intended functional category (more details are found in the syntax part), in particular
a) with declension forms (↑23–63) like μαργαρίτας, which as an accusative (plural of μαργαρίτης *pearl*; ↑26) in this text is best connected with the role of a direct object (answering the question "Whom or what [here: was he searching for]?" (↑23), and
b) with conjugation forms (↑64–125) like ἠγόρασεν, which as a finite verb form has the predicator role representing the core information of the sentence/clause (i.e. the action the subject entity [here: the merchant referred to] is said to be doing; ↑22f) and due to its classification as a 3rd person singular aorist indicative active (of ἀγοράζω *to buy*; ↑76 in combination with 92d and 96.5) points to the person spoken about (3rd person singular [↑64d], the subject entity [here: the merchant]) who is said to have done something in the past (here: bought [that one pearl of great value]; ↑64–65).

The focus of Part 3 **Syntax** (↑126–290) is on the grammatical side of the third level of text structures, i.e. the level of sentences/clauses or propositions (content of sentences/clauses, "situations"; these are the most important structural components of a text as text (↑298); one of the greatest challenges of text interpretation is to understand these and to infer from them the overall content to be communicated by the text. This is the reason why the syntax part is as lengthy as it is; it tells us inter alia about
a) the function that words and phrases may have in Ancient Greek sentences (↑129–252), in the syntax of case forms (↑146–182) e.g. about the fact that dative noun phrases like ἀνθρώπῳ ἐμπόρῳ *a*

50 (Lexical) content is indicated by (lexical) content words such as the noun μαργαρίτης *pearl*, the adjective καλός *beautiful/good/fine* or the verb ζητέω *to search*, (grammatical) functions by function words such as the article ὁ/ἡ/τό or conjunctions as δέ *but* and καί *and*. Information about what may be indicated by content and function words is found in lexicons, information about function words also in the syntax and (if available) textgrammar parts of the grammar.

merchant may occur as objects not only of verbs, but also of certain adjectives such as ὅμοιος *like* (↑179b), or in the section on the syntactic use of participles (↑227–240) about non-articular participles like εὑρών (ptc. aor. act. mask. nom. sg. of εὑρίσκω *to find*) frequently occurring as adverbial adjuncts (very frequently with a temporal nuance [↑229a–231d], here *when he found* … or the like [he sold everything …]),
b) the sentences and their constituents in Ancient Greek (↑253–265), e.g. about attributive modifiers of the head of noun phrases answering questions like "What kind of entity is the entity referred to by the head noun?" (↑260b–260n) and in what form it may occur in texts, inter alia as genitive noun phrase like [ἡ βασιλεία] τῶν οὐρανῶν *[the kingdom] of heaven*, as an adjective phrase showing concord like καλοὺς [μαργαρίτας] *fine [pearls]*, as a participle phrase showing concord like [ἀνθρώπῳ ἐμπόρῳ] ζητοῦντι … *[a merchant] searching* … or even as a relative clause (↑next paragraph), and
c) the types of sentences/clauses occurring in Ancient Greek and the ways they may be combined (↑266–290), inter alia about independent declarative (main) clauses (↑267) like the ἐστίν-clause in Mt 13:45 and the sentence with the two predicators πέπρακεν *(he) sold* and ἠγόρασεν *(he) bought*, also about dependent (subordinate) clauses (serving as sentence constituents or attributive modifiers of a superordinate construction; ↑270ff), e.g. about relative clauses like [πάντα] ὅσα εἶχεν *[everything] that he had* (↑289a).

Part 4 **Textgrammar** (↑297–353; also ↑p. 569) is about the highest level of text structures, that of the text. It is to show in what ways a text is different from the sum of its sentences/clauses as well as the ways in which the distinctive features of the grammatical (↑316–348) and the content (↑349–353) sides of the text structure relate to the coherence of Ancient Greek texts, here of a NT text, inter alia (for further details on our example ↑301; 303; 307):
a) connectives (↑354) like the adverb πάλιν *again/furthermore* (↑325c) that joins our text to the larger speech context and helps us towards recognizing its communicative function; or like the conjunctions δέ *but* (↑338a) and καί *and* (↑312c; 325c; 327) that serve to join the sentences/clauses or propositions/"situations" in question and help us to infer the intended content relations (↑352); similarly also (clause-like) participle phrases (↑312c) like ζητοῦντι … *searching* … , εὑρών … *finding/when he found* … and ἀπελθών *going away/he went away and*; moreover, comparable to some extent, function words that refer back, "anaphorically", or point forward, "cataphorically", (↑346–348) like the article ἡ *the* [kingdom of heaven] or the personal pronoun αὐτόν [bought] *it*, which indicate what exactly (i.e. what specific concepts or entities) the speaker/writer refers to and which within the text establish a dense network of relationships that contributes decisively to the coherence of the text;
b) content words that may be connected with one particular domain of meaning (or "frame"; ↑313) and that relate to one another in a way that is relevant to conveying the text content, like ἔμπορος *merchant*, πιπράσκω *to sell* and ἀγοράζω *to buy* (commerce domain/frame) or also ἡ βασιλεία τῶν οὐρανῶν *the kingdom of heaven*, an expression that, in the light of the wider context, is to be understood as a technical term; especially, however, the discernible (hierarchical) structure of the propositions/"situations" that the text content is made up of (↑312e for a corresponding display of Mt 13:45f).

1 Writing System and Phonology

Part 1 deals with the elements of the lowest level of text structures (↑p. 12f): the letters of the alphabet, the sounds and syllables they represent (↑1–4), then diacritical and punctuation marks (↑5–7), finally "sound laws" that help to explain grammatical peculiarities more easily (↑8–20).

1.1 Writing system and sounds of Ancient Greek

The alphabet and its pronunciation (↑BR §1f; CAGL: 25ff; 85ff; Horrocks: 160ff; Allen: 12ff) 1

Introductory remarks: 1a

1. The alphabet introduced here is used for any kind of Greek texts, both ancient and modern. In Ancient Greek "the heaven and the earth", e.g., would be written as ὁ οὐρανὸς καὶ ἡ γῆ ("polytonic" script with all the traditional diacritics being used), in Modern Greek as ο ουρανό και η γη ("monotonic" script with one accent only, indicating the tone syllable of polysyllabic words).

2. In modern editions of Ancient Greek texts small letters ("minuscules") are used in most cases, while capitals ("uncials") tend to be restricted to the first letter of names and paragraphs.

3. The alphabet in use today basically goes back to the minuscule script that emerged in the 4th century A.D. and was the standard one from about the 8th century. This minuscule script replaced a purely uncial one, which was mostly written without leaving spaces between words and sentences ("scriptio continua"), e.g. the first part of Jn 1:1 *In the beginning was the Word, and the Word was …*:

Ἐν ἀρχῇ ἦν ὁ λόγος, καὶ ὁ λόγος ἦν …	ЄΝΑΡΧΗΗΝΟΛΟΓΟϹΚΑΙΟΛΟΓΟϹΗΝ…
(modern form of the minuscule script)	(uncial script; ↑Codex Sinaiticus, 4th century)

4. The uncial script is a descendant of the Ionic Alphabet, which by the 4th century B.C. had become the general standard alphabet for writing Greek.

5. The letters of this alphabet started off, essentially, by representing well-defined Ancient Greek sounds. Gradually the system of sounds changed, in some cases to a considerable extent. Traditional spelling, however, was largely preserved: the words were spelled the same, but pronounced differently. As a result, older texts were read as if they were new ones. So, in the age of the Renaissance humanism (15th/16th centuries A.D.) people, when reading Ancient Greek texts, including the NT, made use of the pronunciation of the day, i.e. of the then current form of Greek ("Modern" Greek). Some scholars, however, set out to reconstruct the original pronunciation in order to correct the one in general use. One of the more striking of these "corrections" concerned the letter eta (Η/η): in Modern Greek it stood for the sound /ī/ (as in *feet*), in Ancient Greek for something like /ē/ (as in ***bear***). Because of this, some use the terms "itacism" or "itacistic" to refer the more recent (Modern Greek) pronunciation and "etacism" or "etacistic" to refer to the reconstructed (Ancient Greek) pronunciation. As Erasmus favoured the "etacistic" (Ancient Greek) pronunciation, many call it "Erasmian" pronunciation (↑p. 9).

Four alternative pronunciations are listed below: (a) "recommended" pronunciation (based on pragmatic considerations), (b) "Classical" pronunciation (4th century B.C.; here only differences from the "recommended" one are mentioned), (c) pronunciation reconstructed for the "NT" (1st century A.D.; mainly following Horrocks), (d) "Modern Greek" pronunciation.

1b The twenty-four letters of the alphabet

LETTERS (on the sounds ↑2/3)			transliteration	PRONUNCIATION [1] – options recommended		CG	NT (?)	modern
Α α	alpha	Ἄλφα	ă ā	[a] [aː]	***Gaga/cat*** *father*		[a] –	[a] –
Β β [2]	beta	Βῆτα	b	[b]	***bee***		[β][3]	[v][4]
Γ γ	gamma	Γάμμα	g	[g]	***go***		[ɣ/j][5]	[ɣ/j][5]
Δ δ	delta	Δέλτα	d	[d]	***do***		[d]	[ð][6]
Ε ε	epsilon	Ἒ ψῖλόν [7]	ĕ	[ɛ]	*pet*		[ɛ]	[ɛ]
Ζ ζ	zeta	Ζῆτα	z	[dz]	***buds***	[zd][8]	[z][9]	[z]
Η η	eta	Ἦτα	ē	[ɛː]	***air***		[i]	[i]
Θ θ/ϑ [10]	theta	Θῆτα	th	[θ]	***th**ing*	[t^h][11]	[t^h]	[θ]
Ι ι	iota	Ἰῶτα	ĭ ī	[i] [iː]	*belfry/bit* *beat*		[i/j] –	[i/j] –
Κ κ/ϰ [10]	kappa	Κάππα	k	[k]	*s**k**ill*		[k]	[k/k^j][12]
Λ λ	lambda	Λάμβδα	l	[l]	***l**oud*		[l]	[l]
Μ μ	mu	Μῦ	m	[m]	***m**a**n***		[m]	[m]
Ν ν	nu	Νῦ	n	[n]	***n**u**n***		[n]	[n]
Ξ ξ	xi	Ξῖ (Ξεῖ)	x	[ks]	*bo**x***		[ks]	[ks]
Ο ο	omikron	Ὂ μικρόν [13]	ŏ	[ɔ]	*pot*		[ɔ]	[ɔ]
Π π	pi	Πῖ (Πεῖ)	p	[p]	*s**p**ot*		[p]	[p]
Ρ ρ	rho	Ῥῶ	r	[r]	***r**ot* [14]		[r]	[r]
Σ σ/ς [15]	sigma	Σῖγμα	s	[s]	***s**ing*	[s/z][16]	[s/z]	[s/z]
Τ τ	tau	Ταῦ	t	[t]	*s**t**op*		[t]	[t]
Υ υ [2]	upsilon	Υ̓͂ ψῖλόν [17]	y̆ ȳ	[u] [uː]	*book* *root*	[y] [yː][18]	[i] –	[i] –
Φ φ/ϕ [10]	phi	Φῖ (Φεῖ)	ph	[f]	***f**all*	[p^h][11]	[p^h]	[f]
Χ χ	chi	Χῖ (Χεῖ)	ch	[k^h/ x]	***k**ill*/Scottish *lo**ch***	[k^h][11]	[k^h]	[x/ç]
Ψ ψ	psi	Ψῖ (Ψεῖ)	ps	[ps]	*la**ps**e*		[ps]	[ps]
Ω ω	omega	Ὦ μέγα [13]	ō	[ɔː]	*saw*		[ɔ]	[ɔ]

(1) The bold letters of the English words correspond (approximately) to the sounds mentioned to the left (referred to by symbols of the International Phonetic Alphabet within square brackets).
(2) Note that ϐ may at times be used for β, and ϒ quite frequently for Υ.
(3) As in *vase* (bilabial).
(4) As in ***v**ase*. For word-initial [b] Modern Greek uses μπ.
(5) γ before [a, ɔ, u] = [ɣ] ≈ [x] roughly as in Scottish *lo**ch***, but voiced, otherwise [j] as in *yard*.
(6) As in *wi**th***. For word-initial [d] Modern Greek uses ντ.
(7) “Simple” *e* as opposed to the “compounded” *e*, i.e. αι (pronounced like ε in post-CG).
(8) In CG apparently the sound [zd] was used as it is found in English *wi**sd**om* (perhaps, however, rather a voiced [dz] as suggested in the recommended option).
(9) The sound [z] would correspond to the *s* in *ro**s**e* or to the *z* in ***z**one*.
(10) These are equally acceptable alternatives.
(11) CG aspirated (↑3 on aspirates): theta like the *t* in ***t**an*, phi like the *p* in ***p**an*, and chi like the *k* in ***k**ill*.
(12) Before [i, ɛ] as [k^j], i.e. a *k* combined with the sound [j], comparable to the word-initial sound combination in *cute* [**kju**:t].
(13) Omikron (lit. “small” [short] o) and omega (lit. “large” [long] o) both stand for the short sound [ɔ] in post-CG; the traditional names distinguishing the two letters are a comparatively late invention (↑Re 1:8 that for *I am the Alpha and the **Omega*** has Ἐγώ εἰμι τὸ ἄλφα καὶ τὸ **ὦ**).
(14) An *r* articulated with the tip of the tongue as is typical of Scottish.
(15) ς is regularly used at the end and σ at the beginning of or inside a word, e.g. **σ**ει**σ**μό**ς** *earthquake*; some replace the σ by a ς in compounds at the end of a prefix, e.g. εἰ**ς**άγω for (the more common) εἰ**σ**άγω *to lead in*. Some prefer ϲ to both σ and ς, e.g.: ϲειϲμόϲ *earthquake*.
(16) Rarely also [z] before voiced consonants as in Σμύρνα [ˈzmyrna] *Smyrna*.
(17) “Simple” *i* (pronunciation of υ from late Byzantine times) as opposed to the “compounded” *i*, i.e. οι (also pronounced as [i] from late Byzantine times).
(18) Approximately like French *u* in ***lu**ne* (short) “moon” and in ***ru**se* (long) “ruse/trick” or German *ü* in *M**ü**ller* (short) “miller” and *M**üh**le* (long) “mill”.

Digraphs 1c

γγ		gg	[ŋg] *fi**ng**er*		[ŋg]	
γκ		gk	[ŋk] *ba**nk***		[ŋk]	
γχ		gch	[ŋk^h] *bro**nch**itis*	[ŋk^h]	[ŋk^h]	
γξ		gx	[ŋks] *ly**nx***		[ŋks]	
αι	diphthongs (↑2a)	ai	[ai] ***ai**sle*		[ɛ]	[ɛ]
αυ		au	[au] ***n**ow*		[aɸ] [1]	[af/av]
ει		ei	[ei] *v**ei**n*	[e:] [2]	[i]	[i]
ευ		eu	[ju:] ***eu**logy*	[eu] [3]	[ɛɸ] [1]	[ɛf/ɛv]
οι		oi	[ɔi] *b**oi**l*		[y]	[i]
ου		ou	[u:] *l**oo**sen*	[u:] [4]	[u]	[u]
υι		ui	[wi] *q**ui**z*	[yi] [5]	[y]	[ij]

ηυ	ēu	[juː] *eulogy*	[ɛːu] [6]	[iɸ] [1]	([if]) [7]
ᾳ	ā(i)	[aː] *father*	[aː] [8]	[a]	[a]
ῃ	ē(i)	[ɛː] *air*	[ɛː] [9]	[i]	[i]
ῳ	ō(i)	[ɔː] *saw*	[ɔː] [10]	[ɔ]	[ɔ]

(1) [ɸ] an f-sound articulated using one's lips (bilabially).
(2) CG as the *e* in German *Lehrer* "teacher" (↑Engl. *fiancé*), pre-Class, however, [ei] as in ***vein***.
(3) Something like ***every*** with the *v* being pronounced as *w*.
(4) Pre-CG [ou] close to the diphthong in ***show***.
(5) CG as the *ui* in French ***huit*** "eight".
(6) Like ευ, the first part, however, being longer.
(7) Occurs to a limited extent only.
(8) Pre-CG [aːi] like αι, the first part, however, being longer.
(9) Pre-CG [ɛːi] like ει, the first part, however, being longer.
(10) Pre-CG [ɔːi] like οι, the first part, however, being longer.

1d **Diacritical marks** (↑5)

᾿	"smooth" breathing[1]	–	[–] *and*		[–]	not used
῾	"rough" breathing	h	[h] ***hand***		[–]	not used
´	acute	´	stress [ˈ…]	↑5b	stress	stress
`	grave	´	stress [ˈ…]	↑5d	stress	not used
῀/⁀ [2]	circumflex	´	stress [ˈ…]	↑5c	stress	not used

(1) ↑19/20 for two diacritical marks that look the same as this, but have different functions.
(2) These are equally acceptable alternatives.

1e Further noteworthy points on the alphabet:

1. Using the recommended (and Classical) pronunciation ι, **iota**, must always be **pronounced** as [i], never as [j] (i.e. never as English *y* in ***yard***), e.g.: Ἰουδαῖος /**iu**ːˈdaios/ not /**ju**:…/ *Judean/Jew*.

2. Early Ancient Greek also had the sound [w] (like *w* in English ***well***), no longer in use in CG times. The letter corresponding to this was ϝ; because of its form it is called "**digamma**", i.e. "double gamma"). There was also the sound **[j]**, corresponding to *y* in *yoke*; in Greek (or Proto-Indo-European) studies it is transcribed as "**i̯**". By the end of the 2nd millennium it disappeared from Greek [CAGL: 176]; so, no alphabetic letter was introduced. For traces of both the ϝ and the **i̯** ↑12.

3. While the Greek alphabet introduced here (the Ionic Alphabet; ↑1a) is an Eastern variety, it is a Western variety of this alphabet that our alphabet (and all the other Latin-based ones) is descended from. The most striking differences between the two are:

Greek alphabet:
H → long *e*, e.g. Ἠλίας ***Elias*** (Elijah)
X → *ch* (k), e.g. Χριστός ***Christ***

English (Latin-based) alphabet:
H → *h*, e.g. in ***H**ouse of Commons*;
X → *x*, e.g. in *Max*.

4. The letters of the alphabet, supplemented by a few other signs, were also used to refer to numbers. On this ↑62.

Vowels (↑BR §3; BDF §22–28)

2

Pure vowels ("monophthongs"; for further pronunciation options also ↑1b) 2a

always SHORT (approximately as in:)	always LONG (approximately as in:)	SHORT or LONG (approximately as in:)
ε e [ɛ] *pet*	**η** ē [ɛː] *air*	**ᾰ/ᾱ**[1] ă/ā [a]/[aː] *Gaga*[2]*/father*
ο o [ɔ] *pot*	**ω** ō [ɔː] *saw*	**ῐ/ῑ** ĭ/ī [i]/[iː] *belfry/beat*
		ῠ/ῡ y̆/ȳ [u]/[uː][3] *book/root*

(1) In this grammar long vowels are often marked by ¯ ("macron"), short vowels by ˘ ("micron"). Note that these signs are not part of Greek spelling (unlike breathing marks and accents!).
(2) Short *a* as in the name *Lady Gaga*.
(3) Or rather [y]/[yː] as in French *lune/ruse* or German *Müller/Mühle*.

Diphthongs ("double sounds"; for further pronunciation options also ↑1c) 2b

SHORT DIPHTHONGS (the first vowel is short) (approximately as in:)				LONG DIPHTHONGS (the first vowel is long) (in CG already mostly monophthongs; approximately as in:)			
αι	ai	[ai]	*aisle*	**ᾳ/Αι**[1]	ā(i)	[aː]	*father*[2]
αυ	au	[au]	*now*	**ῃ/Ηι**[1]	ē(i)	[ɛː]	*air*[3]
ει	ei	[ei]	*vein*[4]	**ῳ/Ωι**[1]	ō(i)	[ɔː]	*saw*[5]
ευ	eu	[juː]	*eulogy*[6]	**ηυ**	ēu	[juː]	*eulogy*[7]
οι	oi	[ɔi]	*boil*				
ου	ou	[uː]	*loosen*[8]				
υι	ui	[wi]	*quiz*[9]				

(1) With silent iota, written underneath small letters ("iota subscript"), but beside capitals ("iota adscript"), a spelling established as standard only in the Byzantine period (↑p.9), e.g.: ᾅδης/**Ἀι**δης *Hades*, **ᾖ**δον/**Ἦι**δον *I sang*, ᾠδή/**Ὠι**δή *song*.
(2) Pre-CG [aːi] like αι, the first part, however, being longer.
(3) Pre-CG [ɛːi] like ει, the first part, however, being longer.
(4) So in pre-CG, in CG, however, as the *e* in German *Lehrer* "teacher" (↑Engl. *fiancé*).
(5) Pre-CG [ɔːi] like οι, the first part, however, being longer.
(6) More accurately something like ***every*** with the *v* being pronounced as *w*.
(7) CG [ɛːu], i.e. like ευ, the first part, however, being longer.
(8) Pre-CG [ou] close to the diphthong in *show*.
(9) Or rather (CG) as the *ui* in French *huit* "eight".

Note that the **diphthongs** listed above in principle all count as **long**, word-final -αι and -οι in inflectional forms, however, as short (↑23e; 74d), with two exceptions: (1) in the optative (↑74c), e.g. παιδεύ-**οι** *may he train*; (2) as an output syllable of contracted verbs (↑82a; 89a), e.g. δηλ**οῖ** < δηλόει *he makes clear*.

2c With regard to vowels (monophthongs and diphthongs) the following points need to be noted:

1. Post-CG eventually had only short vowels. Furthermore the sound [i] was represented by ι, ει, η/ῃ or (since Late Byzantine times) also by οι or υ/υι ("itacism"; ↑1a) and the sound [ɛ] by αι or ε.

2. Distinguishing two kinds of ει makes it easier to understand certain grammatical peculiarities: (a) a real ει, an ι diphthong, one originally pronounced as [ei] like the *ei* in ***vein***; (b) a false ει, one going back to a compensatory lengthening (↑10) or a contraction without an [i] sound ever being involved (↑11) and from the beginning being pronounced as [e:] as in German *Lehrer* "teacher" (↑ also English ***fiancé*** without [ɪ] element!). As early as CG times both were pronounced the same (as [e:]) and so were written the same, e.g. (↑70):

real ει		false ει	
παιδεύ-**ει**	*he trains*	παυδεύ-**ει**ν (< ε + εν)	*to train*

The iota of the real ει is preserved in the course of contractions with o- or a-sounds (↑11), but not the one of the false ει (↑84b[2]; 87c[3]; 89a[3]), e.g.:

real ει			false ει		
δηλό-ει	> δηλ**οῖ**	*he makes clear*	δηλό-ειν	> δηλ**οῦ**ν	*to make clear*
ἀγαπά-ει	> ἀγαπ**ᾷ**	*he loves*	ἀγαπά-ειν	> ἀγαπ**ᾶ**ν	*to love*

Note that there is also a real ου, in pre-CG pronounced as [ou], and a false ου (like the false ει going back to a compensatory lengthening [↑10] or a contraction [↑11]), in CG both pronounced as [u:].

3 Consonants (↑BR §2; BDF §32–35)

Overview of the Classical inventory of consonants
(especially relevant to a great variety of grammatical explanations):

place of articulation ↓	manner of articulation: STOPS			CONTINUANTS		
	UNVOICED UNASPIRATED	VOICED STOP	UNVOICED ASPIRATE	FRICATIVE[1]	VOICED NASAL	LIQUIDS[2]
LABIAL (lips are pressed together)	**π** [p]	**β** [b]	**φ** [p^h][3] as in ***pan***		**μ** [m]	
DENTAL (tongue touches upper teeth)	**τ** [t]	**δ** [d]	**θ** [t^h][3] as in ***tan***	**σ** [s]	**ν** [n]	**λ** [l] **ρ** [r]
VELAR (back of tongue touches soft palate)	**κ** [k]	**γ** [g]	**χ** [k^h][3] as in ***kill***		**γ** before **γ/κ/χ/ξ** [ŋ]	

(1) The sound [h] represented by the rough breathing (↑5a) is a fricative, too.
(2) μ, ν, λ, and ρ are often classified as liquids in a wider sense (↑36/37; 97ff).
(3) Post-CG: fricatives [f], [θ] and [x/ç] as in ***f**all*, ***th**ing* and (Scottish) *lo**ch***; ↑1b[11].

Further noteworthy points on the consonant inventory of Ancient Greek: 3a

1. The letters ξ, ψ and ζ stand for two consonants each (they are referred to as "twin consonants" in this grammar): [ks], [ps] and [dz]/[zd] (↑1b; 15g).

2. Pre-CG also had (↑1e) the (non-syllabic) semivowels [w] (labial) written as ϝ, and [j] (velar) referred to by specialists as i̯ (no ancient alphabetic letter existing). On traces left by these ↑12.

Syllables (↑BR §6f) 4

1. **Syllable length** (i.e. quantity or weight of syllable sounds) 4a

a) Syllables with a short vowel (↑2a) followed by a single consonant count as **short** by nature, e.g.:[1]

νό-μος *law* φέ-ρο-μεν *we carry* πο-τα-μός *river*

b) Syllables with a long vowel or a diphthong (↑2a/2b) count as **long** by nature, e.g.:

μή-τηρ *mother* ση-μεί-οις *for signs* οὕ-τως *thus*

c) Syllables with a (naturally) short vowel count as long by **"position"** (i.e. by convention) when the vowel is followed by more than one consonant[1] or by a twin consonant (↑3a), e.g.:

ὀ-φθ**α**λ-μός *eye* δ**ε**-σμός *fetter*
ὕ-μνος *hymn* **ὄ**-ψ**ε**-σθε *you* (pl.) *will see*

Note that syllable length by position affects neither accentuation nor pronunciation. It plays an important role in Ancient Greek versification (quantifying meter; ↑BR §316ff; CAGL: 370ff), which, however, is as good as unattested in the NT. ↑50a, however, on comparative and superlative forms.

2. Orthographic **syllabification**[2] 4b

A single consonant connects with the vowel after it. A syllable may, however, begin with two or three consonants provided the cluster in question may occur at the beginning of a Greek word, e.g.:[3]

ἄ-ρο-**τρ**ον *plough* ἀ-**γρ**ός *field*
δε-**σπ**ό-της *master* ἑ-**σπ**έ-ρα *evening*
πρε-**σβ**ύ-τε-ρος *older, elder* ἀν-**δρ**ά-σιν *for men*

Compounds (↑21f; 358a) on the other hand are split into their components, e.g.:

ὥσ-τε *so that, therefore* συν-άγω *I gather (in)*

---

1 In Attic/CG a stop before a liquid (in the wider sense; ↑3[2]) counts as a single consonant; ↑BR §6f; Lejeune: 290.

2 The relevant "rules" were fixed only in the Byzantine period ("National Grammar"; ↑p.9). They lack consistency in several respects. Nor have they been consistently applied in the transmission of Ancient Greek texts (↑Schwyzer I: 235).

3 These clusters may occur at the beginning of words (↑Kühner-Blass I: 254ff; Lejeune §310ff): labial/velar + dental; stop + liquid; μν; σ + stop/μ; twin consonants; σ + unvoiced stop + liquid/ν.

1.2 Diacritical marks

The diacritical marks introduced in this section ultimately go back to the Alexandrian grammarian Aristophanes of Byzantium (ca. 257–180 B.C.; ↑p. 8). From the 2nd/3rd centuries A.D. they started being used in a more systematic manner when writing literary texts. Around A.D. 400 the system of diacritical marks reached its final form as we know it. It has been in general use, however, only since the 9th and 10th centuries.[4] In the early manuscripts of the NT diacritical marks are used only very sparsely if at all (↑Metzger 2005: 21, 41; for details ↑e.g. Nestle: 53f).[5]

5 Breathings and accents (↑BR §4; 8f)

5a 1. **Breathings**

Every word-initial vowel or diphthong carries a breathing mark.

a) ‛ – the **rough breathing** indicating the [h] sound as in ***h**ouse* (↑3[1]), e.g.:

ὁδός **ho**dós	*way*	**ὥ**ρα **hṓ**rā	*hour*

b) ’ – the **smooth breathing** indicating the absence of the [h] sound, e.g.:

ἐγώ **e**gṓ	*I*	**οἶ**κος **oí**kos	*house*

Every word-initial ρ carries a rough breathing, too, e.g.:

ῥήτωρ **rh**ḗtōr	*orator*	**ῥ**ῆμα **rh**ē̃ma	*word*

On the sound represented by ῥ- ↑Allen: 41–45.
In former times -ρρ- inside a word was sometimes written as -ῤῥ- (↑Kühner-Blass I: 67), e.g. instead of the usual Πύρρος (↑Ac 20:4) sometimes as Πύῤῥος *Pyr**rh**us* (↑also *Pyr**rh**ic victory*).

5b 2. **Accents**

Three accents serve to indicate which syllable of a word has the tone or stress:[6]

a) ´ – the **acute** (↑Lat. *acutus* "sharp/pointed") can be:

- on short or long syllables, e.g.:

δ**ό**ξα	*glory*	χ**ώ**ρα	*land/country*
λ**έ**γω	*I say*	σωτ**ή**ρ	*saviour*

---

4 Schwyzer I: 374. In Modern Greek spelling the diacritics treated in ↑5a–5e are not used except for the acute, called "tónos" (hence the term "monotonic" Greek; ↑1a; also below footnote 6).

5 Very early, however, nouns referring to God ("nomina sacra", sg. "nomen sacrum") were regularly written as abbreviations with a horizontal line above them marking them as such, e.g. in Papyrus 66 (ca. A.D. 200) inter alia in: Jn 1:1 $\overline{\text{ΘC}}$ = θεός *God*; in 6:10 $\overline{\text{IC}}$ = Ἰησοῦς *Jesus*; 7:26 $\overline{\text{XP}}$ = χριστός *Christ*; 11:12 $\overline{\text{KЄ}}$ = κύριε *Lord!*; 14:26 $\overline{\text{ΠΝΑ}}$ = πνεῦμα *Spirit* and $\overline{\text{ΠΗΡ}}$ = πατήρ *Father* (↑Trobisch: 4f).

6 Originally pitch was of primary importance. In Hellenistic times (from ca. 300 B.C.; ↑p. 4), as the distinction between long and short vowels gradually disappeared (↑2c), the primary pitch accent gave way to a primary stress accent (Horrocks: 169). In order to preserve the traditional pronunciation, accent marks were introduced: the acute for the rising tone, the grave for the falling tone, and the circumflex for the rising-falling tone. In Modern Greek the "tónos" (a sign that looks the same as the acute) indicates the stressed syllable. ↑also above footnote 4.

• only on one of the last three syllables, on the last but two (the antepenultimate) only if the vowel of the last syllable (the ultimate) is short, e.g.:

on the ultimate (the last):	Χριστ**ό**ς	*Christ*
on the penultimate (the last but one):	λ**ό**γος	*word*
on the antepenultimate (the last but two):	**ἄ**νθρωπος	*human being*

b) ˜/ ˆ [7] – the **circumflex** (↑Lat. *circumflexus* "bent around") can be: 5c

• only on naturally long (↑4a) syllables, e.g.:

φ**ῶ**ς	*light*	δ**εῖ**πνον	*(main) meal*
β**ῆ**μα	*tribunal*	πλ**οῖ**ον	*ship*

• only on one of the last two syllables, on the penultimate only if the vowel of the ultimate is short; if the vowel of the ultimate is short, an accented penultimate containing a long vowel MUST in fact have a circumflex (↑second row below), e.g.:

οὖς	*ear*	π**ῦ**ρ	*fire*
δ**ῶ**ρον	*gift*	σ**ῶ**μᾰ	*body*

c) ` – the **grave** (↑Lat. *gravis* "heavy") can only be on the last syllable, where it replaces the acute unless it is followed by a punctuation mark (↑7b) or by an enclitic (↑6e), e.g.: 5d

Πέπεισμαι δ**έ**, ἀδελφ**οί** μου, κα**ὶ** αὐτ**ὸ**ς ἐγ**ὼ** περ**ὶ** ὑμῶν …	*But I myself am convinced about you, my brothers …* (Ro 15:14)

Often a **change of accent** occurs. Thus, when the quantity of the final syllable changes (↑28) the acute frequently moves to another syllable or replaces the circumflex, e.g.:

ἄνθρωπ**ος** (short)	*(a) human being*	**οἶ**κ**ος** (short)	*(a) house*
ἀνθρ**ώ**π**ῳ** (long)	*for a human being*	**οἴ**κ**ῳ** (long)	*for a house*

3. **Position** of breathings and accents 5e

When breathings and accents appear in combination, the breathing is written before the acute or grave, but underneath the circumflex, e.g.:

εἴδωλον *image/idol* **εἶ**ναι *to be* **ὥ**ρα *hour* **ὧ**ραι *hours*

Breathings and accents are written:

a) above small letters, e.g.:

ὁ λ**ό**γος **ἦ**ν πρ**ὸ**ς τ**ὸ**ν θε**ό**ν.	*The Word was with God.* (Jn 1:1)

b) before capitals, e.g.:

Ἀβραάμ *Abraham* **Ἡ**ρῴδης *Herod* **Ἄ**γαβος *Agabus* **Ὧ**δε *here* (Re 13:18)

c) above the second component of diphthongs, e.g.:

αἷμα *blood* **Εὐ**οδία *Euodia* ποι**οῦ**σιν *they do* **υἱ**ός *son*

d) before the first component of a long diphthong appearing as a capital (↑2b[1]), e.g.:

Ἅιδης (but **ᾅ**δης) *Hades* **Ἦι**δον (but **ᾖ**δον) *I sang*

7 These are equally acceptable alternatives.

6 Proclitics and enclitics (↑BR §10f)

"Proclitics" (<προκλίνω *to lean forward*) and "enclitics" (< ἐγκλίνω *to lean on*) are words with accentuation peculiarities: a proclitic has no tone/stress of its own (↑6a), an enclitic on the other hand may have one, but often throws it back to the word before it (↑6b).

6a I. **Proclitics** are a closed class of monosyllabic words with the following members:

1. four forms of the article (↑24): ὁ, ἡ and οἱ, αἱ
2. three prepositions (↑184): ἐκ/ἐξ *out of*, εἰς *into*, ἐν *in*
3. two conjunctions (↑252.19/252.61): εἰ *if*, ὡς *as/that* (CG also prep. *to*)
4. the negative particle (↑252.47): οὐ/οὐκ/οὐχ *not*

A proclitic, however, sometimes has an acute:

a) generally before an enclitic (↑6b), e.g.:

εἴ τις λαλεῖ … *If anyone speaks* … (1Pe 4:11)

b) οὐ before a punctuation mark (↑7b), e.g.:

ἔξεστιν … δοῦναι ἢ **οὔ**; *Is it right … to pay or not?* (Lk 20:22)

II. **Enclitics**

6b 1. A number of mono- or disyllabic words strongly depend (lean) on the preceding word (a process being called "enclisis"); as a result, their tone/stress is weakened to such an extent that it is lost altogether or is thrown back to the word before it.

6c 2. The following rule applies (also ↑6e):

- monosyllabic enclitics have no accent of their own;
- disyllabic enclitics have an accent on the second syllable, but only when the preceding word has an acute on the penultimate.

6d 3. The following words or word forms are used as enclitics:

a) The short forms of the personal pronoun 1st and 2nd person singular (↑54a/54b/54d):

1st person singular: μου, μοι, με *of me, for me, me*
2nd person singular: σου, σοι, σε *of you* (sg.), *for you* (sg.), *you* (sg.)

b) The indefinite pronoun in all its forms (↑60a), e.g.:

τις *anyone* τι *anything*

c) The ind. pres. forms of εἰμί *to be* except for the 2 sg. (↑125a):

εἰμί, –, ἐστίν *I am, –, he/she/it is*
ἐσμέν, ἐστέ, εἰσίν *we are, you* (pl.) *are, they are*

d) The ind. pres. forms of φημί *to say* except for the 2 sg. (↑125d):

φημί, –, φησίν *I say, –, he/she/it says*
φαμέν, φατέ, φασίν *we say, you* (pl.) *say, they say*

e) The indefinite adverbs (↑61a/61c):

πoυ, ποτέ, πως etc. *somewhere, sometime, somehow* etc.

f) The following particles (↑252):

γε	*"at least"*	τε	*and*

CG also τοι *then/surely*, νυν *then/therefore*, περ *at all events*, πω *yet/at all* as well as (-)δε (↑58a).

4. Accentuation in word combinations with enclitics (↑6c): 6e

a) with monosyllabic enclitics:		b) with disyllabic enclitics:	
ἀδελφ**ός** τις	*a brother*	ἀδελφ**οί** τινες	*some brothers*
ἵππος τις	*a horse*	**ἵ**πποι τιν**ές**	*some horses*
κ**ύ**ρι**ός** τις	*an owner*	κ**ύ**ρι**οί** τινες	*some owners*
τοῦ θε**οῦ** μου	*of my God*	τοῦ θε**οῦ** ἐστιν	*is of God*
τὸ δ**ῶ**ρ**όν** μου	*my present*	τὸ δ**ῶ**ρ**όν** ἐστιν	*the present is*

5. Further noteworthy points: 6f

a) If two enclitics follow each other, the first enclitic has the acute, e.g.:

φίλοι **μού ἐστε.** — *You are my friends.* (Jn 15:14)

b) At the beginning of a sentence enclitics have an accent, e.g.:

εἰσὶν ἡμῖν ἄνδρες τέσσαρες … — *We have four men …* (Ac 21:23)

c) If the syllable expected to receive the accent of the enclitic is deleted (↑19: "elision"), the enclitic keeps its accent, e.g.:

ἀλλ' **εἰσὶν** ὡς ἄγγελοι … — *But they are like angels …* (Mk 12:25)

Further diacritics including punctuation marks (↑BR §5) 7

1. **Diaeresis** (< διαίρεσις *separation*) 7a

Two dots are placed over ι or υ to indicate that the two vowel letters standing next to each other are not to be read as a diphthong, but as two separate vowels, e.g.:

ἀΐδιος	to be read as:	**a-í**dios	*eternal*
πρ**αΰ**της	to be read as:	pr**a-ý**tēs	*gentleness*

2. **Punctuation marks** (also ↑316[31]) 7b

The comma and the full stop (or period) are largely the same as in English. In Greek ";" is used as a question mark. The raised dot "·" has three counterparts in English: semi-colon ";", colon ":", and (typically before direct speech) ",":

Greek	,	.	;	·
English	,	.	?	; : ,

Example:

Εἶπεν δὲ ὁ ἀρχιερεύς**·** εἰ ταῦτα οὕτως ἔχει**;** ὁ δὲ ἔφη**·** Ἄνδρες ἀδελφοὶ καὶ πατέρες**,** ἀκούσατε**.** …

*Then the high priest asked**,** "Are these things true**?**" He replied**:** "Brothers and fathers**,** listen to me**.** …"* (Ac 7:1f)

7c 3. On the **apostrophe** (**μεθ'** ἡμῶν *with us*) and the **coronis** (κ**ἀ**γώ *I, too*) corresponding to the smooth breathing (↑5a) in form, but not in function ↑19/20.

1.3 Important sound changes ("sound laws")

1.3.1 Sound changes affecting vowels (↑BDF §29–31)

8 Ablaut (↑BR §27f)

I. Different members of a word-family or different forms of a word in many cases have a different root or stem vowel (↑21a), a phenomenon called **"ablaut"** (sometimes also "vowel gradation"):[8]

8a 1. The ablaut is typically about the **quality** of the vowel:

ε > ο (↑8e) ει > οι (↑8e) et al.

↑ English *to sing* and *song* or *sing, sang, sung.*

8b 2. The ablaut may concern the vowel **quantity**:

ε > η, ο > ω etc., e.g.:

πάτ**ε**ρ (voc.) *father!* πατ**ή**ρ (nom.) *father* (↑8e)

II. The following **ablaut grades** may be distinguished:

8c 1. In the case of a **qualitative ablaut**:

a) e-grade, e.g.:	λ**έ**γ-ω *to say*	μ**έ**ν-ω *to remain*
b) o-grade, e.g.:	λ**ό**γ-ος *word*	μ**ο**ν-ή *room*

8d 2. In the case of a **quantitative ablaut**:

a) full grade: the normal grade of the e- or o-vowel, e.g.:

πάτ**ε**ρ (voc.; ↑38)	*father!*	**ἔ**θος	*custom*

b) lengthened grade: movement from short e- or o-vowel to the long one, e.g.:

πάτ**ε**ρ > πατ**ή**ρ (↑38)	*father* (nom.)	**ἔ**θος > **ἦ**θος	*custom* (synonym)

c) zero-grade (or weak grade): absence of the e- or o-vowel (or weakening of the e- or o-diphthong to ι or υ), e.g.:

λ**εί**π-ω (↑108e)	*I leave behind*	> ἔ-λ**ι**π-ον	*I left behind*
φ**εύ**γ-ω (↑105c)	*I flee*	> ἔ-φ**υ**γ-ον	*I fled*
ἐ-**γεν**-όμην (↑112.7)	*I became*	γί-**γν**-ομαι (CG)	*I become*

8 This type of sound change (a "morpho[phono]logical" one: connected with word-formation or inflection) is on a different plane from the "sound laws" properly called so (for which ↑9ff).

Fairly frequently so-called “syllabic” liquids and nasals are involved here (generally marked by ̥), i.e. consonants that occur alone (without a vowel) to form a syllable (as in English *button* [bʌtn̥] or *little* [lɪtl̥]). In Greek such Proto-Indo-European sounds appear either as a simple α (e.g. the alpha privative [↑367b] <*n̥) or as an α that precedes or follows the consonant in question, e.g.:

πατ**ρά**σι (↑38) (< *πατr̥σι)	*to/for the fathers*	ἔστ**αλ**μαι (↑100/101) (< *ἐστl̥μαι)	*I have been sent* Also ↑107d; 113.9.

III. **Synopsis** of some important sets of ablaut grades

Note that many sets that are theoretically possible lack complete attestation.

1. Ablaut of the short vowels ε > ο 8e

FULL GRADE e-grade	 o-grade	LENGTHENED GRADE	ZERO-GRADE
ἐ-γ**ε**ν-όμην *I became*	γέ-γ**ο**ν-α *I have become*		γί-**γν**-ο-μαι (CG) *I become* (↑112.7)
γ**έ**νος *race/kind* (↑39)	οἱ γ**ο**νεῖς *the parents* (↑45b[4])		
πάτ**ε**ρ (voc.) *father!*		πατ**ή**ρ (nom.) *father* (↑38)	πατ**ρ**ός (gen.) *of a father*

2. Ablaut of the diphthongs ει > οι 8f

λ**εί**π-ω *I leave behind*	λέ-λ**οι**π-α (pf. 2) *I have left behind* (↑108)		ἔ-λ**ι**π-ον (aor. 2) *I left behind* (↑105)
π**εί**θ-ω *I persuade*	πέ-π**οι**θ-α *I trust* (↑96.1)		π**ι**σ-τός (< π**ι**θ-τος) *trusting, trustworthy*

3. Ablaut of the diphthongs ευ > ου 8g

σπ**εύ**δ-ω *I hasten*	σπ**ου**δ-ή *haste/zeal*		
φ**εύ**γ-ω *I flee*			ἔ-φ**υ**γ-ον (aor. 2) *I fled* (↑105c) φ**υ**γ-ή *flight*

Quantitative metathesis (↑BR §13) 9

In certain cases, we encounter a sound change called “quantitative metathesis”, i.e. the quantity (length) of two vowels that follow each other is exchanged: an expected ηο (long–short) is replaced by εω (short–long) and an expected ηᾰ (long–short) is replaced by εᾱ (short–long). This regularly happens in the case of vowel and diphthong stems of the third declension (↑40/41), e.g.:

(πολη[i̯]ος >)	πόλ**ηος**	> πόλ**εως**	gen. sg.[1] of πόλις	*city*
(βασιλῆϝος >)	βασιλ**ῆος**	> βασιλ**έως**	gen. sg. of βασιλεύς	*king*
	βασιλ**ῆᾰ**	> βασιλ**έᾱ**	acc. sg. of βασιλεύς	

(1) Note that here the acute remains on the antepenultimate "against" the rule (↑5b/5d).

10 Compensatory lengthening for deleted consonants (↑BR §14)

When a vowel is lengthened to make up for one or two deleted consonants it is customary to speak of "compensatory lengthening": a short vowel is replaced by a long one (followed by only one consonant); in this case the long counterparts of ο and ε are represented in writing by the "false" diphthongs ου and ει (↑2c):

10a 1. Deletion of ν or ντ before a σ (↑25; 28/29; 36; 48; 70):

a) -ᾰνς and -ᾰντς > -ᾱς, e.g.:

οἰκι**ᾰ-νς**	> οἰκί**ᾱς**	*houses*	ἱμ**ᾰντ-ς**	> ἱμ**ᾶς**	*straps*
μελ**ᾰν-ς**	> μέλ**ᾱς**	*black*	παιδευσ**ᾰντ-ς**	> παιδεύσ**ᾱς**	
			one who trains/trained (ptc. aor. act.)		

b) -ονς and -οντς > -ους, e.g.:

λογ**ο-νς**	> λόγ**ους**	*words*	πιστευ-**οντ-σ**ιν	> πιστεύ-**ουσ**ιν
			to/for believing ones (ptc. pres. act.)	

c) -ενς and -εντς > -εις, e.g.:

λυ-θ**εντ-ς** > λυ-θ**είς** *one who is/was loosened* (ptc. aor. pass.)

10b 2. Deletion of a σ after a liquid or a nasal (↑13h; 98b–98d), e.g.:

ἠγγ**ελ-σ**α	> ἤγγ**ειλ**α	*I announced*
ἐσπ**ερ-σ**α	> ἔσπ**ειρ**α	*I sowed*
ἐμ**εν-σ**α	> ἔμ**ειν**α	*I remained*

10c 3. Deletion of a σ before a liquid or a nasal (↑13h), e.g.:

ἐσ-μι > **εἰμ**ί (↑125a) *I am*

10d 4. Deletion of a i̯ after a ν or ρ (↑12c; 97c), e.g.:

κρ**ῐν-i̯**ω	> κρ**ῑ́ν**ω	*I judge*
τ**εν-i̯**ω	> τ**είν**ω	*I stretch out*

11 Vowel contraction (↑BR §15; BDF §31)

Two vowels or a vowel and a diphthong standing next to each other are regularly united into a single vowel or diphthong; this process is termed "vowel contraction".

1. Generally the following **rules** apply (for the effect on accentuation ↑83):

a) Two vowels of the same or related kind contract to their long counterparts; note that -εε contracts to -ει and -οο to -ου (to "false" diphthongs; ↑2c), e.g.: 11a

ε + ε	> ει	πόλ**ε-ες**	>	πόλ**εις** (↑40)	*cities*
ε + η	> η	ποι**έ-η**τε	>	ποι**ῆ**τε (↑87)	*(if) you* (pl.) *do*
η + ε	> η	**ἔζη-ε**	>	ἔζ**η** (↑84c)	*he lived*
η + ει	> ῃ	**ζή-ει**	>	ζ**ῇ** (↑84c)	*he lives*
ο + ο	> ου	**νό-ος**	>	ν**οῦς** (↑31)	*mind*
ο + ω	> ω	δηλ**ό-ω**μεν	>	δηλ**ῶ**μεν (↑89a)	*(if) we make clear*
α + α	> ᾱ	ἱστ**ά-α**σιν	>	ἱστ**ᾶ**σιν (↑115b)	*they set/place*

b) Diphthongs swallow up short vowels, provided the first vowel of the diphthong is of the same or related kind, e.g.: 11b

ε + ει	> ει	ποι**έ-ει**	>	ποι**εῖ** (↑87)	*he does*
ε + ῃ	> ῃ	ποι**έ-ῃ**	>	ποι**ῇ** (↑87)	*you* (sg.) *do for yourself*
ο + οι	> οι	δηλ**ό-οι**μεν	>	δηλ**οῖ**μεν (↑89a)	*may we make clear*
ο + ου	> ου	δηλ**ό-ου**σιν	>	δηλ**οῦ**σιν (↑89a)	*they make clear*
α + αι	> αι	μν**ά-αι**	>	μν**αῖ** (↑27)	*mines* (monetary unit)
α + ᾳ	> ᾳ	μν**ά-ᾳ**	>	μν**ᾷ** (↑27)	*(to/for a) mine* (dat.)

c) O-sounds prevail when combined with e-sounds (whatever their sequence), e.g.: 11c

ο + ε	> ου	δηλ**ό-ε**τε	>	δηλ**οῦ**τε (↑89a)	*you* (pl.) *make clear*
ο + η	> ω	δηλ**ό-η**τε	>	δηλ**ῶ**τε (↑89a)	*(if) you* (pl.) *make clear*
ο + ει[1]	> οι	δηλ**ό-ει**	>	δηλ**οῖ** (↑89a)	*he makes clear*
ο + ῃ	> οι	δηλ**ό-ῃ**	>	δηλ**οῖ** (↑89a)	*you* (sg.) *make clear for yourself*
ε + ο	> ου	ποι**έ-ο**μεν	>	ποι**οῦ**μεν (↑87)	*we do*
η + ο	> ω	**ζή-ο**μεν	>	ζ**ῶ**μεν (↑84c)	*we live*
ε + ω	> ω	ποι**έ-ω**μεν	>	ποι**ῶ**μεν (↑87)	*we want to do*
ε + οι	> οι	ποι**έ-οι**το	>	ποι**οῖ**το (↑87)	*may he do for himself*
ε + ου	> ου	ἐποι**έ-ου**	>	ἐποι**οῦ** (↑87)	*you* (sg.) *did for yourself*
ε + ῳ	> ῳ	*χρυσ**έ-ῳ**	>	χρυσ**ῷ** (↑44)	*(to/for a) golden*

(1) Note that this is a "real" ει (↑2c); ο/α + "false" ει > ου/ᾱ (↑2c; 89a[3]; 84b[2]).

d) O-sounds also prevail when combined with a-sounds, e.g.: 11d

α + ο	> ω	ἀγαπ**ά-ο**μεν	>	ἀγαπ**ῶ**μεν (↑84)	*we love*
α + ω	> ω	ἀγαπ**ά-ω**	>	ἀγαπ**ῶ** (↑84)	*I love*
α + οι	> ῳ	ἀγαπ**ά-οι**το	>	ἀγαπ**ῷ**το (↑84)	*may he be loved*
α + ου	> ω	ἠγαπ**ά-ου**	>	ἠγαπ**ῶ** (↑84)	*you* (sg.) *were loved*
ο + α	> ω	μείζ**ο**(σ)**α**	>	μείζ**ω** (↑52)	*larger*

11e e) When a-sounds and e-sounds contract, the first sound prevails, e.g.:

α + ε > ᾱ	ἀγαπά-**ετε**	>	ἀγαπ**ᾶ**τε (↑84)	*you* (pl.) *love*
α + η > ᾱ	ἀγαπά-**η**τε	>	ἀγαπ**ᾶ**τε (↑84)	*(if) you* (pl.) *love*
α + ει > ᾳ	ἀγαπ**ά-ει**	>	ἀγαπᾷ (↑84)	*he loves*
α + ῃ > ᾳ	ἀγαπ**ά-ῃ**	>	ἀγαπᾷ (↑84)	*(if) he loves*
ε + α > η	γέν**ε-α**	>	γέν**η** (↑39)	*races/kinds*

11f 2. **Contraction tables**:

a) The output vowels produced by the various types of vowel combinations:

1st VOWEL	2nd VOWEL a-sound			e-sound				o-sound				
	-α	-αι	-ᾳ	-ε	-ει	-η	-ῃ	-ο	-οι	-ου	-ω	-ῳ
α	ᾱ	αι	ᾳ	ᾱ	ᾳ	ᾱ	ᾳ	ω	ῳ	ω	ω	
ε	η	(ῃ)		ει	ει	η	ῃ	ου	οι	ου	ω	ῳ
η				η	ῃ	η	ῃ	ω	ῳ			
ο	ω			ου	οι	ω	οι	ου	οι	ου	ω	(ῳ)

b) Possible vowel combinations behind the various types of output vowels:

OUTPUT VOWEL	possible ORIGINAL VOWEL COMBINATIONS
ᾱ (ᾳ)	αα αε αη (αᾳ αῃ αει)
η (ῃ)	εα εη ηε ηη ([εαι] εῃ ηει ηῃ)
ω (ῳ)	αο αω αου εω ηο οα οη οω (αοι εῳ [οῳ] ηοι)
αι	ααι
ει	εε εει
οι	εοι οει οῃ οοι
ου	εο εου οε οο οου

11g Change from ᾱ to η (↑BR §12; BDF §43)

In KG/NT as in Ionic-Attic Greek (but not in other dialects such as Doric Greek; ↑p.3) Proto-Greek long ᾱ is generally replaced by η. It is retained, however, when it follows an ε, ι or ρ (this ε/ι/ρ rule applies to Attic, but not to Ionic Greek). ↑25f; 44a/44b; 48e[1]; 84d; 85.4–85.8; 98b. E.g.:

Proto-Greek:	**KG/NT** (= Ionic-Attic):	Proto-Greek:	**KG/NT** (= Attic):	Ionic:
νῑκ**ᾱ**	> νίκ**η** *victory*	θυρ**ᾱ**	θύρ**α** *door*	> θύρ**η**

1.3.2 Sound changes affecting consonants (↑BDF §32–35)

Traces of original ϝ and i̯ (↑BR §17; 21) 12

Original ϝ (digamma) and i̯ (↑1e; 3a) have left certain traces in Ancient Greek. Some of the more important ones are as follows:

1. The ϝ appears as υ before a consonant or at the end of a word, e.g.: 12a
βασιλ**εύ**ς *king*, βασιλ**εῦ** *(O) king*, st. βασιλ**εϝ**- > βασιλ**ευ**- (↑41; also 46a)

2. In rare cases ϝ appears as a rough breathing before a word-initial vowel, e.g.: 12b

ἑσπέρα	< **ϝε**σπερα *evening*	(↑Lat. *vesper*)

not so, however, in most other cases, e.g.:

οἶνος	< **ϝοῖ**νος *wine*	(↑Lat. *vinum*)

3. Original i̯ is involved in the formation of the present stem of stop verbs (↑91b) 12c
and of liquid verbs (↑97c; 110.1) and in a number of other word forms, e.g.:

		verb stem	present stem		
κi̯, χi̯	> σσ (Att. ττ)	φυλακ-	φυλα**κi̯**ω	> φυλά**σσ**ω	*to guard*
		ταραχ-	ταρα**χi̯**ω	> ταρά**σσ**ω	*to stir up*
(γi̯ rarely	> σσ [Att. ττ]	ταγ-	τα**γi̯**ω [↑95.16; also 95.10; 95.11; 95.13–95.15] BR §99)	> τά**σσ**ω	*to put in place* [↑below]
πi̯, φi̯, βi̯	> πτ	κλεπ-	κλε**πi̯**ω	> κλέ**πτ**ω	*to steal*
		θαφ-	θα**φi̯**ω	> θά**πτ**ω	*to bury*
		βλαβ-	βλα**βi̯**ω	> βλά**πτ**ω	*to harm*
γi̯, δi̯	> ζ	σφαγ-	σφα**γi̯**ω	> σφά**ζ**ω	*to slaughter*
		ἐλπιδ-	ἐλπι**δi̯**ω	> ἐλπί**ζ**ω	*to hope*
γi̯ rarely	> σσ (Att. ττ)	ταγ-	τα**γi̯**ω	> τά**σσ**ω	*to put in place* (↑above)
λi̯	> λλ	στελ-	στε**λi̯**ω	> στέ**λλ**ω	inter alia *to send*
νi̯/ρi̯	> ν/ρ	+ compensatory lengthening of the preceding vowel (↑10d)			
		σπερ-	σπ**ερi̯**ω	> σπ**είρ**ω	*to sow* (↑2c)
		κριν-	κρ**ĭνi̯**ω	> κρ**ῑν**ω	*to judge*
however, e.g.:					
ανi̯/αρi̯	> αιν/αιρ (i̯ "leaps" to preceding syllable by "epenthesis" [insertion] of an ι):				
		φαν-	φα**νi̯**ω	> φ**αίν**ω	*to shine*
		ἀρ-	ἀ**ρi̯**ω	> **αἴρ**ω	*to lift up*
τi̯, θi̯	> σ (or σσ)	παντ-	παν**τi̯**α (fem. nom. sg.)	> παν**σ**α >	πᾶσα *every, all* (↑10a; 13h)

4. Combination of ϝ and i̯ (↑80.9; 80.10), e.g.: 12d

ϝi̯	> ι	καυ-/καϝ-	κα**ϝi̯**ω	> κ**αί**ω	*to burn sth.*

Note that the same generally applies to combinations of σ and i̯ (↑48e); however, in such cases both the σ and the ι may be deleted (↑80.1; 86.3; 88.1; 88.2).

13 The deletion of consonants (↑BR §16; 18–20)

13a 1. Before σ a dental (δ, τ, θ) is deleted without trace (↑35; 92a), so is ν in part (↑36), e.g.:

stem	+ σ			
ἐλπιδ-	ἐλπι**δ-ς**	>	ἐλπί**ς**	*hope* (nom. sg.)
	ἐλπι**δ-σ**ιν	>	ἐλπί**σ**ιν	*(to/for) hopes*
σωματ-	σωμα**τ-σ**ιν	>	σώμα**σ**ιν	*(to/for) bodies* (of τὸ σῶμα)
πειθ-	πει**θ-σ**ω	>	πεί**σ**ω	*I will persuade* (πείθω fut.)
(ποιμεν-	ποιμε**ν-σ**ιν	>	ποιμέ**σ**ιν	*shepherds* [of ποιμ-ήν/ένος]

Note that the short ε here is due to morphological factors [inflection], not to any sound law [↑13h].)

13b 2. Before σ a ντ is deleted with compensatory lengthening (↑10a; 36; 46c; 48), e.g.:

stem	+ σ			
ἀρχοντ-	ἀρχ**οντ-σ**ιν	>	ἄρχ**ουσ**ιν	*(to/for) rulers* (of ἄρχ-ων/οντος)
λυθεντ-	λυθ**εντ-ς**	>	λυθ**είς**	*one who is/was loosened*
	λυθ**εντ-σ**ιν	>	λυθ**εῖσ**ιν	*(to/for) such who are/were loosened* (λύω ptc. aor. pass.)
πᾰντ-	πᾰ**ντ-σ**ιν	>	π**ᾶσ**ιν	*(to/for) all* (of πᾶς/παντός)

13c 3. Before κ a dental is deleted (↑92b; 96; in analogy to the vowel verbs; BR §19), e.g.:

stem	+ κ			
ἐλπιδ-	ἤλπι**δ-κ**α	>	ἤλπι**κ**α	*I have hoped* (ἐλπίζω pf.)
ἁγιαδ-	ἡγια**δ-κ**α	>	ἡγία**κ**α	*I have sanctified* (ἁγιάζω pf.)

4. The σ is deleted (↑BR §16):

13d a) at the beginning of a word, in prehistoric Greek already, mostly leading to an aspiration of the vowel following it (represented by a rough breathing in writing), e.g.:

σι-στημι > **ἵ**-στημι — *to set/place* (↑115a)
σεχω > **ἕ**χω (< **ἔ**χω, fut. **ἕ**ξω) — *to have* (↑113.5)

13e b) between vowels inside a word (↑39; 52; 98a), e.g.:

γεν**εσ-ος** > γεν**ε-ος** > γέν**ους** — *(of a) race/kind* (of τὸ γένος)

Note that when CG and post-CG words have a σ between vowels, e.g. παιδεύσω *I will train* (↑76), the σ is not original: it was introduced after the sound change described here.

13f c) between two consonants (2nd person pl. and inf. pf. mid.-pass. of stop and liquid verbs; ↑93 and 99), e.g.:

τε-τα**χ-σθ**ε > τέ-τα**χ-θ**ε — *you* (pl.) *are put in place* (of τάσσω)

13g d) in stem-final position before σ, e.g.:

γενε**σ-σ**ιν > γένε**σ**ιν — *(to/for) races/kinds* (of τὸ γένος; ↑39)
σπα**σ-σ**ω > σπά**σ**ω — *I will draw (a sword)* (σπάω fut.; ↑86.5)

e) after a nasal or liquid inside a word when followed by a vowel, with compensatory lengthening of the short vowel in the preceding syllable (↑10b; 98b–98d), e.g.: 13h

ἐ-κρῐ**ν-σα** > ἔ-κρῑ**ν**-α *I judged* (κρίνω aor. act.)

Note that σ + nasal: either (earlier) > compensatory lengthening + nasal (↑10c; so **ἐσμι** > **εἰμί** *I am* [↑125a]), or (later) > nasal + nasal (present stem assimilation; ↑15f; e.g. ἀμφιέ**σ**νυμι > ἀμφιέ**νν**υμι *to clothe* [↑124.1–124.3]).

Aspirate dissimilation (↑BR §22) 14

1. When two syllables that follow each other both begin with an aspirate (θ, φ, χ), in most cases the first of these aspirates is replaced by the corresponding (unvoiced) unaspirated stop (τ, π, κ), a process termed "aspirate dissimilation", e.g.: 14a

ἐ-**θ**υ-**θ**η	> ἐ-**τ**ύ-**θ**η	*he was sacrificed* (aor. pass.; ↑80.12)
θι-**θ**η-μι	> **τ**ί-**θ**η-μι	*to place* (↑115a)
φε-**φ**ανερωται	> **π**ε-**φ**ανέρωται	*he has been manifested* (φανερόω pf.; ↑72c)
ἐκ-**χ**έ-**χ**υται	> ἐκ-**κ**έ-**χ**υται	*it has been poured out* (ἐκχέω pf.; ↑72c)

2. At the beginning of an ending an unaspirated stop may similarly replace an aspirate, e.g.: 14b

παιδευ-**θ**η-**θ**ι > παιδεύ-**θ**η-**τ**ι *be trained!* (imp. aor. pass.; ↑79b; 107b)

3. In the various forms of a word family only one root aspirate may be retained, e.g.: 14c

root:	dissimilation:			
θρε**φ**-	**τ**ρέ**φ**ω	*to feed*	**τ**ρο**φ**-ή	*food* (↑94.11)
θα**φ**-	**θ**ά**π**τω	*to bury*	**τ**ά**φ**-ος	*tomb* (↑94.14)

As soon as, however, the second aspirate is removed in the course of inflection, the first root aspirate (re-)emerges, e.g.:

root:	dissimilation:		(re-)emergence of the first root aspirate:	
θρι**χ**- (↑42b)	**τ**ρι**χ**-ός	*(of a) hair*	**θ**ρί**ξ** (nom. sg.)	**θ**ρι**ξ**ίν (dat. pl.)

This similarly applies e.g. to (ἐχ < σεχ-; ↑13d):

ἐχ-	**ἔ**χω	*to have*	**ἕξ**ω (fut.)

4. Apparent exceptions: certain forms may have two aspirates next to each other (in NT as well as Attic Greek), e.g.: 14d

ἐξ-ε-**χ**ύ-**θ**η *it was poured out* (↑88.12; 88.13)

Note that aor. and pf. pass. forms of velar and labial stems that (on the basis of sound laws) contain -χθ- or -φθ- are not affected by aspirate dissimilation (as the first aspirate is not found at the beginning of a syllable; ↑90–93).

5. Conversely there is sometimes an aspirate assimilation (↑15): before a rough breathing an unaspirated stop (in the case of elision; ↑19) turns into an aspirate, e.g.: 14e

με**τ**ά + **ὑ**μῖν	> με**θ**' **ὑ**μῖν	*with you* (pl.)
ἀ**π**ό + **ἵ**ημι	> ἀ**φί**ημι	*to let go*

15 Assimilation of consonants (↑BR §18–20; BDF §19)

When one of two successive consonants influences the articulation of the other one generally speaks of “assimilation”. The more important types in Ancient Greek are:

15a 1. Two stops standing next to each other, will have the same manner of articulation:

voiced	βδ	γδ
unaspirated	πτ	κτ
aspirate	φθ	χθ

examples:

ἑ**πτ**ά	ἕ**βδ**ομος	(↑62)	*seven/seventh*
ὀ**κτ**ώ	ὄ**γδ**οος	(↑62)	*eight/eighth*
γέγρα**πτ**αι	γέγρα**φθ**ε	(↑93)	*it is written/you* (pl.) *are written*

Exception: ἐκ *out of* remains unchanged before labials and velars in compounds, e.g.:
ἐκ-δίδωμι *to let out for hire* **ἐκ-θ**αμβέομαι *to be very excited*

15b 2. ν before a velar (γ, κ, χ) changes to γ (a nasal, pronounced as [ŋ]; ↑1c; 3), e.g.:

ἐν-καλέω	> **ἐγ-κ**αλέω	**ἐν-ε**-κάλουν	*to accuse/I* or *they accused*
συν-γράφω	> **συγ-γ**ράφω	**συν-έ**-γραφον	*to write down/I* or *they write down*

↑73c.

15c 3. ν before a labial (β, π, φ) changes to μ, e.g.:

ἐν-βλέπω	> **ἐμ-β**λέπω	**ἐν-έ**-βλεπον	*to look at/I* or *they looked at*
συν-βάλλω	> **συμ-β**άλλω	**συν-έ**-βαλλον	*to meet/I* or *they met*

↑73c.

15d 4. ν before a liquid (λ, ρ) changes to λ or ρ respectively, e.g.:

συν-λαμβάνω	> **συλ-λ**αμβάνω	**συν-ε**-λάμβανον	*to seize/I* or *they seized*
πᾶ**ν ῥ**ῆσις	> πα**ρρ**ησία	*outspokenness*	

[λ + ν > λλ

ἀπ-ο**λ-ν**υμι	> ἀπ-ό**λ-λ**υμι	(↑123.7)	*to ruin*]

15e 5. ν before a σ changes to σ (in compounds [↑368d]; for other cases ↑13h), e.g.:
συ**ν-σ**ωμος > σύ**σ-σ**ωμος *belonging to the same body* (σύν/σῶμα)

15f 6. A labial (β, π, φ) or a ν before a μ changes to μ (↑92a; 93; 99), e.g.:

τε-θλι**β-μ**αι	> τέ-θλι**μ-μ**αι	pf. pass. θλίβω	*to press*
κε-κλε**π-μ**αι	> κέ-κλε**μ-μ**αι	pf. pass. κλέπτω	*to steal*
γε-γρα**φ-μ**αι	> γέ-γρα**μ-μ**αι	pf. pass. γράφω	*to write*
με-μια**ν-μ**αι	> με-μία**μ-μ**αι	pf. pass. μιαίνω	*to defile*

For σ before a nasal ↑13h.

7. Note that the changes involved in the use of the twin consonants (↑3a) ξ and ψ are not due to assimilation, but to spelling conventions (↑34; for ζ ↑12c): 15g

velar (γ, κ, χ) + σ > ξ [ks]
labial (β, π, φ) + σ > ψ [ps]

examples:

stem:	nominative sg.:		
θωρακ-	θωρα**κ+ς**	> θώρα**ξ**	*breastplate*
σαλπιγγ-	σαλπιγ**γ+ς**	> σάλπι**γξ**	*trumpet*
Ἀραβ-	Ἀρα**β+ς**	> Ἄρα**ψ**	*Arab*

Combinations of consonants: synopsis of changes (↑BR §18–20) 16

Consonant clusters which are hard to pronounce are in many cases simplified, mainly through the deletion (↑13), dissimilation (↑14), and assimilation (↑15) of consonants. The changes most relevant to inflection may be summarized as follows: 16a

I. **Stops** before other consonants 16b

1. Changes with stops before another consonant:

	+ μ	+ σ	+ τ	+ θ
labial (β, π, φ)	μμ	ψ	πτ	φθ
velar (γ, κ, χ)	γμ	ξ	κτ	χθ
dental (δ, τ, θ)	σμ	σ	στ	σθ

2. Note that the σ in a three consonant cluster with a σ in the middle is deleted, whilst for the two remaining consonants the above rules apply (↑13f; 92a; 93).

II. **Nasals** and **liquids** before other consonants 16c

1. The ν assimilates to subsequent consonants in the following way (↑99; 100):

ν	+ velar			+ labial			+ liquid		+ nasal
	κ	γ	χ	β	π	φ	λ	ρ	μ
	γκ	γγ	χγ	μπ	μβ	μφ	λλ	ρρ	μμ

2. Nasal or liquid + σ (μσ, νσ, λσ, ρσ): inside a word the σ is deleted before a vowel, leading to a compensatory lengthening of the preceding short vowel (↑13h; 98; but also 13a and 15a).

On other sound changes also ↑12–15.

1.3.3 Word-final sound changes

17 Possible word-final consonants (↑BR §23)

Only ν, ρ, and σ (ξ, ψ = velar and labial respectively + σ) are possible as word-final consonants in regular Ancient Greek. Using **Νηρεύς** *Nereus* (sea-god) as a mnemonic we refer to this as the "Nereus" rule.

There are some exceptions: ἐ**κ** *out of* and οὐ**κ**/**χ** *not*; in NT/LXX Greek (non-Hellenized) Semitic names such as Ἀβραά**μ**, Ναζαρέ**τ** etc.

Note that when factors of word-formation or inflection lead to a form that would violate the above rule, the unacceptable consonants are deleted, e.g.:

stem	nom. sg. (ntr.: without case ending; ↑32b/32e)		
γραμματ-	γραμμα**τ**	> γράμμα_	*letter* (of the alphabet; ↑35d)
γαλακτ-	γαλα**κτ**	> γάλα_	*milk* (↑42b)
παντ-	παν**τ**	> πᾶν_	*every, all* (↑46c)

18 Movable word-final consonants (↑BR §24; BDF §20f)

18a I. ν mobile

The (word-final) ν mobile occurs especially before a word beginning with a vowel or at the end of a clause or a sentence, as part of the following endings:

- 3rd person sg. endings in -ε or -σι and 3rd person pl. endings in -σι (↑70; 114d), e.g.:

ἐπαίδευε(ν)	*he/she trained*	εἰσί(ν)	*they are*
παιδεύουσι(ν)	*they train*	ἐστί(ν)	*he/she/it is*

- pl. dat. endings in -σι(ν) (↑32b), e.g.:

πᾶσι(ν)	*(to/for) all*	πνεύμασι(ν)	*(to/for) spirits*

Especially noteworthy points:

(1) In NT manuscripts the ν mobile is widely used, even before consonants.

(2) In the present grammar it is typically included without brackets.

(3) There never is a ν mobile in 3rd sg. ipf. act. forms of contracted verbs and verbs in -μι (↑82; 114d), e.g.:

ἠγάπ**α**_	*he/she loved*	ἐδίδο**υ**_	*he gave*

(4) In the NT the numeral "20" never has a ν mobile εἴκοσ**ι**_.

18b II. Movable σ and movable velar

These movable consonants are connected with the negation οὐ *not* and with the preposition ἐκ *out of* respectively. The final sound of these words depends on the initial sound of the word or other element that follows:

1. before consonants the final sound is:

οὐ_ **π**ιστεύει	*he/she does not believe*	ἐ**κ**_**τ**οῦ οἴκου	*out of the house*
		ἐ**κ**-**β**άλλω	*to cast out*

2. before vowels the final sound is (inter alia ↑73b):

οὐ**κ** **ἀ**κούει	*he/she does not hear*	ἐ**ξ** **οἴ**κου	*out of a/the house*
		ἐ**ξ**-**έ**ρχομαι	*to go out*

3. before a rough breathing the final sound is:

οὐ**χ** **ἡ**μεῖς	not we	ἐ**ξ** **ὕ**δατος	*out of [the] water*

Elision of short word-final vowels (↑BR §25; BDF §17) 19

The elision (↑Lat. *elidĕre* "to crush out"), i.e. deletion of short word-final vowels before a word beginning with a vowel occurs much less frequently in NT than in Classical Greek.
Elisions are indicated by the "apostrophe" (< ἀπόστροφος lit. "turned away"): ’, which has the same form as the smooth breathing (↑5a).
Examples (before the rough breathing unaspirated stops turn into aspirates; ↑14e):

ἀπὸ πάντων	ἀ**π’** **αὐ**τῶν	ἀ**φ’** **ὑ**μῶν	*from all / them / you* (pl.)
ἐπὶ πάντας	ἐ**π’** **αὐ**τούς	ἐ**φ’** **ὑ**μᾶς	*on all / them / you* (pl.)
μετὰ πάντων	με**τ’** **αὐ**τῶν	με**θ’** **ὑ**μῶν	*with all / them / you* (pl.)
ὑπὸ πάντων	ὑ**π’** **αὐ**τῶν	ὑ**φ’** **ὑ**μῶν	*by all / them / you* (pl.)

Analogously also:

ὑπο-μένω	*I endure*	ὑ**π**-**έ**μεινα	*I endured* (aor.)
ἀπό + ἵημι	*from + to send* >	ἀ**φ**-**ί**ημι	*to let go*

Crasis (↑BR §26; BDF §18) 20

The term "crasis" (< κρᾶσις lit. "a mixing") refers to the following process: certain short words ending in a vowel may merge with a subsequent word that begins with a vowel to form one word. The article, the relative pronoun, καί *and*, and πρό *before* are the words most frequently involved. Crasis is typical of conversational and poetic speech. In the NT it is limited to a small number of fixed combinations.
In writing crasis is indicated by the coronis (< κορωνίς lit. "[something] curved"): ’, which, again, has the same form as the smooth breathing (↑5a), e.g. (the first four combinations are fairly well-attested in the NT/LXX):

κ**ἀ**γώ	= καὶ ἐγώ	*and I, I also, I for my part* (for inflection↑54a)
κ**ἀ**κεῖνος	= καὶ ἐκεῖνος	*and/also that one* (for inflection↑58c)
κ**ἀ**κεῖ	= καὶ ἐκεῖ	*and there*
κ**ἄ**ν	= καὶ ἄν	*even if, if only/at least*
το**ὐ**ναντίον	= τὸ ἐναντίον	*on the contrary* (4× in NT/LXX)
το**ὔ**νομα	= τὸ ὄνομα	*(by) the name* (in NT/LXX only Mt 27:57)

2 Structure of Words – Morphology

Part 2 deals with the second level of the structure of texts: the structure of words. It is of crucial importance to text interpretation. Most importantly this part presents us with the various inflectional patterns ("paradigms") enabling us to identify the specific word-forms of a text and to connect them with the intended functional category.

2.1 Word structure: basics

Word structure is studied under the heading of morphology. The focus of such studies can be either on the structure changes of existing words (inflection, i.e. declension, conjugation, and comparative forms; ↑25ff) or on the creation of new words on the basis of existing ones (word-formation; ↑357ff), e.g.:

inflection (example of verb inflection or conjugation):

σῴζω *to save* → σῴζω *I save* σῴζεις *you save*, σῴζει *he/she/it save* etc.

word-formation:

σῴζω *to save* → σωτήρ *saviour*, σωτηρία *salvation*, σωτήριος *saving*

When dealing with inflection and word-formation it is helpful to break down the words into their grammatical components. These will be the topic of the next paragraph (↑21), to be followed by paragraphs on the various word-classes (↑22).

Grammatical components of words (↑BR §297; CAGL: 104ff) 21

Some of the typical grammatical components are found in the following form:[1]

<table>
<tr><td>κρι-</td><td>-μάτ-</td><td>-ων</td></tr>
<tr><td>ROOT</td><td>ROOT AFFIX (here: suffix)</td><td>ENDING (here: case ending)</td></tr>
<tr><td colspan="2">STEM</td><td></td></tr>
<tr><td></td><td colspan="2">TERMINATION</td></tr>
</table>

The various types of grammatical word components explained:

1. **"Root"**: this is the core component of a word stripped of any suffixes or endings; 21a
it is the element that is common to all the members of a word family as far as their word-formation is concerned and whose essential meaning is typically shared by all of them, e.g.:

λύ-ω	*to loosen*	**λυ**-τρό-ομαι	*to redeem*
λύ-τρο-ν	*redemptive price*	ἀπο-**λύ**-τρω-σις	*redemption*

1 κριμάτων is the gen. pl. of κρίμα *judgement*. Note that the English noun form "judgements" can be analysed in a similar way: *judge-* (root), *-ment-* (suffix), *-s* (ending).

21b 2. **“Root affix”**: one or more elements (“affixes”) may be added to the root at the end (“suffix”), at the beginning (“prefix”) or inside (“infix”), e.g.:

λύ-**τρω-σι**-ς		*redemption*	(2 suffixes)
εὐ-αγγέλ-**ιο**-ν		*good news*	(1 prefix, 1 suffix)
ἔ-λεγ-**ες**		*you* (sg.) *said*	(1 prefix, 1 suffix)
μανθ-**άν**-ομεν	(root: μαθ-)	*we learn*	(1 infix, 1 suffix)

Note that affixes utilized in word-formation (↑357ff) are called “derivational affixes” (e.g. -σι[ς] and -ιο[ν] in the above examples are derivational suffixes).

21c 3. **“Stem”**: this is the base element shared by all forms of a particular word (note that the stem of a word may be identical with its root), e.g.:

σωτήρ	*saviour* (nom. sg.)	**σωτῆρ**-ι	*saviour* (dat. sg.)
σωτῆρ-ος	*saviour* (gen. sg.)	etc.	

On the basis of the stem-final sound the inflection of nouns, “declension”, can be divided into three classes:

- First declension: stems in -α (i.e. -ᾱ/-η or -ᾰ/-η; ↑25ff)
- Second declension: stems in -ο (↑28ff)
- Third declension: stems in consonants, -ι, -υ, and diphthongs (↑34ff)

Something similar is possible with certain parts of verb inflection, “conjugation”, notably in the case of the thematic conjugation (verbs in -ω):

- Vowel verbs: stems in vowels (↑76ff)
- Stop verbs: stems in stops, i.e. in labials, dentals or velars (↑90ff)
- Liquid verbs: stems in liquids (↑97ff)

21d 4. **“Ending”**: this is the closing component of a word; it expresses differences of case, person etc., e.g.:

λόγο-**ν**	*word* (acc. sg.)	λέγ-ο-**μεν**	*we say* (1 pl.; ↑66)

21e 5. **“Termination”**: this refers to the final component of the stem (here: a suffix and, in the verb form, a thematic vowel) plus the ending of the word, e.g.:

λόγ-**ον**	*word* (acc. sg.)	λέγ-**ομεν**	*we say* (1 pl.; ↑66)

Due to vowel contraction and other changes terminations and endings may be hard or impossible to distinguish, e.g. in the case of λόγ-**ῳ** *word* (dat. sg.). So “**ending**” is frequently used **more broadly** with reference to terminations: in the above examples the -**ῳ** would then be called “dat. sg. ending”, the **-ον** “acc. sg. ending” and the **-ομεν** “1 pl. (act. ind. pres.) ending”, λόγ- and λέγ- perhaps best “stem” (the bit unaffected by inflection, “Wortstock” in German).

21f 6. **“Compound”**: this is a word that is typically made up of two or more existing words (or roots, stems), also called “**complex word**” as opposed to “**simplex word**” (↑Lieber: 4), e.g.:

compounds/complex words:		simplex words:	
βαρύ-τιμος	*very precious*	τίμιος	*precious*
ἀπο-θήκη	*storehouse, barn*	θήκη	*sheath (of a sword)*
κατα-γελάω	*laugh at, ridicule*	γελάω	*to laugh*

Word-classes (↑Givón I: 49–103; Crystal and Bussmann under relevant head words) 22

In Ancient Greek there are three basic types of word-classes,[2] two types of word-classes that are inflected (primarily by declension or conjugation) and one type of word-classes that are uninflected. Apart from grammatical properties (regarding word form and syntactic behaviour) membership in a particular word-class in most cases is also connected with semantic or functional properties:

1. Word-classes inflected by **declension** ("declinable" ones; ↑23ff)

1.1 **Noun** (↑Lat. *nomen* "name"):[3] 22a

a) Grammatical properties:

- It expresses gender (in most cases): masculine, feminine or neuter.
- The inflected ("declined") forms (↑23ff) express number and case, with case signalling the syntactic role a particular form has when used in a text (↑146ff), e.g.:

		gender/number:	case:	typical syntactic role:
πούς	*foot*	masc./sg.	nom.	→ subject
χερσίν	*(to/for) hands*	fem./pl.	dat.	→ object
ὠτός	*(of an) ear*	ntr./sg.	gen.	→ attributive modifier

b) Semantic properties:

The use of nouns is determined by a great variety of meaning-related factors. Describing even the typical ones would go beyond the scope of a grammar.

For a very helpful treatment of lexical semantics (alas in German) ↑Leisi 1975: 27ff, or Leisi 1985: 47ff; the observations presented there, though primarily referring to German and English, are by no means restricted to these languages. Also (in English) ↑Givón I: 50ff, where in principle every existing language-type is taken into account. For a more recent general treatment of lexical semantics ↑Murphy.

The core semantic function of nouns is to denote a particular segment of the reality referred to by the communicator (↑312a). A number of semantic properties, however, need to be mentioned here because they may affect the grammatical (syntactic) behaviour of nouns to a considerable extent (e.g. regarding the use of the article [↑132–134] or concord [↑261–265]):

---

2 Traditionally referred to as "parts of speech".

3 Sometimes called "substantive" (↑Lat. *substantivum* "[a word] existing by itself").

• Concrete nouns refer to tangible entities and abstract nouns to intangible entities, e.g.:

concrete nouns:		abstract nouns:	
ἄρτος	*bread*	πίστις	*faith*
σῶμα	*body*	ἀγάπη	*love*

• The referents of nouns can be animate (especially persons, but also "higher" animals) or inanimate entities (including plants and "lower" animals), e.g.:

animate referents:		inanimate referents:	
ἄνθρωπος	*human being*	τράπεζα	*table*
βοῦς	*head of cattle, ox*	συκῆ	*fig tree*

• Proper names in principle refer to specific individual entities (as personal, place or other types of geographical names), whereas common nouns refer to classes and (in the singular) typically to a member of the class in question, e.g.:

proper names:		common nouns:	
(ὁ) Πέτρος	*Peter*	μαθητής	*pupil, disciple*
(ἡ) Κόρινθος	*Corinth*	πόλις	*city, town*

• Collectives (or "collective nouns") typically refer to a plurality of entities (in the singular), "individuatives", on the other hand, typically to individual entities, e.g.:

collectives:		"individuatives":	
ποίμνη	*flock*	πρόβατον	*(a) sheep*
στράτευμα	*army*	στρατιώτης	*soldier*

What was said above about collectives applies to the majority of cases (the so-called "group nouns"). Another (minor) type of collectives ("generic nouns" or "class nouns") can refer to either a plurality of entities (a "genus", a class; as it does in most cases) or sometimes to just one entity (one class member), e.g. σπέρμα in the sense of *offspring* may, depending on the situation, refer to one or more descendants (incidentally the English equivalent *offspring*, too). The "mass nouns" may be viewed as a further type of collectives, usually referring to an unbounded mass, e.g. γάλα *milk*, οἶνος *wine* etc. (↑Leisi 1975: 32ff; also Murphy: 154ff).

22b 1.2 **Adjective** (↑Lat. *adiectivum* "an added [word]"):

a) Grammatical properties (apart from declinability):

• It always accompanies a noun (as a "noun concomitant"[4]) or a noun substitute (i.e. a pronoun or another nominalized expression; ↑22d; 132d); its syntactic role is

---

4 In this grammar "**noun concomitant**" is used as an umbrella term for words that accompany nouns (typically) agreeing with them in gender, number, and case, such as adjectives, pronouns, participles and the article; their syntactic role may be either attributive (modifier) or non-attributive (e.g. complement or adjunct).

either attributive or non-attributive (mostly predicative; ↑137). In both cases the adjective agrees with it in gender, number, and case (↑263ff), e.g.:

attributive, concomitant of a noun:	predicative, concomitant of a noun substitute:
καλὸς στρατιώτης	τοῦτο **καλόν**
a good soldier (2Tm 2:3)	*This [is] good.* (1Tm 2:3)

• Gradable adjectives (↑b below) can inflect for comparison (↑50ff), e.g.:

basic form:	comparative form:	superlative form:
τίμιος	τιμιώτερος (LXX)	τιμιώτατος
precious	*more precious*	*most precious*

b) Semantic properties:

Adjectives typically denote properties of the entity referred to, in many cases gradable ones (↑a above). They also express various types of relations or class membership (and numeric adjectives have a quantifying function; ↑22e)[5], e.g.:

properties:		relations/class membership:	
μικρός	λευκός	κοσμικός	προφητικός
small	*white*	*worldly, earthly*	*prophetic*

1.3 **Pronoun** (↑Lat. *pro-nomen* "a [word] taking the place of a noun"): 22c

a) Grammatical properties (apart from declinability):

• The various types of pronouns (↑54ff) all express case and number, most of them also gender, personal and possessive pronouns person as well (↑54–55; 57), e.g.:

		case/number	gender:	person:
ταύταις	*(to/for) these*	dat./pl.	fem.	–
ὅν	*whom/that*	acc./sg.	masc.	–
σοί	*(to/for) you* (sg.)	dat./sg.	–	2 sg.
σεαυτήν	*yourself*	acc./sg.	fem.	2 sg.
ὑμέτεροι	*your* (pl.)	nom./pl.	masc.	2 pl.

• Syntactically (↑139–144) they serve either as substitutes (as pronouns in the real sense of the word) or as attributive or non-attributive concomitants of nouns, agreeing with these in case and number and, if applicable, in gender (↑262ff), e.g.:

		noun substitute/noun concomitant:	
εἶδον **αὐτόν**.	*He saw him.*	substitute (direct object)	(Re 1:17)
ὁ **αὐτὸς** κύριος	*the same Lord.*	attributive concomitant	(1Cor 12:5)
αὐτὸς ὁ κύριος	*the Lord himself*	non-attributive concomitant	(1Th 4:16)
τίνα ζητεῖς;	*Whom are you seeking?*	substitute (direct object)	(Jn 20:15)
τίς βασιλεὺς …;	*What king …?*	attributive concomitant	(Lk 14:31)

5 For further factors that may determine the use of adjectives ↑Leisi 1985: 53ff, and Givón I: 81ff, also Murphy: 222f.

b) Essentially pronouns have the following characteristic functions (for details ↑54ff; 139ff; 347–348):

Some pronouns point to an entity (a person or thing) mentioned elsewhere in the text or to one in the in the real world being referred to; others have an interrogative function, still others (inter alia) a quantifying one.

The following types may be distinguished (types 1–3 are used as noun substitutes only):

(1) A **personal pronoun** (↑54; 139) refers or points to a specific entity: to the speaker(s) (1 sg./pl.), to the addressee(s) (2 sg./pl.) or to an entity mentioned elsewhere in the text, either by an antecedent expression or by one that comes later (3 sg./pl.).
(2) A **reflexive pronoun** (↑55; 139) refers or points to such an entity and equates it with the subject entity.
(3) A **reciprocal pronoun** (↑56; 139) refers or points to more than one such entity indicating a mutual relationship.
(4) A **possessive pronoun** (↑57; 140) refers or points to such an entity as the possessor of another entity mentioned in the text.
(5) A **demonstrative pronoun** (↑58; 61b; 141) points to an entity identified earlier or later in the text or to one in the real world referred to (present in the immediate situation).
(6) A **relative pronoun** (↑59; 61b; 142) typically refers back to an entity mentioned earlier in the text and at the same time serves as a sentence constituent (subject, object etc.) of the relative clause it introduces.
(7) An **interrogative pronoun** (↑60; 61b; 143) introduces an interrogative clause and is used to ask questions about the identity, dimension, quantity or quality of entities.
(8) An **indefinite pronoun** (↑60; 61b; 144) characterizes entities as unspecified regarding their identity, dimension, quantity or quality.

Examples:

ἐγώ εἰμι Ἰησοῦς **ὃν σὺ** διώκεις.	*I am Jesus whom you are persecuting.* (Ac 9:5)

These pronouns are all noun substitutes: the personal pronouns ἐγώ and σύ point to the speaker and the addressee; the relative pronoun ὅν refers back to Ἰησοῦς mentioned earlier and serves as the direct object of the relative clause it introduces.

πλὴν **τοῦτο** γινώσκετε ὅτι ἤγγικεν ἡ βασιλεία τοῦ θεοῦ.	*Yet you must know this: The kingdom of God is near.* (Lk 10:11)

The demonstrative pronoun τοῦτο here serves as a noun substitute: it points to something identified later in the text, i.e. the “situation” mentioned in the ὅτι-clause.

πόσους ἄρτους ἔχετε;	*How many loaves do you have?* (Mt 15:34)

The interrogative pronoun πόσους introduces an interrogative clause and (here as a noun concomitant) asks about the quantity of the entities referred to.

εἰς νῆσον δέ **τινα** δεῖ ἡμᾶς ἐκπεσεῖν.	*But we must run aground on some island.* (Ac 27:26)

The indefinite pronoun τινά characterizes (here as a concomitant of the noun form νῆσον) the entity referred to as unspecified regarding its identity.

1.4 **Article** (↑ Lat. *articulus* "joint"):[6] 22d

As far as its grammatical properties and its semantic-functional properties (as well as its historical background) are concerned the article is closely related to the pronouns:

a) It is inflected (↑24) for gender, number, and case. For the most part it serves as an attributive concomitant of a noun fully agreeing with it in gender, number, and case (↑263); but to some extent it also functions as a noun substitute (↑132d); e.g.:

		noun substitute/noun concomitant:	
τῷ κυρίῳ	*(in) the Lord*	concomitant of κυρίῳ	(Ac 5:14)
ταῖς ἐκκλησίαις	*(to) the churches*	concomitant of ἐκκλησίαις	(Ga 1:22)
ἡ δὲ εἶπεν …	*But she said …*	substitute	(Mt 15:27)

b) As a noun concomitant it marks the entity referred to by the noun (phrase) as sufficiently identified or "determined" ([intra]textually or extratextually; for further details ↑132–136; 347–348), e.g.:

ἐξέδετο αὐτὸν γεωργοῖς … καὶ ἀπέστειλεν πρὸς **τοὺς** γεωργοὺς τῷ καιρῷ δοῦλον ἵνα … *He leased it to tenants … At the proper time he sent a servant to the tenants to …* (Mk 12:1f)

(τοὺς) γεωργούς is "determined" by the antecedent γεωργοῖς (textually; anaphoric article).

ἡ δὲ περιοχὴ τῆς γραφῆς ἣν ἀνεγίνωσκεν … *Now the passage of the Scripture that he was reading …* (Ac 8:32)

(ἡ) περιοχή is "determined" by the relative clause ἥν … that functions as its attributive modifier (textually; cataphoric article).

ὁ κύριος μετὰ σοῦ. *The Lord is with you.* (Lk 1:28)

(ὁ) κύριος is "determined" by the presupposed world knowledge (extra-textually).

1.5 **Numeral** (↑ Lat. *numerale*): 22e

The words that the term "numeral" stands for, grammatically speaking, belong to a variety of different word-classes. For semantic reasons, however, they are subsumed under one category: they all express a precise number (↑62–63; 145).[7]

Cardinal and ordinal numerals may be classified as adjectives (they agree with these as far as their syntactic use is concerned). But only the ordinal numerals are fully inflected, as are a few cardinal ones ("one" to "four" and those designating the hundreds and the thousands). Numerals answering the question ποσάκις; *how often?* may be called "(multiplicative) adverbs".[8] E.g.:

---

6 As there is no indefinite article in Ancient Greek the term "article" implies definiteness.

7 Words referring to an indefinite number like *some*, *numerous* etc. are not included here.

8 So e.g. Fortson 2010: 147.

		numeral type; inflected/not inflected:	
ἄνδρες **τέσσαρες**	*four men*	cardinal; inflected	(Ac 21:23)
πέντε ἄνδρας	*five men*	cardinal; not inflected	(↑Jn 4:18)
ὥρα **τρίτη**	*(the) third hour*	ordinal; inflected	(Mk 15:25)
τρίς	*three times*	adverb; not inflected	(Mt 26:34)

Various adjectives and nouns are part of the numeral category, too, e.g.:

		numeral type	
διπλῆς τιμῆς	*(of) double honour*	adjective	(1Tm 5:17)
πόσαι **μυριάδες**	*how many thousands*	noun	(Ac 21:20)

22f 2. Word-class inflected by conjugation: the **verb** (↑Lat. *verbum* "word"):

a) Grammatical properties:

• Finite verb forms are inflected/conjugated for voice, "tense"/aspect, mood, number and person, the non-finite ones for voice and "tense"/aspect only (participles are also fully declinable, infinitives only when used in combination with the article; ↑64–125; 188–240), e.g. the following forms of the verb πιστεύω *to believe*:

Note that the basic (dictionary or "lexical") form of Ancient Greek verbs is typically cited in the 1 sg. pres. ind. act. So, though the literal meaning of πιστεύω would be *I believe*, functionally, however, it corresponds to English *to believe*.

		parsing	
πιστεύ**εις**	*you* (sg.) *believe*	2 sg. pres. ind. act.	(Ac 26:27)
ἐπιστεύ**θη**	*it was believed*	3 sg. aor. ind. pass.	(1Tm 3:16)
πίστευ**σον**	*believe!* (sg.)	2 sg. aor. imp. act.	(Lk 8:50)
πιστεύ**οντες**	*believing ones*	ptc. pres. act., nom. m. pl.	(Ac 5:14)
πιστεῦ**σαι**	*(to) believe*	inf. aor. act.	(He 11:6)

• Verb forms are typically in the predicator role of a sentence (or clause). In most cases they represent the core of the information expressed by it, of its "proposition" (used in communication to refer to a state of affairs or "situation"[9] in the real world, in the form of a statement, directive or question). As each verb (or each of its uses) is connected with a particular sentence pattern (due to its valency), verb forms largely determine the way sentences are structured (↑254c; 256; 258d). E.g.:

ὁ Χριστὸς (S) **ἠγάπησεν** (P) ἡμᾶς (Od). *Christ loved us.* (Eph 5:2)

The verb form ἠγάπησεν is the predicator, the core of the proposition. *ὁ Χριστὸς ἡμᾶς would be a mere word chain, but not a sentence; it would not express any information that could refer to a "situation". The verb ἀγαπάω *to love* is connected with the sentence pattern S+P+Od (↑258d,2) which explains the structure of the above sentence.

9 "State of affairs", usually called "situation" in this grammar, is a term for all that is referred to by a verb and its sentence pattern in a particular context. This applies to verbs of any kind, to "dynamic" ones (denoting events, processes, or actions) as well as to "static" ones (denoting states).

b) Semantic properties:

The use of verbs (like the use of nouns) is determined by a great variety of meaning-related factors.[10] The core semantic function of verbs in most cases is to denote different types of change (events, processes, especially actions), less frequently states (↑312a).[11] E.g.:

events:	processes:	actions:	states:
πίπτω *to fall*	αὐξάνω *to grow*	ὑπάγω *to go*	ὑγιαίνω *to be well*

Certain groups of verbs with related meanings typically occur in specific syntactic constructions. So (in several ways agreeing with English usage) verbs of perception are typically linked to the "accusative with participle" (Lat. "accusativus cum participio": "ACP"; ↑233b) and verbs of volition and some others to the "accusative with infinitive" (Lat. "accusativus cum infinitivo": "ACI"; ↑218). ↑also Subject Index "verbs".

3. **Uninflected word-classes** 22g

Note that some use "particles" (↑Lat. *particula* "little part" [of speech]) as an umbrella term for all of the uninflected word-classes. In this grammar, however, it designates (as is more common) just one of these (↑22k), i.e. the one comprising different types of uninflected words with little or no lexical meaning, typically used to modify in various ways the communicative force of the text in which they occur.

3.1 **Adverb** (↑Lat. *ad-verbium* "[a word] added to the verb"; ↑53; 241/242; 320ff): 22h

Grammatically adverbs are a rather heterogeneous group of words in various ways overlapping with other word-classes.

Many adverbs go back to the neuter form of adjectives (↑157; 365) or are derived from members of other word-classes via addition of derivational suffixes such as -ως, -ω, -θεν etc. (↑53; 366). There are also "adverbs" that at the same time serve as prepositions (↑185a) or conjunctions (e.g. ↑252.29). Though in principle adverbs are not inflectable many of them in fact have comparative and superlative forms; these, however, are derived from adjective forms (↑53). There are also correlative groups of adverbs closely similar to the system of correlative pronouns with interrogatives, indefinites, demonstratives and relatives being interrelated.

Semantically or functionally, however, adverbs clearly constitute one category: in most cases they modify verb meanings informing us about the circumstances of the events, processes, actions or states referred to, i.e. they answer questions such as Where?, When?, How?, Why? etc. (↑258c; 259b). Apart from this they may also modify adjectives, other adverbs, nouns, quite often even whole sentences or text passages. E.g.:

ὀρθῶς (ModA) ἔκρινας. *You have judged correctly.* (Lk 7:43)

The adverb ὀρθῶς modifies the verb meaning of ἔκρινας in terms of a manner adjunct.

---

10 On these ↑Leisi 1985: 60ff, and Givón I: 69ff, also Murphy: 201ff.

11 Any of these kinds of verb meaning is often simply called "action" for short in this grammar.

ἦν δὲ **ἐγγὺς** (TempC) τὸ πάσχα. *The Passover was near.* (Jn 6:4)
The adverb ἐγγύς modifies the meaning of ἦν/τὸ πάσχα in terms of a temporal complement.

ὄντως (Attr) ἐλεύθεροι ἔσεσθε. *You will be truly free.* (Jn 8:36)
The adverb ὄντως modifies the adjective ἐλεύθεροι in terms of an "attributive modifier".

ἀληθῶς (EvalA) ἐξ αὐτῶν εἶ. *Surely you are one of them.* (Mk 14:70)
The adverb ἀληθῶς modifies the sentence as a whole in terms of an evaluative adjunct.

22i 3.2 **Preposition** (↑Lat. *praeponĕre* "to place before [something]"; ↑184–187):

a) Prepositions are uninflected words (most of them being originally adverbs) that (1) in principle stand almost always in front of a noun phrase[12] and (2) "govern" its case. A number of prepositions are used with more than one case, though usually connected with a change of meaning (↑184), e.g.:

with one case only (here: gen.):	with two different cases (here: gen./acc.):
ἐκ τῆς οἰκί**ας** *out of the house* (Mt 24:17)	**μετὰ σοῦ**/… **σέ** *with you/after you* (Ac 27:24; Ru 4:4 LXX)

b) Syntactically preposition phrases generally speaking have very similar functions to those of noun phrases in the oblique cases[13] without preposition:[14] informing us about the place, the time or other details (such as manner, cause, purpose etc.) of a situation or entity they may be used as objects (Op), adjuncts or complements or (less frequently) as attributive modifiers (↑183c), e.g.:

ἐκ τοῦ κόσμου (Op) ἐξελθεῖν *to leave the world* (1Cor 5:10)

ἐκ τοῦ πλοίου (LocA) ἐδίδασκεν … *He taught … from the boat.* (Lk 5:3)

τὴν ἀνάστασιν τὴν **ἐκ νεκρῶν** (Attr) *the resurrection of the dead* (Ac 4:2)

22j 3.3 **Conjunction** (↑Lat. *coniūnctio* "linking"; ↑250–251; 271ff; 318):

Conjunctions are uninflected words that link words, phrases or sentences. Semantically there are some similarities with prepositions; unlike these, however, they never govern a particular case (also ↑250b on ways they differ from adverbs). E.g.:

καὶ πολλοὶ ἐπίστευσαν εἰς αὐτὸν ἐκεῖ. *And many believed in him there.* (Jn 10:42)
The conjunction καί links this sentence to the previous one; it does not govern any case, unlike the preposition εἰς which is followed by the accusative (here: αὐτόν).

ἦσαν Μωϋσῆς **καὶ** Ἠλίας. *They were Moses and Elijah.* (Lk 9:30)
The conjunction καί here links two words (or noun phrases), two parts of a sentence/clause constituent (a composite subject).

---

12 I.e. a phrase whose head is a noun, a nominalized expression or a noun substitute. More rarely prepositions stand in front of adverbs, e.g. ἀπὸ μακρόθεν *from afar* (Mk 5:6).

13 The umbrella term for genitive, dative and accusative (↑23c).

14 Quite often preposition phrases and prepositionless case phrases are in competition with each other (↑187).

Conjunctions that link sentences/clauses may be divided into two classes: (1) coordinating conjunctions,[15] i.e. conjunctions that link main sentences/clauses, as above in the case of Jn 10:42, and (2) subordinating conjunctions, i.e. conjunctions that introduce subordinate clauses. Such subordinate clauses ("conjunctional clauses"; ↑271ff) in most cases serve as the sentence constituent of a (superordinate) sentence, frequently as an adverbial clause, e.g.:

Οὐκ οἴδατε **ὅτι** ναὸς θεοῦ ἐστε;	*Do you not know that you are God's temple.* (1Cor 3:16)

The subordinating conjunction ὅτι introduces a subordinate clause (here: an object clause; ↑271).

γρηγορεῖτε καὶ προσεύχεσθε, **ἵνα** μὴ ἔλθητε εἰς πειρασμόν·	*Watch and pray so that you will not enter into temptation.* (Mk 14:38)

The subordinating conjunction ἵνα introduces a subordinate clause (here: an adverbial clause, more specifically a purpose clause; ↑278).

3.4 **Particles** (↑252; on this term↑22g) 22k

Particles are uninflected words that cover a variety of functions. Inter alia there are "scalar" particles (indicating the intensity e.g. of a property), "focus" particles (highlighting the constituent with the greatest communicative weight), "negative" particles, "evaluative" particles (hinting at the attitude of the speaker/writer), "conversation" particles (controlling the flow of dialogues), and "interjections" (expressing emotions), e.g.:

πλούσιος **σφόδρα** (scalar particle)	*very rich* (Lk 18:23)
μόνον (focus particle) πίστευσον.	*Only believe.* (Lk 8:50)
σὺ Ῥωμαῖος εἶ; … **ναί** (conversation particle)	*Are you a Roman citizen? … Yes!* (Ac 22:27)
Ὦ (interjection) βάθος πλούτου …·	*Oh, the depth of the riches …* (Ro 11:33)

A **short overview** of the subject matter of the remainder of this grammar:

The first major topic of Part 2 on **morphology** will be the inflection of nouns and adjectives (including participles), i.e. declension (↑23–49). Next we will deal with the comparative forms of the adjective (↑50–52) and with the adverb and its comparative forms (↑53). The section on declension will be concluded by a treatment of pronouns (↑54–61) and numerals (↑62–63).
The basic concepts connected with declension including the paradigm of the article are introduced in the initial paragraphs devoted to the declension of nouns and adjectives (↑23–24). The largest (and concluding) chapter of Part 2 on morphology deals with verb inflection, i.e. conjugation (↑64–125).

15 Note that a number of "coordinating conjunctions" such as γάρ *for* and οὖν/ἄρα *then/accordingly* (↑251d/251e) are better classified as "particles" (↑22g), inter alia because they are not prepositives (as would be typical of conjunctions), but postpositives (↑128b section c; 128c).

Part 3 entitled **syntax** will be on the functions which inflected and uninflected word-classes may fulfil as part of a sentence (↑126–252).

The functions various word-classes or word-forms may assume above the level of the sentence will be shown in Part 4 on **textgrammar** (↑318ff).

Ways in which new words were made on the basis of existing ones in Ancient Greek will be the topic of the section on **word-formation** in a second appendix (↑357ff).

2.2 Declension of nouns and adjectives

On nouns and adjectives as word-classes ↑22a and 22b.

23 Declension basics (↑BR §29; Langslow: 393–464)

I. Declension involves three semantic or functional categories: gender, number, and case:

23a 1. There are three grammatical **genders** (on gender concord ↑263):

gender:	typically refers to:
MASCULINE	male beings (human or non-human) as well as inanimate entities such as (especially) rivers or streams, winds, months, e.g. ὁ Ἰορδάνης *the Jordan*, ὁ Κεδρών *the Kidron*, ὁ νότος *the south wind*, ὁ Ξανθικός *[the month of] Xanthikos* (↑2Macc 11:30), but also to abstract concepts, e.g. ὁ ἁγιασμός *sanctification*
FEMININE	female beings (human or non-human) as well as inanimate entities such as (especially) fruit-trees, countries, islands, cities, e.g. ἡ συκῆ *the fig-tree*, ἡ Συρία *Syria*, ἡ Κύπρος *Cyprus*, ἡ Ἀντιόχεια *Antioch*, but also to abstract concepts, e.g. ἡ πίστις *faith*
NEUTER	phenomena without natural gender, fairly frequently also to male or female beings in diminutives (↑361b), e.g. τὸ θυγάτριον *the little daughter*, but also to abstract concepts, e.g. τὸ θέλημα *what is willed* (also ↑132a)

There are also nouns that may refer to either male or female beings, sometimes called by the Latin term "nomina communia" (sg.: "nomen commune"); the intended gender is indicated solely by noun concomitants such as the article; in the rare case of "nomina mobilia" (sg.: "nomen mobile") both uses are attested (↑361a), e.g.:

nomen commune:	**ὁ** παῖς	*the boy*	**ἡ** παῖς	*the girl*
nomen mobile:	**ὁ** θεός	*the god, God*	**ἡ** θεός/θεά	*the goddess*

2. In KG including NT Greek two grammatical **numbers** are in use (on number agreement ↑262–264): 23b

number:	typically refers to:
SINGULAR	one discrete entity, but collectives (typically) to a plurality of entities, e. g. ποίμνη *a flock* (for details ↑22a; 265; also 129)
PLURAL	more than one entity, in rare cases apparently to a single entity, e. g. τὰ γενέσια *the birthday* (also ↑129)

In Classical Greek there is a further grammatical number:

DUAL	refers to two entities, e. g. δύο νεανίσκ**ω** *two young men* (Xenophon, Anabasis 4.3.10), **τὼ** πόλ**εε** τούτ**ω** *these two cities* (Isocrates 12.156)

↑also Horrocks: 73; 138; BR §74. BDF §2. On the dual number of the verb ↑64d.

3. There are five **cases** in Ancient Greek: 23c

case:	typical roles: (also ↑146):	typical questions answered by case form:	examples of some possible correspondences in English:
NOMINATIVE (↑147)	subject	Who …?	***He*** *left.*
GENITIVE (↑158ff)	attributive modifier object	Whose …? Of what …?	***Bill's*** *car/the car* ***of Bill*** *They approve* ***of my idea.***
DATIVE (↑173ff)	indirect object adjunct of: • interest • instrument • time	To whom …? For whom …? By what means …? When …?	*We gave it* ***to him.*** *They did it* ***for him!*** *He fastened it* ***with a nail.*** *He came* ***in the morning.***
ACCUSATIVE (↑149ff)	direct object	Whom/What …?	*I saw* ***him/it.***
VOCATIVE (↑148)	addressing hearer		*Do it,* ***John!***

Genitive, dative and accusative are called "**oblique cases**", as opposed to the nominative (including the vocative, by many not counted separately) named "**casus rectus**".

Note that frequently a case form is embedded in a **preposition phrase**. The meaning or function of the preposition will then always have priority over the meaning or function of the case involved.

When dealing with case forms the following points should be kept in mind:

- vocative: in the pl. always = nom., in the sg. often, too
- neuter: nom. = acc. = voc.
- neuter pl.: nom./acc./voc. always in -ᾰ (but σ-stems in -η [contracted]; ↑39)

II. Three **classes of declension** may be distinguished (↑21c): 23d

- First declension: stems in -α/-η (↑25ff)
- Second declension: stems in -ο (↑28ff)
- Third declension (↑32ff)

23e III. **Accentuation** of declension forms:

1. The accent remains on the tone syllable of the nom. sg. as long as the accentuation rules (↑5b–5d) will allow; -αι and -οι (though diphthongs) count as short (↑5).

There are a number of exceptions, inter alia (↑25d [and 46/48], 26, and 33) the following vocatives (in several cases the accent of vocatives is retracted; ↑Chantraine §10):

δέσποτα	*master* (↑26b)	πάτερ etc.	*father* (↑38)
σῶτερ	*saviour* (↑37)	γύναι	*woman* (↑42a)

2. Long accented genitive and dative endings take the circumflex (e.g. ↑24).

24 Article (↑BR §30; Langslow: 555–588)

There is only a definite article in Ancient Greek (on the word-class ↑22d); indefiniteness is inferable from the context. ἡ ἡμέρα e.g. would (usually) correspond to our *the day* and ἡμέρα to either *a day* or *day* (for details ↑130ff; 348a).

		masc.	fem.	ntr.	
sg.	nom.	ὁ	ἡ	τό	*the*
	gen.	τοῦ	τῆς	τοῦ	*of the*
	dat.	τῷ	τῇ	τῷ	*to/for the*
	acc.	τόν	τήν	τό	*the*
pl.	nom.	οἱ	αἱ	τᾰ́	*the*
	gen.	τῶν	τῶν	τῶν	*of the*
	dat.	τοῖς	ταῖς	τοῖς	*to/for the*
	acc.	τούς	τᾱ́ς	τᾰ́	*the*

2.2.1 Declension of nouns

2.2.1.1 First declension: stems in -α/-η

Basically, these stems end in -ᾱ or -ᾰ; but the sg. frequently has -η instead of -α (↑11g). First declension nouns can be feminine (↑25) or masculine (↑26).
Synopsis of **case endings** (in the nom./gen. sg. the masculine ones are bracketed):

	nom.	gen.	dat.	acc.	voc.	stem-final sound (on i̯ ↑12c)	after ε ι ρ?	tables with examples:
sg.	-η (-ης)	-ης (-ου)	-ῃ	-ην	-η (-η/-ᾰ)	ᾱ	no	↑25c (26a/26c)
	-α (-ᾱς)	-ᾱς (-ου)	-ᾳ	-αν	-α (-ᾱ)	ᾱ/(i̯)ᾰ (ᾱ)	yes	↑25a (26a/26c)
	-ᾰ	-ης	-ῃ	-ᾰν	-ᾰ	(i̯)ᾰ	no	↑25b
pl.	-αι (short; ↑23e)	-ῶν (always accented! <-άων [↑11d])	-αις	-ᾱς	-αι			↑25–26

Also ↑44; 46–49 for the declension of adjectives and participles.

First declension: feminine nouns (↑BR §31; 32; BDF §43; MH: 117f) 25

1. Stems in -α throughout the singular (after ε ι ρ) 25a

a) -ᾱ

b) -ᾰ in the nom./acc. sg.

stem →	ἡμέρα *the day* ἡμερᾱ-	ἐκκλησία *assembly* ἐκκλησιᾱ-	γενεά *generation* γενεᾱ-	ἐνέργεια *power* ἐνεργειᾰ-
sg. n./v.	ἡ ἡμέρ-α	ἐκκλησί-α	γενε-ά	ἐνέργει-ᾰ
g.	τῆς ἡμέρ-ας	ἐκκλησί-ας	γενε-ᾶς	ἐνεργεί-ᾱς
d.	τῇ ἡμέρ-ᾳ	ἐκκλησί-ᾳ	γενε-ᾷ	ἐνεργεί-ᾱͅ
a.	τὴν ἡμέρ-αν	ἐκκλησί-αν	γενε-άν	ἐνέργει-ᾰν
pl. n./v.	αἱ ἡμέρ-αι	ἐκκλησί-αι	γενε-αί	ἐνέργει-αι
g.	τῶν ἡμερ-ῶν	ἐκκλησι-ῶν	γενε-ῶν	ἐνεργει-ῶν
d.	ταῖς ἡμέρ-αις	ἐκκλησί-αις	γενε-αῖς	ἐνεργεί-αις
a.	τὰς ἡμέρ-ᾱς	ἐκκλησί-ᾱς	γενε-ᾱ́ς	ἐνεργεί-ᾱς

2. Stems in -α after consonants other than ρ: nom./acc. sg.: -ᾰ; gen./dat. sg.: -η replacing -α 25b

stem →	25b θάλασσα *the sea* θαλασσᾰ-	γλῶσσα *tongue* γλωσσᾰ-
sg. n./v.	ἡ θάλασσ-ᾰ	γλῶσσ-ᾰ
g.	τῆς θαλάσσ-ης	γλώσσ-ης
d.	τῇ θαλάσσ-ῃ	γλώσσ-ῃ
a.	τὴν θάλασσ-ᾰν	γλῶσσ-ᾰν
pl. n./v.	αἱ θάλασσ-αι	γλῶσσ-αι
g.	τῶν θαλασσ-ῶν	γλωσσ-ῶν
d.	ταῖς θαλάσσ-αις	γλώσσ-αις
a.	τὰς θαλάσσ-ᾱς	γλώσσ-ᾱς

3. Stems in -η (< ᾱ) throughout the sg. (↑11g) 25c

25c ἐπιστολή *letter* (sent) ἐπιστολᾱ-	νίκη *victory* νῑκᾱ-
ἐπιστολ-ή	νίκ-η
ἐπιστολ-ῆς	νίκ-ης
ἐπιστολ-ῇ	νίκ-ῃ
ἐπιστολ-ήν	νίκ-ην
ἐπιστολ-αί	νῖκ-αι
ἐπιστολ-ῶν	νικ-ῶν
ἐπιστολ-αῖς	νίκ-αις
ἐπιστολ-ᾱ́ς	νίκ-ᾱς

Notes on the above paradigms:

1. The gen. pl. ending of all first declension nouns (and many fem. participles; ↑48b–48e) is always -ῶν (<-άων; ↑11d); apart from this, gen. and dat. endings take the circumflex only if they are accented (↑23e). 25d

2. In the first declension the acc. pl. ending is always long: -ᾱς (<-ανς; ↑10a). 25e

25f 3. Regarding -α and -η in the sg.:

a) The -α after ε, ι or ρ is long (↑11g), unless ruled out by the accent (↑5b), e.g.:

ἁμαρτίᾱ *sin* σκιᾰ́ *shadow* ἀλή**θειᾰ** *truth*

b) The -α after consonants other than ρ is always unaccented and short, e.g.:

δόξ**ᾰ** *glory* μέριμν**ᾰ** *anxiety* ῥίζ**ᾰ** *root*

c) A long ("pure") -ᾱ remains unchanged in the sg. A short -ᾰ after ε, ι or ρ is replaced by a long -ᾱ in the gen. and dat. sg., after other sounds by an -η (ε/ι/ρ rule; ↑11g).

In KG (and NT Greek) even after the -ρ the short -ᾰ is sometimes replaced by an -η in the gen. and dat. sg. (in agreement with sound changes in the Ionic dialect; also ↑48e), e.g.:

μάχαι**ρ-ᾰ**, μαχαί**ρ-η**-ς, μαχαί**ρ-ῃ**, μάχαι**ρ-ᾰ**-ν etc. *sword* (↑BDF §43.1)

d) Nouns in -η in the nom. sg. keep the -η throughout the sg.

25g 4. Stems in -ᾰ go back to stems in -ι̯ᾰ (↑12c).

26 First declension: masculine nouns (↑BR §33; BDF §43; MH: 119)

Paradigms of nouns in -ᾱς (↑26a) and -ης/-της (↑26b)

1. Masculine nouns in -ᾱς — 2. Masculine nouns in -ης/-της(1)

26a
26b

stem →	26a *the* ὁ νεανίας *young man* νεανιᾱ-	26b ὁ προφήτης *prophet* προφητᾱ-	ὁ τελώνης *tax collector* τελωνᾱ-
sg. n.	ὁ νεανί-α-ς	προφήτ-η-ς	τελών-η-ς
g.	τοῦ νεανί-ου	προφήτ-ου	τελών-ου
d.	τῷ νεανί-ᾳ	προφήτ-ῃ	τελών-ῃ
a.	τὸν νεανί-α-ν	προφήτ-η-ν	τελών-η-ν
v.(2)	νεανί-ᾱ	προφῆτ-ᾰ	τελών-η
pl. n./v.	οἱ νεανί-αι	προφῆτ-αι	τελῶν-αι
g.	τῶν νεανι-ῶν(3)	προφητ-ῶν(3)	τελων-ῶν(3)
d.	τοῖς νεανί-αις	προφήτ-αις	τελών-αις
a.	τοὺς νεανί-ᾱς	προφήτ-ᾱς	τελών-ᾱς

(1) On typical meanings (inter alia denoting an occupation or position) ↑361c; 362a; 368c.

(2) The voc. sg. is usually (1) = nom. without the final ς, (2) in the case of nouns in -της and nouns denoting nationality in -ης, however, -ᾰ.

In the case of ὁ δεσπ**ό**της *the master* the accent is retracted: δέσποτᾰ *(O) master.* ↑23e. For third declension nouns in -ης/-της ↑35e, and for personal names in -ης (σ-stems) ↑45b.

(3) Always -ῶν (↑25d).

3. Personal names in -ᾶς and -ης 26c

	Ἠλίας *Elijah*	Ἰωάννης *John*
n.	Ἠλί-α-ς	Ἰωάνν-η-ς
g.	Ἠλί-ου	Ἰωάνν-ου
d.	Ἠλί-ᾳ	Ἰωάνν-ῃ
a.	Ἠλί-α-ν	Ἰωάνν-η-ν
v.	Ἠλί-α	Ἰωάνν-η

There are also (Greek and non-Greek) personal names in -ᾶς with a gen. in -ᾶ and a dat. in -ᾳ (labelled "Doric" because in the Doric dialect [↑p.5] the -α is not replaced by -η; ↑11g), e.g. Λουκᾶς *Luke,* Κηφᾶς *Cephas,* Βαρναβᾶς *Barnabas.* A few personal names with a different stem-final vowel are inflected analogically, e.g. Ἰησοῦς *Jesus/Joshua* and Λευίς *Levi.* For mainly class. names in -ης (σ-stems) ↑45b; for details on the NT names ↑BDF §55; MH: 143ff; BDAG s.vv.: 26d

	"Doric" names:			analogical:			
n.		Λουκᾶς	Κηφᾶς		Ἰησοῦς		Λευίς (or Λευί)
g.		Λουκᾶ	Κηφᾶ		Ἰησοῦ	(LXX:	Λευί
d.		Λουκᾷ	Κηφᾷ		Ἰησοῦ	Ἰησοῖ)	*Λευί
a.		Λουκᾶν	Κηφᾶν		Ἰησοῦν		Λευίν
v.		Λουκᾶ	*Κηφᾶ		Ἰησοῦ		*Λευί

First declension: contracted nouns (↑BR §34; BDF §45; MH: 119f) 27

There are also a number of contracted nouns: the stem-final -ᾱ and the preceding vowel (ε or α) contract (↑11; here all the endings have the circumflex):

stem →	ἡ γῆ *the earth* γεᾱ- > γη-	ἡ συκῆ *the fig tree* συκεᾱ- > συκη-		ἡ μνᾶ *the mina* (monetary unit) μναᾱ- > μνᾱ-	
n./v.	ἡ γῆ	ἡ συκῆ	αἱ συκαῖ	ἡ μνᾶ	αἱ μναῖ
g.	τῆς γῆς	τῆς συκῆς	τῶν συκῶν	τῆς μνᾶς	τῶν μνῶν
d.	τῇ γῇ	τῇ συκῇ	ταῖς συκαῖς	τῇ μνᾷ	ταῖς μναῖς
a.	τὴν γῆν	τὴν συκῆν	τὰς συκᾶς	τὴν μνᾶν	τὰς μνᾶς

2.2.1.2 Second declension: stems in -o

Here all stems end in -ο. Most of these words are either masculine (-ος) or neuter (-ον; in the case of the article [↑24] and the pronouns [↑54–61], however, -ο). A number of nouns in -ος are feminine. Certain adjectives (mainly compounds; ↑44d) in -ος are combined with both masculine and feminine nouns (referred to as "two-termination adjectives", i.e. -ος m./f. and -ον ntr.). ↑44; 47–49 for the paradigms of adjectives and participles.

Synopsis of **case endings**:

		nom.	gen.	dat.	acc.	voc.	examples:
sg.	masc./(fem.) ntr.	-ος -ον (-ο)	-ου -ου	-ῳ -ῳ	-ον -ον (-ο)	-ε -ον (-ο)	↑28/30 ↑29 (24/54ff)
pl.	masc./(fem.) ntr.	-οι (short; ↑23e) -ᾰ	-ων -ων	-οις -οις	-ους -ᾰ	-οι -ᾰ	↑28/30 ↑29

28 Second declension: masculine nouns (↑BR §36; MH: 120ff)

	ὁ λόγος *the word* λογο-	ὁ ἀγρός *field* ἀγρο-	ὁ ἄνθρωπος *human being* ἀνθρωπο-	ὁ οἶκος *house* οἰκο-
stem →				
sg. n.	ὁ λόγ-ο-ς	ἀγρ-ό-ς	ἄνθρωπ-ο-ς	οἶκ-ο-ς
g.	τοῦ λόγ-ου	ἀγρ-οῦ	ἀνθρώπ-ου	οἴκ-ου
d.	τῷ λόγ-ῳ	ἀγρ-ῷ	ἀνθρώπ-ῳ	οἴκ-ῳ
a.	τὸν λόγ-ο-ν	ἀγρ-ό-ν	ἄνθρωπ-ο-ν	οἶκ-ο-ν
v.	ὦ λόγ-ε		ἄνθρωπ-ε	οἶκ-ε
pl. n./v.	οἱ λόγ-οι	ἀγρ-οί	ἄνθρωπ-οι	οἶκ-οι
g.	τῶν λόγ-ων	ἀγρ-ῶν	ἀνθρώπ-ων	οἴκ-ων
d.	τοῖς λόγ-οις	ἀγρ-οῖς	ἀνθρώπ-οις	οἴκ-οις
a.	τοὺς λόγ-ους(1)	ἀγρ-ούς(1)	ἀνθρώπ-ους(1)	οἴκ-ους(1)

(1) ↑10a.

See also notes after 29–30.

Second declension: feminine and neuter nouns (↑BR §36; MH: 120ff)

	29 ἡ ἄμπελος *the vine* ἀμπελο-	30 τὸ τέκνον *the child* τεκνο-	τὸ πλοῖον *ship* πλοιο-	τὸ τάλαντον *talent* ταλαντο-
stem →				
sg. n.	ἡ ἄμπελ-ο-ς	τὸ τέκν-ο-ν	πλοῖ-ο-ν	τάλαντ-ο-ν
g.	τῆς ἀμπέλ-ου	τοῦ τέκν-ου	πλοί-ου	ταλάντ-ου
d.	τῇ ἀμπέλ-ῳ	τῷ τέκν-ῳ	πλοί-ῳ	ταλάντ-ῳ
a.	τὴν ἄμπελ-ο-ν	τὸ τέκν-ο-ν	πλοῖ-ο-ν	τάλαντ-ο-ν
v.	ὦ ἄμπελ-ε	ὦ τέκν-ο-ν		
pl. n./v.	αἱ ἄμπελ-οι	τᾰ̀ τέκν-ᾰ	πλοῖ-ᾰ	τάλαντ-ᾰ
g.	τῶν ἀμπέλ-ων	τῶν τέκν-ων	πλοί-ων	ταλάντ-ων
d.	ταῖς ἀμπέλ-οις	τοῖς τέκν-οις	πλοί-οις	ταλάντ-οις
a.	τᾱ̀ς ἀμπέλ-ους (↑10a)	τᾰ̀ τέκν-ᾰ	πλοῖ-ᾰ	τάλαντ-ᾰ

Notes on the paradigms of 28–30:

1. All nom. pl. endings in -οι count as short; for this reason, accentuation looks like this (↑2): **οἶκοι** *houses,* **δοῦλοι** *slaves,* ἄνθρωπ**οι** *human beings,* ἄγγελ**οι** *angels.*

2. The gen. and dat. endings of nouns with an accented final syllable always take the circumflex both in the sg. and the pl. (↑23e).

3. The names of islands and cities with a stem in -ο are feminine (↑23a), e.g.: **ἡ** Ῥόδ**ος** *Rhodes,* **ἡ** Ἔφεσ**ος** *Ephesus.*

4. τὸ σάββατον *week* and τὸ δάκρυον *tear* have a third declension ending in the dat. pl. (↑32b): σάββα-**σιν**, δάκρυ-**σιν**.

5. For the inflection of Ἰησοῦς *Jesus/Joshua* ↑26b.

Ancient Greek also has the so-called **"Attic"** (second) **declension** with stems in -(ε)ω (↑BR §40):

ὁ νεώς *the temple*	τοῦ νεώ	τῷ νεῴ	τὸν νεών
οἱ νεῴ	τῶν νεών	τοῖς νεῴς	τοὺς νεώς

This declension is no longer used in popular Hellenistic Greek. So, in the NT νεώς *temple* is replaced by ναός and λεώς *people* by λαός. The only NT representative of this declension is the adjective ἵλεως *gracious* (used as part of an idiomatic expression in Mt 16:22 and in He 8:12 [LXX quotation]). The LXX also uses ἅλως *threshing floor,* which in the NT is replaced by the third declension form ἅλων, ωνος (ἡ). ↑also BDF §44.1; MH: 121.

Second declension: contracted nouns (↑BR §38; BDF §45; MH: 120f) 31

Contracted nouns of the second declension are rare in the NT. The most important one is ὁ νοῦς (< νόος) *the mind.* Note, however, that NT Greek, unlike CG, here uses third declension endings in the gen. and dat. sg. (↑41):

	NT (no plural forms attested) (gen./dat.: third declension):	CG (throughout contracted second declension forms; ↑11):				
ὁ	νοῦς	νοῦς	< νόος	οἱ	νοῖ	< νόοι
τοῦ	νο-ός	νοῦ	< νόου	τῶν	νῶν	< νόων
τῷ	νο-ΐ	νῷ	< νόῳ	τοῖς	νοῖς	< νόοις
τὸν	νοῦν	νοῦν	< νόον	τοὺς	νοῦς	< νόους

Also ↑44c for paradigms of adjectives.

2.2.1.3 Third declension

Introductory remarks (↑BR §41; BDF §46ff; MH: 128ff) 32

1. Third declension **stems** 32a

Consonant stems all fall into this category (↑34–39), as do vowel and diphthong stems in -ι, -υ, -ευ, and -ου (↑40–41). Third declension nouns can be masculine, feminine or neuter. The stem-types do not always connect with a particular gender.

In most cases the stem can be found by taking off the gen. sg. ending -ος, e.g.:

nom. sg.:		gen. sg.:	stem:
φύλαξ	*guard*	φύλακ-ος	φυλακ-

Identifying σ-, ι- and diphthong stems (↑39–41) is more difficult due to formation peculiarities. Sometimes the dat. pl. offers certain clues, e.g.:

nom. sg.:		dat. pl.:	stem:
γένος	*race/kind*	γένε-σιν	γενεσ- and γενος
πόλις	*city*	πόλε-σιν	πολε(ι̯)- and πολι-
βασιλεύς	*king*	βασιλεῦ-σιν	βασιλευ-

32b 2. Synopsis of **case endings**:

	sg. masc./fem.	sg. ntr.	pl. masc./fem.	pl. ntr.
nom.	-ς or –	–	-ες (-εις)	-ᾰ
gen.	-ος (-εως)	-ος	-ων	-ων
dat.	-ῐ	-ῐ	-σῐν(1)	-σῐν(1)
acc.	-ᾰ or (after a vowel) -ν	–	-ᾰς (-εις)	-ᾰ
voc.	= nom. or –	–	= nom.	= nom.

(1) ν mobile (↑18a).

Notes on case endings:

32c 1. -ᾰ and-ᾰς are always short (↑25 regarding first declension), so are -ῐ and-σῐν.

32d 2. The nom. sg. of masc./fem. nouns either ends in -ς ("sigmatic" formation), e.g. ἐλπίς (< ἐλπιδς; ↑35a) *hope*, or it does not ("asigmatic" formation). When it does not, in many cases the stem vowel is lengthened, e.g. ἀ**ή**ρ (stem: ἀερ-; ↑37b) *air* (↑8d/8e; 36–38).

32e 3. Nom./acc./voc. sg. ntr. forms usually correspond to the stem, provided the stem-final sound is admissible at the end of a word (↑17 "Nereus" rule; ↑39 and 35c).

32f 4. Voc. sg. masc./fem. forms correspond to the nom. sg. (↑34) or else to the stem, provided the stem-final sound is admissible at the end of a word (↑17; 38).

Also ↑45–48 for paradigms of adjectives and participles.

33 Accentuation of third declension nouns (also ↑23e; BR §41.6)

33a Monosyllabic stems generally have accented gen. and dat. sg. and pl. endings, e.g.:

nom. sg.:		gen. sg.:	
ἡ θρίξ	*hair*	τριχ**ός**	(τριχ- < θριχ-; ↑14c)
ὁ μήν	*month*	μην**ός**	(μην-)
ἡ σάρξ	*flesh*	σαρκ**ός**	(σαρκ-)

Exceptions to the above rule:

1. The gen. pl. of the following words has the accent on the stem syllable (↑35): 33b

nom. sg.:		gen. sg. etc.:	but gen. pl.:
παῖς	*boy/girl, servant*	παιδ**ό**ς etc.	π**αί**δων
οὖς	*ear*	ὠτ**ό**ς etc.	**ὤ**των (↑42a)
φῶς	*light*	φωτ**ό**ς etc.	φ**ώ**των (↑35d)

2. πᾶς, stem παντ-, masc. and ntr., have the accent on the gen. and dat. endings in the sg., but on the stem syllable in the gen. and dat. pl. (↑46c): 33c

nom. sg.:		gen./dat. sg.:	gen./dat. pl.:
πᾶς/πᾶν	*every, all*	παντ**ό**ς/παντ**ί**	π**ά**ντων/π**ᾶ**σιν

3. Participles (m./ntr.) with a monosyllabic stem have the accent on the stem syllable in the all the case forms, e.g.: 33d

ὤν, **ὄ**ντος, **ὄ**ντι etc.	ptc. m. of εἰμί	*to be* (↑125a)
στ**ά**ς, στ**ά**ντος, στ**ά**ντι etc.	ptc. m. of ἔστην	*I stood* (↑106e; 118a)

(i) Third declension consonant stems

(a) Stop-final stems

Labial and velar stems (↑BR §43; MH: 130ff) 34

The combination of a labial or velar as a stem-final stop with the σ of a nom. sg. or dat. pl. ending is written as a ψ and as a ξ respectively (↑15g; 16c).

For velar stems with peculiarities ↑42a.

Paradigms of regular (1) labial (↑34a) and (2) velar (↑34b) stems:

1. Labial stems (π/β/φ + σ > ψ; ↑15g): 2. Velar stems (κ/γ/χ + σ > ξ; ↑15g): 34a 34b

		34a ἡ λαῖλαψ *the whirlwind* λαιλαπ-	34b ὁ κῆρυξ *the herald* κηρυκ-
stem →			
sg.	n./v.	ἡ λαῖλαψ	ὁ κῆρυξ
	g.	τῆς λαίλαπ-ος	τοῦ κήρυκ-ος
	d.	τῇ λαίλαπ-ῐ	τῷ κήρυκ-ῐ
	a.	τὴν λαίλαπ-ᾰ	τὸν κήρυκ-ᾰ
pl.	n./v.	αἱ λαίλαπ-ες	οἱ κήρυκ-ες
	g.	τῶν λαιλάπ-ων	τῶν κηρύκ-ων
	d.	ταῖς λαίλαψῐν	τοῖς κήρυξῐν
	a.	τὰς λαίλαπ-ᾰς	τοὺς κήρυκ-ᾰς

35 Dental stems (↑BR §44; MH: 131ff)

Paradigms of typical (a) dental stems (↑35a), (b) of nouns in -ις with unaccented stem-final syllable (↑35b), and (c) of neuter nouns (↑35c):

35a a) typical dental stems
35b b) nouns in -ις with an unaccented stem-final syllable
35c c) neuter nouns

		35a ἡ ἐλπίς *the hope*	35b ἡ χάρις *grace*	35c τὸ σῶμα *the body*
stem →		ἐλπιδ-	χαριτ-	σωματ-
sg.	n./v.	ἡ ἐλπίς	χάρις	τὸ σῶμα
	g.	τῆς ἐλπίδ-ος	χάριτ-ος	τοῦ σώματ-ος
	d.	τῇ ἐλπίδ-ῐ	χάριτ-ῐ	τῷ σώματ-ῐ
	a.	τὴν ἐλπίδ-α	χάρι-ν	τὸ σῶμα
pl.	n./v.	αἱ ἐλπίδ-ες	χάριτ-ες	τὰ σώματ-ᾰ
	g.	τῶν ἐλπίδ-ων	χαρίτ-ων	τῶν σωμάτ-ων
	d.	ταῖς ἐλπίσῐν	χάρισῐν	τοῖς σώμασῐν
	a.	τὰς ἐλπίδ-ᾰς	χάριτ-ᾰς	τὰ σώματ-ᾰ

Notes on the above paradigms:

35d 1. The stem-final dental is dropped before the σ of dat. pl. endings, and (where applicable) before the ς of nom. sg. endings (↑13a; 16c).

35e 2. Neuter nouns are generally without an ending in the nom. and acc. sg. (↑32b). However, a form like *σωμα**τ** being inadmissible (↑17), the dental is dropped, too: σῶμα (a form being in line with the "Nereus" rule).

There are only a small number of neuter dental stems with a nom. and acc. sg. in -ς, e.g.:

τὸ τέρας τέρατος	*miracle*	τὸ φῶς φωτός	*light* (↑33b)

35f 3. Nouns in -ις with an unaccented stem-final syllable have an acc. sg. in -ιν (as do the stems in -ι and -υ; ↑40). Apart from χάρις the NT has three nouns of this type:

nom. sg.:		gen. sg.:	acc. sg.:
ἡ ἔρις	*strife*	ἔριδ-ος	ἔρι-ν
ἡ ἶρις	*rainbow*	ἴριδ-ος	ἶρι-ν
ἡ προφῆτις	*prophetess*	προφήτιδ-ος	προφῆτι-ν

Note that twice the NT has the KG form χάρ**ιτα** for χάρ**ιν**: Ac 24:27 and Jd 4.

35g 4. Dental nouns ending in -της are feminine abstract nouns (↑361d) and follow the paradigm of 35a, e.g.:

ἡ ἁγιότης	*holiness*	ἁγιότητ-ος	ἁγιότητ-α

Stems in -μα(τ) (↑35c) are all neuter and often refer to the result of an "action" ("result nouns" or "nomina rei actae"; ↑362c), e.g.:

τὸ γράμμα	*letter* (of the alphabet) γράμματ-ος	< γράφω *to write*

5. The following are dental stems in -κτ (-κτσ > -κσ [↑13a] > -ξ): 35h

nom. sg.:		gen. sg.:	dat. pl.:
ἡ νύξ	*night*	νυκτ-ός	νυξίν
τὸ γάλα (↑17; 42b)	*milk*	γάλακτ-ος	γάλαξιν (NT no pl.)

6. For words with an unusual nom. sg. ↑42a. 35i

7. The only participle with a dental stem is the ptc. pf. act. masc./ntr.: λελυκ-ώς/λελυκ-ός λελυκ-ότος *having loosened* (↑48). 35j

8. For stems in -ντ ↑36. 35k

(b) ν-, ντ- and liquid stems

ν- and ντ-stems (↑BR §45f; MH: 134ff) 36

Notes on the paradigms below (↑36b): 36a

1. ν-stems: ν is dropped before σ of dat. pl. without compensation (↑13a):
   -εν/ον-σιν > **-ε/ο-σ**ιν
   ντ-stems: ντ is dropped before the σ with compensatory lengthening of the preceding syllable (↑10a; 13b):
   -οντ-ς/**-οντ-σ**ιν > **-ου-ς**/**-ου-σ**ιν
2. ν-stems in nom./voc. sg. -μεν or -μον (*e*- or *o*-grade; ↑8) have in the -μην and -μων (lengthened grade) respectively

If the final syllable is unaccented, CG voc. sg. = stem, e.g. ὦ δαῖμον of ὁ δαίμων δαίμονος *demon*.

3. The comparative forms in -ιων/-ων (↑52) are ν-stems, too, as are τίς/τίνος *who?*, τις/τινός *anyone* (↑60a) and οὐδείς/οὐδενός μηδείς/μηδενός *no one* (↑63b).

Also ↑45/46; 48 for paradigms of adjectives and participles.

Paradigms of ν- and ντ- stems: 36b

		ὁ ποιμήν *the shepherd*	ὁ ἡγεμών *the leader*	ὁ αἰών *the age*	ὁ ἄρχων *the ruler*	ὁ ὀδούς *the tooth*
stem →		ποιμεν-	ἡγεμον-	αἰων-	ἀρχοντ-	ὀδοντ-
sg.	n./v.	ποιμήν	ἡγεμών	αἰών	ἄρχων	ὀδούς
	g.	ποιμέν-ος	ἡγεμόν-ος	αἰῶν-ος	ἄρχοντ-ος	ὀδόντ-ος
	d.	ποιμέν-ῐ	ἡγεμόν-ῐ	αἰῶν-ῐ	ἄρχοντ-ῐ	ὀδόντ-ῐ
	a.	ποιμέν-ᾰ	ἡγεμόν-ᾰ	αἰῶν-ᾰ	ἄρχοντ-ᾰ	ὀδόντ-ᾰ
pl.	n./v.	ποιμέν-ες	ἡγεμόν-ες	αἰῶν-ες	ἄρχοντ-ες	ὀδόντ-ες
	g.	ποιμέν-ων	ἡγεμόν-ων	αἰών-ων	ἀρχόντ-ων	ὀδόντ-ων
	d.	ποιμέ-σῐν	ἡγεμό-σῐν	αἰῶ-σῐν	ἄρχου-σῐν	ὀδοῦ-σῐν
	a.	ποιμέν-ᾰς	ἡγεμόν-ᾰς	αἰῶν-ᾰς	ἄρχοντ-ᾰς	ὀδόντ-ᾰς

37 Liquid stems (in -ρ, -λ) (↑BR §42; MH: 136ff)

37a Notes on the paradigms below (↑37b):

1. ρ-stems in: -ερ or -ορ (*e*- or *o*-grade; ↑8) have in the
   nom. sg. -ηρ and -ωρ (lengthened grade) respectively, but not in the voc.
2. The voc. sg. σῶτερ is irregular (the stem being σωτηρ- !); ↑23e.
3. The λ-stems are rare, attested only outside the NT.
4. For exceptional cases ↑42a.

37b Paradigms of ρ- and λ- stems:

			ὁ σωτήρ *the saviour* σωτηρ-	ὁ ἀήρ *the air* ἀερ-	ὁ ῥήτωρ *the orator* ῥητορ-	ὁ ἅλς[(1)] *the salt* ἁλ-
stem →						
sg.	n.	ὁ	σωτήρ	ἀήρ	ῥήτωρ	ἅλ-ς
	g.	τοῦ	σωτῆρ-ος	ἀέρ-ος	ῥήτορ-ος	ἁλ-ός
	d.	τῷ	σωτῆρ-ῐ	ἀέρ-ι	ῥήτορ-ῐ	ἁλ-ΐ
	a.	τὸν	σωτῆρ-ᾰ	ἀέρ-ᾰ	ῥήτορ-ᾰ	ἅλ-ᾰ
	v.	ὦ	σῶτερ !		ῥῆτορ	
pl.	n./v.	οἱ	σωτῆρ-ες	ἀέρ-ες	ῥήτορ-ες	ἅλ-ες
	g.	τῶν	σωτήρ-ων	ἀέρ-ων	ῥητόρ-ων	ἁλ-ῶν
	d.	τοῖς	σωτῆρ-σῐν	ἀέρ-σῐν	ῥήτορ-σῐν	ἁλ-σΐν
	a.	τοὺς	σωτῆρ-ᾰς	ἀέρ-ᾰς	ῥήτορ-ᾰς	ἅλ-ᾰς

(1) CG (inter alia also LXX and Josephus); in the NT it is replaced by τὸ ἅλας ἅλατος (↑35d) *salt*.

(c) Other types of consonant stems

38 Stems in -ρ involving three *ablaut* grades (↑BR §47; MH: 136f)

38a Notes on the paradigms below (↑38b):

1. Inflecting πατήρ *father*, μήτηρ *mother* and θυγάτηρ *daughter* involves three *ablaut* grades (↑8e): -τερ (*e*-grade), -τηρ (lengthened grade) and -τρ (zero-grade).

2. All the forms of ἀνήρ *man* (apart from the nom. and voc. sg.) show a zero-grade (the δ is inserted for easier pronunciation; ↑BR §20 Note 2).

3. In the voc. sg. the accent is retracted to the first stem-syllable (↑23e).

4. A similar dat. pl. form is used for ἀστήρ *star* (↑42a): ἀστρᾰ́-σιν.

38b Paradigms of ὁ πατήρ *the father*, ἡ μήτηρ *the mother*, ἡ θυγάτηρ *the daughter*, ὁ ἀνήρ *the man*:

stem →	ὁ πατήρ *the father* πατερ-	ἡ μήτηρ *the mother* μητερ-	ἡ θυγάτηρ *the daughter* θυγατερ-	ὁ ἀνήρ *the man* ἀνερ-
sg. n.	πατήρ	μήτηρ	θυγάτηρ	ἀνήρ
g.	πατρ-ός	μητρ-ός	θυγατρ-ός	ἀνδρ-ός
d.	πατρ-ῐ́	μητρ-ῐ́	θυγατρ-ῐ́	ἀνδρ-ῐ́
a.	πατέρ-ᾰ	μητέρ-ᾰ	θυγατέρ-ᾰ	ἄνδρ-ᾰ
v.	πάτερ !	μῆτερ !	θύγατερ !	ἄνερ !
pl. n./v.	πατέρ-ες	μητέρ-ες	θυγατέρ-ες	ἄνδρ-ες
g.	πατέρ-ων	μητέρ-ων	θυγατέρ-ων	ἀνδρ-ῶν
d.	πατρᾰ́-σῐν	μητρᾰ́-σῐν	θυγατρᾰ́-σῐν	ἀνδρᾰ́-σῐν
a.	πατέρ-ᾰς	μητέρ-ᾰς	θυγατέρ-ᾰς	ἄνδρ-ᾰς

σ-stems (↑BR §48; MH: 138ff) 39

Paradigm of σ-stem nouns: 39a

stem →		τὸ γένος *the race/kind* γενος (o-grade [↑8e]: n./a./v. sg.), γενεσ- (e-grade: remainder)	
sg. n./v.	τὸ	γένος	
g.	τοῦ	γένους	< γενε(σ)-ος
d.	τῷ	γένει	< γενε(σ)-ῐ
a.	τὸ	γένος	
pl. n. v.	τᾰ̀	γένη	< γενε(σ)-ᾰ
g.	τῶν	γενῶν	< γενε(σ)-ων
d.	τοῖς	γένε-σῐν	< γενε(σ)-σῐν
a.	τᾰ̀	γένη	< γενε(σ)-ᾰ

Notes on the above paradigm (↑39a) 39b

1. The original σ is dropped between two vowels and before another σ (↑13e/13g); the vowels that remain are contracted (↑11): ε-ι > ει, ε-ο > ου, ε-ω > ω, ε-α > η.

2. There is, however, no contraction in the gen. pl. termination of (↑BDF §48)
τὸ ὄρος *the mountain* ὀρ**έ-ων** τὸ χεῖλος *the lip* χειλ**έ-ων**

3. The nouns of the above type are all neuter.

4. For the corresponding adjective type ↑45b.

5. In the NT there are also a small number of stems in -οσ- and -ασ- (↑BDF §47; MH: 140):
ἡ αἰδώς *modesty*, αἰδοῦς (< αἰδο[σ]ος), αἰδοῖ (< αἰδο[σ]ῐ), αἰδῶ (< αἰδο[σ]ᾰ).
τὸ κρέας *meat*, κρέως (< κρεα[σ]ος), nom./acc. pl. κρέᾱ (< κρεα[σ]α) *pieces of meat*.

(ii) Vowel and diphthong stems

40 Vowel stems (↑BR §49–51; MH: 140ff)

	ι-stems (with lengthened grade)(1)	υ-stems: (pure υ-stem)		(with lengthened grade)(1)
	ἡ πόλις *city*	ὁ ἰχθύς *fish*		ὁ πῆχυς *cubit*
stem →	πολῐ-, πολε(i̯)-	ἰχθῡ-		πηχῠ-, πηχε(ϝ)-(2)
sg. n.	πόλι-ς	ἰχθύ-ς	(CG -ῦ-ς)	πῆχυ-ς
g.	πόλε-ως(1)	ἰχθύ-ος		πήχε-ως(1)
d.	πόλει (< πολε-ῐ)	ἰχθύ-ι		πήχει (< πηχε-ῐ)
a.	πόλι-ν	ἰχθύ-ν	(CG -ῦ-ν)	πῆχυ-ν
v.	πόλι			πῆχυ
pl. n./v.	πόλεις (< πολε-ες)(3)	ἰχθύ-ες		πήχεις (< πηχε-ες)(3)
g.	πόλε-ων(4)	ἰχθύ-ων		πήχε-ων(4)
d.	πόλε-σῐν	ἰχθύ-σῐν		πήχε-σῐν
a.	πόλεις(5)	ἰχθύ-ᾰς	(CG -ῦ-ς)	πήχεις(5)

(1) In the gen. sg. forms (↑8d): πολη(i̯)-ος/πήχη(ϝ)-ος, with quantitative metathesis (the accent remaining unchanged; ↑9): πόλε-ως/πήχε-ως.
(2) Analogously: CG τὸ ἄστῠ ἄστεως (inter alia Josephus/Philo: -εος) *city* (n./a. pl. ἄστη [<ἀστε-α]).
(3) Contraction (↑11a).
(4) Accentuation adapted to the gen. sg.
(5) Acc. pl. form adapted to the nom. pl.

Note that ι-stems are almost exclusively feminine. They tend to refer to "activities" ("action nouns" or "nomina actionis"; ↑362b), e.g. ἡ καύχησις *boasting* (< καυχά-ομαι *to boast*).

41 Diphthong stems (ϝ-stems) (↑BR §52f; MH: 142f)

41a Notes on the paradigm of ευ-stem nouns (↑41b; on the ϝ ↑12a):

1. There is a quantitative metathesis in gen./acc. sg. forms:

lengthened grade (↑8d):		quantitative metathesis (↑9):
βασιλ**ῆϝος**	> βασιλ**ῆ-ος**	> βασιλ**έως**
βασιλ**ῆϝᾰ**	> βασιλ**ῆ-ᾰ**	> βασιλ**έᾱ**

2. In all the other case forms the long vowel is shortened.

3. Nouns in -εύς are all masculine and are accented on the final stem-syllable. They typically designate occupations or status (↑361c).

Paradigms of ευ- and ου-stem nouns: 41b

stem →	ὁ βασιλεύς *king* βασιλευ- < βασιλεϝ- βασιληυ- < βασιληϝ-	ὁ βοῦς *head of cattle* βου-, βο- < βοϝ-
sg. n. g. d. a. v.	βασιλεύ-ς βασιλέ-ως βασιλεῖ (< βασιλε-ῐ) βασιλέ-ᾱ βασιλεῦ	βοῦ-ς βο-ός βο-ΐ βοῦ-ν (βοῦ)
pl. n./v. g. d. a.	βασιλεῖς (CG also βασιλῆς [<-ηϝες]) βασιλέ-ων βασιλεῦ-σῐν βασιλεῖς (CG βασιλέ-ᾱς)	βό-ες βο-ῶν βου-σΐν βό-ᾰς (CG βοῦς)

Particularly in Attic Greek the following ϝ-stem nouns play a prominent role (↑BR §53): 41c

1. Ζεύς *Zeus* (Δι̯ευ- [< Δι̯ηυ-], Δι[ϝ]; δι̯ > ζ [↑12c]; LXX 3×; NT 2×: Ac 14:12f):

Ζεύς (v. Ζεῦ) Δι-ός Δι-ΐ Δί-α

2. ἡ ναῦς *ship* (ναυ-, νη[ϝ] < νᾱϝ; LXX 17×; NT 1×: Ac 27:41):

ναῦ-ς νε-ώς νη-ΐ ναῦ-ν νῆ-ες νε-ῶν ναυ-σΐν ναῦς (!)

(iii) Peculiarities and overview of important stems

Irregular third declension nouns (↑BR §55; 44.3; 75) 42

I. In the inflection of the following nouns **more than one stem** is involved: 42a

1. ὁ ἀστήρ *star*, st. ἀστερ-, ἀστέρ-ος etc., but **ἀστρᾰ́**-σῐν in the dat. pl. (↑38a).

2. τὸ γόν**υ** (!) *knee*, st. of the other forms: γονατ-, γόνατ-ος etc.

3. ἡ γυνή *woman*, st. γυναικ-. Although this is a two-syllable stem, the accent is on the gen. and dat. endings as in the case of monosyllabic stems (↑33; for the voc. ↑23e):

γυν**ή**	γυναικ-**ός**	γυναικ-**ί**	γυν**αῖκ**-α	γ**ύ**ναι
γυν**αῖκ**-ες	γυναικ-**ῶν**	γυναιξ**ίν**	γυν**αῖκ**-ας	

4. ὁ κύων *dog* involves three ablaut grades (↑8): *o*-grade in the voc., lengthened grade in the nom. sg., and zero-grade in the remaining cases:

κύων	**κυν**-ός	κυν-ί	κύν-α	κύον
κύν-ες	κυν-ῶν	κυ-σίν	κύν-ας	

5. ὁ μάρτυς *witness*, st. μαρτυ- (nom. sg./dat. pl.) and μαρτυρ- (other cases):

μάρτυ-ς	**μάρτυρ**-ος	μάρτυρ-ι	μάρτυρ-α
μάρτυρ-ες	μαρτύρ-ων	**μάρτυ**-σιν	μάρτυρ-ας

6. τὸ **οὖς** (!) *ear*, st. of the other forms: **ὠτ-**, ὠτ-ός etc. (also ↑33b).

7. ὁ **πούς** (!) *foot*, st. of the other forms: **πόδ-**, ποδ-ός etc.

8. τὸ **ὕδωρ** (!) *water*, st. of the other forms: **ὑδατ-**, ὕδατ-ος etc.

9. τὸ **φρέᾱρ** *well*, st. of the other forms: **φρεᾱτ-**, φρέᾱτ-ος etc.

10. ἡ **χείρ** *hand*, st. **χειρ-**, χειρ-ός etc., but **χερ**-σίν in the dat. pl.

42b II. In spite of their unusual look they are in perfect line with the sound laws:

1. τὸ γάλ**α** *milk*, st. γαλακτ-, γάλακτ-ος, γάλαξιν (↑35h).

2. ἡ **θ**ρίξ *hair*, st. τριχ- < θριχ-, **τ**ριχ-ός, **θ**ριξίν (↑14c).

42c III. In the NT only one οι-stem is attested (↑BR §54; MH: 143):
ἡ πειθώ *persuasiveness*, st. πειθοι-/πειθο(i̯)-:

πειθώ   πειθοῦς   πειθοῖ (1Cor 2:4 Var.)   πειθώ

43 Terminations of important third declension stems

(including adjectives and participles)

nom. in:	stem-final sound	nom. sg.		gen. sg.	
-α	-ακτ	τὸ γάλα	*milk*	γάλακτ-ος	(↑35h)
	-ατ	τὸ σῶμα	*body*	σώματ-ος	(↑35)
-αις	-αιδ	ὁ παῖς	*boy/girl, servant*	παιδ-ός	(↑35; 33b)
-αν	-ᾰν	μέλαν	*black*	μέλᾰν-ος	(↑46b)
	-αντ	τὸ πᾶν	*whole*	παντ-ός	(↑46c)
-ᾰς	-αδ	ἡ λαμπάς	*torch*	λαμπάδ-ος	(↑35a)
	-ατ	τὸ τέρας	*miracle*	τέρατ-ος	(↑35e)
	-ασ	τὸ κρέας	*meat*	κρέως	(↑39b)
-ᾱς	-αν	μέλας	*black*	μέλᾰν-ος	(↑46b)
	-αντ	ὁ ἱμάς	*strap*	ἱμάντ-ος	(↑36)
-αυς	-αυ/-η	ἡ ναῦς	*ship*	νε-ώς	(↑41c)
-ειρ	-ειρ	ἡ χείρ	*hand*	χειρ-ός	(↑42a)
-εις	-εντ	λυθείς	*loosened*	λυθέντ-ος	(↑48d)
	-εν/ἑν	οὐδ-είς/εἷς	*none/one*	οὐδ-εν-ός/ἑν-ός	(↑63)
	-ειδ	ἡ κλείς	*key*	κλειδ-ός	(↑35)
-εν	-εντ	λυθέν	*loosened*	λυθέντ-ος	(↑48d)
	-εν	ἄρσην	*male*	ἄρσεν-ος	(↑36)
-ες	-ες	ἀληθές	*true*	ἀληθοῦς	(↑45b)
-ευς	-ηυ/-ευ	ὁ βασιλεύς	*king*	βασιλέ-ως	(↑41)
	-ευ/-ι	Ζεύς	*Zeus*	Δι-ός	(↑41c)
-ην	-εν	ὁ ποιμήν	*shepherd*	ποιμέν-ος	(↑36)
	-ην	ὁ Ἕλλην	*Greek*	Ἕλλην-ος	(↑36)
-ηρ	-ερ	ὁ ἀήρ	*air*	ἀέρ-ος	(↑37)

	-ερ	ὁ πατήρ	*father*	πατρ-ός	(↑38)
	-ηρ	ὁ σωτήρ	*saviour*	σωτῆρ-ος	(↑37)
-ης	-ητ	ὁ σής	*moth*	σητ-ός	(↑35)
		ἡ πραΰτης	*gentleness*	πραΰτητ-ος	(↑35)
	-ες	ἀληθής	*true*	ἀληθοῦς	(↑45b)
-ι	-ιτ	τὸ μέλι	*honey*	μέλιτ-ος	(↑35)
	-ε/-ει	τὸ σίνᾱπι	*mustard*	σινάπε-ως	(↑40)
-ις	-ι	ἡ πόλις	*city*	πόλε-ως	(↑40)
	-ιδ	ἡ ἐλπίς	*hope*	ἐλπίδ-ος	(↑35)
	-ιτ	ἡ χάρις	*grace*	χάριτ-ος	(↑35)
	-ιθ	ὁ/ἡ ὄρνις	*bird*	ὄρνιθ-ος	(↑35d)
-ξ	-κ	ὁ φύλαξ	*guard*	φύλακ-ος	(↑34b)
	-γ	ἡ φλόξ	*flame*	φλογ-ός	(↑34b)
		ἡ σάλπιγξ	*trumpet*	σάλπιγγ-ος	(↑34b)
-ον	-ον	σῶφρον	*sensible*	σώφρον-ος	(↑45a)
	-οντ	λῦον	*loosening*	λύοντ-ος	(↑48b)
-ος	-ες	τὸ γένος	*race/kind*	γένους	(↑39)
	-οτ	πεπαιδευκός	*having trained*	πεπαιδευκότ-ος	(↑48e)
-ους	-οντ	ὁ ὀδούς	*tooth*	ὀδόντ-ος	(↑36)
	-οδ	ὁ πούς	*foot*	ποδ-ός	(↑42a)
	-ο(υ)	ὁ /ἡ βοῦς	*head of cattle*	βο-ός	(↑41b)
	-ώτ	τὸ οὖς	*ear*	ὠτ-ός	(↑42a)
-υ	-υ	τὸ ἄστυ	*city*	ἄστε-ως	(↑40)
		βαθύ	*deep*	βαθέ-ως	(↑46a)
-υν	-υντ	δεικνύν	*showing*	δεικνύντ-ος	(↑48b/48f)
-υς	-υντ	δεικνύς	*showing*	δεικνύντ-ος	(↑48b/48f)
	-υ	ὁ ἰχθύς	*fish*	ἰχθύ-ος	(↑40)
		ὁ πῆχυς	*cubit*	πήχε-ως	(↑40)
		πραΰς	*gentle*	πραέ-ως	(↑46a)
	-υδ	ἡ χλαμύς	*cloak*	χλαμύδ-ος	(↑35)
-υξ	-υκτ	ἡ νύξ	*night*	νυκτ-ός	(↑35h)
-ψ	-π	ἡ λαῖλαψ	*whirlwind*	λαίλαπ-ος	(↑34a)
		ὁ Αἰθίοψ	*Ethiopian*	Αἰθίοπ-ος	(↑34a)
	-β	ὁ Ἄραψ	*Arab*	Ἄραβ-ος	(↑34a)
		ἡ φλέψ	*vein*	φλεβ-ός	(↑34a)
-ω	-οι	ἡ πειθώ	*persuasiveness*	πειθοῦς	(↑42c)
-ων	-ον	ὁ ἡγεμών	*leader*	ἡγεμόν-ος	(↑36)
	-ων	ὁ ἀγών	*contest*	ἀγῶν-ος	(↑36)
	-οντ	ὁ ἄρχων	*ruler*	ἄρχοντ-ος	(↑36)
-ωρ	-ορ	ὁ ῥήτωρ	*orator*	ῥήτορ-ος	(↑37)
-ως	-ος	ἡ αἰδώς	*modesty*	αἰδοῦς	(↑39b)
	-οτ	πεπαιδευκώς	*having trained*	πεπαιδευκότ-ος	(↑48e)

2.2.2 Declension of adjectives and participles (↑BR §56f; BDF §59)

44 First/second declension adjectives (class 1) (↑28; 25; also BR §37; 39)

Four types are distinguishable here:

Type a: three-termination adjectives with fem. sg. in -ᾱ (↑44a)
Type b: three-termination adjectives with fem. sg. in -η (↑44b)
Type c: three-termination adjectives contracted (↑44c)
Type d: two-termination adjectives (↑44d)

44a
44b

		44a Type a: fem. sg. in -α[1] ἅγιος, -ίᾱ, -ιον *holy*			44b Type b: fem. sg. in -η[1] καινός, -ή, -όν *new*		
		masc.	fem.	ntr.	masc.	fem.	ntr.
sg.	n.	ἅγι-ος	ἁγί-ᾱ	ἅγι-ον	καιν-ός	καιν-ή	καιν-όν
	g.	ἁγί-ου	ἁγί-ᾱς	ἁγί-ου	καιν-οῦ	καιν-ῆς	καιν-οῦ
	d.	ἁγί-ῳ	ἁγί-ᾱͅ	ἁγί-ῳ	καιν-ῷ	καιν-ῇ	καιν-ῷ
	a.	ἅγι-ον	ἁγί-ᾱν	ἅγι-ον	καιν-όν	καιν-ήν	καιν-όν
	v.	ἅγι-ε	ἁγί-ᾱ	ἅγι-ον	καιν-έ	καιν-ή	καιν-όν
pl.	n./v.	ἅγι-οι	ἅγι-αι	ἅγι-ᾰ	καιν-οί	καιν-αί	καιν-ᾰ́
	g.	ἁγί-ων	ἁγί-ων[2]	ἁγί-ων	καιν-ῶν	καιν-ῶν[2]	καιν-ῶν
	d.	ἁγί-οις	ἁγί-αις	ἁγί-οις	καιν-οῖς	καιν-αῖς	καιν-οῖς
	a.	ἁγί-ους	ἁγί-ᾱς	ἅγι-ᾰ	καιν-ούς	καιν-ᾱ́ς	καιν-ᾰ́

(1) Fem. sg. in -ᾱ after ε, ι, ρ, (type a), otherwise in -η (type b; ↑25a/25f; also 11g]).
(2) Accentuation of fem. follows the masc. in the nom. and (against the rule of 25d) gen. pl. ↑49c.

44c
44d

		44c Type c: contracted (rare) χρυσοῦς, -ῆ, -οῦν *golden*[1]			44d Type d: two-termination[2] ἄφθαρτος, -ον *imperishable*	
		masc.	fem.	ntr.	masc./fem.	ntr.
sg.	n.	χρυσ-οῦς	χρυσ-ῆ	χρυσ-οῦν	ἄφθαρτος	ἄφθαρτον
	g.	χρυσ-οῦ	χρυσ-ῆς	χρυσ-οῦ	ἀφθάρτου	
	d.	χρυσ-ῷ	χρυσ-ῇ	χρυσ-ῷ	ἀφθάρτῳ	
	a.	χρυσ-οῦν	χρυσ-ῆν	χρυσ-οῦν	ἄφθαρτον	ἄφθαρτον
	v.	χρυσ-οῦς	χρυσ-ῆ	χρυσ-οῦν	ἄφθαρτε	ἄφθαρτον
pl.	n.	χρυσ-οῖ	χρυσ-αῖ	χρυσ-ᾶ	ἄφθαρτοι	ἄφθαρτᾰ
	g.	χρυσ-ῶν	χρυσ-ῶν	χρυσ-ῶν	ἀφθάρτων	
	d.	χρυσ-οῖς	χρυσ-αῖς	χρυσ-οῖς	ἀφθάρτοις	
	a.	χρυσ-οῦς	χρυσ-ᾶς	χρυσ-ᾶ	ἀφθάρτους	ἄφθαρτᾰ

(1) Stem χρυσεο-/χρυσεα-/χρυσεο- (↑11; 27; 31), ↑Homeric χρύσεος/χρυσέα /χρύσεον.

(2)Note that the majority of type d adjectives are compounds (↑367a); the most common prefix is the "alpha privative" (ἀ- before consonants, ἀν- before vowels; ↑367b), e.g. ἀ-χάριστος *ungrateful*. A number of two-termination adjectives are not compounds (or are not easily recognized as such, with some of these fluctuating between three- and two-termination use; ↑BDF §59), e.g.:

αἰώνιος, -ον	*eternal* (NT: f. 2× in -ᾱ)	φρόνιμος, -ον	*thoughtful*
δόκιμος, -ον	*approved*	ὠφέλιμος, -ον	*useful*
οὐράνιος, -ον	*heavenly*		

Third declension adjectives (class 2: -ν/-σ) (↑36; 39; also BR §45; 48) 45

There are two types here, both of them two-termination adjectives (masc. = fem.):
Type a: ν-stems (↑45a)
Type b: σ-stems (↑45b)

45a

	Type a: ν-stems (↑36); v. sg. = n. sg.(1) σώφρων, σῶφρον *sensible*, st. σωφρον-					
		masc. /fem.	ntr.		masc./fem.	ntr.
n.	sg.	σώφρων	σῶφρον	pl.	σώφρον-ες	σώφρον-ᾰ
g.		σώφρον-ος	σώφρον-ος		σωφρόν-ων	σωφρόν-ων
d.		σώφρον-ῐ	σώφρον-ῐ		σώφρο-σῐν	σώφρο-σῐν
a.		σώφρον-ᾰ	σῶφρον		σώφρον-ᾰς	σώφρον-ᾰ

(1) In CG the voc. sg. masc./fem. is usually identical with the nom./acc. sg. ntr. (i.e. the stem).

For the special paradigm of comparative forms in -ιων/-ων ↑52.

45b

	Type b: σ-stems (↑39); v. sg. = n. sg.(1) ἀληθής, ἀληθές *true*, st. ἀληθεσ-					
		masc./fem.	ntr.		masc./fem.	ntr.
n.	sg.	ἀληθής	ἀληθές	pl.	ἀληθεῖς <ἀληθέ(σ)ες	ἀληθῆ <ἀληθέ(σ)α
g.		ἀληθοῦς <ἀληθέ(σ)ος			ἀληθῶν <ἀληθέ(σ)ων	
d.		ἀληθεῖ <ἀληθέ(σ)ι			ἀληθέσιν <ἀληθέ(σ)σιν	
a.		ἀληθῆ <ἀληθέ(σ)α	ἀληθές		ἀληθεῖς (= nom.)	ἀληθῆ

(1) In CG the voc. sg. masc./fem. is usually identical with the nom./acc. sg. ntr. (i.e. the stem).

Notes on above paradigm (↑45b):

1. The accent is always on the last syllable.

πλήρης, πλῆρες *full* is an exception.
Note that πλήρης is used as a particle (i.e. uninflected; ↑22g) twice in the NT (Jn 1:14; Ac 6:5).

2. Note that πένης, πένητ-ος *poor* is a dental stem (↑35), being used as a one-termination (!) adjective.

3. In CG the ntr. pl. usually ends in -ᾶ, not in -ῆ when there is a vowel before the -εσ- element, e.g.:

ὑγιής, ὑγιές	*well, healthy*	ntr. pl.: CG ὑγιᾶ	KG ὑγιῆ

4. In the NT the dat. pl. of συγγενής, συγγενές *related/akin to* is not συγγενέσιν, but συγγενεῦσιν (by analogy with γονεῖς *parents* [sg. *γονεύς γονέως; ↑41b], τοῖς γονεῦσιν *to the parents*; ↑BDF §47.4).

5. CG also uses σ-stems for personal names (↑BR §48; a type rarely found in the NT), e.g.:

ὁ Σωκράτης	τοῦ Σωκράτους	τῷ Σωκράτει	τὸν Σωκράτη	ὦ Σώκρατες
ὁ Περικλῆς	τοῦ Περικλέους	τῷ Περικλεῖ	τὸν Περικλέᾱ	ὦ Περίκλεις

46 Mixed third and first declension adjectives (class 3) (↑BR §50; 45.4; 46; MH: 155ff)

There are three types here, all of them three-termination adjectives. Masc. and ntr. forms connect with the third declension, the fem. ones with the first declension. Note that the accentuation of the fem. agrees with 25d, not with 44! (↑49c):

Type a (↑46a): stems in -υ and -ε (<-εϝ; ↑12a) fem. in -ειᾰ (< -εϝι̯α; ↑12c)
Type b (↑46b): stems in -ᾰν fem. in -αινᾰ (< -ανι̯α)
Type c (↑46c): stems in -ᾰντ fem. in -ασᾰ (< -ανσα < -αντι̯α)

46a

		Type a (masc./ntr. ↑40; v. sg. = st.): βαθύς, βαθεῖᾰ, βαθύ *deep*, st. βαθυ-, βαθε- (<βαθεϝ-), βαθειᾰ- (<βαθεϝι̯α)						
		masc.	fem.	ntr.		masc.	fem.	ntr.
n.	sg.	βαθύ-ς	βαθεῖᾰ	βαθύ	pl.	βαθεῖς[(1)]	βαθεῖαι	βαθέ-ᾰ
g.		βαθέ-ως[(2)]	βαθείᾱς	βαθέως[(1)]		βαθέ-ων	βαθειῶν	βαθέ-ων
d.		βαθεῖ	βαθείᾳ	βαθεῖ		βαθέ-σῐν	βαθείαις	βαθέ-σῐν
a.		βαθύ-ν	βαθεῖᾰν	βαθύ		βαθεῖς	βαθείᾱς	βαθέ-ᾰ

(1) < βαθεες (contraction; ↑11b) < βαθεϝες.
(2) CG: βαθέος.

46b

		Type b (masc./ntr. ↑36; v. sg. = st.): μέλᾱς, μέλαινᾰ, μέλᾰν *black*, st. μελᾰν-, μελαινα- (< μελανι̯α-; ↑12c)						
		masc.	fem.	ntr.		masc.	fem.	ntr.
n.	sg.	μέλᾱς	μέλαινᾰ	μέλᾰν	pl.	μέλᾰν-ες	μέλαιναι	μέλᾰν-ᾰ
g.		μέλᾰν-ος	μελαίνης	μέλᾰν-ος		μελᾰ́ν-ων	μελαινῶν	μελᾰ́ν-ων
d.		μέλᾰν-ῐ	μελαίνῃ	μέλᾰν-ῐ		μέλᾰ-σῐν	μελαίναις	μέλᾰ-σῐν
a.		μέλᾰν-ᾰ	μέλαινᾰν	μέλᾰν		μέλᾰν-ᾰς	μελαίνᾱς	μέλᾰν-ᾰ

46c

		Type c (masc./ntr. ↑36; v. = n.): πᾶς, πᾶσα, πᾶν *every, all*, st. πᾰντ-, πᾱσα- (<πανσα- <παντι̯α-; ↑12c; 13h)						
		masc.	fem.	ntr.		masc.	fem.	ntr.
n.	sg.	πᾶς[(1)]	πᾶσᾰ	πᾶν[(2)]	pl.	πᾰ́ντ-ες	πᾶσαι	πᾰ́ντ-ᾰ
g.		πᾰντ-ός	πᾱ́σης	πᾰντ-ός		πᾰ́ντ-ων	πᾱσῶν	πᾰ́ντ-ων
d.		πᾰντ-ῐ́	πᾱ́σῃ	πᾰντ-ῐ́		πᾶ-σῐν[(1)]	πᾱ́σαις	πᾶ-σῐν[(1)]
a.		πᾰ́ντ-ᾰ	πᾶσᾰν	πᾶν		πᾰ́ντ-ᾰς	πᾱ́σᾱς	πᾰ́ντ-ᾰ

(1) Nom. sg. < πᾰντ-ς, dat. pl. < πᾰντ-σιν (↑13b).
(2) < πᾰντ (↑17).

Notes on paradigm of type c (↑46c):

1. The accentuation of the gen. and dat. pl. masc./ntr. is irregular (↑33).
2. Regarding its use note (for details ↑136d):

πᾶσα ἡ πόλις	*the whole city*	πᾶσαι αἱ πόλεις	*all the cities*
πᾶσα πόλις	*every city*		

3. ↑48 for paradigms of participles with analogous stems.

4. CG uses similarly inflected adjectives in -εις (-εντος), -εσσα (-εσσης), -εν (-εντος) [dat. pl. masc./ntr. however: -εσιν], e.g. χαρίεις -εσσα -εν *beautiful, attractive* (BR §46; MH: 158); ↑4Macc 8:3 for a LXX example, also Josephus, War 5.226.

Adjectives with more than one stem (↑BR §57) 47

st. →	1. μέγας *great* μεγα-[1], μεγαλο-; μεγαλᾱ- masc.	fem.	ntr.
sg. n.	μέγα-ς[2]	μεγάλη	μέγα
g.	μεγάλου	μεγάλης	μεγάλου
d.	μεγάλῳ	μεγάλῃ	μεγάλῳ
a.	μέγα-ν	μεγάλην	μέγα
pl. n.	μεγάλοι	μεγάλαι	μεγάλᾰ
g.	μεγάλων	μεγ**ά**λων[3]	μεγάλων
d.	μεγάλοις	μεγάλαις	μεγάλοις
a.	μεγάλους	μεγάλᾱς	μεγάλᾰ

st. →	2. πολύς *much, many* πολυ-[1], πολλο-; πολλᾱ- masc.	fem.	ntr.
sg. n.	πολύ-ς	πολλή	πολύ
g.	πολλοῦ	πολλῆς	πολλοῦ
d.	πολλῷ	πολλῇ	πολλῷ
a.	πολύ-ν	πολλήν	πολύ
pl. n.	πολλοί	πολλαί	πολλᾰ́
g.	πολλῶν	πολλῶν	πολλῶν
d.	πολλοῖς	πολλαῖς	πολλοῖς
a.	πολλούς	πολλᾱ́ς	πολλᾰ́

(1) The stems μέγα- and πολυ- are used exclusively in the nom. and acc. sg. of the masc./ntr., μεγαλο-/μεγαλᾱ- and πολλο-/πολλᾱ- respectively in all the other forms.
(2) The voc. sg. masc. is μεγάλε.
(3) ↑44a; 49c.

Participles (↑BR §46b; 44.6) 48

Participles are inflected: 48a

1. always with three terminations;
2. like first/second declension adjectives (↑44; note the fem. pl. is always -μ**έ**νων): ptc. pres. mid./pass., fut. mid. and pass., aor. mid., pf. mid./pass.: -μεν-ος, -η, -ον;
3. like mixed third and first declension adjectives, masc./ntr. with ντ-stems (↑46c): ptc. pres./fut./aor. I/aor. II act., as well as aor. pass. (paradigms ↑48b, 48c, 48d);
4. with a mixed third and first declension pattern, masc./ntr. with τ-stems (↑35): ptc. pf. act. (paradigm ↑48e)

λύω *loosen* (v. = n.)

48b

	ptc. pres. act. λύ-ων, λύ-ουσα, λῦ-ον *loosening* st. λυοντ-, λυουσα- (<λυονσα- <λυοντι̯α-; ↑12c; 13h)							
		masc.	fem.	ntr.		masc.	fem.	ntr.
n.	sg.	λύων	λύουσᾰ	λῦον	pl.	λύοντ-ες	λύουσαι	λύοντ-ᾰ
g.		λύοντ-ος	λυούσης	λύοντ-ος		λυόντ-ων	λυουσῶν	λυόντ-ων
d.		λύοντ-ῐ	λυούσῃ	λύοντ-ῐ		λύου-σῐν	λυούσαις	λύου-σῐν
a.		λύοντ-ᾰ	λύουσᾰν	λῦον		λύοντ-ᾰς	λυούσᾱς	λύοντ-ᾰ

48c

	ptc. aor. act. λύσ-ᾱς, λύσ-ᾱσα, λῦσ-ᾰν *loosening/having loosened* st. λυσ-ᾰντ-, λυσ-ᾱσα- (<λυσ-ᾰνσα- <λυσ-ᾰντι̯α-; ↑12c; 13h)							
		masc.	fem.	ntr.		masc.	fem.	ntr.
n.	sg.	λύσᾱς	λύσᾱσᾰ	λῦσᾰν	pl.	λύσᾰντ-ες	λύσᾱσαι	λύσᾰντ-ᾰ
g.		λύσᾰντ-ος	λυσᾱ́σης	λύσᾰντ-ος		λυσᾱ́ντ-ων	λυσᾱσῶν	λυσᾱ́ντ-ων
d.		λύσᾰντ-ῐ	λυσᾱ́σῃ	λύσᾰντ-ῐ		λύσᾱ-σῐν	λυσᾱ́σαις	λύσᾱ-σῐν
a.		λύσᾰντ-ᾰ	λύσᾱσᾰν	λῦσᾰν		λύσᾰντ-ᾰς	λυσᾱ́σᾱς	λύσᾰντ-ᾰ

48d

	ptc. aor. pass. λυθ-είς, λυθ-εῖσα, λυθ-έν *being/having been loosened* st. λυθ-εντ-, λυθ-εισα- (<λυθ-εντι̯α- <λυθ-ενσα-; ↑12c; 13h)							
		masc.	fem.	ntr.		masc.	fem.	ntr.
n.	sg.	λυθείς	λυθεῖσᾰ	λυθέν	pl.	λυθέντ-ες	λυθεῖσαι	λυθέντ-ᾰ
g.		λυθέντ-ος	λυθείσης	λυθέντ-ος		λυθέντ-ων	λυθεισῶν	λυθέντ-ων
d.		λυθέντ-ῐ	λυθείσῃ	λυθέντ-ῐ		λυθεῖ-σῐν	λυθείσαις	λυθεῖ-σῐν
a.		λυθέντ-ᾰ	λυθεῖσᾰν	λυθέν		λυθέντ-ᾰς	λυθείσᾱς	λυθέν-τᾰ

48e

	ptc. pf. act. masc. and ntr. always τ-stem λελυκ-ώς, λελυκ-υῖα, λελυκ-ός *having loosened*, st. λελυκ-οτ-, -υια- (<-υσι̯α-; ↑12d; 13e)							
		masc.	fem.(1)	ntr.		masc.	fem.	ntr.
n.	sg.	λελυκώς	λελυκυῖᾰ	λελυκός	pl.	λελυκότ-ες	λελυκυῖαι	λελυκότ-ᾰ
g.		λελυκότ-ος	λελυκυίας	λελυκότ-ος		λελυκότ-ων	λελυκυιῶν	λελυκότ-ων
d.		λελυκότ-ῐ	λελυκυίᾳ	λελυκότ-ῐ		λελυκό-σῐν	λελυκυίαις	λελυκό-σῐν
a.		λελυκότ-ᾰ	λελυκυῖᾰν	λελυκός		λελυκότ-ᾰς	λελυκυίᾱς	λελυκότ-ᾰ

(1) Against the general rule (↑11g) KG prefers -υί-**ης** to -υί-**ας** in the gen. sg. (↑25f); so in Ac 5:2 we read συνειδ-υί-ης *with (his wife's) knowledge*. In the LXX both are attested.

48f Additional notes on the paradigms of the participles:

1. The ptc. aor. II act. inflects like 48b, but with a slight accent difference (↑105):

βαλών, βαλοῦσα, βαλόν	*throwing* (from βάλλω *to throw*)

The adjectives ἑκών, ἑκοῦσα, ἑκόν *willing(ly)* (Ro 8:20; 1Cor 9:17) inflect the same way, not, however, the related adjective ἄκων, ἄκουσα, ἆκον *unwilling(ly)* (1Cor 9:17).

2. The ptc. pres. act. of ἵστημι *to place* and the ptc. (root) aor. of ἵσταμαι *to stand (up)* (↑115b; 118) inflect like 48c, as does the ptc. (root) aor. of βαίνω *to go* (↑106):

ἱστάς, ἱστᾶσα, ἱστάν/στάς, στᾶσα, στάν	*placing/standing (still)*
βάς, βᾶσα, βάν	*going*

3. The ptc. pres./aor. act. of δίδωμι *to give* (↑115/116) and the ptc. (root) aor. of γινώσκω *to know* (↑106) inflect like the noun ὀδούς *tooth* ↑36:

(δι)δούς, (δι)δοῦσα, (δι)δόν	*giving*
γνούς, γνοῦσα, γνόν	*knowing*

4. The ptc. pres./aor. act. of τίθημι *to lay* and ἵημι *to send* (↑115/116) inflect like 48d:

(τι)θείς, (τι)θεῖσα, (τι)θέν	*laying*
(ἱ)είς, (ἱ)εῖσα, (ἱ)έν	*sending*

5. The ptc. pres. act. of δείκνυμι *to show* (↑122) inflects as a ντ-stem, too (↑48b–48d):

δεικνύς, δεικνῦσα, δεικνύν	*showing*

(masc./ntr. gen. sg. -νύντος, dat. pl. -νῦσιν; ↑122)

6. The voc. of participles is always identical with the nom.

Overview of adjectives and participles (↑BR §56) 49

1. **Three-termination** adjectives and participles: 49a

a) Most of the first/second declension adjectives and all participles in -μεν-ος (-η, -ον): ↑44; 48a.

b) Adjective stems in -αν (↑46b, type b):

μέλας, μέλαινα, μέλαν	(gen. sg. masc./ntr. μέλαν-ος) *black*

c) Adjective stems in -αντ (↑46c, type c):

πᾶς, πᾶσα, πᾶν	(gen. sg. masc./ntr. παντός) *every, all*

d) Participles (↑48b–48f) in

-ων:	λύ-ων -ουσα -ον	(-οντ-)	pres. act.	(λύω)	*loosening*
	λύσ-ων -ουσα -ον	(-οντ-)	fut. act.	(λύω)	*loosening in the future*
-ών:	βαλ-ών -οῦσα -όν	(-οντ-)	aor. II act.	(βάλλω)	*throwing*
-ας:	λύσ-ας -ασα -αν	(-αντ-)	aor. I act.	(λύω)	*loosening/having loosened*
-άς:	ἱστάς ἱστᾶσα ἱστάν	(-αντ-)	pres. act.	(ἵστημι)	*placing*
	στάς στᾶσα στάν	(-αντ-)	root aor.	(ἵσταμαι)	*standing (up)*
	βάς βᾶσα βάν	(βαντ-)	root aor.	(βαίνω)	*going*
-είς:	λυθ-είς -εῖσα -έν	(-εντ-)	aor. pass.	(λύω)	*being loosened/having been loosened*
	(τι)θείς (τι)θεῖσα (τι)θέν	(-εντ-)	pres./aor. act.	(τίθημι)	*laying*
	(ἱ)είς (ἱ)εῖσα (ἱ)έν	(-εντ-)	pres./aor. act.	(ἵημι)	*sending*

-ους:	(δι)δούς (δι)δοῦσα (δι)δόν	(δοντ-) pres./aor. act.	(δίδωμι)	*giving*
	γνούς γνοῦσα γνόν	(γνοντ-) root aor.	(γιγνώσκω)	*knowing/having known*
-ύς:	δείκ-ν-υς -ῦσα -ύν	(-υντ-) pres. act.	(δείκνυμι)	*showing*
-ως:	λελυκ-ώς -υῖα -ός	(-οτ-) pf. act.	(λύω)	*having loosened*

e) Adjective stems in -υ (↑46a, type a), e.g.:

βαθύς, βαθεῖα, βαθύ (gen. sg. masc./ntr. βαθέως) *deep*

49b 2. **Two-termination** adjectives:

a) In most cases o-stem compounds: ↑44d, type d.

b) Adjective stems in -ν (↑45a, type a), e.g.:

σώφρων, σῶφρον (gen. sg. σώφρονος) *sensible*

↑52 for the special paradigms of comparative forms in -ιων -ιον/-ων -ον.

c) Adjective stems in -σ (↑45b, type b), e.g.:

ἀληθής, ἀληθές (gen. sg. ἀληθοῦς) *true*

49c Note that the **accent of feminine forms** of three-termination words in the nom. and gen. pl. depends on the declension of the masc. and ntr.:

masc./ntr. 2nd declension?	accent of fem. in nom./gen. pl.	examples: masc.	fem.	
yes →	= masc.	**ἅ**γιοι/ἁγ**ί**ων λυ**ό**μενοι/λυομ**έ**νων	**ἅ**γιαι/ἁγ**ί**ων λυ**ό**μεναι/λυομ**έ**νων	*holy* *being loosened*
no →	= fem. nouns (nom. pl. = sg.; gen. pl.: **-ῶν**)	βαθεῖς/βαθέων λύοντες/λυόντων	βαθ**εῖ**αι/βαθει**ῶ**ν λ**ύ**ουσαι/λυουσ**ῶ**ν	*deep* *loosened*

2.3 Comparison of adjectives

Comparative and superlative forms (↑BR §59–61; BDF §60–62; MH: 164ff; ↑138 on syntax)

Preliminary remarks:

Most adjectives (that are gradable; ↑22b) have "regular" three-termination comparative forms falling into the category of the first/second declension adjectives type a (↑44a). On the other hand, there is a small group of adjectives with "irregular" two-termination forms using a special third declension paradigm (↑52); these few adjectives are basic to linguistic communication and so are very widely used in Ancient Greek texts.

The superlatives of these two categories have three-termination forms inflecting as first/second declension adjectives type b (↑44b).

basic form	comparative form	superlative form

1. “**Regular**” comparative and superlative forms: 50

adjective stem	-τερος, -τέρᾱ, -τερον	-τατος, -τάτη, -τατον

a) These terminations in principle are added to the stem: 50a

In the case of o-stems the quantity of the preceding syllable may be relevant:
If it is long (naturally or by “position”; ↑4a), the -o- remains short,
if it is short, the -o- is lengthened to -ω-. Note that in KG/NT this rule is often disregarded.

μωρό-ς *foolish*	μ**ωρό**-τερος	μ**ωρό**-τατος
σοφό-ς *wise*	σ**οφώ**-τερος	σ**οφώ**-τατος
βαθύ-ς *deep* (↑46a)	βαθύ-τερος	βαθύ-τατος
ἀκριβής *exact* (↑45b)	ἀκριβέσ-τερος	ἀκριβέσ-τατος

b) ον-stems (↑45a) have an additional -εσ- between the stem and the termination: 50b

σώφρων *sensible* (st. σώφρον-)	σωφρον-έσ-τερος	σωφρον-έσ-τατος

2. “**Irregular**” comparative and superlative forms: 51

a) The three forms have related stems (so are not really irregular): 51a

μέγας *great* (↑47)	μείζων (< μεγι̯ων; ↑12c)	μέγιστος
πολύς *much* (↑47)	πλείων (ntr. πλεῖον/πλέον)	πλεῖστος
ταχύς *quick* (↑46a)	ταχ-ῑ́ων[1]	τάχ-ιστος

(1) In the NT only as adverbs: τάχιον, superlative: τάχιστα; CG (LXX in part): θᾱ́ττων for ταχίων.

b) There is a combination of different stems (really irregular): 51b

ἀγαθός *good*	κρείσσων/κρείττων	κράτιστος
	βελτῑ́ων[1]	–
κακός *bad*	χείρων[2] *worse*	–
	ἥσσων (Att. ἥττων) *weaker*	
μῑκρός *small, little*	ἐλᾱ́σσων/ἐλᾱ́ττων	ἐλάχιστος[3]
ὀλίγος *few, little*	ἐλᾱ́σσων/ἐλᾱ́ττων	ἐλάχιστος[4]

(1) Once in the NT (2Tm 1:18); CG also uses ἀμείνων, and as superlatives ἄριστος (often in the sense of “most capable”) and (rarely LXX) βέλτιστος (especially referring to moral quality).
(2) CG also uses κακῑ́ων, as superlatives κάκιστος and χείριστος, also ἥκιστα (as an adverb) as superlative of ἥττων.
(3) In the case of μικρός regular forms are in use, too (↑50a).
(4) In the case of ὀλίγος CG also uses μείων and ὀλίγιστος.

51c Additional notes on the irregular forms:

1. In CG (at times in the LXX) the terminations -ῑ́ων and -ιστος are also used for:

ἡδ-ύς *sweet/pleasant* (in the NT only the superlative as an adverb ἥδιστα *most gladly* [2Cor 12:9.15])
καλ-ός *good/beautiful* (in the NT only the comparative as an adverb κάλλιον *better* [Ac 25:10])
αἰσχ-ρός *ugly* as well as ἐχθ-ρός *hostile*

CG further uses (the LXX very occasionally):

ῥᾴδιος *easy*, comparative ῥᾴων/ῥᾷον, superlative ῥᾷστος.

2. The forms with Attic -ττ- (for -σσ-; ↑12c) are the standard forms in CG

3. The following comparative forms are used as contrastive pairs:

βελτῑ́ων	↔ χείρων	μείζων	↔ ἐλάσσων
κρείσσων	↔ ἥσσων	πλείων	↔ ἐλάσσων

4. In the NT there are two cases of double comparatives (used for emphasis, more frequently in the KG than in earlier periods; BDF §61.2):

ἐλαχιστότερος	*(the) very least* (Eph 3:8)	from the superlative ἐλάχιστος *(the) least*
μειζότερος	*greater* (3Jn 4)	from the comparative μείζων *greater*

52 Comparative forms in -ῑων -ῑον/-ων -ον (↑BR §45.5; MH: 164f)

The paradigm of these comparative forms has some special features:
On the one hand, there are -(ο)ν-stem forms as we find them in the paradigm of σώφρων, σῶφρον *sensible* ↑45a.
On the other hand, to various of these forms there are alternatives (frequently used in the NT, too) that are based on -(ο)σ-stems. As in the case of other σ-stems (↑39; 45b) the original σ is dropped between two vowels, and the vowels that remain are contracted (↑11).

Example: μείζων, μεῖζον *greater* (comparative of μέγας; ↑51a)				
	sg. (v. = st.)		pl. (v. = n.)	
	masc./fem.	ntr.	masc./fem.	ntr.
n.	μείζων	μεῖζον	μείζον-ες/μείζους(1)	μείζον-ᾰ/μείζω(2)
g.	μείζον-ος	μείζον-ος	μειζόν-ων	μειζόν-ων
d.	μείζον-ῐ	μείζον-ῐ	μείζο-σῐν	μείζο-σῐν
a.	μείζον-ᾰ/μείζω(2)	μεῖζον	μείζον-ᾰς/μείζους(3)	μείζον-ᾰ/μείζω

(1) (μείζ)**ους** < (μειζ)**οες** < (μειζ)**οσες** (↑13e; 11).
(2) (μείζ)**ω**< (μειζ)**οα** < (μειζ)**οσα** (↑13e; 11).
(3) μείζους: adjustment to the nom.

2.4 Adverbs

Adverbs and their comparison (↑BR §62f; BDF §102ff; MH: 163f; ↑241/242 on syntax) 53

Overview of typical adverbs derived from adjectives with comparison forms: 53a

adjective nom. sg.		gen. pl.	adverb basic form -**ως** (Engl. *-ly*)	comparative = adj.ntr.acc.sg.	superlative = adj.ntr.acc.pl.
δίκαιος	*upright*	δικαίων	δικαίως	δικαιό-τερον	δικαιό-τατα
σώφρων	*sensible*	σωφρόνων	σωφρόνως	σωφρον-έσ-τερον	σωφρον-έσ-τατα
εὐσεβής	*devout*	εὐσεβῶν	εὐσεβῶς	εὐσεβέσ-τερον	εὐσεβέσ-τατα
ταχύς	*quick*	ταχέων	ταχέως	τάχ-ιον	τάχιστα

Notes on the above overview (on adverbs as a word-class also ↑22h):

1. The formation of **adverbs in -ως**: 53b

Adverbs typically end in -ως, mostly being derived from adjectives (very much like English adverbs in *-ly*).[16] The adverb termination -ως as it were replaces the termination -ων of the gen. pl. form of the adjective, adopting its accentuation.

The regular adverb of ἀγαθός *good* has a different stem: εὖ (↑Engl. *good* – *well*). The CG comparative and superlative forms ἄμεινον *better* and ἄριστα *the best* are not attested in the NT.

2. For the **comparison** of such adverbs (if gradable) forms like these are used (↑50): 53c

adj. comparative	acc. sg. ntr.	= adv. comparative	σοφώτερον	*more wisely*
adj. superlative	acc. pl. ntr.	= adv. superlative	σοφώτατα	*most wisely*

The superlative of the comparative adverb μᾶλλον *more/rather* is μάλιστα *most of all/especially*. The CG basic form μάλα *very/exceedingly* does not occur in the NT (but λίαν/σφόδρα instead).

3. There are **other types of adverb formation**, inter alia (for details ↑365–366): 53d

a) Formation of adverbs in -ω:

ἄνω *above* ἔξω *outside* ὀπίσω *behind*

b) Formation of adverbs with case-like terminations:

• adverbs with the suffix -θεν (answering the question From where?):

ἄνω-θεν *from above* μακρό-θεν *from far away* ἔν-θεν *from here*

CG also widely used the suffixes -θι (Where?) and -σε (To where?):

ἄλλο-θι *elsewhere* ἄλλο-σε *to another place* ἄλλο-θεν *from another place*

• acc. sg. forms in -ν (↑157):

πλησίον *near* δωρεάν *freely/without charge* μακράν (sc. ὁδόν; ↑260c) *far away*

Also ↑61c for correlative adverbs.

16 Some from participles, e.g. ὄντως *really* (common) < ὤν (ptc. of εἰμί) *being*; ὁμολογουμένως *admittedly* (1Tm 3:16) < ὁμολογούμενος (ptc. pres. pass. of ὁμολογέω) *being acknowledged*.

2.5 Pronouns (↑BR §64ff; BDF §64, 277ff; MH: 178ff; ↑22c on word-class; ↑139–144 on syntax)

54 Non-reflexive personal pronouns (↑BR §64; BDF §277ff; MH: 179ff; ↑139a–139e on syntax)

54a Paradigm of the non-reflexive personal pronouns:

	1st person	↓enclitic		2nd person	↓enclitic		3rd person(1)			
sg.										
n.	ἐγώ		*I*	σύ		*you*	αὐτός	αὐτή	αὐτό	*he/she/it*
g.	ἐμοῦ	μου	*of me*	σοῦ	σου	*of you*	αὐτοῦ	αὐτῆς	αὐτοῦ	*of him/her/it*
d.	ἐμοί	μοι	*to me*	σοί	σοι	*to you*	αὐτῷ	αὐτῇ	αὐτῷ	*to him/her/it*
a.	ἐμέ	με	*me*	σέ	σε	*you*	αὐτόν	αὐτήν	αὐτό	*him/her/it*
pl.										
n.	ἡμεῖς		*we*	ὑμεῖς		*you*	αὐτοί	αὐταί	αὐτᾰ́	*they*
g.	ἡμῶν		*of us*	ὑμῶν		*of you*	αὐτῶν	αὐτῶν	αὐτῶν	*of them*
d.	ἡμῖν		*to us*	ὑμῖν		*to you*	αὐτοῖς	αὐταῖς	αὐτοῖς	*to them*
a.	ἡμᾶς		*us*	ὑμᾶς		*you*	αὐτούς	αὐτᾱ́ς	αὐτᾰ́	*them*

(1) The nom. is often used in the sense of "he himself/she herself/it itself" and "they themselves".

Notes on the above paradigm (also ↑139a–139e):

54b 1. On ἐγώ *I* and σύ *you*:
In the gen., dat. and acc. sg. the non-enclitic forms (first column) are used only:
a) for emphasis, inter alia when a contrast is intended, e.g.:

ὁ ἀκούων ὑμῶν ἐμοῦ ἀκούει. — *The one who listens to you listens to me.* (Lk 10:16)

b) usually when they are part of a preposition phrase, e.g.:

ὁ κύριος μετὰ σοῦ. — *The Lord is with you.* (Lk 1:28)

In all the other contexts the enclitic forms are the rule (↑6d).

54c 2. On αὐτός, -ή, -ό (↑BR §65f; BDF §288):
Its status as a personal pronoun is limited:
a) Primarily it is a pronoun inflecting like an adjective (↑44b), except that the nom. and acc. sg. ntr. end in -ό (not -όν; ↑p. 56). It is used in two different ways (↑139d):

- Used by itself or outside the article and the noun it has the meaning *self*, e.g.:

αὐτὸς ἐγώ — *I myself* (Ro 7:25)
αὐτὸς ὁ κύριος — *the Lord himself* (1Th 4:16)

- Used after the article ("attributive" position) it has the meaning *the same*, e.g.:

ὁ αὐτὸς κύριος — *the same Lord* (1Cor 12:5)

Crasis (↑20) with the article in CG leads to forms like αὑτός, ταὐτό (often ταὐτ**όν**) etc. (↑BR §65.1c).

b) In the gen., dat. and acc. it had the role of a personal pronoun (replacing the original 3rd person personal pronoun no longer in use in CG; ↑54d), e.g.:

εἶδεν αὐτὸν ἄλλη. *Another girl saw him.* (Mt 26:71)

c) In post-CG it is frequently used as a personal pronoun even in the nom., e.g.:

αὐτοὶ παρακληθήσονται. *They will be comforted.* (Mt 5:4)

In CG the nom. of ἐκεῖνος *that (there)* (↑58c) or οὗτος *this* (↑58b) has this role instead, for emphasis also the cases outside the nom. This CG use is attested in the NT, too.

3. When the subject of the superordinate sentence is referred to ("indirect reflexive" relation) CG may use for the 3rd person (especially in the dat.) the following forms (as in the 1st and 2nd person sg. [↑54b] there are non-enclitic and enclitic forms): 54d

–	*he/she/it*	σφεῖς	*they*
οὗ, οὑ	*of him*	σφῶν	*of them*
οἷ, οἱ	*to him*	**σφίσιν**	*to them*
ἕ, ἑ	*him*	σφᾶς	*them*

Reflexive personal pronouns (↑BR §66; BDF §64.1; MH: 180f; ↑139f–139l on syntax) 55

For all three persons there are reflexive pronouns in the gen., dat. and acc.: 55a

		1st person		2nd person	
sg.	g.	ἐμ-αυτοῦ, -ῆς, -οῦ	*of myself*	σε-αυτοῦ,(1) -ῆς, -οῦ	*of yourself*
	d.	ἐμ-αυτῷ, -ῇ, -ῷ	*to myself*	σε-αυτῷ, -ῇ, -ῷ	*to yourself*
	a.	ἐμ-αυτόν, -ήν, -ό	*myself*	σε-αυτόν, -ήν, -ό	*yourself*
pl.	g.	ἡμῶν αὐτῶν or ἑαυτῶν(2)	*of ourselves*	ὑμῶν αὐτῶν or ἑαυτῶν(2)	*of yourselves*
	d.	ἡμῖν αὐτοῖς, -αῖς, -οῖς or ἑαυτοῖς, -αῖς, -οῖς(2)	*to ourselves*	ὑμῖν αὐτοῖς, -αῖς, -οῖς or ἑαυτοῖς, -αῖς, -οῖς(2)	*to yourselves*
	a.	ἡμᾶς αὐτούς, -άς, -ά or ἑαυτούς, -άς, -ά(2)	*ourselves*	ὑμᾶς αὐτούς, -άς, -ά or ἑαυτούς, -άς, -ά(2)	*yourselves*
		3rd person			
sg.	g.	ἑαυτοῦ,(1) -ῆς, -οῦ	or αὑτοῦ, -ῆς, -οῦ	*of himself, of herself, of itself*	
	d.	ἑαυτῷ, -ῇ, -ῷ	or αὑτῷ, -ῇ, -ῷ	*to himself, to herself, to itself*	
	a.	ἑαυτόν, -ήν, -ό	or αὑτόν, -ήν, -ό	*himself, herself, itself*	
pl.	g.	ἑαυτῶν(3)		*of themselves*	
	d.	ἑαυτοῖς, -αῖς, -οῖς		*to themselves*	
	a.	ἑαυτούς, -άς, -ά		*themselves*	

(1) In CG also contracted to σαυτοῦ etc., so the 3rd pers. ἑαυτοῦ etc. to αὑτοῦ etc.

(2) The NT almost exclusively uses the second option.

(3) For ἑαυτῶν etc. CG also uses the personal pronoun (↑54d) + αὐτός: σφῶν αὐτῶν etc.

55b Notes on the above paradigm:

1. In the NT the 1st and 2nd person pl. forms are almost exclusively replaced by what originally was the 3rd pl. of the reflexive pronoun, i.e. the second option above.

2. αὐτοῦ, an alternative to ἑαυτοῦ in Ancient Greek, occurs rarely in NT manuscripts (↑p.22), and never in modern standard editions (↑139h).

3. Note that the ntr. acc. sg. form ends in -ό (not in -όν; ↑p.56).

4. The reflexive pronoun refers or points to an entity and equates it with the subject entity, e.g.:

ἐταπείνωσεν ἑαυτόν. *He humbled himself.* (Php 2:8)

56 ἄλλος and the reciprocal pronoun (↑BR §65; BDF §287; MH: 179, 181; ↑139m–139n on syntax)

56a 1. ἄλλος, ἄλλη, ἄλλο *other* is a pronoun that inflects like αὐτός, αὐτή, αὐτό (↑54a; for ntr. sg. ↑p.56).

56b 2. The reciprocal pronoun ἀλλήλων *each other/one another* is based on a reduplication of the stem ἀλλο- (there are no forms outside the gen., dat. and acc. pl.!):

	masc.	fem.	ntr.	
g.	ἀλλήλων	ἀλλήλων	ἀλλήλων	*of each other/one another*
d.	ἀλλήλοις	ἀλλήλαις	ἀλλήλοις	*to each other/one another*
a.	ἀλλήλους	ἀλλήλᾱς	ἄλληλᾰ (accent!)	*each other/one another*

3. On the use of the reciprocal pronoun and possible alternatives ↑139m–139n.

57 Possessive pronouns and alternatives (↑BR §67; BDF §284ff; MH: 181; ↑140 on syntax)

There are possessive pronouns only for the 1st and 2nd persons:

masc.	fem.	ntr.	
ἐμός	ἐμή	ἐμόν	*my*
σός	σή	σόν	*your* (sg.)
ἡμέτερος	ἡμετέρα	ἡμέτερον	*our*
ὑμέτερος	ὑμετέρα	ὑμέτερον	*your* (pl.)

They are inflected and used like ordinary adjectives (↑44; 136a). In their most frequent role as attributive modifiers they appear in the "attributive" position, e.g.:

ἡ ἐμὴ χαρά / ἡ χαρὰ ἡ ἐμή *my joy* (2Cor 2:3; Jn 15:11)

Typically, possessive pronouns are used to put a special emphasis on the possessor(s). Mostly the gen. of personal pronouns is used, in the 3rd person so regularly, e.g.:

ὁ ἀδελφός μου/σου *my/your* (sg.) *brother* (Jn 11:21; Ro 14:15)
ὁ ἀδελφὸς αὐτοῦ/αὐτῆς *his/her brother* (Mt 22:24; ↑Jn 11:5)
ὁ ἀδελφὸς ἡμῶν/ὑμῶν/αὐτῶν *our/your*(pl.)*/their brother* (↑Re 12:10; Ac 3:22; He 7:5)

Demonstrative pronouns (↑BR §68; BDF §64.2; 289ff; MH: 178f; ↑141 on syntax) 58

CG has three types of demonstrative pronouns; in KG and NT Greek the first type (↑58a) is used only to a limited extent:

1. ὅδε, ἥδε, τόδε *this*, pointing to what follows in the text (catadeictic use) or what is present in the situation (used only few times in the NT) – inflecting like the article (↑24) with an enclitic (-)δε (↑6d) added (note the acute in the nom. masc./fem.!): 58a

ὅδε	ἥδε	τόδε	οἵδε	αἵδε	τᾰ́δε
τοῦδε	τῆσδε	τοῦδε	τῶνδε	τῶνδε	τῶνδε
τῷδε	τῇδε	τῷδε	τοῖσδε	ταῖσδε	τοῖσδε
τόνδε	τήνδε	τόδε	τούσδε	τᾱ́σδε	τᾰ́δε

2. οὗτος, αὕτη, τοῦτο *this* (frequently used in the NT): 58b
This, too, is linked with the article, the forms of the pronoun agreeing with it as to
• both the word initial sound: rough breathing or τ- like the article (↑24)
• and the diphthong after it: ου → the o-sound, αυ → a/e-sound of the article:

		masc.	fem.	ntr.		masc.	fem.	ntr.
n.	sg.	οὗτος	αὕτη	τοῦτο	pl.	οὗτοι	αὗται	ταῦτᾰ
g.		τούτου	ταύτης	τούτου		τούτων	τούτων	τούτων
d.		τούτῳ	ταύτῃ	τούτῳ		τούτοις	ταύταις	τούτοις
a.		τοῦτον	ταύτην	τοῦτο		τούτους	ταύτᾱς	ταῦτᾰ

3. ἐκεῖνος, ἐκείνη, ἐκεῖνο (widely used in the NT) *that*. Note that ntr. nom. and acc. sg. forms also end in -ό (not -όν; ↑p.56). 58c

4. Note the special word-order: the demonstrative pronoun is placed before or after the article and the noun it modifies, never between them (↑136c; 141b), e.g.: 58d
οὗτος ὁ ἄνθρωπος/ὁ ἄνθρωπος οὗτος *this human-being* (Jn 11:47; Ac 6:13)

5. The article and the (specific) relative pronoun, too, are used with a demonstrative force in set phrases (↑131; 142h): 58e

ὁ μέν – ὁ δέ, ὃς μέν – ὃς δέ	*this one – that one* (1Cor 7:7; 11:21)
ὁ δέ, ὃς δέ	*but this one/but he* (Mk 15:2.23)

6. These are compounds linked with and inflected like οὗτος (↑61b): 58f

τοσοῦτος, τοσαύτη, τοσοῦτο(ν)	*so large/so great/so much*
τοσοῦτοι, τοσαῦται, τοσαῦτα	*so many*
τοιοῦτος, τοιαύτη, τοιοῦτο(ν)	*of such a kind/such as this*
τηλικοῦτος, τηλικαύτη, τηλικοῦτο	*so large/so great/so important*

Note that these are used like ordinary adjectives (unlike simple forms ↑137; 58d).

CG also uses compounds linked with ὅδε etc. (↑58a): τοσόσδε, τοσήδε, τοσόνδε etc., τοιόσδε, τοιάδε, τοιόνδε; τηλικόσδε etc.

59 Relative pronouns (↑BR §69; BDF §64.3; 293ff; MH: 179; ↑142 on syntax)

There are two types of relative pronouns: (a) the specific (simple) one, (b) the indefinite (compound) one:

59a 1. ὅς, ἥ, ὅ *who, which* (for ntr. sg. ↑p.56).

n.	sg. ὅς	ἥ	ὅ	pl. οἵ	αἵ	ἅ
g.	οὗ	ἧς	οὗ	ὧν	ὧν	ὧν
d.	ᾧ	ᾗ	ᾧ	οἷς	αἷς	οἷς
a.	ὅν	ἥν	ὅ	οὕς	ἅς	ἅ

59b 2. ὅστις, ἥτις, ὅ τι *whoever/anyone who, whatever/anything which.*

It is a combination of the simple relative pronoun (whose accentuation is adopted without change!) with enclitic τις *someone/anyone* (↑60). Both elements are inflected. ὅ τι is (generally) written to avoid confusion with ὅτι *that/because.*
Note that in the NT only the nom. is used (often in place of ὅς, ἥ, ὅ).

n.	sg. ὅστις	ἥτις	ὅ τι	pl. οἵτινες	αἵτινες	ἅτινᾰ
g.	οὗτινος	ἧστινος	οὗτινος	ὧντινων	ὧντινων	ὧντινων
d.	ᾧτινῐ	ᾗτινῐ	ᾧτινῐ	οἷστισῐν	αἷστισῐν	οἷστισῐν
a.	ὅντινᾰ	ἥντινᾰ	ὅ τι	οὕστινᾰς	ἅστινᾰς	ἅτινᾰ

For οὗτινος/ᾧτινῐ CG also uses ὅτου/ὅτῳ, for ὧντινων/οἷστισῐν also ὅτων/ὅτοις.
In CG the indefinite relative pronoun was also used as an interrogative (↑60b).

59c 3. The demonstrative pronouns of 58f have these relative counterparts (↑61b):

ὅσος, ὅση, ὅσον	*as large as/as great as/as much as*
ὅσοι, ὅσαι, ὅσα	*as many as*
οἷος, οἵα, οἷον	*of what kind as*
ἡλίκος, ἡλίκη, ἡλίκον	*what size/how great/how small*

For indefinite relatives ὁπόσος *however large* etc. ↑60c.

60 Interrogative and indefinite pronouns (↑BR §70; BDF §64.5; 298ff; MH: 179; ↑143–144 on syntax)

60a Interrogative pronoun: always acute on 1st syllable; indefinite pronoun: enclitic (↑6d):

	interrogative pronoun *who? what? which?* sg.		pl.		indefinite pronoun *someone, anyone, some, any* sg.		pl.	
n.	τίς;	τί;	τίνες;	τίνᾰ;	τις	τι	τινές	τινᾰ́
g.	τίνος;		τίνων;		τινός		τινῶν	
d.	τίνῐ;		τίσῐν;		τινῐ́		τισῐ́ν	
a.	τίνᾰ;	τί;	τίνᾰς;	τίνᾰ;	τινᾰ́	τι	τινᾰ́ς	τινᾰ́

Notes on the above paradigm (also ↑143/144):

1. In CG ὅστις, ἥτις, ὅ τι (↑59b) may also introduce indirect questions …, *who/what/which*. 60b

2. for:	CG uses also:	for:	CG uses also:
τίνος/τινός	τοῦ/του	οὗτινος	ὅτου
τίνι/τινί	τῷ/τῳ	ᾧτινι	ὅτῳ
τινά (ntr. pl.)	ἅττᾰ (not enclitic)	ἅτινᾰ	ἅττᾰ
ὧντινων	ὅτων	οἷστισῖν	ὅτοις

3. Further interrogatives (↑61b): 60c

direct interrogatives (may also introduce indirect questions; ↑143):

(CG uses these as enclitics with indefinite force; πηλίκος, however, is always non-enclitic)

πόσος; πόση; πόσον;	*how large?*	(ποσός	*of a any largeness*)
πόσοι; πόσαι; πόσα;	*how many?*	(ποσοί	*of a any number*)
ποῖος; ποία; ποῖον;	*of what kind?*	(ποιός	*of a any kind*)
πηλίκος; πηλίκη; πηλίκον;	*of what size?*	(πηλικος	*of a any size*)

indirect interrogatives (within brackets are the ones attested only outside the NT):

(ὁπόσος, ὁπόση, ὁπόσον	… *how large*)
(ὁπόσοι, ὁπόσαι, ὁπόσα	… *how many*)
ὁποῖος, ὁποία, ὁποῖον	… *of what kind*

The indirect interrogatives are also used as indefinite relatives (↑59c).

Correlative pronouns and adverbs (↑BR §71f; BDF §64.4, 304ff, 106; ↑22c, 22h on word-classes) 61

There are pronouns and adverbs (called “pronominal adverbs”) appearing in groups 61a
whose members are interrelated in terms of function and (in many cases) of form:
there is a certain correlation between them, hence the term “correlative” pronouns
and adverbs. This is the typical correlation characterizing these groups:

word-initial sound(s):	function of word:
π-	interrogative (if enclitic [↑6d]: indefinite)
ὁπ-	indirect interrogative
τ-	demonstrative
ὁ-	relative

Note that pronouns and adverbs attested only outside the NT are in brackets in the following table.

interrogative (inflection ↑60) direct and indirect	indirect	indefinite (inflection ↑60) enclitic	demonstrative (inflection ↑58)	relative (inflection ↑59) specific	indefinite

61b a) **Correlative pronouns**

τίς; *who?*	(ὅστις *who*)	τις *someone/any-one*	ὅδε/ οὗτος *this* ἐκεῖνος *that*[1]	ὅς *who*	ὅστις *whoever*
ποῖος; *of what kind?*	ὁποῖος *of what kind*	(ποιός *of any kind*)	τοιοῦτος *of such a kind*	οἷος *of what kind as*	ὁποῖος *of whatever kind*
πόσος; *how large?*	(ὁπόσος *how large*)	(ποσός *of any largeness*)	τοσοῦτος *so large*	ὅσος *as large as*	(ὁπόσος *of whatever largeness*)
πόσοι; *how many?*	(ὁπόσοι *how many*)	(ποσοί *of any number*)	τοσοῦτοι *so many*	ὅσοι *as many as*	(ὁπόσοι *of whatever number*)
πηλίκος; *of what size/ how great?*		(πηλίκος *of any size*)	τηλικοῦτος *so large/ so great*	ἡλίκος *of what size/ how great*	(2)

(1) In answer to τίς; also ἄλλος *another one* (↑56a), οὐδείς *no one*, ἕκαστος *every/each* (↑145c/145e).
(2) Of the following CG group only remnants occur in the NT (↑BR §71; BDF §64.6, 306):

πότερος; *which of two?*	ὁπότερος *which of two*	ὁ ἕτερος *the one/the other of two*	ὁπότερος *which of two*	ὁπότερος *whichever of two*

61c b) **Correlative adverbs** (pronominal adverbs)

ποῦ;[1] *where/to where?*	ὅπου *where/to where*	που *somewhere/ anywhere/to somewhere/to anywhere*	ἐνθάδε/ὧδε *here/to here* ἐκεῖ *there/to there* αὐτοῦ *there/here* ἐκεῖσε *to there*	οὗ *where/to where*	ὅπου *wherever/ to wherever*
πόθεν; *from where?*	(ὁπόθεν *from where*)	(ποθέν *from anywhere/ from some-where*)	ἐντεῦθεν/ ἔνθεν *from here* ἐκεῖθεν *from there*	ὅθεν *from where*	(ὁπόθεν *from where/from wherever*)
πότε; *when?*	(ὁπότε *when*)	ποτέ *at some time* πώποτε *ever*	τότε *then, at that time* νῦν/νυνί *now*	ὅτε *when*	ὁπότε *when/ whenever* (NT only in Var.)
ποσάκις; *how often?*				ὁσάκις *as often as*	
πῶς; *how?*	ὅπως *how* (NT 1×)	(πως *somehow*)	οὕτως *thus, in this way* (CG also ὧς/ὥς)	ὡς/ὥσπερ *how*	(ὅπως *how/however*) (2)

(1) CG distinguishes groups answering Where? and those answering To where? more clearly:

ποῦ;	ὅπου	ἐνθάδε	αὐτοῦ	ἐνταῦθα/ἐκεῖ	οὗ/ἔνθα/ὅπου
where?	*where*	*here*	*at the very place*	*there*	*where*
ποῖ;	ὅποι	ἐνθάδε	αὐτόσε	ἐνταῦθα/ἐκεῖσε	οἷ/ἔνθα/ὅποι
to where?	*to where*	*to here*	*to the very place*	*to there*	*to where*

(2) CG also uses the following group of correlative adverbs (↑BR §72):

πῇ;	ὅπῃ	τῇδε		ταύτῃ
how/where/to where(?)		*here/thus*		*there/thus* etc.

2.6 Numerals (↑22e on word-class; 145 syntax)

Cardinals, ordinals and adverbs (↑BR §73; BDF §63; MH: 167ff; BNP s.v. "Numerals") 62

Table of cardinals, ordinals and multiplicative adverbs: 62a

signs		cardinals (inflection "1–4" ↑63)	ordinals (inflection ↑44a/44b)	multiplicative adverbs
question answered →		πόσοι; *how many?*	πόστος; *which?*	ποσάκις *how often?*
α´	1	εἷς μία ἕν *one*	πρῶτος *first*	ἅπαξ *once*
β´	2	δύο etc.	δεύτερος etc.	δίς etc.
γ´	3	τρεῖς τρία	τρίτος	τρίς
δ´	4	τέσσαρες -ρα (CG -ττ-)	τέταρτος	τετράκις
ε´	5	πέντε	πέμπτος	πεντάκις
ς´	6	ἕξ	ἕκτος	ἑξάκις
ζ´	7	ἑπτά	ἕβδομος	ἑπτάκις
η´	8	ὀκτώ	ὄγδοος	ὀκτάκις
θ´	9	ἐννέα	ἔνατος	ἐνάκις
ι´	10	δέκα	δέκατος	δεκάκις
ια´	11	ἕνδεκα	ἑνδέκατος	ἑνδεκάκις
ιβ´	12	δώδεκα	δωδέκατος	etc.
ιγ´	13	δεκατρεῖς -τρία	τρισκαιδέκατος	
ιδ´	14	δεκατέσσαρες -ρα	etc.	
ιε´	15	δεκαπέντε		
ις´	16	δεκαέξ		
ιζ´	17	δεκαεπτά		
ιη´	18	δεκαοκτώ		
ιθ´	19	δεκαεννέα(1)		

κʹ	20	εἴκοσι (↑18a)	εἰκοστός	
λʹ	30	τριᾰ́κοντα	τριᾱκοστός	
μʹ	40	τεσσερᾰ́κοντα(2)	τεσσερᾰκοστός	
νʹ	50	πεντήκοντα	πεντηκοστός	
ξʹ	60	ἑξήκοντα	etc.	
οʹ	70	ἑβδομήκοντα		ἑβδομηκοντάκις
πʹ	80	ὀγδοήκοντα		
ϟʹ	90	ἐνενήκοντα		
ρʹ	100	ἑκατόν		
ρνγʹ	153	ἑκατὸν πεντήκοντα τρεῖς (↑Jn 21:11)		
σʹ	200	διακόσιοι -αι -α		
σοςʹ	276	διακόσιοι ἑβδομήκοντα ἕξ (↑Ac 27:37)		
τʹ	300	τριᾱκόσιοι -αι -α		
υʹ	400	τετρᾰκόσιοι -αι -α		
φʹ	500	πεντᾰκόσιοι -αι -α		
χʹ	600	ἑξᾰκόσιοι -αι -α		
χξςʹ	666	ἑξακόσιοι ἑξήκοντα ἕξ (Re 13:18)		
ψʹ	700	ἑπτᾰκόσιοι -αι -α		
ωʹ	800	ὀκτᾰκόσιοι -αι -α		
ϡʹ	900	ἐνᾰκόσιοι -αι -α		
͵α	1.000	χῑ́λιοι -αι -α, ↑ also ἡ χῑλιάς χῑλιάδος *(the number) one thousand*		
͵β	2.000	δισχῑ́λιοι -αι -α		
͵γ	3.000	τρισχῑ́λιοι -αι -α		
͵δ	4.000	τετρακισχῑ́λιοι -αι -α		
͵ε	5.000	πεντακισχῑ́λιοι -αι -α or χῑλιάδες πέντε		
͵ι	10.000	μῡ́ριοι -αι -α or δέκα χῑλιάδες ↑ also ἡ μῡριάς μῡριάδος *(the number) ten thousand*		
͵ιβ	12.000	δώδεκα χῑλιάδες		
͵κ	20.000	εἴκοσι χῑλιάδες		
͵ν	50.000	μῡριάδες πέντε		

(1) CG: 13–19 τρεῖς (τρία) καὶ δέκα etc. (from 15 in one word), 13.–19. τρίτος καὶ δέκατος etc.
(2) KG/LXX τεσσ**α**ρᾰ́κοντα.

62b Notes on the above the table:

1. Note that the above list is not limited to numerals attested in the NT (↑ e.g. BDAG).

2. Letters of the alphabet are used as **numeric signs** (increasingly from the 3rd century B.C.), marked by additional strokes (up to one thousand on the top right side, from one thousand on the bottom left side). These are supplemented by older signs:

ς for 6 ("stigma", the sign for [st], formerly for ϝ, ↑Hebr. *waw*), ϟ for 90 ("koppa", ↑Hebr. *qof*; alternative [older] graph: ϙ) and ϡ for 900 ("sampi"). The standard text editions of the NT use numerals throughout. This also applies to many, some fairly early manuscripts such as the Codex Sinaiticus (4th century). In the papyri, however, the use of numeric signs is dominant, so in P66 (about A.D. 200).

Inflection of cardinals from one to four (↑BR §73; BDF §63; MH: 169ff) 63

63a

	1. *one* (↑46b) masc.	fem.	ntr.	
n.	εἷς	μία	ἕν	*one*
g.	ἑνός	μιᾶς	ἑνός	*of one*
d.	ἑνί	μιᾷ	ἑνί	*to/for one*
a.	ἕνᾰ	μίαν	ἕν	*one*

	2. *two*	3. *three* masc./fem.	ntr.	4. *four* masc./fem.	ntr.
n.	δύο	τρεῖς	τρίᾰ	τέσσαρες	τέσσαρᾰ(1)
g.	δύο(2)	τριῶν		τεσσάρων	
d.	δυσί(ν)(2)	τρισί(ν)		τέσσαρσι(ν)	
a.	δύο(3)	τρεῖς	τρίᾰ	τέσσαρᾰ	τέσσαρᾰ(1)

(1) For τέσσαρᾰ we frequently find τέσσερᾰ, e.g. in LXX manuscripts.
(2) CG δυοῖν (dual).
(3) In CG ἄμφω *both* inflects like δύο (in the NT ἄμφω is replaced by ἀμφότεροι).

The following compounds containing the negative particles οὐδέ or μηδέ (↑243) inflect like εἷς, "not" + "one" = "none" (outside the NT plural forms occur; "none" unlike "one" can refer to more than one entity in English, too): 63b

οὐδείς	< οὐδὲ εἷς	μηδείς	< μηδὲ εἷς
οὐδεμία	< οὐδὲ μία	μηδεμία	< μηδὲ μία
οὐδέν	< οὐδὲ ἕν	μηδέν	< μηδὲ ἕν

Note that sometimes οὐ**θ**είς/μη**θ**είς etc. replace οὐδείς/μηδείς etc. in certain texts.

	masc.		fem.		ntr.		pl. masc.	
n.	οὐδ-είς	*none*	οὐδε-μία	*none*	οὐδ-έν	*none*	οὐδ-ένες	*none*
g.	οὐδ-ενός	*of none*	οὐδε-μιᾶς	*of none*	οὐδ-ενός	*of none*	οὐδ-ένων	*of none*
d.	οὐδ-ενί	*to none*	οὐδε-μιᾷ	*to none*	οὐδ-ενί	*to none*	οὐδ-έσι(ν)	*to none*
a.	οὐδ-ένᾰ	*none*	οὐδε-μίαν	*none*	οὐδ-έν	*none*	οὐδ-ένᾰς	*none*

2.7 Verbs (↑22f on word-class)

2.7.1 Verbal system: basics

64 Categories of verbal system (↑BR §76; Duhoux §101ff; BDF §65; CAGL: 110–119, 137–142)

64a The verbal system of Ancient Greek is **rich in categories and forms.**

Most of these categories have their counterparts in English and Latin (though their functions often differ in intriguing ways), but in addition to these Ancient Greek has three more:
a) the "middle" voice in addition to the active and the passive (↑64b)
b) the "optative" mood in addition to the indicative, the subjunctive[17] and the imperative (↑64d)
c) the "aorist" "tense" (really a misnomer) in addition to the present/imperfect, the perfect/pluperfect and the future (↑64c; Ancient Greek differs significantly in its "tense" uses from English and Latin).

In the Hellenistic Greek variety (↑p. 5) represented in the NT a number of categories of the verbal system of Classical Greek are of minor or of no importance at all: the future perfect (not used very much even in earlier times) has disappeared almost completely (↑201d); and the optative plays a rather modest role (↑211). Furthermore, in the NT there are no forms of the subjunctive and optative perfect nor of the optative future; and there are only three (or four) instances of the imperative perfect passive. Still a great variety of forms and functions are attested (more than 1840 verbs are in use).

The inflection of the verb, conjugation, involves four classes of semantic or functional categories: (1) voice, (2) "tense"/aspect, (3) categories of the finite verb (person, number, mood), and (4) nominal forms of the verb (infinitive and participle with declension categories coming in as well).

64b I. In Ancient Greek there are three types of **voice**[18] indicating the relationship between the "action" and the subject: the active and the passive voice with the middle "between" the two as it were:

voice:	typically(1) indicates the "action":	
ACTIVE	as being performed by the subject entity (agent; ↑189), e.g.:	
	παιδεύω αὐτόν	*I train him*
MIDDLE	as being performed by the subject entity (agent), however, with greater subject-affectedness (↑190), e.g.:	
	παιδεύομαι αὐτόν	*I train him for me*
PASSIVE	as the subject entity undergoing it, experiencing it, (as "patient"; ↑191) "enduring" it	
	παιδεύομαι	*I am (being) trained*

(1) Note that only a small number of verbs are used with all of these in their typical function.

17 Hardly ever expressed by a special form of the verb in English, e.g. *I insist that she come, too.*
18 The term inherited from antiquity is "diathesis": διάθεσις inter alia *disposition.*

Note that for a fairly large number of verbs no active forms are attested. Traditionally such verbs are called **"deponents"** or "deponent verbs" (< Lat. *dēpōnens* "[a verb] putting away [some of its parts]"), also "middle deponents" or "passive deponents" depending on whether the aorist stem has a middle or a passive form (some verbs actually have both!). Regardless of their non-active form, such verbs usually call for an active rendering in English (e.g. χαρίζομαι *to grant*, not *to be granted*; ↑96.17). Somewhat confusingly, certain verbs have a present stem that is non-active in form but an aorist stem that, for instance, is active in form (e.g. ἔρχομαι *to come/go*; ↑113.3); and a verb may have both an active present stem and a non-active aorist stem (e.g. χαίρω *to rejoice*; ↑103.2[1]).

II. In Ancient Greek there are four "tenses", i.e. more precisely three **aspects** (inherited from Proto-Indo-European) and one **tense** (added later), each one with an aspect- or tense-stem of its own: 64c

1. Three **aspects**, indicating the ways in which the speaker or writer views and presents the "action" of the verb as being unfolded in a particular instance (the common term "tense" is misleading, as solely indicative forms typically serve to place the "action" in time [outside the future tense; ↑64d]; ↑65):

aspect ("tense"):	typically presents the "action" (here illustrated by means of the inf. pass.):	
DURATIVE:	as something ongoing, e.g.:	
"present" stem (↑194a–194d)	παιδεύεσθαι	*to be trained* (*continuously/at the moment* etc.)
AORIST stem (↑194e–194j)	simply as something that is done (without reference to continuation or result), e.g.:	
	παιδευθῆναι	*to be trained*
RESULTATIVE:	with a special focus on its result, e.g.:	
perfect stem (↑194k)	πεπαιδεῦσθαι	*to have been trained*, i.e. *to be a trained person*

2. One real **tense** (all forms of the stem refer to placement in time; ↑65):

tense:	typically presents the "action"	
FUTURE stem (↑202; 206c; 206h)	as something going on in the future or subsequently, e.g.:	
	παιδευθήσομαι	*I will be trained*
	παιδευθήσεσθαι	*to be trained* (*subsequently*)

III. Categories of the **finite verb** (i.e. verb forms with a personal ending): 64d

1. As in English, French, Latin etc. three **persons** are distinguished; they typically serve to identify the subject of the verb (note that Ancient Greek personal endings will generally be translated by English personal pronouns; ↑255d/255f and 348b):

person:	typically identifies as the subject of the "action":	
FIRST person	the speaking person(s)/communicator(s), e.g.:	
	παιδεύω, παιδεύομεν	*I train, we train*
SECOND person	the person(s) spoken to/the addressee(s), e.g.:	
	παιδεύεις, παιδεύετε	*you* (sg.) *train, you* (pl.) *train*

THIRD person	the person(s) or thing(s) spoken about, e.g.:	
	παιδεύει, παιδεύουσιν	*he/she/it trains; they train*
	αὐξάνει, αὐξάνουσιν	*he/she/it grows, they grow*

2. In the verbal system (as with nouns and adjectives; ↑23b), KG and NT Greek distinguish two **numbers** (for concord peculiarities regarding number ↑262–264):

number:	typically identifies the subject of the "action" as consisting in:	
SINGULAR	one entity, e.g.:	
	παιδεύ-ω, -εις, -ει	*I train, you* (sg.) *train, he/she/it trains*
PLURAL	more than one entity, e.g.:	
	παιδεύ-ομεν, -ετε, -ουσιν	*we, you* (pl.), *they train*

In the CG verbal system, too (↑23b), there is a third grammatical number (↑BR §141):

DUAL	two entities, e.g.:	
	δύο … προσελθόν**τε** … διελεγέ**σθην**	*… two came to … and discussed …* (Thucydides 5.59)
	(ptc. aor. II act. nom. dual masc. and 3rd pers. dual ipf. mid./pass.)	

3. In Ancient Greek four **moods** are distinguished: indicative, subjunctive, optative (comparatively rare in the NT), and imperative (note that for lack of corresponding grammatical categories in English, these moods very frequently need to be paraphrased when translated):

mood:	typically presents the "action":	
INDICATIVE	as something factual, e.g.:	
(↑209)	εἰσήλθομεν	*we entered*
	in certain cases, as something non-factual, e.g.:	
	εἰσήλθομεν ἄν	*we would enter/we would have entered*
SUBJUNCTIVE	as something intended or subjectively expected, e.g.:	
(↑210)	εἰσέλθωμεν·	*Let us enter!*
	ἵνα εἰσέλθωμεν	*so that we can/may/might enter*
OPTATIVE	in terms of an attainable wish, e.g.:	
(↑211)	εἰσέλθοι τις	*May someone enter!*
	as a possibility merely in the thoughts of the speaker/writer, e.g.:	
	εἰσέλθοι τις ἄν	*someone might/could enter*
IMPERATIVE	in terms of a command (directive), e.g.:	
(↑212)	εἴσελθε· εἰσελθέτω·	*Enter! Let he/she/it enter!*

4. In the Ancient Greek verbal system there are six categories whose basic use is to locate the "action" of the verb in time. So, these are **tenses** in the real sense of the term. Among the forms of the "present" (more accurately durative), the aorist and the perfect stems, the indicative forms alone belong here. These serve not only to express the aspect of the stem in question, but also to indicate the placement of the

"action" in time.[19] In the future stem, however, all forms, indicative and non-indicative ones, typically serve to locate the "action" in time (↑64c).
The six time-related indicative forms may be divided into (a) three indicatives without augment and (b) three augment indicatives:

time-related ind.:	typically locates the "action":	
a) Indicative forms **without augment**:		
ind. PRESENT (↑197)	in the present, e.g.: ἀναβαίνει εἰς τὸ ἱερόν	*he is going/he goes up to the temple*
ind. FUTURE (↑202)	in the future, e.g.: ἀναβήσεται εἰς τὸ ἱερόν	*he will go up to the temple*
ind. PERFECT (↑200)	in the present as a result of what happened previously, e.g.: ἀναβέβηκεν εἰς τὸ ἱερόν	*he has gone up to the temple*, i.e. *he is up in the temple*
b) Indicative forms **with augment** (also "augment tenses"):		
IMPERFECT = augment ind. present (↑198)	in the past as something that was taking place or used to take place, e.g.: ἀνέβαινεν εἰς τὸ ἱερόν	*he was going/used to go up to the temple*
(augment) ind. AORIST (↑199)	in the past as something that took place (for which the ind. aor. is the standard form), e.g.: ἀνέβη εἰς τὸ ἱερόν	*he went up to the temple*
PLUPERFECT = augment ind. perfect (↑201)	in the past as a result of what had taken place in a situation previous to that, e.g.: ἀνεβεβήκει εἰς τὸ ἱερόν (post-CG: ἀναβεβήκει)	*he had gone up to the temple*, i.e. *he was up in the temple*

On the periphrastic conjugation ↑203.

IV. In the case of the **non-finite verb** (i.e. verb forms without personal endings) or (alternatively) "nominal forms" of the verb there are basically two categories or forms: the infinitive and the participle. Both of these occur in all of the three voice types and all of the four of the tense-aspect stems. As non-indicative forms, neither the infinitive nor the participle in and of themselves (outside the future stem) refer to the time of the "action" (↑footnote 19): 64e

19 Non-indicative forms (subj., opt., imp., inf. and ptc.) of these stems do not in and of themselves indicate the time of the "action". The linguistic and non-linguistic context in which these forms appear will show how exactly the "situation" in question is meant to relate to other "situations" in terms of placement in time (↑Part 4 on textgrammar, inter alia 308ff).

nominal form:	(apart from voice and aspect/tense) typically refers to:		
INFINITIVE (↑213ff)	the "action" itself, e.g. infinitive of παιδεύω *to train* inter alia:		
	παιδεῦσαι	aor. act.	*to train*
	παιδευθῆναι	aor. pass.	*to be trained*
	παιδεύειν	pres. act.	*to train* (*continuously* etc.)
	παιδεύεσθαι	pres. pass.	*to be trained* (*continuously* etc.)
	παιδεύσασθαι	aor. mid.	*to train for o.s.*
PARTICIPLE (↑48; 227ff)	the "action" as a property (either actual or potential) of an entity (the participle inflects like an adjective in case, number and gender), e.g. nom. sg. masc. of παιδεύω *to train* inter alia:		
	παιδεύσας	aor. act.	*one who trains/trained*
	παιδευθείς	aor. pass.	*one who is/was trained*
	παιδεύων	pres. act.	*one who trains/is* (or *was*) *training*
	παιδευόμενος	pres. pass.	*one who is* (or *was*) *being trained*
	παιδευσάμενος	aor. mid.	*one who trains/trained for himself*

In the CG verbal system there are also two **verbal adjectives** (↑BR §72; 92.2h; 249): one in -τός and one in -τέος (↑Latin gerundive; Sihler: 625), e.g. of the verb γράφω *to write*:

γραπ-τός	*written*

(however e.g. βατός [of βαίνω *to go/to pass*] *passable*; ↑Xenophon, Anabasis 4.6.17)

γραπ-τέον (↑Lat. *scribendum*)	*something to be written = something that must be written*
γραπ-τέον τινί (↑176c)	*somebody must write* (↑Xenophon, Horsemanship 2.1)

In the NT the verbal adjective in -τέος occurs once only (Lk 5:38). Those in -τός are normal ("lexicalized") adjectives, e.g. ἀγαπητός *beloved*. For further details ↑360a.

65 Aspect and tense (↑192ff)

Users of languages like English and German and certainly users of Latin tend to associate verb forms above all with tense, in the sense of placement in time (i.e. in terms of "absolute" time; ↑192b). In fact, placement in time is important, in many cases predominant when it comes to choosing verb forms in these and other languages; choices are made typically on the basis of whether the "action" or "situation" referred to should be understood as being in the present, past or future (in relation to a specific reference point, typically the moment of speaking or writing). The verbal system of Ancient Greek, however, is rather different: the predominant factor involved in choosing verb forms is not placement in time, but aspect (formerly also called "aktionsart", a term used in a different way nowadays; ↑194m).

Aspect has to do with the way the speaker/writer views and presents the "action" of the verb regarding its unfolding in time (for details ↑192ff):
1. as something ongoing: **durative** (aspect), expressed by forms of the "present"[20] stem (more accurately "durative" stem);

20 From now on this term is written without quotation marks for practical reasons.

2. simply as something that is done (without reference to continuation or result): **aorist** (i.e. the unspecified/unmarked aspect),[21] expressed by forms of the aorist stem (this is the most striking peculiarity of the Ancient Greek verbal system; yet aorist forms in most cases are the least conspicuous options [they are generally the standard ones], so the indicative aorist e.g. is the dominant form in narratives); or
3. with a special focus on its result: **resultative** (aspect), expressed by forms of the perfect stem.

The forms of these aspect stems (traditionally "tense" stems) may be either indicative or non-indicative (↑64d/64e). All of these typically have aspect meaning due to their connection with a particular aspect stem.[22]
But only **indicative forms** (typically) express **placement in time** in and of themselves: augment indicative forms usually place the "action" in the past, and those without augment in the present.

Unlike the above aspect stems the **future stem**, a real tense stem, typically serves to locate the "action" in time, i.e. in the future (or as something subsequent). Future forms, however, do not have any aspect meaning (↑202[50]).

Synopsis of the components of finite verb forms 66

The following types of components occur in finite verb forms (on mood signs ↑69):

augment ↑71; 73	tense-aspect stem ↑68a–68d			termination (BR §80.3)		
	reduplication ↑72/73	verb stem ↑67	tense-aspect sign ↑68d	thematic vowel ↑68e	character vowel ↑68f	personal ending ↑70
			formative syllable ↑68g			
		παιδεύ-		-ο-		-μεν *we train*
ἐ-		παιδεύ-		-ο-		-μεν *we trained* (ipf.)
ἐ-		παιδεύ-	-σ-		-α-	-μεν *we trained* (ind. aor.)
		παιδεύ-	-σ-	-ο-		-μεν *we will train*
	πε-	παιδεύ-	-κ-		-α-	-μεν *we have trained*
ἐ-	πε-	παιδεύ-	-κ-		-ει-	-μεν *we had trained*

21 BDF §318 and many others use the misleading term "punctiliar" (or "momentary"); ↑194e. – Note that the terminological pair "imperfective" (for durative) and "perfective" (for aorist), current among aspect theorists, is not being used in the present grammar, inter alia to avoid confusion with terms like "imperfect" and "perfect" which have a different meaning.

22 In the case of the indicative present, however, the aspect meaning seems to be largely neutralized (for lack of alternatives when referring to a "situation" in the present; ↑197).

67 Verb stems (↑BR §79; Duhoux §14)

67a 1. The verb stem is the **base element** shared by all forms of a verb. It may be identical with its root (↑21c), e.g.:

λυ-	in λύ-ω	*to loosen*

Or a derivational suffix is added to the root in order to form a verb stem (↑21b), e.g.:

παιδευ-	in παιδεύ-ω	*to train*
παιδ-	root (↑παῖς παιδός *boy/girl*; ↑33b)	
-ευ-	derivational suffix of verbs typically denoting a state or activity connected with something the noun refers to (↑363b)	

67b 2. Verb stems are **classified** on the basis of their stem-final sound:

	present/lexical form:	verb stem:	
a) vowel stems:	λύ-ω	λ**υ**-	*to loosen*
	παιδεύ-ω	παιδ**ευ**-	*to train*
b) consonant stems:	ἄγ-ω	ἄ**γ**-	*to lead*
	μέν-ω	μέ**ν**-	*to remain*

68 Tense-aspect stems (↑BR §80; Duhoux §22; CALG: 110f, 185f)

68a I. **Tense-aspect stems** (↑65) are derived from the verb stem, e.g. from παιδευ-:

(1) present/durative stem (act./mid./pass.)	**παιδεύ**-ω	*I train*
(2) active and middle future stem	**παιδεύσ**-ω	*I will train*
(3) active and middle aorist stem	ἐ-**παίδευσ**-α	*I trained*
(4) active perfect stem	**πεπαίδευκ**-α	*I have trained*
(5) middle-passive perfect stem	**πεπαίδευ**-μαι	*I have been trained*
(6) passive aorist stem	ἐ-**παιδεύθ**-η-ν	*I was trained*
(passive future stem always based on [6]:	**παιδευθήσ**-ομαι	*I will be trained*)

Notes on the tense-aspect stems:

68b a) The tense-aspect stems of a verb are the so-called “principal parts”; knowing these is indispensable for a meaningful reading of Ancient Greek texts (↑79c; 80; 84d; 85/86; 87b; 88; 89c; 92d; 94–96; 100–103; 106; 110–113; 120/121; 123/124).

b) For the middle and passive voice, the present/durative and the perfect stems have the same forms, the aorist and the future stems, however, different ones.

68c c) Often the tense-aspect stem is the same as the verb stem, as in the above example παιδεύω *to train* Sometimes, however, different *ablaut* grades (↑8) are involved, e.g. (↑94.4):

e-grade:	zero-grade:	*o*-grade:	
λειπ-	**λιπ-**	**λοιπ-**	
(1) λείπ-ω			*I leave behind*
(2) λείψ-ω			*I will leave behind*
(3)	ἔ-λιπ-ον		*I left behind*
(4)		λέλοιπ-α	*I have left behind*
(5) λέλειμ-μαι			*I am left behind*
(6) ἐ-λείφ-θην			*I was left behind*

In most cases the verb stem is expanded to form the tense-aspect stems:

- by means of suffixes, to form the stems of the fut. act./mid., aor. act./mid., pf. act., aor. pass. and fut. pass., e.g. in the above example παιδεύω *to train*, and partly also λείπω *to leave behind*; or
- by means of reduplication, especially to form the perfect stems (↑72), e.g. in the above examples.

Sometimes even the formation of the present stem involves an expansion of the verb stem (↑75; particularly 110ff; 120/121; 123/124). Such changes are restricted to the present stem.

d) Suffixes characterizing tense-aspect stems may be termed "**tense-aspect signs**": 68d

tense-aspect sign	tense-aspect stem:		
-σ-	fut. act./mid.	παιδεύ**σ**-ω	*I will train*
	aor. act./mid.	ἐ-παίδευ**σ**-α	*I trained*
-κ-	pf. act.	πεπαίδευ**κ**-α	*I have trained*
-θ-	aor. pass.	ἐ-παιδεύ**θ**-η-ν	*I was trained*
(aor. pass. >: θ+ησ	fut. pass.	παιδευ**θήσ**-ομαι	*I will be trained*)

There are aor. and pf. stems that lack the above tense-aspect signs. These are called "strong" stems, those mentioned above "weak" stems; alternatively one may speak of "second aor."/"second pf. act." or "aor. II/pf. II act." (for the strong variety) and "first aor."/"first pf. act." or "aor. I/pf. I act." (for the weak one); ↑104–107.

II. In a number of cases there is a vowel (or diphthong) between the tense-aspect stem and the ending proper (↑70).

1. The forms of the present stem of the verbs in -ω and all the forms of the future and of the second aorist act./mid. have a so-called **"thematic" vowel** between the stem and the endings proper: 68e

- ο before μ and ν as well as in the opt., e.g.:

παιδεύ-**ο**-μεν	*we train*	ἐ-παίδευ-**ο**-ν	*I/they trained*
παιδεύ-**ο**-ι	*may he train!*		

- ε before σ, τ (and vowels as well as /–/), e.g.:

παιδεύ-**ε**-τε	*you* (pl.) *train*	παιδεύ-**ε**-σθε	*you* (pl.) *are trained*
(παιδεύ-**ε**-εν > -ειν	*to train*	παίδευ-**ε**[-/–/]	*train* [sg.]*!*)

The use and non-use of thematic vowels in present/durative forms have led to the following basic division in the verb inflection:
a) thematic conjugation (verbs in -ω; ↑75–113) and
b) athematic conjugation (verbs in -μι; ↑114–125).

68f 2. The vowel characterizing other forms of the tense-aspect system may be termed **"character" vowel** (in BR §80.3 the term "Kennvokal" is used):

- α characterizing forms of the weak aor. act./mid. and of the pf. act., e.g.:

ἐ-παιδεύσ-**α**-μεν *we trained* πεπαιδεύκ-**α**-μεν *we have trained*

- ει (CG pl.: ε) characterizing forms of the pluperfect act., e.g.:

ἐ-πεπαιδεύκ-**ει**-μεν *we had trained* (CG ἐ-πεπαιδεύκ-**ε**-μεν)

- η (before vowels or -ντ: ε) characterizing forms of the aor. pass., e.g.:

ἐ-παιδεύθ-**η**-μεν *we were trained* παιδευ-**θέ**ντος *of one who was trained*

68g III. Sometimes it is helpful to view the tense-aspect sign and the thematic or character vowel together as one category characterizing forms outside the present stem under the term **"formative syllable"**:

formative syllables	tense-aspect	examples
-σο/-σε	fut. act./mid.	παιδεύ-**σο**-μεν, παιδεύ-**σε**-τε
-σα	aor. act./mid.	ἐπαίδευ-**σα**, ἐπαιδεύ-**σα**-μεν
-κα	pf. act.	πεπαίδευ-**κα**
-κει	plpf. act.	ἐπεπαυδεύ-**κει**-ν
-θη	aor. pass.	ἐπαιδεύ-**θη**-μεν
-θε before vowel or -ντ		παιδευ-**θε**-ίη; παιδευ-**θέ**-ντος
-θη-σο/-σε	fut. pass.	παιδευ-**θη-σό**-μεθα, παιδευ-**θή-σε**-σθε
without formative syllable	pf./plpf. mid./pass.	πεπαίδευ-μαι, ἐπεπαιδεύ-μην
-το	verbal adjectives	ἀγαπη-**τό**-ς *beloved*
-τεο	(↑64e)	βλη-**τέο**-ς *one to be thrown*

69 Mood signs (↑BR §81; CALG: 111f, 186f)

Mood signs are vowel suffixes added to the tense-aspect stem to distinguish subjunctive and optative forms (↑76ff; 114c) from indicative (and imperative) ones:

1. **subjunctive** signs:(1)
(note that these replace thematic/character vowels the aor. using pres. terminations)

- ω before μ and ν, e.g.:

indicative (pres.) λύομεν λύουσιν (<-οντι; ↑70) *we/they loosen*
subjunctive (pres.) λύ**ω**μεν λύ**ω**σιν *(if) we/they loosen*

- η before σ, τ, also before vowels and /–/, e.g.:

indicative (pres.) λύετε (pl.) λύεις (sg.) *you loosen*
subjunctive (pres.) λύ**η**τε (pl.) λύ**ῃ**ς (sg.) *(if) you loosen*

2. **optative** signs: ιη or ῑ, combined with preceding vowels: ειη/ει, οιη/οι, αιη/αι, e.g.:

indicative (aor. pass.)	ἐλύθητε (pl.)	ἐλύθης (sg.)	*you were loosened*
optative (aor. pass.)	λυθε**ίη**τε (pl.)	λυθε**ίη**ς (sg.)	*may you be loosened*

(1) Translations of subjunctive word forms imply the use of ἐάν *if* (↑252.18) in Part 2.

Personal endings and terminations of nominal forms (↑BR §82; BDF §80ff; CALG: 112ff) 70

There are three types of personal endings:

1. the so-called “primary” endings used for the indicative forms without augment (ind. pres., fut. and pf.) and the subjunctive forms;

2. the so-called “secondary” endings used for the augment indicative forms (ipf., ind. aor., plpf.) and for the optative forms (except for 1 sg. opt. act., usually in -μι);

3. the endings of the imperative forms.

Synopsis of personal **endings** or terminations (not including some special cases):

	active (also aor. pass.)				**middle/passive**[1]		
person ↓	without augment		with aug.	imperative	without aug.	with aug.	imperative
sg. 1	ω[2]/[3]	μι	ν[4]		μαι	μην	
2	εις[3]	ς (< σι)	ς	–[5], θι/ς	σαι[6]	σο[6]	(σ)ο[5]/[6]
3	ει[3]	σιν[7] (< τι)	–[4]	τω	ται	το	σθω
pl. 1	μεν		μεν		μεθα	μεθα	
2	τε		τε	τε	σθε	σθε	σθε
3	σιν[7] (< ντι)[8]		ν[9]	τωσαν[10]	νται	ντο	σθωσαν[10]
	terminations of nominal forms (↑48 for paradigms of the ptc.):						
inf.	-ειν (< ε-εν)[3], -(ε)ναι, -σαι				-σθαι		
ptc.	-ντ-, pf. -οτ-/-υια (for details ↑48)				-μεν-ος/η/ον		

(1) The aor. pass. uses the endings and terminations of the active.

(2) In the pf. -(α)–.

(3) In the endings -ω, -εις, -ει, -ειν the thematic vowel is included (↑11).

(4) 1 sg. ind. aor. I act. -(α)–, 3 sg. -(ε)–.

(5) In the aor. I act.: παίδευ-σον, mid. παίδευ-σαι.

(6) Due to the dropping of σ between vowels (↑13e) and vowel contraction (↑11) -(ε)σαι is usually replaced by -ῃ (occasionally by -ει), -(ε)σο by -ου, -(α)σο by -ω (↑77/78; also ↑121.4/121.7).
-σαι is used in the pf. (↑77/78), rarely in the thematic pres. (↑85a), in the fut. (↑110.3; 113.4), typically in the athematic pres. (↑117; 121.5; 122; 125e; 125f).

(7) ν mobile, ↑18a.

(8) -ντι > νσι; ν is dropped and the syllable is lengthened (↑10a); KG/NT pf. sometimes in -ν.

(9) -σαν in the aor. pass.: ἐπαιδεύθη-**σαν** *the were trained*;
in the ipf. of verbs in -μι: ἐδίδο-**σαν** *they gave* (↑115), ↑ind. aor.;
ipf. (and ind. aor. II) in post-CG (especially in the LXX) also -**οσαν**, e.g. εἴχ-**οσαν** *they had* (↑113.5; 87c; 110.13; 112.1), apparently by analogy (in the LXX) also in the opt. (↑76; 105d).
(10) CG -ντων (act.) and -σθων (mid./pass.), in post-CG expanded by -σα-.

71 Augment (↑BR §83; BDF §66f; MH: 188ff; CALG: 185)

71a 1. The augment ("increase") is a **past tense marker** prefixed to (augment) indicative forms (↑65), i.e. to the imperfect (present stem), the indicative aorist and (in principle) to the pluperfect (resultative stem).

2. There are two types of augments:

71b a) the **syllabic augment**: if the stem begins with a consonant, the syllable ε is prefixed (note that if this consonant is a ρ it is doubled), e.g.:

lexical form (pres. ind.)		augment indicative form (here ipf.):	
παιδεύω	*to train*	**ἐ**-παίδευον	*I/they trained*
(ῥίπτω	*to throw*	**ἔ**-ρριπτον	*I/they threw*)

71c b) the **"temporal" augment**:[23] if the stem begins with a vowel, this vowel is lengthened (in the case of a diphthong, the first of its elements is lengthened; ι as a second element is then written as an iota subscript; ↑2b[1]), as follows:

lengthening type:	lexical form (pres. ind.):	augment indicative form (here mostly ipf.):	
α > η	ἄγω	**ἦ**γον	*I/they led*
ε > η	ἐλπίζω	**ἤ**λπιζον	*I/they hoped*
ο > ω	ὀνομάζω	**ὠ**νόμαζον	*I/they named*
ῐ > ῑ	ἰσχύω	**ἴ**σχυον	*I was/they were strong*
ῠ > ῡ	ὑβρίζω	**ὕ**βριζον	*I/they mistreated*
αι > ῃ	αἴρω	**ᾖ**ρον	*I/they lifted*
ᾳ > ῃ	ᾄδω	**ᾖ**δον	*I/they sang*
αυ > ηυ	αὐξάνω	**ηὔ**ξανον	*I/they grew/increased*
ευ > ηυ (but ↑71f)	εὑρίσκω	**ηὕ**ρισκον	*I/they found*
οι > ῳ (but ↑71g)	οἰκοδομέω	**ᾠ**κοδόμησα (aor. ind.)	*I built*

Clarifying points and peculiarities:

71d • A number of stems beginning with an ε have ει (not η) as an augment, e.g.:[24]

ἔχω (↑113.5)	**εἶ**χον	*I/they had*
ἕλκω (↑112.14)	**εἷ**λκον	*I/they drew*
ἐάω (↑85.4)	**εἴ**ων	*I/they let/permitted*
ἐργάζομαι (↑96.7)	**εἰ**ργαζόμην (also **ἠ**-)	*I/they worked*
ἐθίζω (outside NT)	**εἴ**θιζον	*I/they got used*

23 The quantity or *time* ("tempus") of the word appears to increase (↑Kühner-Blass II: 10).

24 Originally the stem-initial sound of these verbs was a σ (↑13d) or a ϝ (↑12), e.g.: ἐ-**σ**εχ-ον > ἐ-εχ-ον > εἶχ-ον *I/they had*.

- Some verbs have a double augment (a syllabic and a temporal one; ↑123.3), e.g.: 71e

	ἀνοίγω (↑95.2)	ἀν**έῳ**ξα (aor.ind.)	*I opened*
	ὁράω (↑113.8)	**ἑώ**ρων	*I/they saw*
• Note:	η < α, ε	ῃ < αι, ᾳ	

- Verbs beginning with ευ- are rarely augmented, the few with ει- hardly ever, e.g.: 71f

εὐδόκησα (aor.ind.)	*I am delighted*	(Mt 3:17)
εὐλόγησεν (aor.ind.)	*he blessed (it)*	(Lk 24:30)
εἴξαμεν (of εἴκω)	*we surrendered*	(Ga 2:5)

some counter-examples are (also Mk 14:55; Ac 7:11; 17:21; 27:29; Ro 9:3; He 11:5):

ηὐδόκησαν (aor.ind.)	*they decided*	(Ro 15:26 Var.)
ηὐφράνθη (aor.ind.)	*(my heart) rejoiced*	(Ac 2:26)

3. **No augment** is added to verbs beginning with a long vowel or ου-, e.g.: 71g

	ἡγέομαι	**ἡ**γησάμην (aor.ind.)	*I considered*
	ὠφελέω	**ὠ**φέλησα (aor.ind.)	*I helped*
(outside NT [rarely]:	οὐτάζω *to wound*	**οὐ**τάζοντο	*they were wounded*)

in KG/NT sometimes also to verbs beginning with οι-[25], e.g.:

οἰκοδομέω usually: **ᾠ**κοδόμησεν (aor.ind.) *he built* (Mt 7:26)
also: **οἰ**κοδόμησεν (aor.ind.) *he built* (Ac 7:47)
οἰκοδομήθη (aor.ind.) *it was built* (Jn 2:20)

less frequently also to verbs beginning with αι- (only 2Tm 1:16 in the NT):

ἐπ-αισχύνομαι ἐπ-**αι**σχύνθη (aor.ind.) *he was ashamed*

Reduplication (↑BR §84, 86; BDF §68; MH: 188ff; CALG: 117f; 186) 72

Reduplication is a **characteristic** of the **perfect stems** (with all the pf. and plpf. forms). Unlike the augment, which is restricted to (augment) indicative forms (↑71a), reduplication is found in both the indicative and the non-indicative forms (such as the inf. and the ptc.). ε is the reduplication vowel here (↑72b–72e). 72a

In some cases, there is reduplication also in other tense-aspect stems:

- in the present/durative stem (the reduplication vowel being ι), e.g.:

γι-γνώ-σκ-ω (CG) *to know* (verb stem: γνώ[σ]-, ↑111.8; also ↑75f; 111.9–111.13; 113.10/113.11; 115a; 121.1/121.2; 121.7)

- in the aorist act./mid. stem (the complete stem being reduplicated), e.g.:

ἤγ-αγ-ον (st. **ἀγ**-αγ-) of ἄγω *to lead* (↑95.1)

I. The initial sound of the verb stem results in different types of reduplication:

(initial sound of verb stem:) (perfect reduplication type:)

1. Verb stems with an **initial consonant** are connected with the following subtypes:

25 Analogically so in the case of reduplication (↑72g).

72b	a) a single consonant (apart from ρ)		→ consonant + ε + consonant:	
	παιδεύω	*to train*	**πε**-παίδευκα	*I have trained*
	λύω	*to loosen*	**λέ**-λυκα	*I have loosened*
72c	b) aspirate (φ/θ/χ; ↑3; 14a)		→ unaspirated stop (π/τ/κ) + ε + aspirate:	
	φανερόω	*to reveal*	**πε**-φανέρωκα	*I have revealed*
	θεάομαι	*to see*	**τε**-θέαμαι	*I have seen*
	χαρίζομαι	*to grant*	**κε**-χάρισμαι	*I have granted*
72d	c) stop + liquid/nasal (λ/ρ/μ/ν; ↑3; 4b)		→ stop + ε + stop + liquid/nasal:	
	κλείω	*to shut*	**κέ**-κλεικα	*I have shut*
	γράφω	*to write*	**γέ**-γραφα	*I have written*
	χρίω (also ↑72c)	*to anoint*	**κέ**-χρικα	*I have anointed*
	ἀπο-**θν**ῄσκω	*to die*	**τέ**-θνηκα	*I am dead*
	exception (st. **γν**ω[σ]-; ↑111.8):		simply ἐ- (↑72e) + stop + liquid/nasal	
	γι(γ)νώσκω	*to know*	**ἔ**-γνωκα	*I have known*
72e	d) two and more consonants or ρ (note that digraphs are included here)		→ no doubling, simply prefixed ἐ- (it has the same form as the augment; ↑71b):	
	στρέφω	*to turn*	**ἔ**-στροφα (↑94.7)	*I have turned*
	ῥίπτω	*to throw*	**ἔ**-ρριμμαι[1] (↑94.19)	*I have been thrown*
	ζητέω	*to seek*	**ἐ**-ζήτηκα	*I have sought*

(1) Initial ρ is usually doubled, as in the case of the augment (↑71b; also ↑BR §83.2; BDF §11.1).

72f	e) special cases (↑110.12/110.13)		→ εἰ- replaces the reduplication syllable:	
	λαμβάνω	*to take*	**εἴ**-ληφα	*I have taken*

2. Verb stems with an **initial vowel** are connected with the following types:

72g	a) standard case		→ "reduplication" = temporal augment (↑71c):	
	ἀγαπάω	*to love*	**ἠ**γάπηκα	*I have loved*
	b) certain verbs		→ the two stem-initial sounds are prefixed to a temporal augment ("Attic" reduplication):	
	ἀκούω	*to hear* (↑80.1)	**ἀκ-ή**κοα	*I have heard*
	ἐγείρω	*to raise* (↑103.5f)	**ἐγ-ή**γερμαι	*I am raised*
	ἀπ-όλλυμι	*to ruin* (↑123.7)	ἀπ-**ολ-ώ**λεκα	*I have ruined*
	ἀπ-όλλυμαι	*to get lost* (↑123.8)	ἀπ-**όλ-ω**λα	*I am lost*
	(φέρω)	*to carry* (↑113.14)	**ἐν-ή**νοχα (st. ἐνεκ-)	*I have carried*

72h II. Augment of the **pluperfect** (augment indicative of the perfect-stem):

(augmentless indicative perfect:) (pluperfect, i.e. augment indicative:)

1. When the perfect-stem has a real reduplication (↑72b–72d), in principle an additional syllabic augment is prefixed, however, rarely so in KG/NT, e.g.:

πεπαίδευκ-α	*I have trained*	**ἐ-πε**παιδεύκ-ειν	*I had trained*
γέγραπ-ται	*it is written*	**ἐ-γέ**γραπ-το	*it was written*

In Mk 14:44, however, there is no augment (plpf. solely identifiable by endings):

δέδωκ-εν	*he has given*	**δε**δώκ-ει	*he had given*

2. When the reduplication of the perfect-stem has the form of an augment (↑72e; 72g), no augment is added (plpf. being solely identifiable by its endings), e.g.:

ἔστροφ-α (↑94.7)	*I have turned*	**ἐ**στρόφ-ειν	*I had turned*
ἔρριμ-μαι (↑94.19)	*I have been thrown*	**ἐ**ρρίμ-μην	*I had been thrown*
ἠγάπηκ-α	*I have loved*	**ἠ**γαπήκ-ειν	*I had loved*

Augment and reduplication in compounds (↑BR §85; BDF §69; MH: 192) 73

(lexical form [pres. ind.]:) (form with augment or reduplication:)

1. When the compounded verb has a **prepositional prefix**, the uncompounded verb is augmented and reduplicated. The preposition behaves in the following ways:

a) Prepositions ending in a (stable) consonant remain unchanged, applicable to εἰς *into*, πρός *to/towards* and ὑπέρ *over*, e.g.: 73a

προ**σ**-κυνέω	*to worship*	προ**σ-ε**-κύνησα	*I worshipped*

b) Before an augment (↑71) or an augment-like reduplication (↑72e; 72g) ἐκ *out of/ from is* replaced by ἐξ (↑18b), e.g.: 73b

ἐκ-βάλλω	*to put out*	**ἐξ-έ**-βαλεν	*he put out*
ἐκ-στρέφω (↑72e)	*to pervert*	**ἐξ-έ**-στραπται	*he is perverted*

c) Before an augment (↑71) or an augment-like reduplication (↑72e; 72g) ἐν *in* and σύν *with* regain their original (i.e. unassimilated) form (↑15b/15c), e.g.: 73c

ἐμ-βλέπω	*to look at*	**ἐν-έ**-βλεψα	*I looked at*
ἐγ-καλέω	*to accuse*	**ἐν-ε**-κάλεσα	*I accused*
συλ-λέγω	*to collect*	**συν-έ**-λεξαν	*they collected*
συλ-λαμβάνω (↑72e)	*to conceive*	**συν-εί**-ληφεν	*she conceived*

Note that ἐκ-, ἐξ-, ἐν- or ἐπ- at the beginning of a verb form may be an augment prefixed to a stem-initial consonant rather than a prepositional prefix, e.g.:

ἐξήρανεν	(Jas 1:11)	→	**ἐ-ξ**ήρανεν	*it dried/dries (it) up*
ἐναυάγησα	(2Cor 11:25)	→	**ἐ-ν**αυάγησα	*I suffered shipwreck*
ἐπίομεν	(Lk 13:26)	→	**ἐ-π**ίομεν	*we drank*

d) Most prepositions ending in a vowel, drop this vowel before an augment or an augment-like reduplication (↑19), e.g.: 73d

ἀπ**ο**-λύω	*to release*	**ἀπ-έ**-λυον	*I/they released*
ἐπι-γινώσκω (↑72b)	*to know*	**ἐπ-ε**-γνωκέναι	*to have known*

This does not, however, apply to περί *about/around* and πρό *before*, e.g.:

περι-λάμπω	*to shine around*	**περι-έ**λαμψεν	*it shone around*
προ-ορίζω	*to predetermine*	**προ-ώ**ρισεν	*he predetermined*

In CG the ο in προ- and the augment often contract to -ου-, e.g. Plato, Charmides 162b:

προ-βάλλω	*to present*	προ-έβαλεν: πρ**ού**βαλεν/πρ**οὔ**βαλεν *he presented*

The augment of the following verb is mostly placed at the beginning (presumably because to most people the base word προφήτης *prophet* seems to have been more of a simplex word; the only NT occurrence of προ-ε-φ … is Jd 14; ↑BDF §69.4), e.g.:

προφητεύω	*to prophesy*	**ἐ**-προφήτευσεν	*he prophesied*

The following verb (↑120.5) with a double prepositional prefix has two augments in KG/NT, one after each prefix:

ἀπο-καθ-ίστημι	*to restore*	ἀπ-**ε**-κατ-**ε**-στάθη	*it was restored*

73e 2. Compounded verbs with a **non-prepositional prefix**:

a) If it is an alpha privative (↑367b) there is a temporal augment (↑71c; 72g), e.g.:

ἀδικέω	*to do wrong*	**ἠ**δίκησεν	*he did wrong*

b) If the first part is a noun stem (↑370), the augment is placed at the beginning, e.g.:

ψευδομαρτυρέω	*to bear false witness*	**ἐψευδο**μαρτύρουν	*they testified falsely*

The following verb has its augment (and its reduplication) after its prefix (an adverb; ↑53b):

εὐ-αγγελίζομαι	*to bring good news*	εὐ-**η**γγελισάμην	*I brought good news*

74 Accentuation of verb forms (↑BR §87f)

I. **Basic rules** (↑79b on how accentuation affects the meaning of verb forms):

74a 1. The accent of **finite verb forms** is as far to the left as possible (↑5b–5d), but never before the augment or the reduplication, e.g.:

ὑπ-**ά**γω *to go* **ὕ**π-αγε *go!* ὑπ-**ῆ**γον *I/they went* (ipf.)

For a number of special cases ↑121.6; 125c; 125e.

74b 2. To the accent of **nominal verb forms** the following rules apply:

a) **Active** (and aor. pass.): the accent of the infinitive is on the last but one syllable, in the thematic aorist II (↑105b), however, on the last syllable, the accent of the corresponding participles is on the same part of the word, e.g. (also ↑76; 78):

inf. pres.	παιδ**εύ**ειν	*to train*
ptc. pres.	παιδ**εύ**ων/παιδ**εύ**ουσα/παιδ**εῦ**ον	*training*
inf. aor. I	παιδ**εῦ**σαι	*to train*
ptc. aor. I	παιδ**εύ**σᾱς/παιδ**εύ**σᾱσα/παιδ**εῦ**σαν	*training*
inf. pf.	πεπαιδευκ**έ**ναι	*to have trained*
ptc. pf.	πεπαιδευκ**ώ**ς/πεπαιδευκ**υῖ**α/πεπαιδευκ**ό**ς	*having trained*
inf. aor. II	βαλ**εῖ**ν	*to throw*
ptc. aor. II	βαλ**ώ**ν/βαλ**οῦ**σα/βαλ**ό**ν	*throwing*

b) **Middle-passive** (except for the aor. pass.; ↑above): the accent is as far to the left as possible (↑5b–5d), in the pf. and the thematic inf. aor. II (middle; ↑105b), however, it is on the last but one syllable, e.g.:

inf. pres.	παιδ**εύ**εσθαι	*to be trained*

ptc. pres.	παιδευ**ό**μενος/παιδευομ**έ**νη/ παιδευ**ό**μενον	*being trained*
inf. pf.	πεπαιδ**εῦ**σθαι	*to have been trained*
ptc. pf.	πεπαιδευμ**έ**νος/πεπαιδευμ**έ**νη/ πεπαιδευμ**έ**νον	*having been trained*
inf. aor. II	βαλ**έ**σθαι	*to throw for o.s.*
ptc. aor. II	βαλ**ό**μενος/βαλομ**έ**νη/βαλ**ό**μενον	*throwing for o.s.*

II. Some special points to be noted:

1. Final -οι and -αι count as long exclusively in the optative, e.g.: 74c

παιδ**εύ-οι** (pres.) παιδ**εύ-σαι** (aor.) *may he train*

In all the other inflected forms, however, they count as short (↑2b), e.g.:

παιδ**εῦ-σαι** (aor.) *to train* πα**ί**δευ-**σαι** (aor.mid.) *train for yourself!*

2. The accent of contracted verb forms is on the contraction syllable, provided it would be on one of the vowels involved in the vowel contraction (↑83), e.g.: 74d

τιμ**ά**ει > τιμ**ᾷ**	*he honours*	τιμ**αέ**τω > τιμ**ά**τω	*he must honour!*
ἐτ**ί**μαε > ἐτ**ί**μα (ipf.)	*he honoured*	τ**ί**μαε > τ**ί**μα	*honour!* (sg.)

Similarly, the accent of the subj. aor. pass. (↑78[4]) is on the syllable containing the mood sign; the same applies to the subj. of the major four verbs in -μι (↑115ff; but also ↑121.5), e.g.:

λυθ**ή**ῃ > λυθ**έ**ῃ > λυθ**ῇ** *(if) he is loosened* διδ**ώ**ῃ > διδ**ῷ** *(if) he gives*

Some of the optative forms have a similar accentuation (↑84b; 87c; 89a).

3. The accent of participles (like nouns and adjectives; ↑105f) remains on the tone syllable of the nom. sg. masc. as long as the accentuation rules allow (↑5b–5d; 48; for the gen. pl. fem. also 49c). 74e

4. The accent of the 2 sg. imp. aor. II act. of some (simplex) verbs (↑105f) is irregular, not, however, the accent of their compounded counterparts, e.g.: 74f

ἐλθ**έ** (↑113.3)	*go!* (sg.)	εἰπ**έ** (↑113.7)	*say!* (sg.)
εἴσελθε	*enter!* (sg.)	πρ**ό**ειπε(1)	*predict!* (sg.)

(1) Attested outside the NT.

Also ↑110.13; 111.4;113.8.

Overview of conjugation classes 74g

At the most basic level there is a division into two conjugation classes:

1. thematic conjugation or verbs in -ω, i.e. ind. pres. forms typically have a thematic vowel between the stem and the endings proper (↑68e), in other words the 1 sg. act. (lexical form) ends in -ω (deponents in -ομαι ↑70), and
2. athematic conjugation or verbs in -μι, i.e. ind. pres. forms have no thematic vowel, the 1 sg. act. ending in -μι (deponents in -μαι).

These are subdivided mainly on the basis of the final sound of verb stems:

1. **Thematic** conjugation or verbs in -ω (↑75–113)

a) Vowel verbs (verb stems in vowels)

(1) Uncontracted vowel verbs (↑76–80)

(2) Contracted verbs (with vowel contraction in forms of the present/durative; ↑81–89)

b) Stop verbs (verb stems in labials, dentals or velars) (↑90–96)

c) Liquid/nasal verbs (verb stems in -λ, -ρ, -μ or -ν) (↑97–103)

d) Strong tense-aspect stems (↑104–109)

e) "Irregular" verbs of the thematic conjugation (↑110–113)

2. **Athematic** conjugation or verbs in -μι (↑114–125)

a) Verbs in -μι with a reduplicated present/durative stem (↑115–121)

b) Verbs in -νυμι/-ννυμι (nasal presents; ↑122–124)

c) Root presents in -μι (↑125)

2.7.2 Thematic conjugation or verbs in -ω

75 Preliminaries: present stem formation (↑BR §89f; BDF §73; CAGL: 115ff)

The present stem, i.e. the lexical form without -ω or -ομαι, may be formed in a variety of ways on the basis of the verb stem (↑67; 68):

(present stem:)		(verb stem:)

75a I. The present stem is **the same as the verb stem**:

πιστεύ-ω	*to believe*	πιστευ- (↑79a)
βλέπ-ω	*to see*	βλεπ- (↑91a)
μέν-ω	*to remain*	μεν- (↑97b)

II. The present stem is formed by adding an **affix to the verb stem**:

75b 1. Originally an i̯ is affixed:

i̯-presents:

a) Present stems going back to verb stems in -ϝ ("digamma-stems") with an i̯ being affixed (↑12a–12d; 80.9/80.10), e.g.:

καί-ω < κα**ϝi̯**-ω	*to burn sth.*	καϝ-, καυ-	↑καῦμα *heat*

b) Present stems in -πτω, -σσω and -ζω going back to verb stems in stops with an i̯ being affixed (↑12c; 91), e.g.:

κόπτω < κο**πi̯**ω	*to strike*	κοπ-	↑κόπος *blow/labour*

c) Present stems going back to verb stems in liquids/nasals with an i̯ being affixed (applies to all liquid/nasal verbs except for μένω and δέρω; ↑12c; 97), e.g.:

ἀγγέλλω < ἀγγε**λi̯**ω	*to announce*	ἀγγελ-	↑ἄγγελος *messenger*

d) Present stems going back to verb stems in -σ with an i̯ being affixed ("sigma-stems"; ↑12d; 13e; 80.1; 86.3; 88.1/88.2), e.g.:

ἀκούω < ἀκου**σi̯**ω	*to hear*	ἀκουσ-	

2. ν, αν, or νε is affixed to the verb stem, or a ν-infix combined with an αν-affix: 75c
nasal-presents (↑110; 114b; 122), e.g.:

τέμ-**ν**-ω	*to cut*	τεμ-	↑τομή *(a) cut*
ἁμαρτ-**άν**-ω	*to sin*	ἁμαρτ-	↑ἁμαρτία *(a) sin*
ἀφ-ικ-**νέ**-ομαι	*to come (to)*	ἱκ-	↑ἱκέτης *suppliant*
μα-**ν**-θ-**άν**-ω	*to learn*	μαθ-η-	↑μαθητής *pupil*

3. σκ or ισκ is affixed to the verb stem: 75d
σκ-presents (↑111), e.g.:

γι-(γ)νώ-**σκ**-ω	*to know*	γνω(σ)- (↑72a; 75f)	↑γνῶσις *knowledge*
εὑρ-ί**σκ**-ω	*to find*	εὑρ(ε/η)-	↑εὑρετής *inventor*

4. ε is affixed to the verb stem (for paradigm ↑87): 75e
part of the so-called **e-class** (↑112), e.g.:

δοκ-**έ**-ω	*to think/to seem*	δοκ-	↑δόγμα *decision*
γαμ-**έ**-ω	*to marry*	γαμ-	↑γάμος *marriage*

5. There is a reduplication of the verb stem: 75f
reduplicated present (↑72a; 111; 113; 114e), e.g.:

γί(γ)ν-ομαι	*to come to be/become*	γεν-, γν-	↑γένος *race/kind*
μιμνῄ-σκ-ομαι	*to remember*	μνη- (also ↑75d)	↑μνήμη *remembrance*

2.7.2.1 Vowel verbs

(i) Uncontracted vowel verbs: paradigm of παιδεύω

↑Paradigms on pages 106–110.

Note:
The **auxiliary translations** of forms given **in the tables** are a rather incomplete and, in many ways, imprecise reflection of the meanings conveyed. For these the corresponding sections of Part 3 on syntax (3.2.2) need to be consulted (↑188–240).

76 Active: παιδεύω "I train/I am training (s.o.)" (↑BR §91)

		INDICATIVE augmentless indicative	augment indicative	SUBJUNCTIVE mood sign ω/η replacing thematic/character v.
PRESENT/		*I train* etc.	*I trained* etc. IPF.	*(if) I train* etc.
DURATIVE	sg. 1	παιδεύ-ω	ἐ-παίδευ-ο-ν	παιδεύ-ω
STEM	2	παιδεύ-εις	ἐ-παίδευ-ε-ς	παιδεύ-ῃς
thematic	3	παιδεύ-ει	ἐ-παίδευ-εν	παιδεύ-ῃ
vowel ε/ο	pl. 1	παιδεύ-ο-μεν	ἐ-παιδεύ-ο-μεν	παιδεύ-ω-μεν
	2	παιδεύ-ε-τε	ἐ-παιδεύ-ε-τε	παιδεύ-η-τε
	3	παιδεύ-ουσιν[(1)]	ἐ-παίδευ-ο-ν[(2)]	παιδεύ-ω-σιν
FUTURE		*I will train* etc.		
STEM	sg. 1	παιδεύ-σ-ω		
tense sign σ	2	παιδεύ-σ-εις		
+ thematic	3	παιδεύ-σ-ει		
vowel ε/ο	pl. 1	παιδεύ-σ-ομεν		
	2	παιδεύ-σ-ετε		
	3	παιδεύ-σ-ουσιν		
AORIST I			*I trained* etc.	*(if) I train* etc.
STEM	sg. 1		ἐ-παίδευ-σα	παιδεύ-σ-ω
tense sign σ	2		ἐ-παίδευ-σα-ς	παιδεύ-σ-ῃς
+character v.	3		ἐ-παίδευ-σεν	παιδεύ-σ-ῃ
mostly α	pl. 1		ἐ-παιδεύ-σα-μεν	παιδεύ-σ-ω-μεν
	2		ἐ-παιδεύ-σα-τε	παιδεύ-σ-η-τε
	3		ἐ-παίδευ-σα-ν	παιδεύ-σ-ω-σιν
PERFECT I		*I have trained* etc.	*I had trained* etc. PLPF.	*(if) I have trained* etc.
STEM	sg. 1	πε-παίδευ-κα	ἐ-πε-παιδεύ-κει-ν	
reduplication	2	πε-παίδευ-κα-ς	ἐ-πε-παιδεύ-κει-ς	CG πε-παιδεύ-κω
+tense sign κ	3	πε-παίδευ-κεν	ἐ-πε-παιδεύ-κει	πε-παιδεύ-κῃς
+character v.	pl. 1	πε-παιδεύ-κα-μεν	ἐ-πε-παιδεύ-κει-μεν[(3)]	etc., or
mostly α or	2	πε-παιδεύ-κα-τε	ἐ-πε-παιδεύ-κει-τε[(3)]	πε-παιδευ-κὼς
plpf. ει (ε)	3	πε-παιδεύ-κα-σιν[(4)]	ἐ-πε-παιδεύ-κει-σαν[(3)]	ὦ, ᾖς etc.

(1) -ουσι < -ονσι (↑68e; 70).
(2) In post-CG occasionally -οσαν (↑113.5; 70[9]).
(3) In CG pl. -κε-.
(4) In KG/NT sometimes -κα-ν.

For a synopsis of endings and terminations ↑70.

OPTATIVE mood signs (ο)ι, (α)ι, (ε)ι, (ε)ιη	IMPERATIVE	INFINITIVE and PARTICIPLE
may I train etc. παιδεύ-οι-μι παιδεύ-οι-ς παιδεύ-οι παιδεύ-οι-μεν παιδεύ-οι-τε παιδεύ-οι-εν	 παίδευ-ε *train!* (sg.) παιδευ-έ-τω *let him train!* παιδεύ-ε-τε *train!* (pl.) παιδευ-έ-τω-σαν[1]	*to train* παιδεύ-ειν *one who trains* etc. παιδεύ-ων -οντος παιδεύ-ουσα -ούσης παιδεῦ-ον -οντος
… *(that) I will/would train* etc. CG παιδεύ-σοι-μι παιδεύ-σοι-ς etc. (↑211h)		*to train in the future* παιδεύ-σ-ειν *one who will train* etc. παιδεύ-σ-ων -σ-οντος παιδεύ-σ-ουσα -σ-ούσης παιδεῦ-σ-ον -σ-οντος
may I train etc. παιδεύ-σαι-μι παιδεύ-σαι-ς (-σειας)[2] παιδεύ-σαι (-σειεν)[2] παιδεύ-σαι-μεν παιδεύ-σαι-τε παιδεύ-σαι-εν (-σειαν)[2]	 παίδευ-σον *train!* (sg.) παιδευ-σά-τω *let him train!* παιδεύ-σα-τε *train!* (pl.) παιδευ-σά-τω-σαν[3]	*to train* παιδεῦ-σαι *one who trains/trained* etc. παιδεύ-σᾱς -σᾰ-ντος παιδεύ-σᾱ-σα -σᾱ́-σης παιδεῦ-σαν -σᾰ-ντος
may I have trained etc. CG πε-παιδεύ-κοι-μι πε-παιδεύ-κοι-ς etc., or πε-παιδευ-κὼς εἴην, εἴης etc.		*to have trained* πε-παιδευ-κέ-ναι *one who has trained* etc. πε-παιδευ-κώς -κότος πε-παιδευ-κυῖα -κυίᾱς[4] πε-παιδευ-κός -κότος

(1) *Let them train!* in CG παιδευ-ό-ντων.

(2) In KG the "Aeolic" forms of the opt. aor. (-σειας/-σειεν/-σειαν) are hardly used at all. The LXX often uses -σαισαν for -σαιεν (aor. II also -οισαν for -οιεν).

(3) *Let them train!* in CG παιδευ-σά-ντων.

(4) In KG also -(κ)υίης (so in the NT; ↑48e).

77 Middle: παιδεύομαι "I train/I am training (s.o.) for myself" (↑BR §91)

		INDICATIVE augmentless indicative	augment indicative	SUBJUNCTIVE mood sign ω/η replacing thematic/character v.
PRESENT/		*I train for myself* etc.	*I trained for myself* etc. IPF.	*(if) I train for myself* etc.
DURATIVE	sg. 1	παιδεύ-ο-μαι	ἐ-παιδευ-ό-μην	παιδεύ-ω-μαι
STEM	2	παιδεύ-ῃ[1]/[2]	ἐ-παιδεύ-ου[1]	παιδεύ-ῃ[3]
thematic	3	παιδεύ-ε-ται	ἐ-παιδεύ-ε-το	παιδεύ-η-ται
vowel ε/ο	pl. 1	παιδευ-ό-μεθα	ἐ-παιδευ-ό-μεθα	παιδευ-ώ-μεθα
	2	παιδεύ-ε-σθε	ἐ-παιδεύ-ε-σθε	παιδεύ-η-σθε
	3	παιδεύ-ο-νται	ἐ-παιδεύ-ο-ντο	παιδεύ-ω-νται
FUTURE		*I will train for myself* etc.		
STEM	sg. 1	παιδεύ-σ-ομαι		
tense sign σ	2	παιδεύ-σ-ῃ		
+ thematic	3	παιδεύ-σ-ε-ται		
vowel ε/ο	pl. 1	παιδευ-σ-ό-μεθα		
	2	παιδεύ-σ-ε-σθε		
	3	παιδεύ-σ-ο-νται		
AORIST I			*I trained for myself* etc.	*(if) I train for myself* etc.
STEM	sg. 1		ἐ-παιδευ-σά-μην	παιδεύ-σ-ω-μαι
tense sign σ	2		ἐ-παιδεύ-σω[1]	παιδεύσ-ῃ
+character v.	3		ἐ-παιδεύ-σα-το	παιδεύ-σ-η-ται
mostly α	pl. 1		ἐ-παιδευ-σά-μεθα	παιδευ-σ-ώ-μεθα
	2		ἐ-παιδεύ-σα-σθε	παιδεύ-σ-η-σθε
	3		ἐ-παιδεύ-σα-ντο	παιδεύ-σ-ω-νται
PERFECT I		*I have trained for myself* etc.	*I had trained for myself* etc.	*(if) I have trained for myself* etc.
STEM	sg. 1	πε-παίδευ-μαι	ἐ-πε-παιδεύ-μην PLPF.	CG πε-παιδευ-μένος ὦ, ᾖς etc.
reduplication	2	πε-παίδευ-σαι	ἐ-πε-παίδευ-σο	
without	3	πε-παίδευ-ται	ἐ-πε-παίδευ-το	
tense sign or	pl. 1	πε-παιδεύ-μεθα	ἐ-πε-παιδεύ-μεθα	
character v.	2	πε-παίδευ-σθε	ἐ-πε-παίδευ-σθε	
	3	πε-παίδευ-νται	ἐ-πε-παίδευ-ντο	

(1) -ῃ < -ε-σαι; -ου < -ε-σο; -σω < -σα-σο (↑70[6]).
(2) In late Attic indicative also -ει, so regularly βούλει *you* (sg.) *want*, οἴει *you* (sg.) *think*, δέει *you* (sg.) *need* (also fut. ὄψει *you* [sg.] *will see* [but in the NT always ὄψῃ]) BR §91; BDF §27; 87.
(3) -ῃ < -η-σαι; -σῃ < -ση-σαι.
For a synopsis of endings and terminations ↑70.

OPTATIVE mood signs (ο)ι, (α)ι, (ε)ι, (ε)ιη	IMPERATIVE	INFINITIVE and PARTICIPLE
may I train for myself etc. παιδευ-οί-μην παιδεύ-οι-ο[1] παιδεύ-οι-το παιδευ-οί-μεθα παιδεύ-οι-σθε παιδεύ-οι-ντο	 παιδεύ-ου[1] *train for yourself!* παιδευ-έ-σθω *let him train for himself!* παιδεύ-ε-σθε *train f. yourselves!* παιδευ-έ-σθω-σαν[2]	*to train for o.s.* παιδεύ-ε-σθαι *one who trains for himself* etc. παιδευ-ό-μενος παιδευ-ο-μένη παιδευ-ό-μενον etc.
… *(that) I will/would train for myself* etc. CG παιδευ-σοί-μην παιδεύ-σοι-ο etc. (↑211h)		*to train for o.s. in the future* παιδεύ-σε-σθαι *one who will train for himself* etc. παιδευ-σό-μενος παιδευ-σο-μένη παιδευ-σό-μενον etc.
may I train for myself etc. παιδευ-σαί-μην παιδεύ-σαι-ο[1] παιδεύ-σαι-το παιδευ-σαί-μεθα παιδεύ-σαι-σθε παιδεύ-σαι-ντο	 παίδευ-σαι *train for yourself!* παιδευ-σά-σθω *let him train for himself!* παιδεύ-σα-σθε *train f.y.-selves!* παιδευ-σά-σθω-σαν[3]	*to train for o.s.* παιδεύ-σα-σθαι *one who trains/trained for himself* etc. παιδευ-σά-μενος παιδευ-σα-μένη παιδευ-σά-μενον etc.
may I have trained for my-self etc. CG πε-παιδευ-μένος εἴην, εἴης etc.	(something like *prove yourself to be* s.o.'s *trainer* etc.:) πε-παίδευ-σο πε-παιδεύ-σθω πε-παίδευ-σθε	*to have trained for o.s.* πε-παιδεῦ-σθαι *one who has trained for himself* etc. πε-παιδευ-μένος πε-παιδευ-μένη πε-παιδευ-μένον etc.

(1) -οι-ο < -οι-σο; -ου < -ε-σο; -σαι-ο < -σαι-σο (↑70[6]).

(2) *Let them train for themselves!* in CG παιδευ-έ-σθων.

(3) *Let them train for themselves!* in CG παιδευ-σά-σθων.

78 Passive: παιδεύομαι "I am (being) trained" (↑BR §91)

		INDICATIVE		SUBJUNCTIVE
		augmentless indicative	augment indicative	mood sign ω/η replacing thematic/character v.
PRESENT/ DURATIVE STEM thematic vowel ε/ο		*I am (being) trained* etc.	*I was (being) trained* etc. IPF.	*(if) I am trained* etc.
	sg. 1	παιδεύ-ο-μαι	ἐ-παιδευ-ό-μην	παιδεύ-ω-μαι
	2	παιδεύ-ῃ[(1)/(2)]	ἐ-παιδεύ-ου[(1)]	παιδεύ-ῃ[(3)]
	3	παιδεύ-ε-ται	ἐ-παιδεύ-ε-το	παιδεύ-η-ται
	pl. 1	παιδευ-ό-μεθα	ἐ-παιδευ-ό-μεθα	παιδευ-ώ-μεθα
	2	παιδεύ-ε-σθε	ἐ-παιδεύ-ε-σθε	παιδεύ-η-σθε
	3	παιδεύ-ο-νται	ἐ-παιδεύ-ο-ντο	παιδεύ-ω-νται
FUTURE STEM "tense sign" θη-σ + thematic vowel ε/ο		*I will be trained* etc.		
	sg. 1	παιδευ-θή-σομαι		
	2	παιδευ-θή-σῃ		
	3	παιδευ-θή-σεται		
	pl. 1	παιδευ-θη-σόμεθα		
	2	παιδευ-θή-σεσθε		
	3	παιδευ-θή-σονται		
AORIST I STEM tense sign θ + character v. η/ε			*I was trained* etc.	*(if) I am trained* etc.
	sg. 1		ἐ-παιδεύ-θη-ν	παιδευ-θῶ[(4)]
	2		ἐ-παιδεύ-θη-ς	παιδευ-θῇ-ς
	3		ἐ-παιδεύ-θη	παιδευ-θῇ
	pl. 1		ἐ-παιδεύ-θη-μεν	παιδευ-θῶ-μεν
	2		ἐ-παιδεύ-θη-τε	παιδευ-θῆ-τε
	3		ἐ-παιδεύ-θη-σαν	παιδευ-θῶ-σιν
PERFECT I stem reduplication without tense sign or character v.		*I have been trained* etc.	*I had been trained* etc. PLPF.	*(if) I have been trained* etc.
	sg. 1	πε-παίδευ-μαι	ἐ-πε-παιδεύ-μην	CG πε-παιδευ-μένος ὦ, ᾖς etc.
	2	πε-παίδευ-σαι	ἐ-πε-παίδευ-σο	
	3	πε-παίδευ-ται	ἐ-πε-παίδευ-το	
	pl. 1	πε-παιδεύ-μεθα	ἐ-πε-παιδεύ-μεθα	
	2	πε-παίδευ-σθε	ἐ-πε-παίδευ-σθε	
	3	πε-παίδευ-νται	ἐ-πε-παίδευ-ντο	

(1) -ῃ < -ε-σαι; -ου < -ε-σο (↑70[6]).
(2) In late Attic indicative also -ει (↑BR §91; BDF §27; 87).
(3) -ῃ < -η-σαι.
(4) -θῶ < -θέ-ω < -θή-ω (↑11).
For a synopsis of endings and terminations ↑70.

OPTATIVE mood signs (ο)ι, (α)ι, (ε)ι, (ε)ιη	IMPERATIVE	INFINITIVE and PARTICIPLE
may I be trained etc. παιδευ-οί-μην παιδεύ-οι-ο[1] παιδεύ-οι-το παιδευ-οί-μεθα παιδεύ-οι-σθε παιδεύ-οι-ντο	 παιδεύ-ου[1] *be trained!* (sg.) παιδευ-έ-σθω *let him be trained!* παιδεύ-ε-σθε *be trained!* (pl.) παιδευ-έ-σθω-σαν[2]	*to be trained* παιδεύ-ε-σθαι *one who is trained* etc. παιδευ-ό-μενος παιδευ-ο-μένη παιδευ-ό-μενον etc.
... *(that) I will/would be trained* etc. CG παιδευ-θη-σοί-μην παιδευ-θή-σοι-ο etc. (↑211h)		*to be trained in the future* παιδευ-θή-σεσθαι *one who will be trained* etc. παιδευ-θη-σό-μενος παιδευ-θη-σο-μένη παιδευ-θη-σό-μενον etc.
may I be trained etc. παιδευ-θείη-ν παιδευ-θείη-ς παιδευ-θείη παιδευ-θείη-μεν[3] παιδευ-θείη-τε[3] παιδευ-θείη-σαν[3]	 παιδεύ-θη-τι *be trained!* (sg.) παιδευ-θή-τω *let him be trained!* παιδεύ-θη-τε *be trained!* (pl.) παιδευ-θή-τω-σαν[4]	*to be trained* παιδευ-θῆ-ναι *one who is/was trained* etc. παιδευ-θείς -θέντος παιδευ-θεῖσα -θείσης παιδευ-θέν -θέντος
may I have been trained etc. CG πε-παιδευ-μένος εἴην, εἴης etc.	(something like *prove yourself to have been trained!* etc.:) πε-παίδευ-σο πε-παιδεύ-σθω πε-παίδευ-σθε	*to have been trained* πε-παιδεῦ-σθαι *one who has been trained* etc. πε-παιδευ-μένος πε-παιδευ-μένη πε-παιδευ-μένον etc.

(1) -οι-ο < -οι-σο; -ου < -ε-σο; -σαι-ο < -σαι-σο (↑70[6]).
(2) *Let them be trained!* in CG παιδευ-έ-σθων.
(3) CG pl. usually -θεῖ-μεν, -θεῖ-τε, -θεῖε-ν.
(4) *Let them be trained!* in CG παιδευ-θέ-ντων.

79 Explanatory notes on the paradigm of παιδεύω (↑BR §92)

79a I. **General remarks**

1. The present stem is the same as the verb stem παιδευ- (↑68; 75).

2. The thematic vowels (↑68e)
-ε- (before σ, τ, vowels as well as /–/) and
-ο- (before μ and ν) are most clearly visible in middle-passive indicative (partly also imperative) forms (↑77/78).

3. On the personal endings ↑70.
Note that various 3rd person indicative and subjunctive forms have a ν mobile (within brackets; ↑18a).

4. On the mood signs of the subjunctive and optative ↑69.

79b II. On **tense-aspect stems** and their forms (for more details ↑68):

(tense-aspect stem:)	(stem formation/tense-aspect sign + thematic/character vowel [formative syllable; ↑68g]:)	(especially noteworthy:)
1. **fut. act./mid.**	σ + ε/ο	no subj./imp. are used, KG no opt. either
2. **aor. I act./mid.**	σ + mostly α	**accentuation** affects the meaning (↑74):
παίδευσον	2. sg. imp. aor. act.	*train!* (sg.)
παιδεῦσον	ptc. fut. act. sg. ntr.	*one* (ntr.) *that will train*
παίδευσαι	2. sg. imp. aor. mid.	*train for yourself!*
παιδεῦσαι	inf. aor. act.	*to train*
παιδεύσαι	3. sg. aor. opt. act.	*may he train*

Sometimes this applies only partly or not at all, e.g. in the case of λῡ́ω *to loosen* and κλέπτω *to steal*:
λῦσον *loosen!* (sg.) or *one* (ntr.) *that will loosen*
λῦσαι *loosen for yourself!* or *to loosen*
λῡ́σαι *may he loosen*
κλέψον *steal!* (sg.) or *one* (ntr.) *that will steal*
κλέψαι *steal for yourself!* or *to steal* or *may he steal*

3. **pf. I act.** (plpf. act.)	reduplication + κ + mostly α (ει/[ε])	the **accent** of the inf. and the ptc. is on the vowel after the tense-aspect sign κ (↑74a)

In CG subj. and opt. have the same terminations as in the present or else they are formed by periphrasis with εἰμί (↑125a; 203a).

4. **pf. mid./pass.** (plpf. mid./pass.)	reduplication	endings are joined directly to the stem; the **accent** of the inf. and the ptc. is on last but one syllable (↑74b)

In CG subj. and opt. are formed by periphrasis with εἰμί (↑125a; 203a).

5. **aor. I pass.**	θ + η/ε	-θι of imp. (↑70) changes to -τι: **dissimilation** due to the tense-aspect sign -θ- ↑14b)
6. **fut. pass.**	θη-σ + ε/ο	

III. The "**principal parts**" of a verb are the basis for all its forms (↑68b); those of παιδεύω *to train* are: 79c
παιδεύω, παιδεύσω, ἐπαίδευσα, πεπαίδευκα, πεπαίδευμαι, ἐπαιδεύθην

Note that the principal parts listed in the following are not limited to the NT (↑p.xv). The ones **in brackets** are not attested in the standard editions of the NT and the LXX, though usually in authors such as Philo and Josephus, certainly, however, in Hellenistic or Classical texts. Gaps point to the fact that the expected forms are not or only rarely encountered in Ancient Greek.

Uncontracted vowel verbs with peculiarities (↑BR §121.1ff; BDF §101) 80

pres.	verb stem	fut.	aor. act./mid. aor. pass.	pf. act. pf. mid./pass.

I. σ-stems in the pf. mid./pass. and the aor. pass.

a) Original σ-stems (↑12d):

ἀκούω *to hear*	ἀκοϝ-, ἀκου(**σ**)-	ἀκούσω or ἀκούσομαι	ἤκουσα ἠκούσθην	ἀκήκοα(1) ἤκου**σ**μαι	80.1
σείω *to shake*	σει(**σ**)-	σείσω	ἔσεισα ἐσεί**σ**θην	σέσεικα (σέσει**σ**μαι)	80.2
χρίω *to anoint*(2)	χρῑ(**σ**)-	χρίσω	ἔχρισα ἐχρί**σ**θην	κέχρικα κέχρι**σ**μαι(3)	80.3

(1) "Attic" reduplication (↑72g); pf. II (↑108).
(2) κυλίω *to roll* and μεθύω *to be drunk* (↑μεθύσκομαι *to get drunk*) have analogical forms.
(3) In CG also κέχριμαι. Note that χρῑστός *anointed* is the verbal adjective of this verb (↑64e).

b) Secondary σ-stems (formations analogical to those mentioned above):

κελεύω *to command*	κελευ(**σ**)-	(κελεύσω)	ἐκέλευσα ἐκελεύ**σ**θην	(κεκέλευκα) (κεκέλευ**σ**μαι)	80.4
κλείω *to shut*	κλει(**σ**)-	κλείσω	ἔκλεισα ἐκλεί**σ**θην	κέκλεικα κέκλει**σ**μαι	80.5
κρούω *to knock*	κρου(**σ**)-	κρούσω	ἔκρουσα ἐκρού**σ**θην	(κέκρουκα) (κέκρου**σ**μαι)	80.6
ῥύομαι *to rescue*	ῥυ(**σ**)-	ῥύσομαι	ἐρρυσάμην ἐρρύ**σ**θην		80.7
λούω *to wash*, mid. *to bathe o.s.*	λου(**σ**)-	λούσω	ἔλουσα ἐλού(**σ**)θην	λέλου(**σ**)μαι	80.8

II. Original ϝ-stems (before a consonant ϝ > υ; ↑12a; on the pres.-stem ↑75b)

80.9	καίω (< καϝjω) *to burn sth.*	καϝ-, καυ-	κα**ύ**σω	ἔκα**υ**σα ἐκα**ύ**θην[1]	(κέκα**υ**κα) κέκα**υ**μαι
80.10	κλαίω (<κλαϝjω) *to weep*	κλαϝ-, κλαυ-	κλα**ύ**σω	ἔκλα**υ**σα ἐκλα**ύ(σ)**θην	(κέκλα**υ**κα) (κέκλα**υ**μαι)

(1) Also ἐκάην (NT; Ionic; Epic); analogically ἐπάην (fut. παήσομαι) of παύομαι *to cease.*

III. Shortened stem-vowel from the pf. act. onwards (quantitative ablaut; ↑8)

80.11	ἐνδῡ́ω[1] *to clothe*	δῡ-, δῠ-	ἐνδῡ́σω	ἐνέδῡσα	ἐνδέδ**ῠ**κα ἐνδέδ**ῠ**μαι
80.12	θῡ́ω *to sacrifice/slaughter*	θῡ-, θῠ-	θῡ́σω	ἔθῡσα ἐτ**ῠ́**θην (↑14a)	τέθ**ῠ**κα τέθ**ῠ**μαι
80.13	λῡ́ω *to loosen*	λῡ-, λῠ-	λῡ́σω	ἔλῡσα ἐλ**ῠ́**θην	λέλ**ῠ**κα λέλ**ῠ**μαι

(1) Mostly mid. *to clothe o.s. (in),* analogically also other compounds such as ἐκδῡ́ω *to take off (sth.).* The following are related to these, overlapping with them in their form (↑LSJ s.v.; BDF §101): δῡ́νω (and δύω) act. *to go down,* (especially of the sun) *to set,* δέδῠκα, ἔδῡν (root aor. [↑106d]; inf. δῦναι; subj. δύω, 3.sg. δύῃ [2Sm 3:35 LXX]); ἐνδῡ́νω *to slip in* (2Tm 3:6); παρεισέδῡσαν (from -έδῡν or -έδῡσα) *they have secretly slipped in* (Jd 4).
Compare also φύω *to grow* (Att. *to bring forth* [LSJ]), (φύσω/φυήσω), aor. ἐφύην *grew* (subj. φυῶ [in Mt 24:32/Mk 13:28 we should perhaps read ἐκφυῇ *grow/sprout out*; ↑BDF §76.2]; Att. uses a root aor. here: ἔφυν [↑106d]; subj. φύω).

(ii) Contracted verbs

81 Contracted verbs: preliminaries (↑BR §93; BDF §70; 74; 80–91)

81a 1. **Term**: contracted verbs are verbs whose present stem ends in α (rarely in η), ε or ο; these vowels contract with the initial vowel of the termination following the rules of ↑11 (NB: this applies only to the forms of the present stem).

81b 2. **Lexical form**: most lexicons list contracted verbs in their uncontracted form (1 sg. ind. pres.); and it is in this form that these verbs should be learnt.

81c 3. **Frequency**: verbs in -έω are the most frequent ones (ca. 392 verbs in the NT), followed by those in -όω (ca. 115 verbs) and those in -άω (ca. 113 verbs, though attested in more forms than those in -όω).

In the NT there are some forms (KG) showing a mixture of -άω- and -έω- types (BDF §90):

ἐλε-ῶντος (< -άοντος, "for" -οῦντος < -έοντος)	*(God) who shows mercy* (Ro 9:16)
ἐλε-ᾶτε (< -άετε, "for" -εῖτε < -έετε)	*have* (pl.) *mercy!* (Jd 22f)
ἐλλόγ-α (< -αε, "for" -ει < -εε)	*charge* (sg.) *(it) to (my) account!* (Phm 18)

Output vowels as pointers to the stem-type (↑11f) 82

1. Found in only **one type** are (↑82d on the translation of the examples): 82a

1.1 **α/ᾳ**	only verbs in -άω, e.g.:		
< α + e-sound	τιμ**ᾶ**τε	< τιμ**άε**τε	*you* (pl.) *honour*
	τίμ**α**	< τίμ**αε**	*honour!* (sg.)
	τιμ**ᾷ**ς	< τιμ**άει**ς	*you* (sg.) *honour*
1.2 **ει** and **η/ῃ**	only verbs in -έω,[1] e.g.:		
< ε + ε	ποι**εῖ**τε	< ποι**έε**τε	*you* (pl.) *do*
	ποί**ει**	< ποί**εε**	*do!* (sg.)
< ε + ει	ποι**εῖ**	< ποι**έει**	*he/she/it does*
< ε + η/ῃ	ποι**ῆ**τε	< ποι**έη**τε	*(if) you* (pl.) *do*
	ποι**ῇ**	< ποι**έῃ**	*(if) he/she/it does*
1.3 **οι**	only in -όω verbs (in NT),[2] e.g.:		
< ο + ει/ῃ	δουλ**οῖ**ς	< δουλ**όει**ς	*you* (sg.) *enslave*
	δουλ**οῖ**	< δουλ**όει**	*he/she/it enslaves*
	or	< δουλ**όῃ**	*(if) he/she/it enslaves*
< ο + οι	δουλ**οῖ**μεν	< δουλ**όοι**μεν	*may we enslave!*

(1) **η/ῃ** also in the very small number of verbs in -ήω: η/ῃ < η + ε/ει/η/ῃ (↑84c).
(2) Outside the NT also opt. pres. act. and pass. forms of verbs in -έω (↑87c).

2. Found in **two types** are: 82b

ου	only in -έω or -όω verbs, e.g.:		
< ε + ο	ἐποί**ου**ν	< ἐποί**εο**ν	*I/they did*
< ε + ου	ἐποι**οῦ**	< ἐποι**έου**	*you did for yourself*
< ο + ε	δουλ**οῦ**τε	< δουλ**όε**τε	*you* (pl.) *enslave*
< ο + ο	δουλ**οῦ**μεν	< δουλ**όο**μεν	*we enslave*
< ο + ου	δουλ**οῦ**σιν	< δουλ**όου**σιν	*they enslave*

3. Found in all of the **three types** are: 82c

ω/ῳ	e.g.:		
< α + o-sound[1]	τιμ**ῶ**	< τιμ**άω**	*I honour*
	τιμ**ῶ**μεν	< τιμ**άο**μεν	*we honour*
	τιμ**ῶ**σιν	< τιμ**άου**σιν	*they honour*
	τιμ**ῷ**μεν	< τιμ**άοι**μεν	*may we honour!*
< ε + ω	ποι**ῶ**	< ποι**έω**	*I do*
	ποι**ώ**μεθα	< ποι**εώ**μεθα	*let's do for ourselves*
< ο + ω	δουλ**ῶ**	< δουλ**όω**	*I enslave*
< ο + η	δουλ**ῶ**τε	< δουλ**όη**τε	*(if) you* (pl.) *enslave*

(1) The same applies to the very small number of verbs in -ήω: ω/ῳ <η + o-sound (↑84c).

4. Vowel contraction increases the number of **homonymous forms** (i.e. forms with a different meaning that look alike; only one variant is translated in the above examples). Thus, νικῶ may have the following meanings (depending on the context): 82d

a) νικῶ as 1 sg. ind. pres. act.[26] *I conquer*
b) νικῶ as 1 sg. subj. pres. act. *(if) I conquer*
c) νικῶ as 2 sg. imp. pres. pass. *be conquered!* (↑Ro 12:21)

82e 5. The 3 sg. ipf. act. of contracted verbs **never** has a **ν mobile** (↑18a; 79a), e.g.:

ἠγάπα	*he loved* (Jn 11:5)	ἐδήλου	*he indicated* (1Pe 1:11)
ἐποίει	*he did* (Jn 5:16)	[↑ἔλεγε**ν**	*he said* (Mk 6:10)]

83 Accentuation of contracted verb forms (↑5b–5d; 74d)

83a 1. The **contraction syllable** has an accent, provided there was one on the vowels involved in the contraction according to the relevant rules (↑5b–5d; note that the second vowel may be a diphthong), e.g.:

ἀγαπ**αέ**τω	> ἀγαπ**ά**τω	*let him/her love!*
ἀγαπ**άου**σιν	> ἀγαπ**ῶ**σιν	*they love*

In every other case the accent is on the syllable that the uncontracted form would have it on, e.g.:

ἐπο**ί**εες	> ἐπο**ί**εις	*you* (sg.) *did it*
ἀγαπαομ**έ**νη	> ἀγαπωμ**έ**νη	*one* (f.) *who is loved*

Accented contraction syllables carry the following type of accent:

83b 2. a **circumflex**, provided the first of the two contracted vowels was accented, e.g.:

ἀγαπ**άει**	> ἀγαπ**ᾷ**	*he/she loves*
δουλ**όε**ται	> δουλ**οῦ**ται	*he/she/it is being enslaved*

83c 3. an **acute**, provided the second of the two contracted vowels was accented, e.g.:

ἐτιμ**αό**μην	> ἐτιμ**ώ**μην	*I was honoured*
ποι**εό**μεθα	> ποι**ού**μεθα	*we do for ourselves*

(a) Contracted verbs in -άω

84 Present/durative forms of ἀγαπάω "to love" (↑BR §93–95; BDF §88; 90)

84a 1. Contraction rules (↑11; 82):

α + e-sound (ε, η, ει, ῃ)	> ᾱ/ᾳ
α + o-sound (ο, ω, οι, ου)	> ω/ῳ

2. Paradigm:[27]

26 Note that the forms a and b are homonymous even without contraction.
27 Note that in the opt. act. there are special sg. terminations (↑76): -οίην, -οίης and -οίη.

84b

ἀγαπάω 84b *to love*			ACTIVE contracted	uncontracted	MIDDLE/PASSIVE contracted	uncontracted
IND. PRES.	sg.	1	ἀγαπ-ῶ	-άω	ἀγαπ-ῶμαι	-άομαι
		2	ἀγαπ-ᾷς	-άεις	ἀγαπ-ᾷ	-άῃ
		3	ἀγαπ-ᾷ	-άει	ἀγαπ-ᾶται	-άεται
	pl.	1	ἀγαπ-ῶμεν	-άομεν	ἄγαπ-ώμεθα	-αόμεθα
		2	ἀγαπ-ᾶτε	-άετε	ἀγαπ-ᾶσθε	-άεσθε
		3	ἀγαπ-ῶσιν	-άουσιν	ἀγαπ-ῶνται	-άονται
IPF.	sg.	1	ἠγάπ-ων	-αον	ἠγαπ-ώμην	-αόμην
		2	ἠγάπ-ας	-αες	ἠγαπ-ῶ	-άου
		3	ἠγάπ-α	-αε	ἠγαπ-ᾶτο	-άετο
	pl.	1	ἠγαπ-ῶμεν	-άομεν	ἠγαπ-ώμεθα	-αόμεθα
		2	ἠγαπ-ᾶτε	-άετε	ἠγαπ-ᾶσθε	-άεσθε
		3	ἠγάπ-ων	-αον	ἠγαπ-ῶντο	-άοντο
SUBJ.	sg.	1	ἀγαπ-ῶ	-άω	ἀγαπ-ῶμαι	-άωμαι
		2	ἀγαπ-ᾷς	-άῃς	ἀγαπ-ᾷ	-άῃ
		3	ἀγαπ-ᾷ	-άῃ	ἀγαπ-ᾶται	-άηται
	pl.	1	ἀγαπ-ῶμεν	-άωμεν	ἀγαπ-ώμεθα	-αώμεθα
		2	ἀγαπ-ᾶτε	-άητε	ἀγαπ-ᾶσθε	-άησθε
		3	ἀγαπ-ῶσιν	-άωσιν	ἀγαπ-ῶνται	-άωνται
OPT.	sg.	1	ἀγαπ-ῴην	-αοίην !	ἀγαπ-ῴμην	-αοίμην
		2	ἀγαπ-ῴης	-αοίης !	ἀγαπ-ῷο	-άοιο
		3	ἀγαπ-ῴη	-αοίη !	ἀγαπ-ῷτο	-άοιτο
	pl.	1	ἀγαπ-ῷμεν	-άοιμεν	ἀγαπ-ῴμεθα	-αοίμεθα
		2	ἀγαπ-ῷτε	-άοιτε	ἀγαπ-ῷσθε	-άοισθε
		3	ἀγαπ-ῷεν	-άοιεν	ἀγαπ-ῷντο	-άοιντο
IMP.	sg.	2	ἀγάπ-α	-αε	ἀγαπ-ῶ	-άου
		3	ἀγαπ-άτω	-αέτω	ἀγαπ-άσθω	-αέσθω
	pl.	2	ἀγαπ-ᾶτε	-άετε	ἀγαπ-ᾶσθε	-άεσθε
		3	ἀγαπ-άτωσαν(1)	-αέτωσαν	ἀγαπ-άσθωσαν(1)	-αέσθωσαν
INF.			ἀγαπ-ᾶν	-άειν(2)	ἀγαπ-ᾶσθαι	-άεσθαι
PTC.	masc./ntr.		ἀγαπ-ῶν	-άων/-άον	ἀγαπ-ώμενος/-ον	-αόμενος/-ον
	gen.		ἀγαπ-ῶντος	-άοντος	ἀγαπ-ωμένου	-αομένου
	fem.		ἀγαπ-ῶσα	-άουσα	ἀγαπ-ωμένη	-αομένη
	gen.		ἀγαπ-ώσης	-αούσης	ἀγαπ-ωμένης	-αομένης

(1) CG uses -ώντων for -άτωσαν and -άσθων for -άσθωσαν (↑70).

(2) Here ει does not stand for a diphthong, but for an e-sound (i.e. the ι is written, but no ι-sound is expressed). For this reason, there is no iota subscript in the contracted form. (↑2c; 11e; 70).

84c 3. The verbs in -ήω (↑86.1f; 86.7f;106e; 114c) ζήω *to live* and χρήομαι *to use* compare with those in -άω as follows: when ω is the outcome vowel the two types agree; but whenever the outcome vowel verbs in -άω is α, those in -ήω have an η:

pres.: ζῶ	ζ**ῇ**ς	ζ**ῇ**	ζῶμεν	ζ**ῆ**τε	ζῶσιν	ζ**ῆ**ν (inf.)
ipf.: ἔζων	ἔζ**η**ς	ἔζ**η**	ἐζῶμεν	ἐζ**ῆ**τε	ἔζων	
pres.: χρῶμαι	χρ**ῇ**	χρ**ῆ**ται	χρώμεθα	χρ**ῆ**σθε	χρῶνται	χρ**ῆ**σθαι (inf.)
ipf.: ἐχρώμην	ἐχρῶ	ἐχρ**ῆ**το	ἐχρώμεθα	ἐχρ**ῆ**σθε	ἐχρῶντο	

Note that in most lexicons these verbs are listed as ζ**ά**ω (or ζῶ) and χρ**ά**ομαι.

84d 4. In the tense-aspect stems **outside the present** the short stem-final vowel is lengthened, α becoming η, after ε, ι, ρ, however, ᾱ (ε/ι/ρ rule: ↑11g):

	future:	aorist:	perfect:
active:	ἀγαπ**ή**σω	ἠγάπ**η**σα	ἠγάπ**η**κα
middle:	ἀγαπ**ή**σομαι	ἠγαπ**η**σάμην	ἠγάπ**η**μαι
passive:	ἀγαπ**η**θήσομαι	ἠγαπ**ή**θην	ἠγάπ**η**μαι

Examples with long ᾱ (instead of η): ἰάομαι, θεάομαι, κατ-αράομαι ↑85.4–85.8. Occasionally we encounter a contracted fut. in -α ↑96.5[1]; 110.2; 124.5.

85 Regular contracted verbs in -άω (↑BR §95; 121.4f.8; BDF §101)

pres.	verb stem	fut.	aor. act./mid. aor. pass.	pf. act. pf. mid./pass.

1. With stem-final -η outside the present stem:

	pres.	verb stem	fut.	aor. act./mid. aor. pass.	pf. act. pf. mid./pass.
85.1	γεννάω *to beget/ to give birth*	γεννα-	γενν**ή**σω	ἐγένν**η**σα ἐγενν**ή**θην	γεγένν**η**κα γεγένν**η**μαι
85.2	ἐρωτάω *to ask*	ἐρωτα-	ἐρωτ**ή**σω	ἠρώτ**η**σα(1) ἠρωτ**ή**θην	(ἠρώτ**η**κα) ἠρώτ**η**μαι
85.3	νικάω *to conquer*	νικα-	νικ**ή**σω	ἐνίκ**η**σα ἐνικ**ή**θην	νενίκ**η**κα νενίκ**η**μαι

(1) Alongside this CG uses the aor.II mid. ἠρόμην (inf. ἐρέσθαι; for paradigm ↑105).

85a Note the follow peculiarity:
In the case of καυχάομαι *to boast* and ὀδυνάομαι *to suffer pain* (otherwise regular) the ending of the 2 sg. ind. pres. mid./pass. is not -ῃ, but -σαι (↑70):

καυχᾶ**σαι**	*you* (sg.) *boast* (Ro 2:17.23; ↑Ro 11:18; 1Cor 4:7)
ὀδυνᾶ**σαι**	*you* (sg.) *suffer pain* (Lk 16:25)

II. Verbs with ε, ι, ρ before stem-final α (> ᾱ; ↑11g; 25d; 113.8)

ἐάω *to permit* ipf. act. **εἴ**ων	ἐᾰ-, ἐᾱ- (↑71d)	ἐᾱ́σω	εἴᾱσα εἰᾱ́θην	(εἴᾱκα) εἴᾱμαι	85.4
θεάομαι *to see*	θεᾰ-, θεᾱ-	(θεᾱ́σομαι)	ἐθεᾱσάμην ἐθεᾱ́θην	τεθέᾱμαι	85.5
ἀγαλλιάομαι *to exult*	ἀγαλλιᾰ-, ἀγαλλιᾱ-	ἀγαλλιᾱ́σομαι	ἠγαλλιᾱσάμην		85.6
ἰάομαι *to heal*	ἰᾰ-, ἰᾱ-	ἰᾱ́σομαι ἰᾱθήσομαι	ἰᾱσάμην ἰᾱ́θην	ἴᾱμαι (mid. and pass.)	85.7
καταράομαι *to curse*	κατ-αρᾰ-, κατ-αρᾱ-	καταρᾱ́σομαι	κατηρᾱσάμην κατηρᾱ́θην	κατήρᾱμαι[1]	85.8

(1) In the LXX also κεκατήρᾱμαι (↑augmenting of προφητεύω *to prophesy*; ↑73d).

Contracted verbs in -άω with peculiarities (↑BR §97f; 121.15–17; BDF §70; 101) 86

I. Verbs in -η (in most lexicons listed as -άω/-άομαι; ↑84c)

ζήω *to live*	ζη-	ζήσω and ζήσομαι	ἔζησα		86.1
χρήομαι *to use*	χρη(**σ**)-[1]	χρήσομαι	ἐχρησάμην ἐχρή**σ**θην	κέχρημαι	86.2

(1) Analogical σ (e.g. ↑86.3), encountered also in the verbal adjective χρη**σ**τός *useful, good.*

II. Verbs with a short -ᾰ throughout, pf. mid./pass. and aor. pass. with an extra σ

γελάω (<γελασι̯ω) *to laugh*	γελᾰ(**σ**)-[1]	γελ**ά**σω (↑13g)	ἐγέλ**ασ**α ἐγελ**άσ**θην	(γεγέλ**ασ**μαι)	86.3
κλάω *to break*	κλᾰ(**σ**)-[2]	κλ**ά**σω	ἔκλ**ασ**α ἐκλ**άσ**θην	(κέκλ**ασ**μαι)	86.4
σπάω (< σπάσω) *to draw (the sword)*	σπᾰ(**σ**)-[1]	σπ**ά**σω (↑13g)	ἔσπ**ασ**α ἐσπ**άσ**θην	(ἔσπ**α**κα) ἔσπ**ασ**μαι	86.5
χαλάω *to let down*	χαλᾰ(**σ**)-[2]	χαλ**ά**σω	ἐχάλασα ἐχαλ**άσ**θην	κεχάλ**ασ**μαι	86.6

(1) Original σ-stem (↑12d).
(2) Analogical σ (e.g. ↑86.3).

III. Verb with a long ᾱ in the fut. and the aor. (act.)

86.7	πεινάω *to hunger*	πεινα-	πεινᾱ́σω	ἐπείνᾱσα	

Note that

a) in CG this verb is used with a different stem-final vowel:

NT:	πεινάω	πεινα-	πεινάσω	ἐπείνασα	
CG:	πεινήω	πεινη- (↑84c)	πεινήσω	ἐπείνησα	πεπείνηκα

b) in NT and CG the notionally related verb διψάω *to thirst* has the same stem-final vowel outside the present stem:

86.8	NT:	διψάω	διψα-/διψη-	διψήσω	ἐδίψησα	δεδίψηκα
	CG:	διψήω	διψη- (↑84c)	διψήσω	ἐδίψησα	δεδίψηκα

(b) Contracted verbs in -έω

87 Present/durative forms of ποιέω "to do" (↑BR §93; BDF §89f)

87a 1. Contraction rules (↑11; 82):

ε + ε > ει

ε + ο > ου

ε disappears before a long vowel or diphthong

87b 2. Outside the present the stem-final ε is replaced by η:

	future:	aorist:	perfect:
active:	ποιήσω	ἐποίησα	πεποίηκα
middle:	ποιήσομαι	ἐποιησάμην	πεποίημαι
passive:	ποιηθήσομαι	ἐποιήθην	πεποίημαι

For verbs in -έω with peculiarities ↑88.
On the contracted future ↑92f; 98a.

3. Paradigm:

Note that in the opt. act. there are special sg. terminations (↑84b; also footnote 27): -οίην, -οίης and -οίη.

87c

ποιέω 87c *to do*		ACTIVE contracted	uncontracted	MIDDLE/PASSIVE contracted	uncontracted
IND. PRES.	sg. 1	ποι-ῶ	-έω	ποι-οῦμαι	-έομαι
	2	ποι-εῖς	-έεις	ποι-ῇ	-έῃ
	3	ποι-εῖ	-έει	ποι-εῖται	-έεται
	pl. 1	ποι-οῦμεν	-έομεν	ποι-ούμεθα	-εόμεθα
	2	ποι-εῖτε	-έετε	ποι-εῖσθε	-έεσθε
	3	ποι-οῦσιν	-έουσιν	ποι-οῦνται	-έονται
IPF.	sg. 1	ἐποί-ουν	-εον	ἐποι-ούμην	-εόμην
	2	ἐποί-εις	-εες	ἐποι-οῦ	-έου
	3	ἐποί-ει	-εε	ἐποι-εῖτο	-έετο
	pl. 1	ἐποι-οῦμεν	-έομεν	ἐποι-ούμεθα	-εόμεθα
	2	ἐποι-εῖτε	-έετε	ἐποι-εῖσθε	-έεσθε
	3	ἐποί-ουν	-εον[1]	ἐποι-οῦντο	-έοντο
SUBJ.	sg. 1	ποι-ῶ	-έω	ποι-ῶμαι	-έωμαι
	2	ποι-ῇς	-έῃς	ποι-ῇ	-έῃ
	3	ποι-ῇ	-εῃ	ποι-ῆται	-έηται
	pl. 1	ποι-ῶμεν	-έωμεν	ποι-ώμεθα	-εώμεθα
	2	ποι-ῆτε	-έητε	ποι-ῆσθε	-έησθε
	3	ποι-ῶσιν	-έωσιν	ποι-ῶνται	-έωνται
OPT.	sg. 1	ποι-οίην	-εοίην !	ποι-οίμην	-εοίμην
	2	ποι-οίης	-εοίης !	ποι-οῖο	-έοιο
	3	ποι-οίη	-εοίη !	ποι-οῖτο	-έοιτο
	pl. 1	ποι-οῖμεν	-έοιμεν	ποι-οίμεθα	-εοίμεθα
	2	ποι-οῖτε	-έοιτε	ποι-οῖσθε	-έοισθε
	3	ποι-οῖεν	-έοιεν	ποι-οῖντο	-έοιντο
IMP.	sg. 2	ποί-ει	-εε	ποι-οῦ	-έου
	3	ποι-είτω	-εέτω	ποι-είσθω	-εέσθω
	pl. 2	ποι-εῖτε	-έετε	ποι-εῖσθε	-έεσθε
	3	ποι-είτωσαν[2]	-εέτωσαν	ποι-είσθωσαν[2]	-εέσθωσαν
INF.		ποι-εῖν	-έειν[3]	ποι-εῖσθαι	-έεσθαι
PTC.	masc./ntr.	ποι-ῶν/-οῦν	-έων/-έον	ποι-ούμενος/-ον	-εόμενος/-ον
	gen.	ποι-οῦντος	-έοντος	ποι-ουμένου	-εομένου
	fem.	ποι-οῦσα	-έουσα	ποι-ουμένη	-εομένη
	gen.	ποι-ούσης	-εούσης	ποι-ουμένης	-εομένης

(1) Post-CG for -εον also -έοσαν (>-οῦσαν, e.g. εὐλογοῦσαν *they blessed* Ps 61:5 LXX; ↑70[9]).
(2) CG uses -ούντων for -είτωσαν and -είσθων for -είσθωσαν (↑70).
(3) This ει does not stand for a real diphthong (but ει < εε; ↑2c; 70).

88 Contracted verbs in -έω with peculiarities (↑Zinsmeister §133; BR §94; BDF §101)

88a I. Monosyllabic stems in -έω (↑88.5–88.7; 88.11–88.13; 112.8) contract only if the outcome is -ει (in the NT only a few actual cases are attested; in the LXX sometimes such forms are left uncontracted), e.g.: πλέω *to travel by sea* and δέομαι *to ask for sth.* (note that δέω *to tie* [↑88.7] in principle contracts like ποιέω!):

ind. pres.:	πλέω	πλεῖς	πλεῖ	πλέομεν	πλεῖτε	πλέουσιν
inf./ptc.:	πλεῖν		πλέων/πλέουσα/πλέον			
ipf.:	ἔπλεον	ἔπλεις	ἔπλει	ἐπλέομεν	ἐπλεῖτε	ἔπλεον
subj. pres.:	πλέω	πλέῃς	πλέῃ	etc.		
opt. pres.:	πλέοιμι	etc.	(opt. of monosyllabic stems is left uncontracted)			
ind. pres.:	δέομαι	δέῃ	δεῖται	δεόμεθα	δεῖσθε	δέονται
inf./ptc.:	δεῖσθαι		δεόμενος etc.			

pres.	verb stem	fut.	aor. act./mid. aor. pass.	pf. act. pf. mid./pass.

II. Contracted verbs in -έω with a short stem-final sound throughout

a) with an original σ-stem (↑12d)

	pres.	verb stem	fut.	aor. act./mid. aor. pass.	pf. act. pf. mid./pass.
88.1	ἀρκέω (<ἀρκεσi̯ω) *to be enough*, pass. *to be content*	ἀρκε(**σ**)-	ἀρκ**έσ**ω	ἤρκ**ε**σα ἠρκ**έσ**θην	
88.2	τελέω (<τελεσi̯ω) *to complete*	τελε(**σ**)-	τελ**έ**σω, (CG τελῶ)	ἐτέλ**ε**σα ἐτελ**έσ**θην	τετέλ**ε**κα τετέλ**εσ**μαι

b) with a short stem-final sound, but without σ in the pass. (as far as attested)

	pres.	verb stem	fut.	aor. act./mid. aor. pass.	pf. act. pf. mid./pass.
88.3	αἰνέω *to praise*	αἰνε-	αἰν**έ**σω	ᾔν**ε**σα (ᾐν**έ**θην)	(ᾔν**ε**κα)
88.4	φορέω *to bear*	φορε-	φορ**έ**σω	ἐφόρ**ε**σα	
	Note that the compounds are regular (in CG also the simplex ones).				

III. Contracted verbs in -έω with an original ϝ-stem (before a consonant ϝ > υ; ↑12a; in some cases an analogical σ is added; also ↑88.11–88.13)

	pres.	verb stem	fut.	aor. act./mid. aor. pass.	pf. act. pf. mid./pass.
88.5	πλέω (<πλεϝω) *to travel by sea*	πλεϝ-, πλευ-	(πλε**ύ**σ-ομαι, also -οῦμαι/-ω)	ἔπλε**υ**σα	(πέπλε**υ**κα)
88.6	πνέω (< πνεϝω) *to blow*	πνεϝ-, πνευ-	(πνε**ύ**σ-ω, CG -ομαι)	ἔπνε**υ**σα (ἐπνε**ύ**[σ]θην)	(πέπνε**υ**κα) (πέπνε**υ**[σ]μαι)

IV. Contracted verbs in -έω with quantitative ablaut (↑8d)

δέω *to tie*	δη-, δε-[(1)]	δήσω δ**ε**θήσομαι	ἔδησα ἐδ**έ**θην	δέδ**ε**κα δέδ**ε**μαι	88.7
καλέω *to call*	καλε-, κλη-[(2)]	καλ**έ**σω, (CG καλῶ)	ἐκάλ**ε**σα ἐ**κλή**θην	κέ**κλη**κα κέ**κλη**μαι[(3)]	88.8
ἐπικαλέω mostly ἐπικαλέομαι *to call upon*	↑88.8	 ἐπικαλ**έ**σομαι	ἐπεκάλ**ε**σα ἐπεκαλ**ε**σάμην ἐπε**κλή**θην	 ἐπικέ**κλη**μαι (mostly pass.)	88.9
παρακαλέω *to plead/appeal to*	↑88.8	παρακαλ**έ**σω	παρεκάλ**ε**σα παρε**κλή**θην	(παρακέ**κλη**κα) παρακέ**κλη**μαι	88.10
ῥέω (< ῥεϝω) *to flow*	ῥεϝ-, ῥευ-, ῥυη-	ῥ**εύ**σω, ῥ**υή**σομαι (CG)	ἐρρ**ύη**ν (root-aor. ↑106d)	ἐρρ**ύη**κα	88.11
χέω (< χεϝω) *to pour*	χεϝ-, χε-, χῠ-	χ**εῶ** (χεεῖς), (CG χέω)	ἔχ**εα**[(4)] ἐχ**ύ̆**θην	κέχ**ῠ**κα κέχ**ῠ**μαι	88.12
ἐκχέω (or -χύννω) *to pour out*	↑88.12	ἐκχ**εῶ**	ἐξέχ**εα**[(4)] ἐξεχ**ύ̆**θην	ἐκκέχ**ῠ**κα ἐκκέχ**ῠ**μαι	88.13

(1) From the pf. act. onwards with a short stem-final sound.
In the NT/LXX present/durative forms are rarely used, if at all (on contraction ↑88a).
(2) Zero-grade (↑8). The verbal adjective is κλητός *invited, called.*
(3) On the meaning of this form ↑200b.
(4) Note that this is an aor. I without a sigma (↑105h); consequently the inf. act. is -χ**έαι**.

V. There are a number of “irregular” verbs in -έω, including

αἱρέω (↑113.1f) *to take* δέομαι (↑112.8) *to ask for sth.* 88.14
ὠθέω (↑112.2) *to push* Also ↑112.1; 112.3–112.5

VI. In NT Greek διακονέω *to serve* is used with a temporal augment η (as if it were *δι-ακονέω [↑δι**η**πόρει (ipf. of δι-**α**πορέω) *he was perplexed* Lk 9:7]; ↑71c; Attic uses ἐδια- correctly connecting it with the simplex διάκονος *servant*; ↑BDF §69.4):

δι**η**κόνουν ipf. δι**η**κόνησα aor. act. δι**η**κονήθην aor. pass. 88.15

(c) Contracted verbs in -όω

Present/durative forms of δηλόω “to make clear” (↑BR §93; 121.7; BDF §91; 101) 89

1. Paradigm (↑89a):

Note that in the opt. act. there are special sg. terminations (↑84b; also footnote 27): -οίην, -οίης and -οίη.

89a

δηλόω *to make clear*			ACTIVE contracted	uncontracted	MIDDLE/PASSIVE contracted	uncontracted
IND. PRES.	sg.	1	δηλ-ῶ	-όω	δηλ-οῦμαι	-όομαι
		2	δηλ-οῖς	-όεις	δηλ-οῖ	-όῃ
		3	δηλ-οῖ	-όει	δηλ-οῦται	-όεται
	pl.	1	δηλ-οῦμεν	-όομεν	δηλ-ούμεθα	-οόμεθα
		2	δηλ-οῦτε	-όετε	δηλ-οῦσθε	-όεσθε
		3	δηλ-οῦσιν	-όουσιν	δηλ-οῦνται	-όονται
IPF.	sg.	1	ἐδήλ-ουν	-οον	ἐδηλ-ούμην	-οόμην
		2	ἐδήλ-ους	-οες	ἐδηλ-οῦ	-όου
		3	ἐδήλ-ου	-οε	ἐδηλ-οῦτο	-όετο
	pl.	1	ἐδηλ-οῦμεν	-όομεν	ἐδηλ-ούμεθα	-οόμεθα
		2	ἐδηλ-οῦτε	-όετε	ἐδηλ-οῦσθε	-όεσθε
		3	ἐδήλ-ουν	-οον	ἐδηλ-οῦντο	-όοντο
SUBJ.	sg.	1	δηλ-ῶ	-όω	δηλ-ῶμαι	-όωμαι
		2	δηλ-οῖς	-όῃς	δηλ-οῖ	-όῃ
		3	δηλ-οῖ	-όῃ	δηλ-ῶται	-όηται
	pl.	1	δηλ-ῶμεν	-όωμεν	δηλ-ώμεθα	-οώμεθα
		2	δηλ-ῶτε[(1)]	-όητε	δηλ-ῶσθε[(1)]	-όησθε
		3	δηλ-ῶσιν	-όωσιν	δηλ-ῶνται	-όωνται
OPT.	sg.	1	δηλ-οίην	-οοίην !	δηλ-οίμην	-οοίμην
		2	δηλ-οίης	-οοίης !	δηλ-οῖο	-όοιο
		3	δηλ-οίη	-οοίη !	δηλ-οῖτο	-όοιτο
	pl.	1	δηλ-οῖμεν	-όοιμεν	δηλ-οίμεθα	-οοίμεθα
		2	δηλ-οῖτε	-όοιτε	δηλ-οῖσθε	-όοισθε
		3	δηλ-οῖεν	-όοιεν	δηλ-οῖντο	-όοιντο
IMP.	sg.	2	δήλ-ου	-οε	δηλ-οῦ	-όου
		3	δηλ-ούτω	-οέτω	δηλ-ούσθω	-οέσθω
	pl.	2	δηλ-οῦτε	-όετε	δηλ-οῦσθε	-όεσθε
		3	δηλ-ούτωσαν[(2)]	-οέτωσαν	δηλ-ούσθωσαν[(2)]	-οέσθωσαν
INF.			δηλ-οῦν	-όειν[(3)]	δηλ-οῦσθαι	-όεσθαι
PTC.	masc./ntr.		δηλ-ῶν/-οῦν	-όων/-όον	δηλ-ούμενος/-ον	-οόμενος/-ον
	gen.		δηλ-οῦντος	-όοντος	δηλ-ουμένου	-οομένου
	fem.		δηλ-οῦσα	-όουσα	δηλ-ουμένη	-οομένη
	gen.		δηλ-ούσης	-οούσης	δηλ-ουμένης	-οομένης

(1) NT 2× -οῦ-: Ga 4:17 ζηλ**οῦ**τε *(that) you are zealous,* 1Cor 4:6 φυσι**οῦ**σθε *(that) you are puffed up.*

(2) CG uses -ούντων for -ούτωσαν and -ούσθων for -ούσθωσαν (↑70).

(3) Here ει does not stand for a diphthong, but for an e-sound (i.e. the ι is written, but no ι-sound is expressed). For this reason there is no iota subscript in the contracted form (↑2c; 11e; 70).

2. Contraction rules (↑11; 82): 89b

ο + short vowel (ε, ο) or ου	> ου
ο + long vowel (η, ω)	> ω
ο + ι-diphthong (ει, οι, ῃ)	> οι

3. Outside the present the stem-final lengthened, ο becoming ω: 89c

	future:	aorist:	perfect:
active:	δηλ**ώ**σω	ἐδήλ**ω**σα	δεδήλ**ω**κα
middle:	δηλ**ώ**σομαι	ἐδηλ**ω**σάμην	δεδήλ**ω**μαι
passive:	δηλ**ω**θήσομαι	ἐδηλ**ώ**θην	δεδήλ**ω**μαι

2.7.2.2 Stop verbs

Stop verbs: preliminaries (↑BR §99; BDF §71) 90

90a 1. Stop verbs are verbs whose stem-final sound is a stop (↑3). Three classes may be distinguished:

a) Labial stems, i.e. stems in π, β, φ, e.g.:

βλέ**π**ω *to see* θλί**β**ω *to press* γρά**φ**ω *to write*

b) Velar stems, i.e. stems in κ, γ, χ, e.g.:

διώ**κ**ω *to persecute* ἄ**γ**ω *to lead* δέ**χ**ομαι *to receive/welcome*

c) Dental stems, i.e. stems in δ, θ (there are none in τ), e.g.:

ψεύ**δ**ομαι *to lie* πεί**θ**ω *to persuade*

2. The **present stem** of many stop verbs differs from their verb stem; in most cases this is due to the fact that originally it had an i̯-affix (↑75b). 90b

3. The **tense/aspect stems** of stop verbs **outside the present** are derived from the verb stem in principle the same way as are those of παιδεύω (↑76–79). The stem-final stops, however, in agreement with regular sound laws change in various ways depending on the consonants that follow them (↑16c; 92). 90c

Present stems of stop verbs (↑BR §99; BDF §73) 91

I. The present stem may be **the same as the verb stem** (↑75a), e.g.: 91a

present stem:		verb stem:
βλέπ-ω	*to see*	βλεπ-
διώκ-ω	*to persecute*	διωκ-
πείθ-ω	*to persuade*	πειθ-

91b II. More frequently the **present stem differs from the verb stem**, due to the fact that it originally had an i̯-affix (↑75b; 12c), e.g.:

present stem:		i̯-stem:	rule:		verb stem		
κλέ**πτ**ω	*to steal*	κλε**πi̯**ω	πτ	< labial + i̯	κλεπ-	↑κλοπή	*theft*
φυλά**σσ**ω	*to guard*	φυλα**κi̯**ω	σσ [1]	< κi̯/χi̯; τi̯/θi̯	φυλακ-	↑φυλακή	*guard*
ἐλπί**ζ**ω	*to hope*	ἐλπι**δi̯**ω	ζ	< δi̯	ἐλπιδ-	↑ἐλπίς -ίδος	*hope*
κρά**ζ**ω	*to cry out*	κρα**γi̯**ω	ζ	< γi̯	κραγ-	(↑κραγέτης *screamer* [rare])	

(1) Attic/CG has ττ instead of σσ.

92 Stop verbs: tense-aspect stems outside the present (↑BR §100; BDF §74)

92a I. When the stem of stop verbs is combined with consonant-initial terminations the stem-final sound will change as follows (↑16c):

	+ μ	+ σ	+ τ	+ (σ)θ	[+κ]
labial (β, π, φ)	μμ	ψ	πτ	φθ	[φ]
velar (γ, κ, χ)	γμ	ξ	κτ	χθ	[χ]
dental (δ, τ, θ)	σμ	σ	στ	σθ	[κ]

Notes on the above table:

92b 1. The column on the far right (+ κ) is about the perfect active stem. Note that the changes indicated there do not depend on any sound laws (hence the brackets). Labial and velar stems have a "strong"/"second" perfect active: it is without the regular tense-aspect sign κ (↑68d; 108d). In the case of dental stems the perfect active stem is formed analogically: the stem-final dental is replaced by -κ (in analogy to the vowel verbs; ↑13c; BR §100).

92c 2. The columns +μ, +σ, +τ, +(σ)θ also apply to the perfect mid./pass. paradigm (↑93).

92d II. **Typical principal parts** of stop verbs:

principal parts	(↑92a)	labial stem βλεπ-	velar stem πρᾱγ-	dental stem ἁγιαδ-
pres. act.		βλέπω *to see*	πρᾱ́σσω *to do*	ἁγιάζω *to sanctify*
fut. act.	(+ σ)	βλέ**ψ**ω	πρᾱ́**ξ**ω	ἁγιά**σ**ω
aor. act.	(+ σ)	ἔβλε**ψ**α	ἔπρᾱ**ξ**α	ἡγία**σ**α
pf. act.	[(+ κ)]	(βέβλε**φ**α)	(πέπρᾱ**χ**α)	(ἡγία**κ**α)
pf. mid./pass.	(+ μ)	βέβλε**μμ**αι	πέπρᾱ**γμ**αι	ἡγία**σμ**αι
aor. pass.	(+ θ)	ἐβλέ**φθ**ην	ἐπρᾱ́**χθ**ην	ἡγιά**σθ**ην

Notes on the above table:

1. Many verbs with a labial or velar stem have a “strong” aorist stem, a 2nd active/ middle aorist (↑105) or a 2nd passive aorist stem (monosyllabic labial stems with an ε replace the ε by an α; ↑107). Also ↑92b on the pf. act. (↑108c–108f). Further ↑94/95. 92e

2. Verbs in -ίζω (< -ιδi̯ω; ↑91b) with two or more stem syllables have a contracted future act./mid. (also called “Attic future”; ↑98a). It inflects like the present of ποιέω *to do* (↑87c): 92f

fut. act. ending in -ιῶ fut. mid. ending in -ιοῦμαι

KG frequently uses a sigmatic future act./mid. instead. Also ↑96.11–96.18.

Stop verbs: forms of the perfect middle-passive stem (↑BR §101) 93

	labial stem γραφ- γράφω *to write*	velar stem πραγ- πράσσω *to do*	dental stem πειθ- πείθω *to persuade*	↑92a
IND. PF.				
sg. 1	γέγρα**μ-μ**αι	πέπρα**γ-μ**αι	πέπει**σ-μ**αι	+ μ
2	γέγρα**ψ**αι	πέπρα**ξ**αι	πέπε**ι-σ**αι	+ σ
3	γέγρα**π-τ**αι	πέπρα**κ-τ**αι	πέπει**σ-τ**αι	+ τ
pl. 1	γεγρά**μ-μ**εθα	πεπρά**γ-μ**εθα	πεπεί**σ-μ**εθα	+ μ
2	γέγρα**φ- θ**ε(1)	πέπρα**χ- θ**ε(1)	πέπε**ι-σθ**ε(1)	+ σθ
3	γεγρα**μ-μ**ένοι εἰσίν(2)	πεπρα**γ-μ**ένοι εἰσίν(2)	πεπει**σ-μ**ένοι εἰσίν(2)	+ μ
PLPF.				
sg. 1	ἐ-γεγρά**μ-μ**ην	ἐ-πεπρά**γ-μ**ην	ἐ-πεπεί**σ-μ**ην	+ μ
2	ἐ-γέγρα**ψ**ο	ἐ-πέπρα**ξ**ο	ἐ-πέπε**ι-σ**ο	+ σ
3	ἐ-γέγρα**π-τ**ο	ἐ-πέπρα**κ-τ**ο	ἐ-πέπει**σ-τ**ο	+ τ
pl. 1	ἐ-γεγρά**μ-μ**εθα	ἐ-πεπρά**γ-μ**εθα	ἐ-πεπεί**σ-μ**εθα	+ μ
2	ἐ-γέγρα**φ- θ**ε(1)	ἐ-πέπρα**χ- θ**ε(1)	ἐ-πέπε**ι-σθ**ε	+ σθ
3	γεγρα**μ-μ**ένοι ἦσαν(2)	πεπρα**γ-μ**ένοι ἦσαν(2)	πεπει**σ-μ**ένοι ἦσαν(2)	+ μ
INF. PF.	γεγρά**φ- θ**αι(1)	πεπρᾶ**χ- θ**αι(1)	πεπε**ῖ-σθ**αι	+ σθ
PTC. PF.	γεγρα**μ-μ**ένος	πεπρα**γ-μ**ένος	πεπει**σ-μ**ένος	+ μ

(1) Between two consonants the σ is dropped (↑13f; 16c; 92a).

(2) The personal endings -νται, -ντο cannot be combined with a stem that ends in a consonant; the resulting consonant cluster would be hard or impossible to pronounce. Consequently the 3rd person plural is always formed by periphrasis (↑200j; 203): the ptc. pf. pass. is combined with εἰσίν *they are* to express the ind. pf. or with ἦσαν *they were* to express the plpf. respectively. Note that such periphrasis is often used in other persons and with other verb types as well.

94 Principal parts of important labial verbs (↑BR §121.32–42; BDF §101)

I. Verbs with an unextended present stem

	pres.	verb stem	fut.	aor. act./mid. aor. pass.	pf. act. pf. mid./pass.
94.1	βλέπω *to see*	βλεπ-	βλέψω	ἔβλεψα (ἐβλέφθην)	(βέβλεφα) (βέβλεμμαι)
94.2	γράφω *to write*	γραφ-	γράψω	ἔγραψα ἐγράφην[(1)]	γέγραφα γέγραμμαι
94.3	θλί̄βω *to press*	θλῑβ-, θλῐβ-	θλί̄ψω	ἔθλῑψα ἐθλί̆βην[(1)/(2)]	τέθλῐφα τέθλῑμμαι
94.4	λείπω *to leave behind*	λειπ-, λιπ-, λοιπ-	λείψω	ἔλιπον[(1)/(3)] ἐλείφθην	λέλοιπα[(4)] λέλειμμαι
94.5	ἐγκαταλείπω – *to forsake* (like λείπω)				
94.6	πέμπω *to send*	πεμπ-, πομπ-	πέμψω	ἔπεμψα ἐπέμφθην	πέπομφα[(4)] πέπεμμαι
94.7	στρέφω *to turn sth.*; pass. *to turn (o.s.)*	στρεφ-, στροφ-, στραφ-	στρέψω	ἔστρεψα ἐστράφην[(1)] (↑189b; 191e)	ἔστροφα[(4)] ἔστραμμαι
94.8	ἐπιστρέφω *to turn around/to go back* (act. trans. and intr.; pass. mostly intr.: *to turn [o.s.] around*; ↑189b; 191e)	↑94.7	ἐπιστρέψω	ἐπέστρεψα ἐπεστράφην[(1)]	
94.9	τρέπω *to turn sth.*	τρεπ-, τροπ-, τραπ-	τρέψω	ἔτρεψα ἐτράπην[(1)/(5)]	(τέτροφα)[(4)] τέτραμμαι
94.10	ἐπιτρέπω *to permit*	↑94.9	ἐπιτρέψω	ἐπέτρεψα ἐπετράπην[(1)]	
94.11	τρέφω *to feed/ to rear*	θρεφ-, θροφ-, θραφ-	θρέψω (↑14c)	ἔθρεψα ἐτράφην[(1)]	(τέτροφα)[(4)] τέθραμμαι

(1) Aor. II (↑105; 107).

(2) Analogically: τρί̄βω *to rub*, τρί̄ψω, ἔτρῑψα, (τέτρῐφα), τέτρῑμμαι, ἐτρί̆βην.
In the aor. pass. of both sets we also encounter aor. I forms (↑92d), though only outside the NT.

(3) In post-CG also ἔλειψα. Partly similar to this set is (the pf forms are not used in the NT): ἀλείφω *to anoint*, ἀλείψω, ἤλειψα, (ἀλήλιφα), (ἀλήλιμμαι)/ἤλειμμαι, ἠλείφθην.

(4) Pf. II with ablaut (↑92a/92b; 108).

(5) Comparable to this is (but pf. act. without aspiration of labial) σήπω *to cause to rot*, σήψω, (ἔσηψα), σέσηπα *I am rotten* (↑189c), (σέσημμαι), ἐσάπην.

II. Verbs with a present stem in -πτω (↑91b)

ἅπτω *to light*; mid. *to touch/hold*	ἁφ-	ἅψω	ἧψα (ἥφθην)	 (ἧμμαι, ἧψαι)	94.12
βάπτω *to dip (in)*	βαφ-	βάψω	ἔβαψα ἐβάφην[1]	 βέβαμμαι	94.13
θάπτω *to bury*	θαφ- (↑14c)	θάψω	ἔθαψα ἐτάφην[1]	 (τέθαμμαι)	94.14
καλύπτω *to cover with*	καλυβ-	καλύψω	ἐκάλυψα ἐκαλύφθην	κεκάλυφα κεκάλυμμαι	94.15
ἀποκαλύπτω – *to disclose/reveal* (like καλύπτω)					94.16
κλέπτω *to steal*	κλεπ-, κλοπ-, κλαπ-	κλέψω	ἔκλεψα ἐκλάπην[1]	(κέκλοφα)[2] κέκλεμμαι	94.17
κόπτω *to cut/beat*	κοπ-	κόψω	ἔκοψα ἐκόπην[1]	(κέκοφα) κέκομμαι	94.18
ῥί̄πτω *to throw* (also ῥῑπτέω)	ῥῑπ-	ῥί̄ψω	ἔρρῑψα ἐρρί̄φην[1]	(ἔρρῑφα) ἔρρῑμμαι	94.19
κρύπτω *to hide*	κρυφ-	κρύψω	ἔκρυψα ἐκρύβην[1]	 κέκρυμμαι	94.20

(1) Aor. II (↑105; 107). Outside the NT (regularly in CG) ἐρρί̄φην (94.19) and ἐκρύβην (94.20) may be replaced by aor. I forms (↑92d).
(2) Pf. II with ablaut (↑92a/92b; 108f).

Principal parts of important velar verbs (↑BR §121.43–55; BDF §101) 95

(also ↑113.11; 123.1–123.6)

pres.	verb stem	fut.	aor. act./mid. aor. pass.	pf. act. pf. mid./pass.

I. Verbs with an unextended present stem

ἄγω *to lead* (rarely *to go*; ↑189b)	ἀγ-	ἄξω	ἤγαγον[1] ἤχθην	(ἦχα) ἦγμαι	95.1

(1) Aor. II (↑105; 107). Note that here the complete verb stem is reduplicated: ἀγαγ- (↑72a). The aor. I occurs very rarely, thus in 2Pe 2:5 -άξας = -αγαγών.

95.2	ἀνοίγω *to open* (CG also ἀνοίγνῡμι; for paradigm ↑122)	-οιγ-	ἀνοίξω	ἤνοιξα/ ἀνέῳξα/ ἠνέῳξα ἠνοίχθην/ ἀνεῴχθην (CG)/ ἠνεῴχθην/ ἠνοίγην[1]	ἀνέῳγα[2] *I stand open* (↑189c)[3] ἀνέῳγμαι (↑71e) or ἠνέῳγμαι
95.3	ἄρχω *to rule*	ἀρχ-	ἄρξω	ἦρξα ἤρχθην	(ἦρχα) ἦργμαι
95.4	ἄρχομαι mid. *to begin*		ἄρξομαι	ἠρξάμην	ἦργμαι
95.5	δέχομαι *to receive/welcome*	δεχ-	δέξομαι	ἐδεξάμην ἐδέχθην	δέδεγμαι
95.6	διώκω *to persecute*	διωκ-	διώξω (CG mid.)	ἐδίωξα ἐδιώχθην	(δεδίωχα) δεδίωγμαι
95.7	ἐκλέγομαι *to choose*	-λεγ-	ἐκλέξομαι	ἐξελεξάμην (ἐξελέχθην)/ ἐξελέγην[1]/[4]	ἐκλέλεγμαι/ (ἐκείλεγμαι)
95.8	προσεύχομαι *to pray*	-ευχ-	προσεύξομαι	προσηυξάμην	[5]
95.9	φεύγω *to flee*	φευγ-, φυγ-	φεύξομαι	ἔφυγον[1]	πέφευγα[2]/[6]

(1) Aor. II (↑105; 107); inf. ἀνοιγῆναι; Aor. I inf. ἀνεῳχθῆναι/ἀνοιχθῆναι.
(2) Pf. II with the stem-final velar remaining unchanged (↑92b; 108c).
(3) CG uses a transitive pf. II (with an aspirate stem-final velar) ἀνέῳχα *I have opened.*
(4) διαλέγομαι *to converse* has analogous principal parts, similarly also συλλέγω *to collect/gather,* συλλέξω, συνέλεξα, (συνείλεχα/συνείλοχα), συλλέλεγμαι etc. But also ↑113.7.
(5) For εὔχομαι *to pray/to vow* there is also a pf. ηὖγμαι *I am under a vow.*
(6) In the case of the following velar verbs the present stem is unextended, too:
πλέκω *to weave/plait,* (πλέξω), ἔπλεξα, (πέπλεχα), πέπλεγμαι, ἐπλάκην/(ἐπλέχθην);
πνίγω *to choke/strangle,* (πνίξω), ἔπνιξα, –, (πέπνιγμαι), ἐπνίγην;
τήκω *to melt sth.,* τήξω, ἔτηξα, τέτηκα, (τέτηγμαι), ἐτάκην;
ψύχω *to make cold/cool,* ψύξω, ἔψυξα, ἔψυχα, (ἔψυγμαι), ἐψύγην/(ἐψύχθην).

II. Verbs with a present stem in -σσω (↑91b)

95.10	ἀλλάσσω [1] *to change sth.*	ἀλλαγ-	ἀλλάξω	ἤλλαξα ἠλλάγην[2]	ἤλλαχα ἤλλαγμαι

(1) Analogous: σπαράσσω *to shake to and fro,* σπαράξω, ἐσπάραξα, ἐσπάραγμαι, ἐσπάραχθην.
(2) Aor. II (↑105; 107). Outside the NT/LXX we also encounter the aor. I ἠλλάχθην.

καταλλάσσω *to reconcile;* ↑καταλλαγή *reconciliation*			κατήλλαξα κατηλλάγην[1]		95.11
κηρύσσω *to proclaim;* ↑κῆρυξ κήρυκ-ος *herald*	κηρυκ-	(κηρύξω)	ἐκήρυξα ἐκηρύχθην	(κεκήρυχα) (κεκήρυγμαι)	95.12
πλήσσω *to strike;* ↑πληγή *blow/stroke*	πλήγ-	(πλήξω)	ἔπληξα ἐπλήγην[1]	πέπληγα[2] πέπληγμαι	95.13
ἐκπλήσσομαι *be amazed/astounded*	πληγ-, πλαγ-	(ἐκπλήξομαι/ ἐκπλαγήσομαι)	ἐξεπλάγην[1]	(ἐκπέπληγμαι)	95.14
πρᾱ́σσω *to do* (α always long)	πρᾱγ-	πρᾱ́ξω	ἔπρᾱξα ἐπρᾱ́χθην	πέπρᾱχα πέπρᾱγμαι	95.15
τάσσω *to put in place*	ταγ-	τάξω	ἔταξα ἐτάγην[1]	τέταχα τέταγμαι	95.16
φυλάσσω *to guard;* ↑φύλαξ φύλακ-ος *guard*	φυλακ-	φυλάξω	ἐφύλαξα ἐφυλάχθην	πεφύλακα[2] πεφύλαγμαι	95.17

(1) Aor. II (↑105; 107).
(2) Pf. II without the stem-final velar changing (↑92b; 108c); for πεφύλακα CG uses πεφύλαχα.

III. Verbs with a present stem in -ζω (↑91b; also 96.22)

βαστάζω *to carry/bear* ↑verbal adjective δυσβάστακτος -ον *hard to bear*	βασταγ-, βασταδ-	βαστάσω/ (βαστάξω)	ἐβάστασα/-αξα ἐβαστάχθην		95.18
κράζω *to cry out*	κραγ-	κράξω	ἔκραξα/ ἔκραγον (CG)[1]	κέκραγα (↑200c)	95.19
σαλπίζω *to blow the trumpet,* σαλπιγγ-, widely (NT/LXX always) treated as a dental stem					95.20
στενάζω *to sigh*	στεναγ-	στενάξω	ἐστέναξα	(ἐστέναγμαι)[2]	95.21
στηρίζω *to strengthen*	στηριδ-, NT mostly: στηριγ-	στηρίξω/ (LXX:)-ίσω/-ιῶ	ἐστήριξα/-ισα ἐστηρίχθην	(ἐστήρικα)[3] ἐστήριγμαι	95.22
σφάζω (CG σφάττω) *to slaughter;* ↑σφαγή *slaughter*	σφαγ-	σφάξω	ἔσφαξα ἐσφάγην	ἔσφαγμαι	95.23

(1) Aor. II (↑105). For ἔκραξα/ἔκραγον in Ac 24:21 ἐκέκραξα is used, mostly in the LXX, too, though sometimes ἐκέκραγον (aor. II; ↑105). For κράξω the LXX uses κεκράξομαι (CG; derived from the pf. II that generally has a present meaning [↑92b; 108c] κέκραγα; ↑Thackeray:273).
(2) Verbs with similar velar stems: νυστάζω *to nod/doze*, νυστάξω, ἐνύσταξα; ἐμπαίζω *to ridicule* ἐμπαίξω, ἐνέπαιξα, ἐμπέπαιχα, ἐμπέπαιγμαι, ἐνεπαίχθην (Attic often treats -παίζω as dental).
(3) Outside the NT/LXX ἐστήρικα may be used instead of ἐστήριχα.

96 Principal parts of important dental verbs (↑BR §121.56–65; BDF §101)

	pres.	verb stem	fut.	aor. act./mid. aor. pass.	pf. act. pf. mid./pass.

I. Verbs with an unextended present stem

	pres.	verb stem	fut.	aor. act./mid. aor. pass.	pf. act. pf. mid./pass.
96.1	πείθω *to persuade,* pass. *to be persuaded, to obey*	πειθ-[1]	πείσω	ἔπεισα ἐπείσθην	(πέπεικα)[1] πέπεισμαι[1] *I am certain*
96.2	φείδομαι *to spare*	φειδ-	φείσομαι	ἐφεισάμην	
96.3	ψεύδομαι *to lie*	ψευδ-	ψεύσομαι	ἐψευσάμην	ἔψευσμαι

(1) Note the cognate pf. II πέποιθα *to trust* (↑189c; 200b); on the meaning of πέπεισμαι also ↑200b.

II. Verbs with a present stem in -ζω (↑91b; 363a; a great number are attested)

a) with a present stem in -άζω:

	pres.	verb stem	fut.	aor. act./mid. aor. pass.	pf. act. pf. mid./pass.
96.4	ἁγιάζω *to sanctify*	ἁγιαδ-	ἁγιάσω	ἡγίασα ἡγιάσθην	ἡγίακα ἡγίασμαι
96.5	ἀγοράζω *to buy*	ἀγοραδ-	ἀγοράσω[1]	ἠγόρασα ἠγοράσθην	(ἠγόρακα) ἠγόρασμαι
96.6	δοξάζω *to praise/to glorify*	δοξαδ-	δοξάσω	ἐδόξασα ἐδοξάσθην	(δεδόξακα) δεδόξασμαι
96.7	ἐργάζομαι *to work* (aug. εἰ- or ἠ-; ↑71d)	ἐργαδ-	ἐργάσομαι[1]	εἰργασάμην εἰργάσθην	εἴργασμαι
96.8	δοκιμάζω *to test* analogically[1]				
96.9	ἑτοιμάζω *to prepare* analogically				
96.10	θαυμάζω *to be amazed/to marvel* analogically				

(1) The LXX occasionally (against the Attic rule) uses ἀγορῶ, -ᾷς etc. (contracted future [↑92f; 98a], however, inflected like the present of ἀγαπάω [↑84b]) instead of ἀγοράσω etc., regularly also ἐργῶμαι, -ᾷ etc. instead of ἐργάσομαι etc. (96.7) and δοκιμῶ, -ᾷς etc. instead of δοκιμάσω etc. (96.8).

b) with a present stem in -ίζω with two or more syllables (↑92f):

• with a contracted future in -ιῶ (inflected like the present of ποιέω *to do*; ↑87c):

ἐλπίζω [(1)] *to hope*	ἐλπιδ-	ἐλπιῶ, -εῖς	ἤλπισα ἠλπίσθην	ἤλπικα ἤλπισμαι	96.11
ἐγγίζω *to draw near*	ἐγγιδ-	ἐγγιῶ, -εῖς	ἤγγισα	ἤγγικα	96.12
καθαρίζω *to cleanse*	καθαριδ-	καθαριῶ/ (καθαρίσω)	ἐκαθάρισα ἐκαθαρίσθην	 κεκαθάρισμαι	96.13

(1) Analogous: ῥαντίζω *to sprinkle*, ῥαντιῶ, ἐρράντισα, ἐρράντισμαι/ῥεράντισμαι, ἐρραντίσθη.

• usually with a sigmatic future (↑92f):

βαπτίζω *to dip/baptize*	βαπτιδ-	βαπτίσω	ἐβάπτισα ἐβαπτίσθην	(βεβάπτικα) βεβάπτισμαι	96.14
γνωρίζω *to make known*	γνωριδ-	γνωρίσω/ γνωριῶ	ἐγνώρισα ἐγνωρίσθην	(ἐγνώρικα) (ἐγνώρισμαι)	96.15
εὐαγγελίζομαι *to bring good news*	-αγγελιδ-	εὐαγγελίσομαι/ εὐαγγελιοῦμαι	εὐηγγελισάμην εὐηγγελίσθην	εὐηγγέλισμαι	96.16
χαρίζομαι *to grant*	χαριδ-	χαρίσομαι	ἐχαρισάμην ἐχαρίσθην	κεχάρισμαι	96.17

c) with a present stem in -ίζω with only one syllable (sigmatic future; ↑92f):

κτίζω [(1)] *to create*	κτιδ-	κτίσω	ἔκτισα ἐκτίσθην	(ἔκτικα) ἔκτισμαι	96.18

(1) Comparable: πρίζω (CG πρίω) *to saw*, aor. act. ἔπρισα, aor. pass. ἐπρίσθην (↑He 11:37).

d) with a present stems in -ύζω:

γογγύζω *to grumble*	γογγυδ-	γογγύσω	ἐγόγγυσα		96.19

III. Dental verb with a present stem in -σσω (isolated case; ↑91b)

πλάσσω *to form*	πλαθ-	πλάσω	ἔπλασα ἐπλάσθην	(πέπλακα) πέπλασμαι	96.20

IV. Verbs with two different verb stems (one dental, the other non-dental)

96.21	σῴζω *to save*	σῳ(δ)-, σω-	σώσω	ἔσωσα ἐσώθην	σέσωκα σέσῳσμαι
96.22	ἁρπάζω *to rob* (↑95.18ff)	ἁρπαδ- ἁρπαγ-	ἁρπάσω ἁρπαγήσομαι	ἥρπασα ἡρπάσθην ἡρπάγην(1)	ἥρπακα ἥρπασμαι

(1) Aor. II (↑105; 107).

2.7.2.3 Liquid verbs

97 Present stems of liquid verbs (↑BR §103; BDF §72f)

97a I. Liquid verbs are verbs whose stem-final sound is a liquid (-λ, -ρ, -μ or -ν; ↑3).

II. The **present stem** may be the same as the verb stem; in most cases, however, it goes back to an extended form that originally had an i̯-affix (↑75a–75f):

97b 1. Liquid verbs (very few) with a present stem that is the same as the verb stem:

present stem:		verb stem:
μέν-ω	*to remain/stay*	μεν-
δέρ-ω	*to beat/whip*	δερ-

97c 2. Most liquid verbs have a present stem that originally had an i̯-affix (↑12). The deletion of this affix led to the following types of changes (↑12c; 10d; 75b):

present stem: i̯-stem: verb stem:

a) λ is doubled:

ἀγγέ**λλ**-ω *to announce* < ἀγγε**λi̯**-ω ἀγγελ- (↑ἄγγελος *messenger*)

b) the short stem vowel (of the only or the second syllable) is lengthened, alternatively "epenthesis" (insertion) of an ι (↑12c):

• the short stem vowel is lengthened (ει [↑10d] < ε and ῑ < ῐ):

τ**είν**-ω	*to stretch*	< τε**νi̯**-ω	τεν-	(↑ἐκτενής *extended/earnest*)
ἐγ**είρ**-ω	*to raise*	< ἐγε**ρi̯**-ω	ἐγερ-	(↑ἔγερσις *raising*)
κρ**ῑ́ν**-ω	*to judge*	< κρῐ**νi̯**-ω	κρῐν-	(↑κρῐνῶ fut.)

• epenthesis of an ι (αι < α; the i̯ leaps as it were to the preceding syllable):

καθ**αίρ**-ω *to cleanse* < καθα**ρi̯**-ω καθαρ- (↑καθαρός *clean*)

Future and aorist active/middle stems of liquid verbs (↑BR §104f) 98

1. For the **future active/middle** the liquid verbs have contracted forms (contracted future; ↑92f): the verb stem has an ε-affix, e.g.: 98a

ἀγγελ**έσω** (↑13e) > ἀγγελ**έω** > ἀγγελ**ῶ** *I will announce*

The **paradigm** is the same as the one of the present of ποιέω *to do* (↑87c for the inf., ptc. and the opt.; note that the future is without imp. and subj.), e.g. of στέλλω inter alia (active) *to send*:[28]

	active		middle	
sg. 1	στελ-ῶ	*I will send*	στελ-οῦ-μαι	*I will send for myself*
2	στελ-εῖς	etc.	στελ-ῇ	etc.
3	στελ-εῖ		στελ-εῖ-ται	
pl. 1	στελ-οῦ-μεν		στελ-ού-μεθα	
2	στελ-εῖ-τε		στελ-εῖ-σθε	
3	στελ-οῦσιν		στελ-οῦ-νται	

2. The **aorist active/middle** stem of liquid verbs is without the tense-aspect sign σ (↑68d); as a result there is a compensatory lengthening of the vowel in the preceding syllable (↑10b; 13h), e.g.: 98b

present		verb stem	aorist act./mid.	lengthening rules		
φαίνω	*to shine*	φ**ᾰ**ν-	ἔ-φ**ᾱ**ν-α	ᾰ	>	ᾱ(1)
ποιμαίνω	*to shepherd*	ποιμ**ᾰ**ν-	ἐ-ποίμ**ᾱ**ν-α	ᾰ	>	ᾱ(1)
ἀγγέλλω	*to announce*	ἀγγ**ε**λ-	ἤγγ**ει**λ-α	ε	>	ει
σπείρω	*to sow*	σπ**ε**ρ-	ἔ-σπ**ει**ρ-α	ε	>	ει
κρΐνω	*to judge*	κρ**ῐ**ν-	ἔ-κρ**ῑ**ν-α	ῐ	>	ῑ
σκληρΰνω	*to harden*	σκληρ**ῠ**ν-	ἐ-σκλήρ**ῡ**ν-α	ῠ	>	ῡ

(1) In CG this rule applies only after ε, ι, ρ, otherwise > η (so it uses ἔφ**η**να, not ἔφ**ᾱ**να and ἐποίμηνα, not ἐποίμᾱνα); ↑11g.

Note that apart from the missing σ this aorist active/middle is regular with the normal aor. I terminations being used (↑76/77 and 98c/98d). For the various types of aor. II ↑104ff.

---

28 Note that while verbs in -ίζω with two or more stem syllables usually have this type of contracted future act./mid., too (↑92f; 96.11ff), there are a number of verbs in -άζω that in the LXX are used with a contracted future (↑96.5ff; similarly 124.4[1]) that, however, inflects like the present of ἀγαπάω (↑84b). ↑also 110.2; 124.5 for certain other verbs with such a contracted future in CG.

3. The **paradigm** of στέλλω inter alia *to send* in the aorist active and middle:

98c a) **Aorist active** ἔστειλα inter alia *I sent* (for further details on the paradigm ↑76):

		INDICATIVE	SUBJUNCTIVE	OPTATIVE	IMPERATIVE
sg.	1	ἔ-στειλ-α	στείλ-ω	στείλ-αι-μι	
	2	ἔ-στειλ-α-ς	στείλ-ῃς	στείλ-αι-ς	στεῖλ-ον
	3	ἔ-στειλ-ε-ν	στείλ-ῃ	στείλ-αι	στειλ-ά-τω
pl.	1	ἐ-στείλ-α-μεν	στείλ-ω-μεν	στείλ-αι-μεν	
	2	ἐ-στείλ-α-τε	στείλ-η-τε	στείλ-αι-τε	στείλ-α-τε
	3	ἔ-στειλ-α-ν	στείλ-ω-σιν	στείλ-αι-εν	στειλ-ά-τω-σαν(1)
		INFINITIVE στεῖλ-αι	PARTICIPLE	στείλας στείλασα στεῖλαν	-αντος -άσης -αντος

(1) CG uses στειλ-άντων instead of στειλ-ά-τω-σαν (↑70).

98d b) **Aorist middle** ἐστειλάμην inter alia *I sent for myself* (for details ↑77):

		INDICATIVE	SUBJUNCTIVE	OPTATIVE	IMPERATIVE
sg.	1	ἐ-στειλ-ά-μην	στείλ-ω-μαι	στειλ-αί-μην	
	2	ἐ-στείλ-ω	στείλ-ῃ	στείλ-αι-ο	στεῖλ-αι
	3	ἐ-στείλ-α-το	στείλ-η-ται	στείλ-αι-το	στειλ-ά-σθω
pl.	1	ἐ-στειλ-ά-μεθα	στειλ-ώ-μεθα	στειλ-αί-μεθα	
	2	ἐ-στείλ-α-σθε	στείλ-η-σθε	στείλ-αι-σθε	στείλ-α-σθε
	3	ἐ-στείλ-α-ντο	στείλ-ω-νται	στείλ-αι-ντο	στειλ-ά-σθω-σαν(1)
		INFINITIVE στείλ-α-σθαι	PARTICIPLE	στειλ-ά-μενος στειλ-α-μένη στειλ-ά-μενον	

(1) CG uses στειλ-άσθων instead of στειλ-ά-σθω-σαν (↑70).

Liquid verbs: forms of the perfect middle-passive stem (↑BR §106) 99

	ἀγγέλλω *to announce* (st. ἀγγελ-)	μιαίνω *to defile* (st. μιαν-)
IND.PF. sg. 1	ἤγγελ-μαι *I am announced*	με-μίαμ-μαι[1] *I am defiled*
2	ἤγγελ-σαι etc.	(με-μίαν-σαι) etc.
3	ἤγγελ-ται	με-μίαν-ται
pl. 1	ἠγγέλ-μεθα	με-μιάμ-μεθα[1]
2	ἤγγελ- θε[2]	με-μίαν- θε[2]
3	ἠγγελ-μένοι εἰσίν (↑93[2])	με-μιαμ-μένοι[1] εἰσίν (↑93[2])
PLPF. sg. 1	ἠγγέλ-μην *I was announced*	ἐ-με-μιάμ-μην[1] *I was defiled*
2	ἤγγελ-σο etc.	(ἐ-με-μίαν-σο) etc.
3	ἤγγελ-το	ἐ-με-μίαν-το
pl. 1	ἠγγέλ-μεθα	ἐ-με-μιάμ-μεθα[1]
2	ἤγγελ- θε[2]	ἐ-με-μίαν- θε[2]
3	ἠγγελ-μένοι ἦσαν (↑93[2])	με-μιαμ-μένοι[1] ἦσαν (↑93[2])
INF. PF.	ἠγγέλ- θαι[2] *to be announced*	με-μιάν- θαι[2] *to be defiled*
PTC. PF.	ἠγγελ-μένος *announced*	με-μιαμ-μένος[1] *defiled*

(1) ν + μ > μμ (↑15f; 16c); CG > σμ (against the rule), ↑BR §20.1(3); BDF §72.
(2) Between two consonants the σ is deleted (↑13f; 16b; 92a).

Typical principal parts of liquid verbs (↑BR §105; 121.66ff; BDF §76; 101) 100

pres.act.	μιαίνω *to defile*	ἀγγέλλω *to announce*	στέλλω *to send*	σπείρω *to sow*	αἴρω *to lift*	δέρω *to beat*
st.	μιαν-	ἀγγελ-	στελ-	σπερ-	ἀρ-	δερ-
fut.act.	μιανῶ, -εῖς	ἀγγελῶ, -εῖς	στελῶ, -εῖς	σπερῶ, -εῖς	ἀρῶ, -εῖς	δερῶ, -εῖς
aor.act.[1]	ἐμίᾶνα	ἤγγειλα	ἔστειλα	ἔσπειρα	ἦρα	ἔδειρα
pf.act.	μεμίαγκα[2]	ἤγγελκα	ἔσταλκα[3]	ἔσπαρκα[3]	ἦρκα	δέδαρκα[3]
pf.mid./pass.	μεμίαμμαι[4]	ἤγγελμαι	ἔσταλμαι	ἔσπαρμαι	ἦρμαι	δέδαρμαι
aor. pass.	ἐμιάνθην	ἠγγέλην[5]	ἐστάλην[5]	ἐσπάρην[5]	ἤρθην	ἐδάρην[5]

(1) Inf.: μιᾶναι, ἀγγεῖλαι, στεῖλαι, σπεῖραι, ἆραι, δεῖραι.
(2) Stem-final ν before κ becomes γ (a velar nasal; ↑3; 16c).
(3) Monosyllabic stems with an ε replace the ε by an α from the pf. act. onwards (ablaut; ↑8, especially 8d; 107d; 108e/108f).
(4) Stem-final ν before μ becomes μ (↑16c).
(5) Aor. II pass. (↑107, especially 107j); CG uses ἠγγέλθην (aor.I) instead of ἠγγέλην.

101 Liquid verbs with stems in -λ (also ↑123.7; BR §121.79f.77; BDF §101)

	pres.	stem	fut.	aor. act./mid. aor. pass.	pf. act. pf. mid./pass.
101.1	ἀπαγγέλλω *to report*	-αγγελ-, (↑100)	ἀπαγγελῶ, -εῖς	ἀπήγγειλα ἀπηγγέλην[1]/ (ἀπηγγέλθην)	ἀπήγγελκα (ἀπήγγελμαι)
101.2	ἐπαγγέλλομαι *to promise*	-αγγελ-		ἐπηγγειλάμην (ἐπηγγέλθην)	ἐπήγγελμαι
101.3	βάλλω *to throw*	βαλ-, βλη-[2]	βαλῶ, -εῖς	ἔβαλον[1] ἐβλήθην	βέβληκα βέβλημαι
101.4	ἀποστέλλω *to send off*	-στελ-, -σταλ- (↑100[3])	ἀποστελῶ, -εῖς	ἀπέστειλα ἀπεστάλην[1]	ἀπέσταλκα ἀπέσταλμαι
101.5	ἐντέλλομαι[3] *to command*	-τελ-, -ταλ- (↑100[3])	ἐντελοῦμαι, -ῇ	ἐνετειλάμην	ἐντέταλμαι
101.6	ἅλλομαι *to leap*	ἁλ-	ἁλοῦμαι, -ῇ	ἡλάμην/ (ἡλόμην)[1]	

(1) Aor. II (↑105; 107, especially 107j).
(2) Zero-grade (↑8); so in (↑64e) βλητέον *must be put* (Lk 5:38) and ἀπό-βλητος *rejected* (1Tm 4:4).
(3) Other verbs belonging here are: ἀνατέλλω *to (cause to) rise* (especially of the sun), ἀνατελῶ -εῖς, ἀνέτειλα, ἀνατέταλκα; ἐπικέλλω *to bring* (a ship) *to land*, aor. ἐπέκειλα (↑Ac 27:41).

A further liquid verb is θάλλω, *to (cause to) bloom*, θαλλήσω, ἔθηλα/ἔθαλον (↑Php 4:10), τέθηλα.

102 Liquid verbs with stems in -ν (also ↑123.8; BR §121.71–73.78–80; BDF §101)

	pres.	stem	fut.	aor. act./mid. aor. pass.	pf. act. pf. mid./pass.

I. Verb stems in ν without ablaut (↑8; 100[3])

a) Verb stem is unextended in the present, in the perfect active an η is affixed:

102.1	μένω *to remain*	μεν(η)-(↑112.13)	μενῶ, -εῖς	ἔμεινα	μεμένηκα

b) Verb stem with a short α (CG has -σμαι instead of -μμαι in the pf. mid./pass.):

102.2	εὐφραίνω *to make glad*, pass. *to be glad*	-φρᾰν-	εὐφρᾰνῶ, -εῖς	ηὔφρᾱνα ηὐφράνθην	

μιαίνω *to defile*	μιᾰν-	μιᾰνῶ, -εῖς	ἐμίᾱνα ἐμιᾰ́νθην	(μεμίᾰγκα) μεμίᾰμμαι	102.3
ξηραίνω *to dry sth.*; pass. *to become dry*	ξηρᾰν-	ξηρᾰνῶ, -εῖς	ἐξήρᾱνα ἐξηρᾰ́νθην	ἐξήρᾰμμαι	102.4
ποιμαίνω *to shepherd*	ποιμᾰν-	ποιμᾰνῶ, -εῖς	ἐποίμᾱνα(1) ἐποιμᾰ́νθην		102.5
σημαίνω *to indicate*	σημᾰν-	σημᾰνῶ, -εῖς	ἐσήμᾱνα(1) ἐσημᾰ́νθην	(σεσήμᾰγκα) σεσήμᾰμμαι	102.6
φαίνω(2) *to shine*; pass. *to appear*, also = act.	φᾰν-	φᾰνῶ, -εῖς φᾰνήσομαι	ἔφᾱνα(1) ἐφᾰ́νην	(πέφᾰγκα) (πέφᾰσμαι)	102.7
κερδαίνω *to gain*	κερδη- (usual LXX/NT stem), κερδᾰν-	κερδήσω/ (κερδᾰνῶ)	ἐκέρδησα/ ἐκέρδᾱνα(1) ἐκερδήθην	(κεκέρδηκα) (κεκέρδημαι)	102.8

(1) CG has an η instead of an α in the aor. act./mid. stem (↑98b[1]).

(2) CG: φαίνω *to show* φᾰνῶ ἔφηνα πέφᾰγκα πέφᾰσμαι ἐφᾰ́νθην
φαίνομαι *to shine/appear* φᾰνοῦμαι/φᾰνήσομαι ἐφᾰ́νην πέφηνα/πέφᾰσμαι

c) Verb stem with a short ι; the pf. act., pf. mid./pass. and aor. pass. stems have no ν:

κλῑ́νω *to cause to bend/to bow*	κλῐν-, κλῐ-	κλῐνῶ, -εῖς	ἔκλῑνα ἐκλῐ́θην	κέκλῐκα κέκλῐμαι	102.9
κρῑ́νω(1) *to judge*	κρῐν-, κρῐ-	κρῐνῶ, -εῖς	ἔκρῑνα ἐκρῐ́θην	κέκρῐκα κέκρῐμαι	102.10

(1) The following compound is widely used: ἀποκρίνομαι *to answer*, ἀποκριθήσομαι/(Att. ἀποκρινοῦμαι, -ῇ), ἀπεκρίθην/(Att.; relatively rare in the NT:) ἀπεκρινάμην, ἀποκέκριμαι.

d) Verb stem with a short υ:

σκληρῡ́νω *to harden*	σκληρῠν-	σκληρῠνῶ, -εῖς	ἐσκλήρῡνα ἐσκληρῠ́νθην		102.11

II. Verb stems in ν with ablaut (↑100[3]; 108e):

ἀποκτείνω, also -κτέννω *to kill*	-κτεν-, -κτον-, -κταν-	ἀποκτενῶ, -εῖς	ἀπέκτεινα ἀπεκτάνθην(1)	(ἀπέκτονα)/ (LXX:) ἀπέκταγκα	102.12

(1) CG uses ἀπέθανον (lit. *I died*) for ἀπεκτάνθην and τέθνηκα (lit. *I am dead*) as a pf. pass. (↑111.3).

103 Liquid verbs with stems in -ρ (↑BR §121.66–68.75f; BDF §101)

pres.	stem	fut.	aor. act./mid. aor. pass.	pf. act. pf. mid./pass.

I. With α in stem-final syllable, without ablaut (↑8; 100[3]):

	pres.	stem	fut.	aor. act./mid. aor. pass.	pf. act. pf. mid./pass.
103.1	αἴρω *to lift up*	ἀρ-	ἀρῶ, -εῖς	ἦρα (inf. ἆραι) ἤρθην	ἦρκα ἦρμαι
103.2	καθαίρω(1) *to make clean*	καθαρ-	καθαρῶ, -εῖς	ἐκάθᾱρα ἐκαθάρθην	(κεκάθαρκα) (κεκάθαρμαι)

(1) The following verb belongs here, too, though it is irregular in some respects: χαίρω *to rejoice*, χαρήσομαι (fut.pass.; ↑107g; the LXX also uses the mid. χαροῦμαι -ῇ) *I will rejoice* (!), ἐχάρην (aor.II pass.; ↑107j) *I rejoiced* (!); CG: fut. χαιρήσω, pf. κεχάρηκα.

II. With α instead of ε from pf. act. onwards (↑100[3]; aor. II pass.; ↑107j):

	pres.	stem	fut.	aor. act./mid. aor. pass.	pf. act. pf. mid./pass.
103.3	δέρω *to beat*	δερ-, δαρ-	(δερῶ, -εῖς)	ἔδειρα ἐδάρην	(δέδαρκα) (δέδαρμαι)
103.4	σπείρω *to sow*	σπερ-, σπαρ-	σπερῶ, -εῖς	ἔσπειρα ἐσπάρην	ἔσπαρκα ἔσπαρμαι

III. With ε in stem-final syllable (CG partly ablaut; on pf. reduplication ↑72g):

	pres.	stem	fut.	aor. act./mid. aor. pass.	pf. act. pf. mid./pass.
103.5	ἐγείρω *to awaken/to raise* (ἔγειρε *stand up!*; ↑212e)	ἐγερ-	ἐγερῶ, -εῖς	ἤγειρα ἠγέρθην	(ἐγήγερκα) ἐγήγερμαι
103.6	ἐγείρομαι *to wake up/ to stand up*	ἐγερ-, ἐγρ-, ἐγορ- (↑8e)	ἐγερθήσομαι	ἠγέρθην/ (CG ἠγρόμην; ↑105)	ἐγήγερμαι/(CG:) ἐγρήγορα *I am awake* (↑189c)

2.7.2.4 Strong tense-aspect stems (aorist II/perfect II)

Strong tense-aspect stems: preliminaries (↑BR §108) 104

Tense-aspect stems that are formed on the basis of the verb stem without specific tense-aspect sign are called "strong"/"second" tense-aspect stems (↑68d). Apart from the perfect mid./pass. stem, which is always strong, the following belong to this class:
a) second thematic aorist active/middle stem (↑105);
b) root aorist stem (↑106);
c) second aorist passive stem and the future passive stem based on it (↑107)
d) second perfect active stem (↑108);
e) less frequent types of perfect stems: root perfect stems and οἶδα (↑109).

Strong thematic aorist active/middle (↑BR §109; BDF §75; 81) 105

1. Here the **thematic vowels** (↑68e) ε/ο are added to the verb stem (before the ending), in the case of βάλλω *to throw* for instance to the verb stem βαλ-: 105a

ἔ-**βαλ-ο**-ν	*I threw*	ἔ-**βαλ-ε**-ς	*you* (sg.) *threw*

Note that the present stem in most cases differs from the verb stem (↑75), sometimes only slightly, here only in having an additional λ; so the imperfect (the augment indicative of the present stem) looks very similar to the indicative aorist active (both having augment and using the same terminations; ↑105b):

ἔ-**βαλλ-ο**-ν	*I threw*	ἔ-**βαλλ-ε**-ς	*you* (sg.) *threw*

2. The **terminations** are the same as those of the **present stem**, i.e. in the indicative the same as those of the imperfect (augment form of the present stem), in the non-indicative forms the same as their present correspondences (↑70; 76–79). 105b

Four forms, however, have a different **accentuation** (this applies to compounds as well; ↑74):

(present)		(aorist II)	
• active infinitive and participle:			
β**ά**λλειν	*to throw*	βαλ**εῖ**ν	*to throw*
β**ά**λλων	*one who throws*	βαλ**ώ**ν	*one who throws/threw*
• middle infinitive and 2 sg. imperative:			
β**ά**λλεσθαι	*to throw for o.s.*	βαλ**έ**σθαι	*to throw for o.s.*
β**ά**λλου	*throw for yourself!*	βαλ**οῦ**	*throw for yourself!*

3. Many verbs have a zero-grade aorist active/middle stem (↑8d–8g): 105c

λ**εί**πω	*to leave behind*	ἔ-λ**ι**π-ον	*I left behind*
φ**εύ**γω	*to flee*	ἔ-φ**υ**γ-ον	*I fled*

105d STRONG THEMATIC AORIST ACTIVE ἔβαλον *I threw* etc.

	INDICATIVE	SUBJUNCTIVE	OPTATIVE	IMPERATIVE	PARTICIPLE
sg. 1	ἔβαλον	βάλω	βάλοιμι		βαλ**ῶ**ν
2	ἔβαλες	βάλῃς	βάλοις	βάλε	-**ό**ντος
3	ἔβαλεν	βάλῃ	βάλοι	βαλέτω	βαλ**οῦ**σα
pl. 1	ἐβάλομεν	βάλωμεν	βάλοιμεν		-ούσης
2	ἐβάλετε	βάλητε	βάλοιτε	βάλετε	βαλ**ό**ν
3	ἔβαλον[1]	βάλωσιν	βάλοιεν[1]	βαλέτωσαν[2]	-**ό**ντος
	INFINITIVE βαλ**εῖ**ν (< -έεν)				

(1) Post-CG (especially LXX) 3 pl. ind. also ἐβάλοσαν, opt. also βάλοισαν (↑70[9]).
(2) CG uses βαλόντων instead of βαλέτωσαν (↑70[10]).

105e STRONG THEMATIC AORIST MIDDLE ἐβαλόμην *I threw for myself* etc.

sg. 1	ἐβαλόμην	βάλωμαι	βαλοίμην		βαλόμενος
2	ἐβάλου	βάλῃ	βάλοιο	βαλ**οῦ**	βαλομένη
3	ἐβάλετο	βάληται	βάλοιτο	βαλέσθω	βαλόμενον
pl. 1	ἐβαλόμεθα	βαλώμεθα	βαλοίμεθα		etc.
2	ἐβάλεσθε	βάλησθε	βάλοισθε	βάλεσθε	
3	ἐβάλοντο	βάλωνται	βάλοιντο	βαλέσθωσαν[1]	
	INFINITIVE βαλ**έ**σθαι				

(1) CG uses βαλέσθων instead of βαλέσθωσαν (↑70[10]).

105f The **most important verbs** with a second aorist active/middle stem in the NT:

present/lexical form:			aor. II act./mid.:	noteworthy points:
ἄγω	*to lead*	(↑95.1)	ἤγαγον	
αἱρέω	*to take*	(↑113.1)	εἷλον	inf. ἑλεῖν
ἁμαρτάνω	*to sin*	(↑110.7)	ἥμαρτον	also aor. I ἡμάρτησα
ἀποθνῄσκω	*to die*	(↑111.3)	ἀπέθανον	
βάλλω	*to throw*	(↑101.3)	ἔβαλον	
γίνομαι	*to become*	(↑112.7)	ἐγενόμην	
ἔρχομαι	*to come*	(↑113.3)	ἦλθον	imp. 2 sg. ἐλθ**έ**[1]
ἐσθίω	*to eat*	(↑113.4)	ἔφαγον	
εὑρίσκω	*to find*	(↑111.4)	εὗρον	CG imp. 2 sg. εὑρ**έ**[1]
ἔχω	*to have/hold*	(↑113.5)	ἔσχον	st. σχ- (without ε-!)[2]
λαμβάνω	*to take*	(↑110.13)	ἔλαβον	CG imp. 2 sg. λαβ**έ**[1]

(1) Compounds, however, have the regular accentuation (↑74a): **εἴ**σελθε *enter!* (sg.) CG **ἔ**ξευρε *find out!* παρ**ά**λαβε *take along!*
(2) Imp. 2 sg. with unusual ending: σχέ**ς** (!) *hold!* (sg.), πρόσχε**ς** *pay attention!*; ↑119b.

λέγω	*to say*	(↑113.7)	εἶπον	imp. 2 sg. εἰπέ(1)
λείπω	*to leave behind*	(↑94.4)	ἔλιπον	also aor. I ἔλειψα
μανθάνω	*to learn*	(↑110.18)	ἔμαθον	
ἀπόλλυμαι	*to perish*	(↑123.7)	ἀπωλόμην	
ὁράω	*to see*	(↑113.8)	εἶδον	CG imp. 2 sg. ἰδέ(1)
πάσχω	*to suffer*	(↑113.9)	ἔπαθον	
πίνω	*to drink*	(↑110.3)	ἔπιον	
πίπτω	*to fall*	(↑113.10)	ἔπεσον	
τίκτω	*to give birth*	(↑113.11)	ἔτεκον	
φέρω	*to carry*	(↑113.14)	ἤνεγκον	also ἤνεγκα (↑105h)
φεύγω	*to flee*	(↑95.9)	ἔφυγον	

(1) CG **ἄ**νειπε *proclaim!* **εἴ**σιδε *look into (it)!*

Additional remarks:

1. In KG (to some extent also in CG) the terminations of the aor. I with the character vowel α (↑68f; 76–79) are sometimes appended to the second thematic aor. act./mid. stem rather than the regular thematic ones (↑BR §114; BDF §81). In the NT this happens quite frequently with the aor. act. of λέγω *to say*, εἶπον *I said*: 105g

εἶπ-α	instead of	εἶπ-ο-ν	*I said*
εἶπ-α-ς	instead of	εἶπ-ε-ς	*you* (sg.) *said*
εἴπ-α-μεν	instead of	εἴπ-ο-μεν	*we said*
εἴπ-α-τε	instead of	εἴπ-ε-τε	*you* (pl.) *said*
εἶπ-α-ν	instead of	εἶπ-ο-ν	*they said* (occurs very frequently)
εἰπ-ό-ν (accent!)	instead of	εἰπ-έ	*say!* (sg.; Mk 13:4; Ac 28:26/Is 6:9 LXX)
εἴπ-α-ς	instead of	εἰπ-ών	*one who says/said*
inf., however, always		εἰπ-εῖν	*to say*

This happens fairly frequently also in the case of ἔρχομαι (ἦλθον) *to come* (↑113.3), much less frequently, however, in the case of αἱρέω (εἷλον) *to take* (↑113.1), βάλλω (↑101.3) *to throw* (ἔβαλον), εὑρίσκω (εὗρον) *to find* (↑111.4), πίπτω (ἔπεσον) *to fall* (↑113.10), ὁράω (εἶδον) *to see* (↑113.8).

2. The aor. act./mid. forms of a small number of verbs have the character vowel α (so terminations of the aor. I), but not the tense-aspect sign σ (↑68d): 105h

χέω	*to pour*	(↑88.11f)	ἔ-χε-α
φέρω	*to carry*	(↑113.14)	ἤνεγκ-α (but also ἤνεγκ-ο-ν; ↑105f)

compare also (↑116; 119a):

τίθημι	*to lay*	ἔ-θηκ-α (but only ind. act.; CG only sg.)
ἵημι	*to send*	ἧκ-α (but only ind. act.; CG only sg.)
δίδωμι	*to give*	ἔ-δωκ-α (but only ind. act.; CG only sg.)

106 Root aorist (↑BR §110; BDF §95)

106a 1. The **tense-aspect stem** in this case corresponds fully to the **"root"** (↑21a), i.e. to a verb stem primarily with a long stem-final vowel.

106b 2. The **endings** are joined **directly** to the long stem-final vowel, so without formative syllable (i.e. without tense-aspect sign and character or thematic vowel; ↑68g):

present/lexical form:		"root":	root aorist:	
ἵσταμαι	*to stand (up)*	στη-	ἔ-στη-ν	*I stood (up)*
βαίνω	*to go*	βη-	ἔ-βη-ν	*I went*
γινώσκω	*to know*	γνω-	ἔ-γνω-ν	*I knew*

The long vowel, however, is shortened (η → α; ω → ο) before -ντ (i.e. in participles; ↑48), but also before a vowel (i.e. before the mood sign of the optative; ↑69):

participle (example for gen.sg. masc./ntr.):(1)		optative:	
στ**ά**-ντ-ος	*of one who stands/stood still*	στ**α**ίη-ν	*may I stand still!*
β**ά**-ντ-ος	*of one who goes/went*	β**α**ίη-ν	*may I go!*
γν**ό**-ντ-ος	*of one who knows/knew*	γν**ο**ίη-ν	*may I know!*

(1) Note that certain forms of the imperative at times may be affected, too (↑106e[1/2]).

106c 3. The **inflection of the indicative** agrees with the one of the aor. pass. (↑78; 70[1]). For the non-indicative forms ↑paradigm under 106e:

ind. sg.		pl.	
1	-ν	1	-μεν
2	-ς	2	-τε
3	–	3	-σαν

106d 4. Very occasionally the NT uses the root aorist of the following verbs:

present/lexical form:		stem:	future:	root aorist (subj. not contracted):	
δύνω	*to go down*	δυ-	δύσω	ἔδυν	(↑80.11[1])
ῥέω	*to flow*	ῥεϝ, ῥευ-, ῥυη-	ῥεύσω	ἐρρύην	(↑88.10; aug. ↑71b)
φύομαι	*to grow* (Att./LXX)	φυ-	(φύσομαι)	ἔφυν (NT?)	(↑80.11[1])

106e 5. **Paradigm** of the root aorists of ἵσταμαι *to stand (up)* (↑118), βαίνω *to go* and γινώσκω *to know* (note that the subjunctive forms involve vowel contraction!):

stem →			ἔστην *I stood (up)* στη-, στα-	ἔβην *I went* βη-, βα-	ἔγνων *I knew* γνω-, γνο-
IND.	sg.	1	ἔστην	ἔβην	ἔγνων
		2	ἔστης	ἔβης	ἔγνως
		3	ἔστη	ἔβη	ἔγνω
	pl.	1	ἔστημεν	ἔβημεν	ἔγνωμεν
		2	ἔστητε	ἔβητε	ἔγνωτε
		3	ἔστησαν	ἔβησαν	ἔγνωσαν

SUBJ.	sg.	1	στῶ (< στήω)	βῶ (< βήω)	γνῶ (< γνώω)
		2	στῇς (↑84c)	βῇς (↑84c)	γνῷς (↑11)
		3	στῇ	βῇ	γνῷ/γνοῖ[1]
	pl.	1	στῶμεν	βῶμεν	γνῶμεν
		2	στῆτε	βῆτε	γνῶτε
		3	στῶσιν	βῶσιν	γνῶσιν
OPT.	sg.	1	σταίην	βαίην	γνοίην
		2	σταίης	βαίης	γνοίης
		3	σταίη	βαίη	γνοίη
	pl.	1	σταίημεν/σταῖμεν	βαίημεν/βαῖμεν	γνοίημεν/γνοῖμεν
		2	σταίητε	βαίητε	γνοίητε
		3	σταῖεν	βαῖεν	γνοῖεν
IMP.	sg.	2	στῆθι also -στα[2]	βῆθι also -βα[2]	γνῶθι
		3	στήτω	βήτω also -βάτω[2]	γνώτω
	pl.	2	στῆτε	βῆτε also -βατε[2]	γνῶτε
		3	στήτωσαν[3]	βήτωσαν[3]	γνώτωσαν[3]
INF.			στῆναι	βῆναι	γνῶναι
PTC.	masc.		στάς	βάς	γνούς
(↑48f)	gen.		στάντος	βάντος	γνόντος
	fem.		στᾶσα	βᾶσα	γνοῦσα
	gen.		στάσης	βάσης	γνούσης
	ntr.		στάν	βάν	γνόν
	gen.		στάντος	βάντος	γνόντος

(1) In the NT (and the LXX) we also encounter γνοῖ (instead of γνῷ).

(2) These alternatives (going back to the Attic dialect) are sometimes used in KG (including the NT/LXX); note, however, that they occur only in compounds.

(3) CG uses στάντων, βάντων, γνόντων instead of στήτωσαν, βήτωσαν, γνώτωσαν (↑70[10]).

The **principal parts** of the most important verbs with a root aorist are: 106f

present:	future:	aorist:	perfect:	
ἵσταμαι	στήσομαι	ἔστην	ἕστηκα	(↑120.5)
βαίνω	βήσομαι	ἔβην	βέβηκα	(↑110.1)
γινώσκω[1]	γνώσομαι	ἔγνων	ἔγνωκα	
		ἐγνώσθην	ἔγνωσμαι	(↑111.8)

(1) The CG form is γιγνώσκω (↑72a; 111.8).

107 Second aorist passive and the future derived from it (↑BR §111; BDF §76)

107a 1. The strong/second aorist passive is **without the tense-aspect sign θ** marking its weak/first counterpart (↑68d). The formative syllable (↑68g) consists of the character vowel -η only, which before vowels and before -ντ is shortened to ε (↑68f), e.g.:

	aor. pass.:		present/lexical form:	
strong (second):	ἐ-κρύβ **-η**-ν	*I hid myself*	κρύπτω	*to hide*
weak (first):	ἐ-φυτεύ**θ-η**-ν	*I was planted*	φυτεύω	*to plant*

107b 2. The **imperative 2 sg.** usually has the (original) **ending -θι** (because there is no tense-aspect sign θ, an aspirate calling for a dissimilation, -θι > -τι; ↑79b), e.g.:

strong (second):	κρύβ -η-**θι**	*hide yourself!*
weak (first):	φυτεύ-**θ**-η-**τι**	*be planted!* (sg.)

Sometimes, however, even the second aor. pass. may have the ending -τι instead of -θι (the dissimilation being due not to the tense-aspect sign, but to the stem-final aspirate), e.g.:

not dissimilated:	ἐπιστράφ-η-θι	*turn back!* (sg.) (Epictetus, Encheiridion 3.17.1)
dissimilated:	ἐπιστράφ-η-τι	*turn back!* (sg.) (Ru 1:15 LXX)

107c 3. The **stem-final sound** of the verb stem usually appears unchanged in the second aorist passive stem (compare the corresponding noun forms), e.g.:

present/lexical form:	aor. pass.:	verb stem:	noun:
καταλλάσσω	κατ-ηλλά**γ**-η-ν	-αλλα**γ**-	ἡ καταλλα**γ**ή
to reconcile	*I was reconciled*		*the reconciliation*
θάπτω	ἐ-τά**φ**-η-ν (↑14c)	-θα**φ**-	ὁ τά**φ**ος (↑14c)
to bury	*I was buried*		*the tomb*

107d 4. The ε of **monosyllabic** verb stems here is replaced by an α (due to zero-grade ablaut; ↑8d; 100[3]; also 94.8–94.11; 103.3f), e.g. in the case of στρέφω *to turn (o.s.)*:

στρ**έ**φω	ἐ-στρ**ά**φ-η-ν	στρ**α**φ < στρ̥φ (↑8d)

107e 5. The aorist passive (weak or strong) of a number of verbs frequently is used with a **non-passive meaning** (often alongside the passive one, e.g. (also ↑191e):

ὑποτάσσω	ὑπετάγην	(e.g. ↑Ro 8:20 [pass.]; 10:3 [non-pass.])
to subject	alongside *I was subjected* (pass.) also *I submitted* (non-pass.)	

107f 6. Only verbs without a second aorist active/middle have a second aorist passive.

7. The second aorist passive occurs only with labial, velar and liquid verbs.

107g 8. As the **future passive** stem is derived from the aorist passive stem (↑68a), verbs with a second aorist passive also have a second future passive (without θ), e.g.:

present/lexical form:	aor. II pass.:	fut. II pass.:
γράφω	ἐ-γράφ-η-ν	γραφ-ή-σο-μαι
to write	*I was written*	*I will be written*

9. **Important verbs** with a second aorist passive:

present/lexical form:			aor. II pass.:	
a) Labial verbs (↑94)				107h
γράφω	*to write*	(↑94.2)	ἐγράφην	
θάπτω	*to bury*	(↑94.14)	ἐτάφην	
θλίβω	*to press*	(↑94.3)	ἐθλίβην	
κλέπτω	*to steal*	(↑94.17)	ἐκλάπην	
κόπτω	*to cut/beat*	(↑94.18)	ἐκόπην	
κρύπτω	*to hide*	(↑94.20)	ἐκρύβην	outside NT also aor. I
ῥίπτω	*to throw*	(↑94.19)	ἐρρίφην	outside NT also aor. I
στρέφω	*to turn sth./o.s.*	(↑94.7)	ἐστράφην	
τρέπω	*to turn sth.*	(↑94.9)	ἐτράπην	
τρέφω	*to feed/rear*	(↑94.11)	ἐτράφην	
b) Velar verbs (↑95)				107i
ἀλλάσσω	*to change sth.*	(↑95.10)	ἠλλάγην	outside NT also aor. I
ἁρπάζω	*to rob*	(↑95.22)	ἡρπάγην	
ἀνοίγω	*to open*	(↑95.2)	ἠνοίγην	also aor. I
πλήσσω	*to strike*	(↑95.13)	ἐπλήγην	
ἐκπλήσσομαι	*to be amazed*	(↑95.14)	ἐξεπλάγην	
σφάζω	*to slaughter*	(↑95.10)	ἐσφάγην	
c) Liquid verbs (↑100–103)				107j
ἀγγέλλω	*to announce*	(↑101.1)	ἠγγέλην	outside NT also aor. I
ἀποστέλλω	*to send off*	(↑101.4)	ἀπεστάλην	
δέρω	*to beat*	(↑103.3)	ἐδάρην	
σπείρω	*to sow*	(↑103.4)	ἐσπάρην	
φαίνομαι	*to appear*	(↑102.7)	ἐφάνην	
χαίρω	*to rejoice*	(↑103.2[1])	ἐχάρην *I rejoiced* (!)	
d) Verbs in -μι (↑123)				107k
κατάγνυμι	*to break sth.*	(↑123.3)	κατεάγην	
πήγνυμι	*to fix*	(↑123.5)	ἐπάγην	
ῥήγνυμι	*to tear in pieces*	(↑123.6)	ἐρράγην	

Strong perfect active (↑BR §112; BDF §101) 108

1. **General remarks**: 108a

a) The strong/second perfect active stem is **without the tense-aspect sign κ** (↑68d). The formative syllable (↑68g) consisting of the character vowel -α/ει is appended to the reduplicated verb stem (↑72).

	ind. pf./plpf. act.:			present/lexical form:	
strong (second):	γε-γραφ	**-α**	*I have written*	γράφω	*to write*
	ἐ-γε-γράφ	**-ει**-ν	*I had written*		
weak (first):	πε-φύτευ**κ**	**-α**	*I have planted*	φυτεύω	*to plant*
	ἐ-πε-φυτεύ**κ**	**-ει**-ν	*I had planted*		

b) The second perfect active is found almost exclusively with labial, velar and liquid verbs.

c) The **endings** or **terminations** of the second perfect (including the pluperfect) are identical with those of the weak perfect (↑76), e.g. in the case of γράφω *to write*:

ind. pf. act.:	γέγραφα, γέγραφας, ... γεγράφασιν	*I have written* etc.
plpf. act.:	ἐγεγράφειν, ἐγεγράφεις, ... ἐγεγράφεισαν	*I had written* etc.
inf. pf. act.:	γεγραφέναι	*to have written*
ptc. pf. act.:	γεγραφώς, -ότος; -υῖα, -υίας; -ός, -ότος	*one who has written* etc.

108b 2. The second perfect active stem mostly **differs in form** from the verb stem:
- due to aspiration: aspirates replace the non-aspirate stem-final labials or velars,
- due to ablaut: short vowel in the stem-final syllable changes its ablaut grade, or
- due to both aspiration and ablaut.

3. **Examples** of second perfect active stems of regular verbs:

present/lexical form:			verb stem:	pf. II act.:
108c a) the final sound of the verb stem remains **unchanged** in the pf. II act. (↑94/95):				
γράφω	*to write*	(↑94.2)	γρα**φ**-	γέ-γρα**φ**-α
κράζω	*to cry out*	(↑95.19)	κρα**γ**-	κέ-κρα**γ**-α
108d b) the final sound of the verb stem is replaced by a **aspirate** (↑92a/92b; 94/95):				
κόπτω	*to cut/beat*	(↑94.18)	κο**π**-	κέ-κο**φ**-α
πράσσω	*to do*	(↑95.15)	πρα**γ**-	πέ-πρα**χ**-α
τάσσω	*to put in place*	(↑95.16)	τα**γ**-	τέ-τα**χ**-α
108e c) the short vowel in the stem-final syllable changes its **ablaut** grade (↑8; 94; 100[3]; 103.2f; 107d):				
ἀποκτείνω	*to kill*	(↑102.12)	-κτ**ε**ν-	ἀπ-έ-κτ**ο**ν-α
λείπω	*to leave behind*	(↑95.4)	λ**ει**π-	λέ-λ**οι**π-α
στρέφω	*to turn (o.s.)*	(↑94.7)	στρ**ε**φ-	ἔ-στρ**ο**φ-α
τρέφω	*to feed/rear*	(↑94.11)	θρ**ε**φ-	τέ-τρ**ο**φ-α
108f d) the pf. II. act. stem is affected both by **aspiration** and **ablaut** (↑8; 94):				
πέμπω	*to send*	(↑94.6)	π**ε**μ**π**-	πέ-π**ο**μ**φ**-α
τρέπω	*to turn sth.*	(↑94.9)	τρ**επ**-	τέ-τρ**οφ**-α

4. A perfect active stem is in use, but **no present stem**: 108g

εἴωθα *I am accustomed* (pres. ptc. ἔθων is used in Homer)
ἔοικα *I am like*/(CG also) *I seem* (ipf. εἶκε is used in Homer)

↑80.1; 96.1; 110.12–110.14; 110.17; 111.5; 112.7; 113.3; 113.9; 113.14; 123.3; 123.5–123.7; on the pf. meaning also ↑189c.

Root perfect and οἶδα (↑BR §113; 115; 131,3; BDF §96; 99.2) 109

Two rarer types of strong perfect active stems still need to be mentioned: (1) the root perfect encountered with a small number of verbs and (2) the very widely used "perfect" οἶδα *to know*, consistently used with a purely present stem meaning.

1. The **root perfect** is an older type of perfect active encountered with a very small number of verbs whose stem ends in a vowel; in fact, it serves as an alternative to the "normal" weak perfect active. Endings or terminations are directly joined to the reduplicated "root" (↑106b on the root aorist).

ἵσταμαι, st. στη-, στα-, *to set/place o.s. (somewhere), to stand (up)* (↑120.5) is the most important verb that alongside the "normal" pf. I ἕστηκα *I stand (somewhere)* also uses forms of the root perfect: 109a

pf. I act.:		root perfect:	
Attested in the NT (and the LXX):			
ἑ-στη-κέ-ναι	*to stand*	ἑ-στά-ναι	infinitive
ἑ-στη-κώς/-κότος	*one who stands*	ἑ-στώς/-στῶτος	participle
ἑ-στη-κυῖα/-κυίας		ἑ-στ**ῶσα**/-στ**ώσης**	
ἑ-στη-κός/-κότος		ἑ-στ**ός**/-στ**ῶ**τος	
		(outside NT/LXX also ἑστ**ώς** instead of ἑστ**ός**)	
Not attested in the NT (and the LXX; for further forms ↑BR §131.3):			
ἑ-στή-κα-μεν	*we stand*	ἕ-στα-μεν	
ἑ-στή-κα-τε	*you* (pl.) *stand*	ἕ-στα-τε	
ἑ-στή-κα-σιν	*they stand*	ἑ-στᾶσιν (< ἑ-στα-ασιν)	

ἀποθνῄσκω, st. θνη-, θνα-, *to die* (↑111.3), alongside the pf. I, τέθνηκα *I am dead*, also has a root perfect. The infinitive is the only form attested in the NT (1× in Byz.): 109b

τε-θνη-κέ-ναι *to be dead* τε-θνά-ναι (Ac 14:19 Var.)

This form is also found in the standard edition of the LXX (2×), apart from this also the following (1×):

τε-θνή-κα-σιν *they are dead* τε-θνᾶσιν (4Macc 12:3)

The isolated perfect **δέδοικα** *to fear* (lexical form usually *δείδω) is not attested in the NT, but represented by a few weak forms in the LXX; it is used in CG where there are also root perfect forms:

δε-δοί-κα-σιν	*they fear*	δε-δί-ασιν
δε-δοι-κέ-ναι	*to fear*	δε-δι-έναι
δε-δοι-κώς -κότος etc.	*one who fears*	δε-δι-ώς -ότος etc.

109c 2. The "perfect" **οἶδα** *to know*, is a special case in several respects:
• It is without reduplication (it may never have been a perfect at all; ↑CAGL: 117).
• The verb stem appears in three different ablaut grades: ϝοιδ-, ϝιδ-, ϝειδ(ε)-;[29] hence the rather complicated system of forms.
• It is not used like a perfect, but like a present/durative stem, the (non-augmented) indicative "perfect" like an indicative present and the "pluperfect" like an imperfect. Unlike "normal" perfects οἶδα does not only have well-established non-indicative forms (subj., imp., inf., ptc. and opt.), but also a corresponding future.

IND. "PF." (PRESENT) *I know* etc.	(CG:)(1)	SUBJUNCTIVE *(if) I know* etc.	IMPERATIVE *know!* etc.	"PLPF." (IMPERFECT) *I knew* etc.	(CG:)
οἶδα	οἶδα	εἰδῶ (<εἰδέω)		ᾔδειν	ᾔδη
οἶδας	οἶσθα	εἰδῇς	ἴσθι	ᾔδεις	ᾔδησθα
οἶδεν	οἶδεν	εἰδῇ	ἴστω	ᾔδει	ᾔδει
οἴδαμεν	ἴσμεν	εἰδῶμεν		ᾔδειμεν	ᾔδεμεν
οἴδατε	ἴστε	εἰδῆτε	ἴστε	ᾔδειτε	etc.
οἴδασιν	ἴσασιν	εἰδῶσιν	ἴστωσαν(2)	ᾔδεισαν	
INFINITIVE	εἰδέναι *to know*				
PARTICIPLE	εἰδώς, -ότος; εἰδυῖα, -υίας/-υίης; εἰδός, -ότος *one who knows* etc.				
OPTATIVE	εἰδείην *may I know!* etc.				
FUTURE	εἰδήσω (CG εἴσομαι) *I will know*				

(1) Occasionally the forms typical of CG also occur in the NT or in the LXX:
οἶσθα (2× LXX), ἴστε (ind.: 2× NT, 1× LXX; imp. [possibly ind.]: Jas 1:19), ἴσασι (Ac 26:4).
(2) CG ἴστων.

2.7.2.5 Thematic conjugation: "irregular" verbs

This section is on verbs whose present stems are characterized by a visible extension (↑75c–75f) and on verbs whose principal parts are made up of stems that in most cases are etymologically unrelated (on etymology ↑p.658[3]):
a) Verbs with a nasal affix in the present stem (↑110);
b) Verbs with a σκ-affix in the present stem (↑111);
c) The so-called e-class verbs (↑112);
d) The mixed class verbs (suppletive verbs; ↑113).

29 It is related to εἶδον (st. ϝιδ-; inf. ἰδεῖν) aor. II of ὁράω *to see* (↑113.8). Still οἶδα in actual usage does not mean "I have seen", but simply *I know* (↑357b).

Verbs with a nasal affix in the present stem (↑75c; BR §123; BDF §101) 110

pres.	stem	fut.	aor. act./mid. aor. pass.	pf. act. pf. mid./pass.	

I. Verbs with a verb stem ending in a vowel

pres.	stem	fut.	aor. act./mid. aor. pass.	pf. act. pf. mid./pass.	
βαί**ν**ω *to go* (< βανι̯ω; ↑12c)	βη-, βα-	βήσομαι	ἔβην (root aor.; ↑106)	βέβηκα (CG also root pf. ↑109)	110.1
ἐλαύ**ν**ω *to drive/to row*	(ἐλαϝ-), ἐλαυ-, ἐλα-	ἐλάσω (CG ἐλῶ, -ᾷς; ↑84d)	ἤλασα ἠλάθην	ἐλήλακα (↑72g) ἤλα(σ)μαι (LXX) (CG ἐλήλαμαι)	110.2
πί**ν**ω *to drink*	πι-, πω-, πο-	πίομαι, 2.sg. πίεσαι	ἔπιον[1]/[2] ἐπόθην	πέπωκα (πέπομαι)	110.3
τί**ν**ω *to pay/undergo a penalty*	τει-, τι- (↑2c)	τείσω (LXX/CG)/ τίσω (NT)	ἔτεισα	(τέτεικα) (τέτ[ε]ισμαι)	110.4
φθά**ν**ω *to precede/arrive*	φθα-, φθη-	φθάσω (φθήσομαι)	ἔφθασα (ἔφθην; ↑106)	ἔφθακα	110.5

(1) Aor. II (↑105).
(2) Inf. in the NT alongside πιεῖν also πεῖν.

II. Verbs with a verb stem ending in a consonant or a vowel

pres.	stem	fut.	aor. act./mid. aor. pass.	pf. act. pf. mid./pass.	
αἰσθά**ν**ομαι *to perceive*	αἰσθ-, αἰσθη-	αἰσθήσομαι[1]	ᾐσθόμην[2]	(ᾔσθημαι)	110.6
ἁμαρτά**ν**ω[3] *to sin*	ἁμαρτ-, ἁμαρτη-	ἁμαρτήσω (CG mid.)	ἥμαρτον[2]/ ἡμάρτησα (ἡμαρτήθην)	ἡμάρτηκα (ἡμάρτημαι)	110.7
αὐξά**ν**ω *to grow/cause to grow*	αὐξ-, αὐξη-	αὐξήσω/ αὐξανῶ (LXX)	ηὔξησα ηὐξήθην	(ηὔξηκα) (ηὔξημαι)	110.8
κάμ**ν**ω *to grow weary* (CG *labour*)	καμ(ε)-, κμη-	(καμοῦμαι, -ῇ; ↑98a)	ἔκαμον[2]	κέκμηκα	110.9
τέμ**ν**ω *to cut*	τεμ(ε)-, τμη-	τεμῶ, -εῖς (↑98a)	ἔτεμον[2] ἐτμήθην	τέτμηκα τέτμημαι	110.10

(1) In the LXX also αἰσθηθήσομαι (↑Is 33:11) and αἰσθανθήσομαι (↑Is 49:26).
(2) Aor. II (↑105).
(3) Similarly βλαστάνω (instead of this Mk 4:27: βλαστάω [↑84]) *to sprout/produce*, βλαστ(η)-, βλαστήσω, ἐβλάστησα (Att. ἔβλαστον [↑105]), (βεβλάστηκα).

III. Stop verbs with a present in -άνω and a nasal stem infix (ν, μ, γ)

110.11	θι**γγάν**ω *to touch*	θιγ-	(θίξω)	ἔθιγον[1]	
110.12	λα**γχάν**ω *to obtain/receive*	λαχ-, ληχ-	(λήξομαι)	ἔλαχον[1]	εἴληχα[2]
110.13	λα**μ**β**άν**ω *to take*	λαβ-, λη(μ)β-	λήμψομαι[3]	ἔλαβον[1]/[4] ἐλήμφθην[3]	εἴληφα[2] εἴλημμαι
110.14	λα**ν**θ**άν**ω *to be hidden*	λαθ-, ληθ-	λήσω	ἔλαθον[1]	λέληθα
110.15	ἐπιλα**ν**θ**άν**ομαι *to forget*	↑110.14	ἐπιλήσομαι	ἐπελαθόμην[1] ἐπελήσθην (LXX)	ἐπιλέλησμαι
110.16	πυ**ν**θ**άν**ομαι παρά τινος *to inquire of/learn from*	πυθ-, πευθ-	(πεύσομαι)	ἐπυθόμην[1]	(πέπυσμαι)

(1) Aor. II (↑105).
(2) ↑72f.
(3) In CG these stems are without μ: λήψομαι, ἐλήφθην.
(4) CG imp. λαβ**έ** (↑105f); post-CG also uses (↑70[9]) ἐλάβ**οσαν** (↑2Th 3:6; so frequently in the LXX) instead of ἔλαβ**ον** 3 pl.

IV. Verbs with a varying verb stem final sound, but a present stem like those of III.

110.17	τυ**γχάν**ω *to meet/attain* (CG *happen to be*)	τυχ-, τευχ-, τυχη-	τεύξομαι	ἔτυχον[1]/[2]	τέτυχα (He 8:6) (KG τέτευχα) (CG τετύχηκα)
110.18	μα**ν**θ**άν**ω *to learn*	μαθ-, μαθη-	μαθήσομαι	ἔμαθον[1]	μεμάθηκα

(1) Aor. II (↑105).
(2) As a inf. aor. mid. 2Macc 15:7 and 3Macc 2:33 have τεύξασθαι.

V. Velar verb with a νε-affix in the present stem (only NT verb of this type)

110.19	ἀφικνέομαι *to reach*	-ἱκ-	ἀφίξομαι	ἀφικόμην[1]	(ἀφῖγμαι)

(1) Aor. II (↑105).

Verbs with a σκ-affix in the present stem (↑75d; 75f; BR §124f; BDF §101) 111

111a There are a number of verbs whose verb stem (if ending in a vowel) is extended by a σκ-affix or (if ending in a consonant) is extended by an ισκ-affix in present stem (note that 111.5 is an exception). In addition to this some verbs have a reduplication in the present stem (↑72a; 75f). ↑also 113.9.

pres.	stem	fut.	aor. act./mid. aor. pass.	pf. act. pf. mid./pass.

I. Verbs without reduplication in the present stem

pres.	stem	fut.	aor. act./mid. aor. pass.	pf. act. pf. mid./pass.	
ἀρέ**σκ**ω *to please*	ἀρε-	ἀρέσω	ἤρεσα		111.1
γηρά**σκ**ω *to grow old*	γηρᾰ-/ᾱ-	γηρᾱ́σω (CG γηρᾱ́σομαι)	ἐγήρᾱσα	γεγήρᾱκα	111.2
ἀποθνῄ**σκ**ω (<*-θνηίσκω) *to die*	θαν-, θνη-	ἀποθανοῦμαι, -ῇ (↑98a)	ἀπέθανον[1] (also ↑102.12)	τέθνηκα *I am dead* (↑109b; 200b)	111.3
εὑρ**ίσκ**ω *to find* (ipf.: ηὕ-/ηὑ-)	εὑρ-, εὑρη-, εὑρε-	εὑρήσω/ (εὑρήσομαι)	εὗρον[1]/[2] εὑρέθην	εὕρηκα[2] εὕρημαι	111.4
διδά**σκ**ω *to teach*	διδαχ-	διδάξω	ἐδίδαξα ἐδιδάχθην	δεδίδαχα δεδίδαγμαι	111.5
ἀνᾱλ**ίσκ**ω/ ἀναλόω[3] *to destroy/consume*	ϝαλ-, -αλ-, -αλω-	ἀνᾱλώσω	ἀνήλωσα ἀνηλώθην	(ἀνήλωκα) ἀνήλωμαι	111.6
ἱλά**σκ**ομαι *to expiate/propitiate*	ἱλα(σ)-	ἱλάσομαι	ἱλασάμην ἱλάσθην[4]		111.7

(1) Aor. II (↑105). On 111.4 note that in CG the imp. 2 sg. (of the simplex) is εὑρέ (↑105f).
(2) On augment and reduplication ↑71f/72g.
(3) The second option occurs only rarely in the NT/LXX.
(4) Analogical σ (↑80.4ff); ἱλάσθητί μοι *Be reconciled with me!/Have mercy on me!* (Lk 18:13).

II. Verbs with a reduplication in the present stem (↑72a; 75f)

pres.	stem	fut.	aor. act./mid. aor. pass.	pf. act. pf. mid./pass.	
γῑνώσκω (CG **γῐ**γνώ**σκ**ω) *to know*	γνω(σ)-	γνώσομαι	ἔγνων (root aor.; ↑106) ἐγνώσθην[1]	ἔγνωκα ἔγνωσμαι[1]	111.8
ἐπιγινώσκω *to recognize/know* like 111.8					111.9

(1) Analogical σ (↑80.4ff).

111.10	ἀναμιμνῄ**σκ**ω (<μιμνη**ισκ**ω) τινά τι *to remind s.o. of sth.*	-μνη(σ)-	ἀναμνήσω	ἀνέμνησα ἀνεμνήσθην[(1)]	(ἀναμέμνημαι)
111.11	ὑπομιμνῄσκω *to remind* like 111.10				
111.12	μιμνῄσκομαί τινος *to remember sth.*	↑111.10	μνησθήσομαι	ἐμνήσθην	μέμνημαι *I think of* (↑200b)
111.13	πιπρᾱ́**σκ**ω also ἀποδίδομαι (mid., mainly aor.; ↑117/118; 120)	πρᾱ-	ἀποδώσομαι	ἀπεδόμην ἐπρᾱ́θην	πέπρᾱκα πέπρᾱμαι
	to sell (in Mt 13:46 the pf. probably replaces the aor. [Z §289]; ↑200f). Note that in the NT the usual verb with this meaning is πωλέω (inflection ↑87).				

(1) Analogical σ (↑80.4ff).

For further verbs with a reduplication in the present stem ↑112.7; 113.10f; 115a.

112 The so-called e-class verbs (↑75e; BR §126; BDF §101)

An e-affix is added to the verb stem, partly in the present only (for inflection ↑87), partly in several or all of the tense-aspect stems.

	pres.	stem	fut.	aor. act./mid. aor. pass.	pf. act. pf. mid./pass.
	I. Verbs with an e-affix only in the present stem (↑87)				
112.1	δοκ**έ**ω[(1)] *to think/to seem*	δοκ-, δοκε-	δόξω	ἔδοξα	
	δοκεῖ μοι *it seems (best) to me, I think/decide*			ἔδοξεν	δέδοκται
	Note that the principal parts of εὐδοκέω *to take delight (in), to decide* correspond to those of ποιέω *to do* (↑87).				
112.2	ὠθ**έ**ω *to push* LXX: simplex 7×; NT: only compounds, ↑111.3f.	ὠθ-, ὠθε-	(ὤσω)	ἔωσα ἐώσθην	(ἔωκα) ὦσμαι/(ἔωσμαι)
112.3	ἀπωθ**έ**ομαι *to push aside/to reject*; ↑111.2		ἀπώσομαι	ἀπωσάμην ἀπώσθην	ἀπῶσμαι
112.4	ἐξωθ**έ**ω *to push out*; ↑111.2		ἐξώσω	ἐξῶσα/ἐξέωσα ἐξώσθην/ (ἐξεώσθην)	(ἐξέωκα) ἐξῶσμαι/ (ἐξέωσμαι)

(1) Hermas Similitude 9.9.5 for ἐδόκουν *they seemed* uses ἐδοκοῦσαν (< ἐδοκέοσαν; ↑70[9]; 87c[1]).

II. Verbs with an e-affix in the present and in the other tense-aspect stems (↑87)

γαμ**έ**ω *to marry/get married* CG: act.: a man to a woman mid.: a woman to a man NT: act.: both cases; a woman to a man also pass.	γαμ-, γαμε-, γαμη-	γαμ**ῶ**, -**εῖς** (↑98a) γαμ**οῦ**μαι, -**ῇ**	ἔγημα ἐγάμ**η**σα (KG) ἐγημάμην ἐγαμ**ή**θην (KG)	γεγάμ**η**κα (γεγάμ**η**μαι) (↑ὁ γάμος *wedding*)	112.5

III. Verbs with an e-affix in every tense-aspect stem except for the present

βούλομαι *to wish* (βούλ**ει** *you* [sg.] *wish*; ↑77[2])	βουλ-, βουλη- (aug. also ἠ-)	βουλ**ή**σομαι	ἐβουλ**ή**θην	(βεβούλ**η**μαι) (↑ἡ βουλή *plan/decision*)	112.6
γίνομαι (CG γίγνομαι) *to come into being, become, happen*	γεν(η)-, γον-, γν-	γεν**ή**σομαι meaning: aor. mid. ≈ aor.pass., pf. act. ≈ pf. pass.	ἐγενόμην ἐγεν**ή**θην (KG)	γέγονα γεγέν**η**μαι	112.7
δέομαι[(1)] *to ask for sth.* (inflection ↑88a)	δε-, δεη-	δεηθήσομαι (CG δε**ή**σομαι)	ἐδε**ή**θην	δεδέ**η**μαι	112.8
θέλω[(2)] *to wish* ipf.: **ἤ**θελον	θελ-, θελη-	θελ**ή**σω[(2)]	ἠθέλ**η**σα	ἠθέλ**η**κα/ τεθέλ**η**κα (LXX)	112.9
μέλλω *to be about (to)/to intend/to be destined*; ipf.: **ἤ**μελλον (rarely **ἔ**μελλον)	μελλ-, μελλη-	μελλ**ή**σω	ἐμέλλ**η**σα		112.10
μέλει μοί τινος (ipf.: ἔμελεν) *sth. is of concern to me/I care for sth.*	μελ-, μελη-	(μελ**ή**σει)	(ἐμέλ**η**σεν)	(μεμέλ**η**κε)	112.11
μετα-μέλομαι *to regret*; ipf.: μετ-εμελόμην	↑112.11	-μελ**η**θήσομαι (CG -μελ**ή**σομαι)	-εμελ**ή**θην (CG -εμελ**η**σάμην)		112.12

(1) CG also *to be in need of sth.*, for δέ**η** *you ask for/are in need of sth.* also δέ**ει** (↑77[2]). – Also take note of the related impersonal δεῖ (3 sg. ind. act.) *it is necessary* (ipf. ἔδει *it was necessary*; subj. δέῃ *[if] it is necessary*; inf. δεῖν *to be necessary*).

(2) Note that CG uses **ἐ**θέλω instead of θέλω and **ἐ**θελήσω instead of θελήσω.

IV. Verb with an e-affix only in the pf. act. stem

μένω *to remain* (↑102.1 listed as a liquid verb)	μεν-, μενη-	μενῶ, -εῖς (↑98a)	ἔμεινα	μεμέν**η**κα	112.13

112.13a V. The following verbs belonging to the e-class are important in CG (in part also in the LXX):

μάχομαι *to fight* (fairly well-attested in the LXX)	μαχ-, μαχε-, μαχη-	(μαχ**οῦ**μαι ↑87; CG)/ μαχ**ή**σομαι (KG)	ἐμαχ**ε**σάμην (ἐμαχ**ή**θην [un-CG])	(μεμάχ**η**μαι)
οἴομαι/οἶμαι *to think/suppose* (fairly well-attested in the LXX; 3× [pres.] in the NT; also ↑77[2])	οἰ-, οἰη-	(οἰ**ή**σομαι)	ᾠ**ή**θην	
οἴχομαι *to be gone* (fairly well-attested in the LXX) In the NT 1× παροίχομαι *to have gone by*: Ac 14:16 ptc. pf. παρῳχημένοι *gone by/past*	οἰχ-, οἰχη-	οἰχ**ή**σομαι		(ᾤχ**η**μαι)
ἄχθομαι *to be annoyed* (not attested in LXX/NT)	ἀχθ-, ἀχθεσ-	ἀχθ**έσ**ομαι	ἠχθ**έσ**θην	

VI. Verb with an υ-affix except for the present (note that this verb does not belong to the e-class, it has, however, similar peculiarities; on the εἰ- augment and reduplication ↑71d)

112.14	ἕλκω *to draw/drag*	ἑλκ-, ἑλκυ(σ)-	ἑλκ**ύ**σω	εἵλκ**υ**σα εἱλκ**ύσ**θην[1]	(εἵλκ**υ**κα) εἵλκ**υσ**μαι[1]

(1) Analogical σ (↑80.4ff).

113 The mixed class verbs (suppletive verbs) (↑BR §127; BDF §101)

These are verbs with principal parts made up of two or three different tense-aspect stems that are mostly unrelated etymologically:

	pres.	stem	fut.	aor. act./mid. aor. pass.	pf. act. pf. mid./pass.
113.1	αἱρέω (↑87) *to take* mid. *to take for o.s./to choose* (in the NT/LXX only used as mid.) ipf. act. ᾕρουν, mid./pass. ᾑρούμην	αἱρε-, αἱρη-, ἑλ-<σελ-(↑13d)	αἱρήσω αἱρήσομαι	εἷλον(↑105d–105f) εἱλόμην (inf. ἑλεῖν/-έσθαι) (augment ↑71d) ᾑρέθην	ᾕρηκα ᾕρημαι ᾕρημαι
113.2	ἀναιρέω[1] *to remove,* mostly *to kill*	↑113.1	ἀνελῶ, -εῖς (↑98a) (CG ἀναιρήσω)	ἀνεῖλον (↑105d–105f) ἀνῃρέθην	(ἀνῄρηκα) (ἀνῄρημαι)

(1) Other compounds such as διαιρέω *to distribute/divide* have analogous principal parts.

ἔρχομαι *to come/go* There are many compounds, inter alia with prefix ἀπ-, εἰσ-, ἐξ-, προσ-, συν-.	ἐρχ-, ἐλευθ-, ἐλυθ-, ἐλθ-	ἐλεύσομαι (< ἐλεύθσομαι) (especially CG also εἶμι; ↑125c)	ἦλθον(↑105d/105g) (inf. ἐλθεῖν) imp. ἐλθ**έ** (↑105f) **εἴ**σελθε	ἐλήλυθα (redup. ↑72g) plpf.: ἐληλύθειν	113.3
ἐσθίω (also ἔσθω, βιβρώσκω) *to eat*	ἐδ-, ἐσθ(ι)-, φαγ-, βρω-,	φάγομαι (2 sg. φάγ**εσαι**) ἔδομαι (CG/LXX)	ἔφαγον (↑105) ἐβρώθην	βέβρωκα βέβρωμαι	113.4
ἔχω *to have/hold* ipf. εἶχον (augment ↑71d) (3 pl. also εἴχ**οσαν** [Jn 15:22.24; LXX; ↑70[9]])	ἐχ- < ἑχ- < σεχ-, σχ-, σχη- (↑13d)	ἕξω/ (CG also σχήσω)	ἔσχον (↑105d/105f) (inf. σχεῖν) subj. σχῶ imp. σχ**ές** (↑105f) πρ**ό**σχες	ἔσχηκα	113.5
ἔχομαι		ἕξομαι	ἐσχόμην	ἔσχημαι	
A fair number of compounds are attested, too (apart from 113.6), e.g. κατέχω *to prevent, to hold to*; παρέχω *to present/offer, to grant*; ἀπέχω *to be receive in full*, ἀπέχομαι *to be distant.*					
ἀνέχομαι *to endure/put up with* ipf. ἀνειχόμην (LXX also ἠνειχ-)		ἀνέξομαι	ἀνεσχόμην imp. ἀνάσχου	(ἀνέσχημαι)	113.6
λέγω *to say* φημί (ipf. ἔφην) (↑125d) (CG also ἀγορεύω)	λεγ-, φη-/φα-, ϝειπ-, ϝερ-, ϝρη- (CG also ἀγορευ-)	ἐρῶ, -εῖς (↑98a)	εἶπον(↑105d/105g) (inf. εἰπεῖν) imp. εἰπ**έ** **ἄ**νειπε (rarely εἰπ**όν**)	εἴρηκα	113.7
		ῥ**η**θήσομαι	ἐρρ**έ**θην	εἴρημαι	
The following compounds have analogous principal parts: ἀντιλέγω *to contradict/oppose* and προλέγω *to tell before.*			(inf. ῥ**η**θῆναι, ptc. ῥ**η**θείς)		
Other compounds of λέγω have regular principal parts (those of velar stems; ↑95), e.g.: ἐκλέγομαι *to choose*, διαλέγομαι *to converse*, συλλέγω *to collect/gather* (↑95.7 including 95.7[4]).					
ὁράω *to see* (↑84) ipf. ἑώρων (aug. ↑71e)	ὁρᾱ- < (ϝ)ορᾱ-, ὀπ-, ἰδ- < (ϝ)ιδ- (Lat.: *video*)	ὄψομαι (Att. for 2 sg. ὄψῃ also ὄψει; ↑77[2])	εἶδον (↑105d/105g) (inf. ἰδεῖν)[1] imp. ἴδε[2] ὤφθην often *I appeared* (↑191g)	ἑώρᾱκα/ ἑόρᾱκα (CG)[3] (redup. ↑72e) ἑώρᾱμαι/ ἑόρᾱμαι (CG)[3]	113.8

(1) Note that Php 2:23 has ἀφίδω for ἀπίδω (subj.).

(2) In CG the imp. 2 sg. (of the simplex) is ἰδ**έ** (↑105f).

On the particle ἰδού "behold!"(< imp. mid. ἰδοῦ) ↑252.63,8.

Very rarely an aorist form related to the future ὄψομαι is encountered: ὠψάμην (Lk 13:28 ὅταν ὄψησθε [subj.] *when you* [pl.] *see*; Var. ind. fut.: … ὄψεσθε).

(3) CG pf. also ὄπωπα and ὦμμαι. A LXX/NT verb derived from these is ὀπτάνομαι *to appear*. (1× in the NT: Ac 1:3).

113.9	πάσχω *to suffer* (<παθ-σκω; ↑111; 13a; 15a)	παθ-<πn̥θ-, πενθ-, πονθ- (↑8d)	πείσομαι (<πένθσομαι; ↑13a/h)	ἔπαθον (↑105) (↑τὸ πένθος *mourning*, τὸ πάθος *suffering/passion*)	πέπονθα
113.10	πίπτω[1] *to fall*	πετ-, πεσ(ε)-, πτ-, πτω-	πεσοῦμαι, -ῇ (↑98a)	ἔπεσον (↑105d/105g)	πέπτωκα
113.11	τίκτω (<τιτκω)[1] *to give birth*	τεκ-, τκ-, τοκ-	τέξομαι	ἔτεκον (↑105) ἐτέχθην	τέτοκα
113.12	τρέχω *to run*	θρεχ- (↑14c), δραμ(η)-	δραμοῦμαι, -ῇ (↑98a)	ἔδραμον(↑105)	(δεδράμηκα)
113.13	τύπτω *to strike*	τυπ-	(τυπτήσω)		
	LXX/NT use only the present stem, otherwise the following verbs (so mostly CG; ↑BDF §101):				
	πατάσσω	παταγ-	πατάξω	ἐπάταξα	
	πλήσσω(↑95.13)	πληγ-		pass.: ἐπλήγην	
	also παίω			ἔπαισα	πέπαικα
113.14	φέρω *to carry*	φερ-, οἰ(σ)-, ἐνεγκ-, ἐνεκ-	οἴσω	ἤνεγκον/ἤνεγκα (↑105d/105g/105h) (inf. ἐνεγκεῖν/ ἐνέγκαι) imp. ἔνεγκε/ ἔνεγκον ptc. ἐνέγκας ἠνέχθην	ἐνήνοχα (redup. ↑72g) ἐνήνεγμαι

(1) There is a reduplication in the present stem (↑72a; 75f; 111.8–113.13).

Important in CG (LXX 4×; NT 1×: Ac 20:4 συνείπετο ipf. of συν-έπομαι *to accompany*) is:

113.15	ἕπομαι *to follow* (ipf. εἱπόμην; ↑71d)	ἑπ- (῾ < σ-), σπ-	ἕψομαι	ἑσπόμην (inf. σπέσθαι)	

2.7.3 Athematic conjugation or verbs in -μι

Athematic conjugation or verbs in -μι: preliminaries (↑BR §128; BDF §92f) 114

I. General remarks

1. The **thematic vowel** 114a

a) The so-called “verbs in -μι” are verbs that in the 1 sg. ind. pres. act. have the personal ending -μι; the term “athematic” conjugation is due to the fact that the forms of the present stem and in many cases of the strong/second aorist are without a thematic vowel (↑68e), e. g.:

δίδ**ο**-**τε** (st. διδο-) *you* (pl.) *give* (↑115b) **φη**-**μί** (st. φη-) *I say* (↑125d)

b) The ind. pres. act. and mid./pass. forms are most clearly athematic (↑115ff).

c) The thematic vowel is used, however, in some forms of the “athematic” conjugation such as those of the ipf. act. and the 2 sg. imp. pres. act. (↑115ff). As a result there is the kind of vowel contraction that occurs regularly with verbs in -όω (↑89) and -έω (↑87), e. g.:

ἐ-δίδουν (st. διδο-) *I gave* ≈ ἐ-δήλ-ουν (<-ο**ο**ν) *I showed*
ἐ-δίδους *you* (sg.) *gave* ≈ ἐ-δήλ-ους (<-ο**ε**ς) *you* (sg.) *showed*
ἐ-δίδου *he/she/it gave* ≈ ἐ-δήλ-ου (<-ο**ε**) *he/she/it made clear*
δίδου *give!* (sg.) ≈ δήλ-ου (<-ο**ε**) *show!* (sg.)

ἐ-τίθεις (st. τιθε-) *you* (sg.) *placed* ≈ ἐ-ποί-εις (<-ε**ε**ς) *you* (sg.) *did*
ἐ-τίθει *he/she/it placed* ≈ ἐ-ποί-ει (<-ε**ε**) *he/she/it did*
τίθει *place!* (sg.) ≈ ποί-ει (<-ε**ε**) *do!* (sg.)

ἵει-ς etc. (st. ἱε-) *you* (sg.) *sent* ≈ ἐ-ποί-εις (<-ε**ε**ς) *you* (sg.) *did*

2. In the ind. pres. act. **stem-final vowel** is long in the sg., but short in the pl. (quantitative ablaut [↑8d]; in the mid./pass. it is short both in the sg. and in the pl.), e. g.: 114b

τίθ**η**-μι *I place* τίθ**ε**-μεν *we place*
φ**η**-μί *I say* φ**ᾰ**-μέν *we say*

3. The verbs in -μι have the same **mood signs** as the verbs in -ω (↑69). Those marking the subj. (η/ω) contract with the stem-final vowel (↑11), though not with a stem-final -υ or -ι (↑122ff; 125c), e. g.: 114c

τιθ**η**-**ω** > τιθ**ῶ** *(if) I place* (↑84c)
διδ**ω**-**η**-σθε > διδ**ῶ**-σθε *(if) you* (pl.) *are given*
δεικν**ύ**-**ῃ** > δεικν**ύ**-**ῃ** *(if) he/she/it shows*

4. For the personal **endings** and **terminations** of nominal forms ↑70. 114d

114e 5. **Three types** of verbs in -μι are distinguishable:
a) verbs in -μι with a reduplication in the present stem (↑115–121; 75f);
b) verbs in -μι with a nasal affix in the present stem (nasal-presents): verbs in -νυμι/-ννυμι such as δείκ-νυ-μι *to show* (↑122–124; 75c);
c) verbs in -μι whose present stem is the same as the verb stem/root: the root presents in -μι such as φη-μί *to say* (↑125).

II. **KG** developments

There is a growing **influence of** the predominant **thematic conjugation** on the formation and inflection of the verbs in -μι:

114f 1. Among verbs that traditionally follow the rules of the athematic conjugation a considerable number of thematic forms are being used. This is especially true of verbs in -νυμι/-ννυμι (a tendency attested already in Att.), e.g.:

δεικ-νύ-**εις**	instead of (↑123.1)	δείκ-νυ-**ς**	*you* (pl.) *show*
ἐστρώννυ-**ον**	instead of (↑124.7)	ἐστρώννυ-**σαν**	*they spread*

In the NT only one thematic form is attested of the first of the following verbs and only a few more of the second one:

ὄμνυμι	*to swear* (↑123.8)	συν-ίημι	*to understand* (↑120.4)

In some cases the stem vowel is replaced by a thematic vowel (↑117[1] and 118[2]) in the NT (and the LXX), e.g. Mt 21:33 (also 1Macc 10:58; regular form Ex 2:21):

ἐξ-έ-δ**ε**το	instead of	ἐξ-έ-δ**ο**το	*he gave/handed over*

114g 2. In the NT (and the LXX) several verbs that traditionally belong to the athematic category are **supplemented by younger formations in -ω**, e.g. (↑120.5[1]):

συν-ιστάνω	supplementing	συν-ίστημι	*to (re)commend*
παρ-ιστάνω	supplementing	παρ-ίστημι	*to present*
ἱστάνω	supplementing	ἵστημι	*to set/place*

114h 3. In the NT (and the LXX) verbs in -μι are frequently **replaced by verbs in -ω with synonymous meaning**, e.g.:

χορτάζω	replacing	κορέννυμι	*to satiate* (↑124.2[1])
σκορπίζω	replacing	σκεδάννυμι	*to scatter* (↑124.4[1])
πληρόω/γεμίζω	replacing	πίμπλημι	*to fill* (↑121.2)
ῥήσσω	replacing	ῥήγνυμι	*to tear/break* (↑123.6)

2.7.3.1 Verbs in -μι with present reduplication (↑BR §129; BDF §94f)

In Ancient Greek four verbs in -μι are used very frequently. Sometimes these are called the "Big Four". Their special feature is a reduplication in the present stem: to form the present stem the verb stem is extended by a reduplication with ι serving as reduplication vowel (↑72a; 75f). This reduplication is characteristic of the present stem distinguishing it from all the other tense-aspect stems. This feature is relevant especially when it comes to telling the present stem forms from their counterparts in the aorist act./mid. stem: in many cases the only difference between the two sets of forms is the presence or absence of the reduplication (↑115b and 116 as well as 117 and 118).

Especially noteworthy points:

(1) The special athematic conjugation presented here **exclusively** concerns the forms of the **present** stem **and** those of the (strong/second) **aorist active/middle** stem.

(2) The **paradigms** applicable to these are given below in ↑115b–118. They include a great deal more forms than are actually attested in the NT or the LXX (for the reasons ↑p. xv).

(3) For the **forms outside** the **present** and the **aorist active/middle** stems the paradigms given for the verbs in -ω are applicable (especially ↑76–78).

(4) The **principal parts** of the "Big Four" are given in ↑120 (also ↑121).

Present/durative forms of the "Big Four" in -μι (↑BR §128; BDF §92f) 115

The present/durative active and middle/passive forms (↑115b/116) as well as the aorist active and middle forms (↑117/118) of the "Big Four" in -μι are based on the following stems: 115a

	lexical form:		present stem (act./mid./pass.):[(1)]	verb/aor. act./mid. stem:
1.	τίθη-μι	*to place*	τιθη-/τιθε-[(2)]	θη-/θε-
2.	ἵη-μι[(3)]	*to send*	ἱη-/ἱε-	ἡ-/ἑ-
3.	δίδω-μι	*to give*	διδω-/διδο-	δω-/δο-
4.	ἵστη-μι	*to set/place*	ἱστη-/ἱστα-[(4)]	στη-/στα-

(1) On the reduplication in the present stem ↑72a.

(2) Aspirate dissimilation (↑14a; 72c).

(3) In the NT (and in the LXX) this verb is attested only in compound form, most frequently ἀφ-ίημι inter alia *to let go/cancel*.

(4) ἱστη-/ἱστα- <*σιστη-/*σιστα- (↑13d).

115b

stem →	τίθημι *to place* τιθη-, τιθε-	ἵημι *to send* ἱη-, ἱε-	δίδωμι *to give* διδω-, διδο-	ἵστημι *to set/place* ἱστη-, ἱστα-
IND. PRES. sg. 1	τίθη-μι	ἵη-μι	δίδω-μι	ἵστη-μι
2	τίθη-ς	ἵη-ς[1]	δίδω-ς	ἵστη-ς
3	τίθη-σιν	ἵη-σιν	δίδω-σιν	ἵστη-σιν
pl. 1	τίθε-μεν	ἵε-μεν	δίδο-μεν	ἵστα-μεν
2	τίθε-τε	ἵε-τε	δίδο-τε	ἵστα-τε
3	τιθέ-ᾱσιν	ἱᾶ-σιν (<ἱέασι[ν])	διδό-ᾱσιν	ἱστᾶ-σιν (<ἱστάασι[ν])
IPF. sg. 1	ἐτίθη-ν	ἵει-ν (aug. ↑71c)	ἐδίδου-ν[2]	ἵστη-ν (aug. ↑71c)
2	ἐτίθει-ς[2]	ἵει-ς[2]	ἐδίδου-ς[2]	ἵστη-ς
3	ἐτίθει[2]	ἵει[2]	ἐδίδου[2]	ἵστη
pl. 1	ἐτίθε-μεν	ἵε-μεν	ἐδίδο-μεν	ἵστα-μεν
2	ἐτίθε-τε	ἵε-τε	ἐδίδο-τε	ἵστα-τε
3	ἐτίθε-σαν[3]	ἵε-σαν	ἐδίδο-σαν[3]	ἵστα-σαν
SUBJ. sg. 1	τιθῶ (<τιθήω)	ἱῶ (<ἱήω)	διδῶ (<διδώω)	ἱστῶ (<ἱστήω)
2	τιθῇ-ς	ἱῇ-ς	διδῷ-ς	ἱστῇ-ς
3	τιθῇ	ἱῇ	διδῷ	ἱστῇ
pl. 1	τιθῶ-μεν	ἱῶ-μεν	διδῶ-μεν	ἱστῶ-μεν
2	τιθῆ-τε	ἱῆ-τε	διδῶ-τε	ἱστῆ-τε
3	τιθῶ-σιν	ἱῶ-σιν	διδῶ-σιν	ἱστῶ-σιν
OPT. sg. 1	τιθείη-ν	ἱείη-ν	διδοίη-ν	ἱσταίη-ν
2	τιθείη-ς	ἱείη-ς	διδοίη-ς	ἱσταίη-ς
3	τιθείη	ἱείη	διδοίη	ἱσταίη
pl. 1	τιθείη-μεν[4]	ἱείη-μεν[4]	διδοίη-μεν[4]	ἱσταίη-μεν[4]
2	τιθείη-τε[4]	ἱείη-τε[4]	διδοίη-τε[4]	ἱσταίη-τε[4]
3	τιθείη-σαν[4]	ἱείη-σαν[4]	διδοίη-σαν[4]	ἱσταίη-σαν[4]
IMP. sg. 2	τίθει[2]	ἵει[2]	δίδου[2]	ἵστη
3	τιθέ-τω	ἱέ-τω	διδό-τω	ἱστά-τω
pl. 2	τίθε-τε	ἵε-τε	δίδο-τε	ἵστα-τε
3	τιθέ-τωσαν[5]	ἱέ-τωσαν[5]	διδό-τωσαν[5]	ἱστά-τωσαν[5]
INF.	τιθέ-ναι	ἱέ-ναι	διδό-ναι	ἱστά-ναι
PTC. masc./ntr.	τιθείς/-έν	ἱείς/-έν	διδούς/-όν[3]	ἱστάς/-άν
gen.	τιθέντος	ἱέντος	διδόντος	ἱστάντος
fem.	τιθεῖσα	ἱεῖσα	διδοῦσα	ἱστᾶσα
gen.	τιθείσης	ἱείσης	διδούσης	ἱστάσης

(1) CG for ἵης also ἵεις; a form derived from this (BDF §94.2) is (ἀφ)εῖς (Re 2:20; Ex 32:32).
(2) -ει- <-εε-, -ου- < -οε/ει- (↑114a). For ἵει the NT has only **ἤφ**-ιεν *he permitted* (Mk 1:34; 11:16).
(3) For CG ἐτίθεσαν/ἐδίδοσαν in NT also ἐτίθ**ουν**/ἐδίδ**ουν**, for διδ**ό**ν in Re 22:2 -διδ**οῦ**ν (BDF §94.1).
(4) CG opt. pl. mostly without η: -εῖμεν, -εῖτε, -εῖεν; -οῖμεν, -οῖτε, -οῖεν; -αῖμεν, -αῖτε, -αῖεν.
(5) CG uses -ντων instead of -τωσαν (↑70).

Strong aorist active forms of the "Big Four" in -μι (↑BR §129.2; BDF §95) 116

	τίθημι *to place* τιθη-, τιθε-	ἵημι *to send* ἱη-, ἱε-	δίδωμι *to give* διδω-, διδο-	ἵστημι *to set* ἱστη-, ἱστα-
IND.	ἔθηκα (↑119a) ἔθηκα-ς ἔθηκε-ν (CG:) ἐθήκα-μεν ἔθε-μεν ἐθήκα-τε ἔθε-τε ἔθηκα-ν ἔθε-σαν	ἧκα (↑119a) ἧκα-ς[1] ἧκεν (CG:) ἥκα-μεν εἷ-μεν ἥκα-τε εἷ-τε ἧκα-ν εἷ-σαν	ἔδωκα (↑119a) ἔδωκα-ς ἔδωκε-ν (CG:) ἐδώκα-μεν ἔδο-μεν ἐδώκα-τε ἔδο-τε ἔδωκα-ν ἔδο-σαν	(ἔστησα etc. [weak aorist; ↑76])
SUBJ.	θῶ (<θήω) θῇ-ς θῇ θῶ-μεν θῆ-τε θῶ-σιν	ὧ (<ἥω)[2] ᾗ-ς ᾗ ὧ-μεν ἧ-τε ὧ-σιν	δῶ (<δώω) δῷ-ς or δοῖς (NT) δῷ or δοῖ/δώῃ (NT) δῶ-μεν δῶ-τε δῶ-σιν	(στήσω etc.)
OPT.	θείη-ν θείη-ς θείη θείη-μεν[3] θείη-τε[3] θείη-σαν[3]	εἵη-ν εἵη-ς εἵη εἵη-μεν[3] εἵη-τε[3] εἵη-σαν[3]	δοίη-ν or δῴην (NT; Ion.) δοίη-ς or δῴης (NT; Ion.) δοίη or δῴη (NT; Ion.) δοίη-μεν[3] δοίη-τε[3] δοίη-σαν[3]	(στήσαιμι etc.)
IMP.	θέ-ς (↑119b) θέ-τω θέ-τε θέ-τωσαν[4]	ἕ-ς (↑119b) ἕ-τω ἕ-τε ἕ-τωσαν[4]	δό-ς (↑119b) δό-τω δό-τε δό-τωσαν[4]	(στῆσον etc.)
INF.	θεῖ-ναι (<θε-έναι)	εἷ-ναι (<ἑ-έναι)	δοῦ-ναι (<δο-έναι)	(στῆσαι)
PTC.	θείς/θέν θέντος θεῖσα θείσης	εἵς/ἕν ἕντος εἷσα εἵσης	δούς/δόν δόντος δοῦσα δούσης	[στήσας etc.]

(1) Re 2:4 ἀφ-ῆκες (Var. ἀφ-ῆκ**ας**).
(2) He 13:5 ἀνῶ (ἀνίημι *to loosen, to let go*).
(3) CG opt. pl. mostly without η: θεῖμεν, θεῖτε, θεῖεν; εἷμεν, εἷτε, εἷεν; δοῖμεν, δοῖτε, δοῖεν.
(4) CG uses -ντων instead of -τωσαν (↑70).

117 Present/durative mid./pass. forms of the “Big Four” in -μι (↑BR §129.3; BDF §94)

stem →	τίθημι *to place* τιθη-, τιθε-	ἵημι *to send* ἱη-, ἱε-	δίδωμι *to give* διδω-, διδο-	ἵστημι *to set* ἱστη-, ἱστα-
IND. PRES. sg. 1	τίθε-μαι	ἵε-μαι	δίδο-μαι	ἵστα-μαι
2	τίθε-σαι	ἵε-σαι	δίδο-σαι	ἵστα-σαι
3	τίθε-ται	ἵε-ται	δίδο-ται	ἵστα-ται
pl. 1	τιθέ-μεθα	ἱέ-μεθα	διδό-μεθα	ἱστά-μεθα
2	τίθε-σθε	ἵε-σθε	δίδο-σθε	ἵστα-σθε
3	τίθε-νται	ἵε-νται	δίδο-νται	ἵστα-νται
IPF. sg. 1	ἐτιθέ-μην	ἱέ-μην	ἐδιδό-μην	ἱστά-μην
2	ἐτίθε-σο	ἵε-σο	ἐδίδο-σο	ἵστα-σο
3	ἐτίθε-το	ἵε-το	ἐδίδο-το(1)	ἵστα-το
pl. 1	ἐτιθέ-μεθα	ἱέ-μεθα	ἐδιδό-μεθα	ἱστά-μεθα
2	ἐτίθε-σθε	ἵε-σθε	ἐδίδο-σθε	ἵστα-σθε
3	ἐτίθε-ντο	ἵε-ντο	ἐδίδο-ντο	ἵστα-ντο
SUBJ. sg. 1	τιθῶ-μαι	ἱῶ-μαι	διδῶ-μαι	ἱστῶ-μαι
2	τιθῇ	ἱῇ	διδῷ	ἱστῇ
3	τιθῆ-ται	ἱῆ-ται	διδῶ-ται	ἱστῆ-ται
pl. 1	τιθώ-μεθα	ἱώ-μεθα	διδώ-μεθα	ἱστώ-μεθα
2	τιθῆ-σθε	ἱῆ-σθε	διδῶ-σθε	ἱστῆ-σθε
3	τιθῶ-νται	ἱῶ-νται	διδῶ-νται	ἱστῶ-νται
OPT. sg. 1	τιθεί-μην	ἱεί-μην	διδοί-μην	ἱσταί-μην
2	τιθεῖ-ο	ἱεῖ-ο	διδοῖ-ο	ἱσταῖ-ο
3	τιθεῖ-το	ἱεῖ-το	διδοῖ-το	ἱσταῖ-το
pl. 1	τιθεί-μεθα	ἱεί-μεθα	διδοί-μεθα	ἱσταί-μεθα
2	τιθεῖ-σθε	ἱεῖ-σθε	διδοῖ-σθε	ἱσταῖ-σθε
3	τιθεῖ-ντο	ἱεῖ-ντο	διδοῖ-ντο	ἱσταῖ-ντο
IMP. sg. 2	τίθε-σο	ἵε-σο	δίδο-σο	ἵστα-σο
3	τιθέ-σθω	ἱέ-σθω	διδό-σθω	ἱστά-σθω
pl. 2	τίθε-σθε	ἵε-σθε	δίδο-σθε	ἵστα-σθε
3	τιθέ-σθωσαν(2)	ἱέ-σθωσαν(2)	διδό-σθωσαν(2)	ἱστά-σθωσαν(2)
INF.	τίθε-σθαι	ἵε-σθαι	δίδο-σθαι	ἵστα-σθαι
PTC. masc.	τιθέ-μενος	ἱέ-μενος	διδό-μενος	ἱστά-μενος
fem.	τιθε-μένη	ἱε-μένη	διδο-μένη	ἱστα-μένη
ntr.	τιθέ-μενον	ἱέ-μενον	διδό-μενον	ἱστά-μενον

(1) Also -εδίδετο (↑114f), e.g. δι-εδίδετο (Ac 4:35), παρ-εδίδετο (1Cor 11:23); also ↑116[1] and 118a[2].

(2) CG uses -σθων instead of -σθωσαν (↑70).

Strong aorist middle forms of the "Big Four" in -μι (↑BR §129.4; BDF §95) 118

118a

	τίθημι *to place* τιθη-, τιθε-	ἵημι *to send* ἱη-, ἱε-	δίδωμι *to give* διδω-, διδο-	ἵστημι *to set/place* στη-/στα-(1)
IND.	ἐθέ-μην ἔθ**ου** (< ἔθεσο) ἔθε-το ἐθέ-μεθα ἔθε-σθε ἔθε-ντο	εἵ-μην εἷ-σο εἷ-το εἵ-μεθα εἷ-σθε εἷ-ντο	ἐδό-μην ἔδ**ου** (< ἔδοσο) ἔδο-το(2) ἐδό-μεθα ἔδο-σθε ἔδο-ντο	ἔστη-ν ἔστη-ς ἔστη ἔστη-μεν ἔστη-τε ἔστη-σαν
SUBJ.	θῶ-μαι θῇ θῆ-ται θώ-μεθα θῆ-σθε θῶ-νται	ὧ-μαι ᾗ ἧ-ται ὥ-μεθα ἧ-σθε ὧ-νται	δῶ-μαι δῷ δῶ-ται δώ-μεθα δῶ-σθε δῶ-νται	στῶ (< στήω) στῇ-ς στῇ στῶ-μεν στῆ-τε στῶ-σιν
OPT.	θεί-μην θεῖ-ο θεῖ-το θεί-μεθα θεῖ-σθε θεῖ-ντο	εἵ-μην εἷ-ο εἷ-το εἵ-μεθα εἷ-σθε εἷ-ντο	δοί-μην δοῖ-ο δοῖ-το δοί-μεθα δοῖ-σθε δοῖ-ντο	σταίη-ν σταίη-ς σταίη σταίη-μεν/σταῖ-μεν(3) σταίη-τε σταίη-σαν
IMP.	**θοῦ** (< θέσο) θέ-σθω θέ-σθε θέ-σθωσαν(4)	**οὗ** (< ἕσο) ἕ-σθω ἕ-σθε ἕ-σθωσαν(4)	**δοῦ** (< δόσο) δό-σθω δό-σθε δό-σθωσαν(4)	στῆ-θι also -στα στή-τω στῆ-τε στή-τωσαν(4)
INF.	θέ-σθαι	ἕ-σθαι	δό-σθαι	στῆ-ναι
PTC.	θέ-μενος θε-μένη θέ-μενον	ἕ-μενος ἑ-μένη ἑ-μένον	δό-μενος δο-μένη δό-μενον	στάς στάντος στᾶσα στάσης στάν στάντος

(1) Root aorist (↑106; like ἔβ**η**ν root aor. of βαίνω *to go*).
(2) Also -έδ**ε**το (↑114f), e.g. ἀπ-έδ**ε**το (He 12:16; MH: 212).
(3) CG opt. pl. is typically without η: -αῖμεν, -αῖτε, -αῖεν.
(4) CG uses -σθων instead of -σθωσαν and στά-ντων instead of στή-τωσαν (↑70).

118b Note that the **accentuation of compounds** is the same as in the case of the simplex (↑74) and that only strong aorist forms may have an accented prepositional prefix (↑74a), e.g.:

ἐπ**ί**-θες	*lay on!* (sg.)	πρ**ό**σ-θες	*add!* (sg.)
ἐπ**ί**-θεσθε	*lay on!* (pl.)	ἀπ**ό**-θεσθε	*put off!* (pl.)

After a monosyllabic prefix, however, θοῦ, δοῦ and οὗ may keep their accent, e.g. (attested in CG, but not in the NT or LXX):

προσ-θ**οῦ**	*add for yourself!*	ἀφ-**οῦ**	*let go!* (sg.)

119 Explanatory notes on the paradigms of the "Big Four" in -μι (↑BR §130; BDF §94f)

1. The verbs δίδωμι *to give*, τίθημι *to place*, ἵημι *to send* share a number of features:

119a a) In the **ind. aor. act.** they have an unusual **tense-aspect sign κ** (unlike CG also in the pl.; ↑105h):

ἔδω-**κα**	*I gave*	ἔδω-**καν**	*they gave*
ἔθη-**κα**	*I placed*	ἔθη-**καν**	*they placed*
ἧ-**κα**	*I sent*	ἧ-**καν**	*they sent*

119b b) **2 sg. imp. aor. act.** forms end in -ς (↑70; 114d; ↑σχές imp. of ἔσχον, ↑113.5):

θέ**ς** *place!* (sg.) ἕ**ς** *send!* (sg.) δό**ς** *give!* (sg.)

119c c) The termination of the **inf. aor. act.** is -έναι (↑70; 114d):

θε-**έναι**	> **θεῖναι**	(↑11a)	*to place*
ἑ-**έναι**	> **εἷναι**	(↑11a)	*to send*
δο-**έναι**	> **δοῦναι**	(↑11c)	*to give*

119d d) The **sg. ipf. act.** and the **2 sg. imp. pres. act.** show some influence of the **thematic** conjugation. On this ↑114a as well as the footnotes to the paradigms.

119e 2. The verb **ἵστημι** *to set/place* has a regular **weak aorist** ἔστησα *I set/placed*. The "middle" forms given in ↑118 (the actual voice of this aorist is hard to determine) ἔστην (root aorist; ↑106) means *I stood (up)* (lit. *I set/placed myself*, as a direct middle), not *I set/placed (sth./s.o.) for myself* (as an indirect middle); for the latter meaning the weak form ἐστησά-μην is available (in CG, not in the NT, but in the LXX to some extent). Also ↑120.5.

120 Principal parts of the "Big Four" in -μι (↑BR §131; BDF §97; 96)

1. First three verbs of the "Big Four" in -μι:

present	future	aorist	perfect	
1. τίθημι *to place* mid. → pass. →	θήσω θήσομαι τεθήσομαι[1]	ἔθηκα ἐθέμην ἐτέθην[1]	τέθεικα/(CG: τέθηκα) τέθειμαι κεῖμαι[2]/τέθειμαι	120.1
2. δίδωμι *to give* mid. → pass. →	δώσω δώσομαι δοθήσομαι	ἔδωκα ἐδόμην ἐδόθην	δέδωκα δέδομαι δέδομαι	120.2
3. ἵημι[3] *to send* mid. → pass. →	ἥσω ἥσομαι ἑθήσομαι	ἧκα εἵμην εἵθην	εἶκα εἶμαι εἶμαι	120.3
4. ἀφίημι[4] *to let go* mid. → pass. →	ἀφήσω ἀφήσομαι ἀφεθήσομαι	ἀφῆκα ἀφείμην ἀφέθην/(CG: ἀφείθην)	(ἀφεῖκα) (ἀφεῖμαι) ἀφέωμαι[5]/ἀφεῖμαι	120.4

(1) Dissimilation of the aspirate (↑14a).
(2) Paradigm ↑125e.
(3) CG principal parts (in the NT/LXX only compounds are attested; ↑120.4).
(4) Principal parts of the most frequent compound (in the NT/LXX) as an example for all the others. Note that in the pres. act. thematic forms are used quite frequently (-ίω for -ίημι; ↑114f).
(5) This pf. pass. (a dialect variant; ↑BDF §97.3) occurs almost exclusively in the NT, more precisely (6×) in the 3 pl.: ἀφέωνται *they are forgiven*. However, He 12:12 (τὰς παρειμένας χεῖρας *the weak hands*) and all the LXX instances are based on (the CG) -εῖμαι.

2. ἵστημι *to set/place*

	TRANSITIVE (with Od in the act./mid.)			INTRANSITIVE (without Od)	120.5
	ACTIVE *to set/ place*	(INDIRECT) MIDDLE *to set/place sth. for o.s.* (not attested in the NT)	PASSIVE *to be set/placed*	(DIRECT) MIDDLE *to put/place o.s. (somewhere) = to stand (up)* (used very frequently)	
present	ἵστημι	ἵσταμαι	ἵσταμαι	ἵσταμαι	
future	στήσω	στήσομαι	σταθήσομαι	στήσομαι/ (post-CG:) σταθήσομαι	
aorist	ἔστησα	ἐστησάμην	ἐστάθην	ἔστην/ (post-CG:) ἐστάθην	
perfect[1]	(↑189c)			ἕστηκα[2] *I stand*	
plpf.				**εἱ**στήκειν *I stood*	

(1) Rarely (post-CG; really pf. act. of -ιστάνω [↑114f]) -έστᾰκα *I have set/placed* (↑Ac 8:11).
(2) Alongside the regular pf. forms (↑76) there are also root perfect forms (↑109a): inf. ἑστάναι, ptc. ἑστώς -ῶτος, ἑστῶσα -ώσης, ἑστός (outside NT/LXX also -ώς) -ῶτος. KG/NT: for ἕστηκα the younger synonym (pres.) στήκω may be used (e.g. in Jn 8:44; ↑Var.).

121 Verbs that are conjugated like ἵστημι (↑BR §132; BDF §101)

	pres.	stem	fut.	aor. act./mid. aor. pass.	pf. act. pf. mid./pass.
121.1	ὀνίνημι *to benefit* ὀνίναμαι mid. *to draw a benefit from*	ὀνη-, ὀνα-[(1)] NT 1× (Phm 20): ὀναίμην opt. aor. mid.	ὀνήσω	(ὤνησα) ὠνάμην/(CG ὠνήμην) (CG ὠνήθην; LXX: 1× ὠνάσθην)	
121.2	πίμπλημι[(1)/(2)] *to fill*	πλη(σ)-, πλα-	πλήσω (↑80.4ff) →	ἔπλησα ἐπλή**σ**θην	(πέπληκα) πέπλη**σ**μαι
121.3	δύναμαι *can/to be able*, ↑121.5	δυνη-, δυνα(σ)- (aug. ἠ- or ἐ-)	δυνήσομαι (↑80.4ff) →	ἠδυνήθην/ ἠδυνά**σ**θην	(δεδύνημαι)
121.4	ἐπίσταμαι[(3)] *to understand/know*	ἐπιστη-, ἐπιστα-	(ἐπιστήσομαι)	(ἠπιστήθην)	

(1) A rather complicated reduplication in the present stem (↑72a), also ↑121.7.
(2) The NT also uses πληρόω and γεμίζω to express this meaning (↑114h).
(3) ipf. **ἠ**πιστάμην, 2 sg. alongside **ἠ**πίστ**ασο** (CG/LXX) also **ἠ**πίστ**ω** (↑70[6]).

121.5		IND. PRES.	IMPERFECT (aug. also ἠ-)	SUBJUNCTIVE	OPTATIVE
	sg. 1	δύνα-μαι	ἐδυνά-μην	δύνω-μαι	δυναί-μην
	2	δύνα-σαι (CG)/δύνῃ (post-CG)	ἐδύνα-σο (CG ἐδύνω; ↑70[6])	δύνῃ	δύναι-ο
	3	δύνα-ται	ἐδύνα-το	δύνη-ται	δύναι-το
	pl. 1	δυνά-μεθα	ἐδυνά-μεθα	δυνώ-μεθα	δυναί-μεθα
	2	δύνα-σθε	ἐδύνα-σθε	δύνη-σθε	δύναι-σθε
	3	δύνα-νται	ἐδύνα-ντο	δύνω-νται	δύναι-ντο
	INF.	δύνα-σθαι			
	PTC.	δυνά-μενος, δυνα-μένη, δυνά-μενον			

Additional points to note:

121.6 1. In the subj. and opt. the accent of deponents is retracted (unlike in case of ἵστημι; ↑115b):

δ**ύ**νωμαι	δ**ύ**νῃ	δ**ύ**νηται	subj.
	δ**ύ**ναιο	δ**ύ**ναιτο	opt.

121.7 2. In the NT the following verbs (inflected analogically) occur occasionally:

πίμπρημι *to burn sth.*	πρη(σ)- πρα-	(πρήσω) (↑80.4ff) →	ἔπρησα (ἐπρή**σ**θην)	(πέπρηκα) (πέπρη**σ**μαι)
κίχρημι *to lend*	χρη-		ἔχρησα (↑Lk 11:5)	(κέχρηκα) (κέχρημαι)

2.7.3.2 Verbs in -νυμι/-ννυμι (nasal-presents) (↑114e)

Present/durative forms of δείκνυμι “to show” (↑BR §133; BDF §92) 122

δείκνυμι *to show*, verb stem: δεικ-, present stem (↑114e): δείκ-νῡ/νῠ- (↑114b)

ACTIVE		IND. PRES.	IMPERFECT	SUBJUNCTIVE	IMPERATIVE (1)
sg.	1	δείκνῡ-μι	ἐδείκνῡ-ν	δεικνύ-ω	
	2	δείκνῡ-ς	ἐδείκνῡ-ς	δεικνύ-ῃς	δείκνῡ
	3	δείκνῡ-σιν	ἐδείκνῡ	δεικνύ-ῃ	δεικνύ-τω
pl.	1	δείκνυ-μεν	ἐδείκνυ-μεν	δεικνύ-ωμεν	
	2	δείκνυ-τε	ἐδείκνυ-τε	δεικνύ-ητε	δείκνυ-τε
	3	δεικνύ-ᾱσιν	ἐδείκνυ-σαν	δεικνύ-ωσιν	δεικνύ-τωσαν(2)
INF.		δεικνύ-ναι			
PTC. (↑48f)		δεικνῡ́ς, -νύντος; δεικνῦσα, -σης; δεικνύν, -νύντος			
MIDDLE/PASSIVE					
sg.	1	δείκνυ-μαι	ἐδεικνύ-μην	δεικνύω-μαι	
	2	δείκνυ-σαι	ἐδείκνυ-σο	δεικνύῃ	δείκνυ-σο
	3	δείκνυ-ται	ἐδείκνυ-το	δεικνύῃ-ται	δεικνύ-σθω
pl.	1	δεικνύ-μεθα	ἐδεικνύ-μεθα	δεικνυώ-μεθα	
	2	δείκνυ-σθε	ἐδείκνυ-σθε	δεικνύῃ-σθε	δείκνυ-σθε
	3	δείκνυ-νται	ἐδείκνυ-ντο	δεικνύω-νται	δεικνύ-σθωσαν(2)
INF.		δείκνυσθαι			
PTC.		δεικνύμενος, δεικνυμένη, δεικνύμενον			

(1) Opt. act. δεικνύ-οιμι etc., mid./pass. δεικνυ-οίμην etc. (as in the case of παιδεύω; ↑76–78).
(2) CG uses δεικνύ-ντων instead of δεικνύ-τωσαν, δεικνύ-σθων instead of δεικνύ-σθωσαν (↑70).

Principal parts of the verbs in -νυμι (↑BR §135; BDF §92; 101) 123

pres.	stem	fut.	aor. act./mid. aor. pass.	pf. act. pf. mid./pass.

1. Velar stems (↑90ff; 95)

δείκ-νυμι/-νύω *to show* (↑114f)	δεικ-	δείξω	ἔδειξα ἐδείχθην	δέδειχα δέδειγμαι	123.1

123.2	ζεύγνυμι *to connect*	ζευγ-	ζεύξω	ἔζευξα (ἐζεύχθην)	ἔζευγμαι
123.3	ἄγνυμι, κατάγνυμι *to break*	(ϝ)αγ-, -έαγ-	κατάξω (CG)/ κατεάξω	κατέαξα κατεάγην[1](CG)/ κατεάχθην	(κατέαγα) *I am broken* (↑189c)
123.4	μ(ε)ίγνυμι or μ(ε)ιγνύω (↑114f) *to mix*	μειγ-/μιγ- (↑2c)	μ(ε)ίξω	ἔμ(ε)ιξα ἐμ(ε)ίχθην/ ἐμίγην[1]	(μέμιχα) μέμ(ε)ιγμαι
123.5	πήγνυμι *to fix*	πηγ-, παγ-	πήξω	ἔπηξα ἐπάγην[1]	πέπηγα *I am firm* (↑189c)
123.6	ῥήγνυμι *to tear in pieces/ break/burst*	ῥηγ-, ῥαγ-	ῥήξω ῥαγήσομαι	ἔρρηξα ἐρράγην[1]	-έρρηχα (LXX), mostly ἔρρωγα *I am torn* (↑189c; 200b)

(1) Aor. II (↑107k; 105f).

2. Liquid stems (↑97ff)

123.7	ἀπόλλυμι (<-ὀλνυμι; ↑15d) *to ruin/destroy* ἀπόλλυμαι *to be ruined/perish/get lost*	-ὀλ-, -ὀλε-	ἀπολέσω/(CG:) ἀπολῶ, -εῖς (↑98a) ἀπολοῦμαι, -ῇ (↑98a)	ἀπώλεσα ἀπωλόμην[1]	ἀπολώλεκα (↑72g) ἀπόλωλα *I am ruined* (↑189c/200b)
123.8	ὄμνυμι *to swear*	ὀμ-, ὀμο-	ὀμοῦμαι, ὀμῇ (↑98a)	ὤμοσα	ὀμώμοκα (↑72g)
	Note that the NT mostly uses ὀμνύω instead of ὄμνυμι (the inf. pres. act. ὀμνύναι being the only athematic representative of this verb in the NT; ↑114f).				

(1) Aor. II (↑107k; 105f).

Principal parts of the verbs in -ννυμι (-νν- < -σν-) (↑BR §134f; BDF §92; 101) 124

pres.	stem	fut.	aor. act./mid. aor. pass.	pf. act. pf. mid./pass.	

1. Verb stems in -σ (on the present stem; ↑13h; on -σσ > -σ of fut./aor.; ↑13g)

pres.	stem	fut.	aor. act./mid. aor. pass.	pf. act. pf. mid./pass.	
ἀμφιέ**νν**υμι (< ἀμφιέ**σν**υμι) ἀμφιέννυμαι *to clothe* (act.), *to clothe o.s.* (mid.)	ἑσ- <(ϝ)εσ-	(ἀμφιῶ, -εῖς; ↑92f) (ἀμφιέσομαι)	ἠμφίεσα ἠμφιεσάμην	 ἠμφίεσμαι	124.1
σβέ**νν**υμι[1] (< σβέ**σν**υμι) *to extinguish/quench/put out* σβέννυμαι *to be extinguished/ go out*	σβεσ-, σβη-	σβέσω (σβήσομαι CG) (↑ἄσβεστος *inextinguishable*)	ἔσβεσα ἐσβέσθην (ἔσβην CG)[2]	 ἔσβεσμαι (ἔσβηκα CG)	124.2
ζώ**νν**υμι (< ζώ**σν**υμι) or ζωννύω (↑114f) *to gird* (act.), *to gird o.s.* (mid.)	ζωσ-	ζώσω	ἔζωσα (ἐζώσθην) (CG without σ)	 (ἔζωσμαι) (CG without σ)	124.3

(1) Analogical: κορέννυμι *to satiate*, κορεσ-, (κορέσω), (ἐκόρεσα), ἐκορέσθην, κεκόρεσμαι. ↑114h.
(2) Root aorist (↑106) like ἔ-βη-ν *I went*, but opt. σβ**ε**ίη-ν etc. and ptc. σβ**ε**ίς σβ**έ**ντος etc., the fut. σβήσομαι being derived from it.

2. Verb with stem-final vowel

pres.	stem	fut.	aor. act./mid. aor. pass.	pf. act. pf. mid./pass.	
κεράννυμι[1] *to mix (wine)* (↑ἄκρατος *unmixed/undiluted*)	κερα(σ)-, κρα-	(κεράσω)	ἐκέρασα ἐκρά(σ)θην	 κεκέρασμαι/ (CG κέκραμαι)	124.4
κρεμάννυμι *to hang sth.*	κρεμα(σ)-	κρεμάσω (CG κρεμῶ, -ᾷς; ↑84)	ἐκρέμασα ἐκρεμάσθην	(Philo κεκρέμακα) (κρέμᾱμαι[2] *to be hanging*)	124.5
(ῥώννυμι) *to make strong* – mostly imp. pf. pass. ἔρρωσο/ἔρρωσθε *farewell!*	ῥω(σ)-	(ῥώσω)	(ἔρρωσα) (ἐρρώσθην)	 ἔρρωμαι (↑212e)	124.6
στρώ-ννυμι/ -ννύω (↑114f) *to spread sth.*	στρω-	στρώσω	ἔστρωσα ἐστρώθην	ἔστρωκα (1× LXX) ἔστρωμαι	124.7

(1) Analogical (LXX): σκεδάννῡμι (compounds; ↑114h) *to scatter*, σκεδα(σ)-, σκεδάσω (σκεδῶ/ -ᾷς; ↑84), ἐσκέδασα, (ἐσκέδασμαι), (ἐσκεδάσθην); πετάννυμι *to spread out*, aor. pass. ἐπετάσθην.
(2) Without reduplication, really a pres. stem (inflecting like ἵσταμαι; ↑117; 121), used as pf. pass. of κρεμάννυμι (↑BR §132).

2.7.3.3 Root presents in -μι (↑114e)

125 εἰμί, εἶμι, φημί, κεῖμαι and κάθημαι (↑BR §137–139; BDF §98–100)

125a 1. **εἰμί** *to be* (root ἐσ-, ↑Lat. *esse* "to be"): ↑table next page.[30]

125b Except for εἶ, all (augmentless) ind. pres. forms are enclitic (↑6d; 6f). However, in certain cases the 3 sg. has the accent on the first syllable (ἔστιν): (1) when the verb is used with the meaning *to be there, to exist*; (2) after a οὐκ, ὡς, εἰ, καί, τοῦτ' or ἀλλ' in all its meanings, e.g.:

... πιστεῦσαι ... ὅτι **ἔστιν**.	... *believe that he exists.* (He 11:6)
οὐκ ἔστιν ἄλλος πλὴν αὐτοῦ·	*There is no other but him.* (Mk 12:32)
οὐκ ἔστιν ὧδε.	*He is not here.* (Mk 16:6)

Important compounds (on the accent ↑74a):

ἄπειμι *to be absent*	πάρειμι *to be present*
ἔνειμι *to be in* sth.	ἔξεστιν *it is right, it is possible*

ἔνεστιν *it is possible* (also ἔνι; in the NT, e.g. Jas 1:17 οὐκ ἔνι *there is not*)

125c 2. **εἶμι** in the (augmentless) ind. *I will go* etc. (root ει-, ι-), all the other forms being without future meaning (↑113.3). In the NT only compounds occur (without future meaning!); in the LXX there are a few simplex forms: ↑table next page.[30]

Accentuation of compounds (↑74a):

ἔξειμι *I go/come out*, but:	ἐπι**ώ**ν -ι**οῦ**σα -ι**ό**ν *following*

125d 3. **φημί** *to say* (root φη-, φᾰ-; ↑113.7): ↑table next page.[30]

Note that

(1) Except for the 2 sg. all (augmentless) ind. pres. forms are enclitic (↑6d).

(2) The NT uses 1 sg./3 sg./3 pl. (augmentless) ind. pres. and the 3 sg. ipf. (being used synonymously with aor. ind. εἶπεν *he/she said*).

(3) In the NT the ptc. of φημί may be replaced by that of φάσκω (φάσκων etc.).

(4) The LXX and Josephus also have an aorist I form: ἔφησεν *he/she said*.

125e 4. **κεῖμαι** *to lie, to be laid* (root κει-): ↑table next page.[30]

Note that

(1) This verb has the role of the pf. pass. of τίθημι *to place* (↑120.1).

(2) Only the ind. and imp. of compounds retract the accent (↑74), e.g.:

ἐπικ**εῖ**σθαι *to lie upon*	ἀντ**ί**κειμαι *I am opposed to*

125f 5. **κάθημαι** *to sit, to be seated* (root καθη-, καθησ-): ↑table next page.[30]

30 The forms not occurring in the NT and the LXX are indented and printed in a narrower font.

	εἰμί (st. ἐσ-) *to be*	εἶμι (st. εἰ/ἰ-) *to go*	φημί *to say*	κεῖμαι *to lie*	κάθημαι *to sit*
IND. PRES. sg. 1	εἰμί (↑10c)	εἶμι	φημί	κεῖμαι	κάθημαι
2	εἶ	εἶ	φῄς/φής	κεῖσαι	κάθῃ (CG:)-ησαι
3	ἐστίν	εἶσιν	φησίν	κεῖται	κάθηται
pl. 1	ἐσμέν	ἴμεν	φαμέν	κείμεθα	καθήμεθα
2	ἐστέ	ἴτε	φατέ	κεῖσθε	κάθησθε
3	εἰσίν	ἴᾱσιν	φᾱσίν	κεῖνται	κάθηνται
IPF. sg. 1	ἤμην CG ἦν/ἦ	ᾖειν/(CG also ᾖα)	ἔφην	ἐκείμην	ἐκαθήμην
2	ἦς CG ἦσθα	ᾖεις	ἔφησθα	ἔκεισο	ἐκάθησο
3	ἦν	ᾖει	ἔφη	ἔκειτο	ἐκάθητο
pl. 1	ἦμεν (CG)/ἤμεθα	ᾖμεν	ἔφαμεν	ἐκείμεθα	ἐκαθήμεθα
2	ἦτε CG also ἦστε	ᾖτε	ἔφατε	ἔκεισθε	ἐκάθησθε
3	ἦσαν	ᾖεσαν/(CG ᾖσαν)	ἔφασαν	ἔκειντο	ἐκάθηντο
SUBJ. sg. 1	ὦ (< ἐσω)	ἴω	φῶ		καθῶμαι
2	ᾖς	ἴῃς	φῇς		καθῇ
3	ᾖ	ἴῃ	φῇ		etc.
pl. 1	ὦμεν	ἴωμεν	φῶμεν		(↑117)
2	ἦτε	ἴητε	φῆτε		
3	ὦσιν	ἴωσιν	φῶσιν		
OPT. sg. 1	εἴην	ἴοιμι	φαίην		καθοίμην/
2	εἴης	ἴοις	φαίης		καθῄμην
3	εἴη	ἴοι	φαίη		etc.
pl. 1	εἴημεν	ἴοιμεν	φαίημεν		(↑117)
2	εἴητε	ἴοιτε	φαίητε		
3	εἴησαν(1)	ἴοιεν	φαίησαν(1)		
IMP. sg. 2	ἴσθι	ἴθι	φάθι	κεῖσο	κάθου/(CG)-ησο
3	ἔστω (CG)/ἤτω	ἴτω	φάτω	κείσθω	καθήσθω
pl. 2	ἔστε(2)	ἴτε	φάτε	κεῖσθε	κάθησθε
3	ἔστωσαν(3)	ἴτωσαν(3)	φάντων	κείσθων	καθήσθων
INF.	εἶναι	ἰέναι	φάναι	κεῖσθαι	καθῆσθαι
PTC.	ὤν ὄντος οὖσα οὔσης ὄν ὄντος	ἰών ἰόντος ἰοῦσα ἰούσης ἰόν ἰόντος	φᾱ́ς φάντος φᾶσα φᾱ́σης φᾰ́ν φάντος	κείμενος κειμένη κείμενον	καθήμενος καθημένη καθήμενον
FUT.	ἔσομαι etc., but 3 sg.: ἔ**σ**ται		φήσω etc.	κείσομαι etc.	καθήσομαι (CG καθεδοῦμαι) etc.

(1) CG usually εἶεν and φαῖεν, 1/2 pl. also εἶμεν/εἶτε and φαῖμεν/φαῖτε.
(2) In the NT this is replaced by the 2 pl. fut. ind. ἔσεσθε (e.g. Mt 5:48) or γίνεσθε (↑112.7).
(3) CG uses ἔστων instead of ἔστωσαν and ἴτωσαν as well as ἰόντων.

125g Important especially for CG (↑BR §138; BDF §358):

χρή (sc. ἐστίν)	*it is necessary* (in the NT only Jas 3:10, in the LXX Pr 25:27)		
	ipf.	χρῆν	(< *χρὴ ἦν), also ἔχρην
	inf.	χρῆναι	(< *χρὴ εἶναι)
	subj.	χρῇ	(< *χρὴ ᾖ)
	opt.	χρείη	(< *χρὴ εἴη)
	ptc. (uninflected)	(τὸ) χρεών	(< *χρὴ ὄν)

3 Syntax

The focus of Part 3 is on the grammatical side of the third level of text structures, i.e. on the grammatical side of propositions, called "sentences" (↑p. 12f). Sentences are the most important structural components of a text as text (↑298); one of the greatest challenges of text interpretation is to understand these and to infer from them the content communicated by the text as a whole. Hence this detailed treatment of the syntactic regularities governing Ancient Greek, particularly of those relevant to the study of the NT.

3.1 Basics of syntax

Definition and organization of syntax (↑BR p. 162; Bussmann s.v.; Crystal s.v.) 126

Syntax (< σύνταξις *putting together, arrangement*), as defined here, is the part of grammar that is devoted to the study of the regularities governing sentences. Within syntax three major subdivisions may be distinguished, which inter alia describe
a) the function that words and phrases may have within sentences (↑129–252),
b) how words and phrases are combined to form sentences (↑253–265), and
c) the types of sentences and combinations of sentences that occur (↑266–296).

Sentence and its constituents (↑Givón I: 8; DuG9: 782–791) 127

A **sentence** is made up of words; these are arranged in a particular way (sentence form) and typically express some information, i.e. (in traditional terms) "a complete thought" (sentence content, "proposition", used in communication to refer to a "situation" in the real world; ↑312a), especially a statement, a directive or a question; e.g.: 127a

αἱ ἀλώπεκες φωλεοὺς ἔχουσιν.	*The foxes have dens.* (Mt 8:20)
(sentence form)	(sentence content; here indicated by translation)

Note that in most cases, words in and of themselves merely convey concepts, i.e. they may be used to point to segments of the reality referred to (↑22a), e.g. ἀλώπηξ *fox*, φωλεός *den*, ἔχω *to have*. A sentence, a particular arrangement of words and word forms, is required to express information (suitable for use in linguistic communication), as shown in the above example.

The three types of information, i.e. statement, directive, and question, are the basis for the most important content-oriented subdivision of sentences into declarative, desiderative, and interrogative sentences/clauses. Alongside this there are also important form-oriented subdivisions, such as the distinction between independent (or main) and dependent (or subordinate) clauses (based on the syntactic usability of the sentence). For a detailed treatment of sentence/clause types ↑266ff.

127b 2. When studying sentences, the focus may be on word-classes and the grammatical form and interaction of sentence elements. In this case **phrases** are of central importance. Phrases, as the term is used here, are the words or word forms of a sentence; each phrase may be made up of one single word form or of a group of words. The grammatically dominant word of a phrase is termed **head**. On the basis of the word-class of the head (↑22) different types of phrases are distinguished, such as "noun phrases", "adverb phrases", "preposition phrases", etc. In Mt 2:15 (↑below) e.g. after the conjunction καί and the verb form ἦν there is an adverb phrase ("AdvP") ἐκεῖ (one single word), followed by the preposition phrase ("PpP") ἕως τῆς τελευτῆς Ἡρῴδου, made up of a (grammatically interdependent) group of word forms. τῆς τελευτῆς Ἡρῴδου is the noun phrase ("NP") governed by the preposition phrase and thus embedded in it; τελευτῆς is the head of the noun phrase; it has two expansions, τῆς, the article as a determiner, and Ἡρῴδου, an embedded (modifying) noun phrase:

καὶ ἦν ἐκεῖ ἕως τῆς τελευτῆς Ἡρῴδου·	*And he stayed there until the death of Herod.* (Mt 2:15)

When analysing sentences, the focus is regularly on the syntactic function that sentence elements have in expressing the information of the sentence, especially sentence elements termed **sentence constituents** (sometimes "clause constituents") in this grammar. Sentence constituents are discrete sentence elements that have distinct roles in conveying the information of sentences; typically, these are phrases, but in many cases also subordinate clauses. In principle sentence constituents may be placed anywhere in a sentence and so are movable (on word-order ↑128b). The most important sentence constituents are (for details ↑254ff):

a) The **subject** ("S"): it typically indicates the "theme"[1] (i.e. what the sentence or clause is "about") and, in sentences with a non-passive verb (↑64b), the agent performing the "action"; in most cases it is a noun phrase in the nominative, e.g. αἱ ἀλώπεκες *the foxes* in Mt 8:20 (↑127d); quite often, however, it is simply referred to by the personal ending of the verb form, as in ἦν *[he]* … in Mt 2:15 (↑above).

b) The **predicate**: it typically indicates the core information of the sentence (the core of its proposition; ↑127a), the "rheme",[1] i.e. what is being said about the theme (the "situation" the subject entity is said to be involved in; ↑22f[9]); it is mostly expressed by a verb phrase, its head (the predicate verb/the "predicator" ["P"]) being a verb form, (due to its "valency"; ↑254c) often accompanied by complements, e.g. ἦν ἐκεῖ *stayed there* (↑above) and φωλεοὺς ἔχουσιν *have dens* in Mt 8:20 (↑127d).

c) The **object** ("O"): a complement typically referring to the entity targeted (more or less directly) by the "action", mostly a noun phrase in the accusative, the "direct object" ("Od"), in non-passive sentences, usually indicating the "patient", i.e. the entity directly targeted by the "action" or experiencing it, e.g. φωλεούς *dens* in Mt 8:20 (↑127d). Less frequently objects are in the dative (the "indirect object"/"Oi" or "da-

1 Note that instead of "theme" and "rheme" many use the pair "topic" and "comment".

tive object"/"O^{dat}") or, more rarely still, in the genitive (the "genitive object"/"Og"); in many cases it is a preposition phrase (↑22i; the "prepositional object"/"Op").

d) The **adverbial** ("Advl"): this is a sentence constituent that modifies the information of the sentence by specifying the place, the time, the manner, or other circumstances of the "situation" the verb form refers to; it is often an adverb phrase (↑22h), e.g. ἐκεῖ *there* in Mt 2:15 (↑above), or a preposition phrase (↑22i) like ἕως τῆς τελευτῆς Ἡρῴδου *until the death of Herod* also in Mt 2:15.

e) Another important type of sentence element is the **attributive modifier** ("Attr"): this is not a sentence constituent itself, but part of one (mostly of a noun phrase), modifying it in some way (↑260); the attributive modifier is usually an adjective or a noun phrase, e.g. Ἡρῴδου *of Herod* in Mt 2:15 (↑above), a noun phrase modifying τῆς τελευτῆς *the death* (a noun phrase embedded in the PpP ἕως ... *until* ...).

3. Generally sentences have a **subject** (S; ↑255) and a **predicate** with at least a verb form as a predicator (P; ↑256), e.g. (due to its valency the sentence pattern is S+P): **127c**
ἐδάκρυσεν (P) ὁ Ἰησοῦς (S). *Jesus wept.* (Jn 11:35)

4. As predicators most verbs (i.e. their valency) also call for a complement in the form of an object (O; ↑254d) in well-formed sentences. By and large objects and other complements being part of the predicate are **obligatory sentence constituents**, i.e. without them the sentence would normally not be considered well-formed (↑254b), e.g. (due to the valency of the verb/predicator the sentence pattern is S+P+Od): **127d**
αἱ ἀλώπεκες (S) φωλεοὺς (Od) ἔχουσιν (P). *The foxes have dens.* (Mt 8:20)

The Od φωλεούς *dens* is dependent on the predicate verb ἔχουσιν *have*, i.e. the valency of ἔχω *to have* calls for a Od as its complement; it is an obligatory sentence constituent, normally indispensable for the sentence to be considered well-formed (or "grammatical").

5. The adverbial (↑254e) modifies the information conveyed by the subject and predicate (the predicator and its complements); it does so by indicating various types of circumstances (for details ↑259a–259o). In most cases adverbials are **optional sentence constituents**, i.e. they are not called for by the valency of the verb/predicator; without them the sentence would still be well-formed ("grammatical"). An optional adverbial is called (adverbial) **adjunct** in the present grammar (↑259b). In the following example (due to the valency of the verb/predicator) the sentence pattern is S+P+Od. The sentence constituent ἐκεῖ *there* indicating the place (as a local adverbial) is not obligatory from a grammatical point of view: if it were deleted, the sentence would still be well-formed (though an informational element would be missing, of course); so, it may be classified as a local adjunct ("LocA"): **127e**
ἐκεῖ (LocA) ἐσταύρωσαν (P/S) αὐτόν (Od). *There they crucified him.* (Lk 23:33)

There are also obligatory adverbials, i.e. adverbials called for by the valency of certain verbs; they are termed "(adverbial) complements". ἐκεῖ *there* in Mt 2:15 of 127b e.g. is a local complement ("LocC").

For details on the various types of sentence constituents and attributive modifiers, especially on the grammatical forms these may be expressed in ↑254–260.

128 Means of expressing syntactic relationships (↑BR §143–145; MB: S202–215)

The ways in which words, phrases, and sentences relate to one another syntactically are expressed by various means in Ancient Greek, the major ones being as follows:

128a 1. **Inflectional endings** (↑23ff; 64ff): these serve to mark the essential sentence constituents and attributive modifiers (↑127b–127e) and to indicate which words or phrases belong to one another in terms of concord (↑261–265).

128b 2. **Word-order**: being defined as the way that sentence constituents are arranged (on other elements ↑below section c), the word-order of Ancient Greek[2] (and Latin) was considerably freer than that of most modern European languages such as English and German, at least as far as grammatical constraints are concerned: in Ancient Greek (and Latin) a great number of inflectional endings were in use indicating the intended syntactic relationships to a very large extent (↑128a).

In English, e.g., the subject generally precedes the predicator (verb) in declarative sentences, the normal word-order being S-V-O (↑Carter §472), e.g. *He* (S) *loves* (P[V]) *football* (O). And in German the finite part of the predicator is always the second element in a declarative main clause (↑DuG9: 872f), e.g. *Auf den Bus* (O) ***hat*** (P[V]/1st [finite] part) *Otto* (S) *schon sehr lange* (TempA) ***gewartet*** (P[V]/2nd [non-finite] part) ("Otto has been waiting for the bus for a very long time already").

Ancient Greek, by contrast, did not seem to need any comparable grammatical constraints regarding the order of sentence constituents.

Note, however, that there is a clear distinction between (a) the "attributive" and (b) the "predicative" position (for details ↑136, for attributive modifiers in general ↑260), e.g. (the AdjP being either inside or outside the bracket formed by the article and the noun phrase it determines):

[ὁ ἀληθινὸς θεός**]** (inside: attributive)	*the true God* (1Jn 5:20)
ἀληθιναὶ [αἱ ὁδοί σου**]** (outside: predicative)	*Your ways are true.* (Re 15:3)

Though grammatically conditioned word-order is only of limited importance in Ancient Greek, the following regularities or tendencies should be taken into account:[3]

a) Word-order depends on a whole range of factors. Among these textgrammatical or **textpragmatic** factors seem to play a central role (↑298ff, especially 301c on

---

2 Inter alia ↑BR §144; MB: S209–215; CAGL: 148f; EAGLL s. v. "Word Order"; Boas-Rijksbaron: 702ff; Reiser 1984: 46–98; Porter/Pitts 2012: 312–346; word-order in general ↑Givón I: 233–284.

3 Note that (a) our knowledge regarding these matters is in many ways incomplete (MB: S209.2: "vielfach lückenhaft"); this is true of both CG and post-CG including NT Greek (for NT Greek the studies by Reiser 1984 and, more recently, by Pitts in Porter/Pitts 2012: 312–346, appear to be important, for CG now Boas-Rijksbaron: 702ff, especially 709–721); (b) there may be fairly significant differences regarding word-order between simple subordinate clauses and complex sentences containing various types of subordinate clauses and constructions; (c) what is being said here, applies mainly to prose; poetry (important in CG) appears to allow for much greater freedom (↑BR §144.7).

theme and rheme functions): sentence constituents may have their typical ("unmarked") position within a sentence (as perhaps suggested by frequency); for text-grammatical or textpragmatic reasons they may, however, be moved to a particular ("marked") position, often to the beginning of the sentence ("fronting"). "Emphases" expressed in this way (also ↑315 on other means) contribute to the coherence of a text, with regard either to what follows or (apparently more often) to what is before within the text in question ("cataphoric/catadeictic" and "anaphoric/anadeictic" relations; ↑346ff).

Other factors that appear to affect word-order are inter alia the length of phrases (the shorter ones tend to precede the longer ones), their semantic-communicative weight (↑MB: S213), and the concern for euphony (especially ease of pronunciation) and rhythm (↑BR §143f).

b) In Classical Greek literature the **predicator** (predicate verb) tends to have a middle position in main clauses (with a full lexical verb in the predicate role), the typical sequences being as follows:

- subject-**predicator**-object (the subject is given special weight),
- object-**predicator**-subject (the object is given special weight), or else quite often
- adverbial (especially if expressed by a subordinate clause)-**predicator**-subject-...

In directives and, if textpragmatically relevant (↑ above a; ↑CAGL: 148f), in other types of utterances, even in Classical Greek, the predicator may easily be fronted:

- **predicator**-...

In the **NT**, especially in **narratives**, the **predicator** is found in the **front position** much **more frequently** than in Classical Greek. This need not be regarded as a Semitism; it is best classified as a normal KG phenomenon, widely attested in popular and non-classicizing narrative literature of the Hellenistic period (a type of literature whose style is close to that of NT narratives; ↑Reiser 1984). E.g.:

Διετίας δὲ πληρωθείσης **ἔλαβεν** διάδοχον ὁ Φῆλιξ Πόρκιον Φῆστον.	*After two years had passed, Felix received a successor, Porcius Festus.* (Ac 24:27)

middle position (like CG): adverbial (with particle)-**predicator**-object-subject (-apposition).

ἔλαβεν οὖν τοὺς ἄρτους ὁ Ἰησοῦς.	*Then Jesus took the loaves.* (Jn 6:11)

front position: **predicator**(-particle)-object-subject, like in popular and non-classicizing narratives.

On the relevance of word-order regarding the **subject complement** and the subject it belongs to ↑135a; 256c/256d; 258a/258b.

c) As we look at the **position of word classes** rather than sentence constituents, we encounter words that can only occur in a fixed position within the syntactic unit they belong to (i.e. the sentence, clause, or phrase; ↑CAGL: 148):

- **Prepositives**: these are words that regularly occur at the beginning of the unit, i.e. the article (↑22d), relative and interrogative pronouns and adverbs (↑22c; 60–61), prepositions (↑22i), conjunctions (↑22j), negative particles (for details ↑243–249), and a number of mostly connective particles (↑252), e.g.:

τίνα (inter.) **τῶν** (art.) προφητῶν **οὐκ** (neg.) ἐδίωξαν **οἱ** (art.) πατέρες ὑμῶν; **καὶ** (conj.) ἀπέκτειναν **τοὺς** (art.) προκαταγγείλαντας **περὶ** (prep.) **τῆς** (art.) ἐλεύσεως **τοῦ** (art.) δικαίου, **οὗ** (rel.) νῦν ὑμεῖς προδόται **καὶ** (conj.) φονεῖς ἐγένεσθε	*Which one of the prophets did your fathers not persecute? And they killed those who had previously announced the coming of the Righteous One, whose betrayers and murderers you have now become* (Ac 7:52)

• **Postpositives**: these are words that regularly appear as the second word of a unit regardless of any elements that normally belong to each other (thus often leading to separation by "hyperbaton"; ↑292c), i.e. most of the remaining particles (↑252), as well as the enclitics (↑6b–6f), e.g.:

ὁ **γὰρ** ζυγός μου χρηστός.	*For my yoke is easy.* (Mt 11:30)

The particle γάρ separates the article from its noun phrase.

εἴ **τί** ἐστιν ἐν τῷ ἀνδρὶ ἄτοπον …	*If there is anything wrong about the man* … (Ac 25:5)

The (enclitic) indefinite pronoun τι, though belonging to ἄτοπον, appears immediately after εἰ.

Non-emphatic pronouns are often affected by this tendency, too, (↑BDF §473.1), in the NT inter alia as part of the following epistolary formula (Ro 1:7 et pass.):

χάρις **ὑμῖν** καὶ εἰρήνη …	*Grace and peace to you …!*

d) For emphasis the subject or (less frequently) the object may be placed before the subordinate clause it belongs to, a phenomenon called **prolepsis** or "anticipation" (↑292b), e.g.:

καταμάθετε **τὰ κρίνα τοῦ ἀγροῦ** πῶς αὐξάνουσιν.	*Consider the lilies of the fields how they grow. = See how the lilies of the field grow.* (Mt 6:28)

128c 3. **Function words** (as opposed to [lexical] content words), i.e. words that indicate the relationship between words or phrases, sentence constituents, and sentences:
a) inflected (declinable) word-classes: the article (↑22d; 130–136); demonstrative, relative, and certain interrogative pronouns (↑22c; 141–143);
b) uninflected word-classes: prepositions (↑22i; 184–186); "pronominal" adverbs (↑61a; 241a); conjunctions (↑22j; 251); particles (↑22k; 241b).

Noteworthy points regarding particles:

• the following words count as particles, too (↑22j[15]): (1) adverb-like function words such as οὐ and μή (negative particles/negations), also ἄν *"possibly"*, γε *"at least"*, οὖν *then/accordingly*, δή *now/indeed*; (2) "conjunctions" such as τε *and*, γάρ *for*; (3) sentence-like expressions (fossilized imperatives) such as ἰδού *lo/behold!*;

• they may belong to a whole sentence (e.g. ἄν) or to a sentence constituent (e.g. γε); moreover they may indicate that elements belong to one another (e.g. τε *and*) or that there is some logical relationship between them (e.g. ἤ – ἤ *either – or*), in this way functioning as "connectives" that help texts to be coherent (↑316ff);

• the bulk of them are postpositives (↑128b section c).

3.2 Words and phrases as sentence elements

3.2.1 Syntax of declinable words and their phrases

For a basic introduction to the categories of declinable words, i.e. gender, number, and case, ↑23. The functions of case forms and of preposition phrases are especially relevant to text interpretation; they are treated in some detail (↑146–187) subsequent to the sections on peculiarities of number use (↑129), the article (↑130–136), the adjectives (↑137–138), the pronouns (↑139–144), and the numerals (↑145). For questions of concord ↑261–265.

Peculiarities of number use (↑BDF §139–142; also ↑23b; Langslow: 126ff) 129

1. The **singular** of noun phrases (in NT as well as CG) sometimes (atypically) refers to more than one entity of a class of phenomena: 129a

a) The "generic" (or "collective") singular: a noun phrase in the singular is used in a generalizing way with reference to the entire class, e.g.:

Τί οὖν τὸ περισσὸν τοῦ Ἰουδαίου ...; *Then what advantage does the Jew have ...? = ... do the Jews have ...?* (Ro 3:1)

Paul does not refer to a particular Jew, but to Jews in general (↑132b): in v. 2 there is a plural verb form referring back to τοῦ Ἰουδαίου: ἐπιστεύθη**σαν** *they **were** entrusted* (notional concord; ↑265).

b) The "distributive" singular: a noun phrase in the singular refers to more than one entity, and each one of these is to be connected – in a distributive manner – with the various persons (or things) in view (as prompted by the presupposed world knowledge; ↑309d), e.g.:

ἄνδρες δύο ἐπέστησαν αὐταῖς ἐν ἐσθῆτι ἀστραπτούσῃ. *Two men in dazzling garments stood by them.* (Lk 24:4)

The sg. refers to more than one garment, each of them to be connected with the two men mentioned. Note that by means of renderings such as "clothes" (appearing only in a pl. form [a "plurale tantum"]) or "apparel" (a collective; ↑22a) this peculiarity can be hidden in a translation into English.

Generally speaking, however, Ancient Greek prefers to use the pl. in such cases (like Lat. and Engl.). In principle this is also true of NT Greek (note that in Ac 1:10 a comparable phrase has the pl., as does the Var. of Lk 24:4); but the distributive sg. does occur, probably facilitated by Ancient Hebrew usage (that has both constructions; ↑GKC §124r/s), typically so in Hebraizing complex prepositions with πρόσωπον *face* or χείρ *hand* (↑185c).

2. Unlike English, Ancient Greek sometimes uses the **plural** in the following ways: 129b

a) concrete (↑22a) plural nouns:

- referring to "right" and "left" or, in part, to cardinal points, e.g.:

ἐκ δεξιῶν ... ἐξ εὐωνύμων/ἐξ ἀριστερῶν *on the right ... on the left* (Mt 20:21/Mk 10:37)

ἀπὸ ἀνατολῶν (pl.) καὶ δυσμῶν (pl.) καὶ ἀπὸ βορρᾶ (sg.) καὶ νότου (sg.) *from the east and the west and from the north and the south.* (Lk 13:29)

- many of those referring to festivals (especially in CG; typically ntr. pl.), e. g.:

τὰ ἐγκαίνια	*festival of rededication* (Jn 10:22)
τὰ γενέσια (CG τὰ γενέθλια)	*birthday* (↑Mt 14:6/Mk 6:21)
τὰ ἀνθεστήρια "Anthesteria"	*Feast of Flowers* (in Athens; ↑OCD s. v.)

b) abstract (↑22a) nouns in the plural referring to concrete manifestations, e. g.:

θυμός → θυμοί	*rage* → *fits of rage* (2Cor 12:20; Ga 5:20)
πλεονεξία → πλεονεξίαι	*greed* → *greedy acts* (Mk 7:22)

3.2.1.1 Syntax of the article (↑22d on word-class, ↑24 on forms)

The article is first of all the **most important concomitant of the noun** (or nominalized expression), whenever possible, fully agreeing with it in gender, number, and case; as a prepositive it always stands at the beginning of the noun phrase (↑128b section c), serving as a determiner of the head in a noun phrase (it is one type of attributive modifier of the noun; ↑260b), in particular marking the entity referred to as sufficiently identified or "determined" ([intra]textually or extratextually; for further details ↑130–136; 347–348). Due especially to its intratextual (anaphoric and cataphoric) connections the article contributes significantly to the coherence of a text (↑346; 348a).
To some extent, the article also functions as a (pronominal) noun substitute (on this ↑131).
The following sections describe the regularities governing the use of the article (also ↑Wallace 1996: 206–254, for a very helpful treatment for anyone involved in NT exegesis, though at times the role of the article seems to be over-emphasized).

The following points are especially relevant to a correct interpretation of texts: (a) the differences in the use of the article between Ancient Greek and English (↑130); (b) the cases in which the noun may have to be regarded as "determined" though there is no article (↑133 and for a number of points 134–135); (c) the role of the article in telling the "attributive" from the "predicative" use of phrases (↑136).

130 Usage differences between Ancient Greek and English (↑BR §148f)

130a I. Cases in which **Ancient Greek does not** use the article, while English does:

1. Unlike English Ancient Greek has no indefinite article. Indefiniteness is generally implied when a noun phrase, that may have the article, is without one. The indefiniteness is sometimes made explicit by means of the indefinite pronoun (↑60; 144a), rarely (in the NT/LXX) by means of the numeral εἷς (↑63a; 145b), e. g.:

ἀνήρ τις ≈ ἀνήρ	*a man* (Ac 25:14; Jas 2:2)
rarely: εἷς γραμματεύς, ἄρχων εἷς	*a scribe, a ruler* (Mt 8:19; 9:18)

2. Frequently before a subject (or object) complement, with contextual factors indicating that the noun phrase refers to something definite (↑135), e. g.:

_ φῶς εἰμι τοῦ κόσμου. (SC)	*I am the light of the world.* (Jn 9:5; but with art. e. g. 8:12)
ὁ πατὴρ ἀπέσταλκεν τὸν υἱὸν _ σωτῆρα τοῦ κόσμου. (OC)	*The Father has sent his Son as/to be the Saviour of the world.* (1Jn 4:14)

3. Often before a noun phrase embedded in a preposition phrase (↑133a), e.g.:

παρὰ _ θάλασσαν — *by the sea* (Ac 10:6)
ἐκ _ νεκρῶν — *from the dead* (Ac 17:31)

4. Occasionally when a unique entity is referred to (↑133b), e.g.:

_ ἡλίου δὲ ἀνατείλαντος … — *But when the sun rose …* (Mt 13:6)

II. Cases in which **Ancient Greek uses** the article, while English does not: 130b

1. Regularly when certain pronouns occur as concomitants of the noun (↑131):

a) possessive pronouns (used as attributive modifiers; ↑57; 136a; 140a), e.g.:

ἡ ἐμὴ χαρά — *my joy* (2Cor 2:3)

b) demonstrative pronouns (used as attributive modifiers; ↑58; 136b; 141b), e.g.:

οὗτος **ὁ** τελώνης — *this tax-collector* (Lk 18:11)

c) typically the dual pronoun ἀμφότεροι *both* (as an attributive modifier; ↑61c; 63a; 136c; regularly so CG ἄμφω *both*, ἑκάτερος *each of two/either*, and frequently ἕκαστος *every/each [one]*), e.g.:

ἀμφότερα **τὰ** πλοῖα — *both boats* (Lk 5:7)

d) before noun phrases in apposition (↑260h) to personal pronouns ($1^{st}/2^{nd}$ pers.), e.g.:

ἱλάσθητί μοι **τῷ** ἁμαρτωλῷ — *be merciful to me a sinner* (Lk 18:13)

↑also Mk 7:6; Jn 6:70; Ac 4:11; Ro 15:1; 1Cor 4:9; 8:10; Ga 6:1; Eph 1:12.19; 2:11.13; 3:1; Php 3:3; 1Th 2:10; 1Jn 5:13; Re 2:24.

e) before a noun phrase referring to a possessed item after a relative pronoun in the possessive genitive (↑159; also ↑59; 142e), e.g.:

ἦν τις βασιλικὸς οὗ **ὁ** υἱὸς ἠσθένει … (↑French *dont* ***le*** *fils*) — *… there was an official whose son was ill* (Jn 4:46)

2. Proper names (↑134):

a) before names of persons that the speaker/writer intends to mark as known (either because of an earlier mention or as generally known; ↑134a; 348a), e.g.:

ἀπεκρίθη αὐτοῖς **ὁ** Ἰωάννης … — *John answered them …* (Jn 1:26)

Note that Hebrew agrees with English here, but e.g. Swiss German (not High German) with Greek:

De *Johannes hät ene die Antwort ggä …* — *wayya'an 'ōṯām _ Yôḥānān …* (↑Delitzsch)

b) usually before names of regions or countries, rarely of towns or villages (↑134c).

3. Before noun phrases in the nominative used as vocatives (KG; ↑148b), e.g.:

δίκαιαι καὶ ἀληθιναὶ αἱ ὁδοί σου, **ὁ** βασιλεὺς τῶν ἐθνῶν. — *Just and true are your ways, O King of the nations.* (Re 15:3)

The pronominal use of the article (↑BR §146; BDF §249–251) 131

The Ancient Greek article originally had the role of a demonstrative pronoun (↑141e). This role has survived in the following pronominal uses: the article serves as a **noun substitute**, sharing several functions with demonstrative or personal pronouns when these are used as sentence constituents (mainly as subjects or objects; ↑54; 139c; 141e; 255b; 257b; also 146ff/184ff on cases and prepositions):

1. Used in pairs (referring to known or unknown entities), at times also in combinations with more than two elements, e.g.:

ὁ μέν – ὁ δέ	*one – another, one – the other* (1Cor 7:7; Ga 4:23)
οἱ μέν – οἱ δέ	*some – others/some, these – those others* (Ac 14:4; 17:32; 28:24; Php 1:16f)
οἱ μέν – οἱ δέ (– οἱ δέ etc.)	*some – others (– others)* (↑Eph 4:11)

Phrases with a closely similar use: ὁ μὲν ἕτερος – ὁ δ' ἕτερος; in the NT also (ὁ) εἷς – (ὁ) ἕτερος/εἷς, Mt 6:24; 20:21; Lk 18:10 (BDF §247.3), inter alia also οἱ μέν – ἄλλοι δέ, τινές – οἱ δέ Mt 16:14; Ac 17:18 (BDF §250; also ↑144a).

2. Without a subsequent second element (NT only in Ac), e.g.:

οἱ μὲν (οὖν ἐπορεύοντο…)	*So they (left …)* (Ac 5:41)

3. The following phrase-types frequently occur (in the NT only in the Gospels and in Ac), pointing to entities mentioned earlier in the text (anaphoric/anadeictic); e.g.:

ὁ δέ, οἱ δέ	*but he, but they* (i.e. … *the latter one/ones*)

Note that often δέ is used without its slightly adversative force (↑252.12), e.g.:

ὁ δὲ εἶπεν …	*(But/And) he said* … (Mt 12:3)
ἡ δὲ εἶπεν …	*(But/And) she said* … (Mk 6:24)
οἱ δὲ εἶπαν …	*(But/And) they said* … (Lk 5:33)

The (specific) relative pronoun is frequently used analogously (especially in KG/NT; ↑54; 142h; the relative pronoun, too, used to have a demonstrative role), e.g.:

ὅς μέν – ὅς δέ	*one – the other:*
ἐσταύρωσαν … ὃν μὲν ἐκ δεξιῶν ὃν δὲ ἐξ ἀριστερῶν	*they crucified … one on his right, the other on his left.* (Lk 23:33)

↑also Mt 25:15; Ro 14:5; 2Cor 2:16; 2Tm 2:20.

132 Standard use of the article (↑BR §147; BDF §252; 263–267; Z §165–171; Wallace: 207–254)

The standard use of the Ancient Greek article agrees by and large with the use of the English definite article.[4] It makes clear that this person/thing or these persons/things are being referred to, and not just such and such; it marks the entity/entities referred to by the noun (phrase) as sufficiently identified or "determined" (definite). It does so by pointing to relevant information given inside the text (intratextually) found either earlier (anaphoric/anadeictic use) or later (cataphoric/catadeictic use)

4 ↑Carter §539: "[…] determiner […] used with a noun to define and specify entities projected as known to speaker/writer and listener/reader." Unlike the English definite article, the Ancient Greek article, of course, agrees (whenever possible) with the noun it determines in gender, number, and case.

in the text; in many cases it points to something outside the text (extratextually), often to information connected with the presupposed world knowledge. The standard use of the article may be divided into three subcategories:
(1) individualizing use (↑132a/132c);
(2) generic use (↑132b);
(3) nominalizing use (↑132d).

1. The **individualizing** article points to a particular entity or group of entities, 132a

a) identified earlier in the text (anaphoric/anadeictic [≈ demonstrative] use), e.g.:

λαβὼν **τοὺς** πέντε ἄρτους καὶ **τοὺς** δύο ἰχθύας …	*Taking the five loaves and the two fish …* ≈ *… these five … these two …* (Mk 6:41)

The articles point back to the "five loaves" and the "two fish" introduced in v. 38.

b) identified later in the text (cataphoric/catadeictic [≈ demonstrative] use), e.g.:

… καὶ κρατεῖτε **τὰς** παραδόσεις ἃς ἐδιδάχθητε …	*… and hold fast to the* (≈ *those*) *traditions that you were taught …* (2Th 2:15)

The article points forward to the information given in the relative clause ἃς … *that …*

c) outside the text in the real world referred to, e.g.:

πλανᾶσθε μὴ εἰδότες **τὰς** γραφάς …	*You are in error because you do not know the Scriptures …* (Mt 22:29)

αἱ γραφαί/ἡ γραφή is one NT way of referring to the Jewish Bible/the OT (↑presupposed world knowledge); ↑inter alia Jn 7:38; Mt 26:54; also BDAG s.v.

… ἐν **τῷ** ἱερῷ ἐκαθεζόμην διδάσκων	*… I sat in the temple teaching* (Mt 26:55)

τὸ ἱερόν in the NT regularly refers to the temple in Jerusalem (↑presupposed world knowledge).

Note that the Ancient Greek article (again in view of the presupposed world knowledge) may be used with a possessive force (in ways similar to possessive pronouns or personal pronouns in the possessive genitive; ↑57; 140d), though in KG/NT far less frequently than in CG, e.g.:

… ἔδειξεν **τὰς** χεῖρας καὶ **τὴν** πλευρὰν αὐτοῖς.	*… he showed them his hands and his side.* (Jn 20:20)
ὁ δὲ υἱὸς τοῦ ἀνθρώπου οὐκ ἔχει ποῦ **τὴν** κεφαλὴν κλίνῃ.	*But the Son of Man has nowhere to lay his head.* (Lk 9:58)
… οὔτε **τῷ** πατρὶ οὔτε **τῷ** ἀδελφῷ ἐπεκοινώσω …	*but you consulted neither with your father nor with your brother …* (Plato, Protagoras 313b/c)

2. One may speak of a **generic** use of the article, 132b

a) when it determines a noun phrase in the singular, in a generalizing way referring to an entire class of phenomena rather than to one particular entity (this is an instance of the generic singular; ↑129a), e.g.:

ἄξιος **ὁ** ἐργάτης τοῦ μισθοῦ αὐτοῦ.	*The worker deserves his pay* (≈ *Those who work deserve their pay*) (1Tm 5:18)

also when the head of the phrase is a nominalized participle (↑237; also 135). e.g.:

ὁ πιστεύων εἰς τὸν υἱὸν ἔχει ζωὴν αἰώνιον.	*The one who/Everyone who/Whoever believes in the Son has eternal life.* (Jn 3:36)
… **ὁ** διψῶν ἐρχέσθω …	… *let the one who/let anyone who is thirsty come* … (Re 22:17)

b) when it determines a noun phrase in the plural, in a generalizing way referring to a whole class rather than simply a plurality of entities, e.g.:

οἱ Ἰουδαῖοι	*the Jews* (Jn 1:19)
οἱ Φαρισαῖοι	*the Pharisees* (Mt 23:2)
οἱ τελῶναι	*the tax collectors* (Mt 5:46)

Note that such generic reference (also called "generic quantification") may be expressed in a variety of ways: not only by singular and plural noun phrases with the article, as exemplified above, but also by noun phrases without the article, generic reference being inferable from the context. By quantifiers such as πᾶς *every*/πάντες *all* this may be made more explicit. E.g.:

οὐκ ἔστιν _ δοῦλος μείζων τοῦ κυρίου αὐτοῦ.	*A servant is not greater than his master (≈ Servants are not greater than their master).*(Jn 15:20)
_ Δούλους ἰδίοις δεσπόταις ὑποτάσσεσθαι …	*Slaves are to be subject to their masters* … (Tt 2:9)
πᾶς γὰρ _ οἶκος κατασκευάζεται ὑπό τινος	*For every house is built by someone.* (He 3:4)
… **πᾶς ὁ** πιστεύων εἰς αὐτόν …	… *everyone who believes in him* … (Jn 3:16)
πάντες δὲ **οἱ** θέλοντες εὐσεβῶς ζῆν …	*but all who want to live godly lives* … (2Tm 3:12)
ἐν ᾧ εἰσιν **πάντες οἱ** θησαυροί … ἀπόκρυφοι.	*in whom are hidden all the treasures* … (Col 2:3)

132c Noteworthy points on the use of the article in **combinations of two coordinated noun phrases**:

(1) If the article is repeated in the second noun phrase, the two noun phrases refer to two distinguishable entities (or groups of entities). If, however, only the first noun phrase has the article, the two entities (or groups of entities) are combined into some kind of conceptual unity; in certain cases they may even be equated (↑BDF §276): a case of "coreference" (the two have the same reference; ↑350); e.g.:

Ἀνέστη τε **ὁ** βασιλεὺς καὶ **ὁ** ἡγεμών …	*The king and the governor* … *rose* … (Ac 26:30)
ἔξελθε εἰς **τὰς** ὁδοὺς καὶ φραγμούς.	*Go out to the roads and country lanes.* (Lk 14:23)

↑also 1Th 1:7f (Z §184).

(2) "Granville Sharp's Rule": in Ancient Greek the combination art.+sg.-NP+ καί+sg.-NP (only the first sg.-NP having the article!) implies that the two noun phrases refer to one and the same person. Note, however, that this rule applies only if (a) neither noun phrase refers to a non-person, (b) neither is in the plural, and (c) neither is a personal name, e.g.:

… **ὁ** υἱὸς τῆς Μαρίας **καὶ** ἀδελφὸς Ἰακώβου …;	*(Is not this the carpenter,) the son of Mary and brother of James …?* (Mk 6:3)

One and the same person (Jesus, the carpenter) is referred to; analogously in the following example:

κατανοήσατε **τὸν** ἀπόστολον **καὶ** ἀρχιερέα τῆς ὁμολογίας ἡμῶν Ἰησοῦν.	*Fix your thoughts on Jesus, the apostle and high priest of our confession.* (He 3:1)

Especially ↑Wallace 1996: 270–290, and Wallace 2009 for a thorough study and presentation of this rule, a rule frequently misunderstood and overrated by exegetes and theologians.

132d 3. The **nominalizing** use of the article: in Ancient Greek all kinds of different words, phrases, and extended expressions could assume the role of the head of a noun phrase, i.e. could as it were turn into a noun or be "nominalized" (going beyond what English usage allows). This is typically done with the article being placed before the phrase or the extended expression in question.[5] As the article is declinable, it indicates (sometimes as the only element of the phrase) not only the case, thus the syntactic role of the phrase, but also the number and notably the gender of the entities referred to (also ↑136 on the article of attributive modifiers). These examples will illustrate the most important nominalizing uses of the article:

a) adjective phrases (↑137d), e.g.:

ὁ πτωχός	*the poor man/person* (↑Lk 16:22)
οἱ πτωχοί	*the poor (persons)* (↑Ga 2:10)
ὁ πλούσιος	*the rich man/person* (Lk 16:22)
οἱ πλούσιοι	*the rich (persons)* (↑1Tm 6:17)
τὸ μωρόν	*what is foolish* = *foolishness* (1Cor 1:25)
τὰ μωρά	*the foolish things* (1Cor 1:27)

In Ancient Greek nominalized phrases in the ntr. sg. typically refer to abstract concepts, so τὸ μωρόν *what is foolish = (the) foolishness*, those in the ntr. pl. typically to concrete "things", i.e. manifestations of the abstract concept in question, so τὰ μωρά *the foolish things* (↑Menge-Thierfelder-Wiesner: 97; Humbert §71). In the NT there are a fair number both of ntr. sg. and ntr. pl. instances; still only in a few cases contrasts between the two constructions seem exegetically relevant.

The abstract use of the ntr. sg. (adj. or ptc. [↑b)]) at times refers (in NT as in CG) to persons: in such cases the focus is not on an individual, but on the quality expressed (↑BDF §138.1), e.g.:

τὸ γεγεννημένον ἐκ τῆς σαρκὸς σάρξ ἐστιν.	*That which is born of the flesh is flesh ≈ Those born by human beings are human beings.* (Jn 3:6)

↑also Jn 6:37; 17:2; 1Jn 5:4.

b) participle phrases (↑237), e.g.:

οἱ κατοικοῦντες	*the inhabitants* (Ac 2:9)
τὰ ὑπάρχοντα	*the possessions* (↑Mt 19:21)

c) infinitive/ACI phrases (↑223ff), e.g.:

τὸ … θέλειν … **τὸ** δὲ κατεργάζεσθαι …	… *the desire … but the doing* … (Ro 7:18)

d) adverb phrases (↑241c), e.g.:

τὸ νῦν, e.g. in ἀπὸ **τοῦ** νῦν	*this time*, e.g. *from this time on* (Lk 1:48)
τὸ πέραν	*the other side (of the lake)* (Mt 8:18)
ὁ πλησίον	*the neighbour* (↑Ro 15:2)

e) preposition phrases (↑183c), e.g.:

οἱ μετ᾽ αὐτοῦ	*those with him/his companions* (Mt 12:3)
τὰ κατ᾽ ἐμέ	*my circumstances/situation* (Php 1:12)

---

5 At times, however, adjectives or participles are nominalized without the article (when indefiniteness is involved; ↑137d; 237b): due to the inflectional endings of such expressions their syntactical role is sufficiently clear even without the article, not so e.g. in the case of articular infinitives (↑223) and adverbs (↑132d[d]), which usually require the article for a correct interpretation of their role. – Also ↑361–362 for nominalization by way of word-formation.

f) particles (↑252), e.g.:

τὸ ναί … **τὸ** οὔ	*the* (*my*) *yes* … *the* (*my*) *no* (2Cor 1:17)

g) numerals (↑145), e.g.:

οἱ δώδεκα	*the twelve* (Lk 9:12 et pass.)

h) a clause, sentence (e.g. ↑273b), or quotation, e.g.:

τὸ εἰ δύνῃ …	*the [word] "If you can"* (Mk 9:23)
ἐν **τῷ**· ἀγαπήσεις τὸν πλησίον σου ὡς σεαυτόν	*in the [commandment]: "You shall love your neighbour as yourself"* (Ga 5:14)

i) a genitive noun phrase (governed by the nominalizing article; ↑159b/159c), e.g.:

οἱ τοῦ Χριστοῦ	*those who belong to Christ* (1Cor 15:23)
τὰ τοῦ θεοῦ	*the things/concerns of God* (Mt 16:23)
τὰ Καίσαρος	*the things that are Caesar's* (Mt 22:21)

j) Note that a few adjectives, when nominalized by the article, may vary in meaning, e.g. (↑51a):

πολλοί *many*	οἱ πολλοί (apart from *the many* also:) *the great majority, most people* (Mt 24:12)
πλείονες *in larger numbers*	οἱ πλείονες *the majority/most* (1Cor 15:6)
πλεῖστοι *in largest numbers, a great many*	οἱ πλεῖστοι *the majority/most* (Ac 19:32 Var.)

133 Definiteness without the article (↑BR §149.2–5; BDF §252–259; Z §171–183)

I. Certain types of phrases lacking the article may still refer to something definite:

133a 1. This often applies to noun phrases embedded in **preposition** phrases (↑184–186), in CG mainly to phrases used as adverbs, in KG/NT, however, more generally, e.g.:

ἀπ' _ ἀρχῆς	*from the beginning* (1Jn 2:7)
ἐκ _ νεκρῶν	*from the dead* (Ac 17:31)
ἐκ _ χειρὸς ἐχθρῶν	*from the hand of our enemies* (Lk 1:74)
παρὰ _ πατρός	*from the Father* (Jn 1:14)
ὑπὲρ _ ἁγίων	*for the saints* (Ro 8:27)
πρὸς _ κέντρα	*against the goads* (Ac 26:14)

133b 2. Occasionally this is the case with phrases referring to a **unique entity**, e.g.:

δόξα _ ἡλίου … δόξα _ σελήνης …	*one glory of the sun … another glory of the moon …* (1Cor 15:41)
… θεὸς ἦν ἐν Χριστῷ _ κόσμον καταλλάσσων ἑαυτῷ …	*… in Christ God was reconciling the world to himself …* (2Cor 5:19)

133c 3. Quite regularly **abstract** nouns are used along these lines (though Ancient Greek generally agrees with English here, English seems somewhat more restrictive), occasionally also some other nouns (apparently used with an abstract force), e.g.:

_ ἀγάπη καλύπτει πλῆθος ἁμαρτιῶν — *love covers a multitude of sins* (1Pe 4:8)
… _ ἀγάπην δὲ μὴ ἔχω … — *… but I do not have love …* (1Cor 13:1–3)

But with anaphoric/anadeictic article (↑133a):

Ἡ ἀγάπη μακροθυμεῖ … — *Love is patient …* or (more accurately) *The love just referred to is patient …* (1Cor 13:4)

_ νόμον οὖν καταργοῦμεν διὰ τῆς πίστεως; μὴ γένοιτο· ἀλλὰ _ νόμον ἱστάνομεν. — *Do we then nullify the law through this faith? Not at all! Rather we uphold the law.* (Ro 3:31)

A further use, perhaps best mentioned here, is that of **book titles** typically having no article, e.g.:

_ Ἀρχὴ τοῦ εὐαγγελίου … — *The beginning of the good news …* (Mk 1:1)
_ Ἀποκάλυψις Ἰησοῦ Χριστοῦ … — *The revelation from Jesus Christ …* (Re 1:1)

4. Sometimes this use is found in combinations of phrases reflecting a **Hebrew construct chain** (where the governing ["construct"] noun never has the article; ↑GKC §125a; Z §182; also ↑136e/136f): 133d

NP_1 (in the "construct": **without article**) + determined NP_2 (in the genitive), e.g.:

_δόξα κυρίου = כְּבוֹד יהוה *kəḇôḏ Yhwh* — *the glory of the Lord* (Lk 2:9; ↑Eze 3:23)

Yhwh "Yahweh" is a Hebrew personal name; it is without the article because Hebrew personal names never have the article; based on this use, its LXX substitute κύριος has no article either.

5. Such is regularly the case, also in the following type of phrase combination: 133e

NP_1 (without article) + **NP_2** (in the genitive; **without article** because NP_1 has none), e.g.:

λόγος _ θεοῦ — *the word of God* (1Th 2:13)

↑But: ὁ λόγος τοῦ κυρίου (both have the article) — *the word of the Lord* (1Th 1:8)

II. In the NT the article with the nouns **θεός** *god/God* and **κύριος** *lord/Lord* (↑BDF §254) makes clear that the phrase is meant to refer to the one God/Lord, who revealed himself in Jesus Christ and previously to Israel. However, even with such a reference these nouns may be without the article in the following cases: 133f

- frequently when embedded in a preposition phrase (↑133a), e.g.:

ἐν _ θεῷ / ἐκ _ θεοῦ / ὑπὸ _ θεοῦ / παρὰ _ θεοῦ etc.

- in the genitive, governed by a noun phrase without article (↑133e), e.g.:

ῥῆμα _ θεοῦ — *the word of God* (Lk 3:2)
δικαιοσύνη _ θεοῦ — *the righteousness of God* (2Cor 5:21)

Further noteworthy points:

(1) In the NT the combination κύριος ὁ θεός is mostly found in OT quotations, e.g. Mt 4:7.10.

(2) ὁ κύριος usually refers to Jesus as the exalted Lord. However, even with such a reference there may be no article when the noun is embedded in a preposition phrase, e.g. πρὸς _ κύριον *to the Lord* (2Cor 3:16).

(3) τὸ ἅγιον πνεῦμα, τὸ ἅγιον τὸ πνεῦμα, and ἅγιον πνεῦμα in the NT are best translated as *the Holy Spirit* (no semantic differences seem discernible) ↑BDAG sub πνεῦμα 5cα/β; also BDF §257.2.

133g Important points relevant to **text interpretation** (↑Z §176ff):

1. It is not unusual for an abstract noun to have no article; however, when it does have one, this generally suggests that the article was used for a specific purpose and that the determination thus expressed is exegetically significant (↑133c), e.g. in Jn 14:6.

2. When concrete nouns are used without the article, this may be significant: indefiniteness is generally indicated (↑130a). However, in the following cases something definite may be referred to, even though the NP is without the article:
a) if the NP is used as a subject complement or an object complement (↑135a/135c; 258a/258b);
b) if it is a personal name (in the NT; ↑134b);
c) if it is embedded in a preposition phrase (↑133a);
d) if it is the first (the governing) NP within a phrase combination reflecting the Hebrew construct chain (in NT/LXX Greek; ↑133d);
e) if it is the second NP in the genitive after a NP that is without the article (↑133e).

134 The article and proper names (↑BR §148.1; BDF §260–262; 254)

I. **Names of persons** (↑132a on the individualizing article):

134a 1. In Ancient Greek the following general rule applies:

The article is used with names of persons that the speaker/writer intends to mark as known, either because of an earlier mention in the text or as generally known (an appositional noun phrase following the name has the article; ↑260h), otherwise the article is not used. E.g.:

μετά … ῥήτορος _ Τερτύλλου τινός	*with … a lawyer, a certain Tertullus* (Ac 24:1)

Tertullus is mentioned for the first time here: there is no article.

ἤρξατο κατηγορεῖν **ὁ** Τέρτυλλος	*Tertullus began to accuse him* (Ac 24:2)

The name has the article, because Tertullus was mentioned earlier in the text: ὁ Τέρτυλλος "the aforementioned Tertullus" or *the Tertullus just mentioned.*

ὁ Μιχαὴλ καὶ οἱ ἄγγελοι αὐτοῦ …	*Michael and his angels …* (Re 12:7)

The Michael is referred to, the one assumed as generally known (↑presupposed world knowledge).

134b 2. In the NT the article is not used in any consistent way with names of persons (in CG the "rule" was not strictly followed either). Frequently there is no article where the above rule would make us expect one. No doubt this tendency can be explained by the Semitic background influencing NT usage, either directly or (via LXX) indirectly: personal names never had the article in Ancient Hebrew nor the determination ending in Ancient Aramaic (↑GKC §125c; Segert: 334).

In the Synoptic gospels the name "Jesus" nearly always has the article: ὁ Ἰησοῦς, whereas in John it is frequently without. "Paul" is mostly written as ὁ Παῦλος; "Peter", however, as ὁ Πέτρος or Πέτρος (about half the instances each).

Uninflected names, notably Semitic ones (↑17), which are normally without the article, sometimes take one making clear in what case it is intended to be, e.g.:

ἐγεῖραι τέκνα **τῷ** Ἀβραάμ	*to raise up children for Abraham* (Mt 3:9)

II. **Geographical** and **ethnographic** names: 134c

1. The names of geographical regions and countries (↑23a) typically have the article, as they go back to adjectives modifying the nouns χώρα *land/country* or γῆ *earth/land* (ellipsis; ↑260c; 293c; 361f), e.g.:

ἡ Ἰουδαία	*Judea* (↑Mt 2:22)
ἡ Γαλιλαία	*Galilee* (↑Mt 2:22)
ἡ Ἀσία	*Asia* (the Roman province; ↑Ac 16:6)

2. The names of rivers (↑23a) have the article, e.g.:

ὁ Ἰορδάνης	*the Jordan* (↑Lk 4:1)
ὁ Εὐφράτης	*the Euphrates* (↑Jr 28:63 LXX; Re 16:12)

3. Names of ethnic or cultural groups occur with and without the article, e.g.:

(οἱ) Ἰουδαῖοι — *the Jews*

(in the Gospels and Acts [especially Jn] with the article, in Paul usually without)

(οἱ) Ἕλληνες — *the Greeks* (in the NT rarely with article)

4. Place names (↑23a) in the majority of instances are without the article, e.g.:

(τὰ) Ἱεροσόλυμα, (ἡ) Ἰερουσαλήμ	*Jerusalem*
(ἡ) Καφαρναούμ	*Capernaum* (hardly ever with the article)

Article use with complements and adverbials (↑BR §149.1; BDF §273; Z §172–175) 135

I. Subject and object **complements** that have an identifying role (SC^{id}/OC^{id}) with either the subject/object entity being equated (more or less extensively) with another entity or being classified (↑258a/256c/256d): 135a

1. Generally speaking, such a complement is without the article, regardless of whether it is intended to classify or to equate (↑132b; which of these is intended, can be inferred from the linguistic and non-linguistic context; ↑308ff), e.g.:

οὐκοῦν **βασιλεὺς** (SC^{id}) εἶ σύ; — *So, you are a king?* (Jn 18:37)

The question is about classifying the subject entity.

εἰ ὁ θεὸς **πατὴρ ὑμῶν** (SC^{id}) ἦν … — *If God were your father …* (Jn 8:42)

This clause is about equating the subject entity with another entity.
↑also Jn 9:5; 10:36.

εἰ οὖν με ἔχεις **κοινωνόν** (OC^{id}) … — *So, if you consider me your partner …* (Phm 17)

This clause is about classifying the object entity.

… σὺ ἄνθρωπος ὢν ποιεῖς σεαυτὸν **θεόν** (OC^{id}). — *… you, only a human being, are making yourself God.* (Jn 10:33)

This statement is about equating the object entity with another entity.

2. Sometimes, however, the complement does have the article, in which case there is typically an emphasis on the equivalence of the two entities involved (↑the individualizing article; ↑132a), i.e.

a) when the speaker/writer presupposes that the complement entity is generally known (↑348a), e.g.:

ὁ προφήτης (SC^{id}) εἶ σύ; *Are you the Prophet?* (Jn 1:21)

The question is about the prophet generally known and expected on the basis of Dt 18:15. ↑also Mk 6:3.

b) when the complement is meant to refer to a unique entity, e.g.:

σὺ εἶ **ὁ χριστὸς ὁ υἱὸς τοῦ θεοῦ τοῦ ζῶντος** (SC^{id}). *You are the Messiah, the Son of the living God!* (Mt 16:16)

For this very reason the subject complement has the article in almost all the self-testimonies of Jesus in the Gospel of John, e.g.:

ἐγώ εἰμι **ὁ ἄρτος τῆς ζωῆς** (SC^{id}). *I am the bread of life.* (Jn 6:35)
ἐγώ εἰμι **τὸ φῶς τοῦ κόσμου** (SC^{id}). *I am the light of the world.* (Jn 8:12)

c) in definitions where the subject and its complement are expressly said to have the same reference, e.g.:

ἡ ἁμαρτία ἐστὶν **ἡ ἀνομία** (SC^{id}). *Sin is lawlessness.* (1Jn 3:4)

3. Word-order appears to be a relevant factor, too (↑BDF §273):

a) If the complement phrase with virtually equating function comes after the subject phrase (which is the standard word-order), it has the article in the great majority of NT instances:

S+(P)+**art.+SC^{id}/NP** (↑128b), e.g.:

ἐγώ (S) εἰμι (P) **τὸ φῶς τοῦ κόσμου** (SC^{id}). *I am the light of the world.* (Jn 8:12)

b) However, if it precedes the subject phrase (which is the less frequent word-order), it typically does not have the article:

(no art.)+SC^{id}/NP+(P)+S, e.g.:

… _ **φῶς** (SC^{id}) εἰμι (P/S) **τοῦ κόσμου** (attributive modifier of SC^{id}). … *I am the light of the world.* (Jn 9:5)

Note that when this latter pattern is used, it does not necessarily follow that the two entities are meant to be equated; often only classification is involved (the linguistic and non-linguistic context shows what is actually intended; ↑135a[1]).

135b II. **Adjective** and **participle** phrases used as **adverbials** (↑259c) never have the article:

1. adjective phrases used as adverbials (↑137e), e.g.:

ὁ ἄλλος μαθητής … ἦλθεν _ **πρῶτος** εἰς τὸ μνημεῖον. *The other disciple … came to the tomb first.* (Jn 20:4)

2. participle phrases used as adverbials (or as predicative elements; ↑229b), e.g.:

_ **ἀκούσας** δὲ ὁ βασιλεύς … *And when the king heard …* (Mt 2:3)

135c Important points relevant to **text interpretation**:

1. Sometimes it is hard to tell which of two noun phrases in the nominative is the **subject** and which should be considered its complement (SC^{id}). In such a case the following points may be helpful:

a) Typically, subject phrases are (notionally) definite, complements (SC^{id}) are not or less "strongly" so. A variety of different types of expressions may be regarded as definite (i.e. the person who uses such expressions presupposes that by them it becomes sufficiently clear what is being referred to). The "strength" of their definiteness may, however, vary. Bearing this in mind, four types of expressions may be distinguished (in decreasing order of "strength"; 1–3 are as it were inherently definite). Note that when assigning the subject role to a noun phrase, the "stronger" types have priority over the "weaker" ones (e.g. [1] over [2] in 1Cor 6:11, [2] over [3] in Mt 14:2 and [3] over [4] in 1Jn 5:5):

(1) Personal pronouns (**S**) or personal endings of the finite verb (P/**S**), e.g.:

ὑμεῖς (**S**) δὲ γένος ἐκλεκτόν (SC^{id}).	*But you are a/the chosen race.* (1Pe 2:9)
θεοῦ οἰκοδομή (SC^{id}) ἐστε (P/**S**).	*You are God's building.* (1Cor 3:9)

(2) Demonstrative pronouns (sometimes also relative pronouns) as noun substitutes, e.g.:

Οὗτός (**S**) ἐστιν ὁ μαθητὴς ὁ … (SC^{id})	*This is the disciple who …* (Jn 21:24)
… ἅ (**S**) ἐστιν σκιά (SC^{id}) …	*… these are a shadow …* (Col 2:17)
ταῦτα (SC^{id}) … ἦτε (P/**S**[1]).	*… you used to be that.* (1Cor 6:11)

(3) Proper names (with or without the article), e.g.:

ὁ πατὴρ ἡμῶν (SC^{id}) Ἀβραάμ (**S**) ἐστιν.	*Abraham is our father.* (Jn 8:39)
σὺ (**S**[1]) εἶ Πέτρος (SC^{id}).	*You are Peter.* (Mt 16:18)
οὗτός (**S**[2]) ἐστιν Ἰωάννης ὁ βαπτιστής (SC^{id}).	*This is John the Baptist.* (Mt 14:2)

(4) Common nouns (↑22a) explicitly made definite (by means of the article; also ↑133b; 134b), e.g.:

ῥίζα (SC^{id})… ἐστιν ἡ φιλαργυρία (**S**).	*The love of money is a/the root …* (1Tm 6:10)
ὁ ἔχων τὴν νύμφην (**S**) νυμφίος (SC^{id}) ἐστίν.	*He who has the bride is the bridegroom.* (Jn 3:29)
ὑμεῖς (**S**[1]) γάρ ἐστε ἡ δόξα ἡμῶν (SC^{id}).	*For you are our glory.* (1Th 2:20)
Οὗτός (**S**[2]) ἐστιν ὁ μαθητὴς ὁ … (SC^{id}).	*This is the disciple who …* (Jn 21:24)
Ἰησοῦς (**S**[3]) ἐστιν ὁ υἱὸς τοῦ θεοῦ (SC^{id}).	*Jesus is the Son of God.* (1Jn 5:5)

b) If both noun phrases have the same "strength" of definiteness (similarly if both are indefinite), the first is typically the subject and the second the subject complement (SC^{id}).

If the two phrases differ with regard to the grammatical person, the following criterion is to be taken into account (already done so in the above examples): The phrase that agrees with the finite verb form, is to be regarded as the subject, e.g.:

ἡ ἐπιστολὴ ἡμῶν (SC^{id}) ὑμεῖς (**S**) ἐστε.	*You yourselves are our letter.* (2Cor 3:2)
οὐ τὸ ἔργον μου (SC^{id}) ὑμεῖς (**S**) ἐστε ἐν κυρίῳ;	*Are you not my work in the Lord?* (1Cor 9:1)
σὺ (**S**) εἶ ὁ χριστός (SC^{id}).	*You are the Messiah.* (Mk 8:29)
ὑμεῖς (**S**) ἐστε τὸ ἅλας τῆς γῆς (SC^{id}).	*You are the salt of the earth.* (Mt 5:13)
σὺ (**S**) εἶ ὁ ἐρχόμενος (SC^{id});	*Are you the one who is to come?* (Mt 11:3)
οὗ πάντες ἡμεῖς (**S**) ἐσμεν μάρτυρες (SC^{id}).	*Of that we are all witnesses.* (Ac 2:32)
ἡμεῖς (**S**) γάρ ἐσμεν ἡ περιτομή (SC^{id}).	*For we are the [true] circumcision.* (Php 3:3)

When the grammatical person is the same, a sentence may be syntactically ambiguous, e.g.:

ὁ δὲ κύριος τὸ πνεῦμά ἐστιν.	*Now the Lord is the Spirit.* (2Cor 3:17)

When faced with this type of ambiguity, in fact when dealing with text interpretation in general, we often need to go beyond a purely grammatical level and look at things from a more semantic-communicative perspective. In this particular case taking into account the **theme–rheme distinction** (on this ↑301c) has proved helpful: Basically a sentence is made up of two information units, (1) the "theme", i.e. the part of information that is thought to be known, (2) the "rheme", i.e. the part of information that is new. Generally speaking, the theme is communicated by the grammatical subject and the rheme by the grammatical predicate (↑127b). Quite often, however, it is the other way round.

Among the above examples this is true inter alia of 1Cor 6:11, Jn 8:39, 2Cor 3:2, and Mt 11:3, where (as indicated by the context) the subject complement (SC[id]) corresponds to the theme and the subject to the rheme. Locating the theme (known information) and the rheme (new information) of a sentence is usually more helpful in interpreting texts than a purely grammatical analysis of sentence constituents. In the following sentence, for instance, the grammatical analysis of the sentence constituents is indisputable; only a careful analysis of the linguistic and non-linguistic contexts, however, will show which part of the sentence is to be regarded as the theme or the rheme respectively:

… ὅτι Ἰησοῦς (S) ἐστιν ὁ χριστός (SC[id]) … — *… that Jesus is the Messiah …* (Jn 20:31)

2. **Adjective** or **participle** phrases **without the article** rarely serve as attributive modifiers of noun phrases (↑136). They may, however, do so, when the head of the noun phrase is indefinite. In such a case the context normally indicates the intended syntactic role (adverbial or attributive; ↑229b). When adjective or participle phrases have the article they are always used as attributive modifiers or else (with the head being nominalized, noun substitutes) as noun phrases (↑132d; 136a; 229b).

For a thorough and exegetically helpful treatment of the above subject–complement problem (including "Colwell's Rule" connected with it) ↑Wallace 1996: 256–270.

On questions of concord ↑263 and 265.

136 Article use and the attributive and predicative positions

(↑BR §150–153; BDF §269–272; Z §186–192.)

136a 1. An attributive modifier (variously expressed; ↑260c–260m) that modifies a definite head noun regularly appears as it were "bracketed", either

a) between the article and the head noun, e.g.:

τὸ **ἀκάθαρτον** πνεῦμα	*the "impure"/evil spirit* (Mt 12:43)
ἡ **εἰς Χριστὸν** πίστις	*the/your faith in Christ* (↑Col 2:5)

or

b) after the head noun with the article being repeated, e.g.:

τὸ πνεῦμα **τὸ ἀκάθαρτον**	*the "impure"/evil spirit* (Mk 1:26)
ἡ πίστις … **ἡ πρὸς τὸν θεόν**	*the/your faith in God* (1Th 1:8)

This "bracket" position (↑a/b above) is called **attributive** position (also ↑136c/136d).

The repeated article (↑b above) may be absent, when there is more than one attributive modifier, especially when its head is a verbal noun (i.e. one referring to an activity or relation; ↑BDF §269.1), e.g.:

τὴν ἐμὴν ἀναστροφήν _ **ποτε ἐν τῷ Ἰουδαϊσμῷ**	*my former way of life in Judaism* (Ga 1:13)
τὴν ὑμῶν ἀγάπην _ **ἐν πνεύματι**	*your love [given] by the Spirit.* (Col 1:8)

When there is already an adjective or participle phrase between the article and the head, a further attributive modifier placed after the head need not have the article repeated (↑BDF §269.5), e.g.:

ἐκ τῆς ματαίας ὑμῶν ἀναστροφῆς _ πατροπαραδότου	*from your futile way of life handed down from your ancestors* (1Pe 1:18)

In such cases the repeated article may still be used, particularly when there is a special emphasis on the attributive modifier placed after its head noun (BDF §269.2), e.g.:

ὁ πιστὸς οἰκονόμος **ὁ φρόνιμος**	*the faithful [and] prudent manager* (Lk 12:42)

On the use of the article with the attributive modifier in the genitive ↑136e.

The attributive modifier of an indefinite head noun in most cases has no article. At times, however, the attributive modifier placed after its head does have one (especially in KG, it seems; ↑BDF §270 Note 3); in such a case the attributive function of the phrase is made explicit; e.g.:

καλὸν ἔργον	*a good deed* (Mk 14:6)
χαρὰν **μεγάλην**	*great joy* (Lk 2:10)
_ στολὴν **τὴν πρώτην**	*a first-class robe* (Lk 15:22)

2. Adjective (↑137) and participle phrases (↑229ff; 259o) that are used neither as attributive modifiers nor as noun phrases are without the article (they are outside the "bracket" position; ↑136a), i.e. either 136b

a) before the article of a noun phrase, e.g.:

μακάριοι (SC) οἱ πτωχοὶ τῷ πνεύματι.	*Blessed are the poor in spirit.* (Mt 5:3)

or

b) after the noun phrase, e.g.:

ἡ ἐντολὴ **ἁγία καὶ δικαία καὶ ἀγαθή** (SC).	*The commandment is holy, righteous and good.* (Ro 7:12)

An example containing an object complement (S+P+Od+OC; ↑258a/258b; 259n):

ὁ … τὸ αἷμα τῆς διαθήκης **κοινὸν** (OC) ἡγησάμενος	*the one who … has regarded as unclean the blood of the covenant* (He 10:29)

Adjective and participle phrases used in this way mostly have the role of a complement. As complements are also called "predicative" elements, this position is known traditionally as **predicative** position (↑136a/136c; 259o; on term ↑254c[3]).

3. In a number of cases attributive modifiers appear in the same position as the uses of 136b. Traditionally the term "predicative" position is used here as well, clearly a misnomer: the form is the same, but its syntactic function is quite different. This use is (grammatically) obligatory with the following types of attributive modifiers: 136c

a) the possessive genitives of non-reflexive personal pronouns (in most cases placed after the head noun; ↑57; 140b[10]), e.g.:

τὸ ὄνομα **αὐτοῦ**	*his name* (Mt 1:21)

Note that the possessive genitives of reflexive personal pronouns may be in this "predicative" position, but more frequently (CG regularly) they are placed between the article and the head noun, e.g.:

τὰ πρωτοτόκια **ἑαυτοῦ**	*his (own) birthright* (He 12:16)
τὸ **ἑαυτοῦ** σῶμα (more frequent position)	*his own body* (Ro 4:19)

↑also Jd 16.18.

At times the same applies to demonstrative pronouns in the possessive genitive, e.g.:

τὸ **ἐκείνου** θέλημα	*his (the former one's) will.* (2Tm 2:26)
τὸ τέλος **ἐκείνων**	*their end/the end of those things* (Ro 6:21)

b) the demonstrative pronouns (↑58; 141), e.g.:

οὗτος ὁ τελώνης	*this tax collector* (Lk 18:11)
ὁ ἄνθρωπος **οὗτος**	*this man/person* (Lk 23:47)

Note that demonstratives like τοσοῦτος *so much* etc. (↑58f) are used like ordinary adjectives, e.g.:

ὁ **τοσοῦτος** πλοῦτος ("bracket" position; ↑136a)	*this great wealth* (Re 18:17)

c) partitive genitives (↑166; also ↑136f), e.g.:

τοὺς πλείονας **τῶν ἀδελφῶν** — *the majority of the brothers* (Php 1:14)

d) typically the (rarely occurring) dual pronoun ἀμφότεροι *both* (↑61c; 63a; regularly so CG ἄμφω *both*, ἑκάτερος *each of two/either*, and frequently ἕκαστος *every/each [one]*), e.g.:

ἀμφότερα τὰ πλοῖα — *both boats* (Lk 5:7)

136d 4. There are some words that may appear either in the "attributive" or "predicative" position, which, however, affects their meaning or function:

a) **πᾶς** (or "intensified" ἅπας, CG also σύμπας) and ὅλος, in the sg. *(the) whole*, in the pl. *all* (↑BDF §275; Z §188–191; for details ↑BDAG s.v.):

- "predicative" position (predominant; standard/unmarked NT/LXX position), e.g.:

πᾶσα ἡ κτίσις — *the whole creation* (Ro 8:22)
πάντα τὰ ἔθνη — *all (the) nations* (Mt 28:19)

- "attributive" position (less frequent; unusual/marked NT/LXX position); said to emphasize completeness as a unity (BR §153: "Vollständigkeit als einer Einheit"), e.g.:

ὁ **πᾶς** νόμος — *the whole/entire law* (Ga 5:14)
οἱ **πάντες** ἄνδρες — *the total number of men* (Ac 19:7)

In the sg. without the article it corresponds to *every*, especially with uncountable head nouns also to *every/any kind of* or *all*, in the pl. to *all/any*, e.g.:

πᾶν πνεῦμα — *every spirit* (1Jn 4:2)
πᾶσα πικρία — *every kind of/all bitterness* (Eph 4:31)
πάντες ἄνθρωποι — *all human beings/everybody* (↑Php 4:5)

In post-CG, however, especially (based on Hebrew usage) with LXX/NT names (↑134c), the sg. without the article occasionally corresponds to *the whole/all* (↑BDF §275 Note 4), e.g.:

πᾶς Ἰσραήλ — *all Israel* (Ro 11:26)
πᾶσα οἰκοδομή (Var. πᾶσα ἡ οἰκοδομή) — *the whole building* (Eph 2:21)

In a nominalized sg. participle phrase (↑237) it corresponds to *every(one)* (not to *the whole*), e.g.:

πᾶς ὁ ἀκούων — *everyone who hears* (Mt 7:26)

b) **αὐτός** (↑54c; 139d):

- "predicative" position, e.g.:

αὐτὸς ὁ κύριος — *the Lord himself* (1Th 4:16)

- "attributive" position, e.g.:

τὸ **αὐτὸ** πνεῦμα — *the same Spirit* 1Cor 12:11)

c) In CG also a number of adjectives with a locative meaning (↑BR §152):

- "predicative" position (the adjective denotes one part of the entity referred to by the noun), e.g.:

ἡ πόλις **μέση** / **μέση** ἡ πόλις — *the middle of the city* (↑similarly Eze 9:4 LXX)

- "attributive" position, e.g.:

ἡ **μέση** πόλις — *the middle town* (↑2Kgs 20:4 LXX)

5. For **genitive** noun phrases functioning as **attributive modifiers** (↑158b) there are four possible positions in NT Greek (a and b agree with CG usage as does 136f[1]); the phrase may be placed 136e

a) between the article and the head noun (↑136a), e.g.:

τὸ **τῆς μεγάλης θεᾶς Ἀρτέμιδος** ἱερόν — *the temple of the great goddess Artemis* (Ac 19:27)

b) after the head noun with the article repeated (↑136a), e.g.:

τὴν διδασκαλίαν **τὴν τοῦ σωτῆρος ἡμῶν θεοῦ** — *the teaching of God, our Saviour* (Tt 2:10)

c) after the head noun without any repeated article that would mark it as an attributive modifier:

- the head noun has the article, the attributive modifier in the genitive does not (KG usage), e.g.:

ἡ γὰρ ἀγάπη **τοῦ Χριστοῦ** συνέχει ἡμᾶς. — *For the love of Christ controls us.* (2Cor 5:14)

Phrases of the following type occur very frequently in the NT:

ἡ βασιλεία **τοῦ θεοῦ** — *the kingdom of God* (Mk 1:15 et pass.)
ἡ βασιλεία **τῶν οὐρανῶν** — *the kingdom of Heaven* (Mt 3:2 et pass.)
τὸ καταπέτασμα **τοῦ ναοῦ** — *the curtain of the temple* (Mk 15:38) etc.

- the head noun is without the article (as the genitive noun phrase functioning as its attributive modifier is without it; ↑133e), e.g.:

_ δικαιοσύνη γὰρ **θεοῦ** ἐν αὐτῷ ἀποκαλύπτεται. — *For in it the righteousness of God is revealed.* (Ro 1:17)

Frequently we also encounter phrases of the following kind:

_ φίλος θεοῦ — *God's friend* (Jas 2:23)
_ πλῆθος ἁμαρτιῶν — *a multitude of sins* (1Pe 4:8)

Further noteworthy points: 136f

(1) **Partitive genitives** (↑166) are never in the "attributive" position (but in an attributive role!), e.g.:

οἱ λοιποὶ **τῶν ἀνθρώπων** — *the other human beings/other people* (Lk 18:11)

(2) A genitive attributive modifier without repeated article may itself be modified by a preposition phrase, which in such a case need not have the article repeated either (↑BDF/BDR §269.1), e.g.:

ὑπὲρ τῶν ἀδελφῶν μου τῶν συγγενῶν _ μου _ κατὰ σάρκα — *for my brothers, my kinsmen according to the flesh* (Ro 9:3)

↑also Php 1:5; Col 1:4; 2Th 3:14.

On questions of concord ↑263 and 265.

3.2.1.2 Syntax of the adjective (↑22b on word-class, ↑44–49 on forms, ↑147ff on cases)

Adjective phrases and their use (↑BR §150–153; 260f; BDF §241–243; 263f; 270; Z §140–142) 137

I. Adjectives serve as the head of **adjective phrases**. Frequently the head stands alone. In many cases, however, it is expanded, if so: (a) mostly by the article; (b) but also by certain types of attributive modifiers; (c) more rarely by a complement (a "second degree object"; ↑254c) due to the valency of the adjective involved, e.g.: 137a

καινὴ (AdjP: adj. alone) κτίσις — *a new creation* (Ga 6:15)
ὁ οἶνος **ὁ νέος** (AdjP with art.) — *the new wine* (Lk 5:37)
ὄρος **ὑψηλὸν λίαν** (AdjP with Attr) — *a very high mountain* (Mt 4:8)

πάσης ἀποδοχῆς ἄξιος (AdjP with Og/2nd) — *worthy of full acceptance* (1Tm 4:9)

II. Adjective phrases may have the following **syntactic roles**:

137b 1. as an **attributive** modifier of the head of a noun phrase, occurring in four possible types of word-order (↑260; 136a/136d):

a) between the article and the head noun, e.g.:

ὁ **δίκαιος** κριτής — *the righteous judge* (2Tm 4:8)
ἡ **καινὴ** διαθήκη — *the new covenant* (Lk 22:20)

b) after the head noun with the article (the one of the head noun being repeated), e.g.:

ὁ ποιμὴν **ὁ καλός** — *the good shepherd* (Jn 10:11)
τὸ φῶς **τὸ ἀληθινόν** — *the true light* (Jn 1:9)

c) after the head noun without the article (like the head noun; occurs frequently; but ↑136a), e.g.:

ζωὴ **αἰώνιος** — *eternal life* (Ro 6:23)
ἔργον … **καλόν** — *a good deed* (Mt 26:10)

d) before the head noun without the article (occurs somewhat less frequently), e.g.:

καλὸς στρατιώτης — *a good soldier* (2Tm 2:3)
μικρὸν μέλος — *a small member* (Jas 3:5)

137c 2. as a **predicative** element (↑258b; 136b; predicative position):

a) as an object complement (OC, S+P+Od+OC; ↑258b, 259p), e.g.:

ἐγὼ δὲ ἔχω τὴν μαρτυρίαν **μείζω** (= μείζονα, OCprop) = ἡ μαρτυρία ἣν ἐγὼ ἔχω μείζων ἐστίν / ἐγὼ ἔχω μαρτυρίαν ἣ μείζων ἐστίν. — *"I have the testimony as a greater one" = The testimony that I have is greater ≈ I have a greater testimony.* (Jn 5:36; BDF §270.1; Z §186)

↑also Mt 12:10 (Var.); He 7:24; similarly also 1Cor 11:5.

Analogously also the participle perfect passive in its adjective use:

πεπωρωμένην (OCprop) ἔχετε τὴν καρδίαν ὑμῶν; (↑233d) — *"Do you have your heart as a hardened one?" ≈ Do you have a hardened heart? ≈ Is your heart hardened?* ↑Fr. (TOB:) *Avez-vous le cœur endurci?* (Mk 8:17)

↑also Mk 3:1; Eph 1:17f.

b) as a subject complement (SC, S+[P]+SC; ↑258a) with or without copula verb εἰμί *to be* or γίνομαι *to become* (↑256c/256d; also ↑231k), e.g.:

ἡ ἐντολὴ **ἁγία καὶ δικαία καὶ ἀγαθή** (SC). — *The commandment is holy, righteous, and good.* (Ro 7:12)
γίνου **πιστὸς** (SC) ἄχρι θανάτου. — *Be faithful until death!* (Re 2:10)

137d 3. It may also be **nominalized**:

a) With or without the article (in the latter case frequently with an adjectival noun concomitant; also ↑132d, especially with regard to the meaning of the neuter), e.g.:

τοῖς **ἁγίοις**	*to the saints* (Eph 1:1)
κλητοῖς **ἁγίοις**	*to "called saints" = to persons called to be saints* (Ro 1:7; 1Cor 1:2)
τὸ **κακόν**	*(the) wrong = what is wrong* (Ro 13:4)
κακόν	*a wrong = anything wrong* (Ro 13:10)
τὰ **κακά**	*(the) evil things = evil* (Ro 3:8)
κακά	*evil things = evil* (1Pe 3:12)

b) Due to frequent nominalization many adjectives tend to be viewed no longer as adjectives, but as nouns (↑260c), e.g.:

ἡ ἔρημος (sc. χώρα/γῆ *land*)	*the wilderness/desert* (↑ e.g. Mt 3:3)

On this ellipsis and the one of ἡμέρα *day*, ὥρα *hour* etc.↑260c; 293c (↑BDF §241).

c) Especially Paul seems to have a liking for the neuter singular of an adjective taking the place of an abstract noun (↑132d; also CG and literary KG), e.g.:

τὸ **χρηστὸν** τοῦ θεοῦ = ἡ χρηστότης …	*God's kindness* (Ro 2:4)
τὸ **δυνατὸν** αὐτοῦ = τὴν δύναμιν αὐτοῦ	*his power* (Ro 9:22)

4. There are a number of adjectives that may be used as **adverbials**: in such a case the adjective phrase does not (as an attributive modifier) modify the noun phrase it shows concord with, but the "action" referred to by the verb (↑259a–259m, 259q; 258c; for the very frequent analogous use of participles also ↑230–232); note that adjective phrases used in this way never have the article (↑135b), e.g.: 137e

δευτεραῖοι (TempA) ἤλθομεν …	*on the second day we arrived* … (Ac 28:13)

↑also Lk 24:22 (ὀρθριναί *early in the morning*).

εἰ γὰρ **ἑκὼν** (ManA) τοῦτο πράσσω … εἰ δὲ **ἄκων** (ManA) …	*For if I do this voluntarily …; if not voluntarily* … (1Cor 9:17)

↑also Lk 1:6 (ἄμεμπτοι *blamelessly*); Mk 4:28/Ac 12:10 (αὐτομάτη *by itself*); Ac 27:19 (αὐτόχειρες *with their own hands*); 2Cor 8:17 (αὐθαίρετος *of his own accord*).

ὅπου αὐτὸν ἐσταύρωσαν, καὶ μετ᾽ αὐτοῦ ἄλλους δύο …, **μέσον** (LocA) δὲ τὸν Ἰησοῦν.	*There they crucified him, and with him two others …, and Jesus in the middle.* (Jn 19:18)

↑also Lk 22:55; 23:45; Jn 1:26; Ac 1:18.

σκηνοῦμεν **ὑπαίθριοι** (LocA).	*We are encamped under the open sky.* (Xenophon, Anabasis 5.5.21)

On terminology ↑259o.
On questions of concord ↑261–265; on pleonastic καί ↑252.29,8.
On possible complements to be expected with certain adjectives (due to their valency) ↑163b; 165; 219; 225a; 254d; 258d.
Note that in the NT noun phrases in the genitive of quality may replace an adjective phrase. On this ↑162; 260c/260e.

138 Comparison (↑50–52 on forms; ↑BR §253.21; 183, BDF §244–246; Z §143–153)

Properties are typically denoted by (basic form) adjectives. When entities are compared with regard to a gradable property, a higher degree is generally expressed by **comparative** forms and the highest degree by **superlative** forms. Sometimes a very high degree rather than the highest is expressed by forms otherwise used as superlatives, which may be called "**elative**" (or "absolute" superlative, i.e. one without involving any comparison; ↑138b). – On sentence/text level comparisons ↑287; 343ff.

138a I. Comparative forms are generally connected with an element that in English is introduced by "than". In Ancient Greek there are two ways of marking the **"than" element** (an attributive modifier of the comparative adjective [or adverb]; ↑260o):

1. Mostly it is marked by the genitive of comparison (↑170), e.g.:

μείζων ἐστὶν ὁ θεὸς **τῆς καρδίας ἡμῶν**	*God is greater than our heart.* (1Jn 3:20)
μὴ ἰσχυρότεροι **αὐτοῦ** ἐσμεν;	*Are we stronger than he?* (1Cor 10:22)

↑also Lk 7:26; 21:3; Jn 1:50; 13:16; 1Cor 15:10.

2. Less frequently the particle ἤ *than* is used, e.g.:

μείζων ἐστὶν ὁ ἐν ὑμῖν **ἢ ὁ ἐν τῷ κόσμῳ**.	*The one who is in you is greater than the one who is in the world.* (1Jn 4:4)

↑also 1Cor 14:5; comparing inf./ACI phrases (ἤ *than for s.o. to …*): Mt 19:24; Mk 10:25.

138b Further noteworthy points:

1. In rare cases the comparison construction is without the second element; in a translation into English this needs to be replaced by something like "that of" or else be supplied from the context, e.g.:

Ἐγὼ δὲ ἔχω τὴν μαρτυρίαν μείζω **τοῦ Ἰωάννου**.	*The testimony that I have is greater than [that of John]/… than John's.* (Jn 5:36; ↑137c)
τὸ μωρὸν τοῦ θεοῦ σοφώτερον **τῶν ἀνθρώπων** ἐστίν …	*The foolishness of God is wiser than [the wisdom of] human beings.* (1Cor 1:25; ↑132d)

2. When no comparison is involved, a superlative form (or its substitute; ↑138c/138d) may (as in other languages) have an **elative** force, e.g.:

ἐκ ξύλου **τιμιωτάτου**	*of most valuable wood/of very expensive wood.* (Re 18:12)

3. The comparative form may be reinforced by πολλῷ or πολύ "to a large extent" = *much/many* (dative of difference/measure [↑178b] and adverbial accusative respectively [↑157] of πολύς *much*), serving as an attributive modifier of the comparative adjective or adverb (often of μᾶλλον *more*; ↑260o), e.g.:

καὶ **πολλῷ** (Attr) πλείους (comp. adj.) ἐπίστευσαν.	*And many* (lit. "to a large extent") *more believed.* (Jn 4:41)
… νυνὶ δὲ **πολὺ** (Attr) σπουδαιότερον (comp. adj.) …	*… who is now much more eager …* (2Cor 8:22)

4. ὡς with a superlative has the force of *as … as possible* (↑252.61 [similarly 252.46]) only 1× in the NT (2× in the LXX):

ὡς τάχιστα (adj. form used as an adv.; ↑53)	*as soon as possible* (Ac 17:15)

5. In a number of instances, the comparative is not expressed by an inflected form but by means of μᾶλλον *more* (in a way comparable to the English construction; ↑BDAG s.v. 1), e.g.:

μακάριόν ἐστιν **μᾶλλον** διδόναι ἢ λαμβάνειν. — *It is more blessed to give than to receive.* (Ac 20:35)

↑also Mk 9:42; 1Cor 9:15; Ga 4:27.

Occasionally the two possibilities are combined (pleonastically; ↑294x; also 51c), e.g.:

πολλῷ γὰρ **μᾶλλον κρεῖσσον** — *For [that is/would be] far better.* (Php 1:23)

↑also 1Cor 12:22; 2Cor 7:13.

6. On the special uses of (οἱ) πλείονες and (οἱ) πλεῖστοι ↑132d(3j).

II. Comparison peculiarities in Biblical Greek (LXX and NT):

1. Peculiarities due to **Semitic** influence: Hebrew and Aramaic have no compara- 138c
tive forms (↑GKC §133; Segert: 342), which has affected Biblical Greek usage; thus, the **basic form** of adjectives (and adverbs) sometimes has

a) a comparative function (as indicated by the context), e.g.:

καλόν ἐστίν σε εἰσελθεῖν εἰς τὴν ζωὴν χωλὸν **ἢ** τοὺς δύο πόδας ἔχοντα βληθῆναι εἰς τὴν γέενναν. — *It is better for you to enter life lame than with two feet to be thrown into hell.* (Mk 9:45)

Note that the comparative form or the basic form having a comparative function in the context may be combined with ἤ *than* as in the above case(s) or else (frequently so in the LXX) with
παρά + acc. *in comparison to, more than* (Lk 3:13; He 11:4; ↑184m) or
ὑπέρ + acc. *over and above, than* (Lk 16:8, He 4:12; ↑184r).

When such preposition phrases occur with certain nouns or verbs the resulting construction may have a comparative force even without μᾶλλον, e.g.:

δοκεῖτε ὅτι οἱ Γαλιλαῖοι οὗτοι **ἁμαρτωλοὶ παρὰ** πάντας τοὺς Γαλιλαίους ἐγένοντο; — *Do you think these Galileans were worse sinners than* (< "sinners more than") *all the other Galileans?* (Lk 13:2)

… **ἔχρισέν** σε ὁ θεός … **παρὰ** τοὺς μετόχους σου — *… God has anointed you … more than/beyond your companions* (He 1:9)

↑also Lk 18:14.

b) a superlative function, e.g.:

ποία ἐντολὴ **μεγάλη** ἐν τῷ νόμῳ; — *Which is the greatest commandment in the Law?* (Mt 22:36)

Note that some think that comparative constructions may at times express exclusion (as would be possible in Semitic constructions with מִן *min*) rather than a difference in degree (e.g. … θεῷ μᾶλλον ἢ ἀνθρώποις … *God, not human beings,* rather than … *God more/rather* (lit. "to a greater degree") *than human beings* [Ac 5:29], ↑BDAG sub μᾶλλον 3c). However, none of the examples listed nor extra-biblical usage (↑BDR §246.2_4) seem to justify the introduction of such a secondary (grammatical) function for this construction; on the other hand, this type of interpretation might occasionally be prompted by contextual factors (textpragmatically).

2. Peculiarities due to **popular** usage in **KG**: in popular KG there was a tendency 138d
for superlative forms to be replaced by comparative forms. Thus, in the NT the

comparative form in addition to its normal comparative function sometimes had a superlative or elative (↑138b) function (indicated by the context), the superlative form having become relatively rare:

a) with a superlative function, e.g.:

μείζων δὲ τούτων (partitive gen.; ↑166) ἡ ἀγάπη.	*But the greatest of these is love.* (1Cor 13:13)

b) with an elative function, e.g.:

σπουδαιότερος δὲ ὑπάρχων αὐθαίρετος ἐξῆλθεν πρὸς ὑμᾶς.	*Since he was very eager, he went off to you of his own accord.* (2Cor 8:17)

On πρῶτος with the sense "earlier (than)" ↑145a.

Note that the syntactic rules applicable to the comparison of adjectives in principle apply to gradable adverbs as well. ↑53; 242.

3.2.1.3 Syntax of pronouns (↑22c on word-class, ↑54–61 on forms; also ↑Langslow: 494ff)

Pronouns are used either as **noun substitutes** (as pronouns in the real sense of the word) or as attributive or non-attributive **concomitants of nouns**. As such they occur in a variety of different syntactic roles, as shown not only in the following paragraphs (↑138–144), but also in the sections dealing with the syntax of case forms and preposition phrases (↑146ff; 184ff). On their relevance to the coherence of texts ↑319 and 346–348.

Regarding the use of pronouns Biblical/KG differs from Classical Greek mainly in two respects:
1. They are used more frequently, quite often pleonastically (↑139a–139c; 140d; 289i; 294x).
2. The more subtle CG distinctions are disregarded (↑139g–139j/139l; 141c; 142a/142b; 143b).

139 Personal and reciprocal pronouns

(↑22c[b] on word-class, ↑54–56 on forms; ↑BR §64–66; 154; BDF §277–283; 287f; Z §195–212; Langslow: 143ff)

139a I. The **non-reflexive personal pronoun** (↑22c[b.1]; 54; 348b; also 130b with App)

1. The **nominative** form as a noun substitute (as a subject; ↑255a/255d; also 135c):

a) Generally speaking, it occurs with the predicate verb (predicator) only for emphasis, especially in contrasts, e.g.:

ἐγὼ χρείαν ἔχω ὑπὸ σοῦ βαπτισθῆναι, καὶ **σὺ** ἔρχῃ πρός με;	*I need to be baptized by you, and do you come to me = I am the one who needs to be baptized by you, and you are the one who comes to me?* (Mt 3:14)
καὶ **σὺ** ἐξ αὐτῶν εἶ.	*You, too, are one of them.* (Lk 22:58)

b) However, in some NT instances no special emphasis appears to be intended, e.g.:

ἔθηκα ὑμᾶς ἵνα **ὑμεῖς** ὑπάγητε …	*I appointed you to go* (lit. *that you should go*) … (Jn 15:16)

↑BDF §277.2; Z §198.

2. The **non-enclitic forms** ἐμοῦ etc., σοῦ etc. (3rd pers. ↑139c), too, are used for emphasis (for use of oblique cases and preposition phrases ↑146ff; 184ff), namely 139b

a) in contrasts, e.g.:

εἰ **ἐμὲ** ἐδίωξαν, καὶ **ὑμᾶς** διώξουσιν.	*If they persecuted me, they will persecute you, too.* (Jn 15:20)

b) usually when they are part of a preposition phrase (↑183b), e.g.:[6]

μάθετε ἀπ᾽ **ἐμοῦ**.	*Learn from me!* (Mt 11:29)

In other contexts, the enclitic forms are generally preferred. In agreement with the trends of popular KG (Semitic influence seems to be less important) they are more frequent in the NT than in CG (which uses them mainly when considered necessary for clarity's sake), sometimes occurring pleonastically, e.g.:

ἐὰν θέλῃς δύνασαί **με** καθαρίσαι.	*If you are willing, you can make me clean.* (Mt 8:2)

Note that in CG the pronoun could be combined with γε for added emphasis:

ἔγωγε (note accentuation!)	*I at least/I at any rate* … (↑252.10; 269c), e.g.:
αἰτίας οὖν **ἔγωγε** τρεῖς εἶναι νομίζω φυγῆς.	*I at least think that there are three reasons for the flight.* (Philo, Fuga 1.3)

3. The **third person** (on textgrammatical role ↑348b): 139c

a) αὐτός is used as a personal pronoun of the 3rd pers., in post-CG and NT Greek (unlike CG) also in the nominative (for the nominative CG uses ἐκεῖνος *that* [sometimes the NT, too] or οὗτος *this* [↑58; 141d]), e.g.:

αὐτὸς γὰρ σώσει … (un-CG)	*For he will save* … (Mt 1:21)
ἐκράτησαν **αὐτόν**. (= CG)	*They arrested him.* (Mk 14:46)
ποῦ ἐστιν **ἐκεῖνος**; (= CG)	*Where is he?* (Jn 7:11)

b) Often a very similar function is encountered with the pronominal use of the article and the analogous use of the relative pronoun (↑131; 142h; generally anaphoric/anadeictic; ↑346–348b), e.g.:

Οἱ μὲν οὖν ἐπορεύοντο …	*Then these/they left* … (Ac 5:41)

c) In CG the personal pronouns οὗ (οὑ), οἷ (οἱ), ἕ (ἑ), σφεῖς, σφῶν etc. (↑54d) were used referring to the subject of the superordinate sentence (indirect-reflexive; ↑139f–139j), e.g.:

… κοινωνὸν **σφίσι** (refers to S) τῆς τύχης μένειν ἱκέτευον (S)	*… they entreated him to remain sharing with them in their fortune* (Josephus, War 3.202)

4. **αὐτός** etc. is used in three different ways in NT/KG (BDF §288; 277.3): 139d

---

6 Note, however, that in the NT πρός με *to me* is more frequent (25×) than πρὸς ἐμέ (6×), similarly so in the LXX, Philo, and Josephus.

a) as a non-attributive noun concomitant ("predicative" position; ↑136b/136d): *-self*, e.g.:

αὐτὸς ὁ κύριος … καταβήσεται ἀπ' οὐρανοῦ.	*The Lord himself will come down from heaven* … (1Th 4:16)
αὐτὸς ἐγώ … δουλεύω …	*I myself serve* … (Ro 7:25)

↑also Lk 2:35 (σοῦ αὐτῆς τὴν ψυχήν *the soul "of yourself" = your own soul*).

Note that especially in Luke and Acts the simple αὐτός (in the "predicative" position) is sometimes used in a way similar to αὐτὸς οὗτος (ἐκεῖνος) ὁ *this (that) same* or *this (that) very*, e.g.:

ἐν **αὐτῇ τῇ** ἡμέρᾳ	*on the day itself = on the same day = on that very day* (Lk 24:13)

Also: (ἐν) αὐτῇ τῇ ὥρᾳ *in that very hour/moment* (also: *immediately*) Lk 2:38; 10:21; 12:12; 13:31; 20:19; Ac 16:18; with other expressions of time: Lk 13:1; 23:12; with other noun phrases: Mt 3:4; Mk 6:17; Lk 10:7; αὐτὸ τοῦτο *this very (thing)*: 2Cor 7:11; Ga 2:10 etc.

b) as an attributive noun concomitant (↑136a/136d; also nominalized [↑132d]): ὁ αὐτός *the same*, e.g.:

διαιρέσεις διακονιῶν εἰσιν, καὶ **ὁ αὐτὸς** κύριος	*There are varieties of ministries, but the same Lord.* (1Cor 12:5)
τὰ αὐτὰ (nominalized) ἐπάθετε.	*You suffered the same things.* (1Th 2:14)

c) as a noun substitute, i.e. as a 3rd pers. personal pronoun: *he, of him, to him, him* etc. (↑139c).

139e 5. **Special uses** of personal pronouns:

a) The **"authorial"** (also "literary") **plural** (or "pluralis sociativus"), used not only in the NT, but also widely in other Ancient Greek and non-Greek texts: the speaker/writer uses ἡμεῖς *we* for ἐγώ *I* (or the 1st pers. pl. for the 1st pers. sg. of the finite verb), referring to himself, but at the same time in some ways involving his readers/hearers in what he is doing (↑BDF §280; Langslow: 134–136; Z §8), e.g.:

πῶς ὁμοιώσ**ωμεν** τὴν βασιλείαν τοῦ θεοῦ;	*With what can we compare the kingdom of God?* (Mk 4:30)

↑also He 5:11; 6:1.3.9.11; 1Jn 1:4.

Note that the authorial plural seems to be used by Paul only occasionally (e.g. 2Cor 10:11ff).

b) Depending on the context the 1st pers. pl. may be understood in terms of either an "**inclusive we**" or an "**exclusive we**" (by no means limited to NT usage; some languages even have two different "we" forms): The persons referred to by the "we" may either include or exclude the addressees, e.g.:

Εἰ ζ**ῶμεν** πνεύματι, πνεύματι καὶ στοιχ**ῶμεν**.	*If we* (inclusive) *live by the Spirit, let us* (inclusive) *also keep in step with the Spirit.* (Ga 5:25)
προελέγ**ομεν** ὑμῖν ὅτι μέλλ**ομεν** θλίβεσθαι …	*we* (exclusive) *told you in advance that we* (inclusive) *would suffer affliction.* (1Th 3:4)

c) The 1st sg. (or pl.↑255f) and 2nd pers. sg. may have **generic reference** (to people in general), a use found in English and many other languages (attested in Ancient Greek since the Late Classical Period), approximately corresponding to the generic personal pronoun "one" in English (↑Carter §60b) or in certain cases to τις *someone, one* (↑144a; 255f). A number of instances are found with Paul (↑BDF §281), e.g.:

εἰ γὰρ ἃ κατέλυσ**α** ταῦτα πάλιν οἰκοδομ**ῶ** …	*For if I am building up again those things I once destroyed …* (Ga 2:18)
Εἰ δὲ **σὺ** Ἰουδαῖος ἐπονομάζ**ῃ** καὶ ἐπαναπαύ**ῃ** νόμῳ …	*But if you call yourself a Jew and rely on the law* … (Ro 2:17)

↑also Ro 11:17; possibly Ro 7:9.16.20.25; 8:2.

On the genitive of the personal pronoun in the role of a possessive pronoun ↑140b.

On questions of concord ↑261–265.

II. The **reflexive personal pronoun** (↑22c[b.2]; 55)[7]

1. The use of the Ancient Greek reflexive pronoun (a subtype of the personal pronoun) is closely similar to the use of the English reflexive pronoun, *myself, yourself,* etc.: the entity designated by the reflexive pronoun is equated with the subject entity, the reflexive pronoun **refers back to the subject** (anaphorically/anadeictically),[8] e.g.: 139f

ἐὰν ἐγὼ μαρτυρῶ περὶ **ἐμαυτοῦ** …	*If I testify about myself …* (Jn 5:31)

The entity designated by ἐμαυτοῦ is equated with the subject entity (here the speaker): ἐμαυτοῦ refers back to the subject.

Non-reflexive example:

ἄλλος ἐστὶν ὁ μαρτυρῶν περὶ **ἐμοῦ**.	*There is another who testifies about me.* (Jn 5:32)

The entity designated by the (non-reflexive) personal pronoun ἐμοῦ (here the speaker) is different from the subject entity ("another"): ἐμοῦ does not refer back to the subject.

Note that one may distinguish (as is relevant to CG syntax; ↑139c) between
a) direct-reflexive, when the subject of the same sentence/clause is referred back to,
b) indirect-reflexive, when the subject of the superordinate sentence/clause is referred back to.

2. Noteworthy points on the **forms** of the reflexive pronoun (↑55): 139g

a) The three persons of the **plural** nearly always have the same form in KG: the ones used for the 3rd pers. pl. in CG. For the 1st and 2nd pers. pl. CG combines the non-reflexive personal pronoun with αὐτός instead (ἡμῶν αὐτῶν etc., ὑμῶν αὐτῶν etc.).

b) The **contracted forms** of the 3rd pers. reflexive pronoun encountered in CG (αὑτοῦ for ἑαυτοῦ etc.; ↑55) are not used in modern standard editions of the NT (the 25th NA edition of 1963 e.g. still had αὑτῷ in Lk 12:21, αὑτόν in Ac 14:17, and αὑτούς in Re 8:6 [in the early manuscripts of the NT diacritics are used very sparsely; ↑p.22]), and only rarely in the LXX (e.g. Eze 22:3). This similarly applies to the 2nd pers. σαυτοῦ etc.: these do not occur in any of the current editions of the NT (including those based on the Byz.), however, 19× in the LXX (e.g. Dt 21:11; Eze 4:9). 139h

7 For a thoroughgoing comparative study ↑Langslow: 512–520.

8 Note that the Ancient Greek reflexive pronoun is not used for emphasis as is its English counterpart in *I **myself*** … etc.; αὐτός in the "predicative" position is used in this way (↑139d).

139i c) Examples:

- singular:

… ἐγὼ μαρτυρῶ περὶ **ἐμαυτοῦ**.	*… I testify about myself.* (Jn 5:31)
τί λέγεις περὶ **σεαυτοῦ**;	*What do you say about yourself?* (Jn 1:22)
πᾶς ὁ ὑψῶν **ἑαυτὸν** ταπεινωθήσεται.	*Everyone who exalts himself will be humbled.* (Lk 14:11)

- plural:

Ἀρχόμεθα πάλιν **ἑαυτοὺς** συνιστάνειν;	*Are we beginning to commend ourselves again?* (2Cor 3:1)
οὐ γὰρ **ἑαυτοὺς** κηρύσσομεν.	*For we proclaim not ourselves.* (2Cor 4:5)
… παραστήσατε **ἑαυτοὺς** τῷ θεῷ …	*… present yourselves to God …* (Ro 6:13)
πορεύεσθε μᾶλλον … καὶ ἀγοράσατε **ἑαυταῖς**.	*Instead, go … and buy for yourselves.* (Mt 25:9)
ἐφ᾽ **ἑαυτὰς** κλαίετε.	*Weep for yourselves!* (Lk 23:28)
Τεκνία, φυλάξατε **ἑαυτὰ** ἀπὸ τῶν εἰδώλων.	*Little children, keep yourselves from idols.* (1Jn 5:21)

↑also Ac 13:46, Ro 12:16.19.

… **ἑαυτοὺς** ἔδωκαν πρῶτον τῷ κυρίῳ …	*… they gave themselves first to the Lord …* (2Cor 8:5)
αἱ ἅγιαι γυναῖκες … ἐκόσμουν **ἑαυτάς** …	*… the holy women … adorned themselves …* (1Pe 3:5)
τὰ θηρία … δύνανται ἐκφυγόντα εἰς σκέπην **ἑαυτὰ** ὠφελῆσαι.	*The animals … fleeing to a shelter are able to help themselves.* (EpJer 1:67)

139j 3. Reflexive relationship left **unexpressed**:

According to the Classical rule a reflexive pronoun is to be used whenever the personal pronoun to be added designates the same entity as the subject (↑139f), e.g.:

γνῶθι **σαυτόν** (= σεαυτόν)·	*Know yourself!* (inscription on the temple of Apollo at Delphi; ↑Pausanias 10.24)

Generally, the reflexive relationship is carefully taken into account by the authors of the NT. At times, however, the reflexive relationship is left unexpressed, most frequently when the personal pronoun is in the possessive genitive (corresponding to a possessive pronoun in English; ↑159b), especially so in the 3rd person.

While in KG this phenomenon is widely attested, in Biblical Greek the Semitic background appears to provide an added incentive to resort to it (neither in Hebrew nor in Aramaic is there a grammatical distinction between non-reflexive and reflexive relationships).

Examples (the more words there are between the subject and the pronoun, the less likely the reflexive pronoun appears to be used):

… ἀπαρνησάσθω **ἑαυτὸν** καὶ ἀράτω τὸν σταυρὸν **αὐτοῦ** …	*… let him deny himself and take up his cross …* (Mt 16:24)

ἐβαπτίζοντο ὑπ' αὐτοῦ ἐν τῷ Ἰορδάνῃ ποταμῷ ἐξομολογούμενοι τὰς ἁμαρτίας **αὐτῶν**.	*They were baptized by him in the river Jordan, confessing their sins.* (Mk 1:5)
ἄξιος ὁ ἐργάτης τοῦ μισθοῦ **αὐτοῦ**	*The worker deserves his pay.* (1Tm 5:18)
… παράλαβε μετὰ **σοῦ** ἔτι ἕνα ἢ δύο …	*… take one or two others with you …* (Mt 18:16)
Τῇ ἐπαύριον βλέπει τὸν Ἰησοῦν ἐρχόμενον πρὸς **αὐτόν**.	*The next day he saw Jesus coming towards him.* (Jn 1:29)

↑also Mk 2:6; 14:33; Lk 23:12; 1Jn 3:15; Re 13:16.

Due to this use, in a handful of instances, more than one interpretation appears to be possible, e.g.:

… διὰ τοῦ σταυροῦ, ἀποκτείνας τὴν ἔχθραν ἐν **αὐτῷ**.	*… through the cross, putting to death the hostility through it* (i.e. through the cross)*/in himself* (i.e. in his own person). (Eph 2:16)

↑also Col 1:20; 1Jn 5:10; Jas 5:20.

4. ἑαυτῶν also functions as a reciprocal pronoun, like ἀλλήλων *each other* (↑139n). 139k

5. In Hebrew נֶ֫פֶשׁ *nēpeš "soul"/life* may have the function of a reflexive pronoun (HALOT s.v.). In a few cases ψυχή is used in a similar way in Biblical Greek, e.g. in Lk 9:24f: 139l

τὴν ψυχὴν αὐτοῦ ≈ ἑαυτόν:	*his "soul" / his life ≈ himself:*
ἀπολέσῃ **τὴν ψυχὴν αὐτοῦ**	*(whoever) loses his "soul" / life* (v. 24)
→ **ἑαυτὸν** δὲ ἀπολέσας	→ *(but) loses himself* (v. 25)

↑BDF §283; Z §212.

On the genitive of the reflexive pronoun in the role of a possessive pronoun ↑140b.
On questions of concord ↑261–265.

III. The **reciprocal pronoun** (↑22c[b.3]; 56) 139m

When a mutual relationship is to be expressed between two or more subject entities involved in the "action" of a verb, for which English typically uses *each other* or *one another*, Ancient Greek uses either the regular reciprocal pronoun or an alternative construction indicating a mutual relationship (also ↑190f).

1. Examples with the regular reciprocal pronoun:

οἱ ποιμένες ἐλάλουν πρὸς **ἀλλήλους** …	*The shepherds said to one another …* (Lk 2:15)
… ἵνα ἀγαπᾶτε **ἀλλήλους** …	*… that you love another …* (Jn 13:34)
ἱνατί ἀδικεῖτε **ἀλλήλους**;	*Why do you wrong each other?* (Ac 7:26)
ὅτι ἐσμὲν **ἀλλήλων** μέλη	*for we are members of one another* (Eph 4:25)

2. Examples with an alternative construction indicating a mutual relationship: 139n

a) The reflexive pronoun ἑαυτῶν (↑139k) used like ἀλλήλων (also CG), e.g.:

εἰρηνεύετε ἐν **ἑαυτοῖς**.	*Live in peace with each other!* (1Th 5:13)

ἀλλὰ παρακαλεῖτε **ἑαυτοὺς** καθ᾽ ἑκάστην ἡμέραν	*But exhort one another every day.* (He 3:13)

b) Very rarely εἷς τὸν ἕνα "one another" for ἀλλήλους (perhaps a Semitism; ↑145b):[9]

οἰκοδομεῖτε **εἷς τὸν ἕνα.**	*Build up/Strengthen one another!* (1Th 5:11)

On the use of related ἄλλος, ἄλλη, ἄλλο *other* ↑145e (last paragraph; on form ↑56a).

140 The possessive pronoun and its alternatives

(↑22c on word-class, ↑57 on forms; ↑BR §67; BDF §284–286; Z §195ff)

140a 1. The **possessive pronoun** itself (normally emphasizing the possessor) is not used much in the NT (ca. 121×), most frequently ἐμός *my/mine (*ca. 76×). The personal pronoun in the possessive genitive (↑140b) is typically used instead.
Syntactically it is used like an adjective (↑137; thus also "possessive *adjective*"); when it is an attributive modifier (so in most cases), its head mostly has the article, e.g.:

ἡ βασιλεία **ἡ ἐμή**	*my kingdom* (Jn 18:36)
διὰ **τὴν σὴν** λαλιάν	*because of your words* (Jn 4:42)

On rare occasions the head has no article, which may affect the meaning of the noun phrase in the following way (but also ↑133 on definiteness without the article):

_ **ἐμὸς** φίλος	*my friend = a friend of mine* (↑BR §67)
… μὴ ἔχων _ **ἐμὴν** δικαιοσύνην.	*… having a righteousness of my own.* (Php 3:9)

The possessive pronoun sometimes indicates a relationship that is not strictly possessive, but one that is typical of an objective genitive relationship (↑160e; applicable to CG, too):

εἰς **τὴν ἐμὴν** ἀνάμνησιν	*in remembrance/memory of me* (1Cor 11:24f)

↑also Ro 11:31; 15:4; 1Cor 15:31.

140b 2. Typically the possessive pronoun is replaced by **the personal pronoun in the possessive genitive** (in the 3rd pers. nearly always), by the non-reflexive form (without emphasis) or (less frequently) by the reflexive form (with some emphasis; ↑159b):[10]

non-reflexive:		reflexive:	
μου	*my*	ἐμαυτοῦ	*my (own)*
σου	*your*	σεαυτοῦ	*your (own)*
αὐτοῦ, -ῆς	*his/its, her*	ἑαυτοῦ, -ῆς	*his/its, her (own)*
(or ἐκείνου –ης/τούτου, ταύτης)			
ἡμῶν	*our*	ἑαυτῶν	*our (own)*
ὑμῶν	*your*	ἑαυτῶν	*your (own)*
αὐτῶν	*their*	ἑαυτῶν	*their (own)*
(or ἐκείνων/τούτων with some emphasis)		(↑54–55/139 for CG forms)	

9 According to BDF §247.4 this is an Aramaism; ↑e.g. Targum of Eze 3:13: *[the sound of the living beings touching]* (חַד לְחַד *ḥad ləḥad* "one to/towards one") *each other* (LXX: ἑτέρα πρὸς τὴν ἑτέραν). ↑also Ex 37:9; 2Sm 14:6; Eze 33:30. Note, however, that there are a number of comparable CG constructions with εἷς (↑LSJ s.v. 1e–g or BDAG s.v. 5a).

10 The non-reflexive one (despite its attributive role) is mostly in the "predicative" position (↑136c), the reflexive one in the "attributive" position (CG; NT sometimes has the "predicative" position).

3. The NT fairly frequently uses the adjective **ἴδιος** *(one's) own* like a personal pro- 140c
noun in the possessive genitive, especially like a reflexive one (typically with the possessor being emphasized), e.g.:

ἐκάλεσεν τοὺς **ἰδίους** δούλους (with no emphasis on the possessor).	*He called his servants.* (Mt 25:14)
↑ἀπέστειλεν τοὺς δούλους **αὐτοῦ**.	*He sent out his servants.* (Mt 22:3)
κοπιῶμεν ἐργαζόμενοι ταῖς **ἰδίαις** χερσίν (with emphasis on the possessor).	*We work hard with our own hands.* (1Cor 4:12)

↑also Lk 6:41; Jn 4:44; 10:3; Eph 5:22; 1Th 2:14.

4. In Ancient Greek (unlike in English) a naturally given possessive relationship may be expressed sim- 140d
ply by means of the article, though in KG/NT far less frequently than in CG (↑132a), e.g.:

ἐκτείνας **τὴν** χεῖρα ἥψατο αὐτοῦ.	*He stretched out his hand* (lit. "the hand") *and touched him.* (Mt 8:3)

On the occasional (KG) use of κατά + acc. comparable to a possessive pronoun ↑184k.

5. Examples: 140e

a) **non-reflexive use**:

• without emphasis on possessor: personal pronoun in the possessive genitive (↑140b):

ὁ παῖς **μου**	*my servant* (Mt 8:6)
ἡ δόξα **ἡμῶν**	*our glory/pride* (1Th 2:20)
ἡ ἀριστερά **σου**	*your left hand* (Mt 6:3)
τὸ φῶς **ὑμῶν**	*your light* (Mt 5:16)
τὰ ἔργα **αὐτοῦ**	*his deeds* (2Tm 4:14)
ὁ λόγος **αὐτῶν**	*their talk/teaching* (2Tm 2:17)

• with emphasis on possessor: possessive pronoun/3rd pers. demonstrative pronoun in the possessive genitive (↑140a/140b):

εἰς τὸ **ἐμὸν** ὄνομα	*in MY name* (Mt 18:20)
εἰς τὴν **ἡμετέραν** διδασκαλίαν	*for OUR instruction* (Ro 15:4)
ὁ λόγος ὁ **σός**	*YOUR word* (Jn 17:17)
ὁ καιρὸς ὁ **ὑμέτερος**	*YOUR time* (Jn 7:6)
τοῖς **ἐκείνου** γράμμασιν	*HIS writings* (Jn 5:47)
εἰς τὸ **ἐκείνων** ὑστέρημα	*for THEIR need* (2Cor 8:14)
τῇ **τούτων** ἀπειθείᾳ	*because of THEIR disobedience* (Ro 11:30)

b) **reflexive use** (for which KG also uses non-reflexive forms; ↑139j):

• without emphasis on the reflexive relationship (it is left unexpressed): possessive pronoun (↑140a):

οὐ ζητῶ τὸ θέλημα τὸ **ἐμόν**.	*I do not seek my own will.* (Jn 5:30)

κατὰ τὸν **ἡμέτερον** νόμον ἠθελήσαμεν κρίνειν.	*We wanted to judge him according to our own law.* (Ac 24:6 Var.)
… τὴν δὲ ἐν τῷ **σῷ** ὀφθαλμῷ δοκὸν οὐ κατανοεῖς;	*… but you do not notice the log in your own eye?* (Mt 7:3)

• with emphasis on the reflexive relationship (it is expressed): reflexive pronoun in the possessive genitive/ἴδιος (↑140b/140c), e.g.:

… μὴ ζητῶν τὸ **ἐμαυτοῦ** σύμφορον.	*… not seeking my own advantage.* (1Cor 10:33)
εὐδοκοῦμεν μεταδοῦναι ὑμῖν … τὰς **ἑαυτῶν** ψυχάς.	*We were delighted to share with you … our own lives.* (1Th 2:8)
σῷζε τὴν **σεαυτοῦ** ψυχήν.	*Save your own life!* (Gn 19:17 LXX)
τὴν **ἑαυτῶν** σωτηρίαν κατεργάζεσθε.	*Continue to work out your own salvation!* (Php 2:12)
ὁ ἀγαπῶν τὴν **ἑαυτοῦ** γυναῖκα …	*He who loves his own wife …* (Eph 5:28)
… θάψαι τοὺς **ἑαυτῶν** νεκρούς.	*… to bury their own dead.* (Mt 8:22)
… ἵνα μὴ … ἐκπέσητε τοῦ **ἰδίου** στηριγμοῦ.	*… so that you do not … fall from your secure position.* (2Pe 3:17)
εὑρίσκει … τὸν ἀδελφὸν τὸν **ἴδιον**.	*He finds … his own brother* (Jn 1:41)
… ὑποτασσόμεναι τοῖς **ἰδίοις** ἀνδράσιν.	*… they submitted themselves to their own husbands.* (1Pe 3:5)

141 Demonstrative pronouns

(↑22c word-class, ↑58 forms, ↑346ff functions; ↑BR §68; 156; BDF §289ff; Z §213f; Langslow: 528ff; Givón I: 97)

141a 1. In **Ancient Greek** there are three major types of demonstrative pronouns (on "anadeictic/catadeictic/deictic" role also ↑346/347b/348c), two to point to what is near, and one to point to what is distant, whether in space, time or emotional distance:

Pointing to what for the speaker/writer is **near**:[11]

(1) **ὅδε/ἥδε/τόδε** (NT: 10×)	*this (here)*
• typically points to	what is present at the moment of speaking/writing (pure deixis) or what is identified later in the text (catadeictic use)

11 Note that in Ancient Greek type 2 is used at least 12× more frequently than type 1 and its function appears to be less clearly fixed. It would, therefore, seem advisable to treat type 2 as the unmarked (normal) option and type 1 as the marked (special) one.

(2) **οὗτος/αὕτη/τοῦτο** (NT: ca. 1390×) — *this* (also *this here*)

- typically points to — what is identified earlier in the text (anadeictic use; especially in CG, and there mostly in contrast to ὅδε etc.) or
- (especially in post-CG/NT Greek) — what is present at the moment of speaking/writing (pure deixis) or what is identified later in the text (catadeictic use)

Pointing to what for the speaker/writer is more **distant**:

(3) **ἐκεῖνος/ἐκείνη/ἐκεῖνο** (NT: ca. 260×) — *that* (anadeictic or catadeictic use, or pure deixis)

2. When any of the above demonstrative pronouns are used as attributive modifiers (rather than as noun substitutes), they are in the so-called **"predicative" position** (a misnomer!; ↑136c), e.g.: 141b

ὅδε ὁ λόγος / ὁ λόγος **ὅδε**	*this word* (i.e. the one at the moment of speaking/writing) or the one that follows in the text)
οὗτος ὁ ἀνήρ / ὁ ἀνὴρ **οὗτος**	*this man* (i.e. the one just mentioned, the one here, or the one to be mentioned)
ἐκείνη ἡ ἡμέρα / ἡ ἡμέρα **ἐκείνη**	*that day*

Rarely a demonstrative pronoun is a concomitant of a noun that is without the article. In such a case the demonstrative pronoun functions as a subject or object, whilst the noun serves as a subject/object adjunct (SA/OA), which in an English rendering may often be introduced by the preposition *as* (↑259n; also ↑137c; BDF §292 or BR §258–262), e.g.:

τοῦτο (O) _ **ἀληθὲς** (nominalized; OA) εἴρηκας. — *You have said this "as something true" ≈ What you have said is true.* (Jn 4:18)

↑also Lk 2:2 (αὕτη [S] ἀπογραφὴ πρώτη [SA] ἐγένετο *This took place as a first registration ≈ This was the first registration*); 24:21 (τρίτην [Attr of OA] ταύτην [O] ἡμέραν ἄγει [OA] *[one] passes this as a third day ≈ it is now the third day*); Jn 2:11 (Ταύτην [O] ἐποίησεν ἀρχὴν [OA] τῶν σημείων [gen. Attr of OA] ὁ Ἰησοῦς … *Jesus did this as a beginning of his signs … ≈ What Jesus did … was the first of his signs*; ταύτην shows concord with ἀρχήν in a way analogous to the use referred to in 263e).

3. The demonstrative pronouns in KG and **NT Greek** 141c

a) In KG ὅδε etc. is used more rarely (still) than in CG (↑141a on relative frequency). As a result: οὗτος etc. by now has become (more) clearly the standard (unmarked) demonstrative pronoun pointing to what is near. Its functional domain has expanded and increasingly includes the CG special use of ὅδε etc. In the NT οὗτος etc. (↑141a and 346–348c) thus regularly points not only to what is identified earlier in the text (anadeictic use), but also to what is present at the moment of speaking/writing (pure deixis) or to what is identified later in the text (catadeictic use).

b) Examples:

(1) ὅδε/ἥδε/τόδε (NT: 10×):

τάδε (here noun substitute; Od; catadeictic) λέγει … — *These things/The following things/Thus says* … (Ac 21:11 and 7× in Re)

↑also Lk 10:39 (un-CG anadeictic use); Jas 4:13: εἰς τήνδε τὴν πόλιν *in this/in such and such a city* (starting from pure deixis, generalizing; according to BDF §289 Hellenistic usage).

(2) οὗτος/αὕτη/τοῦτο (NT: ca. 1390×):

• Pointing to what is identified earlier in the text (anadeictic; typical in CG), e.g.:

οὗτος γάρ ἐστιν ὁ ῥηθείς … — *For this is the one spoken of* … (Mt 3:3)

ταῦτα λελάληκα ὑμῖν ἵνα ἡ χαρὰ ἡ ἐμὴ ἐν ὑμῖν ᾖ. — *These things I have spoken to you so that my joy may be in you.* (Jn 15:11)

• Pointing to what is present at the moment of speaking/writing (pure deixis), e.g.:

τίνος ἡ εἰκὼν **αὕτη** καὶ ἡ ἐπιγραφή; — *Whose image and inscription is this (here)?* (Mk 12:16)

↑also Mt 3:9; 4:3; 17:20; 20:14; Mk 11:23; Ac 3:24; 4:10; 7:7; 11:12; 13:17; 20:34; 22:3; 28:20.

• Pointing to what is identified later in the text (catadeictic), e.g.:

ἀκούσατε τοὺς λόγους **τούτους**· — *Listen to these words!* (Ac 2:22)

τοῦτο δὲ λέγω· — *But I mean this (what follows):* (Ga 3:17)

(3) ἐκεῖνος/ἐκείνη/ἐκεῖνο (NT: ca. 260×; anadeictic/catadeictic, or pure deixis), e.g.:

πολλοὶ ἐροῦσίν μοι ἐν **ἐκείνῃ** τῇ ἡμέρᾳ· (probably pure deixis) — *Many will say to me on that day,* (Mt 7:22)

↑also Ro 14:14 (anadeictic); He 6:7 (catadeictic).

141d 4. Demonstrative pronouns may be used catadeictically (in NT and CG)

a) before a relative clause (↑142; 289d), e.g.:

τίς **οὗτός** ἐστιν ὃς …; — *Who is this, who …?* (Lk 7:49)

↑also Lk 19:15; Jn 13:26; He 6:7.

b) especially τοῦτο *this* before a clause subordinated by ὅτι (↑271; 318e), e.g.:

Οἶδας **τοῦτο**, ὅτι ἀπεστράφησάν με πάντες … — *You are aware of this/of the fact that all … have turned away from me.* (2Tm 1:15)

↑also Lk 10:11; Ro 2:3; Php 1:6; 1Th 4:15.

Analogously also before a clause subordinated by ἵνα *that* (↑272a; 288a) or before an inf./ACI phrase (↑222; 224b; 225a/225f).

c) before a purpose clause subordinated by ἵνα (↑278; 272; 288a; 318e), e.g.:

διὰ τοῦτο ἠλεήθην, ἵνα … — *For this reason I found mercy, in order that* … (1Tm 1:16)

↑also 1Jn 3:8.

d) For οὗτος *this* and ἐκεῖνος *that*, functioning as the 3rd pers. personal pronoun (especially in CG, ἐκεῖνος sometimes also in the NT) ↑54/55; 139c; 140b.

141e 5. Article and (specific) relative pronoun with demonstrative force in set phrases:

a) In set phrases the **article**, too, has the force of a demonstrative pronoun (↑131):

ὁ μέν – ὁ δέ *(this) one – (that) one* (1Cor 7:7)

ὁ δέ *But/And this one/the latter/he* (Mt 12:3)

b) The (specific) **relative pronoun** is frequently used analogously (especially in KG/NT; ↑142h), e.g.:

ὃς μέν – ὃς δέ *(this) one – (that) one* (Lk 23:33)

On the demonstratives in correlation ↑61, on their textgrammatical relevance ↑345. On questions of concord ↑261–265.

Relative pronouns 142

(↑22c on word-class, ↑59ff on forms, ↑289–290/319/348d on functions; ↑BR §157; 292; BDF §293; Z §215–220)

The (declinable) relative pronouns (↑59; 61b) belong to a larger category termed "relatives" (↑319) that also includes (uninflected) relative adverbs (↑61c). The major syntactic functions of relatives are:

(1) They subordinate dependent clauses (↑289–290) and so are (inter-clausal) connectives similar to conjunctions (↑319). Unlike these, however, they are noun substitutes and as such also serve as sentence constituents of the relative clause they introduce.

(2) They may (as they frequently do) refer back (anaphorically) to an element, usually a phrase (the "antecedent [phrase]"), in the superordinate construction.

I. Relative pronouns and their functions 142a

1. In Ancient Greek two types of relative pronouns predominate:

a) the **simple** or **specific** relative pronoun, typically referring back to a specific entity identified usually by an antecedent phrase in the superordinate construction:

ὅς/ἥ/ὅ *who/which/that*, e.g.:

… ὁ Ἰησοῦς (antecedent) **ὃν** (rel. pron.; Od of rel. clause) ἐγὼ καταγγέλλω ὑμῖν. *… Jesus, whom I am proclaiming to you* (Ac 17:3)

b) the **compound** or **indefinite** relative pronoun, typically referring to indefinite entities or a class, often without antecedent phrase in the superordinate construction (the indefinite force may be enhanced by means of ἄν/ἐάν + subj.; ↑252.3; 290e):

ὅστις/ἥτις/ὅ τι *whoever/whatever, any(one) who/ any(thing) that* (also ↑142b), e.g.:

ὅστις (rel. pron.; S of rel. clause) δὲ ὑψώσει ἑαυτὸν ταπεινωθήσεται. *But whoever exalts himself will be humbled.* (Mt 23:12)

Note that there are also special and indefinite varieties of (correlative) **pronouns** and **adverbs** for a listing of these ↑61), e.g.:

ἔσται γὰρ τότε θλῖψις μεγάλη **οἵα** (rel. pron.; S of rel. clause) οὐ γέγονεν … *For then there will be great distress, such as has not occurred …* (Mt 24:21)

ὁποῖοί (rel. pron.; SC of rel. clause) ποτε ἦσαν οὐδέν μοι διαφέρει· *Whatever kind of people they were makes no difference to me.* (Ga 2:6)

ἐπλήρωσεν ὅλον τὸν οἶκον **οὗ** (rel. adv.; LocC of rel. clause) ἦσαν καθήμενοι.	*It filled the entire house where they were sitting.* (Ac 2:2)
ὅπου (rel. adv.; LocC of rel. clause) γὰρ ζῆλος …, ἐκεῖ ἀκαταστασία …	*For where there is envy …, there will be disorder* … (Jas 3:16)

Noteworthy points on the compound/indefinite relative pronoun ὅστις/ἥτις/ὅ τι:

- It may have a **qualitative** force, i.e. the relative clause indicates what qualifies the antecedent as a member of the class referred to: *inasmuch as/who as such*, e.g.:

… ἀνδρὶ φρονίμῳ (class referred to: ἄνδρες **φρόνιμοι**), **ὅστις** ᾠκοδόμησεν …	… *a wise man, inasmuch as he/who as such* (i.e. as a WISE man) *built* … (Mt 7:24)

- In the NT this pronoun occurs only in the nominative (↑59b); so only in this case are possible semantic distinctions between the two types worth considering (also ↑142b).

On the compound/indefinite relatives being regularly used as indirect interrogatives ↑143a and 319c. On their rare use as indefinite pronouns ↑144b.

142b 2. Note that in **KG** the compound/indefinite relative pronoun quite often functions like its simple/specific counterpart, e.g.:

… εἰς πόλιν Δαυὶδ (specific entity) **ἥτις** (= ἥ) καλεῖται Βηθλέεμ.	… *to the city of David, which is called Bethlehem.* (Lk 2:4)

↑also Lk 7:37; Jn 8:53 et pass.

II. Further points **relevant to text interpretation** (also ↑289c–289f):

142c 1. In many cases the relative pronoun presupposes functionally the presence of a demonstrative pronoun as an antecedent (↑289d), e.g.:

… **ὃν** (= οὗτος ὃν) φιλεῖς ἀσθενεῖ.	… *the one whom you love is ill.* (Jn 11:3)

↑also Jn 6:29; 10:36; Ro 8:24f.

142d 2. Prepositions and relative pronouns (also ↑289e/289f):

a) A preposition before the relative pronoun may govern the "presupposed" demonstrative pronoun or the relative pronoun or both, e.g.:

… ἵνα πιστεύητε **εἰς ὃν** (= εἰς τοῦτον ὃν) ἀπέστειλεν ἐκεῖνος.	… *that you believe in the one whom he has sent.* (Jn 6:29)
Πῶς οὖν ἐπικαλέσωνται **εἰς ὃν** (= τοῦτον εἰς ὃν) οὐκ ἐπίστευσαν;	*How, then, can they call on the one in whom they have not believed?* (Ro 10:14)

↑also Ac 24:13.

τί βλασφημοῦμαι **ὑπὲρ οὗ** (= ὑπὲρ τούτου ὑπὲρ οὗ) ἐγὼ εὐχαριστῶ;	*Why am I denounced because of that for which I give thanks?* (1Cor 10:30)

b) A preposition governing the antecedent need not be repeated before the relative pronoun (a form of ellipsis, ↑293b; ↑Z §21), e.g.:

… εἰς τὸ ἔργον **ὃ** (= εἰς ὃ) προσκέκλημαι αὐτούς.	… *for the work to which I have called them.* (Ac 13:2)

↑also Ac 1:21.

3. When the relative pronoun is in the possessive genitive (↑159), the noun phrase that follows (referring to the possessed item) takes the article (↑130b), e.g.: 142e

… τῶν λοιπῶν συνεργῶν μου, **ὧν τὰ** ὀνόματα ἐν βίβλῳ ζωῆς (Fr. *dont **les** noms*).	… *my other co-workers, whose names are in the book of life.* (Php 4:3)

↑also Lk 3:16; 13:1; Jn 10:12; 11:2; Ro 3:8.14.

4. The relative pronoun may also introduce an indirect question (↑143b; 273b), e.g.: 142f

… μὴ εἰδὼς **ὃ** λέγει.	… *not knowing what he said.* (Lk 9:33)
↑οὐ γὰρ ᾔδει **τί** ἀποκριθῇ.	*For he did not know what to say.* (Mk 9:6)

On the other hand, the interrogative pronoun sometimes (especially in KG) introduces a relative clause (↑143b).

In CG relatives (not interrogatives) may introduce exclamative sentences (↑266a; BR §157.2), e.g.:

Οἷα ποιεῖς, ὦ ἑταῖρε.	*What kind of things you are doing, dear friend!* (Plato, Euthyphron 15e)

In the NT it is interrogatives that in part may have such a function (BDF §304), e.g.:

πόσην κατειργάσατο ὑμῖν σπουδήν …	*What eagerness this has produced in you …!* (2Cor 7:11)

5. Sometimes a relative pronoun occurs at the beginning of a new sentence, adopting a coordinating function. So, when used in this way, we call it **"continuative relative"** in this grammar (↑289g; also ↑130; 141d; 142h). In English it may usually be rendered as a personal pronoun, e.g.: 142g

Ἀλέξανδρος … πολλά μοι κακὰ ἐνεδείξατο· … **ὃν** καὶ σὺ φυλάσσου …	*Alexander … did me much harm … You too should be on your guard against him …!* (2Tm 4:14f)

↑also Ac 11:23; 16:24; 1Pe 5:9 et pass.

6. In set phrases the simple/specific relative pronoun like the article may be used with a demonstrative force (especially in KG/NT; ↑131; 139c; 141e), e.g.: 142h

ὃς μέν – ὃς δέ	*(this) one – (that) one* (Lk 23:33)

On the so-called "attraction" of the relative ↑289e/289f.

On the relatives in correlation ↑61, on their textgrammatical relevance also 345.

On questions of concord ↑261–265.

143 Interrogative pronouns

(↑22c on word-class, ↑60ff on forms, also ↑269/273 on functions; ↑BR §158; BDF §298–300; 436/437; Z §221–223)

143a 1. Interrogatives, i.e. interrogative pronouns and adverbs (↑61), are used to ask questions (the pronouns functioning as noun substitutes or as noun concomitants):

a) either **direct** or **indirect** ones (↑269d):

	as noun substitutes:	as noun concomitants:
τίς; / τί;	*who? / what?*	*what (…)? / which (…)?*

analogously the following interrogative pronouns and adverbs:

interrogative pronouns (functioning as noun substitutes or as noun concomitants):

πόσος;	*how large (…)?*	πόσοι;	*how many (…)?*
ποῖος;	*what kind of (…)?* (for this the NT sometimes uses post-CG ποταπός;)		
πηλίκος;	*what size/how great (…)?*		

interrogative adverbs:

ποῦ;	*where/to where?*	πόθεν;	*from where?*
πότε;	*when?*	ποσάκις;	*how often?*
πῶς;	*how?*		

b) **indirect** questions (↑273b), the same form as compound/indefinite relatives (↑142a; 319c), mainly CG (in the NT only occasionally: 4× ὁποῖος, 1× ὅστις, 1× ὅπως):

indirect interrogative pronouns (functioning as noun substitutes or as noun concomitants):

ὅστις / ὅ τι	*who (…)/what (…)*		
ὁπόσος	*how large (…)*	ὁπόσοι	*how many (…)*
ὁποῖος	*of what kind*		

indirect interrogative adverbs:

ὅπου	*where/to where*	ὁπόθεν	*from where*
ὁπότε	*when*		
ὅπως	*how* (1×; otherwise *in order that*)		

c) Examples:

(1) **direct questions** (↑269d):

εἶπαν οὖν αὐτῷ· **τίς** εἶ;	*Then they said to him, "Who are you?"* (Jn 1:22)
πῶς δύνασθε ὑμεῖς πιστεῦσαι …;	*How can you believe …?* (Jn 5:44)

(2) **indirect questions** (↑273b):

ὁ δὲ ἰαθεὶς οὐκ ᾔδει **τίς** ἐστιν	*But the man who had been healed did not know who it was.* (Jn 5:13)
λαληθήσεταί σοι **ὅ τί** σε δεῖ ποιεῖν. (very rare use of ὅ τι in the NT; ↑BDF §300.1)	*You will be told what you are to do.* (Ac 9:6)
… ἐπερωτήσας ἐκ **ποίας** ἐπαρχείας ἐστίν.	*… he asked from what (kind of) province he was.* (Ac 23:34)

ἀπαγγέλλουσιν **ὁποίαν** εἴσοδον ἔσχομεν πρὸς ὑμᾶς.	*they report what kind of reception we had among you.* (1Th 1:9)

↑also 1Cor 3:13; Ga 2:6; Jas 1:24 (↑BDF §300.1).

… καὶ **πῶς** ἐπεστρέψατε πρὸς τὸν θεὸν ἀπὸ τῶν εἰδώλων.	*… and how you turned to God from idols.* (1Th 1:9)
(οὐκ ἔγνως …) **ὅπως** τε παρέδωκαν αὐτόν … οἱ ἄρχοντες ἡμῶν …	*(Have you not heard …) and how … our leaders handed him over …* (Lk 24:20)

(only NT instance with ὅπως meaning *how* [otherwise *in order that*]; ↑BDF §300.1).

2. Indirect questions and relative clauses being similar in function, **interrogative** and **relative pronouns** may replace each other (KG; CG only in part; ↑142f): 143b

a) Interrogative pronouns replacing relative pronouns (especially in KG; ↑289a), e.g.:

ἀλλ᾽ οὐ **τί** ἐγὼ θέλω ἀλλὰ **τί** σύ (Var.: οὐχ **ὃ** ἐγὼ θέλω ἀλλ᾽ **ὃ** σὺ θέλεις).	*Yet not what I will, but what you will.* (Mk 14:36)

↑also Lk 17:8 / Mt 15:32 (τί) and Lk 11:6 (ὅ).

b) Relative pronouns replacing interrogative pronouns (= CG; ↑273b), e.g.:

οἶδεν … ὑμῶν **ὧν** χρείαν ἔχετε.	*… [he] knows what you need.* (Mt 6:8)
↑οὐκ οἴδατε **τί** αἰτεῖσθε.	*You do not know what you ask.* (Mt 20:22)

3. Further examples illustrating the use of interrogatives such as τίς and τί: 143c

a) τίς/τί (similarly e.g. ποῖος) as an **attributive noun concomitant**:

τίς βασιλεύς …;	*What king …?* (Lk 14:31)
τί σημεῖον δεικνύεις ἡμῖν …;	*What sign do you show us …?* (Jn 2:18)
ποίῳ δὲ σώματι ἔρχονται;	*With what kind of body will they come?* (1Cor 15:35)

b) τί "what" used adverbially:

(1) as *why?* quite often for διὰ τί (= CG; ↑156/157), e.g.:

τί μεριμνᾶτε …;	*Why do you worry …?* (Mt 6:28)

(2) as *how!* occasionally in exclamations (↑266a; probably a Semitism [↑Hebr. מַה *mah*; HALOT s.v.]), e.g.:

τί στενὴ ἡ πύλη …	*How narrow the gate …!* (Mt 7:14)

For interrogatives in correlation ↑61.
On questions of concord ↑261–265.

Indefinite pronoun (↑22c on word-class, ↑60/61 on forms; ↑BR §159; BDF §301–303) 144

1. Indefinites, i.e. indefinite pronouns and adverbs (↑61), characterize persons or things as unspecified (with regard to identity, dimension, quantity or quality). The most important indefinite pronoun in Ancient Greek is the enclitic τις/τι (the identity of persons or things referred to is marked as unspecified); it is used as either 144a

a noun substitute or a noun concomitant. Some of the typical English renderings are: *someone, anyone, something, anything, some, any, a certain.*
Within this domain of meaning τις is sometimes used like the English generic personal pronoun "one" (↑139e; 255f), similarly also like ὁ μέν (… ὁ δέ; ↑131).

Examples:

a) **τις** *someone/anyone, some/any*:

• as a **noun substitute**, also translatable as *one/a certain one*, in the pl. as *certain individuals/some*, e.g.:

πῶς δύναταί **τις** εἰσελθεῖν …;	*How can anyone enter …?* (Mt 12:29)
καί **τινες** κατελθόντες …	*And certain individuals/some came down* … (Ac 15:1)
… καθότι ἄν **τις** χρείαν εἶχεν.	… *as any(one) had need.* (Ac 4:35)

• as an **attributive noun concomitant** (↑260b); as such it may have the role of the English indefinite article "a" (↑130a), e.g.:

ἱερεύς **τις** ὀνόματι Ζαχαρίας	*a priest named Zechariah.* (Lk 1:5)
γυναῖκές **τινες** … ἐξέστησαν ἡμᾶς	*some women … astounded us.* (Lk 24:22)
εἴ **τίς** ἐστιν ἐν ὑμῖν λόγος παρακλήσεως …	*if you have any word of exhortation* … (Ac 13:15)

The indefiniteness expressed may have either a softening or an intensifying force (↑context), e.g.:

… εἰς τὸ εἶναι ἡμᾶς ἀπαρχήν **τινα** τῶν αὐτοῦ κτισμάτων.	… *that we might be a kind of* (softening) *firstfruits of all he created.* (Jas 1:18)
… φοβερὰ δέ **τις** ἐκδοχὴ κρίσεως …	… *but only* (intensifying) *a fearful expectation of judgment* … (He 10:27)

b) **τι** *something/anything, some/any*:

• as a **noun substitute**, e.g.:

… ὅτι ὁ ἀδελφός σου ἔχει **τι** κατὰ σοῦ.	… *that your brother has something against you.* (Mt 5:23)
… ὅτι λήμψεταί **τι** παρὰ τοῦ κυρίου	… *that he will receive anything from the Lord* (Jas 1:7)

• as an **attributive noun concomitant**; as such it may be used like the English indefinite article, in the pl. also like *some/any/certain*, e.g.:

νησίον δέ **τι** ὑποδραμόντες …	*Running under the lee of a small island* … (Ac 27:16)
… **τι** ἀγαθὸν ἤ φαῦλον …	… *anything good or bad* (Ro 9:11)
ἦλθον ἐπί **τι** ὕδωρ	*They came to some water.* (Ac 8:36)
μή **τι** προσφάγιον ἔχετε;	*Do you not have any fish?* (Jn 21:5)
ζητήματα δέ **τινα** … εἶχον	*Instead, they had certain points of dispute* … (Ac 25:19)

On the frequent combination with a partitive genitive ↑166b (in such cases, there is sometimes a Semitizing ellipsis of τις/τι).

2. In a way **similar to τις** indefiniteness is sometimes expressed by: 144b

a) **εἷς** *one*, here: *a* (sometimes in NT [popular KG] Greek narratives; occasionally combined as εἷς τις; ↑130a), e.g.:

εἷς γραμματεύς	*a scribe* (Mt 8:19)

b) **ἄνθρωπος** *a human being*, here: *a/some* (also CG; also like the generic personal pronoun *one*; ↑255f [BDAG s.v. 4]; also ↑260j), e.g.:

ἐχθρὸς **ἄνθρωπος**	*an enemy/some enemy* (Mt 13:28)

c) **ἀνήρ** *man*, here: *someone/anyone* (similarly CG; also ↑Hebr. אִישׁ *’îš man*, similarly Aram. אֱנָשׁ *’ĕnāš human being* [HALOT s.v.]; also ↑260j), e.g.:

Μακάριος **ἀνὴρ** ὃς ὑπομένει πειρασμόν	*Blessed is anyone who endures testing.* (Jas 1:12)

d) **πᾶς** *every/all*, here: inter alia *any/any kind of* (↑136b), e.g.:

παρακαλεῖν τοὺς ἐν **πάσῃ** θλίψει	*to comfort those in any trouble.* (2Cor 1:4)

e) **ὅστις** *whoever*, also *any(one) who*, similarly **ὃς ἄν/ἐάν** (↑142a; 290e; BDF §303), e.g.:

ὅστις σε ῥαπίζει εἰς τὴν δεξιὰν σιαγόνα	*if anyone slaps you on the right cheek* (Mt 5:39)
ὃς ἂν τόπος μὴ δέξηται ὑμᾶς	*if any place will not welcome you* (Mk 6:11)

3. **Negations** such as *no one/none, nobody, nothing* may be expressed not only by **οὐ/μή … τις/τι** 144c
(as may be expected), but also by:

a) **οὐδείς** or **μηδείς** *no one/nobody*, ntr. *nothing* (very frequently; ↑63; 145), e.g.:

οὐδεὶς δύναται …	*No one/Nobody can …* (Mt 6:24)
μηδὲν αἴρετε εἰς τὴν ὁδόν	*Take nothing for your journey!* (Lk 9:3)

b) In the NT at times by **οὐ/μή … πᾶς** agreeing with Hebrew usage (↑ לֹא … כֹּל *lō’… kōl*; ↑249a), e.g.:

… **οὐκ** ἂν ἐσώθη **πᾶσα** σάρξ.	… *no one* (lit. "no flesh", rather than "not all flesh") *would be saved.* (Mt 24:22)
ὅτι **οὐκ** ἀδυνατήσει παρὰ τοῦ θεοῦ **πᾶν** ῥῆμα.	*For nothing* (lit. "no thing", rather than "not every thing") *will be impossible with God.* (Lk 1:37)
ὅπως **μὴ** καυχήσηται **πᾶσα** σάρξ	*so that no one might boast* (1Cor 1:29)
But ↑e.g. **οὐ πάντες** χωροῦσιν τὸν λόγον τοῦτον.	*Not all can accept this word.* (Mt 19:11)

c) Occasionally in a comparable way by **εἷς … οὐ** *not one* (= CG and Semitic usage), e.g.:

ἓν … οὐ πεσεῖται	*Not one … will fall* (Mt 10:29)
ἰῶτα **ἓν** ἢ **μία** κεραία **οὐ μὴ** παρέλθῃ …	*not one iota, not one stroke, will pass …* (Mt 5:18)

On the indefinites in correlation ↑61.

On questions of concord ↑261–265.

3.2.1.4 Syntax of numerals

145 Important points on numeral use

(↑22e on word-class, ↑62/63 on forms; ↑BDF §247f; Z §154–159)

Ancient Greek numerals, by and large, are used in the same way as English numerals, mostly as attributive modifiers of a noun phrase (↑260b), but at times nominalized (↑132d). However, there are a few peculiarities that need to be mentioned:[12]

145a 1. **πρῶτος** *first*:

a) When referring to "the first day of the week"[13] (i.e. our Sunday) the NT idiomatically uses the cardinal rather than the ordinal one (un-CG; like Hebr. [↑HALOT sub אֶחָד *'eḥād*]);[14] in agreement with general Greek usage (↑260c) the word ἡμέρα *day* is not expressed, but is to be understood ("sc."), e.g.:

τῇ **μιᾷ** (sc. ἡμέρᾳ) τῶν σαββάτων	*on the first day of the week* (Mk 16:2)
κατὰ **μίαν** (sc. ἡμέραν) σαββάτου	*on the first day of every week* (1Cor 16:2)

↑also Mt 28:1; Lk 24:1; Jn 20:1.19; Ac 20:7.

Not so Mk 16:9 (with ordinal): πρωῒ πρώτῃ (sc. ἡμέρᾳ) σαββάτου *early on the first day of the week.*

Note that μίαν for πρώτην in Tt 3:10 appears to have a purely Greek background, as does μία in Re 9:12 (BDAG sub εἷς 4).

Outside the above idiom the NT uses the (CG) ordinal to express "first", e.g.:

ἀπὸ τῆς **πρώτης** ἡμέρας ἄχρι τοῦ νῦν	*from the first day until now* (Php 1:5)

b) Combined with the genitive of comparison (↑170) πρῶτος means "earlier (than)" (↑BDF §62), e.g.:

ὁ ὀπίσω μου ἐρχόμενος ἔμπροσθέν μου γέγονεν, ὅτι **πρῶτός μου** ἦν.	*He who comes after me ranks before me, because he existed earlier than/before me.* (Jn 1:15; ↑1:30)

c) In CG for "[the] first (of more than two)" πρῶτος was used, and for "[the] first (of two)" πρότερος. In KG and NT Greek πρῶτος may be used for "[the] first (of two or more than two)"; πρότερος in NT Greek simply means "earlier/former" (a meaning current in CG, too; ↑BDF §62), e.g.:

ἦσαν δὲ παρ' ἡμῖν ἑπτὰ ἀδελφοί· καὶ ὁ **πρῶτος** (like CG) γήμας ἐτελεύτησεν …	*Now there were seven brothers among us. The first married and died …* (Mt 22:25)
ἄνθρωπος εἶχεν τέκνα δύο. καὶ προσελθὼν τῷ **πρώτῳ** (un-CG) εἶπεν …	*A man had two sons; he went to the first and said …* (Mt 21:28)

↑also (= CG) Lk 16:5; 19:16; (un-CG) Ac 1:1; 12:10 et pass.

---

12 On the order of numerals above "10" ↑62a.

13 Note (1) that the word for "week" σάββατον (Hebr. שַׁבָּת *šabbāṯ*; Aram. שַׁבְּתָא *šabbəṯā'*) can mean either "Sabbath" or "week" and (2) that in principle it has a sg. meaning no matter whether its form is in the sg. or in the pl. (τὰ σάββατα appears to go back to the Aram. *šabbəṯā'*, which NB is a sg. form).

14 As noted in BDF §247.1, Josephus (Antiquities 1.29) felt that this use (probably regarded as a Hebraism) called for an explanation, similarly Philo (Opificio mundi 1.15).

2. **εἷς/μία/ἕν** *one* may replace the following pronouns: 145b

a) the indefinite pronoun τις (↑130a; 144b), e.g.:

ἰδὼν συκῆν **μίαν** (= συκῆν τινα) … *Seeing a fig tree* … (Mt 21:19)

εἷς τις, however, means *a certain one* (e.g. Mk 14:47) agreeing with CG usage.

b) occasionally the reciprocal pronoun ἀλλήλους (perhaps a Semitism; ↑139n), e.g.:

οἰκοδομεῖτε **εἷς τὸν ἕνα**. *Build up/Strengthen one another!* (1Th 5:11)

↑also 131: ὁ εἷς – ὁ ἕτερος / εἷς *one – the other.*

3. In **distributive** expressions involving numerals we find: 145c

a) ἀνά or κατά before a numeral (= CG; ↑184c/184k), e.g.:

ἀνὰ πεντήκοντα *fifty each* (Lk 9:14)

κατὰ δύο ἢ … τρεῖς *two or … three each time* (1Cor 14:27)

b) the cardinal doubled (KG and Semitic usage; GKC §134q and Dalman §23.4), e.g.:

δύο δύο *two by two / in pairs* (Mk 6:7)

(also **ἀνὰ** δύο δύο Lk 10:1)

Occasionally the doubling of other expressions is used in a similar way, e.g. (↑BDF §493.2):

… ἀνακλῖναι πάντας **συμπόσια συμπόσια** … καὶ ἀνέπεσαν **πρασιαὶ πρασιαὶ** κατὰ ἑκατὸν καὶ κατὰ πεντήκοντα. … *all to sit down in groups* (lit. "groups of diners [beside] groups of diners") … *So they sat down in groups* (lit. "garden plot [beside] garden plot") *by hundreds and by fifties.* (Mk 6:39f)

ἕκαστος *each* may be used with a distributive force (at times εἷς added for emphasis) in combination with a plural subject (= CG), e.g.:

… ἐὰν μὴ ἀφῆτε **ἕκαστος** τῷ ἀδελφῷ αὐτοῦ ἀπὸ τῶν καρδιῶν ὑμῶν. … *if each of you does not forgive your brother or sister from your heart.* (Mt 18:35)

Inter alia also ↑Jn 16:32; Ac 2:6 (εἷς ἕκαστος).

4. To express **approximation** ὡς/ὡσεί *about* (↑252.61) may be used with numerals, e.g.: 145d

ὡς δισχίλιοι *about two thousand* (Mk 5:13)

↑also Mt 14:21; Lk 1:56; 3:23 et pass.

5. Further peculiarities of numeral use: 145e

a) **"The third time"** etc. may be expressed in more than one way:
(1) τρίτον/τὸ τρίτον (e.g. Mk 14:41; Lk 23:22; ↑157]) or (2) ἐκ τρίτου (Mt 26:44).

b) **ἑβδομηκοντάκις ἑπτά** in Mt 18:22 may be understood in two different ways:
(1) as *seventy-seven times* or (2) as *seventy times seven (times).*

Mt 18:22 is likely to refer to Gn 4:24, where the Hebrew expression agrees with 1 (↑HALOT sub שֶׁבַע *šéḇaʿ* 3; apparently favoured by BDF §248.2). On the other hand, nearly all the ancient versions have 2 both in Gn 4:24 and Mt 18:22. Though it may not be quite certain whether the LXX expression (basis of the NT instance) belongs to 1 (↑Septuaginta deutsch) or 2 (↑NETS), the non-literal sense (↑314h) of the Mt 18:22 expression is clear: "innumerable times"/"without counting".

c) **ἓν τριάκοντα** etc. in Mk 4:8.20:

ἕν is widely considered an Aram. meaning *-fold* (ἓν τριάκοντα … *thirtyfold* …; ↑חַד *ḥaḏ* [lit. "one"] in Dn 3:19; ↑BDF §248.3). Understanding it in terms of Greek usage, however, seems possible (↑G. Lohfink, *Biblische Zeitschrift* 30, 1986: 45; also ↑BDAG sub εἷς 5a/b; Kühner-Gerth II: 272):

καὶ ἔφερεν ἓν τριάκοντα καὶ ἓν ἑξήκοντα καὶ ἓν ἑκατόν. *and one (seed) yielded thirty (pieces of grain), the other sixty, and the other one hundred.*

d) **ἡμέρας δεκαπέντε** "fifteen days" in Ga 1:18:

This almost certainly means "two weeks" (inclusively counted as in French "quinze jours") corresponding to English "a fortnight" (↑BDAG sub δέκα – δεκαπέντε for extra-biblical instances).

e) **μετὰ τρεῖς ἡμέρας** "after three days" Mt 27:63; Mk 8:31:

Here, too, inclusive counting is presupposed. The expression has the same meaning as (ἐν) τῇ τρίτῃ ἡμέρᾳ / τῇ ἡμέρᾳ τῇ τρίτῃ "on the third day" (↑BDAG sub μετά B2a and τρεῖς as well as τρίτος with references to extra-biblical sources).

f) **ἑξακόσιοι ἑξήκοντα ἕξ** "666" in Re 13:18: For the numerous attempts to trace the intended meaning scholarly commentaries need to be consulted.

On the dual pronoun ἀμφότεροι *both* ↑63a; 130b.

For ἕτερος *the one/the other of two*, which in the NT (un-CG) is not always distinguishable from ἄλλος *another*, ↑61c[1/2]. Note that ἄλλος inter alia occurs in the CG idiom: ἄλλοι ἄλλο (τι) *some one thing, some another* (↑Ac 19:32; 21:34). For details ↑BDF §305f.

3.2.1.5 Syntax of case forms

(↑22a/23c for basics, ↑321 on textgrammatical relevance; ↑BR §160–194; BDF §143–202; Z §25–74)

146 Syntax of case forms: preliminaries (↑BR §160; Langslow: 371ff)

146a 1. The cases of nouns and other declinable words (article, pronouns, adjectives, and some numerals) indicate the syntactic role of the phrase they are part of (↑22a/23c; also ↑254c/258d with regard to sentence patterns). The **syntax of case forms**, as it is presented here, will show how the five cases of Ancient Greek (above all in the NT) may affect the functions of a noun, adjective or participle phrase when its head appears in a particular case form. Note that only the case forms without prepositions are in view here. Cases are sometimes relevant to the meaning of a preposition phrase, but in principle not to its syntactic role. For the roles of preposition phrases ↑183–186.

Proto-Indo-European, the parent language of Greek (↑p. 1), appears originally to have had eight cases (preserved in Classical Old Indic [Sanskrit]). In Ancient Greek, as it is accessible to us, only five cases are still in use; the functions of the three lost ones have been taken over by other cases:

lost Proto-Indo-European case:		in Ancient Greek its function is taken over by:
a) ablative (answering the question "From where?")	→	genitive (preserved in Lat. with additional functions)
b) locative (answering the question "Where?")	→	dative (in Lat. taken over by the ablative)
c) instrumental (answering the question "By what means?"; still preserved in Mycenaean Greek [↑p. 2])	→	dative (in Lat. taken over by the ablative)

2. Regarding the syntax of case forms **CG** and **KG** usage mainly differ as follows: 146b

CG:			KG/NT:	
a) For several CG prepositionless case noun phrases KG uses **preposition phrases**				
• either **exclusively** (note, however, that these CG constructions had a fairly limited use):				
accusative of goal		→	εἰς + acc. (↑149b), e.g.:	
οἴκ**αδε** (ἦλθεν)	*(he went) home*		**εἰς** τὸν οἶκον (…)	*(…) home*
Ἀθήν**αζε** (<Ἀθήν**ασδε**)	*to Athens*		**εἰς** Πέργην	*to Perga*
dative of place		→	ἐν + dat. (↑173c), e.g.:	
Ἀθήν**ησιν**	*in Athens*		**ἐν** Πέργῃ	*in Perga*
• or **frequently**:				
partitive genitive/genitive of separation/place (↑167; 169; 171)		→	genitive or frequently ἐκ + gen. (in some cases ἀπό + gen.)	
dative of instrument/cause/manner (↑177; 180)		→	dative or frequently or predominantly ἐν + dat. as well as other prepositions	
b) Answering the question "In what respect?":				
accusative standard, dative rare		→	dative standard, accusative rare (↑149b)	
c) Genitive of quality (↑162):				
restricted use		→	used more widely	

3. The syntax of case forms will be **treated** in the following **order**: 146c

case:	typical roles of NP (or AdjP/PtcP):
a) Nominative (↑147)	S, also SC/SA (AdjP/PtcP also Attr, Advl)
b) Vocative (↑148)	addressing hearer or reader
c) Accusative (↑149–157)	Od, also OC/OA, Attr, Advl
d) Genitive (↑158–172)	Attr, also Og, Advl
e) Dative (↑173–182)	Oi/O^{dat}, also Advl, Attr

Also ↑187 for an overview of phrases indicating space, time etc.
On questions of concord ↑261–265.

(i) Nominative and vocative

Nominative (↑BR §162; BDF §143–145; Z §25–34) 147

1. The nominative may have the following syntactic roles: 147a

a) A **nominative noun phrase** (its head being in the nominative, as also any expansions showing concord) functions

• mostly as a subject (S; ↑255), e.g.:

ἡ χήρα αὕτη ἡ πτωχὴ (S) πλεῖον πάντων ἔβαλεν·	*This poor widow has put in more than all the others.* (Lk 21:3)

• also as a subject complement (SC, infrequently as a SA; ↑258a/258b,259q), e.g.:

Αὕτη (S) ἐστὶν **ἡ ἐντολὴ ἡ ἐμή** (SC[id]) *This is my commandment.* (Jn 15:12)

The NT (not CG) may use γίνομαι *to become* and εἰμί *to be* with a SC[id] not in the nominative, but (chiefly in OT quotations) one in the form of an εἰς PpP (↑Hebr. לְ *lə*, HALOT s.v. 13; ↑258a), e.g.:

ἔσονται οἱ δύο **εἰς σάρκα μίαν** (SC[id]) (לְבָשָׂר אֶחָד *ləḇāśār ʼeḥāḏ*). *The two shall become one flesh.* (Mk 10:8)

↑also Lk 20:17 (= Ps 117:22 LXX: γίνομαι + εἰς PpP; ↑Lk 23:12: γίνομαι + nom.).
For an analogous phenomenon regarding object complements (OC[id]) ↑153b/258a.

b) A **nominative adjective** (or participle) **phrase** functions (↑137)

• frequently as an attributive modifier (embedded in a NP; ↑260b/260c), as in the case of πτωχή *poor* in Lk 21:3 above;

• also as a subject complement (SC, more rarely SA; ↑258a/258b, 259n/259o), e.g.:

πέντε δὲ ἐξ αὐτῶν (S) ἦσαν **μωραί** (SC) *But five of them were foolish* (Mt 25:2)

εἱστήκεισαν **ἐνεοί** (SA). *They stood there speechless.* (Ac 9:7)

• with some adjectives, very often with participles as an adverbial (↑259b/259c), e.g.:

ἥτις **αὐτομάτη** (ManA) ἠνοίγη αὐτοῖς. *It opened for them by itself.* (Ac 12:10)

ὃς ἐληλύθει **προσκυνήσων** … (PurpA). *He had come … to worship.* (Ac 8:27)

147b 2. The nominative is sometimes used without a particular syntactic role:

a) as a "nominativus pendens" ("hanging" nominative), e.g.:

ὁ νικῶν … δώσω αὐτῷ … *The victorious one…: I will give him…* (Re 2:26)

The phrase that would normally be in the dative is moved to the beginning of the sentence, for emphasis, in the form of a nominative ("hanging" because, naturally classified as a subject, it is not followed by the expected predicate; it is an "anacoluthon" construction [↑292e]).
↑also Jn 7:38; 17:2; Ac 7:40.

b) in exclamations (in the form of ellipses; ↑293a]), e.g.:

ποταποὶ λίθοι καὶ ποταπαὶ οἰκοδομαί. *What large stones and what large buildings!* (Mk 13:1)

c) replacing a vocative (↑148b).

d) in lists, e.g. Mt 10:2–4; 1Chr 25:1f LXX (also inscriptions; ↑BR §162 Note 1).

e) in book titles, e.g. Mt 1:1; Mk 1:1; Re 1:1.

148 Vocative (↑BR §161; BDF §146f; Z §33–35; ↑23e; 26; 28; 37b; 38; 42a; 47 for forms)

148a 1. A vocative noun phrase expresses a direct address to the hearer(s)/reader(s). Its function is comparable to the 2nd person personal pronoun (↑348b); such a pronoun is frequently added to enhance the vocative force when the phrase is translated into English. Grammatically speaking, a vocative phrase is outside the surrounding sentence structure (it is parenthetical; ↑254e/292d). It has no syntactic role (as a sentence constituent); it does, however, have a communicative function: it (deictically) points to an entity in the extralinguistic situation (on deixis also ↑347b), e.g.:

ὑποκριτά, ἔκβαλε πρῶτον … *You hypocrite, first take …* (Mt 7:5)

KG vocative noun phrases are normally without the interjection ὦ (typical of Att./CG); by ὦ an emotional nuance is generally added, e.g.:

Σὺ δέ, **ὦ ἄνθρωπε θεοῦ** …·	*But you, O man of God …!* (1Tm 6:11)

Noteworthy points relevant to **text interpretation**:
CG: Since ὦ is normally used with vocatives, its absence is exegetically relevant: its absence signals emotional distance or even contempt.
KG/NT: The converse applies here: ὦ is normally absent; if it is used, it generally adds an emotional nuance (but in Ac ὦ is used a few times without such a nuance: e.g. 1:1; 18:14; 27:21).

2. Nominative noun phrases used as vocatives: 148b

a) Vocative forms that are recognizable as such due to a characteristic ending are not uncommon in the NT, especially in the Gospels, e.g. κύριε *lord*, διδάσκαλε *teacher*, δοῦλε *servant*, υἱέ *son*, δέσποτα *master*, γύναι *woman*, βασιλεῦ *king*.

b) Frequently, however, noun phrases with a nominative head are used as vocatives, even in the case of nouns with a clearly marked vocative form, e.g.:

ναὶ **ὁ πατήρ** …	*Yes, Father …* (Lk 10:21)
ἐξέλθατε **ὁ λαός μου**.	*Come out of her, my people!* (Re 18:4)

Note that the vocative form θεέ occurs very rarely (so in Mt 27:46; 2Sm 7:25 LXX; Josephus, Antiquities 14.24); ὁ θεός is generally used instead (BDF §147.3).

c) When nominative noun phrases are used as vocatives (especially in cases where vocative forms exist), KG typically adds the article (↑130b), e.g.:

ὁ κύριός μου καὶ **ὁ θεός μου**	*My Lord and my God!* (Jn 20:28)
μὴ φοβοῦ, **τὸ μικρὸν ποίμνιον**.	*Do not be afraid, little flock!* (Lk 12:32)

3. An adjective as an attributive (↑137a) modifier of a vocative noun will, according to concord rules (↑263a), be in the vocative as well (if such a form exists), e.g.: 148c

πάτερ ἅγιε	*Holy Father* (Jn 17:11)

↑also Mt 25:21.

Interestingly, in the vocative exclamation of Mt 23:37 and Lk 13:34 πρὸς αὐτήν *to her* is used to refer (anaphorically) to the vocative rather than the expected πρὸς σέ *to you*:

Ἰερουσαλὴμ Ἰερουσαλήμ, ἡ ἀποκτείνουσα τοὺς προφήτας καὶ λιθοβολοῦσα τοὺς ἀπεσταλμένους πρὸς αὐτήν …	*Jerusalem, Jerusalem, you who kill the prophets and kill those sent to you …*

(ii) Accusative

Accusative: preliminaries (↑BR §163; BDF §148ff; Z §66ff) 149

1. The Ancient Greek accusative has mainly three syntactic roles: 149a

a) An accusative noun phrase (its head being in the accusative, as also any expansions showing concord) first of all functions as a direct object (Od; answering the question “Whom/What …?”): the “**object accusative**” (↑150–154). The Od noun phrase usually refers to the notionally closest entity, directly targeted by the "action", dative and genitive objects to less directly targeted entities (↑257b), e.g.:

Ἀνὴρ δέ τις … ἐπώλησεν **κτῆμα** (Od)	*But a man … sold some property* (Ac 5:1)

b) Frequently accusative noun phrases function as the subject of infinitive phrases: the "**subject accusative**" (ACI-S; ↑216–226), e.g.:

εἰς τὸ περιπατεῖν **ὑμᾶς** (ACI-S) ἀξίως …	*that you lead a life worthy …* (1Th 2:12)

c) Accusative noun phrases may also be used in a more independent, "free" way, not showing any concord with other sentence constituents, mainly as an optional adverbial (adjunct [↑259a–259m]; rarely as an obligatory one [↑259c]), at times as an attributive modifier (↑260g): the "**free use accusative**" (↑155–157), e.g.:

ἔμεινεν ἐκεῖ **δύο ἡμέρας** (TempA)	*He stayed there for two days.* (Jn 4:40)

Note that various **sentence elements**, whether part of the Od/ACI-S noun phrase (Attr) or outside it, may **show concord** with it and so are in the accusative (↑259q; 261–265; by many called "predicative accusative", ↑153b; on the term "predicative" as used in this grammar ↑254c[3]):

(1) adjective or participle phrases as attributive modifiers (↑260a–260c; 136a), e.g.:

εἶδον οὐρανὸν (head of Od) **καινόν** (Attr)	*I saw a new heaven.* (Re 21:1)
τὸν **κοπιῶντα** (Attr) γεωργὸν (head of ACI-S) δεῖ πρῶτον τῶν καρπῶν μεταλαμβάνειν.	*The hard-working farmer ought to be the first to have a share of the crops.* (2Tm 2:6)

(2) noun or adjective phrases as object/subject complements (↑259a/259b; 233; also ↑147a), e.g.:

ὑμᾶς (Od) δὲ εἴρηκα **φίλους** (OC[id]).	*But I have called you friends.* (Jn 15:15)
λέγω γὰρ Χριστὸν (ACI-S) **διάκονον** (head of SC[id]) γεγενῆσθαι περιτομῆς	*For I tell you that Christ became a servant to the circumcised …* (Ro 15:8)

(3) participle phrases as adverbial adjuncts (↑259a–259m/258c; ↑137d; 229–232), e.g.:

ἀπέστειλεν αὐτὸν (Od) **εὐλογοῦντα ὑμᾶς** (PurpA).	*He sent him (for him) to bless you.* (Ac 3:26)
Βούλομαι οὖν προσεύχεσθαι τοὺς ἄνδρας (ACI-S) ἐν παντὶ τόπῳ **ἐπαίροντας ὁσίους χεῖρας** (ManA)	*So I want the men in every place to pray, lifting up holy hands* (1Tm 2:8)

(4) adjective or noun phrases as object/subject adjuncts (↑259n/259o; also ↑147a), e.g.:

αὐτὸν (Od) … ἀπέστειλαν **κενόν** (OA).	*They … sent him away empty-handed.* (Mk 12:3)
πρέπον ἐστὶν γυναῖκα (ACI-S) **ἀκατακάλυπτον** (SA) τῷ θεῷ προσεύχεσθαι;	*Is it proper for a woman to pray to God unveiled?* (1Cor 11:13)

On nominalization of expressions making possible a variety of syntactic functions ↑132d (and chapters on the syntax of declinable words in general).
On accusative of invoked deity etc. ↑252.33; on accusative absolute ↑230f.
On prepositions + accusative ↑183/184.

149b 2. Regarding the free use accusative **CG** and **KG** differ as follows:

CG:		KG/NT:
a) Accusative of extent (question "For how long?"):		
accusative	→	accusative standard, at times dative (↑182b)
b) Accusative of respect (question "In what respect?"; ↑156):		
accusative standard, dative rare	→	accusative rare, dative standard (↑178a)
c) Accusative of goal (question "Where?" in terms of movement to/towards; ↑BR §173 Note 2):		
restricted use (PpP more frequently used)	→	accusative not used, always PpP instead (↑187b)

(a) Object accusative

Accusative of direct external object (↑BR §163ff) 150

1. In this most typical use, the accusative noun phrase refers to the person(s) or thing(s) directly targeted or affected by the "action": the "affected" object, e.g.: 150a

ὁ γὰρ πατὴρ φιλεῖ **τὸν υἱόν** (Od).	*For the Father loves the Son.* (Jn 5:20)
κατέκλασεν **τοὺς ἄρτους** (Od).	*He broke the loaves.* (Mk 6:41)

2. It may also refer to the entity resulting from the "action": sometimes called "effected" object, e.g.: 150b

ἄνθρωπος … ᾠκοδόμησεν **πύργον** (Od).	*A person … built a tower.* (Mt 21:33)

↑also the objects of verbs such as ἐργάζομαι *to work* (τὰ ἔργα *the works*, Jn 9:4), κατασκευάζω *to prepare*, ποιέω *to do*, γράφω *to write* (ἐπιστολήν *a letter*).

Accusative of direct internal object (↑BR §163; 170; BDF §153) 151

This is the term for direct object phrases with a head closely related to the verb in form ("cognate accusative"; "figura etymologica" construction; ↑294h) or in meaning.

1. The head of such a noun phrase is typically accompanied by an **attributive modifier** (either an adjective phrase or a relative clause; ↑260a/260c/260n), potential tautologies (unnecessary repetition of the same thing) thus being avoided, e.g.: 151a

ὡμολόγησας **τὴν καλὴν ὁμολογίαν** (Od)	*You made the good confession* (1Tm 6:12)
ἐφοβήθησαν **φόβον μέγαν** (Od)	*They were absolutely terrified* (Mk 4:41)

↑also Mt 2:10; Lk 11:46; Jn 7:24; 2Tm 4:7; Re 16:9.

δύνασθε … **τὸ βάπτισμα ὃ ἐγὼ βαπτίζομαι** (Od) βαπτισθῆναι;	*Can you … be baptized with the baptism that I am baptized with?* (Mk 10:38)

↑also Jn 17:26; Eph 2:4.

2. Examples with an internal object that is closely related to the verb in meaning, in terms of **synonymy** (rarely found in the NT): 151b

… **ὅρκον ὃν** (Od) ὤμοσεν …	… *(to remember) the oath that he swore* … (Lk 1:73)
… μὴ φοβούμεναι **μηδεμίαν πτόησιν** (Od)	… *if you do not fear anything that is frightening* (1Pe 3:6)

3. Sometimes noun phrases are used **without an attributive modifier** to make clearer what meaning exactly the verb is intended to convey in the context, e.g.: 151c

… φυλάσσοντες **φυλακάς** (Od) …	… *keeping watch* … (Lk 2:8)
… ἀνθρώπῳ οἰκοδομοῦντι **οἰκίαν** (Od) …	… *a man building a house* … (Lk 6:48)

152 Simple object accusative (S+P+Od; ↑258d; ↑BR §164–167; BDF §148–154; Z §66–70)

152a 1. Generally speaking, in Ancient Greek the simple object accusative (Od) is found with the same types of verbs as in English. There are, however, transitive verbs (i.e. with a Od, the sentence pattern being S+P+Od) in Ancient Greek, that in many cases are best **translated** as a construction **with something other than a Od**, such as:

a) certain verbs of affective behaviour, such as ἐλεέω τινά *to have compassion/mercy on s.o.* or ἐπιποθέω τινά *to long for s.o.*, e.g.:

υἱὲ Δαυίδ, ἐλέησόν **με** (Od).	*Son of David, have mercy on me!* (Mk 10:48)
ἐπιποθῶ **πάντας ὑμᾶς** (Od).	*I long for all of you.* (Php 1:8)

b) ζηλόω τι *to strive for sth.*, φρονέω τι *to set one's mind on sth.*, e.g.:

ζηλοῦτε δὲ **τὰ πνευματικά** (Od).	*Strive eagerly for the spiritual gifts!* (1Cor 14:1)
οὐ φρονεῖς **τὰ τοῦ θεοῦ** ἀλλὰ **τὰ τῶν ἀνθρώπων** (Od).	*You are not setting your mind on God's interests, but man's.* (Mt 16:23)

152b 2. The simple object accusative often combines with verbs signifying *to fear/be afraid of, to flee, to be on one's guard against sth./s.o.*: φοβέομαι, φεύγω, φυλάσσομαι (thus with the sentence pattern S+P+Od), e.g.:

οὐκ ἐφοβήθησαν **τὸ διάταγμα τοῦ βασιλέως** (Od)	*They were not afraid of the king's edict* (He 11:23)
↑also Lk 22:2; Jn 9:22.	
Φεύγετε **τὴν πορνείαν** (Od).	*Flee from sexual immorality!* (1Cor 6:18)
but also with ἀπό-Op:	
φεύγετε **ἀπὸ τῆς εἰδωλολατρίας** (Op).	*Flee from idolatry!* (1Cor 10:14)
↑also Lk 3:7.	
ὃν (Od) καὶ σὺ φυλάσσου.	*You too should be on your guard against him!* (2Tm 4:15)
but also with ἀπό-Op:	
φυλάσσεσθε **ἀπὸ πάσης πλεονεξίας** (Op).	*Be on your guard against all greed!* (Lk 12:15)

152c 3. Not infrequently **intransitive** verbs (i.e. verbs without a Od), especially in the compound form, may **also** be used as **transitive** ones (sentence pattern S+P+Od):

a) verbs of motion with a prepositional prefix, e.g.:

διέρχομαι	*to go/pass through*	προάγω	*to go before/ahead of*
παρέρχομαι	*to go/pass by*	προέρχομαι	*to go before*

διήρχετο δὲ **τὴν Συρίαν καὶ τὴν Κιλικίαν** (Od).	*He went through Syria and Cilicia.* (Ac 15:41)
ὁ ἀστήρ … προῆγεν **αὐτούς** (Od).	*The star … went ahead of them.* (Mt 2:9)

b) ἐνεργέω *to activate/produce* (intr. *to be active*), e.g.:

πάντα δὲ **ταῦτα** (Od) ἐνεργεῖ τὸ ἓν καὶ τὸ αὐτὸ πνεῦμα.	*But one and the same Spirit produces all these things.* (1Cor 12:11)
↑also Ga 3:5; Php 2:13.	

c) μένω *to wait for* (intr. *to remain*); ἀναμένω *to wait for*; ὑπομένω *to endure/bear*; κατηχέω *to teach/instruct* (ἠχέω intr. *to resound*; also ↑153a), e.g.:

ἔμενον **ἡμᾶς** (Od) ἐν Τρῳάδι.	*They waited for us in Troas.* (Ac 20:5)
ἀναμένειν **τὸν υἱὸν αὐτοῦ** (Od) …	*to wait for his Son …* (1Th 1:10)
πάντα (Od) ὑπομένω …	*I endure everything/I am willing to put up with anything …* (2Tm 2:10)

… ἵνα καὶ **ἄλλους** (Od) κατηχήσω. *… that I may instruct others as well.* (1Cor 14:19)

↑also Ac 18:25.

4. Several verbs in the NT are used with an object **either** in the **accusative or** in the **dative**, the dative one occurring more frequently (↑174c): 152d

a) εὐαγγελίζομαι, *to announce good news,* mostly: *to proclaim the good news/gospel,* with the accusative referring to the addressees (sometimes to the things announced; also ↑174c), e.g.:

εὐηγγελίζετο **τὸν λαόν** (Od). *He proclaimed the good news to the people.* (Lk 3:18)

↑also Ac 8:25.40; Ga 1:9; 1Pe 1:12.

Addressee referred to by accusative ca. 11×, by dative ca. 15× (e.g. Lk 2:10; 4:43; Ro 1:15; 1Cor 15:1f).

b) προσκυνέω *to pay homage to, to worship* (with accusative ca. 13× [= CG], with dative ca. 31×), with the accusative e.g.:

κύριον τὸν θεόν σου (Od) προσκυνήσεις. *You must worship the Lord your God.* (Mt 4:10)

↑also Jn 4:22f; Re 13:8.12.

Double accusative (S+P+Od+Od/OC; ↑258d; ↑BR §168f; 171; BDF §155–158; Z §72) 153

1. The double accusative occurs with verbs whose sentence pattern includes two direct (accusative) objects (both directly targeted or affected; ↑150a), **one** referring to a **person**, the **other** referring to a **thing**. The following verbs often connect with such a pattern (S+P+Od[person]+Od[thing]): 153a

a) διδάσκω τινά τι *to teach s.o. sth.* (sometimes similarly κατηχέω), ἀναμιμνῄσκω/ὑπομιμνῄσκω τινά τι *to remind s.o. of sth.*, e.g.:

ὁ δὲ παράκλητος … **ὑμᾶς** (Od[person]) διδάξει **πάντα** (Od[thing]) καὶ ὑπομνήσει **ὑμᾶς** (Od[person]) **πάντα** (Od[thing]). *The Helper … will teach you all things and remind you of everything …* (Jn 14:26)

↑also Ac 21:21; 1Cor 4:17; He 5:12.

b) ἐρωτάω/αἰτέω τινά τι *to ask s.o. about sth., to ask s.o. for sth.*, e.g.:

ἠρώτων **αὐτὸν** (Od[person]) οἱ περὶ αὐτόν … **τὰς παραβολάς** (Od[thing]). *Those around him … asked him about the parables.* (Mk 4:10)

ἐάν **τι** (Od[thing]) αἰτήσητέ **με** (Od[person]) ἐν τῷ ὀνόματί μου ἐγὼ ποιήσω. *If you ask me for anything in my name, I will do it.* (Jn 14:14)

↑also Mt 21:24; Mk 6:22f; Jn 11:22; 16:23; 1Pe 3:15.

c) περιβάλλω/ἐνδύω *to dress s.o. in sth.* and ἐκδύω τινά τι *to strip s.o. of sth.*, e.g.:

ἱμάτιον **πορφυροῦν** (Od[thing]) περιέβαλον **αὐτόν** (Od[person]). *They dressed him in a purple robe.* (Jn 19:2)

ἐξέδυσαν **αὐτὸν** (Od[person]) **τὴν πορφύραν** (Od[thing]) καὶ ἐνέδυσαν **αὐτὸν** (Od[person]) **τὰ ἱμάτια αὐτοῦ** (Od[thing]). *They stripped him of the purple cloak and dressed him in his own clothes.* (Mk 15:20)

d) causative verbs such as the counterparts to πίνω *to drink* and φέρω *to carry*: ποτίζω τινά τι *to give s.o. sth. to drink* (lit. *to cause s.o. to drink sth.*);

φορτίζω τινά τι *to load s.o. with sth.* (lit. *to cause s.o. to carry sth.*), e.g.:

γάλα (Od[thing]) **ὑμᾶς** (Od [person]) ἐπότισα. *I gave you milk to drink/I fed you with milk.* (1Cor 3:2)

φορτίζετε **τοὺς ἀνθρώπους** (Od [person]) **φορτία δυσβάστακτα** (Od[thing]) … *you load people with burdens difficult to bear …* (Lk 11:46)

153b 2. The double accusative also occurs with verbs whose sentence pattern includes two accusative noun phrases, one in the role of a **direct object** (an affected one; ↑150a), the other in the role of an **object complement** (↑258a/258b; sometimes of a object adjunct [↑259n/259o]). The following verbs are of this type (often connecting with the pattern S+P+Od+OC, in some cases S+P+Od + an [optional] OA):

a) ὀνομάζω/καλέω/λέγω τινά τι *to name/call s.o.* (also: "s.o.'s name") *sth.*, e.g.:

οὐκ ἐπαισχύνεται **ἀδελφοὺς** (OC[id]) **αὐτοὺς** (Od) καλεῖν. *He is not ashamed to call them brothers and sisters.* (He 2:11)

ὑμᾶς (Od) δὲ εἴρηκα **φίλους** (OC[id]). *But I have called you friends.* (Jn 15:15)

↑also Mt 1:21; Mk 10:18; Lk 1:13; 6:14; Jn 10:35; Ac 14:12; Ro 9:25.

b) ἡγέομαι τινά τι *to regard s.o./sth. as sth.* or *to consider s.o./sth. as sth.*, e.g.:

ταῦτα (Od) ἥγημαι … **ζημίαν** (OC[id]). *I now regard these as loss …* (Php 3:7)

↑also Ac 26:2; Php 2:3.6; 1Tm 1:12; He 11:26.

c) ποιέω τινά τι *to make s.o./sth. sth.*, e.g.:

καὶ ποιήσω **ὑμᾶς** (Od) **ἁλιεῖς ἀνθρώπων** (OC[id]). *And I will make you fishers of people.* (Mt 4:19)

↑also Mt 21:13; Jn 4:46; Ac 2:36; 2Cor 5:21; 1Jn 1:10; Re 1:6; 3:12 et pass.

d) παρίστημί τί τι (when offering a sacrifice) *to present sth. as sth.* (S+P+Od here + an [optional] OA), e.g.:

… παραστῆσαι **τὰ σώματα ὑμῶν** (Od) **θυσίαν ζῶσαν ἁγίαν** (OA) … *… to present your bodies as a living and holy sacrifice …* (Ro 12:1)

e) καθίστημί/τίθημί τινά τι *to appoint/make s.o. sth.*, e.g.:

τίς **με** (Od) κατέστησεν **κριτήν** (OC[id]) …; *Who appointed me a judge …?* (Lk 12:14)

↑also Lk 20:43; Ac 7:10; Ro 4:17; He 1:2.

Note that in the NT (not in CG), under Semitic influence, such an OC[id] is at times preceded by the prep. εἰς or (very rarely) by the conj. ὡς (↑Hebr. לְ *lə*, HALOT s.v. 13, and כְּ *kə*, חשב *ḥšb* sub 3), e.g.:

εἰς (Var. **ὡς**) **προφήτην** (OC[id]) **αὐτὸν** (Od) εἶχον. *They regarded him as a prophet.* (Mt 21:46)

↑also (+ εἰς:) Ac 7:21; 13:22.47; (+ ὡς:) Ro 8:36; Mt 14:5.

For an analogous phenomenon regarding subject complements (SC[id]) ↑147a/258a.

153c 3. In CG many transitive verbs have two Od, an internal (↑151) and external one. Such a sentence pattern is at times found in the NT, too, e.g.:

κατακλίνατε **αὐτοὺς** (external Od) **κλισίας** (internal Od). *Make them sit down in groups.* (Lk 9:14)

On the ACP (the first accusative element followed by one in the form of a PtcP) ↑233.

Accusative and passive transformation (↑BR §205; BDF §159; Z §72f) 154

1. When an active construction is transformed into a passive one (↑191) the sentence pattern **S+P+Od+OC** (with a double accusative; ↑153b) is replaced by the pattern **S+P+SC** (with a double nominative: S and SC; also ↑218g on the NCI), e.g.: 154a

αὐτοὶ (S) **υἱοὶ θεοῦ** (SC[id]) κληθήσονται (P). *They will be called sons of God.* (Mt 5:9)

A corresponding active construction might run as follows (↑153b; ↑Ro 9:25):

***αὐτοὺς** (Od) **υἱοὺς θεοῦ** (OC[id]) καλέσει (P/S). *He will call them sons of God.*

2. If, however, a verb with two direct objects is involved in the passive transformation, the pattern **S+P+Od(person)+Od(thing)** changes to **S(person)+P+Od(thing)**: the direct object referring to a person (as expected) is changed into a subject (in the nominative), but the one referring to a thing remains unchanged, e.g.: 154b

οἱ σοφώτατοι … (S[person]) … ἐδιδάχθησαν … (P) **τὰς ἀρχάς** (Od[thing]) …	*The wisest … were taught … the principles …* (Josephus, Apion 2.168)

A corresponding active construction might possibly run as follows (↑153a):

***τοὺς σοφωτάτους** … (Od[person]) … ἐδίδαξεν (P/S) **τὰς ἀρχάς** (Od[thing]) …	*… he taught the wisest … the principles …*

↑also Mk 1:6; Lk 16:19; Ga 6:6; 2Th 2:15; similarly Ac 18:25.

3. In the case of some verbs with the sentence pattern **S+P+Od(thing)+Oi(person)** in the active, the pattern may change to **S(person)+P+Od(thing)** when the verb is used in the passive (↑191c): the dative element referring to a person (Oi) is changed into a subject (in the nominative), whilst the Od(thing) remains unchanged (similar to English usage in the case of certain types of verbs such as *to give sth. to s.o.*), e.g.: 154c

οἰκονομίαν (Od[thing]) πεπίστευμαι (P/S [person]).	*I have been/I am entrusted with a commission.* (1Cor 9:17)

A corresponding active construction might run as follows (↑Lk 16:11):

*πεπίστευκέν (P/S) **μοι** (Oi[person]) **οἰκονομίαν** (Od[thing]).	*He has entrusted to me a commission/He has entrusted me with a commission.*

↑also Ga 2:7; 1Th 2:4.

4. Accusative noun phrases as those occurring in Jn 11:44 and He 10:22 are best classified as accusatives of respect (↑156): 154d

δεδεμένος **τοὺς πόδας καὶ τὰς χεῖρας** (ManA) κειρίαις	[he was] *bound with linen strips in respect to his feet and hands ≈ his feet and hands* [were] *bound with linen strips.* (Jn 11:44)
ῥεραντισμένοι **τὰς καρδίας** (ManA)	[we must be] *sprinkled clean in respect to our hearts ≈ with our hearts sprinkled clean.* (He 10:22)

(b) Free use accusative

155 Accusative of extent ("How far/long?", mostly LocA/TempA; ↑259d/259e; ↑BR §173; BDF §161)

155a 1. Noun phrases in the accusative of **spatial extent** answer the question **"How far?"** (rarely encountered in the NT), e.g.:

ἐληλακότες οὖν ὡς **σταδίους εἴκοσι πέντε ἢ τριάκοντα** (LocA) …	*Now, when they had rowed about twenty-five or thirty "stades"/furlongs* (ca. three or four miles/five or six kilometres) … (Jn 6:19)
εἰς κώμην ἀπέχουσαν **σταδίους ἑξήκοντα ἀπὸ Ἰερουσαλήμ** (LocA) …	*to a village … which was sixty "stades"/furlongs* (ca. seven miles/twelve kilometres) *from Jerusalem.* (Lk 24:13)

155b 2. Noun phrases in the accusative of **temporal extent** answer the question **"How long?"** (well-attested in the NT), e.g.:

νηστεύσας **ἡμέρας τεσσεράκοντα καὶ νύκτας τεσσεράκοντα** (TempA) …	*After fasting for forty days and forty nights …* (Mt 4:2)
καὶ εἶδον τὰ ἔργα μου **τεσσεράκοντα ἔτη** (TempA).	*And they saw my works for forty years.* (He 3:9f)

↑also Ac 21:7; 28:12; Re 20:4.

Note that in the NT such accusative noun phrases sometimes answer the question "When?", for which far more frequently dative noun phrases or ἐν preposition phrases are used (these, on the other hand, infrequently answer the question "How long?"; ↑182; 187g), e.g.:

ἐχθὲς **ὥραν ἑβδόμην** (TempA)	*yesterday at the seventh hour* (at one in the afternoon) (Jn 4:52)
τὴν ἡμέραν τῆς πεντηκοστῆς (TempA).	*on the day of Pentecost* (Ac 20:16)

↑also Re 3:3.

Also ↑187a–187i, and 259d/259e for an overview of constructions indicating space and time.

156 Accusative of respect ("In what respect?"; ↑BR §172; BDF §160; Z §74)

Accusative noun phrases answering the question "In what respect?" (in the role of an attributive modifier [↑260g] or a manner adverbial [↑259f]) are to be classified here. There are, however, only a few instances of the accusative of respect in the NT, its function in most cases being expressed by the dative of respect instead (↑178a; 187k), e.g.:

ἄνθρωπος πλούσιος ἀπὸ Ἁριμαθαίας, **τοὔνομα** (= τὸ ὄνομα; ↑20) (Attr) Ἰωσήφ	*a rich man from Arimathea, named* (lit. "in respect to the name") *Joseph* (Mt 27:57)

… πιστὸς ἀρχιερεὺς **τὰ πρὸς τὸν θεόν** (Attr)	*a … faithful high priest in things* (lit. "in respect to the things") *relating to God* (He 2:17)
ἀνέπεσαν οὖν οἱ ἄνδρες **τὸν ἀριθμὸν** (Attr) ὡς πεντακισχίλιοι.	*So the men sat down, about five thousand in number* (lit. "in respect to the number"). (Jn 6:10)
διαπαρατριβαὶ διεφθαρμένων ἀνθρώπων **τὸν νοῦν** (Attr) …	*unending disputes by people who are corrupted in their minds* (lit. "in respect to the mind") … (1Tm 6:5)
τὰ νῦν (ManA ≈ TempA)	*in respect to the present situation ≈ now* (Ac 4:29; 5:38; 17:30; 20:32; 27:22)

For an overview of possible constructions answering the question "In what respect?" ↑187k; also 259f.

Adverbial accusative (↑BR §174; BDF §160; Z §74) 157

The (ancient) adverbial accusative is preserved in the NT mainly in the form of neuter adjectives (which in part had become adverbs; ↑53; 241). Such accusative phrases are used as either manner adjuncts (↑259f) or attributive modifiers (↑260m/260o), e.g.:

λοιπόν or τὸ λοιπόν	*furthermore, still, finally* (1Cor 4:2; Mk 14:41)
πολλά, πολύ	*much, very* (Mk 9:26; 12:27; also ↑138b)
οὐδέν or οὐθέν	*in no respect, in no way.* (Ga 4:1; Ac 15:9)
τὸ καθόλου (nominalized adverb; ↑132d)	*entirely, at all.* (Ac 4:18)

At times this use also occurs in the form of comparatives and superlatives (neuter; ↑53) and some other types of phrases or constructions, e.g.:

τάχιον	*more quickly, soon* (He 13:19.23)
τὸ πλεῖστον (also without the article)	*at the most* (1Cor 14:27)
πλεῖον or πλέον	*more, to a greater extent* (Lk 7:42; Jn 21:15)
κρεῖσσον	*better* (1Cor 7:38)
τὸ νῦν ἔχον	*for now* (Ac 24:25)
ὃν τρόπον (↑287a; 289g)	*in the manner in which, (just) as* (Lk 13:34)
τὸ καθ' ἡμέραν (also without the article)	*every day* (Lk 11:3; ↑184k)

(iii) Genitive

158 Genitive: preliminaries (↑BR §175; BDF §162ff; Z §36ff)

158a 1. In Ancient Greek the genitive covers the functions of two Proto-Indo-European cases (↑146a). Thus, genitive noun phrases may

a) in terms of the "**genitive proper**" (as used in Proto-Indo-European), indicate (↑159–168) the (notional) **domain** that something belongs to, or the entity targeted by the "action", indirectly or in part (↑149a);

Note that this use with its various subdivisions is not always easy to delimit clearly; hence the differences between available grammars.

b) replacing the **ablative** (↑Latin), indicate (↑169–171) a **departure point**, either a spatial departure point (separation) or to a metaphorical one (e.g. in comparisons).

Note that use a and use b are not always easy to distinguish.

158b 2. A genitive noun phrase may depend on (or be "governed" by)

- a noun or (less frequently) an adjective, or sometimes an adverb (i.e. it is embedded in a noun/adjective/adverb phrase; ↑159–166; 167c; 169a; 170; 172), or
- a verb (i.e. on its valency, or serving as an adjunct; ↑163; 167–169; 171).

Ancient Greek genitive noun phrases (the head being in the genitive, as also any expansions showing concord) may have the following syntactic roles:

a) They mainly serve as **attributive modifiers** (↑260a/260e) of the head of a noun phrase (↑159–162; 164–166; 168b; 170; 172), e.g.:

ὁ λόγος **τοῦ θεοῦ** (Attr)	*the word of God* (Ac 6:7)

On the use of the article and the position of genitive attributive modifiers ↑136e/136f.

b) At times they have the role of a **predicative element**, i.e. a subject or object complement (SC/OC; ↑258b; perhaps an OA; ↑259n; on the GCP ↑233), dependent on a verb (mostly on its valency) or as part of a verbless clause (↑159b; 168c; 293c), e.g.:

ὑμεῖς δὲ **Χριστοῦ** (SC).	*But you belong to Christ.* (1Cor 3:23)

c) Quite often they serve as an **object** (Og; ↑257b), dependent on a verb (i.e. its valency; ↑163; 167; 169; also 160a) or on certain adjectives or adverbs (↑163b), e.g.:

ἥψατό **μού** (Og) τις	*Someone touched me.* (Lk 8:46)

d) They may also have the role of an **adverbial** (i.e. an adjunct [↑259a–259m] or, less frequently, a complement [↑258c]; ↑163; 167e–169; 171), e.g.:

... τῶν βοώντων αὐτῷ **ἡμέρας καὶ νυκτός** (TempA)	... *who cry to him day and night* (Lk 18:7)

On nominalization of expressions making possible a variety of syntactic functions ↑132d (and chapters on the syntax of declinable words in general).

On prepositions + genitive ↑184–185.

On the infinitive with the genitive article τοῦ ↑225.

On the rare GCI ↑216d.

On the genitive absolute ↑230.

On the genitive dependent on compounds ↑BR §185; BDF §181.

3. Regarding the use of the genitive **CG** and **NT Greek** mainly differ as follows: 158c
In the NT verbs connect much less frequently with genitive noun phrases; very often preposition phrases are used instead (especially with ἐκ/ἐξ or ἀπό; ↑161; 163; 164; 166; 169; 171). On the other hand, the genitive of quality, under Semitic influence, is used more widely in the NT than in CG (↑162).

(a) Genitive proper

The genitive proper (of domain) may be divided into three major subdivisions:
(aa) genitive of appurtenances ("genitivus pertinentiae"; ↑159–165);
(ab) partitive genitive (↑166–167);
(ac) genitive of time (↑168).

(aa) Genitive of appurtenances ("genitivus pertinentiae"; "Belonging to what domain?"; ↑BR §176)

A noun phrase in the genitive of appurtenances ("genitivus pertinentiae") indicates the domain that the referent of the head noun (the superordinate expression) belongs to. The genitive of appurtenances may be subdivided into a variety of different genitive types depending on the domain type that the head noun referent may be seen to belong to in a particular context. The most important ones are as follows:

Note that when interpreting texts, it may often be sufficient to classify a concrete instance simply as a genitive of appurtenances. For a detailed treatment of possible NT nuances of this and other genitives ↑Wallace 1996: 78–136.

- genitive of originator or possessor (↑159);
- subjective and objective genitive (↑160);
- genitive of material or content (↑161);
- genitive of quality (↑162);
- genitive of value or price (↑163);
- genitive of direction or purpose (↑164);
- genitive of explanation or apposition (↑165).

Genitive of originator or possessor ("Whose?"; ↑BR §176a; BDF §162; 183; Z §36–39) 159

1. The originator or origin of the head noun referent (superordinate expression) is 159a
one possible domain type indicated by the genitive of appurtenances. In this case one may speak of "**genitive of originator**" ("genitivus auctoris"); it serves as an attributive modifier (↑260e), e.g.:

εὐαγγέλιον **θεοῦ** — *the gospel of God* (Ro 1:1)

God is the originator of the message of salvation (↑Ro 15:16 and 1Th 2:2).

Genitive noun phrases modifying nominalized verbal adjective phrases (↑132d), too, may denote the originator, e.g.:

ἐκλεκτοὶ **τοῦ θεοῦ**	*God's chosen ones/people chosen by God* (Col 3:12)
ἀγαπητοῖς **θεοῦ**	*beloved of God/those loved by God* (Ro 1:7)
↑ ἀδελφοὶ ἠγαπημένοι **ὑπὸ τοῦ θεοῦ**	*brothers and sisters loved by God* (1Th 1:4)
οἱ κλητοὶ **τοῦ Αδωνιου**	*Adonijah's guests/those invited by Adonijah* (1Kgs 1:49 LXX)
κλητοὶ **Ἰησοῦ Χριστοῦ**	*those called by Jesus Christ* (Ro 1:6)

↑BDAG sub κλητός; most EVV, however, have *called to belong to Jesus Christ* (↑159b).

For an overview of possible phrases with causal meaning ↑187m.

159b 2. The possessor of the head noun referent is a further domain type the genitive noun phrase very frequently indicates, thus a possessive relationship being involved; hence the term **"genitive of possessor"** or **"possessive genitive"**:

a) Such genitive noun phrases are mostly used as **attributive** modifiers of the head of a noun phrase (↑260e), e.g.:

ἐν τῇ οἰκίᾳ **τοῦ πατρός μου**	*in the house of my Father/in my Father's house* (Jn 14:2)

↑also Mt 13:27.

The head noun may be represented merely by a nominalizing article (↑132d), e.g.:

ἀπόδοτε **τὰ Καίσαρος** Καίσαρι καὶ **τὰ τοῦ θεοῦ** τῷ θεῷ.	*Give to Caesar the things that are Caesar's, and to God the things that are God's.* (Lk 20:25)

↑also 2Cor 12:14.

b) Possessive genitive noun phrases sometimes have the role of a **predicative** complement, i.e. subject complement (S+[P]+SC; ↑258b), e.g.:

τοῦ κυρίου (SC) ἐσμέν.	*We belong to the Lord.* (Ro 14:8)
οὐχ **ὑμῶν** (SC) ἐστιν γνῶναι χρόνους ἢ καιρούς.	*It is not for you* (lit. *not your business/affair/concern* or the like) *to know times or dates.* (Ac 1:7)

↑also He 12:11.

The copula verb "to be" may be left unexpressed (↑256d), e.g.:

… πάντα **ὑμῶν** (SC), ὑμεῖς δὲ **Χριστοῦ** (SC), Χριστὸς δὲ **θεοῦ** (SC).	*… all belong to you, but you belong to Christ and Christ belongs to God.* (1Cor 3:22.23)
οὐ … **πάντων** (SC) ἡ πίστις.	*Faith is not everyone's business ≈ Not everyone has faith.* (2Th 3:2)

↑also Mt 5:3; Ro 9:16.

More rarely γίνομαι *to become* is combined with the possessive genitive:

ἐγένετο ἡ βασιλεία τοῦ κόσμου **τοῦ κυρίου ἡμῶν καὶ τοῦ χριστοῦ αὐτοῦ** (SC).	*The kingdom of the world now belongs to our Lord and his Christ* (lit. … *world has become our Lord's and his Christ's/ world has become [the kingdom] of our Lord and his Christ*). (Re 11:15)

↑also Lk 20:14; 2Pe 1:20; Re 12:10.

On the alternative construction involving the dative and the typical difference of meaning between the two constructions ↑176b.

The predominant construction expressing possessive relationships is the one with the possessive genitive of the personal pronoun in the 1st, 2nd, and 3rd sg. and pl. (↑140b).

On the occasional (KG) use of κατά + acc. comparable to a possessive pronoun ↑184k.

3. Certain constructions expressing **kinship relations** are best classified as instances of the possessive genitive (serving as attributive modifiers), too, e.g.: 159c

οἱ υἱοὶ **Ζεβεδαίου**	*the sons of Zebedee* (Mk 10:35)
ἡ μήτηρ **τοῦ κυρίου μου**	*the mother of my Lord* (Lk 1:43)
Ἰωάννα γυνὴ **Χουζᾶ**	*Joanna, the wife of Chuza* (Lk 8:3)

Note that if the genitive noun phrase is the name of a person, the head noun (of the superordinate expression) may be unexpressed and the intended meaning "son", "mother", "wife", "household" or the like will have to be supplied in thought, a **conventional ellipsis** in Ancient Greek (↑293c; also 132d[i]; 260e):

a) "son" to be supplied, with the father's name being in the genitive, e.g.:

Ἰάκωβος **ὁ τοῦ Ζεβεδαίου**	*James the one/[son] of Zebedee* (Mt 10:2)
οἱ τοῦ Ζεβεδαίου	*the ones/[sons] of Zebedee* (Jn 21:2)
εἶδεν Λευὶν **τὸν τοῦ Ἁλφαίου**.	*He saw Levi the one/[son] of Alphaeus.* (Mk 2:14)

b) "mother" to be supplied, with the son's/daughter's name being in the genitive, e.g.:

Μαρία **ἡ τοῦ Ἰακώβου**	*Mary the one/[mother] of James* (Mk 16:1 or [without τοῦ] Lk 24:10)

c) "wife" to be supplied, with the husband's name being in the genitive, e.g.:

Μαρία **ἡ τοῦ Κλωπᾶ**	*Mary the one/[wife] of Clopas* (Jn 19:25)

d) "people/members of the household" or the like to be supplied (reference to slaves?; ↑BDAG sub Χλόη; BDF §162.5), with the name of the leading person of the household being in the genitive, e.g.:

ἐδηλώθη … **ὑπὸ τῶν Χλόης** …	*it has been reported … by those/[people/ members of the household] of Chloe …* (1Cor 1:11)

↑also Ro 16:10.11 (ἐκ PpP for genitive NP)

e) in Ancient Greek "brother" is sometimes to be supplied (↑Kühner-Gerth I: 265), e.g.:

Τιμοκράτης **ὁ Μητροδώρου**	*Timocrates the one/[brother] of Metrodorus* (Alciphron 4.17 [formerly: 2.2])

possible (ambiguous) NT examples (↑Robertson: 501; BDF §162.4):

Ἰούδας **Ἰακώβου**	*Judas the one/[brother] of James* (↑Jd 1) or (more widely accepted) *Judas the one/[son] of James* (Lk 6:16; Ac 1:13)

159d 4. υἱός *son* or τέκνον *child* is also **used metaphorically** in line with a Hebrew or Semitic idiom denoting a close relationship with a person, thing, or quality (↑BDF §162.6; Z §42–44; GKC §128s–v; Segert: 338f), e.g.:

οἱ υἱοὶ τῆς βασιλείας	*"the sons of the kingdom" = those for whom the kingdom was prepared/those belonging to the kingdom* (Mt 8:12; 13:38)
υἱὸς εἰρήνης	*"son of peace" = a peace-loving person* (Lk 10:6)
υἱὲ διαβόλου	*"[you] son of the devil" = one who belongs to the devil and obeys him* (Ac 13:10)
υἱὸν γεέννης	*"son/child of hell" ≈ one fit for hell* (Mt 23:15)
οἱ υἱοὶ τοῦ νυμφῶνος	*"the sons of the wedding hall/of the bridal chamber" = the bridegroom's attendants,* i.e. the wedding guests standing closest to the bridegroom and playing an essential part in the ceremony (Mt 9:15)
τέκνα φωτός	*"children of the light" = people who belong to the light* (i.e. to God's character and truth) *and who are determined by it* (Eph 5:8)
τέκνα ὑπακοῆς	*"children of obedience" = obedient "children", people who are obedient* [to God] (1Pe 1:14)

↑also Lk 16:8; 20:36; Jn 17:12; Ac 4:36; Ga 4:28; Eph 2:2f; Col 3:6; 1Th 5:5; 2Pe 2:14.

160 Subjective and objective genitive (↑BR §176a note; BDF §163; Z §36–39)

160a One of the domain types indicated by the genitive of appurtenances is about the relationship between an event (or a relation) and those participating in it: the head (the superordinate expression) is typically a verbal noun such as λυτρωτής *redeemer* (agent noun; ↑160b[a]) or λύτρωσις *redemption* (action noun; ↑160b[b]); the genitive noun phrase may (in the role of an attributive modifier; ↑260e) refer to either

a) the "performing" entity (agent; ↑255), the subject of the corresponding (active) verbal sentence; this use is called **"subjective genitive"**, e.g.:

ἡ ἀγάπη **τοῦ θεοῦ**	*the love of God*, i.e. the love that God has for s.o., e.g. *God's love for us* (1Jn 4:9)

corresponding (active) verbal sentence, e.g.:

ὁ θεὸς (S) ἠγάπησεν ἡμᾶς.	*God loved us.* (1Jn 4:11), or

b) the "targeted" entity (patient; ↑257), the object of the corresponding (active) verbal sentence; this use is called **"objective genitive"**, e.g.:

ἡ ἀγάπη **τοῦ θεοῦ**	*the love for God* (1Jn 5:3)

corresponding (active) verbal sentence, e.g.:

τὸν θεὸν (O) ἀγαπῶμεν.	*We love God.* (1Jn 5:2)

For an overview of causal phrases (similar to the subjective genitive) ↑187m.

Noteworthy points relevant to **text interpretation**:

1. In most of the relevant instances the genitive noun phrase is to be understood as an **objective genitive**. This applies especially when the head refers to an event that naturally involves a targeted entity (an object in the corresponding [active] verbal sentence; ↑254c). The head noun very frequently is either 160b

a) an **agent noun** (one referring to the agent, the "performing" entity) such as κρίτης *judge*, κλέπτης *thief* etc. (on these also ↑362a), or

b) an **action noun** (one referring to an "action") such as ἐπίγνωσις *knowledge*, κτίσις *creation*, καταβολή *foundation*, ῥαντισμός *sprinkling* etc. (on these also ↑362b), e.g.:

κριτὴς **ζώντων καὶ νεκρῶν**	*judge of the living and the dead* (Ac 10:42)
ὁ σωτὴρ **τοῦ κόσμου**	*the Saviour of the world* (Jn 4:42)
ἐπίγνωσις **ἁμαρτίας**	*knowledge of sin* (Ro 3:20)
ἀπὸ κτίσεως **κόσμου**	*since the creation of the world* (Ro 1:20)
ἀπὸ καταβολῆς **κόσμου**	*from the foundation of the world* (Mt 25:34)
εἰς … ῥαντισμὸν **αἵματος Ἰησοῦ Χριστοῦ**	*for the sprinkling with the blood of Jesus Christ* (1Pe 1:2)

When no targeted entity is involved in the event referred to (when the corresponding [active] verbal sentence is without an object), the genitive noun phrase is (as expected) a **subjective genitive**, e.g.:

ἡ ἔλευσις **τοῦ δικαίου**	*the coming of the Righteous One* (↑Ac 7:52)

2. In **ambiguous instances** the intended nuance may (as always) be inferred from the linguistic and non-linguistic **context**, e.g.: 160c

αὕτη γάρ ἐστιν ἡ ἀγάπη **τοῦ θεοῦ**, ἵνα τὰς ἐντολὰς αὐτοῦ τηρῶμεν.	*For this is love for God: that we keep his commandments.* (1Jn 5:3)

The ἵνα-clause explains in what way the ἀγάπη τοῦ θεοῦ is expressed, which makes clear that *love for God* (objective genitive) is the most likely understanding of the phrase.

μὴ ἡ ἀπιστία αὐτῶν τὴν πίστιν **τοῦ θεοῦ** καταργήσει;	*Their unfaithfulness will not nullify God's faithfulness, will it?* (Ro 3:3)

The contrasting phrase "their unfaithfulness" shows that the intended meaning of τὴν πίστιν τοῦ θεοῦ here is "God's faithfulness" (subjective genitive), and not "faith in God" (as in other instances).

160d 3. Sometimes, especially in Paul's letters, choosing one of the two alternatives does not seem to do justice with what is being communicated (↑172); a **combination** of the two seems preferable, e.g.:

ἡ γὰρ ἀγάπη τοῦ Χριστοῦ συνέχει ἡμᾶς.	*For the love of Christ/Christ's love controls us.* (2Cor 5:14)

As indicated by the context, the love shown by Christ dying a substitutionary death is what is meant in the first place (so a subjective genitive); yet, with regard to the driving force in the apostle's life the phrase would no doubt refer to the apostle's reciprocating love for Christ, too (as a sort of objective genitive).

160e 4. Sometimes the **possessive pronoun** occurs with the force of an objective genitive (↑140a), e.g.:

τοῦτο ποιεῖτε εἰς **τὴν ἐμὴν** ἀνάμνησιν.	*Do this in remembrance/memory of me.* (Lk 22:19/1Cor 11:24; similarly v. 25)

160f 5. In many cases the **objective genitive** noun phrase needs to be **translated** as a clarifying preposition phrase rather than by the usual (ambiguous) "of" construction, e.g.:

ἡ φιλία **τοῦ κόσμου** ἔχθρα **τοῦ θεοῦ** ἐστιν.	*friendship with the world means enmity against God.* (Jas 4:4)

161 Genitive of material or content ("Of what material?"/"With what content?"; ↑BR §176b; BDF §167)

The material or (more frequently) the content of the head noun referent is another possible domain type indicated by the genitive of appurtenances. This use is generally called "genitive of material or content" ("genitivus materiae"), typically having the role of an attributive modifier (↑260e), e.g.:

τὸ θυσιαστήριον **τοῦ χρυσοῦ**	*the golden altar* (↑Re 9:13)
κεράμιον **ὕδατος**	*a jar of water* (Mk 14:13)
ἀλάβαστρον (acc.) **μύρου**	*an alabaster jar of perfume* (Lk 7:37)
τὸ δίκτυον **τῶν ἰχθύων**	*the net full of fish* (Jn 21:8)
γόμον (acc.) **χρυσοῦ** καὶ **ἀργύρου** καὶ **λίθου τιμίου** …	*a cargo of gold, silver, jewels* … (Re 18:12 with a total of eight genitive NP)

↑also Re 20:10.

Note that for the genitive of material preposition phrases with ἐκ/ἐξ or ἀπό may be used instead (↑184h/184e) or, more frequently, adjective phrases, e.g.:

πλέξαντες στέφανον **ἐξ ἀκανθῶν**	*[they] wove a crown of thorns* (Jn 19:2)
πλέξαντες **ἀκάνθινον** στέφανον	*[they] wove a crown of thorns* (Mk 15:17)
εἶχεν τὸ ἔνδυμα αὐτοῦ **ἀπὸ τριχῶν καμήλου** καὶ ζώνην **δερματίνην**	*he wore a garment of camel's hair and a leather belt* (Mt 3:4)

Genitive of quality ("Of what kind or quality?"; ↑BR §176c; BDF §165; 162.6; Z §40f; 42–44) 162

1. The **property** or **quality** of the head noun referent is a further possible domain type indicated by the genitive of appurtenances. This use is generally called "genitive of quality"; it mostly has the role of an attributive modifier (↑260e). 162a
In CG it is used almost exclusively with reference to measurements or to a person's age (typically as a predicative element; ↑168c), NT example of this use:

ἦν γὰρ **ἐτῶν δώδεκα**	*For she was twelve years old.* (Mk 5:42)

Influenced by Semitic usage, where adjectives occur rather sparsely, NT authors make use of it fairly frequently in a variety of different contexts (GKC §128p; Segert: 415; also ↑295s on "enallage"). Very often its function is largely the same as that of an (attributive) adjective, so that it is usually best translated as an adjective, e.g.:

ἐπῄνεσεν ὁ κύριος τὸν οἰκονόμον **τῆς ἀδικίας** (≈ τὸν **ἄδικον** οἰκονόμον) …	*The master commended the unrighteous/dishonest manager …* (Lk 16:8)
ἐκ τοῦ μαμωνᾶ **τῆς ἀδικίας**	*by means of the unrighteous mammon* (= worldly money/resources) (Lk 16:9)
ἀκροατὴς **ἐπιλησμονῆς** (≈ ἀκροατὴς **ἐπιλήσμων**)	*a forgetful listener* (Jas 1:25; Vulgate: *auditor obliviosus*)

similarly also:

… φέρων τε τὰ πάντα τῷ ῥήματι **τῆς δυνάμεως αὐτοῦ**.	*… and he sustains all things by his powerful word.* (He 1:3)

2. On some noteworthy NT instances of the genitive of quality: 162b

a) Several times Paul uses the genitive of quality to characterize the human σῶμα *body*, e.g.:

τὸ σῶμα **τῆς ἁμαρτίας**	*the body of sin ≈ the body ruled by sin* (Ro 6:6)
ἐκ τοῦ σώματος **τοῦ θανάτου** τούτου	*from this body of death ≈ from this body subject/doomed to death* (Ro 7:24)
τὸ σῶμα **τῆς ταπεινώσεως** ἡμῶν	*the body of our lowliness ≈ our lowly bodies* (Php 3:21)
τῷ σώματι **τῆς δόξης** αὐτοῦ	*[like] the body of his glory ≈ his glorious body* (Php 3:21)

b) It is also used in expressions referring to the "Last Day":

ἐν ἡμέρᾳ **ὀργῆς** καὶ **ἀποκαλύψεως** δικαιοκρισίας τοῦ θεοῦ	*on the day of wrath and revelation of the righteous judgment of God ≈ on the day of God's wrath, when his righteous judgment will be revealed* (Ro 2:5)
εἰς ἡμέραν **ἀπολυτρώσεως**	*for the day of redemption* (Eph 4:30)

c) Further examples of the genitive of quality:

προσερχώμεθα … τῷ θρόνῳ **τῆς χάριτος**.	*Let us approach … the throne of grace (≈ throne of our gracious God)!* (He 4:16)
ῥίζα **πικρίας**	*a root of bitterness ≈ a bitter root* (He 12:15)
καρδία πονηρὰ **ἀπιστίας**	*an evil heart [full] of unbelief ≈ an evil, unbelieving heart* (He 3:12)
βάπτισμα **μετανοίας**	*a baptism of repentance ≈ a baptism as a sign of repentance* (Mk 1:4)

162c 3. Less frequently we encounter the **reverse situation** as it were: The head (superordinate expression) denotes a property/quality of the entity referred to by the genitive noun phrase. In such constructions greater emphasis is probably placed on the property/quality (↑BDF §165; Robertson: 496; also ↑295s), e.g.:

… μηδὲ ἠλπικέναι ἐπὶ πλούτου **ἀδηλότητι**	*… nor to set their hopes on the uncertainty of wealth ≈ … on so uncertain a thing as wealth* (1Tm 6:17)

↑also Lk 1:48; Ac 2:46; Ro 6:4; Eph 6:5; Col 3:22; perhaps (interpretation as genitive of quality equally possible) 1Th 4:5.

On the idiom (Semitism) υἱός *son* or τέκνον *child* denoting a close relationship with a person, thing, or quality ↑159d.

For an overview of possible phrases referring to quality ↑187jff; 260b–260n.

163 Genitive of value or price (“Of what value?”/“For/At how much?”; ↑BR §176d; BDF §179; 182.2)

The value or price of the head noun referent is another possible domain type indicated by the genitive of appurtenances; hence the term “genitive of value or price” (“genitivus pretii”).

163a 1. Such genitive noun phrases are regularly dependent on **verbs** (or their valency) signifying *to buy/acquire, to sell, to value* or the like (serving as adverbial adjuncts/complements [↑259e–259m; 258c] or as an object [↑257b]; in KG sometimes an ἐκ/ἐξ PpP is used instead [↑184h]), such as:

ἀγοράζω	*to buy*	κτάομαι	*to acquire*
πωλέομαι	*to sell*	ἀξιόω	*to consider worthy*

Examples:

ἀγοράσωμεν **δηναρίων διακοσίων** (ManA) ἄρτους;	*Shall we buy bread for two hundred denarii?* (Mk 6:37)
καταξιωθῆναι … **τῆς βασιλείας τοῦ θεοῦ** (Og)	*to be considered worthy of the kingdom of God* (2Th 1:5)

↑also Mt 10:29; Ac 5:8; 7:16; 22:28; 1Cor 6:20; 7:23; 2Th 1:11; 1Tm 5:17; He 3:3; 10:29.

2. The genitive of value or price may also be dependent on the **adjective** ἄξιος *worthy/deserving* (its valency calling for a Og of the 2nd degree; ↑254c; similarly ἀξίως *in a worthy manner*, the adverb derived from it), e.g.: 163b

πιστὸς ὁ λόγος καὶ **πάσης ἀποδοχῆς** (Og/2nd) ἄξιος.	*The saying is trustworthy and worthy/deserving of full acceptance.* (1Tm 1:15; 4:9)

↑also 1Cor 16:4; 1Tm 6:1; He 11:38. ἀξίως: Ro 16:2; Eph 4:1; Php 1:27; Col 1:10.

Genitive of direction or purpose ("With what direction or purpose?"; ↑BDF §166) 164

The **direction** or **purpose** of the head noun referent is a further possible domain type indicated by the genitive of appurtenances; hence the term "genitive of direction or purpose" (serving as an attributive modifier; ↑260e), e.g.:

τὴν **τῶν ἁγίων** ὁδόν	*the way into the sanctuary* (He 9:8)
ὁδοὺς **ζωῆς**	*paths of/to life* (Ac 2:28)
θύραν **πίστεως**	*the door of faith/to believe* (Ac 14:27)
τὴν κλεῖδα **τῆς γνώσεως**	*the key to knowledge* (Lk 11:52)
… εἰς ἀνάστασιν **ζωῆς** … εἰς ἀνάστασιν **κρίσεως**	*[come out]…to a resurrection of life…to a resurrection of condemnation =…rise to live…rise to be condemned* (Jn 5:29)
τὸ φῶς **τῆς ζωῆς**	*the light of life ≈ the light that leads to life* (Jn 8:12)

↑also Mt 1:11; 10:5; Jn 6:35; 10:7; Ac 16:17; Ro 3:17; 5:18; 8:2.15.36; 9:22; 14:19; Eph 6:15; He 12:24; Re 22:1.

The infinitive with τοῦ expressing purpose probably belongs here, too (↑225).

For an overview of possible phrases indicating space or the like ↑187b/187n.

Genitive of explanation or apposition 165

("What kind of?"/"Consisting in what?"; ↑BDF §167; Z §45f)

Sometimes the genitive (of appurtenances) noun phrase expresses an **explanation** of the head noun referent (functioning as an attributive modifier; ↑260e/260h; on the explanatory function also ↑341, especially 341c). This use may be called "genitive of explanation" or (due to its functional proximity to the apposition; ↑260h) "genitive of apposition" ("genitivus epexegeticus/explicativus/appositivus").

1. Frequently such genitive noun phrases serve to **explain some imagery** (↑295x), e.g.: 165a

ἐκεῖνος δὲ ἔλεγεν περὶ τοῦ ναοῦ **τοῦ σώματος αὐτοῦ**.	*But he was speaking about the temple of his body. = But the temple he was speaking about was his body.* (Jn 2:21)

τὸν στέφανον **τῆς ζωῆς**	*the (victor's) crown of (= crown consisting in) life = life as your (victor's) crown* (Jas 1:12 / Re 2:10)

↑also 2Tm 4:8.

ἑορτάζωμεν μὴ ἐν ζύμῃ παλαιᾷ μηδὲ ἐν ζύμῃ **κακίας** καὶ **πονηρίας** ἀλλ᾽ ἐν ἀζύμοις **εἰλικρινείας** καὶ **ἀληθείας**.	*Let us keep the Festival, not with the old leaven, the leaven of (= leaven consisting in) malice and wickedness, but with the unleavened bread of (= unleavened bread consisting in) sincerity and truth!* (1Cor 5:8)

↑also 2Cor 5:5; Eph 6:14.16f; He 12:11.

165b 2. There are, however, many instances without imagery, e.g.:

ἡ δωρεὰ **τοῦ ἁγίου πνεύματος**	*the gift of (= gift consisting in) the Holy Spirit* (Ac 10:45; ↑2:38)
… ἵνα γένηται ἡ προσφορὰ **τῶν ἐθνῶν** εὐπρόσδεκτος	*…so that the offering of (= offering consisting in) the Gentiles may become acceptable = so that the Gentiles may become an acceptable offering* (Ro 15:16)

↑also Mk 15:22 / Jn 19:17; Lk 4:33; 11:29; Jn 11:13; Ac 2:33; Ro 4:11; 2Cor 8:2; He 6:1.

165c 3. Occasionally this genitive is also found in the names of cities/towns and countries (= CG usage [agreeing with English usage!]), e.g.:

πόλεις (acc.) **Σοδόμων** (gen.) καὶ **Γομόρρας** (gen.)	*the cities of Sodom and Gomorrah* (2Pe 2:6)

↑also Ac 13:17.19.

In Ancient Greek such names may, however, also be used (without genitive) as apposition showing concord with the word for "city/town" (↑260h), e.g.:

πόλις (nom.) … **Λασαία** (nom.)	*the town of Lasea* (Ac 27:8)

(ab) Partitive genitive

This is the second major subdivision of the genitive proper (of domain; ↑p.235). The partitive genitive noun phrase denotes the whole of an entity. It typically serves as an attributive modifier (↑166), whose head refers to part of that entity. In addition to this typical (attributive) use there is (according to the traditional approach) the use as a genitive object of certain verbs (due to their valency; ↑167).

166 Partitive genitive modifying noun phrases ("Part of what?"; ↑BR §177; BDF §164)

Typically, a partitive genitive modifies a noun phrase (being embedded in it as its attributive modifier). While the genitive phrase itself denotes the whole of an entity (the whole of the domain), the **head** modified by it **refers to part** of that entity. In other words it is the head that refers to part of something, not the genitive noun phrase which actually refers to the whole of an entity.[15]

Note that
(a) in KG the partitive genitive is quite frequently replaced by preposition phrases with ἐκ/ἐξ (↑184h) and sometimes with ἀπό (↑184e);
(b) though partitive genitive noun phrases are typically attributive modifiers (↑260e), they are never in the "attributive" position (↑136f);
(c) they may occasionally occur as subject complements (↑258b).

1. **Names of countries or regions** regularly appear in this genitive with the head referring to a place within the country/region in question (also called "chorographic" genitive), e.g.: 166a

ἐν Κανὰ **τῆς Γαλιλαίας**	*at Cana in Galilee* (Jn 2:1.11)
εἰς Σάρεπτα **τῆς Σιδωνίας**	*to Zarephath in Sidonia* (Lk 4:26)

↑also Mt 2:5; Ac 22:3.

2. The **indefinite pronoun** τις/τι usually combines with it (↑144a; sometimes τις/τι needs to be supplied in thought [ellipsis influenced by Semitic usage; ↑293c]), e.g.: 166b

τινὲς **τῶν γραμματέων**	*some of the scribes* (Mt 9:3)
τινὰς **τῶν μαθητῶν αὐτοῦ**	*some of his disciples* (Mk 7:2)
συνῆλθον δὲ καὶ (sc. τινὲς) **τῶν μαθητῶν ἀπὸ Καισαρείας**.	*Some of the disciples from Caesarea also came along.* (Ac 21:16)

The construction with an ἐκ/ἐξ (↑184h; at times ἀπό; ↑184e) preposition phrase occurs as well, e.g.:

τινὲς **ἐξ αὐτῶν** ἐπείσθησαν.	*Some of them were persuaded.* (Ac 17:4)
εἶπαν οὖν (sc. τινες) **ἐκ τῶν μαθητῶν αὐτοῦ** …	*Some of his disciples said …* (Jn 16:17)

↑also (without ellipsis:) Jn 7:25; (with ellipsis:) Mt 23:34; Lk 11:49; 21:16; Jn 7:40; Ac 2:30; 19:33. ἀπό preposition phrase (without ellipsis:) Mt 27:21; (with ellipsis:) Mk 12:2.

3. It is used after **ἕκαστος** *each*, e.g.: 166c

ἕνα ἕκαστον **τῶν χρεοφειλετῶν τοῦ κυρίου ἑαυτοῦ**	*each one of his master's debtors* (Lk 16:5)

4. It is often used after **εἷς/μία/ἕν** *one*, e.g.: 166d

ἓν **τῶν μελῶν σου**	*one of your members* (Mt 5:29)

5. It combines with **expressions denoting quantities**, e.g.: 166e

Ἰουδαίων τε καὶ **Ἑλλήνων** πολὺ πλῆθος	*a great number of both Jews and Greeks* (Ac 14:1)

15 To avoid any confusion, some prefer (at least for didactic reasons) to call this genitive "wholative" rather than "partitive" (↑Wallace 1996: 84).

167 Verbs combining with partitive genitive objects (↑BR §177.2; 178; BDF §169–178; 182.1)

Certain **verbs** (due to their valency) combine with a genitive noun phrase as their **object** (referring to an entity more or less directly targeted by the "action"; Og; ↑257b) typically connected with the sentence pattern S+P+Og (↑258d). In most cases a partitive meaning may be assumed: the genitive noun phrase denotes the whole of an entity, part of which is affected by the "action" referred to by the verb. Genitive objects may be combined with the following types of verbs:

167a 1. certain verbs of **perception**:

a) ἀκούω *to hear/to listen to*, with the genitive of the person that one hears speaking, quite frequently with the genitive of the voice that one hears, e.g.:

ὁ ἀκούων **ὑμῶν** (Og) **ἐμοῦ** (Og) ἀκούει.	*The one who hears you hears me/who listens to you listens to me.* (Lk 10:16)
ἐὰν **τῆς φωνῆς αὐτοῦ** (Og) ἀκούσητε …	*If you hear his voice …* (He 3:7)

Overview of **standard use** of ἀκούω (BR §178; BDF §173; Z §69; ↑Turner 1965: 87–90):

1. with the **genitive** of person or thing that one hears speaking or making noises (**source**) (also [CG] with παρά/ἀπό or the like + gen. or [un-CG] ἀπὸ/διὰ/ἐκ τοῦ στόματος + gen.):
a) "typical" meaning: *to hear s.o./sth.*;
b) derived from this (*to hear attentively*): *to listen to, to obey*;

2. with the **accusative** of thing:
a) the thing that one hears (the noise, the **acoustic** side of an utterance): *to hear sth.* or
b) the thing (also the person) that one hears someone talking about (content of an utterance): *to hear sth.* or *to hear sth. about s.o.*

Note that:
a) the accusative of thing is often used alongside the genitive of source;
b) certain nouns may occur either in the genitive or the accusative: not only λόγοι *words*, but especially φωνή, which may have the following meanings:
- *sound, noise* (acoustic, 2a);
- *voice* (source, 1), *shout/cry* (acoustic, 2a);
- *utterance* (acoustic or content, 2a/b)

(in Jn the following applies: ἀκούω φωνῆς *to obey*, ἀκούω φωνήν *to hear*; for "to hear a sound/noise" CG normally uses the genitive: ἀκούω φωνῆς or the like)

On the GCP ↑233, with a predicative participle phrase having the role of a Og.

b) ἅπτομαι *to touch, to take hold of*, e.g.:

τίς **μου** (Og) ἥψατο;	*Who touched me?* (Mk 5:31)

↑also Lk 22:51.

c) γεύομαι *to taste, to partake of*, e.g.:

οὐδείς … γεύσεταί **μου τοῦ δείπνου** (Og).	*None … will taste/will get a taste of my banquet.* (Lk 14:24)

2. verbs signifying *to take hold of, to grasp, to catch*: 167b

a) ἐπιλαμβάνομαι *to take hold of*, e.g.:

ἐπιλαβοῦ **τῆς αἰωνίου ζωῆς** (Og).	*Take hold of the eternal life!* (1Tm 6:12)

↑also Mk 8:23; Lk 20:20.26; He 8:9.

b) κρατέω *to take hold of, to grasp/seize* with the genitive if part of an entity (NT mainly χείρ *hand*) is in view (the accusative if it is the whole of the entity), e.g.:

ἐκράτησεν **τῆς χειρὸς αὐτῆς** (Og).	*He took her by the hand.* (Mt 9:25)
ποῖον ἔθνος … οὐκ ἐκράτησεν **τῶν σκύλων αὐτῆς** (Og);	*What nation … has not taken some of her spoils?* (1Macc 2:10)

3. often verbs signifying *to fill* or *to be full*: πίμπλημι/πληρόω *to fill*, γέμω *to be full* 167c
(occasionally with the adjectives μεστός/πλήρης *full*), e.g.:

ἐπλήσθησαν ἅπαντες **τοῦ ἁγίου πνεύματος** (Og).	*They were all filled with the Holy Spirit.* (Ac 4:31)
ὧν τὸ στόμα **ἀρᾶς** καὶ **πικρίας** (Og) γέμει.	*Their mouths are full of cursing and bitterness.* (Ro 3:14)

↑also Ac 13:52.

4. verbs signifying *to have a share, to partake*: μετέχω *to have a share, to partici-* 167d
pate, μεταλαμβάνω *to have/receive a share*, e.g.:

οὐ δύνασθε **τραπέζης κυρίου** (Og) μετέχειν καὶ **τραπέζης δαιμονίων** (Og).	*You cannot take part in the Lord's table and the table of demons.* (1Cor 10:21)

↑also Ac 2:46.

5. verbs signifying *to aspire to, to desire* (↑169a for cases not always easy to distin- 167e
guish from the ones mentioned here): ὀρέγομαι *to aspire to*, ἐπιθυμέω *to desire*, e.g.:

Εἴ τις **ἐπισκοπῆς** (Og) ὀρέγεται, **καλοῦ ἔργου** (Og) ἐπιθυμεῖ.	*If anyone aspires to the office of overseer, he desires a noble task.* (1Tm 3:1)

Occasionally also with semantically related nouns, thus in Ro 15:23 (↑225a/225f).

6. μιμνῄσκομαι/μνημονεύω *to remember, to think of*, e.g.: 167f

καὶ ἐμνήσθη ὁ Πέτρος **τοῦ ῥήματος Ἰησοῦ** (Og).	*Then Peter remembered the word of Jesus.* (Mt 26:75)

↑also Lk 1:54.72; 17:32; Ga 2:10; Col 4:18.

7. verbs of affective behaviour such as ἀνέχομαι *to endure, to put up with*, e.g.: 167g

ἕως πότε … ἀνέξομαι **ὑμῶν** (Og);	*How long shall I … endure you?* (Lk 9:41)

↑also Eph 4:2; He 13:22.

8. verbs signifying *to dominate* such as κυριεύω *to be lord over, to dominate*, κατα- 167h
κυριεύω *to gain dominion, to subdue*, e.g.:

ἁμαρτία γὰρ **ὑμῶν** (Og) οὐ κυριεύσει.	*For sin will have no dominion over you.* (Ro 6:14)

↑also Mk 10:42.

167i Noteworthy points (↑BR §180f; BDF §178):

Especially CG also uses a type of the genitive proper often termed **"genitive of respect"** (English *in respect to* or *over/for/with*; Og [↑257b] or CausA/CausC [↑259g]), particularly combined with

a) **judicial expressions**, e.g. (NT only 1× gen., otherwise περί + gen.):

τῆς οἰκίας (Og) ἐδικαζόμην.	*I was at law over the house.* (Lysias 17.5)
δώρων (CausA) ἐκρίθησαν.	*They were tried for taking bribes.* (Lysias 27.3f)
ἐγκαλεῖσθαι **στάσεως** (CausA)	*being charged with rioting* (Ac 19:40)

b) expressions of **affective behaviour**, e.g.:

ζηλῶ σε **τοῦ νοῦ** (CausA).	*I admire you for your prudence.* (Sophocles, Electra 1027)

According to others this genitive is classified as a subtype of the ablative genitive (sometimes called "genitive of crime" or "genitive of cause").

↑187k/187m on phrases with similar meanings.

(ac) Genitive of time

The genitive of time (apparently of partitive origin) may be classified as the third major subdivision of the genitive proper (of domain; ↑p. 235):

168 Genitive of time ("When?" or "Within which time span?"; ↑BR §179; 178; BDF §186.2)

Noun phrases in the genitive of time refer to the time (in a general way) or to the **time span within which** something takes place (typically as a TempA/TempC; ↑259e). In the NT this use occurs mainly

168a 1. in **fixed phrases** without article, e.g.:

ἡμέρας καὶ νυκτός	*by day and by night* (Lk 18:7)
νυκτὸς καὶ ἡμέρας	*by night and by day* (1Th 2:9; 3:10)
χειμῶνος	*in winter* (Mt 24:20; Mk 13:18)

168b 2. also with **distributive force** dependent on a multiplicative adverb (↑62a; the genitive as an attributive modifier of an adverb phrase; ↑260o), e.g.:

ἑπτάκις **τῆς ἡμέρας**	*seven times a day* (Lk 17:4)
δὶς **τοῦ σαββάτου**	*twice a week* (Lk 18:12)
ἅπαξ **τοῦ ἐνιαυτοῦ**	*once a year* (He 9:7)

168c Note that the following kind of genitive noun phrases do not belong here, but to the genitive of quality (↑162a; in the role of a predicative element: SC; ↑258b):

ἦν γὰρ **ἐτῶν δώδεκα** (SC).	*For she was twelve years old.* (Mk 5:42)
ἐγένετο **ἐτῶν δώδεκα** (SC).	*He had turned twelve/He was twelve years old.* (Lk 2:42)

For an overview of possible constructions indicating time ↑187e–187i and 259e.

(b) Ablative genitive (genitive of departure point)

This second main type of the Ancient Greek genitive (↑158a) may be divided into three categories:

- genitive of separation (spatial departure point; ↑169)
- genitive of comparison (metaphorical departure point; ↑170)
- genitive of place (↑171)

Genitive of separation ("Away from where?"; ↑BR §182; BDF §180; 182.3) 169

1. The functions of the Proto-Indo-European **ablative** case (< Lat. *ablātus* inter alia "removed from") were taken over by the genitive in Ancient Greek (↑158a): it may refer to the departure point of an event (or relation) and is thus usually called "ablative genitive". In its standard use as genitive object (↑257b) of certain verbs and a small number of adjectives (normal sentence patterns: S+P+Og and S+P+SC+Og/2nd degree respectively; ↑258d) it typically indicates a spatial departure point, more precisely a separation from something; hence the term **"genitive of separation"**. Note, however, that in the NT this genitive is mostly replaced by preposition phrases with ἀπό (↑184e) or ἐκ/ἐξ (↑184h). 169a

a) The following fairly well-attested verbs (or uses) always or mostly have a (prepositionless) genitive object:

ἀπέχομαί τινος *to keep away from sth.* (e.g. 1Pe 2:11; also with ἀπό);
δέομαί τινος (τι) *to ask s.o. (for sth.)* (e.g. 2Cor 8:4);
διαφέρω τινός *to differ from sth., to be more value than sth./s.o.* (e.g. 1Cor 15:41);
ὑστερέω τινός *to lack sth.* (e.g. Lk 22:35);
φείδομαί τινος *to spare s.o./sth.* (e.g. 2Cor 1:23);
χρῄζω τινός *to need sth.* (e.g. Lk 12:30; 2Cor 3:1); analogously χρείαν τινὸς ἔχω *to need sth.* (e.g. Mt 9:12).

b) The following expressions are used this way only once or twice in the NT: 169b

- verbs:

ἀφίσταμαί τινος *to depart from sth.* (Lk 2:37; otherwise ἀπό);
ἀστοχέω τινός *to stray from sth., to swerve from sth.* (1Tm 1:6);
βραδύνω τινός *to be slow about sth.* (2Pe 3:9);
κωλύω τινά τινος *to keep s.o. from (doing) sth.* (Ac 27:43);
λείπομαί τινος *to lack sth.* (Jas 1:5; 2:15);
προσδέομαί τινος *to need sth.* (Ac 17:25).

- adjectives:

ἀκατάπαυστός τινος *unable to stop sth.* (2Pe 2:14);
ἀπείραστός τινος *unable to be tempted by sth.* (Jas 1:13);
ξένος τινός (being) *stranger to sth.* (Eph 2:12).

Examples:

δεήθητε οὖν **τοῦ κυρίου τοῦ θερισμοῦ** (Og) …	*Therefore ask the Lord of the harvest …* (Mt 9:38)
πολλῶν στρουθίων (Og/ManC?) διαφέρετε ὑμεῖς.	*You are of more value than many sparrows.* (Mt 10:31)

μή **τινος** (Od) ὑστερήσατε;	*Did you lack anything?* (Lk 22:35)
ὅς γε **τοῦ ἰδίου υἱοῦ** (Og) οὐκ ἐφείσατο …	*He who did not spare his own Son …* (Ro 8:32)
ὁ γὰρ θεὸς ἀπείραστός ἐστιν **κακῶν** (Og/2nd).	*For God cannot be tempted by evil.* (Jas 1:13)

169c 2. The following verbs signifying *to loosen, to liberate* or the like are always construed with a preposition Phrase in the NT (in CG with a genitive):

ἐλευθερόω ἀπό τινος *to liberate from sth.* (e.g. Ro 8:21);
λύω ἀπό/ἔκ τινος *to free from sth.* (e.g. Re 1:5);
ῥύομαι ἀπό/ἔκ τινος *to rescue from sth.* (e.g. 2Tm 4:17);
σῴζω ἀπό/ἔκ τινος *to save from sth.* (e.g. Jn 12:27);
χωρίζω ἀπό τινος *to separate from sth.* (e.g. Ro 8:35).

NT example:

σωθησόμεθα … **ἀπὸ τῆς ὀργῆς** (Op).	*We will be saved … from God's wrath.* (Ro 5:9)

CG example:

σωθῆναι **κακῶν** (Og)	*be rescued from troubles* (Euripides, Orestes 779)

For an overview of possible constructions indicating place ↑187a–187d and 259d.

170 Genitive of comparison ("… than what?"; ↑BR §183f; BDF §185)

This metaphorical use of the ablative genitive (↑p.249) is the standard way of marking the "than" element connected with comparative forms (↑138a) or other expressions used analogously (e.g. ↑145a); such genitive noun phrases have the role of an attributive modifier of the adjective or adverb phrase expressing the comparison (↑260o), e.g.:

ὁ πατὴρ μείζων (AdjP) **μού** (Attr) ἐστιν.	*The Father is greater than I.* (Jn 14:28)
ἀγαπᾷς με πλέον (AdvP) **τούτων** (Attr);	*Do you love me more than these?* (Jn 21:15)

↑also Jn 1:50; Ac 17:11; He 1:4; 11:26.

171 Genitive of place ("From where?" or "Where?"; ↑BR §182 Note 1; 179 Note; BDF §186; LocA/C [↑259d])

This (prepositionless) genitive of place answering the question "From where" or "Where?" is almost exclusively restricted to poetic use even in CG. In the NT there are only occasional traces of it, e.g.:

ὅτι **ἐκείνης** (sc. ὁδοῦ; ↑260c) (LocA) ἤμελλεν διέρχεσθαι.	*He was going to pass that way.* (Lk 19:4)

↑also Lk 5:19 (ποίας [sc. ὁδοῦ] *by what way*).

In both CG and post-CG this use is mostly replaced by preposition phrases with ἐκ/ἐξ (sometimes ἀπό). For these and other possible constructions indicating place ↑187a–187d and 259d.

(c) Special cases of genitive use

Combinations of different types of genitives (↑BDF §168; Z §47) 172

Interpreters of texts, particularly those of Paul, will quite often encounter combinations of different types of genitives that are not always easy to unravel (↑ also the note on p. 235 about keeping the classification of concrete instances fairly general), e.g.:

τὸν φωτισμὸν **τοῦ εὐαγγελίου** (1st gen.) **τῆς δόξης** (2nd gen.) **τοῦ Χριστοῦ** (3rd gen.) — *the light of the gospel of the glory of Christ* (2Cor 4:4)

The first genitive is best classified as a genitive of originator (↑159a): the gospel is the originator/origin of the light; the gospel diffuses this light.
The second genitive is an objective genitive (↑160) or a genitive of material or content (↑161): the glory of Christ is the "object" or content of the gospel message.
The third genitive could be classified as a subjective genitive (↑160) or as a genitive of possessor (↑159b): Christ radiates this glory and he "possesses" it, it is his glory.

ἵνα ἀναπληρώσῃ τὸ **ὑμῶν** (subjective gen.; ↑160) ὑστέρημα **τῆς πρός με λειτουργίας** (objective gen.; ↑160) — *to complete your lack of the service to me = to make up for the help you yourselves could not give me.* (Php 2:30)

Cases such as Eph 1:6.18; 1Th 1:3 would seem easier to explain.

(iv) Dative

Dative: preliminaries (↑BR §186; BDF §187ff; Z §51ff) 173

1. The Ancient Greek dative covers the functions of three Proto-Indo-European cases (↑146a). Thus a dative noun phrase (its head being in the dative, as also any expansions showing concord; ↑260c; 259q) may 173a

a) in terms of the **"dative proper"** (as used in Proto-Indo-European) refer to

- entities targeted by the "action" ("To whom?"/"Whom?" [Oi/O^{dat}]; ↑174/175) or
- entities to whose advantage or disadvantage something is done ("For whom?" [IntA]; ↑176);

b) replacing the **instrumental case** (in Lat. covered by the ablative)[16] refer to

- entities by which or by whom something is done ("By what means?" or the like [InstrA]; ↑177/178) or
- entities in company with whom something is done ("Together with whom?" or the like [ManA/ManC] ↑179/180);

c) replacing the **locative case** (in Lat. covered by the ablative) refer to

- the place ("Where?" [LocA/LocC]; ↑181) or
- the time ("When?" [TempA/TempC]; ↑182) of the event/state expressed by the verb.

16 The two subcategories may be subsumed under the term "instrumental-sociative" case.

Note that available grammars distinguish and name the dative uses in a variety of different ways. For a detailed treatment of possible NT dative nuances again ↑Wallace 1996: 140–175.

173b 2. So Ancient Greek dative noun phrases occur in the following syntactic roles:

a) very often as an **object**, frequently as an indirect object (Oi) alongside a direct object (Od), but also as the (generally) sole object (O^{dat}), the typical sentence patterns being S+P+Od+Oi and S+P+O^{dat} (↑174/175; 179; 257b); e.g.:

ἔδωκεν αὐτὸν (Od) **τῇ μητρὶ αὐτοῦ** (Oi).	*He gave him to his mother.* (Lk 7:15)
λατρεύω **τῷ πατρῴῳ θεῷ** (O^{dat})	*I serve the God of our fathers.* (Ac 24:14)

b) sometimes as a **subject complement** (SC, particularly as a "possessive dative", ↑176b; 258b; possibly OC/OA; ↑258b/259n), e.g.:

λαός (S) ἐστί **μοι** (SC) πολύς (Attr of S) …	*Many people are mine/I have many people …* (Ac 18:10)

c) frequently as an **adverbial** (↑176–182; typically as an adjunct, sometimes as an [adverbial] complement; ↑259a–259m/254d/258c), e.g.:

Μηδεὶς ὑμᾶς ἀπατάτω **κενοῖς λόγοις** (InstrA).	*Let nobody deceive you with (by means of) empty words!* (Eph 5:6)

d) sometimes as an **attributive modifier** (Attr; ↑260f/260o), showing no concord with the modified head (↑178), e.g.:

οἱ πτωχοὶ (modified head) **τῷ πνεύματι** (Attr)	*the poor in spirit* (Mt 5:3)

On nominalization of expressions making possible a variety of syntactic functions ↑132d (and chapters on the syntax of declinable words in general).

On prepositions + dative ↑183/184.

On the rare DCI ↑216d.

On the very rare casus pendens involving the dative ↑292e.

173c 3. Regarding the use of the dative **CG** and **KG** differ as follows:

CG:		KG/NT:
a) dative of instrument or cause ("By what means?"/"Owing to what?"; ↑177; also 187m/187o):		
dative	→	dative, but more often ἐν + dat. as well as other prepositions such as διά + gen.
b) dative of manner ("How?"; ↑180; also 187j; partly applicable also to dative of association; ↑179a):		
dative	→	dative, frequently ἐν + dat. as well as μετά + gen.
c) dative of place ("Where?"; ↑181; also 187a):		
dative (in a number of expressions)	→	almost exclusively ἐν + dat.
d) dative of time (↑182; also 187e/187g–187i):		
answering the question "When?"	→	mostly answering the question "When?", but at times the question "How long?"
e) dative of respect ("In what respect?"; ↑178; also 187k):		
dative rare, accusative standard (↑156)	→	dative standard, accusative rare

(a) Dative proper

The dative proper (↑173a) may be subdivided as follows:

- objective dative (↑174: dependent on verbs; ↑175: dependent on adjectives);
- dative of interest (↑176).

Note that occasionally noun phrases in the dative proper seem to be replaced by preposition phrases with ἐν + dat. in the NT, e.g. (↑BDF §220.1):

… δεδομένον **ἐν** ἀνθρώποις … *…given among men/given to mankind…* (Ac 4:12)

↑possibly also Ac 13:15; Ro 1:19; 10:20 Var.; 2Cor 4:3; 8:1; Ga 1:16.

Objective dative ("To whom/Whom?"; ↑BR §187; BDF §187; 202 [compound verbs]) 174

There are mainly two types of objects indicated by the objective dative: (1) the indirect object (↑174a) occurring alongside a (predominant) direct object, and (2) the dative object used as the (typically) sole object of a sentence (↑174b).

Note that the objective dative unlike most of the other dative uses (e.g. ↑176) is an obligatory sentence constituent, one normally required by the verb (i.e. its valency; ↑127d; 257; 254c). This typically applies to the dative of association as well, which also occurs in the object role (↑179).

1. The objective dative first of all functions as the **indirect object** (Oi) answering the question "To whom?". It typically occurs alongside a predominant direct object (Od) answering the question "Whom/What?", thus in sentence patterns connected with certain transitive verbs (i.e. verbs with a Od; ↑152a). In such a sentence pattern, S+P+Od+Oi (↑258d), the Od normally refers to the notionally closest entity, the one directly targeted by the "action", whilst the Oi refers to an entity that is notionally more remote, less directly affected, typically a person, e.g.: 174a

δίδωμι **αὐτοῖς** (Oi) ζωὴν αἰώνιον (Od). *I give them eternal life.* (Jn 10:28)

ἄφες **ἡμῖν** (Oi) τὰ ὀφειλήματα ἡμῶν (Od)· *Forgive us our debts!* (Mt 6:12)

The following verbs, inter alia, are often used with this sentence pattern:

παρέχω *to grant* sth. to s.o. | ἐμφανίζω *to make* sth. *visible* to s.o.
χαρίζομαι *to grant* (also *forgive*) sth. to s.o. | φανερόω *to reveal* sth. to s.o.
δείκνυμι *to show* sth. to s.o. | γνωρίζω *to make* sth. *known* to s.o.
ἀποκαλύπτω *to disclose/reveal* sth. to s.o.

Generally also verbs signifying *to say, to announce* or *to write*, e.g.:

λέγω *to say* sth. to. s.o. (also πρός + acc. for Oi) | λαλέω *to say* sth. to s.o. (also μετά + gen. for Oi)
γράφω *to write* sth. to s.o. | ἐπιστέλλω *to write* sth. to s.o. (by letter; ↑293c)
ἀναγγέλλω *to report* sth. to s.o.

2. Quite frequently objective dative noun phrases function as the typically sole object of sentences with certain intransitive verbs (i.e. verbs without a Od; ↑152b). When used in this way, the dative noun phrase refers to an entity that seems directly targeted by the "action", the sentence pattern being S+P+O^{dat}. Though such objects are functionally close to direct objects, the term **"dative object"** (O^{dat}) is preferred in this grammar, mainly for two reasons: (a) dative objects typically refer to persons 174b

only, direct objects, however, very often to things; (b) direct objects are conventionally associated with the accusative case (kept distinct grammatically from the dative in Ancient Greek). Nevertheless, both the O^dat and the Od of Ancient Greek texts tend to be translated as an English Od,[17] e.g.:

Οὐδεὶς δύναται **δυσὶ κυρίοις** (O^dat) δουλεύειν.	*No one can serve two masters.* (Mt 6:24)

The following verbs frequently occur with such a dative object (referring to persons):

a) verbs signifying *to serve, to minister*: δουλεύω, διακονέω, λατρεύω

b) verbs signifying *to believe, to trust*: πιστεύω, πέποιθα
(πιστεύω 39× with O^dat, 48× with εἰς+acc., 22× with ὅτι-clause, less frequently with ἐπί/ἐν, ↑BDAG s. v.)

c) verbs signifying *to obey*: ὑπακούω, πείθομαι

d) verbs signifying *to command*: ἐπιτάσσω, παραγγέλλω

174c 3. Several NT verbs have an object (of person) either in the accusative or dative (also ↑152d):

a) εὐαγγελίζομαι, *to announce good news*, mostly: *to proclaim the good news/gospel*; note that the pattern involving a dative is mostly S+P+Od+Oi (↑174a), less frequently S+P+O^dat (↑174b), e.g.:

εὐηγγελίσατο εἰρήνην (Od) **ὑμῖν τοῖς μακρὰν** (Oi) καὶ εἰρήνην (Od) **τοῖς ἐγγύς** (Oi).	*He proclaimed peace to you who were far away and peace to those who were near.* (Eph 2:17)
εὐηγγελισάμην **ὑμῖν** (O^dat) τὸ πρότερον.	*I first proclaimed the gospel to you.* (Ga 4:13)

b) προσκυνέω *to pay homage to, to worship*, e.g.:

οἱ ἀληθινοὶ προσκυνηταὶ προσκυνήσουσιν **τῷ πατρὶ** (O^dat) ἐν πνεύματι …	*The true worshippers will worship the Father in spirit …* (Jn 4:23)

↑also Jn 4:21; 9:38; Ac 7:43; 1Cor 14:25; Re 4:10; 7:11; 11:16 (Mt and Re mostly dative, Jn mixed).

↑260f/260o on the use of this dative as an attributive modifier.

175 Objective dative with adjectives (↑BR §187 Note 4; 202.2)

There are also adjectives whose valency calls for a dative noun phrase: a second degree object, the sentence pattern most frequently being S+P+SC+O^dat/2nd or S+P+Od+OC+O^dat/2nd (↑254c; 258d). These are mainly adjectives that are related to verbs occurring with a dative object, e.g.:

πιστὴν (OC) **τῷ κυρίῳ** (↑πιστεύω τινί)	*believing in the Lord* (Ac 16:15)
γονεῦσιν ἀπειθεῖς (OC) (↑ἀπειθέω τινί)	*disobedient to parents* (Ro 1:30)
εὐάρεστοι (SC) **αὐτῷ** (↑εὐαρεστέω τινί)	*pleasing to him* (2Cor 5:9)
τὰ ἀρεστὰ (OC) **αὐτῷ** (↑ἀρέσκω τινί)	*what is pleasing to him* (Jn 8:29)
τίμιος (SC) παντὶ **τῷ λαῷ**	*respected by all the people* (Ac 5:34)
… οὐδὲν ἐναντίον (Od) ποιήσας **τῷ λαῷ** …	*… although I had done nothing against the (Jewish) people ….* (Ac 28:17)

17 Due to the fact that Modern English generally has just one form for what some languages, such as Ancient Greek, Latin, and German, use two distinct forms, i. e. the accusative and the dative.

Dative of interest ("For whom?"/"To whose advantage or disadvantage?"; ↑BR §188; BDF §188ff; Z §55ff) 176

The dative of interest is the second major subtype of the dative proper (↑p.253). Its basic use is introduced in the next paragraph (↑176a), an important subtype, often called "possessive dative", in the paragraph after that (↑176b).

176a 1. Noun phrases in the dative of interest ("dativus commodi et incommodi") basically refer to **entities in whose interest** something is done, either to their advantage or to their disadvantage. Unlike noun phrases in the objective dative (↑174) the ones in the dative of interest are typically optional sentence constituents, **adverbial adjuncts** (↑259a–259m; 258c), the subtype "possessive dative" being an exception (↑176b). The term used in this grammar is "adjunct of interest" ("IntA"; ↑259m).

↑260f/260o on the use of this dative as an attributive modifier.

Examples (advantage "+"; disadvantage "-"):

εὑρήσετε ἀνάπαυσιν **ταῖς ψυχαῖς ὑμῶν** (+)	*you will find rest for your souls* (Mt 11:29)
πορεύομαι ἑτοιμάσαι τόπον **ὑμῖν** (+).	*I am going to prepare a place for you* (Jn 14:2)
ὁ … θεὸς ἐμαρτύρησεν **αὐτοῖς** (+)	*God … bore witness to them* (Ac 15:8)
ὥστε μαρτυρεῖτε **ἑαυτοῖς** (-) ὅτι υἱοί ἐστε τῶν φονευσάντων τοὺς προφήτας.	*So you witness against yourselves that you are the descendants of those who murdered the prophets.* (Mt 23:31)

Paul fairly frequently uses this dative when referring to the objective of living the Christian life, e.g.:

οὐδεὶς γὰρ ἡμῶν **ἑαυτῷ** (+) ζῇ … ἐάν τε γὰρ ζῶμεν, **τῷ κυρίῳ** (+) ζῶμεν …	*For none of us lives for himself … For if we live, we live for the Lord …* (Ro 14:7f)

↑also Ro 6:11; 1Cor 6:13; 9:20–22; 2Cor 2:15; 5:15.

For an overview of possible constructions answering the question "In whose interest?" ↑187p; 259m.

176b 2. In combination with εἰμί *to be*, γίνομαι *to become*, ὑπάρχω *to be* (sometimes unexpressed; ↑256d) the dative of interest often indicates a possessive relationship, a use frequently called **"possessive dative"** or "dative of possessor". Such dative noun phrases mostly have a predicative role as a subject complement (SC; ↑258b), occasionally the role of an attributive modifier (↑260f/260o), e.g.:

ἃ δὲ ἡτοίμασας, **τίνι** (SC) ἔσται;	*And the things you have accumulated – whose will they be?* (Lk 12:20)
ἐὰν γένηταί **τινι ἀνθρώπῳ** (SC) ἑκατὸν πρόβατα …	*If someone has/owns a hundred sheep …* (Mt 18:12)
ἀργύριον καὶ χρυσίον οὐχ ὑπάρχει **μοι** (SC) …	*I have no silver or gold …* (Ac 3:6)
πόθεν **τούτῳ** (SC) (sc. ἐστὶν) ταῦτα …;	*Where does he have these things from?* (Mk 6:2)

Some more examples with εἰμί + poss. dat. with the function of "to have sth.": Lk 9:13; Ac 18:10.

αὐτὸς ἔσται **μοι** (Attr) υἱός.	*He will be my son.* (Re 21:7)
↑υἱός μου (Attr) εἶ σύ.	*You are my Son.* (inter alia He 1:5 [Ps 2:7 LXX])

The possessive genitive (↑159b) and the possessive dative (↑above) are used in a closely similar way. Their use differs typically as follows (↑BDF §189.1):
With the **genitive** the focus is generally on the **possessor**,
with the **dative** on the **item possessed** (as with the frequent ἔχω construction), e.g.:

καὶ **ἡμῶν** (gen.) ἔσται ἡ κληρονομία.	*And the inheritance will belong* TO US/ *will be* OURS. (Mk 12:7)
οὐκ εἰσὶν **ἡμῖν** (dat.) πλεῖον ἢ ἄρτοι πέντε καὶ ἰχθύες δύο.	*We have no more than* FIVE LOAVES *and* TWO FISH. (Lk 9:13)
↑οὐκ ἔχομεν ὧδε εἰ μὴ πέντε ἄρτους καὶ δύο ἰχθύας.	*We have nothing here but five loaves and two fish.* (Mt 14:17)

176c 3. A number of additional dative uses, mainly relevant to CG, are best classified here (↑BR §189):

a) The **"sympathetic dative"** ("dativus sympatheticus"), functionally very close to the possessive genitive (IntA [↑259m], ↑BDF §473), e.g.:

ἥ τε καρδία πηδᾷ **μοι**.	*And my heart is leaping* (lit. *And the heart is leaping to/for me*). (↑Plato, Symposium 215e)

b) The **"ethical dative"** ("dativus ethicus"), used almost exclusively in the 1st and 2nd person of the personal pronoun (IntA [↑259m]), e.g.:

καί **μοι** μὴ θορυβήσητε.	*And don't interrupt me!* (lit. *don't make a noise to/for/against me!*) (↑Plato, Apology 20e)

c) The **"dative of agent"** ("dativus auctoris") indicating the originator of an "action" (CausA [↑259g]):

- Combined with the verbal adjective (↑64e): standard in CG, e.g.:

ἡμῖν γ' ὑπὲρ τῆς ἐλευθερίας ἀγωνιστέον.	*We at least must defend our liberty.* (Demosthenes 9.70)

- Combined with the passive, especially in the perfect, in place of ὑπό + gen.: often encountered in CG, in the NT, however, only in one indisputable instance (↑BDF §191; Z §59):

οὐδὲν ἄξιον θανάτου ἐστὶν πεπραγμένον **αὐτῷ**.	*Nothing deserving death has been done by him.* (Lk 23:15)

On the passive ↑191a. For an overview of possible phrases with causal meaning ↑187m.

d) The **"dative of standpoint"**, translatable as "in s.o.'s sight", "before s.o.", "in the eyes of s.o." or the like (used as an adverbial [↑259m] or an attributive modifier [↑260f/260o]), by many seen as part of the ethical dative, e.g.:

… ἄσπιλοι καὶ ἀμώμητοι **αὐτῷ** εὑρεθῆναι ἐν εἰρήνῃ.	*… to be found without spot or blemish before him/in his sight, at peace.* (2Pe 3:14)

↑also Mt 18:17; Ac 4:32; 7:20; 23:1; 1Cor 8:6; 2Cor 10:4; Jas 2:5.

↑παρά + dat., a construction with a closely similar use (↑187m).

(b) Instrumental dative

The instrumental dative is the first main division (↑footnote 16) of the Ancient Greek replacement of the Proto-Indo-European instrumental case (↑146a/173a; covered by the ablative in Lat.), the second one being the sociative dative (↑179/180). The instrumental dative may be subdivided as follows:

- dative of instrument or cause (↑177);
- dative of respect (↑178).

Dative of instrument or cause ("By what means?"/"Owing to what?"; ↑BR §191.1/2; BDF §195f; Z §58; 64) 177

1. A noun phrase in the (instrumental) dative very often refers to the instrument or to the means by which the "action" expressed by the verb takes place, a use called **"dative of instrument"** (mostly an InstrA; ↑259l). In KG it is quite frequently replaced by preposition phrases with ἐν + dat. (due to Semitic influence expanded use in the NT; ↑184i) and διά + gen. (↑184f; 187o). E.g. (note that the English "with" is here used in the sense of "by means of" [for the sense "together with" ↑179]): 177a

ἐργαζόμενοι **ταῖς ἰδίαις χερσίν** (InstrA)	*working with our own hands* (1Cor 4:12)

↑also Eph 4:28.

λελουσμένοι … **ὕδατι καθαρῷ** (InstrA)	*washed with pure water* (He 10:22)
αὕτη δὲ **τοῖς δάκρυσιν** (InstrA) ἔβρεξέν μου τοὺς πόδας καὶ **ταῖς θριξὶν αὐτῆς** (InstrA) ἐξέμαξεν.	*But she has wet my feet with her tears and wiped them with her hair.* (Lk 7:44)

The dative of instrument and the instrumental use of **ἐν + dat.** may occur interchangeably, e.g.:

ἀνεῖλεν δὲ Ἰάκωβον … **μαχαίρῃ** (InstrA).	*And he killed James … with the sword.* (Ac 12:2)
κύριε, εἰ πατάξομεν **ἐν μαχαίρῃ** (InstrA);	*Lord, shall we strike with the sword?* (Lk 22:49)
ἐγὼ ἐβάπτισα ὑμᾶς **ὕδατι** (InstrA).	*I have baptized you with water.* (Mk 1:8)
Ἐγὼ μὲν ὑμᾶς βαπτίζω **ἐν ὕδατι** (InstrA).	*I baptize you with water.* (Mt 3:11)

↑also Mt 3:12 / Re 18:8; Ac 10:38 / Lk 3:16.

Phrases with **διά + gen.** are sometimes used with a similar force, e.g.:

διὰ τοῦ αἵματος	*with the blood* (Ac 20:28)

↑also (διά + gen.:) Eph 1:7; Col 1:20; He 9:12; (instrumental ἐν:) Eph 2:13; He 10:19; Re 1:5.

2. Another subtype of the instrumental dative is a use called **"dative of cause"**. A noun phrase in the dative of cause refers to the reason, the motive, or the occasion leading to the "action" expressed by the verb (usually CausA; ↑259g), e.g.: 177b

λιμῷ (CausA) ὧδε ἀπόλλυμαι.	*here I am dying from hunger* (Lk 15:17)
τῇ ἀπιστίᾳ (CausA) ἐξεκλάσθησαν.	*they were broken off because of (due to) their unbelief.* (Ro 11:20)
νεκροὺς **τοῖς παραπτώμασιν** (CausA)	*dead because of (due to) your transgressions* (Eph 2:1)
πυνθάνομαι οὖν **τίνι λόγῳ** (CausA) μετεπέμψασθέ με;	*Now may I ask for what reason/why you sent for me?* (Ac 10:29)

οὕτως καὶ οὗτοι νῦν ἠπείθησαν **τῷ ὑμετέρῳ ἐλέει** (CausA).	*So they too have become disobedient as a result of the mercy (to be) shown to you.* ([↑140a; BDF §196]; Ro 11:31)

For an overview of constructions with possible instrumental or causal uses ↑187m/187o and 259g/259l.

178 Dative of respect ("In what respect?"; ↑BR §191.3; BDF §197; Z §53)

178a 1. The **"dative of respect"** is a further subtype of the instrumental dative (↑p. 257). In the NT it occurs quite frequently, much more frequently than the functionally similar accusative of respect (↑156). Answering the question "In what respect?" it mostly serves as an attributive modifier (↑260f/260o) or a manner adjunct (↑259f), e.g.:

Note that in the NT it occasionally is replaced by a preposition phrase with ἐν (↑184i).

οἱ πτωχοὶ **τῷ πνεύματι**	*the poor in spirit* (Mt 5:3)
οἱ καθαροὶ **τῇ καρδίᾳ**	*the pure in heart* (Mt 5:8)
ταπεινὸς **τῇ καρδίᾳ**	*humble in heart* (Mt 11:29)
Κύπριος **τῷ γένει**	*a Cypriot as to his origin, a native of Cyprus* (Ac 4:36)
σκηνοποιοὶ **τῇ τέχνῃ**	*tentmakers by trade* (Ac 18:3)
ἀνὴρ **ὀνόματι** Ἰωσήφ	*a man by the name of Joseph* (Lk 23:50)
τῇ ἡλικίᾳ μικρὸς ἦν.	*He was small in stature.* (Lk 19:3)
μὴ παιδία γίνεσθε **ταῖς φρεσὶν** ἀλλὰ **τῇ κακίᾳ** νηπιάζετε, **ταῖς** δὲ **φρεσὶν** τέλειοι γίνεσθε.	*Stop thinking like children. In respect to evil be infants, but in your thinking be adults.* (1Cor 14:20)

178b 2. A use called **"dative of difference"** or **"dative of measure"** is probably best classified here, too. It indicates to what extent something is different from something else, the degree or measure of the difference expressed in comparative constructions (↑138b), answering the question "By how much?" (BR §191.4; Moule: 44); it typically serves as an attributive modifier of the comparative adjective or adverb (↑260o). In the NT it is limited to a small number of phrases such as πολλῷ *(by) much*[18] or πόσῳ *(by) how much* (very often followed by μᾶλλον *more*), e.g.:

πολλῷ μᾶλλον οἱ … βασιλεύσουσιν.	*much more will those … reign* (Ro 5:17)

↑also (πολλῷ:) Mt 6:30; Mk 10:48; Lk 18:39; Jn 4:41; Ro 5:9f.17; 1Cor 12:22; 2Cor 3:9.11; Php 1:23; 2:12. (πόσῳ:) Mt 7:11; 10:25; 12:12; Lk 11:13; 12:24.28; Ro 11:12.24; Phm 16; He 9:14; 10:29.

… **τοσούτῳ** κρείττων γενόμενος τῶν ἀγγέλων **ὅσῳ** διαφορώτερον παρ᾽ αὐτοὺς κεκληρονόμηκεν ὄνομα.	*… he became as much superior to the angels as the name he has inherited is more excellent than theirs.* (He 1:4)

18 πολύ (adverbial accusative of πολύς *much*) may be used with the same force (↑138b; 157).

CG example:

ὁ δὲ βασίλειος πῆχυς τοῦ μετρίου ἐστὶ πήχεως μείζων **τρισὶ δακτύλοις**.	*The royal cubit is larger by three fingers' breadth than the common cubit.* (↑Herodotus 1.178)

For an overview of possible constructions answering the question "In what respect?" ↑187k and 259f.

(c) Sociative dative

The sociative dative is the second main division (↑footnote 16) of the Ancient Greek replacement of the Proto-Indo-European instrumental case (↑146a/173a; covered by the ablative in Lat.); it may be subdivided as follows:

- dative of association (↑179);
- dative of manner (↑180).

Dative of association ("Together with whom?"; ↑BR §190; BDF §193f; 202) 179

The **"dative of association"** is the first (and standard) subtype of the sociative dative. Noun phrases in the dative of association refer to entities that are associated with, accompany, connect or meet with something (in a friendly or hostile manner). Functionally this dative corresponds to the Lat. preposition *cum* + ablative "together with". It typically occurs as the object (↑257b; 254d; on the term "dative object" ↑174b) of certain verbs (↑179a) and adjectives (↑179b):

1. O^{dat} of certain **verbs**, S+P+O^{dat}: 179a

ἀκολούθει **μοι**.	*Follow me!* (Mt 9:9)
ἐγγίσατε **τῷ θεῷ**.	*Come near to God!* (Jas 4:8)
κατηλλάγημεν **τῷ θεῷ**	*we were reconciled to God* (Ro 5:10)
ἀλλ' οὐκ ἐχρησάμεθα **τῇ ἐξουσίᾳ ταύτῃ**	*But we did not use this right.* (1Cor 9:12)

The most important NT verbs with the dative of association are (note that some of them have additional kinds of objects such as Od):

ἀκολουθέω *to follow s.o.*;
ἐγγίζω *to approach s.o.*;
καταλλάσσομαι (Pass.) *to be reconciled with/to s.o.*;
κοινωνέω (also + gen.) *to have a share in sth.* (Ga 6:6; 1Pe 4:13 etc.);
κολλάομαι *to join s.o., to be united to s.o.* (1Cor 6:17 etc.);
ὁμοιόω *to make the same as sth./s.o., to compare with/to sth./s.o.* (He 2:17 etc.);
προσέρχομαι *to approach sth./s.o.* (He 7:25 etc.);
χρήομαι/χράομαι (↑84c) *to make use of sth.*

2. O^{dat} of certain **adjectives**, e.g. S+P+SC+$O^{dat}/2^{nd}$ or S+P+Od+OC+$O^{dat}/2^{nd}$ (↑254c): 179b

ὅμοιοι (SC adj.) **αὐτῷ** ἐσόμεθα.	*we shall be like him* (1Jn 3:2)
ἴσους (OC adj.) **ἡμῖν** αὐτοὺς ἐποίησας	*you made them equal to us* (Mt 20:12)

180 Dative of manner ("How?"/"Under what attendant circumstances?"; ManA/C; ↑BR §190.5; BDF §198; Z §60ff)

180a 1. Noun phrases in the **"dative of manner"** (a subtype of the sociative dative; ↑p. 259) refer to the manner or the attendant circumstances of the "action" expressed by the verb, typically as manner adjuncts (ManA), sometimes as manner complements (ManC), e.g.:

παρρησίᾳ (ManA) τὸν λόγον ἐλάλει.	*he spoke openly about this* (Mk 8:32)

This same is also expressed by ἐν παρρησίᾳ (e.g. Eph 6:19) or μετὰ παρρησίας (e.g. Ac 4:29.31).

οἱ δὲ ἐπέκειντο **φωναῖς μεγάλαις** (ManA) αἰτούμενοι …	*But with loud voices they insistently demanded …* (Lk 23:23)
πλὴν ὅτι **παντὶ τρόπῳ** (ManA), εἴτε **προφάσει** (ManA) εἴτε **ἀληθείᾳ** (ManA), Χριστὸς καταγγέλλεται.	*Only that in every way, whether in pretence or in truth, Christ is being proclaimed.* (Php 1:18)
μάστιξιν (ManA) ἀνετάζεσθαι	*to be examined by flogging* (Ac 22:24)

Note that in the NT (KG) attendant circumstances (ManA) are frequently expressed by a preposition phrase with ἐν or μετά (+ gen.) or else by an adverbial participle phrase (↑187j; 259f), e.g.:

… τὸ δωδεκάφυλον ἡμῶν **ἐν ἐκτενείᾳ** (ἐν PpP) … λατρεῦον	*… as our twelve tribes earnestly worship …* (Ac 26:7)
εὐθὺς **μετὰ χαρᾶς** (μετά PpP) λαμβάνουσιν αὐτόν.	*They immediately receive it with joy.* (Mk 4:16)
ἐπορεύετο … τὴν ὁδὸν αὐτοῦ **χαίρων** (PtcP)	*he went on his way rejoicing.* (Ac 8:39)

For an overview of possible constructions indicating manner ↑187j and 259f.

180b 2. The NT verbs of motion πορεύομαι, στοιχέω, περιπατέω often occur with a dative of manner, when used metaphorically (prompted by LXX usage) signifying **"to walk"** (in its archaic use), i.e. *to live/behave in a specific way* (↑COED sub "walk"); the dative of manner is one important way of expressing the manner complement (ManC) called for by the valency of these verbs (and similarly of ἀναστρέφομαι attested inside and outside Biblical Greek), e.g.:

Ἡ μὲν οὖν ἐκκλησία … εἶχεν εἰρήνην … πορευομένη **τῷ φόβῳ τοῦ κυρίου** (ManC) …	*So the church … experienced peace … "walking"/living in the fear of the Lord …* (Ac 9:31)
Εἰ ζῶμεν πνεύματι (CausA), **πνεύματι** (ManC) καὶ στοιχῶμεν.	*If we live/have life by the Spirit, let us also behave in accordance with the Spirit.* (Ga 5:25)
οὐ **τῷ αὐτῷ πνεύματι** (ManC) περιεπατήσαμεν;	*Did we not behave in the same spirit?* (2Cor 12:18)
εὐσχημόνως (ManC) περιπατήσωμεν	*Let us live decently.* (Ro 13:13)
… **πῶς** (ManC) δεῖ ἐν οἴκῳ θεοῦ ἀναστρέφεσθαι	*… how one ought to behave in the household of God* (1Tm 3:15)

↑also Ac 14:16; Ro 4:12; Ga 5:16; 6:16.

180c 3. In the LXX and the NT (mainly in OT quotations) the dative of manner is also used (as is the manner participle; ↑240) to render the **Hebrew infinitive absolute** (an intensifying verb form; GKC §113; Conybeare-Stock §61; 81/82), e.g.:

מוֹת תָּמוּת *môṯ* (inf.abs.) *tāmûṯ* (Hebr.) **θανάτῳ** (dat. of manner) ἀποθανεῖσθε (LXX)	*You will certainly die.* (LXX lit. "You will die by death") (Gn 2:17)
ἐπιθυμίᾳ (dat. of manner) ἐπεθύμησα … Delitzsch: נִכְסֹף נִכְסַפְתִּי *niḵsōp̄* (inf.abs.) *niḵsap̄tî*	*I have eagerly desired …* (Lk 22:15)

παραγγελίᾳ (dat. of manner) παρηγγείλαμεν ὑμῖν … *We strictly charged you* … (Ac 5:28)
Delitzsch: צַוֹּה צִוִּינוּ *ṣawwōh* (inf.abs.) *ṣiwwînû*

↑also Jn 3:29; Ac 2:30; 23:14; Jas 5:17. OT quotations: Mt 13:14/Ac 28:26; Mt 15:4/Mk 7:10; Ac 2:17.

(d) Locative dative

The the locative dative (↑173a) may be subdivided as follows:
- dative of place (↑181);
- dative of time (↑182).

Dative of place ("Where?"; LocA/C; ↑259d; ↑BR §192; BDF §199; Z §57) 181

In both CG and post-CG this use is almost entirely replaced by preposition phrases. In the NT it has survived only in one fixed expression, the adverb κύκλῳ *in a circle, around* (Mk 3:34; 6:6; Ro 15:19; for its use as an improper preposition ↑185a.25).

The most frequent NT construction answering the question "Where?" is the preposition phrase with ἐν + dat. (↑184i), e.g.:

ἐν τοῖς Ἱεροσολύμοις	*in Jerusalem* (Jn 2:23)
↑also Jn 4:20f.45; Ac 8:1.14 etc.	
ἐν τῇ Ἀσίᾳ	*in [the Province of] Asia.* (Ac 16:6; 2Cor 1:8)
ἐν Ῥώμῃ	*in Rome.* (Ro 1:7.15)

Preposition phrases with ἐπί, παρά etc., too, may answer the question "Where?". For these and other possible constructions indicating place ↑187a–187d and 259d.

Dative of time ("When?"; TempA/C; ↑259e; ↑BR §193; BDF §200f; Z §54; 64) 182

1. The dative of time is a fairly well-attested subtype of the (locative) dative. Noun phrases in this dative typically answer the question "When?" indicating a point of time, e.g.: 182a

τῇ τρίτῃ ἡμέρᾳ	*on the third day* (Mt 16:21)
τῇ ἐνάτῃ ὥρᾳ	*at the ninth hour* (Mk 15:34)
τετάρτῃ … φυλακῇ τῆς νυκτός	*in the fourth watch of the night* (Mt 14:25)
τοῖς σάββασιν / τῷ σαββάτῳ	*on the Sabbath* (Mt 12:10/Lk 13:14)

Frequently (even in CG) preposition phrases with ἐν + dat. (↑184i) are used instead, e.g.:

ἐν τῷ σαββάτῳ	*on the Sabbath* (Lk 6:7)
ἐν τῷ αἰῶνι τούτῳ	*in the present age* (Eph 1:21)

2. Infrequently a noun phrase in the dative of time answers the question "How long?" (un-CG in place of the accusative of temporal extent; ↑155a), e.g.: 182b

χρόνοις αἰωνίοις	*for long ages* (Ro 16:25)

↑also Lk 1:75; 8:27.29; Jn 2:20; 14:9; Ac 8:11; 13:20; also ἐν + dat. (↑184i), e.g. Ac 27:7.

For an overview of constructions indicating time ↑187e–187i; 259e.

3.2.1.6 Prepositions (↑22i on word-class, ↑321 on their textgrammatical relevance)

(↑BR §195–198; BDF §203–240; Z §78–135; Langslow: 589ff)

183 Syntax of prepositions: preliminaries

(↑BR §195f; BDF §203; Z §78–111)

183a 1. Prepositions are uninflected words (most of them originally being adverbs, some of them, however, adjectives or nouns; ↑185). They typically stand in front of a noun phrase and determine, "govern" (↑22i), its case.[19] Generally speaking preposition phrases may have the same kind of syntactic roles as (prepositionless) genitive, dative or accusative noun phrases (compare ↑183c with 146a).[20] Preposition phrases (involving "proper" and "improper" prepositions) occur much more frequently than these. Due to this and to the fact that prepositions have lexical meanings of their own, preposition phrases are capable of expressing a wider range of semantic-functional relationships than prepositionless case noun phrases: as shown by the overview of possible phrases indicating space, time etc. in 187, where preposition phrases clearly predominate, whereas prepositionless case noun phrases seem to play a marginal role only.

The following paragraphs describe (1) the syntactic functions preposition phrases may have, generally speaking (↑183c), and (2) the most important[21] semantic-functional nuances conveyed by the individual prepositions (↑184–186).

183b 2. Two types of prepositions are usually distinguished for Ancient Greek:

a) **"proper"** prepositions – characteristics:

- they are used as prefixes, especially in the formation of verbs (↑184; 369), e.g.:

ἀπό *(away) from* ἀπο-κόπτω *to cut away/off* (↑184e);

b) **"improper"** prepositions – characteristics:

- they are not used as prefixes;
- they almost exclusively "govern" (↑22i) the genitive;
- they mostly occur also as adverbs, some as conjunctions or nouns (↑185). E.g.:

μέχρι *until* (prep. + gen.; conj.) μέχρι does not occur as a prefix.

Especially for the NT (and the LXX) a further distinction is possible: between

- **simple** prepositions, i.e. most of those mentioned in 184–185, and
- **complex** (improper) prepositions, post-CG (↑185a.26) and Hebraizing ones (↑185c), e.g.:

πρὸ προσώπου (τινός) *before the face (of s.o./sth.)* ≈ πρό (τινος) *before (s.o./sth.).*

---

19 Less frequently they stand in front of adverbs, e.g. ἀπὸ τότε *since then* (Lk 16:16); ↑also Mt 4:17; 27:51; Mk 9:19.21; 14:54; Lk 23:5; Jn 2:7.10; Ac 10:16; 28:23; 1Cor 4:13; 2Cor 3:15; Re 6:10.

20 Quite often preposition phrases and case noun phrases "compete" with each other (↑187).

21 For more details see standard dictionaries such as BDAG (for the NT and early Christian Literature), Muraoka (for the LXX) and LSJ or Montanari (for Ancient Greek in general); due to their special emphasis these works offer more information on the use of prepositions than grammars.

Note that most of the proper prepositions originally derive from independent adverbs. Their function as adverbs is attested especially in the language of Homer, Herodotus, and Attic poetry, but hardly ever in CG prose. A few traces of it survive in the following NT phrases:

ἀνὰ εἷς ἕκαστος	*each one (of the gates)* (Re 21:21)
τὸ καθ' εἷς	*with regard to one, individually* (Ro 12:5)
ὑπὲρ ἐγώ	*I even more* [i.e. than they] (2Cor 11:23)
εἷς κατὰ εἷς	*one by one* (Mk 14:19; ↑Jn 8:9)

↑Z §10; BDF §305.

3. Preposition phrases may have the following syntactic roles: 183c

a) the role of an **object** (Op [↑257b]; also Op/2nd [↑254c; 258d,2.3]), e.g.:

πολλοὶ ἐπίστευσαν **εἰς αὐτόν** (Op).	*Many believed in him.* (Jn 7:31)

b) the role of a **subject complement** (SC; ↑258b), e.g.:

οὐκ εἰσὶν **ἐκ τοῦ κόσμου** (SC).	*they do not belong to the world.* (Jn 17:14)

c) frequently the role of an **adverbial** (usually as an [optional] adjunct, sometimes as an [obligatory] adverbial complement; ↑259a–259m/254d/258c), e.g.:

Καὶ **ἐν ἐκείναις ταῖς ἡμέραις** (TempA) ἦλθεν Ἰησοῦς …	*In those days Jesus came …* (Mk 1:9)

d) rarely the role of a **subject/object adjunct** (SA/OA; ↑259n/258b), e.g.:

χωρὶς ἐμοῦ (SA) οὐ δύνασθε ποιεῖν οὐδέν.	*Apart from me you can do nothing.* (Jn 15:5)

e) the role of an **attributive modifier** (↑260l), e.g.:

ἄνδρα **ἐκ φυλῆς Βενιαμίν** (Attr)	*a man of the tribe of Benjamin* (Ac 13:21)

f) when nominalized (↑132d), they may have any of the roles encountered with noun phrases (↑129ff), e.g. that of a subject:

ἀσπάζονται ὑμᾶς … **οἱ ἐκ τῆς Καίσαρος οἰκίας** (S).	*… those of the Caesar's household greet you.* (Php 4:22)

4. Differences between **CG** and **KG/NT** usage: 183d

CG:	KG/NT:
a) For several CG prepositionless case noun phrases KG tends to use preposition phrases:	
• partitive genitive/genitive of separation/place → (↑167; 169; 171; 187)	frequently ἐκ + gen. (in some cases ἀπό + gen.)
• dative of instrument/cause/manner/place/time → (↑177; 180; 181; 182; 187)	frequently or predominantly ἐν + dat. as well as other prepositions such as διά + gen.
b) The proper prepositions are fewer in number and have a less varied grammatical use (↑184):	
• 19 prepositions are in use →	ἀμφί and ὡς are unattested in the NT ἀνά and ἀντί have only a restricted use in the NT πρό is not used much in the NT (regularly improper prepositions replacing it)
• 6 prepositions with 3 cases are in use →	only 3 prepositions with 3 cases are in use

c) Improper prepositions increase in number and frequency (↑185); in addition to these the NT also uses Hebraizing complex prepositions (↑185c) e.g.:

πρό + gen. *before/in front of* (of place) → mostly ἔμπροσθεν or the like (in the NT also inter alia πρὸ προσώπου [↑Hebr. לִפְנֵי *lip̄nê*])

d) Prepositions with comparable meanings are increasingly "confused" (↑184):

- ἐκ *out of, from* (indicating a matter of origin)
ὑπό + gen. *by* (the agent)
παρά + gen. *from* (a person)
NT: these three are sometimes "replaced" by ἀπό *from, away from*
- ὑπέρ + gen. *for (the sake of)*
kept distinct from:
περί + gen. *about, concerning*
NT: these two are sometimes "confused"
- ἀντί *instead of, for*
kept distinct from:
ὑπέρ + gen. *on behalf of*
NT: these two are sometimes "confused"
- εἰς *into*
kept distinct from:
πρός + acc. *towards, to*
NT: these two are sometimes "confused"
- εἰς *into*
kept distinct from ἐν *in*
KG: the two are generally "confused"
NT: they are "confused" only in part: so in Mk, Lk/Ac, rarely in Jn, not, however, in Mt, the Epistles, and Re

Apart from 184 also ↑187 (overview of possible phrases with adverbial force). On questions of concord ↑261–265.

184 Proper prepositions

184a I. **Principal meanings** of proper prepositions (↑BR §196; also footnote 21)

	+ GENITIVE	+ DATIVE	+ ACCUSATIVE
ἀνά		CG poetry *on, upon*	*up, throughout*
ἀντί	*instead of, for*		
ἀπό	*from, away from*		
διά	*through*, (time:) *after*		*on account of*
εἰς			*into*
ἐκ/ἐξ	*out of, from*		
ἐν		*in, at* (place/time)	
ἐπί	*on, in the time of*	*on, at, on the basis of*	*upon, onto*
κατά	*against, down from*		*according to, throughout*
μετά	*with, together with*	CG poetry *among, amid*	*after* (time/place)
παρά	*from* (a person)	*beside, by the side of*	*contrary to, to the side of*
περί	*concerning*	CG *around*	*around, about*

	+ GENITIVE	+ DATIVE	+ ACCUSATIVE
πρό	*before* (time/place)		
πρός	*in the interest of* (NT 1×) CG *from/on the part of*	*near* CG *in addition to*	*towards/to, against*
σύν		*(in company) with*	
ὑπέρ	*on behalf of*		*over and above, beyond*
ὑπό	*by* (agency) CG also *under, from under*	CG *under, subject to*	*under* (NT: position/direction)

CG also uses:
ἀμφί + acc. *around, about* (in poetry also + gen. or dat.);
ὡς + acc. *to* (only of people) (could be classified as improper preposition; ↑183b; 185).

II. **Major uses** of proper prepositions

↑BR §197; BDF §203–213; 218–240; Z §82–135; especially ↑individual entries in lexical works such as BDAG (↑footnote 21); on their function as prefixes ↑MH: 294–328.

For an overview of phrases indicating space, time etc. (with or without prepositions) ↑187.

ἀμφί core meaning[22] "on both sides", "around/about" (↑BDF §203) 184b

In the NT and the LXX used only as the prefix of compounds:

CG:

1. + gen. and dat. almost exclusively poetic *about/concerning* = περί + gen. and dat.
2. + acc. *around* = περί + acc.
3. as a PREFIX "around": ἀμφι-βάλλω *to cast* (a circular fishing net).

ἀνά core meaning "up" (↑adv. ἄνω *above*; opposite of κατά) (↑BDF §204) 184c

In the NT and the LXX used only in fixed phrases and as the prefix of compounds:

CG (in prose rarely used outside Xenophon):

1. + dat. only in poetry *up on*
2. + acc. *up, throughout*

a) indicating space, e.g.:

ἀνὰ τὸν ποταμόν — *upstream* (Herodotus 2.96)

b) indicating time, e.g.:

ἀνὰ τὸν πόλεμον τοῦτον — *throughout this war* (Herodotus 8.123)

---

22 The term "core meaning" here refers to the meaning that is common to the various meanings of a particular preposition. This must not be confused with its "original" (etymological) meaning, which is difficult or impossible to track down (↑357b[3]).

c) metaphorical, e.g.:

ἀνὰ λόγον	*proportionately* (Plato, Phaedo 110d)
ἀνὰ πέντε (distributive use)	*five each* (Xenophon, Anabasis 4.6.4)

In the NT, e.g.:

ἀνὰ μέσον τοῦ σίτου (prep.; ↑185a.26)	*among the wheat* (Mt 13:25)
ἀνὰ μέρος (distributive adv.)	*each in turn* (1Cor 14:27)
ἀνὰ δύο (distributive adv.)	*two by two/in pairs* (Lk 10:1; ↑145c)
ἀνὰ εἷς ἕκαστος (distributive adv.)	*each one (of the gates)* (Re 21:21; ↑183b)

3. as a PREFIX:

a) "up", e.g.:	ἀνα-βαίνω *to go up*
b) "back", "again/anew", e.g.:	ἀνα-γεννάω *to beget/give birth (to) again*

On the traces of its use as an adverb in the NT ↑183b.

184d **ἀντί** core meaning "over against/in front of" (↑BDF §208; Z §91–95)

1. + GENITIVE *instead of, for* (NT also = *on behalf of*; ↑ὑπέρ + gen.), e.g.:

ἀντὶ ἰχθύος ὄφιν	*instead of a fish a snake* (Lk 11:11)
λύτρον **ἀντὶ πολλῶν**	*a ransom for many* (= *on behalf of many*) (Mt 20:28)

↑ἀνθ᾽ ὧν = ἀντὶ τούτων ὅτι *in return for which* = *because* (↑251h; 277a; 289e).
Also ↑226 on the articular infinitive with ἀντί.

2. as a PREFIX:

a) "against/in opposition" (highest frequency), e.g.:

ἀντι-τάσσομαι *to oppose, resist* ἀντι-λέγω *to speak against, contradict*

b) reciprocal use, e.g.:

ἀντι-καλέω *to invite in return*

c) occasionally "instead of, for", e.g.:

ἀντ-ανα-πληρόω *to fill up representatively/* (or else *to fill up on one's part*) (Col 1:24)

184e **ἀπό** core meaning "(away) from" (↑Lat. *ab* [↑prefix e.g. of *ab-errant*])

(↑also BDF §209–211; Z §132f)

CG: ἀπό for separation from the surface; ἐκ for separation from within.
NT: ἀπό and ἐκ sometimes "confused"; ἀπό phrases frequently replace the genitive of separation ("Away from where?"; ↑169) and at times the genitive of material or content ("Of what material?"/ "With what content?"; ↑161).

1. + GENITIVE *from, since*:

a) indicating space (with verbs of motion, including such with prefixed ἐκ), e. g.:

ἦλθεν Ἰησοῦς **ἀπὸ Ναζαρέτ** — *Jesus came from Nazareth* (Mk 1:9)
ἐξῆλθεν Λὼτ **ἀπὸ Σοδόμων** — *Lot went out from Sodom.* (Lk 17:29)

b) indicating time, e. g.:

ἀπ᾽ ἐκείνης … **τῆς ἡμέρας** — *from that day on* (Jn 11:53)
ἀπὸ κτίσεως κόσμου — *since the creation of the world* (Ro 1:20)
ἀπό … **ἕκτης ὥρας** — *from the sixth hour onwards* (Mt 27:45)

↑ἀφ᾽ οὗ = ἀπὸ τοῦ χρόνου ὅτε/ἀφ᾽ ἧς = ἀπὸ τῆς ἡμέρας ᾗ *since* (↑251g; 276a; 289e).

c) metaphorical use:

(1) indicating separation (in the NT sometimes in ways unattested in CG), e. g.:

ἀνάθεμα … **ἀπὸ τοῦ Χριστοῦ** — *cursed … – cut off from Christ* (Ro 9:3)

(2) indicating origin, e. g.:

οἱ **ἀπὸ τῆς Ἰταλίας** — *those from Italy* (He 13:24)

(3) indicating cause, reason, originator (also replacing ὑπό + gen.; ↑184s/191a), e. g.:

ἀπὸ τοῦ φόβου ἔκραξαν. — *They cried out in fear.* (Mt 14:26)
καί … **ἀπὸ τοῦ ὄχλου** — *but because of the crowd …* (Lk 19:3)
τόπον ἡτοιμασμένον **ἀπὸ τοῦ θεοῦ** — *a place prepared by God* (Re 12:6)

(4) partitive use (KG), corresponding to a partitive genitive (↑166), e. g.:

τίνα θέλετε **ἀπὸ τῶν δύο** ἀπολύσω …; — *Which of the two do you want me to release …?* (Mt 27:21)

Also ↑185c on ἀπὸ προσώπου + gen. in the NT replacing ἀπό or παρά + gen.

2. as a PREFIX:

a) "(from) away", "off", e. g.: — ἀπο-κόπτω *to cut off/away*
b) "back", "in return", e. g.: — ἀπο-δίδωμι *to give back, to return*
c) "completely" (↑Schwyzer II: 445), e. g.: — ἀπο-στερέω *to rob* s.o. (completely)

διά core meaning "through" (↑also BDF §222–223; Z §112–115) 184f

1. + GENITIVE *through, by way of* (↑Lat. *per*):

a) indicating space (with verbs of motion, including such with prefixed ἐκ), e. g.:

διέρχεσθαι **διὰ τῆς Σαμαρείας** — *to pass through Samaria* (Jn 4:4)

b) indicating time *through, throughout, after,* KG/NT also *during, within,* e. g.:

δι᾽ ὅλης νυκτός — *throughout the whole night* (Lk 5:5)
διὰ δεκατεσσάρων ἐτῶν … ἀνέβην. — *After fourteen years I went up …* (Ga 2:1)
ὅραμα **διὰ τῆς νυκτός** — *a vision during/in the night* (Ac 16:9)

διὰ τριῶν ἡμερῶν οἰκοδομῆσαι	*to build within three days* (Mt 26:61)

c) metaphorical use:

(1) indicating intermediate agent, instrument, means *through, by means of* or (in the NT comparatively rare) indicating cause, originator (↑191a) *by*, e.g.:

εἰρήνην ἔχομεν πρὸς τὸν θεὸν **διὰ τοῦ κυρίου ἡμῶν Ἰησοῦ Χριστοῦ**.	*we have peace with God through our Lord Jesus Christ.* (Ro 5:1)
Ἐν ᾧ ἔχομεν τὴν ἀπολύτρωσιν **διὰ τοῦ αἵματος αὐτοῦ**.	*In him we have redemption through his blood.* (Eph 1:7)
ἥτις ἀρχὴν λαβοῦσα λαλεῖσθαι **διὰ τοῦ κυρίου** …	*It was first announced by the Lord …* (He 2:3)

(2) indicating manner, e.g.:

δι᾽ ὑπομονῆς ἀπεκδεχόμεθα.	*we wait for it with patience.* (Ro 8:25)

2. + ACCUSATIVE *because of, for the sake of* (Lat. *propter*; CG poetry also *through*):

a) CG poetry (NT 1×: Lk 17:11): indicating space or time *through*.

b) indicating reason, e.g.:

διὰ τοῦτο	*for this reason/therefore* (Col 1:9 et pass.)
δι᾽ ὑμᾶς ἐπτώχευσεν.	*For your sake he became poor.* (2Cor 8:9)

Also ↑226 on the articular infinitive with διά.

Improper prepositions indicating "because of": ἕνεκα/ἕνεκεν/εἵνεκεν, χάριν + gen. (↑185; 187m).

3. as a PREFIX:

a) indicating space "through", e.g.:
δια-πορεύομαι *to travel/pass through*

b) indicating time "through", e.g.
δια-πλέω *to sail through/across*

c) indicating separation, division (↑Lat. *dis-*, [↑prefix e.g. of *dis-mantle*]), e.g.:
δια-κρίνω "to separate one from another" inter alia signifying *to make a distinction*, mid./pass. "to fall apart"/"to disagree" (with others:) *to dispute*, (with o.s.:) *to doubt*

d) indicating the completeness of the "action": "through and through", e.g.:
δια-φθείρω *to spoil/destroy utterly*

184g **εἰς**[23] core meaning "into", "to" (↑Lat. *in* + acc.; opposite of ἐκ) – proclitic (↑6a)

(↑also BDF §205–207; 218; Z §99–111)

CG: εἰς "into", ἐν "in".

---

23 CG also ἐς. εἰς < ἐν (↑184i) + ς (originally: ἐν + acc. *into*).

KG: εἰς and ἐν generally "confused", but in the NT only in part (in Mk, Lk/Ac; rarely in Jn), not in Mt, the Epistles, and Re.

1. + ACCUSATIVE *into, to, towards, against,* e.g.:

a) typically indicating space (mostly goal) *into, in, to,* e.g.:

ὑπάγετε **εἰς τὴν πόλιν**.	*Go into the city!* (Mk 14:13 et pass.)
… ὡς ἂν πορεύωμαι **εἰς τὴν Σπανίαν**.	… *when I go to Spain.* (Ro 15:24; ↑v. 28)

b) sometimes indicating time (a specific point in time up to which sth. continues or for which sth. happens) *until/to, in, at, for,* e.g.:

ὁ δὲ ὑπομείνας **εἰς τέλος** …	*But the one standing firm to the end* … (Mt 10:22)

c) metaphorical use (well-attested in the NT):

(1) indicating the purpose of an "action" *for* (in part ≈ dat. of interest; ↑176a), e.g.:

εἰς κρίμα ἐγὼ … ἦλθον …	*For judgment I have come* … (Jn 9:39)
… εἰ μήτι … ἡμεῖς ἀγοράσωμεν **εἰς πάντα τὸν λαὸν τοῦτον** βρώματα.	… *unless we … buy food for all these people.* (Lk 9:13)

On the related result indicating use especially with inf./ACI phrases ↑226a; 334b.

(2) indicating friendly or hostile attitude *for, towards, to, at,* e.g.:

τὴν ἀγάπην … **εἰς πάντας τοὺς ἁγίους**	*the love … for all the saints* (Col 1:4)
ἔχθρα **εἰς θεόν**	*hostility towards God* (Ro 8:7)
μετενόησαν **εἰς τὸ κήρυγμα Ἰωνᾶ**.	*They repented at the preaching of Jonah.* (Lk 11:32)

(3) indicating reference to sth. *with respect to, with reference to, concerning,* e.g.:

Δαυίδ … λέγει **εἰς αὐτόν** …	*David says concerning him* … (Ac 2:25)

Occasionally (Mt 5:35) εἰς is used in the sense of "by" in oaths; ↑252.33.

(4) mainly in LXX/NT Greek (↑Hebr. לְ *lə*) used as a non-CG replacement of the nominative expressing a subject complement (SC^{id}; ↑147a), less frequently of the accusative expressing an object complement (OC^{id}; ↑153b), e.g.:

ἐγένετο **εἰς δένδρον**.	*It became a tree.* (Lk 13:19)
τέθεικά σε **εἰς φῶς ἐθνῶν**	*I have made you a light for the Gentiles.* (Ac 13:47)

Also ↑226 on the articular infinitive with εἰς.

2. as a PREFIX (of a small number of compounds) mostly indicating space signifying "into", e.g.:

εἰσ-άγω *to lead into*	εἰσ-έρχομαι *to enter*
εἰσ-φέρω *to bring in* (i.e. into an area)	

184h **ἐκ/ἐξ** core meaning "out of" (↑Lat. *ex* + ablative; opposed to εἰς) – proclitic (↑6a)

(↑also BDF §212; Z §134f)

CG:
ἐκ separation from within; ἀπό separation from the surface.

NT (KG):

a) ἐκ and ἀπό sometimes "confused";

b) ἐκ phrases frequently replace:

- partitive genitive ("Part of what?") (↑166);
- genitive of separation ("Away from where?") (↑169);
- genitive place ("From where?" or "Where?") (mostly replaced even in CG prose; ↑171).

c) ἐκ phrases sometimes replace also:

- genitive of material ("Of what material?"; ↑161);
- genitive of value or price ("Of what value?"/"For/At how much?"; ↑163).

1. + GENITIVE *out of, from,* e.g.:

a) typically indicating space, e.g.:

ἐκβάλω τὸ κάρφος **ἐκ τοῦ ὀφθαλμοῦ σου.**	*Let me take the speck out of your eye.* (Mt 7:4)
πάντας ἐξέβαλεν **ἐκ τοῦ ἱεροῦ.**	*He drove all out of the temple.* (Jn 2:15)

In certain expressions a state ("Where?") rather than a movement ("Where from?") is implied, e.g.:

ἐκ δεξιῶν / **ἐξ εὐωνύμων**	*at s.o.'s right / at s.o.'s left.* (Mt 20:21.23)

b) sometimes indicating time *from, since,* e.g.:

ἐκ νεότητός μου	*from/since my youth* (Mk 10:20)

Also note (↑145e):

ἐκ τρίτου	*(for) the third time* (Mt 26:44)

c) metaphorical use (well-attested):

(1) indicating origin, cause (↑191a), reason, motivation, also rule, standard, material (↑161) or the like, *from, of, on the basis of, by, by reason of, according to,* e.g.:

ἐπερωτήσας **ἐκ ποίας ἐπαρχείας** ἐστίν …	*he asked him what province he was from* … (Ac 23:34)
Ἑβραῖος **ἐξ Ἑβραίων**	*a Hebrew of Hebrews* (Php 3:5)
πᾶς ὁ ὢν **ἐκ τῆς ἀληθείας**	*everyone who is of/belongs to the truth* (spiritual kinship; Jn 18:37)
ἐκ γὰρ **τῶν λόγων σου** δικαιωθήσῃ.	*For on the basis of/by your words you will be acquitted.* (Mt 12:37)
καὶ γὰρ ἐσταυρώθη **ἐξ ἀσθενείας**, ἀλλὰ ζῇ **ἐκ δυνάμεως θεοῦ.**	*For he was crucified by reason of/in weakness, but lives because of/by the power of God.* (2Cor 13:4)
ἐκ γὰρ **τοῦ καρποῦ** τὸ δένδρον γινώσκεται.	*For the tree is known by its fruit.* (Mt 12:33)

ἐκ τῶν ἰδίων λαλεῖ — *he speaks according to his own nature* (Jn 8:44)

φραγέλλιον **ἐκ σχοινίων** — *a whip of/from cords* (Jn 2:15)

(2) sometimes indicating manner, e.g.:

ἐκ μέρους — *in part* (1Cor 13:12)

(3) partitive use (KG), corresponding to a partitive genitive (↑166), e.g.:

τινὲς **ἐκ τῶν Ἱεροσολυμιτῶν** — *some of the inhabitants of Jerusalem* (Jn 7:25)

(4) occasionally (KG) corresponding to a genitive of value or price (↑163a), e.g.:

ἠγόρασαν **ἐξ αὐτῶν** τὸν ἀγρὸν τοῦ κεραμέως. — *They bought with them the potter's field.* (Mt 27:7)

Also ↑Mt 20:2; Ac 1:18.

Also ↑226 on the articular infinitive with ἐκ.

2. as a PREFIX:

a) "out", "from", "away", "off", e.g.:

ἐξ-έρχομαι *to go/come out/away*

b) "completely" (intensifying force), e.g.:

ἐξ-απορέομαι *to be at a complete loss, to despair*

ἐκ-θαυμάζω *to be utterly amazed*

ἐν core meaning "in", "at" (↑Lat. *in* + ablative) – proclitic (↑6a) 184i

(↑also BDF §205f; 218–220; Z §116–121)

CG:

ἐν "in", εἰς "into".

KG:

a) εἰς and ἐν generally "confused", but in the NT only in part (in Mk, Lk/Ac; rarely in Jn), not in Mt, the Epistles, and Re.

b) ἐν phrases frequently replace:

- dative of instrument or cause ("By what means?"/"Owing to what?") (↑177; also 187o/187m);
- dative of manner ("How?"/"Under what attendant circumstances?") (↑180; also 187j);
- dative of place ("Where?") (replaced with hardly any exception; ↑181; also 187a);

c) in the NT ἐν phrases less frequently replace:

- dative of respect ("In what respect?"; ↑178a; 187k);
- occasionally the dative proper (↑p. 253).

1. + DATIVE *in, at*, e.g.:

a) indicating space (position) *in, within, at, by, on; among* (a group), e.g.:

ἐγένετο δὲ πολλὴ χαρὰ **ἐν τῇ πόλει ἐκείνῃ**. — *There was much joy in that city.* (Ac 8:8)

οἱ πατέρες ἡμῶν **ἐν τῷ ὄρει τούτῳ** προσεκύνησαν·	*Our ancestors worshipped on this mountain.* (Jn 4:20)
ζήτησον **ἐν οἰκίᾳ Ἰούδα** … Ταρσέα	*at the house of Judas look for a man of Tarsus …* (Ac 9:11)
ὁ λόγος … ἐσκήνωσεν **ἐν ἡμῖν**.	*The Word … dwelt among us.* (Jn 1:14)

b) indicating time *in, at, during*, e.g.:

δοθήσεται γὰρ ὑμῖν **ἐν ἐκείνῃ τῇ ὥρᾳ** …	*For it will be given to you in that hour/at that time …* (Mt 10:19)
μὴ **ἐν τῇ ἑορτῇ** …	*Not during the festival …* (Mt 26:5)

Frequently (= CG and non-CG) ἐν phrases replace the dative of time ("When?"; ↑182; 187e/187g).

c) metaphorical use (well-attested):

(1) indicating a state/condition or situation, e.g.:

ἐν θλίψεσιν, ἐν ἀνάγκαις, ἐν στενοχωρίαις … ἐν φυλακαῖς …	*in afflictions, in hardships, in distresses, … in imprisonments …* (2Cor 6:4f)

in the NT relating also to the new existence brought about by God's salvific activity, particularly as used by John and Paul, *in* (perhaps ≈ *united with* or the like), e.g.:

μείνατε **ἐν ἐμοί** …	*Remain in me …* (Jn 15:4 ↑v. 5)
ἐν Χριστῷ (Ἰησοῦ) / **ἐν κυρίῳ** or the like	*in Christ (Jesus) / in the Lord* (Ro 12:5; Ga 5:6; Php 4:4 et pass.)

(2) in KG also indicating instrument or cause, corresponding to the dative of instrument or cause (↑177; in the NT facilitated by the use of Hebr./Aram. בְּ *bə*, HALOT, Jastrow s.v.) *with, by means of, through, by, because/on account of*, e.g.:

Ἐποίησεν κράτος **ἐν βραχίονι αὐτοῦ**.	*He has performed mighty deeds with his arm.* (Lk 1:51)
δικαιωθέντες … **ἐν τῷ αἵματι αὐτοῦ**	*… we have been declared righteous by his blood* (Ro 5:9)
μέλλει κρίνειν τὴν οἰκουμένην … **ἐν ἀνδρί** …	*he will judge the world … by a man …* (Ac 17:31)

Occasionally (Mt 5:34ff; Re 10:6) ἐν is used in the sense of "by" in oaths; ↑252.33.

↑ἐν ᾧ = ἐν τούτῳ ὅτι *because* (↑251h; 277a; 289e).

(3) in KG indicating manner, corresponding to the dative of manner (↑180) *in, with*, e.g.:

… ἕως ἂν ἴδωσιν τὴν βασιλείαν τοῦ θεοῦ ἐληλυθυῖαν **ἐν δυνάμει**.	*… until they see that the kingdom of God has come in/with power.* (Mk 9:1)

(4) in the NT occasionally used like a dative of respect (↑178a), e.g.:

προβεβηκότες **ἐν ταῖς ἡμέραις αὐτῶν**	*advanced with respect to their days [of life] = very old* (Lk 1:7)

Also ↑Lk 1:18; 2:36.

Also ↑226 on the articular infinitive with ἐν.

2. as a PREFIX:

a) indicating space "in" or "into" (= CG and non-CG), e.g.:

ἐν-οικέω *to live/dwell in*	ἐμ-πίπτω (↑15c) *to fall into*

b) metaphorical use (hostile attitude), e.g.:

ἐγ-καλέω (↑15b) *to accuse*	ἐν-αντίος *opposed, opponent*

ἐπί core meaning "on", "upon", "over" (opposed to ὑπό) (↑BDF §233–235; Z §122–129) 184j

1. + GENITIVE, DATIVE, ACCUSATIVE indicating a) space, b) time, c) used metaphorically:

In KG the CG distinctions tend to be blurred.

a) indicating **SPACE** (ἐπί + gen. and + acc. occur much more frequently than ἐπί + dat.; ἐπί phrases may replace the dative of place; ↑181; 187a):

(1) + GENITIVE *on, upon,* also *at, in* (mostly of position, but also of movement), e.g.:

ἐπὶ γῆς εἰρήνη	*peace on earth* (Lk 2:14)
βάλῃ τὸν σπόρον **ἐπὶ τῆς γῆς**	*(someone) scatters seed on the ground* (Mk 4:26)

(2) + DATIVE *on, at,* also *near, in* (CG of position, KG/NT also of movement), e.g.:

ἠνέχθη ἡ κεφαλὴ αὐτοῦ **ἐπὶ πίνακι**	*his head was brought on a dish* (Mt 14:11)
οὐδεὶς δὲ ἐπιβάλλει ἐπίβλημα ῥάκους ἀγνάφου **ἐπὶ ἱματίῳ παλαιῷ**.	*No one sews a patch of unshrunk cloth on an old garment* (Mt 9:16)

(3) + ACCUSATIVE *onto, towards, to* (CG of movement, KG/NT also of position), e.g.:

πορεύου … **ἐπὶ τὴν ὁδόν** …	*Go … to the road …* (Ac 8:26)
ἐπὶ τὸ προσκεφάλαιον καθεύδων	*sleeping on a cushion* (Mk 4:38)

b) indicating **TIME**:

(1) + GENITIVE *during, during the reign of, in the time of,* e.g.:

ἐγένετο **ἐπὶ Κλαυδίου**.	*(This famine) took place during the reign of Claudius.* (Ac 11:28)
πολλοὶ λεπροὶ ἦσαν … **ἐπὶ Ἐλισαίου τοῦ προφήτου**.	*There were many lepers … in the time of the prophet Elisha.* (Lk 4:27)

(2) + DATIVE (only a few NT instances) *during, at* (CG also *subsequently, after*), e.g.:

νυνὶ δὲ ἅπαξ **ἐπὶ συντελείᾳ τῶν αἰώνων** … πεφανέρωται.	*But now he has appeared once for all at the culmination of the ages …* (He 9:26)

(3) + ACCUSATIVE *for, during* ("How long?"), in the NT also *at, on* ("When?"), e.g.:

ἐκλείσθη ὁ οὐρανὸς **ἐπὶ ἔτη τρία καὶ μῆνας ἕξ**.	*The sky was shut for three years and six months.* (Lk 4:25)

ἐπὶ τὴν αὔριον ἐκβαλὼν ἔδωκεν δύο δηνάρια τῷ πανδοχεῖ. — *The next day he took out two denarii and gave them to the innkeeper.* (Lk 10:35)

c) **METAPHORICAL** use (well-attested with a considerable variety of functions):

(1) + GENITIVE, some of the more frequent uses being:

• *over, of, in charge of* (relating to authority or supervision; also used in CG; ↑ἐπί + acc. below [3]), e.g.:

ἐπὶ τούτων ὁ δεύτερος θάνατος οὐκ ἔχει ἐξουσίαν. — *The second death has no power over them.* (Re 20:6)

• *on the basis of, based on, in accordance with,* e.g.:

ὁ λαὸς γὰρ **ἐπ᾽ αὐτῆς** νενομοθέτηται — *for on that basis* (i.e. on the basis of the Levitical priesthood) *the law was given* (He 7:11)

ἐπ᾽ ἀληθείας τὴν ὁδὸν τοῦ θεοῦ διδάσκεις. — *You teach the way of God in accordance with the truth* (= *truly*). (Mk 12:14)

(2) + DATIVE:

• most frequently indicating reason, grounds, basis, typically in combination with expressions of affective behaviour *over, at, because of* (on ἐφ᾽ ᾧ for *this reason, because* ↑277a), e.g.:

οὕτως χαρὰ ἐν τῷ οὐρανῷ ἔσται **ἐπὶ ἑνὶ ἁμαρτωλῷ** μετανοοῦντι ἢ … — *In the same way there will be more rejoicing in heaven over one sinner who repents than …* (Lk 15:7)

Also ↑Lk 1:14; 15:10.

ἐξεπλήσσοντο οἱ ὄχλοι **ἐπὶ τῇ διδαχῇ αὐτοῦ**. — *The crowds were amazed at his teaching.* (Mt 7:28)

also in combination with expressions indicating belief, trust, and hope, *in, on,* e.g.:

πᾶς ὁ πιστεύων **ἐπ᾽ αὐτῷ** οὐ καταισχυνθήσεται. — *No one who believes/trusts in him will be put to shame.* (Ro 10:11)

ἠλπίκαμεν **ἐπὶ θεῷ ζῶντι**. — *We have our hope set on the living God.* (1Tm 4:10)

… ἵνα μὴ πεποιθότες ὦμεν **ἐφ᾽ ἑαυτοῖς**. — *… that we might not rely on ourselves.* (2Cor 1:9)

Also note the NT/LXX idiom ἐπὶ τῷ ὀνόματί τινος (it occurs much less frequently than the quasi-synonymous NT/LXX idiom ἐν τῷ ὀνόματί τινος) relating to acting *in the name of s.o.* ≈ "on behalf of s.o.", sometimes "invoking the name of s.o.", with expressions such as διδάσκω *to teach,* λαλέω *to speak,* βαπτίζω *to baptize,* e.g.:

καὶ βαπτισθήτω ἕκαστος ὑμῶν **ἐπὶ τῷ ὀνόματι Ἰησοῦ Χριστοῦ**. — *and be baptized every one of you in the name of Jesus Christ.* (Ac 2:38)

… μὴ λαλεῖν **ἐπὶ τῷ ὀνόματι τοῦ Ἰησοῦ**. — *… not to speak in the name* (≈ *on behalf*) *of Jesus.* (Ac 5:40)

↑also ἐφ᾽ ᾧ = ἐπὶ τούτῳ ὅτι *because* (↑251h; 277a; 289e).

- also indicating addition (so also CG) *to*, e.g.:

προσέθηκεν καὶ τοῦτο **ἐπὶ πᾶσιν**. *He still added this to them all.* (Lk 3:20)

- also indicating purpose or result (so also CG), e.g.:

κτισθέντες ἐν Χριστῷ Ἰησοῦ **ἐπὶ ἔργοις ἀγαθοῖς** *created in Christ Jesus for good works/ to do good works* (Eph 2:10)

- also indicating conditions (CG; ↑280b): ἐφ' ᾧ/ἐφ' ᾧτε + inf./ACI (or ind. fut.) *on condition that* (also *in order that*; ↑278a); ↑also 277a.

(3) + ACCUSATIVE:

- (rule) *over* (probably a Semitism, ↑מָלַךְ עַל *mālaḵ ʿal*, HALOT s.v.; ↑ἐπί + gen. above [1]), e.g.:

βασιλεύσει **ἐπὶ τὸν οἶκον Ἰακὼβ** εἰς τοὺς αἰῶνας. *He will reign over the house of Jacob for ever.* (Lk 1:33)

Also ↑Lk 19:14.

ἔδωκεν αὐτοῖς δύναμιν καὶ ἐξουσίαν **ἐπὶ πάντα τὰ δαιμόνια**. *He gave them power and authority over all demons.* (Lk 9:1)

- also like ἐπί + dat. indicating basis of belief/faith or trust (↑174b), e.g.:

… τοῖς πιστεύουσιν **ἐπὶ τὸν ἐγείραντα Ἰησοῦν** … ἐκ νεκρῶν. … *[us] who believe in the one who raised Jesus … from the dead.* (Ro 4:24)

- also indicating hostility *against*, e.g.:

συνήχθησαν … **ἐπὶ τὸν ἅγιον παῖδά σου Ἰησοῦν**. … *they gathered together against your holy servant Jesus.* (Ac 4:27)

Also ↑226 on the articular infinitive with ἐπί + dat. (CG).

2. as a PREFIX (inter alia):

a) indicating space "(up)on", "to", "towards", e.g.:

ἐπι-τίθημι *to lay/put upon* ἐπ-έρχομαι *to come to/upon*

ἐπι-σπείρω *to sow on top*

b) metaphorical use "in addition", e.g.:

ἐπι-κερδαίνω *to gain in addition*

κατά core meaning "down(wards)" (↑adv. κάτω *down*; opposed to ἀνά) 184k

(↑also BDF §224f; Z §130f)

1. + GENITIVE:

a) indicating space *down (from)* (a sense rarely found in the NT), KG/NT frequently *throughout*, CG sometimes also *under*, e.g.:

ὥρμησεν πᾶσα ἡ ἀγέλη **κατὰ τοῦ κρημνοῦ**. *The whole herd rushed down the steep bank.* (Mt 8:32)

γνωστὸν δὲ ἐγένετο **καθ' ὅλης τῆς Ἰόππης**.	*It became known throughout all Joppa.* (Ac 9:42)
… οὔτε … τιμῆς τινος ἠξίωσε τὸν **κατὰ γῆς**.	*… nor ever deemed worthy of any honour the one beneath the earth.* (Xenophon, Cyropaedia 4.6.5)

b) metaphorical use in a hostile sense *against* (occasionally also in the sense of "by" in oaths; ↑252.33), e.g.:

ἡ γὰρ σὰρξ ἐπιθυμεῖ **κατὰ τοῦ πνεύματος**.	*For the flesh has desires against the Spirit.* (Ga 5:17)

2. + ACCUSATIVE (in the NT used much more frequently than κατά + gen.):

a) indicating space *down(wards), throughout, on, along,* KG/NT also *to(wards),* e.g.:

πάντες δὲ διεσπάρησαν **κατὰ τὰς χώρας τῆς Ἰουδαίας καὶ Σαμαρείας**.	*They were all scattered throughout the regions of Judea and Samaria.* (Ac 8:1)

b) indicating time (rarely) *at (about), on, during,* e.g.:

Κατὰ δὲ **τὸ μεσονύκτιον** Παῦλος καὶ Σιλᾶς προσευχόμενοι ὕμνουν τὸν θεόν.	*About midnight Paul and Silas were praying and singing hymns to God.* (Ac 16:25)

c) metaphorical use (well-attested with a considerable variety of functions):

(1) indicating a standard *in accordance with, according to* (occurs frequently; opposed to παρά + acc. *contrary to*; ↑184m), e.g.:

ὡς ἐτέλεσαν πάντα **κατὰ τὸν νόμον κυρίου** …	*When they had completed everything according to the Law of the Lord …* (Lk 2:39)
τότε ἀποδώσει ἑκάστῳ **κατὰ τὴν πρᾶξιν αὐτοῦ**.	*Then he will repay each person according to their deeds.* (Mt 16:27)

(2) with distributive force (noun phrases in the sg., also similarly in the pl.), e.g.:

διώδευεν **κατὰ πόλιν καὶ κώμην**.	*He went on through towns and villages/from one town and village to another.* (Lk 8:1)
διήρχοντο **κατὰ τὰς κώμας**	*They went through the villages/from village to village* (Lk 9:6)
καθ' ἡμέραν ἤμην πρὸς ὑμᾶς ἐν τῷ ἱερῷ. (also ↑157)	*Day after day I was with you in the temple.* (Mk 14:49)

(3) *in relation to, with respect to, concerning,* e.g.:

κατὰ μὲν **τὸ εὐαγγέλιον** ἐχθροὶ δι' ὑμᾶς	*As far as the gospel is concerned, they are enemies for your sake* (Ro 11:28)

(4) indicating manner or quality (functionally similar to adverbs/adjectives), e.g.:

καθ' ὑπερβολὴν … ἐβαρήθημεν	*we were excessively burdened …* (2Cor 1:8)

σύν … ἀνδράσιν τοῖς **κατ' ἐξοχὴν τῆς πόλεως**	*with … the prominent men of the city* (Ac 25:23)

(5) with possessive force (↑140; 159b; KG usage), e.g.:

ἀκούσας τὴν **καθ' ὑμᾶς** πίστιν …	*I have heard of your faith …* (Eph 1:15)

3. as a PREFIX (inter alia):

a) "down", e.g.:

κατα-βαίνω *to come/go down*

b) "down" (destructively), e.g.:

κατα-σκάπτω *to tear down, to raze to the ground*

c) "completely" (intensifying force; ↑Lat. *con-*), e.g.:

κατ-αναλίσκω *to consume*

d) "against" (hostile force), e.g.:

κατα-λαλέω *to speak (evil) against*

On the traces of its use as an adverb in the NT ↑183b.

μετά core meaning "amidst", "among" (↑BDF §226f) 184l

1. + GENITIVE *with, in company with, together with; among*, e.g.:

ἐξῆλθεν … **μετὰ τῶν δώδεκα**.	*He left … with the Twelve.* (Mk 11:11)
ἐγὼ **μεθ' ὑμῶν** εἰμι.	*I am with you.* (Mt 28:20)
ἦν συγκαθήμενος **μετὰ τῶν ὑπηρετῶν**.	*He sat among the guards.* (Mk 14:54)

Also ↑Ac 18:10; 2Cor 13:13.

quite often also combined with abstract concepts indicating attendant circumstances of an activity, e.g.:

ἀπελθοῦσαι ταχὺ ἀπὸ τοῦ μνημείου **μετὰ φόβου καὶ χαρᾶς μεγάλης** …	*They hurried away from the tomb, (filled) with fear and great joy …* (Mt 28:8)
δουλεύων τῷ κυρίῳ **μετὰ πάσης ταπεινοφροσύνης καὶ δακρύων καὶ πειρασμῶν** …	*serving the Lord with all humility and with tears, and with trials …* (Ac 20:19)

2. + DATIVE (only CG poetry) *among, amid*.

3. + ACCUSATIVE *after* (Lat. *post*; CG poetry also *through*): in the NT indicating time, only He 9:3 indicating space *behind* (in CG of space, time or order in a sequence), e.g. (well-attested):

μετὰ δὲ **πολὺν χρόνον** ἔρχεται ὁ κύριος τῶν δούλων ἐκείνων.	*After a long time the master of those slaves came.* (Mt 25:19)

Also ↑226 on the articular infinitive with μετά + acc.

4. as a PREFIX (inter alia):

a) indicating sharing "with", e.g.:

μετα-λαμβάνω *to have/receive a part in* μετ-έχω *to have a part, to participate*

b) indicating change, e.g.:

μετα-βαίνω *to pass on/over* ("to change place/position")
μετα-νοέω *to change one's attitude/behaviour, to repent*

184m **παρά** core meaning "near", "alongside", "by" (in Att. mostly relating to persons; so in the NT in the case of παρά + gen. and + dat.)

(↑BDF §236–238; Z §90)

1. + GENITIVE *from (the side of), from* (of movement from; also ↑191a), e.g.:

ἐγὼ **παρὰ τοῦ θεοῦ** ἐξῆλθον.	*I came from God.* (Jn 16:27)
ἐξῆλθεν δόγμα **παρὰ Καίσαρος** …	*A decree went out from Caesar …* (Lk 2:1)

Also ↑185c on ἀπὸ προσώπου + gen. in the NT replacing ἀπό or παρά + gen.

2. + DATIVE indicating space (position) *at/by (the side of), near, beside, with* (may replace the dative of place; ↑181; 187a), less frequently in a metaphorical sense *in the sight of* (↑176c), e.g.:

Εἱστήκεισαν δὲ **παρὰ τῷ σταυρῷ τοῦ Ἰησοῦ** ἡ μήτηρ αὐτοῦ …	*Near the cross of Jesus stood his mother …* (Jn 19:25)
οὐ γὰρ οἱ ἀκροαταὶ νόμου δίκαιοι **παρὰ τῷ θεῷ** …	*For it is not the hearers of the law who are righteous in God's sight …* (Ro 2:13)

3. + ACCUSATIVE (CG of movement to, KG/NT also of position [of things]) *near (the side of), close to, towards,* KG/NT also *at (the side/edge of), along, by*:

a) indicating space, e.g.:

ἐξήλθομεν ἔξω τῆς πύλης **παρὰ ποταμόν** …	*We went outside the city gate to (the side of) the river …* (Ac 16:13)
Περιπατῶν δὲ **παρὰ τὴν θάλασσαν τῆς Γαλιλαίας** …	*As he was walking along the shore of/by the Sea of Galilee …* (Mt 4:18)

b) indicating time *during, for, in the course of* (not attested in the NT), e.g.:

παρὰ πάντα τὸν χρόνον	*for the whole of life* (Demosthenes 18.10)

c) metaphorical use (inter alia):

(1) with adversative force "past the side/limit of" *in contrast with, contrary to, against* (opposed to κατά + acc. *in accordance with*; ↑184k), e.g.:

παρὰ φύσιν ἐνεκεντρίσθης εἰς καλλιέλαιον.	*Contrary to nature you were grafted into a cultivated olive tree.* (Ro 11:24)

(2) with comparative force *in comparison with, more than, beyond* (↑138c; 242b), e.g.:

δοκεῖτε ὅτι οἱ Γαλιλαῖοι οὗτοι ἁμαρτωλοὶ **παρὰ πάντας τοὺς Γαλιλαίους** ἐγένοντο;	*Do you think these Galileans were worse sinners than* (< "sinners more than") *all the other Galileans?* (Lk 13:2)

4. as a PREFIX (inter alia):

a) "to(wards) the side/presence of", e.g.:

παρα-γίνομαι *to come (to)* παρα-λαμβάνω *to take to o.s., to receive*

b) "past the side/presence of", e.g.:

παρ-έρχομαι *to go/pass by*

c) "contrary to", e.g.:

παρα-βαίνω *to transgress, to violate*

περί core meaning "all around" (≈ ἀμφί; ↑184b) (↑BDF §228f; Z §96) 184n

1. + GENITIVE *around, about, concerning* (especially in the NT also *for [the sake of]*; ≈ ὑπέρ + gen.; ↑184r): indicating the thing or person an activity is about (especially the subject matter of what is being said or perceived), e.g.:

προϊδὼν ἐλάλησεν **περὶ τῆς ἀναστάσεως τοῦ Χριστοῦ**.	*Foreseeing this he spoke about the resurrection of the Messiah.* (Ac 2:31)
ἤκουσεν αὐτοῦ **περὶ τῆς εἰς Χριστὸν Ἰησοῦν πίστεως**.	*He listened to him as he spoke about/concerning faith in Christ Jesus.* (Ac 24:24)
τί ὑμῖν δοκεῖ **περὶ τοῦ χριστοῦ**;	*What do you think about the Messiah?* (Mt 22:42)
Πρῶτον μὲν εὐχαριστῶ τῷ θεῷ μου … **περὶ πάντων ὑμῶν**.	*First, I thank my God … for all of you.* (Ro 1:8; in Eph 1:16 with ὑπέρ)
προσεύχεσθε καὶ **περὶ ἡμῶν**.	*Pray for us, too!* (1Th 5:25; in Mt 5:44 with ὑπέρ)

2. + DATIVE (CG; mainly in poetry) *around, about* (indicating place or used metaphorically).

3. + ACCUSATIVE *around*:

a) indicating space, e.g.:

ζώνην δερματίνην **περὶ τὴν ὀσφύν**	*a leather belt around his waist* (Mt 3:4)
οἱ **περὶ αὐτόν**	*those around him* (Mk 4:10)

The reference of such phrases may include the person that a group is centred around (CG and NT), e.g.:

οἱ **περὶ Παῦλον** ἦλθον εἰς Πέργην τῆς Παμφυλίας.	*Paul and his companions came to Perga in Pamphylia.* (Ac 13:13)

b) indicating time, e.g.:

περὶ τρίτην ὥραν εἶδεν … *about the third hour he saw* … (Mt 20:3)

c) metaphorical use (occurs rarely in the NT):

(1) *with regard to, with respect to,* e.g.:

περὶ πάντα *in every respect* (Tt 2:7)

(2) *(occupied) with,* e.g.:

οὓς συναθροίσας καὶ τοὺς **περὶ τὰ τοιαῦτα** ἐργάτας … *He called a meeting of these and the workers occupied with similar crafts* … (Ac 19:25)

Also ↑226 on the articular infinitive (CG) with περί.

4. as a PREFIX (inter alia):

a) indicating space "around", "about", e.g.:

περι-έρχομαι *to go about*

b) metaphorical use "over and above", "more than", and "exceedingly", e.g.:

περι-λείπομαι *to remain over, to survive*
περι-γίνομαι *to be superior, to survive* (LXX/Josephus)
περί-λυπος *very sad, deeply grieved*

184o **πρό** core meaning "before" (↑Lat. *prō* and *ante*) and CG also "for" (↑Lat. *prō*) (↑BDF §213)

1. + GENITIVE *before, in front of* (CG also *for/on behalf of*):

a) indicating space (used infrequently in the NT), e.g.:

φύλακές τε **πρὸ τῆς θύρας** ἐτήρουν τὴν φυλακήν. *and sentries in front of the door were guarding the prison.* (Ac 12:6)

b) indicating time, e.g.:

ἠγάπησάς με **πρὸ καταβολῆς κόσμου** *you loved me before the creation of the world* (Jn 17:24)

c) metaphorical use:

(1) indicating priority, e.g.:

πρὸ πάντων τὴν εἰς ἑαυτοὺς ἀγάπην ἐκτενῆ ἔχοντες. *Above all, keep loving each other deeply!* (1Pe 4:8)

(2) in CG also *in defence of, for/on behalf of* (≈ ὑπέρ), e.g.:

… **πρὸ τῆς πατρίδος** … ἀποθνῄσκειν … *to die … for their country* (Lycurgus 107)

… οὔτε ἐγὼ ἀρκέσω πράττων τι **πρὸ ὑμῶν** …; *… I shall not be good enough to do anything on your behalf …?* (Xenophon, Cyropaedia 4.5.44)

Also ↑226 on the articular infinitive with πρό.

2. as a PREFIX:

a) indicating space "ahead", "forward", e.g.:

προ-άγω *to go ahead* προ-βαίνω *to go forward, to advance*

b) indicating time (most frequently in the NT) "ahead of time", "beforehand", e.g.:

προ-γινώσκω *to know/choose beforehand*

προ-ορίζω *to decide beforehand, to predetermine*

For improper prepositions such as ἐνώπιον etc. frequently replacing πρό, especially in the NT ↑185c; 187a.

πρός core meaning "in addition", "towards", "in the face of" (↑BDF §239f; Z §97f) 184p

1. + GENITIVE *from/on the part/side of*, (1× in the NT:) *in the interest of*:

a) indicating space (occurring infrequently in CG prose and not at all in the NT), e.g.:

τά … ὑποζύγια ἔχοντες **πρὸς τοῦ ποταμοῦ**	*keeping the beasts of burden on the side next to the river* … (Xenophon, Anabasis 2.2.4)

b) metaphorical use *from the part of*, e.g. in CG indicating originator (*by*; ↑191a), correspondence (*in line with*), or used in oaths (*by/in the presence of*; ↑similarly 252.33), in both the NT and CG indicating advantage, e.g. (1× in the NT):

τοῦτο γὰρ **πρὸς τῆς ὑμετέρας σωτηρίας** ὑπάρχει.	*For this is in the interest of your safety.* (Ac 27:34)

2. + DATIVE *near, at, by* (7× in the NT):

a) indicating space (position), e.g.:

εἱστήκει **πρὸς τῇ θύρᾳ** ἔξω.	*He stood outside at the door.* (Jn 18:16)

b) metaphorical use (unattested in the NT) *in addition to*, e.g.:

καὶ **πρὸς τούτοις** ἕνδεκα στατῆρας	*and in addition to these, eleven staters.* (Plutarch, Lysander 18.2)

3. + ACCUSATIVE *to, towards*:

a) indicating space (movement/direction), e.g.:

(1) with verbs of motion, e.g.:

ἐάν τις διψᾷ ἐρχέσθω **πρός με**.	*If anyone is thirsty, let him come to me!* (Jn 7:37)

(2) in the NT sometimes indicating a state or a position in a place, replacing παρά + dat. *at/by (the side of), near, beside* (↑184m), with verbs such as εἰμί (rarely γίνομαι) *to be*, κεῖμαι *to lie/to be laid*, e.g.:

καὶ αἱ ἀδελφαὶ αὐτοῦ οὐχὶ πᾶσαι **πρὸς ἡμᾶς** εἰσιν;	*Are not all his sisters with us?* (Mt 13:56)

(3) indicating time (not frequently used in the NT):

- *towards* (1× in the NT), e.g.:

πρὸς ἑσπέραν ἐστίν. — *It is towards/near evening.* (Lk 24:29)

- *during, for*, e.g.:

οἳ **πρὸς καιρὸν** πιστεύουσιν — *they believe only for a while* (Lk 8:13)

πρὸς ὀλίγας ἡμέρας κατὰ τὸ δοκοῦν αὐτοῖς ἐπαίδευον. — *They disciplined us for a short time as it seemed best to them.* (He 12:10)

b) metaphorical use (inter alia):

(1) indicating purpose/goal or result, e.g.:

πρὸς τὴν ἔνδειξιν τῆς δικαιοσύνης αὐτοῦ ἐν τῷ νῦν καιρῷ — *(in order) to demonstrate his righteousness in the present time* (Ro 3:26)

↑also Mt 23:5; 2Cor 4:6; Eph 4:12; 2Tm 3:16.

(2) *with a view to, according to, with reference/regard to* or the like, e.g.:

οὐκ ὀρθοποδοῦσιν **πρὸς τὴν ἀλήθειαν τοῦ εὐαγγελίου**. — *They were not acting in line with the truth of the gospel.* (Ga 2:14)

… ὅτι **πρὸς αὐτοὺς** τὴν παραβολὴν εἶπεν. — *… that he had spoken the parable with reference to them.* (Mk 12:12)

(3) indicating a friendly or hostile relationship, e.g.:

εἰρήνην ἔχομεν **πρὸς τὸν θεὸν** διὰ τοῦ κυρίου ἡμῶν Ἰησοῦ Χριστοῦ. — *We have peace with God through our Lord Jesus Christ.* (Ro 5:1)

βλασφημίας **πρὸς τὸν θεόν** — *blasphemies against God* (Re 13:6)

Also ↑226 on the articular infinitive with πρός.

4. as a PREFIX (inter alia):

a) "towards", "to", e.g.:

προσ-έρχομαι *to come/go to, to approach*

b) "in addition", e.g.:

προσ-τίθημι *to add (to)*

c) "beside", e.g.:

πρόσ-μένω *to remain/stay with*

184q **σύν** (CG also ξύν) (↑BDF §221)

1. + DATIVE: indicating association or addition *(in company) with* (↑Lat. *cum*):

a) mainly relating to persons, infrequently to things, e.g.:

εἰσῆλθεν **σὺν αὐτοῖς** εἰς τὸ ἱερόν. — *He went into the temple with them.* (Ac 3:8)

… ἐγὼ ἐκομισάμην ἂν τὸ ἐμὸν **σὺν τόκῳ**. — *… I would have received what was my own with interest.* (Mt 25:27)

b) also relating to spiritual bonds with Christ, e.g.:

ἡ ζωὴ ὑμῶν κέκρυπται **σὺν τῷ Χριστῷ** ἐν τῷ θεῷ. — *Your life is hidden with Christ in God.* (Col 3:3)

2. as a PREFIX:

a) "together (at the same time)", e.g.: συν-άγω *to gather together*

b) "(along) with", e.g.: συν-εργέω *to work together with*

c) "completely" (intensifying force; ↑Lat. *con-*), e.g.:

συγ-καλύπτω (↑15b) *to cover completely* συν-τελέω *to complete*

ὑπέρ core meaning "above", "beyond" (↑BDF §230f; Z §91–96) 184r

1. + GENITIVE *above* (↑Lat. *super*) and *for/on behalf of* (↑Lat. *prō*):

a) indicating space (CG), e.g.:

ὑπὲρ γὰρ **τῆς κώμης** γήλοφος ἦν. — *For above the village there was a hill.* (Xenophon, Anabasis 1.10.12)

b) metaphorical use *for = on behalf of; because of, for the sake of*; also (a small number of instances in the NT) *in place of, instead of*; also (= περί + gen., especially in Paul's letters; ↑184n) *about, concerning*, e.g.:

ὑπὲρ ἡμῶν πάντων παρέδωκεν αὐτόν. — *He gave him up for us all.* (Ro 8:32; also ↑2Cor 5:15)

διὸ εὐδοκῶ ἐν ἀσθενείαις … **ὑπὲρ Χριστοῦ**· — *That is why I am content with/I delight in weaknesses … for Christ's sake.* (2Cor 12:10)

Ἠσαΐας δὲ κράζει **ὑπὲρ τοῦ Ἰσραήλ** (Var. περὶ τοῦ Ἰσραήλ)· — *Isaiah cries out concerning Israel:* (Ro 9:27)

Note the differences between CG and NT usage:

CG:
ὑπέρ + gen. metaphorical use: chiefly *for (the sake of)*, ἀντί + gen. chiefly *for, instead of*;
ὑπέρ + gen. metaphorical use: chiefly *for (the sake of)*, περί + gen. chiefly *about, concerning*.

NT:
ὑπέρ + gen. and ἀντί + gen. as well as ὑπέρ + gen. and περί + gen. are sometimes "confused".

2. + ACCUSATIVE *on, above, over, beyond* (↑Lat. *supra/ultra*):

a) CG: indicating space (movement/direction), e.g.:

τοῖς Θρᾳξὶ τοῖς **ὑπὲρ Ἑλλήσποντον** οἰκοῦσι — *with the Thracians who live beyond the Hellespont* (Xenophon, Anabasis 1.1.9)

b) CG: indicating time (↑c below), e.g.:

οἱ **ὑπέρ** … **πεντήκοντα** … γεγονότες ἔτη — *the men who are over … fifty* (Plato, Laws 665b)

c) metaphorical use: indicating what goes beyond a certain measure (also used in comparisons ↑138c) *over and above, more than*, e.g.:

τῆς καθ᾽ ὑπερβολὴν **ὑπὲρ δύναμιν** ἐβαρήθημεν — *we were burdened excessively, beyond our strength* (2Cor 1:8)

Also ↑226 on the articular infinitive with ὑπέρ (CG).

3. as a PREFIX:
"over", "beyond measure", "exceedingly", e.g.:
ὑπερ-βαίνω *to go beyond, to transgress* ὑπερ-αυξάνω *to grow exceedingly*

On the traces of its use as an adverb in the NT ↑183b.

184s **ὑπό** core meaning "under" (opposed to ἐπί) (↑BDF §232)

1. + GENITIVE CG/NT *by* (originator/cause; ↑Lat. *ab* with pass.), only CG *under* (position from or position):

a) CG (rarely used in prose): indicating space *under* (position from or position).

b) metaphorical use: indicating agency *by* (originator/cause chiefly with pass. verbs or other pass. expressions; sometimes replaced by ἀπό + gen.; ↑184e/191a), e.g.:

πάντα μοι παρεδόθη **ὑπὸ τοῦ πατρός μου**. — *All things have been handed over to me by my Father.* (Lk 10:22)

2. + DATIVE only CG *under* (position) (↑Lat. *sub* + ablative):

a) indicating space (position), e.g.:

ἑστάναι … **ὑπό τινι δένδρῳ**. — *to stand … under a tree* (Plato, Philebus 38c)

b) metaphorical use: under the power of, e.g.:

… **ὑφ᾽ ἑαυτῷ** ποιήσασθαι — *to bring … under his control* (↑Herodotus 7.157)

3. + ACCUSATIVE *under* (direction, in the NT also position):

a) indicating space, e.g.:

οὐκ εἰμὶ ἱκανὸς ἵνα **μου ὑπὸ τὴν στέγην** εἰσέλθῃς. — *I am not worthy to have you come under my roof.* (Mt 8:8)

ὄντα **ὑπὸ τὴν συκῆν** εἶδόν σε. — *I saw you under the fig-tree.* (Jn 1:48)

b) indicating time (only 1× in the NT), e.g.:

εἰσῆλθον **ὑπὸ τὸν ὄρθρον** … — *At daybreak they entered …* (Ac 5:21)

c) metaphorical use, e.g.:

Ταπεινώθητε οὖν **ὑπὸ τὴν κραταιὰν χεῖρα τοῦ θεοῦ**. — *Humble yourselves, therefore, under God's mighty hand!* (1Pe 5:6)

4. as a PREFIX:

a) "under", e.g.: ὑπο-τάσσω *to subject, to subordinate*
b) "back", e.g.: ὑπο-στέλλω *to draw back*
c) "in secret", e.g.: ὑπο-βάλλω *to persuade secretly*

ὡς + ACCUSATIVE (CG; could be classified as an improper preposition) *to* (↑Lat. *ad*; only relating to persons in combination with verbs of motion), e.g.: 184t

πρέσβεις πέπομφεν **ὡς βασιλέα**.	*He has sent ambassadors to the King.* (Demosthenes 4.48)

Also ↑252.61.

Improper prepositions 185

(↑BR §198; BDF §214–217; also 184; Z §83f; BDAG s.vv.)

For an overview of phrases indicating space, time etc. ↑187.

I. Improper prepositions attested in the NT 185a

(the uses within brackets do not occur in the NT; prepositions occurring less than 4× are marked by °)

WORD:	PREPOSITIONAL USE (+ gen., unless otherwise stated):	NON-PREPOSITIONAL USE (adv., unless otherwise stated):
1. ἅμα	*together with* (+ dat.)	*at the same time, together*
°2. ἄνευ (↑ἄτερ, χωρίς)	*without*	–
°3. ἄντικρυς	*opposite* (Ac 20:15)	*straight on, right on, openly*
°4. ἀντιπέρα (post-CG)	*opposite* (Lk 8:26)	*on the other side*
5. ἀπέναντι (KG/NT, ↑ἔναντι, κατέναντι, ἐναντίον)	*opposite; against*	–
°6. ἄτερ (CG: not in prose; ↑ἄνευ, χωρίς)	*without*	–
7. ἄχρι(ς) (↑μέχρι[ς], ἕως; excluding or including endpoint, ↑187h)	*until* (of time or space or extent)	(*to the uttermost, utterly*) conj. (also + οὗ) *until*
8. ἐγγύς	*near, close to* (+ gen. or dat.) (of space or time or metaphorical use)	*near*
9. ἐκτός (↑παρεκτός, πλήν)	*outside*; (NT) *except*	conj. ἐκτὸς εἰ μή *unless, except*
10. ἔμπροσθεν	*in front of, before* (of space or rank) (favoured in the NT probably due to Semitic usage; ↑185c)	*in front, ahead*
°11. ἔναντι (LXX) (↑ἀπέναντι, κατέναντι, ἐναντίον)	*opposite; before, in the presence of* (Lk 1:8; Ac 8:21)	(*in front*)
12. ἐναντίον (↑ἀπέναντι, ἔναντι, κατέναντι)	*before, in the sight of*	adj. ntr. sg. *facing; opposed*
13. ἕνεκα/ἕνεκεν/εἵνεκεν (↑χάριν)	*because of, on account of*	↑226 on the articular inf.
°14. ἐντός	*inside; among* (Mt 23:26; Lk 17:21)	(*inside*)

15. ἐνώπιον (LXX/NT) (↑κατενώπιον) (also ↑185b)	*in the presence of, before* (of space or metaphorical use), *in the opinion of*; NT sometimes replacing dat. with certain verbs (BDAG s.v.)	(adj. ntr. sg. *facing, standing opposite*)
16. ἔξω	*outside* (of position or direction)	*outside*
17. ἔξωθεν	*outside*	*from outside, on the outside*
18. ἐπάνω	*over, above* (of space or rank)	*above, more than* (of space or quantity)
°19. ἐπέκεινα	*beyond* (Ac 7:43 = Am 5:27)	(*further on, beyond*)
°20. ἔσω (also εἴσω, not so NT/LXX)	*inside* (NT only Mk 15:16)	*inside*
21. ἕως (prep. use post-CG) (↑ἄχρι[ς], μέχρι; excluding or including endpoint, ↑187h)	*until, up to* (of space or time, also of order in a sequence and measure)	conj. (also + οὗ or ὅτου) *until, so long as* ↑226 on the articular inf.
22. κατέναντι (NT and LXX) (↑ἀπέναντι, ἔναντι, ἐναντίον)	*opposite* (of space); *in the sight of* (metaphorical use)	*facing, opposite*
°23. κατενώπιον (↑ἐνώπιον)	*before, in the presence/sight of* (3× in the NT; 6× in the LXX)	–
°24. κυκλόθεν	*(in a circle) around* (Re 4:3f)	*all around, from all sides*
°25. κύκλῳ	*around*	*in a circle* (<adj. dat. of place; ↑181)
°26. μέσον (prep. use post-CG)	*in the middle/midst of, between*; ↑: ἀνὰ μέσον + gen. *among*, διὰ μέσου + gen. *along between*, ἐν μέσῳ + gen. *in the middle of* (↑Hebr. בְּתוֹךְ *bəṯôḵ* מִתּוֹךְ *mittôḵ*, ↑HALOT sub תָּוֶךְ *tā́weḵ*)	adj. ntr. sg. *(being) in the middle*; adv. *in the middle*
27. μεταξύ	*among, between* (of space, reciprocal relation or difference)	*between* (of space or time), *afterwards, in the meantime*
28. μέχρι (NT: 3× μέχρις) (↑ἄχρι[ς], ἕως; excluding or including endpoint, ↑187h)	*as far as, until, to the point of* (of space, time or degree/measure)	conj. (also + οὗ) *until* (CG also *as long as*)
°29. ὄπισθεν	*behind* s.o.	*(from) behind*
30. ὀπίσω	*behind, after* (of space or time) (NT/LXX usage)	*behind, backwards*
°31. ὀψέ	*after* (NT: Mt 28:1)	*at a late hour, late, in the evening*
°32. παραπλήσιον	*near* (+ dat. or gen.) (NT: Php 2:27)	adj. ntr. sg. *coming near, similar*
°33. παρεκτός (↑ἐκτός, πλήν)	*except for*	*outside*
34. πέραν (CG also πέρα)	*on the other side*	*on the other side/shore*
°35. πέριξ	*around* (Ac 5:16; ↑BDF §474.8)	*all around*
36. πλήν (↑ἐκτός, παρεκτός)	*except, excluding*	(adv. >) conj. *but; only* (+ ὅτι *except that*)

°37. πλησίον	*near*	*nearby*; ὁ πλησίον *the neighbour*
°38. ὑπεράνω	*above, high above*	*high up*
°39. ὑπερέκεινα	*beyond* (2Cor 10:16)	(*beyond*)
°40. ὑπερεκπερισσοῦ	*immeasurably more than* (Eph 3:20)	*quite beyond all measure* (1Th 3:10; 5:13)
41. ὑποκάτω	*under*	*under, below*
42. χάριν (↑ἕνεκα etc.)	*for the sake of, on behalf of, because* (mostly follows its head)	noun (acc. sg. of χάρις *grace*; ↑35b)
43. χωρίς (↑ἄνευ, ἄτερ)	*without, apart from*	*separately, apart*

Attested inter alia in the "Apostolic Fathers":

δίχα	*without*	*separately, apart*
μακράν	*far from*	*a long way, far*

In CG the following are important, too:

κρύφα, λάθρα	*without the knowledge of*	*in secret*
πόρρω/πρόσω	*far from*	*forwards, onwards*

Note on the improper prepositions signifying "before" (BDF §214.6): 185b

ἐνώπιον and nearly all of the prepositions signifying "before" are often used in ways comparable to the Hebrew expressions לִפְנֵי *lip̄nê*, בְּעֵינֵי *bəʿênê*, נֶגֶד *néḡeḏ* (↑HALOT sub פָּנֶה *pāneh*, עַיִן *ʿáyin*, נֶגֶד *néḡeḏ*), quite frequently in contexts where CG would use a simple dative (or in some cases a simple genitive) construction. ↑185c and 187a.

On ὡς + acc. *to* ↑184t.

II. Hebraizing complex prepositions (↑BDF §217) 185c

Two nouns are often embedded in preposition phrases functioning as (complex) prepositions (↑183b) in ways typical of Hebrew (but not of Greek outside the LXX/NT). In the sg. these nouns generally occur with a "distributive" force (↑129a):

1. πρόσωπόν τινος " s.o.'s face" (↑HALOT sub פָּנֶה *pāneh*):

a) ἀπὸ προσώπου "from s.o.'s face" (↑מִפְּנֵי *mippənê*)	≈ ἀπό or παρά + gen. *from* (↑184e; 184m)
b) πρὸ προσώπου "before s.o.'s face"	≈ πρό *before, in front of* (↑184o)
c) κατὰ πρόσωπον "to(wards) s.o.'s face"	≈ *before*

2. χείρ/χεῖρές τινος "s.o.'s hand(s)" (↑HALOT sub יָד *yāḏ*):

a) εἰς χεῖρας "into s.o.'s hands" (↑בְּיַד *bəyaḏ* [in Hebr. mostly sg.!])	≈ *into s.o.'s power, to*
b) ἐκ χειρός "from s.o.'s hand" (↑מִיַּד *miyyaḏ*)	≈ *from s.o.'s power*
c) ἐν χειρί "in s.o.'s hand" and διὰ χειρός "through s.o.'s hand" (↑בְּיַד *bəyaḏ*)	≈ διά + gen. *through* (↑184f)

186 Prepositional prefixes

(↑BR §307.4; 308.1; BDF §116; MH: 292–332)

186a 1. Prepositional prefixes ("preverbs") quite frequently do not affect the meaning of the simplex word in any discernible way (the standard dictionaries need to be consulted about the meaning actually attested). So, e.g., the compound noun ἔπ-αινος (11× in the NT) simply means *praise* as does its simplex counterpart αἶνος (2× in the NT). And the two preverbs of a double compound do not necessarily both add something to the meaning of the word. Thus in the case of the verb προ-ϋπ-άρχω *to exist/be present before* only προ- ("before") does so, but not ὑπό- (ὑπάρχω means *to exist/be present*).

186b 2. In many cases, however, the preverbs of a double compound are both relevant to the meaning of the word in question, e.g.:

ἀντι-παρ-έρχομαι	*to pass by* (παρ-) *on the opposite side* (ἀντ-)
παρ-εισ-έρχομαι	*to come in* (εισ-) *beside* (παρ-) = *to slip in*
συμ-παρα-λαμβάνω	*to take along* (παρα-) *with o.s.* (συμ-)

187 Overview of phrases indicating space, time etc. (↑BR §200f)

(noun phrases and preposition phrases)

Note that only the more frequent improper prepositions (↑185a) are taken into account here.
On the KG (and NT) tendency to use preposition phrases in place of prepositionless case noun phrases ↑inter alia 146b; 183d.
On the various ways of expressing adverbials ↑259c–259m.

I. Phrases indicating SPACE (also ↑259d)

187a 1. Answers to the question **"Where?"** in terms of **position** may be expressed by[24]

a) a preposition phrase (standard phrase type)

• with a proper preposition (↑184):

[ἀμφί	+ gen./dat.	*about/concerning*	CG almost exclusively poetic]
[ἀνά	+ dat.	*up on*	CG only poetry]
διά	+ gen. (CG poetry also +acc.)	*through*	
εἰς	+ acc.	*in*	so KG/NT in part
[ἐκ	+ gen., rarely, e.g.:	*at (s.o.'s right)]*	
ἐν	+ dat.	*in, within*	
ἐπί	+ gen./dat. (KG/NT also + acc.)	*on, at*	

24 At times Ancient Greek phrases indicating space seem to refer (in ways unexpected by us) to a movement to or from a place rather than to a position. ↑BR §199.

κατά	+ gen.	*in* (CG *rarely under*)	
κατά	+ acc.	*throughout, on*	
μετά	+ gen.	*with, among*	
[μετά	+ dat.	*among, amid*	CG only poetry]
μετά	+ acc.	*behind*	
παρά	+ dat. (KG/NT also + acc.)	*at, by the side of*	
[περί	+ dat.	*around, about*	CG mainly poetry]
περί	+ acc.	*around*	
πρό	+ gen.	*before*	
πρός	+ dat. (NT often + acc.)	*near, at, by*	
[σύν	+ dat. (possibly)	*with]*	
ὑπέρ	+ gen.	*above*	CG
ὑπό	+ gen./dat.	*under*	CG
ὑπό	+ acc.	*under*	NT

• with an improper preposition (↑185a), inter alia:

ἀπέναντι		*opposite*	so KG/NT
ἐγγύς	+ gen./dat.	*near, close to*	
ἐκτός		*outside*	
ἔμπροσθεν		*in front of, before*	
ἐναντίον		*before, in the sight of*	
ἐνώπιον		*in the presence of, before*	so LXX/NT
ἔξω		*outside*	
ἔξωθεν		*outside*	
ἐπάνω		*over, above*	
κατέναντι		*opposite*	so NT/LXX
μεταξύ		*among, between*	
ὀπίσω		*behind, after*	
πέραν		*on the other side*	
ὑποκάτω		*under*	

• with a Hebraizing complex preposition (↑185c):

πρὸ προσώπου / κατὰ πρόσωπον	*before, in front of*	so LXX/NT

[b) a (prepositionless) case noun phrase (hardly any NT instances):

• gen. of place (↑171)	CG almost exclusively in poetry
• dat. of place (↑181)	CG/post-CG hardly attested]

2. Answers to the question “**Where?**” in terms of **movement to** or **towards** (“To where?”) may be expressed by 187b

a) a preposition phrase (chiefly)

• with a proper preposition (↑184):

ἀμφί	+ acc.	*around*	CG

ἀνά	+ acc.	*up, throughout*	CG
διά	+ gen. (CG poetry also + acc.)	*through*	
εἰς	+ acc.	*into*	
ἐν	+ dat.	*into*	so KG/NT in part
ἐπί	+ gen./acc. (KG/NT also + dat.)	*on, onto, to(wards)*	
κατά	+ gen.	*down* KG/NT also *throughout*	
κατά	+ acc.	*down(wards), through-out, on, along* KG/NT also *to(wards)*	
παρά	+ acc.	*near (the side of), to* KG/NT also *along, by*	
περί	+ acc.	*around*	
πρός	+ acc.	*to, towards,*	
ὑπέρ	+ acc.	*above, over, beyond*	
ὑπό	+ acc.	*under*	
ὡς	+ acc.	*to*	CG (only relating to persons)

• with an improper preposition (↑185a), inter alia:

ἔξω	*outside*
ὀπίσω	*behind, after*
πέραν	*on the other side*

Also ↑186a (in part also used to answer question "Where?" in terms of movement to or towards).

b) a (prepositionless) case noun phrase:

• gen. of direction or purpose (↑164; attributive modifier of nouns))

[• acc. of goal (↑149b) limited use in CG poetry]

187c 3. Answers to the question **"From where?"** (movement from) may be expressed by

a) a preposition PHRASE (chiefly)

• with a proper preposition (↑184):

ἀπό	+ gen.	*from*	
διά	+ gen. (CG poetry also + acc.)	*through, by way of*	
ἐκ	+ gen.	*out of, from*	
κατά	+ gen.	*down (from)*	
παρά	+ gen.	*from (the side of), from*	
πρός	+ gen.	*from the part/side of*	CG (rarely used in prose)
ὑπό	+ gen.	*(from) under*	CG (rarely used in prose)

• with an improper preposition (↑185a), inter alia:

ἀπὸ προσώπου	*from*

Also ↑186a (in part also used to answer question "From where?").

b) a (prepositionless) case noun phrase:

• gen. of separation (mainly with verbs; ↑169)

[• gen. of place (↑171) — CG almost exclusively in poetry]

4. Answers to the question **"How far?"** or the like may be expressed by 187d

a) a preposition phrase (↑184/185)

διά	+ gen. (CG poetry also + acc.)	*through*	
ἄχρι(ς)/μέχρι/ἕως + gen.		*until*	

b) a (prepositionless) case noun phrase:

• acc. of spatial extent (↑155a) — rarely used in the NT

II. Phrases indicating TIME (also ↑259e)

1. Answers to the question **"When?"** may be expressed by 187e

a) a (prepositionless) case noun phrase:

• dat. of time (↑182)	indicates a point of time
• gen. of time (↑168)	indicates time in a general way (mainly in fixed phrases)
• acc. of temporal extent (↑155a)	in NT sometimes in answer to "When?"

b) a preposition phrase

• with a proper preposition (↑184):

διά	+ gen. (CG poetry also + acc.)	*after*	
ἐν	+ dat.	*in, at*	
ἐπί	+ gen.	*in the time of*	
ἐπί	+ dat.	*at*; CG also *after*	
ἐπί	+ acc.	*at*	so in the NT
κατά	+ acc.	*at (about)*	rarely used so
μετά	+ acc.	*after*	
περί	+ acc.	*about*	
πρό	+ gen.	*before*	
πρός	+ acc.	*towards*	infrequently used so
ὑπό	+ acc.	*at*	

• with an improper preposition (↑185a), inter alia:

ὀπίσω	*after*

2. Answers to the question **"Within which time span?"** may be expressed by 187f

a) a preposition phrase (↑184):

διά	+ gen.	*during, within*	so KG/NT
ἐν	+ dat.	*in, during*	
ἐπί	+ gen.	*in the time of*	
ἐπί	+ dat.	*during*; CG also *after*	
κατά	+ acc.	*at (about), during*	rarely used so

παρά	+ acc.	*during*	so CG

b) a (prepositionless) case noun phrase:

• gen. of time (↑168)	(mainly in fixed phrases)
• acc. of temporal extent (↑155a)	in NT at times in answer to "Within which time span?"

Also ↑187e.

187g 3. Answers to the question **"How long?"** may be expressed by

a) a (prepositionless) case noun phrase:

• acc. of temporal extent (↑155a)	in NT at times in answer to "How long?"
• dat. of time (↑182)	un-CG, rarely used so in the NT

b) a preposition phrase (↑184):

ἀνά	+ acc.	*throughout*	CG
διά	+ gen. (CG poetry also + acc.)	*through, throughout*	
εἰς	+ acc.	*until, for*	
ἐν	+ dat.	*during*	infrequently used so
ἐπί	+ acc.	*during*	
παρά	+ acc.	*during*	so CG, not in the NT
πρός	+ acc.	*during, for*	infrequently used so in the NT
ὑπέρ	+ acc.	*over*	CG

187h 4. Answers to the question **"Until when?"** may be expressed by

a preposition phrase (↑184/185)

εἰς + acc.	*until* (including endpoint, e.g. Mt 1:17; Lk 16:16; or exclud-
ἄχρι(ς)/μέχρι/ἕως + gen.	ing endpoint, e.g. Mt 11:13, Ro 5:14; ↑BDF §216.3)

187i 5. Answers to the question **"Since when?"** may be expressed by

a) a (prepositionless) case noun phrase:

• acc. of temporal extent (↑155b)	"How long?"
• gen. of time (↑168)	"Within which time span (of the past until now)?"

b) a preposition phrase (↑184):

ἀπό	+ gen.	*from, since*
ἐκ	+ gen.	*from, since*

Also ↑187g (with similar nuances).

III. Phrases indicating MANNER etc.

187j 1. Answers to the question **"How?"/"In what manner?"** may be expressed by

a) a (prepositionless) case noun phrase:

• dat. of manner (↑180a)	"How?" or "Under what attendant circumstances?"
• gen. of quality (↑162)	"Of what or quality?" (attributive modifier of nouns)

• adverbial acc. (↑157)		"How?" (in NT mainly in the form of ntr. adjectives)	

b) a preposition phrase (↑184):

διά	+ gen.	*with*	
ἐκ	+ gen.	*in*	
ἐν	+ dat.	*in, with*	frequently so in KG/NT
κατά	+ acc.	*with, -ly*	
μετά	+ gen.	*with*	

2. Answers to the question **"In what respect?"** may be expressed by 187k

a) a (prepositionless) case noun phrase:

• acc. of respect (↑156)	only a few NT instances
• dat. of respect (↑178a)	
• gen. of respect (↑167i)	especially in CG (with judicial expressions and expressions of affective behaviour)

b) a preposition phrase (↑184):

εἰς	+ acc.	*with respect to*	
ἐν	+ dat.	*with respect to*	occasionally so in the NT
κατά	+ acc.	*in relation to*	
περί	+ gen. (CG poetry also + dat.; KG/NT also + acc.)	*about, concerning*	
πρός	+ acc.	*with a view to*	
ὑπέρ	+ gen.	*about, concerning*	NT (especially in Paul's letters)

3. Answers to the question **"According to what/whom?"** may be expressed by 187l

a preposition phrase (↑184)

ἐκ	+ gen.	*according to*	
κατά	+ acc.	*in accordance with*	used frequently
πρός	+ gen.	*in line with*	CG
πρός	+ acc.	*according to*	

4. Answers to the question **"Why?"/"Owing to what?"** may be expressed by 187m

a) a (prepositionless) case noun phrase:

• dat. of cause (↑177b)	"Owing to what?"
• dat. of agent (↑176c)	mainly CG (originator with verbal adjective and pf. pass.)
• gen. of originator (↑159b, ↑subjective gen.; ↑160)	originator/agent (attributive modifier of nouns)
• gen. of respect (↑167i)	especially in CG (with judicial expressions and expressions of affective behaviour)

b) a preposition phrase (chiefly)

• with a proper preposition (↑184):

ἀπό	+ gen.	*because of, by* (cause, reason, originator)

διά	+ gen.	*through* (cause, originator)	comparatively rarely so in the NT
διά	+ acc.	*because/for the sake of*	frequently so
ἐκ	+ gen.	*from, by reason of* (cause, reason, motivation)	
ἐν	+ dat.	*on account/because of*	quite frequently so in KG/NT
ἐπί	+ dat.	*over, at* (with verbs of affective behaviour)	
πρός	+ gen.	*by* (originator)	CG
ὑπέρ	+ gen.	*for the sake/because of*	
ὑπό	+ gen.	*by* (originator with pass.)	

• with an improper preposition (↑185a), inter alia:

ἕνεκα/ἕνεκεν/εἵνεκεν	*because/on behalf of*
χάριν (mostly follows its head)	*for the sake/because of*

187n 5. Answers to the question **"With what goal"/"For what purpose?"** may be expressed by

a) a preposition phrase (↑184/185):

εἰς	+ acc.	*for* (purpose)
ἐπί	+ dat.	*for* (purpose or result)
πρός	+ acc.	*for* (purpose)
χάριν (mostly follows its head)		*for the sake/purpose of*

b) a (prepositionless) case noun phrase:

• gen. of direction or purpose (↑164; attributive modifier of nouns))

187o 6. Answers to the question **"By what means?"** may be expressed by

a) dat. of instrument (↑177a) "By what means?"

b) a preposition phrase (↑184/185c):

διά	+ gen.	*through* (intermediate agent, instrument)	
ἐν	+ dat.	*with, by*	frequently so in KG/NT
ἐν χειρί/διὰ χειρός + gen.		*through*	Hebraizing complex preposition

187p 7. Answers to the question **"In whose interest?"** may be expressed by

a) dat. of interest "To whose advantage or disadvantage?" (↑176)

b) a preposition phrase (↑184):

ἀντί	+ gen.	*for, on behalf of*	so in the NT
εἰς	+ acc.	*for*	
περί	+ gen.	*for, on behalf of*	especially so in the NT
πρό	+ gen.	*in defence of, for*	CG
πρός	+ gen.	*for, in the interest of*	
ὑπέρ	+ gen.	*for, on behalf of*	

8. Answers to the question **"Against whom or what?"** may be expressed by 187q

a preposition phrase (↑184/185):

εἰς	+ acc.	*for, to, towards, at*	of friendly or hostile attitude
ἐπί	+ acc.	*against*	
κατά	+ gen.	*against*	
παρά	+ acc.	*against, contrary to*	opposed to κατά + acc. *in accordance with* (↑187l)
πρός	+ acc.	*to, towards, against*	of friendly or hostile attitude
ἀπέναντι	+ gen.	*opposite, against*	

3.2.2 Syntax of verb forms (↑22f on word-class, ↑64 on categories of the verbal system)

Understanding verb forms and their function is central to well-founded text interpretation: verb forms serve as the predicator of a sentence; in most cases they indicate the core information conveyed by the sentence (i.e. the core of its proposition, typically used to refer to a "situation" in the real world; ↑127a; 127b; 256); and sentences are the most important structural components of a text as text (↑298). So interpreters of texts have to determine on the one hand what form categories a particular verb form belongs to (↑Morphology 64–125). On the other hand they need to clarify carefully what function or functions it has, or, in other words, what exactly it is capable of contributing to the information conveyed by the sentence on the basis of the grammatical rules applicable to it (↑Syntax 188–240); this will help them to infer what the speaker/writer intends to communicate by means of the form chosen when producing their text.

3.2.2.1 Voice (↑64b on definition; 316 on textgrammatical relevance; EAGLL s.v. "Voice")

(↑also BR §203–205; 116–118; BDF §77–79; 307–317; Z §225–236)

Voice: preliminaries (↑BR §203; BDF §307ff; 77–79; Z §225ff) 188

1. The category voice is about the **relation between the subject and the "action"** expressed by the verb, indicating in what ways the subject entity is meant to be involved in the "action". 188a

2. At the beginning of **the history of Ancient Greek** two **types of voice** (inherited from Proto-Indo-European) were in use: the active and the middle voice; the middle voice had a primarily reflexive function, but it also served to express passive relationships. 188b
The passive voice was added later on the basis of the middle, which led to the classical threefold division into active, middle, and passive voice.
The distinction between the middle and the passive voice, however, remained incomplete (there were only clearly distinguishable forms in the aorist and the future). As a result, the two gradually merged again in the post-Classical period. Modern Greek has only an active and a passive voice.

This merging tendency in the post-Classical period helps to explain a number of (comparatively small) **differences between CG and KG usage**, e.g. the fact that KG usage seems to avoid increasingly the CG middle forms of some verbs in the future and in the aorist: 188c

CG:		KG/NT:
a) the CG middle future forms of certain verbs are frequently replaced by active ones in KG, e.g.:		
• ἁμαρτάνω *to sin*		ἁμαρτάνω *to sin*
ἁμαρτή**σομαι** *I will sin*	→	ἁμαρτή**σω** *I will sin*
• ἀκούω *to hear*		ἀκούω *to hear*
ἀκού**σομαι** *I will hear*	→	ἀκού**σω** *I will hear* (mid. is sometimes used, too)
however:		
• γιγνώσκω *to know*		γινώσκω *to know*
γνώ**σομαι** *I will know*	→	γνώ**σομαι** *I will know*

b) deponent verbs (↑64b) with middle future and aorist forms in CG tend to be used with passive forms in KG instead (in a few cases the opposite applies):

• ἀπεκρίν**ατο** *he answered*	→	ἀπεκρί**θη** *he answered* (mid. less frequently)
ἀποκριν**εῖται** *he will answer*	→	ἀποκρι**θήσεται** *he will answer*

Also ↑191e–191g.

c) In various cases in which CG would normally use middle voice forms KG simply uses active forms (↑189e).

188d 3. In connection with the syntax of verbs the **distinction** between **transitive** and **intransitive** verbs or uses is often referred to. This distinction should **not** be confused with **voice distinctions**. Transitive verbs or uses are simply verbs or uses that (due to their valency; ↑127d) connect with a direct object, as opposed to intransitive verbs or uses that do not, but either have no object at all or connect with a Og, O^{dat}, Op or any other kind of complement (↑254d). Any of these types of verbs or uses may in principle occur in the active, middle, or passive voice:

a) Direct objects may be encountered in the active, the middle, or the passive voice, e.g.:

κατέκλασεν (act.) τοὺς ἄρτους.	*He broke the loaves.* (Mk 6:41)
ὃν καὶ σὺ **φυλάσσου** (mid.).	*You too should be on your guard against him!* (2Tm 4:15)
ἦν κατηχημένος (pass.) τὴν ὁδὸν τοῦ κυρίου.	*He had been instructed in the way of the Lord.* (Ac 18:25)

b) Transitive verbs (i.e. verbs with a Od at least in the active), such as τίθημι *to place*, may in principle be used in the active, middle, or passive voice, e.g.:

… ὃν **ἔθηκεν** (act.) κληρονόμον πάντων.	*… whom he appointed heir of all things.* (He 1:2)
… ὑμᾶς τὸ πνεῦμα τὸ ἅγιον **ἔθετο** (mid.) ἐπισκόπους …	*… the Holy Spirit has appointed you overseers …* (Ac 20:28)
εἰς ὃ **ἐτέθην** (pass.) ἐγὼ κῆρυξ καὶ ἀπόστολος.	*For this I was appointed herald and apostle.* (1Tm 2:7)

c) Intransitive verbs (i.e. without a Od) are connected with the three voice types in a variety of ways, many occurring only in the active, some only in the passive (though mostly with a middle future; ↑64b on the deponent verbs), and a few only in the middle voice, e.g.:

καθεύδω *to sleep*	
βούλομαι *to wish*	ἐβουλήθην *I wished* (βουλήσομαι *I shall wish*)
χρηστεύομαι *to be kind*	ἐχρηστευσάμην *I was kind* (↑1Clement 13:2)

d) Often the same active forms are used both transitively and intransitively, i.e. with or without a Od (↑189; also 152c/152d).

↑also 189b–189f; 191e–191g.

Important points relevant to **text interpretation**:
In view of the complexities and inconsistencies of voice use in Ancient Greek interpreters of texts ought to resist the temptation to appeal to voice nuances simplistically. The standard dictionaries should always be consulted to clarify whether the middle form (to take the most relevant case) of a particular verb does in fact convey a special nuance, and if so, what this might be in the context under consideration.

4. Ancient Greek (and Latin) did not have a standard verb to express **causation** in 188e
the sense of English *to make/have s.o. do sth.* or *to have sth. done*. In contexts that presuppose causation, the usual active or middle forms are used, the causative sense being inferable from the context, e.g.:

ὁ Πιλᾶτος … **ἐμαστίγωσεν**.	*Pilate … had him flogged.* (Jn 19:1)
ἀνεῖλεν δὲ Ἰάκωβον …	*He had James … killed …* (Ac 12:2)
… **κειράμενος** ἐν Κεγχρεαῖς τὴν κεφαλήν …	*… At Cenchreae he had his hair cut …* (Ac 18:18)
βάπτισαι καὶ **ἀπόλουσαι** τὰς ἁμαρτίας σου.	*Be baptized/Have yourself baptized and have your sins washed away!* (Ac 22:16)

There are, however, a small number of verbs, that are sometimes used with a causative sense, thus (especially LXX/NT) ἀποστέλλω (usually *to send off s.o.*; ↑238) and πέμπω (usually *to send s.o.*, so also e.g. in Xenophon, Cyropaedia 3.1.6; similarly μεταπέμπομαι, e.g. in Xenophon, Anabasis 1.1.2) sometimes also ποιέω (usually *to make*, here *to bring about that*; used in CG, too), e.g.:

ἀποστείλας ἀνεῖλεν πάντας τοὺς παῖδας …	*He had all the male children killed …* (Mt 2:16)
Also ↑Mk 6:17; Gn 31:4 LXX.	
… **πέμψας** ἀπεκεφάλισεν τὸν Ἰωάννην …	*… He had John beheaded …* (Mt 14:10)
ποιήσατε τοὺς ἀνθρώπους ἀναπεσεῖν.	*Make/Have the people sit down.* (Jn 6:10)

On the passive with a causative sense ↑191h.

The active voice (↑64b; BR §203–205; BDF §308–310; also 97 and 101; Z §227ff) 189

1. Active voice forms typically present the "action" (or event, process, state etc. de- 189a
noted by the verb) as being performed or primarily caused by the **subject** entity, i.e. as its **agent** or as its leading participant (↑127b; 255). Many verbs denoting an action or a relation (a type of state) are transitive, i.e. they (due to their valency) require a direct object (the sentence pattern being S+P+Od; ↑127d). Event, process and most state verbs are usually intransitive (i.e. without a Od; ↑188d; 257/258):

2. In the active certain verbs may be used in a way **comparable to the middle** voice:

a) The active forms of a number of transitive verbs, especially verbs of motion, may 189b
also occur with an intransitive use (a use generally more typical of the middle voice; ↑190), in the NT most frequently:

	transitive	intransitive
ἄγω and compounds (NT: only in part intr.)	*to lead s.o./sth.*	*to go* (in the NT only the form ἄγωμεν *let us go!* Mk 14:42 et pass.)

ὑπάγω	*to lead under sth.* (CG; NT –)	*to go, to go away* (standard verb for "to go" in popular KG)
βάλλω	*to throw sth.*	*to throw o.s.* (very rare in the NT)
ἐπιβάλλω	*to throw/put sth. on*	*to throw o.s. on*
στρέφω and compounds (NT: only in part intr.)	*to turn sth.*	*to turn (o.s.)*
ἐπιστρέφω	*to turn sth. back* (infrequent use)	*to turn (o.s.) back, to return (o.s.)*
etc.		
similarly also:		
ἔχω	*to have/hold sth.*	combined with an adv. *to be in a certain condition,* e.g. κακῶς ἔχω *to be ill/sick* (Mk 1:32 et pass.)
προσέχω + dat. (CG often + τὸν νοῦν)	–	*to pay attention to s.o./sth.* ("to turn one's mind to s.o./sth.")

189c b) A number of transitive verbs have a strong perfect active that is used intransitively (a use generally more typical of the middle; ↑190):

pres. act.	pf. I	pf. II	
κατάγνυμι *I break sth.*	–	κατέαγα (CG) *I am broken*	(↑123.3)
ἀνοίγω *I open sth.*	ἀνέῳχα (CG) *I have opened sth.*	ἀνέῳγα (post-CG) *I am open* (ἀνέῳγμαι is used for this in CG and often in the NT)	(↑95.2)
ἐγείρω *I awaken s.o.*	ἐγήγερκα *I have awakened s.o.*	ἐγρήγορα (CG) *I am awake*	(↑103.6)
ἵστημι *I set/place*	[-ἑστᾰκα (post-CG) *I have set/placed*]	ἕστηκα[(1)] *I stand*	(↑120.5)
ἀπόλλυμι *I ruin/destroy*	ἀπολώλεκα *I have ruined*	ἀπόλωλα *I am ruined/lost*	(↑123.7)
πείθω *to persuade*	πέπεικα *I have persuaded*	πέποιθα (↑200b) *I trust in*	(↑96.1)
πήγνυμι *I fix*	[πέπηχα (post-CG; NT –) *I have fixed*]	πέπηγα (↑CG) *I am firm*	(↑123.5)
ῥήγνυμι *I tear in pieces*	[ἔρρηχα (LXX) *I have torn in pieces*]	ἔρρωγα *I am torn*	(↑123.6)
σήπω *I cause to rot*	–	σέσηπα *I am rotten*	(↑94.9[5])

↑also φαίνω: *I shine* (CG *I show*; ↑102.7)

(1) ↑also aor. I ἔστησα *I set/placed* – root-aor. ἔστην *I stood (up)*.

c) The active forms of certain verbs that had only a transitive function in CG, could also have an intransitive one (more typical of the middle-passive) in the NT, inter alia: 189d

	CG	NT
αὐξάνω	*to (cause to) grow sth.*	chiefly *to grow (become greater)* (the pass. is used for this in CG and sometimes in the NT)
βρέχω	*to wet/soak sth.*	βρέχει *it rains o.s.* (also *he causes to rain*)

d) The NT uses active forms in some cases in which CG uses the middle voice, e.g.: 189e

	CG	NT
to find (for o.s.)/obtain	εὑρίσκ**ομαι**	εὑρίσκ**ω** (almost exclusively)

A similar difference seems to apply to ποιέω *to do* when combined with a verbal noun (↑362b) (BDF §310; Z §227–228: in the NT the "distinction was still observed … in general"):

Distinction between the active and the middle voice with regard to this CG idiom:

- ποιέ**ω** (**act.**) + verbal noun → to cause the action denoted by the noun, e.g.:
  … ποιήσαντες συστροφήν — … *they formed a conspiracy* (Ac 23:12)
- ποιέ**ομαι** (**mid.**) + verbal noun → to perform the action oneself (the idiom replaces the regular verb, apparently for emphasis), e.g.:
  … ταύτην τὴν συνωμοσίαν ποιησάμενοι (≈ συνομοσάμενοι) — … *who formed this plot* (Ac 23:13) (↑Josephus, Antiquities 15.282)

In a number of NT passages, however, the active is used like a (CG) middle, e.g.:

ποιήσει μετ' αὐτῶν πόλεμον — *[the beast] will make war on them* (Re 11:7; ↑12:17; 13:7; 19:19)

At times the converse applies: the middle "replaces" the expected active (↑190i).

e) Active voice forms may be used (in CG and the NT) together with a reflexive pronoun (↑139f–139l) in a way comparable to certain uses of the middle voice (↑190): to express that the subject entity not only performs the "action" (as its agent), but is also affected by it, e.g.: 189f

λέντιον **διέζωσεν** (act.) **ἑαυτόν** (refl. pron.) — *he tied a towel around himself* (Jn 13:4)

↑… τῷ λεντίῳ ᾧ **ἦν διεζωσμένος** (direct refl. mid.) — … *with the towel he had tied around himself* (Jn 13:5)

This construction expresses the (reflexive) reference back to the subject entity with greater emphasis than a simple use of middle voice forms. Many verbs, however, are without attested middle forms; when active forms of these verbs are combined with a reflexive pronoun to express a reflexive relationship, it would, of course, be problematic to speak of "greater" emphasis. It should further be noted that a reflexive relationship indicated by a middle voice form may be stressed by the addition of a reflexive pronoun. E.g.:

ἐζώννυες (act.) **σεαυτόν** (refl. pron.). — *you used to gird/dress yourself.* (Jn 21:18)

ζῶσαι (imp. mid.). — *Gird/Dress yourself!* (Ac 12:8)

… ἵνα … **ἀγοράσωσιν** (act.) **ἑαυτοῖς** (refl. pron.) βρώματα. — … *so that they may … buy food for themselves.* (Mt 14:15)

Note that ἀγοράζω *to buy* hardly ever occurs in the middle voice (never so in the LXX/NT).

ἐζήτησα νύμφην **ἀγαγέσθαι** (mid.) **ἐμαυτῷ** (refl. pron.). — *I desired to take her as a bride for myself/as my bride.* (Wsd 8:2)

189g 3. The **passive** forms of certain verbs were **replaced by the active** forms of another verb in **CG**, e.g.:

passive forms of ἀποκτείνω *to kill* → ἀποθνῄσκω (ὑπό τινος) *to be killed* (lit. *to die [at s.o.'s hands]*):

There is no uncontested instance of this use in the NT. However, the following replacement is attested both in **CG and** the **NT** (↑120.1; 125e):

the perfect passive of τίθημι *to put/place* → κεῖμαι *I have been placed* (otherwise *to lie*; often replacing the post-CG pf. mid./pass. τέθειμαι):

189h 4. On the **causative sense** connected with active voice forms ↑188e.

190 The middle voice (↑64b; BR §204; BDF §316f; Z §226–235)

190a 1. Middle voice forms typically have a double function: (a) Like active forms (↑189a) they present the "action" (or whatever the verb denotes) as being primarily caused by the subject entity (as its agent). (b) In addition to this they indicate **greater subject-affectedness**. This subject-affectedness is difficult to explain in terms of English usage. The following uses are among the more important ones:

190b a) Frequently middle voice forms indicate that the "action" (or whatever the verb denotes) is performed ***for* the subject entity** (i.e. in his or her own interest). This is often called **"indirect reflexive middle"** (↑dative of interest; 176a), e.g.:

τέσσαρσιν … **φυλάσσειν** (inf. act.) αὐτόν. — *to four squads … to guard him* (Ac 12:4)

ὃν καὶ σὺ **φυλάσσου** (imp. mid.). — *You too should be on your guard against him (in your own interest)!* (2Tm 4:15)

Note, however, that many verbs used in the middle voice are without an active counterpart in the NT (nor in many cases outside the NT), counting as deponent verbs (↑64b). Though the middle voice of such verbs may (in many cases) be classified as indirect reflexive, one should not make too much out of the indirect reflexive element of meaning when interpreting texts (↑p.297; also ↑189f), e.g.:

μεταπέμπομαί τινα — *to send for s.o.* (e.g. Ac 10:29)

ἐκλέγομαί τινα/τι — *to choose s.o./sth.* (e.g. Jn 15:16; Lk 14:7)

190c b) Sometimes middle voice forms indicate that the "action" is performed **on the subject entity's own body**, e.g.:

ἤρξατο **νίπτειν** (inf. act.) τοὺς πόδας τῶν μαθητῶν. — *He began to wash the disciples' feet.* (Jn 13:5)

… χρείαν … τοὺς πόδας **νίψασθαι** (inf. mid.). — *… needs … to wash his (own) feet!* (Jn 13:10)

Without τοὺς πόδας (Od) νίψασθαι would be a "direct reflexive middle" (↑190e).

c) When the active counterpart refers to the subject entity as giving sth., the middle form may present him or her as **receiving** sth., e.g.: 190d

δαν(ε)ί**ζω** (act.)	*to lend (money)* (e.g. Lk 6:34f)
δαν(ε)ί**ζομαι** (mid.)	*to borrow (money)* (e.g. Mt 5:42)
κομί**ζω** (act.)	*to bring* (e.g. Lk 7:37; 1Esd 9:40)
κομί**ζομαι** (mid.)	*to get back, to receive* (e.g. 2Cor 5:10)

d) Middle forms may indicate that the subject entity, the agent, is also its patient (↑257b), i.e. he or she is directly affected, "targeted" by the "action" or experiences it, a (direct) reflexive relationship being expressed (↑139f–139l). This use is therefore often termed **"direct reflexive middle"**. Note that very frequently this use will call for a non-reflexive construction in a translation into English, e.g.: 190e

ἀναπαύ**ω** (act.) τινά	*to cause s.o. to rest* (e.g. Mt 11:28)
ἀναπαύ**ομαι** (mid.)	*to cause o.s. to rest = to rest* (Mk 6:31)
ὕπαγε **νίψαι** (imp. mid.) … καὶ **ἐνίψατο** (ind. mid.)	*Go, wash (yourself) … and he washed (himself)* (Jn 9:7)

↑190c for the "indirect reflexive middle" involving a direct object.

e) At times the middle form indicates a **reciprocal** relationship (↑139m), e.g.: 190f

διαλέγομαί τινι	*to converse with s.o.* (e.g. Ac 18:19)
διαλογίζομαι	*to consider and discuss* (e.g. Mk 9:33)

f) In certain cases, the middle form appears to indicate a **metaphorical** sense, e.g.: 190g

ἀποδίδω**μι** (act.)	*to give back, to render* (e.g. Lk 19:8)
ἀποδίδο**μαι** (mid.)	*to sell* (e.g. Ac 5:8)

2. Generally speaking, the **distinction** between the **active** and the **middle** voice is preserved in the NT. The following points should, however, be noted: 190h

a) Occasionally, the middle form is used instead of the expected active one, e.g.: 190i

καταλαμβάνομαι (mid.; CG: act. with this sense)	*to understand* (e.g. Ac 10:34)

On the converse case ↑188d/188e.

b) No distinction between the active and the middle voice seems to be made in the case of a small number of NT verbs, so apparently between: 190j

αἰτέω and αἰτέομαι	*to ask, to ask for, to demand*

According to Z §234, however, a clear distinction between the active and the (indirect reflexive) middle voice is probably presupposed at least in Mk 6:23f, Jas 4:2f and 1Jn 5:15f.

c) Quite often there is no discernible difference between the active and the middle voice (CG and NT), thus in the case of active verbs that have a middle future, e.g.: 190k

βαίνω *I go*	βήσομαι *I will go* (↑110.1)

ἀποθνῄσκω *I die*	ἀποθανοῦμαι *I will die* (↑111.3)
γινώσκω *I know*	γνώσομαι *I will know* (↑111.8)
λαμβάνω *I take*	λήμψομαι *I will take* (↑110.13)

Nor does any typical middle meaning seem to be attached to many of the deponent verbs (↑64b), e.g.:

ἕπομαι *to follow* (↑113.15)	βούλομαι *to wish* (↑112.6)
γίνομαι *to become* (↑112.7)	θεάομαι *to see* (↑85.5)

Often no meaning difference is discernible between middle and passive forms; ↑191e–191g; also 188c.

190l 3. On the **causative sense** connected with middle voice forms ↑188e.

191 The passive voice (↑64b; BR §205; 116–118; BDF §311–315; 159 232.2; 191; 78f; Z §227–236; 72f)

191a 1. Passive forms typically present the **subject** entity (↑255) as the **patient** (↑257b) of the "action" (or whatever is denoted by the verb), i.e. the entity undergoing, experiencing, or enduring it (being "targeted" by it). In many cases the agent is not mentioned. When it is mentioned, it is usually expressed by a preposition phrase with ὑπό + gen. (English *by*, Lat. *ab* + ablative, Spanish *por*, French *par*, German *von*, Italian *da*) in the role of a causal adjunct (CausA; ↑259g). E.g.:

πάντα μοι παρεδόθη ὑπὸ τοῦ πατρός μου.	*All things have been handed over to me by my Father.* (Lk 10:22)

Subject/patient (who or what is presented as undergoing the "action"?):

πάντα	*all things*

CausA/agent (who is the one causing the "action"?):

ὑπὸ τοῦ πατρός μου	*by my Father*

↑also Lk 21:16f; Jn 14:21; Ac 10:22 et pass.

Less frequently the role of ὑπό + gen. is taken on (↑187m) by ἀπό + gen. (in CG also by ἐκ, παρά, and πρός + gen.), in the NT occasionally by διά + gen. (so in 2Cor 1:11):

ἄνδρα ἀποδεδειγμένος ἀπὸ τοῦ θεοῦ εἰς ὑμᾶς	*a man attested to you by God* (Ac 2:22)

The dat. of agent (↑176c) is regularly used in CG to indicate the agent of the pf. pass. (only 1× in the NT: Lk 23:15) and of the verbal adjective (↑64e).

Note that when an active construction with two direct objects, one personal and one impersonal, is transformed into a passive one, the sentence pattern changes as follows: S+P+Od(person)+Od(thing) → S(person)+P+Od(thing). For details ↑154b.

2. On the **distribution of passive forms** in Ancient Greek:

191b a) In principle passive forms may occur with any kind of transitive verb, whether its regular form is in the active or in the middle voice (↑188d), e.g.:

ἦλθον … ἵνα **σώσω** (act.) τὸν κόσμον.	*I came … to save the world* (Jn 12:47)

ταῦτα λέγω ἵνα ὑμεῖς **σωθῆτε** (pass.).	*I say this that you may be saved* (Jn 5:34)
ἰάσατο (mid.) αὐτόν.	*He healed him.* (Lk 22:51)
ἰάθη (pass.) ὁ παῖς αὐτοῦ.	*His servant was healed.* (Mt 8:13)

b) As pointed out in 154c, there are some intransitive verbs in Ancient Greek involving a Og or O^{dat} that may be used in a **personal passive** construction, e.g. διακονέω τινί *to serve s.o.*: 191c

ὁ υἱὸς τοῦ ἀνθρώπου οὐκ ἦλθεν **διακονηθῆναι** (O^{dat} of act. → S of pass.)	*The Son of Man did not come to be served* (Mt 20:28)

↑Mt 27:12 (Og of the act. → S of pass.); also ↑example given in 154c.

c) ↑189g on some verbs whose passive forms are replaced by the active form of another verb. 191d

3. Quite frequently **passive forms** are used **without a passive meaning**:

a) Especially the aorist passive forms (often also the future passive forms) of many verbs expressing a physical, mental or affective movement is very often used (intransitively) without a passive meaning, e.g.: 191e

pres. act.	pres. mid./pass.	aor. pass. (in part also used with a passive sense)	
στρέφω *I turn sth./turn (myself)*	στρέφομαι *I turn (myself)*	ἐστράφην *I turned (myself)*	(↑94.7; 189b)
πλανάω *I lead astray*	πλανάομαι *I go astray*	ἐπλανήθην *I went astray* (also *I was led astray*)	(↑191h)
ἐκπλήσσω *I amaze s.o.* (CG *I shock s.o.*)	ἐκπλήσσομαι *I am amazed* (CG *I am shocked*; non-passive sense)	ἐξεπλάγην *I was amazed* (CG *I was shocked*; non-passive sense)	(↑95.14)
πείθω *I persuade/convince*	πείθομαι *I obey* (also *I am convinced*)	ἐπείσθην *I obeyed* (also *I was convinced*)	(↑96.1)

b) Somewhat comparable uses occur with many passive deponents and with the aorist (sometimes also with the future) of many middle deponents (↑64b), e.g.: 191f

pres.	fut.	aor.	
βούλομαι *I wish*	βουλήσομαι *I will wish*	ἐβουλήθην *I wished*	(↑112.6)
ὀργίζομαι *I am angry*	ὀργισθήσομαι (LXX) *I will be angry* (CG also ὀργιοῦμαι)	ὠργίσθην *I was angry*	(CG also act.)
πορεύομαι *I travel/go*	πορεύσομαι *I will travel/go*	ἐπορεύθην *I travelled/went*	(CG also act.)
γίνομαι *I become*	γενήσομαι *I will become*	ἐγενόμην/ἐγενήθην *I became* ↑γέγονα/γεγένημαι *I have become* (↑112.7)	(CG mid.)

191g c) The (intransitive) use of passive forms of ὁράω *to see* (↑113.8) is of special relevance to the study of the NT (and the LXX): they are used without the standard passive meaning, but apparently with a causative or "tolerative" sense (↑191h):

ὤφθην (aor.) / ὀφθήσομαι (fut.) + dat. of person (O^{dat} or IntA?; ↑173b/176a)	*I appeared / I will appear to s.o.* (chiefly so in the NT and the LXX, hardly ever with the sense *I was seen / I will be seen*)

↑Hebr. נִרְאָה *nir'āh* or Aram. אתיחמה *'tyḥmh he was seen* or *he appeared* (HALOT sub רָאָה *rā'āh*; Jastrow sub חֲמָא *ḥămā'*), a use (at times) found in extra-Biblical Greek, too (↑Montanari s.v.).

191h 4. Like active and middle forms (↑188e) passive forms were sometimes used with a **causative** sense inferable from the context, e.g.:

οἱ ἐξουσιάζοντες … εὐεργέται **καλοῦνται**.	*Those in authority … are called* (= *cause themselves to be called*) *'Benefactors'* (Lk 22:25)

↑Lk 3:7; Ac 2:38 for further possible instances of this use, which occurs rarely in the NT.

Passive forms may also occur with a **"tolerative"** (or "permissive") sense, e.g.:

διὰ τί οὐχὶ μᾶλλον **ἀποστερεῖσθε**;	*Why not rather let yourselves be cheated?* (1Cor 6:7)
συναρπασθέντος δὲ τοῦ πλοίου … **ἐφερόμεθα**.	*When the ship was caught up in it … we let ourselves be driven along.* (Ac 27:15)

↑255f for the passive voice with the sense of the generic personal pronouns "one" or "you" in English (↑Carter §60b and 147b).

↑296b on the "divine passive".

3.2.2.2 Aspects and tenses (↑64c; 315)

(i) General points on aspects and tenses

192 Preliminary remarks about aspects and tenses

(↑Crystal: 38; Huddleston/Pullum: 117–124; Carter §217ff; BR §77/206; Langslow: 165ff; Adrados 1992: 380–402; MB: S313–317; Duhoux §122–128; CAGL: 140ff; BDF §318; Z §240f; Turner 1963: 59f; Runge/Fresch: 13–80)

The aspects and tenses of the Ancient Greek verb is a subject that has aroused considerable interest in recent years, especially among New Testament scholars (on issues discussed and bibliographical details ↑Campbell 2007/2008a+b and Runge/Fresch). In the light of this and as this is both a basic and a complex part of the syntax of the verb, a fairly detailed treatment seems advisable.

192a I. Important points of **terminology**

The system of Greek verb forms involves two interrelated grammatical categories: (1) tense (past, present, and future) and (2) aspect (durative, aorist, and resultative). Traditionally both of these have been treated as one category under the somewhat confusing term "tense". For clarity's sake and in order to make it easier to deal with these categories appropriately, we shall now briefly define some of the more important terms using English examples for illustration:

1. The **tense** of a verb, as a grammatical category, serves to locate the "action" in time, in relation to a specific reference point, typically the moment of speaking or writing. It shows whether from the vantage point of the speaker/writer a particular "situation" is meant to be placed in the present, the past, or the future, e.g.: 192b
Today, I ***am*** *at home.* (to be placed in the present)
Yesterday, I ***was*** *at work.* (to be placed in the past)
Tomorrow, I ***will be*** *back.* (to be placed in the future)

This kind of time reference (present, past, and future) may be called **"absolute"** tense or time.[25] Its counterpart, **"relative"** tense or time, is about the relationship between two "actions" taking place (in the present, past, or future), either at the same time ("simultaneity"), or one preceding the other ("anteriority"), or one following the other ("posteriority"), e.g. (in this example both "actions" are presented as taking place in the past):
While I ***was preparing*** *my lesson, I* ***was listening*** *to music.* (simultaneity)
After I ***had prepared*** *my lesson, I listened to music.* (anteriority: first "action" in relation to second)
I prepared my lesson ***before I listened*** *to music.* (posteriority: second "action" in relation to first)

It should be noted that time relations between a specific reference point and a particular "situation" (a meaning relation also called "temporality") may be expressed not only grammatically, i.e. by tense, but also by lexical means, e.g.:
Today's *performance …* ***Yesterday's*** *break …* ***Tomorrow's*** *journey …*
Frequently the intended time relation (especially regarding relative time) will be inferable only from the context (on this ↑322a).

2. The **aspect**[26] of a verb, as as grammatical category, has to do with the way the speaker/writer views and presents the "action" of the verb regarding its unfolding in time. He or she may present it in its totality, viewed as a complete whole, so to speak, from the outside, without highlighting any of the phases of its unfolding ("perfective" aspect). Or they do not present it in its totality, viewed, as it were, from within, with certain characteristics of its unfolding such as its progression or continuation being highlighted ("imperfective" aspect). English is a language that distinguishes grammatically between these two possibilities (non-progressive and progressive/continuous),[27] e.g. (in this example, too, the "actions" are again presented as taking place in the past): 192c
When Jane arrived, John ***got*** *up.* (non-progressive)
When Jane arrived, John ***was getting*** *up.* (progressive/continuous)

It should be noted that the use of the aspects of a verb is closely connected with its lexical meaning, especially regarding its "aktionsart" (↑194m). In English (as also in Ancient Greek; ↑194a[32]) there are verbs such as *to turn up* used to refer to one single act without any perceptible extension in time; due to this, only the non-progressive aspect would seem grammatically acceptable in the above example: *John* ***turned*** *up*, not, however, the progressive/continuous one: **John* ***was turning*** *up*. In the case of *to get up*, on the other hand, either aspect appears to be acceptable as this verb is used of a whole series of acts that typically extend over a certain length of time. 192d

25 ↑Comrie: 36–55 (absolute tense) and 56–82 (relative tense).

26 Formerly also called "aktionsart", a term used in a different way nowadays (↑194m). The definitions of aspect given here owe much to Huddleston/Pullum: inter alia 124.

27 Note that English and Ancient Greek agree only partially regarding aspect use. ↑below.

As aspect has to do with the way the speaker/writer views and presents a particular "action" ("situation") it is to be expected that in aspect use textgrammatical or textpragmatic factors (inter alia concern for coherence) play an important role (↑297ff).

192e It was pointed out above (↑192b) that time relations ("temporality"), typically expressed by (grammatical) tense, may also be expressed by other means. Something similar applies to meaning relations that are typically expressed by (grammatical) aspect (called "aspectuality"), which may also be expressed by means other than aspect forms such as lexical phrases e.g. to express progressive aspectuality (but here obviously with additional elements of meaning indicating emphasis):
*When Jane arrived, John was **in the very act of** getting out of bed.*
As the Ancient Greek aspect system differs considerably from the English one, English constructions without aspect forms will often be called for, when Ancient Greek aspects are to be translated accurately into English, e.g. a *used to* paraphrase in the following case (for details ↑194–195):

ἐζώννυες (ipf.: durative-iterative) σεαυτόν — *You used to gird/dress yourself.* (Jn 21:18)

Note that the progressive aspect would be unacceptable here: **You were girding/dressing …*, while the non-progressive past form would not be accurate enough: *You girded/dressed …*

192f 3. Languages that use the grammatical category tense, but lack aspect forms (aspectuality being expressed by non-grammatical means) are sometimes called "tense languages" or "non-aspect languages" (e.g. German), while languages that use aspect forms are known as "aspect languages". It must, however, be noted that in the grammatical system of many **"aspect languages"** aspects do not stand alone, but are expressed in combination with (grammatical) tense. This clearly applies to English. As recent studies have shown (↑Runge/Fresch), in the verbal system of Ancient Greek, too, aspect and tense are used in combination, with aspect, however, playing a predominant part (↑193a).

192g II. **Ancient Greek** is **basically** an **aspect language**: among the four stems, traditionally called "tense" stems (better "tense-aspect" stems; ↑64c), only the future stem is a tense stem in the real sense of the term: all of its forms typically locate a particular "action" ("situation") in the future (or mark it as something subsequent). The other three "tense" stems are actually "aspect" stems. This means inter alia:

1. **The present/durative, the aorist and the perfect stems do not, in themselves, express any tense values** (↑192b),
a) neither in terms of "absolute" tense or time, i.e. they do not – apart from indicatives – expressly locate the "action"/"situation" in the present or the past (↑193a),
b) nor in terms of "relative" tense or time, i.e. they do not express simultaneity, anteriority or posteriority with regard to two "actions"/"situations" (↑193b).

2. **The present/durative, the aorist and the perfect stems, basically express only aspect**; by choosing a particular aspect stem the speaker/writer may indicate the way in which he or she views and means to present the "action" of the verb (the "situation") regarding its unfolding in time,
a) as something ongoing: **durative** aspect (present/durative stem);
b) simply as something that is done or takes place (without reference to continuation or result): **aorist** (i.e. the unspecified) aspect;[28] or
c) with a special focus on its result: **resultative** aspect (perfect stem). ↑193–194.

28 BDF §318 and many others use the misleading term "punctiliar" or "momentary" (↑194e). On aspect terminology used in the present grammar ↑65[21].

Note that the aorist aspect (occurring more frequently than its alternatives) is generally the least conspicuous (the "unmarked") aspect. The durative and resultative aspects, on the other hand, are usually more conspicuous ("marked" and thus especially relevant to text interpretation).

Synopsis of aspect forms with and without tense value 193

(↑BR §207; Duhoux §129f; BDF §318; Z §240f; Turner 1963: 59f; Humbert §226–228; Runge/Fresch: 122–160)

1. All forms of the present/durative, the aorist, and the perfect stems basically express the aspect in question. Among these the **indicative forms**, and only these, typically express an **additional** (absolute) **tense value**; non-indicative forms, on the other hand, do not, in themselves, express any tense value. The linguistic and non-linguistic context in which non-indicative forms appear will show how exactly the "action"/"situation" in question is meant to relate to other "situations" in terms of placement in time (↑Part 4 on textgrammar, inter alia 308ff): 193a

aspect stem	aspect	with additional (absolute) tense value (↑192b)	
a) **present/durative** stem	durative	–	(↑194a–194d; 195)
• INDICATIVE FORMS:	durative	PRESENT/PAST TENSE	(↑209)
without aug.: "ind. pres."	durative[(1)]	present	(↑197)
with aug.: "ipf."	durative	past	(↑198)
• non-indicative forms:	durative	–	(↑204)
subj./opt./imp./inf./ptc.	durative	–	(↑210–214; 228)
b) **aorist** stem	aorist	–	(↑194e–194j; 195)
• INDICATIVE FORM: "ind. aor."	aorist	PAST TENSE	(↑199; 209)
• non-indicative forms:	aorist	–	(↑204)
subj./opt./imp./inf./ptc.	aorist	–	(↑210–214; 228)
c) **perfect** stem	resultative	–	(↑194k/194l; 195)
• INDICATIVE FORM:	resultative	PRESENT/PAST TENSE	(↑209)
without aug.: "ind. pf."	resultative	present (result of past "action")	(↑200)
with aug.: "plpf."	resultative	past	(↑201)
• non-indicative forms:	resultative	–	(↑204)
subj./opt./(imp.)/inf./ptc.	resultative	–	(↑210–214; 228)

(1) In the case of the indicative present, however, the aspect meaning seems to be largely neutralized (for lack of alternatives when referring to a "situation" in the present; ↑197).

In more **recent discussions** about verbal aspect in Ancient Greek a number of scholars (e.g. Porter and Campbell; ↑Campbell 2007/2008a+b) tried to show that not only the non-indicative, but also the indicative forms of these aspect stems express only aspect, the intended placement of particular "actions" in the present or the past being indicated solely by contextual (pragmatic) factors. Though this theory became fairly popular, especially among New Testament scholars, many (including the author of the present grammar) considered the evidence presented by its proponents insufficient to seriously call into question the consensus view held by specialists of Ancient Greek and Proto-Indo-European that indicative forms do in fact have an additional tense value (↑among others Adrados 1992, MB, and Duhoux, so also the New Testament scholar and aspect expert Fanning). And recent research by a whole range of specialists (representing a variety of relevant fields such as general linguistics, classics, applied linguistics, textlinguistics) published in 2016 (↑Runge/Fresch) has shown that the Porter-Campbell approach to the indicative forms had better be discarded in favour of the consensus view just mentioned.

193b Unlike Latin verb forms, Ancient Greek verb forms (belonging to the three aspect stems), in themselves, **never express relative tense** or time (↑192b/192g); the (grammatically conditioned) "consecutio temporum" (sequence of tenses), so important in Latin usage,[29] is foreign to Ancient Greek. Whether two "actions"/"situations" are to be understood as taking place at the same time (simultaneity) or as one preceding the other (anteriority) or as one following the other (posteriority), in principle, is not indicated by a specific verb form, but by contextual factors. Thus, aorist indicative forms, typically used like the past tense in English, quite frequently need to be translated as past perfect (pluperfect) forms on contextual grounds, e.g.:

ἀνήγγειλάν τε ὅσα ὁ θεὸς **ἐποίησεν** … *And they reported all that God had done* … (Ac 15:4)

↑205//206 on verb forms seemingly used with (absolute or relative) tense value.

194 The three aspects: detailed explanation

↑BR §208; Duhoux §123f; BDF §318; Z §240–291; Turner 1963: 59ff; Humbert §228–231; Runge-Fresch 122–160)

The aorist is the most frequent of the three aspects in Ancient Greek.[30] For this reason alone it will have to be regarded as the basically inconspicuous or "unmarked" aspect; this also ties in with its use. The durative and the resultative, on the other hand, occur not only much less frequently, but they are usually also more specific regarding the way the speaker/writer may view and present the "action"/"situation"; they are usually more conspicuous or "marked" and thus especially relevant to text interpretation.

29 ↑Pinkster: 555.

30 In the NT the aorist is two to four times as frequent as the durative, depending on the grammatical category it occurs in (not taking into account either comparisons with ind. pres. forms [lacking truly functional parallels in the aor. these are irrelevant here] or the verb εἰμί *to be* that does not occur in the aor.). The durative for its part is about four times as frequent as the resultative. Similar ratios appear to be found also in Josephus, Philo, the "Apostolic Fathers", and the LXX. Also ↑Duhoux §129f.

1. The **durative** (the durative[31] aspect) is expressed by forms of the present/durative stem. The speaker/writer typically chooses[32] such forms when he or she views and means to present the "action"/"situation" (viewed as it were from the inside) as something ongoing or incomplete regarding its unfolding in time, e.g.: 194a

ἀπέθνῃσκεν (ipf./aug.-ind. pres.)	*she was dying* (Lk 8:42)
ἀποθνῄσκων (ptc. pres.)	*(when) dying* (He 11:21)

Depending on the lexical meaning of the verb (inter alia its aktionsart; ↑194m/194n) **and the context** the durative aspect may be interpreted in a variety of concrete ways. To translate the intended aspectual nuance of verb forms adequately into English, these will frequently need to be paraphrased (often involving additional adverbial expressions; ↑192e). Note that it is not always easy (or even necessary) to distinguish between the linear and the iterative nuances when interpreting texts:

a) **linear** nuance: the "action"/"situation" is presented as something continuing, basically uninterrupted (the most frequently occurring nuance of the durative), e.g.: 194b

——————→

ἐζήτει (ipf./aug.-ind. pres.)	*he sought (continuously)* (Mt 26:16) also e.g. *he was seeking* (↑Mk 14:55)
ζητεῖν (inf. pres.)	*to seek (continuously)* (Ac 17:27) also *to be seeking, to search for* (Mt 2:13)

31 ↑Maier 1967: 67–76, for an early (modern) introduction to the aspects of Ancient Greek (and their relationship to "aktionsart") that proved to be a helpful starting point for what is being said here, especially regarding terminological issues and the drawings visualizing aspect uses. Note that others (such as BR) use the term "linear" in place of "durative" (in the present grammar "linear" denotes a subcategory); Duhoux uses "progressif".

32 It needs to be remembered that choosing presupposes having a choice, of course. When speakers/writers intend to indicate that a "situation" is to be placed in the present, there is basically no alternative to the indicative present available to them; they have no choice but to use this form. So, when an ind. pres. form occurs in a text, it would usually be rather unwise to assume that it was used to express a specific aspectual nuance (the rare conative use perhaps being an exception; ↑194d). Still, in particular contexts an ind. pres. form may refer to a "situation" that at the same time is referred to by other forms of the present stem with clearly durative force; from this we would have to infer that the "situation" is to be understood as something ongoing (even though this is not expressed by the ind. pres. form itself). A case in point would seem to be οὐχ ἁμαρτάνει *he does not sin* in 1Jn 3:6: the "situation" referred to is probably to be understood as something ongoing, calling for a paraphrase such as *he does not keep on sinning* (↑ESV and NIV), indicated, however, not by the ind. pres. form, but by other (non-indicative) present forms with clearly durative force, i.e. by the participles in verses 4, 6b, and 10 as well as the infinitive in verse 9. On the aspectually neutral force of the indicative present ↑Runge-Fresch: 73.
Something similar would also apply to verbs that never occur in the aorist (e.g. εἰμί *to be*) or only rarely so (e.g. βλέπω to see, unlike e.g. ἀναβλέπω *to look up; to regain sight*). ↑Duhoux §124, and §135–142 (on choosing aspects).

194c b) **iterative** nuance (↑Lat. *iterāre* "to repeat"): the "action"/"situation" is presented as something repeated, also habitual, e.g.:

ἔφερον (ipf./aug.-ind. pres.)	*they* (i.e. each one) *brought, they would bring* (Ac 4:34), in other contexts also *they were bringing* (linear) (↑Lk 18:15), *they tried to bring* (conative) (↑Ac 7:26)
προσεύχεσθαι (inf. pres.)	*to pray (regularly)* (1Tm 2:8), also *to be praying* (↑Lk 9:29)

194d c) **conative** nuance (↑Lat. *conārī* "to attempt"):[33] the "action"/"situation" is presented as something whose accomplishment is attempted (very often repeatedly) without the endpoint being reached. This nuance (applying only when clearly indicated by the context) does not occur very frequently, most frequently with the ipf., sometimes also with the ind. pres., more rarely with participles and infinitives. E.g.:

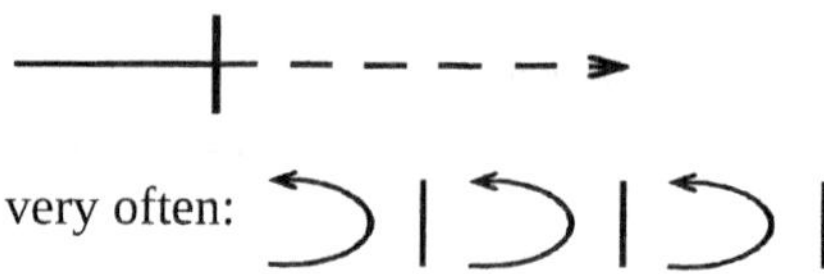

ἐδίδουν (ipf./aug.-ind. pres.)	*they tried to give, they offered* (Mk 15:23), in most contexts, however, *they were giving* (linear) (↑Ac 4:33) or *they would give* (iterative) (↑Ac 4:35)
δικαιοῦσθε (ind. pres.)	*you are trying to be justified* (Ga 5:4), standard use: *you are justified* (↑Jas 2:24)

Note that the present/durative and the perfect/resultative stems are functionally close to one another. ↑194l.

194e 2. The **aorist** aspect (or simply "aorist") is expressed by forms of the aorist stem. It is generally to be regarded as the default aspect, as the inconspicuous, unmarked one, as unspecified.[34] Speakers/writers typically choose aorist forms when they present the "action"/"situation" as a complete whole (viewed as it were from the outside),[35] as something that is done or takes place without reference to continua-

33 Some scholars further posit an "inceptive" nuance (mainly for the imperfect), on which ↑198e.

34 A role connecting well with the inherited term "aorist" < ἀόριστος (χρόνος) = (regarding continuation and result) "indefinite" tense form (↑LSJ s.v.; BR §77).

35 In fact fitting the aspect category usually called "perfective" (↑192c), a term not being used in this grammar inter alia to avoid confusion with the term "perfect" (↑65[21]).

tion or result. The concrete "action"/"situation" referred to may or may not actually be something ongoing or something with an important result; in this respect aorist forms in and of themselves (in most cases) have nothing to say. For details and examples ↑194g and 194h.

In certain contexts the aorist forms of some verbs appear to be used to highlight the beginning or the end point of the "action"/"situation" referred to (rather than presenting it as a complete whole), for which ↑194i and 194j.

As the aorist in its various uses presents the "action"/"situation" as it were in the form of a "point" in time (or as something "momentary"), it has traditionally been called **"punctiliar"** (or "momentary") aspect by many (↑e.g. BDF §318; ↑65[21]). This term, however, has often been misinterpreted as implying that the aorist always refers to something necessarily taking place only once, to something meant to be unrepeatable, in other words always to a "point" in time (or a "moment"). Of course, in order to refer to something unrepeatable, a speaker/writer will naturally use the aorist, because as the indefinite or unmarked aspect it is the most suitable for this purpose. In fact, due to its indefiniteness, aorist forms very frequently refer to something unrepeatable. Yet, just as frequently they may refer to something ongoing or repeated. Thus, the term **"aorist"** is preferred in this grammar as being both perfectly adequate and less confusing.

a) The standard use of the aorist may also be termed **"global"** (in the sense of considering all the parts of a "situation" together).[36] The speaker/writer presents the "action"/"situation" simply as something that is done or takes place; in actual fact it may be something either ongoing or not ongoing (the lexical meaning of the verb [↑194m/194n] and the context making clear what is applicable in a particular instance). He or she views it globally (as it were from the outside) presenting it as a complete whole (in the form of a point in time): 194f

• When the speakers/writers refer to an "action"/"situation" that (both on the basis of the lexical meaning of the verb and in the context concerned) consists in **one single act** without any perceptible extension in time, clearly a point in time, using the (global) aorist comes to them quite naturally, e.g.: 194g

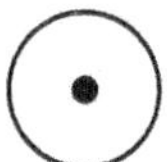

εὗρον (ind. aor.)	*they found* (Lk 2:46)
ἐμνήσθη (ind. aor.)	*he remembered* (Mt 26:75)
παραλαβεῖν (inf. aor.)	*to take (to oneself)* (↑Mt 1:20)
κερδῆσαι (inf. aor.)	*to gain* (Mk 8:36)

36 ↑Z §253. Other possible terms are "constative" (↑Fr. *constater* "to notice"/"to state" a "situation"), "complexive" (i.e. comprising the whole of the "situation" referred to; ↑Lat. *complectī* "to embrace"/"to comprise") or a combination of these "constative-complexive" (↑Zerwick-Grosvenor I/II: xii).

194h • Speakers/writers very frequently use the aorist also to refer to an "action"/"situation" that (as indicated by the lexical meaning of the verb or by the context concerned or both) is **something ongoing** or consists in a **series of acts** or is **repeated**. In such a case the aorist simply presents the "action"/"situation" as a complete whole, as something to be viewed comprehensively (globally) as it were through reverse binoculars,[37] as something compressed into one single point in time, e.g.:

ποσάκις ἠθέλησα (ind. aor.) …	*How often have I desired …!* (Mt 23:37)
πάντοτε ἐδίδαξα (ind. aor.) …	*I always taught …* (Jn 18:20)
πάντοτε δὸς (imp. aor.) ἡμῖν τὸν ἄρτον τοῦτον.	*Always give us this bread!* (Jn 6:34)

In addition to the standard (global) **use**, the aorist forms of a relatively small number of verbs may in certain contexts be used to highlight the beginning or the end point of the "action"/"situation" referred to (rather than presenting it as a complete whole):

194i b) The **inceptive**[38] aorist, highlighting the beginning of the "action"/"situation" referred to, typically occurring with aorist forms of verbs whose predominant lexical meaning is about something ongoing, e.g.:

ἔζησεν (ind. aor. ζήω/ζάω *to live*)	*he came to life* (Re 2:8)
ἐπίστευσαν (ind. aor. πιστεύω *to believe*)	*they became believers/they believed* (Ac 13:48)

194j c) The **effective**[39] aorist used to highlight the end point (the "effect") of the "action"/"situation" referred to, typically occurring with aorist forms of telic verbs (i.e. verbs denoting an activity with a clear end point), e.g.:

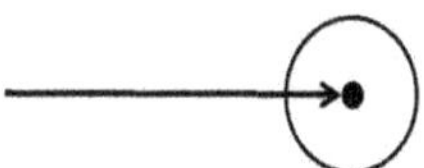

ἔφυγον (ind. aor. φεύγω *to flee*) στόματα μαχαίρης.	*they escaped the edge of the sword.* (He 11:34)

Note that verbs occurring in the effective aorist, may also occur with global or (at times) even inceptive force, e.g. ἔφυγον *they fled* (global; Mk 16:8) and *they ran off* (inceptive; Lk 8:34). Also ↑195.

37 This comparison goes back to Werner Jäkel 1962: Methodik des altsprachlichen Unterrichts (Heidelberg: Quelle & Meyer): 166, quoted by Maier 1967: 73.

38 Also called "ingressive" (↑Lat. *ingredī* "to enter") or "inchoative" (↑Lat. *inchoāre* "to begin").

39 Also called "resultative" by some (↑Turner 1963: 72); to avoid confusion with the resultative aspect of the perfect stem it would seem better not to use this term.

3. The **resultative** aspect (or simply "resultative") is expressed by forms of the perfect stem. Speakers/writers typically choose such forms when they present the "action"/"situation" with a special focus on its result. Generally speaking, both the completed "action"[40] or "situation" and its outcome are indicated; its outcome is especially **highlighted**, however, as a **result that continues** to be present at the time of speaking or writing (so in the case of the augmentless indicative) or at some other reference point (in the case of other forms; ↑194l on similarity with durative), e.g.: 194k

κεκάθικεν (ind. pf.)	*he sat down (and now is seated)* (He 12:2)
ἐγήγερται (ind. pf.) τῇ ἡμέρᾳ τῇ τρίτῃ	*he was raised on the third day (and now is alive)* (1Cor 15:4)
ἐλήλυθεν (ind. pf.) ἡ ὥρα	*the hour has come (and now is here)* (Jn 17:1)
ἐληλύθει (plpf.: aug.-ind. pf.)	*he had come (and then was there)* (Ac 8:27)

There are a small number of perfect forms (inherited from earliest times) that are used **solely** of **something that continues** to be present at the time of speaking or writing without perceptible reference to any "action" that might have led to it, inter alia πέποιθα *to trust/to be confident* (pf. II of πείθω *to persuade*; ↑189c), e.g.:

πεποίθαμεν (ind. pf.) δὲ ἐν κυρίῳ ἐφ᾽ ὑμᾶς …	*We are confident about you in the Lord* … (2Th 3:4)

Note that the resultative (perfect stem) and the durative (present stem) are both typically used of something that continues, something ongoing, the resultative (generally) of a result and the durative of an ongoing (or repeated) "action"/"situation". 194l

4. Textgrammatical or textpragmatic factors (↑297ff) will largely determine what aspect speakers/writers choose and in what way they want it to be understood in a particular context. A similarly important role is played by the lexical meanings of the words involved, above all by the meaning of the verb to be used and its **"aktionsart"** (German for "type of action"; plural: "aktionsarten"),[41] which is an essential feature when distinguishing the lexical meanings of verbs. "Aktionsart" is about the way the "action" assigned to a verb by the lexicon typically unfolds in time (in the real world), regardless of any speaker's/writer's view or presentation; it is an integral part of a verb's lexical meaning. Thus, there are verbs with a "punctual" (or "punctive") aktionsart: the "action" is one single act 194m

40 I.e. the event, process or action referred to by the verb outside the perfect stem.

41 This used to be the term for what is now called "aspect" (also e.g. in BDF). In current usage aktionsart depends on the kind of verb (with its lexical meaning) one chooses, whilst aspect depends on the "tense" (grammatical category). "Aktionsart" is also called "lexical aspect", "situation aspect" or "kind of situation" (↑Aarts: 273; Murphy: 201ff).

or event without any perceptible extension in time; a telling example is εὑρίσκω *to find*. The aktionsart of other verbs is said to be "durative": the "action" consists in a whole series of acts or an activity, typically extending over a certain length of time, e.g. ζητέω *to seek/to search*. Using these two verbs we shall briefly illustrate how the (lexical) aktionsart of a verb may be related to the use of (grammatical) aspects and the specific nuances connected with these (textgrammatical or textpragmatic factors likewise relevant are not taken into account here):

example	AKTIONSART of the verb (lexical)	ASPECT of the chosen form (grammatical)	SPECIFIC ASPECTUAL NUANCE, as "action"/"situation" is meant to unfold
ἐζήτει εὐκαιρίαν. (Lk 22:6)	durative (act series)	durative (ipf./aug.-ind. pres.)	linear: *He sought/looked for an opportunity* (over am extended period).
σπουδαίως **ἐζήτησέν** με. (2Tm 1:17)	durative (act series)	aorist (ind. aor.)	(no specific nuance:) *He eagerly searched for me.*
οὐχ **ηὕρισκον** χορτάσματα. (Ac 7:11)	punctual (single act/event)	durative (ipf./aug.-ind. pres.)	iterative: *They found/could find no food* (wherever they searched).
εὗρον καὶ βωμὸν ἐν ᾧ ἐπεγέγραπτο … (Ac 17:23)	punctual (single act/event)	aorist (ind. aor.)	(no specific nuance:) *I also found an altar with the inscription …*

194n A further distinction has proved helpful in dealing with the lexical meaning and aspect use of verbs: telic versus atelic. Many verbs are **telic**[42] verbs: these denote an "action"/event/activity connected with a specific endpoint (a "telos", i.e. a purpose or result), that is relevant to a meaningful use of the verb. ζητέω *to seek/to search*, e.g., is a telic verb: the act series, whatever its precise nature, must always be determined by a purpose, that of finding or getting hold of something or somebody. There are other telic verbs that not only need to be connected with a specific endpoint for them to be used meaningfully, but this endpoint must also be reached; e.g. ἀποκτείνω *to kill* is used meaningfully only if the person/animal to be killed is dead as a result of the activity referred to. The "action" of atelic verbs, by contrast, need not be connected with any specific endpoint as a requirement of meaningful use; e.g. περιπατέω *to go about/to behave* may be used meaningfully even if no endpoint is in view.

Possible relevance for dealing with aspects: When in a particular situation the main focus is on the telos, the effective aorist nuance may be applicable (in the case of certain telic verbs; ↑194j). When the standard telos is not achieved in spite of the appropriate activity taking place, certain telic verbs may be used with the conative nuance of the durative (forms of the present stem; ↑194d).

42 ↑τέλος inter alia "end/purpose/result".

Overview: examples of typical aspect use (↑BR §209) 195

The following overview is to show what speakers/writers typically intend to express when rather than opting for the inconspicuous or unmarked aorist they choose (↑194a[32] on choice limitations) a form of the more conspicuous or marked durative or resultative aspect (i.e. a form of the present or perfect stem):

Note that in most cases a marked aspect is used to highlight grammatically what is part of the concrete "situation" in the real world referred to (as indicated by the lexical meaning of the verb [inter alia its aktionsart; ↑194m/194n] or by the context or both), but would not specifically be expressed by the (unmarked) aorist.

AORIST (unmarked) (presented as a complete whole)	DURATIVE (marked) (presented as something ongoing, incomplete) RESULTATIVE (marked) (presented with a special focus on the result)

1. **Standard uses**

<table>
<tr><td>ἔζησα (ind.) Φαρισαῖος.
I lived as a Pharisee. (Ac 26:5)</td><td>… ὅτε ἐζῆτε (ipf.: linear) ἐν τούτοις.
… when you lived/were living/used to live in these (sins). (Col 3:7)</td><td>195a</td></tr>
<tr><td colspan="2">The verb refers to something essentially ongoing (indicated lexically; durative aktionsart), which is further highlighted grammatically by the durative aspect (ipf.), but not by the (global) aorist.</td><td></td></tr>
<tr><td>μόνον πίστευσον (imp.).
Only believe! (Lk 8:50)</td><td>μόνον πίστευε (imp. pres.: linear).
Only (continue to) believe! (Mk 5:36)</td><td></td></tr>
<tr><td colspan="2">Again, the durative (imp. pres.), unlike the aorist, further highlights the essentially ongoing character of the "action" (durative aktionsart) indicated by the lexical meaning of the verb.</td><td></td></tr>
<tr><td>ζητησάτω (imp.) εἰρήνην.
Let him seek peace. (1Pe 3:11)</td><td>τὰ ἄνω ζητεῖτε (imp. pres.: linear).
(Always) seek the things above! (Col 3:1)</td><td></td></tr>
<tr><td colspan="2">Analogous to the case just mentioned.</td><td></td></tr>
<tr><td>ζητῆσαι (inf.) … τὸ ἀπολωλός
to seek … the lost. (Lk 19:10)</td><td>ζητεῖν (inf. pres.: linear) τὸν θεόν
so that they would search for God. (Ac 17:27)</td><td></td></tr>
<tr><td colspan="2">Again, the durative (inf. pres) further highlights grammatically the essentially ongoing character of the "action" (durative aktionsart) indicated lexically.</td><td></td></tr>
<tr><td>οὐδὲν αἴτιον θανάτου εὗρον (ind.) ἐν αὐτῷ.
I have found in him no grounds for the death penalty. (Lk 23:22)</td><td>οὐχ ηὑρίσκετο (ipf.: iterative; also ↑198l)
he was not found (probably: in spite of repeated searches). (He 11:5)</td><td>195b</td></tr>
<tr><td colspan="2">Both "situations" were probably preceded by repeated, but unsuccessful searches, a fact which is hinted at by the durative, but left unexpressed by the aorist.</td><td></td></tr>
</table>

<table>
<tr><td></td><td>τῷ αἰτοῦντί σε δός (imp.).
Give to the one who asks you! (Mt 5:42)</td><td>παντὶ αἰτοῦντί σε δίδου (imp. pres.: iterative).
Give to everyone who asks you! (Lk 6:30)</td></tr>
<tr><td></td><td colspan="2">Both sentences express a directive to give each time one is asked to do so. This iterative element inferable from the context is further expressed grammatically by the durative, but not by the aorist.</td></tr>
<tr><td></td><td>ἔξεστιν δοῦναι (inf.) κῆνσον Καίσαρι ἢ οὔ;
Is it right to pay taxes to Caesar or not? (Mt 22:17)</td><td>κωλύοντα φόρους Καίσαρι διδόναι (inf. pres.: iterative).
forbidding us to pay taxes to Caesar (Lk 23:2)</td></tr>
<tr><td></td><td colspan="2">This is about the regular payment of taxes as indicated by both contexts. Here, too, the iterative element is further expressed grammatically by the durative, but not by the aorist.</td></tr>
<tr><td>195c</td><td>εὗρον (ind.) τὴν δραχμὴν ἣν ἀπώλεσα.
I have found the coin that I had lost! (Lk 15:9)</td><td>εὑρήκαμεν (ind. pf.: result present at the time of speaking) τὸν Μεσσίαν.
We have found the Messiah! (Jn 1:41)</td></tr>
<tr><td></td><td colspan="2">After both finding events there is a result (a party in the case of the lost coin). The resultative expresses grammatically that there is a result present at the time of speaking, but the aorist does not.</td></tr>
<tr><td></td><td>εἰς τὴν ἡμετέραν διδασκαλίαν ἐγράφη (ind.).
It was written for our instruction. (Ro 15:4)</td><td>ταῦτα δὲ γέγραπται (ind. pf.: result present as Jn 20 is being composed).
But these have been written/are written. (Jn 20:31)
ἐπ᾽ αὐταῖς ἐγέγραπτο (plpf.: result present in past context referred to) πάντες οἱ λόγοι.
On them had been written/were all the words. (Dt 9:10 LXX)</td></tr>
<tr><td></td><td colspan="2">As indicated by the three contexts the writing activity in each case led to a result: something written is available when three authors composed their texts. The resultative (ind. pf. and plpf.) expresses grammatically that this result is present in the relevant contexts, but the aorist does not.</td></tr>
</table>

2. **Less frequent uses** (conative nuance of durative; inceptive and effective nuances of aorist)

<table>
<tr><td>195d</td><td>ἔπεισαν (ind.) τοὺς ὄχλους …
They persuaded the crowd … (Mt 27:20)</td><td>ἔπειθέν (ipf.: CONATIVE) τε Ἰουδαίους καὶ Ἕλληνας
He tried to persuade Jews and Greeks (Ac 18:4)</td></tr>
<tr><td></td><td colspan="2">The conative nuance of the durative aspect allows us to assume that the "action" this telic verb (↑194n) refers to here consisted in a series of unsuccessful attempts, the context definitely calling for such an interpretation. The aorist, on the other hand, indicates that the attempts were successful.</td></tr>
<tr><td>195e</td><td>ὥστε πιστεῦσαι (inf.: INCEPTIVE) … πολὺ πλῆθος
so that a great number … came to believe (Ac 14:1)</td><td>ἐν τῷ πιστεύειν (inf. pres.: linear)
believing/as you believe (Ro 15:13)</td></tr>
<tr><td></td><td colspan="2">The context of the aorist example indicates a focus on the beginning of the "action"/"situation" referred to (with a durative aktionsart), so it seems legitimate to speak of an inceptive aorist. The durative (inf. pres.) example clearly belongs to the standard linear use.</td></tr>
</table>

ἔφυγον (ind.: EFFECTIVE) στόματα μαχαίρης. *They escaped the edge of the sword.* (He 11:34)	ἔφευγον (ipf.: apparently iterative) ἐπὶ πᾶσαν ὁδόν … *They fled by every path* … (Jdth 15:2)	195f
The context of the aorist example indicates a focus on the endpoint of the "action"/"situation" referred to (telic verb with a durative aktionsart), so it seems legitimate to speak of an effective aorist. The durative (ipf.) example, on the other hand, is apparently iterative (there were repeated movements of individuals running off; cf. plural form and expression "by every path").		

Note that when (telic) verbs of demanding or the like are used in the NT, the durative (ipf.) very frequently appears as the marked counterpart to the unmarked aorist (ind.; ↑198l), in fact, predominantly in cases where the purpose is not achieved, the demand not being met (↑conative use; 194d/195d). When the purpose is achieved, the ind. aor. is the form typically used (↑effective use; 194j), only rarely the ipf. (because viewed "from the inside", the details of the "action"/"situation" are then given more attention). On this ↑Z §272 and BDF §328. 195g

Important points relevant to **text interpretation**:

1. Generally speaking, the durative (forms of the present stem) and the resultative (forms of the perfect stem), being conspicuous or marked aspects, have greater relevance for text interpretation than the mostly inconspicuous or unmarked aorist (↑194[30]). 195h

2. To find out the intended aspectual nuance, one needs to take into account carefully both the lexical meaning of the verb in question (inter alia regarding its aktionsart; ↑194m/194n) and the context in which it is used (particularly other signals pointing to the same "situation"). 195i
Normally speakers/writers express the intended aspectual nuance not merely by grammatical means (by a particular aspect form), but often add inter alia adverbial expressions to underline what they mean.

3. An aspectual nuance should be regarded as intended only in cases where the speaker/writer had a choice about what aspect to use. In the following cases, e.g., he or she would have had no or only a limited choice (↑194a[32]): 195j

a) With the ind. pres.
b) With all the forms of the pres. stem of εἰμί *to be*, for which there are no real aorist alternatives.
c) With οἶδα *to know*, which has neither an aorist nor (at least as far as its form is concerned) a durative/present (↑109c).
d) With a fair number of verbs such as βλέπω *to see*, that hardly ever seem to be used in the aorist.

In order to achieve solid results, one needs to consult scholarly lexicons (or better still electronic databases) to determine what aspect forms actually occur for a particular verb, in other words what choices a speaker/writer may have had.

(ii) Indicative verb forms

Indicative forms: preliminaries (↑BR §210; Duhoux §129; 131–134; 153–163) 196

a) As indicated earlier (↑193), all forms of the present/durative, aorist, and perfect stems[43] express the **aspect** in question, but indicative forms alone typically have an

43 The future stem, however, in all its forms typically has only tense value (↑64c; 192g).

additional (absolute) **tense value**, placing the "action"/"situation" in the present or the past. This standard use of the indicative is found in narratives (by some called "narrative" use or, when the "action" is placed in the past, "historic" use) as well as in isolated statements (by some called "constative" use).

b) Indicative forms sometimes are used in general statements, without the "action"/"situation" being placed in time. This **timeless** use frequently occurs in proverbs and maxims (γνῶμαι; ↑LSJ s. v. III3), so it is also called "gnomic" use. ↑197b; 199l.

On the indicative as one of the four moods ↑209.

197 Indicative present (↑BR §213; Duhoux §302–312; BDF §319–324; Z §278)

The Ancient Greek use of the indicative present largely agrees with the use of the progressive and simple present tense in English, but at times with that of the present perfect. As a form of the durative (present) aspect stem it should in principle be taken as having durative meaning (↑194a–194d); this, however, seems to be largely neutralized, for lack of alternatives when referring to a "situation" in the present (↑195j). For possible aspectual nuances to be expressed in English one will, therefore, have to rely more than usual on the lexical meaning of the verb and the context.

197a 1. Indicative present: "action"/"situation" to be placed in the **present** (typically as seen from the moment of speaking or writing; ↑192b), standard use (the intended nuances are primarily inferable from the context; ↑195j):

a) **linear** (↑194b): of a "situation" best referred to either by an English progressive or a simple present, at times[44] by the present perfect (depending on the aktionsart of the verb and the context; ↑194m), e.g.:

αἱ λαμπάδες ἡμῶν **σβέννυνται.** — *Our lamps are going out.* (Mt 25:8)
ἰδοὺ … **προσεύχεται.** — *… he is praying.* (Ac 9:11)
πιστεύεις τοῦτο; — *Do you believe this?* (Jn 11:26)
ἱλαρὸν γὰρ δότην **ἀγαπᾷ** ὁ θεός. — *For God loves a cheerful giver.* (2Cor 9:7)
πᾶσα ἡ κτίσις **συστενάζει** — *all creation has been groaning* (Ro 8:22)

b) **iterative** (↑194c): of a repeated/habitual "action" (simple present in English), e.g.:

νηστεύω δὶς τοῦ σαββάτου. — *I fast twice a week.* (Lk 18:12)
ὁσάκις γὰρ ἐὰν ἐσθίητε τὸν ἄρτον τοῦτον καὶ τὸ ποτήριον πίνητε, τὸν θάνατον τοῦ κυρίου **καταγγέλλετε** ἄχρι οὗ ἔλθῃ. — *For whenever you eat this bread and drink this cup, you proclaim the Lord's death until he comes.* (1Cor 11:26)

c) **conative** (↑194d): the achievement of an "action" is attempted, but its endpoint (its purpose or result; ↑194n) is not reached (least frequent use), e.g.:

οὗτοι **ἀναγκάζουσιν** ὑμᾶς … — *These are trying to force you …* (Ga 6:12)

44 Apart from Ro 8:22 ↑also Lk 15:29; 2Cor 12:19; 1Jn 3:8.

διὰ ποῖον αὐτῶν ἔργον ἐμὲ **λιθάζετε**;	*For which of these works are you trying to stone me?* (Jn 10:32)

↑also Jn 13:6; Ac 7:25; Ro 2:4; Ga 5:4.

Sometimes the indicative present is used in cases where the utterance and the "action" take place simultaneously. Some speak of **"aoristic"** (indicative) present (↑Burton §13 and BDF §320). It might perhaps be best to subsume this use under the linear nuance. If a special category is seen to be necessary (because a simple present is always called for in English), a preferable term might be something like **"performative"** indicative present. E.g.:

ἐπιτρέπεταί σοι περὶ σεαυτοῦ λέγειν	*You are permitted to speak for yourself.* (Ac 26:1)

↑also Mt 9:2.5 = Mk 2:5.9 (≠ Lk 5:20.23 [pf. instead of pres.]); Ac 9:34; 16:18; Ro 16:21.23a.b etc.

2. The **timeless** (or "gnomic") indicative present (↑196): the speaker/writer presents the "action"/"situation" as something to be considered true in general, in the present, the past, and the future (unlike the gnomic aorist [↑199l] this use occurs fairly frequently); in English this is typically expressed by the simple present, e.g.: 197b

a) referring to natural processes, e.g.:

πᾶν δένδρον ἀγαθὸν καρποὺς καλοὺς **ποιεῖ**.	*Every healthy tree bears good fruit.* (Mt 7:17)

b) referring to principles of spiritual life, e.g.:

πᾶς ὁ ὢν ἐκ τῆς ἀληθείας **ἀκούει** μου τῆς φωνῆς.	*Everyone who belongs to the truth listens to my voice.* (Jn 18:37)
ὅσοι γὰρ πνεύματι θεοῦ **ἄγονται**, οὗτοι υἱοὶ θεοῦ εἰσιν.	*All who are led by the Spirit of God, these are the sons of God.* (Ro 8:14)

↑also Lk 9:62; 14:26f; 1Jn 1:7; 3:3; 5:4 etc.

3. Sometimes (more frequently in the NT than in CG) speakers/writers use the indicative present to place the "action"/"situation" in the **future**, referring to something in the immediate future, to something probable, certain, or threatening. Especially ἔρχομαι *to come/go* is quite frequently used in this way in the NT (sometimes in combination with real future forms), e.g.: 197c

πάλιν **ἔρχομαι** (ind. pres.) καὶ παραλήμψομαι (ind. fut.) ὑμᾶς πρὸς ἐμαυτόν.	*I will come again and take you to be with me.* (Jn 14:3)
Ἠλίας μὲν **ἔρχεται** (ind. pres.) καὶ ἀποκαταστήσει (ind. fut.) πάντα.	*Elijah is indeed coming and will restore all things.* (Mt 17:11)
τῇ τρίτῃ **τελειοῦμαι** (ind. pres.).	*on the third day I will reach my goal.* (Lk 13:32)

↑also Mt 26:2 / Mk 9:31; 1Cor 15:32.

Note that the (augmentless) indicative present of the CG simplex εἶμι (↑125c) is generally used with a future meaning *I will go* etc.

4. In Ancient Greek narratives the (augmentless) indicative present fairly frequently refers to something in the past; it then largely functions like an (augment) indic- 197d

ative aorist. This use is generally termed "**historic**" or "narrative" **present** (limited to the indicative present!). Departing from its standard function (of placing the "action" in the present), it is a more conspicuous (marked) use of the indicative present; it typically serves to make hearers/readers pause drawing their attention to something that is new or particularly relevant to what is being communicated and in this way contributing to its vividness.[45] In the NT it most frequently occurs in Mk (ca. 151×, of which 72× verbs of communication), only rarely in Lk (ca. 9×). In most instances it is best translated as an English past tense form, e.g.:

Καὶ **ἔρχονται** εἰς Βηθσαϊδάν. Καὶ **φέρουσιν** αὐτῷ τυφλὸν καὶ **παρακαλοῦσιν** αὐτὸν ἵνα αὐτοῦ ἅψηται.	*They came to Bethsaida. Some people brought a blind man to him and begged him to touch him.* (Mk 8:22)

↑also Mk 9:2; 11:1; 14:37 etc.

It often alternates with indicative aorist (↑199b) and imperfect forms (↑198), e.g.:

καὶ νεανίσκος τις **συνηκολούθει** (ipf.) αὐτῷ περιβεβλημένος σινδόνα ἐπὶ γυμνοῦ, καὶ **κρατοῦσιν** (ind. pres.) αὐτόν· ὁ δὲ καταλιπὼν τὴν σινδόνα γυμνὸς **ἔφυγεν** (ind. aor.).	*A certain young man was following him, wearing nothing but a linen cloth. They caught hold of him, but he left the linen cloth and ran off naked.* (Mk 14:51f)

↑also Mk 10:49; 11:7; 14:53 etc.

197e 5. Sometimes **indicative present forms** of certain verbs are used with a **perfect-like**, i.e. resultative force (↑200). In the NT this applies to the following verbs:
ἀκούω *I hear*, occasionally (likewise in English) ≈ *I have heard* and
πείθομαι lit. *I am being persuaded*, at times (like πέπεισμαι) = *I am convinced/certain*; e.g.:

ἀκούω σχίσματα ἐν ὑμῖν ὑπάρχειν.	*I hear* (≈ *I have heard*) *that there are divisions among you.* (1Cor 11:18)
πειθόμεθα (= πεπείσμεθα) γὰρ ὅτι καλὴν συνείδησιν ἔχομεν.	*For we are certain/sure that we have a clear conscience.* (He 13:18)

↑also Lk 9:9; 16:2; 1Cor 5:1; Ac 26:26.

In CG this applies also to the following verbs:
αἰσθάνομαι *I perceive* = *I have perceived*; μανθάνω *I understand* = *I have come to understand*; πυνθάνομαι *I hear/learn (that)* = *I have heard/learned (that)*

Comparable to this is the use of the indicative present introducing a quotation, e.g.:

Ἠσαΐας … **λέγει**· εὑρέθην …	*Isaiah … says* (= *said*), *"I was found …"* (Ro 10:20)

Note that there are also verbs that occur with such a "perfect-like" use in **all forms of the present** stem (apparently lexically conditioned) thus in the NT:
ἀδικέω *I do wrong*, occasionally (Ac 25:11) *I am in the wrong, I am guilty*, and
νικάω *I conquer*, also (inter alia Re 2:7) *I am victorious* (= *have won the victory*).
In CG also:
φεύγω *I flee*, also *I am exiled*; ἡττάομαι *I am being defeated*, also *I am defeated.*

45 ↑BR §213.3; also Runge/Fresch: 350.

These two NT verbs **always** have a "perfect-like", i.e. resultative meaning (lexically conditioned):
• ἀπέχω (= ἀπείληφα/ἔσχηκα) *I have received* (frequently used as a commercial term in KG; used alongside the intransitive ἀπέχω *I am far [from]*) and
• ἥκω (NT/LXX 3 pl. ἥκασιν [ἥκουσιν only as a Var.]) *I have come/I am present* (= ἐλήλυθα) (in the ipf. – unattested in the NT – it means *I had come/I was present*, analogously οἴχομαι [↑112.13] pres. ind. *I have gone/I am gone*, ipf. *I had gone/I was gone*), e.g.:

ἀπέχουσιν τὸν μισθὸν αὐτῶν.	*They have received their reward.* (Mt 6:2)
ὁ ἀδελφός σου **ἥκει**.	*Your brother has come.* (Lk 15:27)

6. In indirect speech or dependent declarative clauses (↑271; 274) indicative pres- 197f
ent forms typically agree with the superordinate verb/expression regarding the way the "actions" are placed in time (↑271d). As a result, such indicate present forms often call for a past tense form when translated into English, e.g.:

ἐπέγνωμεν (past tense form) ὅτι Μελίτη ἡ νῆσος **καλεῖται**.	*we learned that the island was called Malta.* (Ac 28:1)

On the periphrastic present ↑203a.

Imperfect (↑BR §214; Duhoux §313–319; BDF §325–330; 358–361; 367; Z §270–276) 198

As an augment indicative of the present/durative stem (↑64d p.91) the imperfect basi- 198a
cally combines the **durative** aspect (↑194a–194d) with the **past tense** (↑198b–198g and 198k–198l), typically used as the durative (marked) counterpart of the (unmarked) indicative aorist (↑199), though at times apparently with toned down aspect meaning (↑198l). Also ↑193ff.
In certain constructions it may also refer to something non-factual (198h–198j).

I. The imperfect serves to place the "action"/"situation" in the **past** (typically as seen from the moment of speaking or writing; ↑192b), standard use (the intended nuances are inferable from the aktionsart of the verb and the context; ↑194m):

1. **linear** (↑194b): as something continuing for some time or else as something tak- 198b
ing place in a particular situation intercepted by "actions" typically expressed by (historic) indicative aorist (↑199b) or historic (indicative) present (↑197d) forms:

a) something **continuing for some time** (in English typically simple past), e.g.:

ἔμενεν παρ᾽ αὐτοῖς, καὶ **ἠργάζετο**·	*He stayed and worked with them.* (Ac 18:3)

b) something **taking place in a particular situation** intercepted by "actions" (in English typically progressive past connected with simple past tense forms), e.g.:

ἤσθιον (ipf.), **ἔπινον** (ipf.), **ἐγάμουν** (ipf.), **ἐγαμίζοντο** (ipf.), ἄχρι ἧς ἡμέρας εἰσῆλθεν (ind. aor.) Νῶε εἰς τὴν κιβωτὸν καὶ ἦλθεν (ind. aor.) ὁ κατακλυσμὸς καὶ ἀπώλεσεν (ind. aor.) πάντας.	*They were eating and drinking, and marrying and being given in marriage, until the day Noah entered the ark, and the flood came and destroyed all of them.* (Lk 17:27)

… αὐτὴ **ἀπέθνησκεν** (ipf.) … ἔρχεταί (historic ind. pres.) τις … ὁ δὲ Ἰησοῦς … ἀπεκρίθη (ind. aor.) …	… *she was dying … someone came … But Jesus … replied …* (Lk 8:42.49f)

198c 2. **iterative** (↑194c): as something repeated/habitual (in English mostly constructions with *used to* or *would* or with *kept* + *-ing* form), e.g.:

αἱ ἅγιαι γυναῖκες … **ἐκόσμουν** ἑαυτάς …	*The holy women … used to adorn themselves* (1Pe 3:5)
ἐν ταῖς ἀγοραῖς **ἐτίθεσαν** τοὺς ἀσθενοῦντας καὶ **παρεκάλουν** αὐτόν …	*they would place the sick in the marketplaces and would ask him …* (Mk 6:56)
ἤρχετο πρὸς αὐτὸν λέγουσα· ἐκδίκησόν με …	*She kept coming with the plea, "Grant me justice …"* (Lk 18:3)
πολλοὶ πλούσιοι **ἔβαλλον** (ipf.) πολλά … χήρα πτωχὴ ἔβαλεν (ind. aor.) λεπτὰ δύο.	*Many rich people put in large sums … a poor widow put in two small coins.* (Mk 12:41f)

↑also Lk 23:21; Jn 12:6; 1Th 3:4.

In KG subordinate clauses the imperfect (or the indicative aorist; ↑199f) combined with ἄν or ἐάν (↑252.3) was used with the function of the CG "iterative" optative (without ἄν; ↑211i). In the NT this use (termed "hellenistisches Nebensatziterativpräteritum" [Hellenistic preterite iterative of the subordinate clause] by Debrunner; ↑BDAG sub ἄν Iαα; BDR §367$_2$) sometimes occurs in relative (↑290f) and temporal clauses (ὅτε + ἄν > ὅταν; ↑276e/276i), e.g.:

καὶ ὅπου **ἂν εἰσεπορεύετο** … ἐτίθεσαν τοὺς ἀσθενοῦντας.	*And wherever he would go … they would place the sick …* (Mk 6:56)

↑also Mk 3:11.

198d 3. **conative** (↑194d): the achievement of an "action" was attempted, but its endpoint (its purpose or result; ↑194n) was not reached (least frequent use), e.g.:

ὁ δὲ Ἰωάννης **διεκώλυεν** αὐτόν …	*But John tried to prevent him …* (Mt 3:14)
ἐπόρθουν αὐτήν.	*I tried to destroy it.* (Ga 1:13)
συνήλλασσεν αὐτοὺς εἰς εἰρήνην.	*He tried to reconcile them.* (Ac 7:26)

↑also Mk 15:23; Lk 1:59.

Note that in most other contexts these verbs are used with a linear or iterative nuance. ↑194a–194d.

198e A further use is perhaps to be added here: the "inceptive" imperfect (as it is termed by some), i.e. one that serves to highlight the beginning of an "action"/"situation" that is continuing for some time (in contradistinction to the inceptive aorist that highlights a beginning, but is non-committal about a possible continuation of the "action"/"situation"; ↑199d), e.g.:

ἡ δὲ πρύμνα **ἐλύετο**	*the stern began to break up* (inceptive) *… was breaking up* (linear) *… threatened to break up* (conative) (Ac 27:41)
ἐδίδασκεν αὐτούς	*he began to teach them* (inceptive) *he taught them (extensively)* (linear) (Mt 5:2)

Grammarians of Ancient Greek have differing views on the legitimacy of such a category:

In favour of an inceptive ipf., (less frequently, also of an analogous ind. and inf. pres.) are among others: Smyth §1900, Moule: 9, Robertson: 880/885, and Wallace 1994: 554f.
Clearly against it is: Schwyzer II: 277 (20th century standard work on Ancient Greek).
It is ignored among others by: Kühner-Gerth, Burton, Wackernagel, Humbert, BR, and Z.

Since almost all the examples cited in support of the legitimacy of such a category can easily be explained in terms of existing categories, it would seem unnecessary to introduce an additional, inceptive one. Nevertheless, it might at times seem best, on contextual or stylistic (textpragmatic) grounds, to translate forms of the durative aspect by a paraphrase involving the verb *to begin* or the like. That is possibly behind the suggestions made by BDF §326 (on Ac 27:41), Zerwick-Grosvenor: xxi (on Lk 5:7 with an infinitive present), and Turner 1963: 65/67 (on Mk 1:31 with an imperfect).

II. The imperfect used of "actions"/"situations" completed prior to some past reference point (↑"past perfect"/"pluperfect" in English) and some other rare uses:

1. As a (grammatically conditioned) sequence of time is foreign to Ancient Greek (↑193b), the imperfect (as the indicative aorist) may in certain contexts refer to something prior to some past reference point and thus call for a **past perfect** form when translated into English. This happens frequently when the imperfect (or indicative aorist) occurs in indirect speech or dependent declarative clauses with the superordinate construction (especially verbs of perception or cognitive attitude) referring to the past point of time in question (↑271d; 273d; 274d; 206), e.g.: 198f

Οὐκ ἐπίστευσαν … ὅτι **ἦν** τυφλός.	*They did not believe … that he had been blind* (Jn 9:18)
ἐπεγίνωσκόν τε αὐτοὺς ὅτι σὺν τῷ Ἰησοῦ **ἦσαν**.	*And they recognized that they had been with Jesus.* (Ac 4:13)

2. The counterpart of the "perfect-like" (resultative) indicative present (↑197e) is the "past perfect-like" (past resultative) imperfect (unattested in the NT), e.g.: 198g

ἐνίκων Ἀθηναῖοι.	*The Athenians had the victory.* (Thucydides 1.105)

III. The imperfect may also refer to something **non-factual** (modal use; ↑207d):

1. The imperfect (or any other augment form; ↑209h), combined **with ἄν** (↑252.3; with οὐ when negated), expresses the "**irrealis**", used by speakers/writers to present something as counterfactual (epistemic modality). This use regularly occurs in the *then*-clause (apodosis) of a remote conditional case (↑284; English mostly *would/would have* phrases); in the corresponding *if*-clause (protasis) subordinated by **εἰ**, the imperfect (or another augment form) is used, too, but without ἄν (English typically [modal] past/past perfect forms) e.g.: 198h

εἰ μὲν ἐκείνης **ἐμνημόνευον** …, **εἶχον ἄν** καιρὸν ἀνακάμψαι.	*If they had been thinking of that [land] … they would have had opportunity to return.* (He 11:15)

2. The imperfect (without ἄν; with οὐ when negated) of mostly **impersonal expressions signifying necessity** (deontic modality), may indicate that something is or 198i

was necessary, but in fact does not or did not take place (↑English *should, could* or *should have, could have* or the like). Whether this necessity is meant to belong to the present or to the past, is inferable solely from the context. E.g.:

ταῦτα δὲ **ἔδει** ποιῆσαι κἀκεῖνα μὴ ἀφιέναι. — *These you should practice/should have practiced without neglecting the others.* (Mt 23:23)

↑also Mt 18:33; 25:27; 26:9; Mk 14:5; Jn 9:33 and 11:37 (personal); Ac 24:19; 26:32 (personal; ↑284c); 27:21.

There are also some NT instances of such a use, where CG would have preferred the ind. pres., e.g.:

… ἃ οὐκ **ἀνῆκεν** …. — *… which are not fitting …* (Eph 5:4)

↑also 209k.

198j 3. In the NT the imperfect (or the indicative aorist) sometimes (↑209j) expresses **wishes** (deontic modality) idiomatically (with μή when negated; ↑244; also ↑268 on desiderative sentences):

a) ὄφελον + imperfect (or indicative aorist; ↑199h) expresses a typically unobtainable wish, e.g.:

ὄφελον ἀνείχεσθε … — *If only you would put up with …!* (2Cor 11:1)

b) ἐβουλόμην or ἤθελον without ἄν + infinitive expresses unobtainable or obtainable wishes, e.g.:

ἐβουλόμην καὶ αὐτὸς τοῦ ἀνθρώπου ἀκοῦσαι. — *I would like to hear the man myself.* (Ac 25:22)

ἤθελον δὲ παρεῖναι πρὸς ὑμᾶς ἄρτι. — *I wish I were present with you now.* (Ga 4:20)

Occasionally (Ro 9:3) ηὐχόμην is used in a similar way.

Note that CG uses ἐβουλόμην ἄν for unobtainable wishes and βουλοίμην ἄν for obtainable wishes.

↑199l on the occasional use of the imperfect (or indicative aorist) as an equivalent to the timeless "perfect" in Hebrew.

IV. Differentiation between **imperfect** and **indicative aorist**:

198k 1. The **basic** difference in meaning between the imperfect and the indicative aorist is about the **aspect** (↑examples in 195a–195b/195d/195f–195g):

IMPERFECT (typically):	INDICATIVE AORIST (typically):
• marked durative (↑194a–194d)	• unmarked/unspecified (↑194e–194h)
• past tense	• past tense

198l 2. On the other hand, Ancient Greek usage always allowed **some flexibility** in differentiating between the two options, in the NT, however, not more than in CG.

Unlike the Latin imperfect the Ancient Greek imperfect is used not infrequently in accounts about events placed in the past, often apparently without rigid dependence on aspect differences. This use may be called **"historic"** or "narrative" **imperfect**. Generally speaking, the indicative aorist (↑199b) briefly mentions the essential elements of a story (now and again interrupted by the historic present [indicative]; ↑197d), whilst the imperfect ("viewed from the inside"; ↑194a) tends to draw the hearer's/reader's attention more to particulars, often describing them in graphic detail (↑BR §214.2). One NT example would be:

Οἱ δὲ ἀκούσαντες **ἐδόξαζον** τὸν θεόν, **εἶπόν** τε αὐτῷ … (↑BDF §327)	*When they heard this, they praised God (for some time and in various ways) until they (finally) said …* (Ac 21:20)

Still, it is not uncommon for an imperfect to occur in contexts where an indicative aorist would seem equally possible as far as aspect use is concerned. In the NT this applies especially to verbs of motion and verbs of demanding or the like. The imperfect frequently occurs in situations where the demand is not or not yet met (↑195g). ↑BR §214.2;[46] BDF §327–329; Turner 1963: 64–68.

↑203a on the periphrastic imperfect.

Indicative aorist (↑BR §211–212; Duhoux §337–344; BDF §331–334; Z §242–269) 199

As an augment form of the aorist stem (↑64d p.91) the indicative aorist basically combines the **aorist** (i.e. unspecified/unmarked) aspect (↑194e–194h) with the **past tense** (↑199b–199c). In addition to this use, it may, in certain contexts in the case of some verbs, highlight the beginning (inceptive; ↑194i) or the end point (effective; ↑194j) of an "action". 199a
In rare cases the indicative aorist may refer to something timeless, and in certain construction not infrequently to something non-factual (↑199g–199n).
On the imperfect as its durative counterpart ↑198, especially 198k–198l (also 194–195).

I. The indicative aorist as a **past tense form**

1. **Standard use** (global nuance; ↑194f): 199b

a) The indicative aorist is used above all as the unspecified/unmarked **past tense form**. As such it serves to place the "action"/"situation" in the past (typically as seen from the moment of speaking or writing; ↑192b), without reference to any possible continuation or result (↑194e). This global (standard) use of the indicative aorist (↑194e–194h) is also called "**historic**" or "narrative" (indicative) **aorist**. It typically corresponds to a simple past in English (but also ↑195c; 199c). E.g.:

Ἔπειτα μετὰ ἔτη τρία **ἀνῆλθον** εἰς Ἱεροσόλυμα … καὶ **ἐπέμεινα** … ἡμέρας δεκαπέντε, ἕτερον … οὐκ **εἶδον** … Ἔπειτα **ἦλθον** εἰς … Ἔπειτα … πάλιν **ἀνέβην** … καὶ **ἀνεθέμην** αὐτοῖς … ἀλλ' οὐδὲ Τίτος … **ἠναγκάσθη** …	*The after three years I went up to Jerusalem … and I stayed … two weeks; I did not see any other … Then I went into … Then … I went up again … and I laid before them … But even Titus … was not compelled …* (Ga 1:18–2:3)

46 ↑Herodotus 1.30–31, Thucydides 2.49–52, Xenophon, Anabasis 1.4.9–13, and Lysias 1.6–21, CG examples cited by BR.

In accounts of past events the historic indicative aorist may alternate with the historic indicative present (↑197d) and with the corresponding imperfect (↑198l).

In the NT the historic indicative aorist is used inter alia to indicate the great **facts of the history of salvation**, e.g.:

ἑαυτὸν ἐκένωσεν	*he emptied himself* (Php 2:7)
ἐταπείνωσεν ἑαυτόν	*he humbled himself* (Php 2:8)
ἀπέστειλεν	*he sent* (e.g. Jn 6:57)
ἐπεφάνη	*(the grace of God) appeared* (Tt 2:11; ↑3:4)
ἐφανερώθη	*he was revealed* (1Tm 3:16; 1Jn 1:2)
ἔδωκεν	*he gave* (Jn 3:16)
παρέδωκεν	*he handed over* (Ro 8:32)
ἀπέθανεν	*he died* (1Cor 15:3)
ἑαυτὸν προσήνεγκεν	*he offered himself* (He 9:14)
ἤγειρεν	*he raised* (e.g. Ac 3:15)
ἠγέρθη	*he was raised* (e.g. Ro 6:4)
ἐδόξασεν	*he glorified* (Ac 3:13)
ὑπερύψωσεν	*he highly exalted* (Php 2:9)
etc.	

Note that the resurrection of Jesus is also referred to by means of an indicative perfect (ἐγήγερται, thus in 1Cor 15:4), which puts a special focus on its (ongoing) result (↑200d).

199c b) As the unspecified/unmarked past tense form the indicative aorist by itself does not indicate whether or not the past "situation" referred to was something ongoing or repeated. Fairly frequently, however, the "situation" referred to is in fact to be understood as something ongoing or repeated, indicated as such by the lexical meaning of the verb (especially its aktionsart; ↑194m/194n) and contextual factors such as adverbial expressions. In this kind of situations the **global** (constative-complexive) character (↑194f[36]) of the aorist aspect stands out **most clearly** (↑194h; 195a/195b):

- something **ongoing** (↑linear durative indicative forms; 197a; 198b), e.g.:

Τεσσεράκοντα καὶ ἓξ ἔτεσιν (TempA) **οἰκοδομήθη** ὁ ναὸς οὗτος.	*This temple has been under construction for forty-six years.* (Jn 2:20)

↑also Lk 13:16; Ac 7:42; 19:10; He 3:9f; Re 20:4.

- something **repeated** (↑iterative imperfect; 198c), e.g.:

πολλάκις (TempA) με **ἀνέψυξεν**	*He often refreshed me.* (2Tm 1:16)

↑also Mt 23:37; Lk 7:21; 13:34; Jn 4:12; 2Cor 11:25; 12:8.

2. **In addition to the standard** (global) **use**, the indicative aorist may, in certain contexts in the case of some verbs, highlight the beginning (inceptive) or the end point (effective) of a past "action"/"situation", which becomes particularly apparent in contrast to situations with corresponding imperfect forms (also ↑195e/195f):

a) **inceptive** indicative aorist (the beginning is highlighted; ↑194i), e.g.: 199d

ἐπίστευσαν (ind. aor.) πολλοὶ ἐπὶ τὸν κύριον.	*Many came to believe in the Lord.* (Ac 9:42)
↑οὐδὲ γὰρ οἱ ἀδελφοὶ αὐτοῦ **ἐπίστευον** (ipf.: linear) εἰς αὐτόν.	*For not even his own brothers believed in him.* (Jn 7:5)
↑also Ac 13:48; 17:12.34;18:8; 2Cor 8:9.	
Χριστὸς ἀπέθανεν καὶ **ἔζησεν** (ind. aor.).	*Christ died and came to life [again].* (Ro 14:9)
↑ἐγὼ δὲ **ἔζων** (ipf.: linear) χωρὶς νόμου ποτέ.	*Once I was alive apart from the law.* (Ro 7:9)

The so-called "dramatic" indicative aorist (↑199m) probably belongs here.

b) **effective** indicative aorist (the end point is highlighted; ↑194j), e.g.: 199e

ἐπείσαν (ind. aor.) τοὺς ὄχλους.	*They persuaded the crowds.* (Mt 27:20)
↑**ἔπειθον** (ipf.: linear) αὐτοὺς προσμένειν τῇ χάριτι τοῦ θεοῦ.	*They urged them to continue in the grace of God.* (Ac 13:43)

Note that the above verbs used in the inceptive or effective indicative aorist also occur in the standard (global) indicative aorist. ↑194i/194j.

In KG subordinate clauses the indicative aorist (or the imperfect; ↑198c) combined with ἄν or ἐάν (↑252.3) was used with the function of the CG "iterative" optative (without ἄν; ↑211i). In the NT this use ("hellenistisches Nebensatziterativpräteritum"; ↑198c) sometimes occurs in relative (↑290f) and temporal clauses (ὅτε + ἄν > ὅταν; ↑276e/276i), e.g.: 199f

ὅσοι **ἂν ἥψαντο** αὐτοῦ ἐσῴζοντο.	*As many as touched it were made well.* (Mk 6:56)

II. The indicative aorist may also refer to something **non-factual** (modal use; ↑207d):

1. The indicative aorist (or any other augment form; ↑209h), combined **with ἄν** (↑252.3; with οὐ when negated), expresses the "**irrealis**", used by speakers/writers to present something as counterfactual (epistemic modality). This use regularly occurs in the *then*-clause (apodosis) of a remote conditional case (↑284; English mostly *would/would have* phrases); in the corresponding *if*-clause (protasis) subordinated by **εἰ**, the indicative aorist (or another augment form) is used, too, but without ἄν (English typically [modal] past/past perfect forms), e.g.: 199g

εἰ γὰρ **ἔγνωσαν**,	*If they had understood it,*
οὐκ **ἂν** τὸν κύριον τῆς δόξης **ἐσταύρωσαν**.	*they would not have crucified the Lord of glory.* (1Cor 2:8)

2. In the NT the indicative aorist (or the imperfect; ↑198j) combined with **ὄφελον** expresses a typically unobtainable wish (deontic modality) idiomatically (with μή when negated; ↑209j; also ↑268 on desiderative sentences), e.g.: 199h

καὶ **ὄφελόν** γε **ἐβασιλεύσατε** …	*I wish that you had become kings* … (1Cor 4:8)

3. In CG **ὀλίγου/μικροῦ** in the sense of *all but/almost* + indicative aorist (without ἄν) was used to refer to something counterfactual in the past (Lat. *paene/prope* with ind. pf. [↑Pinkster: 395]; ↑209l), e.g.: 199i

ὀλίγου εἷλον (τὴν πόλιν)	*they but took/had almost taken (the city).* (Thucydides 8.35)

III. **Less common uses** of the indicative aorist in the NT (with largely rhetorical/textpragmatic categories, in part connected with varying definitions and terms; ↑BDF §333f):

199j 1. The **epistolary** (indicative) **aorist** (also used in CG): when the writer chooses a tense for the "action"/"situation", he does not do so (as is customary in English) with reference to his own vantage point (the present or future tense), but with reference to the addressee's (the past tense), e.g.:

ὃν **ἀνέπεμψά** σοι … — *I am sending him back to you …* (Phm 12)

↑also Php 2:28; Col 4:8 (from Paul's vantage point the "action"/"situation" is to take place in the immediate future).

199k 2. The **proleptic** (i.e. anticipating) or futuristic indicative **aorist**: something that from the speaker's/writer's vantage point is to take place later or after something else, in anticipation of it, is presented as if it had already taken place, e.g.:

ἐὰν μή τις μένῃ ἐν ἐμοί, **ἐβλήθη** ἔξω … καὶ **ἐξηράνθη**. — *If anyone does not remain in me, he will be/he is thrown out … and will wither/withers.* (Jn 15:6)

In the Vulgate ἐβλήθη ἔξω is translated as a future *mittetur foras* "will be thrown out".
↑also verse 8 ἐδοξάσθη *he is glorified.*
↑also Mt 5:28; 18:15 (ἐκέρδησας Vulgate *lucratus eris* "you will have gained"); Mk 11:24; Jn 13:31; 1Cor 7:28.

There is a comparable (rhetorically conditioned) use outside Ancient Greek: the so-called "prophetic perfect" in Ancient Hebrew (↑Joüon-Muraoka §112h): typically a past tense form, the Hebrew "perfect" at times refers to something meant to take place in the future, presenting it as if it had already taken place and thus indicating that it is certain to take place. This is probably the way the indicative aorist forms in Lk 1:51–54 are to be understood, also the ones in the OT quotations of Mt 4:16; 8:17 and Ac 8:32f.

199l 3. A fairly common use in CG is the "**gnomic**" (indicative) **aorist**: it frequently occurs in proverbs and maxims (↑196) expressing a **timeless truth based on experience**; unlike the timeless/gnomic indicative (↑197b) present, this use is attested only in a few NT instances, thus in some comparisons, e.g.:

οὗτος ἔοικεν ἀνδρὶ κατανοοῦντι τὸ πρόσωπον τῆς γενέσεως αὐτοῦ ἐν ἐσόπτρῳ· **κατενόησεν** γὰρ ἑαυτὸν καὶ ἀπελήλυθεν καὶ εὐθέως **ἐπελάθετο** ὁποῖος ἦν. — *He is like a man who looks at his face in a mirror: He looks at himself, goes away and immediately forgets what he looked like.* (Jas 1:23f)

Further possible examples are: Lk 7:35; Jas 1:11; 1Pe 1:24. Since in Jas 1:11 and 1Pe 1:24 there are allusions to Is 40:6/7 LXX, it is possible, however, to interpret the indicative aorist forms not in terms of the gnomic (indicative) aorist but as overly literal renderings of the Biblical Hebrew "perfect" in its timeless use (mainly found in poetic or proverbial contexts; ↑Joüon-Muraoka §112d). This may similarly apply to Ac 4:26 (Ps 2:2 LXX): συνήχθησαν *they band together* corresponding to the timeless "perfect" in Hebrew, παρέστησαν *they rise up* to a comparably used "imperfect" (↑Joüon-Muraoka §113d). In Ac 2:25f (Ps 15:8f LXX; Ps 16:8f MT) the timeless Hebrew "perfect" forms (in one case even a "waw-imperfect") are translated not only as indicative aorist forms, but apparently also as a (Greek) imperfect form.
The following expressions are best interpreted in an analogous way: ὡμοιώθη = ὅμοιός ἐστιν *it is like* (Mt 13:24; 18:23; 22:2); ἐν σοὶ εὐδόκησα *with you I am well pleased* (Mk 1:11; ↑also Mt 3:17; 17:5; Lk 3:22; 2Pe 1:17); ἠγαλλίασεν τὸ πνεῦμά μου *my spirit rejoices* (Lk 1:47).

199m 4. One more use needs to be mentioned that often occurs in the CG dramas and so is termed "dramatic" (indicative) aorist by many. According to BR §211 page 218 it is a variety of the inceptive indicative aorist (↑199d): The 1st pers. sg. indicative aorist refers to an affective reaction previously caused by the communication partner (BR page 218 [emphasis in the original]: “eine vom Gesprächspartner *vorher ausgelöste Gemütsbewegung*”), which usually needs to be translated as an English present tense form. A possible NT example is:

ἔγνων τί ποιήσω.	*I know what I'll do.* (Lk 16:4)

According to Turner 1963: 74 this instance might have to be connected with the gnomic use, according to Robertson: 827 with the effective use of the indicative aorist.

IV. As a (grammatically conditioned) sequence of time is foreign to Ancient Greek (↑193b), the indicative aorist (as the imperfect) may in certain contexts refer to something prior to some past reference point and thus call for a **past perfect** form when translated into English. This happens frequently in indirect speech or dependent declarative clauses with the superordinate construction (especially verbs of perception or cognitive attitude) referring to the past point of time in question (↑271d; 273d; 274d; 206), similarly also in relative clauses (↑289), e.g.: 199n

ᾔδει γὰρ ὅτι διὰ φθόνον **παρέδωκαν** αὐτόν.	*For he knew that they had handed him over out of envy.* (Mt 27:18)

↑also Mt 16:5; 19:1; 26:1.19.48; 27:3.9.31.55.57.60; 28:15f; Mk 1:32; 5:16; 6:14.17.30 etc.

Indicative perfect (↑BR §215; Duhoux §361–375; BDF §340–346; Z §285–289) 200

1. Generally speaking, the (augmentless) indicative perfect combines the (conspicuous or marked)[47] **resultative** aspect (↑194k) with the **present tense**. Basically, the focus is on a “situation” in the present (as seen from the speaker's/writer's vantage point). In most cases this “situation” is a result: something that took place in the past continues to have an effect in the present, an effect usually connected with either the subject entity or the object entity. With a small number of perfect forms (inherited from earliest times) there is no perceptible reference to any “action” that might have led to it the “situation” in focus (↑200b). Generally speaking, however, the indicative perfect refers not only to the present result but also to the past “action”[48] that has led to it. Still, it should not be regarded as a past tense form (however ↑200f); at any rate it must be clearly kept apart from the Latin (narrative) indicative perfect (↑Pinkster: 442–455); and no tense form in English (or German, French, Italian etc.) can be considered an even close equivalent. 200a

There is, however, some overlap with the English present perfect (↑Huddleston-Pullum: 141, 145), thus in situations where the “action” does not continue into the present (“non-continuative perfect”), but where a continuing result is indicated (“resultative perfect”), e.g.:

κεκοίνωκεν τὸν ἅγιον τόπον τοῦτον.	*He **has defiled** this holy place.* (Ac 21:28)

Here the defiling activity does not continue, but a continuing result (the defilement) is indicated.

Note that, depending on the lexical meaning of the verb (↑194m/194n) and the context, the indicative aorist may sometimes best be translated as an English resultative perfect (↑195c).

47 Thus, it may be called, “the most important, exegetically, of all the Greek Tenses” (MH I:140).

48 I.e. the event, process or action referred to by the verb outside the perfect stem.

There are, however, uses of the English present perfect that are foreign to the Ancient Greek indicative perfect, especially when the English present perfect indicates (as it frequently does) that the activity continues into the present ("continuative perfect"; restricted to atelic "situations" [↑194n]; ↑Huddleston-Pullum: 142, e.g. *He HAS LIVED HERE / VISITED HER regularly ever since they met*). So it would be problematic to interpret any of the NT instances of the indicate perfect along these lines, even though a present perfect rendering may prove to be most suitable.[49] Sometimes, depending on the aktionsart of the verb and the context, a continuative perfect rendering best translates indicative present forms, e.g. (also ↑197a):

τοσούτῳ χρόνῳ μεθ' ὑμῶν **εἰμι**. *Such a long time **I have been** with you.* (Jn 14:9)

Examples of indicative perfect use:

It was said at the court of Herod: Ἰωάννης ὁ βαπτίζων **ἐγήγερται** ἐκ νεκρῶν. *John the Baptist has been raised from the dead.* (Mk 6:14)

The ind. pf. is used here because the miracles that people have been hearing about seem to be the result of the alleged resurrection of John the Baptist, here a result connected with the subject entity:

διὰ τοῦτο ἐνεργοῦσιν αἱ δυνάμεις ἐν αὐτῷ. *That is why these miraculous powers are at work in him.* (Mk 6:14)

πεπληρώκατε τὴν Ἰερουσαλὴμ τῆς διδαχῆς ὑμῶν. *You have filled Jerusalem with your teaching.* (Ac 5:28)

The present resultant state: the object entity, Jerusalem, is full of it.

… ὅτι ἡ ἀγάπη τοῦ θεοῦ **ἐκκέχυται** ἐν ταῖς καρδίαις ἡμῶν. *… because God's love has been poured out into our hearts.* (Ro 5:5)

The effect caused by God's presence: his love (subject entity) gives assurance.

τὸν καλὸν ἀγῶνα **ἠγώνισμαι**,
τὸν δρόμον **τετέλεκα**,
τὴν πίστιν **τετήρηκα**.

I have fought the good fight,
I have finished the race,
I have kept the faith. (2Tm 4:7)

The result affecting Paul (the subject entity), continuing in the present (as seen from his vantage point), is stated in verse 8:

λοιπὸν ἀπόκειταί μοι ὁ τῆς δικαιοσύνης στέφανος. *Now there is in store for me the crown of righteousness.*

Similarly also:

ὁ Ἰησοῦς εἶπεν· **τετέλεσται**. *Jesus said, "It is finished!".* (Jn 19:30)

↑also Mk 11:21; Lk 13:12f; Ro 3:21; 5:2; 1Cor 2:11; 4:4; 7:14f; 2Cor 6:11; He 7:14; 9:26; 1Jn 5:9f.

200b 2. There are a small number of indicative perfect forms (inherited from earliest times) whose focus is almost exclusively on a "situation" in the present, clearly a result of a past "action". This is, however, not referred to in any perceptible way by the indicative perfect form. It is best called (indicative) "**perfect with a present force**" (Wallace 1996: 579). It mainly occurs with the following verbs:

49 On the other hand perfect forms of atelic verbs interestingly seem to occur only rarely or not at all in Ancient Greek.

present/lexical form:		indicative perfect (also ↑189c)		
ἵσταμαι	*to stand (up)*	ἕστηκα	*I stand*	(↑120.5)
ἀποθνῄσκω	*to die*	τέθνηκα	*I am dead*	(↑111.3)
μιμνῄσκομαι	*to remember*	μέμνημαι	*I think of*	(↑111.12)
καλέω	*to call*	κέκλημαι	*I am called/named*	(↑88.8)
πείθω	*to persuade*	πέπεισμαι	*I am convinced/certain*	cognate:
		πέποιθα	*I trust in*	(↑96.1)
ἀπόλλυμαι	*to be ruined/to perish*	ἀπόλωλα	*I am ruined*	(↑123.7)
κτάομαι	*to acquire*	κέκτημαι	*I own* (inter alia LXX/Philo)	
A very untypical, but important "perfect" (↑109c):		οἶδα	*I know*	

Examples:

ἰδοὺ **ἕστηκα** ἐπὶ τὴν θύραν.	*Look! I stand at the door.* (Re 3:20)
ἡ δέ … ζῶσα **τέθνηκεν**.	*But she … is dead even while she lives.* (1Tm 5:6)
πέπεισμαι …	*I am convinced/certain …* (Ro 8:38)
ἀπόλωλεν Αἴγυπτος.	*Egypt lies in ruins.* (Ex 10:7 LXX)

Some (mostly older) perfects with present force occur (mainly in CG) without apparently being connected with any preceding activity at all. In fact, they are used with the same (or almost the same) meaning as the corresponding indicative present, though the indicative perfect seems to express a kind of intensification, hence the term "intensive perfects" used by some (↑BR §215 page 223). E. g.: 200c

indicative present:	indicative perfect:
Ἠσαΐας … **κράζει**. *Isaiah … cries/cried out.* (Ro 9:27)	Ἰωάννης … **κέκραγεν** *John … cries/cried out.* (Jn 1:15)
σπουδάζεις … καταβαλεῖν *You are eager to overthrow …* (Josephus, Antiquities 7.289)	… γάμος ἐφ' ὃν **ἐσπούδακας** … *the marriage you are so eager about.* (Josephus, Antiquities 1.282)

3. The **indicative perfect** and the **indicative aorist** are clearly distinguished in the NT with hardly any exception, e.g. (also ↑195c): 200d

πάντα δι' αὐτοῦ ἐγένετο (ind. aor.), καὶ χωρὶς αὐτοῦ ἐγένετο (ind. aor.) οὐδὲ ἓν ὃ **γέγονεν** (ind. pf.). (punctuation ↑Metzger 1994)	*All things were made through him, and apart from him nothing was made that exists.* (Jn 1:3)

The ind. aor. refers to the creating activity, the ind. pf. to the result continuing into the present.

Χριστὸς ἀπέθανεν (ind. aor.) … ἐτάφη (ind. aor.) …**ἐγήγερται** (ind. pf.) …	*Christ died … was buried …was raised … (and now is alive).* (1Cor 15:3f, ↑v. 12 etc.)

The ind. pf. serves to emphasized the continuing reality resulting from Christ's resurrection.

Note that both the indicative aorist and the indicative perfect are capable of referring to an "action"/ "situation" in the past that has led to a result present at the time of speaking or writing. But while the indicative perfect does indicate such a result grammatically, the indicative aorist does not (its presence or absence would be inferable solely from the context). E. g.: 200e

ἐγήγερται	*He was raised (and now is alive)* (1Cor 15:4)
ἠγέρθη (ind. aor.)	*He has been raised.* (Mk 16:6)

200f In the post-Classical period the indicative perfect in its active-transitive use gradually developed into a narrative verb form: more and more it lost its resultative-present character increasingly adopting the role of the narrative indicative aorist. In post-NT times the indicative perfect finally replaced the indicative aorist completely.

It is not entirely clear whether there are early traces of this development in the NT. According to BDF §343 there are "scattered traces" with "unquestionable examples" (§343.1) in a few passages of the Book of Revelation: εἴληφεν = ἔλαβε *he received* (Re 5:7; 8:5) and εἴρηκα/εν = εἶπαν/εν *I/he said* (Re 7:14; 19:3; ↑Byz.). According to Z §289 "the examples alleged nearly all allow of other explanations". As these verb forms are not readily recognizable as having the characteristic reduplication of the perfect stem, in popular speech they were widely classified and used not as perfect forms, but as aorist forms (as exemplified in 1st century papyri; ↑BDR §343$_2$; Duhoux §375).

4. **Less common uses** of the indicative perfect in the NT (at least in part not grammatically, but rhetorically/textpragmatically conditioned):

200g a) In rare cases the indicative perfect is used (analogously to the historic [indicative] present; ↑197d) to refer to a **"situation" in the past** (thus taking the role of the plpf.; ↑201a), e.g.:

ἐν ἑαυτοῖς τὸ ἀπόκριμα τοῦ θανάτου **ἐσχήκαμεν**. (possibly, however, used like an aorist; ↑200f)

We had the sentence of the death within ourselves. (2Cor 1:9)

200h b) Occasionally the indicative perfect refers to a **"situation"** that (from the speaker's/writer's vantage point) is to be placed **in the future** (↑the ind. pres. [↑197c] and the ind. aor. [↑199k]), e.g.:

ὁ πλοῦτος ὑμῶν **σέσηπεν** καὶ τὰ ἱμάτια ὑμῶν σητόβρωτα **γέγονεν**.

Your riches have rotted and your clothes are moth-eaten. (Jas 5:2)

Future "situation": "will prove to have rotted/will prove to be moth-eaten" are presented as if they were a present reality (rhetorically emphasizing its inescapability): *have rotted/are moth-eaten.*

200i c) Occasionally the indicative perfect occurs with a **timeless/gnomic** use corresponding to the timeless/gnomic indicative present (↑197b; also ↑199l on the gnomic indicative aorist), e.g.:

ὃς δ' ἂν τηρῇ αὐτοῦ τὸν λόγον, ἀληθῶς ἐν τούτῳ ἡ ἀγάπη τοῦ θεοῦ **τετελείωται**.

But whoever keeps his word, truly in him the love of God has reached perfection. (1Jn 2:5)

↑also Jas 1:24 (timeless/gnomic ind. pf. alongside gnomic ind. aor.; ↑199l).

200j 5. Note that the **periphrastic conjugation** is always used in the 3rd pers. pl. ind. pf. mid.-pass. of stop and liquid verbs, also in the corresponding forms of the plpf. (↑93/99; 203). However, it occurs with vowel verbs as well. E.g.:

οὗ γάρ **εἰσιν** δύο ἢ τρεῖς **συνηγμένοι** (velar stem) εἰς τὸ ἐμὸν ὄνομα …

For where two or three are gathered in my name … (Mt 18:20)

ὑμῶν δὲ καὶ αἱ τρίχες τῆς κεφαλῆς πᾶσαι **ἠριθμημέναι** (vowel stem) **εἰσίν**.

But even the hairs of your head are all numbered. (Mt 10:30; Lk 12:7 has ἠρίθμηνται)

Fairly frequently the periphrastic conjugation occurs in other persons, too (sometimes also in the active, especially to express the pluperfect [on the subjunctive ↑203a]), e.g.:

ἐὰν ἀγαπῶμεν ἀλλήλους … ἡ ἀγάπη αὐτοῦ ἐν ἡμῖν **τετελειωμένη ἐστίν**.

If we love one another … his love is brought to perfection in us. (1Jn 4:12)

Ind. pf. pass. inter alia: Lk 12:6; 20:6; 24:38; Jn 2:17; 6:31; Ac 2:13; 4:12 Var.; 26:26; Ro 13:1; 1Cor 5:2; 2Cor 4:3; Eph 2:5.8; Col 2:10; He 4:2; 10:10. Ind. pf. act. inter alia: Ac 5:25; 21:33; 25:10; 1Cor 15:19.

αὐτὸς **ἤμην ἐφεστώς**.

I myself stood there. (Ac 22:20)

Plpf. pass. inter alia: Mk 1:33; 15:26; Lk 2:26; 4:16f; 23:19 Var.; Jn 3:24; 12:16; 19:19; Ga 2:11; 4:3; Eph 2:12; Re 17:4. Plpf. act. inter alia: Lk 1:7; 5:1.17; 15:24; 23:55; Jn 18:18.25; Ac 8:16; 16:9; 22:29.

Pluperfect (↑BR §215; Duhoux §385–387; BDF §347; Z §290f) 201

1. As an augment indicative of the perfect stem (↑64d p.91; frequently there is no augment [↑72h]) the pluperfect basically combines the **resultative aspect** (↑194k) with the **past tense** (↑201a–201b), typically used as the past tense counterpart of the indicative perfect (↑200). So, basically the focus is on a "situation" in the past (as seen from the speaker's/writer's vantage point), which in most cases is a result of an activity or event that took place prior to the past situation in view, a result continuing in that situation. As expected, the focus is frequently on the result (preferably translated as a past tense form). Due to the lexical meaning of the verb (↑194m/194n) or the context or both, however, it may be more on the activity or event leading to the result (usually best translated as a past perfect form), e.g.: 201a

… **ἐβέβλητο** πρὸς τὸν πυλῶνα αὐτοῦ.	*At his gate lay (a poor man)* … (Lk 16:20)
… τοῦ ὄρους ἐφ' οὗ ἡ πόλις **ᾠκοδόμητο** αὐτῶν.	… *the hill on which their town was built* (Lk 4:29)
… **συνετέθειντο** οἱ Ἰουδαῖοι …	… *the Jews had agreed* … (Jn 9:22)

↑also Ac 19:32.

2. Note that the Ancient Greek pluperfect (a more accurate term would be "preterite perfect"; ↑BR page 222) is not the same as the pluperfect in Latin or the pluperfect/past perfect in English as in a sentence like *When we arrived, he* ***had*** *already* ***left***. In Ancient Greek there is not (grammatically conditioned) sequence of time. Any one of the three past tense forms, imperfect, indicative aorist and pluperfect may, depending on the context, refer either to something in a past situation or to something prior to it (↑193b; 198f/198g; 199n; 201a). 201b

3. The pluperfect, like the other augment forms (↑209h), though much less frequently, may be combined with **ἄν** (↑252.3) to express the "**irrealis**" (something counterfactual), thus in the *then*-clause (apodosis) of a remote conditional case or without ἄν in the corresponding *if*-clause (protasis) subordinated by **εἰ**, e.g.: 201c

εἰ γὰρ ἐξ ἡμῶν ἦσαν, **μεμενήκεισαν ἂν** μεθ' ἡμῶν.	*For if they had belonged to us,* *they would have stayed with us.* (1Jn 2:19)
ἀπολελύσθαι ἐδύνατο … **εἰ** μὴ **ἐπεκέκλητο** Καίσαρα.	… *he could have been set free,* *if he had not appealed to Caesar.* (Ac 26:32)

4. In CG there is also a **future perfect** (though not used very much), e.g.: 201d

indicative perfect:		pluperfect:		future perfect:	
ἕστηκα	*I stand*	εἱστήκειν	*I stood*	ἑστήξ-ω/-ομαι	*I will stand*
τέθνηκα	*I am dead*	ἐτεθνήκειν	*I was dead*	τεθνήξ-ω/-ομαι	*I will be dead*
κέκληται	*he/she/it is named*	ἐκέκλητο	*he/she/it was named*	κεκλήσεται	*he/she/it will be named*

The last two future perfect stem form are also attested in the LXX.
In the NT the future perfect is always replaced by a periphrastic construction (↑203).

↑200j on the fairly frequent periphrastic conjugation used for the pluperfect (↑203).

202 Indicative future (↑BR §216; Duhoux §399–408; BDF §318; 348–351; Z §277–284; 443)

Being part of the future tense stem (↑64d p.89) the indicative future is a **tense** form **without** expressing **aspect** (↑65 p.93; 192g; 193a).[50]

202a 1. The indicative future **above of all** serves to place the "action" in the **future** (typically as seen from the moment of speaking or writing; ↑192b), e.g.:

ἐπὶ ταύτῃ τῇ πέτρᾳ **οἰκοδομήσω** μου τὴν ἐκκλησίαν.	*On this rock I will/I am going to build my church.* (Mt 16:18)

The building activity appears to be meant as something continuing, similarly the activities referred to in Php 1:6 and Jn 14:26.

πάντες δὲ **ἀλλαγησόμεθα**, ἐν ἀτόμῳ, ἐν ῥιπῇ ὀφθαλμοῦ.	*But we will all be changed, in an instant, in the twinkling of an eye.* (1Cor 15:51f)

The changing process is meant as something very brief (as indicated by the context).

202b 2. In Ancient Greek the indicative future also served to express modality (↑207d), especially **volition**, in English typically expressed by the modal *will* (dynamic or deontic modality) or, less frequently, obligation, in English expressed by modals such as *shall* or *should* (deontic modality). It is, however, not always easy to distinguish between the (primary) use as a future tense and the one expressing modality (as similarly between *will/shall* uses in English; ↑207d).

In NT Greek the modal use of the indicative future appears to have been facilitated (somewhat expanding in scope) by comparable uses (of the "future"/"imperfect") in Ancient Hebrew and Aramaic (Joüon-Muraoka §113l–n; Bauer-Leander §78a/r–u). Thus the indicative future in the NT (and the LXX) could express not only volition, but clearly also obligation, permission (↑*may*) or ability (↑*can*), so various nuances of dynamic, deontic, and epistemic modality (↑207d); all of these are not impossible in CG, but they are usually connected with somewhat different nuances (↑202f[51]) or are less common (↑Z §279f):

202c a) expressing **volition** (closely similar to hortatory subjunctive; ↑210c), e.g.:

ἀκουσόμεθά σου περὶ τούτου καὶ πάλιν.	*We will hear/We would like to hear you again on this subject.* (Ac 17:32)
προσεύξομαι τῷ πνεύματι, **προσεύξομαι** δὲ καὶ τῷ νοΐ·	*I will pray with the spirit, but I will pray with the mind also.* (1Cor 14:15)

↑also Lk 15:18; 19:22; Jn 13:37; Ac 6:3; Ro 15:28; 2Cor 12:5; Php 4:4.

---

50 Some argue that it does express aspect of the same ("perfective") type as it is characteristic of the aorist (↑Campbell 2007: 134–151; Runge-Fresch: 144). Attractive as this view may be to some extent (the future being derived from certain forms of the aorist stem), it seems difficult to maintain: for lack of any alternative when referring to future states of affair, any conceivable aspect meaning will have to be regarded as largely neutralized (↑Duhoux §399; Runge-Fresch: 369–370; also ↑194a[32]).

b) expressing **obligation** or **permission** (somewhat similar to deliberative subjunctive; ↑210d; in CG less frequently than in the NT [BDF §366]), e.g.: 202d

οὐ πολὺ δὲ μᾶλλον **ὑποταγησόμεθα** τῷ πατρὶ τῶν πνευμάτων …;	*Should we not then submit all the more to the Father of spirits …?* (He 12:9)
κύριε, πρὸς τίνα **ἀπελευσόμεθα**;	*Lord, to whom shall/may we go?* (Jn 6:68)

c) expressing **ability**, e.g.: 202e

πῶς **ἐρεῖς** τῷ ἀδελφῷ σου· ἄφες ἐκβάλω …;	*How can you say to your brother, "Let me take the speck out of your eye".* (Mt 7:4)
↑Lk 6:42 (Par.) πῶς δύνασαι λέγειν …;	*How can you say …?*

This use of the indicative future may (in NT and CG) replace the potential optative with ἄν (↑211d; BDF §385[1]), e.g.:

ἐπεὶ πῶς κρινεῖ ὁ θεὸς τὸν κόσμον;	*For then how could God judge the world?* (Ro 3:6)

Note that sometimes obligation/permission and ability are difficult to distinguish, e.g.:

ἐν τίνι ἁλισθήσεται;	*How shall/can it be made salty again?* (Mt 5:13)

d) expressing a strong obligation with **imperative** force (used in place of an imperative or a prohibitive subjunctive; ↑212; 268), mostly in quotations from the legal parts of the OT that express **strict commands** and (+ οὐ; ↑245b) **prohibitions**,[51] similarly in the NT even outside quotations (mostly 2 sg./pl., rarely 3 sg.), e.g.: 202f

οὐ **φονεύσεις**, οὐ **μοιχεύσεις**, οὐ **κλέψεις**, οὐ **ψευδομαρτυρήσεις** … **ἀγαπήσεις** τὸν πλησίον σου ὡς σεαυτόν.	*You shall not murder, you shall not commit adultery, you shall not steal, you shall not give false testimony …, you shall love your neighbour as yourself.* Or *Do not/You must not murder …* (Mt 19:18f)

↑also Mk 10:19 / Lk 18:20 (Par.), where μή + prohibitive subjunctive replaces οὐ + ind. fut.
↑also Mt 5:33; Ro 7:7; He 8:5.

ἔσεσθε οὖν ὑμεῖς τέλειοι.	*Be perfect, therefore.* (Mt 5:48)
οὐκ **ἔσεσθε** ὡς οἱ ὑποκριταί.	*Do not be like the hypocrites.* (Mt 6:5)
ὁ δὲ μείζων ὑμῶν **ἔσται** ὑμῶν διάκονος.	*The greatest among you must be your servant.* (Mt 23:11)

↑also Mt 20:26; 21:3; Mk 9:35; Ac 3:22; 1Pe 1:16.

3. On the prospective conditional case with the indicative future in the *then*-clause (apodosis) ↑282a, similarly temporal clauses with ὅταν (↑276a). 202g

4. The indicative future (more frequently the subj. aor.) may also combine with the particles οὐ μή to express the strongest negation of future "situations"; ↑247a. 202h

5. The indicative future sometimes also expresses the following types of modality: 202i

51 In CG this is at times used to express an almost polite type of directive a much stricter type, however, being expressed in the form of a negated question (οὐ + ind. fut.: strict positive directive; οὐ μή: strict prohibition; ↑Kühner-Gerth I: 176f).

a) Occasionally the indicative future occurs with a gnomic/timeless use to refer to something that is regularly to be expected in certain circumstances (↑197b; dynamic modality: predisposition on the part of the subject entity; ↑Aarts: 284), e.g.:

μόλις γὰρ ὑπὲρ δικαίου **ἀποθανεῖται**.	*For one will scarcely die for a righteous person.* (Ro 5:7)

In rare NT instances the indicative future seems to be patterned on the timeless durative use of the Ancient Hebrew/Aramaic "future"/"imperfect" (↑Joüon-Muraoka §113e; Bauer-Leander §78l), e.g.:

καὶ ὅταν **δώσουσιν** τὰ ζῷα δόξαν … **πεσοῦνται** οἱ … πρεσβύτεροι … καὶ **προσκυνήσουσιν** … καὶ **βαλοῦσιν** …	*And whenever the living creatures give glory … the … elders fall down … worship … and lay down …* (Re 4:9f)

b) There are instances where the indicative future does not, at least not primarily, place the "action"/ "situation" in the future, but expresses a (logical or evidence-based) conclusion (epistemic modality: evidence-based conclusions; ↑Aarts: 282f), sometimes called "logical" future, e.g.:

εἰ ἡμεῖς ὑμῖν τὰ πνευματικὰ ἐσπείραμεν, μέγα εἰ ἡμεῖς ὑμῶν τὰ σαρκικὰ **θερίσομεν**;	*If we have sown spiritual seed among you, is it too much if we reap a material harvest from you?* (1Cor 9:11)

↑also Ro 5:19 (Zerwick-Grosvenor ad loc.); 6:5.

202j 6. The indicative future is used to express a purpose or a result (↑BDF §369.2f):

a) in CG with ὅπως *that* / ὅπως μή *that … not* dependent on expressions that denote *to take care* or the like (↑272d; less frequently the subjunctive is used instead; ↑210g);

b) occasionally (un-CG) in NT clauses subordinated by ἵνα *in order that/that* and (ἵνα) μή *in order that/that … not* or in a καί-clause serving as a continuation of a purpose clause with subjunctive (↑272; 278/279), sometimes in a conditional clause subordinated by ἐάν (↑282a; ↑also 184j; 280b; CG also ἐφ' ᾧ / ἐφ' ᾧτε sometimes with ind. fut. [more frequently inf./ACI] *on condition that* or *in order to/in order that*);

c) in relative clauses of purpose (only occasionally in the NT, but also with subjunctive; ↑290c).

202k 7. The indicative future may be **replaced** by the following constructions:

a) in NT and CG by a **periphrastic** construction involving μέλλω *to be about (to)* + infinitive (also indicative future of εἰμί *to be* + participle present; ↑203a/203b), e.g.:

μέλλει γὰρ ὁ υἱὸς τοῦ ἀνθρώπου **ἔρχεσθαι** ἐν τῇ δόξῃ τοῦ πατρὸς αὐτοῦ.	*For the Son of Man will come in his Father's glory.* (Mt 16:27)

↑17:22; Lk 19:11; Ac 11:28 (+ [intensifying] inf. fut.).

b) in the NT fairly frequently by the **indicative present** (↑197c).

203 Periphrastic conjugation (↑BDF §352–356; BR §242; Z §360–362; Duhoux §246)

203a 1. The finite forms of εἰμί *to be* (↑256c)[52] may be combined with a participle to serve as a periphrasis of finite forms of the present, future and perfect stems. Such constructions were principally acceptable in Ancient Greek; in the NT, however, they are used more widely, apparently under the influence of Hebrew and Aramaic that fairly frequently used comparable constructions (↑Joüon-Muraoka §121e–g;

52 At times of the synonymous ὑπάρχω (+ ptc. pf.), also of γίνομαι *to become* (also ↑203b).

Rosenthal §177). The periphrasis involving the participle present in the NT quite often (in CG regularly) appears to underscore the durative aspect; in many cases, however, it seems to have the same force as the corresponding simple construction (especially so the periphrastic imperfect). Also ↑235 (inter alia on the periphrastic conjugation as one variety of the predicative use of the participle).

a) Periphrasis of finite forms of the **present stem** (ind. [↑197], ipf. [↑198; the most frequent one, particularly in Luke], subj. [↑210], imp. [↑212]): finite present form of εἰμί (very occasionally of γίνομαι; ↑203b) *to be* + participle present, e.g.:

ζῶν εἰμι (≈ ζῶ [ind.]) εἰς τοὺς αἰῶνα … *I am alive for ever* … (Re 1:18)

… πᾶν τὸ πλῆθος **ἦν** τοῦ λαοῦ **προσευχόμενον** (≈ προσηύχετο [ipf.]) ἔξω. … *the whole assembly of the people were praying outside.* (Lk 1:10)

↑also Col 2:23 (ind.); 1:18 (subj.); Mt 5:25 (imp.).

b) Periphrasis of the **indicative future** (↑202k): indicative future of εἰμί *to be* + participle present, e.g.:

ἔσεσθε μισούμενοι (≈ μισηθήσεσθε [ind. fut.], but with durative force) ὑπὸ πάντων … *You will be hated by all* … (Mt 10:22)

↑also Mk 13:25.

c) Periphrasis of finite forms of the perfect stem (ind. [↑200j], plpf. [↑200j/201], also subj. [↑210]) and periphrasis of the future perfect (↑201d): ind. pres., ipf. or subj. pres. and ind. fut. of εἰμί *to be* (occasionally ὑπάρχω) + participle perfect, e.g. (↑also 200j on ind. pf. and plpf.):

ἐὰν μὴ **ᾖ δεδομένον** … (subj. pf.) *unless it is granted him* … (Jn 6:65)

For subj. pf. ↑also Jn 16:24; 17:19.23; 1Cor 1:10; 2Cor 1:9; 9:3; 2Tm 3:17; Jas 5:15; 1Jn 1:4; 2Jn 12. For periphrasis of pf. involving ὑπάρχω: Ac 8:9.16; 19:36; ↑Jas 2:15.

… **ἔσται δεδεμένον** ἐν τοῖς οὐρανοῖς … *will be bound in heaven*
… **ἔσται λελυμένον** … (2× fut. pf.) … *will be loosed* … (Mt 16:19)

Note that the focus is on the resulting state affair continuing in the future situation in view.

↑also Mt 18:18; He 2:13 (OT quotation).

Further note that when the ptc. pf. is combined with the ptc. pres. of εἰμί the continuing character of the resulting "situation" receives additional emphasis, e.g.:

ἐσκοτωμένοι τῇ διανοίᾳ **ὄντες** … *they are darkened in their understanding/their minds are in the dark* … (Eph 4:18)

2. Occasionally εἰμί *to be* is replaced by γίνομαι, which, however, does not have quite the same 203b
meaning; for it typically marks the entry into a "situation", e.g.:

ἐγένετο ἡ βασιλεία αὐτοῦ **ἐσκοτωμένη**. *its kingdom was/became darkened/was plunged into darkness* … (Re 16:10)

↑also Mk 9:3, 2Cor 6:14.

203c 3. In NT and CG there is also a periphrasis of future forms involving μέλλω *to be about (to)* + infinitive (also ↑202k), e.g.:

μέλλει ὁ υἱὸς τοῦ ἀνθρώπου **παραδί-δοσθαι** (≈ παραδοθήσεται [ind. fut.], used e.g. in Lk 18:32) εἰς χεῖρας ἀνθρώπων.	*The Son of Man will be handed over to people.* (Mt 17:22)

↑also Mt 16:27; Lk 19:11; Ac 27:10 (+ inf. fut.).

203d The construction μέλλω *to be about (to)* + infinitive may also be used for the "**future-in-the-past**" (or "past futurate") in English typically expressed by *would* constructions (also *was/were to*; ↑Carter §390a; Aarts: 251f; also ↑206c), e.g.:

ὀδυνώμενοι μάλιστα ἐπὶ τῷ λόγῳ ᾧ εἰρήκει, ὅτι οὐκέτι **μέλλουσιν** τὸ πρόσωπον αὐτοῦ **θεωρεῖν**.	*grieving especially because of what he had said, that they would not see his face again.* (Ac 20:38)
… εἰς τόπον ὃν **ἤμελλεν λαμβάνειν** εἰς κληρο-νομίαν.	*… to a place he would later/he was to receive as an inheritance.* (He 11:8)

↑also Mk 13:4 (with subj. referring to the future [in the role of the impossible subj. fut. form; ↑79b]); Lk 7:2; Ac 25:4; 27:2; 28:6 (with ACI).

Further ways of expressing the "future-in-the-past":
a) Inside indirect speech: (1) ὅτι-clause or εἰ-clause + ind. fut. (↑206b): Mk 3:2; Mt 20:10; Ac 24:26; perhaps Mt 17:11; (2) inf./ACI aor. or fut. (↑206c): Ac 2:30; 3:18; 4:28; He 3:18.
b) Inside a narrative a periphrastic ipf. (↑203a): Ac 21:3.

Note that the periphrastic conjugation serves as a multi-part predicator: (1): (typically) finite part, (2): non-finite part (↑256b, also ↑235a).

(iii) Non-indicative verb forms

204 Overview of non-indicative verb forms (↑BR §218; Duhoux §134)

Non-indicative verb forms (outside the future stem), unlike indicative ones, principally express **no tense value** in themselves (↑193). The basic difference of meaning between the various present/durative, aorist, and perfect non-indicative forms is solely about the **aspect** (↑192–194), the aorist in most cases serving as the inconspicuous, unmarked, unspecified option, while the present/durative and the perfect ones (if there is any choice at all; ↑194a[32]) are conspicuous, marked, and so especially relevant for text interpretation (↑194e–194j).
However, ↑205/206 on forms that seemingly express tense value.

Examples:
1. non-indicative moods of the **finite verb** (details ↑207–212):
a) **subjunctive**:

ἀγαπῶμεν ἀλλήλους (pres.: linear).	*Let us love one another.* (1Jn 4:7)
ποιήσωμεν σκηνὰς τρεῖς (aor.).	*Let us make three tents.* (Lk 9:33)

b) **optative** (disappearing in KG):

ἔχοιμ᾽ ἂν ὑμῖν ἐπιδεῖξαι … (pres.: linear).	*I could prove to you …* (4Macc 1:7)
εὐξαίμην ἂν τῷ θεῷ … (aor.).	*I would pray to God …* (Ac 26:29)

c) **imperative**:

δίδοτε, καὶ δοθήσεται ὑμῖν (pres.: iterative).	*Give, and it will be given to you.* (Lk 6:38)
δότε αὐτοῖς ὑμεῖς φαγεῖν (aor.).	*You give them something to eat.* (Mk 6:37)

2. **non-finite verb** (details ↑213–240):

a) **infinitive**:

οὗτος ὁ ἄνθρωπος ἤρξατο **οἰκοδομεῖν** (pres.: linear).	*This person began to build.* (Lk 14:30)
Τίς γὰρ ἐξ ὑμῶν θέλων πύργον **οἰκοδομῆσαι** οὐχὶ πρῶτον … (aor.).	*For which of you, intending to build a tower, does not first …* (Lk 14:28)
… διὰ τὸ καλῶς **οἰκοδομῆσθαι** αὐτήν (pf. [↑71g/72g]/resultative).	*… because it is well built.* (Lk 6:48)
τίσιν δὲ ὤμοσεν μὴ **εἰσελεύσεσθαι** … (fut.: referring to something subsequent);	*And to what kind of people did he swear that they would not enter …?* (He 3:18)

b) **participle**:

εἶδεν ὁ Ἰησοῦς τὸν Ναθαναὴλ **ἐρχόμενον** πρὸς αὐτόν (pres.: linear).	*Jesus saw Nathanael approaching him.* (Jn 1:47)
εἶδεν ἄνδρα … Ἁνανίαν ὀνόματι **εἰσελθόντα** (aor.).	*He has seen … a man named Ananias come in.* (Ac 9:12)
… ἔγνων δύναμιν **ἐξεληλυθυῖαν** ἀπ᾽ ἐμοῦ (pf./resultativ [the woman is well]).	*… I know that power has gone out from me* (Lk 8:46)
ἰδόντες δὲ οἱ περὶ αὐτὸν τὸ **ἐσόμενον** εἶπαν … (fut.: referring to something subsequent).	*But when his followers saw what was going to happen, they said …* (Lk 22:49)

(iv) Verb forms seemingly expressing a tense value

Absolute tense seemingly expressed by certain verb forms 205

(↑BR §219; Duhoux §130)

Infinitives, **participles**, and **optatives** as non-indicative verb forms (outside the future stem) in principle do not express any tense value in themselves (↑192ff). As part of certain syntactic constructions they may, however, in specific contextual-syntactic circumstances ("internal dependence") refer to "situations" that are from the writer's/speaker's vantage point in the **past** (or to one prior to it): they seem to express absolute tense (↑206 on relative tense frequently connected with them as well).
This often occurs when inf./ACI phrases (↑218f–218k), participle phrases (ACP/GCP; ↑233) or clauses with oblique optative (rare in the NT; ↑211f/211g) express a statement or a question and are (internally)

dependent on a (superordinate) clause with a past tense value. The verb forms used in independent constructions corresponding to internally dependent constructions are typically past tense forms.

complex sentence with internally dependent construction		independent construction
superordinate construction	inf./ACI phrase, ptc. phrase (ACP/GCP) or clause with oblique opt.	
ἔλεγεν *[The crowd] said* (Jn 12:29)	**βροντὴν γεγονέναι**. *that it was thunder.* (ACI)	*βροντὴ ἐγένετο (ἐγεγόνει). *It was thunder.*
ἤκουσαν *They heard* (Jn 12:18)	τοῦτο **αὐτὸν πεποιηκέναι** τὸ σημεῖον. *that he had done this sign.* (ACI)	*τοῦτο ἐποίησε (ἐπεποιήκει) τὸ σημεῖον *He had done this sign.*
ἐπυνθάνετο *He inquired* (Ac 21:33)	**τίς εἴη** καὶ τί ἐστιν πεποιηκώς. *who he was and what he had done* (oblique opt.?)	*τίς ἦν καὶ τί ἦν πεποιηκώς; *Who was he and what had he done?*
*ἠκούσαμεν *We have heard* (↑Lk 4:23)	**σημεῖα γενόμενα**. *that signs had been performed.* (ACP)	σημεῖα ἐγένοντο/ἐγένετο. *Signs had been performed.* (↑Ac 2:43)
ἤκουον *They listened* (Ac 15:12)	**Βαρναβᾶ καὶ Παύλου ἐξηγουμένων** … *to Barnabas and Paul as they related …* (GCP)	*ἐξηγεῖντο/ἐξηγήσαντο … *They related …* (↑Ac 15:14; 21:19)
ᾔδεισαν *They knew* (Lk 4:41)	τὸν χριστὸν **αὐτὸν εἶναι**. *that he was the Messiah.* (ACI)	*ὁ χριστὸς ἦν. *He was the Messiah.*
οἶδα … *I know …* (2Cor 12:2)	**ἁρπαγέντα τὸν τοιοῦτον** ἕως τρίτου οὐρανοῦ. *such a man was caught up to the third heaven.* (ACP)	*ὁ τοιοῦτος ἡρπάγη ἕως τρίτου οὐρανοῦ. *Such a man was caught up to the third heaven.*

Note that in the NT verbs of communication and cognitive attitude (mental perception) mostly combine with a ὅτι *that*-clause containing an indicative (the clause pattern agreeing with the corresponding independent construction; ↑271a–271d); the ACI construction does not occur much, apparently with no uncontested instance of an inf. aor. referring to past "situations" (the inf. pf. clearly doing so instead; ↑206c). On indirect speech ↑274.

For an overview of the more important Ancient Greek constructions frequently corresponding to English *that*-clauses ↑275.

The oblique optative in CG often replacing indicatives (or subjunctives) in subordinate clauses, hardly ever occurs (never as part of ὅτι-clauses) in the NT (↑211f/211g; 270h), e.g. (from BR §219):

Ἤκουον	*I heard*
ὅτι ὁ φίλος διδοίη … (or ACI or ACP with pres. forms),	*that my friend (apparently) gave* (replacing ὅτι δίδωσι) or *had given* … (replacing ὅτι ἐδίδου)
ὅτι ὁ φίλος δοίη … (or ACI or ACP with aor. forms),	*that my friend (apparently) gave* … (replacing ὅτι ἔδωκε)

Note that in CG usage the optative, ACI and ACP constructions replace indicatives typically to indicate that the content of the declaration represents somebody else's view.

Relative tense seemingly expressed by certain verb forms 206

(↑BR §220; Duhoux §130; 134; BDF §339; 350/351; Z §261–267; 282–284; 372)

As pointed out in 193b a (grammatically conditioned) sequence of time is foreign to Ancient Greek. In seeming contradiction to this, there are many situations where an Ancient Greek verb form clearly refers to a "situation" that occurs at the same time as something else (simultaneity) or precedes it (anteriority) or follows it in time (posteriority) calling for a verb form that best expresses the relative time in question (↑192b; 327–330) when translated into English, thus for a past or present form to express simultaneity and a past perfect or present perfect form to express anteriority. It must, however, be remembered that this is to be connected primarily with contextual factors rather than with the grammatical form of the Ancient Greek verb. Still, some general connection seems to be observable between the relative time of the "situations" referred to (in the real world) and the use of Ancient Greek verb forms, a connection that is largely due to the aspect values involved: 206a

"situation" is something:	aspect form mostly used:
SIMULTANEOUS	durative/present or resultative/perfect
ANTERIOR	aorist (in the NT, however, the inf. aor. mostly refers to something posterior)

1. **Indicative forms** in two clauses (with or without syntactic subordination; ↑266b; 327–330): 206b

a) **Main clauses**

- The two "situations" are SIMULTANEOUS, e.g.:

ἐξῆλθον κρατῆσαι αὐτόν·
They went out to seize him,
(main clause 1)

ἔλεγον γὰρ ὅτι ἐξέστη.
for they were saying, "He has gone out of his mind." (main clause 2) (Mk 3:21)

- The second "situation" is ANTERIOR, e.g.:

Καὶ **ἤκουσεν** ὁ βασιλεὺς Ἡρῴδης,
Now King Herod heard about this,
(main clause 1)

φανερὸν γὰρ **ἐγένετο** τὸ ὄνομα αὐτοῦ.
for Jesus' name had become well known
(main clause 2) (Mk 6:14)

b) Two clauses with **syntactic subordination**

- The two "situations" are SIMULTANEOUS, e.g.:

ἡμᾶς **δεῖ** ἐργάζεσθαι …,
We must work … (main clause)

ἕως ἡμέρα **ἐστιν**.
while it is day (subordinate clause) (Jn 9:4)

ὡς δὲ **ἐπλήρου** Ἰωάννης τὸν δρόμον,
And as John was completing his course,
(subordinate clause)

ἔλεγεν …
he said …
(main clause) (Ac 13:25)

- The "situation" referred to by the subordinate clause is ANTERIOR, e.g.:

ζητεῖτέ με *You are looking for me,* (main clause)	οὐχ ὅτι **εἴδετε** σημεῖα … *not because you saw signs* (subordinate clause) (Jn 6:26)
ὅτε οὖν **ἠγέρθη** ἐκ νεκρῶν, *So after he was raised from the dead,* (subordinate clause)	**ἐμνήσθησαν** οἱ μαθηταὶ αὐτοῦ … *his disciples remembered …* (main clause) (Jn 2:22)

Note that in indirect speech or dependent declarative clauses and in dependent interrogative clauses (indirect questions) generally the same verb form is used as in the corresponding direct speech (apart from the required change of grammatical person, of course), regardless of the tense/placement in time of the superordinate expression. ↑271d; 273d/273e; 274d; also ↑203d (future in the past).

206c 2. An **infinitive** or ACI phrase typically occurs with a relative time reference only when it depends on a **verb of saying** (communication) or **thinking/believing** (cognitive attitude) or, especially in the NT, a verb of **showing** or **announcing**, or to some extent a verb of (sensual or mental) perception (↑218f–218k; 275), with the following tendencies to be observed:

"situation" is something:	infinitive/ACI normally used: NT:	CG:
SIMULTANEOUS	inf. pres. or inf. pf.	=
ANTERIOR	inf. pf. (at times inf. pres.)	inf. aor. (at times inf. pres. or inf. pf.)
POSTERIOR	inf. fut. or inf. aor. (!) or inf. pres. with μέλλω (↑202k)	inf. fut.

Note especially that the inf. aor. referring to something anterior appears to be absent from the NT (but also ↑226a with μετά, less frequently with ἐν). In most cases the inf. aor. refers to something posterior (also ↑203d on future in the past).

Also ↑271d (dependent declarative clauses); 273d/273e (dependent interrogative clauses); 274d (indirect speech); 275 (overview of constructions corresponding to English *that*-clauses); ; 327–330 (textgrammar).

Examples:

… περί τινος Ἰησοῦ τεθνηκότος ὃν ἔφασκεν ὁ Παῦλος **ζῆν** (sth. simultaneous: inf. pres.)	*… about a dead man named Jesus who Paul claimed was alive.* (Ac 25:19)
… νομίζοντες αὐτὸν **τεθνηκέναι**. (sth. simultaneous: inf. pf.)	*… thinking that he was dead.* (Ac 14:19)

… λέγουσαι καὶ ὀπτασίαν ἀγγέλων **ἑωρακέναι**. (sth. anterior: inf. pf.)	*… they told us that they had even seen a vision of angels.* (Lk 24:23)
ἐνταῦθα λέγεται Ἀπόλλων **ἐκδεῖραι** Μαρσύαν. (sth. posterior: inf. aor.; CG)	*It is here, so the story goes, that Apollo flayed Marsyas.* (Xenophon, Anabasis 1.2.8)
τίσιν δὲ ὤμοσεν μὴ **εἰσελεύσεσθαι** …; (sth. posterior: inf. fut.)	*And to what kind of people did he swear that they would not enter …?* (He 3:18)
μεθ' ὅρκου ὡμολόγησεν αὐτῇ **δοῦναι** … (sth. posterior: inf. aor.; un-CG)	*he promised on oath to give her …* (Mt 14:7)
οἱ δὲ προσεδόκων αὐτὸν **μέλλειν πίμπρασθαι** …(sth. posterior: inf. pres. with μέλλω)	*They were waiting for him to swell up …* (Ac 28:6)

3. As **participle phrases** occur frequently in Ancient Greek (↑227ff), the (grammatically unexpressed) relative time of the "situation" indicated by the participle (in the real world) in relation to the "situation" indicated by the superordinate verb is a matter of special interest. The following tendencies are observable: 206d

a) **Most frequently** observable relative time:

• Due its aspect of continuation (↑194a–194d; 195a–195b) the **participle present** usually refers to a "situation" that is to be understood as **simultaneous** with the one indicated by the superordinate verb, placed (by the speaker/writer) 206e

in the past, e.g.:

προσῆλθον αὐτῷ **διδάσκοντι** οἱ ἀρχιερεῖς …	*The chief priests … came to him while he was teaching.* (Mt 21:23)

in the present or as something timeless, e.g.:

τίς δὲ ἐξ ὑμῶν **μεριμνῶν** δύναται προσθεῖναι ἐπὶ τὴν ἡλικίαν αὐτοῦ πῆχυν ἕνα;	*And which of you by worrying can add a single moment to his life-span?* (Mt 6:27)

in the future, e.g.:

τότε ὄψονται τὸν υἱὸν τοῦ ἀνθρώπου **ἐρχόμενον** ἐν νεφέλῃ.	*Then they will see the Son of Man coming in a cloud.* (Lk 21:27)

• Due to its aspect of completion (↑194e–194j; 195) the **participle aorist** usually refers to something that is to be understood as preceding, **anterior** to, what is indicated by the superordinate verb, placed (by the speaker/writer) 206f

in the past, e.g.:

τοῦτο δὲ **εἰπὼν** ἐξέπνευσεν.	*And after he had said this, he breathed his last.* (Lk 23:46)

in the present or as something timeless, e.g.:

Εὐχαριστοῦμεν τῷ θεῷ … **ἀκούσαντες** τὴν πίστιν ὑμῶν ἐν Χριστῷ Ἰησοῦ.	*We thank God …, since we heard about your faith in Christ Jesus.* (Col 1:3f)

in the future, e.g.:

καὶ **ἐλθὼν** ἐκεῖνος ἐλέγξει τὸν κόσμον.	*And when he comes* (really: *he will have come*), *he will convict the world.* (Jn 16:8)

206g • Due to its resultative aspect (↑194k–194l) the **participle perfect** mostly refers to a "situation" that is the result of a preceding event, process or action, usually a result to be understood as **simultaneous** with what is indicated by the superordinate verb, e.g.:

Τοσαῦτα δὲ αὐτοῦ σημεῖα **πεποιηκότος** ἔμπροσθεν αὐτῶν οὐκ ἐπίστευον εἰς αυτόν.	*Although he had performed so many signs in their presence, they still did not believe in him.* (Jn 12:37)
οὗ γάρ εἰσιν δύο ἢ τρεῖς **συνηγμένοι** εἰς τὸ ἐμὸν ὄνομα, ἐκεῖ εἰμι ἐν μέσῳ αὐτῶν.	*For where two or three are gathered in my name, I am there among them.* (Mt 18:20)

206h • Due to its particular tense meaning (↑192) the **participle future** indicates (in the NT comparatively rarely) that the "situation" referred to is to be understood as **something posterior** to the one expressed in the superordinate verb, mostly as its purpose, e.g.:

… οὐ τὸ σῶμα τὸ **γενησόμενον** σπείρεις.	*… you do not plant the body that is to be.* (1Cor 15:37)
ἀνέβην **προσκυνήσων** εἰς Ἰερουσαλήμ.	*I went up to Jerusalem to worship.* (Ac 24:11)

206i b) **Less frequently** occurring relative time

In the above examples relative time appears to be indicated by participles. This is (outside the future) primarily due to aspect, which is confirmed by the fact that the participle present sometimes refers to a "situation" that is to be understood as preceding (prior to) the one indicated by the superordinate verb, and the participle aorist to something simultaneous. In the NT the (rarely occurring) participle future may also be replaced by the participle present to refer to something posterior (↑206h); there are, however, no uncontested instances of a participle aorist in the role of a future participle (↑BDF §339; Z §264):

• The **participle present** at times refers to something to be understood as **anterior** (↑BDF §339; Z §264), e.g.:

τυφλὸς **ὢν** ἄρτι βλέπω.	*I was blind, but now I see.* (Jn 9:25)
ὁ **διώκων** ἡμᾶς ποτε νῦν εὐαγγελίζεται τὴν πίστιν …	*He who used to persecute us is now proclaiming the faith …* (Ga 1:23)

↑also Mt 2:7; 23:35; Mk 5:15; Php 3:6; He 10:33; Re 20:10; 22:8.

• The **participle aorist** at times refers to something to be understood as **simultaneous** (the superordinate verb is typically an aorist indicative; ↑BDF §339), e.g.:

προσεύξαμενοι **εἶπαν** …	*They prayed and said …* (Ac 1:24)

Πίστει παρῴκησεν εἰς γῆν τῆς ἐπαγγελίας … ἐν σκηναῖς **κατοικήσας** μετὰ Ἰσαάκ …	*By faith he stayed for a time in the land he had been promised … living in tents with Isaac …* (He 11:9)

↑also Mt 27:4; Ac 6:6; 8:32; 9:25; 11:30; 13:22; 25:13; He 2:10; 5:7.

- The **participle present** may also refer to something to be understood as **posterior** (↑BDF §339), e.g.:

ὁ θεός … ἀπέστειλεν αὐτὸν **εὐλογοῦντα** ὑμᾶς.	*God … sent him to bless you* (= … *sent him so that he would bless you*). (Ac 3:26)

↑also Mt 3:11.

3.2.2.3 Moods (↑64d; 316)

Moods: preliminaries (↑BR §221; Duhoux §143–145; 149; BDF §357; Z §295–298; Langslow: 269ff) 207

207a 1. The four moods of the Ancient Greek verbal system, indicative, subjunctive, optative (disappearing in KG), and imperative (↑64d), may be used by speakers/writers to **express** how the "situation" is meant to relate to reality, i.e. whether it is to be understood as **factual** or as **non-factual** (inter alia as counterfactual, possible, or as something to be expected, wished for, or demanded).

207b 2. The **particle ἄν** (sometimes merged with conjunctions; ↑252.3) in various contexts highlights the intended "modality", i.e. mood meaning.

207c 3. The moods also determine what **negative particle** typically combines with a particular verb form: οὐ is usually negating, μή dismissive (↑243–249).

207d 4. In English there are hardly any (grammatically based) mood distinctions (outside the imperative perhaps). So, very often Ancient Greek moods cannot be **translated into English** as a particular form of the verb in question; instead, the intended mood meaning or modality[53] is typically rendered by the addition of a modal verb such as *will/would, can/could, may/might, must* etc. or by some other lexical means.

In the following a **brief introduction to linguistic modality** is given as a help for text interpretation:

a) **Modality** is about the way speakers/writers may characterize a "situation" in terms of "necessity", "obligation", "permission", "intention", "possibility", "probability", or "ability", so basically as not being factual or not being actualized. If they, for instance, characterize something as "possible", they typically indicate that they do not know whether or not it is a fact at the time of speaking/writing, but that it could be or could become one. Or, if they say someone is "obliged" to do something, they indicate that this person must bring about (actualize) the "situation" in question (↑Aarts: 275). They express such modal meanings in relation to a certain background such as particular norms, ideals, areas of knowledge, factual circumstances etc. (↑DuG9: 511).

53 "Modality" relates to "mood" in the same way as "time (relations)/temporality" to "tense" and "aspectuality" to "aspect" (↑192e). Note that the indicative in its standard use, not expressing any modality, may be classified as an unmodalized verb form (↑Aarts: 278).

b) The world's languages **express** modality by various means (for English ↑Aarts: 277–313):

• **grammatically**: by moods (i.e. particular verb forms such as imperatives, subjunctives or modal past tense forms), so not only in Ancient Greek, but also in many other languages including Latin and its daughter languages, as well as German, however, hardly so in English;

• **lexically** (in English mostly so): by modal verbs (e.g. *will/would, can/could, may/might, must*; ↑δεῖ *it is necessary*), but also by modal idioms (e.g. *had better*; ↑Jn 9:24 δὸς δόξαν τῷ θεῷ lit. "give God the glory" ≈ *I adjure you to tell the truth*), modal nouns (e.g. *necessity, request*; ↑ἀνάγκη *necessity*), modal adjectives (e.g. *essential, willing*; ↑ἕτοιμος *ready/willing*), modal lexical verbs (e.g. *to advise, to suggest*; ↑συμβουλεύω *to advise*), modal adverbs (e.g. *possibly, perhaps*; ↑ἴσως *perhaps/probably*), and "hedges" (e.g. *I would have thought*; ↑Lk 3:23 ὡς ἐνομίζετο *as was supposed*).

c) Modality is a complex category of meaning, extending from absolute necessity to possibility. It is without well-defined boundaries or subdivisions. Many, however, divide it roughly into **three subcategories** (↑Aarts: 276f; Huddleston-Pullum: 177f): deontic, epistemic, and dynamic modality:

• The focus of **deontic** modality is on necessity (↑δέον *what is needful*, ptc. ntr. of δεῖ *it is necessary*) of varying degrees such as obligation or permission, with speakers/writers expressing inter alia:

directives, e.g.:

ἄφετε (imp.) αὐτήν·	*Leave* (imp.) *her alone!* (Mk 14:6)
καὶ ἐάν … ἑπτάκις ἐπιστρέψῃ πρὸς σὲ λέγων· μετανοῶ, **ἀφήσεις** (ind. fut.) αὐτῷ.	*Even if … turns to you seven times saying, "I repent", you must* (modal verb) *forgive him.* (Lk 17:4)
δεῖ (lexical verb) οὖν τὸν ἐπίσκοπον ἀνεπίλημπτον εἶναι	*Therefore an overseer must* (modal verb) *be above reproach.* (1Tm 3:2)

permissions, e.g.:

τὸ νῦν ἔχον **πορεύου** (imp.)	*You may* (modal verb) *go for now.* (Ac 24:25)
οὐκ **ἀφῆκεν** (lexical verb) εἰσελθεῖν τινα σὺν αὐτῷ εἰ μὴ …	*He did not allow* (lexical verb) *anyone to enter with him except …* (Lk 8:51)

• The focus of **epistemic** modality is on the knowledge of speakers/writers (↑ἐπιστήμη *knowledge*), as a basis for their conclusion that a "situation" is possible, probable, necessary, e.g.:

… μήποτε **ἐκλυθῶσιν** (prospective subj.) ἐν τῇ ὁδῷ.	*… or they may* (modal verb) *faint on the way.* (Mt 15:32)
διελάλουν πρὸς ἀλλήλους τί **ἂν ποιήσαιεν** (potential optative) τῷ Ἰησοῦ.·	*They discussed with one another what they might* (modal verb) *do to Jesus.* (Lk 6:11)
ἴσως (adverb) τοῦτον ἐντραπήσονται.	*Perhaps* (adverb) *they will respect him.* (Lk 20:13)
… παρὰ ποταμὸν οὗ **ἐνομίζομεν** (lexical verb) προσευχὴν εἶναι	*… to riverside where we supposed* (lexical verb) *there was a place of prayer.* (Ac 16:13)

Note that the "source" of the necessity and the knowledge that deontic and epistemic modality are about, is typically the speaker/writer, as the above examples illustrate. Moreover, these two types of modality are closely related (the deontic one likely to be primary). Thus, if speakers/writers conclude something on the basis of their knowledge, they may say that they are obliged to do so, sometimes even on logical grounds (e.g. *John killed the fly* entails *The fly must be dead*; Aarts: 277).

• The focus of **dynamic** modality is typically on modal meanings such as volition, predisposition, possibility, and ability of the subject entity of the clause/sentence in question (↑δύναμαι *to be able/strong enough* to do sth.). In other words, the "source" of the necessity or of whatever modal meaning is expressed, is primarily located in the subject entity (sometimes in the circumstances) rather than in the speaker/writer. This is actually the central distinguishing mark of the dynamic type of modality over against the other two which may often appear to have a closely similar meaning (especially in terms of necessity and possibility; ↑table below under d), e.g.:

δύναται (lexical verb) ὁ θεὸς ἐκ τῶν λίθων τούτων ἐγεῖραι τέκνα τῷ Ἀβραάμ. — *God is able* (adjective) *from these stones to raise up children for Abraham.* (Lk 3:8)

ὁ γὰρ θεὸς **ἀπείραστός** (adjective) ἐστιν κακῶν. — *For God cannot* (modal verb) *be tempted by evil.* (Jas 1:13)

Ἡρῴδης **θέλει** (lexical verb) σε ἀποκτεῖναι. — *Herod wants* (lexical verb) *to kill you.* (Lk 13:31)

τί **θέλετέ** (lexical verb) μοι δοῦναι, κἀγὼ ὑμῖν παραδώσω αὐτόν; — *What will* (modal verb) *you give me, if I deliver him over to you?* (Mt 26:15)

d) The (core) **modal verbs**, the predominant way of expressing modality **in English**, may occur in more than one of the three standard subcategories, some also having other uses (↑Aarts: 280–301; "1.", "2.", "3." etc.: decreasing order of frequency):

MODAL VERB	DEONTIC	EPISTEMIC	DYNAMIC	OTHER USES
WILL/would	4. obligation	1. futurity and evidence-based predictions/conclusions	2. volition, 3. predisposition	
SHALL	2. rules and regulations, asking for instructions, self-imposed obligation	1. futurity	3. volition	
should	1. necessity	2. evidence-based supposition		3. mandative/putative uses (1) 4. conditional use(2) 5. purposive use(3)
CAN/could	2. possibility: permission	3. necessity (in negative contexts): knowledge-based conclusion	1. possibility: neutral possibility, ability, and existential meaning(4)	
MAY/might	2. possibility: permission	1. possibility: knowledge-based supposition		3. formulaic use(5)
MUST	1. necessity: obligation	2. necessity: knowledge-based conclusion	3. necessity: a property necessarily attributable to a subject entity, or neutral necessity	

(1) E.g.: I do not mean that others *should* be eased and you burdened … (2Cor 8:13 ESV).
(2) E.g.: If the foot *should* say, "Because I am not a hand … (1Cor 12:15 ESV).
(3) E.g.: We take this course so that no one *should* blame us … (2Cor 8:20 ESV).
(4) E.g.: Don't blame breed, all dogs *can* be aggressive. (↑Aarts: 292, Example 85)
(5) E.g.: *May* the Lord direct your hearts … (2Th 3:5 ESV).

5. Originally the Ancient Greek moods were used in the same way in **subordinate clauses** as in **main clauses**. Gradually, however, special rules were developed for subordinate clauses. For this reason, the rules applying to main and subordinate clauses are treated separately in the following paragraphs. 207e

208 Moods and tense/aspect meanings

As emphasized before (e.g. ↑193), all moods (outside the future) basically express aspect, but **only indicative** forms both aspect and **tense** meanings. But ↑205/206.

209 Indicative (↑BR §222–226; Duhoux §153–163; BDF §358–362; 367–383)

I. Indicative in **main clauses**

209a In its **standard** (unmodalized)[54] use the indicative refers to something that is to be understood as **factual** (in declarative and interrogative clauses; ↑209b–209f). In certain constructions, however, it is **also** used to present something as **non-factual** (expressing various types of modality; in declarative, interrogative, and wish clauses; ↑209g–209l) and (in the future tense) to express modality, especially **volition**, also with **imperative force** (↑209m).

209b 1. In its standard use, referring to something **factual** ("modus realis"), the Ancient Greek indicative, generally speaking, agrees with its counterpart in English (ignoring aspect differences; ↑196–203), i.e. in declarative (↑267) and interrogative (↑269) clauses, the usual negative particle being οὐ (↑244), placing a "situation" (typically as seen from the moment of speaking/writing)

209c a) in the **present**:

- indicative present (standard; ↑197a),
- indicative perfect (mostly result of something that took place in the past; ↑200);
- rarely indicative aorist as epistolary (indicative) aorist (↑199j),

209d b) in the **past**:

- indicative aorist (standard; in certain contexts highlighting the beginning or the end point of the "action"; ↑199b–199f),
- imperfect (durative; ↑198a–198g/198k–198l),
- pluperfect (resultative; ↑201), at times also indicative perfect (↑200d–200g),
- indicative present as historic/narrative (indicative) present (↑197d);

209e c) in the **future**:

- indicative future (standard [↑202]; when negated, frequently οὐ μή + subjunctive aorist instead [↑247a]),
- sometimes indicative present (↑197c), occasionally indicative perfect (↑200h),
- rarely indicative aorist (proleptic aorist; ↑199k),
- CG also future perfect (resultative; ↑201d);

209f d) as **timeless**:

- indicative present (↑197b), occasionally indicative perfect (↑200i),
- (rarely in the NT) indicative aorist as gnomic (indicative) aorist (↑199l),
- occasionally indicative future as gnomic future, in the NT on rare occasions patterned on a comparable use of the Ancient Hebrew/Aramaic "future"/"imperfect" (↑202i).

---

54 ↑207d[53].

2. An **augment indicative** may also refer to something non-factual, especially in main clauses (declarative, interrogative, and wish clauses; ↑267–269]): 209g

a) An **augment indicative** combined **with ἄν** (in the NT occasionally without ἄν; ↑252.3; with οὐ when negated), expresses the "**irrealis**", used by speakers/writers in independent declarative or interrogative clauses to present something as counterfactual (epistemic modality), mostly corresponding to English *would/would have* constructions. Note that the choice of "tense"/aspect forms is due not to time reference, but to aspect. Still, the following tendency (connected with aspect) is observable (on the pluperfect, rarely used in the NT, ↑201c): 209h

augment indicative with ἄν:	non-factual "situation" usually to be placed:
imperfect (↑198h)	in the **present** (or as timeless)
indicative aorist (↑199g)	in the **past**

This use regularly occurs in the *then*-clause (apodosis) of a remote conditional case (↑284; English mostly *would/would have* phrases); in the corresponding *if*-clause (protasis) subordinated by **εἰ**, the augment indicative is used, too, but without ἄν (English typically [modal] past/past perfect forms):

• The "**irrealis of the present**": The "situation" is presented as something that **is** counterfactual, because certain conditions **are** not fulfilled:

Usually the imperfect with ἄν (durative irrealis of the present) is chosen, e.g.:

εἰ γὰρ ἐπιστεύετε Μωϋσεῖ, **ἐπιστεύετε ἂν** ἐμοί. — *For if you believed Moses, you would believe me.* (Jn 5:46)

However, the indicative aorist with ἄν is possible, too, e.g.:

εἰ ᾔδει ὁ οἰκοδεσπότης …, **ἐγρηγόρησεν ἂν** καὶ **οὐκ ἂν εἴασεν** διορυχθῆναι τὴν οἰκίαν αὐτοῦ. — *If the owner of the house knew …, he would stay awake and would not let his house to be broken into.* (Mt 24:43)

• The "**irrealis of the past**": The "situation" is presented as something that **was** counterfactual, because certain conditions **were** not fulfilled:

Usually the indicative aorist with ἄν is chosen, e.g.:

κύριε, εἰ ἦς ὧδε, **οὐκ ἂν ἀπέθανεν** ὁ ἀδελφός μου· — *Lord, if you had been here, my brother would not have died.* (Jn 11:21)

However, the imperfect with ἄν is possible, too (durative), e.g.:

Εἰ γὰρ ἡ πρώτη ἐκείνη ἦν ἄμεμπτος, **οὐκ ἂν** δευτέρας **ἐζητεῖτο** τόπος. — *For if that first covenant had been faultless, no place would have been sought for a second one.* (He 8:7)

• Example of the rare **pluperfect with ἄν**:

εἰ γὰρ ἐξ ἡμῶν ἦσαν, **μεμενήκεισαν ἂν** μεθ' ἡμῶν (↑72h) — *For if they had belonged to us, they would have remained with us.* (1Jn 2:19)

209i In CG this pattern may also have the force of the **Latin potential of the past** (↑Pinkster: 166), e.g.:

… **ἔγνω ἄν** τις …	… *one might have realized* … (Xenophon, Cyropaedia 7.1.38)

↑211d on the "potential of the present" (potential optative).

209j b) The **augment indicative** (**without ἄν**) is sometimes used to express **wishes** (deontic modality) idiomatically (with μή when negated; ↑244; also ↑268 on desiderative sentences):

• There a few NT instances with the particle ὄφελον (originally ὤφελον, ind. aor. of ὀφείλω, *I owed*; in CG used as a verb) being combined with the imperfect (↑198j) or the indicative aorist (↑199h) to express a typically **unobtainable wish**, e.g.:

ὄφελον ἀνείχεσθε …	*If only you would put up with …!* (2Cor 11:1)
καὶ **ὄφελόν** γε **ἐβασιλεύσατε** …	*I wish that you had become kings* … (1Cor 4:8)

• In the NT ἐβουλόμην or ἤθελον without ἄν + infinitive is used to express unobtainable or obtainable wishes (in CG with ἄν to express unobtainable **wishes**, optative with ἄν to express obtainable wishes [potential optative; ↑211d]) or in popular usage ἤθελον + infinitive, e.g.:

ἐβουλόμην καὶ αὐτὸς τοῦ ἀνθρώπου **ἀκοῦσαι**.	*I would like to hear the man myself.* (Ac 25:22)
ἤθελον δὲ παρεῖναι πρὸς ὑμᾶς ἄρτι.	*I wish I were present with you now.* (Ga 4:20)
Ὃν ἐγὼ **ἐβουλόμην** πρὸς ἐμαυτὸν κατέχειν.	*I would have liked to keep him with me.* (Phm 13)

Occasionally (Ro 9:3) ηὐχόμην is used in a similar way.

• In CG the **augment indicative without ἄν**, introduced by εἴθε or εἰ γάρ, could be used to express an **unobtainable wish** (with μή when negated; aspect determining choice of "tense"), e.g.:

εἴθε σοι … τότε **συνεγενόμην** …	*If I had only been your companion then …!* (Xenophon, Memorabilia 1.2.46)

↑211c on the optative of (obtainable) wish.

209k c) The imperfect (without ἄν; with οὐ when negated) of mostly **impersonal expressions signifying necessity** (deontic modality), may indicate that something is or was necessary, but in fact does not or did not take place (↑English *should, could* or *should have, could have* or the like). Whether this necessity is meant to belong to the present or to the past, is inferable solely from the context. E.g.:

ταῦτα δὲ **ἔδει** ποιῆσαι κἀκεῖνα μὴ ἀφιέναι.	*These you should practice/should have practiced without neglecting the others.* (Mt 23:23)

There are also some NT instances of such a use, where CG would have preferred the ind. pres., e.g.:

… ἃ οὐκ **ἀνῆκεν** …	… *which are not fitting* … (Eph 5:4)

↑also 198i.

Note that ἔδει (as other impersonal expressions used analogously) may refer to something factual and so occurs with three different meanings:

• *it was necessary*: something that was necessary actually took place, e.g.:

Ἔδει δὲ αὐτὸν διέρχεσθαι διὰ τῆς Σαμαρείας.	*Now he had to go through Samaria* (and this is what he did). (Jn 4:4)

• *it would be necessary*: something really necessary does not take place/is not the case, e.g.:

οὓς ἔδει … παρεῖναι …	*They ought to be here* … (but are not). (Ac 24:19)

- *it would have been necessary*: something really necessary did not take place, e.g.:

ἔδει σε … βαλεῖν τὰ ἀργύριά μου … … *you should have put my money* … (Mt 25:27)

When ἔδει (or an analogous expression) is combined with ἄν, necessity itself is presented as something counterfactual (↑209h), e.g. (not attested in the NT):

… οὐδὲν ἄν σὲ ἔδει δεῦρο ἰέναι … *there would be* (or *would have been*) *no need for you to come here.* (Plato, Republic 328c)

d) In CG **ὀλίγου/μικροῦ** in the sense of *all but/almost* + indicative aorist (without ἄν) could refer to something counterfactual in the past (Lat. *paene/prope* with ind. pf. [↑Pinkster: 395]; ↑199i), a use also attested in the LXX, e.g.: 209l

μικροῦ ἐκοιμήθη τις … μετὰ τῆς γυναικός σου. *Someone … almost slept with your wife.* (Gn 26:10 LXX)

3. The **indicative future**, too, had non-factual uses in main clauses, serving to express modality, especially volition, often obligation and permission, also with **imperative force** (with οὐ when negated). For details ↑202b–202f. 209m

II. Indicative in **subordinate clauses**

1. In indirect speech or **declarative clauses** subordinated by ὅτι (or ὡς) *that* (↑271) and in dependent interrogative clauses (↑273) **generally** the same indicative form is used **as in a main clause**. On the time relation between such subordinate clauses and their superordinate constructions ↑271d. 209n

2. In **conjunctive clauses** (mostly with adverbial function; ↑270; 288), **too**, the indicative is **generally** used in the same way **as in a main clause**, with the exception of those whose subordinating conjunction or syntactic context requires the use of a subjunctive: 209o

a) in **temporal clauses** (↑276; also 209p) subordinated by:

ὅτε (less frequently ἡνίκα, ὁπότε) post-CG ὅταν (+ aug. ind., otherwise mostly + subj.)	*when, after; whenever* (↑211i)
ὡς (less frequently ἐπειδή; CG also ἐπεί)	*when, after; while*
ἕως (οὗ/ὅτου; in the NT mostly + subj.) ἄχρι(ς)/μέχρι(ς) (οὗ; in the NT less frequently + subj.), CG also ἔστε	*until; as long as* (μέχρι[ς] in the NT only *until*)
ἐν ᾧ	*while, as long as*
πρίν (CG: when main clause is neg., also + ἄν + subj., when affirmative, then + inf./ACI or + ἤ + inf./ACI; NT: usually + inf./ACI or + ἤ + inf./ACI)	*before*
especially CG also ἀφ᾽ οὗ and ἐξ οὗ	*since*

b) in **causal clauses** (↑277) subordinated by:

ὅτι/ἐπεί/ἐπειδή etc.	*because, as/since* (ἐπεί also *[since] otherwise*)

c) at times in **purpose clauses** of the NT subordinated by ἵνα + indicative future instead of subjunctive, occasionally subordinated by ὥστε + finite verb (↑278a).

d) in **result clauses** (↑279a) subordinated by

ὥστε (also + inf./ACI)	*so that* (= *with the result that*)

e) in **conditional clauses** (*if*-clause/protasis) subordinated by:

• εἰ + indicative, when the *then*-clause (apodosis) verb is in any mood without ἄν: **indefinite** case (↑280c/281);

• εἰ + augment indicative, when the *then*-clause (apodosis) verb is an augment indicative with ἄν: **remote** case ("irrealis": counterfactual; ↑280c/284);

• in the NT occasionally ἐάν + indicative (future/pres.) (↑282a) instead of subjunctive (↑210i).

f) in **concessive clauses** (↑286) subordinated by:

εἰ καί — *even if*

g) in **manner clauses** (↑287) subordinated by:

ὡς etc. — *(in such as way) as* (or with other moods as in a main clause)

209p 3. In **relative clauses** (mostly attributive modifiers; ↑289/290):

a) Without ἄν or ἐάν indicatives are used in the same way as in a main clause (↑289a; 290bff).

b) In KG subordinate clauses the imperfect (↑198c) or the indicative aorist (↑199f) combined with ἄν or ἐάν (↑252.3) was used with the function of the CG "iterative" optative (without ἄν; ↑211i). In the NT this use ("hellenistisches Nebensatziterativpräteritum"; ↑198c) sometimes occurs in relative (↑290f) and temporal clauses (↑276e/276i); especially Herodotus makes use of this construction also in main clauses (↑276e).

210 Subjunctive (↑BR §227; 230; Duhoux §168–180; BDF §363–366; 367–383)

210a I. "**Tenses**"/aspects and the subjunctive

As a non-indicative (and non-factual; ↑207a) verb form the subjunctive does **not** express **any tense value** at all. The choice of the aorist, the present or (much less frequently; ↑203a) the perfect has to do with aspect considerations. The linguistic and non-linguistic context in which a subjunctive appears will show how exactly the "action"/"situation" in question is meant to relate to other "situations" in terms of placement in time and how it is best translated into English. ↑192–195; 204; 208.

II. Subjunctive in **main clauses**

210b 1. General observations:

Basically, the modality (↑207d) expressed by the Ancient Greek subjunctive may be understood in terms either

a) of something intended or volitional: "**volitional** subjunctive", or

b) of something subjectively expected: "**prospective** subjunctive".

In post-Homeric Greek the prospective subjunctive is used almost exclusively in subordinate clauses (↑especially 210h; 210i; but also 210f).

2. In main clauses the force of the **volitional subjunctive** may be

210c a) **hortatory**: "hortatory subjunctive" (↑Lat. *hortārī* "to urge"), to express a directive addressed to oneself (↑268), the 1st person, mostly in the plural (with μή when negated; ↑244), typically translated as *Let us …!* (also *We must …*), e.g.:

ἀποθώμεθα οὖν τὰ ἔργα τοῦ σκότους, **ἐνδυσώμεθα** δὲ τὰ ὅπλα τοῦ φωτός … εὐσχημόνως **περιπατήσωμεν** … (aor.)	*So let us lay aside the deeds of darkness and put on the armour of light … Let us live decently …* (Ro 13:12f)
κατέχωμεν τὴν ὁμολογίαν τῆς ἐλπίδος ἀκλινῆ. (pres.: linear)	*Let us hold fast the confession of our hope without wavering.* (He 10:23)

↑also 1Cor 5:8; 2Cor 7:1; Ga 6:10; He 4:11.14.16.

Noteworthy points:

(1) Sometimes the modal indicative future is used in a similar way (↑202c).

(2) In the NT the hortatory subjunctive is sometimes preceded by a short directive (↑252.63):

ἄφες, ἄγετε (CG uses ἄγε, φέρε *come/now/well!*)	*Let me!, Let us!*
δεῦρο (also in CG)	*Come!*

Examples:

ἄφες ἐκβάλω τὸ κάρφος ἐκ τοῦ ὀφθαλμοῦ σου.	*Let me* (lit. *Let me, I must*) *take the speck out of your eye.* (Mt 7:4)
καὶ νῦν **δεῦρο ἀποστείλω** σε εἰς Αἴγυπτον.	*Now come, I will/let me send you to Egypt!* (Ac 7:34; ↑Ex 3:10)

↑272e on the dependent desiderative clauses.

b) **deliberative**: "deliberative subjunctive" (also "dubitative subjunctive"), used in (direct) questions typically addressed to oneself (or to oneself along with others; ↑269a), in the 1st person (mostly in the plural; with μή when negated; ↑244), generally to find out whether or not something is to be done, or else (when introduced by an interrogative pronoun or adverb) to find out about the what or how of the "action" concerned (deontic modality: obligation; ↑207d); in English modals such as *should, shall, must,* or sometimes *could* (or idioms *to be to* or *to have to*) may be used to translate this type of subjunctive, e.g.: 210d

δῶμεν ἢ **μὴ δῶμεν**; (aor.)	*Should we pay them, or shouldn't we?* (Mk 12:14)
σὺ εἶ ὁ ἐρχόμενος ἢ ἕτερον **προσδοκῶμεν**; (pres.: linear)	*Are you the one who is to come or shall we look for another?* (Mt 11:3)
τί ποιῶμεν ἵνα ἐργαζώμεθα τὰ ἔργα τοῦ θεοῦ; (pres.: linear)	*What must we do to do the works God requires?* (Jn 6:28)
πόθεν ἀγοράσωμεν ἄρτους …; (aor.)	*Where are we to buy bread …?* (Jn 6:5)

↑also Mt 6:31; Jn 12:27 (1 sg.); Ro 10:14 (3 pl.).

Noteworthy points:

(1) Fairly frequently the modal indicative future is used in a similar way (↑202c).

(2) The deliberative subjunctive is sometimes preceded (asyndetically) by the following expressions to indicate more clearly who is expected to answer the question (↑293e):

θέλεις/θέλετε (CG βούλει/βούλεσθε) …;	*Do you wish/want …?* (sg./pl.)

Example:

θέλεις … **συλλέξωμεν** αὐτά;	*Do you want us to … pull them up?* (Mt 13:28)

(3) Quite often the deliberative subjunctive occurs in indirect questions; in such cases the 1st person will obviously be replaced by the 2nd or 3rd person. On this ↑273e.

(4) Sometimes the deliberative subjunctive is also used in subordinate clauses that are not interrogative clauses, but may be understood as going back to deliberative questions, e.g.:

ὁ δὲ υἱὸς τοῦ ἀνθρώπου οὐκ ἔχει ποῦ τὴν κεφαλὴν **κλίνῃ** (3 sg. subj.)	*But the Son of Man has nowhere to rest his head.* (Mt 8:20 / Lk 9:58)

The subordinate clause may go back to the following kind of a deliberation question:
*ποῦ τὴν κεφαλὴν **κλίνω**; *Where should/can I rest my head?* or an indirect question:
*(ἠρώτων αὐτὸν) ποῦ τὴν κεφαλὴν **κλίνῃ**. *(They asked him,) where he could rest his head.*
↑also Mt 10:19; 12:14; 15:32; 22:15; 26:54; Mk 3:6; 6:36; 8:1; 9:6; 11:18; 13:11; 14:1.11.40; 15:24; Lk 5:19; 12:5.11.22.29; 22:2.4.11; Ac 4:21; 25:26.

(5) In Lk 11:5.7 a special use occurs (perhaps influenced by Semitic or popular Greek usage): The 3 sg. subj. is used (continuing a modal ind. fut.) in a question with conditional force (↑269d; BDF §366.1):

τίς ἐξ ὑμῶν ἕξει φίλον … καὶ **εἴπῃ** αὐτῷ· … (V. 7:) κἀκεῖνος … **εἴπῃ** … ≈	*Which of you would have a friend … and you would say to him: … and he would answer …:* ≈
(*if*-clause/protasis:) ἐάν τις ὑμῶν φίλον ἔχῃ … καὶ εἴπῃ αὐτῷ· … (*then*-clause/apodosis:) ἐκεῖνος … ἐρεῖ …	*Suppose one of you has a friend … and suppose you say to him … will he answer …?*

↑272e on the dependent desiderative clauses.

210e c) **prohibitive**: "prohibitive subjunctive", used in prohibitions, i.e. negative commands/directives, mostly directed to the 2nd person (less frequently the 3rd person), expressed by the negative particle **μή** (↑244) + **subjunctive aorist**, **replacing the negated imperative aorist** (not used in the 2nd person; ↑212c; 268), e.g.:

Μὴ ἀποβάλητε οὖν τὴν παρρησίαν ὑμῶν	*So do not throw away your confidence!* (He 10:35)
μὴ οὖν **μεριμνήσητε**.	*So do not worry!* (Mt 6:31)

↑also Mk 10:19; Mt 17:9; Ac 16:28; Ro 10:6; He 3:8.

In the NT the prohibitive subjunctive quite often is preceded (asyndetically; ↑293e) by

ὅρα, ὁρᾶτε, βλέπετε	*See to it/Take care/Watch out that* (sg./pl.)

Example:

Ὁρᾶτε μὴ καταφρονήσητε ἑνὸς τῶν μικρῶν τούτων·	*Take care that you do not despise any of these little ones.* (Mt 18:10)

↑272e on the dependent desiderative clauses.

210f d) **οὐ μή** + **subjunctive aorist** (less frequently indicative future; ↑202h) is used to express the **strongest negation of future "situations"** (↑247a and 248a),[55] e.g.:

οἱ δὲ λόγοι μου **οὐ μὴ παρέλθωσιν**.	*But my words will not/never pass away.* (Mt 24:35)

Very occasionally μή (or a compound) + subjunctive is used to express a cautious statement; ↑247c.

55 This use of the subjunctive (with a prospective force) regularly appears in subordinate clauses. It is, however, likely to go back to a subordinate clause use (↑BR §227.2d).

e) Occasionally the volitional subjunctive occurs in an independent ἵνα-clause (in CG more frequently in a ὅπως-clause; ↑268a/272), e.g.: 210g

ἡ δὲ γυνὴ **ἵνα φοβῆται** τὸν ἄνδρα.	*And the wife must respect her husband.* (Eph 5:33)

III. Subjunctive in **subordinate clauses**

1. In **subject-object clauses** the subjunctive may principally be used in the same way as in main clauses (in CG the subjunctive is sometimes replaced by the oblique optative [↑211f/211g], in the NT occasionally by the indicative future [↑202j]). Note, however, that the volitional or prospective subjunctive may occur in the following constructions: 210h

a) in **clauses subordinated by ἵνα** *that* (less frequently by ὅπως; CG by ὅπως + indicative future; in CG less widely used than in KG) replacing infinitive phrases (mostly desiderative clauses; ↑272/213c/217–221; also with explanatory/epexegetical force ↑222; also 225a; ↑BDF §369; 392);

b) in declarative clauses subordinated by μή *that* (or by μὴ οὐ *that … not*; ↑247b) dependent on **expressions of fearing** (sometimes to be supplied in thought; ↑271e) with the prospective subjunctive (less frequently with the indicative, when a past "situation" is the object of fear).

In CG expressions denoting *to take care* or the like (↑272d) were followed by subordinate clauses subordinated by ὅπως/ὅπως μή + subjunctive, but more frequently + indicative future (↑202j).

c) in **interrogative clauses** (indirect questions), when a corresponding direct question would have a **deliberative subjunctive**, with the 2nd or 3rd person obviously replacing the 1st person of the direct question (↑210d; 273a).

2. The **prospective** subjunctive (typically combined with the particle ἄν) or (less frequently) the **volitional** subjunctive is used in the following types of conjunctional clauses (mostly functioning as adverbials; 270; 288): 210i

a) in **temporal clauses** (↑276, in the NT fairly frequently without ἄν) subordinated by

ὅταν (CG also ὁπόταν) (less frequently post-CG also + ind.)	*when, as soon as, whenever* (↑211i)
ἐπάν (infrequently attested)	*as soon as*
ἕως (οὗ/ὅτου), ἕως ἄν (less frequently also + ind.)	*until; as long as*
ἄχρι(ς) (οὗ) (ἄν) (however, mostly + ind.)	*until; as long as*
μέχρι(ς) (οὗ) (in the NT apparently without ἄν)	*until* (CG also *as long as*)
ὡς ἄν (in Pauline texts, though infrequently)	*as soon as*
πρίν (CG: when main clause is neg., + ἄν + subj., or + ind., when affirmative, then + inf./ACI or + ἤ + inf./ACI; NT: usually + inf./ACI or + ἤ + inf./ACI)	*before*

b) in **purpose clauses** (↑278; NT occasionally + indicative future; ↑202j) subordinated by

ἵνα (less frequently ὅπως, CG also ὡς)	*so that* (= *in order that*)
ἵνα μή / ὅπως μή / μή (or μήποτε)	*so that … not* (= *in order that/lest …*)

c) in NT **result clauses** (↑279) subordinated by

ἵνα — *so that* (= *with the result that*)

d) in **conditional clauses** (*if*-clause/protasis; ↑280c; 282) subordinated by ἐάν *if* (with μή when negated): prospective case (in the NT occasionally has the ind. fut./pres. replacing the subj. [↑202j/209o]).

e) in **concessive clauses** (↑286) subordinated by

ἐάν καὶ or κἄν — *even if, even though*

f) in **manner clauses** (↑287; in principle the subj. use is the same as in main clauses).

210j 3. The **prospective** subjunctive also occurs in **relative clauses** (mostly attributive modifiers; ↑289/290):

a) + ἄν or ἐάν after the relative in a relative clause with a conditional force (↑290e).

b) in the NT without ἄν or ἐάν after the relative in a relative clause expressing a purpose or a result (↑290c/290d).

The hortatory subjunctive is used in the same way as in a main clause (↑288a; 290e).

211 Optative (↑BR §228; 230; Duhoux §190–197; BDF §384–386; Z §354–358; 346)

I. General observations:

211a 1. The optative was **disappearing in KG**. In the NT it is used merely ca. 67×, most frequently by Paul in the formulaic expression μὴ γένοιτο *By no means!* (↑211c).

2. As a non-indicative (and non-factual; ↑207a) verb form the optative (outside the future) does **not** express **any tense value** at all. The choice of the aorist, the present or (much less frequently; ↑203a) the perfect has to do with aspect considerations. The linguistic and non-linguistic context in which an optative appears will show how exactly the "action"/"situation" in question is meant to relate to other "situations" in terms of placement in time and how it is best translated into English. ↑192–195; 204; 208.

3. The optative future (unattested in the NT) occurs only as an oblique optative (↑211h).

II. Optative in **main clauses**

211b 1. In main clauses the modality (↑207d) expressed by the optative is to be understood in terms of either

a) an **obtainable wish** (deontic modality): "optative of wish", or

b) a **possibility** merely **in the thoughts of the speaker/writer** (epistemic modality): "potential optative", in CG regularly combined with ἄν in main clauses.

Note that these two uses are not always easy to distinguish (something that generally applies to the category of modality and its subdivisions; ↑207d sub-point c).

In subordinate clauses a number of further optative functions occur (↑211e–211i).

211c 2. The **optative of wish** is used by speakers/writers to express a **wish presented as obtainable**; in English it is typically translated by the addition of the modal *may*. More than half of the NT instances of the optative belongs here. Most frequently they are found in the final benedictions of Paul's letters; μή is used in negated wishes (↑244), e.g.:

Ὁ δὲ θεὸς τῆς ἐλπίδος **πληρώσαι** ὑμᾶς πάσης χαρᾶς καὶ εἰρήνης … — *May the God of hope fill you with all joy and peace …* (Ro 15:13)

Αὐτὸς δὲ ὁ θεὸς τῆς εἰρήνης **ἁγιάσαι** ὑμᾶς ὁλοτελεῖς, καὶ ὁλόκληρον ὑμῶν τὸ πνεῦμα καὶ ἡ ψυχὴ καὶ τὸ σῶμα … **τηρηθείη**. — *Now may the God of peace himself sanctify you completely, and may your whole spirit and soul and body be kept blameless …* (1Th 5:23)

παρακαλέσαι … καὶ **στηρίξαι** …. — *may he comfort … and strengthen …* (2Th 2:17)

Ὁ δὲ κύριος **κατευθύναι** ὑμῶν τὰς καρδίας εἰς τὴν ἀγάπην τοῦ θεοῦ … — *Now may the Lord direct your hearts into God's love …* (2Th 3:5)

Αὐτὸς δὲ ὁ κύριος τῆς εἰρήνης **δῴη** ὑμῖν τὴν εἰρήνην … — *Now may the Lord of peace himself give you peace …* (2Th 3:16)

μὴ αὐτοῖς **λογισθείη**. — *May it not be counted against them!* (2Tm 4:16)

… ἐγώ σου **ὀναίμην** ἐν κυρίῳ — *… may I have/let me have this benefit from you in the Lord!* (Phm 20)

The formulaic μὴ γένοιτο (lit. *may it not become/be!*) belongs here, too. It is used to express a strong negation, rendered e.g. as *By no means!, Not at all!, Never!, Of course not!* (AV/KJV *God forbid!*). Lk 20:16; Ro 3:4.6.31; 6:2.15; 11:1.11 etc.

The optative of wish is also used fairly widely in the LXX, e.g. in Nu 6:24–26 (Priestly Benediction).

In CG the optative of wish is typically preceded by the particle εἴθε or εἰ γάρ *o that!/if only!* (in poetry also by ὡς), e.g.:

εἴθε … φίλος ἡμῖν **γένοιο**. — *O that you … may come to be our friend.* (Xenophon, Hellenica 4.1.38)

On unobtainable wishes ↑209j.

On different types of independent desiderative clauses ↑268b.

3. The **potential optative** is used by speakers/writers to present a "situation" as 211d
something they consider possible in the present (or in the future or always possible), a use some call "potential of the present" (↑209i on the "potential of the past"). In English it is typically translated by the addition of modals such as *can/could* and *may/might* (↑207d sub-point d), sometimes underlined by *possibly*.

CG regularly adds ἄν in main clauses (↑211e; with οὐ, when negated; ↑245). In the NT this optative occurs rarely, almost exclusively in Lk and Ac, e.g.:

πῶς γὰρ **ἂν δυναίμην** ἐὰν μή τις ὁδηγήσει με; — *How could I possibly understand unless someone explains it to me?* (Ac 8:31)

τί **ἂν θέλοι** ὁ σπερμολόγος οὗτος λέγειν; — *What does/may this babbler (possibly) wish to say?* (Ac 17:18)

εὐξαίμην ἂν τῷ θεῷ …	*I (can/may) pray to God …* (Ac 26:29)

The potential optative also occurs in the *then*-clause (apodosis) of the potential conditional case, which is only partially attested in the NT (↑280c; 283).
↑also 211e.

The potential optative with ἄν may be **replaced by the indicative future** (in NT and CG; ↑202e; BDF §385.1), e.g.:

ἐπεὶ πῶς **κρινεῖ** ὁ θεὸς τὸν κόσμον;	*For then how could God judge the world?* (Ro 3:6)

In the LXX there are slightly more instances of the potential optative than in the NT, e.g. Gn 23:15; 33:10; 44:8; Dt 28:67; Job 11:5; 19:23; 4Macc 1:1; Sir 25:3; Is 66:20; Eze 15:2 etc.

III. Optative in **subordinate clauses**

211e 1. In conjunctional subject-object and relative clauses as well as in manner clauses (↑271–275; 289a; 287) the optative may principally be used in the same way as in main clauses. Note that the potential optative occurs also in the εἰ *if*-clause (protasis) of the potential conditional case (only partially attested in the NT), however, without ἄν (↑280b/283; with μή, when negated [↑246]), e.g.:

εἰ δ᾽ ἀναγκαῖον **εἴη** ἀδίκεῖν ἢ ἀδικεῖσθαι (*then*-clause/apodosis:) ἑλοίμην ἂν μᾶλλον ἀδικεῖσθαι ἢ ἀδικεῖν.	*But should it be necessary either to do wrong or suffer wrong,* *I would choose to suffer wrong rather than to do wrong.* (Plato, Gorgias 469c)
εἰ καὶ **πάσχοιτε** διὰ δικαιοσύνην, (*then*-clause/apodosis:) μακάριοι.	*Even if you should suffer for what is right,* *you are blessed.* (1Pe 3:14)

211f 2. The **oblique optative** (i.e. the optative of indirect utterance) may occur, without ἄν, in subordinate clauses, when the predicate verb of the superordinate clause expresses a past tense value (augment indicatives or historic/narrative indicative present). Speakers/writers use it as a replacement for indicatives, typically to indicate that the content of the clause represents someone else's view (usually the view of the subject entity of the superordinate clause). ↑also 205; 270h. It occurs

a) in dependent declarative clauses replacing the indicative (↑271),

b) in dependent desiderative clauses replacing the subjunctive (↑272),

c) in dependent interrogative clauses (indirect questions) replacing the indicative (↑273), sometimes (agreeing with the corresponding direct speech; ↑211e) the potential optative with ἄν (rather than the oblique optative) being used (↑273d, also 211d on NT usage),

d) in the following conjunctional (adverbial) clauses:
- in CG causal clauses replacing the indicative (↑277),
- in CG purpose clauses replacing the indicative (↑278).

When the optative replaces indicatives, οὐ is used as a negative particle, when it replaces a subjunctive, μή is used (↑245a).

211g **In the NT** the oblique optative **occurs very rarely**, if so, only in Lk/Ac, but even there never in ὅτι- or ὡς-clauses, e.g.:

ἀπεκρίθην ὅτι οὐκ ἔστιν ἔθος Ῥωμαίοις χαρίζεσθαί τινα ἄνθρωπον πρὶν ἢ ὁ κατηγορούμενος κατὰ πρόσωπον **ἔχοι** τοὺς κατηγόρους τόπον τε ἀπολογίας **λάβοι** περὶ τοῦ ἐγκλήματος.	*I answered them that it was not Roman practice to hand over anyone before the accused had faced the accusers and been given the opportunity to make a defence against the charge.* (Ac 25:16)

All the other NT instances are indirect questions. In such cases it is possibly better to interpret the optative as potential (the mood agreeing with the corresponding direct question; ↑273d), the omission of the particle ἄν perhaps being due to popular usage (↑Z §346; 339.2).

The **optative future** (without NT or [undisputed] LXX instance) occurs only as an oblique optative; it is used under the syntactic conditions described in 211f, replacing the indicative future, e.g.: 211h

ὁ θεὸς ἀπήγγειλεν **ὡς** παῖς αὐτῷ ἐκ Σάρρας **ἔσοιτο.**	*God announced to him that he would have a child with Sarah.* (Josephus, Antiquities 1.191)

The corresponding independent declarative clause would be:

*παῖς αὐτῷ ἐκ Σάρρας **ἔσται.**	*He will have a child with Sarah.*

3. The **iterative optative** (without ἄν) in a subordinate clause (+ μή, when negated; ↑246b) may refer to a repeated "action"/"situation" typically placed in the past, when the predicate verb of the superordinate clause is a durative verb form (mostly an imperfect), a use sometimes called "preterite/past iterative" (↑276d; on the "present iterative" ↑282b). This use is not found in the NT. In CG it occurs 211i

a) in temporal clauses (↑276e), e.g.:

ἐθήρευεν ἀπὸ ἵππου ὁπότε γυμνάσαι **βούλοιτο** ἑαυτόν	*He used to hunt on horseback whenever he wanted to exercise himself.* (Xenophon, Anabasis 1.2.7)

b) in relative clauses (↑290f), e.g.:

πάντας … ὅσους λάβοιεν … διέφθειρον.	*They would slaughter … all whomever they captured …* (Thucydides 2.67)

As a replacement for the CG iterative optative (without ἄν) NT/KG may use the **augment indicatives** (imperfect and indicative aorist; ↑198c/199f) **combined with ἄν or ἐάν** (↑252.3), a use termed "hellenistisches Nebensatziterativpräteritum" (Hellenistic preterite iterative of the subordinate clause) by Debrunner (↑BDAG sub ἄν Ιaα; BDR §367₂), e.g.:

ὅσοι ἂν ἥψαντο αὐτοῦ **ἐσῴζοντο.**	*All who touched him/it were made well.* (Mk 6:56)

Imperative (↑BR §229; Duhoux §200–205; 172–174; BDF §387; 335–337; Z §242–248; 254; also ↑231b[70]) 212

1. The imperative is used by speakers/writers to express obligations (deontic, but also epistemic modality; ↑207d), more particularly **directives**, i.e. to get somebody to behave in a particular way; these may be directives of the more direct type such as commands/commandments, orders, and instructions, but also directives of the more indirect type such as warnings, requests, advice, suggestions, and permissions.[56] Negated by **μή** (↑244), the imperative expresses **prohibitions**, but also less direct types of negative directives. The predominant 2nd person forms serve to get the listener(s)/reader(s) to behave in a particular way, the less frequent 3rd person ones to affect other entities somehow connected with the listener(s)/reader(s) who may be indirectly urged to take an active role (↑e.g. Mt 6:3 in 212d). Also ↑268b. Note that Ancient Greek imperatives are typically translated as English imperative phrases; quite often, however, they need to be rendered, 3rd person forms regularly so, by means of modals such as *must, should,* or *may/might* or (the 3rd person forms) by the imperative *let.* 212a

56 ↑Carter §412; Huddleston/Pullum: 29; 853.

212b 2. As non-indicative (and non-factual; ↑207a) forms imperatives do **not** express **any tense value** at all. The choice of the aorist, the present or (much less frequently; ↑203a) the perfect has to do with aspect considerations (but ↑212e). ↑192–195; 204; 208.

212c 3. In the **aorist prohibitions** are expressed not by the negated 2nd person imperative, but by the **prohibitive subjunctive** (↑210e). In the 3rd person both the negated imperative (aorist) and the subjunctive are used, the standard **paradigm** for expressing commands (etc.) and prohibitions by aorist and present forms being as follows:

	command etc. 2nd/3rd person	**prohibition** (negative directives) 2nd person	 3rd person
aorist (unmarked form) frequently specific directive	imp. aor.	μή + subj. aor.	μή + imp. aor. or μή + subj. aor.
present (durative) frequently general directive	imp. pres.	μή + imp. pres.	

4. Examples:

212d a) **aorist**: inconspicuous, unmarked form (↑194e–194j; 195), e.g.:

ἐπιδείξατέ μοι τὸ νόμισμα τοῦ κήνσου. (specific)	*Show me the coin used for paying the tax!* (Mt 22:19)
κήρυξον τὸν λόγον, **ἐπίστηθι** εὐκαίρως ἀκαίρως, **ἔλεγξον**, **ἐπιτίμησον**, **παρακάλεσον**, ἐν πάσῃ μακροθυμίᾳ καὶ διδαχῇ. (general; ↑context: εὐκαίρως ἀκαίρως e.g.)	*Proclaim the word, be ready in season and out of season, correct, rebuke, encourage, with great patience and careful teaching.* (2Tm 4:2)
μὴ ὀκνήσῃς διελθεῖν ἕως ἡμῶν (specific)	*Come to us without delay!* (Ac 9:38)
Πρεσβυτέρῳ **μὴ ἐπιπλήξῃς** ἀλλὰ παρακάλει ὡς πατέρα. (general; ↑context: imp. pres.)	*Do not rebuke an older man harshly, but speak to him as to a father.* (1Tm 5:1)
δειξάτω … τὰ ἔργα αὐτοῦ … (general; ↑context)	*Let him show his works …* (Jas 3:13)
ὅς … **μὴ καταβάτω** ἆραι αὐτά. (specific)	*Anyone who … must not come down to get them.* (Lk 17:31)
μὴ γνώτω ἡ ἀριστερά σου τί ποιεῖ ἡ δεξιά σου. (general; ↑context)	*Do not let your left hand* (lit. *Your left hand must not*) *know what your right hand is doing.* (Mt 6:3)

This is also the standard form used in prayers, in the NT almost exclusively (in CG mainly) so, e.g.:

κύριε Ἰησοῦ, **δέξαι** τὸ πνεῦμά μου … κύριε, **μὴ στήσῃς** αὐτοῖς ταύτην τὴν ἁμαρτίαν. (specific)	*"Lord Jesus, receive my spirit."* … *"Lord, do not hold this sin against them."* (Ac 7:59f)

Πάτερ ἡμῶν … **ἁγιασθήτω** … **ἐλθέτω** … **γενηθήτω** … **δός** … **ἄφες** … **μὴ εἰσενέγκῃς** … **ῥῦσαι** … (general; ↑context) — *Our Father … may … be kept holy, may … come, may … be done … give … forgive … do not lead … deliver …* (Mt 6:9–13)

b) **imperative present**: durative form (↑194a–194d; 195a–195b): 212e

• an **ongoing "action"** is to **continue** or, if negated, is to **stop** (linear or iterative), e. g.:

μόνον **πίστευε**. — *Only (continue to) believe.* (Mk 5:36)

μὴ κλαῖε. — *Don't weep/Stop crying!* (Lk 7:13; Re 5:5)

μὴ φοβοῦ. — *Do not fear! Don't be afraid!* (Mk 5:36; Ac 18:9; 27:24)

μή μου **ἅπτου** — *Do not hold on to me/Stop clinging to me!* (Jn 20:17; ↑BDAG sub ἅπτω 2b)

• an **"action"** is **to take place continually** (linear) or **repeatedly** (iterative) or, if negated, **never** (or: not continually/not repeatedly), e. g.:

αἰτεῖτε … **ζητεῖτε** … **κρούετε** … — *Ask (continually) … seek (continually) … knock (continually) …* (Lk 11:9)

… **μὴ προμεριμνᾶτε** τί λαλήσητε. — *… do not (ever) worry beforehand about what to say.* (Mk 13:11)

μὴ θροεῖσθε· — *do not (ever) be alarmed.* (Mk 13:7)

Note that the imperative present of a small number of verbs is used without a durative nuance (↑198l regarding to the imperfect; the imp. pres. is used "perhaps for politeness", so Turner 1963: 75):

ἔγειρε — *stand up!* (interjection-like use; ↑252.63; also ↑103.5)

ἔρχου/ἔρχεσθε — *come!*

πορεύου/πορεύεσθε — *go!*

ὕπαγε/ὑπάγετε — *go!*

φέρε/φέρετε — *bring!* (rarely used in the NT)

c) Very occasionally the NT uses the imperative perfect passive (↑Zerwick-Grosvenor on Mk 4:39):

σιώπα, **πεφίμωσο**. — *Quiet! Be still!* (really *"Be silenced!"*) (Mk 4:39)

ἔρρωσθε (conventional letter closing; ↑124.6) — *Farewell!* (Ac 15:29)

5. Directives may be preceded by the following particles (↑252.63; ↑hortatory subjunctive: 210c): 212f

δεῦρο / δεῦτε — *Come!*

ἄγε (in the NT only Jas 5:1; CG also φέρε) — *Come!*

Example:

δεῦτε ἴδετε τὸν τόπον ὅπου ἔκειτο. — *Come, see the place where he lay.* (Mt 28:6)

Also ↑210e on ὅρα, ὁρατε, βλέπετε *See to it/Take care* (sg./pl.) preceding the prohibitive subjunctive.

6. Note that the indicative future (negated by οὐ; ↑202f), infinitive phrases (218d), participle phrases (↑231k), and independent ἵνα-clauses (↑210g) may serve as replacements for the imperative. On desiderative clauses in general ↑268. 212g

3.2.2.4 Non-finite verb (nominal verb forms) (↑64e; 325ff)

(i) Infinitive

213 Infinitive: preliminaries (↑BR §231; 238; Duhoux §211ff; BDF §388; Z §380ff; 406–411; Langslow: 324ff)

213a 1. The main function of the Ancient Greek infinitive is to refer to the "action" of the verb; like other verb forms, it does so expressing also a particular voice and aspect, as a non-finite form, however, no person, number or mood. As it is a nominal verb form, there is both a verb-like and a noun-like side to its use:

a) **Like other verbs forms** it expresses a particular voice and aspect, e.g.:

voice:	δοῦναι (act.) *to give*	δόσθαι (mid.) *to give for o.s.*	δοθῆναι (pass.) *to be given*
aspect:	διδόναι (pres.) *to give (repeatedly)*	δοῦναι (aor.) *to give*	δεδωκέναι (pf.) *to have given*

Frequently infinitives have the role of a predicator with objects, other kinds of complements or adjuncts, often even with a subject (↑216a) of their own. Such infinitive phrases typically have a sentence-like function: they are used to refer to a real-world "situation", and like subordinate clauses (↑270g), they serve as sentence constituents of the superordinate clause they belong to, e.g. (infinitive phrase with a direct object and a object adjunct, similar to a purpose clause, serving as an adjunct of purpose of the superordinate clause):

δοῦναι (P) **τὴν ψυχὴν αὐτοῦ** (Od) **λύτρον ἀντὶ πολλῶν** (OA) (InfP/PurpA ≈ purpose clause)	*(in order) to give his life as a ransom for many* (Mt 20:28)

b) **Like a noun** (phrase) an infinitive phrase may have the role inter alia of[57]

- a nominative noun phrase (functioning as a subject; ↑217),
- an accusative noun phrase (functioning as an object; ↑218/219), or
- a dative noun phrase (functioning as an optional adverbial [adjunct; ↑220/219], sometimes as an obligatory adverbial [complement; ↑217f/219]).
- Moreover it may be preceded by the neuter article (τό, τοῦ, τῷ), often embedded in a preposition phrase (↑223–226); used in this way, it may have a whole range of syntactic functions (i.e. as sentence constituents or attributive modifiers).

213b 2. **Ancient Greek** infinitive phrases may be translated typically as **English** infinitive phrases (by *to*-infinitive phrases unless ruled out syntactically e.g. by a modal verb like *will/would* etc. [↑207d] preceding them). Quite often, however, they need to be rendered by other means, as the use of the Ancient Greek infinitive is quite different from its English counterpart, the more striking peculiarities being as follows:

57 Keep in mind that infinitives never have any case endings. Their case role is generally inferable from the context, most clearly when they are preceded by the article.

a) ACI constructions are used more widely (↑216);

b) infinitive/ACI phrases with ὥστε *so that* in the role of an adverbial of result (↑221);

c) infinitive/ACI phrases with τοῦ in the role of an attributive modifier, but especially of adverbial of purpose or result or manner (explanatory/epexegetical) (↑225);

d) infinitive/ACI phrases with πρίν (ἤ) *before* (↑276);

e) infinitive/ACI phrases with the neuter article (τό, τοῦ, τῷ), often embedded in a preposition phrase (↑223–226).

In most of the above cases the infinitive/ACI phrases will be translated as subordinate clauses, sometimes also as nominalized *-ing* form (gerund) phrases (↑227b), e.g.:

ἐνόμιζεν δὲ **συνιέναι τοὺς ἀδελφοὺς αὐτοῦ** …	*He thought that his brothers would understand* … (Ac 7:25)
…**μετὰ τὸ παθεῖν αὐτόν** …	… *after his suffering* … (Ac 1:3)

3. Differences between CG and KG usage: 213c

a) **Some** types of **constructions** are used **more widely in KG**, thus the one used as an adverbial of purpose (↑220) and certain articular varieties with or without governing preposition (↑223ff), especially those with τοῦ (↑225).

b) On the other hand, **in KG quite often** infinitive/ACI constructions are replaced by **subordinate clauses** subordinated by ἵνα (less frequently ὅπως) *that* (usually dependent desiderative clauses; ↑272a/278) or by ὅτι *that* (dependent declarative clauses; ↑218g/271).

c) The so-called **"absolute" infinitive**, used quite frequently in a number of CG idiomatic phrases, occurs only once in the NT (↑BR §238; BDF §391/BDR §391.6):

ὡς ἔπος εἰπεῖν	*so to speak, one might even say* (He 7:9; literary style)

In CG also inter alia:

(ὡς) ἐμοὶ δοκεῖν	*as it seems to me, in my opinion*
ὀλίγου δεῖν	*little missing, almost*
τὸ νῦν εἶναι	*for the present*

d) In CG the **particle ἄν** (↑252.3) is often used in infinitive phrases with potential or irrealis force (as a replacement for the potential optative [↑211d/211e] or for augment indicatives with ἄν [↑209h]), a use **unattested in the NT** (↑BR §248; BDF §396), e.g.:

… ὥστε καὶ ἰδιώτην **ἂν γνῶναι** (= ἂν ἔγνω) …	… *so that even a layman could have perceived* … (Xenophon, Anabasis 6.1.31)

Infinitive and tense/aspect meanings 214

As non-indicative forms infinitives (outside the future) do **not** express any **tense value** at all. The choice of the aorist, the present or the perfect has to do with aspect considerations. ↑192–195; 204 (especially the examples listed there).

Note, however, that in specific contextual-syntactic circumstances infinitives may as part of certain constructions **seemingly** express absolute **time**, thus when ACI/infinitive phrases express a declaration or question and are dependent on a (superordinate) clause with a past tense value (↑205). On relative time seemingly expressed by infinitives ↑206c (with overview and examples).

215 Negated infinitive phrases ↑BR §233.1/2 Note 2; 234 Note 4; page 241; BDF §429; Z §440ff)

In the NT infinitive phrases are always negated by μή (↑244; 246c), e.g.:

ἀπεκρίθησαν **μὴ** εἰδέναι πόθεν.	*They answered that they did not know where it came from.* (Lk 20:7)

↑also Ac 20:20; 21:12; Ro 6:6; 1Pe 3:10.

In CG οὐ is used when the infinitive phrase depends (as it does in the above NT example) on a verb of purely cognitive attitude or assertion (↑245d), e.g.:

οἴομαι **οὐκ** εἰδέναι.	*I think that I do not know.* (Plato, Apology 29b)

216 Cases inside infinitive phrases: ACI et al (↑BR §232; 235; BDF §405–410; Z §393–395)

216a 1. When in an infinitive phrase the **subject** (↑255g) of the "action" is expressed, it is **usually** in the (subject) **accusative** (↑149a). Such a construction is termed "ACI" (short for Latin *accusativus cum infinitivo* "accusative with infinitive"). Fairly frequently an Ancient Greek ACI construction may be translated as a comparable English construction (especially when it is dependent on a verb of volition; ↑218), e.g.:

Θέλω δὲ **ὑμᾶς** (ACI-S) **εἰδέναι** …	*Now I want you to realize …* (1Cor 11:3)
ἠρώτησαν **αὐτὸν** (ACI-S) **ἐπιμεῖναι** …	*They asked him to stay …* (Ac 10:48)

In many other cases a subordinate clause (↑213b) will be preferred (very often due to the valency of the superordinate verb or "stylistic" considerations), e.g.:

εὔχομαί **σε** (ACI-S) … **ὑγιαίνειν**	*I pray that … you may be in good health.* (3Jn 2)

This regularly happens also when inf./ACI phrases are combined with the article, especially those embedded in a preposition phrase (↑226), e. g.:

μετὰ τὸ **γενέσθαι με** (ACI-S) ἐκεῖ …	*After I have been there …* (Ac 19:21)

216b 2. The **CG rule** says that the ACI is to be used only when the subject of the infinitive phrase is not already mentioned in the superordinate clause (in Latin it is to be used even when the subject is already mentioned):

Ancient Greek:	Latin:	
νομίζω σε εἰδέναι.	*puto te scire.*	*I think that you know.*
νομίζω __ εἰδέναι.	*puto **me** scire.*	*I think that I know.*

NT examples:

ἐνόμιζεν (S of superordinate clause) δὲ **συνιέναι τοὺς ἀδελφούς** (InfP-S: ACI) …	*He thought that his brothers would understand …* (Ac 7:25)

Εἰ δέ **τις** ἀσχημονεῖν ἐπὶ τὴν παρθένον αὐτοῦ νομίζει … (InfP-S in superordinate clause)	*If anyone thinks he is acting improperly towards his fiancée …* (1Cor 7:36)

↑Vulgate: *Si quis autem turpem* ***se*** *videri existimat super virgine sua …*

3. This **rule** is **not always** followed in the **NT** (nor in KG generally): 216c

a) The subject accusative is sometimes **used** against the CG rule, e.g.:

πέποιθάς τε **σεαυτὸν** ὁδηγὸν εἶναι τυφλῶν.	*And you are confident that you are a guide for the blind.* (Ro 2:19)

↑also Ac 25:4.21; Ro 6:11; Php 3:13.

b) The subject accusative is sometimes **not used** against the CG rule, e.g.:

τότε ὁ Πιλᾶτος ἐκέλευσεν __ ἀποδοθῆναι. (no ACI despite change of S)	*Then Pilate ordered it* (i.e. Jesus' body) *to be handed over.* (Mt 27:58)

↑Vulgate: *Tunc Pilatus jussit reddi* ***corpus****.*

↑also Mt 13:5; 18:13; 23:23; 24:6; 24:24 Var.; 26:54; Mk 1:27; 3:10; 4:5; 13:7; Lk 2:26; 11:8.42; 12:12; Ac 9:43; 12:15.19; 15:2 Var.; 15:29; 17:26f; 18:3; 19:16; 20:35; 26:28; 27:21; He 9:14; 12:10; 1Pe 4:3.

4. In certain cases the subject of the "action" of the infinitive phrase is in the genitive or dative, due to the valency of the superordinate verb. It would thus be possible to speak of a kind of "GCI" (*genitivus cum infinitivo* "genitive with infinitive") and "DCI" (*dativus cum infinitivo* "dative with infinitive"), in the NT at times alternating (partly in a non-classical way) with an ACI, e.g.: 216d

δέομαί **σου ἐπιβλέψαι** ἐπὶ τὸν υἱόν μου. (GCI)	*I beg you to look at my son.* (Lk 9:38)
ἔγραψα **ὑμῖν μὴ συναναμίγνυσθαι** … (DCI)	*I am writing to you not to associate …* (1Cor 5:11)

↑also Ac 11:26 ("DCI" dependent on ἐγένετο).

5. **Case of subject and sentence constituents modifying it** in an ACI (or GCI/DCI): 216e

a) Sentence constituents modifying the subject of an ACI are in the accusative, too, i.e. subject complements ("SC"; ↑258) as well as any other sentence constituent expected to show concord (↑259q),[58] e.g.:

μή τίς **με** (ACI-S) δόξῃ **ἄφρονα** (ACI-SC) **εἶναι**.	*Let no one think that I am a fool.* (2Cor 11:16)

↑also Ac 9:32; 19:16.

Such sentence constituents are, however, in the nominative, when the subject of the superordinate verb is also the subject of the (simple) infinitive phrase dependent on it (a construction called "nominative with infinitive" ["NCI"]; ↑218g), e.g.:

εἴ **τις** (S) δοκεῖ **σοφὸς** (SC) **εἶναι** …	*If anyone thinks he is wise …* (1Cor 3:18)

↑also Jn 7:4; Ro 1:22; 9:3; 2Cor 10:2; Jas 4:4.

---

58 A direct object dependent on the infinitive remains, as one would expect, in the accusative.

b) When the subject of an infinitive phrase is in the **genitive** or **dative** ("GCI" or "DCI"; ↑216d), a sentence constituent modifying it, such as a subject complement or an adverbial participle phrase expected to show concord, **may be** either in the **same case** as the subject **or** in **the accusative**, e. g.:

ἐπίτρεψόν **μοι** (InfP-S) **ἀπελθόντι** (Advl/PtcP dat. like the S) … **θάψαι** …	*… let me go and bury …* (Lk 9:59)

↑also Ac 16:21.

… τοῦ δοῦναι **ἡμῖν** (InfP-S) ἀφόβως ἐκ χειρὸς ἐχθρῶν **ῥυσθέντας** (Advl/PtcP acc. unlike the S) **λατρεύειν** αὐτῷ.	*… to grant us that we, being rescued from the hand of our enemies, might serve him without fear.* (Lk 1:73f)

↑also Mt 18:8.9; Lk 5:7; Ac 11:12; 15:22; 25:27; 26:20.

c) When no subject is expressed in the infinitive phrase, a sentence constituent meant to modify it, is in the accusative, e. g.:

… οὕτως **κοπιῶντας** (ManA/PtcP [meant to modify the unexpressed InfP-S]) δεῖ **ἀντιλαμβάνεσθαι** τῶν ἀσθενούντων.	*… by working hard in this way we must help the weak.* (Ac 20:35)
φιλάνθρωπον (SC meant to modify the unexpressed InfP-S) **εἶναι** δεῖ.	*One must be humane/a lover of human beings.* (Isocrates 2.15)

(a) Non-articular infinitive/ACI

217 Infinitive/ACI phrases as subjects (↑BR §234; Duhoux §214; 224; BDF §393; Z §406–408)

217a Infinitive/ACI (GCI or DCI; ↑216d) phrases may serve as the subject (corresponding to a nominative noun phrase; ↑213a; 255b) of **impersonal verbs** and expressions with a comparable use (in the NT such phrases may be replaced by a clause subordinated by ἵνα *that,* unless a past "situation" is to be referred to; ↑272a):

217b
• ἔξεστιν + inf., DCI / (sometimes) ACI	*it is right, it is permitted*
• δυνατόν ἐστιν, (not in the NT:) ἔστιν	*it is possible*
• ἀδύνατον (with out without ἐστίν)	*it is impossible*

Example:

ἔξεστιν (P) **δοῦναι κῆνσον Καίσαρι** (S) ἢ οὔ;	*Is paying the imperial tax to Caesar right or not?/Is it right to pay the imperial tax to Caesar, or not?* (Mk 12:14)

217c
• δεῖ, δέον ἐστίν, also (NT 1×!) χρή	*it is necessary, one must*
• ἀναγκαῖον (with or without ἐστίν) (similarly ἀνάγκη ↑217f)	*it is necessary* (negated: *it is unnecessary*)
• συμφέρει + inf./DCI/ACI	*it is profitable/useful*

Example:

εἰ οὕτως ἐστὶν ἡ αἰτία τοῦ ἀνθρώπου μετὰ τῆς γυναικός (CondA), **οὐ συμφέρει** (P) **γαμῆσαι** (S).	*If this is the situation between a husband and his wife, marrying is not profitable/ it is better not to marry* (Mt 19:10)

Note that in declarative clauses negated δεῖ means *one must not* (as in English; this applies analogously to negated δέον ἐστίν and χρή, but not to negated ἀναγκαῖον/ἀνάγκη [ἐστίν], which means *it is unnessary/one need not* [unattested in the NT]), e.g.:

... ὅπου **οὐ δεῖ** (ἑστάναι).	*... where it ought not (to stand).* (Mk 13:14)
... **οὐκ ἀναγκαῖον εἶναι** ... τοῦτο ποιεῖν	*... (he said) that it was unnecessary to do this ...* (Josephus, Antiquities 7.319)

However, in rhetorical questions with οὐ (to be understood as affirmations; ↑245b) it means *is it not necessary? = it is necessary/one must*, e.g.:

οὐχὶ ταῦτα **ἔδει** παθεῖν τὸν χριστόν;	*Did not the Messiah have to suffer these things? = The Messiah had to suffer ...* (Lk 24:26)

• καλόν (ἐστίν) + inf./DCI/ACI	*it is good*	217d
• δοκεῖ + DCI	*it seems good*	
• πρέπει + DCI/ACI	*it is fitting/proper*	
• δίκαιον (with or without ἐστίν) + inf./ DCI, also + ACI (not in the NT)	*it is right*	

Example:

ῥαββί, καλόν (SC) ἐστιν (P) **ἡμᾶς ὧδε εἶναι** (S).	*Rabbi, for us to be here is good/it is good for us to be here.* (Mk 9:5)

• γίνεται, mainly CG also συμβαίνει	*it happens/comes about*	217e

Example:

ἐγένετο (P) **αὐτόν ... παραπορεύεσθαι** (S).	*He was passing ...* (lit. *His passing ... came about*) (Mk 2:23)

↑also Mt 18:13; Lk 3:21; 6:1.6; 16:22; Ac 4:5; 9:3.32.37.43; 14:1; 19:1; 21:1.5; 27:44; 28:8.

συνέβη (P) ... **Γέλωνα καὶ Θήρωνα νικᾶν**	*Gelon and Theron won a victory.* (lit. *Gelon's and Theron's winning a victory came about*) (Herodotus 7.166)

↑also Ac 21:35 (only συμβαίνει instance in the NT).

Note that the above use of ἐγένετο agrees with standard Ancient Greek usage. The following construction, however, frequently occurring in the LXX and NT narrative texts, is clearly a Hebraism: /ἐγένετο + adverbial + καί (or without καί) + finite verb form/
(↑/וַיְהִי *wayhî* + adverbial + waw-imperfect/, GKC §111f/g; 114e; BDF §442.4/5; Z §389), e.g.:

Ἐγένετο δὲ ἐν μιᾷ τῶν ἡμερῶν **καὶ** αὐτὸς ἐνέβη εἰς πλοῖον.	*One day he got into a boat.* (lit. *But/And it came about one day that he got into a boat.*) (Lk 8:22)

Delitzsch: ... וַיְהִי הַיּוֹם וַיֵּרֶד *wayhî hayyôm wayyēreḏ* ...

Ἐγένετο δὲ ἐν ταῖς ἡμέραις ἐκείναις ἐξῆλθεν δόγμα παρὰ Καίσαρος Αὐγούστου. — *In those days a decree went out from Caesar Augustus.* (lit. *But/And it came about in those days that a decree* …) (Lk 2:1)

Delitzsch: … וַיְהִי בַּיָּמִים הָהֵם וַתֵּצֵא *wayhî bayyāmîm hāhēm wattēṣē['] …*

↑LXX for instance:[59]

καὶ ἐγένετο μετὰ τὰ ῥήματα ταῦτα καὶ ἐπέβαλεν ἡ γυνὴ τοῦ κυρίου αὐτοῦ … — *After these events his master's wife cast* … (lit. *And it came about after these events that his master's wife cast* …) (Gn 39:7)

Hebr.: … וַיְהִי אַחַר הַדְּבָרִים הָאֵלֶּה וַתִּשָּׂא *wayhî 'aḥar haddəḇārîm hā'ēlleh wattiśśā['] …*

Further NT instances: Mt 7:28; 9:10; 11:1; 13:53; 19:1; 26:1; Mk 1:9; 4:4; Lk 1:8.23.41.59; 2:6.15. 46; 5:1.12.17; 6:12; 8:1; 14:1.

↑226a on the Hebraizing ἐν + τῷ + InfP as part of the above construction.

217f Noteworthy points:

When **noun phrases** connect with a non-articular infinitive/ACI phrase, they may have the role of a subject or object (depending on their case form); the inf./ACI phrase governed by them corresponds to a dative noun phrase (dative of interest; IntC; ↑259m/176a; 219/220),[60] e.g. in constructions like these:

ὥρα (ἐστίν), καιρὸν ἔχω — *it is the hour/time, I have time/opportunity*

Example:

ὥρα (S) … **ὑμᾶς ἐξ ὕπνου ἐγερθῆναι** (IntC). — *It is time … for you to wake up.* (lit. … *for your waking up*) (Ro 13:11)

↑also He 11:15; 1Pe 4:3 (χρόνος *time*).

Comparable expressions: ἀνάγκη/ἀνάγκην *necessity* (↑217c): Mt 18:7; Lk 14:18; Ro 13:5; He 7:27; 9:16.23; Jd 3; ἐξουσία/ἐξουσίαν *authority*: Mt 9:6; Mk 3:15; Lk 12:5; Jn 1:12; 5:27; 10:18; 19:10; Ac 9:14; Ro 9:21; 1Cor 9:4–6; He 13:10; Re 9:10; 11:6; χρεία/χρείαν *need*: Mt 3:14; 14:16; Jn 13:10; 1Th 1:8; 4:9; 5:1; He 7:11; similarly also ὦτα *ears* (↑Dt 29:3 or Is 32:3): Mk 4:9.23; Lk 8:8; 14:35.

In such cases, too, the NT may replace the inf./ACI phrase by a clause subordinated by ἵνα *that* (↑272a), e.g. in Mt 26:16; Jn 16:30; 1Jn 2:27.

218 Infinitive/ACI phrases as objects (↑BR §233; Duhoux §214; 224; BDF §392; 396f; Z §406–408)

Infinitive/ACI (GCI or DCI; ↑216d) phrases may serve as the object of (↑257c):

218a 1. Verbs of **volition** (of will or desire in a narrower and wider sense; with infinitive/ACI phrases corresponding to a desiderative clause; ↑268; 272).

---

59 Interestingly, in the LXX the future counterpart of this Hebrew construction (וְהָיָה *wəhāyā* …) is rendered as (καὶ) ἔσται … (not γενήσεται … or the like), e.g. in Gn 9:14; 12:12. In the NT this idiom occurs only in connection with OT quotations: Ac 2:17ff (Jl 3:1ff); 3:23 (↑Dt 18:19); Ro 9:26 (Ho 2:1).

60 Its function here is not too far removed from that of a genitive attributive modifier (↑260e). For in most cases these noun phrases may also connect with attributive modifiers (↑Adrados 1992: 642) in the form of a genitive of appurtenances (↑159–165) or a genitive of separation (↑169a), e.g. ὥραν τῆς προσευχῆς *hour of prayer* (Ac 3:1), χρείαν … μαρτύρων *need of witnesses* (Mk 14:63); ↑also e.g. ἐξουσίαν τοῦ (!) πατεῖν *authority to tread* (Lk 10:19), on this ↑225.

Typical verbs used in this way are:[61]

βούλομαι; θέλω (CG ἐθέλω) etc.	*to desire, to want*
αἰτέω; αἰτέομαι; παρακαλέω; δέομαι + GCI etc.	*to ask (for), to request*
κελεύω + inf./ACI, παραγγέλλω + inf./DCI etc.	*to give orders, to command*
ἐάω + inf./ACI; ἀφίημι + inf./ACI; ἐπιτρέπω + inf./DCI; δίδωμι + DCI/ACI *to grant (permission/ power), to permit,* at times *to cause* (similarly also χαρίζομαι + DCI)	*to allow, to permit*
κωλύω (↑247a on negation) (also + τοῦ + InfP; ↑225c)	*to stop (s.o. from doing sth.), to prevent, to forbid*
ἀναγκάζω; ἀγγαρεύω (1× ellipsis of inf., 2× + ἵνα-clause)	*to compel, to force*
ποιέω	*to make s.o. do sth.*

Examples:

Βούλομαι οὖν **προσεύχεσθαι τοὺς ἄνδρας ἐν παντὶ τόπῳ** (Od)	*I desire/want the men in every place to pray* (1Tm 2:8)
θέλεις **ὑγιὴς γενέσθαι** (Od);	*Do you want to get well?* (Jn 5:6)
παρεκάλει ὁ Παῦλος **ἅπαντας μεταλαβεῖν τροφῆς** (Od).	*Paul urged all of them to take some food.* (Ac 27:33)
ἄφετε **τὰ παιδία ἔρχεσθαι πρός με** (Od).	*Permit the little children to come to me.* (Mk 10:14)
ποιήσω **ὑμᾶς γενέσθαι ἁλιεῖς ἀνθρώπων** (Od).	*I will make you become fishers of people.* (Mk 1:17)

Note that in KG and in the NT many of these verbs often combine with a clause subordinated by ἵνα 218b
(less frequently by ὅπως) + subj. *that* rather than an inf./ACI phrase (↑210h; 272a).
In CG many verbs combine with ὥστε + inf./ACI (↑221), some of them with ὅπως + ind. fut. (↑202j).

NT examples:

Πάντα οὖν ὅσα ἐὰν θέλητε **ἵνα ποιῶσιν ὑμῖν οἱ ἄνθρωποι …** (Od)	*So whatever you want people to do for you …* (Mt 7:12)
παρακαλοῦσιν αὐτὸν (Od of person) **ἵνα ἐπιθῇ αὐτῷ τὴν χεῖρα** (Od of thing).	*They begged him to place his hand on him.* (Mk 7:32)

Noteworthy points:

(1) Regarding the voice of infinitives depending on verbs signifying *to give orders* or *to prevent* CG 218c
and NT usage differ when the subject of the "action" is not expressed in the infinitive phrase:

61 Note that verbs of communication such as λέγω *to say* sometimes express volition, too (↑218f[62]). At times (1Th 2:12; 3:10; 2Th 2:2) εἰς + τό + InfP serves as a Od (otherwise as an Advl; ↑226).

(a) CG uses the infinitive active, e.g.:

βασιλεύς … ἐκέλευε **παραδιδόναι** (act.) τὰ ὅπλα. ↑Lat.: … *arma **tradi*** (pass.) *iussit.* (BR §233.1 Note 2)	*The King … ordered [us] to give up our arms.* (Xenophon, Anabasis 3.1.27)
ἐκέλευσεν ἔξω βραχὺ τοὺς ἀνθρώπους **ποιῆσαι** (act.; CG usage).	*He gave orders to put the men/… the men to be put outside for a short time.* (Ac 5:34)

↑Vulgate: *iussit foras ad breve homines **fieri*** (pass.).

(b) In the NT the infinitive passive is typically used (like in Latin, and apparently in English), e.g.:

ἐκέλευσεν τὸν Παῦλον **ἀχθῆναι** (pass.).	*He ordered Paul to be brought.* (Ac 25:6)

↑Vulgate: *iussit Paulum **adduci*** (pass.).

218d (2) The so-called **"imperatival" infinitive** may best be mentioned here. It occurred very much in Homer, but rarely in CG prose. It is a use going back to a construction with a verb of volition in the superordinate clause. In the NT there are two instances (↑BR §239; Duhoux §230; BDF §389):

χαίρειν μετὰ χαιρόντων, κλαίειν μετὰ κλαιόντων.	*Rejoice with those who rejoice, weep with those who weep.* (Ro 12:15)
πλὴν εἰς ὃ ἐφθάσαμεν, τῷ αὐτῷ **στοιχεῖν**.	*Only let us live up to what we have already attained.* (Php 3:16)

The infinitive χαίρειν is also used as a standard salutation in Ancient Greek letters, with ἐπιστέλλω *to say (by means of a letter), to write* or λέγω *to say* to be supplied in thought (ellipsis; ↑293c), e.g.:

Κλαύδιος Λυσίας (sc. ἐπέστειλα/ἐπέστειλε or the like) τῷ κρατίστῳ ἡγεμόνι Φήλικι χαίρειν.	*Claudius Lysias [sends] to the most excellent governor Felix, greetings.* (Ac 23:26)

↑also Ac 15:23; Jas 1:1; also inter alia 1Macc 10:18; 2Macc 9:19; also 2Jn 10f (for a greeting outside a letter context, without ellipsis).

In the letters of Paul, also (in a slightly different way) in those of Peter and in the Book of Revelation χαίρειν is replaced by a combination of χάρις *grace* and (שָׁלוֹם *šālôm* >) εἰρήνη *peace.*

↑268 on the desiderative clauses in general.

218e 2. The following types of verbs usually combine with a (simple) infinitive phrase as their object:

a) verbs expressing **ability** or **knowledge**, especially:

δύναμαι, ἰσχύω	*can, to be able*
οἶδα (↑109c) γινώσκω (only Mt 16:3 + inf.) ἐπίσταμαι (not + inf. in the NT)	*to know/understand (how)* (↑218k and 233b on further uses)

b) verbs of **teaching** or **learning**, mainly:

διδάσκω – μανθάνω	*to teach – to learn*

Note that, semantically, verbs of teaching are manifestly connected with verbs of learning, syntactically, however, with verbs of volition (↑218a): an ACI phrase may serve as their object, e.g.:

κύριε, δίδαξον ἡμᾶς προσεύχεσθαι.	*Lord, teach us to pray.* (Lk 11:1)

c) verbs signifying "to **dare**" or "to **hesitate**", mainly:

τολμάω	*to dare*
ὀκνέω (1× in the NT), μέλλω	*to hesitate, to delay*

Note that CG often uses μέλλω like this, so also Ac 22:16 (↑also 4Macc 6:23), in the NT, however, its predominant meaning is *to be about (to)* + inf. (↑202k)

d) verbs indicating an **obligation**, a **habit**, et al:

ὀφείλω	*to be under obligation, must, ought*
εἴωθα (*ἔθω; ↑108g)	*to be accustomed*
ἄρχομαι (in CG also + PtcP)	*to begin*

Note that the fairly frequent use of ἄρχομαι + InfP in the Synoptic gospels (especially Mk, repeatedly its meaning being somewhat toned down) is best not classified as an Aramaism (as suggested by many), but as a normal KG phenomenon, widely attested in popular and non-classicizing narrative literature of the Hellenistic period (↑Reiser 1984: 11–12, especially 43–45, where he demonstrates that Mark's use of ἄρχομαι and other phenomena is anything but a Semitism and that he uses his Greek with absolute confidence ["es sich hier um alles andere als einen Semitismus handelt und Markus sich seines Griechisch durchaus sicher ist"]).

Examples:

Οὐδεὶς δύναται **δυσὶ κυρίοις δουλεύειν** (O).	*No one can serve two masters.* (Mt 6:24)

↑also Lk 6:39; 16:2; Jn 15:4f; Mt 26:40; Lk 16:3.

εἰ οὖν ὑμεῖς … οἴδατε **δόματα ἀγαθὰ διδόναι** (O) …	*If you then … know how to give good gifts …* (Lk 11:13)
μὴ ὀκνήσῃς **διελθεῖν ἕως ἡμῶν** (O).	*Do not delay to come to us/Come to us without delay.* (Ac 9:38; ↑259c, p. 458)
… εἰώθει ὁ ἡγεμὼν **ἀπολύειν ἕνα** … (O).	*… the governor was accustomed to release one …* (Mt 27:15)

3. Verbs of **communication** or **cognitive attitude** (with infinitive/ACI phrases cor- 218f
responding to a declarative clause [↑267; 271]; in the NT this use is more limited than in CG [↑206c]):[62]

a) verbs of **saying** (i.e. of asserting), mainly:

λέγω, φημί	*to say*
ἀπαγγέλλω	*to announce*
μαρτυρέω (in the NT only He 11:4 + inf.)	*to testify*

b) verbs of **thinking** or the like, mainly:

δοκέω, νομίζω, ἡγέομαι (in the NT only Php 3:8 + ACI), οἴομαι (2× in the NT)	*to think, to suppose*
ἐλπίζω	*to hope*
πιστεύω (in the NT rarely + inf.: Ac 15:11)	*to believe* (i.e. *to consider it true*)

62 Note that verbs such as λέγω *to say* may be used in the sense of both "to declare" and "to desire/to give orders", e.g.:

a) ἔλεγον αὐτὸν εἶναι θεόν.	*They said (= declared) he was a god.* (Ac 28:6)

(inf./ACI phrase corresponds to a declarative clause)

b) ἐγὼ δὲ λέγω ὑμῖν μὴ ἀντιστῆναι τῷ πονηρῷ·	*But I tell (= command) you, do not resist the evil-doer.* (Mt 5:39)

(inf. phrase corresponds to a desiderative clause; ↑218a)

Examples:

λέγω γὰρ **Χριστὸν διάκονον γεγενῆσθαι περιτομῆς** (Od) … *For I tell you that Christ has become a servant to the Jews …* (Ro 15:8)

ἐδόκουν **πνεῦμα θεωρεῖν** (Od). *The thought they saw a ghost.* (Lk 24:37)

↑also Jn 5:39; 1Cor 3:18; Jas 1:26.

… νομίζων **ἐκπεφευγέναι τοὺς δεσμίους** (Od) *… because he thought the prisoners had escaped.* (Ac 16:27)

↑also Lk 2:44.

τοῦτον μὲν οὖν ἐλπίζω **πέμψαι** … (Od). *I therefore hope to send him …* (Php 2:23)

c) Additional notes on above uses (↑275 for an overview of alternative constructions):

218g • In the NT verbs of **communication** (i.e. of asserting), apart from a few exceptions even in CG, frequently combine with a clause subordinated by ὅτι *that* et al (↑271b) rather than with an inf./ACI phrase, e.g.:

ὑμεῖς λέγετε **ὅτι ἐγώ εἰμι**. *You say that I am.* (Lk 22:70)

καὶ λέγουσιν **ὅτι Λακεδαιμονίοις δοκεῖ στρατεύεσθαι ἐπὶ Τισσαφέρνην** *And they said that Lacedaemonians had resolved to undertake a campaign against Tissaphernes.* (Xenophon, Anabasis 7.6.1)

CG further uses the following constructions (the NT only occasionally):

(1) The "**nominative with infinitive**" ("NCI"; ↑216e; in Ancient Greek it occurs less frequently than in Latin): a **personal passive** (↑191c) + **infinitive** (↑English *He is said to …*), e.g.:

ἐμαρτυρήθη εἶναι δίκαιος. *He was attested to be righteous.* (He 11:4; singular NT example)

ἐνταῦθα λέγεται Ἀπόλλων ἐκδεῖραι Μαρσύαν. *There Apollo is said to have flayed Marsyas.* (Xenophon, Anabasis 1.2.8)

(2) An **impersonal passive + ACI** (↑Engl. *It is said that …*), e.g.:

ἦν αὐτῷ κεχρηματισμένον ὑπὸ τοῦ πνεύματος τοῦ ἁγίου μὴ ἰδεῖν (sc. αὐτὸν [↑216c]) θάνατον πρὶν ἤ … *It had been revealed to him by the Holy Spirit that he would not see death before …* (Lk 2:26)

λέγεται … ἄνδρα τινά … ἐκπεπλῆχθαι … *It is said … that a certain man … had been struck …* (Xenophon, Cyropaedia 1.4.27)

Other NT instances comparable to the above constructions combine with a ὅτι-clause: a) personal passive: Jn 3:21; 2Cor 3:3; 1Jn 2:19; b) impersonal passive: Mk 2:1 (possibly personal; ↑BDF §405); 1Cor 15:12 (apparently prolepsis [↑292b] of the ὅτι-clause subject: Εἰ δὲ Χριστὸς κηρύσσεται ὅτι … = Εἰ δὲ κηρύσσεται ὅτι Χριστός *But if it is preached that Christ …* [↑BDAG sub ὅτι 1f]).

218h • In CG (in the NT less clearly) verbs of **thinking** regularly combine with an infinitive phrase.

218i • Verbs of **showing** and **reporting** (δηλόω *to make clear, to show*, ἀπαγγέλλω *to report* et al) including the corresponding impersonal expressions also combine with infinitive/ACI phrases in the NT (sometimes with a ὅτι-clause; ↑271b); in CG this is possible, too, though a combination with an ACP phrase is more common (but which is not attested in the NT with this type of expressions; ↑233c), e.g.:

τοῦτο δηλοῦντος τοῦ πνεύματος τοῦ ἁγίου, **μήπω πεφανερῶσθαι τὴν τῶν ἁγίων ὁδόν** (ACI phrase).	*The Holy Spirit was showing by this that the way into the Most Holy Place had not yet been disclosed.* (He 9:8)
πρόδηλον γὰρ **ὅτι ἐξ Ἰούδα ἀνατέταλκεν ὁ κύριος ἡμῶν** (ὅτι-clause).	*For it is clear that our Lord descended from Judah.* (He 7:14)

• The verbs of **sensual** and **mental perception** (ἀκούω *to hear*, ὁράω *to see*, γινώσκω/οἶδα *to know*) may sometimes combine with an inf./ACI phrase, however, more frequently with a ὅτι-clause (↑271b) or with an ACP phrase (in part with a GCP phrase; ↑233b, on possible differences of meaning also ↑167a), e.g.: 218j

ἀκούω **σχίσματα ἐν ὑμῖν ὑπάρχειν** (ACI).	*I hear that there are divisions among you.* (1Cor 11:18)
Ἠκούσατε ὅτι **ἐρρέθη** (ὅτι-NS) …	*You have heard that it was said …* (Mt 5:27)
Ἀκούομεν γὰρ **τινας περιπατοῦντας ἐν ὑμῖν ἀτάκτως** (ACP phrase).	*For we hear that some among you are living undisciplined lives.* (2Th 3:11)

• Occasionally ACI phrases and ὅτι-clauses occur in combination (CG and NT Greek [Ac 27:10]). 218k

• On infinitives seemingly expressing tense when subordinate to a verb of saying (communication), of thinking/believing (cognitive attitude), of showing/announcing or of (sensual or mental) perception, ↑205; 206c; 271d. 218l

Infinitive phrases as complements of adjectives (↑BR §237; Duhoux §215; BDR §393.3) 219

Infinitive phrases[63] may also serve as complements, i.e. as 2nd degree objects (↑254c), of certain adjectives, whose pattern of use typically requires an object (↑158b; 163b; 175; on a similar use of infinitive phrases with τοῦ ↑225a), e.g.:

ἱκανός *sufficient, qualified/fit*	ἄξιος *worthy*

Examples:

… ἱκανὸς (adj.: SC) **τὰ ὑποδήματα βαστάσαι** (O/2nd).	*… I am not qualified/fit to carry his sandals.* (Mt 3:11)
οὐκέτι εἰμὶ ἄξιος (adj.: SC) **κληθῆναι υἱός σου** (Og/2nd).	*I am no longer worthy to be called your son.* (Lk 15:19)

↑also 2Cor 3:5.

↑also: δυνατός *capable*: Lk 14:31; Ac 11:17; Ro 4:21; Tt 1:9; He 11:19; ἐλεύθερος *free*: 1Cor 7:39.

An analogous use occurs with ἔχω + adverb, a construction that is similar in meaning to εἰμί *to be* + a corresponding adjective (BDAG sub ἔχω 10b), e.g.:

ἐγώ … καὶ **ἀποθανεῖν** … **ἑτοίμως** (adv.) **ἔχω**.	*I am ready … even to die.* (Ac 21:13)

63 Based on the original dative function of the infinitive (↑217f; 220a).

ἕτοιμοι (adj.) γάρ ἐσμεν **ἀποθνῄσκειν**.	*For we are ready to die.* (4Macc 9:1)

In the NT the inf./ACI phrase may be replaced by a clause subordinated by ἵνα + subj. *that* (↑272a), e.g.:

οὐ … ἱκανός (adj.: SC) εἰμι **ἵνα ὑπὸ τὴν στέγην μου εἰσέλθῃς** (Og/2nd).	*I am not worthy to have you enter under my roof.* (Lk 7:6)

220 Infinitive/ACI phrases as adverbials of purpose (↑259j)

(↑BR §237; Duhoux §228; BDF §390; Z §381; 392)

220a Infinitive/ACI phrases quite often serve as adverbials of purpose with a function closely similar to purpose clauses subordinated by ἵνα (also ὅπως) + subjunctive *in order that*. This use is sometimes called "**infinitive of purpose**".[64] Usually it is best translated as a *to*-infinitive phrase or (when the subject needs to be mentioned) as an *in-order-that/so-that* clause. The infinitive of purpose occurs more frequently in the NT/KG than in CG, especially after

220b 1. verbs of **motion** (in CG typically with participle future; ↑206h) such as

ἔρχομαι; πορεύομαι	*to come; to go/travel*
ἀναβαίνω; καταβαίνω	*to go up; to go/come down*
ἐπιστρέφω, ὑποστρέφω	*to turn around, to return*
ἐγγίζω	*to come near, to approach*

Examples:

ἀνέβη εἰς τὸ ὄρος **προσεύξασθαι** (PurpA).	*He went up to the mountain to pray.* (Lk 9:28)
ἦλθον δὲ καὶ τελῶναι **βαπτισθῆναι** (PurpA).	*Even tax collectors came to be baptized.* (Lk 3:12)

↑also Mt 5:17; 10:34; 12:42; 20:28; Lk 17:18; Jn 4:7; 1Tm 1:15.

220c 2. verbs of **sending**, **giving** or the like (CG and NT usage) such as

πέμπω, ἀποστέλλω	*to send*
δίδωμι; παραδίδωμι	*to give; to give/hand over*

Examples:

ἔπεμψεν αὐτὸν εἰς τοὺς ἀγροὺς αὐτοῦ **βοσκεῖν χοίρους** (PurpA).	*He sent him to his fields to feed the pigs.* (Lk 15:15)
καὶ ἐδίδου τοῖς μαθηταῖς **παραθεῖναι τῷ ὄχλῳ** (PurpA).	*And he gave them to the disciples to set before the crowd.* (Lk 9:16) (↑Mk 6:41: ἵνα παρατιθῶσιν [purpose clause])

Note that the InfP after verbs of giving or the like sometimes serves as their direct object, e.g.:

---

64 Or "infinitive with dative force": the dative function that the Ancient Greek infinitive apparently had surfaces very clearly here (in terms of the dative of interest; ↑176).

δότε αὐτοῖς ὑμεῖς **φαγεῖν** (Od). | *You give them something to eat!* (Lk 9:13)

↑259j on other constructions expressing purpose.

On cases of infinitives (without ὥστε; ↑221) expressing a result ↑279.

3. In the NT such infinitive phrases are occasionally used like a Hebrew לְ *lə* + infinitive (construct) indicating manner typically rendered as *(by)* + *-ing* form in English (GKC §114 o/p; also ↑225f), e.g.: 220d

ἀντελάβετο Ἰσραὴλ παιδὸς αὐτοῦ, **μνησθῆναι ἐλέους** (ManA; ↑259f). | *He has helped his servant Israel, (by) remembering his mercy.* (Lk 1:54)

On a comparable use of infinitive phrases with τοῦ ↑225f, with εἰς τό or πρὸς τό ↑226b.

Infinitive/ACI phrases as adverbials of result (↑259i) 221

(↑BR §275; Duhoux §227; BDF §391; Z §350–353)

1. Infinitive/ACI phrases may also serve as adverbials of result, a use sometimes called "**infinitive of result**". It is typically introduced by the particle ὥστε (CG also ὡς) *so that* (= *with the result that*), e.g.: 221a

οὐκ ἀπεκρίθη αὐτῷ πρὸς οὐδὲ ἓν ῥῆμα, **ὥστε θαυμάζειν τὸν ἡγεμόνα λίαν.** (ResA). | *He gave him no answer, not even to a single charge, so that the governor was quite amazed.* (Mt 27:14)

↑also Mk 2:12; Ac 16:26; Ro 7:6; 15:19; 2Cor 3:7; Php 1:13.

Example without ὥστε:

οὐ γὰρ ἄδικος ὁ θεὸς **ἐπιλαθέσθαι** ... (ResA). | *For God is not unjust so as to forget …* (He 6:10)

↑also Ac 5:3; 16:14; Ro 1:28.

Note that in KG this construction may not only refer to an actual or conceivable result, but also to an intended result, i.e. a purpose. Due to this, in a few NT instances a purpose is indicated (↑259j), reference to an actual or conceivable result, however, being the norm, e.g.: 221b

ἤγαγον αὐτὸν ἕως ὀφρύος τοῦ ὄρους … **ὥστε κατακρημνίσαι αὐτόν** (PurpA). | *They led him to the brow of the hill … in order to throw him off the cliff.* (Lk 4:29)

↑also Lk 9:52; 20:20.

2. With reference to an actual result ὥστε in CG is followed by the indicative, a use only rarely attested in the NT (↑279a). 221c

3. Infinitive/ACI phrases expressing a result may be replaced by a clause subordinated by ἵνα + subj. *(so) that* (↑279a), e.g.: 221d

τίς ἥμαρτεν … **ἵνα τυφλὸς γεννηθῇ** (ResA); | *Who sinned … that he was born blind?* (Jn 9:2)

↑also Lk 9:45.

4. On the occasional Semitizing uses indicating manner ↑220d. 221e

On infinitive/ACI phrases preceded by the conjunction πρίν (ἤ) *before* ↑276.

On the CG infinitive/ACI phrases preceded by ἐφ᾽ ᾧ or ἐφ᾽ ᾧτε *on condition that* or *in order to/in order that* ↑280b (also 278a); 184j.

222 Explanatory infinitive/ACI phrases as appositions (↑BDF §394; Z §410)

Infinitive/ACI phrases may also have an explanatory role, i.e. to explain ("epexegetically") a noun phrase, quite often specifically a demonstrative pronoun, in this way functioning as an apposition (↑260h), e.g.:

τοῦτο (S) γάρ ἐστιν (P) θέλημα τοῦ θεοῦ (SC[id]), ὁ ἁγιασμὸς ὑμῶν (App 1 to S), **ἀπέχεσθαι ὑμᾶς ἀπὸ τῆς πορνείας** (App 2).	*For this is God's will: your sanctification: that you keep away from sexual immorality.* (1Th 4:3)
θρησκεία καθαρά … (SC[id]) αὕτη (S) ἐστίν (P), **ἐπισκέπτεσθαι ὀρφανούς** … (App).	*Religion that is pure … is this: to look after orphans …* (Jas 1:27)
ὁ δὲ θεός (S), ἃ (↑142c) προκατήγγειλεν διὰ στόματος πάντων τῶν προφητῶν (relative clause = Od) **παθεῖν τὸν χριστὸν αὐτοῦ** (App to Od), ἐπλήρωσεν (P) οὕτως.	*But the things God foretold by the mouth of all the prophets – that his Messiah would suffer – he has fulfilled in this way.* (Ac 3:18)

↑also Ac 15:28f; 20:24; 26:16; 1Cor 7:37; 2Cor 10:13; Eph 1:9f; 3:4–6; 3:8; 4:21–24 (the infinitives explain the οὕτως/τοῦτο to be supplied in thought as an object of ἐδιδάχθητε); He 9:8.

Explanatory infinitive/ACI phrases, too, may be replaced by a clause subordinated by ἵνα + subj. *that* (sometimes by a clause subordinated by ὅτι *that* or some other construction; ↑272a; 288), e.g.:

αὕτη (S) γάρ ἐστιν (P) ἡ ἀγάπη τοῦ θεοῦ (SC[id]), **ἵνα τὰς ἐντολὰς αὐτοῦ τηρῶμεν** (App to S).;	*For the love is this: that we keep his commandments.* (1Jn 5:3)

On a corresponding use with the article τό ↑224b and τοῦ ↑225a/225f.

(b) Articular infinitive/ACI

223 Articular infinitive/ACI phrases: preliminaries

(↑BR page 241; Duhoux §218; BDF §398; Z §382; Turner 1963: 140)

An infinitive/ACI phrase may be preceded by the neuter singular article (τό, τοῦ, τῷ), which highlights its use as a noun phrase (↑213a). As the infinitive itself is without case endings, it is only the article that changes its form in the course of the declension of such infinitive/ACI phrases (inter alia when they are governed by a particular preposition). Generally speaking, such phrases are usually best translated as a subordinate (conjunctional) clause, sometimes by an *-ing* form (gerund) phrase especially those embedded in a preposition phrase (↑216a; 226; 227b). Articular infinitive/ACI phrases are part of higher KG usage. In the LXX they seem to be (comparatively) more frequent than in the NT.

Infinitive/ACI phrases with simple article 224

(↑BR §236.1.2; Duhoux §218; 221; BDF §399; 401; Turner 1963: 140–142)

1. Infinitive/ACI phrases with simple article, i.e. one that is not governed by a preposition, may principally serve as a subject, object or adverbial of the superordinate verb (on the peculiarities of the infinitive/ACI with τοῦ ↑225): 224a

a) as a **subject** (↑255b), e.g.:

τὸ δὲ **ἀνίπτοις χερσὶν φαγεῖν** (S) οὐ κοινοῖ (P) τὸν ἄνθρωπον (Od).	*But eating with unwashed hands does not defile anyone.* (Mt 15:20)

↑also Mk 9:10; 10:40; 12:33; Ro 7:18; 14:21; 1Cor 7:26; 2Cor 7:11; 9:1; Php 1:21.24.29; He 10:31.

b) as an **object** (↑257c), e.g.:

οὐχ ἁρπαγμὸν (OC[id]) ἡγήσατο (S/P) **τὸ εἶναι ἴσα θεῷ** (Od).	*He did not consider equality with God something to cling to.* (Php 2:6)

↑also Mt 20:23; Ac 25:11; 1Cor 14:39; 2Cor 8:10f; 10:2; Php 2:13.

c) as an **adverbial** (↑259c), only 1× in the NT:

… **τῷ μὴ εὑρεῖν με Τίτον τὸν ἀδελφόν μου**. (CausA)	*… because I did not find my brother Titus.* (2Cor 2:13)

(in KG τῷ + InfP may also be used as an instrumental adverbial; ↑177)

2. Infinitive/ACI phrases with the simple article may, moreover, serve as an **apposition** to the preceding noun phrase (↑260h), e.g.: 224b

ἡ ἐπαγγελία (S) …, **τὸ κληρονόμον αὐτὸν εἶναι κόσμου** (App to S)	*The promise … that he would be the heir of the world* (Ro 4:13)

↑also Ro 14:13; 2Cor 2:1.

On a corresponding use of non-articular infinitive/ACI phrases (↑222).

Note that in the NT the infinitive/ACI with simple article is mainly used by Paul.

Infinitive/ACI phrases with τοῦ 225

(↑BR §236 Note 1 page 242; Duhoux §218; BDF §400; Z §383–386; 392; 411)

1. In the NT infinitive/ACI phrases with τοῦ are to be classified mainly as genitives of appurtenances (↑159, especially 164), less frequently as a genitive of separation (↑169). It occurs in a number of **different constructions** such as (it belongs to higher KG usage, but only to limited extent to CG usage): 225a

a) part of a **noun phrase** (as an attributive modifier; ↑260d; also in CG), e.g.:

ὁ χρόνος (αἱ ἡμέραι) **τοῦ τεκεῖν αὐτήν** (Attr)	*the time* (Lk 2:6 *the days*) *for her to give birth* (Lk 1:57)
εὐκαιρίαν **τοῦ παραδοῦναι αὐτόν** (Attr)	*an opportunity to hand him over* (Lk 22:6)

↑also Lk 10:19; 24:25; Ac 9:15; 14:9; 20:3; 27:20; Ro 8:12; 11:8; 15:23; 1Cor 9:10; 2Cor 8:11; Php 3:21; 1Pe 4:17.

This construction, too, may be replaced by a clause subordinated by ἵνα + subj. *that* (↑272a; 288b), e.g.:

ἐλήλυθεν ἡ ὥρα **ἵνα δοξασθῇ ὁ υἱὸς τοῦ ἀνθρώπου** (Attr).
The hour has come for the Son of Man to be glorified. (Jn 12:23)

b) part of an **adjective phrase** (Og/2nd, ↑254c; 163b; also in CG), e.g.:

… βραδεῖς τῇ καρδίᾳ **τοῦ πιστεύειν** … (Og/2nd)
… slow of heart to believe … (Lk 24:25)

ἕτοιμοί ἐσμεν **τοῦ ἀνελεῖν αὐτόν** (Og/2nd)
We are ready to kill him (Ac 23:15)

↑also 1Cor 16:4.

On a comparable use without τοῦ ↑219.

c) connected with a **verb** (mostly serving as an adverbial [↑259c], less frequently as an object [for details ↑225b–225f]; fairly frequently in cases where an infinitive/ACI phrase without τοῦ is attested with a comparable use; in CG acceptable only to a limited extent), e.g.:

… ὃν (Od) κατέστησεν (P) ὁ κύριος (S) ἐπὶ τῆς οἰκετείας αὐτοῦ (Op) **τοῦ δοῦναι αὐτοῖς τὴν τροφὴν ἐν καιρῷ** (PurpA).
… whom his master has put in charge of his household to give them their food at the proper time. (Mt 24:45)

Used as an object: Ac 3:12; 21:12; used as a subject: Lk 17:1; Ac 27:1.

2. **Details** on the function of infinitive/ACI phrases with τοῦ connected with a **verb**:

225b a) In most cases they indicated a **purpose** (as a PurpA; ↑genitive of direction or purpose [↑164]), also apparently fairly frequently with verbs that otherwise connect with non-articular infinitive/ACI phrases, inter alia with verbs of motion (frequently in the NT, rarely in CG; ↑220), e.g.:

μέλλει γὰρ Ἡρῴδης ζητεῖν τὸ παιδίον **τοῦ ἀπολέσαι αὐτό** (PurpA).
For Herod is going to search for the child to kill him. (Mt 2:13)

εἰσῆλθεν **τοῦ μεῖναι σὺν αὐτοῖς** (PurpA).
He went in to stay with them. (Lk 24:29)

↑also Mt 3:13; 11:1; 13:3; Lk 4:42; 5:7; 12:42; Ac 3:2; 13:47; 18:10; 26:18; Php 3:10; He 10:7.

↑259j on other constructions expressing purpose.

225c b) Infinitive/ACI phrases with τοῦ sometimes clearly indicate a **result** (*so that* = *with the result that*; ↑221), especially with verbs of hindering e.g.:

οἱ δὲ ὀφθαλμοὶ αὐτῶν ἐκρατοῦντο **τοῦ μὴ ἐπιγνῶναι αὐτόν** (ResA)
But their eyes were kept from recognizing him (= *… were kept so that they did not recognize him*). (Lk 24:16)

μήτι τὸ ὕδωρ δύναται κωλῦσαί τις **τοῦ μὴ βαπτισθῆναι τούτους** (ResA);
Surely no one can refuse the water for these people to be baptized (= *… water so that these people are not baptized*)? (Ac 10:47)

Note that without μή this infinitive/ACI construction would be equivalent to one in the role of an object (↑218a); ↑e.g. Ro 15:22.

↑also Ac 20:20; Ro 1:24; 7:3; 1Cor 10:13 (really Attr of ἔκβασιν); He 11:5; 1Pe 3:10.

↑259i on other constructions expressing a result.

c) Infinitive/ACI phrases with τοῦ also combine with verbs that (due to their valen- 225d
cy) require a **genitive object** (↑257c; genitive of separation [↑169]; also in CG), e.g.:

… ὥστε ἐξαπορηθῆναι ἡμᾶς καὶ **τοῦ ζῆν** (Og).	… *so that we despaired of life itself.* (2Cor 1:8)

Note that in a fair number of NT instances (especially in Lk and Ac) the preference for an infinitive/ 225e
ACI phrase with (apparently pleonastic) τοῦ may be due to a Hebraizing style of writing: in the LXX this construction frequently stands for Hebrew לְ *lə* + infinitive (construct) phrases. e.g.:

Ὡς δὲ ἐκρίθη **τοῦ** ἀποπλεῖν ἡμᾶς εἰς τὴν Ἰταλίαν …	*And when it was decided that we should sail for Italy …* (Ac 27:1)
↑ἔκρινα __ πέμπειν.	*I decided to send him.* (Ac 25:25)

LXX example:

τοῖς ἀγγέλοις αὐτοῦ ἐντελεῖται περὶ σοῦ **τοῦ** διαφυλάξαι σε.	*He will command his angels concerning you to guard you.* (Lk 4:10 / Ps 90:11)
Hebr.: מַלְאָכָיו יְצַוֶּה־לָּךְ לִשְׁמָרְךָ בְּכָל־דְּרָכֶיךָ	*mal'āḵâw yəṣawweh-lāḵ lišmorḵā bəḵol-dərāḵêḵā*

↑also Ac 3:12; 10:25; 15:20; 21:12; 23:20; Jas 5:17; also examples of ↑225b/225c.

d) Infinitive/ACI phrases with τοῦ may also have an **explanatory** role, i.e. to ex- 225f
plain ("epexegetically") the superordinate expression (a verb, a noun, or a whole construction; ↑222 for a comparable use without τοῦ), e.g.:

ἐκάκωσεν τοὺς πατέρας ἡμῶν **τοῦ ποιεῖν** … (= ποιῶν or καὶ ἐποίει) (ManA [↑259f], perhaps apposition to a clause [↑260k])	*He oppressed our ancestors by forcing them …* (Ac 7:19)

This use appears to be a **Semitism**, too (↑GKC §114 o). In 1Sm 12:17 for instance the Hebrew original and Aramaic (Targum Jonathan) version read as follow:
(*You will realize and see what a great sin you have committed before Yhwh*)
Hebr.:

לִשְׁאוֹל לָכֶם מֶלֶךְ *liš'ôl lāḵem meleḵ*	*by demanding a king for yourself.*

Aram.:
לְמִשְׁאַל לְכוֹן מַלְכָּא *ləmiš'al ləḵôn malkā'*

In such instances the LXX may use an infinitive/ACI phrase with τοῦ (e.g. 1Kgs 2:3) or without τοῦ (e.g. Ex 23:2), often, however, a manner participle phrase instead, thus in 1Sm 12:17 αἰτήσαντες.
↑Z §392.

Articular infinitive/ACI phrases governed by prepositions 226

(↑BR §236.3; Duhoux §218; 221; 226–229; BDF §402–404; Z §387–392; Turner 1963: 142f)

1. An articular infinitive/ACI phrase governed by a preposition usually serves as an 226a
adverbial adjunct of the superordinate clause (↑259aff/258c; 325ff; very occasionally as an object or an attributive modifier). In most cases it is best translated as an adverbial clause. This use occurs more frequently in KG than in CG.

On the various types of adverbial constructions ↑259d–259m (general overview); 276ff (adverbial clauses).

a) In the NT the following prepositions govern articular infinitive/ACI phrases:

preposition	meaning (↑184/185)	English conjunction in standard renderings	adverbial function
διά + acc. (27× in the NT)	*because of*	*because*	causal (↑259g; 277)
εἰς + acc. (63× in the NT)(1)	*into, to*	*in order to, so that/in order that* *so that/with the result that* (also ↑226b)	indicating purpose (↑259j; 278) indicating result (↑259i; 279)
ἐν + dat. (52× in the NT)	*in, during, at* (in most cases) *with, by means of* (at times)(2)	*while* (with inf. PRES.), *when/after* (with inf. AOR.: simultaneity [!] or anteriority; especially Lk/Ac) *by/in* + *-ing* form	temporal (↑259e; 276; not used in CG, probably a Hebraism [↑בְּ *bə* + infinitive construct, GKC §114e], frequently preceded by ἐγένετο [↑וַיְהִי *wayhî*]) indicating manner (↑259f)
μετά + acc. (15× in the NT)	*after*	*after*	temporal (↑259e; 276)
πρό + gen. (9× in the NT)	*before*	*before*	temporal (↑259e; 276)
πρός + acc. (12× in the NT)	*to, towards*	*in order to, so that/in order that* possibly *so that/with the result that* (also ↑226b) possibly *by* + *-ing* form (↑226b)	indicating purpose (↑259j; 278) indicating result (↑259i; 279) indicating manner (↑259f)

(1) Occasionally used as an Od (↑218a[61]).
(2) Occasionally perhaps *because of – because* (cause), ↑Turner 1963: 145f.

Attested only 1× in the NT:

ἀντί + gen.	*instead of*	*instead of* + *-ing* form	Jas 4:15 (also in CG)
διά + gen.	*through*	*during* + *-ing* form	He 2:15 (temporal)
ἐκ + gen.	*out of, according to*	*according to* + *-ing* form	2Cor 8:11 (causal/manner)
ἕνεκεν + gen.	*on account of*	*so that/in order that*	2Cor 7:12 (purpose)
ἕως + gen.	*until*	*until*	Ac 8:40 (temporal)

Note that CG also uses:

ἐπί + dat.	*over, because of*	*because* *so that/in order that*	causal indicating purpose
περί + gen.	*around, concerning*	*so that/in order that*	indicating purpose
ὑπέρ + gen.	*on behalf of*	*so that/in order that*	indicating purpose

b) Examples:

- **διά** + acc. *because of – because*:

… **διὰ τὸ μὴ ἔχειν ῥίζαν** (CausA) — *… because they had no root.* (Mt 13:6)

- **εἰς** + acc. *into, to – in order to, so that/in order that; so that/with the result that* (for occasional alternatives ↑218a[61] and 226b), e.g.:

… **εἰς τὸ δοκιμάζειν ὑμᾶς** (PurpA) — *… so that you may discern* (Ro 12:2)

… **εἰς τὸ εἶναι αὐτοὺς ἀναπολογήτους** (ResA) — *… so that/with the result that they have no excuse.* (Ro 1:20)

- **ἐν** + dat. *in, during – while* (with infinitive present), e.g.:

ἐν δὲ τῷ καθεύδειν τοὺς ἀνθρώπους (TempA) ἦλθεν αὐτοῦ ὁ ἐχθρός … — *But while everyone was sleeping, his enemy came …* (Mt 13:25)

at – when, after (with infinitive aorist, especially Lk/Ac), e.g.:

καὶ **ἐν τῷ εἰσαγαγεῖν τοὺς γονεῖς τὸ παιδίον Ἰησοῦν** (TempA) … — *And when the parents brought in the child Jesus …* (Lk 2:27)

Ἐν δὲ τῷ λαλῆσαι (TempA) ἐρωτᾷ αὐτὸν Φαρισαῖος … — *After he had spoken* (or *As he was speaking*)*, a Pharisee asked him …* (Lk 11:37)

preceded by καὶ ἐγένετο … (a Hebraism in this construction; ↑217e), e.g.:

καὶ ἐγένετο ἐν τῷ ὑπάγειν αὐτοὺς (TempA) ἐκαθαρίσθησαν. — *And (it came about that) as they were going they were cleansed.* (Lk 17:14)

Delitzsch: וַיְהִי בְּלֶכְתָּם וַיִּטְהָרוּ *wayhî b̲əlek̲tām wayyiṭhārû*

LXX/Hebrew example:

καὶ ἐγένετο ἐν τῷ εἰσελθεῖν αὐτὸν πρὸς Δαυιδ καὶ ἔπεσεν ἐπὶ τὴν γῆν. — *And (it came about that) when he came to David, he fell to the ground.* (2Sm 1:2 LXX)

Hebr.: וַיְהִי בְּבֹאוֹ אֶל־דָּוִד וַיִּפֹּל אַרְצָה *wayhî bəb̲ōʼô ʼel-dāwīḏ wayyippōl ʼarṣāh*

with, by means of – by/in + -ing form, e.g.:

… **ἐν τῷ ἀποστρέφειν ἕκαστον** … (ManA) (↑BDAG sub ἀποστρέφω 2a) — *… by turning each of you away/in each of you turning away …* (Ac 3:26)

TempA or ManA: Lk 12:15; Ac 4:30.

- **μετά** + acc. *after – after*, e.g.:

… **μετὰ τὸ ἀναστῆναι αὐτόν** (TempA) — *… after he rose from the dead.* (Ac 10:41)

↑also Mt 26:32; Lk 12:5.

- **πρό** + gen. *before – before*, e.g.:

… **πρὸ τοῦ τὸν κόσμον εἶναι** (TempA) — *… before the world existed.* (Jn 17:5)

↑also Lk 22:15; Ga 3:23.

- **πρός** + acc. *to, towards – in order to, so that/in order that* (↑also 226b), e.g.:

… **πρὸς τὸ θεαθῆναι αὐτοῖς** (PurpA) — *… (in order) to be seen by them.* (Mt 6:1)

↑also Mt 13:30; 2Cor 3:13; Eph 6:11.

226b 2. Note that infinitive/ACI phrases with πρός or εἰς in some cases may possibly be interpreted as indicating manner in analogy with a Hebr. or Aram. לְ *lə* + infinitive (↑225f; 220d; 221), e. g.:

πᾶς ὁ βλέπων γυναῖκα **πρὸς τὸ ἐπιθυμῆσαι αὐτήν** (ManA; ↑259f)	*Everyone who looks at a woman with lust for her/lustfully* (or else in terms of purpose or result:) *… with lustful intent/… in such a way that he feels lust for her*) (Mt 5:28)

↑Z §391; Turner 1963: 144; BDAG sub πρός 3cγ/3eε.

In Lk 18:1 hat πρός + acc. probably has the sense *with a view to, with reference to* (↑184p):

… **πρὸς τὸ δεῖν** πάντοτε προσεύχεσθαι αὐτούς.	*… with a view to the fact/to show that should always pray.*

↑Turner 1963: 144; BDF §402.5.

On (non-articular) infinitive/ACI phrases preceded by the conjunction πρίν (ἤ) *before* ↑276.

On the CG (non-articular) infinitive/ACI phrases preceded by ἐφ' ᾧ or ἐφ' ᾧτε *on condition that* or *in order to/in order that* ↑280b (also 278a); 184j.

(ii) Participle

227 Participle: preliminaries (↑BR §240; Duhoux §242ff; BDF §411; Langslow: 354ff)

227a 1. The main function of the Ancient Greek participle is to present the "action" of the verb as the property (either actual or potential) of an entity, e.g. διδούς *one who gives (repeatedly)* (↑below), i.e. a person with the property of repeated giving. Like other verb forms, it also expresses a particular voice and aspect, as a non-finite form, however, basically no mood or person. Morphologically it is treated like an adjective (↑48), and so inflects for gender, number and case. As it is a nominal verb form, there is both a verb-like and a noun-like side to its use:

a) **Like other verbs forms** it expresses a particular voice and aspect, e.g. (here translated as a nominalized participle; ↑237b):

voice:	δούς (act.) *one who gives/gave*	δόμενος (mid.) *one who gives/gave for himself*	δοθείς (pass.) *one who is/was given*
aspect:	διδούς (pres.) *one who gives (repeatedly)*	δούς (aor.) *one who gives/gave*	δεδωκώς (pf.) *one who has given*

Frequently participles (like infinitives; ↑213a) have the role of a predicator with objects, other sentence constituents, or sometimes even with an explicit subject (↑230d/233) of their own. Such participle phrases typically have a sentence-like function: they are used to refer to a real-world "situation", and like subordinate clauses (↑270g), they serve as sentence constituents of the superordinate construction they belong to, e.g. (participle phrase with a direct object and a object adjunct;

similar to a relative clause, it serves as an attributive modifier of the head of a noun phrase Χριστὸς Ἰησοῦς *Christ Jesus* in Verse 5):

… ὁ δοὺς (P) **ἑαυτὸν** (Od) **ἀντίλυτρον ὑπὲρ πάντων** (OA) …	… *who gave himself as a ransom for all* (1Tm 2:6)

b) As an adjective form of the verb it is connected with nominal word-classes and word forms: Not only does it inflect like an adjective (↑48), but its syntactic use is basically that of an adjective (↑229).

2. Comparison between **Ancient Greek** and **English** as well as Latin usage: 227b

a) Ancient Greek differs from English, and in part also from Latin, regarding the use of participles mainly as follows:

- Ancient Greek uses a great deal more participle **forms** ("+" used, "–" not used):

	ANCIENT GREEK (↑48)			ENGLISH(1)		LATIN(2)	
	act.	mid.	pass.	act.	pass.	act.	pass.
pres.	+	+	+	+	–	+	–
fut.	+	+	+	–	–	+	–
aor.	+	+	+	–	–	–	–
pf.	+	+	+	+	= +	–	+

(1) *-ing* participles, e.g. *working, joining, taking,* and *-ed* participles, e.g. *worked, joined,* (irregular verb with variant form:) *taken* (↑Carter §539).
Note that *-ing* forms may also have the function of a gerund, a nominalized form typically occurring as the head of noun-phrases (often preceded by a preposition); ↑Carter §231. English gerunds fairly frequently correspond to Ancient Greek infinitive/ACI phrases (↑213b; 223).
(2) *vocāns* "calling", *rēctūrus* "about to rule", *acceptus* "accepted" (↑Allen-Greenough §158).

- In Ancient Greek participle phrases occur also with a wider range of **syntactic functions** (in English many of these are, e.g., preferably expressed not by a participle phrase, but by conjunctional adverbial clauses). So, the high frequency of participle phrases in Ancient Greek texts is not surprising.

b) The frequently occurring Ancient Greek "**genitive absolute**" ("gen.abs.") has the same origin and function as the Latin "ablative absolute" (↑146a), and there is also a kind of counterpart in English (↑230d).

c) The use of the "**participle conjunct**" ("p.c.") is essentially the same in Ancient Greek and Latin, and, though to a more limited extent, also in English (↑230c).

d) The "**accusative with participle**" ("ACP") occurs very frequently in Ancient Greek, much less so in Latin, however, quite often in English (↑233).

The "nominative with participle" ("NCP"), used instead of the ACP, when the superordinate verb and the participle phrase have the same subject, occurs in Ancient Greek (in the NT very rarely), but not in Latin nor (with any grammatical clarity) in English (↑233e).

e) In Ancient Greek certain **"modifying" verbs** connect with a (predicative) participle phrase, not so in Latin, however, to some extent also in English (↑234), e.g.:

παῦσαι (modifying verb) **λέγουσα** (ptc.)· *Stop talking!* (Euripides, Hippolytus 706)

f) The "**accusative absolute**" use of certain participles is a peculiarity of Ancient Greek (not used in the NT; ↑230f).

227c 3. **Differences** between **CG** and **KG/NT** usage:

a) The **participle future**, important in CG, occurs only **infrequently** in the NT; it is replaced by the participle present or by alternative constructions expressing purpose (↑259j).

b) The CG **predicative participle** is in the course of **disappearing** in KG usage (↑233c; 234).

c) In the NT the CG "**accusative absolute**" is not used (↑230f).

d) In CG the **particle ἄν** (↑252.3) is used **in participle phrases** with **potential** or **irrealis** force (as a replacement for the potential opt. [↑211d] or for the augment indicative with ἄν [↑209h]), a use unattested in the NT, e.g.:

ὁρῶν τὸ παρατείχισμα …ῥᾳδίως **ἄν** … **ληφθέν** (= **ἄν** … **ληφθείη** [potential opt.]) …	*As he saw that the counter wall … might easily be taken …* (Thucydides 7.42)

↑BR §248; BDF §425.5.

e) In KG μή largely replaces οὐ in participle clauses. ↑227d.

227d 4. In **CG** participle phrases are usually **negated** by means of the particle that would be used in a subordinate clause with a corresponding force:

- μή, when the participle phrase has a **volitional** or **conditional** force, at times also in other cases;
- οὐ in every other case, thus especially when the participle phrase has a declarative (assessing) force or when the meaning of the participle phrase is to be reversed.

In the NT **participle phrases** are **mostly** negated by means of **μή**, a use corresponding to the KG tendency to generally use μή to negate non-indicative forms (↑244; 245d; 246c), e.g.:

ἡ γυνὴ αὐτοῦ **μὴ εἰδυῖα τὸ γεγονὸς** εἰσῆλθεν. (in CG οὐ would be expected)	*His wife came in, not knowing what had happened.* (Ac 5:7)

↑also Lk 24:23; 2Cor 4:18; 5:21; 2Th 1:8; He 9:9; 11:27 etc.

There are only a small number of instances in the NT where οὐ is used in line with CG usage, inter alia in Mt (1×), Lk, Ac and Paul, e.g.:

εἶδεν ἐκεῖ ἄνθρωπον **οὐκ ἐνδεδυμένον ἔνδυμα γάμου**.	*He saw a person there not dressed in a wedding garment.* (Mt 22:11)
… **οὐ στενοχωρούμενοι** … **οὐκ ἐξαπορούμενοι**.	*… not crushed … not driven to despair.* (2Cor 4:8)

228 Participle and tense/aspect meanings

As non-indicative forms participles (outside the future) do **not** express any **tense value** at all. The choice of the aorist, the present or the perfect has to do with aspect considerations. ↑192–195; 204 (especially the examples listed there).

On the other hand, however, there is a clearly noticeable **general tendency** regarding the (grammatically unexpressed) **relative time** of the "situation" indicated by the participle (in the real world) in relation to the "situation" indicated by the superordinate verb (from which we may infer whether the "situation" indicated by the participle is to be understood as being in the past, present, or future, or as timeless):

intended relative time (real world) of the participle's "situation" in relation to the "situation" of the superordinate verb (in the past, present, or future, or as timeless)	participle used	
	predominantly	less frequently
SIMULTANEOUS	ptc. pres. or ptc. pf.	ptc. aor. (the superordinate verb typically ind. aor.)
ANTERIOR	ptc. aor.	ptc. pres.
POSTERIOR	ptc. fut. (CG/NT) ptc. pres. (NT)	

Note that apparently there are no unambiguous instances of the participle aorist referring to something posterior. For more details and examples ↑206d–206i.

On absolute time seemingly expressed in certain contexts ↑205.

Syntactic use of participles (↑Maier 1969: 79ff; Adrados 1992: 631–641; BR §240; BDF §411–425) 229

Syntactically, participle phrases may in principle be used like adjective phrases (↑137); their use as adverbials is, however, not only a minor possibility (as in the case of adjectives), but the predominant one.

The syntactic use of participles is helpfully subdivided into **three types**:

1. **adverbial** participle: the participle phrase serves as an adverbial, i.e. as an (op- 229a
tional) adjunct, less frequently as an (obligatory) complement (↑259a–259m/258c),

a) mainly occurring in two kinds of grammatical constructions,

- **participle conjunct** and
- **genitive absolute** (↑230)

b) with mainly **six** distinguishable adverbial **nuances** (↑231/232);

2. **predicative** participle: the participle phrase serves as an obligatory part of the predicate, i.e. as a subject complement or object complement (↑258a/258b) or as an integral part of a multi-part predicator (↑256b),

a) within "**ACP**" (and "GCP") constructions (↑233),

b) connected with **modifying verbs** (↑234) and

c) the **periphrastic conjugation** and comparable constructions (↑235);

3. **attributive and nominalized** participle (↑236/237): the participle phrase serves

a) as an attributive modifier within a nominal phrase (↑260a–260n) or

b) as the head of a nominal phrase (↑137c; 132d).

229b Note that presence or absence of the **article** is of critical importance when it comes to identifying the intended syntactic role of a participle phrase (↑135/136; 259o):

a) The **presence of the article** clearly points to an **attributive or nominalized** role.

b) The absence of the article generally rules out the attributive (or nominalized) role, unless the head of the attributive modifier is not determined; in this comparatively rare case an attributive role is possible, the context usually making it clear whether an attributive or non-attributive role is intended. ↑260d.

Whether a participle phrase without article is meant to have an adverbial role (which occurs most frequently) or a predicative one, is almost always inferable from the syntactic context.

229c Further noteworthy points:

a) In Latin the syntactic use of participle phrases is less varied and it is impossible to distinguish clearly between the three types mentioned above (due inter alia to the lack of an article determining attributive and non-attributive uses). It would, therefore, be problematic to rely on Latin usage when dealing with the syntax of Ancient Greek participle phrases.

b) The way the syntax of the participle is organized may vary somewhat in relevant publications, sometimes involving a partly different terminology. Rijksbaron, for instance, subsumes the participles that in this grammar are termed "predicative" (Rijksbaron: "as an obligatory constituent") and "adverbial" (Rijksbaron: "as a satellite") under one generic term "predicative participle", contrasted with "attributive participle" (pages 116ff).[65] BR's categories (here translated into English) compare with the ones adopted in the present grammar as follows (minor points are not taken into account):

BORNEMANN-RISCH:	PRESENT GRAMMAR (agreeing e. g. with Adrados):
§241 ptc. as an attributive modifier	attributive (↑236/237)
§242 ptc. as a predicate noun	predicative: periphrastic conjugation (↑235)
§243 ptc. seemingly as a predicate noun	predicative: connected with modifying verbs (↑234)
Complementary ptc. as a predicate adjunct:	
§244 a) in the ACP connected with a Od	predicative: ACP (and GCP) (↑233)
§245 b) connected with the subject of the superordinate verb	occurs very rarely in the NT (↑233e)
§246 sentence expanding ptc. as a participle conjunct (as a predicate adjunct) and in the genitive absolute	adverbial (↑230–232)

(a) Adverbial participle

230 Adverbial participle: "p.c." and "gen.abs."

(↑Maier 1969: 81–88; BR §246; Duhoux §253ff; BDF §417f; 423f; Z §48–50 [gen.abs.])

230a I. Syntactically, Ancient Greek participle phrases most frequently have the role of an adverbial (usually of an [optional] adjunct, at times of an [obligatory] complement; ↑259b; 312c): they modify the information of the superordinate construction by indicating in a general way the circumstances of the "action"/"situation" that the

65 In the present grammar "predicative" is more narrowly defined (↑254c[3]).

verb form (of the superordinate construction) refers to. Though English participle phrases are sometimes used in this way, conjunctional adverbial clauses are generally preferred when translating Ancient Greek adverbial phrases (↑231b). E.g.:

καὶ **ἰδὼν τὴν πίστιν αὐτῶν** (TempA) **εἶπεν** …	*And when he saw their faith, he said …* (Lk 5:20)

"Under what circumstances did he say …?" *When he saw their faith.*

On possible adverbial nuances and ways of translating them ↑231/232.

II. The adverbial participle is **never** accompanied by the **article** (↑135b; 229b); it mainly occurs in two kinds of grammatical constructions: **230b**
(1) as a "participle conjunct" (abbreviated "p.c.") and
(2) as a "genitive absolute" (abbreviated "gen.abs.").

1. The **participle conjunct** ("participium coniunctum"): the participle phrase and the superordinate construction are grammatically conjoined, i.e. the participle phrase is in a particular case that connects it with a sentence element of the superordinate finite verb in the same case[66] (and otherwise showing concord; ↑261ff; on the Book of Revelation ↑261b); it is from this element that the intended subject of the participle phrase may be inferred (the intended placement in time of the "situation" being inferable from the superordinate finite verb; ↑228): **230c**

a) The participle (phrase) is in the **nominative** agreeing with the subject of the superordinate construction (in the majority of p.c. instances),[67] e.g.:

καὶ **μὴ εὑρόντες** (TempA) **ὑπέστρεψαν** (superordinate finite verb) εἰς Ἰερουσαλὴμ …	*And when they did not find him, they returned to Jerusalem …* (Lk 2:45)

The participle is in the nominative, which agrees with the case (and number) of the subject of the superordinate finite verb, from which the intended subject of the participle phrase may be inferred (as well as the intended placement in the past): *not finding (him)→ when **they did** not find him.*

καὶ **ἐλθὼν** (TempA) ἐκεῖνος **ἐλέγξει** (superordinate finite verb) τὸν κόσμον …	*And when he comes, he will prove the world to be in the wrong …* (Jn 16:8)

The participle is in the nominative, which agrees with the case (and number) of the subject of the superordinate finite verb from which the intended subject of the participle phrase may be inferred (as well as the intended placement in the future): *coming →when **he** comes* (= *when he **will** come*).

b) The participle (phrase) is in **some other case** agreeing with any sentence element of the superordinate construction that is in the case in question (much less frequently so in the genitive than in the dative or accusative):

66 Occasionally the p.c. is not in the expected case (probably a type of notional concord; ↑265): Ac 15:23 (nom. for acc./dat.); Eph 3:17 (nom. for gen.); Php 1:30 (nom. for acc./dat.); Col 3:16 (nom. for dat.); 2Pe 3:3 (nom. for acc./dat.; also ↑231k). Also ↑BDF §468.

67 This use (p.c. as an adjunct, in the "nominative" connected with the subject of the superordinate clause) is quite common in English, too, e.g. (↑Aarts: 230f; 234): *Every Tuesday I stood there* ***waiting by the door*** (TempA) = … *there* ***while I was waiting by the door***. Or: ***Dressed in civilian clothes*** (SA) *they gave the impression of being members of a rabble army.*

- **genitive**, e.g.:

τὰ σπλάγχνα **αὐτοῦ** (gen. Attr) περισσοτέρως εἰς ὑμᾶς ἐστιν **ἀναμιμνῃσκομένου τὴν πάντων ὑμῶν ὑπακοήν** (CausA).

And his affection for you is all the greater, as he remembers the obedience of all of you. (2Cor 7:15)

The participle is in the genitive agreeing with the genitive attributive modifier (of the subject) of the superordinate finite verb, from which the intended subject of the participle phrase is inferable (intended placement in time from the finite verb): *remembering … → as* ***he*** *remembers.*

↑also Mt 1:22 (9× in Mt: διὰ τοῦ προφήτου λέγοντος *through the prophet when the latter said/ through the prophet saying*); Ac 17:16 and 27:30 (agreeing with the subject of a gen. abs.); Jas 1:5 (agreeing with the subject of an attributive ptc. in the gen.).

- **dative**, e.g.:

ἢ **ἡμῖν** (O^{dat}) τί ἀτενίζετε **ὡς ἰδίᾳ δυνάμει … πεποιηκόσιν τοῦ περιπατεῖν αὐτόν** (ManA);

Or why do you stare at us, as if by our own power … we have made him walk? (Ac 3:12)

The participle is in the dative, which agrees with the dative object of the superordinate finite verb, from which the intended subject of the participle phrase is inferable (intended placement in time from the finite verb): *as if … making … → as if …* ***we*** *have made* (nuance of an ind. pf.; ↑200a) …

- **accusative**, e.g.:

ἀπέστειλεν **αὐτὸν** (Od) **εὐλογοῦντα ὑμᾶς** (PurpA).

He sent him so that he would bless you. (Ac 3:26)

The participle is in the accusative, which agrees with the case of the direct object of the superordinate finite verb, from which the intended subject of the participle phrase is inferable (placement as a kind of "future in the past" from the finite verb; ↑203d): *blessing you → in order for* ***him*** *to bless you.*

230d 2. The **genitive absolute** ("genitivus absolutus"): the participle phrase and the superordinate construction are not conjoined grammatically, the participle phrase having an explicit subject of its own is independent, "absolute" (↑Lat. *absolutus* "detached"), as far as the grammatical (syntactic) form is concerned. Genitive absolute phrases consist of at least two genitive expressions: a) a participle (predicator of the gen. abs.) and b) a noun phrase (its head being a noun or a noun substitute; subject of the gen. abs.). To be sure, as far as their syntactic (notional) function is concerned genitive absolute phrases are by no means "detached": like p.c. phrases they serve as adverbials, indicating in a general way the circumstances of the "action"/"situation" that the verb form of the superordinate construction refers to,[68] e.g.:

ἔτι **λαλοῦντος** (gen. abs. P) **αὐτοῦ** (gen. abs. S) (TempA) ἐφώνησεν ἀλέκτωρ.

While he was still speaking, the rooster crowed. (Lk 22:60)

The genitive of the ptc. phrase ἔτι λαλοῦντος (gen. abs. P) αὐτοῦ (gen. abs. S) is not connected grammatically with any element of the superordinate clause ἐφώνησεν ἀλέκτωρ. Syntactically (notionally), however, the gen. abs. phrase functions as a TempA of that clause.

---

68 A comparable use is found in English, too (though with an accusative subject), e.g. (↑Aarts: 230f): *We muddled through,* ***him asking questions, me answering the best I could*** (TempA). = … ***while he was asking questions*** and ***while I was answering the best I could.***

In **KG** and in the **NT** the subject entity of the gen.abs. is not infrequently (in CG only occasionally; ↑BR §246.3 Note 1) at the same time referred to by a nominal phrase of the superordinate construction, without the two agreeing in their grammatical form. In other words, a gen.abs. is used where according to CG usage a p.c. would be expected, e.g.:

Καταβάντος δὲ **αὐτοῦ** (TempA) ἀπὸ τοῦ ὄρους ἠκολούθησαν αὐτῷ ὄχλοι πολλοί.	*When he came down from the mountain, large crowds followed him.* (Mt 8:1)

In CG something like ***καταβάντι** δὲ … (p.c.) ἠκολούθησαν **αὐτῷ** ὄχλοι πολλοί would be expected.

↑also Mt 1:18; 18:25; Ac 22:17.

Noteworthy points: 230e

a) Occasionally (both in NT and CG) the subject of a gen.abs. is not expressed, but is inferable from the context, e.g.:

τελειωσάντων (sc. αὐτῶν) τὰς ἡμέρας (TempA) … ὑπέμεινεν Ἰησοῦς ὁ παῖς ἐν Ἰερουσαλήμ.	*After they had completed the festival days … the boy Jesus stayed behind in Jerusalem.* (Lk 2:43)
Ἐκ τούτου θᾶττον προϊόντων (sc. αὐτῶν; TempA) ἀπὸ τοῦ αὐτομάτου δρόμος ἐγένετο τοῖς στρατιώταις.	*And then, as they advanced faster, the troops broke into a run of their own accord.* (Xenophon, Anabasis 1.2.17)

↑also Mt 17:26; Ac 21:10.31; Re 17:8. ↑BDF §423.

b) While in a Latin ablative absolute construction it was possible to replace the participle by an ablative noun (e.g. *Caesare ducente* [ablative ptc.] may be replaced by *Caesare duce* [ablative noun] "with Caesar as a leader"), in an Ancient Greek gen.abs. construction the participle is obligatory (so, as an equivalent of our example we would expect either Καίσαρος **ἡγουμένου** [ptc.] or Καίσαρος **ἡγεμόνος** [noun] **ὄντος** [ptc.]).

III. CG also had a participle use called "**accusative absolute**" occurring in two types of constructions (↑Duhoux §257):[69] 230f

1. Typically, the neuter singular of a participle used as an impersonal expression, e.g.:

δέον, χρεών	*as (when/while/although) it is / was / would be / would have been necessary*
ἐξόν, παρόν	*as (when/while/although) it is / was / would be / would have been possible*
δόξαν, δεδογμένον	*as (when/while/although) it is / was / would be / would have been resolved*

Example:

οὐδεὶς τὸ μεῖζον [κακὸν] αἱρήσεται **ἐξὸν** τὸ ἔλαττον [αἱρεῖσθαι].	*No one will choose the greater [evil] when it is possible to choose the lesser* (Plato, Protagoras 358d)

69 The "dative absolute", apparently used in Old Church Slavonic, cannot be regarded as belonging to Ancient Greek usage. There are a small number of instances in poetic texts that might possibly be classified as such (Adrados 1992: 636f). The participle use found in Mt 14:6 Γενεσίοις δὲ γενομένοις τοῦ Ἡρῴδου … *But when Herod's birthday came* … (perhaps a mixture of a dative of time [↑182a] with a gen.abs. construction [↑230d]; BDF §200.3) would certainly be insufficient to justify the introduction of such a category (a possibility considered e.g. by Porter 1992: 184).

The only somewhat comparable expression in the NT is τυχόν (aor. ptc. act. ntr. sg. of τυγχάνω *to meet/attain*; in CG already used as an adverb) *perhaps/if possible* (< *if it turns out that way*) in 1Cor 16:6 (also Lk 20:13 Var. and Ac 12:15 Var.). ↑BDAG sub τυγχάνω 2c, BDF §424.

2. Occasionally preceded by ὡς used like a gen.abs. with a causal nuance, e.g.:

ἥδεσθε … **ὡς περιεσομένους ἡμᾶς** Ἑλλήνων. (ὡς περιεσομένων ἡμῶν … would be more conventional)	*Rejoice … as we will overcome the Greeks.* (Herodotus 9.42.4)

231 Adverbial participle: adverbial nuances

(↑Maier 1969: 81–88; BR §246; BDF §418; 421; 425).

231a I. The circumstances of the "action"/"situation" indicated (↑230f) by adverbial participle phrases (p.c. or gen.abs. phrases) will typically have to be understood in a more specific way when dealing with particular instances. Thus, a number of specific adverbial nuances are usually distinguished, e.g.:

ἰδὼν αὐτὸν (adv. ptc.: TempA, less likely here ManA/CausA/CondA/ConcA …; ↑231c)	*When he saw him* (less likely *By seeing/ Because/If/Although he saw him*),
ἀντιπαρῆλθεν	*he passed by on the other side.* (Lk 10:31)

Which adverbial nuance is most likely to be intended (as also the intended relative time in relation to the "situation" of the superordinate verb; ↑228; 206), is usually inferable from the context, sometimes facilitated by the addition of particles.

231b II. Adverbial participle phrases sometimes allow for a fairly literal translation, e.g.:

ἰδὼν αὐτὸν ἀντιπαρῆλθεν	*Seeing him, he passed by …* (Lk 10:31)

However, other ways of translating them usually seem to be preferable:

- **as a conjunctional adverbial clause** (standard; ↑231d–231i; TempA):
  When he saw him, he passed by …
- **as a preposition phrase with embedded noun phrase** (TempA):
  At the sight of him, he passed by …
- **as part of a main clause combination** (often involving connectives such as adverbs, in narratives very frequently "and"), the participle being translated as if it had the same grammatical properties as the superordinate verb form),[70] e.g.:
  He saw him; yet, he passed by …
  He saw him and passed by …

Here the adverb *yet* indicates a concessive nuance (assumed for the sake of illustration); it is placed in the second main clause, the one translating the superordinate construction. In other cases, such an indicator is placed in the main clause translating the participle phrase (e.g.↑231e)
Note that as a connective "and" may be understood in various ways (inferable from the context), here maybe: *… and [at the same time/after that/yet] he passed by …* (↑312c[23] and 322a).

70 Inter alia: Ancient Greek **p.c. + (superordinate) imperative** as English **imperative + ["and"] imperative** (typical understanding and translation of such combinations; ↑Kühner-Gerth I: 182).

If a participle clause is intertwined with a relative or interrogative clause (↑289j), it is usually best to make it into the superordinate construction in a translation into English, e.g.:

τί ποιήσας ζωὴν αἰώνιον κληρονομήσω;	*What must I do to inherit eternal life?* (< "Having done what, will I inherit …?"; Lk 10:25)

Occasionally, what is intended as the superordinate proposition is expressed by a participle phrase, whilst the subordinate proposition is expressed by the superordinate construction (in CG this phenomenon is rhetorically conditioned). In such cases, too, it is advisable to translate the participle phrase as a superordinate construction. Possible NT example:

οἱ μαθηταὶ αὐτοῦ ἤρξαντο ὁδὸν **ποιεῖν τίλλοντες** (= ἤρξαντο ὁδὸν ποιοῦντες τίλλειν?) τοὺς στάχυας.	*His disciples began to pick some heads of grain as they made their way.* (Mk 2:23)

↑also He 2:10 (ἀγαγόντα … τελειῶσαι = ἀγαγεῖν … τελειώσαντα?). BDR §339_5; Z §263/376.

III. Six major **adverbial nuances** are usually distinguished (↑259; on textgrammatical distinctions; ↑322ff). 231c

These distinctions are primarily meant as a help for interpreters and translators; native speakers of Ancient Greek in most cases were probably not aware of them.

When dealing with these nuances interpreters of texts should bear in mind the following points:

Adverbial participles (due to their grammatical function) basically indicate in a general way the circumstances of the "action"/"situation" referred to by the superordinate construction (↑230a). What specific part of the range of possible circumstances is most likely to be intended in a particular instance will generally be inferable from relevant contextual (pragmatic) factors. As such a range is bound to be a continuum without well-defined boundaries between its various parts, it will not always be possible to come to an unambiguous conclusion. Quite possibly the speaker/writer did not intend to be unambiguous about it. Had this been the case, a clearer construction such as a conjunctional adverbial phrase would presumably have been chosen. So, some flexibility in dealing with these nuances seems necessary.

adverbial nuance	answering question
1. TEMPORAL (TempA; ↑259e; 276)	"When?" (↑231d)
2. MANNER (ManA; or "modal"; ↑259f)	"How?"/"In what manner?"; "Under what concomitant circumstances?" (↑231e)
3. CAUSAL (CausA; ↑259g; 277)	"Why?"/"For what reason?" (↑231f)
4. CONCESSIVE (ConcA; ↑259k; 286)	"In spite of what?" (↑231g)
5. CONDITIONAL (CondA; ↑259h; 280)	"In what case?", "Under what condition?" (↑231h)
6. INDICATING PURPOSE (PurpA; ↑259j; 278) (only p.c. fut. and [NT] pres.)	"What for?" (↑231i)

The manner and temporal nuances appear to be intended most frequently (BDF §418.5; Turner 1963: 154) and so should be given a high priority when interpreting and translating texts.

A number of idiomatic uses really belong here, too (↑238–240): "graphic" participles, pleonastic participles, and participles relating to the Hebrew infinitive absolute.

231d 1. **Temporal** (“When?”)

clause subordinated by	preposition phrase (often with *-ing* form)	part of a main clause combination	possible particles within the PtcP
a) **simultaneous** (mostly ptc. pres. [or pf.]; ↑228/206e/206g/206i)			
while, as	*during, at*	*(and) meanwhile* (sup.)[(1)]	ἅμα *at the same time* (CG also μεταξύ *in the middle of*)
b) **anterior** (mostly ptc. aor.; ↑228/206f/206i)			
after, when	*after*	*(and) then* (sup.)[(1)]	εὐθύς (CG also αὐτίκα) *at once*; also a subsequent τότε (or εἶτα) *then*

(1) “sup.” = “referring to the superordinate construction”, i.e. the main clause with the adverb listed here translates the superordinate construction.

Example (a use very frequently encountered; TempA):

Περιπατῶν δὲ **παρὰ τὴν θάλασσαν τῆς Γαλιλαίας** (p.c.) εἶδεν δύο ἀδελφούς.	*As he walked/While walking by the Sea of Galilee, he saw two brothers.* (Mt 4:18)
ἅμα ταῦτ᾽ εἰπὼν (p.c.) ἀνέστη.	*As he said this/With these words he got up at once.* (Xenophon, Anabasis 3.1.47)
πολλαχοῦ με ἐπέσχε **λέγοντα μεταξύ** (p.c.).	*It stopped me at many points in the middle of my speech.* (Plato, Apology 40b)
Ἔτι λαλοῦντος τοῦ Πέτρου τὰ ῥήματα ταῦτα (gen.abs.) ἐπέπεσεν τὸ πνεῦμα τὸ ἅγιον ἐπὶ πάντας …	*While Peter was still speaking these words, the Holy Spirit fell on all …* (Ac 10:44)

↑also Ac 4:1; 10:19.

ταῦτα εἰπὼν (p.c.) ἔπτυσεν χαμαὶ καὶ ἐποίησεν πηλὸν ἐκ τοῦ πτύσματος.	*After saying this, he spat on the ground and made mud with the saliva.* (Jn 9:6)

↑also Lk 2:17; 4:17; 5:8.20; 7:9; 23:11; Ac 14:23; 19:19.

καὶ **εἰσελθοῦσα εὐθὺς** (p.c.) … ᾐτήσατο …	*At once she came in … and requested …* (Mk 6:25)
καὶ **δεηθέντων αὐτῶν** (gen.abs.) ἐσαλεύθη ὁ τόπος …	*After they prayed, the place … was shaken.* (Ac 4:31)

↑also Ac 2:6; 13:23f.

In CG the following participles were used in formulaic way:

ἀρχόμενος	*at first*
τελευτῶν	*finally*
ἀρξάμενος ἀπό (ἐκ)	*starting from*
διαλιπὼν χρόνον	*after some time*
ἐπισχὼν πολὺν χρόνον	*after a long time*

Example:

... ἅπερ καὶ **ἀρχόμενος** εἶπον	*... as I said at first.* (Thucydides 4.64)

↑Lk 24:47 (ἀρξάμενοι ἀπό, however, not fully agreeing with CG usage; BDF §419.3).

2. **Manner** (also "modal") ("How?"/"In what manner?"; "Under what concomitant 231e
circumstances?"), frequently best rendered by a plain *-ing* participle phrase, sometimes alternatively by:

clause subordinated by	preposition phrase (often with *-ing* form)	part of a main clause combination	possible particles within the PtcP
a) **manner**: **the way in which** the "action"/"situation" is meant to unfold (is sometimes best translated as an adverb phrase)			
as, in that	*by, in*	*(and) thus/so/thereby* (sup.)[1]	
b) **manner**: specific **concomitant circumstances** or specific characterization of "action"/"situation"			
whereby (at times in contrasts *while*)	*by, in*	*(and) beside that* (for PtcP)	
c) **manner**: imagined **comparison**[2]			
as if, as though			ὡς/ὥσπερ *as if, as though* (↑also 231i)
d) **negated**:			
	not, without (+ *-ing* form)		

(1) "sup." = "referring to the superordinate construction", i.e. the main clause with the adverb listed here translates the superordinate construction.
(2) BR (§246.1,f) has a separate category for this use, Duhoux (§253) includes it in the causal nuance.

Examples (a use also very frequently encountered; ManA):

ἐκεῖ διεσκόρπισεν τὴν οὐσίαν αὐτοῦ **ζῶν ἀσώτως** (p.c.).	*There he squandered his property in wild living.* (Lk 15:13)

↑also Lk 7:29f; 21:12.

δι' ἧς ἐμαρτυρήθη εἶναι δίκαιος, **μαρτυροῦντος ἐπὶ τοῖς δώροις αὐτοῦ τοῦ θεοῦ** (gen.abs.).	*Through this he received approval as righteous, God giving approval to his gifts.* (He 11:4)
καὶ αὐτὸς ἐδίδασκεν ἐν ταῖς συναγωγαῖς αὐτῶν **δοξαζόμενος ὑπὸ πάντων** (p.c.).	*And he taught in their synagogues being praised by all.* (Lk 4:15)

νῦν δὲ καὶ **κλαίων** (p.c.) λέγω …	*And now I tell you even with tears* (lit. *… tell you even weeping*) … (Php 3:18)

↑also Mk 1:41; 15:43; Ac 5:41.

ἦλθαν **σπεύσαντες** (p.c.).	*They came in haste.* (Lk 2:16)
ὑπὸ τῶν ἀκουσάντων εἰς ἡμᾶς ἐβεβαιώθη, **συνεπιμαρτυροῦντος τοῦ θεοῦ σημείοις τε καὶ τέρασιν** … (gen.abs.)	*It was attested to us by those who heard him, God adding his testimony by signs and wonders …* (He 2:3f)
πῶς δύνασαι λέγειν τῷ ἀδελφῷ σου· … **αὐτὸς τὴν ἐν τῷ ὀφθαλμῷ σου δοκὸν οὐ βλέπων** (p.c.);	*How can you say to your brother, … while you yourself do not see the plank in your own eyes?* (Lk 6:42)
τί **ὡς ζῶντες ἐν κόσμῳ** (p.c.) δογματίζεσθε;	*Why do you submit to regulations as if you still lived in the world?* (Col 2:20)

↑also Ac 17:25 (without ὡς); He 11:27 (with ὡς).

μὴ ξενίζεσθε … **ὡς ξένου ὑμῖν συμβαίνοντος** (gen.abs.).	*Do not be surprised … as though something strange were happening to you* (1Pe 4:12)

↑also Ac 2:2 (with ὥσπερ).

ἐξῆλθεν ἀπ’ αὐτοῦ **μηδὲν βλάψαν αὐτόν** (p.c.).	*He/It came out of him without injuring him.* (Lk 4:35)

In CG (rarely in the NT) ἔχων and λαβών are also used in formulaic way signifying *(together) with*, e.g.:

κόλπον δέ τινα κατενόουν **ἔχοντα** αἰγιαλόν.	*But they noticed a bay with a beach.* (Ac 27:39)
ὁ οὖν Ἰούδας **λαβὼν** τὴν σπεῖραν … ἔρχεται.	*So Judas came … with* (?) *an attachment of soldiers …* (Jn 18:3)

231f 3. **Causal** (“Why?”/“For what reason?”)

clause subordinated by	preposition phrase (often with *-ing* form)	part of a main clause combination	possible particles within the PtcP
a) **objective reason**			
because, as, since	*because of, as a result of*	*for* (for PtcP) *(and) therefore* (sup.)[(1)]	CG ἅτε/οἷα/οἷον *as, because*; ἄλλως τε καί *especially as*
b) **subjective reason**			
because (I/you etc. *think that); convinced that*			ὡς *because* (*I/you* etc. *think that*); *convinced that* (↑also 231i; 2Pe 1:3 ὡς = ἅτε)

(1) “sup.” = “referring to the superordinate construction”, i.e. the main clause with the adverb listed here translates the superordinate construction.

Examples (CausA):

πάντες ἐφοβοῦντο αὐτὸν **μὴ πιστεύοντες ὅτι ἐστὶν μαθητής** (p.c.).
And they were all afraid of him, because they did not believe that he was a disciple. (Ac 9:26)

↑also Mt 1:19; 2Cor 4:1; 5:14; He 10:19.

ὁ δὲ Κῦρος **ἅτε παῖς ὢν** (p.c.) … ἥδετο τῇ στολῇ.
And Cyrus was pleased with the dress, as he was a child … (Xenophon, Cyropaedia 1.3.3)

… **τοῦ θεοῦ περὶ ἡμῶν κρεῖττόν τι προβλεψαμένου** (gen.abs.).
… since God had planned something better for us. (He 11:40)

↑also Ac 19:36; 21:34; He 4:2.

γνώμην δὲ δίδωμι **ὡς ἠλεημένος ὑπὸ κυρίου** … (p.c.)
but I give my opinion, convinced that I have been shown mercy by the Lord … (1Cor 7:25)

Ὑπὲρ Χριστοῦ οὖν πρεσβεύομεν **ὡς τοῦ θεοῦ παρακαλοῦντος δι᾽ ἡμῶν** (gen.abs.)
So, we are ambassadors for Christ, convinced that God is making his appeal through us. (2Cor 5:20)

↑also He 13:17.

In CG the following expressions were used in a formulaic way (BR §246.2c note):

τί παθών / τί μαθών
used as an emphatic "Why?" (< *Having experienced/learned what?*), e.g.:

τί μαθόντες ἐμαρτυρεῖθ᾽ ὑμεῖς …;
Why have you testified …? (Demosthenes 45.38)

4. **Concessive** ("In spite of what?") 231g

clause subordinated by	preposition phrase (often with *-ing* form)	part of a main clause combination	possible particles within the PtcP
(al)though, even though	*in spite of, despite*	*(and) yet*[(1)]	καί, καίπερ, καίτοι *though*; CG at times also ὅμως *nevertheless* in the superordinate construction

(1) "sup." = "referring to the superordinate construction", i.e. the main clause with the adverb listed here translates the superordinate construction.

Examples (ConcA):

καίπερ ὢν υἱός (p.c.), ἔμαθεν ἀφ᾽ ὧν ἔπαθεν τὴν ὑπακοήν.
Although he was the Son, he learned obedience from what he suffered. (He 5:8)

ἐδίδασκεν ἀκριβῶς τὰ περὶ τοῦ Ἰησοῦ, **ἐπιστάμενος μόνον τὸ βάπτισμα Ἰωάννου** (p.c.).
He taught accurately the facts about Jesus, though he only knew the baptism of John. (Ac 18:25)

… **καίτοι τῶν ἔργων ἀπὸ καταβολῆς κόσμου γενηθέντων** (gen.abs.).	*… and yet his works were accomplished at the foundation of the world.* (He 4:3)

↑also Mt 7:11; Jn 4:9; Ac 13:28; Ro 1:32; 1Cor 9:19; Php 3:4; He 11:4; 12:17; Jas 3:4.

231h 5. **Conditional** ("In what case?", "Under what condition?")

clause subordinated by	preposition phrase (often with *-ing* form)	part of a main clause combination	possible particles within the PtcP
if, on condition that, provided/ providing (that)	*in case of, in the event of*	*(and) as a consequence*[(1)]	CG at times ἄν negative particle μή
Note that the temporal and conditional nuances are without well-defined boundaries (↑280e/280f).			

(1) "sup." = "referring to the superordinate construction", i.e. the main clause with the adverb listed here translates the superordinate construction.

Examples (CondA):

τί γὰρ ὠφελεῖται ἄνθρωπος **κερδήσας τὸν κόσμον ὅλον ἑαυτὸν δὲ ἀπολέσας ἢ ζημιωθείς** (p.c.);	*For what does it profit a person, if they gain the whole world, but lose or forfeit their very self?* (Lk 9:25) (↑Mt 16:26 ἐάν … κερδήσῃ)
πᾶν κτίσμα θεοῦ καλόν … **μετὰ εὐχαριστίας λαμβανόμενον** (p.c.).	*Everything created by God is good … provided it is received with thanksgiving.* (1Tm 4:4)

↑also Ac 15:29; Ga 6:9; 1Cor 4:12; 11:29; 1Tm 5:9; He 12:25.

πῶς ἡμεῖς ἐκφευξόμεθα **τηλικαύτης ἀμελήσαντες σωτηρίας** … (p.c.);	*How can we escape if we neglect so great a salvation …?* (He 2:3)
μετατιθεμένης γὰρ τῆς ἱερωσύνης (gen.abs.) ἐξ ἀνάγκης καὶ νόμου μετάθεσις γίνεται.	*For if the priesthood is changed, there is necessarily a change of law as well.* (He 7:12)

↑also He 10:26.

231i 6. **Indicating purpose** (also "final") ("What for?")

clause subordinated by	preposition phrase (often with *-ing* form)	part of a main clause combination	possible particles within the PtcP
so that/in order that	*for the sake of; (in order) to* + InfP		ὡς[(1)] *in order/expecting that*; negation: μή
Note that this nuances occurs **only** for the **p.c. future** and (in the NT) **p.c. present** (↑206h/206i)!			

(1) So, ὡς has three functions when combined with participles (↑also 252.61): (a) manner (imagined comparison; ↑231e) *as if/as though*; (b) causal (subjective reason; ↑231f) *because* (*I/you* etc. *think that*); *convinced that*; (c) indicating purpose (with p.c. fut. and in the NT pres.; ↑231i) *in order/expecting that.*

Examples (PurpA):

ἐλεημοσύνας ποιήσων εἰς τὸ ἔθνος μου (p.c.) παρεγενόμην.	*I came to bring my people gifts for the poor.* (Ac 24:17)

↑also Mt 27:49; Ac 8:27; 22:5; 24:11.

οὕτως λαλοῦμεν, **οὐχ ὡς ἀνθρώποις ἀρέσκοντες ἀλλὰ θεῷ** (p.c.).	*That is how we declare it, not to please people, but God.* (1Th 2:4)

↑also Ro 15:15; He 13:17.

ἦλθεν **ὡς εὑρήσων τι** (p.c.).	*He came expecting that he would find something on it.* (Mk 11:13 Var.)

IV. **Less typical uses**, especially occurring with Paul and Peter (↑Z §373f):

1. After a finite verb form **Paul** fairly frequently uses a **participle conjunct** in cases where we would have expected a **finite** verb form: no subordination seems to be involved, e.g.: 231j

οὐ πάλιν ἑαυτοὺς συνιστάνομεν ὑμῖν ἀλλὰ ἀφορμὴν **διδόντες** (for δίδομεν) ὑμῖν καυχήματος ὑπὲρ ἡμῶν.	*We are not trying to commend ourselves to you again, but are giving you the opportunity to take pride in us.* (2Cor 5:12)

↑also 2Cor 6:3; 7:5; 8:19; 9:11.13; 10:4.15 (2×); 11:6.

Especially in **Re** and **Jn**, the **converse** occurs at times: a participle phrase is continued by καί + finite verb form, e.g.:

… τοὺς λέγοντας ἑαυτοὺς ἀποστόλους καὶ οὐκ **εἰσίν** (for ὄντας) …	*… those who claim to be apostles, but are not …* (Re 2:2)

↑also Jn 1:32; 5:44; 15:5; Ac 11:5; 2Jn 2.

2. **Paul** and **Peter** occasionally seem to use participles (as wide-spread in KG) with an **imperative force** (without an imperative form in the superordinate construction requiring it; ↑231b[70]), e.g.: 231k

τὴν ἀναστροφὴν ὑμῶν ἐν τοῖς ἔθνεσιν **ἔχοντες** καλήν.	*Keep your conduct among the pagans honourable!* (1Pe 2:12)

↑also (at times also adjectives thus used) Ro 12:9–19; 1Pe 2:18; 3:1.7.9.15; 2Pe 3:3; similarly He 13:5.

Presumably this use of the participle is to be classified as predicative (rather than adverbial): it may be a case of periphrastic conjugation with ellipsis of the imperative form of εἰμί *to be* (↑235a; 256d). ↑268 on desiderative sentences.

V. Sometimes **two or more adverbial participle phrases** depend on a particular superordinate construction; the relationship between them may be as follows: 231l

1. They may have the **same rank**, typically indicated by connectives such as καί *and*, e.g.:

διερχόμενος γὰρ καὶ **ἀναθεωρῶν** (two PtcP with the same rank: TempA) τὰ σεβάσματα ὑμῶν εὗρον καὶ βωμὸν ἐν ᾧ ἐπεγέγραπτο· Ἀγνώστῳ θεῷ.	*For as I walked around and looked carefully at your objects of worship, I even found an altar with the inscription "To an unknown god"!* (Ac 17:23)

2. They may have a **different rank**, typically so when there is no connective between them ("asyndesis"; ↑293e); which is to be treated as having a higher rank, is inferable from the context, e.g.:

ἐξῆλθεν **διερχόμενος** … **τὴν Γαλατικὴν χώραν** (TempA/rank 1) … **ἐπιστηρίζων πάντας τοὺς μαθητάς** (ManA/rank 2).	*He set out and travelled … throughout the region of Galatia … strengthening all the disciples.* (Ac 18:23)
φοβηθεὶς (CausA/rank 2) **ἀπελθὼν** (TempA/rank 1) ἔκρυψα τὸ τάλαντόν σου ἐν τῇ γῇ.	*Out of fear I went off and hid your talent in the ground!* (Mt 25:25)

↑also Mk 1:41.

232 Adverbial participle: standard ways of translating it (↑Maier 1969: 88)

232a

clause subordinated by	preposition phrase (often with *-ing* form)	part of a main clause combination	possible particles within the PtcP
1. TEMPORAL			
a) **simultaneous** (mostly ptc. pres. [or pf.]; ↑228/206e/206g/206i)			
while, as	*during, at*	*(and) meanwhile* (sup.)[1]	ἅμα *at the same time* (CG also μεταξύ *in the middle of*)
b) **anterior** (mostly ptc. aor.; ↑228/206f/206i)			
after, when	*after*	*(and) then* (sup.)[1]	εὐθύς (CG also αὐτίκα) *at once*; also subsequent τότε (or εἶτα) *then*
2. MANNER (also “modal”; frequently best rendered by a plain *-ing* participle phrase in English)			
a) **manner**: **the way in which** the “action”/“situation” is meant to unfold			
as, in that	*by, in*	*(and) thus/so/thereby* (sup.)[1]	
b) **manner**: specific **concomitant circumstances** or specific characterization of “action”/“situation”			
whereby (at times in contrasts *while*)	*by, in*	*(and) beside that* (for PtcP)	
c) **manner**: imagined **comparison**			
as if, as though			ὡς/ὥσπερ *as if/though*
d) **negated**:			
	not, without + *-ing* form		
3. CAUSAL			
a) **objective reason**			
because, as, since	*because of, as a result of*	*for* (for PtcP) *(and) therefore* (sup.)[1]	CG ἅτε/οἷα/οἷον *as/because*; ἄλλως τε καί *especially as*
b) **subjective reason**			
because (I/you etc. *think that)*; *convinced that*			ὡς *because (I/you* etc. *think that)*; *convinced that*
4. CONCESSIVE			
(al)though, even though	*in spite of, despite*	*(and) yet*[1]	καί/καίπερ/καίτοι *though*; CG also ὅμως *nevertheless* in the superordinate clause
5. CONDITIONAL			
if, provided/providing (that) an the like	*in case of, in the event of*	*(and) as a consequence*[1]	CG at times ἄν negation: μή
6. INDICATING PURPOSE (“final”): only the **p.c. future** and (in the NT) **p.c. present** (↑206h/206i)			
so that/in order that	*for the sake of; (in order) to* + InfP		ὡς *in order/expecting that*; negation: μή

(1) “sup.” = “referring to the superordinate construction”, i.e. the main clause with the adverb listed here translates the superordinate construction.

Noteworthy points: 232b

a) In CG conditional and purpose indicating nuances are negated by means of μή, otherwise by means of οὐ, in KG and in the NT participle phrases are nearly always negated by means of μή (↑227d).

b) On a number of idiomatic uses of the participle ↑238–240.

c) On less typical uses, especially with Paul and Peter ↑231j/231k.

d) ↑also ↑231c.

(b) Predicative participle

Predicative participle: ACP (and GCP) 233

(↑BR §244f; Duhoux §252; Maier 1969: 93–95; BDF §416)

1. The Ancient Greek predicative[71] participle (always without article; ↑135b; 229b) most frequently occurs in a construction called "accusative with participle", abbreviated to "ACP" (<Lat. "accusativus cum participio"), or less frequently "genitive with participle", "GCP" (<Lat. "genitivus cum participio"): a noun phrase in the accusative (or genitive) combines with a participle phrase in the same case. An ACP (or GCP) as a whole has the role of an object, an obligatory sentence constituent dependent on (the valency of) certain verbs and so may be called predicative.[71] Within the ACP (or GCP) phrase the noun phrase serves as the subject and the participle as the predicator of the sentence-like phrase (↑227a). On the accusative ↑149a and 153c, on the genitive ↑158b, 167a and 159b.[72] 233a

Fairly frequently (depending on the valency of the verb and the context in question) an ACP (and GCP) is best translated as an ACP in English (↑227b), sometimes as an ACI (↑216a) or fairly frequently as a subordinate *that*-clause.

2. In the NT there is only one semantic class of verbs having ACP (or GCP) phrases as their object (CG has two; ↑233c): **verbs of sensual perception** and **of cognitive attitude or mental perception**: 233b

a) verbs of **seeing**:

ὁράω (or εἶδον) *to see*	θεωρέω *to look at, to observe*
βλέπω *to see, to look at*	θεάομαι *to look at, to see*

---

71 Note that in this grammar the term "predicative" is used of whatever obligatory sentence constituent is dependent on (the valency of) the predicate verb of a sentence (apart from the subject): objects and other complements (↑254c³).

72 Most of the verbs in view here are used with an ACP, a smaller number with a GCP. Very occasionally certain Ancient Greek verbs (outside the NT) may occur with a "DCP" (<Lat. "dativus cum participio": dative with participle), e.g. Plato, Apology 34b:

συνίσασι	*They know*
Μελήτῳ μὲν ψευδομένῳ ("DCP" 1),	*that Meletus is lying,*
ἐμοὶ δὲ ἀληθεύοντι ("DCP" 2).	*and I am speaking the truth.*

Examples:

εἶδεν (P/S) **σχιζομένους τοὺς οὐρανοὺς** (ACP/Od 1) καὶ **τὸ πνεῦμα … καταβαῖνον** … (ACP/Od 2).	*He saw the heavens splitting apart and the Spirit descending …* (Mk 1:10)

"What did he see?" *The heavens splitting apart …*

βλέπει (P/S) **τὸν λίθον ἠρμένον** (ACP/Od) ἐκ τοῦ μνημείου.	*She saw that the stone had been removed from the tomb.* (Jn 20:1)

↑also Mt 16:28; 25:37–39; Mk 5:15; 14:67; Lk 5:27; 10:18; 21:1.20; Jn 1:33.47; 6:62; Ac 1:11; 3:3; 10:11; 17:16.

Note that a ὅτι-clause may replace the ACP, especially when the verb of seeing itself appears in the form of a participle (↑271b; 275), e.g.:

ἰδὼν **ὅτι ἰάθη** …	*when he saw that he had been healed …* (Lk 17:15)

↑also Mk 2:16; Jn 6:5; 12:19; He 3:19.

Note that sometimes there seems to be an **ellipsis** of the participle of εἰμί *to be* (↑259n), e.g.:

πότε δέ σε εἴδομεν ξένον [ὄντα];	*When did we see you a stranger? / When did we see that you were a stranger?* (Mt 25:38)

↑BR §244.1 Note 1; BDF §416.1.

↑also Mt 14:30; 15:31; Mk 6:20; Ac 17:22; He 11:23 (↑Ex 2:2 LXX); Re 2:19.

Similar cases of ellipsis (↑ellipsis of copula ↑256d; ↑BDF §418.6) occur in Mk 1:23 (p.c./Attr); Lk 4:1 (p.c.); Ac 6:8 (p.c.); 19:37 (p.c.); 27:33 (in the case of διατελέω *to continue (to do/be)* [↑234b; BDF §414.1]), perhaps Ac 14:8 (p.c./Attr).

b) verbs of **hearing**: ἀκούω (+ GCP or ACP)[73]

Examples:

ἀκούομεν (P/S) **λαλούντων αὐτῶν** (GCP/Og) …	*We hear them speaking …* (Ac 2:11)
ὅσα (ACP/Od, part 1) ἠκούσαμεν (P/S) **γενόμενα** (ACP/Od, part 2)	*The things that we have heard were done …* (Lk 4:23)

↑also Mk 12:28 (GCP); Lk 18:36 (GCP); Jn 1:37 (GCP); Ac 22:7 (GCP); 26:14 (ACP); 2Th 3:11 (ACP); 2Pe 1:18 (ACP); Re 11:12 (GCP).

---

73 In place of an ACP/GCP an ACI or, more frequently, a ὅτι-clause may be used, so that ἀκούω (also πυνθάνομαι *to inquire* analogously) occurs with four types of objects (↑218j; 271b/275; also 167a):

a) GCP	when hearing a person
b) ACP	when hearing of an assured fact indirectly (in the NT occasionally when hearing a person)
c) ὅτι-clause	when hearing of an assured fact indirectly
d) ACI	when perceiving a message/a rumour

↑BDF §397.1; 416.1; BR §244.1 Note 3.

c) verbs of **knowing** and **discovering** (verbs of cognitive attitude or of mental perception):[74]

γινώσκω *to know*	ἐπίσταμαι *to know* (ACP extra-biblical)
οἶδα *to know*	εὑρίσκω *to find/discover*

Examples:

ἐγώ … ἔγνων (P) **δύναμιν ἐξεληλυθυῖαν ἀπ᾽ ἐμοῦ** (ACP/Od).	*I noticed that power had gone out from me.* (Lk 8:46)
οἶδα (P/S) … **ἁρπαγέντα τὸν τοιοῦτον** ἕως τρίτου οὐρανοῦ. (ACP/Od).	*I know … that such a person was caught up to the third heaven.* (2Cor 12:2)
εὑρίσκει (P/S) **αὐτοὺς καθεύδοντας** (ACP/Od).	*He found them sleeping.* (Mk 14:40)
οὐ γὰρ ἠπίστατο (P/S) [**αὐτούς**] … **κλαπέντας** (ACP/Od).	*For he did not know that they had been stolen …* (Josephus, Antiquitates 1.342)

↑also γινώσκω + ACP: Ac 19:35; εὑρίσκω + ACP: Lk 7:10 et pass. (especially Synoptic gospels).

3. CG has a second class of **verbs** with ACP phrases as their object: those of **showing** and **reporting**: 233c

δείκνυμι *to show*	ἀποφαίνω *to give evidence of sth.*
δηλόω *to make clear, to show*	ἀγγέλλω *to announce, to report*

Example:

αὐτῷ Κῦρον ἐπιστρατεύοντα (ACP/Od) πρῶτος ἤγγειλα (P/S).	*I was the first to report that Cyrus was marching against him.* (Xenophon, Anabasis 2.3.19)

The NT almost exclusively uses an inf./ACI phrase or a ὅτι-clause instead (↑218i; 271b/275), which was also acceptable in CG (though ACI phrases less frequently). There is, however, one NT instance that appears to belong here:

οἷς καὶ παρέστησεν (P/S) **ἑαυτὸν ζῶντα** (ACP/Od) … ἐν πολλοῖς τεκμηρίοις	*He presented himself to them … and gave many convincing proofs that he was alive.* (Ac 1:3)

Perhaps similarly Ac 9:41.

Verbs that are used with a double accusative (sometimes with an inf./ACI phrase; ↑153; 218) may seemingly occur with an ACP. In such cases the participle phrase is best taken as being nominalized (↑BDF §416.3) in the role of an identifying object complement (OC^{id}; ↑237c; 235b; also 137b), e. g.: 233d

… ἐάν τις αὐτὸν (Od) ὁμολογήσῃ **χριστόν** (OC^{id}: NP).	*… if anyone should acknowledge him as the Messiah.* (Jn 9:22)
πᾶν πνεῦμα ὃ ὁμολογεῖ Ἰησοῦν Χριστὸν (Od) **ἐν σαρκὶ ἐληλυθότα** (OC^{id}: nominalized PtcP)	*Every spirit that acknowledges Jesus Christ (as one) come in the flesh.* (1Jn 4:2)

---

74 In place of an ACP (that is attested rather infrequently in the NT) in principle a ὅτι-clause may be used (semantically = ACP) or (less frequently) an ACI (↑218j; 271b/275; also 233b[73]) so that three types of objects occur (not all of them attested with these verbs in the NT):

a) ACP (rather infrequent in the NT)	*that sth. is the case*
b) ὅτι-clause	*that sth. is the case*
c) ACI	*that sth. is the case,* CG mostly *how to do sth.*

↑BDF §397.1; 416.2; BR §244.1 Note 4.

Eph 1:17f may be interpreted in a similar way:

… ἵνα ὁ θεός … δώῃ ὑμῖν πνεῦμα σοφίας … **πεφωτισμένους** τοὺς ὀφθαλμοὺς τῆς καρδίας ὑμῶν …	*… that God … may give you the Spirit of wisdom … the eyes of your hearts as enlightened ones = … [give you/grant to you] that the eyes of your hearts are enlightened.* (↑Zerwick-Grosvenor)

Alternatively, πεφωτισμένους might replace πεφωτισμένοις as a p.c. connected with ὑμῖν: *… may give you …, as you have /having the eyes of your hearts enlightened* (lit. *as you are/being enlightened with regard to the eyes of your hearts*).
↑also Mk 8:17 (also ↑137b).

233e 4. Note that if the subject at the same time refers to what is perceived or shown, CG puts the predicative participle in the nominative (↑BR §245; whilst the NT uses ὅτι-clauses; ↑218j; 271b/275):

ὁρᾷς ἡμᾶς **ἀποροῦντας** (ACP)	*You see that we are at a loss.*
ὁρῶμεν **ἀποροῦντες** ("NCP")	*We see that we are at a loss.*

NT has something comparable mainly in the personal passive of εὑρίσκω *to find* (↑154a; 191c), e.g.:

εὑρέθη **ἐν γαστρὶ ἔχουσα** (SC/"[N]CP").	*She was found to be pregnant* (lit. … *found as being pregnant*) (Mt 1:18)

↑also further instances with εὑρίσκω: Lk 9:36; 17:18; Ro 7:10 (↑BDAG sub εὑρίσκω 2).
↑also instances with other verbs used comparably (with nominative complements): Mt 6:16 (ὅπως φανῶσιν *so that they may appear as*); 17:3 (ὤφθη *there appeared*); Jn 8:4 (κατείληπται *she was caught*).

234 Predicative participle: modifying verbs

(↑BR §243; Maier 1969: 88–92; BDF §414; 415; 435; Turner 1963: 158–160)

234a I. In Ancient Greek the predicative[75] participle (without article; ↑135b; 229b) fairly frequently occurs as a subject complement of certain verbs that may be called "modifying" verbs: unlike most other verbs they do not refer to the event, process, action or state that the sentence is about, its core information, but they modify it (as is similarly done by adverbials; ↑259b/259c), whilst the **participle** combined with it **expresses** the **core information**. The modifying verb, usually a finite form, plus the (nominative) participle combined with it, constitute a multi-part predicator (↑256b). Often the modifying verb form may be translated as an adverb, the Ancient Greek participle, however, as a finite verb form, though in quite a few cases there is a comparable use in English:

Examples:

ἔλαθόν (finite verb form) τινες **ξενίσαντες** (participle) ἀγγέλους.	*Some have **unknowingly*** (adverb) ***entertained*** (finite verb form) *angels.* (He 13:2)
ὁ ἄνθρωπος οὗτος οὐ **παύεται** (finite verb form) **λαλῶν** (participle) …	*This fellow does not **stop*** (finite verb form) ***saying*** (participle) … (Ac 6:13)

75 On the definition of the term "predicative" in the present grammar ↑254c[3].

ἔτυχον (finite verb form) **καθήμενος** (participle) ἐνταῦθα.	***Coincidentally*** (adverb), ***I was sitting*** (finite verb phrase) *there.* Or better (closer to Greek): *I happened to be sitting there.* (Plato, Euthydemus 272e)

II. In CG this use was widespread; in KG it was disappearing. The CG verbs that belong here may be assigned to the following semantic classes. **In the NT** these verbs are **only rarely** used (marked bold below), and if so, almost exclusively in Lk-Ac and Paul:

1. Modifying verbs that serve as a **blanket modification of the "action"** such as: 234b

τυγχάνω (not used in this way in the NT)	*coincidentally, to happen to*
λανθάνω (He 13:2)	*unknowingly, unseen* (sometimes + acc. *by*)
διαλείπω (Lk 7:45)	*to stop (doing sth.)*
ἐπιμένω (Ac 12:16; Jn 8:7; un-CG)	*to continue (doing sth.)*
διάγω, διαγίγνομαι, διατελέω (CG)	*to continue (doing sth.)*
προφθάνω (Mt 17:25)	*be ahead* (+ acc. *of s.o.*) *(doing sth.)*

NT example:

ὁ δὲ Πέτρος **ἐπέμενεν κρούων**.	*Peter continued knocking.* (Ac 12:16)

Similarly ἐπισχύω *(more) urgently*: Lk 23:5; προϋπάρχω *previously*: Lk 23:12; Ac 8:9.

On the ellipsis of ὤν (ptc. of εἰμί) ↑233b, p.400.

2. Modifying verbs that **highlight certain sub-aspects** of the "action" referred to, particularly: 234c

a) **getting tired** of or **ceasing** the "action" as well as **bearing with** or **beginning** the "action":

ἐγκακέω (Ga 6:9; 2Th 3:13), CG κάμνω	*to grow weary (in doing sth.)*
παύομαι (Lk 5:4 et pass.)	*to stop (doing sth.)*
τελέω (Mt 11:1; un-CG [BDF §414.2])	*to finish (doing sth.)*
ἀνέχομαι (in the NT not with PtcP)	*to endure, to bear with*
ἄρχομαι (in the NT + inf.; ↑218e)	*to begin*

b) **prevailing** or **being defeated** with regard to the "action":

ἡττάομαι (in the NT not with PtcP)	*to be defeated*
νικάω (in the NT not with PtcP)	*to prevail, to conquer*

c) **evaluating** the "action" (by the speaker/writer with regard to a certain norm):

καλῶς ποιέω (e.g. Ac 10:33)	*to act rightly (doing sth.)*
ἀδικέω (in the NT not with PtcP)	*to do wrong, wrongfully*
ἁμαρτάνω (Mt 27:4 according to BDF §414.5)	*to sin (in doing sth.)*

NT examples:

οὐκ **ἐπαυσάμην** μετὰ δακρύων **νουθετῶν** ἕνα ἕκαστον.	*I did not stop warning each one of you with tears.* (Ac 20:31)
καλῶς ἐποίησας παραγενόμενος.	*You were kind enough to come.* (Ac 10:33)

Similarly (simple) ποιέω *to do* with participle in Mk 11:5 and Ac 21:13.

234d 3. Modifying verbs that express an inner **attitude of the subject entity** regarding the "action" (note that in the NT these do not combine with a predicative participle), e.g.:

χαίρω *to rejoice* — ἀγανακτέω *to be indignant*
αἰσχύνομαι *to be ashamed* — μεταμέλομαι *to regret*

Example:

χαίρω διαλεγόμενος τοῖς σφόδρα πρεσβύταις. — *I enjoy talking with the very aged.* (Plato, Republic 328d)

In the NT only the following instances appear to connect with this semantic class:

ἠγαλλιάσατο … **πεπιστευκώς** … — *He rejoiced that he had become a believer* … (Ac 16:34)

δόξας οὐ **τρέμουσιν βλασφημοῦντες**. — *They are not afraid to slander the glorious ones.* (2Pe 2:10)

Comparable: Ac 26:2 (ἥγημαι ἐμαυτὸν μακάριον *I consider myself fortunate*), perhaps also Lk 19:48.

234e Note that in **CG** some of the above verbs combined with either a **participle** phrase or an **infinitive** phrase, the intended meaning typically being affected, e.g. (BR §243 note):

	with a participle phrase:	with an infinitive phrase:
αἰσχύνομαι	*I am ashamed to do sth.* = *I do it with shame*, e.g.: Plato, Gorgias 494e	*I am ashamed to do sth.* = *I refrain from doing it out of shame*, e.g.: Plato, Laws 656a
φαίνομαι	*It is evident that I* …, e.g.: Plato, Apology 22c	*It seems that I* …, e.g.: Plato, Sophist 235d

235 Predicative participle: periphrastic conjugation (↑203)

(↑BR §242; Duhoux §246; BDF §352–356; Z §360–362)

235a 1. In Ancient Greek the predicative participle (without article; ↑135b; 229b) also occurred as part of the periphrastic conjugation (↑203), which serves as a complex, i.e. a multi-part predicator (↑256a/256b; but also ↑235b):
Part 1: (typically) a finite form of εἰμί *to be*;
Part 2: participle; e.g.:

ἔσεσθε (Part 1) **μισούμενοι** (Part 2). — *You will be hated.* (Mt 10:22)

Note that at times it is not easy to decide whether the participle is meant as part of the predicator (of a periphrastic construction) or as an adverbial (↑230–231; 259), e.g.:

… ὅπου (LocA/LocC) ἦν (P) ὁ Ἰωάννης (S) **βαπτίζων** (part of the P or ManA [↑231e]?) — … *where John was baptizing* (part of the P) or … *where John stayed baptizing* (ManA) (Jn 1:28)

↑231k on Paul's and Peter's occasional use of the participle with an imperative force (presumably periphrastic conjugation with ellipsis of imperative of εἰμί *to be*).

235b 2. There is one use of the participle that is closely related to its use as part of the periphrastic conjugation (without well-defined boundary between them): in cases where a nominalized participle phrase (↑237) serves as a subject complement (SC[id]; ↑258a/258b) in combination with a finite form of εἰμί *to be* in the role of a copula verb, e.g.:

εἰ μὴ ἦν (P: copula verb) οὗτος (S) **κακὸν ποιῶν** (SC[id]), οὐκ ἄν σοι παρεδώκαμεν αὐτόν.	*If he were not a criminal, we would not have handed him over to you.* (Jn 18:30)
καὶ ἐκεῖναί (S) εἰσιν (P: copula verb) **αἱ μαρτυροῦσαι** περὶ ἐμοῦ (SC[id], article emphasizing equivalence [↑135a]).	*And these are the ones that bear witness about me.* (Jn 5:39)

So, there is an overlap here between the predicative and attributive/nominalized participles (as these categories are defined in this grammar; ↑229c). ↑237.

(c) Attributive and nominalized participles

Participle phrases as attributive modifiers 236

(↑BR §241; Duhoux §251; Maier 1969: 96f; BDF §412)

Like adjective phrases participle phrases frequently occur as attributive modifiers within a nominal phrase (↑136a/137b; 260a–260n):

1. modifying a **definite head noun** (occurs most frequently): 236a

a) between the article and the head noun, e. g.:

κληρονομήσατε τὴν **ἡτοιμασμένην ὑμῖν** βασιλείαν ἀπὸ καταβολῆς κόσμου. (Attr between art. and head noun)	*Inherit the kingdom (that has been) prepared for you from the foundation of the world.* (Mt 25:34)

b) after the head noun with the article being repeated, e.g.:

εἰς τὸ πῦρ (head) … **τὸ ἡτοιμασμένον τῷ διαβόλῳ καὶ τοῖς ἀγγέλοις αὐτοῦ** (Attr with repeated art.)	*into the fire … (that has been) prepared for the devil and his angels* (Mt 25:41)

similarly after 1st or 2nd pers. personal pronoun (inherently definite) with the participle phrase being in apposition to it (↑130b; 260h), e. g.:

ὑμεῖς (head) **οἱ ἀκολουθήσαντές μοι** (Attr with art.)	*you who have followed me* (Mt 19:28)

↑also 1Th 4:15.17; He 12:25; 1Pe 1:5.

2. modifying a non-determined head noun placed before or after it (occurs less frequently): 236b

a) in principle without article, e.g.:

ἀρχιερέα (head) **μὴ δυνάμενον συμπαθῆσαι** (Attr like head without art.)	*a high priest who is unable to sympathize* (He 4:15)

b) sometimes with the article to indicate definiteness or something as known (or to make the attributive function of the phrase explicit; ↑136a), e.g.:

… χρυσίου (head) **τοῦ ἀπολλυμένου** (Attr with art.)	*… than gold which perishes* (1Pe 1:7)

καὶ ἄλλαι πολλαὶ (head) **αἱ συναναβᾶσαι αὐτῷ εἰς Ἱεροσόλυμα** (Attr with art.)	*and many other women who had come up with him to Jerusalem* (Mk 15:41)

↑also Jas 4:14; 1Pe 1:10; 2Jn 7.

The following formulaic expressions frequently connect with proper names:

ὁ λεγόμενος / ὁ καλούμενος	*who/that is/was (also) called*

Examples:

Σίμων **ὁ λεγόμενος Πέτρος**	*Simon who is (also) called Peter* (Mt 10:2)
ἄνεμος τυφωνικὸς **ὁ καλούμενος εὐρακύλων**	*a violent wind called the Northeaster* (Ac 27:14)

On the ellipsis of ὤν (ptc. of εἰμί) ↑233b, p. 400.

237 Nominalized participle phrases (↑BR §241; Duhoux §244; Maier 1969: 97f; BDF §413; 264.6)

237a 1. Like adjective phrases participle phrases are frequently nominalized serving themselves as heads of nominal phrases, typically with the article preceding it; in such cases they are virtually the same as those serving as attributive modifiers (↑238), yet without (explicit) head noun (↑132d/137d). The article may have either an individualizing or a generic effect (↑132a/132b).

Examples:

a) referring to persons:

ὁ βαπτίζων (individualizing)	*the (well-known) baptizer* (Mk 6:14)
Ὁ ἀκούων ὑμῶν (generic)	*whoever listens to you* (Lk 10:16)
πάντας **τοὺς κακῶς ἔχοντας** (generic)	*all who were ill* (Mt 4:24)

b) referring to things:

… σου **τὰ ὑπάρχοντα** (individualizing)	… *your possessions* (Mt 19:21)
τὸ γεγονός (individualizing)	*what had (just) happened* (Lk 8:34)

237b 2. At times the participle phrase is nominalized without the article (↑132d[5]), e.g.:

ἐπηρώτων δὲ αὐτὸν καὶ **στρατευόμενοι** …	*Soldiers also asked him* … (Lk 3:14)

↑also Mt 5:32; 13:35; Ro 6:13; 2Cor 6:9; Jas 4:17.

237c 3. Nominalized participle phrases, as noun phrases, may have any of the **syntactic roles** typical of these (↑syntax of case forms ; ↑146–182), thus also the role of an identifying subject or object complement (S[id]C/O[id]C; ↑258a/258b; ↑also 255–260), a use where there is an overlap between the predicative and attributive/nominalized participles (as these categories are defined in this grammar; ↑229c; 235; ↑also 233d).

On combinations with πᾶς *every* ↑136d.

(d) Special idiomatic uses of participles

"Graphic" participle 238

(↑BDF §419; Z §363–365; 367; Reiser 1984: 133f; HALOT sub Hebrew or Aramaic equivalents)

In the NT, particularly in narratives, we often come across a special idiomatic use of the adverbial participle, that may be termed "graphic" participle. It mostly refers to an "action" (usually left implicit in English) that naturally **precedes** or **accompanies** the "action"/"situation" indicated by the superordinate verb form. The fact that there are a fair number of semantic-functional parallels in Ancient Hebrew (and Ancient Aramaic) need not imply that this is a Semitism. It can be regarded as a normal KG phenomenon, hardly ever occurring in classic or classicizing literature, but fairly well-attested in popular narrative literature of the Hellenistic period (a type of literature whose style is close to that of NT narratives).

Body movements or postures are frequently referred to, inter alia:

ἀναστάς / ἐγερθείς …	*he got up and …*
πορευθείς / ἀπελθών / προσελθών …	*he went (away/to s.o.) and …*
καθίσας …	*he sat down and …*
λαβών …	*he took (sth.) and …*
ἀνοίξας τὸ στόμα αὐτοῦ …	*he opened his mouth and …*
ἐκτείνας τὴν χεῖρα αὐτοῦ …	*he stretched out his hand and …*
ἀναβλέψας …	*he looked up and*
ἀποστείλας …	*he sent off (s.o.) and (did sth.) = he had sth. done …* (↑188e)

Examples:[76]

Ἐκεῖθεν δὲ **ἀναστὰς** ἀπῆλθεν …	*And from there he set out* (lit. *he got up*) *and went away …* (Mk 7:24)
πορευθέντες δὲ μάθετε …	*Go and learn …* (Mt 9:13)
καθίσας ἐφώνησεν …	*He sat down and called …* (Mk 9:35)
ἀποστείλας ἐκράτησεν τὸν Ἰωάννην.	*He had John arrested.* (Mk 6:17)
ἀναστὰς ἔφυγεν.	*He got up and ran off.* (Philogelos 240)
ἀποστείλας πρὸς τὸν δῆμον ἔφη …	*He sent word to the people/He had the people told …* (Plutarch, Lysander 15.2)

---

76 Delitzsch translates the first two examples as follows, rendering the graphic participle as a finite verb form (in line with the syntactic rules of Ancient Hebrew):
וַיָּקָם מִשָּׁם וַיֵּלֶךְ *wayyāqqom miššām wayyēleḵ* (Mk 7:24; ↑Gn 24:10: MT with a finite verb form, LXX with a graphic participle])
צְאוּ וְלִמְדוּ *ṣə'û wəlimḏû* (Mt 9:13)
Occasionally the Greek NT uses a finite verb (rather than a graphic participle): Ac 8:26 (Var. has a participle instead).

239 Pleonastic participles (↑BDF §420; Z §366; 368; Baum: 21ff)

A further idiomatic use of the adverbial participle may be called "pleonastic" (↑294x): in NT narratives direct speech is frequently introduced by a participle of a verb of communication (saying or answering), sometimes of cognitive attitude (thinking) or the like that seems unnecessary semantically. In spite of numerous functional parallels in Ancient Hebrew and Ancient Aramaic (↑HALOT sub אָמַר/ אֲמַר *'āmar/'ămar*), this use, too, is to be regarded basically as a normal KG phenomenon, hardly ever occurring in classic or classicizing literature, but fairly well-attested in popular narrative literature of the Hellenistic period (a type of literature whose style is close to that of NT narratives). Still, its relatively high frequency in Biblical Greek (LXX and NT) suggests that the Semitic or Biblical background in many cases was probably an important incentive to make use of it in NT narratives:

1. εἶπεν (ἔλεγεν or the like) **λέγων**	*he said,* "…" (Mt 22:1; Lk 7:39 etc.)

Outside the NT ↑e.g. Vita Aesopi 114; Philogelos 202, 234.

Note that functionally the participle corresponds to Hebr. לֵאמֹר *lē'mōr* (לְ *lə* + infinitive construct), e.g.: וַיֹּאמֶר … לֵאמֹר *wayyō'mer … lē'mōr.* LXX Καὶ εἶπεν … λέγων *and … he said,* "…" (Gn 9:8).

2. ἀπεκρίθη **λέγων** (also καὶ εἶπεν / λέγει, especially Jn) or	*he answered,* "…" (Mt 25:9.37 etc.)
ἀποκριθεὶς εἶπεν / ἔφη / λέγει / ἐρεῖ etc. (occurs frequently)	*he answered/answers/will answer,* "…" (Mt 4:4 etc.)

Outside the NT ↑e.g. Philogelos 46, 186.

Note that Hebr./Aram. mostly use two coordinated verb forms (↑Gn 40:18 and Dn 2:26): וַיַּעַן וַיֹּאמֶר *wayya'an wayyō'mer* (Hebr.), עָנֵה וְאָמַר *'ānēh wə'āmar* (Bibl. Aram.), וַאֲתֵיב וַאֲמַר *wa'ăṯêḇ wa'ămar* (Targum Aram.).

Note that in the Book of Revelation quite often there is no concord between the participle and its head. On this ↑261 and BDF §136.4; Z §13.

240 Participle and the Hebrew infinitive absolute (↑BDF §422; Z §369)

The adverbial participle is also used idiomatically in the LXX and as a result in OT quotations within the NT to render the Ancient Hebrew infinitive absolute (an intensifying verb form, ↑GKC §113), e.g. (NT = LXX):

βλέποντες βλέψετε.	*Seeing you will see = you will indeed see/you will be ever seeing* (Mt 13:14)

Is 6:9 Hebr.: וּרְאוּ רָאוֹ *ûrə'û rā'ô*

εὐλογῶν εὐλογήσω σε καὶ **πληθύνων** πληθυνῶ σε.	*I will bless you greatly and give you many descendants.* (He 6:14)

Gn 22:17 Hebr.: בָּרֵךְ אֲבָרֶכְךָ וְהַרְבָּה אַרְבֶּה *bārēḵ 'ăḇārekkā wəharbāh 'arbeh*

On the alternative LXX/NT rendering of the infinitive absolute as a noun in the dative of manner ↑180c.

3.2.3 Uninflected words

In 22g–22k the uninflected word-classes were divided into four groups: adverbs, prepositions, conjunctions and particles. The use of prepositions, closely connected with the syntax of declinable words and phrases, was discussed after the syntax of case forms (↑183–187). The following section is on the remaining groups. Note that a special chapter is devoted to the negatives (these include not only adverbs or particles, but also pronouns and conjunctions), as these are of special relevance to text interpretation. 252 contains an alphabetic list of the most important uninflected words. On the problem of assigning certain uninflected words to particular word-classes ↑250b, on interjections ↑252.63.

3.2.3.1 Adverbs (on word-class ↑22h, on word-formation ↑53; 365–366)

On the use of adverbs (↑53; 61c; also ↑DuG9: 601ff; BDF §434–437) 241

I. Adverbs are not only a rather heterogeneous group of words grammatically, but 241a
they also vary greatly with regard to their meaning, function, scope, and syntax. Classifying them appears to be impossible without certain overlaps. So, the overview below is based on a cross-classification (↑DuG9: 584ff). The main focus is on **meaning** and **function**, particularly on the semantic subdivision of circumstantial adverbs into local, temporal, manner, and (the smallest group) causal adverbs (in a broader sense). These may be assigned either to the class of absolute adverbs or to the class of pronominal adverbs (↑61a) with phoric-deictic (↑348), interrogative or relative functions:

		ADVERBS		
		absolute adverbs	pronominal adverbs	
			phoric-deictic	interrogative/relative(1)
circumstantial adverbs	local	πανταχοῦ *everywhere*	ἐκεῖ *there*	ποῦ/οὗ *where/to where*
	temporal	πάντοτε *always*	τότε *at that time*	πότε/ὅτε *when*
	manner	ταχύ *quickly*	οὕτως *so*	πῶς/ὅπως *how*
	causal	φυσικῶς *by instinct*	διό *therefore*	τί/ὅτι *because*
evaluative adverbs		τάχα *perhaps*		

(1) Note that the bulk of subordinating conjunctions were derived from relative adverbs; so, these two word-classes are without well-defined boundaries between them (↑270c).

1. **Circumstantial** adverbs indicate various kinds of circumstances:

a) **local** adverbs indicate place ("Where?", "To where?", "Where from?"), e.g.:

ἄνω	*above, upwards*	ἄνωθεν	*from above*

b) **temporal** adverbs indicate time ("When?", "How long?" or the like), e.g.:

σήμερον *today* ἀεί *always*

c) **manner** (or "modal") adverbs indicate manner etc. (typical question: "How?"):

• manner adverbs referring to some type of quality, e.g.:

ἀσμένως *gladly* ταχύ *quickly*
ὡσαύτως *likewise* ἄλλως *in another way*

• manner adverbs referring to quantity (↑241b scalar particles), e.g.:

περισσῶς *exceedingly* ὀλίγως *scarcely*

d) **causal** adverbs indicate reasons in a broader sense ("Why?" or the like), e.g.:

εἰκῇ *without cause* ὅθεν *therefore* (↑259c/259g)

2. Absolute and phoric-deictic circumstantial adverbs:

a) **Absolute** (or "autonomous") circumstantial adverbs can in principle be understood without any intra- or extratextual clues, e.g.:

ἐπιμελῶς *carefully* ἀναντιρρήτως *without objection*

b) The **phoric-deictic** circumstantial adverbs (part of the category of pronominal adverbs; ↑61c; 142/143), however, can only be understood when they are seen in relation to relevant entities inside or outside the text, in which they occur (on this also ↑346ff), e.g.:

κατῆλθον εἰς Σελεύκειαν, **ἐκεῖθέν** (loc. adv.) τε ἀπέπλευσαν εἰς Κύπρον. — *They went down to Seleucia, and from there they sailed to Cyprus.* (Ac 13:4)

ἐκεῖθεν *from there* refers or "points" (anaphorically or anadeictically) to Σελεύκεια *Seleucia* occurring just before in the text, which makes it possible to understand what the adverb is to communicate.

ἕκαστος τὴν ἑαυτοῦ γυναῖκα **οὕτως** (mod. adv.) ἀγαπάτω ὡς ἑαυτόν. — *Each man must love his wife as much as he loves himself.* (Eph 5:33)

οὕτως *so/as much* refers or "points" (cataphorically or catadeictically) to ὡς ἑαυτόν *as (he loves) himself* occurring later in the text, which shows how the adverb is to be understood.

σὺ κάθου **ὧδε** (loc. adv.) καλῶς. — *Have a seat here, please.* (Jas 2:3)

By means of ὧδε *here* the speaker "points" (pure deixis) to a concrete seat (not mentioned in any other part of the text, but situated in the real world outside the text), making clear what is intended.

3. These adverbs, too, are part of the category of pronominal adverbs (↑61c; 142/143): **interrogative adverbs** (calling for an answer by an adverbial) and **relative adverbs** (connected with an antecedent; on these ↑also 319a), e.g.:

πόθεν; *from where?* ὅθεν *from where*

4. **Evaluative adverbs** indicate the speaker's or writer's opinion on a "situation" (in a sentence-like way communicating a proposition; ↑311c), e.g.:

ὁμολογουμένως *undeniably* ἀληθῶς *obviously* (Mk 14:70)
τάχα *perhaps* οὐδαμῶς *by no means*

241b 5. Numerous adverbs overlap with other word-classes as far as their function is concerned, the following points being a matter of particular interest:

a) Quite often adverbs serve to link sentences, i.e. propositions/"situations" within a text (thus functioning as "connectives" that help texts to be coherent; on this ↑320; 325ff), in a way similar to that of conjunctions. In such cases the term "**conjunctional adverbs**" is used by some.

b) Various words classifiable as manner or modal adverbs, in view of their function, have more recently tended to be classified as **particles** (↑22g; 22k; 252). Particles may be subdivided inter alia into the following groups (↑DuG9: 600ff; also ↑252):

• **"scalar" particles**, indicating the intensity of a property or of a "situation" (↑manner adverbs; ↑241a), e.g.:

λίαν	*very (much)*	ἔτι	*still, yet*

• **"focus" particles**, marking a sentence element as having the greatest informational weight, e.g.:

καί	*even*	ἤδη	*already* (e.g. Jn 21:14)

• **"negative" particles**, negating the sentence as a whole or some of its elements (on this and on negation in general ↑243–249).

• **"evaluative" particles** (or "modal" particles), hinting at the speaker's/writer's attitude (and so communicating a proposition; ↑311c), e.g.:

γάρ (↑252.9b)	in questions expressing doubt, sympathy or the like, mostly not translatable, though sometimes as an added *then, pray* or a prefixed *What! Why!* (↑BDAG s.v. 1f)
δή (↑252.13a)	giving exhortations or commands greater urgency, mostly not translatable, though possibly sometimes like the prefixed discourse marker colloquial *Well* or *Well now* (↑BDAG s.v. 2, and Carter §76)
μή (↑252.38b)	introducing direct questions marking the expectation of a negative answer, mostly not translatable, sometimes as a negative statement with a positive tag question, e.g. Lk 22:35 μή τινος ὑστερήσατε; *You didn't lack anything, did you?* (↑BDAG s.v. 3a)

• **"conversation" particles**, controlling the flow of dialogues (and so communicating a proposition; ↑311c), especially (↑269c):

ναί	*yes*	οὔ	*no*

• **"interjections"** (expressing emotions); on these ↑252.63; 311c.

Also ↑183b and 185 on adverbs that also occur as prepositions.

II. Circumstantial adverbs (phrases) may have the following **syntactic roles**: 241c

1. mostly as an **adverbial adjunct** (optional sentence constituent; ↑259a–259m):

ἐθεράπευσεν αὐτοὺς **ἐκεῖ** (LocA).	*He healed them there.* (Mt 19:2)
ἀσμένως (ManA) ἀπεδέξαντο ἡμᾶς οἱ ἀδελφοί.	*The brothers and sisters received us warmly.* (Ac 21:17)

2. also as an **adverbial complement** (obligatory sentence constituent; ↑258c):

ὅπου (LocC) γάρ ἐστιν ὁ θησαυρός σου, **ἐκεῖ** (LocC) ἔσται καὶ ἡ καρδία σου.	*For where your treasure is, there your heart will be also.* (Mt 6:21)

When ἔχω and (rarely in the NT) πράσσω combine with an adverb (as quasi-synonyms of εἰμί *to be* + a corresponding adjective) the adverb is used as an adverbial complement (↑BR §166; BDAG sub ἔχω 10b and sub πράσσω2/3), e.g.:

… ταῦτα **οὕτως ἔχει**;	… *are these things so?* (Ac 7:1)
… εἰ **ἔχοι** ταῦτα **οὕτως**.	… *whether these things were so.* (Ac 17:11)
εὖ πράξετε.	*you will do well* or perhaps *you will be fine* (Ac 15:29)

3. as an **attributive modifier**:

a) as an attributive modifier of a noun (the head of a noun phrase; ↑260m; 136a):

ἐν τῷ **νῦν** καιρῷ	*at the present time* (Ro 3:26)
ὁ **τότε** κόσμος	*the world of that time* (2Pe 3:6)

b) as an attributive modifier of an adjective (the head of an adjective phrase (↑260i):

οὕτω μέγας	*so tremendous* (Re 16:18)
εἰς ὄρος ὑψηλὸν **λίαν**	*to a very high mountain* (Mt 4:8)

c) as an attributive modifier of an adverb (the head of an adverb phrase; ↑260o):

οὐ **πολὺ** δὲ μᾶλλον ὑποταγησόμεθα …;	*Should we not much more submit …?* (He 12:9)
περισσοτέρως μᾶλλον ἐχάρημεν …	*we rejoiced even much more …* (2Cor 7:13)

4. It may also be **nominalized** (sometimes even without article, when combined with a preposition) making possible a variety of syntactic functions (↑132d on syntax of declinable words and their phrases; ↑129ff):

πάντα ὑμῖν γνωρίσουσιν **τὰ ὧδε** (Od).	*They will tell you about everything here.* (Col 4:9)
ἐξ ὧν οἱ πλείονες μένουσιν **ἕως ἄρτι** (TempA).	*most of whom are still* (lit. *up to the present time/until now*) *alive.* (1Cor 15:6)

Note that occasionally the adverb οὕτως *thus/in this way* occurs in the role of a subject (↑255b, replacing τοιοῦτος *such as this*) or an object (↑257c, replacing τοιοῦτον *such as this*):

οὐδέποτε ἐφάνη **οὕτως** (S) ἐν τῷ Ἰσραήλ.	*Never has anything like this appeared/happened in Israel.* (Mt 9:33)

↑also Mk 2:12.

On complements ("second degree objects") occurring with certain adverbs ↑254c; 258d.

Comparison of adverbs (↑BDF §244–246) 242

242a I. For (gradable) adverbs in principle the same syntactic rules apply as for the comparison of (gradable) adjectives (↑138). These are a few examples:

1. Marked by the particle ἤ *than* (↑138a):

ἠγάπησαν οἱ ἄνθρωποι **μᾶλλον** τὸ σκότος **ἢ** τὸ φῶς·	*People loved the darkness more* (or *rather*) *than the light.* (Jn 3:19; also ↑138c)

↑also Ac 4:19; 5:29.

2. Marked by the genitive of comparison (↑138a):

ἀγαπᾷς με πλέον **τούτων**;	*Do you love me more than these?* (Jn 21:15)

↑also Mt 5:20; 1Tm 5:9.

3. Semitizing or Hellenistic replacement of forms (↑138c):

… **βέλτιον** (comparative form used as a superlative/elative) σὺ γινώσκεις.	… *you know very well.* (2Tm 1:18)

242b II. At times the adverb μᾶλλον *more* apparently needs to be supplied in thought in conformity with Semitic usage, e.g.:

ἔχρισέν σε ὁ θεός … **παρὰ** (= Hebr. מִן *min*) τοὺς μετόχους σου.	*God has anointed you … more than your companions.* (He 1:9; Ps 44:8 LXX)
χαρά … ἐπί … **ἢ ἐπί** …	*more joy … over … than over …* (Lk 15:7)

3.2.3.2 Negatives

Overview of negatives in Ancient Greek (↑Langslow: 712ff) 243

I. simplex negatives (adverbs/particles)		
not	οὐ/οὐκ/οὐχ (↑18b) (intensified: οὐχί)	μή (in certain cases intensified: μήτι)
II. complex negatives (pronouns, conjunctions, adverbs/particles)		
no one, none / nothing, none (↑63)	οὐδείς/οὐδεμία/ οὐδέν (< οὐδέ εἷς)	μηδείς/μηδεμία/ μηδέν (< μηδέ εἷς etc.)
nor, neither/nor, not even	οὐδέ (< οὐ δέ)	μηδέ (< μή δέ)
neither – nor	οὔτε – οὔτε	μήτε – μήτε
not yet	οὔπω	μήπω
no longer	οὐκέτι	μηκέτι
also note: *no – yes* (↑269c)	οὔ/οὐχί – ναί	

244 Typical use of negatives in KG (↑ BR §250; BDF §426ff; Z §440f)

	οὐ etc. (↑245; 247–249) ≈ Lat. *non* (LXX for לֹא *lō'*)	μή etc. (↑246; 247–249) ≈ Lat. *ne* (LXX for אַל *'al*)
1. nature of negation	objective	subjective
2. negated expressions	a) indicative clauses b) InfP or PtcP (rarely) c) verbless phrases	a) clauses with non-indicative moods (subj., opt., imp.) b) InfP or PtcP (standard use)
3. before direct questions (= CG)	*(do/does …) not?* (expected answer: "yes!")	not translatable (expected answer: "no!")
4. negated expressions CG	with "negative" force: a) declarative clauses b) verbless or ptc. phrases c) InfP depending on a verb of purely cognitive attitude or assertion	with "prohibitive" force: a) desiderative clauses b) clauses, PtcP, and other expressions with conditional force c) InfP (typically)
5. position a) negating a clause (↑128b) b) negating verbless phrases	at the beginning (in a subordinate clause mostly after the connective) or before the finite verb form before the phrase to be negated	

245 Use of the negative particle οὐ (↑BR §250; BDF §427–430; Z §440/441; 443)

245a **οὐ** *not* (in English often *do/does/did/am/are/is/was/were/will/would not* etc.) is used I. to negate **verbless phrases**, e.g.:

οὐκ ἐγὼ ἀλλ᾽ ὁ κύριος	*not I, but the Lord* (1Cor 7:10)
… ἀλλὰ εὐαγγελίζεσθαι, **οὐκ ἐν σοφίᾳ λόγου**.	*… but to preach the gospel – not with clever speech.* (1Cor 1:17)

II. generally to negate a **complete indicative clause** (in CG also one with a potential or oblique optative; ↑211d/211f):

245b 1. a **main clause** (↑209j on a rare exception with μή, ↑also 246a):

a) a declarative clause (↑267), e.g.:

οὐ γὰρ **ἐπαισχύνομαι** τὸ εὐαγγέλιον	*I am not ashamed of the gospel* (Ro 1:16)

b) in the NT one with a modal indicative future expressing a prohibition (↑202f), e. g.:

οὐ φονεύσεις·	*You shall not murder/Do not murder/You must not murder* (Mt 5:21)

c) (οὐ or intensified οὐχί) a direct question (↑Lat. *nonne*), expecting an affirmative answer: "Yes!", cancelling the negation expressed in the question (agreeing with English usage; unlike questions with [untranslatable] μή; ↑246a, 269b), e. g.:

οὐχ οὗτός ἐστιν ὁ τέκτων …;	*Isn't this the carpenter?* (implied: *Yes, he is!*) (Mk 6:3)

2. a **subordinate clause**: 245c

a) a declarative or interrogative clause with indicative (↑271a; 273d [in CG in the second part of an alternative question also μή]), e. g.:

ἐὰν εἴπωμεν **ὅτι οὐχ** ἡμαρτήκαμεν …	*If we say that we have not sinned …* (1Jn 1:10)

b) a temporal, causal or manner clause, in the NT normally also a conditional clause, with indicative (↑276/277; 287; 281), e. g.:

ὡς δὲ **οὐκ** ἐνέβλεπον …	*As/Since I could not see …* (Ac 22:11)
… **ὅτι οὐ** μετενόησαν·	*… because they did not repent* (Mt 11:20)
εἰ δέ τις πνεῦμα Χριστοῦ **οὐκ** ἔχει …	*But if anyone does not have the Spirit of Christ …* (Ro 8:9)
καθὼς τὸ κλῆμα **οὐ** δύναται καρπὸν φέρειν …	*Just as the branch cannot bear fruit …* (Jn 15:4)

c) almost always a relative clause with indicative (↑289a; 290b), e. g.:

… **ὅπου οὐκ** εἶχεν γῆν πολλήν.	*… where they did not have much soil* (Mt 13:5)
θερίζεις **ὃ οὐκ** ἔσπειρας.	*You reap what you did not sow.* (Lk 19:21)

III. to negate a phrase with **non-finite verb forms** (rarely so in the NT): 245d

1. a **participle phrase** (rarely so in the NT) in CG regularly, unless this is used with volitional or conditional force (↑227d), e. g.:

ὃν **οὐκ ἰδόντες** ἀγαπᾶτε. (agrees with CG usage)	*Though you have not seen him, you love him.* (1Pe 1:8)

2. in CG (in the NT) an **infinitive phrase** when it depends on a verb of purely cognitive attitude or assertion (↑215), e. g.:

… λέγοντες **οὐκ εἶναι** (οὔκ ἐσμεν if it were direct speech) αὐτόνομοι …	*… asserting that they were not independent …* (Thucydides 1.67)

246 Use of the negative particle μή (↑BR §250; BDF §427–430; Z §440–442)

μή *not* (in English mostly *do/let/may/should/must not* etc.) is used

I. to negate a **complete clause** (mostly) with a **non-indicative mood**:

246a 1. a **main clause** (mostly) with a **non-indicative mood**:

a) an independent desiderative clause (↑268 with a volitional subjunctive [↑210c–210f], optative of wish [↑211c], imperative [↑212c]), e.g.:

μὴ καθεύδωμεν. (hortatory subj.)	*Let us not sleep.* (1Th 5:6)
μὴ εἰσενέγκῃς ἡμᾶς εἰς πειρασμόν. (prohibitive subj.)	*Do not lead us into temptation.* (Mt 6:13)
μὴ φοβεῖσθε. (imp.)	*Do not be afraid.* (Mt 14:27 et pass.)
μὴ αὐτοῖς **λογισθείη.** (opt. of wish)	*May it not be counted against them.* (2Tm 4:16)

In CG also an augment indicative main clause without ἄν to express an unobtainable wish; ↑209j.

b) an independent (direct) question (269b/269f):

• μή (or intensified μήτι) indicates (↑Lat. *num*; in contrast ↑245b the use of οὐ *not*) that an answer is expected that negates the "situation" referred to in the question; here the negative particle is not translatable, often the question is best rendered as a statement of the intended "situation" together with a tag question (↑BDAG s.v. 3a), e.g.:

μὴ λίθον **ἐπιδώσει** αὐτῷ;	*Will he give him a stone?/He won't give him a stone, will he.* (Mt 7:9)
μὴ οὐκ ἤκουσαν;	*Have they not heard?/They have heard, haven't they.* (Ro 10:18)

For οὐ μή + subj. (less frequently with ind. fut.) ↑247a.

• with deliberative subjunctive (↑210d), e.g.:

δῶμεν ἢ **μὴ δῶμεν;**	*Should we pay them, or shouldn't we?* (Mk 12:14)

246b 2. a **subordinate clause** with a **volitional** or **conditional** force (mainly with volitional or prospective subjunctive; ↑210h–210j):

a) a clause subordinated by ἵνα + subj. *that* replacing an infinitive phrase (in CG less widely used than in KG; ↑210h; 272; on μή after expressions of fearing ↑247b), e.g.:

παρεκάλει αὐτὸν πολλὰ **ἵνα μὴ** αὐτὰ **ἀποστείλῃ** …	*He begged him earnestly not to send them ….* (Mk 5:10)

b) in a dependent declarative or interrogative clause the same as in its independent counterpart, e.g. with deliberative subj. (↑271; 273):

οὐκ οἶδ' **ὅπως φῶ** τοῦτο καὶ **μὴ φῶ.**	*I don't know how I am to say and not to say this.* (Euripides, Iphigenia in Aulis 643)

c) an adverbial clause with subjunctive, e.g.:

Note that in CG the iterative opt. could be used as well, a construction which in KG/NT is replaced by an augment ind. with ἄν (↑211i). In some types of Ancient Greek conditional clauses ind. or opt. occur, too (the NT indefinite case, however, was mostly negated by means of οὐ; ↑276–287).

μὴ κρίνετε, **ἵνα μὴ** κριθῆτε. (purpose clause)	*Do not judge so that you may not be judged.* (Mt 7:1)
… **ἐὰν μὴ** μένῃ ἐν τῇ ἀμπέλῳ. (prospective conditional clause)	*… unless it remains in the vine.* (Jn 15:4)
καὶ **εἰ μὴ** ἐκολόβωσεν κύριος τὰς ἡμέρας … (remote conditional clause)	*If the Lord had not shortened those days* … (Mk 13:20)

d) a relative clause with or without ἄν or (replacing ἄν) ἐάν plus subjunctive (↑290c–290e; mainly with conditional force or expressing purpose, in CG also relative clauses with indicative; on CG also ↑290f), e.g.:

ὃς ἂν μὴ ἔχῃ …	*The one who does not have …* (Lk 8:18)

II. to negate a phrase with **non-finite verb forms** (regularly so in the NT): 246c

1. an **infinitive phrase** (also in CG, unless it depends on a verb of purely cognitive attitude or assertion; ↑215; 245d), e.g.:

αἰτοῦμαι **μὴ ἐγκακεῖν**.	*I ask you not to lose heart.* (Eph 3:13)
… **ὥστε μὴ χρείαν ἔχειν ἡμᾶς** λαλεῖν τι. (a result clause, also ind. with οὐ possible; ↑279a)	*… so that we have no need to speak about it.* (1Th 1:8)

2. a **participle phrase** (μή is standard in the NT; in PtcP of CG it occurred only when a volitional or conditional force was indicated; ↑227d), e.g.:

ὁ **μὴ συνάγων** μετ᾽ ἐμοῦ σκορπίζει.	*Whoever does not gather with me scatters.* (Lk 11:23)

On μή = ἵνα μή *in order that … not* ↑251i; 278.

Peculiar uses of negative particles (↑BR §271 Note 3; 251; BDF §365; 370; Z §444; 344) 247

1. **οὐ μή + subjunctive aorist** (less frequently + indicative future) is used both in CG and KG to express the strongest negation of future "situations" (↑267), e.g.: 247a

ὁ ἀκολουθῶν ἐμοὶ **οὐ μὴ περιπατήσῃ** ἐν τῇ σκοτίᾳ.	*The one who follows me will never walk in darkness.* (Jn 8:12)
οἱ δὲ λόγοι μου **οὐ μὴ παρέλθωσιν**. (Mk 13:31/Lk 21:33 have the ind. fut. παρελεύσονται)	*But my words will never pass away.* (Mt 24:35)

↑also Mt 5:20; 18:3; Mk 9:1; Lk 13:35; 21:18; Jn 6:35; 10:28. With ind. fut.: Jn 4:14; 6:35; He 10:17.

On un-CG οὐδ᾽ (or the like) οὐ μή used in the same way ↑248b.

Originally μή may here have had reference to the speaker's misgivings about something, while the phrase negated by οὐ would indicate that these were unfounded:

οὐ μὴ γένηται τοῦτο.	*There is no* (οὐ) *risk that* (μή) *this happens. This will certainly not happen.* (↑Kühner-Gerth II: 221)

Note that the same construction (though with a different force) also occurs in independent (direct) questions with deliberative subjunctive (↑245b/246a; 269b/269f), e.g.:

οὐ μὴ πίω αὐτό;	*Shall I not drink it?* (expected answer: *Yes, you shall!*) (Jn 18:11)

247b 2. **μή** *that* and **μὴ οὐ** *that … not* after expressions of **fearing** (↑271e), mostly combined with subjunctive (less frequently with indicative, when the object of fear is placed in the past; in CG the oblique optative is possible as well; ↑211f), e.g.:

φοβοῦμαι μή …	*I fear that …* (↑210h; 271e)

In the NT this use occurs only in Ac, with Paul, and in He 4:1, e.g.:

… **φοβηθεὶς** ὁ χιλίαρχος **μὴ** διασπασθῇ ὁ Παῦλος ὑπ᾽ αὐτῶν …	*… the tribune, fearing that Paul would be torn to pieces by them …* (Ac 23:10)

↑also Ga 4:11 with ind.

At times an expression of fearing is to be supplied in thought, e.g.:

ἀνεθέμην αὐτοῖς τὸ εὐαγγέλιον … **μή πως** εἰς κενὸν τρέχω (probably subj.) ἢ ἔδραμον (ind.).	*I presented to them the gospel … for fear that I might be running, or had run, in vain/… in order to make sure that I was not running, or had not run, in vain.* (Ga 2:2)

↑also 1Th 3:5.

247c Fear clauses with μή or μὴ οὐ that lack a superordinate expression of fearing are sometimes used to express a cautious statement (↑267, infrequently so in the NT; Turner 1963: 98), e.g.:

Μὴ ἀγροικότερον **ᾖ** τὸ ἀληθὲς εἰπεῖν.	*[I fear] that it is too rude to tell the truth = It may be too rude to tell the truth.* (Plato, Gorgias 462e)
μήποτε δώῃ αὐτοῖς ὁ θεὸς μετάνοιαν …	*God may perhaps grant them repentance …* (2Tm 2:25)

↑Ac 5:39 (also ↑278b); Mt 25:9 Var.; LXX (MT אוּלַי *'ûlay* "perhaps"): inter alia Gn 27:12.

↑273f on a comparable use of εἰ.

3. Apparently pleonastic οὐ or μή after expressions denoting a negative idea (rarely used in the NT):

247d a) after verbs expressing negative statements ("to deny", "to dispute", "to doubt" or the like): ὅτι- or ὥς-clause, often with non-translatable οὐ or infinitive phrase with non-translatable μή, e.g.:

… ὁ ἀρνούμενος ὅτι Ἰησοῦς **οὐκ** ἔστιν ὁ χριστός.	*… the one who denies that Jesus is the Christ.* (1Jn 2:22)
… ἕως τρίς με ἀπαρνήσῃ **μὴ** εἰδέναι.	*… until you have denied three times that you know me.* (Lk 22:34 Var.)

↑also Lk 20:27.

247e b) especially in CG after certain verbs of negative volition ("to prohibit", "to prevent", "to refuse", "to guard against", or the like): an infinitive phrase combined with a non-translatable μή, when the verb is not negated, with a non-translatable μὴ οὐ, when the verb is negated, e.g.:

… ἀποκωλῦσαι τοὺς Ἕλληνας **μὴ** ἐλθεῖν …	*… to prevent the Greeks from coming …* (Xenophon, Anabasis 6.4.24)
οὐδὲν ἐδύνατο ἀντέχειν **μὴ οὐ** χαρίζεσθαι …	*He could not refuse to grant him the favour …* (Xenophon, Cyropaedia 1.4.2)
τίς ὑμᾶς ἐνέκοψεν τῇ ἀληθείᾳ **μὴ** πείθεσθαι;	*Who prevented you from obeying the truth?* (Ga 5:7)

↑also Ac 10:47; 14:18; 20:20.27; similar use (with subordinate clause): 2Cor 8:20; 2Pe 3:17.

c) in CG after negative expressions denoting something impossible or improper: frequently an infinitive phrase combined with a non-translatable μὴ οὐ, when the "situation" it refers to is meant to be negated, e.g.:

οὐδεὶς οἷός τ᾽ ἐστὶν ἄλλως λέγων **μὴ οὐ** καταγέλαστος εἶναι.	*No one who states it differently is able not to be ridiculous = No one has been able to state it differently without making himself ridiculous.* (Plato, Gorgias 509a)

Double and multiple negatives (↑BR §252; BDF §431; Langslow: 776ff) 248

1. In Ancient Greek double and multiple negatives in most cases strengthen the negation concerned; under specific conditions, however, the negation is cancelled. The following rules apply: 248a

if the last chain element:	then the negation:
a) is complex οὐκ ἦλθεν **οὐδείς**.	is strengthened (standard case) *Not a single one came.*
b) is simple οὐδεὶς **οὐκ** ἦλθεν.	is cancelled (a rather infrequent case) *Every one came.* (lit. *No one did not come.*)

2. Examples:

a) the negation is strengthened:

οὐκ ἔστιν ἐν ἄλλῳ **οὐδενὶ** ἡ σωτηρία.	*There is salvation in no one else.* (Ac 4:12)

↑also Lk 4:2; Jn 5:19; 15:5; Lk 9:36; Jn 3:27; 5:30.

… ὥστε ὑμᾶς **μὴ** ὑστερεῖσθαι ἐν **μηδενὶ** χαρίσματι.	*… so that you do not lack any spiritual gift.* (1Cor 1:7)
ὁ δὲ Ἰησοῦς **οὐκέτι οὐδὲν** ἀπεκρίθη.	*But Jesus gave him no further answer.* (Mk 15:5)

↑also Mk 11:14.

ἔθηκεν αὐτὸν ἐν μνήματι … οὗ οὐκ ἦν **οὐδεὶς οὔπω** κείμενος.	*He laid him in a tomb … in which no one had yet been buried.* (Lk 23:53)

b) the negation is cancelled:

… **οὐ** παρὰ τοῦτο **οὐκ** ἔστιν ἐκ τοῦ σώματος(1)	… *it is not for that reason any the less a part of the body = nevertheless it still belongs to the body.* (1Cor 12:15)
οὐ δυνάμεθα … ἡμεῖς ἃ εἴδαμεν καὶ ἠκούσαμεν **μὴ** λαλεῖν.	*We cannot keep from speaking about what we have seen and heard. = We must speak about what …* (Ac 4:20)

(1) For grammatical reasons it seems best to interpret this as a statement (not as a question as is done by NA); ↑BDAG sub παρά C5 and BDF §236.5.

↑also Lk 8:17; Mt 24:2.

248b 3. The NT and the LXX at times use the un-CG combination οὐδ᾽ (or the like) οὐ μή (instead of οὐδὲ μή) + subjunctive aorist (or indicative future) to express the strongest negation of future "situations" (↑247a): in this case the negation is not cancelled (against the above rule), e.g.:

οὐ μή σε ἀνῶ **οὐδ᾽ οὐ μή** σε ἐγκαταλίπω.	*I will never leave you nor forsake you.* (He 13:5; ↑Dt 31:6 LXX)

249 Negation influenced by Semitic usage (↑BDF §302; 448.1; Z §445f)

249a 1. The following Semitizing use (↑HALOT sub כֹּל *kōl* 11) occurs in the NT:

οὐ (μή) … πᾶς (לֹא/אַל … כֹּל *lō'/'al … kōl*)	= οὐδείς (μηδείς) *no one* (rather than *not … everyone!*) ↑144c.

Examples:

ἐξ ἔργων νόμου **οὐ** δικαιωθήσεται **πᾶσα** σάρξ.	*By works of the law no one* (lit. "no flesh", rather than "not all flesh") *will be justified.* (Ga 2:16)
πᾶς πόρνος … ἢ πλεονέκτης … **οὐκ** ἔχει κληρονομίαν ἐν τῇ βασιλείᾳ τοῦ Χριστοῦ καὶ θεοῦ.	*No sexually immoral … or greedy person has any inheritance in the kingdom of Christ and God.* (Eph 5:5)

↑also Mt 24:22; Lk 1:37; 1Jn 2:21; 3:10; Re 22:3.

249b 2. The hyperbolic (i.e. seemingly exaggerating; ↑295q) use of οὐ (μή) … ἀλλά meant as *not so much … as* (rather than *not … but*) agrees with Semitic usage, too, e.g.:

οὐ γὰρ ἀπέστειλέν με Χριστὸς βαπτίζειν **ἀλλὰ** εὐαγγελίζεσθαι.	*For Christ did not send me to baptize, but to proclaim the gospel = For Christ sent me not so much to baptize as to proclaim …* (1Cor 1:17; ↑Z §445.)

↑also Mt 10:20; Mk 9:37; Jn 7:16; 12:44; similarly also Lk 10:20.

3.2.3.3 Conjunctions (word-class ↑22h, function also ↑271ff; 318)

Conjunctions: preliminaries 250

1. Questions of terminology: 250a

a) **Conjunctions** are neither sentence constituents nor attributive modifiers (↑260), but they link words, phrases, or sentences/clauses (↑22j), which may have the role of sentence constituents or attributive modifiers.

b) What **distinguishes** conjunctions from adverbs and prepositions: 250b

• Sometimes it may be uncertain whether an uninflected word is to be classified as an adverb, conjunction, or preposition, mainly because all of these may be involved in indicating the place, time, manner, and causal relations of "situations" (↑259a–259m on ways of expressing adverbials), e.g.:

adverb:

… εἰσελεύσονται … λύκοι βαρεῖς εἰς ὑμᾶς … **διὸ** γρηγορεῖτε …	*… savage wolves will come in … Therefore be alert …* (Ac 20:29–31)

conjunction:

Ὅτι δέ ἐστε υἱοί, ἐξαπέστειλεν ὁ θεὸς τὸ πνεῦμα …	*And because you are sons, God has sent the Spirit …* (Ga 4:6)

preposition:

τὸ μὲν σῶμα νεκρὸν **διὰ** ἁμαρτίαν …	*the body is dead because of sin …* (Ro 8:10)

• Conjunctions are distinguishable from prepositions and adverbs along the following lines::

Prepositions combine with words that, if declinable, will be in a certain case (↑183a), while conjunctions do not. Some words, however, are used both as prepositions and as conjunctions, e.g.:

ἕως **τῆς ἡμέρας ἐκείνης**	*until that day* (Mk 14:25)

Here ἕως is used as an (improper) preposition + genitive (↑185a).

… ἕως **ἔρχομαι** …	*… until I come …* (Jn 21:22)

Here ἕως is a subordinating conjunction that introduces a temporal clause (↑276a).

Adverbs are used as sentence constituents, i.e. as adverbials (mostly adjuncts), or as attributive modifiers (↑241c), while conjunctions are not. Again, some words belong to the two word-classes at the same time, e.g.:

στρέψον αὐτῷ **καὶ** (direct object [Od]:) τὴν ἄλλην.	*turn the other one to him as well.* (Mt 5:39)

Here καί is a manner adverb/focus particle (↑241b): it highlights the Od as something additional.

Πολυμερῶς **καὶ** πολυτρόπως …	*at many times and in many ways …* (He 1:1)

Here καί is a coordinating conjunction that connects two sentence constituents of the same kind.

• Various uninflected words seem to be so difficult to assign to any of the word-classes under consideration that specialists have not reached any generally accepted solution. In such cases it is probably best to use the term "**particle**" in a grammar with primarily practical objectives (↑22k and 252).

2. Conjunctions (or particles; ↑22j[15]; 250b) may be divided in the following ways: 250c

a) according to their **function**:

• coordinating conjunctions, e.g. καί *and* and ἤ *or*; they connect words, phrases, or sentences/clauses (↑266b) as of the same (syntactic) rank (↑251a–251e).

• subordinating conjunctions, e.g. εἰ *if* and ἵνα *in order that*; they subordinate dependent clauses (↑251f–251m).

b) according to their **form**:
- one-word conjunctions (typical case), e.g. καί *and*, εἰ *if*;
- two-word (correlative) conjunctions, e.g. εἴτε – εἴτε *either – or*.

251 Overview of conjunctions (or particles; ↑250b)

(↑BR §253; 269–286; BDF §442–457; Z §400–477; DuG3: 316ff)

I. **Coordinating** conjunctions or particles
(also ↑252 for an alphabetic list of important uninflected words)

251a 1. **Copulative** conjunctions (simply linking words, phrases, or clauses; ↑266b):

(one-word conjunctions)	(two-word/correlative conjunctions)
καί *and* (as adv./focus particle *also/even*)	καί – καί *both – and*
τε *and* (postpositive, enclitic; ↑6d; 128b)	τε – τε/καί or τε καί *both – and*
οὔτε/μήτε *and not*	οὔτε – οὔτε/μήτε – μήτε *neither – nor*
δέ *and* (more often mildly adversative *but*)	
οὐδέ/μηδέ *and not* (as adv./focus particle *not even*)	

251b 2. **Disjunctive** conjunctions (expressing choice or opposition between two possibilities = "inclusive" or "exclusive" use; ↑e.g. 269e):

(one-word conjunctions)	(two-word/correlative conjunctions)
ἤ *or* (inclusive like Lat. *vel*, exclusive like *aut*)	ἤ – ἤ *either – or*
	εἴτε – εἴτε *either –, or; whether –, or* (↑273a; 280)
	πότερον – ἤ *whether –, or* (↑269e; 273a)

251c 3. **Adversative** or **restrictive** conjunctions (expressing opposition or limitation):

(one-word conjunctions)	(two-word/correlative conjunctions)
ἀλλά *but, yet, rather* (stronger than δέ)	
δέ *but* (often *and*) (postpositive; ↑128b)	μέν – δέ *on the one hand – (but) on the other hand* (both postpositive; ↑128b)
πλήν *but; rather* (+ ὅτι *except that*)	
μέντοι *but, yet* (also *in fact*) (usually postpositive; ↑128b)	

especially CG also (further ↑252.44; 252.34c):
ἀτάρ *but, yet*
καίτοι *and yet* (CG also *and further*)

251d 4. **Explanatory/causal** (coordinating) particle (↑250b):

γάρ (postpositive; ↑128b) *for* (explanatory/indicating reason)

5. **Inferential/consequential** particles (↑250b): 251e

οὖν, ἄρα (postpositive; ↑128b) — *so, therefore*

διό (= δι' ὅ), less frequently διόπερ, ὅθεν — *for which reason, therefore*

less frequently also:

τοιγαροῦν — *for that very reason, therefore*

τοίνυν — *hence, therefore*

II. **Subordinating** conjunctions

(also ↑270 on dependent clauses)

1. Conjunctions subordinating **subject-object clauses**: 251f

a) declarative clauses (↑271):

ὅτι — *that* (also " , '…' " when ὅτι ["recitative"] introduces direct speech)

ὡς (less distinctive than ὅτι; in the NT rarely with this function, more frequently in the sense of *as/how*, in part with the role of πῶς; ↑273b) — *that*

dependent on expressions of fearing (sometimes these need to be supplied in though; ↑247b):

μή mostly + subj. (CG also + oblique opt; ↑211f) — *that* (+ οὐ *that not*)

dependent on expressions of affective behaviour (↑BDAG sub εἰ 2; BDF §454.1):

εἰ — *that*

dependent on oath formulas or the like, agreeing with Hebrew usage (↑BDF §454.5):

εἰ (= אִם *'im*; ↑HALOT s.v. 4) — *certainly not*

b) dependent desiderative clauses (↑272) replacing infinitive/ACI phrases (↑213c; 217–221), with explanatory ("epexegetical") function (↑222; also ↑225a):

ἵνα (less frequently ὅπως) + subj. (sometimes + ind. fut.) — *that* (un-CG use) (+ ἵνα μή or + simple μή *that not*)

CG dependent on expressions that denote *to take care* or the like:

ὅπως + ind. fut. — *that* (ὅπως μή *that not*)

c) dependent interrogative clauses (indirect questions; ↑273):

εἰ — *if/whether* (NT: also before direct questions, translatable as " , '…;' "; on εἰ *[to see* or the like*] whether [perhaps]* ↑273f)

εἴτε – εἴτε — *whether – or*

πότερον (CG also πότερα) – ἤ (CG also εἰ – ἤ or εἰ – εἴτε) — *whether – or*

2. Conjunctions subordinating **adverbial clauses**: 251g

a) **temporal** conjunctions (↑276, especially regarding use of moods):

• in answer to question "When?":

ὅτε (less frequently ἡνίκα, ὁπότε) — *when, after*

ὡς	+ ind. aor. *when, after* + ipf. *while, when*; + ind. pres. (rare) *while/when*

less frequently:

ἐπειδή (only Lk 7:1 in the NT), CG also ἐπεί	*when, after*

+ prospective subj. (↑210i):

ὅταν (< ὅτε ἄν; less frequently ἡνίκα) CG also ὁπόταν	*when, whenever*

less frequently:

ἐπάν (Paul/LXX also ὡς ἄν)	*when, as soon as*
πρίν	*before*

(CG: when main clause is neg., also + ἄν + subj., when affirmative, then + inf./ACI or + ἤ + inf./ACI; NT: usually + inf./ACI or + ἤ + inf./ACI)

CG also (+ iterative opt.; ↑211i):

εἰ (temporal-iterative)	*when = as often as*

• in answer to question “How long?” (most of these conjunctions may also be followed by ἄν + prospective subj. [↑210i, in the NT sometimes without ἄν]):

ἕως (οὗ/ὅτου) (less frequently + ind.) or ἄχρι(ς) (οὗ)	*until, as long as*
μέχρι(ς) (οὗ)	*until* (CG also *as long as*)
also ἐν ᾧ or ἐφ’ ὅσον	*while, as long as*
rarely also ἀφ’ οὗ/ἀφ’ ἧς, ἐξ οὗ, ὡς	*since*
CG also ἔστε	*up to the time that, until, as long as*

251h b) **causal** conjunctions (↑277; 333d):

ὅτι, διότι (= διὰ τοῦτο ὅτι), also ὡς (NT 1×), in the NT also καθώς	*because, since* (sometimes *for* appears to be more adequate contextually)
ἐπεί (↑Lat. *cum*)	*as/since*; also *(since/for) otherwise*
ἐπειδή (and CG ἐπείπερ)	*as/since* (Lk 1:1 ἐπειδήπερ *since*)

less frequently:

ὅπου	*since/because* (mostly adv. *where/to where*; ↑61c)
ἀνθ’ ὧν = ἀντὶ τούτων ὅτι	*in return for which = because* (↑289e)
NT also καθότι (Lk/Ac), at times ἐν ᾧ or ἐφ’ ᾧ	*because* (↑289e)
CG rarely ὅτε and ὁπότε (↑Lat. *quando*)	*since/because, granted that*

251i c) **purpose** indicating conjunctions (↑278):

ἵνα, ὅπως	*in order that* (↑Lat. *ut*)

also (NT rarely): ὡς mostly + inf./ACI phrase;
especially CG at times: ὅπως/ὡς + ἄν

ἵνα μή, ὅπως μή or simple μή/μήποτε	*in order that … not* (↑Lat. *nē*)

Usually + subj. (↑210i); CG mostly + oblique opt., when the superordinate clause refers to the past (↑211f/211g); in the NT at times + ind. fut. replacing subj. (↑202j).

↑KG/NT occasionally: ὥστε + inf./ACI (↑221b) *in order to, in order that*

d) **result** indicating conjunctions (↑279; frequently rendering it as *therefore* [as a main clause] rather than as *so that* appears to be more adequate contextually): 251j

ὥστε (CG less frequently, NT rarely: ὡς) *so that* (= *with the result that*)

+ indicative (rarely attested in the NT) — mostly reference to actual results (neg. οὐ)

+ inf./ACI phrase (in the NT standard; ↑221c) — KG/NT reference to conceivable or actual results; CG mostly reference to conceivable results (neg. μή)

KG/NT less frequently: ἵνα + subj. *so that* (= *with the result that*)

Apparently in questions also ὅτι *(so) that* (= *with the result that*; ↑279a).

e) **conditional** conjunctions (↑280–285; BDF §371–376; Z §299–338; negated by μή [the NT indefinite case mostly by οὐ]): 251k

εἰ *if* (indefinite, remote, or potential case)

+ ind.: indefinite case; + augment ind.: typically remote case; + opt.: potential case

ἐάν (less frequently ἄ̆ν, CG also ἤν) *if* (prospective case)

+ subj., in the NT occasionally + ind. fut./pres. (↑210i; 209)

coordinated conditional clause also:

εἴτε – εἴτε *if – (or/and) if, whether – or*

f) **concessive** conjunctions (↑286; negated by μή): 251l

εἰ καί (or at times ἐὰν καί) *even if, (even) though*

less frequently:
καὶ εἰ or καὶ ἐάν (κἄν) *even if*

(καί, καίπερ, καίτοι + PtcP; ↑231g)

↑after a negation (in exceptive conditional clauses; ↑286):
εἰ μή (ἐὰν μή), also εἰ μήτι, KG/NT also ἐκτὸς εἰ μή *except (that)*

g) **comparative** conjunctions (↑287): 251m

ὡς (intensified ὥσπερ) *(just) as*

CG also (with generalizing force) ὅπως

καθάπερ, καθώς *just as*

less frequently: καθά, καθό, καθώσπερ

with a correlative adverb in the superordinate construction (↑61c):

ὡς (or ὥσπερ/καθώς/καθάπερ) *as* – οὕτως (less frequently καί) *so*

CG also ὥσπερ ἂν εἰ + opt. (conditional comparison) *as if*

252 Alphabetical list of important uninflected words

(↑BR §253; Denniston; BDF §438–457; 107 [also index]; Montanari; BDAG; Z §400–477; Thrall; also ↑318ff)

252a Preliminary remarks:

1. The following types of uninflected words are listed (alphabetically):
a) various kinds of particles (many of these may be classified as manner adverbs; ↑241a/250b);
b) coordinating conjunctions or particles (↑251a–251e);
c) subordinating conjunctions with more than one major function (↑251f–251m);
d) other particles (↑250b) including important interjections (↑252.63).
Note that many particles (though not sentence-like expressions) communicate propositions (↑311c).

2. Words marked by ° are postpositives, typically being the second word of a unit (↑128b p. 180).

3. The translational equivalents for a given word serve to express major functions. For a full coverage of its use standard lexicons need to be consulted. Note also that English usage and contextual factors often call for varied renderings to adequately express what is intended in a particular context.

4. Note that in the language of the NT (or KG) clearly fewer particles are used than in CG, yet, still a fairly large number, when compared to many other languages including English.

5. For a possible Ancient Aramaic influence on the use of relative pronouns, the genitive, ὅτι (*because/that*), ἵνα, ὅτε, and ὥστε (all corresponding to דְּ *də* /דִּי *dî* in Ancient Aramaic) in some NT contexts ↑Z §423–429 or Black 1967: 70–81.

252.1 **ἀλλά** strong adversative particle (stronger than δέ), major functions:

1. typically conjunction: *but*, frequently after a negation (↑Lat. *sed*);

2. sometimes modal particle before a directive: *(but) now/therefore*, e.g.:

ἰδοὺ ἄνδρες τρεῖς ζητοῦντές σε, **ἀλλ᾽** ἀναστὰς κατάβηθι καὶ πορεύου σὺν αὐτοῖς …	*There are three men looking for you. Now/So get up, go down and go with them …* (Ac 10:19f)

3. sometimes modal particle before a statement: *(but) indeed, certainly*, e.g.:

… **ἀλλ᾽** ἐν παντὶ φανερώσαντες ἐν πᾶσιν εἰς ὑμᾶς.	*… indeed, in every way we have been this clear to you in all things.* (2Cor 11:6)

ἀλλ᾽ ἤ *except* (after a negative clause), e.g.:

οὐ γὰρ ἄλλα γράφομεν ὑμῖν **ἀλλ᾽ ἢ** ἃ ἀναγινώσκετε …	*For we write nothing else to you except/than what you read …* (2Cor 1:13)

οὐ μὴν (μέντοι) ἀλλά *nonetheless, notwithstanding, anyway*, e.g.:

οὐ μὴν δὲ ἀλλ᾽ ἐγὼ πρὸς κύριον λαλήσω	*Nonetheless I will speak to the Lord* (Job 13:3 LXX)

252.2 **ἀμήν** particle of affirmation borrowed from Ancient Hebrew (אָמֵן *'āmēn* "surely!", HALOT s.v.; LXX: αμην, mostly, however, γένοιτο *So be it!*) *let it be so, truly, amen!* Usually spoken at the end of doxologies or the like, but also at the beginning of a solemn declaration made by Jesus (in the gospels, in Jn always doubled).

252.3 °**ἄν** (on ἄν = ἐάν ↑252.18; 280b) modal particle "possibly" (the "situation" referred to is conditional in some way), used

1. combined with an augment **indicative**:

a) to express the irrealis (↑209h; 284; in the NT occasionally without ἄν), e.g.:

(εἰ γὰρ ἐπιστεύετε Μωϋσεῖ,) **ἐπιστεύετε ἂν** ἐμοί.	*(If you believed Moses), you would believe me.* (Jn 5:46)

b) Hellenistic preterite iterative of the subordinate clause (replacing the CG iterative opt. [↑198c/199f; 211i] in temporal and relative clauses [↑276e; 290f]), e.g.:

ὅσοι ἂν ἥψαντο αὐτοῦ ἐσῴζοντο. — *All who touched him/it were made well.* (Mk 6:56)

2. combined with prospective **subjunctive** in subordinate clauses (↑210i/210j, in the NT sometimes without ἄν):

a) in temporal (ὅταν etc.; ↑276), conditional (ἐάν; ↑282), concessive (κἄν; ↑286) and comparative (↑287), also mainly in CG purpose clauses (ὅπως ἄν; ↑278), e.g.:

ἴσθι ἐκεῖ **ἕως ἂν εἴπω** σοι. — *Stay there until I tell you.* (Mt 2:13)

b) in relative clauses with a conditional (mostly general-prospective) force (↑290e), in KG frequently ἐάν replacing ἄν, e.g.:

ὃς δ᾽ **ἂν ποιήσῃ καὶ διδάξῃ**, οὗτος μέγας κληθήσεται. — *But whoever does and teaches them will be called great.* (Mt 5:19)

ὃς ἐὰν (= ἄν) οὖν **βουληθῇ** φίλος εἶναι τοῦ κόσμου … — *Therefore whoever wishes to be a friend of the world* … (Jas 4:4)

3. combined with potential **optative** in main clauses (↑211d) as well as in functionally corresponding content (↑271–275) and relative clauses (↑289), also in manner clauses expressing a conditional comparison (↑287), e.g.:

πῶς γὰρ **ἂν δυναίμην** …; — *How could I possibly …?* (Ac 8:31)

(In dependent/indirect questions of the NT the optative occurs without ἄν, perhaps due to popular KG usage, which is probably better than classifying it as an oblique optative; ↑211g.)

4. in **CG** combined with **infinitive** and **participle** phrases corresponding to the irrealis or the potential optative of main clauses (↑213c; 227c).

°**ἄρα** (in the NT also clause-initial), inferential/consequential particle *then, so, therefore* (also intensified by means of γε [↑252.10]: ἄρα γε and ἄραγε), e.g.: 252.4

Οὐδὲν **ἄρα** νῦν κατάκριμα — *Therefore, there is now no condemnation* (Ro 8:1)

In Paul frequently intensified: ἄρα οὖν (↑252.51) *so then/consequently.*

ἆρα interrogative particle (↑Lat. *-nĕ?*, ἆρ᾽ οὐ *nonne*, ἆρα μή *num*; Hebr. הֲ *hă*; only 3 instances in the NT; ↑269b), e.g.: 252.5

ἆρά γε γινώσκεις ἃ ἀναγινώσκεις; — *Do you understand what you are reading?* (Ac 8:30)

ἀτάρ CG adversative particle *but, nonetheless.* 252.6

ἄχρι(ς) temporal conjunction (also + οὗ) *until; as long as* (↑276a); preposition + gen. *until* (of time or space or extent). 252.7

°**αὖ** (also αὖτε/αὖτις/αὖθις) CG particle *again; on the other hand.* 252.8

°**γάρ** explanatory/causal particle: 252.9

1. mostly causal indicating a reason *for, since* (Lat. *enim*):

καὶ γάρ *for (indeed)* (Lat. *etenim*); *indeed, even* (Lat. *nam etiam*)
ἀλλὰ γάρ (CG) *but indeed*

αὐτὸς **γὰρ** σώσει τὸν λαὸν αὐτοῦ … — *For he will save his people* … (Mt 1:21)

2. also as a modal particle (↑241b p. 411) in questions (↑269d) expressing doubt, sympathy or the like, mostly not translatable, though sometimes as an added *then*, *pray* or a prefixed *What! Why!* (↑BDAG s.v. 1f), e.g.:

Τί γὰρ κακὸν ἐποίησεν; — *Why? What crime has he committed?* (Mt 27:23)

Less frequently in the NT (CG):
3. also with a confirmative force in answers (↑269c): *(yes/no) indeed* (originally representing a "yes" or "no" confirmed by a gesture), e.g.:

… καὶ νῦν λάθρᾳ ἡμᾶς ἐκβάλλουσιν; **οὐ γάρ**, ἀλλά … αὐτοὶ ἡμᾶς ἐξαγαγέτωσαν. — *… and now they are going to release us secretly? Certainly not! Let them … escort us out themselves.* (Ac 16:37)

On a number of further uses ↑BDAG/Montanari s.v. and Z §473.

252.10 °**γε** (enclitic; ↑6d) focus particle (↑241b p. 411; frequently not translatable)

1. limitative *at least, in any case*, e.g.:

… διά **γε** τὴν ἀναίδειαν αὐτοῦ ἐγερθεὶς δώσει αὐτῷ ὅσων χρῄζει. — *… at least because of his persistence he will get up and give him as much as he needs.* (Lk 11:8)

2. emphatic (definitive/intensive) *even*, e.g.:

ὅς γε τοῦ ἰδίου υἱοῦ οὐκ ἐφείσατο … — *who did not spare even his own Son …* (Ro 8:32)

3. frequently combined with other particles:

εἴ γε *if indeed/really*, e.g.:

… **εἴ γε** ἐπιμένετε … — *… if indeed you continue …* (Col 1:23)

εἰ δὲ μή γε *otherwise*, e.g.:

εἰ δὲ μή γε, μισθὸν οὐκ ἔχετε … — *Otherwise you have no reward …* (Mt 6:1)

In CG pronouns frequently combine with γε for added emphasis (↑139b; also 269c), e.g.:

ἔγωγε — *I at least/I at any rate*

252.11 **γοῦν** (< γε + οὖν), stronger form of γε.

252.12 °**δέ**

1. adversative *but* (weaker than ἀλλά), ↑Lat. *autem*;

2. often copulative, joining clauses (↑266b; indicating some development in the text): *and, then* (frequently best left untranslated),

also (like καί; ↑252.29,1) with explanatory or intensifying force *namely, that is* (LSJ s.v. II2a; BDF §447.8), e.g. Ro 9:30; Php 2:8; also negated μηδέ;

καί … δέ *and also*;

δὲ καί *but also*;

ὁ δέ, οἱ δέ etc. *but he/they (the latter one/ones)* etc. (↑131).

↑ also 252.34 on combinations with μέν.

252.13 °**δή** focus particle (↑241b p. 411), varying between temporal and consequential significance, it points to something present or conceivable:

1. gives exhortations or commands greater urgency, mostly not translatable, though possibly sometimes like the prefixed discourse marker colloquial *Well* or *Well now* (↑BDAG s.v. 2), e.g.:

διέλθωμεν **δή** … — *Well, let's go …* (Lk 2:15)

2. presents something as known or as a matter of course, *indeed* or the like, e.g.:

… ὃς **δὴ** καρποφορεῖ … — … *who indeed bears fruit* … (Mt 13:23)

3. underlining an idea of time *already, now*, e.g.:

… ἐκ γὰρ **δὴ** πολλῶν χρόνων … — … *actually since many ages already* … (1Clement 42:5)

Attic: νῦν δή *now, as it is*, πάλαι δή *for a long time already*, πολλοὶ δή *many already*.

4. also with inferential/consequential force *therefore*;

5. also to continue a narrative (like δέ) *then*; as well as in combinations such as:

ἔνθα/ἐνταῦθα/τότε δή *right then, at that moment*;
εἰ δή *if truly*;
ὅτε δή *precisely when*;
ὅστις δή *precisely the one that; anyone who*.

δῆθεν *indeed, really* (frequently used ironically), also *allegedly*. 252.14

δήπου (weakened δή) *surely, without doubt* (frequently used ironically), e.g.: 252.15

οὐ γὰρ **δήπου** ἀγγέλων ἐπιλαμβάνεται. — *For surely his concern is not for angels.* (He 2:16; only NT instance)

°**δῆτα** an intensified δή. 252.16

διό (= δι᾽ ὅ) *for which reason, therefore*. 252.17

ἐάν (< εἰ + ἄν) + subjunctive 252.18

1. conditional (less frequently ἄ̆ν, CG also ἤν; NT occasionally + ind. fut. or ind. pres.) *if* (prospective case; ↑282);

2. KG/NT = ἄν in relative clauses with a conditional (mostly general-prospective) force (↑252.3; 290e).

3. Note that (↑286) ἐὰν καί or καὶ ἐάν (κἄν) may correspond not only to *and if* but also to *also if, even if* and *at least*, e.g.:

ὁ πιστεύων εἰς ἐμὲ **κἂν** ἀποθάνῃ ζήσεται. — *The one who believes in me will live even if he dies.* (Jn 11:25)

… ἵνα **κἂν** τοῦ κρασπέδου τοῦ ἱματίου αὐτοῦ ἅψωνται. — … *that they might touch at least the fringe of his robe.* (Mk 6:56)

4. Note also that ἐὰν μή *if not/unless* (↑280b) may also correspond to *except that* (↑286b).

εἰ (proclitic; ↑6a) 252.19

1. conditional *if* (↑280–285):

+ indicative: indefinite case; + augment indicative: remote case;

+ optative: potential case (CG also temporal-iterative *when = as often as*; ↑276e);

Note the compound εἴπερ *if indeed, if it is true that* (↑εἴ γε [252.10]; the assumption introduced by εἴπερ is more certain, in parts almost causal *since*, e.g. Ro 3:30)

2. subordinating declarative clauses dependent on expressions of affective behaviour *that* (↑271e);

Note that dependent on oath formulas or the like agreeing with Hebrew usage (= אִם *'im* ↑HALOT s.v. 4): *certainly not*.

3. subordinating interrogative clauses (indirect questions; ↑273) *if/whether* (on εἰ [*to see* or the like] *whether [perhaps]* ↑273f);
4. in the NT also before direct questions (↑269b), mostly translatable as " , '...;' " (apparently a Hebraism, ↑אִם *'im* HALOT s.v. 5, or הֲ *hă*, which the LXX sometimes renders as εἰ before direct questions).
5. further noteworthy points (↑280b; 286; 273f):
a) εἰ μή/μήτι (= πλήν) (KG/NT also ἐκτὸς εἰ μή) also (apart from *unless*) *but*, after negation *except*, e.g.:

οὐδεὶς ἔρχεται πρὸς τὸν πατέρα **εἰ μὴ** δι᾽ ἐμοῦ.	*No one comes to the Father except by me.* (Jn 14:6)

CG also εἰ μὴ ἄρα *unless perhaps*.
b) εἰ καί (less frequently καὶ εἰ) *even if, although*, e.g.:

εἰ καὶ τὸν θεὸν οὐ φοβοῦμαι ... ἐκδικήσω αὐτήν ...	*Although I don't fear God ... I will grant her justice.* (Lk 18:4f)

252.20 **εἶεν** interjection *well!, so!, come now!* in dialogue especially marking transition (similarly εἶα).

252.21 **εἶτα/ἔπειτα** *then, afterwards.*

252.22 **εἴτε – εἴτε** *either – or; whether –, or* (↑273; 280b).

252.23 **ἐπεί**
1. causal *as/since* (also ἐπειδή; CG also ἐπείπερ); also *(since) otherwise* (↑277);
2. temporal *when, after* (in the NT only ἐπειδή in Lk 7:1 *after*; ↑276a).

252.24 **ἕως** temporal conjunction (also + οὗ/ὅτου) *until; as long as* (↑276a); (post-CG use:) preposition + gen. *until* (of time or space or extent).

252.25 **ἦ** adverb:
1. confirming an assertion (also ironically) *certainly, undoubtedly* (intensified ἦ μήν, KG εἶ μήν, ↑252.39), ἦ που *surely*;
2. in questions *by chance/perhaps?* or untranslated (↑269b).

252.26 **ἤ**
1. disjunctive conjunction *or* (expressing choice or opposition between two possibilities = "inclusive" or "exclusive" use, like Lat. *vel* and *aut* respectively; ↑e.g. 269e);
ἤ – ἤ *either – or;*
πότερον – ἤ *whether –, or* (↑273).
2. comparative particle *than* after comparatives (↑138a; 242) and other expressions of comparison or differentness, e.g.:

... ἐν ἐκκλησίᾳ θέλω πέντε λόγους τῷ νοΐ μου λαλῆσαι ... **ἢ** μυρίους λόγους ἐν γλώσσῃ.	*... in the church I would rather speak five words with my mind ... than ten thousand words in a tongue/in an unknown language.* (1Cor 14:19)
οὐδὲν ἕτερον ... **ἤ**	*in nothing else than ...* (Ac 17:21)

Note that ἤ *than* is often to be supplied in thought after figures or measures (Mt 26:53; Ac 4:22 etc.).
ἀλλ᾽ ἤ *except* (↑252.1);
ἄλλο τι ἤ; *isn't it so?*
↑also 276a on combination with πρίν *before*.

ἤν ≈ ἐάν; ↑252.18; 282a. 252.27

ἵνα conjunction + subj. (↑210i; CG mostly + oblique opt. when superordinate clause 252.28
refers to the past [↑211f/ 211g]; in the NT occasionally ind. fut. for subj. [↑202j]):

1. indicating **purpose** *so that = in order that* (↑278);

also with ellipsis of superordinate construction: ἀλλ' ἵνα *[but this has happened] that = but … must* (↑BDAG sub ἵνα 2f; BDF §448.7), e.g. Mk 14:49;

2. KG/NT less frequently indicating **result** *so that = with the result that* (↑279);

3. KG/NT frequently subordinating dependent desiderative clauses (replacing inf./ ACI phrases in a wide range of functions [↑272a–272d]) *that;*

4. occasionally introducing an independent desiderative clause: a kind of periphrasis of the imperative (↑210g; 268c; BDAG sub ἵνα 2g; BDF §387.3), e.g.:

ἵνα … **ἐπιθῇς** τὰς χεῖρας αὐτῇ …	*Please … lay your hands on her …* (Mk 5:23)

5. CG also used as a relative adverb *where; to where.*

καί *and; also, even* (↑BDF §442; Z §450–465): 252.29

1. coordinating **conjunction** *and*

a) As a **one-word conjunction** it joins words, phrases, or clauses/sentences (the joining of clauses/sentences occurs more frequently in the NT than in CG; this use is quite common in popular Greek literature of the Hellenistic period, its relatively high frequency in NT/LXX narratives, however, is quite likely due to Semitic/Hebrew influence [↑HALOT sub וְ *wə*]; ↑Baum: 27–39; ↑also 266b). καί basically means *and* indicating simple addition, which, however, may be understood in a variety of more specific ways (what exactly is intended by the speaker/writer is inferable [pragmatically] from the context in question; ↑312c[23] and 322a); among these the following nuances are especially worth mentioning (note that frequently *and* may still be retained as a translation of καί!):

(1) 'adversative' καί (≈ δέ; ↑338a): "but", "(and) yet" (occasionally "though": He 3:9; ↑286a), e.g.:

Ἐζήτουν οὖν αὐτὸν πιάσαι **καὶ** οὐδεὶς ἐπέβαλεν ἐπ' αὐτὸν τὴν χεῖρα.	*So they tried to arrest him, but no one laid a hand on him.* (Jn 7:30)

(2) 'consecutive' or 'consequential' καί (↑259i; 259e): "(and) so", "(and) then", "(so) that", a logic or temporal consequence (also 'apodotic' καί, i.e. introducing a *then*-clause; ↑280a); at times it adds something that is meant as temporally simultaneous "and at the same time": Jn 7:4), e.g.:

τοῦτο δὲ ἐγένετο ἐπὶ τρίς, **καὶ** ἀνεσπάσθη πάλιν ἅπαντα εἰς τὸν οὐρανόν	*This happened three times, and then everything was drawn up again into heaven.* (Ac 11:10)

(3) 'final' or 'purpose indicating' καί (↑259j): "in order that", e.g.:

πάλιν ἔρχομαι **καὶ** παραλήμψομαι ὑμᾶς πρὸς ἐμαυτόν.	*I will come again and (= in order that) I will take you to myself.* (Jn 14:3)

(4) 'temporal' καί, i.e. a καί introducing a temporal clause (↑217e; 259e): "when", e.g.:

ἦν δὲ ὥρα τρίτη **καὶ** ἐσταύρωσαν αὐτόν.	*It was the third hour/nine o'clock in the morning when they crucified him.* (Mk 15:25)

(5) 'relative' καί, i.e. a καί introducing a relative clause (↑289a), e.g.:

ἦσαν γὰρ πολλοὶ **καὶ** ἠκολούθουν αὐτῷ.	*For there were many who followed him.* (Mk 2:15)

(6) καί-clause corresponding to a ὅτι-clause or an infinitive phrase (↑271b; 275), e.g.:

ἤκουσεν ὁ βασιλεύς … **καὶ** ἔλεγον …	*The king heard … that people were saying …* (Mk 6:14)

(7) 'epexegetical'/'explanatory' καί (in part also CG): "that is (to say)", "namely" or ":" (↑341a), e.g.:

ὁ δὲ θεὸς δίδωσιν αὐτῷ σῶμα καθὼς ἠθέλησεν, **καὶ** ἑκάστῳ τῶν σπερμάτων ἴδιον σῶμα — *But God gives it a body as he planned, and (= that is) to each kind of seed its own body.* (1Cor 15:38)

(8) seemingly 'pleonastic' καί (↑294x), CG/KG/NT, after πολύς *much* before an adjective phrase, or after a relative pronoun (or after an article with a comparable function), not translatable, e.g.:

Πολλά … **καὶ** ἄλλα σημεῖα … — *… many other signs …* (Jn 20:30)

Ἰούδαν Ἰσκαριώθ, ὃς **καὶ** παρέδωκεν αὐτόν — *Judas Iscariot who betrayed him.* (Mk 3:19)

(9) καί signifying "as/like" with expressions indicating equality or similarity (no NT instances), e.g.:

οὐχ ὁμοίως πεποιήκασι **καὶ** Ὅμηρος. — *They haven't composed their work the same way as Homer.* (Plato, Ion 531d)

↑also 217e.

b) As a **two-word/correlative conjunction** καί – καί *both – and, not only – but also*; at times indicating contrast: *although – yet*, ↑(1) above; occasionally *on the one hand – on the other [hand]* (1Cor 1:22).

2. **adverb/focus particle** (↑241b p. 411) *also/as well* (something additional being highlighted), *even* (something unexpected or extreme being highlighted), e.g.:

στρέψον αὐτῷ **καὶ** τὴν ἄλλην. — *turn the other one to him as well.* (Mt 5:39)

ὑμῶν δὲ **καὶ** αἱ τρίχες τῆς κεφαλῆς πᾶσαι ἠριθμημέναι εἰσίν. — *Even all the hairs on your head are numbered.* (Mt 10:30)

↑also καί used as a particle indicating the concessive nuance of the adverbial participle (↑231g) or introducing a concessive clause (↑286).

Note that as an adverb/focus particle καί occasionally occurs after an interrogative with a use that corresponds to English *at all* or *still*, e.g.:

ἱνατί **καὶ** τὴν γῆν καταργεῖ; — *Why should it still use up the ground?* (Lk 13:7)

3. **Less common** uses of καί:

a) 'alternative' καί signifying *or*, e.g.:

ἐπὶ στόματος δύο μαρτύρων **καὶ** τριῶν … — *by the evidence of two or three witnesses …* (2Cor 13:1 ≈ Dt 19:15 LXX; Hebr. אוֹ *'ô*)

b) in a hendiadys ("one single [concept] referred to by two [coordinated] expressions"; ↑294v), e.g.:

περὶ ἐλπίδος **καὶ** ἀναστάσεως νεκρῶν — *concerning the hope of the resurrection of the dead* (Ac 23:6)

252.30 **καίπερ** indicating concessive nuance of adverbial participle (↑231g) *though.*

252.31 **καίτοι** (also καίτοιγε) adversative-concessive *and yet*, (also with adverbial participle; ↑231g:) *though.*

252.32 **κἄν** = καὶ ἐάν (↑252.18).

252.33 **μά** (related to μέν and μήν) exclamatory particle "indeed!" + accusative of the invoked deity or some other entity appealed to *by* (↑also 252.41).

In the NT this accusative is used (without μά) in Mk 5:7, Ac 19:13 and 2Tm 4:1; sometimes certain prepositions may have the same function: εἰς (↑184g; Mt 5:35), ἐν (↑184i; Mt 5:34ff; 23:16ff; Re 10:6) or (in CG as well) κατά + gen. (Mt 26:63; He 6:13.16; ↑184k), in CG also πρός + gen. (↑184p).

252.34 °**μέν** (shortened form of μήν):

1. combined with other particles to form a two-word/correlative conjunction:

a) μέν – δέ (characteristic of CG usage, much less frequently used in the NT) *(indeed) – but, on the one hand – on the other*, e.g.:

τὸ **μὲν** πνεῦμα πρόθυμον, ἡ **δὲ** σὰρξ ἀσθενής. *The spirit is willing, but flesh is weak.* (Mt 26:41)

↑also 131/142h:

ὁ μέν – ὁ δέ / ὃς μέν – ὃς δέ *one – the other / (this) one – (that) one*;

b) less frequently μέν – ἀλλά/πλήν *(indeed) – but* (e.g. Ac 4:16f; Ro 14:20; Lk 22:22);

2. 'solitary' μέν, i.e. μέν is used without the customary δέ (an anacoluthon construction [↑292e]; not uncommon in the NT, in part against CG usage):

a) In cases where there is a contrast, but it is either not expressed at all (i.e. only inferable from the context) or it is expressed in a way that does not grammatically tie in with the μέν phrase (so that a δέ appears to be dispensable; a phenomenon that occurs in CG, too), e.g.:

ἅτινά ἐστιν λόγον **μὲν** ἔχοντα σοφίας ... _ *These have indeed an appearance of wisdom ...* (sc.: *but in fact are foolish*) (Col 2:23)

Πρῶτον **μέν** ... _ *First ...* (series is discontinued) (Ro 1:8)

πρῶτον **μέν** ..., ἔπειτα (replacing δέ) ... *First ... then ...* (Jas 3:17)

b) in the NT (disregarding good CG usage): there is no correlative δέ, or it is replaced by an expression with καί, e.g.:

ὃ **μέν** ... **καὶ ἕτερον** (un-CG without δέ) ... *Some (seed) ... other seed ...* (Lk 8:5f)

3. μὲν οὖν indicating continuation:

a) *so, then* (especially in Ac), e.g.:

Οἱ **μὲν οὖν** ἐπορεύοντο χαίροντες ἀπὸ προσώπου τοῦ συνεδρίου ... *So they left the presence of the council, rejoicing ...* (Ac 5:41)

b) μὲν οὖν (CG), μενοῦν(γε) (NT clause-initial) enhancing or correcting a previous assertion *certainly, clearly; in fact, actually, rather*, e.g.:

μενοῦν μακάριοι οἱ ἀκούοντες τὸν λόγον τοῦ θεοῦ καὶ φυλάσσοντες. *Blessed rather are those who hear the word of God and obey it.* (Lk 11:28)

4. CG also = μήν:

καὶ μὲν δή *indeed*
ἀλλὰ μὲν δή *but certainly in fact*
οὐ μὲν δέ *certainly not*
πάνυ μὲν οὖν *certainly, undoubtedly* (in responses)

μενοῦν(γε) ↑252.34c. 252.35

°**μέντοι** (μέν [= μήν] intensified by τοι) emphatically affirmative *certainly*; mostly adversative *but, however*, e.g.: 252.36

οὐδεὶς **μέντοι** εἶπεν ... *But no one would speak ...* (Jn 4:27)

μέχρι(ς) temporal conjunction (also + οὗ) *until* (CG also *as long as*; ↑276a); preposition + gen. *until* (of time or space or extent). 252.37

μή (for details ↑244; 246–249) 252.38

1. in Ancient Greek basically "prohibitive" *not* (KG/NT negating non-indicative moods, mostly also infinitive and participle phrases);

2. μή (or μήτι) before direct questions (↑269b) untranslatable (expected answer: "No!");
3. μή = ἵνα μή *in order that … not* (↑278) or *that … not* (↑272a; 272c).
On μηδέ ↑252.48, on μήτε – μήτε ↑252.52.

252.39 °**μήν** (↑μέν, μά, and μέντοι) is used
1. confirming an assertion *surely, certainly,* also (CG) ἦ μήν (KG εἶ μήν, ↑252.25) *surely* (He 6:14; also LXX);
2. with adversative force *but, and yet* (↑252.1 οὐ μὴν ἀλλά);
3. in questions *now, then.*

252.40 **ναί** conversational particle *yes* (↑241b p. 411; 269c).

252.41 **νή** (related to ναί) confirming an assertion *yes, indeed, by* (+ acc., ↑252.33), e.g. (only NT instance):
νὴ τὴν ὑμετέραν καύχησιν … *by my pride in you* … (1Cor 15:31)

252.42 **νῦν** (also νυνί [in poetry also enclitic; ↑6d]), *now*, sometimes *as things now stand* (also nominalized, e.g. τὸ νῦν *this time/the present time* [↑131 p. 187], τὰ νῦν *with respect to the present situation ≈ now* [accusative of respect; ↑156 p. 233]).

252.43 **ὅθεν** (↑61c) *from where* (↑273b; 289a); *for which reason, therefore* (↑259c/259d).

252.44 **ὅμως** *however, nevertheless* (only 3× in the NT; ≠ ὁμῶς: *in the same way*!).

252.45 **ὅπως** basically comparative relative adverb, however, mainly used as:
1. conjunction + subjunctive (↑210i; at times + ἄν, CG mostly + oblique opt., when the superordinate clause refers to the past; ↑211f/211g):
a) subordinating a purpose clause *in order that* (↑278);
b) KG/NT subordinating dependent desiderative clauses (replacing inf./ACI phrase; ↑218b; 272) *that*;
c) CG dependent on expressions that denote *to take care* or the like (+ ind. fut. [↑202j; 272d]) *that*;
d) CG + any mood subordinating a manner clause (↑287a) *in the way that*;
2. adverb (basic use) *how, in what way* (↑61c; in the NT only Lk 24:20!).

252.46 **ὅτι** (going back to the neuter of ὅστις; ↑60b):
1. subordinating a declarative clause (↑271) *that*;
2. introducing direct speech (ὅτι "recitative" [↑274]) rendered as " , '…' ";
3. subordinating a causal clause(↑277) *because, since* (sometimes *for*);
4. occasionally (e.g. Mk 9:11) = (διὰ) τί (↑143c) or < τί (ἐστιν) ὅτι *why …?* (↑Z §222);
5. CG also (like ὡς) + superlative *as … as possible* (↑252.61).
On a possible consequential force of ὅτι *(so) that* (= *with the result that*) in questions ↑279a.

252.47 **οὐ** (proclitic; ↑6a; intensified οὐχί; for details ↑244/245; 247–249):
1. negative *not* (KG/NT generally negating indicative clauses);
2. οὐ before direct questions (↑269b) *(do/does …) not?* (expected answer: "yes!");
3. οὔ/οὐχί conversational particle *no* (↑241b p. 411; 269c).

οὐδέ (analogously μηδέ; ↑243): 252.48
1. preceded by another negative *and not, nor, neither*;
2. intensifying *not even*.

οὐκοῦν (the stress is on οὖν): 252.49
1. CG in questions *(well) then …? … isn't it?* (like Lat. *nonne igitur*);
2. inferential (in declarative clauses mainly post-CG; ↑BR §253.39) *therefore, so*, e.g. (NT/LXX 1×):

οὐκοῦν βασιλεὺς εἶ σύ;	*So you are a king?* (Jn 18:37)

οὔκουν (the stress is on οὐ), used in CG: 252.50
1. giving emphasis *certainly not, in no way*;
2. in questions *isn't it that …? surely not …?* (↑269b).

°οὖν inferential/consequential and temporal (as well as affirming) particle: 252.51
1. inferential/consequential *so, therefore*, e.g.:

μὴ **οὖν** φοβεῖσθε.	*So/Therefore don't be afraid.* (Mt 10:31)

2. temporal: indicating continuation:
a) to resume narrative after a parenthesis *well then, then, so*, e.g.:

Ἔλεγεν **οὖν** τοῖς ἐκπορευομένοις ὄχλοις.	*So he said to the crowds that came out …* (Lk 3:7; resumption after parenthesis of verse 4–6)

b) to mark a transition to something new (especially in the Gospel of John) *then* (sts. ≈ *and*), e.g.:

εἶπαν **οὖν** αὐτῷ· τίς εἶ; …	*Then they said to him, "Who are you? …"* (Jn 1:22)

c) combined with other particles such as ἄρα οὖν (↑252.4), οὐκοῦν/οὔκουν (↑252.49/252.50), and μενοῦν (↑252.34).
3. CG, possibly at times in the NT, too, μὲν οὖν affirmative *surely*, inter alia to correct a previous assertion: *in fact, actually* (↑Montanari μέν 3B), e.g.:

Πολλὰ **μὲν οὖν** καὶ ἄλλα σημεῖα ἐποίησεν ὁ Ἰησοῦς …	*In fact, Jesus made also many other signs …* (Jn 20:30; ↑Zerwick-Grosvenor ad loc.)

οὔτε – οὔτε (μήτε – μήτε, ↑243) *neither – nor*. 252.52

°περ (enclitic [↑6d]; related to περί [↑218b]; originally something like "in excess") 252.53
outside poetry only as an intensifier appended to relatives and particles, e.g.:

ὥσπερ *just as* (↑61c; 287)	εἴπερ *if indeed, if it is true* (↑252.19)
καίπερ *though* (↑252.30)	

πλήν adversative conjunction *but; rather* (+ ὅτι *except that*) *until* (CG also *as long* 252.54
as; ↑276a); preposition + gen. *except, excluding*.

°ποτέ (enclitic; ↑6d): 252.55
1. indefinite temporal adverb *at some time, ever* (↑61c);
2. CG intensifying particle (expressing impassioned urgency) occur with an interrogative, e.g.:

τίς **ποτε** …;	*Who in the world?* (↑LSJ s.v. III3)

°πω (enclitic; ↑6d) *yet* usually after a negative (NT/LXX always appended to it; 252.56
↑243), but also e.g. πώποτε *ever*, after a negative *never*.

252.57 **°τε** (postpositive enclitic; ↑6d; 128b) copulative conjunction *and* (less strong than καί; ↑Lat. *-que/et*):

1. usually joining clauses/sentences (↑269b; 251a), less frequently phrases, e.g.:

ἑτέροις **τε** λόγοις πλείοσιν διεμαρτύρατο …	*And with many other words he bore witness* … (Ac 2:40)

2. τε – τε (clauses/sentences or sentence constituents) *(both) – and*, e.g.:

ἐάν **τε** γὰρ ζῶμεν … ἐάν **τε** ἀποθνῄσκομεν …	*For if we live … and if die* … (Ro 14:8)

3. τε – καί or τε καί *(both) – and*, often simply *and*, mostly joining phrases, e.g.:

… ὅ **τε** στρατηγὸς τοῦ ἱεροῦ **καὶ** οἱ ἀρχιερεῖς …	*… the commander of the temple guard and the chief priests* … (Ac 5:24)

Note that τε being a postpositive it is usually placed after the first word of a phrase (after the article in the above example). When this is a one-word phrase the τε immediately precedes the corresponding καί , e.g.:

… ποιεῖν **τε καὶ** διδάσκειν	*… to do and to teach* (Ac 1:1)

252.58 **°τοι** (enclitic; ↑6d)[77] affirmative *certainly, exactly, believe me*, very frequently (in the NT only) appended to other particles, e.g. καίτοι (↑252.31), μέντοι (↑252.36).

252.59 **τοιγάρ** inferential *well then, (just) so*, strengthened τοιγαροῦν (2× in the NT) *(exactly) so, then, therefore*.

252.60 **τοίνυν** inferential *consequently, hence, so therefore* (3 or 4× in the NT).

252.61 **ὡς** (proclitic; ↑6a) basically a relative and indirect interrogative adverb of manner and comparison meaning "how/as/like" (↑61c), which the various uses go back to:

1. + noun, adjective, adverb, or numeral phrases (also ↑260i; in part ὡσεί for ὡς):

a) + **noun** phrases:

(1) comparative *as/like*, e.g.:

μία ἡμέρα παρὰ κυρίῳ **ὡς** χίλια ἔτη …	*One day is like a thousand years* … (2Pe 3:8)

influenced by Semitic usage *something like* (↑Hebr. כְּ *kə* HALOT s.v. 6), e.g.:

ἐνώπιον τοῦ θρόνου **ὡς** θάλασσα ὑαλίνη.	*In front of the throne there was something like a sea of glass.* (Re 4:6)

(2) indicating a property:

- a real one *as*, e.g.:

τί ἔτι κἀγὼ **ὡς** ἁμαρτωλὸς κρίνομαι;	*Why am I still being judged as a sinner?* (Ro 3:7)

- an objectively false or erroneous one *as though*, e.g.:

ἐπιστολὴ **ὡς** δι' ἡμῶν	*a letter as though from us* (2Th 2:2)

b) + **adjective** or **adverb** phrases (in the NT mostly replaced by πῶς, against CG usage) *how* (in exclamations; ↑266a), e.g.:

ὡς ὡραῖοι οἱ πόδες τῶν εὐαγγελιζομένων τὰ ἀγαθά.	*How beautiful the feet of those who bring good news.* (Ro 10:15; ↑Is 52:7)

---

77 This goes back to an earlier dative form of the 2nd person singular personal pronoun used as an ethical dative (↑176c) "to/for/against you (sg.)".

c) + **superlative** (↑138b; also 252.46) *as … as possible*, e.g. (only NT instance):
ὡς τάχιστα — *as soon as possible* (Ac 17:15)

d) + **numeral** phrases (↑145d) *about/approximately*, e.g.:
ὡς τάχιστα — *about two thousand* (Mk 5:13)

e) in CG used as a preposition + acc. (↑184t) *to* (↑Lat. *ad*; only relating to persons in combination with verbs of motion), e.g.:
ὡς βασιλέα — *to the King* (Xenophon, Anabasis 2.6.1)

2. + constructions with verb forms:

a) + constructions with **finite verb** forms, as a subordinating conjunction of:

(1) dependent declarative clauses	*that* (less distinctive than ὅτι; in the NT rarely used with this function; ↑271);
(2) dependent interrogative clauses	*how* (comparatively rare in the NT; ↑ 273b);
(3) temporal clauses	*when, after, while* (↑276);
(4) causal clauses	*because/since* (= ὅτι, rarely used in the NT; ↑277);
(5) purpose clauses	*in order that* (= ἵνα, occasionally in the NT; ↑278);
(6) result clauses	*so that* (= *with the result that*) (= ὥστε in CG at times, in the NT only occasionally, ↑279);
(7) manner clauses	*as* (strengthened ὥσπερ, CG ὥσπερ ἄν εἰ conditional comparison + opt. *as if*; ↑287).
b) + **infinitive**/ACI phrases indicating result	*so that* (= *with the result that*) (CG = ὥστε; ↑279; in the NT ↑Ac 20:24 [purpose/intended result])

c) + **participle** phrases:

(1) manner (imagined comparison)	*as if/as though* (↑231e);
(2) causal (subjective reason)	*because (I/you etc. think that)* (↑231f);
(3) indicating purpose (with p.c. fut. and in the NT pres.)	*in order/expecting that* (↑231i).

ὥστε + inf./ACI phrase or + subordinate clause with finite verb: 252.62
1. indicating result *so that* (= *with the result that*); + finite verb (rarely attested in the NT): reference to an actual result; + inf./ACI: KG/NT reference to conceivable or actual results, but CG mostly reference to conceivable results (↑279);
2. KG/NT + inf./ACI occasionally indicating purpose *in order to/in order that* (↑278).

Interjections (↑241b p. 411). These express reactive emotions or evaluations, some 252.63
of them also directives. Like vocatives (↑148a), they are, grammatically speaking, outside the surrounding sentence structure (they are parenthetical; ↑254e/292d). They do, however, have a communicative function: as text constituents they convey propositions (↑311c). In the NT the following three (proper) interjections are used, typically with the function of an exclamation (↑266a; ↑BDR §107.2):

1. ὦ mostly + vocative (for details ↑148a), but also to express surprise, joy (thus in Ro 11:33) or pain *oh* (↑LSJ; also written ὤ).

2. οὐαί expresses profound grief, especially in the face of impending disaster *woe to …! ≈ How terrible it will be for …!* (Mt 11:21 etc.), mostly + dat., but also + acc. or voc.

3. οὐά *ah!* expresses scornful amazement amounting to something like "Didn't we know that nothing would come of it" (Mk 15:29).

Alongside these there are adverbs used as interjections:

4. δεῦρο/δεῦτε *Come!* (Mt 28:6 etc.; ↑210c; 212f).

5. εὖ *Well done/Wonderful!* (Mt 25:21.23).

6. καλῶς *Well said/You are right!* (Mk 12:32; Ro 11:20).

Similarly a number of fossilized imperatives (↑210c; 212f) such as:

7. ἄγε *Come!* (Jas 4:13; 5:1).

8. ἰδού (↑ἰδοῦ, imp. aor. mid. [↑105e] of ὁράω *to see* [↑113.8]), sometimes replaced by ἴδε (imp. aor. act. of ὁράω), occurring frequently in the NT/LXX, used along the following lines (being a particle its form always stays the same regardless of whether one or more persons are addressed), in principle in KG/NT the same as in CG (though some NT uses appear to be due to Semitic influence [as reflected in the LXX], thus the frequency of καὶ ἰδού; ↑Hebrew הִנֵּה *hinnēh* HALOT s.v.; Baum: 20–26):

a) Traditionally *behold!, see!, look!*. "In communities accustomed to oral communication, ἰδού would serve to nuance a narrative reduced to writing, especially to focus on exceptional moments in the narrative." (Danker s.v.). It is particularly common in Mt and Lk, where it often occurs after some adverbial construction (e.g. a genitive absolute; ↑230d). Depending on the context it may be rendered in a variety of ways (often it is not translatable at all). E.g.:

Αὐτῶν δὲ ἐξερχομένων (gen.ab.) **ἰδοὺ** προσήνεγκαν αὐτῷ ἄνθρωπον … δαιμονιζόμενον.	*As they were going away, (behold) a man who was demon-possessed … was brought to him.* (Mt 9:32)

b) In verbless clauses it may have the role of a predicate (↑256d; BDAG s.v. 2): *here/there is (are), here/there was (were)* or *there comes (came)* or the like (↑use not only of Hebr. הִנֵּה *hinnēh* and Aram. הָא *hā*ʾ, but also of CG ἰδού as well as of Lat. *ecce*, and e.g. Italian *ecco* and Fr. *voici*), e.g.:

κύριε, **ἰδοὺ** ἡ μνᾶ σου …	*Sir, here is your mina …* (Lk 19:20)

3.3 Sentences and their constituents

Sentences and their constituents: preliminaries (↑BR §254) 253

In 129–252 we saw mainly what functions word-classes and phrases may have within sentences (↑126). In the next section (↑254–260) we will be moving in the opposite direction: starting from functions within sentences, i.e. from the various types of sentence constituents and attributive modifiers (↑127), we will show how these may be expressed by word-classes, phrases, and clauses.
This will be followed (↑261–265) by a section on the rules of grammatical concord (or agreement) of sentence constituents or of attributive modifiers and their heads.
After that there will be a section dealing with the various types of clauses or sentences (↑266–290), while a final section (↑291–296) will be about important peculiarities of sentence structure ("syntactic stylistics") and related questions.

3.3.1 Sentence constituents

Sentence constituents: terminological approach 254

I. On many details of how to classify and define the essential elements of well-formed sentences or clauses and of how to view their functional role there is no agreement among linguists. Most points of disagreement, however, are of merely theoretical concern. The approach adopted here basically follows the one used in the standard German grammar, the Duden-Grammatik, primarily the third edition (DuG3), supplemented with insights found in subsequent editions, especially the ninth one (DuG9). For the English version of the present grammar leading English grammars of a fairly recent date were regularly consulted, particularly those by Aarts, Carter, and Huddleston-Pullum (also the Crystal Dictionary). These works have greatly helped to make sure that the approach adopted in the present grammar is not only reasonably up-to-date as far as the results of general linguistic research are concerned, but also sufficiently accessible to prospective users (typically accustomed to a more traditional approach). At the same time, it was kept in mind that the syntax of Ancient Greek, in spite of basic similarities with the syntax of other languages, has laws and rules of its own and must not be squeezed into the mould of distinctions applicable to German or English syntax. 254a
In 127b–127e there is a brief introduction to the most important syntactic functions that sentence elements may have (major sentence constituents and attributive modifiers). These and a number of further ones will now have to be defined more systematically and illustrated more copiously (↑254b–254e). In particular it will be shown how they are expressed grammatically in Ancient Greek, primarily in the variety used in the NT (↑255–260).

II. To begin with, **sentence constituents** may be divided into **two groups**: 254b

1. Sentence constituents that are typically **obligatory** for sentences to be well-formed or "grammatical": subject and predicate (↑254c–258);

2. Sentence constituents that are **optional**, i.e. not needed for sentences to be well-formed or "grammatical" (not required by the valency of the verb): adverbial adjuncts and subject or object adjuncts (↑259).

Note that an attributive modifier is not a sentence constituent itself, but generally part of one (mostly of a noun phrase), modifying it in some way (↑260).

Example:

νηστεύω (S/P) δὶς τοῦ σαββάτου (ManA). *I fast twice a week.* (Lk 18:12)

νηστεύω *I fast* (subject and predicator) is obligatory for the sentence to be well-formed or "grammatical". Without it there would be a phrase (↑127b), but no sentence capable of conveying any information (↑127a):

δὶς τοῦ σαββάτου *twice a week*

Conversely, δὶς τοῦ σαββάτου *twice a week* (adverbial adjunct) is optional. Without it there would still be a well-formed, "grammatical", sentence:[1]

νηστεύω *I fast* (↑Mt 9:14)

254c III. As stated above (↑254b) the group of **obligatory sentence constituents** is made up of the subject (↑255) and the predicate (↑256).

The term "**predicate**"[2] is meant to refer to

1. the **predicator** (predicate verb; ↑256), rarely occurring alone, but (due to the valency of the verb; ↑below) calling for

2. one or more "**complement(s)**", i.e. typically obligatory (predicative) sentence constituents such as objects, subject/object or adverbial complements (↑254d; 257).[3]

Each verb (or each of its uses) is connected with a particular **sentence pattern** that largely determines the way a sentence/clause is to be structured, i.e. what further constituents, if any, are expected for it to be considered well-formed or "grammatical" (↑258d for an overview of typical sentence patterns).

In this context many linguists make use of the term "**valency**" borrowed from chemistry ("a measurement that shows the combining power of an element, especially as measured by the number of hydrogen atoms it can displace or combine with"; ↑COED s.v.). The sentence pattern of a verb is said to derive from the valency of the verb in question (or of one of its uses): it is the valency of the predicate verb that shows its "combining power", indicating the number of sentence constituents that, if any, it (usually) combines with in a well-formed ("grammatical") sentence/clause.

The concept of valency, a syntactic-semantic phenomenon, may be illustrated by the two examples 1 and 2 below (↑DuG9: 397ff; also ↑Huddleston-Pullum: 218–219):

Example 1: The "action"/"situation" referred to by the verb φεύγω *to run away* (in its typical use) necessarily involves someone who moves "quickly from a point or area in order to avoid presumed difficulty or danger" (↑LN 15.61). This verb may be said to have one semantic role to assign: the role of the agent (the entity performing or primarily causing the "action"), here represented by the subject οἱ βόσκοντες *the herdsmen*. The valency of this verb does not call for any further sentence constituents, its sentence pattern thus being simply S+P.

Example 2: ποιέω with a double accusative (↑153b) refers to an "action"/"situation" that may be defined as *to cause sth./s.o. to be sth./s.o.* This (in its typical use) necessarily involves not only an agent ("causer"), here represented by the subject (ἐγώ *I* [Jesus]), but also an entity or entities caused (to be sth./s.o.), i.e. a "patient" or "patients" (entity/entities targeted or affected by the "action"), here represented by the direct object (ὑμᾶς *you* [the disciples]). Moreover, there must be an entity or entities standing for the "effect" of the "action" (what or who the patient is caused to be), here represented

1 The information conveyed by it would obviously be reduced. Though grammatically speaking, δὶς τοῦ σαββάτου *twice a week* is dispensable, communicationally it is certainly not.

2 ↑Huddleston-Pullum: 24–26; Aarts: 89ff; ↑Carter §276a.

3 Note that in the present grammar whatever is part of the predicate is basically referred to as "predicative".

by the object complement with an identifying function (ἁλιεῖς ἀνθρώπων *fishers of people*). So, this verb, used this way, may be said to have three semantic roles to assign: the roles of agent, patient, and effect. This state of affairs has led to the valency of ποιέω with a double accusative (in the active) usually requiring not only a subject, but also a direct object and an identifying object complement for a sentence to be well-formed ("grammatical"), its sentence pattern being S+P+Od+OC^{id}.

Example 1 with φεύγω *to run away* (valency → sentence pattern S+P; ↑258d,1.1), based on Mt 8:33:

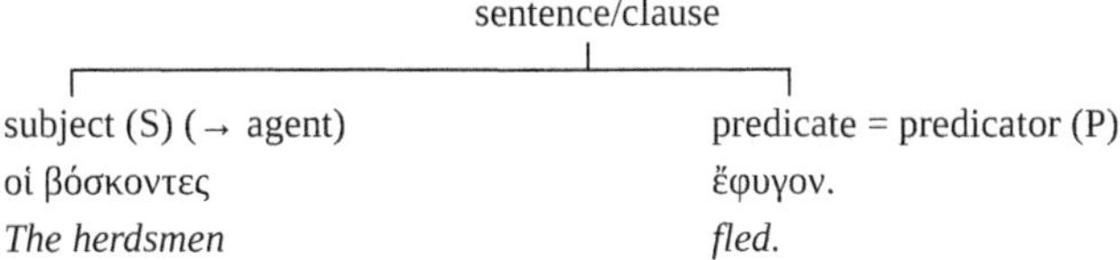

Example 2 with ποιέω + double accusative *to cause sth./s.o. to be sth./s.o.* (valency → sentence pattern S+P+Od+OC^{id}; ↑258d,1.15), based on Mt 4:19:

sentence/clause

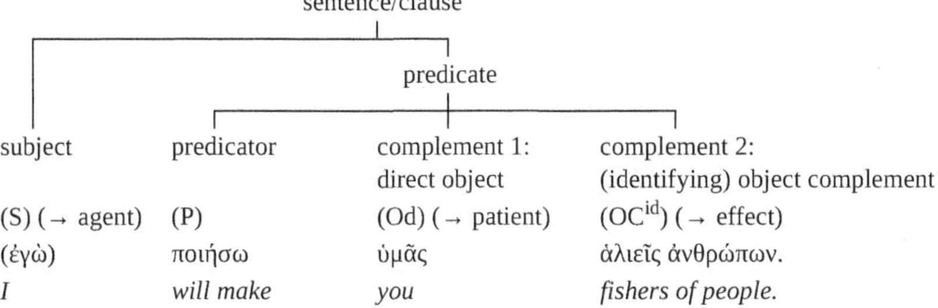

Note that not only verbs, but also some adjectives and adverbs, or even nouns have a valency of their own: some members of these word-classes need to be connected with a certain kind of expression in well-formed ("grammatical") sentences/clauses. This type of valency leads to what may be called a "second degree pattern", the basis of a "composite complement", of which the adjective/adverb or noun in question is "complement part 1", and the "second degree object" called for by the valency of the adjective/adverb or noun (mostly a Og/2nd, sometimes a $O^{dat}/2^{nd}$ or a Op/2nd) "complement part 2" (↑137a; 163b; 169a; 169b; 175; 179b; 183c; 219). ↑example 7 in 254d.

The following sentence constituents count as **complements**: 254d

1. **objects** (↑257), ↑example 6 below, and

2. **other** types of **predicative elements/complements** (↑258):

a) **subject/object complements** (on the less frequent subject/object adjuncts ↑254e), ↑examples 3, 4 and 7;

b) **adverbial complements** (on the more frequent adverbial adjuncts ↑254e), ↑examples 5 and 6.

Examples 3 and 4 (sentence pattern: S+P+SC; ↑258d,1.6), based on Mt 16:16 and Lk 19:2:

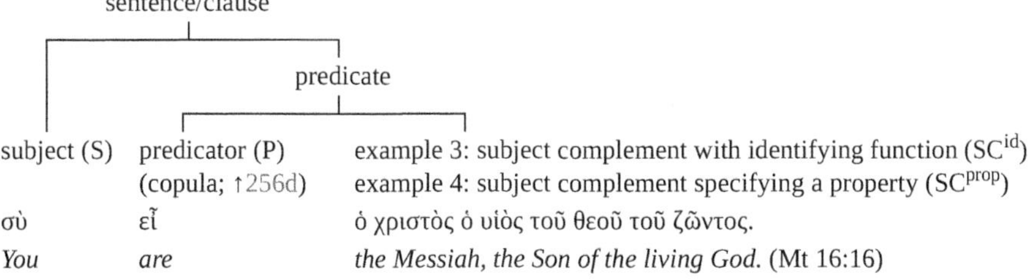

(αὐτὸς) ἦν πλούσιος.
He was rich. (↑Lk 19:2)

Example 5 (sentence pattern S+P+LocC; ↑258d,1.7), based on Ac 10:38:

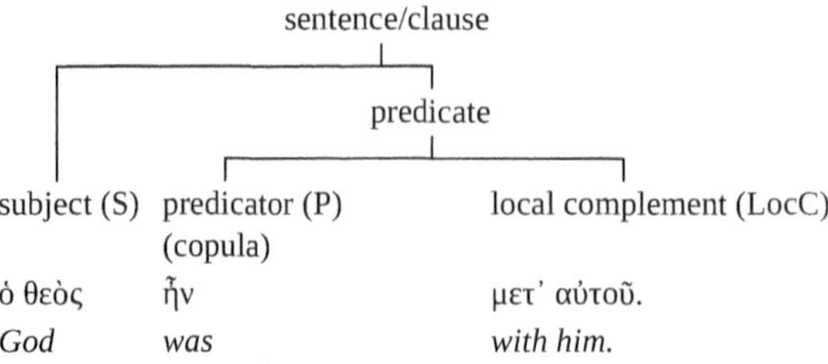

Example 6 (sentence pattern S+P+Od+LocC; ↑258d,1.14), based on Re 1:17:

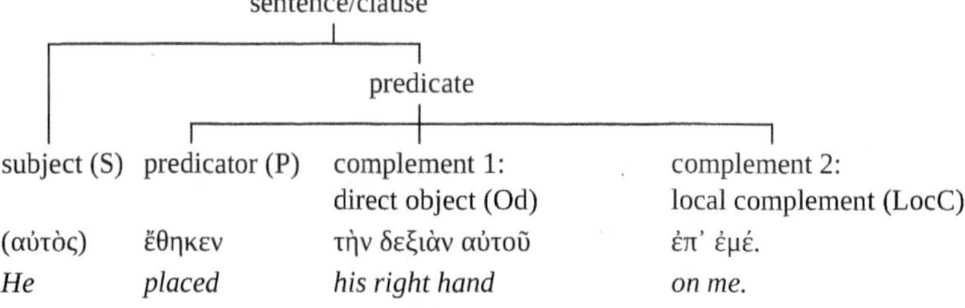

Example 7 (sentence pattern S+P+SC^{prop}+Og/2nd; ↑258d,2.2), based on Mk 3:29:

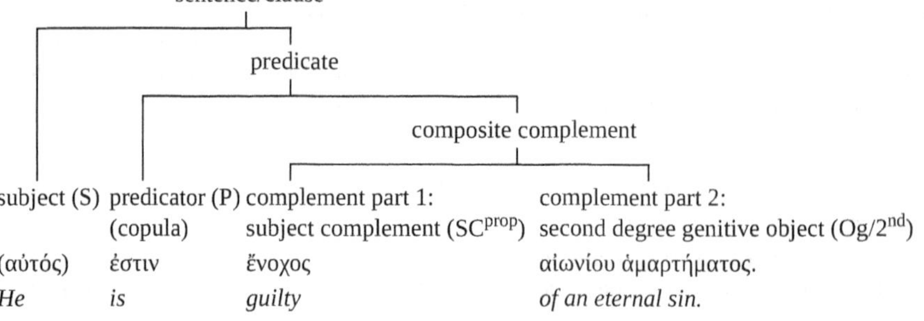

Example with an adverb used with a valency of its own:

περιπατῆσαι (P) **ἀξίως** (adverb/ManC) **τοῦ κυρίου** (Og/2nd) *to live in a manner worthy of the Lord* (Col 1:10)

254e IV. As stated above (↑254b) the group of **optional sentence constituents** is made up of

1. **adverbial adjuncts** (standard function of adverbials; on the less frequent adverbial complements ↑254d also 259a) and
2. **subject or object adjuncts** on the more frequent subject/object complements ↑254d also 259n).

Note that **attributive modifiers** (adding some information to an existing sentence constituent) are usually to be considered optional as well, i.e. grammatically speaking (though necessary in terms of communicational intent; ↑254b[1]), e.g.:

ἐπορεύθησαν εἰς **ἑτέραν** (Attr) κώμην. *They went on to another village.* (Lk 9:56)

The adjective phrase ἑτέραν here functions as an attributive modifier (↑260o). It is part of the local complement εἰς ... κώμην *(in)to ... a village*. It contributes some additional information, which is dispensable grammatically speaking. Without ἑτέραν *another* the sentence/clause would be poorer informationally (in terms of communicational intent), but still be well-formed grammatically.

Also note that the **vocative** phrases (↑148a) and **interjections** (↑252.63) are **outside** the surrounding **sentence structure** (they are parenthetical; ↑292d).

3.3.1.1 Obligatory sentence constituents

(i) Subject

Subject: function and ways of expressing it 255

I. The subject ("S") typically indicates the "theme"[4] (i.e. what the sentence or clause is "about"; also ↑135c) and, in sentences/clauses with a non-passive predicate verb, the entity performing the "action", the agent (↑254d), or its leading participant. 255a

With a passive predicate verb it mostly indicates the entity undergoing, experiencing, or enduring the "action", i.e. the patient (↑254c) which in a non-passive construction appears as the object entity.

Example:

ἔτεκεν υἱόν. *She bore a son.* (Mt 1:25)

subject = agent (the one bearing the son); object = patient (the one born)

ἐτέχθη ... σωτήρ. *A Saviour has been born ...* (Lk 2:11)

subject = patient (the one born); the agent (the one bearing the Saviour) is not mentioned (↑191a).

As the subject is a sentence constituent regularly called for by the predicate verb (by its valency), many classify it as a complement. In the present grammar, however, the term "complement" refers exclusively to sentence constituents of the predicate other than the predicator/predicate verb (↑254c). This seems to be justified inter alia because in several respects the subject may be regarded as having a special status (↑DuG9: 822).

II. The subject may be **expressed** as follows: 255b

1. In **normal clauses/sentences**

a) by a **noun phrase** whose head is in the **nominative** (so also any expansions showing concord; ↑147a) and may be:

- a **noun**

(occasionally preceded by ὡς *something like*; ↑252.61,1a[1]),

4 Note that instead of "theme" and "rheme" many use the pair "topic" and "comment".

• a **pronoun** used as a noun substitute (↑22c; 139, especially 139a), including the pronominal article (↑131)
(in the NT occasionally replaced by an adverb [↑241c]; ↑also 166b on τινές *some* at times to be supplied in thought in a partitive genitive [also ἐκ/ἐξ or ἀπό + gen.] construction),

• any kind of **nominalized** expression: adjective (↑137d), participle (↑237), or infinitive/ACI (↑217; 224) phrases or any other expressions that are nominalized, (typically) by means of the article (↑132d).

Examples:

ἐδάκρυσεν **ὁ Ἰησοῦς** (noun/proper name).	*Jesus wept.* (Jn 11:35)
ἐκεῖνος (pron.: noun substitute) ἐμὲ δοξάσει.	*He will glorify me.* (Jn 16:14)
ἀπέθανεν δὲ καὶ **ὁ πλούσιος** (nominalized AdjP).	*The rich man also died.* (Lk 16:22)
ὁ ἀκούων ὑμῶν (nominalized PtcP) ἐμοῦ ἀκούει.	*The one who listens to you, listens to me.* (Lk 10:16)
τὸ γὰρ **θέλειν** (nominalized InfP) παράκειταί μοι, **τὸ** δὲ **κατεργάζεσθαι τὸ καλὸν** (nominalized InfP) οὔ.	*For the desire [to do] what is good is with me, but not [the ability] to carry it out.* (Ro 7:18)
οἱ δώδεκα (nominalized numeral) εἶπαν αὐτῷ …	*The Twelve said to him …* (Lk 9:12)
Ἀσπάζονται ὑμᾶς **οἱ ἀπὸ τῆς Ἰταλίας**. (nominalized PpP)	*Those from Italy send you greetings.* (He 13:24)

255c Note that the phrase expressing the subject is absent in certain cases (↑BDF §129/130; on the ellipsis phenomenon generally ↑293c), especially

• with verbs referring to the weather,[5] the time of the day or the like, e.g.:

οὐκ ἔβρεξεν (βρέχω; CG prefers ὕω/ὕει).	*It did not rain.* (Jas 5:17)
ἦν δὲ πρωΐ.	*It was early morning.* (Jn 18:28)

• with verbs whose subject is easy to infer, e.g.:

σαλπίσει (3rd sg. fut. act. of σαλπίζω *to sound a trumpet*).	*He* (i.e. the trumpeter) *will sound a trumpet.* (1Cor 15:52; otherwise with explicit subject in the NT)

• in the citation formula λέγει etc., with ὁ θεός *God*, ἡ γραφή *the Scripture* or the like being the implied subject, e.g.:

λέγει γάρ· καιρῷ δεκτῷ ἐπήκουσά σου …	*For God/the Scripture/he* or the like/*it says, "At an acceptable time …"* (2Cor 6:2)

255d b) very frequently (solely) by the **personal ending** of the predicate verb, in which case the subject and the predicate verb are both expressed by one form (the personal pronoun is added usually only for emphasis, especially in contrasts; ↑139a), e.g.:

πιστεύ**ω**.	*I believe.* (Jn 9:38)

5 At times the subject phrase is present. So, the LXX uses CG ὕω 2× (with the subject ἐγώ *I* [Yahweh] *am sending rain*): Ex 9:18; 16:4.

c) a **subordinate clause** in the subject role (↑270a), i.e. a conjunctional declarative, desiderative or interrogative clause (↑270–273) as well as certain relative clauses (↑289b), similarly direct speech (↑274b), e.g.: 255e

συμφέρει ὑμῖν **ἵνα ἐγὼ ἀπέλθω.** (ἵνα-clause)	*It is good for you that I go away.* (Jn 16:7)
"What is good for?" *That I go away.*	
ἠκούσθη **ὅτι ἐν οἴκῳ ἐστίν.** (ὅτι-clause)	*It was heard/reported that he was at home.* (Mk 2:1; also ↑218g)
"What was heard/reported?" *That he was at home.*	
ὃς γὰρ **οὐκ ἔστιν καθ' ἡμῶν** (relative clause), ὑπὲρ ἡμῶν ἐστιν.	*For whoever is not against us is for us.* (Mk 9:40)
ἐρρέθη· **οὐ μοιχεύσεις.** (direct speech)	*It was said, "You shall not commit adultery".* (Mt 5:27)

d) In Ancient Greek there are different ways of expressing a **generic reference**, i.e. to people in general as the subject (↑the generic personal pronoun "one" and a similar use of the 1st and 2nd pers. in English; ↑Carter §60b; also ↑139e; 144a; BDF §130): 255f

• quite often by the 3rd pl. act. (CG verbs of communication; in the NT extended to other types of verbs, apparently influenced by Semitic usage), e.g.:

συνάγουσιν αὐτὰ καὶ εἰς τὸ πῦρ **βάλλουσιν.**	*People* (lit. *They*) *gather them and throw them into the fire.* (Jn 15:6)

↑also inter alia Mt 4:24; 7:16; 9:2; Mk 3:21; 14:12.

Note that in the NT the 3rd pl. act. may also be used for a periphrastic reference to God (↑for more details Z §1ff; ↑also 296b), e.g.:

δώσουσιν εἰς …	*They/One* (i.e. God) *will put* … (Lk 6:38)
… ἵνα … **δέξωνται** ὑμᾶς εἰς τὰς αἰωνίους σκηνάς.	… *so that* … *they/one* (i.e. God) *will welcome you into the eternal homes.* (Lk 16:9)

• also by the passive (when the agent is not mentioned; ↑191a), though generally it may best be translated as a passive, e.g.:

ἠδύνατο γὰρ τοῦτο τὸ μύρον **πραθῆναι** … καὶ **δοθῆναι** τοῖς πτωχοῖς.	*For this ointment could have been sold … and given to the poor/For one could have sold this ointment …* (Mk 14:5)

• very occasionally by an impersonal passive (↑218g), e.g.:

καρδίᾳ γὰρ **πιστεύεται** …, στόματι δὲ **ὁμολογεῖται** …	*For one believes with the heart … and one confesses with the mouth …* (Ro 10:10)

In the NT this construction, too, may be used for a periphrastic reference to God ("divine passive"; ↑296b), e.g.:

ἐν ᾧ μέτρῳ μετρεῖτε **μετρηθήσεται** ὑμῖν.	*With the measure you use, it will be measured to you/ … use, one* (i.e. God) *will measure to you.* (Mt 7:2)

• sometimes by τις *someone/anyone* (↑144a), e.g.:

πόθεν τούτους δυνήσεταί **τις** ὧδε χορτάσαι …;	*How can one feed these people here …?* (Mk 8:4)

τις may be replaced by ἄνθρωπος *a human being* (↑144b), e.g.:

Οὕτως ἡμᾶς λογιζέσθω **ἄνθρωπος** …	*This is how one should regard us …* (1Cor 4:1)

• "by" an unexpressed (accusative) subject of an inf./ACI phrase that is dependent on an impersonal expression (↑217), e.g.:

πειθαρχεῖν δεῖ θεῷ μᾶλλον ἢ ἀνθρώποις. — *One/We must obey God rather than any human beings.* (Ac 5:29)

• sometimes by the 1st pers. pl. (or sg.) and 2nd pers. sg. (↑139e), e.g.:

καὶ ἃ **δοκοῦμεν** ἀτιμότερα εἶναι τοῦ σώματος τούτοις τιμὴν περισσοτέραν **περιτίθεμεν**. — *And on those parts of the body we think/one thinks less honourable, we clothe/one clothes with greater honour.* (1Cor 12:23)

Ἐρεῖς μοι οὖν … (also ↑202e) — *You/One will/might say/object then …* (Ro 9:19)

On the authorial plural ↑139e.

255g 2. In **infinitive phrases**: the subject, if made explicit,[6] is mostly in the **accusative** ("ACI"), less frequently in the genitive or dative (↑216a/216d).

255h 3. In **participle phrases**: the participle and its subject (if made explicit)[6] are in the same case (↑229ff).

On the concord between the subject and other sentence elements ↑261–265.

(ii) Predicate

256 The predicator (↑BR §255; BDF §127/128)

256a I. The predicate typically indicates the **core information** of the sentence (the core of its proposition; ↑127b), its "rheme", i.e. **what is being said** about the theme (↑255a[4]), in communication used to refer to a "situation" in the real world (↑22f[9]; 312a). It is usually expressed by a verb phrase, i.e. a phrase with a verb form as its head, which we call **predicator** ("P"; also "predicate verb"). Depending on the "valency" of the verb (↑254c) the predicator is used alone (in which case the predicator and the predicate are the same) or it is accompanied by one or more complements, making possible a number of different sentence patterns (for some typical ones ↑258d).

256b II. In Ancient Greek there were simple one-part or (at times) multi-part predicators:

1. simple one-part predicators (standard), e.g.:

εὑρήκαμεν τὸν Μεσσίαν. — *We have found the Messiah.* (Jn 1:41)

---

6 Since non-finite verb forms have no personal endings of their own, the subject of the sentence-like construction indicated by infinitive or participle phrases (↑213a; 227a) may be expressed by personal endings at best indirectly, i.e. by the personal ending of the finite verb in the superordinate construction, e.g.:

οὐκ **ἦλθον** (P/S of superordinate construction) **καλέσαι** (P/[S] of InfP) δικαίους (Od of InfP). (personal ending -ον of ἦλθον → S of InfP) — ***I** have not come to call the righteous ≈ that **I** may call the righteous.* (Mk 2:17)

For examples with participles (p.c. in the nominative) ↑inter alia 230c.

2. multi-part predicators in these constructions: a) with modifying verbs (↑234a) and b) in the periphrastic conjugation (↑203d; 236a), e.g.:

ὁ δὲ Πέτρος **ἐπέμενεν** (Part1) **κρούων** (Part2).	*Peter continued knocking.* (Ac 12:16)
ἔσεσθε (Part1) **μισούμενοι** (Part2)	*You will be hated.* (Mt 10:22)

III. The **copula** (↑Carter §539; Crystal s.v.)

1. A predicator/predicate verb that links the subject and the complement of a sentence/clause is called "copula" or "copular verb" (↑258a–258c). The most important verbs having this function in Ancient Greek are εἰμί *to be*, γίνομαι *to become*, and (in KG frequently replacing εἰμί) ὑπάρχω *to be (present)*. 256c

Examples:

a) linking subject and subject complement (S+P+SC; also ↑135c):

ὁ λόγος (S) σὰρξ (SC^id^) **ἐγένετο** (P: copula).	*The Word became flesh.* (Jn 1:14)
πραΰς (SC^prop^) **εἰμι** (P: copula/S).	*I am gentle.* (Mt 11:29)
ἡ ἐπιστολὴ ἡμῶν (SC^id^) ὑμεῖς (S) **ἐστε** (P: copula).	*You yourselves are our letter.* (2Cor 3:2)
ἐγὼ καὶ ὁ πατὴρ (S) ἕν (SC^prop^) **ἐσμεν** (P: copula).	*I and the Father are one.* (Jn 10:30)
οὗτος (S) ἄρχων τῆς συναγωγῆς (SC^id^) **ὑπῆρχεν** (P: copula).	*He was a leader of the synagogue.* (Lk 8:41)

b) linking subject and adverbial complement (here S+P+LocC/TempC):

ἐγὼ (S) μεθ' ὑμῶν (LocC) **εἰμι** (P: copula).	*I am with you.* (Mt 28:20)
ἐγγὺς (TempC) τὸ θέρος (S) **ἐστίν** (P: copula).	*Summer is near.* (Mk 13:28)
ἡμῶν γὰρ τὸ πολίτευμα (S) ἐν οὐρανοῖς (LocC) **ὑπάρχει** (P: copula).	*But our citizenship is in heaven.* (Php 3:20)

2. Such (copular) sentences/clauses may be **without copula** (ellipsis; ↑293c), most frequently without the third person forms ἐστίν *is* or εἰσίν *(they) are*, less frequently without forms in other persons (mostly so when the subject is a personal pronoun) or moods and tenses,[7] thus: 256d

a) often in simple everyday sentences/clauses, especially in vivid and affective utterances, in the NT inter alia in beatitudes/macarisms and (probably in most cases the 3 sg. pres. opt. of wish of εἰμί is to be supplied in thought: εἴη *may … be …*; ↑211c) in doxologies and greetings;

b) with impersonal expressions, especially nouns and adjectives indicating necessity or possibility (↑217b/217c/217f) such as

ἀνάγκη *it is necessary*	ἀδύνατον *it is impossible*;

7 On an occasional ellipsis of the participle of εἰμί *to be* ↑233b.

c) in proverbs and aphorisms;

d) after the interjection ἰδού "behold" = *here/there is (are), here/there was (were)* or *there comes (came)* or the like, which appears to adopt a quasi-predicate role (↑252.63,8 for details on its use in Ancient Greek and other languages).

Such sentences/clauses without copula are often called "verbless clauses" (↑266a).

Examples:

Μακάριοι (SC) οἱ πτωχοὶ τῷ πνεύματι (S).	*Blessed are the poor in spirit.* (Mt 5:3)
θεὸς (S) μάρτυς (SC[id])	*God is our witness.* (1Th 2:5)
Χάρις (S) τῷ θεῷ (IntC).	*Thanks be to God.* (e.g. 2Cor 9:15)
χάρις (S) ὑμῖν (IntC).	*Grace to you.* (e.g. 1Th 1:1)
Ἡ χάρις τοῦ κυρίου ἡμῶν Ἰησοῦ Χριστοῦ (S) μεθ' ὑμῶν (LocC).	*May the grace of our Lord Jesus Christ be with you.* (1Th 5:28)
ἀνάγκη (SC) γὰρ ἐλθεῖν τὰ σκάνδαλα (S).	*For it is necessary that stumbling blocks come.* (Mt 18:7)
πλήρωμα οὖν νόμου (SC[id]) ἡ ἀγάπη (S).	*Love is the fulfilling of the law.* (Ro 13:10)
ἰδοὺ ("P"/[LocC?) ὕδωρ (S).	*(Look), here is water.* (Ac 8:36)

On questions of distinguishing subjects from subject complements with an identifying function ↑135a and 135c.

On questions of concord between the subject and the predicate ↑262 and 265.

257 Complements: objects

257a I. Very frequently the predicator/predicate verb (due to its valency; ↑254c) is accompanied by an object ("O"). This is a complement typically referring to the **entity that is more or less directly "targeted" or affected** by the "action" (↑also 254c/254d on "second degree objects" accompanying certain adjectives/adverbs and nouns).

257b II. Noun phrases with heads in the accusative, genitive, or dative (also expansions showing concord; ↑146c) as well as preposition phrases (↑183c) may have the role of an object in Ancient Greek. So, the following object types may be distinguished (note that various combinations of object types and other types of complements occur in sentence patterns; ↑258d):

1. **Direct object** ("Od"): In its standard form as a noun phrase with a head in the accusative (also expansions showing concord; ↑150–154), it typically refers to the notionally closest entity, directly targeted or affected by the "action" indicated by the predicate verb; in non-passive constructions it has the semantic role of a patient (a role that in passive constructions is usually taken by the subject; ↑254c). Less frequently, as a direct "internal" object (↑151), it may refer to the "action" itself, e.g.:

ἱλαρὸν γὰρ **δότην** (Od) ἀγαπᾷ ὁ θεός.	*For God loves a cheerful giver.* (2Cor 9:7)

τοὺς ἄρτους τῆς προθέσεως (Od) ἔφαγεν	*He ate the sacred loaves.* (Mk 2:26)
τὸν καλὸν ἀγῶνα (Od) ἠγώνισμαι.	*I have fought the good fight.* (2Tm 4:7)

2. **Genitive object** ("Og"): In its standard form as a noun phrase with a head in the genitive (also expansions showing concord), it may refer to an entity that is affected by the "action" in a variety of more or less direct ways (depending on the type of genitive and the type of "action"; ↑163; 167; 169; also ↑160a), e.g.:

μνημονεύετε **τῆς γυναικὸς Λώτ** (Og).	*Remember the wife of Lot.* (Lk 17:32)
γεμίσατε τὰς ὑδρίας (Od) **ὕδατος** (Og).	*Fill the jars with water.* (Jn 2:7)

3. **Indirect object** ("Oi") and **dative object** ("O^{dat}"): A noun phrase with a head in the dative (also expansions showing concord), or its replacement by other expressions (↑257c/257d), may be used a) as indirect objects or b) as dative objects.
a) An indirect object is usually combined with a direct object, referring to the somewhat more remote entity, "indirectly" affected by the "action", a typical sentence pattern being S+P+Od+Oi, e.g.:

ἄφες **ἡμῖν** (Oi) τὰ ὀφειλήματα ἡμῶν (Od).	*Forgive us our debts.* (Mt 6:12)

b) A dative object is (generally) the sole object accompanying the predicator/predicate verb, normally referring to a directly affected entity, a typical sentence pattern being S+P+O^{dat} (↑174/175; 179; 258d,1.3), e.g.:

ὑπακούετε **τοῖς γονεῦσιν** (O^{dat})	*Obey your parents.* (Col 3:20)

4. **Prepositional object** ("Op"): This is a preposition phrase that is called for by the valency of the predicator/predicate verb referring to an entity more or less directly affected by the "action" (depending on the type of "action" and the type of preposition involved; ↑183c), e.g. (for relevant sentence patterns ↑258d,1.5/2.13):

ἀπὸ παντὸς εἴδους πονηροῦ (Op) ἀπέχεσθε.	*Stay away from/Avoid every kind of evil.* (1Th 5:22)
… ἀλλὰ ῥῦσαι ἡμᾶς (Od) **ἀπὸ τοῦ πονηροῦ** (Op).	… *but deliver us from the evil one.* (Mt 6:13)

On the object complements ↑258a/258b.

III. Objects may be **expressed** as follows:

1. by a **noun phrase** with a head in the case form characteristic of the object type (also any expansions showing concord)[8] or a noun phrase embedded in the **preposition phrase** in question (↑257b); the head of the noun phrase involved may be: **257c**

a) a **noun**

(occasionally preceded by ὡς *something like*; ↑252.61,1a[1]),

8 Remember that the case role of infinitive/ACI phrases is generally to be inferred from the context, most clearly when they are preceded by the article (↑223–226).

b) a **pronoun** used as a noun substitute (↑22c; 139, especially 139a), including the pronominal article (↑131)

(in the NT occasionally replaced by an adverb [↑241c]; ↑also 166b on τινές *some* at times to be supplied in thought in a partitive genitive [also ἐκ/ἐξ or ἀπό + gen.] construction),

c) any kind of **nominalized** expression: adjective (↑137d), participle (↑237), or infinitive/ACI (↑217; 224) phrases or any other expressions that are nominalized, (typically) by means of the article (↑132d).

Examples:

οἵτινες **ὑποδείγματι καὶ σκιᾷ** (O^{dat}: noun) λατρεύουσιν …	*They serve a copy and a shadow …* (He 8:5)
τί (Od: pron.) θέλεις;	*What do you want?* (Mt 20:21)
ἄφες **ἡμῖν** (Oi: pron.) **τὰ ὀφειλήματα ἡμῶν** (Od: noun).	*Forgive us our debts.* (Mt 6:12)
ὁ πατὴρ ὑμῶν … δώσει **ἀγαθὰ** (Od: nominalized AdjP) **τοῖς αἰτοῦσιν αὐτόν** (Oi: nominalized PtcP).	*Your Father … will give good things to those who ask him.* (Mt 7:11)
Θέλω δὲ **ὑμᾶς εἰδέναι** (Od: ACI phrase) …	*But I want you to realize …* (1Cor 11:3)
καλοῦ ἔργου (Og: noun) ἐπιθυμεῖ.	*He desires a noble task.* (1Tm 3:1)
πολλοί … δίκαιοι ἐπεθύμησαν **ἰδεῖν** (Og: InfP) …	*Many … righteous people longed to see …* (Mt 13:17)
Τὰ κατ᾽ ἐμὲ πάντα (Od: nominalized PpP) γνωρίσει **ὑμῖν** (Oi: pron.) Τύχικος …	*Tychicus … will give you a full report about my situation.* (Col 4:7)
Τίς **ἡμᾶς** (Od: pron.) χωρίσει **ἀπὸ τῆς ἀγάπης τοῦ Χριστοῦ** (Op: noun);	*Who will/can separate us form the love of Christ?* (Ro 8:35)

257d 2. a **subordinate clause** in the object role (↑270a), i.e. a conjunctional declarative, desiderative or interrogative clause (↑270–273) as well as certain relative clauses (↑289b), similarly direct speech (↑274b), e.g.:

οὐκ ἤθελεν **ἵνα τις γνοῖ** (Od: ἵνα-clause).	*He did not want anybody to know it.* (Mk 9:30)
σὺ οἶδας **ὅτι φιλῶ σε** (Od: ὅτι-clause).	*You know that I love you.* (Jn 21:15f)
δέομαι δέ σου (Og), **ἐπίτρεψόν μοι λαλῆσαι πρὸς τὸν λαόν** (Od: direct speech).	*Now I ask you, "Allow me to speak to the people".* (Ac 21:39)
ἐπηρώτα αὐτόν (Od)· **εἴ τι βλέπεις;** (Od: direct question with εἰ)	*He asked him, "Do you see anything?"* (Mk 8:23)
ἐπηρώτησεν αὐτὸν (Od) **εἰ πάλαι ἀπέθανεν** (Od: indirect question with εἰ).	*He asked him if he had been dead for some time.* (Mk 15:44)
ἐμνήσθησαν … **ὅτι τοῦτο ἔλεγεν** (Og: ὅτι-clause).	*They remembered … that he had said this.* (Jn 2:22)

ὃν γὰρ **ἀγαπᾷ** (Od: relative clause) κύριος παιδεύει.	*For the Lord disciplines the one he loves.* (He 12:6)

IV. An **object** (mainly a pronominal one) is left **unexpressed** (ellipsis) in Ancient Greek more frequently than in English, especially in contexts in which it can easily be supplied in thought (↑293a–293c; BDF §479), e.g.: 257e

Οἱ δὲ ἀκούσαντες [sc. ταῦτα] (Od) διεπρίοντο …	*When they heard this, they were enraged* … (Ac 5:33)
κατέκλασεν τοὺς ἄρτους καὶ ἐδίδου [sc. αὐτοὺς] (Od) τοῖς μαθηταῖς.	*He broke the loaves and gave them to the disciples.* (Mk 6:41)
ἤθελεν γεύσασθαι [sc. τινος/τι] (Og/Od). παρασκευαζόντων δὲ αὐτῶν [sc. τι] (Od) ἐγένετο ἐπ' αὐτὸν ἔκστασις.	*He wanted something to eat. But while they were preparing it, a trance came over him.* (Ac 10:10)

On questions of concord ↑261–265.

Complements: other types of predicative elements 258

As stated in 254d alongside objects the following types of predicative elements, i.e. complements may be distinguished:
- subject and object related complements as well as
- adverbial complements.

I. **Subject and object related complements** ("SC" and "OC") are complements that convey information about the subject and object entities respectively. This information typically concerns either their identity or some of their properties. It is therefore frequently helpful to distinguish between (1) subject/object complements with an identifying function ("SC^{id}"/"OC^{id}") and (2) subject/object complements specifying properties ("SC^{prop}"/"OC^{prop}"; ↑e.g. Aarts: 97ff; on the much less frequent subject/object adjunct ↑259p):

1. Subject/object complements with an identifying function ("SC^{id}"/"OC^{id}"): they **identify the subject/object entity** indicating either full identity or as belonging to a particular class of phenomena. 258a

They may be **expressed** as follows:

a) by a **noun phrase** whose head is in the same case as the subject/object (as also any expansions showing concord; ↑147a; 153b) and may be:[9]

- a **noun**
(occasionally preceded by ὡς *something like*; ↑252.61,1a[1]),
- a **pronoun** used as a noun substitute (↑22c; 139, especially 139a),

9 ↑135c on how to tell which of two noun phrases in the nominative is the subject and which should be considered its complement with identifying function.

• any kind of **nominalized** expression: adjective (↑137d), participle (↑237; 235b), or infinitive/ACI (↑224) phrases or any other expressions that are nominalized, (typically) by means of the article (↑132d).

b) by a **subordinate clause** (↑270a).

In the NT the SC (in the nominative) and the OC (in the accusative) are sometimes replaced (influenced by Semitic usage) by a preposition phrase with εἰς + acc. (for more details on this and some further options ↑147a; 153b): S+P+SC(with εἰς)/S+P+Od+OC(with εἰς).

Examples (for relevant sentence patterns ↑258d,1.6):

οὗτός (S) ἐστιν **ὁ υἱός μου ὁ ἀγαπητός** (SC^id: noun).	*This is my beloved Son.* (Mt 3:17)

Full identity is indicated by the SC^id (with article; ↑135a/135c).

καὶ αὐτὴ (S) ἦν **χήρα** (SC^id: noun).	*She was a widow.* (Lk 7:12)

Classification is indicated by the SC^id (not determined; ↑135a/135c).

ἐκάλουν … τὸν Βαρναβᾶν (Od) **Δία** (OC^id: noun/proper name).	*They called … Barnabas "Zeus".* (Ac 14:12)

Full identity appears to be indicated by the OC^id (proper name; ↑135a/135c).

ὑμᾶς (Od) δὲ εἴρηκα **φίλους** (OC^id: noun).	*But I have called you friends.* (Jn 15:15)

Classification is indicated by the OC^id (not determined; ↑135a/135c).

τοῦτ᾽ (S) ἔστιν **Χριστὸν καταγαγεῖν** (SC^id: InfP).	*That is to bring Christ down.* (Ro 10:6)
… ποιεῖν τὰ βρέφη (Od) **ἔκθετα** (OC^id: nominalized AdjP) αὐτῶν.	*… to abandon their infants* (lit. *to make their infants abandoned ones*). (Ac 7:19)
οὐχ οὗτός (S) ἐστιν **ὃν ζητοῦσιν ἀποκτεῖναι** (SC^id: relative clause);	*Isn't this the one they are trying to kill?* (Jn 7:25)

258b 2. Subject/object complements specifying properties ("SC^prop"/"OC^prop"): they **specify properties** that are ascribed to **the subject/object entities**.

They may be **expressed** as follows (typically in the same case as the subject/object as far as possible):

a) by an adjective phrase (in the "predicative" position; ↑136b; 137b; 259q),

b) by a non-attributive/predicative use of (certain) pronouns, of numerals, or of participle phrases (ACP/GCP ↑233; ↑ also periphrastic conjugation [↑235a]),

c) by a noun phrase with a noun or nominalized expression as its head:

• preceded by ὡς/ὡσεί *as/like* (↑252.61,1a[1]),

• in the genitive or one embedded in a preposition phrase replacing it (↑159b; 166; 168c) or else in the dative of interest/possessor (↑176b), or

d) by a subordinate clause (↑270a).

Examples (for a relevant sentence pattern ↑258d,1.6):

μακάριοί (SC^prop: AdjP) εἰσιν ἐκεῖνοι (S).	*Blessed are they.* (Lk 12:38)

ἰδοὺ **καινὰ** (OC^{prop}: AdjP) ποιῶ πάντα (Od).	*Look, I am making all things new.* (Re 21:5)
… οἵτινες (S) ἔξωθεν μὲν φαίνονται **ὡραῖοι** (SC^{prop}: AdjP).	… *which appear beautiful on the outside.* (Mt 23:27)
ὁ φυτεύων δὲ καὶ ὁ ποτίζων (S) **ἕν** (SC^{prop}: numeral) εἰσιν.	*The one who plants and the one who waters are one.* (1Cor 3:8)
… **ζῶν** (SC^{prop}: ptc.) εἰμι …	… *I am alive* … (Re 1:18)
… ἀλλ᾽ **ὡς ἄγγελοι** (SC^{prop}: ὡς + NP) … εἰσιν.	… *but they are like angels* … (Mt 22:30)
ἐφάνησαν ἐνώπιον αὐτῶν **ὡσεὶ λῆρος** (SC^{prop}: ὡσεί + NP) τὰ ῥήματα ταῦτα (S).	*These words seemed like nonsense to them.* (Lk 24:11)
τοῦ κυρίου (SC^{prop}: NP in the possessive gen.) ἐσμέν.	*We are the Lord's/We belong to the Lord.* (Ro 14:8)
ἦν γὰρ **ἐτῶν δώδεκα** (SC^{prop}: NP in the gen. of quality).	*She was twelve years old.* (Mk 5:42)
οὐκ ἦν **αὐτοῖς** (SC^{prop}: pron. in the dat. of interest) τόπος (S) …	*No room was available for them …/They had no room* … (Lk 2:7)
καὶ σὺ (S) **ἐξ αὐτῶν** (SC^{prop}: PpP replacing partitive gen.) εἶ.	*You, too, belong to them/are one of them.* (Lk 22:58)
χάριτι δὲ θεοῦ εἰμι **ὅ εἰμι** (SC^{prop}: relative clause).	*But by the grace of God I am what I am.* (1Cor 15:10)

↑also 137c for further OC^{prop} examples.
On the subject/object adjuncts ↑259pff.
On questions of concord ↑263 and 265.

II. In contrast to the much more frequent adverbial adjuncts (↑259a–259o), **adverbial complements** are obligatory sentence constituents. They are like objects called for by the valency of certain verbs (↑254c/254d). However, while objects are classified mainly on the basis of their form (Od, Og, Oi, O^{dat}, or Op; ↑257b), adverbial complements on the basis of their function (LocC, TempC, ManC etc.) their form being variable (for some sentence patterns ↑258d,1.7–10 and 258d,2.14/17). 258c

Four major types may be distinguished on the basis of their function:

1. **Local complement** ("LocC"; specifies the place of the "action"), e.g.:

σὺν ὑμῖν εἰμι.	*I am with you.* (Col 2:5)
οὐκ ἤμην **ἐκεῖ**·	*I was not there.* (Jn 11:15)

2. **Temporal complement** (TempC"; specifies the time of the "action"), e.g.:

πότε ταῦτα ἔσται;	*When will these things be?* (Mk 13:4)
ὁ θρόνος σου … **εἰς τὸν αἰῶνα τοῦ αἰῶνος**	*Your throne … is for ever and ever.* (He 1:8)

3. **Manner complement** ("ManC"; specifies the manner of the "action"), e.g.:

Ἐν σοφίᾳ περιπατεῖτε …	*Conduct yourselves wisely* … (Col 4:5)
ἐποίησαν αὐτοῖς **ὡσαύτως**.	*They treated them the same way.* (Mt 21:36)

4. **Causal complement** (specifying a reason for the "action" in the widest sense) with further possible subtypes:

4.1 **causal** (in a narrower sense: "Why?"/"For what reason?"): "CausC"
4.2 **conditional** ("In what case?"/"Under what conditions?"): "CondC"
4.3 indicating **result** ("With what result?"): "ResC"
4.4 indicating **purpose** ("What for?"): "PurpC"
4.5 **concessive** ("In spite of what?"): "ConcC"
4.6 **instrumental** ("By what means?"): "InstrC"
4.7 of **interest** ("For whom?"/"To whose advantage or disadvantage?"): "IntC"

Examples:

τὰ γὰρ πάντα **δι' ὑμᾶς** (CausC/IntC).	*For it is all because of you/for your sake.* (2Cor 4:15)
τὰ δὲ πάντα … **ὑπὲρ τῆς ὑμῶν οἰκοδομῆς** (PurpC).	*And all … for building you up/… to build you up.* (2Cor 12:19)

↑also Ro 10:1 (PurpC).

On the various ways of expressing adverbial complements (in principle corresponding to those of the much more widely occurring adverbial adjuncts) ↑259c–259o.

258d **Overview** of typical **sentence patterns** in the Greek New Testament

Note that this list contains only a limited number of (typical) sentence patterns and that each example contains only one of (usually) many possible verbs (adjectives or adverbs) whose valency calls for the pattern in question (↑254c/254d).

1. Sentence patterns (↑254c/254d)

Sentence without complements:

1. S+P:	ἠρίστησαν (ἀριστάω).	*They had breakfast.* (Jn 21:15)

Sentences with one complement (S+P+C):

2. S+P+Od:	ὁ πατὴρ ἀγαπᾷ τὸν υἱόν.	*The Father loves the Son.* (Jn 3:35)
3. S+P+O^{dat}:	ὑπακούουσιν αὐτῷ.	*They obey him.* (Mk 1:27)
4. S+P+Og:	ἥψατο αὐτοῦ (ἅπτομαι).	*He touched him.* (Lk 5:13)
5. S+P+Op:	πέποιθεν ἐπὶ τὸν θεόν.	*He trusts in God.* (Mt 27:43)
6. S+(P)+SC:	αὐτὴ ἦν χήρα.	*She was a widow.* (Lk 7:12)
7. S+(P)+LocC:	ὁ θεὸς ἐν ὑμῖν ἐστιν.	*God is in your midst.* (1Cor 14:25)
8. S+(P)+TempC:	ὁ θρόνος σου … εἰς τὸν αἰῶνα.	*Your throne … is for ever.* (He 1:8)
9. S+P+ManC:	εὐσχημόνως περιπατήσωμεν.	*Let us behave decently!* (Ro 13:13)
10. S+(P)+CausC:	τὰ πάντα δι' ὑμᾶς.	*All (is/happens) because of you.* (↑2Cor 4:15)

Sentences with two complements (S+P+C+C):

11. S+P+Od+Oi:	δώσω σοι τὸν στέφανον.	*I will give you the victor's crown.* (↑Re 2:10)
12. S+P+Od+Og:	ὑμᾶς ἀξιώσει τῆς κλήσεως.	*He will make you worthy of his call.* (↑2Th 1:11)

13. S+P+Od+Op:	τίς ἡμᾶς χωρίσει ἀπὸ τῆς ἀγάπης;	*Who will separate us from this love?* (↑Ro 8:35)
14. S+P+Od+LocC:	ἔθηκεν αὐτὸν ἐν μνήματι.	*He laid him in a tomb.* (Lk 23:53)
15. S+P+Od+OC:	ὑμᾶς εἴρηκα φίλους.	*I have called you friends.* (↑Jn 15:15)
16. S+P+Od+Od:	ὑμᾶς διδάξει πάντα.	*He will teach you all things.* (Jn 14:26)
17. S+P+O^{dat}+ManC:	ἐποίησαν αὐτοῖς ὡσαύτως.	*They treated him the same way.* (Mt 21:36)
	etc.	

2. Sentences containing second degree patterns (S+P+C+O/^{2nd}; ↑254d)

1. S+(P)+SC+O^{dat}/^{2nd}:	ὁ … εὐάρεστος τῷ θεῷ.	*The one who … is pleasing to God.* (Ro 14:18)
2. S+(P)+SC+Og/^{2nd}:	ἦτε ξένοι τῶν διαθηκῶν.	*You were strangers to the covenants.* (↑Eph 2:12)
3. S+(P)+SC+Op/^{2nd}:	ἐλευθέρα ἐστὶν ἀπὸ τοῦ νόμου.	*She is free from the law.* (Ro 7:3)
4. S+P+ManC+O^{dat}/^{2nd}:	λατρεύωμεν εὐαρέστως τῷ θεῷ.	*Let us offer worship pleasing to God.* (He 12:28?)
5. S+P+ManC+Og/^{2nd}:	περιπατῆσαι ἀξίως τοῦ κυρίου	*to live in a manner worthy of the Lord* (Col 1:10)
	etc.	

3.3.1.2 Optional sentence constituents

Adverbial adjuncts and subject/object adjuncts 259

259a As stated earlier (e.g. ↑254b) there are basically **two types of optional sentence constituents** (i.e. they are not needed for sentences to be well-formed or “grammatical”, not called for by the valency of the predicate verb, and so not part of the sentence pattern; ↑254c):

a) **adverbial adjuncts** (↑259b–259o; on the much less frequent adverbial complements ↑258c),

b) **subject/object adjuncts** (↑259p; on the much more frequent subject/object complements ↑258a/258b).

A. Adverbial adjuncts

259b I. Adverbial adjuncts modify the information of the sentence by specifying the place, the time, the manner, or other circumstances of the “action”/“situation” that the (superordinate) predicator/predicate verb refers to. Like the rather infrequent adverbial complements (↑258c) they are usually subdivided into **four major types**:

More recently other types have been added that (unlike the traditional types) modify the information of the sentence, as it were, from the outside (↑DuG9: 794f, similarly Huddleston/Pullum: 771ff):

• Evaluative adjunct (“EvalA”): it indicates the speaker’s or writer’s opinion on a “situation” (↑241a/241b on evaluative adverbs/particles), e.g.:

ἐπ᾽ ἀληθείας καὶ οὗτος μετ᾽ αὐτοῦ ἦν.	*Certainly this man also was with him.* (Lk 22:59)

• Text adjunct (“TextA”): it serves to highlight connections within the structure of a text, e.g.:

ἀθέτησις **μὲν** γὰρ γίνεται … ἐπεισαγωγὴ **δέ** …	*For there is, on the one hand, the abrogation …, on the other hand, the introduction …* (He 7:18f)
οὗτός ἐστιν ὁ ἄνθρωπος ὁ … διδάσκων, **ἔτι τε** καὶ Ἕλληνας εἰσήγαγεν εἰς τὸ ἱερόν …	*This is the man who teaches … Moreover he even brought Greeks into the temple …* (Ac 21:28)

1. **Local adjunct** ("LocA"): it specifies the place of the "action"/"situation", answering questions such as "Where?", "To where?", "Where from?", "How far?" (also ↑259d), e.g.:

ἐκεῖ (LocA) αὐτὸν ὄψεσθε.	*You will see him there.* (Mt 28:7)

2. **Temporal adjunct** ("TempA"): it specifies the time of the "action"/"situation", answering questions such as "When?", "How long?" (also ↑259e), e.g.:

ἐτέχθη ὑμῖν **σήμερον** (TempA) σωτήρ.	*Today a Saviour has been born for you.* (Lk 2:11)

3. **Manner adjunct** ("ManA"; also called "modal adjunct"): it specifies the manner of the "action"/"situation", answering questions such as "How?"/"In what manner?", also "Under what concomitant circumstances?" (also ↑259f), e.g.:

ἀσμένως (ManA) ἀπεδέξαντο ἡμᾶς οἱ ἀδελφοί.	*The brothers welcomed us warmly.* (Ac 21:17)

4. **Causal adjunct** (specifying a reason for the "action"/"situation" in the widest sense), usually subdivided into the following types (also ↑259g–259m):

4.1 **causal** ("CausA"): in a narrower sense it specifies the reason for the "action"/"situation", answering questions such as "Why?", "For what reason?" (↑259g), e.g.:

διὰ τοῦτο (CausA) λέγω ὑμῖν …	*For this reason I tell you …* (Mt 6:25)

4.2 **conditional** ("CondA"): it specifies the condition that the "action"/"situation" is subject to, answering questions such as "In what case?", "Under what condition?" (↑259h), e.g.:

εἰ ἀρνησόμεθα (CondA), κἀκεῖνος ἀρνήσεται ἡμᾶς.	*If we disown him, he will also disown us.* (2Tm 2:12)

4.3 indicating **result** ("ResA"): it specifies the consequence or result of the "action"/"situation", answering questions such as "With what result?" (↑259i), e.g.:

γίνεται δένδρον, **ὥστε ἐλθεῖν τὰ πετεινά** … (ResA)	*It becomes a tree, so that the birds come* … (Mt 13:32)

4.4 indicating **purpose** ("PurpA", also "final"): it specifies the purpose of the "action"/"situation", answering questions such as "What for?" (↑259j), e.g.:

ἦλθεν … **ἵνα μαρτυρήσῃ περὶ τοῦ φωτός** (PurpA).	*He came … to testify about the light.* (Jn 1:7)

4.5 **concessive** ("ConcA"): it presents the "action"/"situation" as taking place contrary to certain expectations, answering questions such as "In spite of what?" (↑259k), e.g.:

καίπερ ὢν υἱός (ConcA), ἔμαθεν ἀφ' ὧν ἔπαθεν τὴν ὑπακοήν.	*Although he was the Son, he learned obedience from what he suffered.* (He 5:8)

4.6 **instrumental** ("InstrA"): it specifies the means/instrument making the "action"/"situation" possible, answering questions such as "By what means?" (↑259l), e.g.:

ἐν μαχαίρῃ (InstrA) ἀπολοῦνται.	*They will die by the sword.* (Mt 26:52)

4.7 of **interest** ("IntA"): it specifies the entities in whose interest the "action"/"situation" takes place, either to their advantage or to their disadvantage, answering questions such as "For whom?", "To whose advantage or disadvantage?" (↑259m), e. g.:

Σολομὼν δὲ οἰκοδόμησεν **αὐτῷ** (IntA) οἶκον. *Solomon built a house for him.* (Ac 7:47)

II. **Adverbial adjuncts** (also adverbial complements; ↑258c) may be **expressed** as follows (also ↑259g–259m and 317ff): 259c

1. by an **adverb** phrase (↑241c also lexicon), e. g.:

ἔξελθε **ταχέως** (ManA) … *Go out quickly …* (Lk 14:21)

2. by a **preposition** phrase (↑183; 187), e. g.:

ἤρξατο κηρύσσειν **ἐν τῇ Δεκαπόλει** (LocA) ὅσα … *He began to proclaim in the Decapolis how much …* (Mk 5:20)

3. by a noun phrase (its head being a noun, a nominalized expression, or a noun-substitute/pronoun) in one of the following **cases** (↑187):

a) **accusative** (↑149b; 155–157), e. g.:

… ἔμειναν **οὐ πολλὰς ἡμέρας** (TempA; acc. of temporal extent). *… they stayed for a few days.* (Jn 2:12)

b) **genitive** (↑158b; 163; 167–169; 171), e. g.:

εἰ **τοσούτου** (ManA; gen. of value/price) τὸ χωρίον ἀπέδοσθε; *Did you sell the land for this amount?* (Ac 5:8)

c) **dative** (↑173b; 176–182), e. g.:

οὐδείς … ἡμῶν **ἑαυτῷ** (IntA or IntC; dat. of interest) ζῇ. *… none of us lives for himself.* (Ro 14:7)

4. by an **infinitive/ACI** phrase

a) without article (↑220/221), e. g.:

οὐκ ἦλθον **καταλῦσαι** (PurpA) ἀλλὰ **πληρῶσαι** (PurpA). *I have not come to abolish, but to fulfil.* (Mt 5:17)

b) articular

- with simple article (↑224), e. g.:

οὐκ ἔσχηκα ἄνεσιν … **τῷ μὴ εὑρεῖν με Τίτον τὸν ἀδελφόν μου** (CausA). *I had no rest … because I did not find my brother Titus [there].* (2Cor 2:13)

- with τοῦ (↑225b/225c), e. g.:

ἐξῆλθεν ὁ σπείρων **τοῦ σπείρειν** (PurpA). *A farmer went out to sow.* (Mt 13:3)

- with an article governed by a preposition (↑226), e. g.:

καὶ **διὰ τὸ μὴ ἔχειν ῥίζαν** (CausA) ἐξηράνθη. *And since they had no root, they withered.* (Mt 13:6)

5. by a **participle** phrase (↑229b; 230–232; 238–240; also ↑237c and above No. 3):

a) as a participle conjunct (↑230c), e.g.:

ἰδὼν δὲ **Σίμων Πέτρος** (TempA) προσέπεσεν τοῖς γόνασιν Ἰησοῦ.
But when Simon Peter saw this, he fell at Jesus' knees. (Lk 5:8)

b) as a genitive absolute (↑230d), e.g.:

μὴ ξενίζεσθε … **ὡς ξένου ὑμῖν συμβαίνοντος** (ManA: imagined comparison).
Do not be surprised … as though something strange were happening to you. (1Pe 4:12)

c) as an accusative absolute, in CG (↑230f), e.g.:

οὐδεὶς τὸ μεῖζον [κακὸν] αἱρήσεται **ἐξὸν** (TempA) τὸ ἔλαττον [αἱρεῖσθαι].
No one will choose the greater [evil] when it is possible to choose the lesser (Plato, Protagoras 358d)

6. by an **adjective** phrase ("predicative" position; ↑136b; 137b; also ↑259q), e.g.:

… μήποτε … ἐπιστῇ ἐφ' ὑμᾶς **αἰφνίδιος** (TempA) ἡ ἡμέρα ἐκείνη.
… that … that day will not come on you suddenly/unexpectedly. (Lk 21:34)

7. by a **subordinate clause** (↑270a/270c; 276–287 [conjunctional clause]; 289b [relative clause]), e.g.:

ἡμᾶς δεῖ ἐργάζεσθαι … **ἕως ἡμέρα ἐστίν** (TempA).
We must work … as long as it is day. (Jn 9:4)

8. Further noteworthy points:

In the case of certain sentence patterns, the "action"/"situation" is referred to not by a finite, but by a non-finite verb form (by a participle or an infinitive), while the finite verb form indicates circumstances connected with the "action"/"situation" (↑BDF §435):

a) in the case of modifying verbs regularly combined with a (predicative) participle (↑234), e.g.:

ἔλαθόν τινες ξενίσαντες ἀγγέλους.
Some have entertained angels without knowing it. (He 13:2)

b) in the case of certain verbs that combine with an infinitive phrase as their object (↑218e), often agreeing with English usage, such as φιλέω + inf. *to love to do sth./to customarily do sth.* (↑BDAG s.v. 1c), ὀκνέω + inf. *to do sth. with delay,* προλαμβάνω + inf. *to do sth. before the usual time* (↑BDAG s.v. 1a), προστίθεμαι + inf. *to again/still do sth.*,[10] e.g.:

φιλοῦσιν … προσεύχεσθαι.
they love to pray … (Mt 6:5)

μὴ ὀκνήσῃς διελθεῖν ἕως ἡμῶν.
Come to us without delay. (Ac 9:38)

προέλαβεν μυρίσαι τὸ σῶμά μου …
She anointed my body beforehand … (Mk 14:8)

προσέθετο τρίτον πέμψαι.
He sent still a third. (Lk 20:12)

↑also 252.29,1a on comparable uses of sentences/clauses introduced by καί.

On questions of concord ↑261–265.

10 This is a LXX idiom (only occasionally occurring in extra-biblical Greek): προστίθεμαι translates the Hebr. הוֹסִיף *hôsîp̄, to do again/more* (↑HALOT sub יסף *ysp*). NT examples: Lk 20:11f (the parallel in Mk 12:4f uses πάλιν *again* combined with a finite verb form); Ac 12:3. In Lk 19:11 this verb appears as a manner participle (active) combined with a finite verb form (a usage attested in normal extra-biblical Greek).

III. **Overview** of the ways the various **types of adverbial** (optional) adjuncts and adverbial (obligatory) complements may be **expressed** (also ↑259c):

1. **LocA/C** ("Where?", "To where?", "Where from?", "How far?", etc.): 259d

a) by an **adverb** phrase (↑241c, also lexicon), e.g.:

ἅπαντες γάρ ἐσμεν **ἐνθάδε**. *For we are all here.* (Ac 16:28)

b) by a **preposition** phrase (also ↑187a–187d), e.g.:

παρ' αὐτῷ ἔμειναν. *They stayed with him.* (Jn 1:39)

c) by a noun phrase (its head being a noun, a nominalized expression, or a noun-substitute/pronoun) in one of the following **cases** (also ↑187a–187d):

- **accusative** of spatial extent ("How far?"↑155a; rarely used in the NT; ↑149b on CG poetic use of the acc. of goal ["To where?"]), e.g.:

ἦλθον **ἡμέρας ὁδόν**. *They went a day's journey.* (Lk 2:44)

- **genitive** of place ("From where?" or "Where?" ↑171; almost exclusively used in CG poetry, in the NT only in occasional traces), e.g.:

ὅτι **ἐκείνης** (sc. ὁδοῦ) ἤμελλεν διέρχεσθαι. *for he was about to pass that way.* (Lk 19:4)

- **dative** of place ("Where?", in both CG and post-CG almost entirely replaced by PpP; ↑181), e.g.:

d) by an **adjective** phrase (in the "predicative" position; ↑136b; 137b), e.g.:

ὑπαίθριος δὲ ηὐλίζετο. *but he spent the night in the open air.* (Josephus, Antiquities 1.279)

e) by a **subordinate clause** (relative clause; ↑289a/289b), e.g.:

οὗ γάρ **εἰσιν δύο ἢ τρεῖς συνηγμένοι** … ἐκεῖ εἰμι ἐν μέσῳ αὐτῶν. *For where two or three are gathered … I am there among them.* (Mt 18:20)

2. **TempA/C** ("When?", "How long?" or the like): 259e

a) by an **adverb** phrase (↑241c, also lexicon), e.g.:

νῦν χαίρω. *Now I rejoice.* (2Cor 7:9)

b) by a **preposition** phrase (↑also 187e–187i), e.g.:

μετὰ τρεῖς ἡμέρας ἀνέβη … *Three days later he went up …* (Ac 25:1)

c) by a noun phrase (its head being a noun, a nominalized expression, or a noun-substitute/pronoun) in one of the following **cases** (↑also 187e–187i):

- **accusative** of extent ("How long?"; in the NT sometimes "When?"; ↑155b), e.g.:

ἔμειναν οὐ **πολλὰς ἡμέρας**. *they stayed for a few days.* (Jn 2:12)

- **genitive** of time ("When?" or "Within which time span?"; in the NT especially in fixed phrases without article; ↑168), e.g.:

… ἵνα μὴ γένηται **χειμῶνος**. *… that it will not happen in winter.* (Mk 13:18)

- **dative** of time ("When?"; in the NT sometimes "How long?"; ↑182), e.g.:

τῇ τρίτῃ ἡμέρᾳ ἐγερθήσεται. *On the third day he will be raised.* (Mt 17:23)

d) by an **infinitive/ACI** phrase with an article governed by a preposition (↑226):

- ἐν + dat. (NT; not used in CG) mostly *while, as* (inf. pres.), especially Lk/Ac: *when/after* (inf. aor.; simultaneity or anteriority), e.g.:

καὶ **ἐν τῷ σπείρειν αὐτὸν** ἃ μὲν ἔπεσεν … *And as he sowed, some seeds fell …* (Mt 13:4)

• μετά + acc. *after*, e.g.:

μετὰ τὸ γενέσθαι με ἐκεῖ δεῖ με καὶ Ῥώμην ἰδεῖν. *After I have been there I must also see Rome.* (Ac 19:21)

• πρό + gen. *before*, e.g.:

οἶδεν γάρ … **πρὸ τοῦ ὑμᾶς αἰτῆσαι αὐτόν**. *For he knows … before you ask him.* (Mt 6:8)

• διά + gen. *through, during* + *-ing* form (in the NT only He 2:15).

• ἕως + gen. *until* (in the NT only Ac 8:40).

• similarly non-articular inf./ACI phrases preceded by πρίν (ἤ) (↑276a) *before*, e.g.:

κατάβηθι **πρὶν ἀποθανεῖν τὸ παιδίον μου**. *Come down before my child dies.* (Jn 4:49)

e) by a **participle** phrase (p.c. or gen.abs. [↑231d; 232a]; CG also acc.abs. [↑230f]):
• simultaneity (mostly pres. [or pf.]) *while, as*;
• anteriority (mostly aor.) *after, when*, e.g.

ἰδὼν δὲ **Σίμων Πέτρος** προσέπεσεν τοῖς γόνασιν Ἰησοῦ. *But when Simon Peter saw this, he fell at Jesus' knees.* (Lk 5:8)

f) by an **adjective** phrase (in the "predicative" position; ↑136b; 137b; also ↑259q), e.g.:

δευτεραῖοι ἤλθομεν εἰς … *on the second day we arrived …* (Ac 28:13)

g) by a **subordinate clause** (temporal clause; ↑276), e.g.:

… τί ἐποίησεν Δαυὶδ **ὅτε ἐπείνασεν**. *… what David did when he was hungry* (Mt 12:3)

↑also relative clauses with iterative force (referring to past "situations"); ↑290f, also 289b.
↑also 252.29,1a on comparable uses of sentences/clauses introduced by καί.

259f 3. **ManA/C** ("How?"/"In what manner?" or the like)

a) by an **adverb** phrase ("How?"/"In what manner?", "How much", etc. ; ↑241c, also lexicon), e.g.:

Ἐτρέχετε **καλῶς**. *You were running well.* (Ga 5:7)

b) by a **preposition** phrase ("How?"/"In what manner?", "In what respect?", "According to what/whom?"; ↑184/185, also 187j–187l), e.g.:

κεκλεισμένον **ἐν πάσῃ ἀσφαλείᾳ** *securely locked* (Ac 5:23)

c) by a noun phrase (its head being a noun, a nominalized expression, or a noun-substitute/pronoun) in one of the following **cases** (↑187j/187k):

• **accusative** :

adverbial accusative ("How?"; in NT mainly in the form of ntr. adjectives; ↑157), e.g.:

οὐδὲν διαφέρει δούλου. *He differs in no way from a slave.* (Ga 4:1)

accusative of respect ("In what respect?"; only a few instances in the NT; ↑156), e.g.:

ἀπορούμενος δὲ ἐγὼ **τὴν περὶ τούτων ζήτησιν** … *Since I was at a loss regarding the investigation of these things … = Since I was at a loss how to investigate these things …* (Ac 25:20)

• **genitive** ("For/At how much?"; ↑163a), e.g.:

εἰ **τοσούτου** τὸ χωρίον ἀπέδοσθε; *Did you sell the land for this amount?* (Ac 5:8)

• **dative** (↑173b; 176–182),

dative of manner ("How?", "Under what concomitant circumstances?"; ↑180a), e.g.:

παρρησίᾳ τὸν λόγον ἐλάλει. *he spoke openly about this.* (Mk 8:32) dative of respect ("In what respect?"; ↑178a), e.g.:

ἐστερεοῦντο **τῇ πίστει.** — *they were strengthened regarding/in their faith.* (Ac 16:5)

d) by an **infinitive/ACI** phrase ("How?"/"In what manner?")

• without article or with τοῦ occasionally as a ManA/C (↑220d; 225f) in the NT, alongside its typical use of indicating purpose or result, similarly so by the articular inf./ACI governed by the preposition πρός + acc. (↑226b) *by* + *-ing* form;

• with an article governed by the preposition ἐν + dat. occasionally in the NT *by/in* + *-ing* form alongside its typical temporal use (↑226a); 1× in the NT (2Cor 8:11) ἐκ + gen. *according to* + *-ing.*

e) by a **participle** phrase (mainly p.c., sometimes gen.abs.; ↑231e; 232a; "How?"/"In what manner?", "Under what concomitant circumstances?"; occurs frequently), indicating:

• the way in which the "action"/"situation" is meant to unfold, *as/in that* or *by/in* + *-ing* form, e.g.:

διώξουσιν, **παραδιδόντες εἰς** … — *they will persecute you (by) handing you over …* (Lk 21:12)

• specific concomitant circumstances or a specific characterization of "action"/"situation", *whereby* (at times in contrasts *while*) or *by/in* + *-ing* form;

• an imagined comparison (preceded by ὡς/ὥσπερ), *as if/as though*;

• negated, *not, without* (+ *-ing* form).

f) by an **adjective** phrase (in the "predicative" position; ↑136b; 137b), e.g.:

… μήποτε … ἐπιστῇ ἐφ' ὑμᾶς **αἰφνίδιος** ἡ ἡμέρα. — *… that … that day will not come on you suddenly/unexpectedly.* (Lk 21:34)

g) by a **subordinate clause** ("How?", manner clause; ↑287), e.g.:

οὐκ ἔδει καὶ σε ἐλεῆσαι τὸν σύνδουλόν σου, **ὡς κἀγὼ σὲ ἠλέησα**; — *Shouldn't you also have had mercy on your fellow servant, as I had mercy on you?* (Mt 18:33)

↑also 289b (relative clauses).

4. Causal adjuncts and complements (specifying the reason for the "action"/"situation" in the widest sense):

4.1 **CausA/C** ("Why?", "For what reason?", in a narrower sense) 259g

a) by an **adverb** phrase (↑241c, also lexicon), e.g.:

διὸ γρηγορεῖτε. — *Therefore be on the alert.* (Ac 20:31)

b) by a **preposition** phrase (↑187m), especially with διά + acc. *because/for the sake of*, e.g.:

χαίρω **δι' ὑμᾶς**. — *I am glad for your sake.* (Jn 11:15)

c) by a noun phrase (its head being a noun, a nominalized expression, or a noun-substitute/pronoun) in one of the following **cases** (also ↑187m):

• **dative** of cause ("Owing to what?"; ↑177b), e.g.:

τῇ ἀπιστίᾳ ἐξεκλάσθησαν. — *they were broken off because of (due to) their unbelief.* (Ro 11:20)

• **dative** of agent (mainly CG: originator with verbal adjective and pf. pass. [↑176c]; on the agent of the passive ↑191a).

d) by an articular **infinitive/ACI** phrase governed by (↑226a)

• διά + acc. *because*, e.g.:

διὰ τὸ μὴ ἔχειν ῥίζαν ἐξηράνθη. — *Since they had no root, they withered.* (Mt 13:6)

- in the NT occasionally perhaps ἐν + dat. *because*.
- in CG also ἐπί + dat. *because* (also *in order that*).

The NT has one CausA example of an inf./ACI phrase with simple τῷ in 2Cor 2:13 (↑224; 259c).

e) by a **participle** phrase (p.c. or gen.abs.; [↑231f; 232a]; CG also acc.abs. [↑230f]):

- indicating an objective reason *because, as, since*, e.g.:

πάντες ἐφοβοῦντο αὐτὸν **μὴ πιστεύοντες ὅτι ἐστὶν μαθητής**.	*All were afraid, because they did not believe that he was disciple.* (Ac 9:26)

- indicating a subjective reason (preceded by ὡς) *because* (*I/you* etc. *think that*), *convinced that.*

f) by a **subordinate clause** (causal clause; ↑277), e.g.:

πᾶσαν τὴν ὀφειλὴν ἐκείνην ἀφῆκά σοι, **ἐπεὶ παρεκάλεσάς με**.	*I forgave you all that debt because you begged me to.* (Mt 18:32)

259h 4.2 **CondA/C** ("In what case?"/"Under what conditions?"):

a) occasionally by an adverb, a preposition, or a noun phrase (in an appropriate case), if at all, e.g.:

πῶς **οὖν** σταθήσεται ἡ βασιλεία αὐτοῦ;	*How then (in that case) can his kingdom stand?* (Mt 12:26)
οὐ δεδούλωται ὁ ἀδελφὸς ἢ ἡ ἀδελφὴ **ἐν τοῖς τοιούτοις**.	*In such cases the brother or sister is not under bondage.* (1Cor 7:15)

b) in CG by ἐφ᾽ ᾧ / ἐφ᾽ ᾧτε + inf./ACI phrase *on condition that* (↑280b).

c) by a **participle** phrase (p.c. or gen.abs.; [↑231h; 232a]; CG also acc.abs. [↑230f]), e.g.:

εἰ δὲ **ἑαυτοὺς διεκρίνομεν**, οὐκ ἂν ἐκρινόμεθα.	*If we were properly judging ourselves, we would not be judged.* (1Cor 11:31)

d) by a **subordinate clause** (conditional clauses, i.e. *if*-clauses; ↑280–285):

- indefinite case (εἰ + ind.; ↑281).
- prospective case (ἐάν + subj.; ↑282).
- potential case (εἰ + opt.; ↑283).
- remote case (εἰ + augment ind.; ↑284), e.g.:

πάντες ἐφοβοῦντο αὐτὸν **μὴ πιστεύοντες ὅτι ἐστὶν μαθητής**.	*All were afraid, because they did not believe that he was disciple.* (Ac 9:26)

↑also relative clauses with conditional force (↑289e/290f; possibly 289b), also occurring rhetorical questions with a conditional nuance (↑269d).

259i 4.3 **ResA/C** ("With what result?") *so that/with the result that* (when rendered as main clause also *therefore*, leading to overlaps with CausA/C; ↑259g; also 334):

a) for adverb, preposition, noun (in the dative of cause), and participle phrases ↑CausA/C (↑259g) and PurpA/C (↑259j).

b) by an **infinitive/ACI** phrase

- without article preceded by ὥστε (in CG sometimes, in the NT occasionally, also ὡς; ↑221a), e.g.:

ἄρας τὸν κράβαττον ἐξῆλθεν …, **ὥστε ἐξίστασθαι πάντας**.	*He picked up his mat and walked out …, so that all were amazed.* (Mk 2:12)

- KG/NT also with τοῦ (↑225c).
- also with article governed by εἰς/πρός + acc. (↑226a).

c) by a **subordinate clause** (result clause; ↑279):

• subordinated by ὥστε (CG also ὡς) + finite verb (as predicator) *so that/with the result that*, e.g.:

οὕτως γὰρ ἠγάπησεν ὁ θεὸς τὸν κόσμον, **ὥστε τὸν υἱὸν τὸν μονογενῆ ἔδωκεν** …	*For God so loved the world (with the result) that he gave his one and only Son* … (Jn 3:16)

• KG/NT less frequently subordinated by ἵνα or the like, mostly + subj. (↑279a).

Possibly in questions also ὅτι *(so) that* (= *with the result that*; ↑279a).

↑also relative clauses with a similar force (↑290d, also 289b). ↑also 252.29,1a on the 'consecutive' καί.

4.4 **PurpA/C** ("What for?", "For what purpose?"): 259j

a) by an **adverb** phrase (also ↑CausA/C 259g), e.g.:

ἱνατί καὶ τὴν γῆν καταργεῖ;	*Why (= For what purpose) should it still use up the ground?* (Lk 13:7)

b) by a **preposition** phrase (↑187n) with εἰς/πρός + acc. et al. *for* (purpose), e.g.:

εἰς τοῦτο γὰρ ἐξῆλθον.	*For this purpose I have come.* (Mk 1:38)

c) by an **infinitive/ACI** phrase

• without article (↑220), e.g.:

οὐκ ἦλθον **καταλῦσαι** ἀλλὰ **πληρῶσαι**.	*I have not come to abolish, but to fulfil.* (Mt 5:17)

• KG/NT also with τοῦ (↑225b), e.g.:

ἐξῆλθεν ὁ σπείρων **τοῦ σπείρειν**.	*A farmer went out to sow.* (Mt 13:3)

• with an article governed by the preposition (↑226a) εἰς/πρός + acc. *in order to* (CG also ἐπί + dat., ὑπέρ + gen.; in the NT 2Cor 7:13 ἕνεκεν + gen.), e.g.:

ἀπήγαγον αὐτὸν **εἰς τὸ σταυρῶσαι**.	*They led him away to crucify him.* (Mt 27:31)

• KG/NT less frequently with ὥστε (↑221b).

• in CG also by ἐφ' ᾧ / ἐφ' ᾧτε + inf./ACI phrase (also ind. fut. replacing the inf./ACI) *in order to/ in order that* (↑280b; 184j).

d) by a **participle** phrase (only p.c. fut., in the NT also pres.; frequently preceded by ὡς; ↑231e; 232a), e.g.:

ἐληλύθει **προσκυνήσων** εἰς Ἰερουσαλήμ.	*He had come to Jerusalem to worship.* (Ac 8:27)

e) by a **subordinate clause** (purpose clause; ↑278)

• subordinated by ἵνα or the like mostly + subj. *so that/in order that*, e.g.:

τί ἀγαθὸν ποιήσω **ἵνα σχῶ ζωὴν αἰώνιον**;	*What good thing must I do to have eternal life?* Mt 19:16)

• KG/NT less frequently subordinated by ὥστε (ὥστε inf./ACI phrase) *so that/in order that*.

↑also relative clauses indicating purpose (↑290c; also 289b). ↑also 252.29,1a on the 'final' καί.

4.5 **ConcA/C** ("In spite of what?", related to CondA/C [↑259h]): 259k

a) occasionally by an adverb, a preposition, or a noun phrase (in an appropriate case), if at all, e.g.:

ὅμως μέντοι καὶ ἐκ τῶν ἀρχόντων πολλοὶ ἐπίστευσαν εἰς αὐτόν.	*Nevertheless, even among the leaders many believed in him.* (Jn 12:42)

b) by a **participle** phrase (p.c. or gen.abs., quite often preceded by καί/καίπερ/καίτοι [↑231g; 232a]; CG also acc.abs. [↑230f]), e.g.:

… τὰ πλοῖα **τηλικαῦτα ὄντα** … μετάγεται ὑπὸ ἐλαχίστου πηδαλίου.	*… the ships: although they are so large … they are steered by a very small rudder.* (Jas 3:4)

c) by a **subordinate clause** (concessive clause; ↑286) subordinated by εἰ καί, ἐὰν καί, κἄν et al. *even if, even though, although*, e.g.:

ὁ πιστεύων εἰς ἐμὲ **κἂν ἀποθάνῃ** ζήσεται.	*The one who believes in me will live, even if he dies.* (Jn 11:25)

259l 4.6 **InstrA/C** ("By what means?"; related to CausA/C [↑259g] and ManA/C [↑259f]):

a) by a **preposition** phrase (↑187o), especially with ἐν + dat. *with/by* and διά + gen. *through*, e.g.:

… εἰ πατάξομεν **ἐν μαχαίρῃ**;	*… shall we strike with the sword?* (Lk 22:49)

b) by a noun phrase (its head being a noun, a nominalized expression, or a noun-substitute/pronoun) the **case** being typically the dative of instrument ("By what means?"; ↑177a), e.g.:

ἅλατι ἠρτυμένος	*seasoned with salt* (Col 4:6)

c) in KG (not in the NT) by an infinitive/ACI phrase preceded by τῷ (↑224).

d) by a **subordinate clause** (relative clause; ↑289b).

↑also ManA/C and CausA/C (↑259f/259g).

259m 4.7 **IntA/C** ("In whose interest?", "To whose advantage or disadvantage?"):

a) by a **preposition** phrase (↑187p), especially with ὑπέρ + gen. *for, on behalf of*, e.g.:

παρέδωκεν ἑαυτὸν **ὑπὲρ ἡμῶν** προσφορὰν καὶ θυσίαν …	*He gave himself up for us as an offering and sacrifice …* (Eph 5:2)

b) by a noun phrase (with a noun, a nominalized expression, or a noun-substitute/pronoun as its head) the **case** (↑187p) being typically the dative of interest (↑176a; ↑also 176c on the sympathetic and ethical dative or perhaps the dative of standpoint), e.g.:

οὐδεὶς γὰρ ἡμῶν **ἑαυτῷ** ζῇ.	*For none of us lives for himself.* (Ro 14:7)

c) by a **subordinate clause** (relative clause; ↑289b).

259n B. **Subject/object adjuncts** (↑Huddleston-Pullum: 261ff)

The **subject and object related adjuncts** (or simply "subject/object adjuncts"; "SA"/"OA") are the optional counterparts of the (more frequent obligatory) subject/object complements (SC/OC; ↑258). They convey information about the subject and object entities respectively, concerning either their identity ("SA^{id}"/"OA^{id}") or some of their properties ("SA^{prop}"/"OA^{prop}"), and, in principle, they may also be expressed in the same way (↑258a/258b). Closely connected with the "action"/"situation", the SA^{id} and the OA^{id} typically answer the question "In what capacity/As who or as what is the subject or object entity involved in the 'action'/'situation'?", the SA^{prop} and the OA^{prop} "In what condition or endued with what property is the subject or object entity involved in the 'action'/'situation'?". E.g.:

Χριστὸς (S) δὲ παραγενόμενος **ἀρχιερεὺς τῶν … ἀγαθῶν** (SA^{id}) …	*But when Christ came as the high priest of the good things …* (He 9:11)

Here the ἀρχιερεύς NP is optional (not called for by the valency of παραγίνομαι); in He 2:7, e.g., it is obligatory (due to the valency of γίνομαι: SC^{id}).
In the following examples a similar state of affairs applies.

Note that at times the "as" of the SA^{id}/OA^{id} is made explicit by ὡς (e.g. in 1Pe 4:10; also ↑260i).

ὁ πατὴρ ἀπέσταλκεν τὸν υἱὸν (Od) **σωτῆρα τοῦ κόσμου** (OA[id]).	*The Father sent his Son as the world's Saviour.* (1Jn 4:14)
… δοῦναι τὴν ψυχὴν αὐτοῦ (Od) **λύτρον ἀντὶ πολλῶν** (OA[id]).	*… to give his life as a ransom for many.* (Mk 10:45)

↑also Mt 16:26; 19:4; 20:28; Ro 3:25; 4:11; 6:13; 12:1; 1Cor 7:21; 9:5; 2Cor 4:5; 11:2; Eph 5:2; He 6:20.

ἀπέθανεν (P/S) **ἄτεκνος** (SA[prop]).	*He died childless.* (Lk 20:29)

Here the ἄτεκνος AdjP is optional (not called for by ἀποθνῄσκω), not so in Lk 20:28 where it is obligatory due to the valency of εἰμί: SC[prop]). The same rules apply to the following examples.

οἱ δὲ γεωργοὶ ἐξαπέστειλαν αὐτὸν (Od) δείραντες **κενόν** (OA[prop]).	*But the farmers beat him and sent him away empty-handed.* (Lk 20:10)

↑also Mt 20:3 (SA[prop] to ACP-S); Mk 12:3; 14:52; Lk 10:30; Ac 3:11; 4:10; 9:7; 14:10; 16:37; 19:16 (SA to ACI-S); 20:9.12; 1Cor 7:37.

Note that SA/OA[prop] need to be distinguished from **attributive modifiers** ("Attr"; ↑260). Both may inform about properties of subject and object entities. They **differ**, however, from one another at least in two ways:

a) SA/OA[prop] (like SC/OC[prop]) are not preceded by the article, thus adjective and participle phrases with this function are in the "predicative" position (↑136b; 137c), while attributive modifiers are typically in the attributive position (↑260).

b) The properties specified by SA/OA[prop] are closely connected with the "action"/"situation" referred to by the predicator/predicate verb; as stated above, SA/OA[prop] usually answer the question "In what condition or endued with what property is the subject or object entity involved in the 'action'/'situation'?". The properties indicated by an Attr are usually without such a connection; they simply answer questions like "What kind of entity is the entity referred to by the head noun?", "What characterizes it?" (↑260).

Regarding the **terminology** two points need to be added: 259o

a) Subject/object adjuncts as well as complements specifying properties (SA/OA[prop] and SC/OC[prop]; ↑259n; 258b) and adverbials (complements as well as adjuncts) expressed by adjective or participle phrases (↑258c; 259a–259m) may all modify subjects or objects (and show concord with noun phrases that express these) and have one characteristic in common: they are in the "predicative" position (↑136b). In line with this state of affairs many refer to several of these sentence constituents as having a "predicative" use (↑e.g. BDF §243; Schwyzer II: 178f; 618). It is true, of course, that such sentence constituents usually state ("predicate") something about the subject or object entity and so the use of the term "predicative" might be justified. Still, in the present grammar a narrower, perhaps more straightforward, definition of the term has been adopted: whatever is part of the predicate of a sentence/clause is referred to as "predicative" (↑254c[3]).

b) In reference to what in this grammar is called subject/object adjuncts a whole range of different terms (with varying definitions) are used by specialists, as a small selection of examples from Greek, German, and English linguistics indicate:

- "adjectival/substantival adjunct" (BR §260–262: "adjektivisches/substantivisches Adjunkt");
- "state related predicative attributive modifier" (Sommer: 5: "prädikatives Zustandsattribut");
- "apposition"/"verb apposition" (Schwyzer II: 618/178–180: "Apposition"/"Verbalapposition");
- "depictive predicative" (Huddleston-Pullum: 262; DuG9: 803: "depiktives Prädikativ");
- "predicative attributive modifier" (Altmann-Hahnemann: 90: "prädikatives Attribut").

Overview of sentence **elements** connected with the **subject** or the **object**:

sentence element:	points worth noting:	status of sentence element:

259p I. Sentence elements that **modify** the S or the O

1. SC/OC (↑258a/258b): indicating identity (SC^{id}/OC^{id}) or properties (SC^{prop}/OC^{prop})		obligatory sentence constituents
2. SA/OA (↑259n): indicating identity (SA^{id}/OA^{id}) or properties (SA^{prop}/OA^{prop})	S/O identity or property is closely connected with the "action"/ "situation"	optional sentence constituents
3. attribute modifier (↑260)	S/O property is not connected with the "action"/"situation"	part of a sentence constituent

259q II. Sentence elements **showing concord** with the S or the O

1. SC/OC (↑258a/258b): SC^{id}/OC^{id} and SC^{prop}/OC^{prop}	in part expressed by PpP, also by case NP without concord	obligatory sentence constituents
2. AdvlC (↑258c)	adverbial use of AdjP and PtcP (peculiarity of Ancient Greek)	
3. AdvlA (↑259a–259m)		optional sentence constituents
4. SA/OA (↑259n): SA^{id}/OA^{id} and SA^{prop}/OA^{prop}		
5. attribute modifier (↑260)		part of a sentence constituent

On questions of concord ↑261–265.

3.3.1.3 Attributive modifiers

260 Attributive modifiers including apposition

(↑BR §259; BDF §241/242; 268–272; 474.1.4; Turner 1963: 185–222)

260a I. An attributive modifier is not a sentence constituent itself, but part of one, being embedded in the phrase expressing it. Usually occurring as an optional sentence element, it adds **information about the head of the phrase**, characterizing in some way the entity (or property) referred to. It may be embedded in the following phrase types:

1. **mostly** in **noun phrases**, answering questions such as "What kind of entity is the entity referred to by the head noun?", "What characterizes it?",[11] e.g.:

τὸν υἱὸν **τὸν μονογενῆ** ἔδωκεν. *He gave his one and only Son.* (Jn 3:16)

The Attr is embedded in a NP in the role of a Od (τὸν υἱὸν τὸν μονογενῆ); it answers the question "What kind of 'Son' (entity referred to by the head noun υἱόν) is he?": *The one and only* (τὸν μονογενῆ).

2. sometimes in **adjective phrases**,[12] answering questions such as "How …?", e.g.:

ἦν γὰρ πλούσιος **σφόδρα**. *For he was very rich.* (Lk 18:23)

The Attr is embedded in an AdjP in the role of a SC (πλούσιος σφόδρα); it answers the question "How 'rich' (property referred to by the head πλούσιος)?": *Very* (σφόδρα).

3. sometimes in **adverb phrases** (or phrases with a similar function), answering questions such as "To what extent …?", e.g.:

πόσῳ μᾶλλον ὁ πατὴρ ὑμῶν ὁ ἐν τοῖς οὐρανοῖς δώσει ἀγαθὰ τοῖς αἰτοῦσιν αὐτόν. *How much more will your Father in heaven give good things to those who ask him.* (Mt 7:11)

The Attr is embedded in an AdvP in the role of a ManA (πόσῳ μᾶλλον); it answers the question "To what extent 'more' (referred to by the head μᾶλλον)?": *To a great extent/Much* (πόσῳ *How much?* rhetorical for "Much"; dative of difference/measure [↑178b]).

II. Attributive modifiers of the head of **noun phrases** may be expressed as follows ("HN" = head noun):

1. by the (definite) **article** and, corresponding to the English indefinite article, the indefinite pronoun or sometimes the numeral εἷς (↑130a; 144a; 145b), showing concord with the head noun, e.g.: 260b

ὁ (art.) νόμος (HN) καὶ **οἱ** (art.) προφῆται (HN)	*the Law and the Prophets* (Lk 16:16 et pass.)
ἀνήρ (HN) **τις** (indefinite pron.)	*a man* (Lk 8:27)
μία (numeral) παιδίσκη (head)	*a servant-girl* (Mt 26:69)

---

11 Note that attributive modifiers are used with two distinctive functions (which applies especially when they are expressed in the form of relative clauses; ↑260n; for examples ↑319a; ↑Huddleston-Pullum: 1033; DuG9: 1041f; the intended function is inferable from the context):
(a) restrictive function, i.e. limiting the range of entities the head may refer to (identifying role);
(b) non-restrictive, purely descriptive function. In 2Macc 10:34, e.g., we are told about people that utter λόγους **ἀθεμίτους** *forbidden words.* The attributive modifier is used restrictively: the NP refers to forbidden words, not to words in general. In 1Pe 4:3, where we read about **ἀθεμίτοις** εἰδωλολατρίαις *forbidden idolatries,* it is used non-restrictively: idolatries are always forbidden; the attributive modifier has a purely descriptive function.

12 The term "attributive modifier" (or simply "attribute") is used in various ways by grammarians. Many use it with reference exclusively to modifiers connected with the heads of noun phrases (↑Crystal: 43; DuG9: 789f). In the present grammar we follow the approach adopted by many fairly recent linguistic publications (some of the earlier editions of the DuG included) in applying the term "attributive modifier" to modifiers of the heads of other types of phrases such as adjective and adverb phrases as well (↑Bussmann: 41).

2. by the following phrase types

260c a) by an **adjective** phrase (↑137a) or a phrase whose head is used like an adjective (as far as possible showing concord with the head noun [HN], normally in the "attributive" position [↑136a]) such as a participle phrase (↑236), or one with a pronoun (in certain cases in the "predicative" position; ↑139–144), or a numeral (↑62/63; 145) as its head, e.g.:

ἡ **καινὴ** (AdjP) διαθήκη (HN)	*the new covenant* (Lk 22:20)
τὸ φῶς (HN) τὸ **ἀληθινόν** (AdjP)	*the true light* (Jn 1:9)
ὁ **ζῶν** (PtcP) πατήρ (HN)	*the living Father* (Jn 6:57)
λόγια (HN) **ζῶντα** (PtcP)	*living oracles* (Ac 7:38)
τὸ **αὐτὸ** (pers. pron.) πνεῦμα (HN)	*the same Spirit* (1Cor 12:4)
ὁ λόγος (HN) **οὗτος** (dem. pron.)	*this word* (Lk 4:36)
ὁ θάνατος (HN) ὁ **δεύτερος** (numeral)	*the second death* (Re 21:8)

On attributive modifiers in the "predicative" position also ↑136c/136d.

Adjective phrases (at times also adverb phrases; ↑260m) in the role of an "attributive modifier" fairly frequently occur **without a head noun** (apparently easy to supply in thought; a conventional ellipsis; ↑293c; 134c; 137d; BDF §241; ↑also 132d for the related nominalizing use of the article). Frequently in a translation into English such a "head noun" needs to be supplied (e.g. "day"); at times the whole phrase may be rendered by a single noun (phrase), ↑e.g. Mt 3:3 below:

"head nouns" frequently to be supplied:

γῆ/χώρα *land*	ἡμέρα *day*	ὥρα *hour/time*	(ἡ) ὁδός *(the) way*

less frequently inter alia:

χείρ *hand*	μέρος *part*	ὑετόν *rain*	γλῶσσα *language*

Examples:

ἡ ἔρημος (sc. γῆ/χώρα)	*the wilderness/desert* (Mt 3:3 et pass.)
εἰς ὅλην τὴν περίχωρον (sc. γῆν)	*into the whole surrounding region* (Mk 1:28)

↑also Mt 3:5 et pass. (ἡ Ἰουδαία *Judea*); 14:35 et pass. (ἡ περίχωρος … *the region around* …); 23:15 (ἡ ξηρά *the dry land, the land*); Lk 1:39 (ἡ ὀρεινή *the hill country*); 6:17 (ἡ παράλιος *the coastal region*).

τῇ πρώτῃ (sc. ἡμέρᾳ) τῶν ἀζύμων	*the first day of Unleavened Bread* (Mt 26:17)
ἡ αὔριον (sc. ἡμέρα)	*tomorrow* (Mt 6:34 et pass.)

↑also Mt 27:8 (ἡ σήμερον *today*); 27:62 et pass. (ἡ ἐπαύριον *the next day*); Ac 16:11/20:15 (τῇ ἐπιούσῃ *the following day*); 20:15 (τῇ ἑτέρᾳ/τῇ ἐχομένῃ *the next day*); 21:1 (τῇ ἑξῆς *the next day*); 27:19 (τῇ τρίτῃ *on the third day*); 1Cor 16:2 (κατὰ μίαν σαββάτου *on the first day of every week*).

ἡ πρωΐα (sc. ὥρα)	*the morning (hour/time)* (↑e.g. Mt 27:1)

↑also Mt 20:6 (ἡ ἑνδεκάτη *the eleventh hour*); Ac 10:30 (ἡ ἐνάτη *the ninth hour*).

ἔσται τὰ σκολιὰ εἰς εὐθεῖαν (sc. ὁδόν)	*the crooked will become (a) straight (way)* (Lk 3:5)

↑also Mt 8:30 et pass. (μακράν *far [away/off]* [< *a long way/distance away*]; fixed acc. sg. form used as an adv. [↑53d]); Lk 5:19 (ποίας *by what way*); 19:4 (ἐκείνης *there* [< *that way*; ↑171]).

ἡ δεξιά (sc. χείρ) / ἡ ἀριστερά (sc. χείρ)	*the right hand / the left hand* (Mt 6:3)
τὸ τρίτον (sc. μέρος) τῆς θαλάσσης	*the third part of the sea* (Re 8:8)

↑also Jas 5:7 (πρόϊμον [sc. ὑετόν] *the early/autumn rain* / ὄψιμον [sc. ὑετόν] *the late/spring rain*); Re 9:11 (ἡ Ἑλληνική [probably sc. γλῶσσα] *the Greek language*).

b) by a **noun** phrase whose head may not only be a noun, but also a **pronoun** used as a noun substitute (↑22c; ↑139–144) or any kind of **nominalized expression** (↑132d; on participle ↑237, on inf./ACI ↑222; 224b; 225a/225b), mainly in 260d

• the **genitive** (as "genitive attributive modifier"; on possible positions ↑136e): 260e

(1) genitive of originator or possessor (↑159; also 159c [ellipsis of "son" etc.]), e.g.:

… ἀγαπητοῖς (HN) **θεοῦ**	*to … those loved by God …* (Ro 1:7)
οἱ δοῦλοι (HN) **τοῦ οἰκοδεσπότου**	*the slaves of the owner* (Mt 13:27)
ὁ οἶκος (HN) **ὑμῶν**	*your house* (Mt 23:38)

(2) subjective or objective genitive (↑160), e.g.:

τὴν πίστιν (HN) **τοῦ θεοῦ** (subjective)	*God's faithfulness* (Ro 3:3)
πίστιν (HN) **θεοῦ** (objective)	*faith in God* (Mk 11:22)

(3) genitive of material or content (↑161), e.g.:

τὸ δίκτυον (HN) **τῶν ἰχθύων**	*the net full of fish* (Jn 21:8)

(4) genitive of quality (in the NT influenced by Semitic usage; ↑162), e.g.:

σκεῦος (HN) **ἐκλογῆς**	*a chosen instrument* (Ac 9:15)

(5) genitive of direction or purpose (↑164), e.g.:

ὁδὸν (HN) **σωτηρίας**	*the way of/to salvation* (Ac 16:17)

(6) genitive of explanation or apposition (↑165; ↑also 260h), e.g. (↑165a):

περὶ τοῦ ναοῦ (HN) **τοῦ σώματος αὐτοῦ**	*about the temple of his body* (Jn 2:21)

(7) partitive genitive (↑166; not in "attributive" position; ↑136e), e.g.:

οἱ πρῶτοι (HN) **τῶν Ἰουδαίων**	*the leading men of the Jews* (Ac 25:2)
πολλοὶ (HN) δὲ **τῶν ἀκουσάντων τὸν λόγον**	*many of the those who had heard the message* (Ac 4:4)

• the **dative**: 260f

(1) dative proper (↑174–176), e.g.:

εὐχαριστίαν (HN) **τῷ θεῷ**	*thanksgiving to God* (2Cor 9:11)

(2) dative of respect (↑178; ↑also 187k on constructions with a similar use), e.g.:

οἱ καθαροὶ (HN) **τῇ καρδίᾳ**	*the pure in heart* (Mt 5:8)

• the **accusative** (of respect; ↑156; ↑also 187k) infrequently in the NT, e.g.: 260g

ἄνθρωπος (HN) πλούσιος ἀπὸ Ἁριμαθαίας, **τοὔνομα** Ἰωσήφ	*a rich man from Arimathea, named Joseph* (Mt 27:57)

• the same case form as the head noun, a special type of attributive modifier known as **apposition**; communicationally it typically corresponds to a sentence with an identifying subject complement (SC^{id}; ↑258) and mostly follows the head noun; a proper name in the role of a head noun is normally without the article (↑134a), while appositions regularly have the article (especially those modifying a personal pro- 260h noun; ↑130b); before an apposition an expression such as *namely* (viz.) or *that is* (i.e.) may helpfully be supplied in thought, which in writing is regularly indicated by a comma or a colon when translated into English, e.g.:

Ἡρῴδης (HN) **ὁ βασιλεύς**	*Herod,* [viz.] *the King* = (more idiomatic English) *King Herod* (Ac 12:1)

May be traced back to the sentence Ἡρῴδης (S) βασιλεὺς (SC^id^) ἦν *Herod was the king.*

ἐν οἰκίᾳ Σίμωνος (HN) **τοῦ λεπροῦ** …	*in the house of Simon,* [i.e.] *the leper.* (Mt 26:6)

Traceable back to … Σίμωνος, αὐτὸς (S) ἦν ὁ λεπρός (SC^id^) … *of Simon, he was the [former] leper.*

Ἰάκωβος (HN) **ὁ τοῦ Ἁλφαίου** (↑159c)	*James,* [i.e.] *the son of Alphaeus* (Mt 10:3)
Συμεὼν (HN) **ὁ καλούμενος Νίγερ**	*Simeon,* [i.e.] *the one called Niger* (Ac 13:1)
προσήνεγκαν αὐτῷ δῶρα (HN), **χρυσὸν καὶ λίβανον καὶ σμύρναν**.	*They presented him with gifts: gold, frankincense and myrrh.* (Mt 2:11)
… βασιλέα ἕτερον (HN) … εἶναι **Ἰησοῦν**.	… *that there is another king,* [namely] *Jesus.* (Ac 17:7)
ἡ γυνή σου Ἐλισάβετ (HN)	*your wife Elizabeth* (Lk 1:13)

Perhaps fronted for emphasis (↑128b).

Οὐαὶ ὑμῖν (HN) **τοῖς Φαρισαίοις**	*Woe to you Pharisees* (Lk 11:43)

↑also Mk 9:43; Lk 11:42; Jn 14:26; Ac 13:33 (App fronted); 2Cor 11:28; Eph 3:1; Col 3:4; He 3:1; 1Pe 5:1.8; 2Pe 2:6; 1Jn 5:13; Re 12:9; 15:1; etc.; Ac 11:5 (prep. occurs only 1×); 1Jn 3:24 (HN: ἐν … App: ἐκ …); Re 1:5 (App in the nom. "instead" of the gen.; ↑261b).

On explanatory inf./ACI phrases ↑222, similarly 224b (with τό) and 225f (with τοῦ), on appositional subordinate clauses ↑288 (also 260j), on the genitive of explanation or apposition with a comparable function ↑165 (also 260e).

Noteworthy points:

260i (1) Attributive modifiers showing concord with the head noun are sometimes preceded by ὡς (ὡσεί) *as/like* (↑252.61,1a); in such cases one may speak of appositions, too, e.g.:

Χριστὸς (HN) δὲ [πιστὸς] **ὡς υἱὸς** ἐπὶ τὸν οἶκον αὐτοῦ.	*But Christ is faithful as (= in his capacity as) a Son over His house.* (He 3:6)
προφήτην (HN) ὑμῖν ἀναστήσει κύριος ὁ θεὸς ὑμῶν … **ὡς ἐμέ**.	*The Lord God will raise up for you … a prophet like me (= a prophet as I am one)* (Ac 3:22)

Note that there are sentence elements preceded by ὡς comparable with this ὡς-apposition in form, but with a distinct function:

- as a subject/object complement (SC^id^/OC^id^ or SC^prop^/OC^prop^; ↑258a/258b), e.g.:

καὶ σχήματι εὑρεθεὶς **ὡς ἄνθρωπος** (SC^id^ [here: classification]; S: ὅς in verse 6)	*and being found in appearance as a human being* (Php 2:7)
ἐποίησέν με (Od) **ὡς πατέρα Φαραω** (OC^id^)	*he made me as a father to Pharaoh* (Gn 45:8 LXX)
οἱ ὀφθαλμοὶ (S) αὐτοῦ **ὡς φλὸξ πυρός** (SC^prop^).	*His eyes were like blazing fire.* (Re 1:14)

• as a subject/object adjunct (SA/OA; ↑259n) or a manner adjunct (ManA; ↑259b), e.g.:

ὡς σοφὸς ἀρχιτέκτων (SA) θεμέλιον ἔθηκα (P/S). *I laid a foundation as a wise builder* (1Cor 3:10)

Answering the question "In what capacity did I lay a foundation?"

Ἥξει (P) δὲ ἡμέρα κυρίου **ὡς κλέπτης** (ManA). *The day of the Lord will come like a thief* (2Pe 3:10)

Answering the question "In what manner will the day of the Lord come?"

• as an attributive modifier of the head of an adjective phrase (↑260o), e.g.:

αἱ τρίχες λευκαὶ **ὡς ἔριον λευκόν** (Attr of λευκαί). *his hair was white like white wool* (Re 1:14)

Answering the question "How white was his hair?"

(2) Terms denoting status, occupation, origin, etc. are preceded fairly frequently by a general expression such as ἀνήρ *man* (frequently), ἄνθρωπος *human being* (less frequently; then usually in the sense of *man [male]*, so in the NT and outside: BDAG s.v. 3, LSJ s.v. I5]) or γυνή *woman* (comparatively rarely), used pleonastically (seemingly unnecessary; ↑294x) or with the force of a τις *a/some* (↑144b; ↑Kühner-Gerth I: 272), e.g.: 260j

ἀνὴρ προφήτης/Αἰθίοψ/Ἰουδαῖος/Μακεδών etc. *a prophet/an Ethiopian/a Jew/a Macedonian* (Lk 24:19/Ac 8:27/10:28/16:9)

↑also Mt 12:41; Lk 5:8 (ἀνὴρ ἁμαρτωλός *a sinner*); 11:32; Ac 1:11.16; 2:29 (ἄνδρες ἀδελφοί *brothers*); 3:12; 3:14 (ἄνδρα φονέα *a murderer*); 5:35; 7:2; 11:20; 13:6.15f; 15:7; 17:22 (ἄνδρες Ἀθηναῖοι *men of Athens/Athenians* [frequent in CG]); 19:35; 21:28; 22:1.3; 23:1; 28:17.

ἄνθρωπος ἔμπορος/Ῥωμαῖος/τυφλός etc. *a merchant/a Roman* (Mt 13:45/Ac 16:37)

↑also Mt 11:19; 13:24.52; 18:23; 21:33; 27:32; Lk 7:34; Jn 9:16; Ac 21:39; 22:25; Tt 3:10.

γυνὴ χήρα *a widow* (Lk 4:26)

(3) Sometimes appositions (mostly in the nominative or accusative) are **appositive to a whole clause** (↑260n) serving to explain its content (proposition), e.g.: 260k

... ὑπὲρ τῆς ὑπομονῆς ὑμῶν καὶ πίστεως ἐν πᾶσιν τοῖς διωγμοῖς ὑμῶν καὶ ταῖς θλίψεσιν αἷς ἀνέχεσθε, (5) **ἔνδειγμα τῆς δικαίας κρίσεως τοῦ θεοῦ** ... *... about your perseverance and faith in all the persecutions and afflictions that you are enduring: (5) [all this is] evidence of God's righteous judgment ...* (2Th 1:4f)

ἐμέθυον· **ἱκανὴ πρόφασις** ... *I was drunk: excuse enough ...* (Philemon, Comicorum Atticorum Fragmenta 2.531)

Sometimes the converse seems to happen: a word, especially a demonstrative pronoun, is explained by an appositional clause or a clause-like construction: by a subordinate clause (↑272a; 288b) or an inf./ACI phrase (↑222; 224b; 225f).

c) by a **prepositional** phrase (↑183c; 184/185; mostly in the "attributive" position; ↑136a/136e), e.g.: 260l

τῶν **κατὰ φύσιν** κλάδων (HN) *the natural branches* (lit. *the branches corresponding to nature*) (Ro 11:21)

ἡ πίστις (HN) ὑμῶν ἡ **πρὸς τὸν θεόν** *your faith in God* (1Th 1:8)

even when modifying a non-determined head word, it often has the article, e.g.:

πίστει (HN) **τῇ εἰς ἐμέ** *by faith in me* (Ac 26:18)

but e.g.: χαρὰ (HN) **ἐν πνεύματι ἁγίῳ** *joy in the Holy Spirit* (Ro 14:17)

Note that when a prepositional phrase is without the article (as the marker of the attributive function) it is occasionally uncertain whether it is to be understood as an attributive modifier or a sentence constituent (then usually an adverbial). But even in such cases the context usually indicates what function is more likely to be intended (↑229b), e.g. (the second interpretation appears more adequate in the light of the world knowledge presupposed in the text):

Ἔρχεται γυνὴ **ἐκ τῆς Σαμαρείας** ἀντλῆσαι ὕδωρ.	*A woman came from Samaria* (LocA) *to draw water.* Or: *A woman from Samaria* (Attr)/*A Samaritan woman came to draw water.* (Jn 4:7)

260m d) by an **adverb** phrase (↑241c; in the "attributive" position; ↑136a), e.g.:

ἐν τῷ **νῦν** καιρῷ (HN)	*at the present time* (Ro 3:26)

260n 3. by a **subordinate clause** (relative clause [↑289/290], occasionally modifying a whole clause [↑289b]; sometimes also a conjunctional clause [↑288]), e.g.:

τὸ ὕδωρ (HN) **ὃ δώσω αὐτῷ**	*the water that I will give him* (Jn 4:14)

260o III. Attributive modifiers of the head of **adjective**, **adverb**, or functionally similar **phrases** may be expressed as follows:

1. by an **adverb** phrase (↑241c), e.g.:

σεισμὸς **οὕτω** (Attr: AdvP) μέγας (HN: adj.).	*such a great earthquake* (Re 16:18)
οὐ **πολὺ** (Attr: AdvP) μᾶλλον (HN: adv.) ὑποταγησόμεθα …;	*Should we not much more submit …?* (He 12:9)

2. by a **noun** phrase

a) its head being in a certain **case form** (↑149ff), e.g.:

ταπεινὸς (HN: adj.) **τῇ καρδίᾳ**	*humble in heart* (Mt 11:29)

Attr: dative of respect (↑178a).

πόσῳ μᾶλλον (HN: adv.) ὁ πατὴρ ὑμῶν ὁ ἐν τοῖς οὐρανοῖς δώσει ἀγαθὰ τοῖς αἰτοῦσιν αὐτόν.	*How much more will your Father in heaven give good things to those who ask him.* (Mt 7:11)

Attr: dative of measure/difference (↑178b).

πλεῖον (HN: comparative adj.) **πάντων**	*more than all the others* (Lk 21:3)
πάντων ὑμῶν μᾶλλον (HN: comparative adv.)	*more than all of you* (1Cor 14:18)

Attr: genitive of comparison (↑170; 138a; 242a).

ἑπτάκις (HN: adv.) **τῆς ἡμέρας**	*seven times a day* (Lk 17:4)

Attr: genitive of time (↑168b).

b) being embedded in a **prepositional** phrase (↑183ff), e.g.:

φρονιμώτεροι (HN: comparative adj.) **ὑπὲρ τοὺς υἱοὺς τοῦ φωτός**	*more shrewd than the people of the light* (Lk 16:8)

μᾶλλον (HN: comparative adv.) **ὑπὲρ τὴν δόξαν τοῦ θεοῦ**	*more than the praise from God* (Jn 12:43 Var.)

Attr: in both instances a PpP replaces the genitive of comparison (↑138a; 242a).

c) being preceded by the particles ὡς *as/like* (↑252.61,1a), ἤ *than* (↑138a; 242a) or the like, e.g.:

αἱ τρίχες λευκαὶ (HN: adj.) **ὡς ἔριον λευκόν.**	*his hair was white like white wool* (Re 1:14)
ὅτι μείζων (HN: comparative adj.) ἐστὶν ὁ ἐν ὑμῖν **ἢ ὁ ἐν τῷ κόσμῳ.**	*The one who is in you is greater than the one who is in the world.* (1Jn 4:4)
μᾶλλον (HN: comparative adv.) τὸ σκότος **ἢ τὸ φῶς**	*the darkness more/rather than the light* (Jn 3:19)

On questions of concord ↑261–265.

3.3.2 Concord

(↑BR §257; BDF §131–137; Z §9–15; Crystal: 98)

Concord: preliminaries 261

261a The term “concord” refers to the (grammatical) agreement between sentence elements with respect to
a) number (between the subject and the predicator; ↑262; 262) or
b) gender, number, and case (between declinable sentence elements; ↑263).

Note that due to the wealth of inflectional endings available Ancient Greek concord is considerably more complex than its English counterpart (↑e.g. Carter §539, also 195 or 276c).

On the relationship between reflexive pronouns and the subject ↑139f–139j; 140b–140c; on notional concord ↑265.

261b Generally speaking, the same concord rules are followed in the NT as in other Ancient Greek texts. In the **Book of Revelation**, however, written in a simple popular variety, there is a striking number of instances of irregular concord; this applies mostly to the concord involving participles. BDF §136 distinguishes five types of such **solecisms** (↑also Z §13–15):

1. The apposition (↑260h) or the participle conjunct (↑230c) frequently occurs in the nominative, regardless of the case form of its head, e.g.:

… τῷ ἕκτῳ ἀγγέλῳ, **ὁ ἔχων** (for τῷ ἔχοντι) τὴν σάλπιγγα	*… to the sixth angel who had the trumpet* (9:14)

↑also 1:5; 2:20; 3:12; 8:9; 14:12.14; 20:2.

2. At times an accusative or genitive occurs in isolation: 7:9 (acc. for nom.); 21:9 (gen. masc. for acc. fem.).

3. Not infrequently the masculine replaces the feminine or neuter, e.g.:

… αἱ δύο λυχνίαι αἱ … **ἑστῶτες** (for ἑστῶσαι)	*… the two lampstands that stand …* (11:4)

↑also 4:1.7; 5:6.13; 9:14; 13:8.14; 14:19; 17:3.

4. λέγων/λέγοντες *saying* may be used like an (uninflected) particle as it were, e.g.:

εἶδον ἄλλον ἄγγελον … **λέγων** (for λέγοντα) …· φοβήθητε τὸν θεόν …	*I saw another angel …; and he said …, "Fear God …".* (14:6f)

4:1; 5:12; 11:15; similarly ἔχων *having*: 10:2; 21:12.14.

5. Occasionally there is a breach of number concord (↑264/265): 9:12 (a sg. P with a pl. S).

262 Number concord (↑BDF §133)

262a 1. Regarding number concord the basic rule in **Attic** (Classical) Greek was:
A **ntr. pl.** NP in the **subject** role combines with a **sg. predicator**/predicate verb, e.g.:

πάντα … **ἔθνη** (S) ὑπήκοα μέν **ἐστιν** (P)	*all the nations … are subject* (Xenophon, Hellenica 6.1.9)
πρόβατα (S) … οὐκέτι **ἦν** (P)	*there were no more sheep …* (Xenophon, Anabasis 6.4.22)
τὰ πάντα (S) **ῥεῖ** (P)	*Everything flows* ("Heraclitus"; ↑Plato, Theaetetus 182c)

In **Koine** Greek there was an increasing tendency to use the pl. rather than the sg. in such cases. The NT use varies somewhat, also between textual witnesses (e.g. Mk 4:36 ἄλλα πλοῖα ἦν [Var. ἦσαν] μετ᾽ αὐτοῦ *other boats were with him*).

262b 2. In the **New Testament** we encounter the following tendency:

a) There seems to be a preference for a **pl. predicator** when the **ntr. pl.** NP in the subject role refers to persons,[13] especially so in the case of ἔθνη *nations*, less frequently in the case of τέκνα *children*, e.g.:

ἐνευλογηθήσονται (P) ἐν σοι **πάντα τὰ ἔθνη** (S).	*All the nations will be blessed through you.* (Ga 3:8)

↑also Ac 11:1; Re 11:18; 15:4.

τέκνα *children* in the subject role with a sg. predicator, e.g.:

ἐπεὶ ἄρα **τὰ τέκνα ὑμῶν** (S) ἀκάθαρτά **ἐστιν** (P), νῦν δὲ ἅγιά **ἐστιν** (P).	*Otherwise your children are unclean, but now they are holy.* (1Cor 7:14)

↑also Ro 9:8; 1Jn 3:10; 2Jn 13.

b) When the subject entity is a non-person there is mostly a sg. predicator, e.g.:

ἄλλα ἦλθ**εν** (P) **πλοιάρια** (S) …	*other boats came …* (Jn 6:23)
τὰ γὰρ **ἔργα αὐτῶν** (S) ἀκολουθ**εῖ** (P) μετ᾽ αὐτῶν.	*For their deeds follow them.* (Re 14:13)

13 According to Kühner-Gerth I: 65 in such cases even CG very often uses the plural in order to emphasize the personhood of the referent, in line with the principles of notional concord (↑265).

c) In the case of abstract nouns and pronouns in the subject role sg. predicators predominate even more clearly, e.g.:

… **ταῦτα πάντα** (S) προστεθήσ**εται** (P) ὑμῖν. — *… all these things will be given to you as well.* (Mt 6:33; similarly Lk 12:31)

ἐπωρώθ**η** (P) **τὰ νοήματα αὐτῶν** (S). — *Their minds were made dull.* (2Cor 3:14)

↑also 264, on notional concord ↑265.

Gender, number and case concord (↑BDF §131/132; Z §9–15) 263

1. **Attributive modifiers** of noun phrases (↑260) 263a

a) When an adjective phrase or any other phrase with an adjective-like head such as a pronoun or a participle (↑236) is used as an attributive modifier (Attr; ↑260c for further details), it generally shows full gender, number and case concord with the head noun it modifies (HN), e.g.:

προφήτης (HN) μέγ**ας** (Attr) ἠγέρθη ἐν ἡμῖν … — *A great prophet has appeared among us.* (Lk 7:16)

ἡ μαρτυρία (HN) **αὕτη** (Attr) ἐστὶν ἀληθής. — *This testimony is true.* (Tt 1:13)

b) This similarly applies to appositions (App; ↑260h), e.g.:

Παῦλος (HN) δοῦλ**ος** (App) Χριστοῦ Ἰησοῦ … — *Paul, a servant of Christ Jesus, …* (Ro 1:1)

2. **Non-attributive** concomitants of noun phrases (↑259q)

a) When a noun or an adjective phrase is used as a subject/object complement (SC/OC; ↑258a/258b) or (at times) as a subject/object adjunct (SA/OA; ↑259n), the noun in question shows case concord with the subject or object head noun (HN: S/HN: O), while the adjective shows full gender, number and case concord, e.g.: 263b

ὁ λόγος ὁ σὸς (HN: S) ἀλήθει**ά** (SC^{id}) ἐστιν. — *Your word is truth.* (Jn 17:17)

καιν**ὰ** (OC^{prop}) ποιῶ **πάντα** (HN: O). — *I am making all things new.* (Re 21:5)

b) When an (adverbial) participle conjunct phrase or an adjective phrase is used as an adverbial adjunct (AdvlA) or (at times) as an adverbial complement (AdvlC; ↑259a–259m), the participle or adjective in question shows full gender, number and case concord with the subject or object head noun of the superordinate construction (HN: S/HN: O), e.g.:

προσῆλθον **αὐτῷ** (HN: O^{dat}) διδάσκ**οντι** (AdvlA). — *They approached him as he was teaching.* (Mt 21:23)

αὐτὸς (HN: S) πρῶτ**ος** (AdvlA) ἠγάπησεν ἡμᾶς. — *He first loved us.* (1Jn 4:19)

c) Noteworthy points:

263c (1) When a noun or adjective phrase is used as a subject complement within an ACI phrase, the noun or adjective in question is in the accusative (showing concord with the ACI-subject; ↑216e), e.g.:

ἡ ἐπαγγελία … τὸ κληρονόμ**ον** (ACI-SC^{id}) **αὐτὸν** (HN: ACI-S) εἶναι κόσμου …
The promise … that he would be the heir of the world … (Ro 4:13)

263d (2) When in Ancient Greek a subject complement (SC^{prop}) in the form of an AdjP (↑258b) was used in a statement of general scope, the adjective in question fairly frequently was in the ntr. sg. regardless of the form of the subject; there are, however, only a few NT instances of this use, e.g.:

οὐκ ἀγαθ**ὸν** (SC^{prop}) **πολυκοιρανίη** (HN: S).
the rule of many is not good (Homer, Iliad 2.204)

ἡ γὰρ **ψυχὴ** (S) πλεῖ**όν** (SC^{prop}) ἐστιν τῆς τροφῆς.
For life is more than food. (Lk 12:23)

↑also Mt 6:25; 12:41f; Lk 11:31f.

263e (3) When a demonstrative or relative pronoun functions as a subject, it almost exclusively shows concord with its subject complement (mostly a SC^{id} expressed by a NP), e.g.:

αὕτη (S) δέ ἐστιν **ἡ κρίσις** (SC^{id}) …
This is the verdict … (Jn 3:19)

τοῦτό (S) ἐστιν **τὸ σῶμά μου** (SC^{id}).
This is my body. (Lk 22:19)

Note that τοῦτο *this* (in terms of pure deixis; ↑141a) factually points to the bread the speaker (Jesus) was holding in his hands, something that might also have been referred to as οὗτος ὁ ἄρτος.

… μὴ πτυρόμενοι ἐν μηδενὶ ὑπὸ τῶν ἀντικειμένων, **ἥτις** (S) ἐστὶν αὐτοῖς **ἔνδειξις** (SC^{id}) ἀπωλείας, ὑμῶν δὲ σωτηρίας …
… not being intimidated in any way by your opponents. For them this is evidence of their destruction, but of your salvation … (Php 1:28)

↑also Mt 13:32; 22:38; Mk 4:31; 15:16 (but also ↑263f); Ac 16:12; Ga 3:16; Eph 1:13f (Var.; the NA text follows the usage mentioned in 263f); 3:13; 1Tm 3:15.

Occasionally a relative pronoun that functions as a subject complement (SC^{id}) occurs with a subject expressed by a personal pronoun and then (somewhat surprisingly) shows concord with the subject rather than with its antecedent, e.g.:

ὁ γὰρ ναὸς τοῦ θεοῦ ἅγιός ἐστιν, **οἵτινές** (SC^{id}: pl. despite its antecedent ναός) ἐστε **ὑμεῖς** (S: pl.).
For God's temple is holy, which is what you are. (1Cor 3:17)

263f (4) KG/NT explanatory clauses not infrequently are introduced by the formulaic ὅ ἐστιν/τοῦτ' ἔστιν *which/that is* (↑"i.e." in English) with the pronouns being in the ntr. sg. regardless of the form of the head noun to be explained (HN; ↑289e) nor of the subject complement it might be expected to show concord with (↑263e), e.g.:

(Ἐνδύσασθε …) **τὴν ἀγάπην** (HN) **ὅ** (S) **ἐστιν σύνδεσμος** (SC^{id}) **τῆς τελειότητος** (Var. ὅς or ἥτις) …
(Put on …) love, which is the perfect bond of unity … (Col 3:12.14)

ἀναφέρωμεν **θυσίαν** (HN) αἰνέσεως … **τοῦτ'** (S) **ἔστιν καρπὸν** ("SC^{id}") χειλέων
Let us offer a sacrifice of praise, that is the fruit of our lips (He 13:15)

↑also Mt 27:46; Mk 3:17; 7:2.11; Ac 1:19; 19:4; Ro 1:12; Eph 6:17; He 2:14; et pass.

↑also 265 on notional concord.
↑also 289e on the "attraction" of the relative.
↑also 129a on the "distributive" singular.

Phrases joined by means of καί "and" or the like (↑BDF §135; Kühner-Gerth I: 77ff) 264

1. Phrases joined by means of καί *and* (or the like; ↑251a) in the **subject** role, with the number pattern **sg. (+ sg. …) + sg.** or **sg. (+ sg./pl. …) + pl.** combine 264a

a) typically with a pl. predicator (as in English if expressible at all) when it follows the subject, e.g.:

Πέτρος δὲ **καὶ Ἰωάννης** (S) ἀνέβαιν**ον** (P) εἰς τὸ ἱερόν …	*Peter and John were going up to the temple …* (Ac 3:1)
Ἰάκωβος καὶ Κηφᾶς καὶ Ἰωάννης (S) … δεξιὰς ἔδωκ**αν** (P) ἐμοὶ καὶ Βαρναβᾷ …	*James, Cephas and John gave me and Barnabas the right hand …* (Ga 2:9)
ἡ μήτηρ σου καὶ οἱ ἀδελφοί σου (S) ἑστήκ**ασιν** (P) ἔξω.	*Your mother and your brothers are standing outside* (Lk 8:20)
Ἡ οὖν **σπεῖρα καὶ ὁ χιλίαρχος καὶ οἱ ὑπηρέται τῶν Ἰουδαίων** (S) συνέλαβ**ον** (P) τὸν Ἰησοῦν …	*So the detachment of soldiers and their commander and the officers of the Jews arrested Jesus …* (Jn 18:12)

Less typically the predicator may be in the sg. when the subject entities are non-persons (inter alia in the case of abstract nouns) or when they are to be understood as a single unit (inter alia in the case of fixed word pairs), which to some extent is possible in English, too (↑Huddleston/Pullum: 507), e.g.:

… ὅπου **σὴς καὶ βρῶσις** (S) ἀφανίζ**ει** (P)	*… where rust and moth/decay destroy* (Mt 6:19)
ἡ χάρις καὶ ἡ ἀλήθεια (S) διὰ Ἰησοῦ Χριστοῦ ἐγέν**ετο** (P).	*Grace and truth came through Jesus Christ.* (Jn 1:17)
σὰρξ καὶ αἷμα (S) οὐκ ἀπεκάλυψ**έν** (P) σοι …	*Flesh and blood (= a human being) has not revealed this to you …* (Mt 16:17; ↑also 1Cor 15:50)

↑also Mt 12:31 13:22; 24:35 (ὁ οὐρανὸς καὶ ἡ γῆ *heaven and earth = the universe*); Mk 4:41; Ac 4:28.

b) when the predicator precedes the subject, it is usually in the sg., e.g.:

καὶ ἐξεπορεύ**ετο** (P) πρὸς αὐτὸν **πᾶσα ἡ Ἰουδαία χώρα καὶ οἱ Ἱεροσολυμῖται πάντες** (S).	*And people from all the Judean countryside and all of Jerusalem were going out to him.* (Mk 1:5)

↑also Mt 12:3; 28:1; Mk 1:36; 14:1; Lk 6:3; 8:19; Jn 1:35.45; 20:3; Ac 11:14; 16:15.31; 26:30; Col 4:10; 1Tm 1:20; 2Tm 4:21; Tt 1:15; Jas 3:10; 1Pe 4:11; et pass.
There are, however, a few exceptions, e.g. Mk 10:35; Lk 9:30; Jn 21:2; Ro 15:26.

2. When an element would be expected to show concord (↑259q) **with more than one element** (HN), it generally shows concord with 264b

a) the nearest of these element (according to the "proximity principle", apparently applying universally; ↑Givón II: 64), e.g.:

ἀποκριθ**εὶς** (p. c. with S/HN: sg.) δὲ **Πέτρος καὶ οἱ ἀπόστολοι** (S/HN) εἶπ**αν** (P: pl.) … *Peter and the other apostles replied:* "…". (Ac 5:29)

οἱ ταῦροί μου καὶ τὰ σιτιστὰ (S/HN) τεθυμέν**α** (part of P: ptc.: ntr.). *My oxen and my fat calves have been slaughtered.* (Mt 22:4)

↑also Mt 17:3; Mk 4:17; Ac 5:17; Col 3:16; 1Th 5:23; He 1:10f; 9:9.

b) When elements refer to persons the masculine gender is given priority, e.g.:

καὶ **ἦν** (P/part 1: sg.) **ὁ πατὴρ αὐτοῦ καὶ ἡ μήτηρ** (S: HN) θαυμάζ**οντες** (P/part 2: ptc.: masc.) … *And his father and mother were amazed* … (Lk 2:33)

↑also Lk 2:48; Ac 9:2; 17:12; 18:26; Jas 2:15.

264c 3. Note that a single adjective or member of another declinable word-class may be connected semantically with more than one noun phrase. When it comes to concord the two principles just mentioned basically apply (↑264b), regarding number concord (analogously) also what was said about the relationship between the subject and the predicator in 264a. The following types of combinations are frequently of special interest to interpreters of texts:

<table>
<tr><td rowspan="2"></td><td colspan="2">CATEGORIES of heads of involved NOUN phrases:</td><td colspan="2">ADJECTIVE or MEMBER OF OTHER DECLINABLE WORD-CLASS semantically connected with the involved noun phrases usually shows concord with the nearest noun; note however:</td></tr>
<tr><td>the NUMBER is</td><td>the GENDER is</td><td>the NUMBER of non-attributive word or relative pronoun is:</td><td>the GENDER of the word is as follows:</td></tr>
<tr><td>(a)</td><td>pl.</td><td rowspan="2">of any kind</td><td>always pl.</td><td rowspan="2">When persons are referred to masc. is given priority.</td></tr>
<tr><td>(b)</td><td rowspan="2">sg.</td><td rowspan="2">pl., but sg. when entities to be understood as a single unit</td></tr>
<tr><td>(c)</td><td>the same kind</td><td>as the involved nouns</td></tr>
</table>

Examples of

combination (a):

… **δυνάμεσι καὶ τέρασι καὶ σημείοις** (HN: 1× fem., 2× ntr.) **οἷς** (rel. pron.: ntr.) ἐποίησεν … *… by mighty works, wonders and signs, which God did …* (Ac 2:22)

↑also Ac 8:13; Eph 5:19 (?); 2Th 1:4; He 2:4.

combination (b):

… **ἱερεύς τις … καὶ γυνὴ αὐτῷ** (HN) … ἦσαν δὲ δίκαι**οι** ἀμφότερ**οι** ἐναντίον τοῦ θεοῦ … καί … προβεβηκ**ότες** ἐν ταῖς ἡμέραις αὐτῶν (adj./ptc.: mask. pl.). *… a priest … and his wife … Both of them were righteous in the sight of God … and … both were getting on in years …* (Lk 1:5–7)

ἐγὼ γὰρ δώσω ὑμῖν **στόμα καὶ σοφίαν** (HN [↑294v]) **ᾗ** (rel. pron.: sg.) οὐ δυνήσονται ἀντιστῆναι … *For I will give you words and wisdom, which none … will be able to withstand …* (Lk 21:15)

Διονύσιος … καὶ γυνὴ ὀνόματι Δάμαρις (HN) καὶ ἕτεροι σὺν αὐτ**οῖς** (pron.: masc. pl.) *Dionysius … and a woman named Damaris, and others with them.* (Ac 17:34)

καὶ οὐκ ἴσχυον ἀντιστῆναι **τῇ σοφίᾳ καὶ τῷ πνεύματι** (HN [↑294v]) **ᾧ** (rel. pron.: sg.) ἐλάλει. *But they could not stand up against the wisdom and the Spirit with which he spoke.* (Ac 6:10)

↑also Mt 18:8; Lk 10:1; 2Th 2:17.

combination (c):

… **ἰδίᾳ** (Attr) **δόξῃ καὶ ἀρετῇ** (HN) …	… *to his own glory and excellence* … (2Pe 1:3)

↑also Mt 12:25; Lk 21:27; Ac 7:11; 9:31; Ro 1:18; 2Cor 2:4; 12:21; Eph 1:8; 4:31; 5:5.9; 1Tm 2:2; 2Tm 1:9; Phm 5; He 2:2; et pass.

In many cases (if communicationally relevant) the word showing concord is repeated, e.g.:

ἐν παντὶ ἐπλουτίσθητε ἐν αὐτῷ, **ἐν παντὶ λόγῳ καὶ πάσῃ γνώσει.**	*in him you have been enriched in every way, in every kind of speech and every kind of knowledge.* (1Cor 1:5)

↑also Mt 3:5; Ac 13:10; Ro 7:12; 14:11; 1Cor 8:5; Jas 1:17; Re 21:1; et pass.

On instances of irregular concord in the Book of Revelation ↑261b.

Notional concord (↑BR §257.5; BDF §134; 282; Bussmann: 470) 265

Fairly frequently there is "notional" concord (also called "synesis") between Ancient Greek sentence elements, i.e. the expected grammatical agreement (↑261a) with regard to number (↑262) or gender or both is replaced (↑263/264) by an agreement based on meaning (also occurring in English; ↑Quirk: 757ff).

In most cases notional concord concerns the predicator (but sometimes other sentence elements as well): the expected singular is replaced by the **plural**. This frequently happens when a **collective** (noun) is the head of a noun phrase (in the singular) functioning as the subject. A collective (in the singular) typically refers to a plurality of entities (↑22a) and in line with the principles of notional concord very often combines with other inflected sentence elements that are in the plural: predicate verbs, non-attributive and attributive adjective/participle/(pro)noun phrases. Some of the more important collectives are:

ὁ λαός	*the people*	ὁ ὄχλος	*the crowd*
τὸ πλῆθος	*to multitude*	ἡ στρατιά	*the host/army*

Examples:

ὁ δὲ **πλεῖστος ὄχλος** (S/HN: sg.) ἔστρωσ**αν** (P: pl.) ἑαυτ**ῶν** (Attr of Od: refl. pron.: pl.) τὰ ἱμάτια ἐν τῇ ὁδῷ …	*The/A very large crowd spread their cloaks on the road* … (Mt 21:8)
πᾶς ὁ ὄχλος (S/HN: sg.) ἐζήτ**ουν** (P: pl.) ἅπτεσθαι αὐτοῦ.	*The whole crowd was/were trying to touch him.* (Lk 6:19)
Καὶ περιῆγεν **ἐν ὅλῃ τῇ Γαλιλαίᾳ** (HN: sg.) διδάσκων ἐν ταῖς συναγωγαῖς αὐτ**ῶν** (pron.: pl.).	*And he went throughout Galilee teaching in their synagogues* (i.e. in the synagogues of the Galileans). (Mt 4:23)

↑also Mt 1:21; 14:14; Mk 4:1; 5:24; 9:15; Lk 2:13 (στρατιᾶς οὐρανίου corresponds to ἀγγέλων, leading to αἰνούντων; ↑BDF §134); 19:37; Jn 6:2; Ac 3:11 (P: sg., SA/AdjP: pl.); 6:5; 1Th 1:9. For examples from the Book of Revelation ↑261b.

In other cases notional concord leads to the expected grammatical gender being replaced by the **gender** based on factors of meaning, fairly frequently in addition to a “change” in number, particularly in the case of personal and relative pronouns (↑289e/289f), e.g.:

μαθητεύσατε **πάντα τὰ ἔθνη** (HN: ntr.), βαπτίζοντες **αὐτούς** (pron.: masc.) …	*Make disciples of all nations, baptizing them …* (Mt 28:19)
κατελθὼν **εἰς τὴν πόλιν** (HN: fem. sg.) τῆς Σαμαρείας ἐκήρυσσεν **αὐτοῖς** (pron.: masc. pl.) τὸν Χριστόν.	*He went down to the main city of Samaria and proclaimed the Messiah to them* (i.e. to the Samaritans). (Ac 8:5)
… **περὶ τοῦ ἐμοῦ τέκνου** (HN: ntr.) **ὃν** (rel. pron.: masc.) ἐγέννησα …, Ὀνήσιμον …	*… concerning my child Onesimus, whose father I have become …* (Phm 10)
… **πλῆθος πολὺ** (HN: ntr.) τοῦ λαοῦ … **οἳ** (rel. pron.: masc. pl.) ἦλθ**ον** (P: pl.) …	*… a great number of people … who had come …* (Lk 6:17f)
ἰδ**ὼν** (p.c.: masc.) αὐτὸν **τὸ πνεῦμα** (HN: ntr.) …	*When the spirit saw him …* (Mk 9:20; presented as a person; ↑BDF §134)

↑also Mt 25:32; Mk 13:14; Jn 6:9; Ro 2:14; Ga 4:19; Php 2:15; Col 2:15.19; 2Jn 1. For Re ↑261b.

At times a plural is replaced by a singular on the basis of notional concord, e.g.:

… **ἐν οὐρανοῖς** (HN: pl.) … ἐξ **οὗ** (rel. pron.: sg.) (↑BDAG sub ὅς 1cβℵ)	*… in heaven … from it …* (Php 3:20;)

On comparable instances of irregular case concord involving a p.c. ↑230c[66].

3.4 Sentence/clause types

266 Sentence/clause types: preliminaries (↑BR §263; BDF §458)

266a I. Sentences/clauses (↑127a) may be **subdivided** mainly in three ways:

1. Subdivision according to the **type of predicate** (↑254c; 256)

a) **verb clauses** (standard case): the predicate contains a verb (“predicator”/“predicate verb”; ↑256a), e.g.:

ἐδάκρυσεν (P [verb]) ὁ Ἰησοῦς (S).	*Jesus wept.* (Jn 11:35)

b) **verbless clauses**: the predicate contains a subject or adverbial complement, but no verb (these are copular sentences/clauses without copula; ↑256d), e.g.:

κύριος (SC^{id}) _ Ἰησοῦς Χριστός (S).	*Jesus Christ is Lord.* (Php 2:11)

2. Subdivision according to their **syntactic usability**:

a) independent or **main clauses** (↑267–269; on direct speech ↑274b), e.g.:

ἐγώ εἰμι ἡ θύρα.	*I am the door.* (Jn 10:9)

b) dependent or **subordinate clauses** (↑271–293), e.g.:

… ἵνα ζωὴν ἔχωσιν. (expresses a PurpA)	… *so that they may have life.* (Jn 10:10)

3. Subdivision according to the major **communicative function** (content-oriented):

a) **declarative clauses** (independent: ↑267; dependent: ↑271), e.g.:

γινώσκω τὰ ἐμά. (statement)	*I know my own (sheep).* (Jn 10:14)

b) **desiderative clauses** (independent: ↑268; dependent: ↑272), e.g.:

ἀκολούθει μοι. (directive)	*Follow me.* (Mk 2:14)

c) **interrogative clauses** (independent: ↑269; dependent: ↑273), e.g.:

διὰ τί λύετε; (open interrogative clause)	*Why are you untying it?* (Lk 19:31)

Noteworthy points on content-oriented clause types:

(1) Some prefer to divide the desiderative type as defined in the present grammar (↑268) into two distinguishable types: desiderative (or optative) clauses and imperative clauses.

(2) Many treat **exclamative clauses** as a separate (independent) clause type. Exclamative clauses have the form of a declarative, desiderative, or (very frequently) interrogative clause (including indirect questions; ↑273b); they typically serve to express reactive emotions on the part of the speaker/writer, frequently underlined by the use of vocatives, interjections or modal particles (↑Crystal: 177; Bussmann: 158; Carter §294), e.g.:

εὖ, δοῦλε ἀγαθὲ καὶ πιστέ, ἐπὶ ὀλίγα **ἦς** πιστός, ἐπὶ πολλῶν σε **καταστήσω· εἴσελθε** εἰς τὴν χαρὰν τοῦ κυρίου σου. (interjection, vocative, declarative and desiderative clauses)	*Well done, good and faithful servant! You have been faithful with a few things; I will put you in charge of many things. Come and share your master's happiness!* (Mt 25:21)
ἴδετε ποταπὴν ἀγάπην δέδωκεν ἡμῖν ὁ πατήρ … (desiderative clause and indirect question)	*See what kind of love the Father has given us …* (1Jn 3:1)

↑also Mt 6:23; 7:14; 23:37; Jn 11:36; Ro 11:33; Ga 6:11; 2Tm 3:11; He 10:37.

(3) Apart from the clause types a) to c) mentioned above the following content-oriented types of conjunctional **adverbial clauses** are usually distinguished (↑276–287 for details and examples): temporal, causal, purpose, result, conditional, concessive, exceptive conditional, and manner clauses.
Also ↑290 on relative clauses with adverbial force.

II. For sentences/clauses that are closely connected semantically/communicationally two types of combinations are in use (↑Carter §271): 266b

1. The term **compound sentence** refers to a combination of two or more coordinated main clauses (their coordination usually being marked by coordinating conjunctions or particles; ↑250c; 251a–251e). Such coordinating combinations (often called "paratactic" combinations or "parataxis", as opposed to "hypotactic" ones or "hypotaxis", i.e. subordination; ↑2 below) occur frequently in NT narratives, much

less so in CG texts, but are fairly well-attested in popular and non-classicizing narrative literature of the Hellenistic period (↑Reiser 1984: 99ff; for the high frequency in the LXX and in parts of the NT quite likely being influenced by Semitic/Hebrew usage ↑Baum: 27ff), e.g.:

main cl. 1	καὶ ἐξῆλθεν ἐκεῖθεν *And/Then he left from there*
main cl. 2	καὶ ἔρχεται εἰς τὴν πατρίδα αὐτοῦ *and came to his home town,*
main cl. 3	καὶ ἀκολουθοῦσιν αὐτῷ οἱ μαθηταὶ αὐτοῦ. *and his disciples followed him.* (Mk 6:1)

2. A combination of a main clause with one or more subordinate clauses is called **complex sentence**: the main clause is the "governing" or superordinate clause, the other clause or clauses being subordinate to it (typically these are in one way or other subordinate to each other, too). Such a subordination (or "hypotaxis"; ↑1 above) is typically marked (↑270c) by a subordinating conjunction (↑251f–251m) or a relative (pronoun or adverb; ↑59–61; 142; 143b). E.g.:

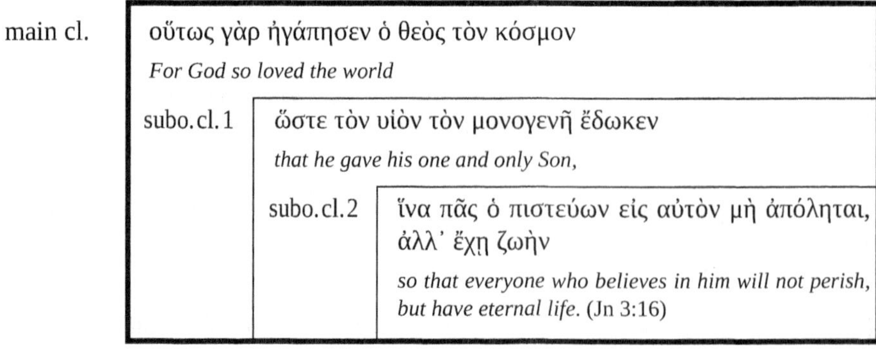

Note that conjunctions or particles (↑250–252) and relatives (↑142/143) serve to mark not only the combination of clauses to form compound and complex sentences, but also the combination of compound or complex sentences to form paragraphs and texts/discourses. Especially coordinating conjunctions or particles may have such a function (↑251a–251e), but also certain adverbials used in a comparable way (↑259a–259m). This function and other aspects of the highest level of text structures (↑p. 12) are treated in Part 4 on textgrammar (↑297–354).

On time relations between the "situations" referred to by the sentences/clauses involved in the above combinations ↑206.

3.4.1 Independent (main) clauses

Independent declarative clauses (↑BR §264) 267

By means of independent declarative clauses (↑266a.3; prototypical clause type) the speaker/writer presents the proposition, i.e. what is being declared,

1. as referring to something that is to be understood as **factual**

a) by means of any indicative form without ἄν (↑209b–209f), e.g.:

ἠγέρθη, οὐκ **ἔστιν** ὧδε. — *He has risen; he is not here.* (Mk 16:6)

b) to express the strongest negation of future "situations", by means of οὐ μή + subj. aor. (less frequently ind. fut.; ↑210f; 247a; ↑also 248b), e.g.:

οἱ δὲ λόγοι μου **οὐ μὴ παρέλθωσιν**. — *But my words will not/never pass away.* (Mt 24:35)

c) very occasionally to express a cautious statement, by means of μή or the like + subj. (mostly aor.) conveying the nuance *maybe/perhaps* (↑247c), e.g.:

μήποτε οὐκ ἀρκέσῃ ἡμῖν καὶ ὑμῖν. (well-supported Var.; NA: μήποτε οὐ μή) — *Perhaps there will not be enough.* (NA: *Certainly there* …; Mt 25:9; ↑BDAG s. μήποτε 4)

2. or as referring to something **non-factual**

a) to something counterfactual (epistemic modality), by means of the "irrealis", i.e. an augment indicative combined with ἄν (in the NT occasionally without ἄν; ↑209h), e.g.:

(εἰ ἠγαπᾶτέ με) **ἐχάρητε ἄν**. — *(If you loved me), you would be happy.* (Jn 14:28)

b) to something that is or was necessary but in fact does not or did not take place, by means of the imperfect (without ἄν) of mostly impersonal expressions signifying necessity (deontic modality; ↑209k), e.g.:

ἔδει σε οὖν βαλεῖν τὰ ἀργύριά μου τοῖς τραπεζίταις. — *Then you should have put my money on deposit with the bankers.* (Mt 25:27)

3. or as referring to something regarded as **possible** in the present or in the future or as always possible, by means of the potential optative (in CG) combined with ἄν (occurring rarely in the NT, sometimes being replaced by the ind. fut.; ↑211d), e.g.:

εὐξαίμην ἄν τῷ θεῷ … — *I (can/may) pray to God …* (Ac 26:29)

4. or (in CG) as referring to something regarded as possible in the past, by means of an augment indicative combined with ἄν (↑209i), e.g.:

… **ἔγνω ἄν** τις … — *… one might have realized …* (Xenophon, Cyropaedia 7.1.38)

οὐ is the negative typically used in independent declarative clauses (↑245b).

268 Independent desiderative clauses

(↑BR §265; BDF §359; 364; 384; 387; 389; Z §242–248; 254; 280, 355, 373; 415; 443)

268a I. Independent desiderative clauses (↑266a.3) may have the following **functions** (expressing volition being central; ↑deontic, but also epistemic modality; ↑207d)[14]

1. **directives**:

a) to do something: directives of the more direct type such as commands/commandments, orders, or instructions as well as directives of the less direct type such as warnings, requests, advice, suggestions, or permissions;

b) not to do something: negative directives such as prohibitions, or admonitions;

2. **wishes** or desires of variable strength (and variable attainability) that something should be done or should take place.

268b II. Independent desiderative clauses may have the following grammatical **forms** (on questions of aspect ↑cross references, also 192–195):

function	form of predicate/predicator
1. **directive to 1st** sg. or (mostly) pl.	hortatory subj. (↑210c) (especially NT also ind. fut.; ↑202c)
ἀγαπῶμεν ἀλλήλους·	*Let us love one another.* (1Jn 4:7)
2. **directive to 2nd or 3rd** sg./pl.	
a) typically	imp. (↑212)
ἆρον …/**ἀράτω** …	*Take …/Let him take …* (Mt 9:6; 16:24)
b) in the NT: mostly in quotations from the legal parts of the OT that express strict commands or prohibitions (in CG an almost polite type of directive)	ind. fut. (↑202f)
ἀγαπήσεις τὸν πλησίον σου	*You shall love your neighbour* (Jas 2:8)
3. **negative** directive, prohibition (↑212c)	
a) **to 2nd** sg./pl.	μή + subj. aor. (prohibitive; ↑210e) or μή + imp. pres. (↑212c)
μὴ θαυμάσῃς …	*Don't be surprised …* (Jn 3:7)
μὴ μεριμνᾶτε …	*Do not worry …* (Mt 6:25)

14 Note that the two categories listed here are without well-defined boundaries or subdivisions.

b) **to 3rd** sg./pl.	μή + imp. aor. or subj. aor. or μή + imp. pres.
ὁ ἐπὶ τοῦ δώματος **μὴ καταβάτω**.	*The one on the housetop must not go down.* (Mk 13:15)
μή τις οὖν αὐτὸν **ἐξουθενήσῃ**.	*So let no one despise him.* (1Cor 16:11)
… ἄνθρωπος **μὴ χωριζέτω**.	*… let no one separate.* (Mt 19:6)
c) in the NT: to express strict prohibitions to 2nd or 3rd sg./pl. (↑above 2b)	οὐ + ind. fut. (↑202f)
οὐ μοιχεύσεις.	*Do not commit adultery.* (Mt 19:18)
4. a **wish** to 1st, 2nd or 3rd sg./pl. presented as **attainable**	optative of wish (↑211c) (on NT usage ↑also below 5a)
γένοιτό μοι κατὰ τὸ ῥῆμά σου.	*Let it happen to me according to your word.* (Lk 1:38)
5. a **wish** to 1st, 2nd or 3rd sg./pl. presented as **unattainable**	augment indicative without ἄν (↑209j)
a) in the NT:	
• a few instances:	particle ὄφελον + ipf. or ind. aor.
ὄφελον ἀνείχεσθε …	*If only you would put up with …!* (2Cor 11:1)
• in the case of an unattainable or attainable wish:	ἐβουλόμην without ἄν/ἤθελον (popular) + inf.
ἐβουλόμην … **κατέχειν**. (similarly Ro 9:3)	*I would have liked to keep …!* (Phm 13)
ἤθελον δὲ παρεῖναι πρὸς ὑμᾶς ἄρτι.	*I wish I were present with you now!* (Ga 4:20)
[CG in the case of an unattainable wish in the case of an attainable wish	ἐβουλόμην + ἄν (irrealis; ↑209h) βουλοίμην (opt.) + ἄν (potential opt.; ↑211d)
Ἐβουλόμην ἄν … οὕτως **ἔχειν**	*I wish it were so …!* (Xenophon, Cyropaedia 7.2.16)
βουλοίμην ἄν … **ἀκούειν**.	*I would … like to hear it!* (Xenophon, Economics 6.12)]
b) CG	augment ind. without ἄν, introduced by εἴθε or εἰ γάρ
Εἴθε σοι … τότε **συνεγενόμην**.	*If I had only been your companion then …!* (Xenophon, Memorabilia 1.2.46)

Note that very occasionally the **imperative** is **replaced** by one of the following constructions: 268c

1. The "imperatival" **infinitive** (rare in the NT and CG prose, but very often in Homer; ↑218d), e.g.:

χαίρειν μετὰ χαιρόντων … *Rejoice with those who rejoice …* (Ro 12:15)

2. A **participle** with an imperative force (without an imperative form in the superordinate construction requiring it [↑231b[70]]; wide-spread in KG), occasionally used by Paul and Peter (↑231k), e.g.:

τὴν ἀναστροφὴν ὑμων … **ἔχοντες** καλήν *Keep your conduct … honourable.* (1Pe 2:12)

3. Occasionally an independent ἵνα-clause (CG more frequently a ὅπως-clause; ↑272; 210g), e.g.:

ἵνα … **ἐπιθῇς** τὰς χεῖρας αὐτῇ …	*Please … lay your hands on her …* (Mk 5:23)

μή is the ("prohibitive") negative typically used in independent desiderative clauses (↑244; 246a), 3c above being an important exception.

269 Independent interrogative clauses (direct questions)

(↑BR §266; BDF §298f; 300.2; 366; 427.2; 432; 440; 441; 446; 451.1; 452.1; Z §401; DuG9: 901f; Aarts: 167–170; Carter §424–432)

269a I. Preliminaries:

1. Interrogative clauses/direct questions (↑266a.3) may be subdivided as follows:

a) **Closed interrogative clauses** (or "*yes-no* questions"): they ask for an answer that either affirms or negates the proposition expressed by the question (↑269c), e.g.:

σὺ Ἠλίας εἶ; (– **οὐκ εἰμί**)	*Are you Elijah? (– I am not.)* (Jn 1:21)

b) **Open interrogative clauses** (or "*wh*-questions"): introduced by an interrogative word (typically translatable as a *wh*-word: *who*, *what* etc.; ↑269d), they ask for "an unrestricted set of answers" (Aarts: 167), mostly for specific information about the participants, circumstances or the nature of the "action"/"situation" referred to), e.g.:

πόθεν εἶ σύ;	*Where are you from?* (Jn 19:9)

c) **Rhetorical questions:** grammatically these are normal interrogative clauses, but contextual (pragmatic) factors make it clear that the speaker/writer does not expect an answer to the "question", but intends to move the addressee to adopt a particular view on the state of affairs concerned. Functionally rhetorical questions correspond to emphatic declarative or desiderative clauses (frequently with exclamative force; ↑266a), e.g.:

οὐκ οἴδατε ὅτι ναὸς θεοῦ ἐστε;	*Do you not know that you are God's temple? ≈ Bear in mind that you are God's temple!* (1Cor 3:16)

2. All of the three types mentioned above may occur as **alternative questions**: the addressee is given the choice between two or more alternatives (↑269e), e.g.:

περὶ τίνος ὁ προφήτης λέγει τοῦτο; περὶ ἑαυτοῦ **ἢ** περὶ ἑτέρου τινός;	*Who is the prophet talking about, about himself or about some one else?* (Ac 8:34)

3. All of the three types mentioned above also occur as **deliberative questions**[15] the predicator/predicate verb being typically in the deliberative subj. (↑210d; further ↑269f): the addressee is asked to tell the speaker/writer what to do, the expected answer generally being a deliberative/imperative clause, e.g.:

15 Or "direction" questions (opposed to "information" questions); Huddleston/Pullum: 876–879.

ἐπιμένωμεν τῇ ἁμαρτίᾳ, ἵνα ἡ χάρις πλεονάσῃ; (– μὴ γένοιτο)	*Should we continue in sin so that grace may increase?* (– *By no means!*) (Ro 6:1)

Note that independent interrogative clauses are often part of direct speech (↑274b).

II. With the exception of their deliberative use (↑269f) **closed interrogative clauses** 269b
(“*yes-no* questions”) correspond to declarative clauses (↑267), as far as their grammatical form is concerned. Fairly frequently the two clause types actually look the same in the NT (less frequently so in CG). In the standard editions, of course, punctuation marks are added (↑p.22) to indicate what is probably intended. Still, in the NT (in CG fairly regularly) questions may be introduced by means of interrogative particles, to a fair extent also indicating whether the addressee is expected to give an affirmative or negative answer. Three cases may be distinguished:

particles	Lat. parallel	expected answer
1. ἆρα (CG also ἦ), in the NT only 3× (LXX: 5×), also εἰ replacing it (↑273 on dependent interrogative clauses; apparently Hebraism, ↑אִם *'im* HALOT s.v. 5, or הֲ *hă-*, in the LXX sometimes translated as εἰ before direct questions)	*-nĕ* (↑Hebr. אִם *'im* or הֲ *hă-*)	
ἆρα (in the NT also **εἰ** [mostly = “:/,”]) πάρεστιν;	*Is he here?* Lat. *adest nĕ?*	

Examples:

ἆρά γε γινώσκεις ἃ ἀναγινώσκεις;	*Do you understand what you are reading?* (Ac 8:30)
(λέγοντες·) **εἰ** ἔξεστιν τοῖς σάββασιν θεραπεῦσαι;	*(they asked him,) “Is it lawful to heal on the Sabbath?”* (Mt 12:10)

↑also (with ἆρα:) Lk 18:8; Ga 2:17; (with εἰ:) Lk 13:23; Ac 1:6.

particles	Lat. parallel	expected answer
2. οὐ (or intensified οὐχί *not*; ↑245b) (CG also ἆρ᾽ οὐ, intensified οὐκοῦν or ἄλλο τι [ἤ])	*nonne*	“Yes!”
οὐ πάρεστιν;	*Isn’t he here?* Lat. *nonne adest?* (expected answer: *Yes, he is!*) (= *He is here, isn’t he?*)	

Example:

οὐκ εἶπόν σοι ὅτι ἐὰν πιστεύσῃς ὄψῃ τὴν δόξαν τοῦ θεοῦ;	*Didn’t I say to you, ‘If you believe, you will see the glory of God?’* (Jn 11:40)

↑also Mt 13:55; Lk 2:49; 11:40; 17:17; 24:26; Ac 9:21; 13:10.

particles	Lat. parallel	expected answer
3. μή (or intensified μήτι) not translatable (on details ↑246a) (CG also μῶν [μή + οὖν]) (μή οὐ [also οὐ μή + subj.] *not*)	*num*	"No!" ("Yes!")
μὴ πάρεστιν;	*Is he here?* Lat. *num adest?* (expected answer: *No, he isn't!*) (= *He isn't here, is he.*)	

Examples:

μὴ καὶ ὑμεῖς θέλετε ὑπάγειν; — *Do you want to leave too?/You don't want to leave too, do you?* (Jn 6:67)

↑also Mt 7:9; 9:15; Lk 17:9; Jn 7:51; 8:53; 21:5; with μήτι: Mt 12:23; Lk 6:39; Jn 4:29; 18:35.

μὴ οὐκ ἤκουσαν; — *Have they not heard?/They have heard, haven't they?* (Ro 10:18)

↑also Ro 10:19; 1Cor 9:4f; 11:22.

οὐ μὴ πίω αὐτό; (↑269f) — *Shall I not drink it?* (expected answer: *Yes, you shall!*) (Jn 18:11)

269c Note that **affirmative and negative answers** may be expressed as follows:

a) by ναί *yes* or οὔ/οὐχί *no*, e.g.:

Συνήκατε ταῦτα πάντα; … **ναί**. — *"Have you understood all these things?"… "Yes."* (Mt 13:51)

↑also Mt 9:28; 21:16; Jn 11:26f; 21:16; Ac 22:27.

θέλεις οὖν ἀπελθόντες συλλέξωμεν αὐτά; … **οὔ**. — *"Do you want us to go and gather them up?"… "No, …"* (Mt 13:28f)

↑also Jn 1:21; 7:12; 21:5.

b) by repetition of the expression in focus or elliptical declarative clauses, e.g.:

δύνασθε πιεῖν τὸ ποτήριον; … **δυνάμεθα**. — *"Can you drink the cup …?" … "We can."* (Mt 20:22)

μήτι ἐγώ εἰμι, ῥαββί; … **σὺ εἶπας**. — *"Rabbi, am I the one?"… "You have said it/ Yes."* (Mt 26:25)

μὴ καὶ σύ … εἶ …; … **οὐκ εἰμί**. — *"Are you also …?"… "I am not."* (Jn 18:17)

ὁ νόμος ἁμαρτία; **μὴ γένοιτο**· (↑211c) — *Is the law sin? Absolutely not!* (Ro 7:7)

προεχόμεθα; **οὐ πάντως**. — *Are we [Jews] better off? … Not at all!* (or *Not entirely!*; ↑commentaries) (Ro 3:9)

c) in CG also by personal pronouns in their emphatic use (e.g. Ἔγωγε, οὐκ ἔγωγε [↑139b]) as well as by assertive particles, in particular also certain adverbs (e.g. πάνυ μὲν οὖν *certainly/undoubtedly* [↑252.34]; πῶς γὰρ οὔ; *How/Why not indeed? = Yes, of course!*) πῶς γάρ; *How/Why indeed? = Of course not!*; ↑also 252.9), e.g.:

εἶχες δήπου ἄν τί μοι εἰπεῖν; … **Ἔγωγε**. — *"You could presumably give me an answer?" … "I could."* (Plato, Meno 72c)

μέμνησαι; … **Πῶς γὰρ οὔ;**	*"Do you remember?"* … *"Yes, of course!"* (Plato, Sophist 250d)

III. **Open interrogative clauses** are introduced by interrogative pronouns or adverbs (↑60/61; 143; on word-order also ↑270e; on "intertwined" clauses ↑289j): 269d

τίς;	*who?*	τί;	*what?*
πόσος;	*how large (…)?*	πόσοι;	*how many (…)?*
ποῖος;	*what kind of (…)?* (NT: for this at times post-CG ποταπός;)		
πηλίκος;	*what size of/how great (…)?*		
ποῦ;	*where?* KG/NT also *to where?*	πόθεν;[1]	*from where?*
πότε;	*when?*	ποσάκις;	*how often?*
πῶς;	*how?*		

(1) CG also ποῖ; *to where?* πῇ; *how? where? to where?*

Examples:

τίνες εἰσὶν οἱ ἀδελφοί μου;	*Who are my brothers?* (Mt 12:48)
πῶς ἐγείρονται οἱ νεκροί;	*How are the dead raised?* (1Cor 15:35)

Sometimes γάρ (↑252.9) occurs in questions as a modal particle expressing doubt, sympathy or the like, mostly not translatable, though sometimes as an added *then, pray* or a prefixed *What! Why!* (↑BDAG s.v. 1f), also in answers with a confirmative force (↑269c): *(yes/no) indeed* (↑BDF §452.2), e.g.:

τί **γὰρ** κακὸν ἐποίησεν;	*Why? What crime has he committed?* (Mt 27:23)

The syntactic structure of open interrogative clauses in NT narratives sometimes deviates markedly from the standard ones used in written Ancient Greek or written English (this may be due to Semitic or popular KG influence); in most cases these clauses function as rhetorical questions (↑269a), e.g.:

τίς ἐστιν ἐξ ὑμῶν ἄνθρωπος, ὃν αἰτήσει ὁ υἱὸς αὐτοῦ ἄρτον, μὴ λίθον ἐπιδώσει αὐτῷ; in "normal" written Ancient Greek something like this: τίς ἐξ ὑμῶν τῷ υἱῷ ἄρτον αἰτοῦντι λίθον ἐπιδώσει; (BDF §469)	*What person is there among you, whose son will ask for bread – will they give him a stone/they will not give him a stone, will they? = Which of you, if your son asks for bread, will give him a stone?/None of you will give your son a stone if he asks for bread.* (Mt 7:9)
τίς ἄνθρωπος ἐξ ὑμῶν ἔχων ἑκατὸν πρόβατα καὶ ἀπολέσας ἐξ αὐτῶν ἓν οὐ καταλείπει τὰ ἐνενήκοντα ἐννέα ἐν τῇ ἐρήμῳ καὶ πορεύεται ἐπὶ τὸ ἀπολωλὸς ἕως εὕρῃ αὐτό;	*What person among you who has a hundred sheep and loses one of them, does not leave the ninety-nine in the wilderness and go after the one that is lost until he finds it? = Suppose one of you has a hundred sheep and loses one of them. Doesn't he leave the ninety-nine …?* (Lk 15:4)

↑also Mt 12:11; 24:45; Lk 11:5.7 (↑210d.5); 12:42; 14:28; 17:7.

269e IV. Grammatically the two or more components of **alternative questions** correspond to independent declarative clauses (↑267) or to deliberative questions (↑269a). The following disjunctive conjunctions/particles (↑251b) are used to introduce them:

Component 1	Component 2 etc.
without particle	ἤ *or*
CG also: πότερον (also πότερα/ἆρα), not translatable (πότερον 1× in the NT, but only in indirect question: Jn 7:17; ↑273a)	ἤ *or*

↑Lat. *utrum – an, ne – an.*

Examples:

ἀπὸ σεαυτοῦ σὺ τοῦτο λέγεις **ἢ** ἄλλοι εἶπόν σοι περὶ ἐμοῦ;	*Are you asking this on your own, or did others tell you about me?* (Jn 18:34)
τίς ἡμᾶς χωρίσει ἀπὸ τῆς ἀγάπης τοῦ Χριστοῦ; θλῖψις **ἢ** στενοχωρία **ἢ** διωγμὸς **ἢ** λιμὸς **ἢ** γυμνότης **ἢ** κίνδυνος **ἢ** μάχαιρα;	*Who can separate us from the love of Christ? Can affliction or distress or persecution or famine or nakedness or danger or sword?* (Ro 8:35)
πότερον θάλασσά εἰμι **ἢ** δράκων …;	*Am I a sea or a dragon …?* (Job 7:12 LXX = CG)

269f V. Closed and open interrogative clauses, in the form of simple or alternative questions (used as real or rhetorical questions), function as **deliberative questions** when the predicator/predicate verb is a deliberative subjunctive (less frequently an indicative future; negated by means of μή; ↑210d; 269a), e.g.:

δῶμεν ἢ **μὴ δῶμεν**;	*Should we pay them, or shouldn't we?* (Mk 12:14)
Τί ποιήσωμεν;	*What should we do?* (Ac 2:37)
οὐ μὴ πίω αὐτό; (↑269b)	*Shall I not drink it?* (Jn 18:11)

3.4.2 Dependent (subordinate) clauses

270 Dependent (subordinate) clauses: preliminaries (↑BR §268; 293)

270a I. Dependent (subordinate) clauses may have a variety of **syntactic functions** in their relation to the superordinate construction as sentence constituents or attributive modifiers. As a result, we may distinguish the following types of dependent (subordinate) clauses (on other kinds of subdivisions ↑266a):

1. Dependent (subordinate) clauses **as sentence constituents**:

a) subject clause (↑255e), e.g.:

ἐκ τοῦ αἰῶνος οὐκ ἠκούσθη **ὅτι ἠνέῳξέν τις ὀφθαλμοὺς τυφλοῦ γεγεννημένου·**	*Since the beginning of time it has never been heard that anyone opened the eyes of a person born blind.* (Jn 9:32)

"What has never been heard since the beginning of time?" *That anyone opened …*

↑271c (ὅτι *that* or the like); 272e (ἵνα *that* or the like); 273c (interrogative clause); 289b/290 (relative clause).

b) complement clauses (↑254c):

- object clause (↑257d), e.g.:

σὺ οἶδας **ὅτι φιλῶ σε.**	*You know that I love you.* (Jn 21:15f)

"Whom or what do you know?" *That I love you.*

↑271c (ὅτι *that* or the like); 272e (ἵνα *that* or the like); 273c (interrogative clause); 289b/290 (relative clause).

- subject or object complement clause (↑258a/258b), e.g.:

οὗτός ἐστιν **ὑπὲρ οὗ ἐγὼ εἶπον** … (SC^{id})	*This is the one of whom I said …* (Jn 1:30)
χάριτι δὲ θεοῦ εἰμι **ὅ εἰμι** (SC^{prop}).	*But by the grace of God I am what I am.* (1Cor 15:10)

↑289b/290 (relative clause).

- adverbial complement clause (↑258c; 259d–259m), e.g.:

… ἵνα **ὅπου εἰμὶ ἐγὼ** (LocC) καὶ ὑμεῖς ἦτε.	*… so that where I am you may be also.* (Jn 14:3)

c) adverbial (adjunct) clause (↑259a–259m), e.g.:

ἐὰν θέλῃς (CondA) δύνασαί με καθαρίσαι.	*If you are willing, you can make me clean.* (Mt 8:2)

↑276–287 (adverbial clauses); 289b (relative clause; ↑also 290).

2. Dependent (subordinate) clauses **as attributive modifiers** (↑260n), e.g.:

τὰ ῥήματα (HN) **ἃ ἐγὼ λελάληκα ὑμῖν** (Attr) πνεῦμά ἐστιν καὶ ζωή ἐστιν.	*The words that I have spoken to you are spirit and are life.* (Jn 6:63)

↑289b (relative clause); 288 (conjunctional clause).

II. In a complex sentence (↑266b) there may be more than one dependent (subordinate) clauses subordinate to the main clause, typically in one way or other subordinate to each other resulting in a hierarchy with **different degrees of subordination** (↑266b,2), e.g.: 270b

main clause:
μετανοήσατε οὖν …
Repent therefore …

subordinate clause/degree 1 (PurpA [↑278a] to main cl.):
ὅπως ἂν ἔλθωσιν καιροὶ ἀναψύχεως … καὶ ἀποστείλῃ τόν … χριστὸν Ἰησοῦν
so that times of refreshing may come … and that he may the send … the Messiah, Jesus,

subordinate clause/degree 2 (Attr of Ἰησοῦν in subo. cl./degree 1):
ὃν δεῖ οὐρανὸν μὲν δέξασθαι ἄχρι χρόνων ἀποκαταστάσεως πάντων
whom heaven must receive until the times of the restoration of all things

subordinate clause/degree 3 (Attr of πάντων in subo. cl./degree 2):
ὧν ἐλάλησεν ὁ θεός …
which God spoke about …

(Ac 3:19–21)

Noteworthy points:

a) An even **more complex hierarchy** may surface, if we take into account the fact that frequently infinitive and participle phrases occur with a sentence/clause-like function (↑213a; 227a; also ↑270g), thus in Ac 3:19–21 a hierarchy with five to six subordinate constructions:

main cl.: μετανοήσατε οὖν … *Repent therefore …*
(1) εἰς inf./ACI phrase (PurpA) with ἐξαλειφθῆναι as "P": *so that … may be wiped out*
(2) ὅπως-clause (PurpA) with ἔλθωσιν and ἀποστείλῃ as P: … *so that … may come … send …*
(3.1) attributive PtcP with προκεχειρισμένον as "P" (Attr): … *who has been appointed …*
(3.2) ὅν-clause with δεῖ as P (Attr): … *whom … it is necessary …*
(4) inf./ACI phrase with δέξασθαι as "P" (S of δεῖ): … *(for heaven to) receive …*
(5) ὧν-clause with ἐλάλησεν as P (Attr): *which … spoke about*

b) The **main clause** is frequently **preceded** and followed by subordinate constructions, e.g. in Jn 10:38:

conditional clause (↑280b):
εἰ δὲ ποιῶ, *But if I do [them],*
concessive clause (↑286a):
κἂν ἐμοὶ μὴ πιστεύητε, *even though you do not believe me,*

main clause:
τοῖς ἔργοις πιστεύετε, *believe the works,*

purpose clause with ἵνα (↑278a):
ἵνα γνῶτε καὶ γινώσκητε *so that you may know and understand*
object clause with ὅτι (dependent declarative clause; ↑271a):
ὅτι ἐν ἐμοὶ ὁ πατὴρ κἀγὼ ἐν τῷ πατρί. *that the Father is in me, and I in the Father.*

III. Dependent clauses are mostly introduced by a **subordinator**, either by a subordinating conjunction (↑251f–251m) or by a relative (pronoun or adverb; ↑59–61; 142; 143b). On this basis one further uses the following distinctions: 270c

1. **Conjunctional clauses** (but ↑273[16]), mostly serving as sentence constituents, either as

a) subject-object clauses (as subject or complement [mostly object]; ↑271–275), e.g.:

οὐκ οἴδατε **ὅτι ναὸς θεοῦ ἐστε** …; (Od) — *Do you not know that you are God's temple?* (1Cor 3:16)

or as

b) adverbial clauses (mostly adverbial adjunct; ↑276–287), e.g.:

ἴσθι ἐκεῖ **ἕως ἂν εἴπω σοι** (TempA). — *Stay there until I tell you.* (Mt 2:13)

c) less frequently as attributive clauses (attributive modifier; ↑288), e.g.:

ἔρχεται ὥρα **ὅτε οὐκέτι ἐν παροιμίαις λαλήσω ὑμῖν** (Attr of ὥρα: "What kind of time/hour?"). — *A time/The hour is coming when I will no longer speak to you in figures of speech.* (Jn 16:25)

2. **Relative clauses**, typically attributive clauses, but also as sentence constituents (↑289b):

a) attribute clauses, when the relative has an antecedent phrase as a head noun/phrase ("HN") in the superordinate construction, e.g.:

πᾶσα **φυτεία** (HN) **ἣν** (rel.) **οὐκ ἐφύτευσεν ὁ πατήρ μου ὁ οὐράνιος** ἐκριζωθήσεται. — *Every plant that my heavenly Father has not planted will be uprooted.* (Mt 15:13)

b) as sentence constituents, when the relative is without an antecedent phrase, e.g.:

οἶδα γὰρ **ᾧ** (rel.) **πεπίστευκα** (Od). — *I know in whom I have faith.* (2Tm 1:12)

Note that the two types of subordinators are principally different regarding their syntactic function: **Relatives** (pronouns and adverbs) as subordinators introduce the subordinate (relative) clause, but at the same time have the role of a sentence constituent of the relative clause (↑22c p. 44), thus in Mt 15:13 ἥν *that* is the direct object of ἐφύτευσεν *has planted*; in 2Tm 1:12 ᾧ *in whom* is the dative object of πεπίστευκα *I have faith.*

Subordinating **conjunctions**, however, do not function as sentence constituents. This may be demonstrated by turning relative and conjunctional clauses into main clauses: relatives will be replaced by the corresponding (personal) pronouns or adverbs, while conjunctions will be deleted, e.g.:

*__αὐτὴν__ οὐκ ἐφύτευσεν ὁ πατήρ μου ὁ οὐράνιος — *my heavenly Father has not planted it*

*__αὐτῷ__ πεπίστευκα — *I have faith in him*

*– ναὸς θεοῦ ἐστε — *you are God's temple* (↑1Cor 3:16)

In Ancient Greek differentiating the two, however, may in part prove problematic, since most subordinating conjunctions were originally relatives (↑319c[35]), e.g. ὅτε *when* (↑276 and 61c), ὡς *how/as/like* (↑271a; 273; 287 and 61c). ↑BR §287/288.

3. As far as **word-order** is concerned note that **subordinators** are principally prepositives, occurring at the beginning of the clause (↑128b p. 179). Occasionally, however, both in the NT and CG elements belonging to the subordinate clause (mainly its subject, less frequently its object) may be placed before the subordinator for emphasis (↑128b p. 180; BDF §475), e.g.: 270d

τυφλὸς δὲ τυφλὸν (S and Od) **ἐὰν** ὁδηγῇ, ἀμφότεροι εἰς βόθυνον πεσοῦνται.	*If a blind person guides a blind person, both will fall into the pit.* (Mt 15:14)
νῦν (TempA) **ὃν** ἔχεις οὐκ ἔστιν σου ἀνήρ.	*The one you have now is not your husband.* (Jn 4:18)

↑also Lk 7:39; 1Cor 3:5; 6:4; 7:17; also in the case of interrogatives (↑269d): Mt 22:28; Mk 14:68; Jn 1:19.

270e Overview of conjunctional and relative clauses based on their syntactic function:

syntactic function	conjunctional clause	relative clause
SUBJECT	↑271–274	↑289b (main cl. without HN)
COMPLEMENT (mostly object)	↑271–274	↑289b (main cl. without HN)
ADVERBIAL (mostly adjunct)	↑276–287 (adverbial cl.)	↑289b (main cl. without HN); ↑also with adverbial nuances 290
ATTRIBUTE MODIFIER	↑288 (infrequent)	↑289b (attributive cl.)

↑245c and 246b on the use of negatives in subordinate clauses.

270f IV. In many cases dependent clauses and **infinitive** or **participle phrases** are mutually exchangeable:

1. Subordinate clauses and **infinitive phrases** in competition with each other:

a) subject-object clauses replacing infinitive/ACI phrases (↑also 275):

• dependent declarative clauses (with ὅτι *that* or the like; ↑271), frequently in CG, but to some extent more frequently still in KG, e.g.:

ὑμεῖς λέγετε **ὅτι ἐγώ εἰμι**.	*You say that I am.* (Lk 22:70)
ἔλεγον **αὐτὸν εἶναι θεόν**.	*They said that he was a god.* (Ac 28:6)

• dependent desiderative clauses (with ἵνα *that* or the like; ↑272), rarely in CG, but extensively in KG, e.g.:

παρήγγειλεν αὐτοῖς, **ἵνα μηδὲν αἴρωσιν εἰς ὁδόν**.	*He ordered them to take nothing for their journey.* (Mk 6:8)
αὐτὸς παρήγγειλεν αὐτῷ **μηδενὶ εἰπεῖν**.	*He ordered him to tell no one.* (Lk 5:14)

b) adverbial clauses and infinitive/ACI phrases with a comparable function in competition (↑259d–259m, on relation to CG usage also 213c and 226b), e.g.:

διὰ τὸ μὴ ἔχειν ῥίζαν ἐξηράνθη.	*Because they had no root they withered* (Mt 13:6)
ὅτι οὐκ εἰμὶ χείρ, οὐκ εἰμὶ ἐκ τοῦ σώματος.	*Because I am not a hand I do not belong to the body.* (1Cor 12:15)

2. Subordinate clauses and **participle phrases** in competition with each other:

a) subject-object clauses replacing participle phrases (↑also ↑275), i.e. dependent declarative clauses with ὅτι *that* (↑271) replacing ACP phrases (↑233b/233c) as the object of

- verbs of sensual perception or cognitive attitude/mental perception (CG and NT)
- verbs of showing and (only outside NT + ACP) of reporting, e.g.:

γινώσκετε **ὅτι ἐγγύς ἐστιν ἡ βασιλεία τοῦ θεοῦ** (ὅτι-clause). — *You know that the kingdom of God is near.* (Lk 21:31)

Γινώσκετε **τὸν ἀδελφὸν ἡμῶν Τιμόθεον ἀπολελυμένον** (ACP). — *You should know that our brother Timothy has been released.* (He 13:23)

b) adverbial clauses and participle phrases (p.c. and gen.abs.) with a comparable function (↑259d–259m), e.g.:

… τί ἐποίησεν Δαυὶδ **ὅτε ἐπείνασεν**. — *… what David did when he was hungry* (Mt 12:3)

ἰδὼν δὲ Σίμων Πέτρος προσέπεσεν τοῖς γόνασιν Ἰησοῦ. — *But when Peter saw it, he fell at Jesus' knees.* (Lk 5:8)

V. Subordinate clauses of any kind may be **internally dependent**, i.e. they depend on a superordinate clause with a past tense value and so appear to refer to "situations" that are in the past or to one prior to it (from the writer's/speaker's vantage point). In such cases CG frequently (the NT very rarely) replaces the ind. or subj. (with or without ἄν) normally found in the subordinate clause by the oblique optative, provided the predicate verb of the superordinate clause expresses a past tense value (augment indicatives or historic/narrative indicative present; ↑205; 211f/211g), e.g.: 270g

ἔγνωσαν … ὅτι κενὸς ὁ φόβος **εἴη** (oblique opt. for ind. pres. after ind. aor.) … — *… they realized that their fear was groundless …* (Xenophon, Anabasis 2.2.21)

VI. Quite often the **mood** of the subordinate clause is **assimilated** to the mood of the superordinate clause: the mood normally found in a subordinate clause is replaced by the opt. without ἄν (after an opt. of wish or a potential opt.), by the augment ind. (after an ind. with non-factual meaning). This happens (in CG usage) especially in the case of relative, temporal, and purpose clauses, e.g.: 270h

πῶς γὰρ ἄν τις, ἅ γε μὴ **ἐπίσταιτο**, ταῦτα σοφὸς εἴη; — *How could anyone be wise about the things that he does not even know?* (Xenophon, Memorabilia 4.6.7)

On time relations between the "situations" referred to by the clauses of complex sentences ↑206.

On subordinate clauses or infinitive and participle phrases intertwined with relative or interrogative clauses ↑289j.

3.4.2.1 Conjunctional clauses (but ↑273[16])

(i) Conjunctional subject-object clauses

271 Dependent declarative (subject-object) clauses (↑BR §269; 271; BDF §324; 330; 370; 454)

271a 1. Dependent declarative clauses (↑266a.3) are subordinated by (↑251f):

ὅτι	*that* (on ὅτι ["recitative"] ↑274b)
also ὡς, though less distinctive than ὅτι; in the NT rarely with this function (e.g. first ὡς in 1Th 2:11), more frequently in the sense of *as/how*, in part with the role of πῶς (↑273b)	
οὐ is the negative typically used, ↑245b; on those after verbs expressing negative statements.	

Example:

independent declarative clause (↑267):	dependent declarative clause:
ἐξουσίαν ἔχω … *I have authority* … (Jn 10:18)	οὐκ οἶδας **ὅτι ἐξουσίαν ἔχω** … *Don't you know* *that I have authority* … (Jn 19:10)

271b 2. They are subordinate to clauses whose predicators are verbs (or other expressions)

a) of **communication** (i.e. asserting) and (in the NT; in CG regularly + inf./ACI phrases) of **cognitive attitude**, e.g. thinking, (also + inf./ACI phrases; ↑218f–218h);
b) of **sensual** and **mental perception** (also + ACP [in part GCP] phrases, less frequently and only in part + inf./ACI phrases; also ↑218j; 233b for comparisons between the various possible constructions);
c) of **showing** and **reporting** (also + inf./ACI phrases, as well as ACP phrases [frequently in CG, rarely in the NT and there limited to verbs of showing]; 218i; 233c).
Examples:

ὑμεῖς λέγετε **ὅτι ἐγώ εἰμι.**	*You say that I am.* (Lk 22:70)
ἐν τούτῳ πιστεύομεν **ὅτι ἀπὸ θεοῦ ἐξῆλθες.**	*Because of this we believe that you have come from God.* (Jn 16:30)
ἤκουσεν **ὅτι ἀσθενεῖ.**	*He heard that he was ill.* (Jn 11:6)
ἰδὼν **ὅτι ἐνεπαίχθη** …	*When he saw that he had been tricked* … (Mt 2:16)
ἐπίστασθε **ὡς ἀθέμιτόν ἐστιν ἀνδρὶ Ἰουδαίῳ** …	*You know that it is unlawful for a Jew* … (Ac 10:28)
οἶδα **ὅτι ἀναστήσεται.**	*I know that he will rise again.* (Jn 11:24)

πάντα ὑπέδειξα ὑμῖν **ὅτι οὕτως κοπιῶντας δεῖ ἀντιλαμβάνεσθαι τῶν ἀσθενούντων.** — *In every way I have shown you that by working hard in this way we must help the weak.* (Ac 20:35)

ἀπήγγειλαν δὲ αὐτῷ **ὅτι Ἰησοῦς … παρέρχεται.** — *They told him that Jesus … was passing by.* (Lk 18:37)

↑also 274 on direct speech.

3. Functionally dependent declarative clauses mostly occur as an **object** (↑257d) of the superordinate construction, less frequently as a **subject** (↑255e), e.g.: 271c

ἐνόμισαν **ὅτι πλεῖον λήμψονται** (Od). — *They thought they would receive more.* (Mt 20:10)

οὐ μνημονεύετε **ὅτι … ταῦτα ἔλεγον ὑμῖν** (Og); — *Don't you remember that … I told you these things?* (2Th 2:5)

πρόδηλον γὰρ **ὅτι ἐξ Ἰούδα ἀνατέταλκεν ὁ κύριος ἡμῶν** (S). — *For it is evident that our Lord descended form Judah.* (He 7:14)

Occasionally such a clause serves as an attributive modifier (↑288a), very rarely also as an adverbial (thus as a ManA [↑259f; 287a] in Ro 5:8: ὅτι = ἐν τούτῳ ὅτι *in that* or *by* + *-ing* form; ↑BDF §394).

4. The same **tense** (!) and **mood** are generally used 271d

a) **as in independent declarative clauses** (↑267)

(when there is internal dependence on a superordinate clause with a past tense value CG may use an oblique opt. instead; ↑205; 211f/211g; 270h),

b) on **time relations** of the "situation" of a dependent declarative clause (subo. cl.) to the "situation" of its superordinate clause (main cl.) note the following (↑206):

time relation to the "situation" of the superordinate clause and verb form used in the subo. cl.	typical translation into English: with *that*
simultaneous: ind. pres. in the subo. cl.:(1)	+ the same time form as the main cl.
λέγει ὅτι χαίρεις.	*He says that you are glad.*
γινώσκει ὅτι χαίρεις.	*He knows that you are glad.*
εἶπεν/ἔλεγεν ὅτι χαίρεις.	*He said that you were glad.*
ἔγνω/ἐγίνωσκε ὅτι χαίρεις.	*He knew that you were glad.*
anterior: past tense form in the subo. cl.:(2)	+ past/past perfect form
λέγει ὅτι ἐχάρης/ἔχαιρες.	*He says that you were glad.*
γινώσκει ὅτι ἐχάρης/ἔχαιρες.	*He knows that you were glad.*
εἶπεν/ἔλεγεν ὅτι ἐχάρης/ἔχαιρες.	*He said that you had been glad.*
ἔγνω/ἐγίνωσκε ὅτι ἐχάρης/ἔχαιρες.	*He knew that you had been glad.*
posterior: ind. fut. in the subo. cl.:(3)	+ future/future in the past
λέγει ὅτι χαρήσῃ.	*He says that you will be glad.*
γινώσκει ὅτι χαρήσῃ.	*He knows that you will be glad.*
εἶπεν/ἔλεγεν ὅτι χαρήσῃ.	*He said that you would be glad.*
ἔγνω/ἐγίνωσκε ὅτι χαρήσῃ.	*He knew that you would be glad.*

(1) ↑271b Lk 22:70 and Lk 18:37
(2) ↑271b Mt 2:16 and 271c 2Th 2:5.
(3) ↑271b Jn 11:24 and 271c Mt 20:10.

On this typical use ↑Duhoux §132. In the NT there are a few exceptions (seeming ones in part), among them Jn 2:25 (ipf. ἦν instead of ind. pres. ἐστίν referring to something simultaneous; but is found not in a dependent declarative, but in an interrogative clause) and Ac 22:2 (ipf. προσεφώνει instead of ind. pres. προσφωνεῖ [so Var.] referring to something simultaneous). ↑BDF §324/330.

271e 5. **Less frequent** forms of dependent declarative clauses (↑251f):

a) dependent on expressions of **fearing** (sometimes these need to be supplied in thought; ↑247b) subordinated by

μή	*that*
μὴ οὐ	*that not*
mostly + subj. (less frequently + indicative, when a past "situation" is the object of fear) (CG also + oblique opt; ↑211f)	

in the NT occurring only in Ac, Paul and He 4:1, e.g.:

… φοβηθεὶς ὁ χιλίαρχος **μὴ διασπασθῇ ὁ Παῦλος ὑπ' αὐτῶν** …	*… the tribune, fearing that Paul would be torn to pieces by them …* (Ac 23:10)

The background to this construction is probably one with an independent desiderative clause: *the tribune was in fear – Paul must by no means be torn to pieces by them! …*; (↑BR §271).

b) dependent on expressions of **affective behaviour** (↑BDAG sub εἰ 2; BDF §454.1) subordinated by

εἰ	*that*

Example:

ὁ δὲ Πιλᾶτος ἐθαύμασεν **εἰ ἤδη τέθνηκεν**.	*Pilate was surprised that he was already dead* (Mk 15:44)

The background to this construction is probably one with a dependent interrogative clause (↑273): *… was surprised [asking] whether he was already dead* (↑second part of the same verse).
↑also Ac 26:23; 2Cor 11:15; 1Jn 3:13.

c) dependent on **oath formulas** or the like, agreeing with Hebrew usage (↑BDF §454.5) subordinated by

εἰ (= אִם *'im*; ↑HALOT s.v. 4)	*(that) certainly not*

Example:

	… ὤμοσα …	*… I swore …*
	εἰ εἰσελεύσονται εἰς τὴν κατάπαυσίν μου.	*They will certainly not enter my rest.* (He 3:11; 4:3.5 = Ps 94:11 LXX)
Hebr.:	… נִשְׁבַּעְתִּי …	*… nišbá'tî …*
	אִם־יְבֹאוּן אֶל־מְנוּחָתִי	*'im-yəḇō'ûn 'el-mənûḥāṯî*

↑also Mk 8:12 (no OT quotation!).

↑275 for an overview of constructions often rendered by "that"-clauses.

Dependent desiderative (subject-object) clauses 272

(↑BR §270; BDF §388; 393; 392; 390; 391; 394; 400; Z §406–408; 381/382; 350–353; 410; 383–386; 392; 411; 415)

1. **ἵνα** (or the like) as a **subordinator** of desiderative and other types of clauses 272a

The **primary** function of ἵνα (or the like; neg. ἵνα μή or μή) in the NT/KG is the standard CG one, i.e. to subordinate purpose clauses (*so that = in order that*; ↑278). And it is this function that makes ἵνα-clauses and inf./ACI phrases natural competitors, at least in part (↑220). In the **post-CG period**, the competition between the two constructions increased, with ἵνα gradually adopting additional functions including the one of subordinating result clauses (↑279). In KG ἵνα-clauses could eventually **replace** almost any **inf./ACI phrase**, provided it referred to a "situation" interpretable as an intended or unintended **consequence** of what was said in the superordinate construction (↑213c; for references to a "situation" to be understood as factual, declarative ὅτι-clauses would be more appropriate; ↑271):

a) an inf./ACI phrase as the subject of impersonal verbs and expressions with a comparable use (non-CG; ↑217a; ↑also 217f), e.g.:

συμφέρει ὑμῖν **ἵνα εἷς ἄνθρωπος ἀποθάνῃ ὑπὲρ τοῦ λαοῦ** …
It is better for you that one man should die for the people … (Jn 11:50)

↑συμφέρει **ἕνα ἄνθρωπον ἀποθανεῖν ὑπὲρ τοῦ λαοῦ**.
It is better that one man should die for the people. (Jn 18:14)

b) an inf./ACI phrase as the object of verbs of volition (non-CG; ↑218a–218d), e.g.:

πάντα οὖν ὅσα ἐὰν θέλητε **ἵνα ποιῶσιν ὑμῖν οἱ ἄνθρωποι** οὕτως καὶ ὑμεῖς ποιεῖτε αὐτοῖς.
So whatever you want people to do for you, do also for them. (Mt 7:12)

↑**οὐδένα** ἤθελεν **γνῶναι**.
He did not want anybody to know it. (Mk 7:24)

↑also Jn 8:56.

c) an inf./ACI phrase as the complement of an adjective (non-CG; ↑219), e.g.:

οὐκ εἰμὶ ἐγὼ ἄξιος **ἵνα λύσω αὐτοῦ τὸν ἱμάντα τοῦ ὑποδήματος**.
I am not worthy to untie the strap of his sandal. (Jn 1:27)

↑… οὐκ ἄξιος … **λῦσαι**
… *not worthy to untie* … (Ac 13:25)

d) an inf./ACI phrase as an adjunct of purpose (CG; ↑220a), e.g.:

οὐ γὰρ ἦλθον **ἵνα κρίνω τὸν κόσμον**.
For I have not come to judge the world. (Jn 12:47)

↑οὐκ ἦλθον **καταλῦσαι** …
I have not come to abolish … (Mt 5:17)

e) an inf./ACI phrase as an adjunct of result (non-CG; ↑221d), e.g.:

τίς ἥμαρτεν … **ἵνα τυφλὸς γεννηθῇ**;
Who sinned … that he was born blind? (Jn 9:2)

↑ἠγέρθη καὶ … ἐξῆλθεν … **ὥστε ἐξίστασθαι πάντας** …
He got up … walked out … so that they were all amazed … (Mk 2:12)

f) an explanatory inf./ACI phrase as an apposition (non-CG; ↑222), e.g.:

τοῦτο γάρ ἐστιν τὸ θέλημα τοῦ πατρός μου, **ἵνα πᾶς ὁ θεωρῶν τὸν υἱὸν καὶ πιστεύων εἰς αὐτὸν ἔχῃ ζωὴν αἰώνιον** …
For this is my Father's will that everyone who sees the Son and believes in him will have eternal life … (Jn 6:40)

↑οὕτως ἐστὶν τὸ θέλημα τοῦ θεοῦ **ἀγαθοποιοῦντας φιμοῦν** …
It is God's will that by doing good you should silence … (1Pe 2:15)

↑also Mk 11:28; Jn 15:8. On χρείαν ἔχω *to need* ↑217f.

g) an inf./ACI phrase with τοῦ (non-CG; ↑225a; ↑also 217f), e.g.:

ἐλήλυθεν ἡ ὥρα **ἵνα δοξασθῇ** …
The hour has come for … to be glorified (Jn 12:23)

↑… ὁ χρόνος **τοῦ τεκεῖν**
… *the time for … to give birth* (Lk 1:57)

Thus, the conjunction ἵνα or the like in KG may basically be translated in three different ways, something that in principle applies to the NT as well (especially to Jn, Mt, and Mk; however, in Lk, Ac, Jas, Pe, and He there are hardly any non-CG instances):

subordinator of →	purpose clauses (↑278; standard use) (CG/KG/NT)	result clauses (↑279) (KG/NT)	other inf./ACI replacements (↑272a/272b) (KG/NT)
ἵνα (less frequently ὅπως)	*in order that/ so that; to*	*with the result that/ so that*	*that; to*
ἵνα μή or μή (also μήποτε)	*in order that not/ so that not; not to*	*with the result that not/ so that not*	*that not; not to*
+ subj. (in the NT occasionally replaced by ind. fut. [↑202j]; CG mostly + oblique opt., when the superordinate clause refers to the past [↑211f/211g])			

272b 2. When subordinate clauses introduced by ἵνα *that* or the like replace inf./ACI phrases, especially in the uses a) to c) above (↑272a), they may mostly be understood more or less clearly as dependent desiderative clauses, e.g.:

independent desiderative clause (↑268):	dependent desiderative clause:
μηδὲν αἴρετε εἰς τὴν ὁδόν. *Take nothing for the journey.* (Lk 9:3)	παρήγγειλεν αὐτοῖς **ἵνα μηδὲν αἴρωσιν εἰς ὁδόν**. *He ordered them* *to take nothing for the journey* (Mk 6:8)
λῦσον … *Untie/Take off* … (Ac 7:33)	οὐκ εἰμὶ ἐγὼ ἄξιος **ἵνα λύσω** … *I am not worthy* *to untie* … (Jn 1:27) (≈ *I am not worthy to be asked to untie* …)
κατάβηθι … *Come down* … (Jn 4:49)	ἠρώτα **ἵνα καταβῇ** … *He asked him* *to come down* … (Jn 4:47)

Note that occasionally the ἵνα-clause (or the ὅπως-clause, more frequently in CG; ↑272c; 210g) is without superordinate construction and so serves as one replacement of the imperative. ↑268c.

272c In CG subordinate clauses introduced by ὅπως (less frequently by ὡς) *that* (negated by means of μή) + ind. fut. (less frequently + subj.; ↑202j) had a comparable use when they were dependent on expressions denoting *to take care* or the like (↑210h), e.g.:

ἔπρασσον **ὅπως τις βοήθεια ἥξει**. *They saw to it that some reinforcement arrived.* (Thucydides 3.4)

Note that in the NT certain types of independent desiderative clauses (↑268b) sometimes have a function similar to that of dependent clauses, though without a subordinator (asyndesis; ↑293e): 272d

a) clauses with hortatory subj. (↑210c) preceded by

ἄφες, ἄγετε (CG uses ἄγε, φέρε *come/now/well!*)	*Let me!, Let us!*
δεῦρο (also in CG)	*Come!*

Example:

ἄφες ἐκβάλω τὸ κάρφος ἐκ τοῦ ὀφθαλμοῦ σου.	*Let me* (lit. *Let me, I must*) *take the speck out of your eye.* (Mt 7:4)

b) clauses with prohibitive subj. (↑210e) preceded by (on negation ↑247e)

ὅρα, ὁρᾶτε, βλέπετε	*See to it/Take care/Watch out that* (sg./pl.)

Example:

ὅρα μηδενὶ εἴπῃς.	*See that you don't tell anyone.* (Mt 8:4)

c) similarly clauses with deliberative subj. (↑210d) preceded by

θέλεις/θέλετε (CG βούλει/βούλεσθε) …;	*Do you wish/want …?* (sg./pl.)

Example:

θέλετε ἀπολύσω ὑμῖν τὸν βασιλέα τῶν Ἰουδαίων;	*Do you want me to release the "King of the Jews" for you?* (lit. *Do you want, shall I …?*) (Mk 15:9)

3. Dependent desiderative clauses subordinated by ἵνα *that* or the like (neg. ἵνα μή or μή) function either as an **object** (↑257d; 272a uses b and c) of the superordinate construction or, less frequently, as a **subject** (↑255e; 272a use a), e.g.: 272e

ἐκήρυξαν **ἵνα μετανοῶσιν** (Od).	*They proclaimed that people should repent.* (Mk 6:12)
συμφέρει ὑμῖν, **ἵνα ἐγὼ ἀπέλθω** (S).	*It is good for you that I go away.* (Jn 16:7)

On the use as an attributive modifier ↑288.

↑275 for an overview of constructions often rendered by "that"-clauses.

Dependent interrogative (subject-object) clauses 273

(↑BR §272; BDF §298f; 300.1; 368; 375; 386.1.2; 396; 440; 454.1; also 267.2; Z §401–403)

Interrogative clauses (questions) of any kind (↑269a) occur not only as independent clauses (direct questions; ↑269b), but also as dependent ones (indirect questions). They may be dependent (typically as objects or, less frequently, as subjects; ↑273c) on verbs of communication (of saying, inquiring), cognitive attitude (of knowing/discovering) or the like. The type of subordinator used varies with the type of interrogative clause to be expressed.[16]

16 Note that only closed interrogative clauses are conjunctional clauses, the open ones being relative clauses (↑273b).

273a 1. Subordinators of **closed interrogative clauses** (*yes-no* questions), simple or alternative questions, in their normal or deliberative use (↑269a):

εἰ	*if/whether*
εἴτε – εἴτε	*if/whether – or*
πότερον (CG also πότερα) – ἤ (CG also εἰ – ἤ, εἰ – εἴτε)	*whether – or* (Jn 7:17 only NT instance)

Examples:

direct question (↑269):	indirect question:
οὐχ … οὗτοί εἰσιν … Γαλιλαῖοι; *Aren't … these … Galileans?* (Ac 2:7)	Πιλᾶτος … ἐπηρώτησεν **εἰ ὁ ἄνθρωπος Γαλιλαῖός ἐστιν.** *Pilate asked if the man was a Galilean.* (Lk 23:6)

↑also Jn 9:25; Ac 4:19; 10:18; 19:2; 1Cor 7:16; 2Cor 13:5.

273b 2. Subordinators of **open interrogative clauses** (actually relative clauses; ↑289):[17]
a) either **the same** interrogative pronouns or adverbs **as** those used to introduce the **independent** counterparts (↑269d)
b) or **indirect** interrogative pronouns or adverbs, to some extent also relative pronouns (↑60/61; 143; 142f):[18]

τίς, τί (NT occasionally τὸ τίς/τὸ τί; ↑132d)	ὅστις, ὅ τι and ὅς/ἥ, ὅ	*who, what*
πόσος, πόσοι	ὁπόσος, ὁπόσοι	*how large, how many*
ποῖος (NT: also post-CG ποταπός)	ὁποῖος	*what kind of*
πηλίκος	–	*what size/how great*
ποῦ	ὅπου	*where,* KG/NT also *to where*
CGποῖ	ὅποι	*to where*
CGπῇ	ὅπῃ	*how/where/to where*
πόθεν	ὁπόθεν	*from where*
πότε	ὁπότε	*when*
ποσάκις	–	*how often*
πῶς (NT occasionally τὸ πῶς; ↑132d)	ὡς, (NT 1×:) ὅπως	*how*

17 On intertwined clauses ↑289j.

18 Note that exclamative clauses (having the form of [independent] declarative, desiderative, or interrogative clauses (↑266a) may be introduced by indirect interrogatives as well, e.g.:
ὡς ἀνεξεραύνητα τὰ κρίματα αὐτοῦ. *How unsearchable are his judgments!* (Ro 11:33)

Examples (indirect question are introduced by the same kind of interrogative):

direct question (↑269):	indirect question:
τίς εἶ; *Who are you?* (Jn 1:22)	εἰπὲ **τίς** ἐστιν … *Tell us* *who it is* … (Jn 13:24 Var.)
ἐν ποίᾳ ἐξουσίᾳ ταῦτα ποιεῖς; *By what authority are you doing these things?* (Mk 11:28)	οὐδὲ ἐγὼ λέγω ὑμῖν **ἐν ποίᾳ** ἐξουσίᾳ ταῦτα ποιῶ. *Neither will I tell you* *by what authority I am doing these things.* (Mk 11:33)

↑also (τίς, τί:) Mk 5:14; Lk 18:6; Jn 6:64; 9:21; 13:28; 18:21; Ac 4:9; 17:19; (πόσος, πόσοι:) Mt 27:13; Ac 21:20; (ποῦ:) Jn 1:39; 3:8; (πόθεν:) Jn 2:9; 8:14; (πότε:) Mt 24:3; Lk 17:20; (πῶς:) Mk 5:16; Lk 8:18; 12:27; Jn 9:15; Ac 12:17; (ποῖος:) Mt 24:42f; Jn 21:19; Ac 23:34; (τὸ τίς/τί/πῶς:) Lk 1:62; 9:46; 19:48; 22:24; Ac 4:21; 1Th 4:1.

Examples (indirect question are introduced by a different kind of interrogative):

ποῖον γὰρ κλέος εἰ …; *For what kind of credit is it if …?* (1Pe 2:20)	ἀπαγγέλλουσιν **ὁποίαν** εἴσοδον ἔσχομεν πρὸς ὑμᾶς. *They report* *what kind of reception we had among you.* (1Th 1:9)
πῶς εἰσῆλθες …; *How did you get in …?* (Mt 22:12)	οὐδὲ τοῦτο ἀνέγνωτε … **ὡς** εἰσῆλθεν … *Haven't you read* *how he entered* … (Lk 6:3f; Var. and Mt 12:4/Mk 2:26: πῶς)
τί λέγεις περὶ σεαυτοῦ; *What do you say about yourself?* (Jn 1:22)	οὗτοι οἴδασιν **ἃ** εἶπον ἐγώ. (rel. pron.) *They know* *what I said.* (Jn 18:21) οὐκ οἶδα **τί** λέγεις. *I don't know* *what you mean.* (Mt 26:70)

Note that dependent interrogative clauses serve as reported clauses of indirect speech, on which ↑274.

273c 3. Dependent interrogative clauses function as either an **object** (↑257d) of the superordinate construction or, less frequently, a **subject** (↑255e), e.g.:

ἐπηρώτησεν αὐτὸν **εἰ πάλαι ἀπέθανεν** (Od). *He asked him if he had been dead for some time.* (Mk 15:44)

λαληθήσεταί σοι **ὅ τί σε δεῖ ποιεῖν** (S). *It will be told you/You will be told what you are to do.* (Ac 9:6)

On the use as an attributive modifier ↑288/289.

4. The same **moods** and **negatives** are used in dependent interrogative clauses as in their independent counterparts: they are largely determined by the expected answer:

273d a) The answer to a **non-deliberative question** generally corresponds to a declarative clause. In this case the following applies to the dependent interrogative clause:

- the **mood** is

(1) either the same as in the independent clause (direct question);

(2) or, when there is internal dependence (↑205), the oblique optative replaces the indicative (only rarely in the NT and only in Lk/Ac; ↑211f/211g), e.g.:

direct question (↑269):	indirect question:
τίς **ἐστιν** ὁ ἄνθρωπος …; *Who is the man …?* (Jn 5:12)	οὐκ ᾔδει τίς **ἐστιν** … *He did not know* *who it was* … (Jn 5:13) ἐπυνθάνετο τίς **εἴη** … *He inquired* *who he was* … (Ac 21:33)

- The usual **negative** is οὐ (in the second component of alternative questions of CG also μή); ↑245c.

- With regard to the **time relations** of the “situation” of a dependent interrogative clause to the “situation” of its superordinate clause the same rules apply as in the case of the dependent declarative clause (↑271d).

273e b) A **deliberative question** is usually answered by means of a desiderative clause. In this case the following applies to the dependent interrogative clause:

- the **mood** is

(1) either a deliberative subjunctive as in the independent clause (obviously the 1st person being replaced by the 2nd or 3rd person; ↑210h);

(2) or, when there is internal dependence (↑205), it is frequently replaced by the oblique optative (in CG, apparently never in the NT; ↑211f/211g), e.g.:

direct question (↑269):	indirect question:
τί **φάγωμεν**; ἢ τί **πίωμεν**; *"What shall we eat?" or "What shall we drink?"* (Mt 6:31)	μὴ μεριμνᾶτε τῇ ψυχῇ ὑμῶν τί **φάγητε** ἢ τί **πίητε** *Do not worry about your life* *what you will eat or what you will drink.* (Mt 6:25)
***παραδῶμεν** Κορινθίοις τὴν πόλιν; *Shall we deliver the city to the Corinthians?*	τὸν θεὸν ἐπήροντο εἰ **παραδοῖεν** Κορινθίοις τὴν πόλιν *They asked the god* *whether they should deliver the city to the Corinthians.* (Thucydides 1.25)

• The usual **negative** is μή (↑246b).

5. Sometimes **εἰ-clauses** that seem to be dependent closed interrogative clauses have in fact a function **similar to** that of **purpose clauses** (↑278). This is the case when the superordinate expression implies (contextually) that the agent makes every effort, hopes or is anxious for the "action" of the εἰ-clause to take place. The conjunction εἰ (sometimes enhanced by the addition of ἄρα[γε] or πως) may then be translated as *to try/to see* [or the like], *if hopefully/perhaps*; sometimes a rendering such as *(in order) to* + infinitive seems more appropriate, e.g.: 273f

διώκω δὲ **εἰ καὶ καταλάβω.**	*But I press on to try/to see if I could indeed take hold of it/But I press on (in order) to take hold of it.* (Php 3:12)
ἦλθεν **εἰ ἄρα τι εὑρήσει ἐν αὐτῇ.**	*He went to see if perhaps he could find anything on it.* (Mk 11:13)
... **εἴ πως παραζηλώσω μου τὴν σάρκα καὶ σώσω τινὰς ἐξ αὐτῶν.**	*... in order somehow to make my own people jealous and save some of them.* (Ro 11:14)
δεήθητι τοῦ κυρίου **εἰ ἄρα ἀφεθήσεταί σοι ...**	*Pray to the Lord [in the hope] that perhaps ... will be forgiven you./Pray to the Lord. Perhaps ... will be forgiven you.* (Ac 8:22)

↑also Lk 6:7; 14:28; Ac 17:11.27; 27:12; Ro 1:10; Php 3:11.

↑also 247c on a comparable use of μή or μήποτε.

Direct and indirect speech (↑BR §294f; BDF §396; 470; Z §346–349; Carter §506f; 539) 274

I. There are basically two ways of conveying what someone has uttered or thought, both typically introduced by a reporting clause, whose predicator is a verb of communication (of saying, reporting etc.) or of cognitive attitude (of thinking, knowing etc.): 274a

1. **direct speech**: the utterance or thought is given directly, word by word;

2. **indirect speech** (or "reported speech"): the utterance or thought is given indirectly, i.e. in a reported clause, which may have the form of an inf./ACI (or some-

times participle) phrase or of any of the subject-object clause types (↑271–273; for details and examples ↑274d), e.g.:

direct speech:	indirect speech: (here in the form of inf./ACI phrases)
ἀποκριθέντες τῷ Ἰησοῦ εἶπαν· *They answered Jesus,* **οὐκ οἴδαμεν**. *"We don't know."* (Mt 21:27)	ἀπεκρίθησαν *They answered* **μὴ εἰδέναι πόθεν**. *that they didn't know where it was from.* (Lk 20:7)
ἀπεκρίθη δὲ ὁ χιλίαρχος· *The tribune answered,* **ἐγὼ πολλοῦ κεφαλαίου τὴν πολιτείαν ταύτην ἐκτησάμην.** *"I acquired this citizenship for a large sum of money."* (Ac 22:28)	ὁ μὲν οὖν Φῆστος ἀπεκρίθη *Festus replied* **τηρεῖσθαι τὸν Παῦλον εἰς Καισάρειαν, ἑαυτὸν δὲ μέλλειν ἐν τάχει ἐκπορεύεσθαι**. *that Paul was being held in custody at Caesarea and that he himself was about to go there shortly.* (Ac 25:4) Festus possibly said something like this: τηρεῖται ὁ Παῦλος … ἐγὼ δὲ μέλλω … *Paul is being held in custody … and I myself am about to …*

274b II. **Direct speech**

1. Direct speech in most cases is a basically independent piece of text (e.g. any kind of independent clause, frequently one or more complex or compound sentences). Still, like dependent clauses, it mostly **functions as an object** of the superordinate reporting clause (or a subject, if that clause is in the passive; ↑255a/255e; 257d). In Mt 21:27 e.g. the direct speech serves as an answer to the question "What did they answer Jesus?" (in the case of a passive construction "What was answered/said?", ↑e.g. Mt 5:27).

Note that occasionally the reporting clause or at least its verb of communication is omitted (an ellipsis; ↑293c).

2. In most cases direct speech is not introduced by any conjunction (there is asyndesis; ↑293e). In the standard text editions it is, however, usually indicated by means of the punctuation mark "·" (↑7b), in some editions it begins with a capital letter (like in English) preceded by a comma. Fairly frequently direct speech (both in the NT and in CG) is introduced by the **ὅτι "recitative"**, which in English cannot be translated by a word, but will have to be rendered simply as " , '…' " (↑251f; 252.46; ↑also Hebr. כִּי *kî* and Aram. דִּי *dî* "that", HALOT s. v.). Note that at times it is not entirely clear whether the ὅτι is meant to introduce direct or indirect speech, e.g.:

ἐκεῖνος ἔλεγεν **ὅτι ἐγώ εἰμι**. (clearly direct speech)	*He kept saying, "I am the one".* (Jn 9:9)
ἄλλοι δὲ ἔλεγον **ὅτι Ἠλείας ἐστίν**. (direct or indirect speech?)	*But others said, "He is Elijah."* Or: *But others said that he was Elijah.* (Mk 6:15)

III. **Indirect speech**

1. Indirect speech (particularly indirect speech in a narrower sense; ↑274d) occurs less frequently in Ancient Greek than in Latin. After starting off with indirect speech speakers/writers tend to switch to direct speech before too long, which in CG is usually indicated by the insertion of ἔφη *he/she said* (↑125d) or of a ὅτι recitative (↑274b), in the NT, however, frequently remains without marker, e.g.: 274c

… παρατιθέμενος ὅτι τὸν χριστὸν ἔδει παθεῖν καὶ ἀναστῆναι ἐκ νεκρῶν καὶ ὅτι οὗτός ἐστιν ὁ χριστὸς ὁ Ἰησοῦς ὃν ἐγὼ καταγγέλλω ὑμῖν.	*… he pointed out that it was necessary for the Messiah to suffer and to rise from the dead and [said], "This Jesus, whom I am proclaiming to you, is the Messiah."* (Ac 17:3)

↑also Mk 6:8f; Lk 5:14; Ac 1:4; 14:22; 23:22; 25:4f (φησίν inserted).

2. There are two types of indirect speech: a) indirect speech in a **wider sense** and b) indirect speech in a **narrower sense** ("oratio obliqua" proper). While in stylistically elevated CG texts both types are used, in narratives of the more popular variety as well as in the NT almost exclusively indirect speech in a wider sense. 274d

a) The reported clause of indirect speech in a **wider sense**, as defined in the present grammar, has the form of a dependent declarative, desiderative, or interrogative (subject-object) clause (↑271–273) or of any of the competing inf/ACI (sometimes participle) phrases that are dependent on a verb of communication (of saying, reporting etc.) or of cognitive attitude (of thinking, knowing etc.), e.g.:

direct speech:	indirect speech:

• dependent declarative clause subordinated by ὅτι that or the like (↑271) and corresponding inf./ACI phrase (↑218f–218h):

ὁ δὲ Ἰησοῦς εἶπεν· **ἐγώ εἰμι**. *Jesus said,* *"I am."*(Mk 14:62)	ὑμεῖς λέγετε **ὅτι ἐγώ εἰμι**. *You say* *that I am.* (Lk 22:70) … λέγων **εἶναί τινα ἑαυτόν**. *… saying/claiming* *that he himself was somebody/to be somebody.* (Ac 5:36)

• dependent desiderative clause subordinated by ἵνα *that* or the like (KG; ↑272) and corresponding inf./ACI phrase (↑218a–218d):

καὶ εἶπεν πρὸς αὐτούς· **μηδὲν αἴρετε εἰς τὴν ὁδόν**. *And he said to them, "Take nothing for the journey."* (Lk 9:3)	παρήγγειλεν αὐτοῖς **ἵνα μηδὲν αἴρωσιν εἰς ὁδόν**. *He ordered them that they should take nothing for the journey/to take nothing …* (Mk 6:8) αὐτὸς παρήγγειλεν αὐτῷ **μηδενὶ εἰπεῖν**. *He ordered him to tell no one.* (Lk 5:14)

• dependent interrogative clause subordinated by interrogative (↑273; also 273d):

ἐπυνθάνετο, **τί ἐστιν ὃ ἔχεις …** *He asked, "What is it that you have …?"* (Ac 23:19)	ἐρώτησον τοὺς ἀκηκοότας **τί ἐλάλησα αὐτοῖς**. *Ask those who heard what I said to them.* (Jn 18:21) ἐπυνθάνετο **τί εἴη τοῦτο**. *He inquired what this meant.* (Lk 18:36)

On tense and mood ↑271d (↑also ↑272a and 273d/273e), on time relations between the "situations" referred to by superordinate and dependent clauses ↑271d and 206a–206c.

274e b) The reported clauses of **indirect speech in a narrower sense** ("oratio obliqua" proper; hardly attested in the NT) may occur in the form of dependent declarative or desiderative clauses or of corresponding inf./ACI phrases (frequently a whole series of these). Characteristically, the reported clauses here depend only indirectly on a reporting clause (with a verb of communication/saying or cognitive attitude/thinking etc.): of course, there is semantic dependence; grammatically, however, the reported clauses will have to be regarded as independent.

Typically, the following relationship may be observed between direct and indirect speech in a narrower sense:

• the **main clauses** of direct speech, within indirect speech appear as inf./ACI phrases (↑218f–218h),
• the **subordinate clauses** of direct speech, within indirect speech appear as subordinate clauses

(1) whose **tense** and **mood** (with or without ἄν) are generally unchanged,

(2) when there is internal dependence on **superordinate clause with a past tense value** the original mood may, however, be replaced by an **oblique optative** (without ἄν; ↑205; 211f/211g; 270g) in CG.

(Note that statements with potential meaning [↑209i] and the "irrealis" [↑209h] remain unchanged!)

Example based on Xenophon, Anabasis 1.6.3 (taken from BR §294):

	direct speech:	indirect speech:
	reporting (superordinate) clause:	
	Ὀρόντας ἔγραψε παρὰ βασιλέα· *Orontas wrote to the King,*	Ὀρόντας ἔγραψε παρὰ βασιλέα τάδε· *Orontas wrote to the King as follows:*
main cl.:	**Ἥξω** ἔχων τοὺς ἱππέας *"I will come with the horsemen*	**Ἥξειν** ἔχων τοὺς ἱππέας *That he would come with the horsemen*
subo. cl.:	οὓς Κῦρός μοι **ἔδωκεν**· *Cyrus has given me;*	οὓς Κῦρος αὐτῷ **ἔδωκεν** (or **δοίη**)· *Cyrus had given him;*
main cl.:	ἀλλά με ὡς φίλον **ὑποδέχου**. *therefore do receive me as a friend."*	ἀλλ' ἐκεῖνον ὡς φίλον **ὑποδέχεσθαι** αὐτόν. *that therefore he should receive him as a friend.*

Overview of constructions often rendered by "that"-clauses (also 323b; ↑BR §273) 275

The combinations within thick borders occur more frequently than those within the thin ones. Note also that in several cases a more idiomatic rendering may be preferable to a "that"-clause.

predicator of superordinate clause:		dependent construction:	
1. verbs of communication, i.e. of **saying/asserting** or the like:			
a) dependent clause subordinated by ὅτι *that* or the like (↑271b)			
λέγεις	*You say*	ὅτι εἴληφα αὐτό.	*that I have received it.*
b) inf./ACI phrase (↑218f/218g; use more restricted in the NT than in CG; ↑206c)			
λέγεις	*You say*	ἐμὲ εἰληφέναι αὐτό.	*that I have received it.*
2. verbs of cognitive attitude, i.e. of **thinking/believing** or the like:			
a) dependent clause subordinated by ὅτι *that* or the like (infrequent in CG; ↑271b)			
νομίζεις	*You think/believe*	ὅτι εἴληφα αὐτό.	*that I have received it.*
b) inf./ACI phrase (↑218f/218g; ↑also 206c)			
νομίζεις	*You think/believe*	ἐμὲ εἰληφέναι αὐτό.	*that I have received it.*
3. verbs of **sensual** or **mental perception** (cognitive attitude):			
a) dependent clause subordinated by ὅτι *that* or the like (↑271b)			
ὁρᾷς/οἶδας	*You see/know*	ὅτι εἴληφα αὐτό.	*that I have received it.*
b) ACP phrase, when the subjects differ (↑233b, also comparison of the various constructions)			
ὁρᾷς	*You see*	ἐμὲ εἰληφότα αὐτό.	*that I have received it.*
c) inf./ACI phrase (occurs less frequently; ↑218j; ↑also 206c)			
ἀκούεις/γινώσκεις	*You hear/know*	ἐμὲ εἰληφέναι αὐτό	*that I have received it.*
d) CG: "NCP" phrase, when the subjects are the same (↑233e)			
ὁρᾷς/οἶσθα	*You see/know*	εἰληφὼς αὐτό.	*that you have received it.*

4. verbs of **showing** or **reporting** or the like:

a) dependent clause subordinated by ὅτι *that* or the like (↑271b)

ὑποδείκνυς	*You show*	ὅτι εἴληφα αὐτό.	*that I have received it.*

b) inf./ACI phrase (↑218f/218g; used in the NT, less so in CG; ↑also 206c)

ὑποδείκνυς	*You show*	ἐμὲ εἰληφέναι αὐτό.	*that I have received it.*

c) CG: ACP phrase, when the subjects differ (↑233c)

ὑποδείκνυς	*You show*	ἐμὲ εἰληφότα αὐτό.	*that I have received it.*

d) CG: "NCP" phrase, when the subjects are the same (↑233e)

ὑποδείκνυς	*You show*	εἰληφὼς αὐτό.	*that you have received it.*

5. verbs/expressions of **affective behaviour**:

a) dependent clause subordinated by εἰ *that* (occurs only infrequently; ↑271e)

θαυμάζεις	*You are surprised*	εἰ εἴληφα αὐτό.	*that I have received it.*

b) "NCP", when the subjects are the same (1× in the NT; ↑234d)

χαίρεις	*You are glad*	εἰληφὼς αὐτό.	*that you have received it.*

6. verbs/expressions of **fearing** (sometimes these need to be supplied in thought; ↑271e):

dependent clause subordinated by μή *that*/μὴ οὐ *that not* (in the NT only in Ac, Paul, and He 4:1)

φοβῇ	*You fear*	μὴ λάβω αὐτό.	*that I will receive it.*

7. **oath** formulas or the like (in the NT, agreeing with Hebrew usage; ↑271e):

dependent clause subordinated by εἰ *(that) certainly not*

ὄμνυς	*You swear*	εἰ λήμψομαι αὐτό.	*that I will certainly not receive it.*

8. verbs/expressions of **volition** or the like (including those of necessity):

a) inf./ACI phrase (↑218a–218e; more generally all of 217–219)

θέλεις	*You wish*	ἐμὲ λαβεῖν αὐτό.	*that I receive it.*

b) dependent clause subordinated by ἵνα *that* or the like (widely used in KG/NT, not in CG; ↑272; CG similarly ὅπως + ind. fut. [sometimes subj.] after expressions denoting *to take care* or the like; ↑272c)

θέλεις	*You wish*	ἵνα λάβω αὐτό	*that I receive it.*

9. the verb forms **θέλεις/θέλετε** and **ὅρα/ὁρᾶτε** (↑272d):

a) asyndeton with deliberative subjunctive

θέλεις	*Do you wish*	λάβω αὐτό;	*that I receive it?*

b) asyndeton with prohibitive subjunctive

ὅρα	*See to it*	μὴ λάβῃς αὐτό.	*that you don't receive it.*

↑also the comparable use of καί with the force of *that*; ↑252.29,1a.

(ii) Conjunctional adverbial clauses

Temporal clauses (↑BR §286; BDF §381–383; 455; 367; 395) 276

1. Temporal clauses typically **function** as temporal adjuncts (↑259b/259e): they specify the time of the "action"/"situation" referred to by the superordinate construction answering questions such as "When?" or "How long?". Sometimes they function also as attributive modifiers (↑288). 276a

Subordinators of temporal clauses (↑251g; on text-level temporal relations 327ff):

a) in answer to the question **"When?"**:

• + **indicative** (CG also + iterative optative; ↑211i):	
ὅτε (less frequently [not in the NT, but inter alia LXX/CG] ἡνίκα, ὁπότε)	*when, after*
ὡς	+ ind. aor. *when, after* + ipf. *while, when*; + ind. pres. (rare) *while/when*
less frequently (otherwise causal; ↑277): ἐπειδή (NT: only Lk 7:1), CG/LXX also ἐπεί	*when, after*
• + prospective **subjunctive** (↑210i):	
ὅταν (< ὅτε ἄν) (less frequently ἡνίκα) CG also ὁπόταν	*when, whenever* (future reference: mostly + subj. aor., present or timeless reference: frequently + subj. pres.; NT at times + ipf./ind. aor.; ↑211i)
less frequently: ἐπάν (Paul/LXX also ὡς ἄν)	*when, as soon as*
πρίν	*before* (1)
(NT: usually + inf./ACI or + ἤ + inf./ACI; CG: negated main cl.: + ind. [single event], or + ἄν + subj. [subjective expectation or general event], affirmative main cl.: + inf./ACI or + ἤ + inf./ACI)	
CG also (+ iterative opt.; ↑211i; others classify this use as conditional; ↑280b; 282b):(2) εἰ (temporal-iterative)	*when = as often as*

(1) In Mt 15:2 ὅταν (contextually conditioned) seems to have the force of *before* (↑Mk 7:2).

(2) In the NT ὁσάκις ἐάν *as often as, whenever* is occasionally used instead (↑61c).

b) in answer to the question **"How long?"**:

+ **indicative** or + prospective **subjunctive** with ἄν (NT sometimes without; ↑210i):	
ἕως (οὗ/ὅτου) (less frequently + ind.) or ἄχρι(ς) (οὗ), CG also ἔστε	*until, as long as*
μέχρι(ς) (οὗ)	*until* (CG also *as long as*)
also ἐν ᾧ (sc. χρόνῳ) or ἐφ' ὅσον (sc. χρόνῳ)(1)	*while, as long as*
rarely also: ἀφ' οὗ (sc. χρόνου) or ἐξ οὗ (sc. χρόνου) (2) ἀφ' ἧς (sc. ἡμέρας; ↑260c; 289e), ὡς	 *since*

(1) ↑LSJ ἐν IVa and BDAG sub ὅσος 1b.
(2) ↑LSJ ἀπό II and ἐκ II2; ↑also 289e; similarly 260c.

Note that in the NT the "then"-clause (superordinate to the temporal clause) is sometimes introduced by means of καί; ↑252.29,1a.

2. Placement in **time** of the "actions"/"situations" referred to by the complex clause and the **verb forms** typically used, particularly the mood of the temporal clause:

	placement in time of "actions"/"situations" referred to by the complex clause:	verb forms typically used:
276b	a) **past**	**subo. cl.**: ind., mostly ind. aor. (↑199b) (neg. οὐ, ↑244), **main cl.**: with past tense value (↑199b)
	ὅτε ἐποίησε τοῦτο, **προσηύξαντο**.	*When he did this,* *they prayed.*
	b) **future** or **timeless** (↑also 282b)	**subo. cl.**: prospective subj. + ἄν (NT sometimes without ἄν; ↑210i) (neg. μή, ↑244),
276c	• a specific **future** "situation"	**main cl.**: with future tense value (including specific directives)
	ὅταν ποιήσῃ/ποιῇ τοῦτο, **προσεύξονται**.	*When/As soon as he does this,* *they will pray.*
276d	• a general **timeless** "situation" (1)	**main cl.**: with present tense value or timeless (including general directives)
	ὅταν ποιήσῃ/ποιῇ τοῦτο, **προσεύχονται**.	*When/Whenever he does this,* *they pray.*

(1) Some call this "present iterative" (on the "preterite/past iterative" ↑276e below), a somewhat imprecise term, as timeless "situations" may include future ones as well. Also ↑282a/282b on the prospective conditional case which in part is used synonymously.

c) something repeated in the **past** (1)	**subo. cl.**: CG: iterative opt. (neg. μή; ↑244); KG/NT: augment ind. (including aor.!) + ἄν/ἐάν (ὅτε + ἄν > ὅταν; ↑198c; 199f (neg. apparently οὐ), **main cl.**: mostly ipf.	276e
ὅτε (ὁπότε, also εἰ) **ποιοίη/ποιήσειεν** τοῦτο (CG)/ ὅταν **ἐποίησε/ἐποίει** τοῦτο (KG/NT), **προσηύχοντο**.	*Whenever he did this,* *they prayed.*	

(1) The CG use is normally called "preterite/past iterative"; for its KG/NT replacement ↑211i. Note that Herodotus also uses ἄν with ipf. (less frequently ind. aor.) in main clauses with iterative force (↑LSJ sub ἄν C).

3. Examples:

a) The subo. cl. "situation" appears as something **anterior** to the main cl. "situation": 276f

• anteriority in the **past**: subo. cl.: *when/after*

subo. cl.: mostly ὅτε or (less frequently, especially Lk, Jn, Ac) ὡς + ind. aor.;
main cl.: verb form with past tense value (↑276b).

ὅτε ἐτέλεσεν ὁ Ἰησοῦς τὰς παραβολὰς ταύτας, μετῆρεν ἐκεῖθεν. — *When Jesus finished these parables, he moved on from there.* (Mt 13:53)

↑also Mt 9:25; 13:26; Mk 7:17; 11:1 (historic pres.; ↑197d); 15:20; Lk 6:13; 23:33; Jn 13:12; 19:30; Ac 8:39; Ga 2:11f etc.

ὡς ἦλθεν ἐπὶ τὸν τόπον, ἀναβλέψας ὁ Ἰησοῦς εἶπεν … — *When Jesus came to the place, he looked up and said …* (Lk 19:5)

↑also Lk 2:39; 5:4; 11:1; Jn 6:12; 7:10; Ac 10:7; 13:29; 19:21 etc.

ἀφ' οὗ *since*: Lk 24:16 (main cl.: in the present); Re 16:18; ἐξ οὗ *since*: 2Chr 31:10 LXX.

• anteriority in the **present** or **timeless**: subo. cl.: *when, whenever*

subo. cl.: mostly ὅταν + subj. aor.;
main cl.: verb form with present tense value or timeless (including general directives; ↑276d; 276i).

Ὅταν δὲ τὸ ἀκάθαρτον πνεῦμα ἐξέλθῃ ἀπὸ τοῦ ἀνθρώπου, διέρχεται δι' ἀνύδρων τόπων … — *When an unclean spirit leaves a person, it passes through waterless regions …* (Mt 12:43)

↑also Mt 13:32; 23:15; 24:32f; Mk 4:15; 13:28; Lk 21:30; Jn 2:10; 10:4.

• anteriority in the **future**: subo. cl.: *when/after/as soon as*

subo. cl.: mostly ὅταν + subj. aor.;
main cl.: verb form with future tense value (↑276c).

Ὅταν δὲ ἔλθῃ ὁ υἱὸς τοῦ ἀνθρώπου … τότε καθίσει ἐπὶ θρόνου δόξης αὐτοῦ· *When the Son of Man comes …, then he will sit on his glorious throne.* (Mt 25:31)

↑also Mt 19:28; Lk 23:42; Jn 4:25; 7:31; 8:28; 13:19; 14:29; 15:26; Ac 23:35; 24:22; 1Cor 13:10 etc.

2× in Paul: ὡς ἄν + subj. aor.:

τοῦτον μὲν οὖν ἐλπίζω πέμψαι **ὡς ἂν** ἀφίδω τὰ περὶ ἐμὲ ἐξαυτῆς· *Therefore I hope to send him as soon as I see how things go with me.* (Php 2:23)

↑also 1Cor 11:34.

ἀφ' οὗ *when once*: Lk 13:25.

276g b) Subo. and main cl. "situations" appear as something (at least partly) **simultaneous**:

• simultaneity in the **past**: subo. cl.: *when/while*

subo. cl.: especially ὅτε or ὡς (also↑276a);
subo. cl./main cl.: verb forms with past tense value (especially ipf.)

ὅτε ἦς νεώτερος, ἐζώννυες σεαυτόν … *When you were younger, you used to gird/dress yourself.* (Jn 21:18)

οὐκ ἦν μετ' αὐτῶν **ὅτε** ἦλθεν Ἰησοῦς. *He was not with them, when Jesus came* (Jn 20:24)

↑also Mk 14:12; 15:41; Jn 12:17; 17:12; Ac 22:20; Ro 6:20; 7:5; 1Cor 13:11 etc.

οὐχὶ ἡ καρδία ἡμῶν καιομένη ἦν ἐν ἡμῖν **ὡς** ἐλάλει ἡμῖν ἐν τῇ ὁδῷ **ὡς** διήνοιγεν ἡμῖν τὰς γραφάς; *Didn't our hearts burn within us while he talked with us on the road, while he opened the Scriptures to us?* (Lk 24:32)

↑also Jn 8:7; 20:11; Ac 1:10; 16:4; 19:9; 22:25.

ἠνάγκασεν τοὺς μαθητὰς ἐμβῆναι εἰς τὸ πλοῖον καὶ προάγειν …, **ἕως οὗ** ἀπολύσῃ τοὺς ὄχλους. *He made the disciples get into the boat and go on ahead …, while he dismissed the crowds.* (Mt 14:22)

• simultaneity in the **present** or **timeless**: subo. cl.: *when, whenever, while*

subo. cl.: mostly ὅταν + subj. pres. (also↑276a);
main cl.: verb form with present tense value or timeless (including general directives; ↑276d; 276i).

ὅταν ἐν τῷ κόσμῳ ὦ, φῶς εἰμι τοῦ κόσμου. *While/As long as I am in the world, I am the light of the world.* (Jn 9:5)

↑also Mt 5:11; Mk 11:25 (subo. cl.: ind. pres.); 14:7; Lk 6:22; 11:34; Jn 8:44; 1Cor 3:4.

less frequently:

ἡμᾶς δεῖ ἐργάζεσθαι … **ἕως** ἡμέρα ἐστίν. *We must work … while it is day.* (Jn 9:4)

… μήποτε ἰσχύει **ὅτε** ζῇ ὁ διαθέμενος.	*… it is not in force as long as the one who made it is alive.* (He 9:17)

Also ἐφ' ὅσον: 2Pe 1:13.

ἴσθι εὐνοῶν τῷ ἀντιδίκῳ σου ταχύ, **ἕως ὅτου** εἶ μετ' αὐτοῦ ἐν τῇ ὁδῷ …	*Come to terms quickly with your accuser while you are on the way to court with him …* (Mt 5:25)

↑also Mt 26:36; Mk 14:32.

παρακαλεῖτε ἑαυτούς …, **ἄχρις οὗ** τὸ σήμερον καλεῖται …	*You must warn each other … as long as it is called "Today", …* (He 3:13)

- simultaneity in the **future**: subo. cl.: *when/while/as long as*

subo. cl.: usually ὅταν + subj. (mostly pres.), also ὅτε/ὡς + ind., moreover signifying "while"/"as long as": ἕως (ὅτου) + subj. with ἄν or + ind. pres., occasionally ἄχρις οὗ + ind. pres.;
main cl.: verb form with future tense value (including specific directives; ↑276c).

ὅταν προσεύχησθε οὐκ ἔσεσθε ὡς οἱ ὑποκριταί …	*When/Whenever you pray, do not be like the hypocrites …* (Mt 6:5)

↑also Mt 6:2.16; 10:23; Mk 13:11; Lk 11:2; 12:11; 1Th 5:3.

ὅταν λέγωσιν· εἰρήνη …, τότε αἰφνίδιος αὐτοῖς ἐφίσταται ὄλεθρος …	*While they are saying, "Peace …", destruction will come on them suddenly …* (1Th 5:3)
ἔρχεται ὥρα **ὅτε** οὐκέτι ἐν παροιμίαις λαλήσω ὑμῖν. (ὅτε-cl.: Attr of ὥρα; ↑288b)	*A time/the hour is coming when I will no longer speak to you in figures of speech.* (Jn 16:25)

↑also Lk 17:22; Jn 4:21.23; 5:25; 9:4; Ro 2:16; 2Tm 4:3.

περιπατεῖτε **ὡς** τὸ φῶς ἔχετε.	*Walk while you have the light.* (Jn 12:35)

↑also Lk 12:58; Jn 12:36; Mt 9:15 (ἐφ' ὅσον).

1× in Paul: ὡς ἄν + subj. pres.:

… ἐπιποθίαν δὲ ἔχων τοῦ ἐλθεῖν πρὸς ὑμᾶς …, **ὡς ἂν** πορεύωμαι εἰς τὴν Σπανίαν	*… I desire … to come to you when I travel to Spain.* (Ro 15:23f)

c) The subo. cl. "situation" appears as something **posterior** to the main cl. "situation": 276h

subo. cl.: *until*

subo. cl.: mostly ἕως (οὗ/ὅτου), less frequently ἄχρι(ς)/μέχρι(ς) (οὗ) (also↑276a)
+ ind aor. or
+ subj. aor., usually + ἄν (indicating that the "situation" is dependent on certain circumstances).

subo. cl.: *before*

subo. cl.: πρίν in the NT mostly + inf./ACI phrase with or without ἤ. (also↑276a).

- posteriority in the **past**:

καὶ οὐκ ἐγίνωσκεν αὐτὴν **ἕως οὗ** ἔτεκεν υἱόν.
He did not have sexual relations with her until she gave birth to a son. (Mt 1:25)

↑also Mt 24:39; Jn 9:18.

ηὔξησεν ὁ λαός … **ἄχρι οὗ** ἀνέστη βασιλεὺς ἕτερος
The people increased in number … until another king came to power (Ac 7:17f)

↑also Ga 3:19.

πρὶν ἢ συνελθεῖν αὐτοὺς εὑρέθη ἐν γαστρὶ ἔχουσα ἐκ πνεύματος ἁγίου.
Before they came together, she was found to be pregnant from the Holy Spirit. (Mt 1:18)

↑also Ac 7:2.

- posteriority in the **present** or **timeless**:

οὐχὶ ἅπτει λύχνον … καὶ ζητεῖ ἐπιμελῶς **ἕως οὗ** εὕρῃ;
Doesn't she light a lamp … and search carefully until she finds it? (Lk 15:8)

τὸν θάνατον τοῦ κυρίου καταγγέλλετε **ἄχρι οὗ** ἔλθῃ.
You proclaim the Lord's death until he comes. (1Cor 11:26)

↑also 1Cor 15:25; μέχρις οὗ + subj. aor.: Ga 4:19; Eph 4:13.

less frequently:

… ὅτι οὐκ ἔστιν ἔθος Ῥωμαίοις χαρίζεσθαί τινα ἄνθρωπον **πρὶν ἢ** ὁ κατηγορούμενος κατὰ πρόσωπον ἔχοι τοὺς κατηγόρους …
… that it was not the Roman custom of the Romans to hand over anyone before the accused has faced the accusers … (Ac 25:16)

νῦν εἴρηκα ὑμῖν **πρὶν** γενέσθαι …
Now I have told you before it happens … (Jn 14:29)

- posteriority in the **future**:

οὐ μὴ ἐξέλθῃς ἐκεῖθεν, **ἕως ἂν** ἀποδῷς τὸν ἔσχατον κοδράντην.
You will never get out until you have paid the last penny. (Mt 5:26)

↑also Mt 5:18; 10:11; 17:9; Mk 6:10; 12:36; Lk 9:27; 13:8; Jn 13:38; Ac 23:12; 1Cor 4:5 etc.

Ἰερουσαλὴμ ἔσται πατουμένη ὑπὸ ἐθνῶν, **ἄχρι οὗ** πληρωθῶσιν καιροὶ ἐθνῶν.
Jerusalem will be trampled on by the Gentiles, until the times of the Gentiles are fulfilled. (Lk 21:24)

Mk 13:30 (μέρχρις οὗ + subj. aor.); Re 2:25 (ἄχρις οὗ + fut.).

πρὶν ἀλέκτορα φωνῆσαι τρὶς ἀπαρνήσῃ με.
Before the cock crows, you will disown me three times. (Mt 26:34)

↑also Mt 26:75; Jn 4:49; Ac 2:20.

d) Subo. and main cl. “situations” appear as **something repeated**: 276i
(↑especially 276e, but in part also the cases with a timeless reference in 276f–276h)

	whenever, as often as
• repetition in the **past**:	
ὅταν αὐτὸν **ἐθεώρουν**, **προσέπιπτον** αὐτῷ …	*Whenever the unclean spirits saw him, they fell down before him …* (Mk 3:11)

↑also Mk 11:19 (subo. cl.: ὅταν + ind. aor.; main cl.: ipf.).

This KG/NT use replaces the following CG combination with iterative optative (↑198c; 199f; 211i):

ἐθήρευεν ἀπὸ ἵππου **ὁπότε** γυμνάσαι **βούλοιτο** ἑαυτόν.	*He used to hunt on horseback whenever he wanted to exercise himself.* (Xenophon, Anabasis 1.2.7)
εἴ πού τι **ὁρῴη** βρωτόν, **διεδίδου** …	*Whenever he saw anything edible, he would distribute it …* (Xenophon, Anabasis 4.5.8)

• repetition in the **present** or **timeless** (↑276d, especially with forms of the present stem [↑194a]):

ὅταν συνέρχησθε, ἕκαστος ψαλμὸν ἔχει …	*Whenever you come together, each one has a hymn …* (1Cor 14:26)

Occasionally with ὁσάκις ἐάν + subj. *as often as*: 1Cor 11:25f; in 2Tm 1:3 with ὡς (+ ind. pres.).

• repetition in the **future** (↑276c, especially with forms of the present stem [↑194a]):

Ὅταν οὖν **ποιῇς** ἐλεημοσύνην, μὴ σαλπίσῃς ἔμπροσθέν σου.	*So whenever you give to the needy, don't sound a trumpet before you.* (Mt 6:2)

↑also Mt 6:5.16.

On constructions often in competition with temporal clauses (especially inf./ACI phrases with an article governed by prepositions and participle phrases) ↑259e; on the functionally related conditional clauses ↑280b/282b.

Causal clauses (↑BR §274; BDF §456; Z §416–422) 277

1. Causal clauses typically **function** as causal adjuncts (in a narrower sense): they specify the reason for the “action”/“situation” referred to by the superordinate construction answering questions such as “Why?”, “For what reason?” (↑259b/259g). At times they function also as attributive modifiers (↑288). 277a

Subordinators of causal clauses (↑251h; on text-level causal relations and their connection with the underlying presupposed If-Then-relationship ↑333; on negation [like main clauses] ↑245b/245c):

ὅτι, διότι (= διὰ τοῦτο ὅτι)(1) CG also ὡς (NT 1×: Ac 22:11), NT also καθώς	*because, since* (sometimes *for* appears to be more adequate contextually)
ἐπεί (↑Lat. *cum*)	*as/since*; also *(since/for) otherwise*
ἐπειδή (and CG ἐπείπερ)	*as/since* (Lk 1:1 ἐπειδήπερ *since*)
less frequently:	

ὅπου (apparently so in 1Cor 3:3)	*since/because* (mostly adv. *where/to where*; ↑61c)
ἀνθ' ὧν = ἀντὶ τούτων ὅτι(2)	*in return for which* = *because* (↑289e)
NT also καθότι (Lk/Ac), at times ἐν ᾧ or ἐφ' ᾧ (= ἐν/ἐπὶ τούτῳ ὅτι; ↑184j; 289e)(3)	*because* (↑289e)
CG rarely ὅτε and ὁπότε (↑Lat. *quando*)	*since/because, granted that*

(1) ↑LSJ s.v.
(2) ↑LSJ sub ἀντί III3.
(3) ↑BDAG sub ἐπί II1bγ and sub ἐν III3a.

Note that occasionally a ὅτι-clause does not serve to give a cause or (logically valid) reason for the "situation" referred to by the superordinate clause, but instead, changing to a **symptom-oriented perspective**, it rather mentions certain facts (signs, indications) that show that such a "situation" does exist, e.g. (↑also 333d):

… ἀφέωνται αἱ ἁμαρτίαι αὐτῆς αἱ πολλαί, **ὅτι** ἠγάπησεν πολύ·	*… her many sins have been forgiven, so/hence/ that's why she has shown great love.* (Lk 7:47)

As suggested by the context, this verse does not mean: Her many sins have been forgiven because (by reason of the fact that) she has shown great love. Rather: The fact that she has shown great love shows that her many sins have been forgiven. So, most EVV correctly render the ὅτι not as "because", but as "for" or (more clearly) as "so", "thus", "hence", "that's why", or the like.

277b 2. Basically, the same moods are used here as in independent declarative clauses (↑267). In CG the oblique opt. may be used instead, when a subjective reason is given and the predicate verb of the superordinate clause expresses a past tense value (↑211f/211g; 270h).

277c 3. Examples:

ὅτι εἶπόν σοι ὅτι εἶδόν σε ὑποκάτω τῆς συκῆς πιστεύεις;	*Do you believe because I told you that I saw you under the fig-tree?* (Jn 1:50)

↑also Lk 13:2; 19:17; Jn 20:29; Ro 5:5; 6:15; 8:29; 10:9; 11:36; 1Cor 12:15f.

οὐκ εἰμὶ ἱκανὸς καλεῖσθαι ἀπόστολος, **διότι** ἐδίωξα τὴν ἐκκλησίαν τοῦ θεοῦ.	*I am unfit to be called an apostle, because I persecuted God's church.* (1Cor 15:9)

↑also Lk 1:13; Ac 18:10; Ro 8:7; Php 2:26; He 11:5.23.

δοῦλε πονηρέ, πᾶσαν τὴν ὀφειλὴν ἐκείνην ἀφῆκά σοι, **ἐπεὶ** παρεκάλεσάς με.	*You wicked servant, I forgave you all that debt because you begged me.* (Mt 18:32)

↑also Mt 21:46; Jn 13:29; 19:31; He 2:14; 11:11.

ἐπειδὴ ἀπωθεῖσθε αὐτόν … ἰδοὺ στρεφόμεθα εἰς τὰ ἔθνη.	*Since you reject it* (God's word) *… we are now turning to the Gentiles.* (Ac 13:46)

↑also Ac 14:12; 1Cor 15:21; Php 2:26.

διώκω δὲ εἰ καὶ καταλάβω, **ἐφ' ᾧ** καὶ κατελήμφθην ὑπὸ Χριστοῦ.	*But I press on to take hold of it because I have also been taken hold of by Christ.* (Php 3:12)

↑also 2Cor 5:4; Ro 5:12; with ἐν ᾧ: Ro 8:3; He 2:18; 6:17.

καθὼς οὐκ ἐδοκίμασαν τὸν θεὸν ἔχειν ἐν ἐπιγνώσει παρέδωκεν αὐτούς … | *And since they did not think it worthwhile to acknowledge God, he gave them over …* (Ro 1:28)

↑also Jn 17:2; 1Cor 1:6; 5:7; Eph 1:4; 4:32; Php 1:7.

οὐκ ἔξεστιν βαλεῖν αὐτὰ εἰς τὸν κορβανᾶν, **ἐπεὶ** τιμὴ αἵματός ἐστιν. | *It is not lawful to put it into the treasury, since it is blood money.* (Mt 27:6)

↑also (ἐπειδή) Lk 11:6; 1Cor 1:22.

Note this special use of ἐπεί *(since/for) otherwise* (instead of *because/since*; ↑280b):

… ἐπὶ δὲ σὲ χρηστότης θεοῦ, ἐὰν ἐπιμένῃς τῇ χρηστότητι, **ἐπεὶ** καὶ σὺ ἐκκοπήσῃ | *… but God's kindness to you, provided you continue in his kindness; otherwise you too will be cut off.* (Ro 11:22)

↑also Ro 3:6; 1Cor 5:10; 7:14

↑259g on constructions often in competition with causal clauses, especially inf./ACI phrases with an article governed by prepositions and participle phrases, but also relative clauses with causal force.

Purpose clauses (↑BR §276; BDF §369; Z §340–345; 351–353) 278

1. Purpose clauses typically **function** as purpose adjuncts: they specify the purpose of the "action"/"situation" referred to by the superordinate construction answering questions such as "What for?" (↑259b/259j). At times they function also as attributive modifiers (↑288). 278a

Subordinators of purpose clauses (↑251i; on text-level purpose relations and their connection with the underlying presupposed If-Then-relationship ↑333):

ἵνα, ὅπως, also (in the NT very occasionally): ὡς mostly + inf./ACI phrase; especially CG at times: ὅπως/ὡς + ἄν	*in order that* (↑Lat. *ut*)
ἵνα μή, ὅπως μή or simple μή/μήποτε	*in order that … not* (↑Lat. *nē*)
Usually + subj. (↑210i); CG mostly + oblique opt., when the superordinate clause refers to the past (↑211f/211g; 270g); in the NT at times + ind. fut. replacing subj. (↑202j).	
↑KG/NT occasionally: ὥστε + inf./ACI (↑221b; 279)	*in order to, in order that*
CG also ἐφ' ᾧ or ἐφ' ᾧτε + inf./ACI phrase (or + ind. fut.)	*in order to/in order that* (more frequently *on condition that*; ↑280b; 184j; 289e)

↑272 on ἵνα-clauses or the like as a KG replacement of inf./ACI phrases; ↑279a on their use with the force of a result clause.

278b 2. Examples:

οὐ γὰρ ἀπέστειλεν ὁ θεὸς τὸν υἱὸν εἰς τὸν κόσμον **ἵνα** κρίνῃ τὸν κόσμον, ἀλλ' **ἵνα** σωθῇ ὁ κόσμος δι' αὐτοῦ.

For God did not sent his Son into the world to condemn the world, but in order that the world might be saved through him. (Jn 3:17)

καὶ ἡγοῦμαι σκύβαλα, **ἵνα** Χριστὸν κερδήσω.

And I count them as rubbish, in order that I may gain Christ. (Php 3:8)

↑also Mt 19:16; Ro 1:13; 5:20; 6:4; 8:4; 15:4; 1Cor 9:25; He 4:16 et pass.

οὕτως λαμψάτω τὸ φῶς ὑμῶν ἔμπροσθεν τῶν ἀνθρώπων, **ὅπως** ἴδωσιν ὑμῶν τὰ καλὰ ἔργα καὶ δοξάσωσιν τὸν πατέρα ὑμῶν τὸν ἐν τοῖς οὐρανοῖς.

In the same way, let your light shine before people, so that they may see your good deeds and give glory to your Father in heaven. (Mt 5:16)

… **ἵνα μὴ** ὑπεραίρωμαι, ἐδόθη μοι σκόλοψ τῇ σαρκί.

… so that I would not exalt myself, I was given a thorn in my flesh. (2Cor 12:7)

↑also Lk 16:28; Jn 3:20; 5:14; 2Cor 4:7; He 3:13; 1Jn 2:1.

… καὶ τὸ πρόσωπόν σου νίψαι, **ὅπως μὴ** φανῇς τοῖς ἀνθρώποις νηστεύων …

… and wash your face, so that your fasting isn't obvious to others … (Mt 6:17f)

↑also Ac 20:16.

ἀλλ' οὐδενὸς λόγου ποιοῦμαι τὴν ψυχὴν τιμίαν ἐμαυτῷ **ὡς** τελειώσω (NA τελειῶσαι) τὸν δρόμον μου.

But I do not count my life of any value to myself; my purpose is to finish my course. (Ac 20:24 Var.)

↑also Lk 9:52.

ἀλλὰ ὑπωπιάζω μου τὸ σῶμα καὶ δουλαγωγῶ, **μή** πως ἄλλοις κηρύξας αὐτὸς ἀδόκιμος γένωμαι.

But I discipline my body and enslave it, so that after proclaiming to others I myself will not be disqualified. (1Cor 9:27)

↑also Mk 13:36 (μή); Ac 27:42 (μή τις); μήποτε: Mt 4:6; Lk 12:58; Ac 5:39 (↑also 247b); He 2:1.

… ἤγαγον αὐτὸν ἕως ὀφρύος τοῦ ὄρους … **ὥστε** κατακρημνίσαι αὐτόν.

… they led him to the brow of the hill … in order to hurl him off the cliff. (Lk 4:29)

↑also Lk 20:20.

↑259j on constructions often in competition with purpose clauses, especially inf./ACI phrases with and without an article governed by prepositions and participle phrases (p.c. fut./pres.), but also relative clauses with causal force. ↑273f on functionally comparable εἰ-clauses.

Result clauses (↑BR §275; BDF §391; Z §350–353) 279

1. Result clauses typically **function** as result adjuncts: they specify the consequence or result of the "action"/"situation" referred to by the superordinate construction answering questions such as "With what result?" (↑259b/259i). At times they function also as attributive modifiers (↑288). 279a

Subordinators of result clauses (↑251j; on text-level result relations and their connection with the underlying presupposed If-Then-relationship ↑333):

ὥστε (CG less frequently, NT rarely ὡς)	*so that (= with the result that)*[(1)]
+ indicative (rarely attested in the NT)	mostly reference to actual results (neg. οὐ; ↑244)
+ inf./ACI phrase (in the NT standard; ↑221c)	KG/NT reference to conceivable or actual results; CG mostly reference to conceivable results (neg. μή; ↑244)
KG/NT less frequently (↑278; 272a): ἵνα + subj.	*so that (= with the result that)*
Apparently in questions also ὅτι *(so) that* (= *with the result that*; ↑279a); ↑Hebr. כִּי *kî*, GKC §107u; BDF §456; Z §420; BDAG s.v. 5c. (↑e.g. He 2:6).	

(1) Frequently also: *so/in such a way/such … that* or the like.

Note that alongside its typical use as a subordinator ὥστε **fairly frequently** serves to introduce **independent clauses** and is then translatable as *for this reason, therefore, so.*[19] This always applies to ὥστε-clauses whose predicator (predicate verb) is an imperative, not infrequently also (as contextually indicated) in the case of indicatives (↑BDAG s.v. 1a/b).

2. Examples:

a) Quite clearly typical use of ὥστε introducing a **subordinate clause**: 279b

οὕτως γὰρ ἠγάπησεν ὁ θεὸς τὸν κόσμον, **ὥστε** τὸν υἱὸν τὸν μονογενῆ ἔδωκεν …	*For God so loved the world that he gave his one and only Son …* (Jn 3:16)

An actual result is indicated (= CG). The only other unambiguous NT instance of this use is Ga 2:13.

Πόθεν ἡμῖν ἐν ἐρημίᾳ ἄρτοι τοσοῦτοι **ὥστε** χορτάσαι ὄχλον τοσοῦτον;	*Where could we get so many loaves to satisfy so great a crowd?* (Mt 15:33)

A conceivable result is indicated (= CG).

ἱκανὸν τῷ τοιούτῳ ἡ ἐπιτιμία αὕτη …, **ὥστε** … μᾶλλον ὑμᾶς χαρίσασθαι καὶ παρακαλέσαι.	*This punishment … is sufficient for that person, so that … you should rather forgive and comfort him.* (2Cor 2:6f)

An expected result is indicated (= CG).

19 οὖν and ἄρα (usually postpositives; ↑128b p. 180) may be used in a comparable way (↑251e).

ἐθεράπευσεν αὐτόν, **ὥστε** τὸν κωφὸν λαλεῖν καὶ βλέπειν.	*He healed the mute man so that he could speak and see.* (Mt 12:22)

An actual result is indicated (≠ CG).
↑also Mt 13:2; 27:14; Mk 4:1; 9:26; Ac 14:1; 16:26; 1Cor 1:7; 5:1; 2Cor 3:7; Php 1:13.

ῥαββί, τίς ἥμαρτεν, οὗτος ἢ οἱ γονεῖς αὐτοῦ, **ἵνα** τυφλὸς γεννηθῇ;	*Rabbi, who sinned, this man or his parents, that he was born blind?* (Jn 9:2)

b) ὥστε more likely to introduce a **main clause** (↑punctuation in text editions):

- imperative as the predicator of ὥστε-clause, e.g.:

τῷ δὲ θεῷ χάρις τῷ διδόντι ἡμῖν τὸ νῖκος διὰ τοῦ κυρίου ἡμῶν Ἰησοῦ Χριστοῦ. **Ὥστε** … ἑδραῖοι γίνεσθε …	*But thanks be to God who gives us the victory through our Lord Jesus Christ. Therefore … be steadfast …* (1Cor 15:57f)

↑1Cor 4:5; Php 2:12.

- indicative as the predicator of ὥστε-clause, e.g.:

… καὶ ἔσονται οἱ δύο εἰς σάρκα μίαν. **ὥστε** οὐκέτι εἰσὶν δύο ἀλλὰ σὰρξ μία.	*"… and the two will become one flesh". So they are no longer two but one flesh.* (Mt 19:5f)

↑also Ro 7:4; 13:2 et pass.

↑259i on constructions often in competition with result clauses, especially inf./ACI phrases even without ὥστε/ὡς, inf./ACI phrases with or without τοῦ as well as such with an article governed by prepositions, but also relative clauses with qualitative-consequential force.

280 Conditional clauses: preliminaries and overview

(↑BR §277; BDF §371–376; 385.2; 360; Z §299–334)

280a 1. Conditional clauses typically **function** as conditional adjuncts: they specify the condition that the "action"/"situation" referred to by the superordinate construction is subject to, answering questions such as "In what case?", "Under what condition?" (↑259b/259h).
Between a conditional (subordinate) clause and the superordinate construction, typically a main clause, there is a particularly close functional connection. For this reason the two clauses involving a conditional relationship are best treated as a whole. Such a complex sentence, here called "**conditional construction**", consists of
a) an ***if*-clause**,[20] the conditional clause, traditionally "protasis"[21], specifying the condition, and

20 In formal English conjunctions such as *if* are sometimes replaced by inversion, e.g. ***Had they** not been so uncooperative, I might have forgiven them and not complained* (↑Carter §458).
21 ↑πρότᾰσις, εως, ἡ, (προτείνω) lit. *putting forward, that which is put forward* (↑LSJ s.v.)

b) a ***then*-clause,**[22] the main clause (which may be a compound sentence) expressing the consequence of the condition being fulfilled, traditionally "apodosis"[23] (mostly placed after the protasis);[24] it is typically a declarative clause, but desiderative or interrogative clauses (including rhetorical questions; ↑269a) are possible as well.

An example of a typical conditional construction is Jn 8:31:

if-clause/protasis (subordinate clause):

ἐὰν ὑμεῖς μείνητε ἐν τῷ λόγῳ τῷ ἐμῷ, — *If you continue in my word,*

The speaker (Jesus) specifies the condition that being his disciples is subject to.

then-clause/conclusion/apodosis (main clause):

ἀληθῶς μαθηταί μού ἐστε. — *[then] you are really my disciples.*

The consequence of the condition being fulfilled is expressed by a declarative clause: the addressees are really Jesus' disciples.

Examples with a desiderative and a interrogative clause functioning as a *then*-clause:

ἐάν ἐμοί τις διακονῇ, ἐμοὶ ἀκολουθείτω. — *If anyone serves me, he must follow me.* (Jn 12:26)

ἐὰν γὰρ ἀγαπήσητε τοὺς ἀγαπῶντας ὑμᾶς, τίνα μισθὸν ἔχετε; — *For if you love those who love you, what reward do you have?* (Mt 5:46)

2. **Subordinators** of conditional clauses (↑251k; on text-level conditional relations 280b
and their connection with the underlying presupposed If-Then-relationship ↑333):

εἰ or ἐάν (< εἰ + ἄν) (less frequently ἄν, CG also ἤν)	*if* (for other translational equivalents ↑280e and 280a[20])
coordinated conditional clauses also (1Cor 12:26; 2Cor 1:6):	
εἴτε – εἴτε	*if – (or/and) if, whether – or*

Generally speaking, *if*-clauses are negated by means of μή, NT usage, however, mostly prefers οὐ in *if*-clauses of the indefinite type. In *then*-clauses, being main clauses, the rules for negating main clauses apply (thus by means of οὐ in declarative clauses and by means of μή in desiderative ones; for details ↑244; 245b; 246a).

22 While the concept of "then" is always presupposed, it is expressed comparatively rarely (for emphasis) both in English (↑Carter §73) and in Ancient Greek (ἄρα ↑251e; 252.4; in the NT sometimes also 'apodotic' καί ↑252.29.1a).

23 ↑ἀπόδοσις, εως, ἡ, (ἀποδίδωμι) lit. *giving what one owes, restoration* (↑Montanari s.v.)

24 Note that as a general rule the *if*-clause expresses the factual condition and the *then*-clause the factual consequence. If the propositions of the two clauses are interchanged a transition takes place from a fact-oriented perspective to a symptom-oriented one (↑331d). ↑DuG9: 1099ff.

εἰ and ἐάν may **combine with other particles**; the most important combinations are:

εἴ γε	*if indeed/really* (↑252.10)
εἴπερ	*if indeed, if it is true* (the assumption here is more certain than in the case of εἴ γε, in parts it is close to the causal meaning *since*; ↑252.19; 252.53)
εἰ μή	*if not/unless*, also *except* (in the NT rarely with a finite verb; ↑286)
CG εἰ μὴ ἄρα	*unless perhaps*
εἰ δὲ μή γε	*otherwise*
εἰ καί	*even if* (↑also 286)
ἐὰν μή	*if not/unless*; also *except that* (with or without finite verb; ↑286b)
ἐὰν καί	*if (even)*
ἐάνπερ	*if indeed, if only, supposing that*

Noteworthy points:

a) In relative clauses of KG ἐάν frequently replaces ἄν (placed after the relative pronoun/adverb, so recognizable as such); on the remaining functions of εἰ and ἐάν ↑252.18/252.19.

b) ἐπεί is used in a special way: on the one hand as a subordinator of causal clauses, translatable as *because/since* (↑277a), on the other with a causal-conditional force, translatable as *(for/since) otherwise* (presupposing the ellipsis [↑293a] of an *if*-clause such as "If it does not/would not happen"). For examples ↑277c p. 519.

c) CG also uses ἐφ᾽ ᾧ or ἐφ᾽ ᾧτε + inf./ACI phrase (or + ind. fut.) translatable as *on condition that* (also *in order to/in order that*; ↑184j; 278a; 289e), e.g.:

ἔφασαν ἀποδώσειν (τοὺς νεκροὺς) ἐφ᾽ ᾧ μὴ καίειν τὰς οἰκίας.	*[The barbarians] said that they would hand over [the dead] on the condition that [the Greeks] should not burn their houses.* (Xenophon, Anabasis 4.2.19)

d) On ὥσπερ ἂν εἰ introducing a conditional comparison (CG) ↑287c.

280c 3. Ancient Greek has a number of fairly clearly definable types of conditional constructions. Based on various conditional functions to be differentiated one usually distinguishes **four major cases**; these are linked to certain grammatical properties, i.e. the subordinator, the verb forms (moods and tenses) used in the *if*-clause and the *then*-clause and the presence or absence of the particle ἄν in the *then*-clause:

if-clause/protasis/subordinate clause	*then*-clause/apodosis/main clause
1. **indefinite** conditional case (also misleadingly called "real"; ↑281): the relationship of the *if*-clause proposition to reality is left open ("indefinite"), the conclusion is, however, presented as (logically) necessary.	
εἰ + ind. of any "tense"/aspect stem	any mood

<table>
<tr><td>εἰ τοῦτο ποιεῖς
(or ποιήσεις/ἐποίησας etc.),

If you do this
(or will do/have done this),

(I leave it open whether or not this is so),</td><td>ἡμᾶς βλάπτεις
(or βλάψεις/ἔβλαψας or βλάψον/μὴ βλάψῃς etc.).
you harm us
(or will harm/have harmed us or harm/don't harm us! etc.)
(I say this thinking that this is bound to follow).</td></tr>
<tr><td colspan="2">2. prospective conditional case (the unmarked case; ↑282):
the if-clause proposition refers to something one can or must expect.
ἐάν + subj. |
frequently subdivided (as a rule of thumb only, well-defined boundaries lacking between them; contextual/pragmatic factors are of primary importance!) into

a) specific prospective conditional case:
the if-clause proposition refers to something one can or must expect in the future.</td></tr>
<tr><td>ἐάν + subj.
("tenses" dependent on aspect considerations)</td><td>mostly verb form with future tense value (also specific directives)</td></tr>
<tr><td>ἐὰν τοῦτο ποιήσῃς (ποιῇς),
If you do this,

(something one can or must expect in the future)</td><td>ἡμᾶς βλάψεις (or e.g. μὴ βλάψῃς).
you will harm us
(or e.g. don't harm us!).</td></tr>
<tr><td colspan="2">b) general prospective conditional case:
the if-clause proposition refers to something one can or must generally expect.</td></tr>
<tr><td>ἐάν + subj.

("tenses" dependent on aspect considerations)</td><td>mostly verb form with present tense value or timeless (also general directives)</td></tr>
<tr><td>ἐάν τις τοῦτο ποιῇ (ποιήσῃ),
If someone does this,
(something one can or must generally expect),</td><td>χαίρουσιν οἱ ἄγγελοι τοῦ θεοῦ.
God's angels rejoice.</td></tr>
<tr><td colspan="2">3. potential conditional case (only partially attested in the NT; ↑283):
the "situation" referred to by the if-clause is presented as possible or as at least conceivable, the conclusion, too, is presented as a mere possibility (however, presented as [logically] necessary when the then-clause predicator is an ind. pres./pf./fut./aor. form).</td></tr>
<tr><td>εἰ + opt.</td><td>opt. with ἄν</td></tr>
<tr><td>εἰ τοῦτο ποιήσαις (ποιοίης),
If you should do this,
(and this something I consider conceivable).</td><td>ἡμᾶς ἂν βλάψαις (βλάπτοις).
you may/might/could harm us .</td></tr>
<tr><td colspan="2">("tenses" dependent on aspect considerations)</td></tr>
</table>

4. **remote** (or "unreal") conditional case (↑284):
the "situation" referred to by the *if*-clause is presented as counterfactual,
the conclusion is, however, as (logically) necessary,
thus the "situation" referred to by the *then*-clause as counterfactual, too.

εἰ + augment indicative	augment indicative with ἄν
εἰ τοῦτο **ἐποίεις** (or **ἐποίησας**, **ἐπεποιήκεις**), *If you did this/had done this,*	ἡμᾶς **ἂν ἔβλαπτες** (or **ἔβλαψας**, **ἐβεβλάφεις**) *you would harm us/you would have harmed us*

(but you do not/did not do it, thus you do not/did not harm us).

("tenses" basically dependent on aspect considerations; but ↑284)

For mixed conditional constructions and special cases ↑285.

4. Additional observations regarding conditional constructions:

280d a) Differences between CG and KG/NT usage:

• In KG the **potential** conditional case was disappearing; and in the NT there are only a handful of incomplete instances (↑211a). The fact that the use of ἐάν-clauses greatly expanded at the cost of εἰ-clauses has likely to do with this process (↑282b).

• On the shift in meaning assumed by some (probably wrongly) with regard to the indefinite conditional case ↑281a.

• On the "preterite/past iterative" and "present iterative" ↑276d/276e (temporal clauses); also ↑282b.

280e b) With regard to conditional constructions **English** and **Ancient Greek** usage agree with each other only to limited extent: the number of grammatically marked conditional cases differs as does the way they are used. When interpreting and translating texts one obviously needs to take due account of such differences.

The following points are especially noteworthy (↑also 331b–331g):

• While in Ancient Greek conditional clauses would normally have been introduced by εἰ or ἐάν, in English not only the standard subordinating **conjunction** ***if*** may be used, but (depending on the context) also expressions such as *providing/provided that, on condition that, in the event that, in case* (↑Carter §456), sometimes in formal contexts also inversion replacing it (↑280a[20]).

• In **English two basic types** of conditional constructions are usually distinguished (↑Aarts: 250; Carter §450):

Type 1: "remote" (also "unreal" or "hypothetical") conditional constructions whose "conditions are not likely to be fulfilled" (↑Aarts: 250) and which occur in two basic patterns (↑Carter §449):

1.1: *if* + simple past tense + modal verb with future-in-the-past reference: "the speaker or writer states that the condition must be fulfilled for the present or future to be different", e.g.:
If he came here, we would offer him some help.

1.2: *if* + past perfect tense + modal verb with future-in-the-past reference + *have* + *-ed* participle: "the speaker or writer is talking about a past event which did not happen, and therefore things are different from how they might have been", e.g.:
If he had come here, we would have offered him some help.

Type 2: "open" (also "real") conditional constructions whose conditions "can realistically be fulfilled" (↑Aarts: 250) and whose basic pattern is (↑Carter §449):
if + present simple tense + modal verb with future reference: "a speaker or writer predicts a likely result in the future if the condition is fulfilled", e.g.:
If he comes here, we will offer him some help.

Depending on the context the above types may be used as renderings of the various conditional cases occurring in Ancient Greek texts. As one might expect, the remote type used in English is nearly always an adequate translation of the Ancient Greek remote case, in certain contexts, however, also of the potential, sometimes even of the prospective case. The open type is generally a good rendering of both the indefinite and the prospective case, sometimes also of the potential one. Further nuances expressed in Ancient Greek texts may frequently be taken into account (lexically) by means of additional expressions such as *perhaps* or *always* and by means of modal verbs (↑207d, p. 347).

c) When interpreting texts, the **fuzziness** of certain **categorical boundaries** needs to be taken into account, too: 280f

(1) Ancient Greek conditional clauses are sometimes hard to distinguish functionally from **temporal clauses**. This applies e.g. to the prospective conditional case (↑temporal clause with ὅταν; ↑276a; 282b).

(2) Conditional clauses sometimes move functionally close to **causal clauses**: in contexts where the condition emerges as obviously fulfilled, e.g.:
If you come along, too, and we know that you will, we are ready to accept the proposal. ≈
Since/As you will come along, too, we are ready to accept the proposal.
↑e.g. 281a/281b.

On other ways of expressing conditional adjuncts/complements ↑259h.

Indefinite conditional case (↑BR §278; BDF §372; Z §303–312) 281

1. Grammatical properties and typical function of the indefinite conditional case: 281a

if-clause/protasis/subordinate clause	*then*-clause/apodosis/main clause
εἰ + ind. of any "tense"/aspect stem (neg.: CG μή, NT generally οὐ; ↑245c; 246b)	any mood
The speaker/writer leaves the relationship of the *if*-clause proposition to reality open ("indefinite"), but presents the conclusion as (logically) necessary:	
If A is true (which I leave undecided),	B is necessarily true too.

This conditional case is sometimes called "real" instead of "indefinite" (especially so in traditional approaches). But this is a rather misleading term, as it has often led people into assuming (erroneously) that here the condition is presented as fulfilled, the proposition of the *if*-clause as being "real". As a matter fact, however, its relationship to reality is principally left open. Whether or not the condition is fulfilled in a particular instance will be indicated by the individual context. The relationship of the *if*-clause proposition to the *then*-clause proposition, the conclusion, on the other hand, is typically presented as (logically) necessary.
It is true that in the NT the condition of the indefinite case frequently appears to be fulfilled, so that the "if" in such instances moves very close to a causal "since". However, this is most probably dependent on contextual factors rather than on the type of conditional construction (↑Z §304–306; Funk §856; Robertson: 1007–1012; contra BDF §371 with its questionable assumption that in NT times the indefinite conditional case had undergone a shift of meaning towards a genuine "realis"). For relevant examples ↑281b below.

281b 2. Examples:

a) εἰ + ind. pres. in the *if*-clause (most frequent pattern):

εἰ δέ τις πνεῦμα Χριστοῦ οὐκ **ἔχει**, οὗτος οὐκ **ἔστιν** αὐτοῦ.	*But if anyone does not have the Spirit of Christ, they do not belong to Christ.* (Ro 8:9)

Whether or not the condition is fulfilled, is left open. The generalizing construction introduced by εἴ τις (↑144a) is functionally similar to relative clauses with a conditional force (↑290e).

↑also 1Cor 8:3; Ga 6:3.

εἰ γὰρ κατὰ σάρκα **ζῆτε**, **μέλλετε ἀποθνῄσκειν**.	*For if you live according to the flesh you will die.*
εἰ δὲ πνεύματι τὰς πράξεις τοῦ σώματος **θανατοῦτε**, **ζήσεσθε**.	*But if you put to death the misdeeds of the body, you will live.* (Ro 8:13)

Whether or not the condition is fulfilled, is left open. This becomes particularly clear when two contrasting propositions are expressed.

↑also Ac 5:39 (fulfilment left open).

εἰ δὲ ἐγὼ ἐν Βεελζεβοὺλ **ἐκβάλλω** τὰ δαιμόνια, οἱ υἱοὶ ὑμῶν ἐν τίνι **ἐκβάλλουσιν**;	*Now if I drive out the demons by Beelzebul, by whom do your disciples drive them out?* (Lk 11:19)
εἰ δὲ ἐν δακτύλῳ θεοῦ ἐγὼ **ἐκβάλλω** τὰ δαιμόνια, ἄρα **ἔφθασεν** ἐφ᾽ ὑμᾶς ἡ βασιλεία τοῦ θεοῦ.	*But if it is by the finger of God that I drive out the demons, then the kingdom of God has come upon you.* (Lk 11:20)

As suggested by the context, the condition of v. 19 is certainly to be regarded as unfulfilled, the one of v. 20, however, as fulfilled.

εἰ πατέρα **ἐπικαλεῖσθε** τὸν ἀπροσωπολήμπτως κρίνοντα … ἐν φόβῳ … **ἀναστράφητε**.	*If you call on a Father who judges impartially … conduct yourselves … in reverent fear.* (1Pe 1:17)

The condition is to be regarded as fulfilled ("if" very close to a causal "since"). Comparably:

Εἰ ζῶμεν πνεύματι, πνεύματι καὶ **στοιχῶμεν**.	*If we live by the Spirit, let us also keep in step with the Spirit.* (Ga 5:25)

b) εἰ + ind. pf. in the *if*-clause:

εἰ κεκοίμηται σωθήσεται.	*If he is asleep, he will be all right.* (Jn 11:12)

The condition is regarded as being fulfilled, on the basis of Jesus' statement (wrongly interpreted).

↑also Ac 16:15 (apparently fulfilled); Ro 6:5 (apparently fulfilled); 1Cor 15:17 (not fulfilled: it is something wrongly asserted by opponents).

c) εἰ + ind. aor. in the *if*-clause:

εἰ οὖν ἐγὼ **ἔνιψα** ὑμῶν τοὺς πόδας …, καὶ ὑμεῖς **ὀφείλετε** ἀλλήλων νίπτειν τοὺς πόδας.	*So, if I … have washed your feet, you also ought to wash one another's feet.* (Jn 13:14)

The condition is fulfilled: it refers to something that has just been put into action (by the speaker).

↑also Lk 19:8; Ro 5:10 (fulfilled).

d) εἰ + ind. fut. in the *if*-clause:

εἰ ἀρνησόμεθα, κἀκεῖνος **ἀρνήσεται** ἡμᾶς·	*If we disown him, he will also disown us.* (2Tm 2:12)

The fulfilment of the condition is left open.

↑also Mt 26:33; 1Cor 3:14f.

Prospective conditional case (↑BR §279; BDF §373; Z §320–322; 325–327; 337) 282

1. The most frequent (unmarked) conditional case of both CG and post-CG: 282a

if-clause/protasis/subordinate clause	*then*-clause/apodosis/main clause
ἐάν + subj. (↑210a) (the choice of "tenses" depending on aspect considerations) (less frequently ἄν, CG also ἤν; NT occasionally + ind. fut./pres.; ↑209o) (neg.: μή; ↑246b)	a) **specific** prospective case: mostly verb form with future tense value (also specific directives) (typically ind. fut. [↑202g], also imp., subj., or opt. [↑268b]) b) **general** prospective case: mostly verb form with present tense value or timeless (also general directives) (typically ind. pres., also e.g. gnomic [ind.] aor. [↑197b; 199l] also imp., subj., or opt. [↑268b])
The *if*-clause proposition refers to something one can or must expect:	
If A is true (which can or must be expected),	B is/will be true too.

282b The following points are especially worth noting:

a) The above division into **specific** prospective and the **general** prospective conditional cases is without well-defined boundaries. It should be treated as no more than a general **rule of thumb** useful as a starting point when dealing with instances of prospective conditional cases. The precise nuance intended in a particular instance will normally be inferable from the specific context (pragmatic factors) rather than from the verb forms used in the conditional construction.

b) The conclusions indicated by the **general** prospective conditional case refer in a generalizing way not only to present "situations", but especially to timeless ones which will (typically) include future ones as well (↑197b).

So, the term "present iterative" that some apply to this use of the prospective conditional case (along with the general use of the temporal clause with ὅταν; ↑276d) is clearly imprecise (on the "preterite/past iterative" ↑276e/276i).

c) Since the use of **ἐάν-clauses** expanded at the expense of εἰ-clauses (↑280d) in **post-CG**, the prospective conditional case here occurs also in contexts, in which CG is likely to have preferred the potential (or perhaps even the remote) case, e.g.:

ἐὰν αὐτὸν θέλω μένειν ἕως ἔρχομαι, τί πρὸς σέ;	*If I want him to remain alive until I come back* (and this would be possible or at least conceivable, but unlikely to be expected [↑v. 23]), *what is that to you?* (Jn 21:22)

↑also 1Cor 4:15; 13:2; Jn 21:23.

d) Conditional clauses with ἐάν are sometimes functionally very close to temporal clauses with ὅταν (↑276c/276d; 280f).

2. Examples:

282c a) specific prospective conditional case (the one most frequently occurring):

ἐάν τις ὑμᾶς **ἐρωτᾷ** (subj. pres.: durative)· διὰ τί λύετε; οὕτως **ἐρεῖτε** …	*If anyone asks you, "Why are you untying it?", say this …* (Lk 19:31)
Ἐὰν μόνον **ἅψωμαι** (subj. aor.) τοῦ ἱματίου αὐτοῦ **σωθήσομαι**.	*If I only touch his cloak, I will be made well.* (Mt 9:21)

↑also Mt 5:13; 21:3; 28:14; Mk 10:12; 11:31; Lk 16:30; Jn 8:24; 11:48; Ro 13:4; Jas 4:15.

ἐὰν μὴ **νίψω** σε οὐκ **ἔχεις** μέρος μετ' ἐμοῦ.	*If I don't wash you, you have no part with me.* (Jn 13:8)

Specific prospective case, but against the "rule" an ind. pres. is used in the *then*-clause.

↑also Jn 8:54.

κἀγὼ **ἐὰν ὑψωθῶ** ἐκ τῆς γῆς, πάντας **ἑλκύσω** πρὸς ἐμαυτόν.	*And I when* (lit. *if*) *I am lifted up from the earth, I will draw all people to myself.* (Jn 12:32)

Functionally close to a specific temporal ὅταν-clause (hence most EVV have *when*).

b) general prospective conditional case: 282d

ἐὰν δὲ καὶ ἀθλῇ (subj. pres.: linear) τις, οὐ **στεφανοῦται** ἐὰν μὴ νομίμως ἀθλήσῃ.	*Also, if anyone competes as an athlete, he is not crowned unless he competes according to the rules.* (2Tm 2:5)
ἐάν τις **περιπατῇ** ἐν τῇ ἡμέρᾳ, οὐ **προσκόπτει.**	*If anyone walks during the day, he does not stumble.* (Jn 11:9)

Functionally close to a general temporal ὅταν-clause.

↑also Mk 3:24; Jn 7:51; 12:24; Ro 7:3; 1Cor 7:39f.

ἐὰν δὲ μὴ **ἀκούσῃ** (subj. aor.), **παράλαβε** μετὰ σοῦ ἔτι ἕνα ἢ δύο …	*But if he does not listen, take one or two others with you ….* (Mt 18:16)
ἐάν τις **θέλῃ** τὸ θέλημα αὐτοῦ (sc. θεοῦ) ποιεῖν **γνώσεται** περὶ τῆς διδαχῆς πότερον ἐκ τοῦ θεοῦ ἐστιν.	*If anyone wants to do God's will, he will know whether the teaching is from God.* (Jn 7:17)

General prospective case, but against the "rule" an ind. fut. is used in the *then*-clause.

↑also Jn 6:51; Mt 15:14.

Potential conditional case (↑BR §280; BDF §371; 385.2; Z §323f) 283

1. While this conditional construction was widely used in Attic Greek (CG), it was disappearing in KG, and thus there are only a handful of incomplete instances attested in the NT: 283a

if-clause/protasis/subordinate clause	*then*-clause/apodosis/main clause
εἰ + opt. (↑211e) (neg. μή; ↑246b)	mostly opt. with ἄν (↑211d)
(the choice of "tenses" depending on aspect considerations)	
The speaker/writer presents the "situation" referred to by the *if*-clause as possible or as at least conceivable, leaving open its relationship to reality. The conclusion is presented as a mere possibility (potential opt. [↑211d]; but if it is to presented as [logically] necessary, the *then*-clause predicator will be an ind. pres./pf./fut./aor. form).	
If A is true (which I consider at least conceivable),	B may/might be true too.

2. Examples: 283b

a) complete CG example (↑also 211e), e.g.:

εἴης φορητὸς οὐκ **ἄν**, **εἰ πράσσοις** καλῶς.	*You might be unbearable, if you should be successful.* (Aeschylus, Prometheus 979)

b) in the NT the opt. occurs only in *if*-clauses:

εἰ καὶ **πάσχοιτε** διὰ δικαιοσύνην, μακάριοι.	*Even if you should suffer for righteousness' sake, you are blessed.* (1Pe 3:14)

↑also Ac 20:16; 1Pe 3:17; with idiomatic εἰ τύχοι *undoubtedly/perhaps* 1Cor 14:10; 15:37.

↑however (*if*-clause: prospective [here ind. fut. replacing subj.; ↑282a]; *then*-clause: potential opt.):

πῶς γὰρ **ἂν δυναίμην** ἐὰν μή τις ὁδηγήσει με;	*How could I possibly understand unless someone explains it to me?* (Ac 8:31)

284 Remote conditional case (↑BR §281; BDF §371; 360; Z §313–319)

284a 1. Grammatical properties and typical function of the remote conditional case:

<table>
<tr><td>if-clause/protasis/subordinate clause</td><td>then-clause/apodosis/main clause</td></tr>
<tr><td>εἰ + augment indicative (↑209a)
(neg.: μή; 246b)</td><td>augment indicative with ἄν (↑209h)
(in the NT sometimes without ἄν)[(1)]</td></tr>
<tr><td colspan="2">The choice of “tenses” in principle depends on aspect considerations, the intended placement in time of the “situations” concerned usually being inferable from the context. Still, the following tendency is observable (note that the pluperfect is rarely used in the NT: ↑209h):
a) ipf. mostly refers to something meant to be placed in the present or to something timeless;
b) ind. aor. mostly refers to something meant to be placed in the past.</td></tr>
<tr><td colspan="2">The speaker/writer presents the “situation” referred to by the if-clause as counterfactual (epistemic modality), the conclusion, however, as (logically) necessary:</td></tr>
<tr><td>If A were true,</td><td>B would necessarily be true too</td></tr>
<tr><td colspan="2">(since, however, A is not true, B is not true either), or</td></tr>
<tr><td>If A had been true,</td><td>B would necessarily have been true too</td></tr>
<tr><td colspan="2">(since, however, A was not true, B was not true either).</td></tr>
</table>

(1) Thus in Jn 8:39; 9:33; 15:22.24; 19:11; Ro 7:7; Ga 4:15 (↑BDF §360.1).

2. Examples:

284b a) referring to something meant to be placed in the present or to something timeless:

- more frequently by means of ipf./ipf., e.g.:

Εἰ τυφλοὶ **ἦτε**, οὐκ **ἂν εἴχετε** ἁμαρτίαν.	*If you were blind, you wouldn't have sin.* (Jn 9:41)
εἰ δὲ ἑαυτοὺς **διεκρίνομεν**, οὐκ **ἂν ἐκρινόμεθα**.	*If we judged ourselves rightly, we would not be judged.* (1Cor 11:31)

↑also Lk 7:39; Jn 5:46; 9:33; Ga 1:10.

- less frequently by means of ind. aor./ind. aor., ipf./ind. aor. or the like, e.g.:

εἰ ᾔδει ὁ οἰκοδεσπότης ποίᾳ φυλακῇ ὁ κλέπτης ἔρχεται, **ἐγρηγόρησεν ἂν** καὶ οὐκ **ἂν εἴασεν** διορυχθῆναι τὴν οἰκίαν αὐτοῦ.	*If a homeowner knew at what time of the night a burglar was coming, he would stay awake and would not let his house be broken into.* (Mt 24:43)

↑also Jn 14:28 (ipf./ind. aor.).

b) referring to something meant to be placed in the past: 284c

• more frequently by means of ind. aor./ind. aor., e.g.:

ὅτι **εἰ** ἐν Τύρῳ καὶ Σιδῶνι **ἐγένοντο** αἱ δυνάμεις αἱ γενόμεναι ἐν ὑμῖν, πάλαι **ἂν** ἐν σάκκῳ καὶ σποδῷ **μετενόησαν**.	*For if the mighty works done in you had been done in Tyre and Sidon, they would have repented long ago in sackcloth and ashes.* (Mt 11:21)
εἰ μὴ κύριος Σαβαὼθ **ἐγκατέλιπεν** ἡμῖν σπέρμα, ὡς Σόδομα **ἂν ἐγενήθημεν** καὶ ὡς Γόμορρα **ἂν ὡμοιώθημεν**.	*If the Lord of Hosts had not left us offspring, we would have become like Sodom, and we would have been made like Gomorrah.* (Ro 9:29 = Is 1:9 LXX)

↑also 1Cor 2:8.

• less frequently by means of ipf/ipf., ipf./ind. aor., ipf./plpf., plpf./ind. aor. or the like, e.g.:

εἰ μὲν ἐκείνης (sc. πατρίδος) **ἐμνημόνευον** … **εἶχον ἂν** καιρὸν ἀνακάμψαι.	*If they had been thinking of that land …, they would have had opportunity to return.* (He 11:15)
εἰ ἦς ὧδε οὐκ **ἂν ἀπέθανεν** ὁ ἀδελφός μου.	*If you had been here, my brother would not have died.* (Jn 11:21)
εἰ γὰρ ἐξ ἡμῶν **ἦσαν, μεμενήκεισαν ἂν** μεθ᾽ ἡμῶν (plpf. here without aug.; ↑72h)	*For if they had belonged to us, they would have stayed with us.* (1Jn 2:19)

↑also Mt 12:7 (plpf./ind. aor.); Jn 14:28 (ipf./ind.aor.); Ac 26:32 (plpf./ipf.; ↑198i).

c) mixed placement in time, e.g.: 284d

εἰ μὴ **ἦν** οὗτος κακὸν ποιῶν, οὐκ **ἄν** σοι **παρεδώκαμεν** αὐτόν.	*If this man were not a criminal, we would not have handed him over to you.* (Jn 18:30)
εἰ γὰρ **ἐδόθη** νόμος ὁ δυνάμενος ζῳοποιῆσαι ὄντως ἐκ νόμου **ἂν ἦν** ἡ δικαιοσύνη.	*For if a law had been given that could impart life, then righteousness would indeed be on the basis of the law.* (Ga 3:21)

↑also Jn 15:22.

Mixed conditional constructions and special cases 285

(↑BR §282; BDF §360, 371; Z §329–334)

1. Sometimes mixed conditional constructions occur (in CG and in NT/KG) with the standard cases being combined in unusual ways, e.g.: 285a

πῶς γὰρ **ἂν δυναίμην ἐὰν** μή τις **ὁδηγήσει** με;	*How could I possibly understand unless someone explains it to me?* (Ac 8:31)

A potential case *then*-clause (↑283) is combined with a prospective case *if*-clause (↑282).

εἰ ἔχετε πίστιν ὡς κόκκον σινάπεως **ἐλέγετε ἂν** τῇ συκαμίνῳ ταύτῃ …	*If you had* (lit. *have*) *faith the size of a mustard seed, you could* (lit. *would*) *say to this mulberry tree …* (Lk 17:6)

An indefinite case *if*-clause (↑281) is combined with a remote case *then*-clause (↑284).

285b 2. Various special cases:

a) remote case *if*-clause after ind. pres. used with the force of an irrealis (↑209h), e. g.:

τί **θέλω εἰ** ἤδη **ἀνήφθη**.	*How I wish it were already kindled/How I would be glad if it were …* (Lk 12:49; ↑BDF §360.4)

b) indefinite conditional case with the force of a remote case, e. g.:

καλόν **ἐστιν** αὐτῷ μᾶλλον **εἰ περίκειται** μῦλος ὀνικὸς περὶ τὸν τράχηλον αὐτοῦ καὶ **βέβληται** εἰς τὴν θάλασσαν.	*It would be better for him if a heavy millstone were hung around his neck and he were thrown into the sea.* (Mk 9:42)

c) incomplete remote conditional case construction: the *then*-clause is left unexpressed (aposiopesis; ↑293f), e. g.:

εἰ ἔγνως ἐν τῇ ἡμέρᾳ ταύτῃ καὶ σὺ τὰ πρὸς εἰρήνην·	*If you only knew* (or *had known*) *this day what would bring peace!* (Lk 19:42)

286 Concessive and exceptive conditional clauses (↑BR §284; BDF §374; 376)

The following clause types can be classified as subtypes of the conditional clauses treated above (↑280–285) each with a restrictive function of its own:

286a 1. **Concessive clauses** typically **function** as concessive adjuncts: they present the "action"/"situation" referred to by the superordinate construction as taking place contrary to certain expectations, answering questions such as "In spite of what?" (↑259b/259k). On a possible function as an attributive modifier ↑288.

a) **Subordinators** (↑251l; on text-level concessive [and similar adversative] relations and their connection with the underlying presupposed If-Then-relationship ↑339):

εἰ καί (or at times ἐὰν καί)	*even if, (even) though, although, in spite of the fact that* or the like
less frequently: καὶ εἰ or καὶ ἐάν (κἄν),[1](Jn 4:2 καίτοιγε)	*even if*
(καί, καίπερ, καίτοι + PtcP; ↑231g)	
(neg. μή; ↑246b)	

(1) For other uses of κἄν ↑252.18; occasionally (He 3:9) καί i.t.s. *though* (↑252.29,1a).

On other ways of expressing concessive adjuncts, most importantly by means of adverbial participle phrases ↑259k.

b) Examples:

εἰ γὰρ **καὶ** τῇ σαρκὶ ἄπειμι, ἀλλὰ τῷ πνεύματι σὺν ὑμῖν εἰμι.	*For though I am absent from you in body, I am with you in spirit.* (Col 2:5)
κἂν δέῃ με σὺν σοι ἀποθανεῖν, οὐ μή σε ἀπαρνήσομαι.	*Even if I have to die with you, I will never disown you.* (Mt 26:35)

↑also Jn 11:25; Ro 9:27; 2Cor 4:16; 7:8; 12:11; Ga 1:8; 6:1; Php 2:17.

2. The less frequently occurring **exceptive conditional clauses** refer to an exception, i.e. to a condition that alone would be sufficient to overturn the proposition expressed by the main clause (↑DuG9: 1102). They overlap both grammatically and functionally with **restrictive clauses** which serve to restrict the validity of utterances (on these ↑342). 286b

a) **Subordinators** (in the NT εἰ μή rarely combines with finite verb forms):

εἰ μή (ἐὰν μή) (also εἰ μήτι, KG/NT also ἐκτὸς εἰ μή)	*except (that)*

b) Examples of exceptive conditional (or restrictive) clauses:

καὶ οὐκ ἐδύνατο ἐκεῖ ποιῆσαι οὐδεμίαν δύναμιν, **εἰ μὴ** ὀλίγοις ἀρρώστοις ἐπιθεὶς τὰς χεῖρας ἐθεράπευσεν.	*And he could do no mighty work there, except that he laid his hands on a few people who were ill and healed them.* (Mk 6:5)
οὐδεὶς δύναται ἐλθεῖν πρός με **ἐὰν μὴ** ὁ πατὴρ ὁ πέμψας με ἑλκύσῃ αὐτόν.	*No one can come to me except/unless the Father who sent me draws him.* (Jn 6:44)

↑also Lk 9:13; Jn 5:19; 1Cor 14:5; 15:2. Without finite verb form: Mt 5:13; 11:27; Lk 4:27; 5:21; 11:29; 18:19; Jn 14:6; Ac 11:19; Ro 13:8; 1Cor 7:5; 12:3; 1Tm 5:19.

Manner clauses (↑BR §285; BDF §453) 287

1. Manner clauses typically **function** as manner adjuncts: they specify the manner of the "action"/"situation" referred to by the superordinate construction, answering basically questions such as "How?" or "In what manner?" (↑259b/259f). 287a

Various subtypes of manner clauses may be distinguished: a) **means-focused** manner clauses, more specifically answering the question "By what means?", b) **comparison-focused** manner clauses, mostly called "comparative clauses", more specifically answering the question in terms of a comparison between the "situations" referred to by the main clause and the subordinate clause, and c) a functionally related, but distinct variety (occurring much less frequently): **proportional clauses**[25] indicating parallel or proportional comparisons between the "situations" referred to by the two clauses.

On other ways of expressing manner adjuncts ↑259f.

25 ↑Quirk: 1111; Huddleston-Pullum: 1135: "correlative comparative construction".

2. **Subordinators** and examples

287b a) For **means-focused** manner clauses there are no standard subordinators in Ancient Greek. Very rarely ὅτι (= ἐν τούτῳ ὅτι) *in that* or *by* + *-ing* form occurs with such a function (↑271c). The leading construction involving verb forms used to express manner adjuncts including means-focused ones (↑259f) is clearly the (adverbial) participle phrase indicating manner (mainly p.c., sometimes gen.abs.; ↑231e; 232a); occasionally infinitive/ACI phrases without article or with τοῦ or with an article governed by prepositions such as πρός + acc., and ἐν + dat. have this function (↑220d; 225f; 226a). On text-level manner and means relations ↑335.

Examples of means-focused manner constructions:

συνίστησιν δὲ τὴν ἑαυτοῦ ἀγάπην εἰς ἡμᾶς ὁ θεός, **ὅτι** (= ἐν τούτῳ ὅτι) ἔτι ἁμαρτωλῶν ὄντων ἡμῶν Χριστὸς ὑπὲρ ἡμῶν ἀπέθανεν. (rare instance with subo. cl.)	*But God shows his love for us in that while we still were sinners Christ died for us./But God shows his love for us by having Christ die for us while we were still sinners.* (Ro 5:8)
ἐκούφιζον τὸ πλοῖον **ἐκβαλλόμενοι** τὸν σῖτον εἰς τὴν θάλασσαν. (typical instance with adverbial PtcP [p.c.])	*They lightened the ship by throwing the wheat into the sea.* (Ac 27:38)
ὑμῖν πρῶτον … ὁ θεός … ἀπέστειλεν αὐτὸν εὐλογοῦντα ὑμᾶς **ἐν τῷ ἀποστρέφειν** ἕκαστον … (rare instance with ἐν + dat. + InfP)	*God … sent him first to you to bless you by turning each of you away …* (Ac 3:26)

287c b) Subordinators of **comparison-focused** manner or comparative clauses (↑251m; on text-level comparative ↑344); in principle the same moods are used as in independent declarative clauses (↑267):

(1) ὡς (intensified ὥσπερ)[1]		*(just) as*
CG also (with generalizing force) ὅπως		(may also introduce dependent interrogative and declarative clauses; ↑273b; 271a; 252.61)
καθάπερ, καθώς (less frequently: καθά, καθό, καθώσπερ)		*just as*
(2) with a correlative adverb in the superordinate construction (↑61c):		
ὡς[1] – (or ὥσπερ, καθώς, καθάπερ)	οὕτως (less frequently καί)	*as – so*
similarly also the correlative pronouns (↑61):		
ὅσος/ὅσοι –	τοσοῦτος/τοσοῦτοι	*as large/as many – so large/so many*
καθ' ὅσον –	οὕτως/κατὰ τοσοῦτο	*as – so*
οἷος –	τοιοῦτος	*of what kind/as – of such kind/so*
CG also: ὥσπερ ἂν εἰ + opt. (conditional comparison; ↑211d)		*as if*

(1) Also ὃν τρόπον/καθ' ὃν τρόπον *(just) as* (< [κατὰ] τὸν τρόπον [καθ'] ὅν *in the manner in which/just as*; ↑142d; 289c).

Examples of comparison-focused manner clauses/comparative clauses:

(1) without correlative adverb in the superordinate construction, e.g.:

ἠγάπησας αὐτοὺς **καθὼς** ἐμὲ ἠγάπησας.
You have loved them just as you have loved me. (Jn 17:23)

… ἠσπάζετο αὐτὸν **ὥσπερ ἂν εἴ** τις … πάλαι φιλῶν **ἀσπάζοιτο**.
… he greeted him as one does … who had long been his friend. (Xenophon, Cyropaedia 1.3.2)

(2) with a correlative adverb in the superordinate construction, e.g.:

… **ὡς** δι' ἑνὸς παραπτώματος εἰς πάντας ἀνθρώπους εἰς κατάκριμα, **οὕτως** καὶ δι' ἑνὸς δικαιώματος εἰς πάντας ἀνθρώπους εἰς δικαίωσιν ζωῆς.
… as through one trespass condemnation came for all people, so also through the one righteous act came justification leading to life for all people. (Ro 5:18)

↑also Jn 7:46 (Byz.)

ὥσπερ γὰρ ὁ πατὴρ ἔχει ζωὴν ἐν ἑαυτῷ, **οὕτως** καὶ τῷ υἱῷ ἔδωκεν ζωὴν ἔχειν ἐν ἑαυτῷ.
For as the Father has life in himself, so he has granted the Son also to have life in himself. (Jn 5:26)

↑also Jn 5:21; Ro 5:19.21; 6:4.19; 1Cor 15:22; Ga 4:29; et pass.

καὶ **καθὼς** ἐγένετο ἐν ταῖς ἡμέραις Νῶε, **οὕτως** ἔσται καὶ ἐν ταῖς ἡμέραις τοῦ υἱοῦ τοῦ ἀνθρώπου.
Just as it was in the days of Noah, so it will be in the days of the Son of Man. (Lk 17:26)

↑also Jn 3:14; 12:50; 15:4; 2Cor 1:5; (καθ') ὃν τρόπον: Ac 1:11; 27:25.

οἷος ὁ χοϊκός, **τοιοῦτοι** καὶ οἱ χοϊκοί, καὶ **οἷος** ὁ ἐπουράνιος, **τοιοῦτοι** καὶ οἱ ἐπουράνιοι.
As was the man of dust, so are those who are of the dust; and as is the man of heaven, so are those who are of heaven. (1Cor 15:48)

↑also He 7:20–22; 9:27f (καθ' ὅσον – κατὰ τοσοῦτο / καθ' ὅσον – οὕτως).

(3) with ellipsis of predicator (predicate verb) in the component introduced by ὡς *as/like* or the like, which occurs frequently, not only in the common case of copula ellipsis (e.g. 1Cor 15:48; ↑256d; 293c), but also in other cases (apo koinou ellipsis; ↑293b; ↑BDAG sub ὡς 1b; which basically agrees with English usage; ↑Aarts: 195), e.g.:

τότε οἱ δίκαιοι ἐκλάμψουσιν **ὡς** ὁ ἥλιος …
*Then the righteous will shine like the sun/shine as the sun [**shines**] …* (Mt 13:43)

Sometimes the construction superordinate to the manner/comparative clause is not expressed (this is a kind of aposiopesis; ↑293f; BDF §482), e.g.:

καὶ οὐ – καθάπερ Μωϋσῆς ἐτίθει κάλυμμα ἐπὶ τὸ πρόσωπον αὐτοῦ …
*And [**we do**] not [**do it**] like Moses who used to put a veil over his face …* (2Cor 3:13)

↑also Mt 25:14/Mk 13:34 (sc. "It is/It will be" or the like).

287d c) Subordinators of **proportional clauses** (↑61; 345)

ὅσῳ (↑178b) –	τοσούτῳ	*(by) as much – (by) so/as much*
ὅσον (↑157) –	μᾶλλον	*the more – the more*

Examples of proportional clauses:

… **τοσούτῳ** κρείττων γενόμενος τῶν ἀγγέλων **ὅσῳ** διαφορώτερον παρ' αὐτοὺς κεκληρονόμηκεν ὄνομα.	*… he became as much superior to the angels as the name he has inherited is more excellent than theirs.* (He 1:4)
ὅσον δὲ αὐτοῖς διεστέλλετο, αὐτοὶ **μᾶλλον** περισσότερον ἐκήρυσσον.	*But the more he ordered them, the more zealously they proclaimed it.* (Mk 7:36)
ὅσῳ μέγας εἶ **τοσούτῳ** ταπείνου σεαυτόν.	*The greater you are, the more you must humble yourself.* (Sir 3:18)

(iii) Conjunctional clauses as attributive modifiers

288 Conjunctional attributive clauses (↑Z §411; 428)

Conjunctional clauses mainly function as the subject, complement (mostly object; ↑271–275) or adverbial (↑276–287) of the superordinate construction. Under certain circumstances, however, they also occur as attributive modifiers (typically) of the head of noun phrases, often in apposition to demonstratives (↑260h/260n):

288a a) "subject-object" clauses functioning as attributive modifiers:

- ὅτι-clause *that …* or the like (dependent declarative clauses; ↑271), e.g.:

… διὰ τὴν χαρὰν **ὅτι ἐγεννήθη ἄνθρωπος** …	*… because of her joy that a human being has been born into the world.* (Jn 16:21)

The ὅτι-clause answers the question "Because of kind of joy?".

↑also Mt 26:54; Mk 14:72; Jn 3:19 (App to αὕτη); Ac 11:16 (ὡς-clause); Ro 2:3.

- ἵνα-clause *that …* or the like (dependent desiderative clause; ↑272), e.g.:

αὕτη ἐστὶν ἡ ἐντολὴ αὐτοῦ, **ἵνα πιστεύσωμεν τῷ ὀνόματι τοῦ υἱοῦ αὐτοῦ** …	*This is his commandment, that we believe in the name of his Son …* (1Jn 3:23)

The ἵνα-clause functions as an attributive modifier/apposition of αὕτη.

↑also Mk 11:28; Jn 15:8.13; Ac 17:15.

- εἰ-clause *if …* (dependent interrogative clause; ↑273), also ὡς-clause *how …*, e.g.:

ἐμνήσθην δὲ τοῦ ῥήματος τοῦ κυρίου **ὡς ἔλεγεν·** …	*And I remembered the word of the Lord how he said, "…"* (Ac 11:16)

The ὡς-clause answers the question "What kind of word of the Lord?".

↑also Mk 14:72 (ὡς *how* … App to τὸ ῥῆμα *the word*); Lk 9:46 (τὸ τίς *[about] who* … App to διαλογισμός *argument*); Ac 4:21 (τὸ πῶς *how* … App to μηδέν *nothing*).

Instances with εἰ-clauses occur outside the NT, e.g. in Josephus, Antiquities 15.135:

ἔστιν οὖν ἔτι ζήτησις ὑμῖν **εἰ δεῖ τοὺς ἀδίκους τιμωρεῖσθαι** …;	*Is it then still a question with you, whether these unjust are to be punished …?*

The εἰ-clause answers the question "What kind of question?".

b) "adverbial" clauses functioning as attributive modifiers, e.g.: **288b**

ἐλεύσονται δὲ ἡμέραι **ὅταν ἀπαρθῇ ἀπ' αὐτῶν ὁ νυμφίος**.	*The time will come when the bridegroom will be taken away from them.* (Mt 9:15)

The temporal clause (↑276) answers the question "What kind of time?".

↑also Mt 26:29. Examples with ὅτε-clause: Mk 14:12; Lk 17:22; Jn 4:21; 9:4; Ro 2:16.

εἰς τοῦτο ἐφανερώθη ὁ υἱὸς τοῦ θεοῦ **ἵνα λύσῃ τὰ ἔργα τοῦ διαβόλου**.	*The Son of God appeared for this purpose: to destroy the devil's works.* (1Jn 3:8)

The purpose clause (↑278) functions as an attributive modifier/apposition of τοῦτο.

↑also BDAG sub ἵνα 1e for further examples.

3.4.2.2 Relative clauses

(↑BR §287–292; BDF §377–380; 386:4; 294–297; 469; Z §335–339)

289 Form and syntactic function of relative clauses

(↑BR §287/288; 291/292; BDF §294–297; 469; Z §16–21; 201–203)

289a I. **Subordinators**

Relative clauses are subordinate clauses that are subordinated by relatives, i.e. relative pronouns and adverbs (↑59–61; 142; 143b; 319):

1. **simple** or **specific** relatives:

(these typically refer back to a specific entity identified usually by an antecedent phrase in the superordinate construction)

ὅς/ἥ/ὅ (↑142) (post-CG also τίς/τί; ↑143b)	*who/which/that*
analogously also (↑59–61):	
ὅσος, ὅσοι	*as large as/as great as/as much as; as many as*
οἷος	*of what kind as*
ἡλίκος	*what size/how great/how small*
οὗ	*where*, KG/NT also *to where*
ὅθεν	*from where*
οἷ (CG)	*to where*
ᾗ/ᾗπερ (CG)	*where/to where* (also *how*)

2. **compound** or **indefinite** relatives:

(these typically refer to indefinite entities or a class, often without antecedent phrase in the superordinate construction; the indefinite force may be enhanced by means of ἄν/ἐάν + subj.; ↑252.3; 290e; in KG, however, they are often used like the simple/specific ones; ↑142b)

ὅστις/ἥτις/ὅ τι (↑142)	*whoever/whatever, any(one) who/ any(thing) that* (also *inasmuch as/who as such*; ↑142a, p.214)
analogously also (↑59–61):	
ὁπόσος, ὁπόσοι	*of whatever largeness, of whatever number*
ὁποῖος	*of whatever kind*
ὅπου	*wherever*, KG/NT also *to wherever*
ὁπόθεν	*from wherever*
ὅποι (CG)	*to wherever*
ὅπῃ (CG)	*wherever/to wherever* (also *however*)

Noteworthy points:

a) ὡς/ὅπως *how/however* and ὅτε/ὁπότε *when/whenever* could have been listed here, too. They have, however, already been treated as subordinators of conjunctional clauses (↑270c; 288), especially in the context of subject-object clauses (↑271a; 272c; 273b) as well as temporal (↑276a), causal (↑277a), purpose (↑278a), result (↑279a) and manner clauses (↑287c).

b) On basic functional overlaps of relatives with conjunctions ↑270c.

c) Dependent open interrogative clauses (subordinated e.g. by τίς *who*) are to be counted as relative clauses, too (they are treated together with the open ones; ↑273).

d) Relative clauses introduced by οὗ/ὅπου *(to) where/(to) wherever* or ὅθεν/ὁπόθεν *from where/from wherever* or the like might also be classified as "local clauses" (↑BR §287; also ↑323a).

e) On the 'relative' καί and the seemingly 'pleonastic' καί after a relative pronoun ↑252.29.1a.

Basically relative clauses have **the same form as main clauses** (↑266–269; on negation ↑245b/245c; 246a/246b). On peculiarities ↑289c–289j; on certain types of relative clauses with adverbial force ↑290.

II. **Syntactic function** 289b

Relative clauses typically function as attributive modifiers (mostly) of the head of a noun phrase within the superordinate construction (attributive clauses; ↑260a/260n); they may, however, also function as sentence constituents (↑270a/270c).

1. A relative clause functions as an **attributive modifier**, i.e. as an attributive clause, when there is an antecedent in the superordinate construction, the head noun ("HN") of the attributive modifier. The relative refers back to a specific entity identified by the antecedent, the relative clause characterizing it in some way (↑260a). E.g.:

ἀληθής ἐστιν **ἡ μαρτυρία** (S/HN) **ἣν μαρτυρεῖ περὶ ἐμοῦ** (Attr).	*The testimony that he bears about me is true.* (Jn 5:32)
… **τὸν αὐτὸν ἀγῶνα** (Od/HN) ἔχοντες, **οἷον εἴδετε ἐν ἐμοί** (Attr) …	*… engaged in the same struggle that you saw I had …* (Php 1:30)
… εὗρεν **τὸν τόπον** (Od) **οὗ ἦν γεγραμμένον** … (Attr)	*… he found the place where it was written …* (Lk 4:17)
καὶ ἔστιν αὕτη **ἡ ἀγγελία** (SC^{id}/HN) **ἣν ἀκηκόαμεν ἀπ' αὐτοῦ** (Attr).	*And this is the message that we have heard from him.* (1Jn 1:5)
ἀπῆλθεν πάλιν … **εἰς τὸν τόπον** (LocA) **ὅπου ἦν Ἰωάννης τὸ πρῶτον βαπτίζων** (Attr).	*He went away again … to the place where John had been baptizing earlier.* (Jn 10:40)

Occasionally the antecedent is not a single word or phrase, but a whole clause (this would be a so-called "**sentential relative clause**"), e.g.:

τοῦτον τὸν Ἰησοῦν ἀνέστησεν ὁ θεός (clause/"HN"), **οὗ πάντες ἡμεῖς ἐσμεν μάρτυρες** (Attr).	*God has raised this Jesus to life, and we are all witnesses of this.* (Ac 2:32)

↑also Ac 3:15; 11:29f; 26:9f; Ga 2:10; Col 1:29; 1Pe 2:8; Re 21:8.

Note that, as indicated earlier (↑260a[11]), attributive modifiers may be **restrictive** (i.e. with an identifying role) or **non-restrictive** (i.e. purely descriptive), something that applies especially to attributive modifiers expressed in the form of relative clauses, e.g.:

ἀφορίσατε δή μοι τὸν Βαρναβᾶν καὶ Σαῦλον εἰς **τὸ ἔργον** (HN) **ὃ προσκέκλημαι αὐτούς**. (restrictive)	*Set apart for me Barnabas and Saul for the work to which I have called them.* (Ac 13:2)
… **ἐλπίδα** (HN) ἔχων εἰς τὸν θεὸν **ἣν καὶ αὐτοὶ οὗτοι προσδέχονται** … (non-restrictive)	*… I have a hope in God, which these men themselves also accept …* (Ac 24:15)

2. When there is no antecedent in the superordinate construction, the relative clause normally functions as a **sentence constituent** (↑also inter alia 289d):

a) as a subject (↑255e), e.g.:

ὅστις δὲ ὑψώσει ἑαυτὸν (S) ταπεινωθήσεται …	*Whoever exalts himself will be humbled.* (Mt 23:12)

"Who will be humbled?" *Whoever exalts himself.*

b) as an object (↑257d), e.g.:

ἀπαγγείλατε Ἰωάννῃ **ἃ εἴδετε καὶ ἠκούσατε** (Od)	*Report to John what you have seen and heard.* (Lk 7:22)

c) as a subject/object complement or as an adverbial complement (↑258a/258b/258c), e.g.:

… ἐγώ εἰμι **ὃν ζητεῖτε** (SC[id]).	*… I am the one you are looking for.* (Ac 10:21)
… ἵνα **ὅπου εἰμὶ ἐγὼ** (LocC) καὶ ὑμεῖς ἦτε.	*… so that where I am you may be also.* (Jn 14:3)

d) as adverbial adjunct (↑259a–259m) or subject/object adjunct (↑259n/259o), e.g.:

θερίζω **ὅπου οὐκ ἔσπειρα** (LocA).	*I reap where I have not sown.* (Mt 25:26)

↑also 290 on the additional adverbial force of certain types of relative clauses.

III. Interplay of relatives and their antecedents (on relatives and prepositions ↑142d)

289c 1. Antecedents are sometimes placed ("incorporated") in the relative clause (a phenomenon found in Lat. too, in the NT less frequently than in CG), in which case it is without its (usual) article, e.g.:

ᾧ γὰρ **μέτρῳ** μετρεῖτε ἀντιμετρηθήσεται ὑμῖν. (= **τῷ** γὰρ **μέτρῳ ᾧ** μετρεῖτε …)	*For* ***with the measure with which*** *you measure will in return be measured out to you.* (Lk 6:38)

↑also Mt 24:44; Mk 6:16; Lk 24:1; Jn 6:14.

2. In many cases the relative pronoun presupposes functionally the presence of a 289d
demonstrative pronoun as an antecedent. In a translation into English the seemingly missing element needs to be supplied (↑142c), e.g.:

ᾧ δὲ ὀλίγον ἀφίεται, ὀλίγον ἀγαπᾷ. (**οὗτος** "missing")	*But **the one to whom** little is forgiven, loves little.* (Lk 7:47)
πῶς δὲ πιστεύσωσιν **οὗ** οὐκ ἤκουσαν. (**τούτῳ** "missing")	*And how can they believe **in him of whom** they have not heard?* (Ro 10:14)

3. The relative pronoun ὅς *who* etc. (not, however, ὅστις) frequently is not only in 289e
the same number and gender as its antecedent (as expected), but also in the same case (↑263), though the predicator of the relative clause (i.e. its valency) might call for another case. As the case of the relative is attracted or assimilated into the case of the antecedent, this phenomenon is called "**attraction of the relative**" (the traditional term) or "assimilation of the relative".

This typically happens when

- the antecedent ("HN") is in the genitive or dative and
- the relative pronoun would normally be in the accusative, e.g.:

μνημονεύετε **τοῦ λόγου** (HN) **οὗ** (= **ὃν**) ἐγὼ εἶπον ὑμῖν.	*Remember the word that I said to you.* (Jn 15:20)
ἤρξατο νίπτειν τοὺς πόδας τῶν μαθητῶν καὶ ἐκμάσσειν **τῷ λεντίῳ** (HN) **ᾧ** (= **ὅ**) ἦν διεζωσμένος.	*He began to wash the disciples' feet and to dry them with the towel he had wrapped around himself.* (Jn 13:5)

↑also Ac 20:18 (ἀπὸ πρώτης ἡμέρας ἀφ' ἧς [ἀφ' ἧς = ᾗ] *from the first day that*).

The antecedent of a construction with attraction of the relative occurs in one of **three possible positions**:

a) The antecedent is placed in the superordinate construction (like in English), e.g.:

… τὸ σῶμα ὑμῶν ναὸς … τοῦ … **ἁγίου πνεύματός** (HN) ἐστιν **οὗ** (= **ὃν**) ἔχετε ἀπὸ θεοῦ.	*… your body is a temple of the Holy Spirit … whom you have from God.* (1Cor 6:19)

↑also Jn 15:20; 21:10; Ac 3:25; 7:17; 9:36; 2Cor 1:6.

… δόξασόν με σύ … τῇ **δόξῃ** (HN) **ᾗ** (= **ἣν**) εἶχον πρὸ τοῦ τὸν κόσμον εἶναι …	*… glorify me … with the glory that I had before the world existed.* (Jn 17:5)

↑also Mk 7:13; Lk 2:20; 24:25; Ac 17:31; Eph 2:10.

b) The antecedent is placed ("incorporated") in the relative clause without the (normal) article (↑289c):

- typical case, e.g.:

ἤρξαντο … αἰνεῖν τὸν θεὸν … περὶ πασῶν **ὧν** εἶδον **δυνάμεων** (HN) (= περὶ πασῶν **τῶν δυνάμεων** [HN] **ἃς** εἶδον).	*they began to praise God … for the mighty works that they had seen.* (Lk 19:37)

↑also Lk 1:4.

- sometimes with the antecedent immediately after the relative, e.g.:

ἄχρι **ἧς ἡμέρας** (HN) … (= ἄχρι **τῆς ἡμέρας** [HN] **ᾗ** …)	*until the day when* … (Mt 24:38; Lk 1:20; 17:27; Ac 1:2)

↑also Lk 1:4.

c) The antecedent in the form of a demonstrative is seemingly missing (↑289d):

- the relative pronoun is a simple case form without preposition, e.g.:

οὐδενὶ ἀπήγγειλαν … **οὐδὲν ὧν** ἑώρακαν (= **οὐδὲν τούτων** [HN] **ἃ** ἑώρακαν).	*They told no one … any of the things which they had seen.* (Lk 9:36)

↑also Jn 7:31; Ac 21:19.24; 25:11; 26:16; 2Cor 12:17.

- the relative pronoun is embedded in a prepositional phrase (on relatives and prepositions ↑142d, also 289f), e.g.:

(ἐρωτῶ) … **περὶ ὧν** δέδωκάς (= **περὶ τούτων** [HN] **οὓς** δέδωκάς μοι).	*(I pray) … for those whom you have given me.* (Jn 17:9)

↑also 2Cor 2:3; 2Tm 3:14.

- in a comparable manner relative clauses introduced by relative adverbs, e.g.:

… συνάγων **ὅθεν** (= **ἐκεῖθεν οὗ**) οὐ διεσκόρπισας.	*… gathering (from) where you did not scatter.* (Mt 25:24)

↑also Mk 2:4; Jn 7:34.

The following conjunction-like phrases go back to combinations of the above type:

ἀνθ᾽ ὧν = ἀντὶ τούτων ὅτι	*because* (Lk 19:44)	(↑277a/277c)
ἀφ᾽ οὗ = ἀπὸ τοῦ χρόνου ὅτε	*since/when once* (Lk 13:25)	(↑276a)
ἀφ᾽ ἧς = ἀπὸ τῆς ἡμέρας/ὥρας ᾗ	*since* (Ac 24:11; Lk 7:45)	(↑276a)
ἐν/ἐφ᾽ ᾧ = ἐν/ἐπὶ τούτῳ ὅτι (NT)	*because* (2Cor 5:4; Ro 8:3)	(↑277a/277c)

↑184d/184e/184i/184j.

289f 4. Less frequently the antecedent is assimilated to the relative pronoun. This is commonly referred to as "**inverse attraction**":

- The antecedent is placed in the superordinate construction, e.g.:

τὸν ἄρτον (HN) **ὃν** κλῶμεν, οὐχὶ κοινωνία τοῦ σώματος τοῦ Χριστοῦ ἐστιν (= **ὁ ἄρτος** [HN] **ὃν** κλῶμεν …);	***The bread that** we break, is it not a sharing in the body of Christ?* (1Cor 10:16)

↑also Mt 21:42; Lk 1:73.

- The antecedent is placed in the relative clause (↑289c; also 142d), e.g.:

ὑπηκούσατε δέ … **εἰς ὃν** παρεδόθητε **τύπον διδαχῆς** (HN) (= **τῷ τύπῳ διδαχῆς** [HN] **εἰς ὃν** παρεδόθητε).	*You obeyed … that standard of teaching to which you were committed.* (Ro 6:17)

↑also Mk 6:16; Ac 21:16.

On further peculiarities of subordinate clauses regarding word-order ↑270d.

On questions of concord ↑262–265, including in particular 263e, 263f and 265.

IV. **Peculiarities** of **adjoining** relative clauses

1. Relative clauses fairly frequently (more frequently in Lat. than in Ancient Greek) do not appear to have their typical function as a subordinate (attributive) clause (↑289b,1), but rather that of a coordinated (main) clause, even though there is an antecedent in a preceding sentence. It then simply serves to continue the text flow, hence the term "**continuative relative clause**" (↑also 142g). In such cases the relative pronoun is best translated as a personal pronoun or demonstrative. Whether or not a particular relative clause is of this type, will basically be inferable from the context (often indicated also by punctuation in text editions), e.g.: **289g**

ὁ ἀντίδικος ὑμῶν … περιπατεῖ ζητῶν τινα καταπιεῖν· **ᾧ** ἀντίστητε στερεοὶ τῇ πίστει …	*Your adversary the devil is prowling around like a roaring lion, looking for anyone he can devour. Resist* ***him****, firm in faith …* (1Pe 5:8f)

Note that relative clauses whose predicator is an imperative are typically continuative.

καὶ ἐξαπέστειλαν Βαρναβᾶν διελθεῖν ἕως Ἀντιοχείας. **ὃς** παραγενόμενος καὶ ἰδὼν τὴν χάριν τὴν τοῦ θεοῦ, ἐχάρη …	*And they sent Barnabas to Antioch. When* ***he*** *arrived and saw the grace of God, he was glad …* (Ac 11:22f)

↑also Mt 3:12; 27:56; Lk 12:1 (ἐν οἷς = τούτοις *meanwhile*); Jn 19:18 (ὅπου = ἐκεῖ *there*); Ac 1:3; 2:24; 3:3; 5:36; 7:20 (ἐν ᾧ καιρῷ = ἐν τούτῳ τῷ καιρῷ *at this time*); 8:10; 9:39; 12:4; 13:31; 16:14.24; 21:32; 24:18; 26:7 (περὶ ἧς ἐλπίδος = περὶ ταύτης τῇ ἐλπίδος *for this hope*); 28:10; 2Cor 11:15; Ga 1:5; Eph 1:13; 1Tm 3:16; 2Tm 1:6 (δι᾽ ἣν αἰτίαν = διὰ ταύτην τὴν αἰτίαν *because of this*; also 1:12, Tt 1:13 and He 2:11); 2:17; 3:8 (ὃν τρόπον = τοῦτον τὸν τρόπον *just as*; ↑157; 287c[1]); 4:15; He 5:11; 9:5; 11:7; 1Pe 1:12; 4:5; 5:12; 2Pe 2:2 etc.

2. When two (or more) **relative clauses** are to be **coordinated** and the second (or third etc.) relative pronoun would require a different case form from the first one, then the second (or third etc.) relative is either dropped or replaced by αὐτός in the required case, e.g.: **289h**

ἡμῖν εἷς θεὸς ὁ πατὴρ **ἐξ οὗ** τὰ πάντα **καὶ** ἡμεῖς **εἰς αὐτόν** (sc. καὶ **εἰς ὃν** ἡμεῖς).	*For us there is one God, the Father,* ***from whom*** *are all things* ***and for whom*** *we exist.* (1Cor 8:6)

↑also Lk 13:4; 2Pe 2:3; Re 17:2.

ὃς ἔσται ἐπὶ τοῦ δώματος **καὶ** τὰ σκεύη **αὐτοῦ** ἐν τῇ οἰκίᾳ, μὴ καταβάτω (sc. καὶ **οὗ** τὰ σκεύη …)	*A person* ***who*** *is on the housetop* ***and whose*** *belongings are in the house must not go down to get them.* (Lk 17:31)
Ἀριαῖος **ὃν** ἡμεῖς ἠθέλομεν βασιλέα καθιστάναι **καὶ** (sc. **ᾧ**) ἐδώκαμεν **καὶ** (sc. **παρ᾽ οὗ**) ἐλάβομεν πιστά … ἡμᾶς … κακῶς ποιεῖν πειρᾶται.	*Ariaeus* ***whom*** *we wanted to make king* ***and whom*** *we gave* ***and from whom*** *we received pledges … is trying to harm us.* (Xenophon, Anabasis 3.2.5)

289i 3. Placed inside NT relative clauses there is sometimes a **pleonastic** (seemingly unnecessary; ↑294x) **personal pronoun** or demonstrative adverb that correlates with the relative of the clause. This use is not entirely foreign to CG and post-CG, but in most NT cases it is probably influenced by Semitic or Biblical usage, e.g.:

γυνή … **ἧς** … τὸ θυγάτριον **αὐτῆς** …	*a woman* ***whose*** (lit. *whose her*) *little daughter* … (Mk 7:25)

↑also Mk 1:7; 9:3 (οἷα … οὕτως *as*); 13:19 (οἵα … τοιαύτη *such as*); Lk 3:16; 13:4; Ac 15:17; Jas 4:17; Re 3:8; 7:2.9; 13:8.12; 16:18; 17:9; 20:8.

… εἰς τὴν ἔρημον **ὅπου** ἔχει **ἐκεῖ** τόπον …	… *into the wilderness* ***where*** (lit. *where … there*) *she had a place* … (Re 12:6)

sometimes similarly after a participle phrase, e.g.:

τῷ νικῶντι δώσω **αὐτῷ** …	*To the one who conquers I will give* ***to him*** … (Re 2:7.17)

↑also Mt 4:16 (OT quotation); 5:40.

Biblical (OT) example (Ec 6:2):

LXX:

ἀνήρ **ᾧ** δώσει **αὐτῷ** ὁ θεὸς πλοῦτον …	*a man* ***to whom*** *God gives wealth* (lit. *to whom … to him*) …

MT:

אִישׁ אֲשֶׁר יִתֶּן־לוֹ הָאֱלֹהִים עֹשֶׁר

ʾîš ***ʾăšer*** *yitten-**lô** hāʾĕlōhîm ʿōšer*

Targum Aram.:

גְּבַר דִּי יְהַב לֵיהּ …

*gəḇar **dî** yəhaḇ **lêh*** …

↑also GKC §155; Bauer-Leander §108.

289j 4. Ancient Greek, like Lat., makes use of "**clause intertwining**", i.e. of relative clause intertwining and of open interrogative clause intertwining: The relative or interrogative word functions as a sentence constituent not of the relative or interrogative clause (as it typically does), but of a construction subordinated to the relative or interrogative clause, i.e. of a subordinate clause, of an infinitive/ACI phrase or of a participle phrase. As a result, the relative or open interrogative clause may be said to be intertwined with that subordinated construction.[26]

a) **Relative clause intertwining** may be illustrated by the following examples.[27] Note that in many cases the Ancient Greek relative pronoun is best translated as a demonstrative or personal pronoun (↑142g; 289g).

---

26 As there is a close affinity between relative and open interrogative clauses (at least in part; ↑269d; 273b) both types clause intertwining are here treated together.

27 ↑Maier 1969: 132–135, to which this presentation is largely indebted.

The relative word may function as the sentence constituent

- of a clause subordinated to the relative clause, e.g.:

ἦσαν γὰρ προεωρακότες Τρόφιμον … ἐν τῇ πόλει σὺν αὐτῷ, **ὃν** (Od of the subordinated ὅτι-clause) ἐνόμιζον **ὅτι εἰς τὸ ἱερὸν εἰσήγαγεν ὁ Παῦλος**. *For they had previously seen Trophimus … in the city with him, and they supposed that Paul had brought him into the temple.* (Ac 21:29)

↑also Mt 7:12; 21:24; Jn 21:25.

- of an infinitive/ACI phrase subordinated to the relative clause, e.g.:

… οἱ μαθηταί σου ποιοῦσιν **ὃ** (Od of the subordinated InfP) οὐκ ἔξεστιν **ποιεῖν** ἐν σαββάτῳ. *… your disciples are doing what is not lawful to do on the Sabbath.* (Mt 12:2)

↑also Mt 3:11; 12:4; Mk 2:26; Lk 6:4; Ac 3:21; 4:12.28; 9:6.16; 13:25; 16:21; 22:10; 24:19; 25:10.19.26; 26:7; 27:39; Tt 1:11; He 13:10.

- of a participle phrase subordinated to the relative clause, e.g.:

ὁμοία ἐστὶν κόκκῳ σινάπεως, **ὃν** (Od of the subordinated PtcP) **λαβὼν** ἄνθρωπος ἔβαλεν εἰς κῆπον ἑαυτοῦ. *It is like a mustard seed that a person took and* (↑231b) *planted in the garden.* (Lk 13:19)

κἀκεῖθεν οἱ ἀδελφοί … ἦλθαν εἰς ἀπάντησιν ἡμῖν … **οὓς** (Od of the subordinated PtcP) **ἰδὼν** ὁ Παῦλος εὐχαριστήσας τῷ θεῷ ἔλαβε θάρσος. *The believers from there … came to meet us … When he saw them, Paul thanked God and took courage.* (Ac 28:15)

↑also Mt 13:31.33.44; Lk 4:23; 12:37.43; 13:21; Ac 11:6; 12:4; 13:22; 15:29; 19:25; 22:5; 23:29; 27:17; 28:7f.13f; 2Cor 8:22; 1Tm 1:6.19; 6:10.21; He 11:29; 12:19; 13:7.9; 1Pe 1:8 (2×); 2:4; 3Jn 6.

b) **Open interrogative clause intertwining** occurs with both dependent and independent interrogative clauses.

The interrogative word may function as the sentence constituent

- of a clause subordinated to the interrogative clause, e.g.:

ἤρξαντο … τοὺς κακῶς ἔχοντας περιφέρειν **ὅπου** (= ἐκεῖ ὅπου [↑289d]; ὅπου is LocC of the subordinated ὅτι-clause) ἤκουον **ὅτι ἐστίν**. *They began to bring those who were ill … to wherever they heard (that) he was.* (Mk 6:55)

- of an infinitive/ACI phrase subordinated to the interrogative clause, e.g.:

ἐξήλθομεν ἔξω τῆς πύλης παρὰ ποταμὸν **οὗ** (LocC of the subordinated ACI phrase) ἐνομίζομεν **προσευχὴν εἶναι**. *We went outside the city gate to the riverside where we thought (that) there was a place of prayer.* (Ac 16:13)

↑also Mt 11:7; 16:13; Mk 8:27.

- of a participle phrase subordinated to the interrogative clause, e.g.:

τί (Od of the subordinated PtcP) **ποιήσας** ζωὴν αἰώνιον κληρονομήσω;	*What must I do to inherit eternal life?* (lit. *Doing/Having done what, will I inherit eternal life?*) (Lk 10:25; 18:18)

290 Relative clauses with adverbial force

(↑BR §289/290; BDF §377–380; 386:4; Z §335–339; Maier 1969: 129–130)

290a As pointed out in 289b, relative clauses basically function as either attributive modifiers or sentence constituents. Alongside theses regular syntactic functions, Ancient Greek relative clauses sometimes have an **additional adverbial force**, with a communicational role that is very similar to that of certain adverbial clauses. One usually distinguishes five types of "adverbial" relative clauses. These can be recognized by specific formal features or (especially) by contextual clues or both. In the NT only the conditional type is fairly well-attested.

290b 1. Relative clauses with an additional **causal** force (↑277; 259g; 333a),

a) recognizable by the **ind.** (expressing facts; neg. οὐ; ↑245c) and by the context,

b) translatable as a relative clause or as a causal clause introduced by *since/for* or the like, e.g.:

Προσέχετε ἀπὸ τῶν ψευδοπροφητῶν, **οἵτινες ἔρχονται** πρὸς ὑμᾶς ἐν ἐνδύμασιν προβάτων, ἔσωθεν δέ εἰσιν λύκοι ἅρπαγες. (≈ … **ὅτι ἔρχονται** …)	*Be on your guard against false prophets who come to you in sheep's clothing but inwardly are ferocious wolves.* (Mt 7:15) (≈ … *since/for they come* …)

↑also Ac 10:47; Eph 3:13.

290c 2. Relative clauses with an additional **purpose** force (↑278; 259j; 336a),

a) recognizable by the **ind. fut.**, in the NT also **subj.** (↑210j), (neg. μή; ↑246b), and by the context,

b) translatable as a relative clause with *to be to* (or some other means of expressing obligation; ↑207d) or as a purpose clause introduced by *so that/in order that* or a *to*-infinitive phrase, e.g.:

ἀποστέλλω τὸν ἄγγελόν μου … ὃς **κατασκευάσει** τὴν ὁδόν σου. (≈ … **ἵνα κατασκευάσῃ** τὴν ὁδόν σου)	*I am sending my messengers … who is to prepare your way.* (Mk 1:2) (≈ … *in order that he may prepare your way/to prepare your way*)
συνῆλθον … ἄγοντες **παρ' ᾧ ξενισθῶμεν** Μνάσωνί τινι Κυπρίῳ … (= … ἄγοντες πρὸς Μνάσωνά τινα … παρ' ᾧ ξενισθῶμεν [inverse attraction; ↑289f]) (≈ … πρὸς Μ. … **ἵνα ξενισθῶμεν** παρ' αὐτῷ)	*Some … came along and brought us to Mnason of Cyprus … with whom we were to stay.* (Ac 21:16) (≈ … *to M. … so that we might stay with him*)
… ἔπεμψα ὑμῖν Τιμόθεον … **ὃς** ὑμᾶς **ἀναμνήσει** τὰς ὁδούς μου τὰς ἐν Χριστῷ Ἰησοῦ … (≈ … **ἵνα** ὑμᾶς **ἀναμνήσῃ** …)	*… I have sent Timothy to you … who will remind you of my ways in Christ Jesus.* (1Cor 4:17) (≈ … *in order that/to remind you* …)

↑Mk 14:14; Lk 22:11 (it may, however, be better to classify these two examples as indirect deliberative questions; ↑273e).

3. Relative clauses with an additional **qualitative-consequential** (or "qualitative-result") force (these indicate a consequence or result of a particular quality ["such that"]); ↑279; 259i; 334a), **290d**

a) recognizable by the **ind.** (neg. οὐ; ↑245c), in the NT also by the **subj.** (↑210j) (neg. μή; ↑246b), and by the context,

b) translatable as a result clause introduced by *that* or as a relative clause (perhaps with *can*), e.g.:

τίς οὗτός ἐστιν **ὃς** καὶ ἁμαρτίας **ἀφίησιν**; (≈ … **ὥστε** … **ἀφιέναι**;)	*Who is this, who even forgives sin?* Or perhaps: *Who is this, who can even forgive sins?* (Lk 7:49)
ἄξιός ἐστιν ᾧ **παρέξῃ** τοῦτο.	*He is worthy that you grant him this/He is worthy for you to grant him this.* (Lk 7:4)
… ἔχειν τι καὶ τοῦτον **ὃ προσενέγκῃ**.	*… have something (that) he can offer/… something to offer.* (He 8:3)

4. Relative clauses with an additional **conditional** force (↑280–285; 259h; 331a), **290e**

a) recognizable (apart from the context):

in CG by the moods that are typical of conditional clauses,

in the NT

- by the prospective **subj.** (↑210j) with **ἄν** or **ἐάν** (!) (↑general prospective case, neg. μή; ↑246b) the clause typically being introduced by

ὅς (ὅστις)/ὅσοι/ὅπου mostly + ἄν/ἐάν + subj.	*whoever/as many as/wherever* (↑282a/282b; ↑also 142a)

- less frequently by the **ind.** (↑indefinite case; ↑281),

b) translatable usually as a relative clause (ἄν/ἐάν often taking into account as *-ever*), sometimes best as a conditional clause, e.g.:

ὃς ἐὰν οὖν **λύσῃ** μίαν τῶν ἐντολῶν τούτων τῶν ἐλαχίστων καὶ **διδάξῃ** οὕτως …, ἐλάχιστος κληθήσεται … (≈ **ἐάν τις** … **λύσῃ**…)	*So, whoever relaxes one of the least of these commands and teaches … will be called least …* (Mt 5:19) (*So, if anyone relaxes …*)
ὃς δ' **ἂν εἴπῃ** … Μωρέ, ἔνοχος ἔσται εἰς τὴν γέενναν τοῦ πυρός. (≈ **ἐάν τις** … **εἴπῃ** …)	*Whoever says, "You fool!" will be liable to the hell of fire.* (Mt 5:22) (*If anyone says …*)
οἶδα ὅτι **ὅσα ἂν αἰτήσῃ** τὸν θεὸν δώσει σοι ὁ θεός. (≈ … **ἐάν τι αἰτήσῃ** …)	*I know that whatever you ask from God, God will give you.* (Jn 11:22) (*… if you ask anything …*)

↑also Mt 10:11.14; 11:6; 12:50; 23:16; Lk 8:18; 9:5; Jn 4:14; Ac 3:23; Ro 9:15; 1Cor 11:27; Jas 2:10 (without ἄν); 1Jn 2:5; 3:17.

ὃς γὰρ (≈ **εἰ** γάρ **τις**) οὐκ ἔστιν καθ' ὑμῶν ὑπὲρ ὑμῶν ἐστιν.	*For the one who is not against you is for you.* (Lk 9:50) (*… if someone is not against you, he …*)

ὅστις (≈ **εἴ τις**) σε ῥαπίζει εἰς τὴν δεξιὰν σιαγόνα σου, στρέψον αὐτῷ καὶ τὴν ἄλλην.	*If someone slaps you on your right cheek, turn the other to him also.* (Mt 5:39)

↑also Mk 6:11; He 9:16 (with ὅπου *where* [≈ *if*]).

Note that a subj. used in a relative clause it does not necessarily imply a conditional force (↑289a, p.541; 290c/290d); it could e.g. be a hortatory subj., so in He 12:28).

290f 5. Relative clauses with an **iterative** (conditional-temporal) force (referring to something in the past; occurring only infrequently in the NT; ↑276e),

a) recognizable (apart from the context):

in CG by the **opt.** (without ἄν; ↑211i; neg. μή; ↑244),

in the NT by the **augment indicative + ἄν** (↑211i; neg. probably οὐ; ↑244),

b) translatable as a relative clause, often with an additional *-ever* element, e.g.:

καὶ **ὅπου ἂν εἰσεπορεύετο** εἰς κώμας … ἐτίθεσαν τοὺς ἀσθενοῦντας καὶ παρεκάλουν αὐτόν … καὶ **ὅσοι ἂν ἥψαντο** αὐτοῦ ἐσῴζοντο.	*And wherever he would go into villages … they would place those who were ill … and would ask him … and all who would touch him/it were made well.* (Mk 6:56)
πάντας … **ὅσους λάβοιεν** … διέφθειρον.	*They would slaughter … all whomever they captured …* (Thucydides 2.67)

3.5 Deviations from syntactic and other "norms"

Deviations as stylistic devices or "figures of speech" 291

I. Speakers/writers of Ancient Greek (as of other languages) often deviate from "normal" usage to achieve certain rhetorical effects. They do so in a variety of ways that affect not only the syntax of a text but in fact every level of text structure: that of writing, sounds, word-forms and syntax involving, of course, the various types of content indicated by these (lexical, propositional and textual). Such deviations are often referred to as "stylistic devices" (also as "rhetorical devices") or by the traditional (somewhat more restricted) umbrella term "figures of speech" (↑291b, 2). The highest text level (the textgrammatical and textpragmatic one) is hardly touched upon in typical accounts of stylistic devices (with their beginnings in Ancient Greece) nor was it possible yet to do any better in the present overview. Moreover, it should be noted that the stylistic devices or figures of speech treated here are to a large extent about what Schwyzer (II: 698) calls "lower" (i.e. standardized) stylistics or "syntactic stylistics"; in other words the bulk of these are commonly used "deviations" (really from typical rather than from "normal" usage), which most native speakers would not even have regarded as deviations. However, between such "lower" stylistics and the "higher" (i.e. not standardized, always intentional, rhetorical) one there are no clearly-defined boundaries. 291a

II. Types of stylistic devices 291b

1. Stylistic devices are associated primarily with either of the **two sides of the elements of linguistic structures** (↑p. 12). This allows us to distinguish between two basic types:

a) stylistic devices that are primarily associated with the **expression side**, i.e. with the grammatical form (writing, sounds, word-forms and syntax);[1]

b) stylistic devices whose focus is on the **content side**, on the kind of contents or content combinations to be conveyed, thus on the semantic side (e.g. in the case of a metaphor and paradox).

2. According to the kind of **deviation from the normal or rather typical usage** (grammatical or semantic) stylistic devices, in most cases "**figures of speech**", which is the traditional rendering of the Ancient Greek term σχήματα, sg. τὸ σχῆμα, may be subdivided as follows:

a) Figures involving word or clause order (↑292),
b) Figures involving omission (↑293),
c) Figures involving repetition and amplification (↑294),
d) Tropes (non-literal use of words; ↑295), and
e) Figures involving paraphrasing, veiling, and unveiling (↑296).

While a) to c) are primarily connected with grammar or syntax, d) and e) are semantic phenomena. These are included in the present overview[2] too for the sake of completeness, though they are explained only briefly.

---

1 A sound-related example is the avoidance of the hiatus (a break between two vowels, a word-final and a word-initial one as in *th**e** **a**pple*) so important in CG (though not in the NT; ↑BDF §486). Another one would be the metre which was basic to CG poetry, but in the NT is almost exclusively limited to a handful of extra-biblical quotations (↑BDF §487).

2 Largely based on Bühlmann-Scherer (a reference work on figures of speech dealing mainly with the usage attested in the Bible, with helpful bibliographical references), which as many of the titles mentioned there owes a great deal to the comprehensive classic by E. W. Bullinger.

292 Figures involving word or clause order

(↑Bühlmann-Scherer: 47–53; BDF §472; LAW on most head words)

292a 1. **Anastrophe** (↑Bühlmann-Scherer: 49f; BDF §472)

When the usual order of two expressions is inverted (frequently for emphasis), one may speak of "anastrophe" (↑ἀναστρέφω *to turn upside down, to invert*; ἀναστροφή *inverted word-order*; other terms in use: "inversio", "perversio", "reversio"), e.g.:

καὶ φόβος (S) ἐπέπεσεν (P) ἐπ' αὐτόν (O).	*And fear fell upon him.* (Lk 1:12)

In NT narratives the predicator is typically found in the front position (↑128b p. 179).

Note that others (BDF §494; Smyth §3011) use this term to refer to the repetition of the final word of sentence (or verse) at the beginning of the subsequent sentence (or verse). ↑294n.

Hysteron proteron (↑Bühlmann-Scherer: 50) is a figure of speech related to the anastrophe: two contents are arranged in a way that reverses its temporal order (↑ὕστερον πρότερον *what is later [is mentioned] first*), rarely occurring in the NT, a possible example being:

ὄψεσθε … τοὺς ἀγγέλους τοῦ θεοῦ **ἀναβαίνοντας** καὶ **καταβαίνοντας** …	*You will see … the angels of God ascending and descending …* (Jn 1:51)

292b 2. **Prolepsis** (↑Bühlmann-Scherer: 50; BDF §476; Z §204–207)

When the subject or (less frequently the object) of a subordinate clause is placed before the clause it belongs to (for emphasis), one usually speaks of "prolepsis" (↑προλαμβάνω *to precede, to anticipate*, πρόληψις; other terms in use: "anticipation", "anticipatio"; ↑128b p. 180), e.g.:

ἀλλὰ **τοῦτον** οἴδαμεν πόθεν ἐστίν.	*But we know where this man is from.* (Jn 7:27)

292c 3. **Hyperbaton** (↑Bühlmann-Scherer: 51; BDF §477)

When two expressions that syntactically belong together are separated by the interposition of one or more expressions, one speaks of "hyperbaton" (↑ὑπερβαίνω *to overstep*, ὑπερβατόν *transposition* [of expressions]); other terms in use: "transiectio", "verbi transgressio"); the hyperbaton occurs especially in CG poetry, less frequently in CG prose and in the NT, e.g.:

οὐκ ἐπίστασθε **τῆς αὔριον** (Attr) ποία **ἡ ζωὴ** (HN) ὑμῶν.	*You do not know what your life of (the day) tomorrow will be like.* (Jas 4:14 Var.; NA: τὸ τῆς αὔριον *what concerns [the day] tomorrow* [Od of ἐπίστασθε])

The attributive modifier τῆς αὔριον *of (the day) tomorrow* is separated from its head noun ζωή *life* (and is placed in the superordinate construction) with ποία *what kind* being interposed.
↑also Ac 11:11; 12:13; He 6:10; 10:11; 12:11; 1Pe 4:2.

292d 4. **Parenthesis** (↑Bühlmann-Scherer: 53; BDF §465)

The term "parenthesis" (↑παρεντίθημι *to insert*, ἡ παρένθεσις *insertion*) refers to a grammatically independent insertion into a text component whose content it is to elucidate (↑341; 352b,30). As it regularly interrupts the flow of a sentence, a parenthesis typically leads to a hyperbaton (↑292c). It occurs fairly frequently in the NT (sometimes against CG usage):

a) mostly as a fairly short insertion easy to identify as such, e.g.:

Ὅταν οὖν ἴδητε τὸ βδέλυγμα τῆς ἐρημώσεως … ἑστὸς ἐν τόπῳ ἁγίῳ, **ὁ ἀναγινώσκων νοείτω**, τότε οἱ … φευγέτωσαν.	*So when you see the abomination of desolation … standing in the holy place (let the reader understand), then those … must flee …* (Mt 24:15f)

↑also Mk 7:2; Eph 2:5; 1Tm 2:7.

b) less frequently as something along the following lines:

πολλάκις προεθέμην ἐλθεῖν πρὸς ὑμᾶς, **καὶ ἐκωλύθην ἄχρι τοῦ δεῦρο**, ἵνα τινὰ καρπὸν σχῶ … *I often planned to come to you (but thus far have been prevented) in order that I might have some fruit …* (Ro 1:13)

The purpose clause is subordinate to προεθέμην ἐλθεῖν … (the parenthesis leads to a hyperbaton). ↑also Ro 7:1; 2Cor 12:2; Mk 2:10.

Note that vocatives and interjections are not rhetorical, but conventional parentheses (↑148a; 252.63; 254e).

5. **Anacoluthon** (↑Bühlmann-Scherer: 52; BDF §466–470; §458.4) 292e

The term "anacoluthon" (↑ἀκολουθέω *to follow*, plus alpha privative as a negating prefix [↑367b]) refers to "a change of construction in a sentence that leaves the initial construction unfinished" (Baldick s.v.), as the speaker/writer suddenly stops in the middle of a sentence (↑ellipsis; ↑293a) or transitions into a different construction. This phenomenon occurs frequently in vivid speech (e.g. in the dialogues of Plato; it would be wrong to classify it, if used with moderation, as a violation of grammatical rules, as a "solecism" [↑LAW sub "Anakoluth"]), e.g.:

ὁ γὰρ Μωϋσ**ῆς** οὗτ**ος** (S without P), ὅς … – οὐκ οἴδαμεν τί ἐγένετο αὐτῷ. *For this Moses who … we don't know what has happened to him = As for this Moses …* (Ac 7:40)

This is an instance of a "casus pendens", here (as mostly) a nominativus pendens (↑147b); the other cases rarely have this function (↑Z §29–31; examples: 2Cor 12:17 [acc.]; Lk 12:48 [dat.]).

↑also Lk 20:18; Ac 8:7; 19:34; 24:5; Ga 2:4; Eph 3:17; Php 1:30; 1Tm 1:3; 2Pe 1:17.

ὁ πιστεύ**ων** (S without P) εἰς ἐμέ … – ποταμοὶ ἐκ τῆς κοιλίας αὐτοῦ ῥεύσουσιν ὕδατος ζῶντος. *The one who believes in me … rivers of living water will flow from his heart = From the heart of the one who believes in me … rivers of living water will flow.* (Jn 7:38)

For more extensive instances of anacoluthon ↑Ro 2:17–19 and 5:12–14. ↑also 252.34.

Figures involving omission (↑Bühlmann-Scherer: 55–59; LAW on most head words) 293

I. **Ellipsis** (↑Bühlmann-Scherer: 56f; BDF §479–481) 293a

The term "ellipsis" (↑ἐλλείπω *to omit*, ἔλλειψις *omission*), sometimes called "omissio", refers to the omission of one or more sentence elements that would normally be required in a well-formed (grammatical) construction. Frequently they are omitted when they can easily be supplied in thought on the basis of the context (↑257e). For an example ↑Mk 13:1 in 147b.

The term "brachylogy" (↑βραχύς *brief/concise*, λέγω *to speak*, βραχυλογία *conciseness*) is by many treated as a synonym of "ellipsis". Those who distinguish between the two terms (e.g. BDF §483), apply the term "brachylogy" more specifically to the omission of elements that in normal usage would be semantically required, but not grammatically, while "ellipsis" would cover both types of omission. Other terms used instead of "brachylogy" are "breviloquentia", "brevitas" or "detractio".

1. The so-called **"apo koinou" construction** (↑ἀπὸ κοινοῦ *in common*) occurs very frequently: an element that is common to two sentences or sentence constituents is not repeated (also ↑257e), e.g.: 293b

εἰ καὶ **πάντες** (S1) **σκανδαλισθήσονται** (P1), ἀλλ' οὐκ ἐγώ (S2) _ (P2). *Even though all fall away, I will not.* (Mk 14:29)

On the basis of the εἰ-clause the predicator (P2) implied by ἐγώ (S2) can easily be supplied in thought: (οὐκ) σκανδαλισθήσομαι *I will (not) fall away* (in Mt 26:33 it is explicit).

… τοῦ ἐπιστρέψαι **ἀπὸ σκότους** εἰς φῶς καὶ _ **τῆς ἐξουσίας** τοῦ σατανᾶ ἐπὶ τὸν θεόν. — *… so that they may turn from darkness to light and [from] the power of Satan to God.* (Ac 26:18)

The preposition ἀπό *from* is not repeated.

↑also e.g. Mt 4:25; also ↑142d on prepositions not being repeated in relative clauses.

Further examples with apo koinou ellipsis: Mt 9:19; Lk 22:36; Jn 6:56; 15:4; Ro 11:16.

The apo koinou ellipsis frequently occurs in comparative constructions (↑287c p.537).

293c 2. There are **formulaic** or **conventional** (non-rhetorical) types of **ellipsis**, particularly:

a) the "omission" of the copula (occurs very frequently; ↑256d), e.g.:

… **ὧν τὰ ὀνόματα** (S) **ἐν βίβλῳ ζωῆς** (LocC) _ (P). — *… whose names are in the book of life.* (Php 4:3)

b) the "omission" of ἐπιστέλλω *to say (by means of a letter), to write* or λέγω *to say* to be supplied in thought; with the dative indicating the addressee, a special use of the objective dative (↑174a), regularly at the beginning of a letter (↑218d), e.g.:

Παῦλος … (sc. ἐπέστειλα/ἐπιστέλλω or ἐπέστειλεν/ἐπιστέλλει) **Τιμοθέῳ** … — *[I] Paul … [am writing]* or *Paul … [is writing] to Timothy …* (1Tm 1:1f)

c) the omission of the reporting clause or at least of its verb introducing direct speech (occurs only occasionally in the NT; ↑274b), e.g.:

Ἀγρίππας δὲ πρὸς τὸν Φῆστον (sc. ἔφη or the like)· ἐβουλόμην καὶ αὐτὸς τοῦ ἀνθρώπου ἀκοῦσαι. — *Then Agrippa [said] to Festus, "I would like to hear the man myself."* (Ac 25:22; ↑26:1)

↑also Ac 5:9; 9:5.11 (but this may be an instance of apo koinou ellipsis; ↑293b); 17:18; 26:28f.

d) the omission of an object (mainly a pronominal one) in contexts in which it can easily be supplied in thought (↑257e; occurs frequently), e.g.:

ἀκούσας δὲ (sc. ταῦτα/τοῦτο) ὁ Ἰησοῦς εἶπεν αὐτῷ· … — *When Jesus heard [this], he said to him, "…"* (Lk 18:22)

e) the omission of the subject in certain cases (↑255c/255f), e.g.:

σαλπίσει (P) _ (S). — *He* (i.e. the trumpeter) *will sound a trumpet.* (1Cor 15:52)

f) the omission of γῆ/χώρα *land*, ἡμέρα *day*, ὥρα *hour/time* etc. (↑134c; 137c; 260c), e.g.:

τῇ ἐπιούσῃ _ — *on the following [day]* (Ac 21:18 etc.)

g) the omission of "son", "mother", "wife", "household" or the like within a combination of two personal names (meant to express a kinship relation), the second one being in the genitive (↑159c), e.g.:

Μαρία ἡ τοῦ Ἰακώβου _ — *Mary the [mother] of James* (Mk 16:1)

h) the omission of "other", "else" or the like (↑BDF §306), e.g.:

Πέτρος καὶ **οἱ _ ἀπόστολοι** εἶπαν … — *Peter and the [other] apostles said …* (Ac 5:29)

Εἴτε οὖν ἐσθίετε εἴτε πίνετε εἴτε **τι** _ ποιεῖτε, πάντα εἰς δόξαν θεοῦ ποιεῖτε. — *So whether you eat or drink, or whatever [else] you do, do it all for the glory of God.* (1Cor 10:31)

i) the occasional omission (influenced by Semitic usage) of τις *some(one)/any(one)* or τι *some(thing)/any(thing)* usually combined with partitive genitive phrases or their replacements with ἐκ/ἐξ (↑166b).

↑also 280b on ἐπεί translatable as *(for/since) otherwise*.

↑also BDF §480 for a more detailed account of the formulaic/conventional use of the ellipsis.

3. **Zeugma** (↑Bühlmann-Scherer 57f; BDF §479.2) is a further variety of the ellipsis (↑ζεύγνυμι *to join together*, ζεῦγμα *what is used for joining together*): two sentence elements (subjects or objects) are used jointly with one other syntactic element (typically the predicate verb), though only one of them in a way that would normally be considered acceptable (syntactically or semantically), e.g.: 293d

γάλα (Od of thing 1) ὑμᾶς **ἐπότισα** (P1), οὐ **βρῶμα** (Od of thing 2) _ (P2).	*I gave you milk to drink, not solid food [to eat].* (1Cor 3:2)

II. **Asyndesis** (↑Bühlmann-Scherer: 58; 30; BDF §459–463) 293e

When the usual connective between words, phrases or sentences/clauses is omitted, one speaks of "asyndesis", the element lacking the usual connective being called "asyndeton" (↑συνδέω *to bind together/to connect*, plus alpha privative prefix [↑367b]: τὸ ἀσύνδετον *the lack of connection*). There is a counterpart called "polysyndesis" ("manifold [πολύς *much/many*] connection"), the repeated use of connectives such as "and", "or" or the like to mark the coordination of individual expressions, typically occurring in ancient languages, but often used deliberately for rhetorical effect, e.g.:

κήρυξον τὸν λόγον, ἐπίστηθι εὐκαίρως _ ἀκαίρως (asyndesis).	*Preach the Word; be persistent [whether] it is convenient [or] inconvenient.* (2Tm 4:2)
… πίστις, _ ἐλπίς, _ ἀγάπη (asyndesis).	*… faith, hope, [and] love.* (1Cor 13:13)
ἔλεος … **καὶ** εἰρήνη **καὶ** ἀγάπη (polysyndesis) …	*Mercy …, (and) peace, and love …* (Jd 2)

↑274b; 272d; 231l; on the asyndesis in a textgrammatical context ↑322a.

III. **Aposiopesis** (↑Bühlmann-Scherer: 59; BDF §482) 293f

When a speaker/writer due to excitement, embarrassment or the like breaks off a sentence in the middle leaving it unfinished, one speaks of "aposiopesis" (↑ἀποσιωπάω *to fall silent*, ἀποσιώπησις *the act of falling silent*; other terms in use: "interruptio", "obticentia", "reticentia"), e.g.:

εἰ δὲ πνεῦμα ἐλάλησεν αὐτῷ …;	*Suppose a spirit has spoken to him …?* (Ac 23:9)

The *then*-clause is not expressed, perhaps something like *what could we do to stop it?* (the Byz adds μὴ θεομαχῶμεν [hortative subj. pres. θεωμαχέω] *let us not fight against God*).

↑also Jn 6:62; Ro 2:17; 9:22; 1Cor 9:15.

A kind of aposiopesis sometimes occurs in clauses superordinate to comparative clauses; ↑287c p. 537.

Figures involving repetition and amplification 294

(↑Bühlmann-Scherer: 15–46; LAW on most head words)

1. **Alliteration** (↑Bühlmann-Scherer: 16–18; BDF §488) 294a

The term "alliteration" (↑Lat. *ad* "to" + *lit[t]era* "letter") refers to the repetition of the same sound or syllable in a sequence of words, especially (but not only)[3] word-initially (other terms in use: "homoioprophoron" [ὁμοιοπρόφορον] and "assiduitas"), e.g.:

Πολυμερῶς καὶ **π**ολυτρόπως **π**άλαι ὁ θεὸς λαλήσας τοῖς πατράσιν ἐν τοῖς προφήταις …	*Long ago God spoke to the fathers by the prophets at different times and in different ways …* (He 1:1)
… ἔμ**αθεν** ἀφ' ὧν ἔπ**αθεν** τὴν ὑπακοήν.	*… he learned obedience from what he suffered.* (He 5:8)

"Alliteration" may refer to consonantal agreement only, "assonance" then to vowels agreement.

3 ↑294b with exclusive word-initial sound agreement.

294b 2. **Homoiokatarkton** (↑Bühlmann-Scherer: 18; BDF §488)

In the case of identity of the word-initial sounds of words, phrases, or sentences/clauses that follow each other immediately or more remotely one may speak of "homoiokatarkton" (ὁμοιοκάταρκτον) or "homoiarkton" (↑ὅμοιος *equal, similar* [κατ]-ἄρχω *to begin*; sometimes called "parhomoion" [παρόμοιον *something closely resembling*]), e.g.:

χαίρειν μετὰ **χ**αιρόντων,	*Rejoice with those who rejoice,*
κλαίειν μετὰ **κλ**αιόντων.	*weep with those who weep.* (Ro 12:15)

294c 3. **Homoioteleuton** (↑Bühlmann-Scherer: 18f; BDF §488)

The repetition of word-final sounds of words, phrases, or sentences/clauses that follow each other immediately or more remotely may be called "homoioteleuton" (ὁμοιοτέλευτον; ↑ὅμοιος *equal, similar*, τελευτή *end*) or "end rhyme", e.g.:

ὃς ἐφανερώ**θη** ἐν σαρκί	*He was manifested in the flesh,*
ἐδικαιώ**θη** ἐν πνεύματι	*vindicated by the Spirit,*
ὤφ**θη** ἀγγέλοις	*seen by angels,*
ἐκηρύχ**θη** ἐν ἔθνεσιν	*proclaimed among the nations,*
ἐπιστεύ**θη** ἐν κόσμῳ	*believed on in the world,*
ἀνελήμφ**θη** ἐν δόξῃ	*taken up in glory.* (1Tm 3:16)

↑Ro 5:16; Ac 17:25.

294d 4. **Paronomasia** (↑Bühlmann-Scherer: 19f; LSJ s.v.; BDF §488)

When the similarity of repeated expressions extends to entire words (and not to syllables only as in the case of alliteration), one may speak of "paronomasia" (↑παρονομάζω *to call by a slightly different name*; παρονομασία *play upon words which sound alike, but have different senses*; other terms in use: παρήχησις [*similarity of sound*], "affictio", "annominatio", "denominatio", "levis immutatio", "supparile"), e.g.:

294e a) words that sound similar (BDF §488.2: "parechesis"), e.g.:

… **λιμοὶ** καὶ **λοιμοὶ** ἔσονται. (also ↑2c,1)	*There will be … famines and plagues.* (Lk 21:11)

294f b) words belonging to the same word-family or having the same stem but differing in sense/function (BDF §488.1: "paronomasia"), e.g.:

ἆρά γε **γινώσκεις** ἃ **ἀναγινώσκεις**;	*Do you understand what you are reading?* (Ac 8:30)

↑Mt 21:41.

294g c) words that are the same, but have a different inflectional form or function (a figure called "polyptoton" [πολύπτωτον; ↑πολύς *much/many*, πτῶσις *inflectional variety/case*], also "figura ex pluribus casibus", "variatio", "declinatio", "derivatio", μεταβολή [*change*], μετάκλισις [*change of position*], παρηγμένον [*something derived*], "traductio"), e.g.:

Ὃς **παρ' ἐλπίδα ἐπ' ἐλπίδι** ἐπίστευσεν …	*In hope against hope he believed …* (Ro 4:18)
ὅτι **ἐξ αὐτοῦ** καὶ **δι' αὐτοῦ** καὶ **εἰς αὐτὸν** τὰ πάντα·	*For from him and through him and for him are all things.* (Ro 11:36)

294h 5. **Figura etymologica** (↑Bühlmann-Scherer: 21f; BDF §153; 488.1a)

When two words are closely related (etymologically) having the same stem, one speaks of "figura etymologica" (some include cases of non-related, but synonymous stems as well). This typically applies to verb forms whose complement is a (cognate) accusative (a direct internal object; ↑151), e.g.:

ἀγωνίζου τὸν καλὸν **ἀγῶνα** τῆς πίστεως.	*Fight the good fight of the faith.* (1Tm 6:12)

6. **Wordplay** (↑Bühlmann-Scherer: 22f; BDF §488.1) 294i

One may speak of "wordplay" (or "pun") when the play on sounds (as in the case of paronomasia) is joined by a play on meanings, e.g.:

πολλοὶ γάρ εἰσιν **κλητοί**, ὀλίγοι δὲ **ἐκλεκτοί**. *For many are called, but few are chosen.* (Mt 22:14)

7. **Leitmotif** (↑Bühlmann-Scherer: 24f) 294j

When words or phrases that highlight the theme of a text are frequently repeated, one may speak of "leitmotif" or "leitmotiv" (from German: "leading motif"); other terms sometimes used in a similar way are "catchword"/"catch phrase", "keyword"/"key phrase"; e.g.:

ἀγάπη, ἀγαπάω, ἀγαπητός … *love, to love, beloved* … in 1Jn 4:7–12

8. **Gemination** (↑Bühlmann-Scherer: 26–29; BDF §493.1; LAW sub "Epanalepse" and "Anadiplose") 294k

When an expression is repeated in the same form and with the same meaning, one may speak of "gemination". Terms sometimes used instead: "reduplicatio", "iteratio", "repetitio", "anadiplosis" (ἀναδίπλωσις *doubling*), "epanalepsis" (ἐπανάληψις *resumption*), παλιλλογία (*repetition*). Frequently, however, the following distinctions are made, e.g.:

a) repetition of words: iteratio, palillogia, e.g.: 294l

Μάρθα, Μάρθα … *Martha, Martha* … (Lk 10:41)

b) repetition of phrases: repetitio, epanalepsis, e.g.: 294m

μεγάλη ἡ Ἄρτεμις Ἐφεσίων, *Great is Artemis of the Ephesians!*
μεγάλη ἡ Ἄρτεμις Ἐφεσίων. *Great is Artemis of the Ephesians!* (Ac 19:34; Codex B)

c) repetition of the preceding word or phrase of a sentence or verse at the beginning of the next: 294n
reduplicatio, anadiplosis, epanadiplosis, epanastrophe (ἐπαναστροφή *return*), e.g.:

Ἐν ἀρχῇ ἦν ὁ **λόγος**, *In the beginning was the Word,*
καὶ ὁ **λόγος** ἦν πρὸς τὸν **θεόν**, *and the Word was with God,*
καὶ **θεὸς** ἦν ὁ λόγος. *and the Word was God.* (Jn 1:1)

This is an instance of "anadiplosis iterata" (also called "catena" [i.e. a chain or connected series; ↑COED], "climax" [BDF §493; Baldick s.v.], or "Stufenrhythmus" [German: "step rhythm"]), e.g.:

ἡ θλῖψις **ὑπομονὴν** κατεργάζεται, *Affliction produces endurance*
ἡ δὲ **ὑπομονὴ δοκιμήν**, *endurance produces proven character,*
ἡ δὲ **δοκιμὴ ἐλπίδα**, *and proven character produces hope.*
ἡ δὲ **ἐλπὶς** οὐ καταισχύνει. *And hope does not put to shame.* (Ro 5:3–5)

d) repetition of an expression for emphasis: *at-taʿkīd* (Arabic "reinforcement [of a meaning]"), e.g.: 294o

ὃ **γέγραφα γέγραφα**. *What I have written, I have written.* (Jn 19:22)

9. **Anaphora** (↑Bühlmann-Scherer: 29f; BDF §489; 491) 294p

When at the beginning of successive lines or sentences/clauses the same expression is used, one may speak of "anaphora"/"epanaphora" (↑[ἐπ]αναφέρω also *to carry back*; [ἐπ]αναφορά *repetition*), e.g.:

μακάριοι οἱ πτωχοί … *Blessed are you who are poor* …
μακάριοι οἱ πεινῶντες νῦν … *Blessed are you who are hungry now* …
μακάριοι οἱ κλαίοντες νῦν … *Blessed are you who weep now* … (Lk 6:20ff)

↑also He 11:3–31 (πίστει *by faith*).

294q 10. **Epiphora** (↑Bühlmann-Scherer: 30; LAW sub "Epipher"; BDF §489; 491)

When at the end of successive lines or sentences/clauses the same expression is used, one may speak of "epiphora" (ἐπιφορά: ↑ἐπιφέρω *to add*); other terms in use: "epistrophe" (↑ἐπιστρέφω *to turn to*) and "antistrophe" (ἀντιστροφή; ↑ἀντίστροφος *turned so as to face one another, counterpart*), e.g.:

Ἑβραῖοί **εἰσιν; κἀγώ.**	*Are they Hebrews? So am I.*
Ἰσραηλῖταί **εἰσιν; κἀγώ.**	*Are they Israelites? So am I.*
σπέρμα Ἀβραάμ **εἰσιν; κἀγώ.**	*Are they offspring of Abraham? So am I.* (2Cor 11:22)

294r 11. **Ploce** (↑Bühlmann-Scherer: 31; BDF §489)

When both at the beginning and the end the same expression is used, one may speak of a "ploce", (Baldick s.v.: "delayed repetition of the same word or words"; ↑πλέκω *to weave,* πλοκή *weaving, web*; somewhat similar to "chiasmus" [↑294ac]); other terms in use: "kyklos" [κύκλος "circle"], "redditio" and "inclusio"), e.g.:

Ἡ ἀγάπη μακροθυμεῖ,	*Love is patient,*
χρηστεύεται **ἡ ἀγάπη.**	*love is kind.* (1Cor 13:4)

294s 12. **Symploce** (↑Bühlmann-Scherer: 31; BDF §489)

When an anaphora and an epiphora are combined or an anaphora is doubled, one may speak of "symploce" (↑σύν *together* + πλέκω *to weave*; συμπλοκή *weaving together*); other terms in use: "complexio", "connexio", "connexum", e.g.:

σπείρεται ἐν φθορᾷ,	*What is sown is perishable;*
ἐγείρεται ἐν ἀφθαρσίᾳ	*what is raised is imperishable.*
σπείρεται ἐν ἀτιμίᾳ,	*It is sown in dishonour;*
ἐγείρεται ἐν δόξῃ.	*it is raised in glory.*
σπείρεται ἐν ἀσθενείᾳ	*It is sown in weakness;*
ἐγείρεται ἐν δυνάμει.	*it is raised in power.*
σπείρεται σῶμα ψυχικόν,	*It is sown a natural body;*
ἐγείρεται σῶμα πνευματικόν.	*it is raised a spiritual body.* (1Cor 15:42–44)

294t 13. **Inclusio** (↑Bühlmann-Scherer: 32)

When a communicationally important word, phrase or sentence/clause occurs in the first and the last part of a section, one speaks of "inclusio" ["enclosing"]), e.g.:

ἀπὸ τῶν καρπῶν αὐτῶν ἐπιγνώσεσθε αὐτούς, μήτι συλλέγουσιν ἀπὸ ἀκανθῶν σταφυλάς … ἄρα γε **ἀπὸ τῶν καρπῶν αὐτῶν ἐπιγνώσεσθε αὐτούς**.	*You will recognize them by their fruit. Grapes are not gathered from thorns … are they? … So then, you will recognize them by their fruit.* (Mt 7:16–20)

294u 14. **Synonymy** (↑Bühlmann-Scherer: 32f)

When expressions with equal or closely similar meanings are linked, one may speak of "synonymy" (↑σύν *together* + ὄνομα [dialectal: ὄνυμα] *name, term*; συνωνυμία *sameness of definition*); other terms in use: "exaggeratio a synonymis" and "communio nominis", e.g.:

καὶ οὐκ οἶδας ὅτι σὺ εἶ ὁ **ταλαίπωρος** καὶ **ἐλεεινὸς** καὶ πτωχὸς καὶ τυφλὸς καὶ γυμνός.	*But you do not realize that you are wretched, pitiful, poor, blind and naked.* (Re 3:17)

15. **Hendiadys** (↑Bühlmann-Scherer: 33f; BDF §442.16; Z §460) 294v

When one single concept (ἕν *one [thing]*) is referred to by (διά) two (δύο) coordinated expressions, one may speak of a "hendiadys" (or "hendiadyoin" ἓν διὰ δυοῖν; ↑63a[2]), e.g.:

πάντα ὅσα **προσεύχεσθε καὶ αἰτεῖσθε** …	*Whatever you ask for in prayer* (lit. … *you pray and ask for*) … (Mk 11:24)

↑also Mt 4:16; 14:9; Lk 6:48; Ac 14:17; 23:6. ↑252.29,3b.

16. **σχῆμα καθ᾽ ὅλον καὶ μέρος** (↑Bühlmann-Scherer: 35; BDR $§159_3$; Schwyzer II: 81) 294w

When two expressions are used in succession one referring to the whole (ὅλον) and the other referring to a part (μέρος), which is mostly done for clarification, one may speak of a σχῆμα καθ᾽ ὅλον καὶ μέρος (*figure involving the whole and its part*), e.g.:

ἐνδυναμοῦσθε **ἐν κυρίῳ** (the whole) καὶ **ἐν τῷ κράτει τῆς ἰσχύος αὐτοῦ** (a part).	*Be strong in the Lord and in his mighty power.* (Eph 6:10)

17. **Pleonasm** (↑Bühlmann-Scherer: 36; BDF §484) 294x

When two expressions are used in succession with the a second one adding little or no new information, in fact indicating something that is (at least seemingly) unnecessary, one may speak of "pleonasm" (↑πλεονάζω *to be more than enough*, πλεονασμός), especially when the construction is not rhetorically prompted, but goes back to common usage (unlike e.g. synonymy [↑294u] and affirmation plus negated denial [↑294y], which, however, some regard as instances of pleonasm), e.g.:

πάλιν ἀνακάμψω πρὸς ὑμᾶς.	*I will return to you again* … (Ac 18:21)
ἐρεῖτε τῷ **οἰκο**δεσπότῃ τῆς **οἰκίας** …	*Say to the (house) owner of the house* … (Lk 22:11)
ἔπειτα μετὰ τοῦτο λέγει …	*Then after this he said* … (Jn 11:7; similarly Plato, Euthyphron 3a)

↑p. 202; 225e; 239; 260j; 289i.

18. **Affirmation plus negated denial** (↑Bühlmann-Scherer: 36f) 294y

In order to emphasize the content of an expression an expression may be added that says the same but does so by negating the opposite (e.g. *bad – not good*; a type of litotes; ↑296h; also 352b,16), e.g.:

ἀλήθειαν λέγω οὐ ψεύδομαι.	*I am telling the truth, I am not lying.* (1Tm 2:7)

19. **Parallelism** (↑Bühlmann-Scherer: 37–42; BDF §485; 489–492) 294z

When there is a particularly far-reaching analogy in form or content between elements of a compound or complex sentence (in poetry between verse elements/lines, verses, couplets or triplets), one usually speaks of "parallelism" or "parallelismus membrorum", i.e. parallelism of members (the elements involved usually being called "members").

Parallelism, one of the most fundamental modes of expression among ancient Semitic people, occurs extremely frequently in Biblical Hebrew (especially in poetic-prophetic contexts). The term "parallelism" goes back to the pioneering work by Robert Lowth, *De sacra poesi Hebraeorum* … (Oxford, 1753; translated by G. Gregory, *Lectures in the Sacred Poetry of the Hebrews*, 1835).

In the NT (outside Old Testament quotations) the Semitic type of parallelism ("parallelismus membrorum") occurs fairly frequently in the Gospels. In the Epistles parallelisms of the Greek tradition are better represented, especially so in the letters of Paul. The Semitic type of parallelism is usually subdivided as follows (↑Lowth):

294aa a) "**Synonymous parallelism**": the content of the first member is essentially repeated, but expressed in a different way, e.g.:

Ἑτοιμάσατε τὴν ὁδὸν κυρίου
εὐθείας ποιεῖτε τὰς τρίβους αὐτοῦ.

Prepare the way for the Lord,
make his paths straight. (Mk 1:3; ↑Is 40:3)

τὸν ἥλιον αὐτοῦ ἀνατέλλει ἐπὶ πονηροὺς καὶ ἀγαθοὺς
καὶ βρέχει ἐπὶ δικαίους καὶ ἀδίκους.

For he makes his sun rise on the evil and on the good,
and sends rain on the just and on the unjust. (Mt 5:45)

↑also 1Cor 1:25.

294ab b) "**Antithetic parallelism**": the content of the first member is made clearer by means of an expression that corresponds to it antithetically (i.e. by indicating the opposite), e.g.:

ὀφθαλμοὶ κυρίου ἐπὶ δικαίους
καὶ ὦτα αὐτοῦ εἰς δέησιν αὐτῶν,
(synonymic parallelism)
πρόσωπον δὲ κυρίου ἐπὶ ποιοῦντας κακά.
(antithetic parallelism)

For the eyes of the Lord are on the righteous,
and his ears are open to their prayer.
But the face of the Lord is against those who do evil. (1Pe 3:12/Ps 33:16f LXX)

(οὐδεὶς δύναται δυσὶ κυρίοις δουλεύειν)
ἢ γὰρ τὸν ἕνα μισήσει καὶ τὸν ἕτερον ἀγαπήσει
ἢ ἑνὸς ἀνθέξεται, καὶ τοῦ ἑτέρου καταφρονήσει.

(No one can serve two masters),
for either he will hate the one and love the other,
or he will be devoted to the one and despise the other. (Mt 6:24)

Some would add a further type: "synthetic parallelism", serving specifically to expand on the content of the first member, e.g.:

מָ֣וֶת וְ֭חַיִּים בְּיַד־לָשׁ֑וֹן
mā́weṯ wəḥayyîm bəyaḏ-lāšôn
וְ֝אֹהֲבֶ֗יהָ יֹאכַ֥ל פִּרְיָֽהּ׃
wə'ēhăḇę́hā yō'ḵal piryāh

Death and life are in the power of the tongue,
and those who love it will eat its fruit. (Pr 18:21)

As no real parallelism is (usually) involved in such "synthetic" instances and as the purpose of a parallelism is principally to expand on the content of the first member, the introduction of a "synthetic" type seems unnecessary.

294ac 20. **Chiasmus** (↑Bühlmann-Scherer: 43–45; BDF §477)

When the order of the constituents of the first member of a parallelism (↑294z) is reversed in the second member, one speaks of "chiasmus", χιασμός. The constituents are arranged crosswise to form the shape of an X, which corresponds to the Greek letter chi, hence the term "chiasmus", the arrangement having e.g. the following pattern:

a b
X
b' a'

The parallelismus membrorum is often chiastic. Generally in Ancient Hebrew and (biblical and extra-biblical) Greek texts, chiasmus frequently occurs as a structuring principle, e.g.:

ἡ γυνὴ (a) τοῦ ἰδίου σώματος οὐκ ἐξουσιάζει (b) ἀλλὰ ὁ ἀνὴρ (c), ὁμοίως δὲ ὁ ἀνὴρ (c') τοῦ ἰδίου σώματος οὐκ ἐξουσιάζει (b') ἀλλὰ ἡ γυνή (a').

For the wife does not have authority over her own body, but the husband does; likewise the husband does not have authority over his own body, but the wife does. (1Cor 7:4)

For the rationale behind the following account of figures of speech connected with lexical semantics being included in the present grammar ↑291b.

Tropes (↑Bühlmann-Scherer: 67–86; Leisi 1985: 176–195; LAW on most head words) 295

When an expression is not used with its normal (literal) meaning, but figuratively (non-literally), one may speak of a "trope" (↑τρέπω *to turn, to direct*; τροπή [rhetorical] *variation*: the expression is "directed away" from its normal content to a different one). 295a

The following uses are among the most important tropes:

1. **Metaphor** (↑Bühlmann-Scherer: 68f; Leisi 1985: 182–190; 207–213; ↑μεταφέρω *to transfer*, μεταφορά): 295b

The denotation of an expression that is used literally and the content denoted by its non-literal use have a number of features in common; certain features, however, appear to be mutually incompatible (breach of "semantic concord"), e.g.:

Ἐν αὐτῇ τῇ ὥρᾳ προσῆλθάν τινες Φαρισαῖοι λέγοντες αὐτῷ· ἔξελθε … ὅτι Ἡρῴδης θέλει σε ἀποκτεῖναι, καὶ εἶπεν αὐτοῖς· πορευθέντες εἴπατε **τῇ ἀλώπεκι ταύτῃ** …	*At that very hour some Pharisees came and said to him, "Get away … for Herod wants to kill you." And he said to them, "Go and tell that fox …"* (Lk 13:31f)

This utterance by Jesus indicates among other things: the fox (as conventionally seen) and Herod share the features of cunning and craftiness. The feature "non-human animal" relevant to the use of the expression "fox" appears in an unacceptable way with reference to a human being (Herod), which leads to a breach of semantic concord (one cannot normally converse with an animal!).

2. **Allegory** (↑Bühlmann-Scherer: 69f; ↑ἄλλο ἀγορεύω *to say sth. different*; ἀλληγορία *allegory*): 295c

A continued application of metaphors (↑295b), e.g. in 1Pe 2:6–8, where, alluding to Is 28:16, Ps 118 (LXX: 117):22 and Is 8:14f, Jesus is referred to as a special building stone for some being precious, but for others a stone that makes them stumble.

Note that the figure of speech "allegory" should not be confused with "allegoresis" which is the allegorizing interpretation of texts, e.g. in Mk 4:13–30 of Mk 4:3–8 (Parable of the Sower) or Ga 4:24–31 of the Genesis accounts of Sarah and Hagar.

3. **Simile** (↑Bühlmann-Scherer: 70): 295d

Similes (unlike metaphors) contain explicit hints such as "like", "is to be compared with" making clear that two things, "situations" or properties are not meant to be the same, but to be similar, e.g.:

ὁ λόγος αὐτῶν **ὡς** γάγγραινα νομὴν ἕξει.	*Their talk will spread like gangrene.* (2Tm 2:17)

4. **Parable** (↑Bühlmann-Scherer: 70–72; ↑παραβάλλω *to compare*; παραβολή *comparison*): 295e

An extended comparison in the form of a brief story that is to be understood metaphorically (↑295b) and whose focal point is about a certain truth to be communicated. ↑especially the parables of Jesus.

5. **Pictorial saying** (German "Bildwort"; ↑Bühlmann-Scherer: 72): 295f

Here, the comparison meant to communicate a certain truth is not presented in the form of a story (as in a parable; ↑295e), but in the form of a proverb or aphorism in pictorial language highlighting a (partially valid) principle observable in the world of experience. In Mk 2:21f e.g. the pictorial saying is about the partially valid principle that what is new is not compatible with what is old:

… καὶ οὐδεὶς βάλλει οἶνον νέον εἰς ἀσκοὺς παλαιούς· εἰ δὲ μή, ῥήξει ὁ οἶνος τοὺς ἀσκοὺς καὶ ὁ οἶνος ἀπόλλυται καὶ οἱ ἀσκοί· ἀλλὰ οἶνον νέον εἰς ἀσκοὺς καινούς.	… *And no one puts new wine into old wineskins. Otherwise, the wine will burst the skins, and the wine is lost as well as the skins. No, new wine is put into fresh wineskins.*

295g 6. **Metonymy** (↑Bühlmann-Scherer: 72ff; Leisi 1985: 190f; Bullinger: 613ff; ↑μετονομάζω *to call by a new name*, μετονομασία *change of name*; another term in use is ὑπαλλαγή *exchange*):

One expression is used in place of another; the meanings of the two are closer to each other than in the case of a metaphor (the concepts of metonymy and metaphor are without well-defined boundaries between them). The following uses will normally come under the umbrella term "metonymy":

295h a) **Synecdoche** (↑συνεκδέχομαι *to comprehend at the same time*, συνεκδοχή *understanding one thing with another*; also known as "comprehensio", "conceptio" or "intellectio"): an expression (normally) denoting a part of something is used to refer to the whole or vice versa:

295i • ***a part for the whole*** ("pars pro toto"), e.g.:

τὸν **ἄρτον** ἡμῶν τὸν ἐπιούσιον δὸς ἡμῖν σήμερον.	*Give us this day our daily bread* ("bread" for "food needed for life"). (Mt 6:11)
ὅτι **σὰρξ καὶ αἷμα** οὐκ ἀπεκάλυψέν σοι.	*For flesh and blood* ("flesh and blood" for "human beings") *did not reveal this to you.* (Mt 16:17)

295j • ***the whole for a part*** ("totum pro parte"), e.g.:

Τότε ἐξεπορεύετο πρὸς αὐτὸν **Ἱεροσόλυμα** καὶ **πᾶσα ἡ Ἰουδαία** …	*Then Jerusalem and all Judea* ("Jerusalem and all Judea" for "a large part of the population of …") … *were going out to him.* (Mt 3:5)

295k • ***the material for the thing made from/of it*** (↑295i), e.g.:

… καὶ ἐνεδιδύσκετο **πορφύραν** καὶ **βύσσον**.	… *who would dress in purple and fine linen* ("purple and …" for "garments made of …"). (Lk 16:19)

b) Other kinds of metonymy:

295l • ***the cause for its effect*** and ***the effect for its cause***, e.g.:

Μὴ νομίσητε ὅτι ἦλθον καταλῦσαι τὸν νόμον ἢ **τοὺς προφήτας**.	*Do not think that I have come to abolish the Law or the Prophets* ("Prophets" to refer to the message proclaimed by them). (Mt 5:17)
ἀθῷός εἰμι ἀπὸ τοῦ **αἵματος** τούτου.	*I am innocent of this man's blood* ("this man's blood" to refer to his murder). (Mt 27:24)

↑also Ac 11:23 ("grace" for its effects).

295m • ***the container for its contents*** (or the place for what is placed in it), e.g.:

ὁσάκις … τὸ **ποτήριον** πίνητε, τὸν θάνατον τοῦ κυρίου καταγγέλλετε …	*As often as … you drink the cup* (i.e. its contents) *you proclaim the Lord's death* … (1Cor 11:26)

295n • ***the abstract for the concrete*** ("abstractum pro concreto") and ***the concrete for the abstract*** ("concretum pro abstracto"), e.g.:

ἕνεκεν γὰρ **τῆς ἐλπίδος τοῦ Ἰσραὴλ** τὴν ἅλυσιν ταύτην περίκειμαι.	*Since it is because of the hope of Israel* (i.e. because of the Messiah Israel hopes for) *that I am wearing this chain.* (Ac 28:20)

ἡ **ἐπιστολὴ** ἡμῶν ὑμεῖς ἐστε. *You yourselves are our letter [of recommendation]* (i.e. our recommendation). (2Cor 3:2)

• ***the instrument for the activity***, e.g.: 295o

Ἐὰν ταῖς **γλώσσαις** τῶν ἀνθρώπων λαλῶ καὶ τῶν ἀγγέλων … *If I speak in the tongues* (i.e. languages) *of human beings and of angels* … (1Cor 13:1)

c) **Metalepsis** (↑μεταλαμβάνω *to exchange*; μετάληψις *exchange*): 295p

In place of an expression one of its synonyms is used which, strictly speaking, does not fit into the context in question. An example from Homer:

νῆσοι θοαί (νήσοισιν … θοῇσιν) *"swift" islands* (i.e. steeply sloping/sharp/pointed islands) (Odyssey 15.299)

θοός (*swift* etc.) sometimes replaces the adjective ὀξύς (*sharp, pointed, steeply sloping* [e.g. of a mountain peak]; *quick, swift*), but normally only when it refers to speed, not to something to be described as "steeply sloping/sharp/pointed".

d) **Hyperbole** (↑ὑπερβάλλω *to go beyond, to exceed*; ὑπερβολή *excess*; ↑Bühlmann-Scherer: 83): 295q

One use of the whole for a part ("totum pro parte"; ↑295j): an exaggeration not meant literally serving to emphasize a certain point (stretching it, as it were, into infinity), e.g.:

ὁδηγοὶ τυφλοί, οἱ διϋλίζοντες τὸν κώνωπα, τὴν δὲ **κάμηλον καταπίνοντες**. *You blind guides! You strain out a gnat but swallow a camel.* (Mt 23:24)

↑Mt 7:3; 18:22; 1Cor 1:17 (↑249b).

e) **Merismus** (↑μερίζω *to split up*; μερισμός *splitting up*; ↑Bühlmann-Scherer: 84f): 295r

One variety of metonymy (↑295g): the whole is referred to by means of two or more of its essential parts, often by polar opposites (also known as "distributio"), e.g.:

ὁ **οὐρανὸς** καὶ ἡ **γῆ** *heaven and earth* (= the universe) (Mt 5:18 et pass.)

οἱ **μικροὶ** καὶ οἱ **μεγάλοι** *the small and the great* (= all) (Re 19:5)

f) **Enallage** (↑ἐναλλάσσω *to swap*, ἐναλλαγή *interchange*; ↑Bühlmann-Scherer: 79f) with two uses: 295s

• contrasting with metonymy (↑295g): replacement of one word-class or inflectional form with another (in the case of metonymy there is typically no such replacement), e.g.:

… διὰ τὸ μὴ ἔχειν **βάθος γῆς**. … *because it had no depth of soil.* (Mt 13:5; Mk 4:5)

A possible attributive adjective (βαθύς *deep*; ↑γῆν πολλήν *much soil* in the previous clause) is replaced by a noun in the object role (βάθος *depth*), and, connected with it, "soil" is not in the object accusative, but in the attributive genitive ("antiptosis": interchange of case form); ↑162c.

ἐπῄνεσεν ὁ κύριος **τὸν οἰκονόμον τῆς ἀδικίας** … *The master commended the unrighteous/dishonest manager* … (Lk 16:8)

A possible adjective (ἄδικος *unrighteous, crooked*) is replaced by a noun in the genitive of quality (↑162a).

• as a subtype of metonymy: here expressions or their relationships are interchanged (not simply replaced; ↑295g), as e.g. in *a good cup of tea* for *a cup of good tea* (the attributive modifier "good" is transferred from the more appropriate to the less appropriate of two heads, from "tea" to "cup"; such use is also called "hypallage"; ↑Baldick s. v.); possible NT example:

λαλεῖτε … τῷ λαῷ **πάντα τὰ ῥήματα τῆς ζωῆς ταύτης**.	*… proclaim to the people all the words of this life* (possibly = *all these words of life*). (Ac 5:20)

295t 7. **Personification** (or "prosopopoeia", ↑πρόσωπον *person* + ποιέω *to make*, προσωποποιία; ↑Bühlmann-Scherer: 75):

Animals, inanimate things, or abstract ideas are referred to as if they were persons that are alive and active (in part going back to the abstract for the concrete, "abstractum pro concreto"; ↑295n), e. g.:

ποῦ σου, **θάνατε**, τὸ νῖκος;	*Where, O death, is your victory?* (1Cor 15:55; ↑Ho 13:14)

While in general stylistics the terms "personification" and "hypostasis" tend to be used interchangeably (↑"hypostasize" = to treat or represent as concrete reality [COED]), in exegesis "hypostasis" typically refers to a quasi-personal entity that is a personification of an activity or a characteristic trait of a deity (so purportedly "Wisdom" in Pr 8:22–31 [חָכְמָה *ḥokmāh*] and Sir 24:1–22 [σοφία]).

295u 8. **Symbol** (↑σύμβολον "tally used for recognition"; ↑Montanari/LSJ s. v.) or "signum", "emblem"; not always distinguishable from the concrete for abstract, "concretum pro abstracto" (↑295n; ↑Bühlmann-Scherer: 77f), e. g.:

ὁ πιστεύων εἰς ἐμέ … ποταμοὶ ἐκ τῆς κοιλίας αὐτοῦ ῥεύσουσιν **ὕδατος ζῶντος**.	*Anyone who believes in me … rivers of living water will flow from his heart.* (Jn 7:38)

The "living water" mentioned here is a symbol of the Holy Spirit (↑verse 39).

295v 9. **Ideogram** (↑ἰδέα *form, concept, idea* + γράμμα *letter* [of the alphabet], *piece of writing*; may also be referred to as "cipher", "secret code", "secret word"; ↑Bühlmann-Scherer: 78f):

This term (more frequently referring to a written sign representing an idea or thing) is here used of a linguistic expression with a function similar to that of a symbol (↑295u); the relationship between the entity normally denoted and the concept actually indicated by such an expression is less natural than in the case of a symbol; it is more or less arbitrary, frequently going back to some historical events, e. g.:

… ἵνα μὴ κενωθῇ ὁ **σταυρὸς** τοῦ Χριστοῦ.	*… so that the cross of Christ will not be emptied of its effect.* (1Cor 1:17)

The expression "the cross of Christ" enciphers the core of the Gospel: on the basis of Christ's suffering and dying a criminal's death on a cross God guarantees salvation to those who believe.

295w 10. **Catachresis** ("incorrect use, misuse"; ↑καταχράομαι *to use*, also *misuse*, κατάχρησις; also called "abusio"; ↑Bühlmann-Scherer: 85):

A variety of metaphor (↑295b) or metonymy (i. e. synecdoche; ↑295h): the misapplication of an expression, or the extension of a meaning in a strictly illogical metaphor (↑Baldick s. v.), typically in cases where no specific expression is a available, e. g. "mouse" to refer to the "small hand-held device which is moved across a flat surface to move the cursor on a computer screen" (COED s. v.):

a) metaphorical catachresis, e. g.:

πνεῦμα	"blast" for "spirit"

b) metonymic-synecdochical catachresis, e. g.:

πατήρ	"father" for "ancestor"
υἱός	"son" for "descendant"

11. **Expanded metaphor** (↑μεταφορὰ πλεονάζουσα, LSJ sub πλεονάζω [I1]; Bühlmann-Scherer: 86: "Annexionsvergleich" [German: comparison involving an annexation]): 295x

The metaphorical expression is expanded with a non-figurative expression being attached ("annexed") which explains the metaphor (especially by means of a genitive of explanation; ↑165), e.g.:

τὸν θώρακα **τῆς δικαιοσύνη** … *the breastplate* (metaphor) *of righteousness* (explanation)

τὸν θυρεὸν **τῆς πίστεως** … *the shield* (metaphor) *of faith* (explanation)

τὴν περικεφαλαίαν **τοῦ σωτηρίου** … *the helmet* (metaphor) *of salvation* (explanation) (Eph 6:14–17)

Figures involving paraphrasing, veiling, and unveiling 296

(↑Bühlmann-Scherer: 87–99; LAW on most head words)

1. **Antonomasia** (↑ἀντονομασία *a common noun in place of a proper name* [or vice versa]; also known as "pronominatio"; ↑Bühlmann-Scherer: 88f): 296a

A concept such as a characteristic feature or an activity of person is referred to in place of his or her proper name (similar to metonymy; ↑295g), e.g.:

πάτερ, ἥμαρτον εἰς τὸν **οὐρανὸν** καὶ ἐνώπιόν σου. *Father, I have sinned against heaven* (= against God) *and in your sight.* (Lk 15:18)

An antonomasia common in contemporary Judaism. ↑also ἡ βασιλεία τῶν οὐρανῶν *kingdom of heaven* in Mt (e.g. 4:17) corresponding to ἡ βασιλεία τοῦ θεοῦ *kingdom of God* in Mk (e.g. 1:15) and Lk (e.g. 4:43).

βλέπει **τὸν μαθητὴν ὃν ἠγάπα ὁ Ἰησοῦς** ἀκολουθοῦντα *He saw the disciple Jesus loved* (= John) *following them.* (Jn 21:20)

This is an instance of antonomasia involving periphrasis (↑296c).

Important forms of antonomasia:

a) ***divine passive*** (or: theological passive; ↑Bühlmann-Scherer: 89; BDF §130; Z §236): in place of a direct reference to God as an agent the passive is used (at times the 3rd pl. act.; ↑255f), e.g.: 296b

μακάριοι οἱ πενθοῦντες ὅτι **αὐτοὶ παρακληθήσονται**. *Blessed are those who mourn, for they will be comforted* (i.e. there is one [God] who will comfort them) (Mt 5:4)

b) ***periphrasis*** ("a roundabout way of referring to something by means of several words instead of naming it directly in a single word or phrase" [Baldick s.v.]; also called "circumlocution" or "circumscriptio"), inter alia when referring to persons (↑Bühlmann-Scherer: 90: "Personenumschreibung" or "Personentausch"), e.g.: 296c

νῦν ἀπολύεις **τὸν δοῦλόν σου**, δέσποτα, κατὰ τὸ ῥῆμά σου ἐν εἰρήνῃ. *Lord, now you can dismiss your servant* (= me) *in peace, as you promised.* (Lk 2:29)

2. **Kenning** (↑Old Norse *kenna* "to make known"; ↑Bühlmann-Scherer: 90f): 296d

A multi-part pictorial periphrasis/circumlocution (↑296c) referring to a thing or a person, e.g.:

τὸ φῶς τοῦ κόσμου τούτου βλέπει. *He sees the light of this world* (= the sun). (Jn 11:9)

296e 3. **Euphemism** (↑εὐφημέω *to use words of good omen, to avoid unlucky words,* εὐφημία [↑LSJ s.v.]; ↑Bühlmann-Scherer: 91f):

Offensive expressions are replaced by less problematic ones, e.g.:

οὐκ **ἐγίνωσκεν αὐτὴν** ἕως οὗ ἔτεκεν υἱόν.

He did not know her (= He did not have intercourse with her; a euphemism attested in and outside the Bible) *until she had given birth to a son.* (Mt 1:25)

… τινὲς δὲ **ἐκοιμήθησαν**.

… but some have fallen asleep (= but some have died/passed away). (1Cor 15:6)

εὐώνυμος, **ἀριστερός**

left (lit. *of a good* [veiled for: *bad*] *name*), *right* (<ἄριστος *best*) (old euphemisms originally connected with superstitious beliefs) (Mt 20:21; 6:3)

296f 4. **Dysphemism** (↑δυσφημέω *to speak ill-omened words,* δυσφημία [Montanari s.v.]) or (↑Bühlmann-Scherer: 92f) “aischrology” (↑αἰσχρολογία *base* or *obscene language* [Montanari s.v.]):

The opposite of euphemism: rude or offensive expressions are used intentionally to refer to a thing or person. E.g. the false god בַּ֫עַל זְבוּל *bá'al zəḇûl* “Baal, the Prince” (?) appears to be referred to as בַּ֫עַל זְבוּב *bá'al zəḇûḇ* “Lord of flies” (2Kgs 1:2.3.6.16; ↑Βεελζεβούλ [Var. Βεελζεβούβ *Beelzebub*] Mt 10:25; 12:24.27; Mk 3:22; Lk 11:15.18f).

296g 5. **Amphibole** (↑ἀμφίβολος *attacked on both* or *all sides*; *hitting at both ends*; *doubtful, ambiguous,* ἀμφιβολία; also called “ambiguity”/“ambiguitas” or “dilogia”; ↑Bühlmann-Scherer: 93f; on linguistic ambiguity in general ↑also von Siebenthal 1984):

The speaker/writer uses a particular expression ambiguously, i.e. without clearly indicating what exactly it is meant to refer to, e.g.:

ἀπεκρίθη Ἰησοῦς καὶ εἶπεν αὐτῇ· εἰ ᾔδεις τὴν δωρεὰν τοῦ θεοῦ καὶ τίς ἐστιν ὁ λέγων σοι· δός μοι πεῖν, σὺ ἂν ᾔτησας αὐτὸν καὶ ἔδωκεν ἄν σοι **ὕδωρ ζῶν**. λέγει αὐτῷ ἡ γυνή· κύριε, οὔτε ἄντλημα ἔχεις καὶ τὸ φρέαρ ἐστὶν βαθύ· πόθεν οὖν ἔχεις **τὸ ὕδωρ τὸ ζῶν**;

Jesus answered her, “If you knew the gift of God, and who it is that is saying to you, ‘Give me a drink,’ you would have asked him, and he would have given you living water.” The woman said to him, “Sir, you have nothing to draw water with, and the well is deep. Where do you get that living water? …” (Jn 4:10f)

ὕδωρ ζῶν “living water” can and typically does refer to spring water; and that is the way the woman understood the expression; Jesus, however, was referring to eternal life.

Note that amphibole, a rhetorically motivated ambiguity, should not be confused with “polysemy” which is about a particular expression having more than one (lexical) meaning (e.g. the English noun *spring* that may refer to 1 a season, 2 curved metal, 3 water, or 4 a sudden jump; ↑Longman s.v.). Such lexical ambiguity is typically resolved by contextual factors. On disambiguation ↑Leisi 1985: 213–216.

296h 6. **Litotes** (↑λιτότης *simplicity;* ≈ “understatement”; ↑Bühlmann-Scherer: 94):

By means of an understatement less is said than what is meant, usually by denying its opposite, e.g.:

ἐν τούτῳ **οὐκ ἐπαινῶ**.

In this matter I do not praise you (= I must rebuke you). (1Cor 11:22)

↑also Lk 15:13; Ac 1:5; 12:18; 14:17.28; 15:2; 17:4; 19:11.23f; 20:12; 21:39; 26:19.26; 27:20; 28:2; Ro 1:13.16; 11:25; 1Cor 10:1; 11:17; 12:1; 2Cor 1:8; 2:11; 2Th 3:2; He 13:17.

7. **Irony** (↑εἰρωνεία *dissimulation, pretence,* εἰρωνεύομαι *to dissimulate, to feign ignorance*; also 296i
called “illusio”, “simulatio” or “permutatio”; ↑Bühlmann-Scherer: 96f; BDF §495):

Something is referred to by an expression indicating its opposite, with the communicational situation making it clear what is actually intended, e.g. referring to an extravagant person as “thrifty”. E.g.:

χαρίσασθέ μοι τὴν ἀδικίαν ταύτην.

Forgive me this wrong (that the Corinthians were inferior to the other churches in one thing only: that Paul had never burdened them). (2Cor 12:13)

8. **Sarcasm** (↑σαρκάζω *to tear flesh like dogs,* σαρκασμός; ↑Bühlmann-Scherer: 97): 296j

Biting mockery by which a person or a thing is ridiculed, e.g. in Is 44:16f, where a man is described who taking a block of wood uses part of it to warm himself and to bake bread and makes the rest into a god to pray to it. A NT example:

Ὅταν οὖν ποιῇς ἐλεημοσύνην, **μὴ σαλπίσῃς ἔμπροσθέν σου**, ὥσπερ οἱ ὑποκριταὶ ποιοῦσιν ἐν ταῖς συναγωγαῖς καὶ ἐν ταῖς ῥύμαις, ὅπως δοξασθῶσιν ὑπὸ τῶν ἀνθρώπων.

So whenever you give to the needy, don’t sound a trumpet before you, as the hypocrites do in the synagogues and on the streets, to be applauded by people. (Mt 6:2)

9. **Paradox** (↑παράδοξος *contrary to opinion,* τὸ παράδοξον *what is contrary to popular opinion*; 296k
↑Bühlmann-Scherer: 98; BDR §$495_{6.7}$):

Two concepts are connected in an astounding, seemingly contradictory way in order to bring to light some more or less hidden truth, e.g.:

ὃς γὰρ ἂν θέλῃ τὴν ψυχὴν αὐτοῦ σῶσαι ἀπολέσει αὐτήν. ὃς δ’ ἂν ἀπολέσῃ τὴν ψυχὴν αὐτοῦ ἕνεκεν ἐμοῦ οὗτος σώσει αὐτήν.

For whoever wants to save his life will lose it, but whoever loses his life because of me will save it. (Lk 9:24)

A figure of speech not easy to distinguish from the paradox is the **oxymoron** (↑ὀξύς *sharp, acute* – μωρός *foolish,* ὀξύμωρος *acutely foolish*) τὸ ὀξύμωρον (Montanari s.v.): *paradoxical union of discordant or contradictory concepts,* according to Bühlmann-Scherer, typically in cases where the meaning of one concept is neutralized by the other, e.g.:

καὶ γὰρ **οὐ δεδόξασται τὸ δεδοξασμένον** ἐν τούτῳ τῷ μέρει …

Indeed, in this case, that first glory was not glorious at all … (2Cor 3:10)

4 Textgrammar

Part 4 is about the highest level of text structures (↑p. 12f), that of the text. It is to show in what ways a text is different from the sum of its sentences/clauses as well as the ways in which the distinctive features of the grammatical (↑316–348) and the content (↑349–353) sides of the text structure relate to the coherence of Ancient Greek texts, especially of those in the NT (↑p. 12f).

Part 4 is subdivided as follows:

Preliminary note:

Texts have been regarded as a legitimate object of linguistic research for a comparatively short time only. People engaged in the discipline of "**textlinguistics**" (or "discourse analysis")[1] throughout the world agree on many essential points. There are, however, a great variety of theoretical and analytical approaches, each with its special terminology. Conceptually and terminologically Part 4 is based largely on the findings of German textlinguistic research as presented by C. Gansel and F. Jürgens (↑GaJü), by T. A. Fritz (↑DuG9) as well as on the typological studies inter alia of T. Givón and K. Callow. At the same time great care was taken, of course, to do justice to the peculiarities of Ancient Greek by consulting relevant publications and by conducting empirical studies of our own. Since textlinguistics in general, especially, however, regarding Ancient Greek has no definitive answers (yet) to many questions, what is said here will to a large extent be rather provisional; at the same time many issues will necessarily have to be left undecided.

1 There seems to be considerable overlap between the two approaches, "and some linguists see very little difference between them" (↑Crystal: 482).

4.1 Text basics

4.1.1 Texts as a linguistic phenomenon

297 Basic characteristics of a text (↑DuG9: 1076ff; GaJü: 35–52; Givón I: 7ff)

As stated in the introduction (↑p. 12), this grammar starts from the idea that linguistic communication (the main function of language) operates by means of texts (involving a wide range of text types); for a text[2] to count as text three features are essential:[3]
1. it must have a specifically organized structure (↑298);
2. its coherence (↑300);
3. a recognizable communicative function (↑302).

4.1.1.1 Text structure

298 The concept of text structure (↑GaJü: 51)

A text, as presupposed so far, is a linguistic entity with a structure that is organized in a specific way; it is a structure with two sides that are clearly distinct, but also clearly interdependent:
a) the grammatical side (i.e. the expression/form side) with the sentence/clause as the most important structural unit;
b) the content side (related to what the text says as a whole) with the proposition (referring to a particular "situation"; ↑127a) as the most important structural unit.

---

2 The category "text" (<Lat. *textus* "tissue"; ↑COED s.v.) here includes both written and spoken utterances (an approach adopted by many linguists; ↑Crystal: 482). Spoken utterances, especially in interactive communication, are often referred to as "discourse" (↑Crystal: 148; also p. 569 above footnote 1). When dealing with Ancient Greek we frequently encounter utterances that originally were "discourses" (e.g. in Mk 14:61f telling us about a dialogue between the high priest and Jesus), now accessible only as written texts.

3 So the widely accepted "integrative" text model combining two approaches: the one focused on the grammatical side of text structures with the one focused on the content or semantic-communicative side (↑Brinker: 17–20). According to this model "a text is a coherent unit of linguistic communication with a recognizable communicative function and a structure that is organized in a specific way" (for the German original ↑GaJü: 51; also ↑Crystal: 482).

Example: text structure of Matthew 13:45f 299

In Mt 13:45f we find the following two-sided text structure (for explanatory comments ↑301, 303 and 307):[4]

grammatical side of the text structure (↑301b): **sentences/clauses** or sentence-like phrases		**content** side of the text structure (↑301d): **propositions** (rendered in bold, functions of connectives in normal type; ↑301b[1])	
main cl. 1	**Πάλιν ὁμοία** (SC^{prop}) **ἐστὶν** (P) **ἡ βασιλεία τῶν οὐρανῶν** (S) **ἀνθρώπῳ ἐμπόρῳ** ($O^{dat}/2^{nd}$)	Again **the kingdom of heaven is like a merchant**,	proposition 1
PtcP (Attr)	**ζητοῦντι** (P) **καλοὺς μαργαρίτας** (Od)	**searching for fine pearls.**	proposition 2
PtcP (AdvlA)	**εὑρὼν** (P) **δὲ ἕνα πολύτιμον μαργαρίτην** (Od)	Then as **he found one pearl of great value,**	proposition 3
PtcP (AdvlA)	**ἀπελθὼν** (P)	**he went away** and	proposition 4
main cl. 2, part A	**πέπρακεν** (P) **πάντα** (Od)	**sold everything**	proposition 5
rel. cl. (Attr)	**ὅσα** (Od) **εἶχεν** (P)	**that he had**	proposition 6
main cl. 2, part B	**καὶ ἠγόρασεν** (P) **αὐτόν** (Od).	and **bought it.**	proposition 7

4.1.1.2 Coherence

The concept of coherence (↑GaJü: 51f; DuG9: 1088f) 300

The most important feature characterizing a text is its coherence (<Lat. *cohaerēre* "to stick together"; ↑COED sub "cohere"): the content elements expressed in a text, in most cases more than one proposition (pointing to "situations"), are connected, cohere, "stick together" meaningfully.[5]

Propositions (pointing to "situations") are (normally) made up of lexical content elements (word meanings) that are meaningfully connected.[6] But the propositions themselves need to be connected meaningfully, too; otherwise they cannot be regarded as making up a text (suited for linguistic communication). It is not enough to string together clauses/sentences or propositions that in themselves are made up of meaningfully connected elements; the resulting structure, too, must be organized in

4 On the syntactic analysis ↑127/254–260 (constituents) and 266ff (sentence/clause types).

5 This is what language users principally assume when faced with a text (↑314f).

6 More than a correct grammatical sentence/clause structure is needed. This may be illustrated by Noam Chomsky's classical example ([1965]: *Aspects of the Theory of Syntax*. Cambridge/MA: MIT: 149): "Colorless green ideas sleep furiously", a sentence with a correct grammatical structure, but without (recognizable) propositional content.

such a way that its propositions are meaningfully connected or coherent. E.g. the following sentences removed from their original context (Jdth 1:14a, 11:8a and 13:12b) in themselves are structured correctly both grammatically and semantically; strung together, however, they lack coherence and so do not make up a text:

ἐκυρίευσε τῶν πόλεων αὐτοῦ.	*He took possession of his cities.*
ἠκούσαμεν γὰρ τὴν σοφίαν σου.	*For we have heard of your wisdom.*
συνεκάλεσαν τοὺς πρεσβυτέρους τῆς πόλεως.	*They summoned the elders of the city.*

301 Example: coherence of Matthew 13:45f

301a Our initial example Mt 13:45f is undoubtedly coherent. The text structure is organized in such a way, both in terms of grammar and content, that propositions 1–7 (Pp. 1–7) may readily be accepted as meaningfully connected. On both sides of the text structure there are elements that contribute to the coherence of the text (along typical lines):

301b a) On the **grammatical** side of the text structure (↑316ff) there are:[7]

(1) Three **connectives** (two coordinating conjunctions and one relative pronoun):[8]
– δέ *then* joins Pp. 1–2 and Pp. 3–7, indicating some development in the text;
– καί *and* joins Pp. 5–6 and Pp. 7, indicating an additive relationship;
– ὅσα *that* joins Pp. 5 and Pp. 6, by reference back to πάντα *everything*.

(2) Three **participle phrases**:[9]
– the one of Pp. 2 provides a connection with Pp. 1,
– the ones of Pp. 3 and Pp. 4 provide a connection with Pp. 5–7.

(3) **Anaphoric** elements (referring back to what was previously said in the text):[10]
– αὐτόν *it*, personal pronoun, direct object of main cl. 2, part B, refers back to ἕνα πολύτιμον μαργαρίτην *one pearl of great value*, which is the direct object of the participle phrase of Pp. 3; αὐτόν functions as the substitute of this direct object and in this way provides a connection between Pp. 3 and Pp. 4–7, specifically between Pp. 3 and Pp. 7.
– the subject indicated or implied by the six verb forms, "he", agent of Pp. 2–7, has an anaphoric role, too, referring back to ἀνθρώπῳ ἐμπόρῳ *a merchant* in Pp. 1 and thus has a connecting function.

(4) The **tense/aspect**, the **voice**,[11] and (in the case of four finite forms) the **mood** of the verb forms that refer to the core concepts of the seven propositions and make sure that these propositions may be understood as being connected meaningfully in the context of the reality indicated by our text:
– Pp. 1 affirms that there is an apparently timeless likeness of the "kingdom of heaven" to the content of the short narrative of Pp. 2–7, as this is expressed by the timeless indicative present (↑197b): (ὁμοία) ἐστίν *is (like)*.

---

7 When grammatical means (including punctuation marks) are used to attain coherence, one normally speaks of "cohesion" (the Lat. participle *cohaesum* of the verb *cohaerēre* "to stick together").

8 On further word-classes functioning as connectives ↑317ff, on the content relations indicated by connectives ↑323ff. On the function of πάλιν in Mt 13:45 ↑307a; 320.

9 Infinitive/ACI phrases may be used in similar ways; ↑312a.

10 Note that the connective ὅσα *that* (Pp. 6), as a relative pronoun, has two functions: a) that of a Od within the relative clause, b) that of an anaphoric element (referring back to its antecedent). On the "(ana/cata)phoric" and the "(ana/cata)deictic" roles of the article and pronouns ↑347–348.

11 There are only active verb forms in our example, an apparently typical case, here at any rate not challenging the coherence of the text; this point will not be discussed any further. But ↑also 316.

– Pp. 2 indicates the background activity as something characterizing the protagonist of the short narrative, being expressed by a participle present, which most frequently is used with a linear nuance, i.e. the "action"/"situation" referred to is presented as something continuing, basically uninterrupted (↑194b); here the participle phrase has the role of an attributive modifier adding some information about ἄνθρωπος ἔμπορος *a merchant* characterizing in some way the entity referred to (↑236b; 260a): ζητοῦντι (καλοὺς μαργαρίτας) *searching for (fine pearls).*
– Pp. 3–7 convey the content of the short narrative:
In Pp. 3–4 we find two adverbial adjuncts; most probably they indicate temporal circumstances, expressed by participles conjunct in the aorist, which here refer to something that (as in most cases) precedes the main "situation" (↑206f; 228): εὑρὼν (ἕνα πολύτιμον μαργαρίτην) *as he found (one pearl of great value)* and ἀπελθὼν *he went away and [then].*
Pp. 5 and Pp. 7 refer to the main events of the short narrative, expressed by two typical narrative forms (↑199b): the indicative perfect (functioning as indicative aorist [↑111.13]) πέπρακεν (πάντα) *he sold (everything)* and the indicative aorist ἠγόρασεν (αὐτόν) *he bought (it)*; in Pp. 6 some background information is inserted, expressed by a (linear) imperfect (↑198b): (ὅσα) εἶχεν *(that) he had.*

The coherence of Mt 13:45f is also evidenced by the "**functional sentence perspective**"[12] (or 301c
"theme-rheme structure") observable in the text. The functional sentence perspective is about the ways in which the known and the new portions of information are expressed and arranged within the sentence/clause or sentence-like phrase concerned, with sentence stress (in spoken linguistic communication) playing an important role.[13] The functional sentence perspective is located, as it were, between the grammatical and the content sides of text structure, as a kind of bridge that leads from one side to the other:

(1) The **theme**,[14] i.e. the portion of information assumed to be known (at the sentence or proposition level), in our text is marked as known or definite (as is typical of thematic entities) by the article or by anaphoric elements (↑347–348) and is expressed, with one exception, by the grammatical subject. There are three "themes" in the seven sentences/clauses or sentence-like phrases of our text:
– theme 1 of Pp. 1 (subject of main cl. 1): ἡ βασιλεία τῶν οὐρανῶν "the kingdom of heaven";
– theme 2 of Pp. 2–7 (subject throughout): "he" (referring back to rhematic ἀνθρώπῳ ἐμπόρῳ "a merchant" [rheme 1; ↑below] of main cl. 1);
– theme 3 (alongside theme 2) of Pp. 6 (direct object): ὅσα "that" (referring back to rhematic πάντα "everything" [rheme 5; ↑below] of main cl. 2, part A).
Note also the following facts relevant to the coherence of our text: a) in Pp. 2–7 the "theme" remains unchanged; b) theme 2 and theme 3 are linked to the rhemes of the preceding sentences (rheme 1 and rheme 5; ↑below).

(2) The **rheme**,[14] the portion of information that is added as something new, the core of the proposition, in our text is expressed in a way that is typical of rhematic entities: by the predicate, i.e. by the predicator/predicate verb plus (mostly) with complement(s) as required by the valency of the verb (↑256a), sometimes accompanied by adjuncts. The rheme (in spoken communication) is typically the sentence component carrying the strongest stress (below in italic):

---

12 ↑e.g. Crystal: 203.

13 In addition to DuG9: 1136ff (on German) ↑e.g. Quirk: 1430–1432 (on English). Nothing is known about sentence stress in Ancient Greek (MB: S214.1). However, English sentence stress may prove to be a useful heuristic aid when translating texts into English, helping us to find an interpretation that is most likely to be intended.

14 The "theme" (<τὸ θέμα *that which is placed* or *laid down*; ↑LSJ s.v.) is the known portion of information of the proposition concerned, the "rheme" (<τὸ ῥῆμα *that which is said* or *spoken*; ↑LSJ s.v.) the new portion.

– rheme 1 of Pp. 1: ὁμοία ἐστίν … ἀνθρώπῳ ἐμπόρῳ "is like … a *mer*chant";
– rheme 2 of Pp. 2: ζητοῦντι καλοὺς μαργαρίτας "searching for fine *pearls*";
– rheme 3 of Pp. 3: εὑρών … ἕνα πολύτιμον μαργαρίτην "… found one pearl *of great* value";
– rheme 4 of Pp. 4: ἀπελθών "went a*way* …";
– rheme 5 of Pp. 5: πέπρακεν πάντα "sold *every*thing";
– rheme 6 of Pp. 6: εἶχεν "*had*";
– rheme 7 of Pp. 7: ἠγόρασεν αὐτόν "*bought* it".

301d b) On the **content** side of the text structure (↑349ff):

The (lexical) content words of Mt 13:45f, via the concepts they denote, point to concrete entities, i.e. to segments of the reality referred to and are combined into meaningful propositions; and the "situations" that these propositions point to present themselves in a way that makes us recognize a meaningful overall content. All of this is possible for us to infer as we tap the various areas of the cultural knowledge presupposed in Mt 13:45f (for details ↑309; note that the elements between " " mentioned below represent the content of the Greek expressions):

(1) By means of the presupposed **lexical knowledge** we are able to recognize the intended concepts as well as the concrete entities that they are meant to refer to and how these are to be combined meaningfully (i.e. to understand what the words used in the text mean here), inter alia:
– in Pp. 1 the "kingdom of heaven" (a technical term of Mt), a "merchant" (a general ordinary language term) and their "being alike" (a common relational concept of ordinary language; ↑312a);
– in Pp. 2 and Pp. 3 "searching" and its correlative "finding" (a common pair of event concepts of ordinary language; ↑312a).
(2) By means of the presupposed **world and action knowledge** we recognize inter alia the meaningful connection between the following concepts/entities or "situations" (↑313):
– between the "merchant" mentioned in Pp. 1 to Pp. 7, his "searching" (Pp. 2), his "finding" (Pp. 3) as well as his subsequent "going away" (Pp. 4), his "selling" (Pp. 5) and his "buying" (Pp. 7);
– between the search object (Pp. 2), "fine pearls" as something valuable, and the merchant's find (Pp. 3), "one pearl of great value", meaningfully triggering off the act series related in Pp. 4–7.

4.1.1.3 Communicative function of texts

302 The concept of communicative function of texts (↑GaJü: 52; 81ff)

302a A text feature closely linked to coherence is its communicative function: a coherent text must have a recognizable communicative function, i.e. those for whom the text is produced need to be able to know the basic objective pursued by the speaker/writer communicating with them. In principle this objective should become clear to them from the text structure itself, above all, however, from the way contextual factors outside and (in the case of a partial text) inside the text are brought into play.

The typical communicative functions of texts (expected to be applicable to every language) are classified in a variety of ways.

There are influential possibilities based on the theory of speech acts, e.g. (↑Crystal: 446; DuG9: 1170): "representatives" (asserting), "directives" (trying to make s.o. to act), "commissives" (making commitments), "expressives" (expressing feelings), "declarations" (bringing about a state of affairs). With somewhat less obvious dependence on the speech-act theory textlinguist K. Brinker proposes (↑DuG9: 1170; also Bussmann: 480) the following classification:

1. **Information**: the text is to convey knowledge. 302b
The type of knowledge to be conveyed varies greatly, as do the text types to be used (↑304/306). Among these are reports (including short ones such as Ac 5:25: the apostle that had been put to prison are no longer there, but are standing in the temple teaching the people), parables (e.g. Mt 13:44), accounts (e.g. Ac 27:1ff: Paul's sea voyage to Rome), speeches (e.g. the Areopagus speech in Ac 17:21ff), letters (e.g. Ac 23:26–30) etc.

2. **Appeal**: the text is to influence s.o.'s attitude or action or both. 302c
A wide range of different types of influence may be in view, as may be the text types to be used. It may be a simple request (e.g. Jn 4:7: Jesus asks the Samaritan woman for a drink) or an invitation to do sth. (e.g. Lk 15:9: a woman invites others to rejoice with her over the recovered coin), detailed instructions (e.g. Lk 15:23f: a father gives instructions on the celebration in honour of his son who was lost and now is found) or more extensive paraeneses (e.g. Ro 12–15) etc.

3. **Commitment**: the text expresses a commitment to a particular attitude or to a particular course of action or to both. 302d
Various types of promises are to be included here (e.g. Mk 6:23: Herod promises the daughter of Herodias to give her whatever she will ask for; Lk 19:8: the chief tax collector Zacchaeus promises compensation for the wrong done in the past), also the many divine promises contained in the NT (e.g. Mt 28:20 ἐγὼ μεθ' ὑμῶν εἰμι πάσας τὰς ἡμέρας … *I am with you always* …; He 13:5 οὐ μή σε ἀνῶ … *I will never leave you* …).

4. **Contact**: the text primarily serves to establish or maintain personal relationships. 302e
To be included here are inter alia personal greetings such as those of Paul (e.g. Ro 16:6ff).

5. **Declaration**: the text creates a new legal state of affairs. 302f
This is the function inter alia of the decisions of certain state agencies (e.g. the decree of the Roman senate by which Herod the Great was made king [Josephus, War 1.346]), verdicts (↑e.g. Ro 5:16f), adoptions (↑e.g. 2Cor 6:18) etc.

6. **Poetry/Entertainment**: the text is to give pleasure by the beauty of language used or simply to entertain. 302g
The words of court jesters no doubt belong here (e.g. the saying by a Tryphon recorded in Josephus, Antiquities 12.212). Poetry plays an extremely important part, of course, in the history of Ancient Greek literature outside the Bible. Though elements of it are certainly present within the Bible, too (not only in the poetic parts of the Old Testament such as Job, Psalms, Proverbs, but also in many sections of the NT, e.g. in Lk 1:47–55, 67–79; 2Tm 2:11–13; Re 4:11; 5:9f etc.), being aesthetically pleasing is obviously not their primary communicative function.

Note that frequently elements of various communicative functions occur side by side. However, one of these functions is typically dominant.[15] 302h

Example: the communicative function of Matthew 13:45f 303

From Mt 13:45f itself and from the way it relates to neighbouring and superordinate texts, it is fairly clear that the communicative function here is first of all information (↑302b). While this widely occurring (typical) function appears to be dominant (↑302h), there can hardly be any doubt (as indicated by the wider context) that appeal (↑302c) is part of the speaker's/writer's objective, too (↑307b).

15 Therefore the "dominance principle" plays an important part in text interpretation: generally speaking, a particular text should be connected with that type of communicative function that can be shown to be dominant (↑GaJü: 89). This principle similarly applies to dealing with other text-related aspects such as text production strategies (↑304) and text types/genres (↑305).

4.1.1.4 Further text-related aspects

304 Text production strategies (↑DuG9: 1163–1175; GaJü: 149ff)

304a There are not only various types of communicative functions of texts, i.e. various types of basic objectives speakers/writers may pursue when producing their texts. There are also various text production strategies, i.e. various possibilities to organize the text structure in a functionally optimal way: to construct propositions, arrange and connect them in such a way that the objectives are achieved as best as possible. The following text production strategies[16] may be distinguished (as proposed by T. A. Fritz in DuG9):

304b 1. **Description**: the propositions refer to particular aspects of a topic (typically viewed in spatial terms) are mostly joined additively (with or without connectives; ↑325). This strategy is behind e.g. Re 21:9–27, where there is a description of the new Jerusalem.

304c 2. **Narration**: the propositions/"situations" are generally arranged chronologically; they are typically connected by means of connectives that are to be interpreted in temporal terms (↑327ff). As far as its content is concerned, each narration step is presented as a change from one (starting) state of affairs to another (end) state of affairs, with the two states of affairs having a significantly different content. (↑DuG9: 1165). When the narration is meant to present certain facts as objectively as possible, the text to be produced is more accurately termed "account" than "narrative" or "story". The Gospels and the Book of Acts consist of texts largely determined by the narration strategy.

304d 3. **Explication**: this is about portraying complex relationships that exist between propositions/"situations". The propositions are typically connected by means of conditional connectives (↑331); sometimes, however, the relationships indicated are to be classified as causal connections in the widest sense (↑332ff). Note that the propositions involved here may be expressed not only by means of sentences/clauses, but also fairly frequently by means of sentence-like preposition phrases, prepositionless noun phrases, participle phrases or infinitive/ACI phrases (↑312a; 317). Explication is found inter alia in Hebrews e.g. in the section about "Melchizedek" (He 7).

304e 4. **Argumentation**: this is about trying to persuade the hearers/readers of the correctness of an idea, action, or a theory and to lead them to take certain actions in view of it (↑DuG9: 1166). Connecting propositions/"situations" by means of conditional or causal connectives (↑331ff; 352b) is a central part in argumentation. Argumentation is found frequently inter alia in the letters of Paul.

304f 5. **Directive**: this aims directly at controlling the hearers'/readers' actions. Argumentation is largely absent even in the case of complex directives. The propositions referring to the various action steps are typically connected in terms of addition, thus e.g. in Mt 10:2ff with Jesus sending out the Twelve.

305 Text types and text genres

305a The communicative function and the text production strategy are connected inter alia with the **text type** to be used. In everyday communication a wide range of different text types are in use: invitations, requests, inquiries, offers, complaints, protests, appeals, birth and marriage announcements, death notices, anecdotes etc.

16 ↑302h[15] on the "dominance principle" similarly applicable here.

The textlinguistic study of text types is a complex area of research, one that needs to take into account a wide range of disciplines and that so far has produced only preliminary results. On this ↑DuG9: 1162ff, especially, however, GaJü: 53ff; on the intriguing question of the relationship between (text-linguistic) "text types" and (literary) "genres" ↑GaJü: 73f, Esser: 75f.[16]

An introduction to the **Ancient Greek text types/genres** used in the NT (basically from a classicist's 305b
perspective) is found in Reiser 2001: 92–194. He speaks of "literary forms" ("Literarische Formen"), which he classifies as follows (for further distinctions and detailed explanations ↑Reiser's volume):

I. **Large forms** (Reiser 2001: 98–130; ↑"macro-texts", ↑306) 305c

1. biographical narrative (Gospels; Reiser 2001: 98–105),
2. historiography (Acts; Reiser 2001: 106–115),
3. letter (apart from 21 independent NT letters there are two inside Acts [15:23–29; 23:26–30] Reiser 2001: 116–125)
4. apocalypse (Reiser 2001: 125–130).

II. **Small forms**, literary patterns, and style types (Reiser 2001: 131–194; ↑"partial texts", ↑306):

1. ***Narration forms*** (Reiser 2001: 132–149): 305d

– anecdote (a short narrative about real people and events, often culminating in a pointed saying; frequently occurring in the Synoptics, e.g. Mk 12:41–44 [The poor widow's offering]);
– miracle story (e.g. Mt 14:22–33 [sinking Peter], Ac 3:1–10 [healing of a paralyzed beggar] etc.; the rigid form characterizing pagan examples does not occur in the NT; on the other hand, the symbolic dimension of NT miracle stories seems to be foreign to the pagan ones);
– parable (e.g. Mt 7:24–27 [wise and foolish builders]; compared with both the Jewish and the Greek parable traditions Jesus' parables stand out as unusually original);
– genealogy (Mt 1:1–17; Lk 3:23–38).

2. ***Narration patterns*** (Reiser 2001: 149f): narration patterns in the style of Old Testament prece- 305e
dents, e.g. the "annunciation scheme" ("Verkündigungsschema") in Lk 1:8–22 (announcement of the birth of John the Baptist), apparently in the style of Gn 16:7–12 (announcement of the birth of Ishmael) and Gn 17:15–19 (announcement of the birth of Isaac).

3. ***Speech forms*** (Reiser 2001: 151–184): 305f

– proem, i.e. a preface or introduction (e.g. Lk 1:1–4; Re 1:1–3);
– aphorism ("gnome" or "sententia"): mostly a short saying concisely expressing an insight that claims to be generally applicable, citable by itself; a large part of Jesus' sayings belong here, in many cases being embedded in an anecdote (e.g. Mk 12:17: τὰ Καίσαρος ἀπόδοτε Καίσαρι … *Give to Caesar the things that are Caesar's …!*);
– farewell speech (e.g. Ac 20:17–38 [Paul at Miletus]);
– catalogue (e.g. Ga 5:19–23 [list of the works of the flesh and the fruit of the Spirit, "vice and virtue catalogue"] or Ro 8:35 [list of adverse circumstances in life, "peristasis catalogue"]);
– household code ("Haustafel"): ethical instructions to the various members of a household (e.g. Eph 5:22–6:9);
– prayer (e.g. Mt 11:25f [Jesus thanking his Father], Ac 1:24f [a group of believers before the appointment of Matthias]);
– hymn: in the NT there are a variety of hymnic texts (e.g. Lk 1:47–55 [The Magnificat] or Re 5:9f.12f ["Worthy is the Lamb"]); it is uncertain, however, whether any of the texts usually termed "hymns" were actually sung in the Early Church;
– liturgical formulae and standard phrases used in prayer (e.g. ἀμήν *Amen!* [Ro 1:25 et pass.], ἁλληλουϊά *Hallelujah!* [Re 19:1 etc.] or ᾧ ἡ δόξα εἰς τοὺς αἰῶνας τῶν αἰώνων *To him be the glory for ever and ever!* [Ga 1:5 etc.]);

– acclamation: a loud expression of demand or approval, especially by a crowd (e.g. Mk 15:13 σταύρωσον αὐτόν *Crucify him!*);
– confession formula (apparently e.g. 1Cor 15:3–5).

305g 4. ***Style types*** (Reiser 2001: 184–188):
– "diatribe": a functional literary style type reflecting a lively conversational kind of discourse; the "diatribe" occurs in different Ancient Greek genres and may deal with diverse topics; Paul makes use of it fairly frequently (e.g. Ro 6:15f Τί οὖν; ἁμαρτήσωμεν, ὅτι οὐκ ἐσμὲν ὑπὸ νόμον ἀλλὰ ὑπὸ χάριν; μὴ γένοιτο. οὐκ οἴδατε ὅτι … *What then? Should we sin because we are not under the law but under grace? Of course not! Don't you know that …?*),
– paraenesis: any kind of exhortation or ethical instruction; in the NT paraenetic texts or text complexes are mostly found in the final parts of letters (e.g. Ro 12–15 or 1Pe 2:11–5:11).

306 Macro-texts and partial texts (↑DuG9: 1073; GaJü: 47)

Texts may not only be different in size (even individual words may have the role of a text; ↑311c); many texts are also made up of multiple smaller texts, of partial texts (or partial text complexes), and so constitute text complexes or "macro-texts".

The Gospel of Matthew e.g. may on the one hand be classified as a macro-text; not only its pericopes may then be regarded as partial texts, one of these being our illustrative example Mt 13:45f, but also larger sections such as Jesus' parable speech in Mt 13:1–53. On the other hand, taking into account the Gospel of Matthew' acceptance into the NT canon, it will at the same time need to be viewed as a partial text (of the NT canon as a whole).

The communicative function and the text production strategy and so the text type/genre of a particular text, whether a partial text or a macro-text, are (usually) to be inferred inter alia from the way the various parts are brought into play in communicating the overall content.

307 Example: further text-related aspects of Matthew 13:45f

307a In Mt 13:45f Jesus "informs" his hearers (as reported by Matthew) about a further characteristic of the "kingdom of heaven",[17] specifically about its outstanding value. In order to convey this knowledge he tells a short story. In other words, he employs narration as his text production strategy (↑304c): The merchant's search for fine pearls (starting state) leads to him owning that pearl of great value (end state). The text type/genre he chooses is undoubtedly the parable (↑305d), as … ὁμοία ἐστίν … *is like* clearly indicates.

307b The **main point of the text** may be inferred quite easily in the light of the presupposed action knowledge (that includes the ability to participate in linguistic communication): as illustrated by the parable, the "kingdom of heaven" is something so outstanding, so valuable, that it is worth giving up everything else in exchange for it. That this is the main point will become more evident linguistically when the hierarchical propositional structure of the text is analysed, as will be shown in 312, especially in 312e.

---

17 ↑the adverb πάλιν *again/furthermore* connecting this text with the preceding ones (functioning as an additive connective; ↑325c).

4.1.2 Text comprehension

(↑GaJü: 162–174; DuG9: 1176–1178)

Text comprehension and text interpretation 308

For NT text interpretation to be optimally transparent and reasonable it is worth getting adequately acquainted with the regularities and procedures of text comprehension. The integrative textlinguistic approach reflected in Part 4 of the present grammar makes it possible for us to combine relevant findings of a variety of disciplines.[18] The following findings appear to be particularly important:

1. Text comprehension presupposes various types of knowledge (↑309).
2. Text comprehension involves the interaction of two distinctive processes, the "bottom-up" process and the "top-down" process (↑310).
3. Text comprehension does not begin at the level of complete sentences only; it rather sets in as soon as we try to come to grips with any of the "text constituents" (↑311).
4. Understanding a text as a whole always leads via understanding its propositions. The overall content of the text emerges from its propositional structure (conceived as a hierarchy). The intended semantic relationship (the "connection") between the propositions is not always indicated by lexical or grammatical means; it is, however, (mostly) inferable from the context (↑312).
5. Text comprehension in many cases is based specifically on the important parts of world and action knowledge that are usually called "frames" (↑313).
6. Text comprehension has to take into account not only content elements that are communicated directly (expressed linguistically), but also those that are communicated indirectly (without being expressed linguistically). This state of affairs is linked decisively with those parts of world and action knowledge that have to do with presuppositions and principles of successful communication (↑314).

Text comprehension – types of knowledge (↑DuG9: 1076f; GaJü: 114ff) 309

It is basic to (successful) linguistic communication that those participating in it have various types of relevant knowledge. Persons producing a text rely on it and expect the hearers/readers do so as well when trying to understand the text. Such types of knowledge allow us to recognize the coherence of a text and to infer everything else relevant to text comprehension. According DuG9: 1076f, the following types of knowledge are relevant to linguistic communication: 309a

1. **Grammatical knowledge** which enables us to connect the word forms and the grammatical function words with the intended syntactic and textgrammatical functions (grammatical side of the text structure; ↑301b).[19] This is done on the basis of closed paradigms: inflectional patterns and the inventory of function words are fixed both in English and Ancient Greek: they cannot (in principle) be changed or augmented. 309b

2. **Cultural knowledge**, which may be subdivided as follows:

– **Lexical knowledge** which enables us to connect the (lexical) content words of the text with the intended content elements. In this case it is possible to speak of open paradigms: the number of lexical words may be increased as the need arises (↑357a). 309c

– **World and action knowledge** which enables us to use our grammatical and lexical knowledge to connect "situations" with each other meaningfully when producing or trying to understand texts. 309d

---

18 In addition to the various branches of linguistics especially cognitive psychology and psycholinguistics (↑GaJü: 163).

19 This is about the part of coherence usually called "cohesion" (301b[7]).

309e – **Text knowledge** which enables us inter alia to deal meaningfully with questions of communicative functions and text types/genres and thus to recognize what is intended by the one producing the text, which includes possible relations of the text with other texts (i.e. the level of "intertextuality", so important in NT interpretation regarding the Old Testament).

310 Text comprehension – interaction of two processes (↑GaJü: 163f)

Text comprehension involves the interaction of two processes that are differently oriented:

310a 1. The **"bottom-up"** process:
As the elements of the grammatical side of the text structure enter our minds as hearers/readers, we identify the functions and content elements assigned to them by the grammar and the lexicon of the language ("parsing"; ↑311) on the basis of the presupposed grammatical and lexical knowledge (↑309b/309c) and then process all of it on the basis of the presupposed world and action knowledge (↑309d), including the presupposed text knowledge (↑309e): from the lowest level of the text structure, that of writing and sounds, we move to the next higher level, that of words and word-forms with the concepts and functions indicated by them, from this level in turn to the third, that of sentences/clauses and sentence-like phrases with the propositions indicated by them, until we reach the highest level, the one of the text itself with the overall content communicated by it.

310b 2. The **"top-down"** process:
We continually compare the findings of the "bottom-up" process with our knowledge (↑309), experience, beliefs, emotions, and abilities, which makes us evaluate and if it is necessary adjust them as it were from the "top". The two processes continually interact with each other (in similar contexts many speak of a "hermeneutical spiral"), our objective all along being to understand what the author of the text means to say and intends to communicate. This process will lead us beyond the text structure itself bringing into focus the communicative situation in which the text was produced.

311 Text comprehension – parsing and text constituents (↑GaJü: 164–166)

311a Identifying the function and the content of text structure elements is usually called "**parsing**". This may actually include every kind of endeavour to understand a text, i.e. to move from the grammatical to the content side of the text structure, whether at the sentence/clause or text level. Such parsing is not only geared to dealing with the text's word-forms, sentence constituents, and word-order to determine in what way these contribute to the content of the sentences and the text, but also to resolving lexical ambiguities and not least to inferring propositions (pointing to particular "situations").

311b A noteworthy fact in this context is that inferring the content of a sentence and the text as a whole does not begin at the level of complete sentences only. Text comprehension sets in as soon as one tries to come to grips with any of the "**text constituents**", i.e. words, phrases, clauses or sentence-like phrases which typically function as sentence constituents. Text constituents are "natural content elements". Apparently, these are to be viewed as psychological realities in text comprehension. Thus, experiments mentioned by the cognitive psychologist J. R. Anderson have shown that Form A of the following text passage e.g. is understood more easily than Form B:[20]

20 ↑Anderson: 408.

Form A	Form B
During World War II even fantastic schemes received consideration if they gave promise of shortening the conflict	During World War II, even fantastic schemes received consideration if they gave promise of shortening the conflict

Text comprehension (normally) begins with the first text constituent that enters our minds (and which we "parse"). It serves as the basis for our first text interpretation hypothesis. This hypothesis is then continually adjusted as further constituents come into play in the course of the "bottom-up" and "top-down" processes (↑310) until we are convinced that we understand (adequately) what the one producing the text intends to communicate.

If text comprehension in fact sets in at the level of text constituents already, we need not be surprised that linguistic communication is possible quite frequently even in cases where incomplete sentences are used: propositions, even the overall content of a text may be conveyed by a single word or phrase that cannot be regarded as a (complete) sentence/clause. The wide (and obviously successful) use of a telegraphic or, more recently, a texting style of communication is clear proof of this fact. This phenomenon also occurs (sanctioned by traditional usage) in titles, headlines, ellipses (↑293c) or the like, also in the case of interjections (e.g. οὐά *ah!* expresses scornful amazement amounting to something like "Didn't we know that nothing would come of it" in Mk 15:29; ↑252.63) or other uninflected words such as evaluative adverbs, evaluative/modal particles etc. (↑241a/241b; 252).[21] 311c

Text comprehension – propositional structure (↑GaJü: 166–169; Callow: 150–155) 312

The most important element of the content side of text structures is the proposition (with a "situation" being represented by it). Text comprehension is essentially about recognizing a text's propositions[22] and the way these are related to each other. 312a

Prototypically a **proposition** corresponds to the content of an independent (affirmative, active) declarative sentence/clause (↑267), e.g. of the following sentence:

Σολομὼν οἰκοδόμησεν αὐτῷ οἶκον. *Solomon built a house for him.* (Ac 7:47)

A proposition is (usually) made up of several concepts (as they are indicated by the [lexical] content words), one of these being the nucleus of the proposition, which in most cases is an
– **event concept**, here "to build".
The nucleus is usually accompanied by one or more
– **entity concepts** such as "Solomon", "house" and (pointed to by means of αὐτῷ) "God".
In place of an event concept there is sometimes a
– **relational concept**, e.g. "to believe" in Ro 4:3, or a
– **state concept**, often joined to a **property concept**, e.g. "to be (state) wise (property)" in Ro 16:19.

21 As is well known, this occurs very frequently in oral communication, e.g. (↑Givón 1995, I: 24): a) *Scalpel!* = "Give me a scalpel!", uttered by a surgeon in the operation theatre; b) *Water!* = "Give me water!", uttered by a person crawling out of the desert; c) *Mummy!* = "Mother, I need you!", uttered by a child.

22 Callow: 155, defines "proposition" as follows (emphases in the original): "In our view, *a proposition represents the interweaving of concepts in the speaker's mind as he relates them together for some communicative purpose* [...]. If the communication is successful (as most are), then the same proposition represents the way in which concepts interrelate in the hearer's mind as he listens."

Further noteworthy points:

(1) The form of the sentence will vary from language to language; the proposition as a content entity, however, is language independent. The sentence may have the following form:
Solomon built a house for him;
Salomon lui bâtit une maison;
Salomo baute ihm ein Haus; or (as in Ac 7:47):
Σολομὼν οἰκοδόμησεν αὐτῷ οἶκον.
The proposition (with the "situation" represented by it) "Solomon built a house for him" is unchanged (provided the context is the same).

(2) A proposition (or the "situation" it points to) such as "Solomon built a house for him" may occur in variously structured sentences of the same language (its content being modified accordingly), e.g.:
Solomon built a house for him (prototypical form: information, affirmative, active),
Did Solomon build a house for him? (*yes-no*-question),
Solomon did not build a house for him (information, negated),
A house was built for him by Solomon (information, affirmative, passive) or
Solomon, build a house for him! (command, affirmative).

Even lexically the same proposition may be expressed in different ways, e.g.:
The King erected a temple for God etc.

(3) Propositions are expressed not only by means of independent sentences (main clauses), but frequently also by means of dependent ones (subordinate clauses) or by means of sentence-like participle or infinitive phrases, sometimes even by means of text constituents without sentence/clause function at all, e.g.:
… *that Solomon built a house for him* (subordinate clause),
Building a house for him [Solomon did such and such] (participle phrase; ↑227ff),
[Solomon did such and such] *to build a house for him* (infinitive phrase; ↑213ff) or
Because of the construction of a house for him [Solomon did such and such] (a sentence constituent without sentence/clause function: preposition phrase with an action noun [↑362b] as the head of the embedded noun phrase).

312b A text is typically made up of several propositions. There is (usually) a particularly close content relationship between two successive propositions. This kind of relationship may be called "**inter-clausal connection**" or, so in the following, simply "**connection**". What type of connection is intended between the following two propositions, can easily be inferred:

μὴ φοβεῖσθε· (Pp. 1)	*Don't be afraid;*
πολλῶν στρουθίων διαφέρετε. (Pp. 2)	*you are worth more than many sparrows.* (Lk 12:7)

This is a causal connection: Pp. 2 gives the grounds for the exhortation of Pp. 1. In this case, as fairly frequently, the intended connection is not indicated by any lexical or syntactic means; it can be inferred without difficulty due to the cultural knowledge we have (↑309c–309e). More frequently, however, there are connectives that expressly indicate it, e.g.:

μὴ φοβοῦ, Μαριάμ, (Pp. 1)	*Do not be afraid, Mary;*
εὗρες **γὰρ** χάριν παρὰ τῷ θεῷ. (Pp. 2)	*for you have found favour with God.* (Lk 1:30)

A connection without connector is called "**asyndesis**" (↑293e), one with a connective "**syndesis**"; accordingly, one may speak of "asyndetic" and "syndetic" connections.

312c There are connections that are somewhat similar functionally to the asyndetic ones: the ones that are grammatically indicated by means of an adverbial participle (↑231–232) or by means of a copulative conjunction such as καί *and* (↑252.29,1a; similarly δέ *but/and* ↑252.12). Thus, **adverbial participles** (lacking grammatically fixed nuances) may in particular contexts indicate a causal connection, similarly (though less frequently) the semantically weak **καί** ***and***,[23] as these examples show:

καὶ κατεγέλων αὐτοῦ (Pp. 1)	*And they laughed at him,*
εἰδότες ὅτι ἀπέθανεν. (Pp. 2/3)	*because they knew that she was dead.* (Lk 8:53)
ἐκλυθήσονται ἐν τῇ ὁδῷ· (Pp. 1)	*… they will collapse on the way;*
καί τινες αὐτῶν ἀπὸ μακρόθεν ἥκασιν. (Pp. 2)	*for some of them have come a long distance.* (Mk 8:3)

In most cases one of the two parts of a connection is communicationally more prominent.[24] Its con- 312d
tribution to the content to be communicated carries more weight; the other part serves above all to supplement or support it. In the above examples Pp. 1 carries more communicative weight. In each case Pp. 1 contains the main part of the information conveyed by the combination, its "nucleus". Pp. 2 and Pp. 2/3 simply have a supplementing or supporting function: to give a reason for Pp. 1. The causal connections of the above examples actually indicate semantic relations that may be termed as follows (small capitals: label referring to the nucleus; ↑323c, for more details 333b and 352b):

Example:	semantic relation:
Lk 12:7 and 1:30	EXHORTATION–grounds
Lk 8:53	RESULT–reason
Mk 8:3	CONCLUSION–grounds

Note that the EXHORTATION, the RESULT or the CONCLUSION, the nucleus, (in this context) carries more weight regarding the content to be communicated by each of these proposition pairs; in fact, it is indispensable. For if the "situation" for which a reason or grounds are to be given is not mentioned, nothing meaningful would (usually) be left: there would be "a reason" or "grounds", but nothing to explain by them! On the other hand, mentioning the "situation" referred to by the nucleus makes good sense even without a reason or grounds being given, thus in our examples: "Don't be afraid"/ "Do not be afraid, Mary", "And they laughed at him", and "… they will collapse on the way".

Texts made up of a single proposition pair do not occur very often. In most cases several such micro- 312e
structures are involved. These are joined to form larger text entities, macro-structures, complete texts. The propositional structures thus formed are (usually) hierarchical, as may be illustrated by the analysis of Mt 13:45f below:[25]

23 Note that "and" basically indicates an addition (↑325), which, however, occurs with a variety of different nuances depending on the individual context: apart from the standard use "and [in addition]" there are other uses inter alia with a temporal nuance such as "and [then]" as well as "and [at the same time]" or a consequential one such as "and [so]" (for further details on καί ↑252.29,1a). In the following example Mk 8:3 a causal nuance occurs.

24 "Prominence" is a property relevant to various levels of text structures; ↑e.g. Callow: 151f.

25 ↑352–353 for more details on the underlying methodology, termed "Semantic and Structural Analysis", where the various interpropositional semantic relations typical of linguistic communication are listed and illustrated.

hierarchical propositional **structure**:

propositions:
(italics: indirectly communicated elements)

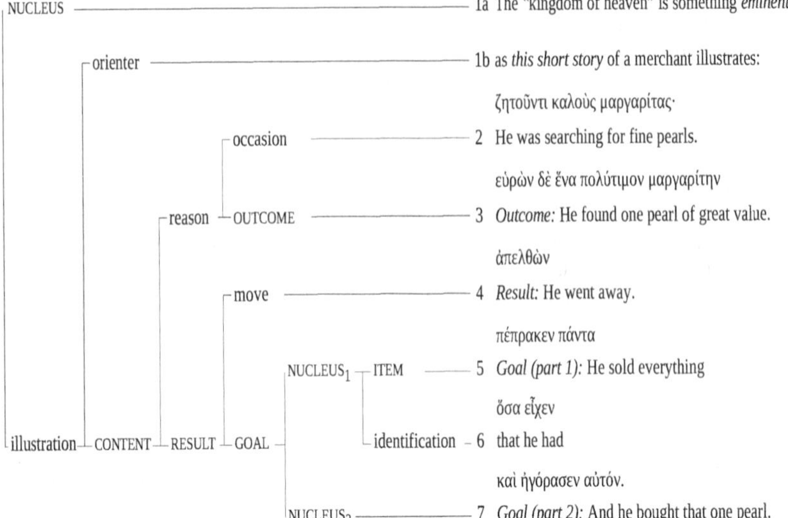

Pp. 6 identifies the (indispensable) ITEM concept "everything". The ITEM concept is part of Pp. 5: "He sold everything". The relative pronoun serves as a connective.

Between Pp. 5 and Pp. 7 there is a NUCLEUS_1–NUCLEUS_2 (sequential) relation; the two parts appear to carry the same communicational weight (they are of equal natural prominence). They are joined by the connective καί "and", as is typical of such relationships.

The connection of Pp. 4 "He went away" with Pp. 5 and Pp. 7 (including Pp. 6) seems best understood in terms of a move-GOAL relation. Since Pp. 5 and Pp. 7 carry equal weight the connecting line of the diagram to the higher hierarchy levels (illustration-CONTENT-RESULT-GOAL-) starts from the middle of these two. Unlike Pp. 4 the complex Pp. 5–Pp. 7 is communicationally indispensable and is therefore the nucleus of this relation. In this case the (interclausal) connection is indicated by an adverbial participle (ἀπελθών *He went away [and]*; ↑301b; 312c).

Pp. 5 and Pp. 7 (including Pp. 4 and Pp. 6 subordinated to them) are placed (one hierarchy level higher) in a reason–RESULT relation to Pp. 3. The connection between them is again indicated by an adverbial participle (εὑρών *He found … [and]*; ↑301b; 312c).

The connection between Pp. 2 and Pp. 3 (one hierarchy level lower) may be interpreted meaningfully as an occasion–OUTCOME relation. The weak adversative δέ "but" functions as a connective, often indicating some development in a text, here indicates the beginning of the short story of Pp. 3–7.

At a higher hierarchy level (one level above the reason–RESULT connection), an orienter–CONTENT relation can be made out between Pp. 1b and the proposition complex Pp. 2–7; it is a connection indicated by an attributive participle (ζητοῦντι *searching for*; ↑301b; 236).

At the highest hierarchy level, we may speak of a NUCLEUS–illustration relation (↑lexical indicator ὁμοία ἐστιν *is like*) existing between Pp. 1a and the remaining propositions of our text.

312f With regard to recognizing or inferring the propositional structure, particularly the intended types of connections (relations), the following needs to be noted:

a) Whatever is expressed by linguistic means needs to be supplemented by content elements derived from the presupposed world, action and text knowledge (↑309d–309e; “top-down” process [↑310b]).
b) Here, too, we have to work with interpretation hypotheses that are to be adjusted continually. As in other situations (↑311b) an important contributive role is played not only by our knowledge, but also by our experience, beliefs, emotions, and abilities.
c) Our objective remains, however, to understand what the author of the text intends to communicate.

Text comprehension – frames (↑DuG9: 1160f; GaJü: 169–171) 313

In many cases our text comprehension, especially our endeavours to recognize or infer the hierarchical propositional structure, will depend on those parts of our world and action knowledge (↑309d) that are termed “frames” or “scripts”. 313a
The term “**frames**” generally refers to those parts of knowledge that concern static relationships, the term “script” to parts of knowledge whose focus is on dynamic relationships, inter alia on individually and socially acceptable and successful behaviour. Since there are no clearly definable boundaries between frames and scripts, it seems advisable to use the term “frames” to cover both domains (a course of action apparently chosen by GaJü).
As soon as our parsing and processing of text constituents (↑311) show that the text is about a particular frame such as “personal computing”, we will be geared to this frame for the rest of the process drawing on what we know about personal computing. Lexically ambiguous words will be disambiguated, being connected (quite naturally) with concepts belonging to the frame of personal computing, e.g. *printer, mouse, directory, document, to boot, to shut down.* As we deal with NT texts frames are no less important. Among these are the frames “temple”, “synagogue”, “ritual purity”, “festivals”, “jurisdiction”, “house construction”, “agriculture”, “animal husbandry”, “fishing”, “seafaring”, “marriage”, “mourning customs” etc.

Text comprehension – implied elements (↑GaJü: 171–173; Akmajian 2001: 370–387) 314

In every phase of the text comprehension process we primarily draw on what is indicated by the grammatical side of the text structure (when parsing; ↑311a); on the other hand, however, we also take into account whatever is to be understood without being expressed, content elements that are implied, to be inferred in the light of the intratextual and extratextual context. We are able to infer such content elements with the help of our cultural knowledge, i.e. our lexical, world, action and text knowledge, as presupposed by the one(s) producing the text (↑309c–309e). Fairly frequently the following two domains are particularly relevant: 314a

1. **Logical or semantic presuppositions**: 314b

These are elements of the presupposed knowledge that are connected with particular expressions or utterances (including their negation) and are activated in the process of text comprehension. According to GaJü: 172f, three types of presuppositions may be distinguished:

a) Existential presupposition: the existence of something is presupposed, implied. e.g.: 314c

expressly indicated:	presupposed, implied:
Καὶ ἐλθὼν ὁ Ἰησοῦς εἰς τὴν οἰκίαν Πέτρου εἶδεν τὴν πενθερὰν αὐτοῦ βεβλημένην καὶ πυρέσσουσαν. *And when Jesus entered Peter’s house, he saw his mother-in-law lying in bed with a fever.* (Mt 8:14)	(1) Peter had a house. (2) Peter had a mother-in-law (and so was married).

314d b) Factive presupposition: the truth of a statement is presupposed, implied. This applies especially to certain types of verbs/predicators that are combined with "that"-clauses (dependent declarative subject-object clauses; in Ancient Greek mainly ὅτι-clauses and infinitive/ACI phrases [↑271]), e.g.:

expressly indicated:	presupposed, implied:
ὅτι δὲ ἀνέστησεν αὐτὸν ἐκ νεκρῶν μηκέτι μέλλοντα ὑποστρέφειν εἰς διαφθοράν, οὕτως εἴρηκεν … *That he raised him from the dead, not to return to corruption, he declared in this way …* (Ac 13:34)	*It is true* that he raised him from the dead, not to return to corruption.

314e c) Categorical presupposition: what is presupposed, implied, is connected with lexical-semantic properties of certain verbs (also called "implicative" verbs), e.g.:

verb:		presupposed, implied:
ἀποκρίνομαι	mostly *to answer*	A person has uttered something beforehand.
σῴζω	*to rescue/save*	The object entity is in (great) danger.
κλέπτω	*to steal*	The object entity belongs to some one else.

314f 2. **Communication principles**:

There are certain communication principles (part of text knowledge; ↑309e) that are of vital importance to text comprehension, particularly when it comes to inferring implied content elements.[26] The highest of these principles is the all-embracing cooperative principle.[27] As Akmajian 2001: 371, puts it,[28] "linguistic communication is a kind of cooperative problem solving. The speaker faces the problem of getting the hearer to recognize the speaker's communicative intentions; so, the speaker must choose an expression that will facilitate such recognition, given the context of utterance. From the hearer's point of view the problem is to successfully recognize the speaker's communicative intention on the basis of the words the speaker has chosen and the context of utterance." Such cooperative problem solving is (usually) successful if and when the participants are at pains to cooperate as needed. Cooperation of this kind is based on a variety of shared beliefs: the speaker/writer and the hearer/reader (usually) start from certain "presumptions"; at the same time they are acquainted with a number of "inferential strategies" providing "communicants with short, effective patterns of inference from what someone utters to what that person might be trying to communicate." In combination these presumptions and inferential strategies "provide the basis for an account of successful communication."

314g a) The ***presumptions*** (according to Akmajian: 371) are:

"*Linguistic Presumption*

Unless there is evidence to the contrary, the hearer is presumed capable of determining the meaning and the referents of the expressions in the context of utterance.

Communicative presumption

Unless there is evidence to the contrary, the speaker is assumed to be speaking with some identifiable communicative intent.

---

26 The present overview of communication principles is based on Akmajian 2001: 370–387 ("Inferential Model of Linguistic Communication"; for details ↑there), which is highly indebted to Paul Grice's foundational work *Logic and Conversation* (originally a 1967 Harvard lecture), most clearly regarding the "Conversational Presumptions" (↑Grice's "maxims").

27 The cooperative principle is more specifically described in terms of relevance by the increasingly influential "Relevance Theory" (↑Wilson-Sperber), a cognitive linguistic approach that overlaps in many respects with the one presented here (↑DuG9: 1178).

28 Note that in our quotations from Akmajian "speaker", "speaking", "hearer", and "hearing" are meant to include the concepts of "writer", "writing", "reader", and "reading" respectively.

Presumption of literalness
Unless there is evidence to the contrary, the speaker is assumed to be speaking literally.

Conversational Presumptions

Relevance:	The speaker's remarks are relevant to the conversation.
Sincerity:	The speaker is being sincere.
Truthfulness:	The speaker is attempting to say something true.
Quantity:	The speaker contributes the appropriate amount of information.
Quality:	The speaker has adequate evidence for what [he or] she says."

b) The following ***inferential strategies*** (based on Akmajian: 372–385) make it possible to infer all of the intended content, i.e. the parts that are expressed explicitly as well as those that are implied: **314h**

DIRECT STRATEGY (parsing; ↑311a):
STEP 1: a text constituent reaches the mind of the hearer/reader.
STEP 2: the intended lexical-grammatical meanings/functions are inferred.
STEP 3: what the speaker/writer refers to concretely (the "reference") is inferred.
STEP 4: what the speaker/writer communicates directly (explicitly and literally) is inferred.

↓

The hearer/reader recognizes,
what the speaker/writer would communicate directly (explicitly),
if it were meant literally
(content without taking into account what might be meant nonliterally or indirectly)

↓ ↓

LITERAL STRATEGY:
STEP 5: literal interpretation appears to be contextually appropriate.
STEP 6: conclusion:
what is said is meant literally.

↓

The hearer/reader recognizes,
what the speaker/writer communicates (directly [explicitly]) and literally
(content without what might be meant indirectly)

NONLITERAL STRATEGY:
STEP 5': literal interpretation appears to be contextually inappropriate.
STEP 6': conclusion:
what is said is not meant literally; it is to be interpreted as a figure of speech (↑291–296).

↓

The hearer/reader recognizes,
what the speaker/writer communicates (directly [explicitly]) and nonliterally
(content without what might be meant indirectly)

↓

INDIRECT STRATEGY:
STEP 7: it would be contextually inappropriate, if the speaker/writer did not mean to communicate something indirectly in addition to what is being communicated directly (explicitly).
STEP 8: what the speaker/writer communicates indirectly (implicitly) is inferred.

↓

The hearer/reader recognizes,
what the speaker/writer also communicates indirectly (implicitly).
The hearer/reader has thus inferred the intended content.

4.2 Coherence and the two sides of text structures

(↑DuG9: 1079–1159)

315 In 301 we showed, using Mt 13:45f as a representative example, how the coherence of a text (↑300) may be tied to elements of both the grammatical side (↑301b) and the content side (↑301d) of text structures; we also introduced the "functional sentence perspective" as a kind of bridge between the two (↑301c). In the following paragraphs a systematic overview is given of the most important factors affecting coherence, first dealing with those on the grammatical side (↑316–348), then with those on the content side (↑349–353) of text structures.[29]

4.2.1 Coherence and the grammatical side of text structures

(↑DuG9: 1079–1135)

316 There are a variety of grammatical means[30] in Ancient Greek (as also in English) to ensure the coherence of texts. Apart from punctuation[31] (not discussed here) these mainly include (as already shown by our example Mt 13:45f in 301b)
1. the connectives (↑317–345) and
2. the phoric or deictic function words (i.e. words that refer to elements inside or outside the text), especially the article and pronouns (↑346–348); also tense/aspect, voice, mood, and non-finite verb form choices (whose textgrammatical role will not be treated any further here).[32]

Note that while these means contribute to coherence already at the sentence level, they (mainly) perform their proper function only at the level of the text. To a large extent they are organized in closed classes (as paradigms) and are part of the presupposed grammatical knowledge (↑309b).

---

29 For lack of adequate empirical data related to Ancient Greek, unfortunately, no further details of the "functional sentence perspective" can be given here beyond what was said in 301c.

30 These coherence-related factors are about what is usually called "cohesion" (↑301b[7]).

31 Punctuation, as described in 7b, became a regular part of Greek orthography only in the 9th century A.D. It cannot be connected with any system known from Antiquity; and it seems to have been used rather haphazardly (↑Nesselrath: 50; LAW: 1388f). In modern standard editions of the NT the use of punctuation seems to be largely dependent on the rules of the primary language of the leading editors, i.e. on German rules (NA and ECM) or on English ones (UBSGNT). The textual segmentation indicated in these, however, goes back to early times. The UBSGNT has a special "Discourse Segmentation Apparatus" informing about important variants. In the Greek New Testament produced at Tyndale House in Cambridge (published in 2017) the paragraphs "are informed by manuscripts, in particular by those from the fifth century or earlier" (THGNT: 512).

32 Apart from the hints given in 301b ↑especially the explanations in Part 3 on syntax: 192ff on tense/aspect, 188ff on voice, 207ff on moods, and 213ff on non-finite verb forms. – For important (extended and partly controversial) discussions of the text/discourse-grammatical/pragmatic roles of some of these choices ↑Runge/Fresch: 163ff; also ↑relevant sections in Runge: inter alia 125ff.

4.2.1.1 Coherence and connectives

(↑DuG9: 1083–1120)

As stated in 312b the content relationship between two successive propositions is termed "interclausal connection" or, so in the following, simply "connection" in the present grammar. A connection that is marked by a connective (the typical case) is called "syndetic" (or "syndesis"), one without a connective "asyndetic" (or "asyndesis").[33] We will now show (i) what kind of forms connectives may have (↑317–321), and (ii) what kind of connections may be marked by them (↑322–345).

(i) Connectives: possible forms

(↑DuG9: 1083ff)

Members of various word-classes or form elements may serve as connectives: **317**
1. conjunctions (↑318);
2. relatives (↑319);
3. adverbs or the like (↑320);
4. prepositions and case forms (↑321).

Connectives: conjunctions (↑DuG9: 1084f) **318**

In the majority of cases connectives are conjunctions (or particles; ↑250b), either **318a**
coordinating or subordinating conjunctions (or particles; ↑22j; 250/251), e.g.:

SYNTACTIC STRUCTURE: (in bold: connective)	CONNECTION TYPE: →type of semantic relationship (↑352b; in bold: proposition that contains the connective)
οὕτως **γὰρ** ἠγάπησεν ὁ θεὸς τὸν κόσμον, *For God so loved the world,*	coordinating, causal conj. (or particle; ↑22j[15]): →[v. 15]–Pp.1(-4): [CONCLUSION]–**grounds**
ὥστε τὸν υἱὸν τὸν μονογενῆ ἔδωκεν, *that he gave his one and only Son,*	subordinating, result indicating conj.: →Pp.1–**Pp.2(-4)**: reason–**RESULT**
ἵνα πᾶς ὁ πιστεύων εἰς αὐτὸν μὴ ἀπόληται, *so that everyone who believes in him will not perish,*	subordinating, purpose indicating conj.: →Pp.2–**Pp.3/4**: move–**GOAL**
ἀλλ' ἔχῃ ζωὴν αἰώνιον. *but have eternal life.* (Jn 3:16)	coordinating, adversative conj.: →Pp.3–**Pp.4**: negative–**POSITIVE**

33 Note that while GaJü: 166, use the term "connection" ("Konnexion") as it is done here, DuG9: 1083, uses it only when the relationship is marked by a connective ("Konnektor").

318b Note that there are also two-word/correlative (coordinating) conjunctions such as μέν – δέ *(on the one hand) – but (on the other hand)* (↑251a–251c):

... πάντες **μὲν** τρέχουσιν, *... all run,*	coordinating, adversative conj./part 1: →**Pp. 1**–: **contrast**–
εἷς **δὲ** λαμβάνει τὸ βραβεῖον. *but only one gets the prize.* (1Cor 9:24)	coordinating, adversative conj./part 2: →–**Pp. 2**: –NUCLEUS

The two-word conjunctions should not be confused with the following (partially similar) uses:

318c 1. Certain (coordinating or subordinating) conjunctions may be combined with a **correlative**, (mostly) an **adverb**, that appears in the other part of the connection and clarifies or supplements the connection, thus in Jn 3:16 (↑318a):

οὕτως ... *... so (much) ...*	adverb: correlates with ὥστε in Pp. 2
ὥστε ... *(with the result) that ...*	conj.: clarified by οὕτως in Pp. 1 (ὥστε could be used alone: *[with the result] that*)
... μή ... *... not ...*	negative: correlates with ἀλλά in Pp. 4
ἀλλά ... *but ...*	conj.: supplemented by μή in Pp. 3 (ἀλλά could not be used alone without change of content)

318d 2. Conjunctional clauses sometimes occur as **attributive modifiers** (typically) of the head of a noun phrase placed in the superordinate sentence/clause (↑288). The proposition expressed by such a clause provides some additional information on the concept referred to by that head (↑341c), a use that is more typical of relative causes (↑319). E.g.:

ἔρχεται νὺξ *Night is coming*	νύξ/"night" in Pp. 1 is the head/concept the ὅτε-clause (Pp. 2) refers to
ὅτε οὐδεὶς δύναται ἐργάζεσθαι. *when no one can work.* (Jn 9:4)	ὅτε-clause is the attributive modifier: **Pp. 2**: additional information on concept "night"

318e Note, however, that a kind of correlative is involved in cases where the conjunctional clause is the attributive modifier or apposition of a demonstrative pronoun or adverb (↑61), which, placed in the superordinate sentence/clause, functions as its **substitute**, e.g.:[34]

καὶ αὕτη ἐστὶν ἡ ἀγάπη, *And this is love*	αὕτη *this* (dem. pron.) in Pp. 1 is the head of the ἵνα-clause (Pp. 2)
ἵνα περιπατῶμεν κατὰ τὰς ἐντολὰς αὐτοῦ· *that we live according to his commandments.* (2Jn 6)	**ἵνα** *that* (conj.) in **Pp. 2** correlates with αὕτη: the ἵνα-clause is an Attr/App of αὕτη (↑222; 272a; 288a)
ὅτε ἐδοξάσθη Ἰησοῦς *When Jesus was glorified,*	**ὅτε** *when* (conj.) correlates with τότε *then*, which is explained by the ὅτε-clause (↑288b)
τότε ἐμνήσθησαν ... *then they remembered ...* (Jn 12:16)	τότε *then* (adv.) in Pp. 2 is the head of the ὅτε-clause (Pp. 1); it clarifies/emphasizes the connection (ὅτε could be used without it).

34 ↑DuG9: 1125.

Connectives: relatives (↑DuG9: 1085f) 319

Relatives, too, function as connectives. This applies to the various relative pronouns (↑59; 61b) and relative pronominal adverbs (↑61c) that serve as subordinators of relative clauses (↑289–290).

Relative clauses typically function as attributive modifiers (↑289b; 260): the relative (mostly) refers back to a specific entity identified by the antecedent (usually the head of a noun phrase in the superordinate construction). To put it another way: the proposition of the relative clause (mostly) provides some additional information on the **concept** (or the entity it represents, the "ITEM") referred to by the **antecedent**, either to identify or to further characterize it (↑341c). e.g.: 319a

SYNTACTIC STRUCTURE: (in bold: connective)	RELATIVE TYPE: →type of semantic relationship (↑352b; in bold: proposition that contains the connective)
εὗρον τὴν δραχμὴν *I have found the coin*	antecedent/concept/entity referred to: τὴν δραχμήν/"the coin"
ἣν ἀπώλεσα. *that I had lost.* (Lk 15:9)	specific (simple) rel. pron.: →Pp. 1–**Pp. 2**: ITEM–**identification**
ὑμεῖς ἐστε ἐν Χριστῷ Ἰησοῦ, *You are in Christ Jesus,*	antecedent/concept/entity referred to: (ἐν) Χριστῷ Ἰησοῦ/"(in) Christ Jesus"
ὃς ἐγενήθη σοφία ἡμῖν ἀπὸ θεοῦ … *who became for us wisdom from God* … (1Cor 1:30)	specific (simple) rel. pron.: →Pp. 1–**Pp. 2**: ITEM–**description**
ἐν Ἱεροσολύμοις ἐστὶν ὁ τόπος *In Jerusalem is the place*	antecedent/concept/entity referred to: ὁ τόπος/"the place"
ὅπου προσκυνεῖν δεῖ. *where people must worship.* (Jn 4:20)	relative adverb: →Pp. 1–**Pp. 2**: ITEM–**identification**
Μὴ θησαυρίζετε ὑμῖν θησαυροὺς ἐπὶ τῆς γῆς, *Don't store up treasures on earth,*	antecedent/concept/entity referred to: (ἐπὶ) τῆς γῆς/"(on) earth"
ὅπου σὴς καὶ βρῶσις ἀφανίζει … *where moth and rust destroy.* (Mt 6:19)	relative adverb: →Pp. 1–**Pp. 2**: ITEM–**description**

All sentences/clauses subordinated by a relative have been classified as relative clauses, including those **without** an **antecedent** in the superordinate construction. This certainly seems legitimate when the "missing" antecedent can easily be supplied in thought. As relative clauses without an antecedent do not function as attributive modifiers, but as sentence constituents (↑289b,2), it would also be possible to classify such relative clauses as subject, object or adverbial clauses. E.g.: 319b

διηγήσαντο αὐτῷ *They reported to him*	Pp. 1 is without (a possible) antecedent (Par. Mk 6:30 has πάντα *all/everything*)
ὅσα ἐποίησαν. *all that they had done.* (Lk 9:10)	rel. cl. (Pp. 2) is a Od ("object clause"): →Pp. 1–**Pp. 2**: orienter–**CONTENT**

θερίζω
I harvest
ὅπου οὐκ ἔσπειρα.
where I didn't sow. (Mt 25:26)

Pp. 1 is without (a possible) antecedent (↑e.g. Jn 11:30: ἐν τῷ τόπῳ ὅπου … *in the place where* …) rel. cl. (Pp. 2) is a LocA ("adverbial clause"): → Pp. 1–**Pp. 2**: NUCLEUS–**circumstance**

Noteworthy points:

319c In Ancient Greek **indefinite relative adverbs** are generally identical in form with **indirect interrogatives** (↑59c; 60c; but above all 61b–61c), e.g.:

ὁπότε	indefinite relative adv.:	*whenever/when* conj. (↑Ps 3:1 LXX)
	indirect interrogative:	*when* (= *at what point of time*) (↑Job 26:14 LXX)

Quite a few authors (e.g. Philo and Josephus), however, generally prefer the direct to the indirect interrogatives even when introducing indirect questions (thus πότε to ὁπότε for *when* = *at what point of time*, which is always possible according to the general rule; ↑273b). This happens in the NT even to a greater extent (↑61b–61c). Regarding NT usage the following state of affairs is worth noting, too: apart from ὅστις *whoever/anyone who* and ὅπου *wherever/to wherever*, which are both well-attested (though ὅστις only in the nom.; ↑59b; 61c), indefinite relatives occur only occasionally.[35]

319d In the case of "sentential relative clauses" (where the antecedent is not a word or phrase, but a whole clause; ↑289b), the proposition of the relative clause provides some additional information on the superordinate proposition, whose function fairly frequently will be that of a "comment" or "parenthesis" (↑341b), e.g.:

μόνον τῶν πτωχῶν ἵνα μνημονεύωμεν,
Only, we were to be mindful of the poor,

No word or phrase in Pp. 1 qualifies as an antecedent; none may be supplied in thought either.

ὃ καὶ ἐσπούδασα αὐτὸ τοῦτο ποιῆσαι.
which was actually what I was eager to do. (Ga 2:10)

The rel. cl. (Pp. 2) refers back to the whole clause of Pp. 1: → Pp. 1–**Pp. 2**: NUCLEUS–**comment**

320 Connectives: adverbs or the like (↑DuG9: 1086–1088)

Certain adverbs and (mainly) multi-word phrases with a similar use, too, may function as connectives. These include pronominal adverbs (↑22h; 61c; 319) that typically refer back to content elements of sentences or texts (anadeictically; ↑347b) as also other types of adverbs. E.g.:

προάγει ὑμᾶς εἰς τὴν Γαλιλαίαν·
He is going ahead of you to Galilee;

"Galilee" is mentioned as the destination of the event of Pp. 1.

ἐκεῖ αὐτὸν ὄψεσθε.
there you will see him. (Mk 16:7)

ἐκεῖ "there" (pronominal adv.) in Pp. 2 refers back to the content "Galilee" of Pp. 1 (anadeictically).

35 One of the exceptions is ὁποῖος *of whatever kind* in Ga 2:6 (↑BDF §303). ὅπως in the NT is used almost exclusively as a conjunction *in order that/that* (↑252.45).
Note that the majority of Ancient Greek conjunctions were originally relatives (↑270c): apart from ὅπως also inter alia ὅτε *when* (↑276) and ὡς *how/as/like* with its various conjunctional functions (↑252.61) and ὥστε *with the result that* (↑252.62), also ὅτι *that/because* (derived from the indefinite relative pronoun ὅ τι *what[ever]*; ↑60b; 252.46).

Πάλιν ὁμοία ἐστὶν ἡ βασιλεία τῶν οὐρανῶν σαγήνῃ … *Again, the kingdom of heaven is like a net …* (Mt 13:47)	πάλιν "again/furthermore" (adverb: a "conjunctional" adverb) connects this text ("additively") with something that precedes it.

↑318c on adverbs that are used as correlatives of conjunctions.

Connectives: prepositions and case forms (↑DuG9: 1088) 321

Prepositions and case forms, too, may be used as connectives, i.e. when the preposition phrase or prepositionless case noun phrase expresses a proposition. This occurs with (embedded) articular infinitive/ACI phrases (↑223–226), but also with (embedded) noun phrases whose head is a verbal noun (↑362b) or a pronominal noun substitute (↑22c). E.g. (on the semantic-communicative relations between propositions ↑352b–352c):

SYNTACTIC STRUCTURE: (in bold: connective)	CONNECTION TYPE: →type of semantic relationship (↑352b; in bold: proposition that contains the connective)
πάντα δὲ τὰ ἔργα αὐτῶν ποιοῦσιν, *They do all their deeds*	Pp. 1: superordinate construction (main cl.)
πρὸς τὸ θεαθῆναι τοῖς ἀνθρώποις· *to be seen by people.* (Mt 23:5)	Pp. 2: preposition phrase: πρὸς τό + InfP →Pp. 1–**Pp. 2**: move–GOAL
οὐκ ἔσχηκα ἄνεσιν … *I had no rest …*	Pp. 1: superordinate construction (main cl.)
τῷ μὴ εὑρεῖν με Τίτον τὸν ἀδελφόν μου. *because I did not find my brother Titus [there].* (2Cor 2:13)	Pp. 2: prepositionless case noun phrase: τῷ + infinitive/ACI phrase →Pp. 1–**Pp. 2**: RESULT–**reason**
κατανοῶμεν ἀλλήλους *Let us watch out for one another*	Pp. 1: superordinate construction (main cl.)
εἰς παροξυσμὸν ἀγάπης καὶ καλῶν ἔργων. *to provoke love and good works.* (He 10:24)	Pp. 2: preposition phrase: εἰς + verbal noun →Pp. 1–**Pp. 2**: move–**GOAL**
εἰς τοῦτο (= ἵνα κηρύξω) *For this purpose (= in order to proclaim the message)*	Pp. 1: preposition phrase: εἰς + pronominal noun substitute
ἐξῆλθον. *I have come.* (Mk 1:38)	Pp. 2: superordinate construction (main cl.) →**Pp. 1**–Pp. 2: **GOAL**–move

τῇ προσευχῇ … *By prayer* …	**Pp.1**: prepositionless case noun phrase: dat. of instrument (↑177a) with verbal noun
τὰ αἰτήματα ὑμῶν γνωριζέσθω πρὸς τὸν θεόν. *let your requests be made known to God.* (Php 4:6)	Pp.2: superordinate construction (main cl.) →**Pp.1**–Pp.2: MEANS–purpose

(ii) Connections

In 317–321 we saw what lexical-grammatical forms may be used as connectives. The following section (↑322–345) is about the kinds of (syndetic) connections that connectives may indicate. After looking at some of the basics for dealing with connections in 322 an introduction to the most important types of connections will be given in 323–345.

322 Basics of connections (↑DuG9: 1088ff)

322a 1. Fairly frequently the intended content relationship between propositions ("situations"), the **connection**, is **obvious** (to cooperative hearers/readers; ↑314f), i.e. it is easy to infer on the basis of the presupposed cultural knowledge (↑309c–309e); in such cases we may encounter (as indicated in 312b–312c)

a) asyndesis (a connection without connectives),

b) copulative connectives such as καί *and*, δέ *but/and* or the like (↑325c; also 312c[23]) or else

c) a connection by means of an adverbial participle phrase (whose intended nuance is sometimes made more specific by means of particles; ↑231–232; 312c).

Note that in the case of **asyndesis** the inferable connection may be: most frequently causal (↑312b; 333c) and explanatory (↑341d), somewhat less frequently consequential (↑334), rarely conditional (↑331e), at times adversative (↑338), additive (↑325f) or alternative (↑326c). Moreover, asyndesis frequently occurs with various types of subject-object clauses, in English renderings indicated by " , '…' " (↑274b) or by "that" (↑272d; 275), with an orienter–CONTENT relation being expressed (↑323b; 352c). For further details on the use of asyndesis ↑Reiser 1984: 138–162.

322b 2. As was emphasized in 312d, one of the two parts of a connection usually carries more communicational weight, being its "nucleus" (or its "content basis"; ↑DuG9: 1089), while the other part has mainly a supplementing or supporting role. Finding out which proposition may be regarded as carrying more communicational weight and (as a result) inferring the intended hierarchical propositional structure of a text as a whole can be quite challenging, and fairly frequently more than one solution seems to be defensible (↑353b). The points mentioned in 312f should always be taken into account.

3. When trying to infer the intended connections one sometimes needs to determine what the supplementing or supporting proposition is concerned with, whether a) exclusively with the "situation" (referred to by the proposition) or b) also with the utterance conveying the nucleus, i.e. mostly by supporting the utterance's affirmative, interrogative, or desiderative character. In case a) one may speak of (exclusive) **"'situation' relatedness"**, in case b) of (additional) **"utterance relatedness"** (DuG9: 1090: "Sachverhaltsbezug" and "Äußerungsbezug").

a) In most cases there is (exclusive) **"situation" relatedness**: Both propositions are part of one and the same utterance, i. e. both the "situation" of the nucleus and the "situation" of the other proposition form integral parts of the affirmation, question, or directive/wish uttered. In such cases the "situation" referred to by the nucleus (and not its utterance) is supplemented or supported by the other proposition (typically expressed by means of a subordinate construction). E. g.: 322c

ἔθυσεν ὁ πατήρ σου τὸν μόσχον τὸν σιτευτόν, *Your father has slaughtered the fattened calf,*	Pp. 1: RESULT (nucleus; main cl.): utterance part 1: affirmation of a "situation"
ὅτι ὑγιαίνοντα αὐτὸν ἀπέλαβεν. *because he has received him back safe and sound.* (Lk 15:27)	Pp. 2: reason (a supplementing/supporting Pp.; subo. cl.): utterance part 2: **the "situation" of Pp. 2 supports** (justifies) **the "situation" of Pp. 1** (itself, and not the fact that it was affirmed).

b) Fairly frequently, however, there is some additional **utterance relatedness** (mainly regarding causal connections in the widest sense; ↑332): The supplement or supporting proposition is to be understood as an independent utterance (typically expressed by a coordinated construction). Such a proposition is not only about the "situation" of the nucleus, but also about its utterance, i. e. its function. In addition to supplementing or supporting the "situation" of the nucleus, it specifically supplements or supports the affirmative, interrogative, or desiderative character of the nucleus being uttered. E. g. (on the semantic-communicative relations between propositions ↑352b–352c): 322d

κύριε, ἤδη ὄζει, *Lord, there will be a terrible smell,*	Pp. 1: RESULT (nucleus; main cl.): 1st utterance: a "situation" is being affirmed
τεταρταῖος **γάρ** ἐστιν. *for he has been dead for four days* (= I am affirming this because he has been dead for four days/ After all, he has been …) (Jn 11:39)	Pp. 2: reason (a supplementing/supporting Pp.; main cl.): 2nd (independent) utterance: **Pp. 2 indicates the reason why the "situation" of Pp. 1 is being affirmed.**
τίνος τῶν ἑπτὰ ἔσται γυνή; *Whose wife will she be of the seven?*	Pp. 1: CONCLUSION (nucleus; main cl.): 1st utterance: a question about a "situation" is being asked.
πάντες **γὰρ** ἔσχον αὐτήν. *For they all had been married to her* (= We are asking this question because all had been married to her [and she cannot possibly live together with all of them at the same time; ↑314]) (Mt 22:28)	Pp. 2: grounds (a supplementing/supporting Pp.; main cl.): 2nd (independent) utterance: **Pp. 2 indicates the grounds for asking the question about the "situation" of Pp. 1.**
λαλεῖτε ἀλήθειαν ἕκαστος μετὰ τοῦ πλησίον αὐτοῦ, *Speak the truth, each one to his neighbour,*	Pp. 1: EXHORTATION (nucleus; main cl.): 1st utterance: a certain "situation" (behaviour) is being demanded.
ὅτι ἐσμὲν ἀλλήλων μέλη. *for we are all members of one body.* (= I demand this because we [Christians] are all members of one body [and must therefore not lie to one another]) (Eph 4:25)	Pp. 2: grounds (a supplementing/supporting Pp.; subo. cl.): 2nd (independent) utterance: **Pp. 2 indicates the grounds for uttering the exhortation of Pp. 1.**

323 Overview of connections (↑DuG9: 1091)

323a The connections that are indicated by connectives, may be divided into seven major types; in most cases these may be subdivided into several subtypes:

copulative	**temporal**	**conditional**	**causal-codirectional** (widest sense)	**causal-contradirectional** (widest sense)	**specifying**	**involving comparisons**
additive alternative	anterior posterior simultaneous		causal (narrow) consequential modal-instru-mental purpose-oriented	adversative concessive	explanatory restrictive	comparative proportional
(↑324–326)	(↑327–330)	(↑331)	(↑332–336)	(↑337–339)	(↑340–342)	(↑343–345)

Two further types might be added:

(1) a "**local**" type applicable to cases where a relative clause with a local relative (ὅπου/οὗ *where* or the like) is used without antecedent (↑289a/319b). However, in most of these cases a temporal or conditional relation (↑327–330; 331) predominates over the local content element. E.g.:

(local) circumstance–NUCLEUS (→ time– NUCLEUS or condition–CONSEQUENCE):

οὗ γάρ εἰσιν δύο ἢ τρεῖς συνηγμένοι εἰς τὸ ἐμὸν ὄνομα,	*For where (≈ when/if) two or three are gathered in my name*
ἐκεῖ εἰμι ἐν μέσῳ αὐτῶν.	*I am there among them.* (Mt 18:20)

323b (2) a "**content**" type applicable to subject-object clauses with ὅτι/ἵνα "that" and the like or εἰ "if" and the like as well as functionally similar constructions such as infinitive/ACI and participle phrases, also asyndesis (including direct and indirect speech; ↑271–274 [for connectives ↑there, on asyndesis also 322a]). E.g.:

orienter–CONTENT (↑352b/352c,6):

οἶδα	*I know*
ὅτι πιστεύεις.	*that you believe.* (Ac 26:27)

323c Note that the integrative text model adopted in the present grammar (↑297[3]) allows us to combine **two complementary approaches to systematizing** the content relations between sentences/clauses or propositions respectively: (1) the above approach that is based on DuG9 whose typology is largely connective-oriented; (2) the clearly semantic-communicative system used among others by Callow where the hierarchical propositional structure receives greater attention (↑312d/312e; 352). This latter approach is being referred to in our examples (e.g. above "circumstance–NUCLEUS" or "orienter–CONTENT"; for a chart of semantic-communicative relations ↑352b).

(a) Copulative connections

(↑DuG9: 1092)

Copulative connectives serve to join propositions (or proposition parts) that (typically) carry the same communicational weight. Two subtypes may be distinguished: **324**
(1) "additive" connection (involving simple addition; ↑325);
(2) "alternative" connection (involving a choice; ↑326).[36]

Additive connection (↑DuG9: 1092–1094) **325**

Preliminaries on the chart of connectives below (↑325b) and those of subsequent sections:

1. The **connectives** are listed in the following order (note, however, that for most connections only part of the possible connective types are actually used): **325a**
a) "c/conj.": coordinating conjunction(s) (↑318).[37]
b) "s/conj.": subordinating conjunction(s) (↑318).
c) "prep.": prepositions, the preposition phrase expressing a proposition, i.e. one with an embedded articular infinitive/ACI phrase or an embedded noun phrase whose head is a verbal noun or a pronominal noun substitute (↑321).
d) "case": prepositionless case noun phrase expressing a proposition, i.e. one with an embedded articular infinitive/ACI phrase or an embedded noun phrase whose head is a verbal noun or a pronominal noun substitute.
e) "inf.": non-articular infinitive/ACI phrase (in the role of a case noun phrase; ↑213a).
f) "rel.": relatives (↑319).
g) "adv.": adverbs and (mostly) multi-word phrases with a similar use (↑320).
h) "ptc.": functionally appropriate participle phrases (↑322a).

2. **Noteworthy** points: **325b**
a) For the connectives listed in the charts only those meanings or functions are mentioned that are specifically in focus. However, many connectives have more than one use and therefore may occur in several connections. For information about the whole range of meanings or functions of such expressions one needs to consult the relevant sections of the present grammar (↑cross-references), the alphabetical list of connectives and the like in 354, and the standard lexicons, especially BDAG.
b) A large number of expressions listed under "adv." are part of the (lexical) content vocabulary which constitutes an open paradigm (↑309c). Therefore, the information given in the present grammar is bound to be incomplete particularly as far as this category of connectives is concerned.
c) Of course, the points made in 322a about asyndesis and copulative connectives always need to be taken into account, too.

---

36 In Ancient Greek connections indicated by καί *and* or ἤ *or* and the like may occur several times in a row. Against typical English usage the connective tends to be repeated (but ↑325b). E.g.:

Φιλήμονι … **καὶ** Ἀπφίᾳ … **καὶ** Ἀρχίππῳ … **καὶ** τῇ … ἐκκλησίᾳ.	*To Philemon … (and) Apphia … (and) Archippus (and) the church* … (Phm 1f)
θλῖψις **ἢ** στενοχωρία **ἢ** διωγμὸς **ἢ** …;	*Trouble (or) distress (or) persecution (or) …?* (Ro 8:35)

37 Under "c/conj." fairly frequently correlative adverbs or similar expressions are mentioned, too (↑318). On several "coordinating conjunctions" that are better classified as "particles" ↑22j[15].

325c Connectives of additive connection (↑325a on connectives in general):

C/CONJ. (↑251a)	καί *and*; τε *and* (postpositive, enclitic); καί – καί, τε – τε/καί or τε καί *both – and*; οὔτε/μήτε *and not*; οὔτε – οὔτε, μήτε – μήτε *neither – nor*; fairly frequently: δέ *and*; οὐδέ/μηδέ *and not*; occasionally οὖν *then* ≈ *and* (↑252.51); οὐ μόνον – ἀλλὰ καί *not only – but also* (2nd Pp. emphasized).
PREP.	σύν *(along) with* (↑184q); μετά + gen. *(along) with* (↑184l); χωρίς + gen. i.t.s. *besides.*
REL.	referring to a whole Pp. (rarely): ὅ *which* (↑319d).
ADV.	καί *also*; πάλιν *again/furthermore*; ἔτι *still/further*; πρὸ πάντων *above all.*
PTC.	p.c./gen.abs. i.t.s. *whereby/(and) beside that …*/plain *-ing* form or negated *without* (+ *-ing* form) … (↑231e; concomitant circumstances, there listed as one type of "manner" nuance).

325d This most straightforward copulative connection **additively** joins one proposition to a further one; typically, they carry the same communicational weight. E.g.:

NUCLEUS$_1$–NUCLEUS$_2$ (simple conjoining; for term ↑352b,3):

ζωὴν αἰώνιον ἔδωκεν ἡμῖν ὁ θεός,	*God has given us eternal life,*
καὶ αὕτη ἡ ζωὴ ἐν τῷ υἱῷ αὐτοῦ ἐστιν.	*and this life is in his Son.* (1Jn 5:11)

There are also certain additive connectives made up of a conjunction plus adverbs (or other similarly used expressions) that may serve to emphasize the second proposition of the connection. E.g.:

NUCLEUS$_1$(adv. element)–**NUCLEUS$_2$**(c/conj.+adv.) (conjoining, the 2nd Pp. being emphasized):

οὐ μόνον ἔλυεν τὸ σάββατον,	*Not only was he breaking the Sabbath,*
ἀλλὰ καὶ πατέρα ἴδιον ἔλεγεν τὸν θεόν …	*but he was even calling God his own Father …* (Jn 5:18)

325e Additive examples with connectives that occur less frequently:

NUCLEUS$_{1\text{-}5}$–NUCLEUS$_6$ (prep.) (conjoining):

πᾶσα πικρία καὶ θυμὸς καὶ ὀργὴ καὶ κραυγὴ καὶ βλασφημία …	*all bitterness, rage, anger, brawling and slander,*
σὺν πάσῃ κακίᾳ (↑312a,3; noun phrases express propositions!)	*along with every form of malice.* (Eph 4:31)

NUCLEUS$_1$[…]–NUCLEUS$_2$[…]–NUCLEUS$_3$ (adv.) (conjoining):

Ἠκούσατε ὅτι … Ἠκούσατε ὅτι …	*You have heard that … You have heard that …* (Mt 5:21.27)
Πάλιν ἠκούσατε ὅτι …	*Again/Furthermore you have heard that …* (Mt 5:33)

NUCLEUS$_1$–NUCLEUS$_2$(p.c.) (conjoining):

διήρχοντο τήν τε Φοινίκην καὶ Σαμάρειαν	*They passed through Phoenicia and Samaria,*
ἐκδιηγούμενοι τὴν ἐπιστροφὴν τῶν ἐθνῶν.	*telling of the conversion of the Gentiles.* (Ac 15:3)

NUCLEUS$_1$–NUCLEUS$_2$(p.c. negated) (conjoining):

αἰτείτω δὲ ἐν πίστει	*But he must ask in faith*
μηδὲν **διακρινόμενος**·	*without doubting/and not doubt.* (Jas 1:6)

An additive connection may be intended in cases of **asyndesis** (↑322a), too. E.g.: 325f

NUCLEUS$_1$–NUCLEUS$_2$(asyndesis) (conjoining):

τὸ αὐτὸ φρονεῖτε,	*Be of one mind,*
εἰρηνεύετε.	*[and] live in peace.* (2Cor 13:11)

Alternative connection (↑DuG9: 1094f) 326

Connectives of alternative connection (also ↑325a): 326a

C/CONJ. (↑251b)	ἤ *or* (inclusive like Lat. *vel*, exclusive like *aut*); ἤ – ἤ *either – or*; εἴτε – εἴτε *either –, or*; *whether –, or*; πότερον – ἤ *whether –, or*.

An **alternative** connection joins propositions as two (or more) basically equal possibilities to choose from. Alternative "or" nuclei may be thought to be either valid/true simultaneously ("inclusive" reading) or to be mutually exclusive ("exclusive" reading). E.g.: 326b

NUCLEUS$_1$–NUCLEUS$_2$(exclusive; c/conj.) (alternation; for term ↑352b,4):

σὺ εἶ ὁ ἐρχόμενος	*Are you the one who is to come*
ἢ ἕτερον προσδοκῶμεν;	*or shall we look for another.* (Mt 11:3)

NUCLEUS$_1$–NUCLEUS$_2$(inclusive; c/conj.) (alternation):

ὃς ἂν ἐσθίῃ τὸν ἄρτον	*Whoever eats the bread*
ἢ πίνῃ τὸ ποτήριον τοῦ κυρίου ἀναξίως …	*or drinks the cup of the Lord in an unworthy manner …* (1Cor 11:27)

NUCLEUS$_1$(c/conj.)–NUCLEUS$_2$(exclusive; c/conj.) (alternation):

ἢ γὰρ τὸν ἕνα μισήσει καὶ τὸν ἕτερον ἀγαπήσει,	*Since he will hate the one and love the other,*
ἢ ἑνὸς ἀνθέξεται καὶ τοῦ ἑτέρου καταφρονήσει	*or he will be devoted to one and despise the other.* (Lk 16:13)

NUCLEUS$_1$(c/conj.)–NUCLEUS$_2$(inclusive; c/conj.) (alternation):

Εἴτε οὖν ἐσθίετε	*So, whether you eat*
εἴτε πίνετε …	*or drink …* (1Cor 10:31)

326c Occasionally, an alternative connection may be intended in cases of **asyndesis** (↑322a), too. E.g.:

NUCLEUS$_1$–NUCLEUS$_2$(asyndesis) (alternation):

(ἐπίστηθι)	*(Be persistent)*
εὐκαίρως	*whether it is convenient*
ἀκαίρως.	*or inconvenient.* (2Tm 4:2)

(b) Temporal connection (↑DuG9: 1095)

327 A temporal connection involves a time relation between the propositions ("situations") it joins. The propositions of a temporal connection may carry either the same or unequal communicative weight: either in terms of NUCLEUS$_1$–NUCLEUS$_2$–[…] or time–NUCLEUS/NUCLEUS–time (↑352b).

The simplest time relation is that of temporally successive propositions ("situations") of equal weight: NUCLEUS$_1$–NUCLEUS$_2$–[…] (sequential). Even a simple "and" (especially καί; occasionally asyndesis) may be understood as "and then" (↑328a; also as "and at the same time"; ↑330a; 252.29,1a), if the propositions involved and their context permit (↑322a; 325c; typical of narration; ↑304c). E.g.:

NUCLEUS$_1$–NUCLEUS$_2$(c/conj.) (sequential):

εἶπεν τῇ θυρωρῷ	*He spoke to the woman watching the gate*
καὶ εἰσήγαγεν τὸν Πέτρον.	*and [then] brought Peter in.* (Jn 18:16)
οἱ βόσκοντες … ἀπήγγειλαν εἰς τὴν πόλιν	*The herdsmen … reported this in the town*
…	…
ἐξῆλθον **δὲ** ἰδεῖν …	*Then people came out to see …* (Lk 8:34f)

Example involving **asyndesis** (↑322a):

ὑπάγετε	*Go*
_ ἴδετε.	*and [then] see.* (Mk 6:38)

↑also 259e for an overview of the various ways temporal adjuncts may be expressed, which, however, also includes non-propositional expressions.

328 Temporal-anterior connection (↑DuG9: 1095f)

328a Connectives of temporal-anterior connection (↑325a on connectives in general):

S/CONJ. (↑276a/276f)	ὅτε or (especially Lk, Jn, Ac) ὡς *when/after* (mostly + ind. aor.);(1) sometimes also ὅταν *when/after* (mostly + subj. aor.).(2)
PREP.	μετά + acc. (↑184l), sometimes διά + gen. (↑184f); μετὰ τὸ + inf./ACI aor. phrase *after*; ἐν + inf./ACI aor. phrase *when/after* (↑226a).
ADV.	τότε (less frequently εἶτα/ἔπειτα; sometimes οὖν [↑252.51]) *then, thereupon.*
PTC.	p.c./gen.abs. (used very frequently) i.t.s. *when/after* … (mostly ptc. aor; ↑231d).

(1) Less frequently ἐπειδή (NT: only Lk 7:1), CG/LXX also ἐπεί.
(2) These connectives also appear in temporal-simultaneous connections, signifying "while"/"as long as"/"as soon as". On the other hand, ↑also 330a[38] for cases where a "when", "since" or "as soon as" clause within a temporal-simultaneous connection may indicate an additional temporal-anterior relation.

A temporal-anterior connection indicates that the "situation" of one proposition precedes the "situation" of the other. Very frequently the connective (s/conj./prep. or ptc.) is integrated into the anterior proposition, which typically leads to a time–NUCLEUS/NUCLEUS–time relation. However, a connective (adv.) may instead be put in the other proposition; in such a case there is usually a NUCLEUS_1–NUCLEUS_2 (sequential) relation (on this also ↑327). Sometimes these two possibilities occur in combination: 328b

ANTERIOR "SITUATION"	(subsequent "situation")
"after" (s/conj./prep.)	"then"/"thereupon" (adv.)
time	– NUCLEUS
or: NUCLEUS	– time
or: NUCLEUS_1	– NUCLEUS_2 (sequential)

Examples:

time(c/conj.)–NUCLEUS:

ὅτε ἐνέπαιξαν αὐτῷ,	*After they had mocked him,*
ἐξέδυσαν αὐτὸν τὴν πορφύραν.	*they stripped him of the purple robe.* (Mk 15:20)

time(prep. + inf./ACI phrase)–NUCLEUS:

μετὰ τὸ γενέσθαι με ἐκεῖ	*After I have been there,*
δεῖ με καὶ Ῥώμην ἰδεῖν.	*I must also visit Rome.* (Ac 19:21)

NUCLEUS_1–NUCLEUS_2(adv.) (sequential):

λέγουσιν αὐτῷ· ναὶ κύριε.	*They said to him, "Yes, Lord."*
τότε ἥψατο τῶν ὀφθαλμῶν αὐτῶν	*Then he touched their eyes.* (Mt 9:28f)

time(p.c.)–NUCLEUS:

ἀσπασάμενος αὐτοὺς	*After greeting them*
ἐξηγεῖτο καθ᾽ ἓν ἕκαστον …	*he reported in detail …* (Ac 21:19)

time(s/conj.)–NUCLEUS (adv.):

ὅτε ἐδοξάσθη Ἰησοῦς	*When Jesus had been glorified,*
τότε ἐμνήσθησαν ὅτι …	*then they remembered that …* (Jn 12:16)

329 Temporal-posterior connection (↑DuG9: 1096f)

329a Connectives of temporal-posterior connection (↑325a on connectives in general):

	focus on a PRECEDING POINT IN TIME	focus on PRECEDING PERIOD OF TIME
S/CONJ. (↑276a/276h)	πρίν with or without ἤ *before* (in the NT mostly + inf./ACI phrase)	ἕως (οὗ/ὅτου), less frequently ἄχρι(ς) (οὗ), μέχρι(ς) (οὗ) + conj. (mostly with ἄν; at times + ind.) *until* (1)
PREP.	πρό + gen., also πρὸ τοῦ + inf./ACI phrase *before* (↑184o; 226a).	ἄχρι(ς)/μέχρι/ἕως + gen. (↑185a; ἕως 1× + inf./ACI phrase; ↑226a); εἰς (↑184g) *until.*
ADV.	(τὸ) πρῶτον *at first*; (rather infrequently:) (τὸ) πρότερον *before*; ποτέ *formerly.*	

(1) In Lk 19:13 apparently also ἐν ᾧ (BDF §383.1); CG also ἔστε.

329b A temporal-posterior connection indicates that the "situation" of one proposition follows the "situation" of the other in time. In the latter proposition the focus may be either on a preceding point in time ("before") or on a preceding period of time ("until"). The s/conj. or prep. functioning as a connective is integrated into the proposition referring to the "situation" that follows, the posterior one, a case that leads to a time–NUCLEUS/NUCLEUS–time relation. However, when the connective is an adverb, it appears in the other proposition, in which case there is usually a NUCLEUS_1–NUCLEUS_2 (sequential) relation (on this also ↑327):

(preceding "situation")		POSTERIOR "SITUATION"
"at first" (adv.)	(focus on point in time)	"before" (s/conj./prep.)
	(focus on period of time)	"until" (s/conj./prep.)
NUCLEUS		– time
or: time		– NUCLEUS
or: NUCLEUS_1		– NUCLEUS_2 (sequential)

Examples:

NUCLEUS(focus on point in time)–time(c/conj.):

κατάβηθι	*Come down*
πρὶν ἀποθανεῖν τὸ παιδίον μου.	*before my little boy dies.* (Jn 4:49)

NUCLEUS(focus on point in time)–time(prep. + inf./ACI phrase):

ἀπ᾽ ἄρτι λέγω ὑμῖν	*I am telling you this now,*
πρὸ τοῦ γενέσθαι.	*before it happens.* (Jn 13:19)

NUCLEUS_1–NUCLEUS_2(focus on point in time; adv.) (sequential):

ἀκολουθήσω σοι, κύριε·	*I will follow you, Lord;*
πρῶτον δὲ ἐπίτρεψόν μοι …	*but first permit me …* (Lk 9:61)

NUCLEUS(focus on period of time)–time(c/conj.):

ἴσθι ἐκεῖ	*Stay there*
ἕως ἂν εἴπω σοι·	*until I tell you.* (Mt 2:13)

NUCLEUS(focus on period of time)–time(prep.):

Ἤκουον δὲ αὐτοῦ	*They listened to him,*
ἄχρι τούτου τοῦ λόγου.	*until he said this.* (Ac 22:22)

Temporal-simultaneous connection (↑DuG9: 1097–1099) 330

Connectives of temporal-simultaneous connection (↑325a: connectives in general):[38] 330a

	the focus of the simultaneity may be on its (1) progress	(2) end	(3) beginning	(4) starting point	(5) iterativeness
S/CONJ. (↑276a/ 276g/ 276i)	ὅτε/ὡς (mostly + ipf.), also ὅταν *when/ while.*(1)	ἕως (οὗ/ὅτου), ἄχρι(ς) (οὗ), *as long as* (mostly + ἄν + subj.).(2)	rarely ἀφ' οὗ, ἐξ οὗ/ἀφ' ἧς *since.*	ὅταν (mostly + subj. aor.) *when/ as soon as.*(3)	ὅταν (often + subj. pres.) *whenever.*(4)
PREP.(5)	ἐν *in/during,* often + inf./ACI phrase; also ἐπί + gen./dat./ acc., διά + gen. (↑184i; 184j; 184f; 226a).(6)		ἀπό *from/ since*; also ἐκ (↑184e; 184h).	ἐν *at,* also (outside the NT) ἐπί + dat. (↑184i; 184j).	at times ἐπί + dat. i.t.s. *whenever* (↑184j).
ADV.	ἅμα *at the same time,* ἐν τῷ μεταξύ *meanwhile.*			εὐθέως/εὐθύς *at once.*	πάντοτε *at all times.*
PTC.	p. c./gen. abs. frequently i.t.s. (mostly pres.) *while* … (often + ἔτι *still*), also *as long as* … and *whenever* … (↑231d)				

(1) Infrequently ἐν ᾧ.
(2) Apart from these also ὅτε as well as ἐν ᾧ/ἐφ' ὅσον, CG also μέχρι(ς) (οὗ) and ἔστε.
(3) Less frequently ἐπάν, occasionally ὡς, Paul/LXX also ὡς ἄν; rarely also ἀφ'οὗ, CG also ὁπόταν.
(4) CG also ὁπόταν; rarely (NT) ἡνίκα (ἄν/ἐάν) or ὁσάκις ἐάν; ↑211i on KG replacement for iter. opt.
(5) To a very limited extent a prepositionless case noun phrase may be possible, too; ↑259e.
(6) CG also παρά + acc. (↑184m); in the NT rarely also κατά + acc. (↑184k), occasionally διά + gen. also + inf./ACI phrase (↑226a).

A temporal-simultaneous connection presents the "situations" of two (or sometimes more) propositions as taking place at the same time, simultaneously: depending on the respective communicative weight of these propositions there is either a time–NUCLEUS/NUCLEUS–time or NUCLEUS_1–NUCLEUS_2 (simultaneous) relation. In 330b

38 Note that in cases where a "when", "since" or "as soon as" clause within a temporal-simultaneous connection refers to a "situation" that is presented as completed, a temporal-anterior relation is indicated in addition to the temporal-simultaneous one (↑328a[2]).

the **prototypical case** of this "while" relationship (case 1 in the chart of 330a) the focus is on the "situations" involved being in progress simultaneously, without reference to their end or beginning:

(1) "situation" Pp. 1 "while" (s/conj./prep.)	"situation" Pp. 2 "at the same time" (adv.)
NUCLEUS	– time
or: time	– NUCLEUS
or: NUCLEUS_1	– NUCLEUS_2 (simultaneous)

Note that
a) Pp. 2 is frequently refers to a rather brief "situation";
b) Pp. 2 may be introduced by an "and" (especially καί; occasionally asyndesis) to be understood as "and at the same time" (Mk 12:37 [↑Mt 22:45]; ↑327).

Examples:

time (c/conj.) – NUCLEUS:

ὅτε ἦμεν πρὸς ὑμᾶς,	*When we were with you,*
τοῦτο παρηγγέλλομεν ὑμῖν.	*we gave you this rule.* (2Th 3:10)

NUCLEUS_1 – NUCLEUS_2 (adv.) (simultaneous):

καὶ ἤρχοντο πρὸς αὐτόν.	*They were on their way to him.*
Ἐν τῷ μεταξὺ ἠρώτων αὐτὸν οἱ μαθηταὶ λέγοντες· ῥαββί, φάγε.	*Meanwhile the disciples kept urging him, "Rabbi, eat something".* (Jn 4:30f)

time (prep. + inf./ACI phrase) – NUCLEUS:

ἐν δὲ τῷ καθεύδειν τοὺς ἀνθρώπους	*But while everyone was sleeping,*
ἦλθεν αὐτοῦ ὁ ἐχθρός …	*his enemy came …* (Mt 13:25)

330c In addition to simultaneity a temporal-simultaneous connection may express iterativeness (case 5 in the chart of 330a), presenting something as being repeated simultaneously ("whenever"), e.g.:

time (c/conj.) – NUCLEUS:

ὅταν θέλητε	*Whenever you want,*
δύνασθε αὐτοῖς εὖ ποιῆσαι.	*you can do good for them.* (Mk 14:7)

NUCLEUS (adv.) – time (p. c.):

Εὐχαριστῶ τῷ θεῷ μου **πάντοτε**	*I thank my God always,*
μνείαν σου **ποιούμενος** ἐπὶ τῶν προσευχῶν μου.	*whenever I mention you in my prayers.* (Phm 4)

In temporal-simultaneous connections there is sometimes (cases 2–4 in the chart of 330a) an indication that the simultaneity has an end ("as long as"), a beginning ("since") or that it starts at a particular point in time ("as soon as"):

Focus on the end of the simultaneity: 330d

(2) "situation" Pp. 1 "as long as" (s/conj./prep.)	"situation" Pp. 2 "at once"
NUCLEUS	– time
or: time	– NUCLEUS
or: NUCLEUS$_1$	– NUCLEUS$_2$ (simultaneous)

Examples:

NUCLEUS–time (s/conj.):

ἴσθι εὐνοῶν τῷ ἀντιδίκῳ σου ταχύ,	*Come to terms quickly with your accuser*
ἕως ὅτου εἶ μετ᾽ αὐτοῦ ἐν τῇ ὁδῷ.	*while/as long as you are on the way to court with him.* (Mt 5:25)

time (adv. and gen. abs.)–NUCLEUS:

ἔτι αὐτοῦ πόρρω **ὄντος**	*While/as long as the other is still far away,*
πρεσβείαν ἀποστείλας ἐρωτᾷ τὰ πρὸς εἰρήνην.	*he sends a delegation and asks for terms of peace.* (Lk 14:32)

Focus on the beginning of the simultaneity: 330e

(3) "situation" Pp. 1 "since" (s/conj./prep.)	"situation" Pp. 2 "since then"
NUCLEUS	– time
or: time	– NUCLEUS
or: NUCLEUS$_1$	– NUCLEUS$_2$ (simultaneous)

Example:

NUCLEUS–time (s/conj.):

… οἷος οὐκ ἐγένετο	*… such as had not occurred*
ἀφ᾽ οὗ ἄνθρωπος ἐγένετο ἐπὶ τῆς γῆς.	*since humankind has been on the earth.* (Re 16:18)

Focus on the starting point of the simultaneity: 330f

(4) "situation" Pp. 1 "as soon as" (s/conj./prep.)	"situation" Pp. 2 "at once" (adv.)
NUCLEUS	– time
or: time	– NUCLEUS
or: NUCLEUS$_1$	– NUCLEUS$_2$ (simultaneous)

Examples:

time (s/conj.)–NUCLEUS:

ὅταν ἤδη ὁ κλάδος αὐτῆς γένηται ἁπαλός …	*When/As soon as its branch gets tender …*
γινώσκετε …	*you know …* (Mt 24:32)

NUCLEUS–time (prep.):

ἀνταποδοθήσεται γάρ σοι	*For you will be repaid*
ἐν τῇ ἀναστάσει τῶν δικαίων.	*at the resurrection of the righteous* (= *as soon as the righteous rise*). (Lk 14:14)

(c) Conditional connection

331 Conditional connection (↑DuG9: 1099–1103)

331a Connectives of conditional connection (↑325a on connectives in general):

S/CONJ. (↑280a/280b)	εἰ or ἐάν *if*;(1) copulative εἴτε – εἴτε *if – (or/and) if, whether – or*.(2)
PREP.	occasionally ἐν *in* (a certain case) (↑184i; 259h).
REL.	ὅς (ὅστις)/ὅσοι/ὅπου (mostly + ἄν/ἐάν + subj.) *whoever/as many as/wherever* ≈ *if any(one)* or the like (↑290e; 323).
ADV.	as an *if*-Pp.: εἰ δὲ μή γε (also ἐπεί) *otherwise*; in the *then*-Pp.: at times ἄρα (occasionally οὖν [↑259h], καί [↑252.29,1a]) *then*.
PTC.	p. c./gen. abs. i.t.s. *if* … (↑231h); rarely nominalized ptc. i.t.s. *whoever* … ≈ *if anyone* … (↑237a).

(1) ἐάν may be replaced (rarely) by ἄν (clause-initially). CG also uses ἐφ' ᾧ or ἐφ' ᾧτε + inf./ACI phrase (or + ind. fut.) translatable as *on condition that*. In Mt 26:15 perhaps also καί (κἀγώ).
(2) There are also important combinations with other particles such as εἴ γε or εἴπερ *if indeed* and ἐάνπερ *if indeed/supposing that* (for details ↑280b).

331b The connectives of a conditional connection indicate an If-Then-relationship between the propositions (and "situations") involved. The *if*-proposition refers to a factual condition, and the *then*-proposition to a closely connected factual consequence. Note that in *then*-propositions the concept of "then" is always presupposed, but comparatively rarely expressed in Ancient Greek as also in English (↑above 331a under "adv.", also 280b[22]). E.g.:

condition (s/conj.)–CONSEQUENCE:

ἐὰν δὲ ἀποθάνῃ ὁ ἀνήρ,	*But if her husband dies,*
ἐλευθέρα ἐστὶν ἀπὸ τοῦ νόμου.	*she is free from that law.* (Ro 7:3)

condition (p.c.)–CONSEQUENCE:

ταῦτα γὰρ **ποιοῦντες**	*For if you do these things,*
οὐ μὴ πταίσητέ ποτε.	*you well never stumble.* (2Pe 1:10)

Important points relevant to text interpretation:

331c 1. The standard case just mentioned does not preclude the possibility of other factual conditions being connected with a particular consequence coming about. Logically, a conditional connection and its inversion do not amount to the same. E.g.:

ἐάν τις εἴπῃ ὅτι ἀγαπῶ τὸν θεὸν καὶ τὸν ἀδελφὸν αὐτοῦ μισῇ,	*If anyone says, "I love God," but hates his brother,*
ψεύστης ἐστίν·	*he is a liar.* (1Jn 4:20)

Since other kinds of factual conditions may equally well be connected with the proposition that someone is to be considered a ψευστής *liar* (↑e.g. 1Jn 2:4), an inversion of the connection would be logically problematic: "If someone is liar, he says, 'I love God,' but hates his brother."

2. However, sometimes the content of the *if*-proposition is exchanged as it were for the content of 331d
the *then*-proposition, in which case a change takes place from a fact-oriented perspective to a symptom-oriented one (↑280a[24]): indicators or symptoms of a factual connection between "situations" come into focus, e.g.:

condition/factual condition–CONSEQUENCE/factual consequence (apparently standard case):

ἐάν τις ἀγαπᾷ με	*If anyone loves me,*
τὸν λόγον μου τηρήσει.	*he will keep my word.* (Jn 14:23)

CONSEQUENCE–"condition"/symptom (apparently symptom-oriented perspective):

ὑμεῖς φίλοι μού ἐστε	*You are my friends*
ἐὰν ποιῆτε ἃ ἐγὼ ἐντέλλομαι ὑμῖν.	*if you do what I command you.* (Jn 15:14)

Examples of *if*-propositions being expressed in ways other than a conditional clause (↑259h): 331e

εἰ δὲ μή γε (*if*-Pp.),	*Otherwise* (i.e. if it is put into old wineskins),
ῥήγνυνται οἱ ἀσκοί.	*the skins burst.* (Mt 9:17)
ἐπεὶ (*if*-Pp.)	*Otherwise* (i.e. if the unbelieving spouse were not made holy by the believing spouse),
ἄρα τὰ τέκνα ὑμῶν ἀκάθαρτά ἐστιν.	*your children would be unclean.* (1Cor 7:14)
ὅστις (rel.) σε ἀγγαρεύσει μίλιον ἕν,	*If anyone forces you to go one mile,*
ὕπαγε μετ' αὐτοῦ δύο.	*go with him two miles.* (Mt 5:41)
ὁ ἔχων (nominalized ptc.) βαλλάντιον	*Whoever has a moneybag*
ἀράτω.	*should take it.* (Lk 22:36)
Κακοπαθεῖ τις ἐν ὑμῖν,	*If anyone among you is suffering,*
προσευχέσθω·	*let him pray.* (Jas 5:13)

Grammatically, this (apparently asyndetic) *if*-Pp. is an interrogative clause (*Is anyone among you suffering?*), apparently also in 1Cor 7:21 and Eph 4:26 (καί i.t.s. "then"); ↑similarly Lk 15:4 (↑269d).

↑also ↑276d/282b on conditional ἐάν-clauses sometimes being functionally close to temporal ὅταν-clauses.

Indicating to what **the extent** a condition **can** be expected to **be fulfilled** (and its 331f
consequence to follow) is of great importance to linguistic communication. Ancient Greek has various means to do so: apart from adverbs or particles, most importantly four or (in KG) three fairly clearly definable types of conditional constructions; e.g. (on details ↑280c–285b; on comparisons with English usage ↑280e):

εἰ ᾔδει ὁ οἰκοδεσπότης ποίᾳ φυλακῇ ὁ κλέπτης ἔρχεται,	*If a homeowner knew at what time of the night a burglar was coming,*
ἐγρηγόρησεν ἂν καὶ **οὐκ ἂν εἴασεν** διορυχθῆναι τὴν οἰκίαν αὐτοῦ.	*he would stay awake and would not let his house be broken into.* (Mt 24:43)

Remote conditional case, counterfactual: the condition is not fulfilled; therefore the consequence does not follow either (↑284a).

Ἐὰν γὰρ **ἀφῆτε** τοῖς ἀνθρώποις τὰ παραπτώματα αὐτῶν,	*For if you forgive other people their offences,*
ἀφήσει καὶ ὑμῖν ὁ πατὴρ ὑμῶν ὁ οὐράνιος.	*your heavenly Father will forgive you as well.* (Mt 6:14)

Prospective conditional case (normal, unmarked case): one can or must expect the condition to be fulfilled and the consequence to follow as well (↑282a).

Note that these main types are defined primarily in terms of grammatical properties, which, however, do not take into account the whole range of content elements relevant to linguistic communication. Here, as always in the text comprehension process, textgrammatical and extratextual factors will have to come into play as well (↑314a). This applies e.g. to the question whether in a particular instance a prospective conditional construction is meant to be interpreted as a specific or general prospective case (↑282b). It is also at the text level only that one is able to decide whether the use of the remote conditional construction in a particular case refers to something counterfactual to be placed in the present or in the past (↑284a). Similarly only the text level reveals whether the condition of an indefinite conditional construction is to be understood as being fulfilled or not fulfilled (↑281a).

In cases where the condition is presented as being fulfilled, some speak of a "factual if" (DuG9: 1102).

Conditional connections are sometimes used in order to highlight the consequences of a particular assertion; in such cases one may speak of an "epistemic if" (one related to the speaker's/writer's knowledge; DuG9: 1102). E.g.:

ὁ καιρὸς τοῦ ἄρξασθαι τὸ κρίμα ἀπὸ τοῦ οἴκου τοῦ θεοῦ· (assertion)	*For it is time for judgment to begin with God's household;*
εἰ ("epistemic if") δὲ πρῶτον ἀφ' ἡμῶν,	*and if it begins with us,*
τί τὸ τέλος τῶν ἀπειθούντων τῷ τοῦ θεοῦ εὐαγγελίῳ;	*what will be the end for those who do not obey the gospel of God?* (1Pe 4:17)

331g There are certain types of *if*-clauses/propositions occurring in connections that may be classified as varieties of the conditional connection. The relationship indicated by these between a factual condition and its factual consequence differs in various ways from that of the standard conditional connection:

1. The rarely occurring **exceptive conditional** clause (↑286a) expresses a condition that alone would be able to overturn the nucleus proposition connected with it. E.g.:

μείζων δὲ ὁ προφητεύων ἢ ὁ λαλῶν γλώσσαις (nucleus Pp.),	*The one who prophesies is greater than the one who speaks in tongues,*
ἐκτὸς εἰ μὴ διερμηνεύῃ. (exceptive conditional cl.)	*unless/except he interprets.* (1Cor 14:5)

In cases where the exceptive condition does not refer to the "situation" itself, but to the utterance, the connection should be classified as a restrictive connection (↑342).

2. One may speak of an "**irrelevance conditional** clause" when one or more conditions are expressed for the very purpose of indicating the irrelevance to the nucleus proposition connected with it. E.g.:

καὶ ἐὰν ἑπτάκις τῆς ἡμέρας ἁμαρτήσῃ εἰς σὲ καὶ ἑπτάκις ἐπιστρέψῃ πρὸς σὲ λέγων· μετανοῶ, (irrelevance conditional clause),	*And if he sins against you seven times in a day, and comes back to you seven times, saying, 'I repent,'*
ἀφήσεις αὐτῷ. (nucleus)	*you must forgive him.* (Lk 17:4)

Irrelevance conditional clauses are closely related to concessive clauses (↑286a/339c).

(d) Causal-codirectional connections in the widest sense (↑DuG9: 1103)

Causal connections in the widest sense are connections that are based on a generally presupposed If-Then-relationship. Such connections may express a codirectional interpretation of the conditional relationship. This applies, on the one hand, to the causal connection in a narrower sense whose propositions mostly appear in a reason–RESULT or RESULT–reason relation (↑333), on the other hand also to the consequential, modal-instrumental, and purpose-oriented connections (all of them causal in a wider sense; ↑334–336). A contradirectional perspective, however, characterizes the adversative and concessive connections: these run counter to the presupposed conditional relationship (↑337–339). 332

Causal connection in a narrower sense (↑DuG9: 1103–1106) 333

Connectives of causal connection in a narrower sense (↑325a: connectives in general): 333a

C/CONJ.	γάρ (postpositive) *for* (explanatory/indicating reason) (↑251d).
S/CONJ. (↑277a)	ὅτι, διότι *because, since* (sometimes *for* more adequate contextually);(1) ἐπεί *as/since*, ἐπειδή *as/since*.(2)
PREP.	διά + acc. *because of, for the sake of* (↑184f), also ἐπί + dat. (↑184j), περί + gen. (↑184n), ὑπέρ + gen. (↑184r) and ἕνεκα/ἕνεκεν/εἵνεκεν, χάριν + gen. (↑185a); ἐκ *on the basis of/by reason of* (↑184h), also ἀπό (↑184e), ἐν (↑184i), εἰς (↑184g) and κατά + acc. (↑184k); διά + gen. *through/by means of* (↑184f); διά + acc. + inf./ACI phrase *because* (↑226a).
CASE	dative of cause *due to/because of* (↑177b; 187m).(3)
REL.	ὅς (or the like) *who ≈ since/for he/she* or the like (infrequently in the NT; ↑290b).
ADV.	ὅθεν *for which reason/therefore*, οὖν *so, therefore*, διὰ τοῦτο, ἐν τούτῳ, διό *for this reason/therefore*.(4)
PTC.	p. c./gen. abs. i.t.s. *because, as, since*, with ὡς *because* (*I/you* etc. *think that*); *convinced that* (↑231f).

(1) Also ὡς (CG; NT 1×), less frequently also καθώς (NT), ἀνθ' ὧν and (Lk/Ac) καθότι, at times (NT) ἐν ᾧ or ἐφ' ᾧ.
(2) CG also ἐπείπερ; Lk 1:1 ἐπειδήπερ *since*; less frequently ὅπου (apparently so in 1Cor 3:3) *since/because*; CG rarely also ὅτε and ὁπότε *since/because, granted that*.
(3) Especially in CG also *for* (= *because of*; ↑167i).
(4) Inter alia also the particle ἄρα *so, therefore*; αὐτὸ τοῦτο *for this very reason* (causal and consequential connections converging here).

↑also 259g for an overview of the various ways causal adjuncts may be expressed, which, however, also includes non-propositional expressions.

333b A connection is **causal** in a narrower sense when the "situation" of one proposition is presented as the reason (or grounds) for the "situation" of the other proposition (the latter in most cases carrying more communicative weight). Depending on whether the hearer/reader is meant to simply understand or to act in some way, either a reason–RESULT/RESULT–reason or a grounds–EXHORTATION/EXHORTATION–grounds relation may be indicated. To put it another way: a potential condition (of the underlying If-Then-relationship; ↑332) appears as a factual "situation", as a reason (or as grounds) to be understood not only as possible or imaginary, but as real. Typically a connective signifying "because", "as/since", "for", "because of", "due to", or the like, is integrated into the reason/grounds proposition; fairly frequently (sometimes additionally) in the result/exhortation proposition there is a connective signifying "therefore" or the like (indicating a consequence or result, typical of the consequential connection; ↑334a). E.g.:

RESULT(adv.)–reason(s/conj.):

διὰ τοῦτο ἐδίωκον οἱ Ἰουδαῖοι τὸν Ἰησοῦν,	*For this reason the Jews were persecuting Jesus,*
ὅτι ταῦτα ἐποίει ἐν σαββάτῳ.	*because he was doing these things on the Sabbath.* (Jn 5:16)

If-Then-basis: If someone did these things on the Sabbath, the Jews persecuted him.

reason(prep. + inf./ACI phrase)–RESULT:

διὰ τὸ ὁμότεχνον εἶναι	*Because he was of the same trade,*
ἔμενεν παρ᾽ αὐτοῖς.	*he stayed with them.* (Ac 18:3)

If-Then-basis: If he was of the same trade, he stayed with them.

EXHORTATION–reason(c/conj.):

ἀγρυπνεῖτε·	*Be alert!*
οὐκ οἴδατε **γὰρ** πότε ὁ καιρός ἐστιν.	*For you don't know when the time will come.* (Mk 13:33)

If-Then-basis: If you don't know when the time will come, you must be alert.

333c For examples of causal propositions being expressed in other ways, including **asyndesis** (↑322a) which is especially well-represented here ↑312b/312c.

333d The reason/grounds proposition, in the standard case shown above, indicates the real cause of the "situation" referred to by the nucleus. Sometimes, however, the causal connection is used in a somewhat different way:

1. In addition to the (standard) "situation" relatedness fairly frequently there is an **utterance relatedness**: The reason/grounds proposition does not only indicate why the "situation" of the nucleus is to be accepted; it especially indicates the reason/grounds for the speaker/writer uttering it (as an affirmation, question or directive/wish; ↑322b–322d for further details). E.g.:

κύριε, ἤδη ὄζει,	*Lord, there will be a terrible smell,*
τεταρταῖος **γάρ** ἐστιν.	*for he has been dead for four days* (= I am affirming this because he has been dead for four days/ After all, he has been …) (Jn 11:39)

2. The reason/grounds proposition occasionally does not indicate the real cause of the "situation" referred to by the nucleus, but instead expresses the cause of knowledge, that which allows us to conclude that the nucleus proposition is true: As was similarly observed in the case of the conditional connection (↑331d) there is a change to a **symptom-oriented perspective** leading to a CONCLUSION–grounds relation. E.g. (↑also 277a):

ἀφέωνται αἱ ἁμαρτίαι αὐτῆς αἱ πολλαί,	*Her many sins have been forgiven [by me],*
ὅτι ἠγάπησεν πολύ·	(which may be concluded from the fact that she has shown [me] great love:) *for/that's why she has shown [me] great love.* (Lk 7:47)

If-Then-basis: If her many sins have been forgiven (by me), she shows (me) great love.
Symptom observation (grounds): She has shown (me) great love. Conclusion: Her many sins have been forgiven (by me).

Consequential connection (↑DuG9: 1106f) 334

Connectives of consequential connection (↑325a on connectives in general): 334a

C/CONJ.	οὖν/ἄρα (mostly postpositive) *so, therefore*; διό (= δι' ὅ) *for which reason, therefore* (↑251e).(1)
S/CONJ.	ὥστε(2) *so that* (= *with the result that*), + ind. (rarely attested in the NT) mostly reference to actual results, + inf./ACI phrase (KG/NT standard) reference to conceivable or actual results (CG mostly to conceivable results); less frequently (KG/NT) ἵνα + subj. *with the result that* (↑221a; 225c; 251j; 279).
PREP.	εἰς *to* (↑184g), especially + inf./ACI phrase *so that/with the result that* (↑226a).(3)
REL.	ὅς (or the like) ≈ ὥστε *that* or the like (rarely so in the NT; ↑290d).

(1) Less frequently διόπερ, ὅθεν; also τοιγαροῦν *for that very reason, therefore*, τοίνυν *hence, therefore*; also ὥστε i.t.s. *for this reason, therefore, so* (↑279).
On the 'consecutive' καί "(and) so", "(and) then", "(so) that" ↑252.29,1a; 322b.
(2) Also ὡς (CG; NT occasionally); apparently in questions also ὅτι.
Inf./ACI phrases sometimes without ὥστε.
τοῦ + inf./ACI phrases, too, sometimes express a result.
(3) Possibly πρός + acc. + inf./ACI phrase (↑226a/226b).
Since there is a close affinity between causal (in a narrower sense; ↑333) and consequential connections, the prepositionless case noun phrases and the preposition phrases mentioned in 187m are likely to be used, at least in part, in consequential connections as well (↑321).

↑also 259i for an overview of the various ways result indicating (consequential) adjuncts may be expressed, which, however, also includes non-propositional expressions.

The If-Then-relationship (↑332) underlying **consequential** connections is to be understood as follows: the "situation" referred to by one proposition appears as a factual initial state of affairs, the "situation" referred to by the other one as its consequence or result leading to a reason–RESULT or an occasion–OUTCOME relation. Thus, the consequential connection shows a close affinity with the causal one 334b (in a narrower sense; ↑333); typically there is, however, a greater focus on the consequence/result here: the connectives signifying “so that/with the result that”, “therefore” or the like are primarily integrated into the result or outcome proposition. The reason/occasion proposition, however, sometimes contain correlative elements signifying “so”, “such” or the like, which makes it possible to express certain nuances. E.g.:

reason–RESULT(c/conj./particle):

ἡ ἀγάπη τῷ πλησίον κακὸν οὐκ ἐργάζεται·	*Love does no harm to a neighbour;*
πλήρωμα **οὖν** νόμου ἡ ἀγάπη.	*therefore love is the fulfilment of the law.* (Ro 13:10)

occasion–OUTCOME(s/conj. + inf./ACI phrase):

… καὶ ἐθεράπευσεν αὐτούς·	*… and he healed them.*
ὥστε τὸν ὄχλον θαυμάσαι …	*So the crowd was a amazed …* (Mt 15:30f)

occasion(adv.)–OUTCOME(s/conj. + inf./ACI phrase):

αὐτούς … λαλῆσαι **οὕτως**	*They spoke in such a way,*
ὥστε πιστεῦσαι … πολὺ πλῆθος.	*that a great number … believed.* (Ac 14:1)

occasion–OUTCOME(prep.):

ἐλυπήθητε	*your sorrow*
εἰς μετάνοιαν·	*led you to repentance.* (2Cor 7:9)

335 Modal-instrumental connection (↑DuG9: 1107f)

335a Connectives of modal-instrumental connection (↑325a on connectives in general):

PREP. (↑187j/187o)	διά + gen. *through/by means of*; manner: *with* (↑184f); ἐν *through/by means of*; manner: *in, with* (↑184i); at times ἐν + inf./ACI phrase *with, by means of* (↑226a).(1)
CASE	dat. of manner *with/in* (↑180) and dat. of instrument *with/by means of* (↑177a).(2)
PTC.	p. c./gen. abs. (used very frequently) i.t.s. *by/in* + *-ing* form (↑231e).

(1) Also Hebraizing complex prepositions ἐν χειρί/διὰ χειρός + gen. *through* (↑185c).
Further possibilities: ἐκ *in* (↑184h), κατά + acc. *-ly, like* (↑184k), μετά + gen. *with* (↑184l).
(2) In KG (outside the NT) also τῷ + inf./ACI phrase (↑224b).
Within certain limits the adverbial acc. may be expected here, too (↑157).

↑also 259f and 259l for an overview of the various ways manner and instrumental adjuncts may be expressed, which, however, also includes non-propositional expressions.

335b The If-Then-relationship (↑332) underlying **modal-instrumental** connections is to be understood as follows: the “situation” referred to by one proposition is presented as the means (instrument or manner) by which the “situation” referred to by the other one is brought about, which typically leads to a RESULT–means/means–RESULT relation. The connectives are primarily integrated into the means proposition;

sometimes, however, there may be additional elements in the result proposition enhancing the intended relation. E.g.:

RESULT–means(prep.):

ἀπόλλυται γὰρ ὁ ἀσθενῶν …	*So the weak person … is ruined*
ἐν τῇ σῇ γνώσει,	*by your knowledge.* (1Cor 8:11)

means(prep. + rel.)–RESULT:

… ἐπεισαγωγὴ δὲ κρείττονος ἐλπίδος	*… a better hope is introduced,*
δι' ἧς ἐγγίζομεν τῷ θεῷ.	*by which we draw near to God.* (He 7:19)

means(case)–RESULT:

… μή πως **τῇ** περισσοτέρ**ᾳ** λύπ**ῃ** καταποθῇ ὁ τοιοῦτος.	*… so that he will not be overwhelmed by excessive sorrow.* (2Cor 2:7)

RESULT–means(p.c.)

ἐκούφιζον τὸ πλοῖον	*They lightened the ship*
ἐκβαλλόμενοι τὸν σῖτον εἰς τὴν θάλασσαν.	*by throwing the wheat into the sea.* (Ac 27:38)

Purpose-oriented connection (↑DuG9: 1109) 336

Connectives of purpose-oriented connection (↑325a on connectives in general): 336a

S/CONJ. (↑278)	ἵνα/ὅπως[(1)] + subj. *in order that* (negated ἵνα μή, ὅπως μή or simple μή/μήποτε)[(2)]
PREP. (↑187n)	εἰς (↑184g), πρός + acc. (↑184p) or ἐπί + dat. (↑184j) *for* (purpose);[(3)] εἰς/πρός + acc.[(4)] + inf./ACI phrase *in order to, so that/in order that* (↑226a); διά + acc. (↑184f), ὑπέρ + gen., (↑184r) ἕνεκα/ἕνεκεν/εἵνεκεν + gen. as well as χάριν + gen. (mostly follows its head) (↑185a) *for the sake/purpose of.*
INF.	non-articular inf. of purpose or with dative force (↑220a[64]; KG/NT also τοῦ + inf./ACI phrase; ↑225b).
REL.	ὅς (or the like) + ind. fut./(NT) subj. *who … [is to]* or the like ≈ *in order that he …* (infrequently so in the NT; ↑290c).
PTC.	p. c. fut. or (NT) pres. i.t.s. *so that/in order that; expecting that* (may be preceded by ὡς; ↑231i).

(1) In the NT very occasionally ὡς; especially CG at times ὅπως/ὡς + ἄν.
(2) KG/NT occasionally ὥστε + inf./ACI i.t.s. *in order that/to* (↑221b; 279).
(3) In certain contexts also prepositionless case noun phrases: gen. of direction or purpose (↑164).
(4) CG also ἐπί + dat.; in the NT 1× ἕνεκεν + gen.

↑also 259j for an overview of the various ways adjuncts of purpose may be expressed, which, however, also includes non-propositional expressions.

336b The If-Then-relationship (↑332) underlying **purpose-oriented** connections is similar to the one underlying the modal-instrumental one: the "situation" referred to by one proposition is presented as the means by which the "situation" referred to by the other one is brought about; however, the "result" here is a goal or purpose to be achieved, the intended effect of the "situation" in question. Note that within a purpose-oriented connection itself there is no indication as to whether or not the goal or purpose is achieved, whether or not that "situation" has the intended effect (other parts of the text may tell us about it). The purpose-oriented connection typically leads to a move–GOAL or a MEANS–purpose relation. The connectives are primarily integrated into the goal/purpose proposition; in the other proposition there may be additional elements enhancing the intended relation. E.g.:

MEANS–purpose/move–GOAL (s/conj.):

ταῦτα λέγω	*I say these things*
ἵνα ὑμεῖς σωθῆτε.	*so that you may be saved.* (Jn 5:34)

If-Then-basis: If I say these things, you will be saved.

MEANS–purpose/move–GOAL (prep.):

τὸ αἷμά μου … τό … ἐκχυννόμενον	*my blood … which is poured out …*
εἰς ἄφεσιν ἁμαρτιῶν.	*for the forgiveness of sins.* (Mt 26:28)

move–GOAL (inf.):

πορεύομαι	*I am going out*
δοκιμάσαι αὐτά·	*to examine them.* (Lk 14:19)

MEANS–purpose (p.c.):

ἔγραψα ὑμῖν …	*I have written to you …*
ὡς ἐπαναμιμνῄσκων ὑμᾶς.	*to remind you of them again.* (Ro 15:15)

(e) Causal-contradirectional connections in the widest sense

(↑DuG9: 1103)

337 Adversative (↑338) and concessive (↑339) connections, too, may be classified as causal connections in the widest sense (↑332). They are based to a large extent on a presupposed If-Then-relationship as well. However, unlike the above causal-codirectional connections they are characterized by a contradirectional perspective, running counter to the presupposed conditional relationship.

Adversative connection (↑DuG9: 1110–1112) 338

Connectives of adversative connection (↑325a on connectives in general): 338a

C/CONJ. (↑251c)	ἀλλά[1] *but, yet, rather*; δέ *but* (weaker than ἀλλά) (postpositive);[2] πλήν[3] *but, rather*; μέν – δέ *on the one hand – (but) on the other hand* (both postpositive).[4]
PREP. (↑187q)	παρά + acc. *against, contrary to* (↑184m); ἀντί *instead of* (↑184d).[5]
ADV.	ὅμως *however, nevertheless* (3× in the NT; ↑252.44)
PTC.	at times p. c./gen.abs. i.t.s. *while* (in contrasts; ↑231e; there listed as one manner nuance).

(1) Occasionally also ἀλλ᾽ ἤ *but (rather).*
(2) Less frequently μέντοι *but, yet,* at times μενοῦν *rather* (↑252.35) and καίτοι *and yet* (↑252.31), especially CG also ἀτάρ *but, yet.*
(3) Occasionally s/conj. + ὅτι *except that.*
(4) ↑ὁ μέν – ὁ δέ or ὃς μέν – ὃς δέ *one – the other* (↑131/142h; 348a).
(5) Jas 4:15 + inf./ACI phrase (↑226a).

An **adversative** connection indicates that its propositions (and their "situations") stand in contrast to one another. Typically, there is a NUCLEUS$_1$–NUCLEUS$_2$ (contrast) relation between them, or (involving a restatement) a negative–POSITIVE or (when clarification is intended) a contrast–NUCLEUS relation. In most cases the connectives signifying "but/however" or the like are integrated into the second proposition; sometimes the other proposition contains additional elements shedding further light on the contrast. E. g.: 338b

NUCLEUS$_1$–NUCLEUS$_2$(c/conj.)(contrast):

… ἐκράτησαν αὐτόν.	*… they arrested him.*
εἷς **δέ** τις … σπασάμενος τὴν μάχαιραν ἔπαισεν …	*But one … drew his sword and cut off …* (Mk 14:46f)

negative–POSITIVE (c/conj.):

ὅς γε τοῦ ἰδίου υἱοῦ οὐκ ἐφείσατο	*He who did not spare his own Son,*
ἀλλὰ ὑπὲρ ἡμῶν πάντων παρέδωκεν αὐτόν …	*but gave him up for as all …* (Ro 8:32)

contrast (c/conj.)–NUCLEUS (c/conj.):

… πάντες **μὲν** τρέχουσιν,	*… all run,*
εἷς **δὲ** λαμβάνει τὸ βραβεῖον.	*but only one gets the prize.* (1Cor 9:24)

contrast –NUCLEUS (p. c.):

πῶς δύνασαι λέγειν τῷ ἀδελφῷ σου …	*How can you say to your brother, …*
αὐτὸς τὴν ἐν τῷ ὀφθαλμῷ σου δοκὸν οὐ **βλέπων**;	*while you yourself do not see the plank in your own eyes?* (Lk 6:42)

338c The “but” proposition may indicate a contrast to something that is not expressed, but merely implied, to be understood in the light of the intratextual and extratextual context (↑314). E.g.:

… αἰτείτω παρὰ τοῦ διδόντος θεοῦ πᾶσιν ἁπλῶς καὶ μὴ ὀνειδίζοντος, καὶ δοθήσεται αὐτῷ.	*… he should ask God, who gives to all generously and ungrudgingly, and it will be given to him,*
αἰτείτω **δὲ** ἐν πίστει …	*But he must ask in faith …* (Jas 1:5f)

The “but” proposition of verse 6 does not stand in contrast to anything expressed in verse 5 or before, but to something that is part of the presupposed world and action knowledge (↑309d): when people pray to God they frequently do so without the necessary faith.

338d Particularly in complex cases the adversative connection clearly emerges as a variety of the causal-contradirectional connections in the widest sense. What exactly is being involved in the contrast, may not be inferable from what is said in the text, but on the basis of an underlying If-Then-relationship. In such a case the “but” proposition does not correct the previous proposition itself, but certain expectations created by it.[39] E.g.:

ὁ μὲν θερισμὸς πολύς,	*The harvest is abundant,*
οἱ **δὲ** ἐργάται ὀλίγοι·	*but the workers are few.* (Mt 9:37)

If-Then-basis: If the harvest is great, many workers are needed.

Note that it is frequently difficult to detect the factors that allow us to fully understand adversative connections. Apparently only in typical cases such an understanding is possible on the basis of an underlying If-Then-relationship that may be called into question or challenged in some other way by the “but” proposition. Frequently such connections will simply qualify as restrictive (↑342c).

339 Concessive connection (↑DuG9: 1112–1114)

339a Connectives of concessive connection (↑325a on connectives in general):

S/CONJ.	εἰ καί (or at times ἐὰν καί)(1) *even if, (even) though* (↑251l; 286a).(2)
PTC.	p. c./gen.abs. i.t.s. *though* or the like (↑231g; καί/καίπερ/καίτοι *though*).(3)

(1) Less frequently καὶ εἰ or καὶ ἐάν (κἄν) *even if*, occasionally καί i.t.s. *though* (↑252.29,1a).
(2) Occasionally (c/conj.) πλήν i.t.s. *nevertheless* (Php 4:14; in Jd 8 perhaps also μέντοι). Occasionally (prep.) ἐν *in* ≈ *in spite of* (e.g. Lk 1:36; 2Cor 8:2; 1Th 1:6).
(3) CG at times also ὅμως *nevertheless* in the other proposition.

↑also 259k for an overview of the various ways concessive adjuncts may be expressed, which, however, also includes non-propositional expressions.

339b Concessive connections, too, correct expectations that arise from an underlying If-Then-relationship. In this case, however, the correction begins with the condition (the If-part of the relationship); a concessive connection usually leads to a concession–CONTRAEXPECTATION or CONTRAEXPECTATION–concession relation. Typically connectives signifying “though/although/even though” or the like are integrated into the concession proposition. The contraexpectation proposition, however, fre-

39 Particularly at this point we will see that there are no well-defined boundaries between the adversative and the concessive connections (↑339c).

quently contains additional elements signifying "nevertheless", "in spite of this" "still", or the like. The correction of expectations that is indicated may be related either to the "situation" or to the utterance (↑322c/322d). When it is related to the utterance, the underlying conditional relation is viewed from a symptom perspective (↑331d; 333d). E.g.:

concession (gen. abs.)–CONTRAEXPECTATION:

Τοσαῦτα δὲ **αὐτοῦ** σημεῖα **πεποιηκότος** ἔμπροσθεν αὐτῶν	*Although he had performed so many signs in their presence,*
οὐκ ἐπίστευον εἰς αὐτόν.	*they did not believe in him.* (Jn 12:37)

If-Then-basis: If someone performs so many signs in their presence, they are expected to believe in him.

concession (s/conj.)–CONTRAEXPECTATION:

κἂν ἀποθάνῃ	*Even if /Although he dies,*
ζήσεται.	*he will live.* (Jn 11:25)

If-Then-basis: If someone dies, he is not expected to be alive any longer.

CONTRAEXPECTATION–concession (prep.):

… δεξάμενοι τὸν λόγον **ἐν** θλίψει πολλῇ μετὰ χαρᾶς …	*… in spite of severe suffering, you welcomed the message with joy …* (1Th 1:6)

If-Then-basis: If people go through severe suffering, we do not expect them to welcome the message with joy …

The concessive connection in many contexts cannot easily be distinguished from the following uses: **339c**

1. Distinguishing it from the **adversative** connection quite often proves to be particularly difficult (↑338d).[40] This is approximately how the two types of connections compare with one another:
Both are based on a (conditional) If-Then-relationship that creates certain expectations, and both indicate a contrast that is meant to correct these expectations in some way.
In the case of the concessive connection the correction clearly and consistently begins with the condition (the If-part of the relationship): Although the "situation" referred to by the condition is to be presumed or conceded (concession), what is indicated by the other proposition (unexpectedly) applies.
The adversative correction is less transparent; it tends to call into question the If-Then-relationship or at least to challenge it in some way: the "situation" of the first proposition is confronted with the "situation" of the "but/however" proposition.
Typically, the connectives of the concessive connections are integrated into the "though" proposition, those of the adversative connection into the "but/however" proposition. Both connection types may also have connectives or other elements in the other proposition, either in place of the "standard" connectives or in order to shed further light on what is to be conveyed by the connection in question.

2. Connections involving **irrelevance conditional** clauses are closely related to the concessive connection as well (↑331g).

3. Sometimes **proportional connections** may be understood in terms of a concessive relation (↑345c).

---

40 ↑e.g. Ro 1:21 and 8:10, that appear to be translatable either as an adversative connection (… *but*) or as a concessive one (*Though* …) without discernible difference of meaning.

(f) Specifying connections (↑DuG9: 1114)

340 Specifying connections serve to convey some additional information (propositions): the explanatory connection (↑341) conveys information that explains the "situation" (or item) indicated by the preceding proposition, the restrictive connection (↑342) information that limits the applicability of the utterance concerned.

341 Explanatory connection (↑DuG9: 1114f)

341a Connectives of explanatory connection (↑325a on connectives in general):

C/CONJ.	'epexegetical'/'explanatory' καί (↑252.29,1a), similarly δέ (↑252.12), i.t.s. *that is (to say), namely* or ":"; τοῦτ' ἔστιν/ὅ ἐστιν (formulaic [conjunction-like] use) *that/which is* (↑263f).
S/CONJ.	ἵνα + subj./ὅτι *(namely) that* or ":" (↑222; 288a).
CASE	gen. of explanation or apposition i.t.s. *consisting in* (↑165).
INF.	explanatory inf./ACI i.t.s. *(namely) that* or the like (↑222; KG/NT also τοῦ + inf./ACI phrase; ↑224b; 225f).
REL.	when referring to a proposition (but also ↑341c): ὅ *which* (↑319d).
ADV.	e.g. μάλιστα inter alia *especially*.(1)

(1) Once (He 7:9) ὡς ἔπος εἰπεῖν *so to speak* (↑213c).

341b In the case of **explanatory** connections the "situation" (or item) referred to in a proposition is explained by a subsequent proposition (sometimes by more than one) conveying additional information. Depending on the context and the "situation" that is to be explained, an explanatory connection may express various types of semantic-communicative relations (↑352b) such as NUCLEUS–equivalent, GENERIC–specific($_1$–specific$_2$ …), generic–SPECIFIC and (at the same time adversative) negative–POSITIVE, also (when the explanation is to be classified as a metatextual element) NUCLEUS–comment or NUCLEUS–parenthesis. Connectives, if any, are always integrated into the explanatory proposition(s). E.g.:

NUCLEUS–equivalent (c/conj.):

ὁ δὲ θεὸς δίδωσιν αὐτῷ σῶμα καθὼς ἠθέλησεν,	*But God gives it a body as he planned,*
καὶ ἑκάστῳ τῶν σπερμάτων ἴδιον σῶμα.	*and (= that is) to each kind of seed its own body.* (1Cor 15:38)

GENERIC–specific$_1$ (s/conj.)–specific$_2$ …:

Ἠκούσατε γὰρ τὴν ἐμὴν ἀναστροφήν ποτε ἐν τῷ Ἰουδαϊσμῷ,	*For you have heard about my former life in Judaism:*

ὅτι καθ᾽ ὑπερβολὴν ἐδίωκον τὴν ἐκκλησίαν τοῦ θεοῦ καὶ ἐπόρθουν αὐτήν …	*I intensely persecuted God's church and tried to destroy it …* (Ga 1:13)

NUCLEUS–equivalent (conjunction-like formula):

Χριστὸς δέ … διὰ τῆς … σκηνῆς οὐ χειροποιήτου,	*But Christ … has entered through that … tent, not made with human hands,*
τοῦτ᾽ ἔστιν οὐ ταύτης τῆς κτίσεως … εἰσῆλθεν.	*that is, not of this creation …* (He 9:11f)

NUCLEUS–comment (rel.):

… ὃν ὁ θεὸς ἤγειρεν ἐκ νεκρῶν,	*… whom God raised from the dead,*
οὗ ἡμεῖς μάρτυρές ἐσμεν.	*of which we are witnesses.* (Ac 3:15)

GENERIC–specific (adv.):

ἐργαζώμεθα τὸ ἀγαθὸν πρὸς πάντας,	*Let us do good to all people,*
μάλιστα δὲ πρὸς τοὺς οἰκείους τῆς πίστεως.	*especially to those in the family of faith.* (Ga 6:10)

Note that frequently a proposition serves to explain only part of a "situation", i.e. a **particular item** belonging to it (one indicated by a concept). Relative clauses in the role of attributive modifiers (↑260a; 289b) are typically used in doing so, similarly also participle phrases (↑236; 260c).[41] Two types of semantic-communicative relations may be distinguished: (1) ITEM–identification, when the explanation serves to identify the entity/item, i.e. to make clear which concrete entity/item is meant of the class of phenomena referred to (restrictive use; 289b), or (2) ITEM–description, when the explanation serves to provide additional information on an entity/item whose identity is already clear (non-restrictive use). For examples ↑319a (involving relative clauses; similarly ↑236 for examples involving participle phrases). Apart from relative clauses and participle phrases there are also other ways of expressing item-related explanations, e.g.: 341c

ITEM–identification (conjunction-like formula):

νῦν δὲ κρείττονος ὀρέγονται,	*But now they desire a better homeland,*
τοῦτ᾽ ἔστιν ἐπουρανίου.	*a heavenly one.* (He 11:16)

ITEM–identification (genitive of explanation or apposition):

δώσω σοι τὸν στέφανον	*the (victor's) crown*
τῆς ζω**ῆς**.	*of (= crown consisting in) life.* (Re 2:10)

An explanatory (or appositional) use is inferable particularly frequently in the case of **asyndesis** (↑260h/260k; 322a). E.g.: 341d

ITEM–identification (conjunction-like formula):

ὁ δὲ γαμήσας μεριμνᾷ τὰ τοῦ κόσμου,	*But the married man is concerned about the affairs of this world,*
πῶς ἀρέσῃ τῇ γυναικί.	*[namely] how to please his wife.* (1Cor 7:33)

41 ↑also 260b–260n for an overview of the various ways attributive modifiers may be expressed, which, however, also includes non-propositional expressions.

342 Restrictive connection (↑DuG9: 1115–1117)

342a Connectives of restrictive connection (↑325a on connectives in general):

C/CONJ.	μέντοι[(1)] *but, yet* (also *in fact*); πλήν *but; rather* (↑251c).
S/CONJ.	εἰ μή/ἐὰν μή[(2)] *except (that)* (εἰ μή rarely with finite verb forms in the NT); infrequently πλὴν ὅτι *except that* (↑286b).
PREP./CASE/ ADV.	παρεκτός + gen. *except for*; πλήν + gen. *excluding*; χωρίς + gen. *apart from* (↑185a); occasionally τὸ (adv. acc.) ἐκ *as far as it depends on* (↑157);[(3)] at times μόνον *only*.

(1) Fairly frequently also δέ (↑252.12), at times also γάρ (↑252.9) or καίτοι(γε) (↑252.31).
(2) Also εἰ μήτι, KG/NT also ἐκτὸς εἰ μή.
(3) Other types of case noun phrases and preposition phrases may be included here as well, perhaps those answering questions such as "In what respect?" (↑187k), "In whose interest?" (↑187p), or "Against whom or what?" (↑187q).

342b A **restrictive** connection serves to limit the applicability of what is uttered. A text component (typically) combined with a restrictive connective indicates that a "situation" asserted by means of other text components (propositions) does not apply to the extent one may have initially assumed. In the case of the restrictive component there is utterance relatedness (↑322d). Typically, the semantic-communicative relation between the propositions involved may be classified as NUCLEUS–amplification or (when the restrictive part is to be classified as a metatextual element) as NUCLEUS–comment/parenthesis. E.g.:

NUCLEUS–(restrictive) amplification (s/conj.):

καὶ οὐκ ἐδύνατο ἐκεῖ ποιῆσαι οὐδεμίαν δύναμιν,	*And he could do no mighty work there,*
εἰ μὴ ὀλίγοις ἀρρώστοις ἐπιθεὶς τὰς χεῖρας ἐθεράπευσεν.	*except that he laid his hands on a few people who were ill and healed them.* (Mk 6:5)

NUCLEUS–(restrictive) amplification (prep.):

εὐξαίμην ἂν τῷ θεῷ ... οὐ μόνον σὲ ἀλλὰ καὶ πάντας ... γενέσθαι τοιούτους ὁποῖος καὶ ἐγώ εἰμι	*I (can/may) pray to God ... that not only you, but also all ... might become what I am,*
παρεκτὸς τῶν δεσμῶν τούτων.	*except for theses chains.* (Ac 26:29)

NUCLEUS–(restrictive) parenthesis (c/conj.; restrictive part is metatextual):

Ὡς οὖν ἔγνω ὁ Ἰησοῦς ὅτι ἤκουσαν οἱ Φαρισαῖοι ὅτι Ἰησοῦς πλείονας μαθητὰς ποιεῖ καὶ βαπτίζει ἢ Ἰωάννης	*Now when Jesus learned that the Pharisees had heard he was making and baptizing more disciples than John*
– **καίτοιγε** Ἰησοῦς αὐτὸς οὐκ ἐβάπτιζεν ἀλλ' οἱ μαθηταὶ αὐτοῦ – ἀφῆκεν τὴν Ἰουδαίαν ...	*(although in fact it was not Jesus who baptized, but his disciples), he left Judea ...* (Jn 4:1–3)

(restrictive)amplification(case)–NUCLEUS:

… **τὸ** ἐξ ὑμῶν,	*… as far as it depends on you,*
μετὰ πάντων ἀνθρώπων εἰρηνεύοντες·	*live at peace with all people.* (Ro 12:18)

Note that restrictive connectives in many cases may also occur in an adversative connection (↑338a), which unlike the restrictive connection is without utterance relatedness. E.g.: 342c

contrast–NUCLEUS(c/conj.):

ὕδωρ μοι ἐπὶ πόδας οὐκ ἔδωκας·	*You gave me no water for my feet,*
αὕτη **δὲ** τοῖς δάκρυσιν ἔβρεξέν μου τοὺς πόδας …	*but she has wet my feet with her tears …* (Lk 7:44)

(g) Connections involving comparisons (↑DuG9: 1117)

There are connections involving comparisons. These indicate similarity relations between the "situations" referred to by the propositions concerned. The similarity may be of a general kind (comparative connection; ↑344) or it may be about a parallel increase or decrease (proportional connection; ↑345). 343

Comparative connection (↑DuG9: 1117–1119) 344

Connectives of comparative connection (↑325a on connectives in general): 344a

S/CONJ.	ὡς (intensified ὥσπερ)[1] *(just) as*; καθάπερ, καθώς[2] *just as*; ὡς[3] – οὕτως (less frequently καί) *as – as* (↑287c). ἤ + inf./ACI phrase (after a comparative) *(more …) than for s.o. to …* (↑138a).
PREP.	πρός + acc. *with a view to*, occasionally i.t.s. *in comparison with* (↑184p).[4]
REL./DEM. (less frequently)	ὅσος/ὅσοι – τοσοῦτος/τοσοῦτοι *as large/as many – so large/so many*; καθ᾽ ὅσον – οὕτως/κατὰ τοσοῦτο *as – so*; οἷος – τοιοῦτος *of what kind/as – of such kind/so* (↑61; 287c).
ADV.	οὕτως *so*; ὁμοίως, ὡσαύτως *likewise*; παραπλησίως *similarly, likewise.*
PTC.	p.c./gen.abs. preceded by ὡς/ὥσπερ i.t.s. *as if, as though* (imagined comparison; ↑231e) [5]

(1) Also ὃν τρόπον/καθ᾽ ὃν τρόπον *(just) as*; CG also (with generalizing force) ὅπως.
(2) Less frequently: καθά, καθό, καθώσπερ; outside the NT with expressions indicating equality or similarity also καί signifying "as/like" (↑252.29,1a).
(3) Or ὥσπερ, καθώς, καθάπερ.
(4) Other preposition phrases such as those answering the question "According to what/whom?" (↑187l) might sometimes be included here as well.
(5) CG also ὥσπερ ἂν εἰ + potential opt. *as if* (conditional comparison; ↑287c).

344b A **comparative** connection indicates a similarity relation of a general kind between two (or more) "situations"; it is typically made up of an "as" proposition and a "so" proposition. In most cases a connective (s/conj., rel. or ptc.) is integrated into the "as" proposition. Frequently in the "so" proposition there is a correlative element (rel.), sometimes an adv. functioning as the sole connective. Various more complex forms of comparative connections occur as well. The semantic-communicative relations comparative connections may point to, can be classified inter alia (↑352b/352c) as NUCLEUS–comparison, NUCLEUS–illustration, CONGRUENCE–standard or NUCLEUS–manner, also (at the same time adversative) contrast–NUCLEUS. E.g.:

comparison(s/conj.)–NUCLEUS(adv.):

καθὼς ἐγένετο ἐν ταῖς ἡμέραις Νῶε,	*Just as it happened in the days of Noah,*
οὕτως ἔσται καὶ ἐν ταῖς ἡμέραις τοῦ υἱοῦ τοῦ ἀνθρώπου.	*so too it will be in the days of the Son of Man.* (Lk 17:26)

standard–CONGRUENCE(adv. as the sole connective):

ὃς ἐὰν οὖν λύσῃ μίαν τῶν ἐντολῶν τούτων τῶν ἐλαχίστων	*So, whoever relaxes one of the least of these commands*
καὶ διδάξῃ **οὕτως** τοὺς ἀνθρώπους …	*and teaches others accordingly …* (Mt 5:19)

comparison–NUCLEUS(c/conj. + inf./ACI phrase):

εὐκοπώτερόν ἐστιν κάμηλον διὰ τρυπήματος ῥαφίδος διελθεῖν	*It is easier for a camel to go through the eye of a needle*
ἢ πλούσιον εἰσελθεῖν εἰς τὴν βασιλείαν τοῦ θεοῦ.	*than for a rich person to enter into the kingdom of God.* (Mt 19:24)

NUCLEUS–comparison(p.c. preceded by ὡς):

τί καυχᾶσαι	*Why do you boast*
ὡς μὴ **λαβών**;	*as if you did not receive it?* (1Cor 4:7)

manner(rel.)–NUCLEUS(dem.):

οἷοί ἐσμεν τῷ λόγῳ δι' ἐπιστολῶν ἀπόντες,	*What we are in word through letters when absent,*
τοιοῦτοι καὶ παρόντες τῷ ἔργῳ.	*that we also are in action when present.* (2Cor 10:11)

manner(rel.)–NUCLEUS(dem.):

ὅσην γὰρ ἡδονὴν ἔχει τὰ ῥήματα ταῦτα τοῖς ποιήσασιν αὐτά,	*For as great as is the pleasure these words have for those doing them,*
τοσαύτην κατάκρισιν ἔχει τοῖς παρακούσασιν.	*so great is the condemnation they have for those disobeying them.* (2Clement 15:5)

Proportional connection (↑DuG9: 1119f) 345

345a Connectives of proportional connection (↑325a on connectives in general):

REL./DEM./ ADV.	ὅσῳ (↑178b) – τοσούτῳ *(by) as much – as;* ὅσον (↑157) – μᾶλλον *the more – the more* (↑61; 287c).

345b The **proportional** connection is about a special kind of similarity: about a parallel increase or decrease in the "situations" that the two propositions refer to. E.g.:

CONGRUENCE(dem.)–standard(rel.):

τοσούτῳ κρείττων γενόμενος τῶν ἀγγέλων	*... he became as much superior to the angels*
ὅσῳ διαφορώτερον παρ' αὐτοὺς κεκληρονόμηκεν ὄνομα.	*as the name he has inherited is more excellent than theirs.* (He 1:4)

contrast(rel.)–NUCLEUS(adv.):

ὅσον δὲ αὐτοῖς διεστέλλετο,	*But the more he ordered them,*
αὐτοὶ **μᾶλλον** περισσότερον ἐκήρυσσον.	*the more zealously they proclaimed it.* (Mk 7:36)

345c Note that a proportional connection i.t.s. "the more – the more" may combine with a conditional relationship (↑331). E.g.:

standard(rel.)–CONGRUENCE(dem.) / condition–CONSEQUENCE:

ὅσῳ μέγας εἶ	*The greater you are,*
τοσούτῳ ταπείνου σεαυτόν.	*the more you must humble yourself.* (Sir 3:18)

4.2.1.2 Coherence and phoric or deictic function words

(↑DuG9: 1120–1125)

346 The connectives (↑317–345) are not the only grammatical means used in Ancient Greek to ensure the coherence of texts (↑316); there are also **phoric** and **deictic function words** that have such a role, i.e. above all the article and certain types of pronouns and pronominal adverbs. While connectives indicate the content relationship between two (sometimes more) successive propositions (with their "situations"), these words mainly refer to items (concepts and their referents) and larger elements introduced elsewhere in the text. In this way a dense network of relations[42] is established that contributes decisively to the coherence of the text. In the following paragraphs (↑347–348) a short overview is given of the phoric and deictic ways of referring to what is introduced elsewhere in the text ("phora" and "deixis") as well as of the words that are used in this process.

42 Here an important part is played by appropriate (lexical) content words as well (↑351–352).

347 Phora and deixis (↑DuG9: 1120f)

347a 1. One may speak of "phora" (↑φορά *[the] carrying* < φέρω *to carry*) in the case of purely intratextual references. Two kinds of references are distinguishable (by the direction in which they may move):

a) **Anaphoric** references, i.e. references that "carry" or lead the hearer/reader to an expression further up or back in the text (↑ἀναφέρω *to carry up/back*): the article or the pronoun refers back to a content word (or the phrase whose head it is), as its antecedent, sometimes also to a larger element, occurring previously in the text. E.g.:

οὐκ ἔστιν δοῦλος (antecedent) μείζων τοῦ κυρίου **αὐτοῦ**.	*A slave is not greater than his master.* (Jn 13:16)

The pron. αὐτοῦ *his* refers anaphorically back to the content word δοῦλος *a slave.*

b) **Cataphoric** references, i.e. references that "carry" or lead the hearer/reader to an expression further down in the text (↑καταφέρω *to carry/bring down*): the article or the pronoun refers to a content word (or the phrase whose head it is), sometimes also to a larger element, occurring further on in the text. E.g.:

πιστὸς **ὁ** λόγος …, ὅτι Χριστὸς Ἰησοῦς ἦλθεν εἰς τὸν κόσμον ἁμαρτωλοὺς σῶσαι.	*The [following] saying is trustworthy…: "Christ Jesus came into the world to save sinners".* (1Tm 1:15)

The article ὁ *the* refers cataphorically to what is expressed in ὅτι-clause.

347b 2. One speaks of "deixis" (↑δεῖξις *[the] showing* < δείκνυμι *to show*) in the case of extratextual references that point to concrete items or "situations" in the real world ("showing" them directly). Specific pronouns and some other types of expressions that are used anaphorically or cataphorically may at the same time be used anadeictically or catadeictically as well, allowing us to distinguish the following types of references:

a) **Anadeictic** references, i.e. references that do not only lead the hearer/reader (anaphorically) to expression elements further up in the text, but at the same time point to a concrete item or "situation" that is mentioned there. E.g.:

τοῦτο ἤδη τρίτον ἐφανερώθη Ἰησοῦς τοῖς μαθηταῖς ἐγερθεὶς ἐκ νεκρῶν.	*This was now the third time Jesus appeared to his disciples after he was raised from the dead.* (Jn 21:14)

The dem. pron. τοῦτο *this* points anadeictically back to a "situation" mentioned further up in the text.

b) **Catadeictic** references, i.e. references that do not only lead the hearer/reader (cataphorically) to expression elements further down in the text, but at the same time point to a concrete item or "situation" mentioned there. E.g.:

Τάδε λέγει ὁ ἔχων τὴν ῥομφαίαν τὴν δίστομον τὴν ὀξεῖαν·	*This is what the one who has the sharp double-edged sword says:* (Re 2:12)

The dem. pron. τάδε *this* points catadeictically down to a "situation" mentioned further down in the text.

Note that phora and deixis do not always move in the same direction. Thus, the demonstrative pronoun ἐκεῖνος *that*, for instance, may refer back anaphorically to something that was mentioned earlier and at the same time point forward catadeictically to some special information given later. E.g.: 347c

μακάριος ὁ δοῦλος **ἐκεῖνος** ὃν ἐλθὼν ὁ κύριος αὐτοῦ εὑρήσει οὕτως ποιοῦντα·	*Blessed is that servant whom his master will find so doing when he comes.* (Mt 24:46)

The dem. pron. ἐκεῖνος *that* refers back anaphorically to the servant topic dealt with earlier and at the same time points forward catadeictically to the special information given later (in the relative clause).

Words used for phora and deixis (↑DuG9: 1121–1125) 348

The function words used to indicate phoric and deictic references are above all:

1. The **article** (the most important concomitant of nouns or nominalized expressions; for details ↑130–136): When speakers/writers use the article as a determiner of a noun phrase, they expect the hearers/readers to be able to easily recognize what entity or "situation" exactly is being referred to. The article typically refers back anaphorically to some information already given earlier in the text.[43] The definiteness indicated by the article may, however, extend to something that is not explicitly mentioned, but is assumed to be known in the situation in which the text is uttered, on the basis of the presupposed world and action knowledge (especially the frames; ↑309d/313), in many cases including text knowledge (inter alia regarding intertextuality; ↑309e). 348a

When a noun phrase, that could have the article, is without one, indefiniteness is generally implied (on important exceptions ↑133–136). Indefiniteness is sometimes made explicit by means of the indefinite pronoun τις *some/any* (when used as an attributive noun concomitant; for occasional alternatives ↑144b). In such cases a cataphoric relationship is typically established. Indefinite expressions often serve to introduce a new entity.[44] E.g.:

Ἦν δέ **τις** μαθητὴς ἐν Δαμασκῷ ὀνόματι Ἀνανίας, καὶ εἶπεν πρὸς αὐτὸν ἐν ὁράματι **ὁ** κύριος· Ἀνανία. **ὁ** δὲ εἶπεν· ἰδοὺ ἐγώ, κύριε.	*Now there was a disciple in Damascus named Ananias. The Lord said to him in a vision, "Ananias," and he replied, "Here I am, Lord."* (Ac 9:10)

The indefinite τὶς μαθητής *a disciple* introduces a new entity with a cataphoric relationship being established: some more specific information about this entity is to be expected in what follows in the text. ὁ κύριος *the Lord* with the article is definite, since the referent can be easily recognized on the basis of the presupposed world or text knowledge. The pronominal use of the article in the expression ὁ δέ *and he* points back anadeictically to Ananias, the entity just introduced.

An example of the article being used cataphorically is found in 347a.

43 The article is used anaphorically also when it precedes an attributive modifier placed after its head (e.g. ὁ οἶνος **ὁ** νέος *the new wine* [Lk 5:37]; ↑136a). In the case of its pronominal use it has an anadeictic role (e.g. **ὁ** μέν – **ὁ** δέ *one – another* [1Cor 7:7]; **οἱ** δέ *And these/they* [Mt 16:14]; ↑131).

44 They generally express the rhematic core of the proposition concerned (↑301c; also 135a).

348b 2. **Personal pronouns** (including possessive forms; for details ↑139–140) as well as the personal endings of finite verb forms (expressing a nominative subject; ↑255d) may refer back anaphorically to content elements occurring earlier in the text. This does not, however, apply to all of them: in the 1st and 2nd person ("I"/ "we"; "you" sg./pl.) they "point" (deictically) to extralinguistic entities, i.e. to the speaker(s) and to the hearer(s) respectively. In typical contexts the 3rd person ("he"/ "she"/"it"/"they") is used anaphorically: a) when it is expressed by the personal ending of a finite verb (as the only element standing for the nominative subject) or b) by oblique case forms (gen., dat. or acc.) of personal pronouns (the use of the nominative of αὐτός will, however, mostly have to be regarded as anadeictic). E.g.:

ἐλθὼν εἰς τὸν οἶκον συγκαλ**εῖ** τοὺς φίλους καὶ τοὺς γείτονας λέγων **αὐτοῖς**· συγχάρη**τέ μοι**, ὅτι εὗρ**ον** τὸ πρόβατόν **μου** τὸ ἀπολωλός.	*When he comes home, he calls together his friends and neighbours, saying to them, 'Rejoice with me, for I have found my sheep that was lost.'* (Lk 15:6)

-εῖ *he* refers (anaphorically) to ἄνθρωπος *a person* in v. 4 and αὐτοῖς *to them* to the entities just mentioned, τοὺς φίλους καὶ τοὺς γείτονας *his friends and neighbours*; -τε (2nd pl. ending of *rejoice*), however, "points" (deictically) to the hearers addressed in the context (friends and neighbours), μοι *with me*, -ον *I* and μου *my* to the speaker (the one who recovered his sheep).

μακάριοι οἱ πεινῶντες καὶ διψῶντες τὴν δικαιοσύνην, ὅτι **αὐτοὶ** χορτασθήσονται.	*Blessed are those who hunger and thirst for righteousness, for they will be filled.* (Mt 5:6)

αὐτοί *they* refers back to οἱ πεινῶντες καὶ διψῶντες τὴν δικαιοσύνην *those who hunger and thirst for righteousness,* either purely anaphorically or perhaps also anadeictically.

The 3rd person personal ending of a finite verb may also refer (cataphorically) to what is expressed later in the text, provided it happens within a reasonably limited space. E.g.:

Εἱστήκεισ**αν** δὲ παρὰ τῷ σταυρῷ τοῦ Ἰησοῦ ἡ μήτηρ αὐτοῦ καὶ ἡ ἀδελφὴ τῆς μητρὸς αὐτοῦ …	*Standing by the cross of Jesus were his mother, his mother's sister …* (Jn 19:25)

-αν *they* (not expressed in English) refers (cataphorically) to ἡ μήτηρ αὐτοῦ καί … *his mother and …*

348c 3. **Demonstratives** (demonstrative pronouns and pronominal adverbs; ↑61) are used in three basic ways (for more details on the pronouns ↑141a):
a) anadeictically (pointing to concrete items or "situations" identified earlier in the text),
b) catadeictically (pointing to concrete items or "situations" identified later in the text) or
c) purely deictically (pointing directly to concrete items or "situations" in the speech context).
Examples of the use of the demonstrative pronoun οὗτος *this* (↑141c):

οὗτοι οὖν προσῆλθον Φιλίππῳ … λέγοντες· κύριε, θέλομεν τὸν Ἰησοῦν ἰδεῖν.	*So these approached Philip … and said, "Sir, we wish to see Jesus."* (Jn 12:21)

οὗτοι *these* points anadeictically to the "Greeks" identified in v. 20.

θρησκεία καθαρὰ καὶ ἀμίαντος παρὰ τῷ θεῷ καὶ πατρὶ **αὕτη** ἐστίν, ἐπισκέπτεσθαι ὀρφανοὺς καὶ χήρας ἐν τῇ θλίψει αὐτῶν …	*Religion that is pure and undefiled before God the Father is this: to look after orphans and widows in their distress …* (Jas 1:27)

αὕτη *this* points catadeictically to the behavioural patterns identfied later in the text.

οὗτός ἐστιν ὁ υἱός μου ὁ ἀγαπητός, ἀκούετε αὐτοῦ.	*This is my beloved Son. Listen to him.* (Mk 9:7)

οὗτος *this* has a purely deictic role, pointing to Jesus who is present in the speech context.

Demonstrative adverbs are used analogously, e.g. ἐκεῖ *there*: a) Mk 6:10 (anadeictic): b) Ps 13:5 LXX (catadeictic [occurring comparatively rarely]); c) Jas 2:3 (purely deictic).

4. **Relatives** (↑142; 289–290; 319) typically have a dual function at the text level: a) as connectives they connect sentences (with relative clauses mostly providing some additional information on a certain entity referred to by an antecedent in the superordinate construction; ↑341); b) as reference words they usually have an anaphoric role. E.g.: 348d

ἄνθρωπός τις ἦν πλούσιος **ὃς** εἶχεν οἰκονόμον …	*There was a rich man who had a manager …* (Lk 16:1)

The relative pronoun ὅς *who* as a connective connects the relative clause with the main clause; at the same time, it refers (anaphorically) to ἄνθρωπός τις … πλούσιος *a rich man*.

Relative adverbs such as ὅπου *where* are used analogously, e.g. in Jn 19:41.

Relatives without an antecedent naturally will not have an anaphoric role (↑319b).

4.2.2 Coherence and the content side of text structures

(↑DuG9: 1151–1159)

The coherence of texts is not only tied to the grammatical side of text structures (↑316–345). It is also hinges very much on the way the content side is structured: Appropriate (lexical) content words conveying concepts have to come into play; and these need to be combined in an adequate way into propositions and proposition complexes (↑312). This allows speakers/writers to indicate what concrete entities they refer to, what they mean to say about them and what their communicative intentions are. They will also take care to choose a text production strategy (with the appropriate text types/genres) that best suits their intentions (↑304–305). When doing so they will rely on the various types of cultural knowledge that linguistic communication depends on: lexical knowledge, world and action knowledge as well as text knowledge (↑309c–309e). In the present grammar only a very small part of the content factors relevant to the coherence of texts may be treated. We shall limit ourselves to two types that seem particularly important: 349

1. Content words (expressing coreferentiality; ↑350–351);
2. Propositional structure (content relations between hierarchically arranged propositions; ↑352–353).

4.2.2.1 Content words

350 Coherence and coreferentiality (↑DuG9: 1154; Crystal: 116f)

Content words by means of coreferentiality contribute to the coherence of texts as is similarly done by phoric or deictic function words (↑346–348): In a text the same concrete persons, things or "situations" may be repeatedly referred to. When words or phrases make reference to the same (concrete extralinguistic) entity one speaks of "coreference"; they are "coreferential"; there is "coreferentiality". E.g.:

Ἐν ἀρχῇ ἦν **ὁ λόγος**, καὶ **ὁ λόγος** ἦν πρὸς τὸν θεόν, καὶ θεὸς ἦν ὁ λόγος. **οὗτος** ἦν ἐν ἀρχῇ πρὸς τὸν θεόν.	*In the beginning was the Word, and the Word was with God, and the Word was God. This [Word]/He was with God in the beginning.* (Jn 1:1f)

The function words ὁ *the* and οὗτος *this* contribute anaphorically/anadeictically to the coherence of the text, the content word λόγος *(the) word* by means of coreferentiality (repetition; ↑351; 294n).

351 Types of coreferentiality (↑DuG9: 1151–1157)

Coreferentiality is brought about in various ways:

a) By **repetition**, i.e. the same content word (or phrase) is repeated, e.g. ἡ ἀγάπη *(the) love* in 1Cor 13:4.8.13 (also ↑294j–294r).

b) By **lexical substitution**, i.e. another expression is used (coreferentially) to refer to the same concrete entity or "situation", either
(1) a "**synonym**" (an expression with the same or very similar lexical meaning), e.g. ἐτήρουν *I protected (them)* and ἐφύλαξα *I guarded (them)* in Jn 17:12 (also ↑352b,11; 294u); with a similar force sometimes a negated "antonym" (an expression that means the opposite lexically), e.g. ἀλήθειαν λέγω οὐ ψεύδομαι *I am telling the truth, I am not lying* in 1Tm 2:7 (also ↑352b,16; 294y), or
(2) a "**hyperonym**" (generic term) or a "**hyponym**" (specific term), e.g. τὰς ἐντολάς μου *my commandments* (hyponym) and τὸν λόγον μου *my word* (hyperonym) in Jn 14:21.23 or εἴπατε *(you must) say* (hyperonym) and κηρύξατε *(you must) proclaim* (hyponym) in Mt 10:27.

4.2.2.2 Propositional structure

Semantic relations between propositions 352

On the grammatical side of text structures connectives play a major role in marking 352a
the ways in which sentences/propositions are related to one another (↑317–321). A systematic overview of the types of content relations (connections) that these may indicate, largely dependent on DuG9: 1091ff, was given above (↑323–345). In that overview continual reference was made to another approach to systematizing content relations (↑323c). While the approach of DuG9 is inseparably tied to the use of grammatical means, particularly connectives, this one, by contrast, is more clearly dependent on **semantic-communicative** considerations: the propositional structure is explored and described mainly from the perspective of the content side of text structures. Going beyond what is explicitly indicated by linguistic means, it is aimed not only at considering individual propositions and their relations to their immediate neighbours, but also at highlighting the way in which they relate to the overall content communicated by the text (also taking into account figures of speech and content elements that are indirectly/implicitly communicated; ↑314h). As it distinguishes between propositions of equal and propositions of unequal communicational weight/prominence this approach allows us to deal in a well-founded manner with the hierarchical propositional structure of a text (↑312d/312e). This approach commends itself for a further reason: it is based on typological studies taking into account a wide range of language types and, though undoubtedly improvable, is likely to be applicable to linguistic communication in general.

The work by Callow (1998) is a serious scholarly, yet accessible introduction to this approach. Introductions that are geared to the concrete needs of those involved in text interpretation and translation are found inter alia in the various volumes of the SIL International series Semantic and Structural Analysis, e.g. by Banker (1996), Deibler (1998), Hart (2001), Johnson (2008), Persson (2016). The chart of semantic-communicative relations between propositions of 352b is taken from these publications.

352b The following **chart** shows how according to this approach the semantic-communicative relations between the propositions of a text may be systematized:

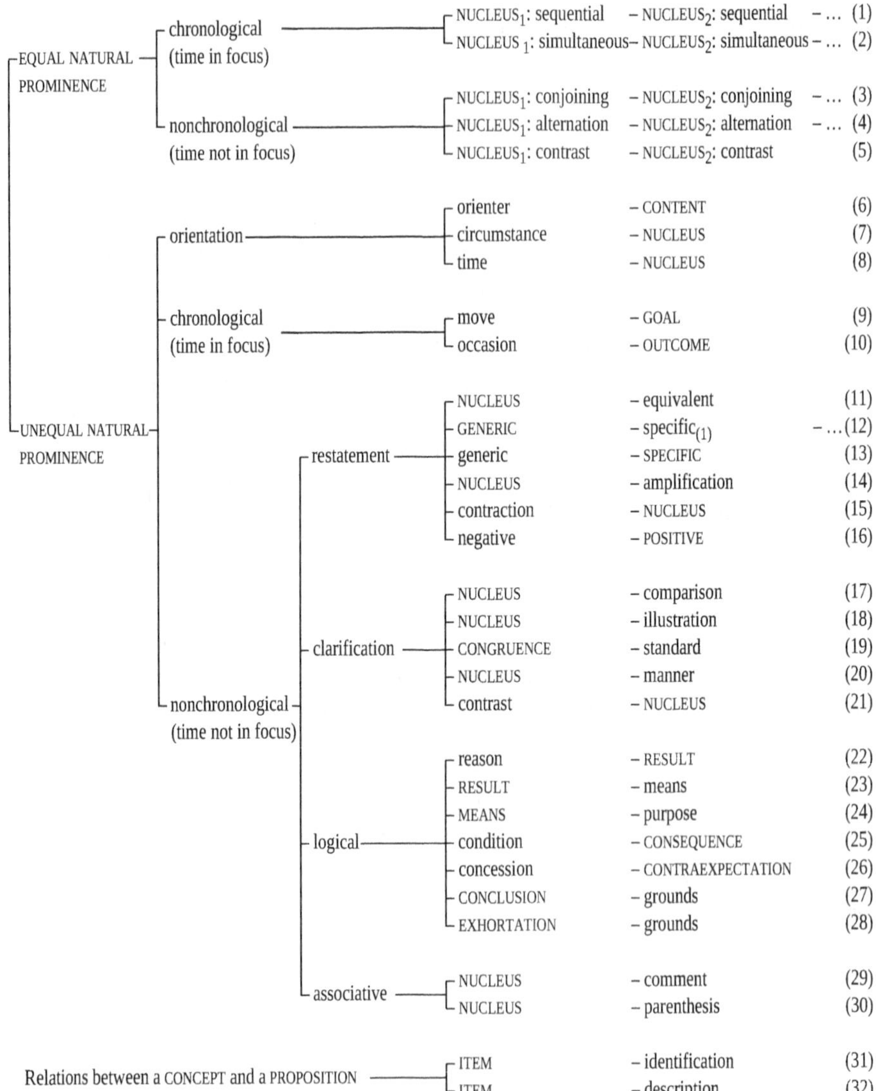

Note that the sequence or the semantic-communicative weight or both may sometimes deviate from what is indicated above (where typical cases are taken into account).

352c **Examples** (a translation into English represents the propositions, which themselves are language independent [↑312a]; in bold: the proposition that carries more communicative weight [in cases of unequal prominence]; square brackets: implied elements):
(1) He spoke to the woman watching the gate and [then] brought Peter in. (Jn 18:16; ↑327)
After they had mocked him, they stripped him of the purple robe. (Mk 15:20; ↑328b)

I will follow you, Lord; but first permit me … (Lk 9:61; ↑329b)
Go and [then] see. (Mk 6:38; ↑327)
(2) They were on their way to him. Meanwhile the disciples kept urging him … (Jn 4:30f; ↑330b)
David himself calls him “Lord”. How can he [at the same time] be his son? (Mk 12:37; ↑330b)
(3) God has given us eternal life, and this life is in his Son. (1Jn 5:11; ↑325d)
Be of one mind, [and] live in peace. (2Cor 13:11; ↑325f)
(4) Whoever eats the bread or drinks the cup of the Lord in an unworthy manner … (1Cor 11:27; ↑326b)
(Be persistent) [whether] it is convenient [or] inconvenient. (2Tm 4:2; ↑326c)
(5) … they arrested him. But one … drew his sword … (Mk 14:46f; ↑338b)
(6) He said to them, “**The harvest is abundant …**” (Lk 10:2; ↑323b)
They said **he was a god**. (Ac 28:6; ↑323b)
Jesus saw **her weeping**. (Jn 11:33; ↑323b)
Believe me **that I am in the Father and the Father is in me.** (Jn 14:11; ↑323b)
It is good **for us to be here**. (Mk 9:5; ↑323b)
(7) Foreseeing this **he spoke about the resurrection of the Messiah**. (Ac 2:31; ↑335)
(8) As they entered the tomb, **they saw a young man …** (Mk 16:5; ↑328)
(9) They do all their deeds **to be seen by people**. (Mt 23:5; ↑321)
(10) Then the rest of the Jews joined his hypocrisy, **so that even Barnabas was led astray by their hypocrisy.** (Ga 2:13; ↑334)
(11) **Be sober-minded**; be watchful. (1Pe 5:8; ↑322a; 341)
(12) **Love your enemies** and pray for those who persecute you. (Mt 5:44; ↑312c; 341)
(13) Treat your slaves in the same way: **Stop threatening them**. (Eph 6:9; ↑322a; 341)
(14) **I have more than enough**; I am fully satisfied, now that I have received from Epaphroditus the gifts you sent. (Php 4:18; ↑322a; 341)
(15) … you hear and see: **the blind receive their sight and the lame walk, lepers are cleansed …** (Mt 11:4f; ↑322a; 341)
(16) … who did not spare his own Son, **but gave him up for us all …** (Ro 8:32; ↑338b)
(17) **The day of the Lord will come** like a thief in the night. (1Th 5:2; ↑344)
(18) **The kingdom of God [grows]** like this: A farmer scatters seed on the ground. He goes to sleep and gets up, night and day; the seed sprouts and grows … (Mk 4:26ff; ↑344)[45]
(19) … **to offer a sacrifice** according to what is specified in the law of the Lord. (Lk 2:24; ↑344)
(20) **Build up/Strengthen one another**, just as you are doing. (1Th 5:11; ↑344)
(21) All run, **but only one gets the prize**. (1Cor 9:24; ↑338b)
(22) Because he was of the same trade, **he stayed with them**. (Ac 18:3; ↑333b)
(23) **He avenged the oppressed man** by striking down the Egyptian. (Ac 7:24; ↑335)
(24) **I have written these things to you** … so that you may know that … (1Jn 5:13; ↑336)
(25) If you do these things, **you will never stumble.** (2Pe 1:10; ↑331)
(26) **Although he had done so many signs in their presence**, they did not believe in him. (Jn 12:37; ↑339b)
(27) **These people are not drunk** … After all, it’s only nine in the morning. (Ac 2:15; ↑322d)
(28) **Don’t be afraid**; you are worth more than many sparrows. (Lk 12:7; ↑312b)
(29) **Only, we were to be mindful of the poor,** which was actually what I was eager to do. (Ga 2:10; ↑319d)
(30) B**ut when you see “the abomination of desolation” standing …**(let the reader understand)… (Mk 13:14; ↑341)
(31) I have found **the coin** that I had lost. (Lk 15:9; ↑319a)
(32) You are in **Christ Jesus**, who became for us wisdom from God… (1Cor 1:30; ↑319a)

45 Note that within this approach parables (↑305d) are part of the illustration category.

353 Example: relational structure of Philippians 2:5–11

353a The **connectives**, the standard signals of text structures on the grammatical side, indicate the following type of content structure:

type of connection:		text (syntactic display; in bold: connectives):
– (asyndesis)	5	Τοῦτο φρονεῖτε ἐν ὑμῖν *Have this mind among yourselves*
explanatory (rel.)		**ὃ** καὶ ἐν Χριστῷ Ἰησοῦ, *which was also in Christ Jesus:*
explanatory (rel.)	6	**ὃς** ↓ *Who,*
concessive (p.c.)		ἐν μορφῇ θεοῦ **ὑπάρχων** *though he was in the form of God,*
		↑οὐχ ἁρπαγμὸν ἡγήσατο *did not consider*
(content; ↑323b)		τὸ εἶναι ἴσα θεῷ, *equality with God something to cling to,*
adversative (c/conj.)	7	**ἀλλ᾽** ἑαυτὸν ἐκένωσεν *rather, he emptied himself*
modal (p.c.)		μορφὴν δούλου **λαβών**, *by taking on the form of a slave*
additive (asyndesis)		ἐν ὁμοιώματι ἀνθρώπων **γενόμενος**· *by coming in human likeness.*
additive (c/conj.)		**καὶ** ↓ *And*
temporal-anterior (p.c.)		σχήματι **εὑρεθεὶς** ὡς ἄνθρωπος *when he appeared in human form,*
	8	↑ἐταπείνωσεν ἑαυτὸν *he humbled himself*
modal (p.c.)		**γενόμενος** ὑπήκοος μέχρι θανάτου, *by becoming obedient to the point of death,*
additive (c/conj.)		θανάτου **δὲ** σταυροῦ. *even death on a cross.*
consequential (c/conj./adv.)	9	**διὸ** καὶ ὁ θεὸς αὐτὸν ὑπερύψωσεν *Therefore also God has highly exalted him*
additive (c/conj.)		**καὶ** ἐχαρίσατο αὐτῷ τὸ ὄνομα τὸ ὑπὲρ πᾶν ὄνομα, *and bestowed on him the name that is above every other name,*
purpose-oriented (s/conj.)	10	**ἵνα** ἐν τῷ ὀνόματι Ἰησοῦ πᾶν γόνυ κάμψῃ ἐπουρανίων καὶ ἐπιγείων καὶ καταχθονίων *so that at the name of Jesus every knee will bow, in heaven and on earth and under the earth,*
additive (c/conj.)	11	**καὶ** πᾶσα γλῶσσα ἐξομολογήσηται ↓ *and every tongue will confess*
(content; ↑323b)		**ὅτι** κύριος Ἰησοῦς Χριστὸς *that Jesus Christ is Lord,*
purpose-oriented (prep.)		↑**εἰς** δόξαν θεοῦ πατρός. *to the glory of God the Father.*

The **semantic-communicative** approach (↑352) may lead to a more detailed (hier- 353b
archical) content structure. For principles applicable to this kind of analysis ↑312e.

The display below is based on Banker: 84. The explicit translation (adjusted to the needs of the analysis) is his. His hierarchical structure is slightly modified here. His "paragraph patterns" (5a: appeal; 5b–11b: motivational bases) have not been taken into account. Note that at various points different solutions are possible (the quality of the analysis depends on the quality of our exegesis; ↑312f).

hierarchical propositional **structure**: | **propositions** (italics: implicit elements; within []: figures of speech labels):

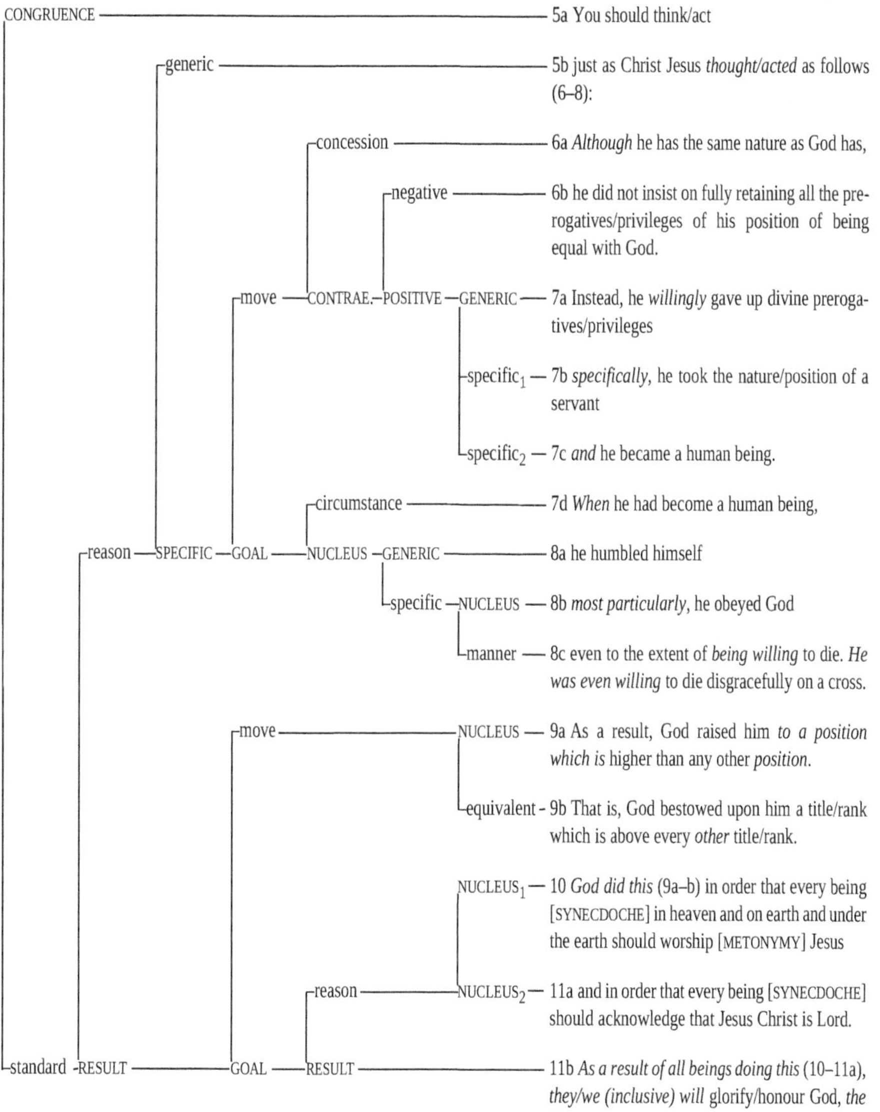

354 Alphabetical list of connectives and the like

Appendix 1 Classical and NT Greek: differences

↑BDF §1–7 (also index sub "Vernacular" and "Semitisms"); Reiser 2001: 16–90; Z §480–494; MH: 413–485; Moule: 171–191; Turner 1963: 1–9 (also index sub "Koine" and "Semitisms"); Debrunner-Scherer §160–199.

As indicated in the introduction to the present grammar (↑p. 5ff), the variety of Ancient Greek used in the NT is basically the vernacular of the Hellenistic period (Koine); it is, however, characterized by a number of Semitizing uses ("Semitisms") that to a large extent are best classified as Septuagintisms (↑p. 7). So, the differences between Classical or Attic (↑p. 3) and NT Greek usage can be divided into two major groups:
(1) peculiarities of the Hellenistic vernacular (↑355/356),
(2) Semitisms (or Septuagintisms, less frequently real Hebraisms or Aramaisms; ↑356): these are marked by an "S" in the inner margin.

It is not always easy to determine whether a particular use is genuine Ancient Greek or a Semitism. It must be kept in mind that "not everything which conforms to Semitic idiom is a Semitism, nor is everything which appears somewhere or sometime in Greek genuine Greek. In numerous instances a phenomenon not unheard of in Greek, but yet unusual, has become a living expression and has replaced the customary idiom because it coincided with Semitic usage. [...] The Semitic element has often supported the tendencies of the more popular levels of the language and abetted them in Jewish-Christian circles" (BDF §4.3). This applies e.g. to the temporal ἐν + τῷ + inf./ACI (↑226a).

There are two major tendencies of NT Greek usage that were favoured by both the popular levels of the Hellenistic Greek (↑p. 4) and the Semitic background. And most of its deviations from Classical Greek arise from these tendencies:
a) the tendency towards greater clarity (e.g. by using pronouns more frequently; ↑p. 202 and 356d);
b) the tendency towards greater simplicity of expression (e.g. by avoiding the reflexive pronoun; ↑139j and 356f).

Phonology and inflectional morphology 355

(Classical Greek) (NT Greek)

A. **Phonology** (↑1–20)

I. Combinations of consonants 355a

1. The Attic -ττ- is mostly replaced by -σσ- (< κι̯, χι̯, occasionally < γι̯) used in other dialects, e.g.:

θάλαττα	*sea*	θάλασσα (↑12c; 25b)
τάττω	*to put in place*	τάσσω (↑95.16)

2. The γ disappears before the ν in the present stem of the following verbs:

γῐγνώσκω	*to know*	γῑνώσκω (↑111.8)
γῐ́γνομαι	*to become*	γῑ́νομαι (↑112.7)

II. Further phonological differences 355b

1. The CG aspirates were later replaced by fricatives (↑1b[11]; 3[3]).
2. In post-CG times the sound [i] came to be represented by ι, ει, η/ῃ or (since Late Byzantine times) also by οι or υ/υι ("itacism") and the sound [ε] by αι or ε (↑2c).

3. Proto-Greek ᾱ is replaced by η at times even when followed by ε, ι, ρ (Ionic; ↑11g; 25f; 44a[1]; 45b,3; 48e[1]); on the other side the ᾱ is preserved throughout in the aor. act./mid. of liquid verbs (↑98b).
4. A few CG enclitics are absent (↑6d).
5. In the NT the movable ν also occurs before consonants (↑18a).
6. The elision of short word-final vowels occurs much less frequently in the NT (↑19).

Also ↑BDF §8–35.

B. **Inflectional morphology** (↑21–125)

355c I. General points

The dual is no longer in use (↑23b; 63a; 64d).

(Classical Greek) (NT Greek)

355d II. Declension of nouns and adjectives

1. Declensions that are not used or only rarely:

a) The so-called "Attic" (second) declension is not used (↑p.57):

ὁ νεώς *temple* → ὁ ναός
ὁ λεώς *people* → ὁ λαός

b) The contract nouns of the second declension are rare; in the gen. and the dat. sg. third declension endings are used (↑31):

ὁ νοῦς *the mind* ≈ ὁ νοῦς
τοῦ **νοῦ**, τῷ **νόῳ** → τοῦ **νοός**, τῷ **νοΐ**

c) In the NT there are also a small number of stems in -οσ- and -ασ- (↑39b): ἡ αἰδώς *modesty* ἡ αἰδώς (NT: 1×; 3Macc: 2×); τὸ κρέας *meat* (NT: 2× acc. pl.; LXX: well-attested).

d) Only one stem in -οι may be attested in the NT (1Cor 2:4 Var.): ἡ πειθώ *persuasiveness* (↑42b).

e) No adjectives in -εις, -εσσα, -εν are used in the NT (↑46c p.71).

2. Some of the more important differences regarding inflectional patterns (paradigms):

a) acc. pl. of the noun stems in -υ (↑40):

ἰχ**θῦς** *fish* (pl.) → ἰχ**θύας**

b) acc. pl. of the noun stems in -ευ and -ου (↑41b):

βασιλ**έᾱς** *kings* → βασιλ**εῖς**
β**οῦς** *heads of cattle* → β**όας**

c) gen. sg. of the adjective stems in -υ and -ε (↑46a):

βαθέ**ος** *deep* → βαθέ**ως**

3. Further differences regarding the declension of nouns and adjectives:

a) ntr. pl. of adjective stems in -σ when there is a vowel before the -εσ- element (↑45b):

ὑγ**ιᾶ** *well, healthy* → ὑγ**ιῆ**

b) ptc. pf. act. fem. (↑48e[1]):

-υ**ίας** etc. → -υ**ίης** etc. (LXX partly = CG, partly = NT)

c) acc. sg. of ἡ χάρις *grace* 2× χάρ**ιτα** (KG) for χάρ**ιν** (↑35e).

355e III. Comparison of adjectives

There are a number of differences regarding "irregular" comparative and superlative forms (↑51).

(Classical Greek) (NT Greek)

IV. Adverbs 355f

Local adverbs with the following case-like terminations occur less frequently (↑53d; also 366):

ἄλλο**θι**	*elsewhere*	–
ἄλλο**σε**	*to another place*	–
ἄλλο**θεν**	*from another place*	ἄλλοθεν

↑also 53c (μάλα *very/exceedingly* → λίαν/σφόδρα).

V. Correlative pronouns and adverbs 355g

1. Fewer groups are in use; moreover, their use is partially more restricted (↑61b[2]; 61c[1/2]):

πότερος;	*which of two?*	occurs only in remnants
πῇ;	*how? where? to where?*	–
ποῖ;	*to where?*	–
ποῦ;	*where?*	ποῦ; *where? to where?*

2. Indefinite forms occur only rarely (↑60c; 61), e.g.:

ποτέ	*at some time*	ποτέ
ποσός	*of any largeness*	–

↑also 36a (voc. of ν-stems); 54c/54d; 55a/55b; 58a; 59b; 60b (pronouns; ↑also 356d–356l).

VI. Numerals 355h

The elements of the cardinals 13–19 are arranged differently in KG and in the NT (↑62a[1] p. 86). ↑also 63a[3] (ἄμφω *both* → ἀμφότεροι; ↑also 130b).

VII. Verbs 355i

1. General points

a) The following categories used in CG are absent (↑64a; 76–79):

fut. pf.	–
subj./opt. pf.	–
opt. fut.	–

b) The opt. plays a rather modest role (↑64a/64b).

c) The verbal adjective is no longer alive as part of the inflection of the verb: the one in -τέος occurs only once, the ones in -τός are normal adjectives (↑64e).

d) The character vowel of the plpf. act. is the same in the pl. as in the sg. (↑68f; 76[3] p. 106), e.g. *I had trained, we had trained*:

ἐπεπαιδεύκ**ειν**	= ἐπεπαιδεύκ**ειν**
ἐπεπαιδεύκ**ε**μεν	→ ἐπεπαιδεύκ**ει**μεν

e) Personal endings:

- The imp. 3 pl. regularly ends in -τωσαν/-σθωσαν, not in -ντων/-σθων (↑70[10]), e.g.: *let them train!, let them be trained!*:

παιδευό**ντων**	→ παιδευέ**τωσαν**
παιδευέ**σθων**	→ παιδευέ**σθωσαν**

- The pf. act. 3. pl. at times ends in -ν rather than in -σ(ιν) (↑70[8]), e.g. *they have seen*:

ἑωράκα**σιν**	at times → ἑώρακα**ν**

- The ipf. (also ind. aor. II) act. 3 pl. occasionally has -οσαν for -ον (↑70[9]), e.g. *they had*:

εἶχ**ον**	occasionally εἴχ**οσαν**

(Classical Greek)	(NT Greek)

f) Augment and reduplication

• Verbs beginning with ευ- are rarely augmented (the few with ει- never; ↑71f), e.g. *I found*:

ηὔρισκον	mostly **εὔ**ρισκον

• The plpf. rarely has an augment (↑72h), e.g. *I had trained*:

ἐπεπαιδεύκειν	mostly **_πεπ**αιδεύκειν

355j 2. Thematic conjugation or verbs in -ω

a) Opt. forms:

• The "Aeolic" forms of the opt. aor. (2 sg. and 3. sg./pl.) are almost entirely absent (↑76[2] p. 107), e.g. *may you* (sg.) *train!*:

παιδεύ**σαις** or παιδεύ**σειας**	almost exclusively παιδεύ**σαις**

• The aor. pass. opt. in the pl. always has -είη- (as in the sg.; ↑78[3] p. 111), e.g. *may I be trained!, may we be trained!*:

παιδευθ**είη**ν	= παιδευθ**είη**ν
παιδευθ**εῖ**μεν (at times **-είη**μεν)	always παιδευθ**είη**μεν

b) Principal parts of thematic verbs

• Principal parts of vowel verbs:

– χρίω *to anoint* (↑80.3) – *I am anointed*:

κέχρ**ισ**μαι or κέχρ**ι**μαι	only κέχρ**ισ**μαι

– καίω *to burn* (↑80.9) – *I was burned*:

ἐκα**ύθην**	ἐκα**ύθην**, also ἐκά**ην**

– "to hunger"/"to thirst" (↑86.7/86.8) – *I will hunger/thirst* etc.:

πειν**ή**ω	διψ**ή**ω	πειν**ά**ω	διψ**ά**ω
πειν**ή**σω	διψ**ή**σω	πειν**ά**σω	διψ**ή**σω
ἐπείν**η**σα	ἐδίψ**η**σα	ἐπείν**α**σα	ἐδίψ**η**σα

– τελέω *to complete* (↑88.2) – *I will complete*:

τελ**ῶ**	τελ**έσω**

– καλέω *to call* (↑88.8) – *I will call*:

καλ**ῶ**	καλ**έσω**

– ῥέω *to flow* (↑88.11) – *I will flow*:

ῥυήσομαι	**ῥεύσω**

– χέω *to pour* (↑88.12) – *I will pour*:

χέω	**χεῶ**

– φορέω *to bear* (↑88.4) – *I will bear* etc.:

φορ**ή**σω etc.	φορ**έ**σω etc.

• Principal parts of stop verbs:

– verbs in -ίζω with two or more stem syllables have (↑92f):

contracted fut. act./mid. (called "Attic future")	in many cases **σ**-fut.

– i̯-present stems of velar verb stems end in (↑91b; also 355a):

-ττ-	**-σσ-**

– θλίβω *to press* (↑94.3) – *I was pressed*:

ἐθλί**φθ**ην	ἐθλί**β**ην

– λείπω *to leave behind* (↑94.4) – *I left behind*:

ἔλ**ιπον**	ἔλ**ιπον**, also ἔλ**ειψα**

– ῥίπτω *to throw* (↑94.19) – *I was thrown*:

ἐρρί**φθ**ην	ἐρρί**φ**ην

(Classical Greek)		(NT Greek)	
– κρύπτω *to hide* (↑94.20) – *I was hidden*:			
ἐκρύ**φθ**ην		ἐκρύ**β**ην	
– ἀνοίγω *to open* (↑95.2):			
ἀνοίγω/**ἀνοίγνυμι**		ἀνοίγω/–	
ἀνέῳχα	***I have opened***	ἀνέῳγα ***I stand open***	
ἀνέῳγμαι	*I stand open*	**ἀ**νέῳγμαι or **ἠ**νέῳγμαι	
ἀνεῴχθην	*I was opened*	**ἠνοί**χθην, **ἠνεῴ**χθην or **ἠνοίγην**	
– διώκω *to persecute* (↑95.6) – *I will persecute*:			
διώξ**ομαι**		διώξ**ω**	
– κράζω *to cry out* (↑95.19) – *I will cry out, I cried out*:			
κράξ**ομαι**		κράξ**ω**	
ἔκρα**γον**		ἔκρα**ξα**, also ἐ**κέ**κραξ**α**	
– σαλπίζω *to blow the trumpet* (↑95.20):			
velar stem, in part also dental stem		always dental stem	
– σφάζω/σφάττω *to slaughter* (↑95.23):			
σφάττω		σφάζω	

• Principal parts of liquid verbs:

– aor. act./mid. liquid verb (↑98b):			
ᾰ > η (except after ε, ι, ρ)		ᾰ > ᾱ	
ἐποίμ**η**να	*I shepherded*	ἐποίμ**ᾱ**να	
– pf./plpf. mid./pass. liquid verb (↑99[1]):			
ν + μ > σμ		ν + μ > μμ	
μεμία**σμ**αι	*I am defiled*	μεμία**μμ**αι	
– ἀγγέλλω *to announce* (↑100[5]) – *I was announced*:			
ἠγγέλ**θ**ην		ἠγγέ**λ**ην	
– φαίνω/φαίνομαι (↑102.7[2]):			
φαίνω	*to show*	φαίνω	*to shine*
φανῶ	*I will show*	φανῶ	*I will shine*
ἔφ**η**να	*to showed*	ἔφ**ᾱ**να	*I shone*
πέφαγκα	*I have shown*	(πέφαγκα	*I have shone*)
πέφασμαι	*I have been shown*	(πέφασμαι	*I have shone for myself*)
ἐφάνθην	*I was shown*	–	
φαίνομαι	*to shine/appear*	φαίνομαι	*to appear*
φαν**οῦμαι**/φαν**ήσομαι**	*I will appear*	φαν**ήσομαι**	*I will appear*
ἐφάνην	*I shone/appeared*	ἐφάνην	*I appeared*
πέφηνα/πέφασμαι	*I have appeared*	(πέφασμαι	*I have appeared*)
– ἀποκτείνω *to kill* (↑102.12) – *I was killed, I have been killed*:			
ἀπέθανον		**ἀπεκτάνθην**	
τέθνηκα		**ἀπέκτονα**	
– χαίρω *to rejoice* (↑103.2[1]) – *I will rejoice*:			
χ**αι**ρήσ**ω**		χ**α**ρήσ**ομαι**	
– ἐγείρομαι *to wake up* (or *to stand up*) (↑103.6) – *I will wake up / I woke up / I am awake*:			
ἐγερθήσομαι		ἐγερθήσομαι	
ἠγρόμην		**ἠγέρθην**	
ἐγρήγορα		**ἐγήγερμαι**	

(Classical Greek)	(NT Greek)

- Strong tense-aspect stems (aorist II/perfect II):

– accentuation of imp. 2 sg. aor. II act. (↑105f) – *find!/take!/see!*:

εὑρ**έ**	**εὗ**ρε
λαβ**έ**	λ**ά**βε
ἰδ**έ**	**ἴ**δε

– aor. II act./mid.: the terminations of the aor. I with the character vowel α are appended to the second thematic aor. stem more frequently (↑105g), e.g. *I said*:

εἶπ**ον**, sometimes εἶπ**α**	εἶπ**ον**, fairly frequently εἶπ**α**

– to certain imp. forms of the root aor. alternatives are sometimes used (originally a peculiarity of the Attic dialect), though only in compounds (↑106e), e.g. *go …!* (sg.) / *let him go …! / go …!* (pl.):

-β**ηθι**	-β**ηθι** sometimes -β**α**
-β**ή**τω	-β**ή**τω sometimes -β**ά**τω
-β**η**τε	-β**η**τε sometimes -β**α**τε

– οἶδα *to know* (↑109c; the NT/LXX occasionally use CG ind. forms):

οἶσθα	*you* (sg.) *know*	οἶδας
ἴσμεν	*we know* etc.	οἴδαμεν
εἴσομαι	*I will know* etc.	εἰδήσω

↑also 108g (ἔοικα *I am like*, not *I seem*); 109a/120.5 (ἕστηκα *I stand*: less frequently strong forms, at times replaced by στήκω]); 109b (τέθνηκα *I am dead*: rarely strong forms; δέδοικα *I fear* absent).

- Principal parts of "irregular" (thematic) verbs:

– βαίνω *to go* (↑110.1): root pf. not in use.

– πίνω *to drink* (↑110.3[2]): inf. aor. alongside πιεῖν also πεῖν.

– τίνω *to pay* (↑110.4) – *I will pay*:

τ**εί**σω	also τ**ί**σω

– ἁμαρτάνω *to sin* (↑110.7) – *I will sin*:

ἁμαρτήσ**ομαι**	ἁμαρτήσ**ω**

– λαμβάνω *to take* (↑110.13[3]) – *I will take, I was taken*:

λή**ψ**ομαι, ἐλή**φ**θην	λή**μψ**ομαι, ἐλή**μφ**θην

– τυγχάνω *to attain* (CG *to happen to be* is not used; ↑110.17) – *I have attained*:

τετ**ύχη**κα	τέτ**υχ**α/τέτ**ευχ**α

– πιπράσκω *to sell*: usually replaced by πωλέω (↑111.13).

– γαμέω *to marry/to get married* (↑112.5):

act. a man to a woman	act. both cases
mid. a woman to a man	pass. also a woman to a man

– δέομαι *to ask for sth.* (↑112.8) – *I will ask for sth.*:

δεή**σομαι**	δεη**θήσομαι**

– *to wish* (↑112.9):

ἐθέλω (fut. **ἐθ**ελήσω)	**θ**έλω (fut. **θ**ελήσω)

– μάχομαι *to fight*, οἴομαι/οἶμαι *to think/suppose*, οἴχομαι *to be gone*, ἄχθομαι *to be annoyed*: not or rarely used (↑112.13a).

– ἀναιρέω *to remove, to kill* (↑113.2) – *I will remove/kill*:

ἀν**αιρήσω**	ἀν**ελῶ**

– ἔρχομαι *to come/go* (↑113.3) – *I will come/go*:

εἶμι	**ἐλεύσομαι**

– ἐσθίω *to eat* (↑113.4) – *I will eat*:

ἔδομαι	**φάγομαι**

(Classical Greek)	(NT Greek)

– ἔχω *to have/hold* (↑113.5) – *I will have/hold*:

ἕξω/**σχήσω**	only ἕξω

– λέγω *to say* (↑113.7): ἀγορεύω hardly ever occurs.

– ὁράω *to see* (↑113.8; also 77[2] p. 108) – *you will see*:

ὄψ**ει**	ὄψ**ῃ**

– τύπτω *to strike* (↑113.13): outside the present stem forms of πατάσσω or the like are used.

– ἕπομαι *to follow* (↑113.15) is used only occasionally.

↑also 355a on γινώσκω and γίνομαι.

3. Athematic conjugation or verbs in -μι **355k**

a) General points

There is a growing influence of the predominant thematic conjugation on the formation and inflection of the verbs in -μι, especially those in -(ν)νυμι (↑114f–114h), e.g.:

δείκν**υς**	*you* (sg.) *show*	δεικν**ύεις**
ἵστ**ημι**	*to set/place*	also ἱστ**άνω**
κορέννυμι	*to satiate*	→ **χορτάζω**

b) The "Big Four" in -μι

• Pres. and aor. act./mid.:

the inflection forms of the aor. act. ind. pl. of τίθημι *to place*, ἵημι *to send*, δίδωμι *to give* conform to the pattern of the sg. (↑116), e.g. *I placed, we placed*:

ἔθ**ηκα**	= ἔθ**ηκα**
ἔθ**εμεν**	→ ἐθ**ήκαμεν**

On individual forms ↑also 115b[1–5]; 116[1–4]; 118[1–4].

• Principal parts of the "Big Four" in -μι:

– τίθημι *to place* (↑120.1):

τέθ**η**κα	*I have placed*	τέθ**ει**κα
κεῖμαι	*I have been placed*	κεῖμαι or **τέθειμαι**

– ἵημι *to send* (↑120.3/120.4; also note that in the NT/LXX only compounds occur):

εἶμαι	*I have been sent*	**ἕω**μαι
εἵθην	*I was sent*	**ἕ**θην

– ἵστημι *to set/place* (↑119e; 120.5; for ἕστηκα also στήκω):

ἵσταμαι		
indirect mid.:	***to set/place for o.s.***	–
direct mid.:	*to stand (up)*	*to stand (up)*
σταθήσομαι	*I will be set/placed*	*I will be set/placed*
	–	also ***I will stand (up)*** (= στήσομαι)
ἐστάθην	*I was set/placed*	*I was set/placed*
		also ***I stood (up)*** (= ἔστην)

↑also 121.1 (ὀνίνημι *to benefit* aor. mid. also with α); 121.2[2] (for πίμπλημι *to fill* also πληρόω and γεμίζω); 121.3/121.5 (for δύν**ασαι** *you* [sg.] *are able* also δύν**ῃ**, for ἐδύν**ω** *you* [sg.] *were able* post-CG ἐδύν**ασο**).

c) Verbs in -νυμι /-ννυμι

– ἀπόλλυμι *to ruin/destroy* (↑123.7) – *I will ruin/destroy*:

ἀπολ**ῶ**	ἀπολ**έσω**

– κεράννυμι *to mix (wine)* (↑124.4) – *I have been mixed*:

κέ**κραμαι**	κε**κέρασμαι**

(Classical Greek)		(NT Greek)

↑also 123.4 (for μείγνυμι *to mix* also μίγνυμι); 123.8 (for ὄμνυμι *to swear* mostly ὀμνύω); 124.3 (pf./aor. pass. of ζώννυμι *to gird* with σ).

d) Root presents in -μι
– εἰμί to be (↑125a):

ἦν/ἦ	*I was*	**ἤμην**
ἦσθα	*you* (sg.) *were*	mostly **ἦς**
ἦμεν	*we were*	also **ἤμεθα**
ἦτε/ἦστε	*you* (pl.) *were*	only **ἦτε**
ἔστω	*let him/her be!*	also **ἤτω**
ἔστε	*be!* (pl.)	**ἔσεσθε**

– Of εἶμι *I will go* there are only compounds (without future meaning; ↑125c).
– Of φημί *to say* only the forms φημί *I say*, φησίν *he/she says*, φασίν *they say* and ἔφη *he/she said* are used (↑125d).
– κάθημαι *to sit, to be seated* (↑125f):

κάθ**ησαι**	*you* (sg.) *are seated*	κάθ**ῃ**
κάθ**ησο**	*be seated!* (sg.)	κάθ**ου**
καθ**εδοῦμαι**	*I will be seated*	καθ**ήσομαι**

– χρή *it is necessary* only in Jas 3:10 (↑125g).

356 Syntax

Note that the examples given below are often invented or are only allusions to original quotations. For authentic examples readers need to turn to the main part of the grammar (↑the cross-references).

356a A. **General points**

Word-order: position of the predicator (predicate verb) in main clauses (↑128b p. 179):

tends to have a middle position (CG literature)	very frequently front position (especially in NT narratives as in non-classicizing KG ones)

B. **Words and phrases as sentence elements**

I. Syntax of declinable words and their phrases

1. Peculiarities of number and gender use

a) The distributive singular occurs (Hebraism; ↑129a): S

men in dazzling garments	*men in **a** dazzling garment* (= *in dazzling apparel*)

b) Diminutives (nouns indicating smallness, when used literally; ↑361b) in the neuter are widely used in popular KG (often non-literally), in the NT not very frequently, and if they are, mostly without diminutive force (so a few times, especially in Mk), e.g. κυνάριον:

little do, puppy	mostly simply *dog*

356b 2. Article

a) Noun phrases embedded in preposition phrases are often without article (↑133a), e.g. *from the city*:

ἀπὸ **τῆς** πόλεως	often ἀπὸ _ πόλεως

b) In spite of its definiteness the head noun of a genitive attributive modifier may be without article, as a Hebrew construct chain is reflected (so regularly in the LXX; ↑133d), e.g. *the glory of God*: S

ἡ δόξα τοῦ θεοῦ (↑also 133e)	_ δόξα τοῦ θεοῦ possible

c) Frequently in such cases even the genitive attributive modifier may be without the article (↑133e):

	in such cases frequently _ δόξα _ θεοῦ

(Classical Greek)	(NT Greek)

S d) Names of persons, to be understood as definite, may be without the article as well (Semitism; ↑134b), e.g. *the aforementioned or generally known Paul*:

ὁ Παῦλος	_ Παῦλος possible

e) Even if the head noun of an attributive modifier is indefinite the attributive modifier placed after it has the article (especially in KG, it seems; ↑136a), e.g. *a first-class robe*:

_ στολὴ _ πρώτη	_ στολὴ **ἡ** πρώτη possible

S f) At times πᾶς (especially, Hebraizing, in the case of proper names) may have the force of *(the) whole* even without the article (↑136d), e.g. *the whole building*:

ἡ πᾶσα οἰκοδομή / πᾶσα **ἡ** οἰκοδομή	at times πᾶσα _ οἰκοδομή

g) A genitive attributive modifier without repeated article may itself be modified by a preposition phrase, which in such a case need not have the article repeated either (↑136e), e.g. *the man of the house near the temple*:

ὁ ἀνὴρ **ὁ τοῦ** οἴκου **τοῦ παρὰ** τῷ ἱερῷ	mostly **ὁ** ἀνὴρ _ **τοῦ** οἴκου **τοῦ παρὰ** τῷ ἱερῷ also **ὁ** ἀνὴρ _ **τοῦ** οἴκου ___ **παρὰ** τῷ ἱερῷ

↑also 130b (dual pron.; vocative nom.); 131 (the pronominal art. is frequently replaced by a rel. pron.); 132a (the possessive of force of the art. is rarer); 136d (μέσος *in the middle of* is not used).

3. Adjective 356c

Comparison peculiarities:

S a) Due to Semitic influence the basic form sometimes has the function of the comparative or superlative (↑138c), e.g. *better, greatest*:

κάλλ**ιον**	sometimes καλ**όν**
μέγ**ιστος**	sometimes μέγ**ας**

b) In line with popular KG usage the comparative often occurs with the force of a superlative or elative (↑138d), e.g. *greatest/very great*:

μέγ**ιστος**	often μεί**ζων**

4. Pronouns

a) General points (↑p. 202): 356d

- They are used more frequently, quite often pleonastically.
- The more subtle CG distinctions are disregarded.

b) Non-reflexive personal pronouns 356e

- Sometimes no emphasis appears to be intended (↑139a), e.g. ὑμεῖς ὑπάγετε:

you (pl.) *go* = *you are the ones who go*	sometimes simply *you* (pl.) *go*

- The (enclitic forms of) personal pronouns occur more frequently (↑139b):

mainly when necessary for clarity's sake	more frequently, often pleonastically

- In reference to the 3rd pers. the following pronouns are used (↑139c):

οὗτος/ἐκεῖνος, αὐτοῦ etc.	typically αὐτός (also in the nom.)

↑also 139b/139c (indirect reflexive οὗ *of oneself* etc. and forms such as ἔγωγε are absent); 139c (the pronominal art. is frequently replaced by a rel. pron.).

c) Reflexive personal pronouns 356f

- The forms of the 1 and 2 pl. are usually the same as those of the 3 pl. (↑139g; 55), so ἑαυτῶν:

of themselves	also *of ourselves*, *of yourselves*

- Contracted forms such as αὑτοῦ for ἑαυτοῦ have lost their importance (↑139h).

S • The reflexive relationship is often unexpressed, most frequently when the pers. pron. is in the possessive gen., especially in the 3rd pers. (KG; NT also Semitizing; ↑139j; 140e), e.g. *He went to his house*:

ἀπῆλθεν εἰς τὸν οἶκον τὸν **ἑαυτοῦ**.	frequently … εἰς τὸν οἶκον **αὐτοῦ**.

(Classical Greek)	(NT Greek)

• In line with Hebrew usage ψυχή *"soul"/life* occasionally replaces the reflexive pers. pron. (↑139l), e.g. *he lost himself* (lit. *his "soul"/life*):

ἑαυτὸν ἀπώλεσε	occasionally **τὴν ψυχὴν αὐτοῦ** ἀπώλεσε

356g d) Reciprocal pronoun
Perhaps a Semitism (↑139n; 145b), *one another*:

ἀλλήλους	sometimes → **εἷς τὸν ἕνα**

356h e) Possessive pronouns
• It is not used much in the NT (↑140a).
• ἴδιος *one's own*, fairly frequently replaces a possessive αὐτοῦ/ἑαυτοῦ (↑140c), e.g. *he calls his sheep*:

τὰ **ἑαυτοῦ** πρόβατα φωνεῖ	fairly frequently τὰ **ἴδια** πρόβατα …

↑also 140d (the possessive of force of the art. is rarer).

356i f) Demonstrative pronouns
ὅδε *this (here)* is disappearing; οὗτος *this* covers the special function of the latter as well (↑141c):

ὅδε and (much more frequently) οὗτος	almost exclusively οὗτος

↑also 141e (the pronominal art. is more frequently replaced by a rel. pron.; ↑356j).

356j g) Relative pronouns
• ὅστις *whoever* quite often functions like ὅς *who* (↑142b):

ὅστις ≠ ὅς	ὅστις quite often = ὅς

• ὅς replaces the pronominal art. more frequently (↑142h; 131; 356b/356e/356i), e.g. *(this) one – (that) one*:

ὁ μέν – ὁ δέ	more frequently also **ὃς** μέν – **ὃς** δέ

↑also 142f (interrogative pronouns replacing a rel. pron.; ↑356k).

356k h) Interrogative pronouns
• They may replace a rel. pron. (↑143b; 142f), e.g. … *what I am doing*:

… **ὃ** ἐγὼ ποιῶ	… **τί** ἐγὼ ποιῶ acceptable

• Probably a Semitism (↑143c):

τί *what? why?*	occasionally also ***how!***

356l i) Indefinite pronouns
Agreeing with Hebrew usage (↑144c):

οὐδείς *no one, none*	at times → οὐ … πᾶς

↑also 144b (τις replaced by εἷς, ↑145b).

356m 5. Numerals
a) The use of εἷς (↑145a/145b):

typically *one*	*first*: only in the Hebraizing idiom "the first day…" sometimes *a* (replacing τις; ↑144b)

b) The use of πρῶτος (↑145a):

[the] first (of more than two)	*[the] first* (of two or more than two)

c) A doubled cardinal may used distributively (KG/Semitism; ↑145c), e.g. *two each/two by two:*

ἀνὰ/κατὰ δύο	also **δύο δύο**

↑also 145e (ἕν *-fold*: hardly an Aramaism; ἄλλος *another* also for ἕτερος *the one/the other of two*).

6. Syntax of case forms

356n a) General points (↑146b): preposition phrases increasingly replace CG prepositionless case noun phrases.

(Classical Greek)	(NT Greek)

b) Nominative

S In line with Semitic usage a SC^{id} in the nominative is sometimes replaced by a PpP with εἰς + acc.; ↑147a), e.g. … *they shall be/become one flesh*:

ἔσονται … **σὰρξ μία**	sometimes … **εἰς σάρκα μίαν**

c) Vocative

KG: Voc. noun phrases are normally without ὦ, nom. noun phrases are used as voc. typically have the art. (↑148a), e.g. (1) *O Lord*, (2) *O child*:

(1) ὦ κύριε	mostly _ κύριε
(2) ὦ παῖ	typically **ὁ** παῖς

d) accusative (↑149b etc.): 356o

• acc. of extent ("For how long?"; ↑155)	infrequently → dat. (↑182) sometimes used to answer the question "When?"
• acc. of respect ("In what respect?"; ↑156)	mostly → dat. (↑178)
• adverbial acc. (↑157)	preserved mainly in the form of neuter adjectives (in part turned into adverbs)

S • In line with Semitic usage an OC^{id} in the acc. is at times preceded by the prep. εἰς or by the conj. ὡς (↑153b; also ↑356n), e.g. *They regarded him as a prophet*:

προφήτην αὐτὸν εἶχον.	at times **εἰς/ὡς** προφήτην αὐτὸν εἶχον.

↑also 152d (object types used with προσκυνέω).

e) Genitive (↑158c etc.): 356p

• partitive gen., gen. of separation or of place (especially when dependent on verbs; ↑166; 169; 171)	very often → PpP, especially with ἐκ/ἀπό + gen. (↑182)

S • gen. of quality is used more widely, under Semitic influence (↑162), e.g. *the dishonest manager*:

ὁ **ἄδικος** οἰκονόμος	ὁ οἰκονόμος **τῆς ἀδικίας** quite possible

S • in line with a Hebrew/Semitic idiom: υἱός *son* or τέκνον *child* + a gen. NP to denote a close relationship (↑159d), e.g.: *"children of the light" = people who belong to the light:*

	τέκνα φωτός

↑also 166b (in phrases like… τινες [ἐκ] τῶν μαθητῶν αὐτοῦ *some of his disciples* τινες sometimes needs to be supplied in thought [influenced by Semitic usage]); 167i (gen. of respect very rare); 168 (gen. of time mainly in fixed phrases without article); 171 (gen. of place only occasional traces left).

f) Dative (↑173c etc.): 356q

S • dat. of instrument or cause ("By what means?"/"Owing to what?"; ↑177)	frequently → PpP with ἐν + dat. or prep. like διά + gen. (expanded use of ἐν in the NT: Semitism)
• dat. of manner ("How?"; ↑180)	frequently → PpP with ἐν + dat. or μετά + gen.
• dat. of place ("Where?"; ↑181)	almost entirely → PpP with ἐν + dat. (even CG)
• dat. of time ("When?"; ↑182)	at times in answer to the question "How long?"
• dat. of respect ("In what respect?"; ↑178): rarely (acc. frequently) used	frequently (acc. rarely; ↑156) used

S • the dat. of manner is also used to render the Hebrew infinitive absolute (↑180c; also 356z), e.g.: *I have eagerly desired:*

	ἐπιθυμίᾳ ἐπεθύμησα

↑also p. 253 (occasionally a dat. NP is replaced by a PpP with ἐν + dat.); ↑174c (object types used with προσκυνέω); 176c (sympathetic/ethical dat. and dat. of standpoint occur only infrequently); 180b (dat. of manner with verbs "to walk/to behave" in LXX/NT).

(Classical Greek)	(NT Greek)

356r 7. Prepositions

a) General points (↑183d):

- Preposition phrases increasingly replace CG prepositionless case noun phrases.
- Phe proper prepositions are fewer in number and have a less varied grammatical use (↑184):

19 prepositions	ἀμφί and ὡς are not in use, ἀνά and ἀντί very restricted, πρό not frequently (improper prepositions instead)

- Improper prepositions increase in number and frequency; in addition to these the NT also uses Hebraizing complex prepositions (↑185), e.g. *before/in front of* (of place): S

πρό + gen.	mostly → ἔμπροσθεν or the like (also πρὸ προσώπου in line with Hebrew usage)

- Prepositions with comparable meanings are increasingly “confused” (↑184):

ἐκ (origin); ὑπό + gen. (agent); παρά + gen. *from*	these three are sometimes → ἀπό
ὑπέρ + gen. *for (the sake of)*; περί + gen. *concerning*	in part ὑπέρ ↔ περί
ἀντί *instead of, for*; ὑπέρ + gen. *on behalf of*	in part ἀντί ↔ ὑπέρ
εἰς *into*; πρός + acc. *towards, to*	in part εἰς ↔ πρός
εἰς *into*; ἐν *in*	in part εἰς ↔ ἐν (in Mk, Lk/Ac, rarely in Jn; not in Mt, the Epistles, and Re)

↑also 183b (original function as adverbs survives in a few set phrases).

b) Proper prepositions

On various more or less important usage differences ↑184a–184t.

c) Improper prepositions

- There are differences in number and to some extent in use (↑185a).
- On Hebraizing complex prepositions involving the nouns πρόσωπόν τινος “s.o.’s face” and χείρ/χεῖρές τινος “s.o.’s hand(s)” ↑185b. S

d) Prepositional prefixes in compounds (↑186)

Compounds with one or more prepositional prefixes (often without affecting the meaning of the simplex word or the compound with a single prepositional prefix) appear to have been more popular in KG than in CG (↑Z §484; BDF §116.1).

↑also 187 for an overview of phrases indicating space, time etc. (noun phrases or preposition phrases) with various more or less important differences.

II. Verb

1. Voice

356s a) General points (↑188c; also 355j/355k):

• fut. mid. of certain active verbs	→ fut. act.
• fut./aor. mid. of middle deponent verbs	tendency: → fut./aor. pass.
• mid.	frequently → act. (↑189e)

b) Active voice

- There are a number of minor differences regarding the middle-like use of the active of certain verbs (↑189b–189d), e.g.:

ἀνέῳχα	*I have opened*	–	
ἀνέῳγμαι	*I stand open*	also ἀνέῳγα	*I stand open*

(Classical Greek) (NT Greek)

• There are hardly any verbs whose passive form could be replaced by the active form of another verb (↑189g), e.g. aor. *I was killed* (of ἀποκτείνω *to kill*):

ἀπέθανον → ἀπεκτάνθην

↑also 189e (act. replacing mid. or vicè versa).

c) Middle voice

• The middle deponent verbs are more numerous (↑190b).

• typically act. ≠ mid. in meaning act. = mid. of certain verbs (↑190h/190j)

d) Passive voice

• The dat. of agent occurs very rarely (↑191a).

• There are some small differences regarding the non-passive use of certain passive forms (in some cases agreeing with Hebrew usage; ↑191e–191g), e.g.:

ἐγενόμην *I became* ἐγενόμην or ἐγενήθην *I became*

S ὤφθην *I was seen* ὤφθην *I was seen*, also *I appeared* (≈ Hebr.)

2. Aspects and tenses

a) Indicative forms 356t

• Indicative present

More frequently than in CG the indicative present refers to something in the immediate future, to something probable, certain, or threatening (↑197c), e.g. ἔρχομαι:

I come/I am coming fairly frequently also *I will come*

↑also 197c (εἶμι: simplex *I will go* absent; ↑125c); 197e (on ind. pres. with a perfect-like force).

• Imperfect (augment indicative present)

↑198c (hellenistisches Nebensatziterativpräteritum; ↑356v); 198g (on past perfect-like force); 198i (impersonal expressions signifying necessity); 198j (wishes: ipf./ind. aor. after ὄφελον or inf. after ἐβουλόμην/ἤθελον); 198l (ipf. ≠ ind. aor.).

• Indicative aorist

S The gnomic ind. aor. occurs rarely, at times rather perhaps as a correspondence to the Biblical Hebrew "perfect" in its timeless use (in poetic or prophetic texts; ↑199l).

↑also 199f (hellenistisches Nebensatziterativpräteritum; ↑356v); 199h (wishes: ind. aor./Ipf. after ὄφελον); 199i (ind. aor. after ὀλίγου/μικροῦ *all but/almost* … is absent); 199m (the "dramatic" ind. aor. occurs very rarely).

• Indicative perfect

In the NT the ind. pf. is not yet a narrative verb form (↑200f).

↑201d (the future perfect is replaced by a periphrastic construction).

• Indicative future

S Facilitated by comparable uses (of the "future"/"imperfect") in Ancient Hebrew and Aramaic the modal use of the ind. fut. future (in the NT/LXX) appears to have been expanding somewhat in scope (202b–202f; 268), quite often expressing also obligation, permission (↑may) or ability (↑can), most strikingly strict commands and prohibitions, e.g. (1) ἔσεσθε …, (2) οὐκ ἔσεσθε …:

(1) *you* (pl.) *will be …* also *you* (pl.) *must be …! be …!*

(2) *you* (pl) *will not be …* also *you* (pl.) *must not be …! Do not be …!*

S ↑also 202i/202j (occasionally with a gnomic/timeless force [in line with Semitic usage]; at times replacing the subj. in purpose or result clauses).

• Periphrastic conjugation

S In line with Ancient Hebrew and Aramaic usage it is used more widely, in many cases with the same force as its non-periphrastic counterpart (↑203a).

(Classical Greek) (NT Greek)

356u b) Verb forms seemingly expressing relative tense

• Inf./ACI in the aor. depending on a verb of saying or thinking/believing or (especially in the NT also a verb of showing/announcing or to some extent a verb of sensual/mental perception; ↑206c; 356y):

(Classical Greek)	(NT Greek)
frequently refers to sth. anterior	apparently never refers to sth. anterior (inf. pf. used instead), but mostly to sth. posterior (for which the rare inf. fut. may be used as well)

• Something posterior is referred to (↑206h/206i):

(Classical Greek)	(NT Greek)
very often by the ptc. fut.	also by the ptc. pres. (replacing the rare ptc. fut.)

↑also 206a.

3. Moods

a) General point

The opt. is disappearing (↑207a).

356v b) Indicative

• The irrealis occasionally occurs without the particle ἄν (↑209h).

• ἄν/ἐάν + augment ind. (hellenistisches Nebensatziterativpräteritum) replaces the "iterative" opt. (↑209p), e.g. … *whenever he wanted* …:

(Classical Greek)	(NT Greek)
… ὁπότε … **βούλοιτο**	… ὁπότε **ἂν ἐβούλετο**

↑also 209e (there is no fut. pf.; ↑201d); 209f (gnomic ind. aor. occurs rare, at times perhaps corresponding to timeless Hebrew "perfect" [↑199l]; ind. fut. occasionally timeless [Semitism; ↑202i]); 209j (wishes: wishes: ipf./ind. aor. after ὄφελον or inf. after ἐβουλόμην/ἤθελον; εἴθε/εἰ γάρ + augment ind. not used); 209k (ipf. of impersonal expressions signifying necessity; ↑198i); 209l (ind. aor. after ὀλίγου/μικροῦ *all but/almost* … is absent; ↑199i); 209o (fairly small differences regarding moods in temporal clauses; ↑276).

356w c) Subjunctive

• Main clauses: slight differences (regarding introductions to hortative and deliberative subj. [↑210c/210j]; occasionally the subj. occurs in an independent ἵνα-clause replacing an imp. [↑210g]).

• Subordinate clauses:

– subject-object clauses subordinated by ἵνα or the like (mostly dependent desiderative clauses) frequently replace inf./ACI phrases (↑210h; 272)

(ὅπως + subj., more often + ind. fut., depending on expressions denoting *to take care*, is absent)

– On rather small differences of subj. use in various dependent clause types ↑210h–210j.

356x d) Optative

• Main clauses:

– The opt. of wish (more than half of NT instances) is never accompanied by εἴθε/εἰ γάρ (↑211c).

– The potential opt. occurs rarely, almost exclusively in Lk and Ac; er may be replaced by the ind. fut. (in CG, too; ↑211d; 202e), e.g. *how could he judge?*:

(Classical Greek)	(NT Greek)
πῶς ἂν κρίνοι;	possible replacement: πῶς κρινεῖ;

• Subordinate clauses:

– The oblique opt. occurs very rarely (never in ὅτι- or ὡς-clauses); when it occurs in indirect question it is possibly better to regard it as potential opt. (the omission of ἄν perhaps being due to popular usage); ↑211g; 356af.

– The "iterative opt." (without ἄν) is replaced by the augment ind. with ἄν/ἐάν (hellenistisches Nebensatziterativpräteritum); ↑211i; 209p; 356v) ↑also 211h (the opt. fut. is not used).

e) Imperative

The imp. pf. pass. occurs very occasionally only (↑212e).

356y 4. Non-finite verb (nominal verb forms)

(Classical Greek)	(NT Greek)

a) Infinitive

• General points (↑213–216):

– Some constructions are used more widely, thus the one used as an adverbial of purpose (↑220) and certain articular varieties with or without preposition (↑223), especially those with τοῦ (↑225).
– On the other hand ἵνα- or ὅτι-clauses often replace inf./ACI phrases (↑272a; 271; 211–222; 225a).
– An absolute inf. occurs only in He 7:9 (ὡς ἔπος εἰπεῖν *so to speak, one might even say*).
– Inf./ACI phrases with ἄν (as a replacement for the potential opt. [↑211d/211e] or for the augment ind. with ἄν [↑209h]) is unattested.
– μή is always used for negation (also when the inf./ACI phrase is dependent on a verb of purely cognitive attitude or assertion; ↑246c), e. g. *You say that he does not exist*:

λέγεις αὐτὸν **οὐ** εἶναι	λέγεις αὐτὸν **μὴ** εἶναι

– ACI et al.: the subject accusative is sometimes absent against the CG rule (↑216c).
↑also 216d.

• Non-articular inf./ACI

S – γίνεται (outside the NT also συμβαίνει) *it happens/it comes about* + inf./ACI phrase agrees with standard Ancient Greek usage, however /ἐγένετο+adverbial+(καί)+finite verb form/ is a Hebraism (↑217e), e. g. *After that he entered …*:

μετὰ ταῦτα τρεῖς ἐνέβη …	Hebraizing καὶ **ἐγένετο** μετὰ ταῦτα (καὶ) ἐνέβη …

– The use of inf./ACI phrases dependent on verbs of communication or cognitive attitude is more limited (↑218f; 356u), thus the inf. aor. may refer:

frequently to sth. anterior	apparently not to sth. anterior (the inf. pf. instead), mostly to sth. posterior (like the rare inf. fut.)
e. g. λέγεις αὐτὸν ἐλθεῖν:	
You say that he came.	*You say that he will come.*

– The nom. with inf. ("NCI": personal pass. + inf.) and the impersonal pass. with ACI occur rarely if at all (↑218g), e. g. (1) *He is said to have come first*, (2) *It is said that he came first*:

(1) λέγεται ἐλθεῖν πρῶτος	–
(2) λέγεται αὐτὸν ἐλθεῖν πρῶτον	↑Lk 2:26

– Inf./ACI phrases indicating a purpose occur more frequently: after verbs of sending, giving etc., as well as of motion (in CG these usually with ptc. fut.; ↑220a/220b), e. g. *He went up … to pray*:

ἀνέβη … προσευξόμενος	frequently ἀνέβη … **προσεύξασθαι**

– Inf./ACI phrases indicating a result introduced by ὥστε may refer not only to a conceivable, but also to an actual result (ὥστε + ind. occur rarely; ↑221c; 279a; 356ah), e. g. (They did it) ὥστε αὐτὸν ἐλθεῖν:

… so that (with the result that) he should come.	also *… so that (with the result that) he came.*

– This construction is occasionally used to express an intended result or purpose (↑220b; 356ah):

	occasionally *… so that (in order that) he came.*

↑also 217c (χρή only 1×); 218c (after verbs signifying *to give orders* or *to prevent*: CG ACI act., NT mostly ACI pass. [as in Lat.]); 218d ("imperatival" inf.); 218e (ἄρχομαι + InfP in the Synoptics in line with popular Greek narrative style); 218i (verbs of showing and reporting + inf./ACI phrase or in part
S + ὅτι-clause, not + ACP); 220d (indicating manner in line with Hebrew usage); 280b (not attested: ἐφ' ᾧ or ἐφ' ᾧτε + inf./ACI phrase [or + ind. fut.] *on condition that* [or *in order to/in order that*]).

• Articular inf./ACI

– Articular infinitive/ACI phrases are part of higher KG usage. In the LXX they seem to be (comparatively) more frequent than in the NT. (↑223).

(Classical Greek) (NT Greek)

– Inf./ACI phrases with τοῦ have a greater variety of uses. Thus they frequently indicate purpose or express other functions of non-articular inf./ACP phrases (Hebraizing style of writing may have led to a change of construction), or have an explanatory role in line with Semitic usage (↑225a/225b/225e/225f). S S

– The frequency of the temporal use of ἐν + τῷ + inf./ACI is probably a Hebraism (↑226a). S

↑also 226a (various CG combinations with prep. are not attested, while some non-CG ones are); 226b (Semitizing use of πρός/εἰς + τό + inf./ACI indicating manner). S

b) Participle

356z • General points (↑227c/227d; 228):

– The ptc. fut. occurs infrequently.

– The CG predicative participle is in the course of disappearing (↑233c; 234).

– Ptc. phrases with ἄν (as a replacement for the potential opt. [↑211d/211e] or for the augment ind. with ἄν [↑209h]) is unattested.

– The "accusative absolute" is not used.

– The negation is mostly μή (not only with conditional and purpose indicating nuances; ↑232b; 356aa).

– The ptc. pres. can refer to sth. posterior, in place of the rarely occurring ptc. fut. (↑356u).

• Adverbial participle

Quite often a gen. abs. replaces a p.c. (↑230d), e.g. *When he came down, they followed him*:

καταβάντι _ ἠκολούθησαν αὐτῷ — quite often **καταβάντος αὐτοῦ** ἠκολούθησαν αὐτῷ

↑also 230f (no accusative absolute); 231d/231e/231f (formulaic use of participles less important); 231f–231h (particles clarifying the intended nuance occur less frequently); 231i (not only ptc. fut., but also ptc. pres. may indicate purpose); 231k (Paul and Peter occasionally use an imperatival ptc.).

• Predicative participle

– ACP phrases do not occur with verbs of showing and reporting (inf./ACI phrases, sometimes ὅτι-clauses, are used instead; ↑233c; 275), e.g. *You show that I have received it*:

ὑποδείκνυς **ἐμὲ εἰληφότα** αὐτό — → … **ἐμὲ εἰληφέναι** αὐτό or … **ὅτι εἴληφα** αὐτό

– NCP phrases occur only occasionally when there is no change of subject (mostly ὅτι-clauses are used instead; ↑233e; 275), e.g. *You see that you have received it*:

ὁρᾷς **εἰληφὼς** αὐτό — almost always → **ὅτι εἴληφας** αὐτό

– Modifying verbs are rarely used (only παύομαι *to stop [doing sth.]* and καλῶς ποιέω *to act rightly [doing sth.]* occur fairly frequently; ↑234), e.g. *I happened to be sitting there*:

ἔτυχον καθήμενος ἐνταῦθα — –

• Special idiomatic uses of the participle

– "Graphic" participle (popular KG narrative style; ↑238), e.g. *He went away*:

ἀπῆλθεν — frequently **ἀναστὰς** ἀπῆλθεν

– Pleonastic participles (especially referring to saying or answering; ↑239), e.g. *He said*:

εἶπεν· — frequently εἶπεν **λέγων**

– Participle used to render the Hebrew infinitive absolute (↑240; 356q), e.g. *I will bless you greatly*: S

εὐλογῶν εὐλογήσω

III. Uninflected words

356aa 1. Adverbs

↑241c (πράσσω + adv. ≈ εἰμί + adj. *to be* … occurs rarely); 242a/242b (adv. comparison like the adj. one; also Semitizing or Hellenistic replacement of forms; occasionally μᾶλλον *more* is omitted). S

(Classical Greek)	(NT Greek)

2. Negatives (NT/KG usage)

a) οὐ occurs in ind. clauses, rarely in InfP or PtcP,
μή occurs in clauses with non-indicative moods, mostly also in InfP and PtcP. (↑244–246).

b) There are hardly any instances of apparently pleonastic οὐ or μή after expressions denoting a negative idea (↑247d/247e), e.g. (1) *I prevented him from coming* and (2) *I am not able not to come* (= *I can't help coming*):

(1) ἐκώλυσα αὐτὸν **μὴ** ἐλθεῖν	mostly → … αὐτὸν _ ἐλθεῖν
(2) οὐ δύναμαι **μὴ οὐ** ἐλθεῖν	mostly → … **μὴ** ἐλθεῖν

↑also 247a/248b (at times οὐδ' [or the like] οὐ μή replaces οὐ μή + subj. aor. to express the strongest
S negation of future "situations"); 249a (οὐ[μή] … πᾶς Semitizing = οὐδείς [μηδείς], ↑356l); 249b (οὐ
S μή … ἀλλά Semitizing also *not so much … as*).

3. Conjunctions

There are various more or less important differences regarding their number and use (↑250/251).

4. Important uninflected words 356ab

a) General points

Clearly fewer particles are used (↑252a).

S For a possible influence of Ancient Aramaic דְּ *də* / דִּי *dî* on the use of relative pronouns, the genitive, ὅτι (*because/that*), ἵνα, ὅτε, and ὥστε ↑references in 252a.

b) On the alphabetic list (↑252.1–252.63)

	• ἄν(↑252.3)	
	augment ind. + ἄν expressing irrealis	} occasionally without ἄν (↑209h; 210i/210j)
	prospective subj. + ἄν	
	rel. clauses + ἄν with a conditional force	frequently ἐάν for ἄν (↑290e)
	inf./ptc. phrases fairly frequently + ἄν	never (↑213c; 227c)
	↑also 356v on hellenistisches Nebensatziterativpräteritum.	
	• εἰ (↑252.19)	Hebraisms:
S	–	dependent on oath formulas *certainly not* (↑271e)
S	–	before direct questions: " , '…;' " (↑269b)
	• ἐπεί (↑252.23)	
	as/since (causal), *(since) otherwise*; and *when, after*	only *as/since, (since) otherwise* (↑277; 276a)
	• ἕως (↑252.24)	
	conjunction *until; as long as*	also prep. + gen. *until* (↑185)
	• ἵνα (↑252.28)	
	so that = in order that (indicating purpose)	also *that* (inf./ACI phrase replacements; ↑356ag) less frequently *so that* (indicating result; ↑356ah)
S	• καί (↑252.29)	mainly popular KG, in parts Semitisms
	and (also: *also/as well, even*)	also with the nuances of "but", "(and) so/then", "(so) that", "in order that", ≈ rel. pron., ≈ ὅτι or inf., "that is to say", pleonastic
	• μέν – δέ (↑252.34)	
	(indeed) – but, on the one hand – on the other	used much less frequently
	• ὅπως (↑252.45)	
	+ subj. *so that (= in order that)*	also *that* (inf./ACI phrase replacements; ↑356ag)
	+ ind. fut. (dependent on expressions that denote *to take care* or the like) *that*	not used (↑356ag)
	how, in what way (adv.; basic use)	only in Lk 24:20 (↑287)

(Classical Greek)	(NT Greek)
• ὡς (↑252.61) “how/as/like”	
+ noun phrases	
–	Semitism *something like*
to (prep. + acc. with verbs of motion)	–
+ verb forms	
that (= ὅτι), *how* (dependent interrogative clause), *because* (= ὅτι), *so that* (purpose/result; = ἵνα/ὥστε)	} rarely or only occasionally used
• ὥστε (↑252.62)	
so that/with the result that (result)	occasionally *so that/in order that* (purpose; ↑278)

↑also 252.1–252.63 for minor differences.

C. Sentences and their constituents

356ac I. Sentence constituents

1. The 3rd pers. pl. act. more frequently refers to people in general (↑generic “one”; ↑255f), apparently influenced by Semitic usage:

λέγουσιν or the like	*people say*	not restricted to verbs of communication

2. The 3rd pers. pl. or the pass. may be used in place of a direct reference to God (↑255f; 296b), e.g. *God/the Lord will give (it) to you*:

ὁ θεὸς / κύριος δώσει ὑμῖν	also δώσουσιν ὑμῖν or δοθήσεται ὑμῖν

3. Sometimes the LXX idiom προστίθεμαι + inf. *to do again/more* is used(↑259c[10]).

↑also 255b (and 257c: a pron. is sometimes replaced by an adv.); 255c (λέγει *[God/the Scripture] says*); 255f (and 258a; a PpP with εἰς + acc., in line with Semitic usage, may replace a SC^{id} in the nom. or an OC^{id} in the acc.; ↑356n/356o); 259c–259m (various differences regarding adverbials, mostly already mentioned above); 260b–260j (various differences regarding attributive modifiers, mostly already mentioned above).

356ad II. Concord

1. A ntr. pl. NP in the subject role increasingly combines with a pl. predicator (↑262a), e.g. *The sheep hear (it)*:

τὰ πρόβατα ἀκούε**ι**	increasingly τὰ πρόβατα ἀκού**ουσιν**

2. There are only a few instances with the subject complement (SC^{prop}) in the form of an AdjP being in the ntr. sg against standard concord rules (↑263d).

D. Sentence/clause types

356ae I. General point

“Paratactic” combinations of sentences occur more frequently in line with popular KG narrative style, the high frequency in the LXX and in parts of the NT quite likely being influenced by Semitic/Hebrew usage (↑266b).

II. Independent (main) clauses

Independent closed interrogative clauses are more frequently without special marker (the particle ἆρα occurs only 3× in the NT [LXX: 5×]; 269b), e.g. *Is he coming?*:

ἆρα ἔρχεται;	almost exclusively _ ἔρχεται;

On various points, mostly already mentioned above ↑267 (independent declarative clauses); 268 (independent desiderative clause) and 269 (independent interrogative clause).

(Classical Greek)	(NT Greek)

III. Dependent (subordinate) clauses

1. General points 356af

The oblique opt. occurs very rarely (↑270g; 356x), e.g. They realized that it was empty:

ἔγνωσαν ὅτι κενὸς **εἴη**	almost exclusively → ἔγνωσαν ὅτι κενός **ἐστιν**

↑also 270f (verbs of showing and reporting + inf./ACI phrase or in part + ὅτι-clause, not + ACP); 270h (mood assimilation is of little importance).

2. Conjunctional clauses 356ag

a) Conjunctional subject-object clauses

• Subordinate clauses introduced by ἵνα *that* or the like frequently replace Inf./ACI phrases; they may mostly be understood more or less clearly as dependent desiderative clauses (↑272a), e.g. *It is better that one man should die*:

συμφέρει **ἕνα ἀποθανεῖν**	frequently also συμφέρει **ἵνα εἷς ἀποθάνῃ**

• Indirect speech in a narrower sense ("oratio obliqua" proper) is hardly attested (↑274d/274e).
↑also 271a (ὡς rarely = ὅτι *that*); 272c/272e (inter alia ὅπως + subj., more often + ind. fut., depending on expressions denoting *to take care*, is not used); 273a/273b (inter alia for ποῖος *what kind of* also ποταπός); 275 (overview of constructions often rendered by "that"-clauses with differences mostly mentioned already above).

b) Conjunctional adverbial clauses 356ah

• Temporal clauses

There are minor differences regarding subordinators and moods (↑276a). Thus, πρίν *before* rarely combines with the ind. (almost exclusively with inf./ACI or with ἤ + inf./ACI).
↑also 276i (CG "iterative opt." [without ἄν] is replaced by the hellenistisches Nebensatziterativpräteritum; ↑356x).

• Causal clauses

There are minor differences regarding subordinators (↑277a).

• Purpose clauses

There are minor differences regarding subordinators and moods (↑278a), the more important ones being:

also ὡς = ἵνα *in order that*	occurs only occasionally
ὅπως/ὡς also + ἄν	not attested
ὥστε + ind. or + inf./ACI *with the result that*	occasionally also *in order that*

↑also 356ag.

• Result clauses

– subordinators (279a):

also ὡς = ὡς = ὥστε	occurs only occasionally
ἵνα + subj. *in order that*	occasionally also *with the result that*
S ὅτι in questions	also (Hebraism?) *(so) that* (= *with the result that*)

– verb forms and semantic nuances (↑279a; 356y):

ὥστε + ind.: mostly actual result	occurs rarely
ὥστε + Inf./ACI phrases: mostly conceivable result	conceivable or actual result

• Conditional clauses

Most important points:

– potential conditional case (with opt.; ↑280c/280d; 283):

widely used	only a handful of incomplete instances

(Classical Greek)	(NT Greek)

– prospective conditional case (with subj.; ↑282b; 280d):

most frequently used (unmarked) conditional case	used even more widely (largely encompassing the domain of the CG potential and, in part, apparently the remote conditional case

↑also 282a (occasionally the ind. fut./pres. replaces the subj.).

– indefinite conditional case (with ind.): negation of the *if*-clause (↑280b; 281a):

by means of μή	mostly by means of οὐ

On the subordinators also ↑280b.

- Concessive and exceptive conditional clauses (↑286a: minor points)
- Manner clauses

There are minor differences regarding subordinators (ὅπως *as, in such manner as* and ὥσπερ ἂν εἰ + opt. *as if* are not used; ↑287a).

356ai 3. Relative clauses

a) There are minor differences regarding subordinators (↑289a). ↑also 289e.

b) Probably influenced by Semitic or Biblical usage relative clauses sometimes contain a pleonastic (seemingly unnecessary) pers. pron. or demonstrative adv. correlating with the relative (↑289i), e.g. S
a woman whose little daughter …:

γυνὴ **ἧς** τὸ θυγάτριον …	γυνὴ **ἧς** τὸ θυγάτριον **αὐτῆς** …

c) With the exception of the relative clause with conditional force relative clauses with adverbial force occur comparatively rarely (↑290a).

↑also 290c/290d/290e (minor differences regarding the use of moods); 290f (hellenistisches Nebensatziterativpräteritum for CG iterative opt.; ↑356v).

356aj E. **Deviations from syntactic and other "norms" (figures of speech)**

I. Sound-related stylistic devices (avoidance of the hiatus and metre) occur only very occasionally in the NT (↑291b).

II. The Semitic type of parallelismus membrorum occurs fairly frequently in the Gospels (↑294z). S

↑also 292c (Hysteron proteron occurs rarely, if at all); 292d (parenthesis occurs fairly frequently, sometimes against CG usage).

Appendix 2 Word-formation

1 Lexical word-formation: preliminaries

Lexical word-formation and text interpretation (↑MB: W302f) 357

1. Interpreters of texts cannot do without the grammatical knowledge that allows them to connect the word forms and the grammatical function words of a text with the syntactic and textgrammatical functions intended by the speaker/writer (↑309b). But equally indispensable is the lexical knowledge that enables them to connect the (lexical) content words of a text with the intended content meanings (↑309b). Now, while grammatical knowledge is about (essentially) closed paradigms (↑inflectional morphology and syntax), lexical knowledge is about open paradigms: inflectional patterns and the inventory of function words are (principally) fixed; the number of lexical words, however, may be increased as the need arises. In English new lexical words keep on being added to the established ones (↑Huddleston/Pullum: 1623ff); the same happened in Ancient Greek. Such processes are subject to certain rules that enable hearers/readers to understand the newly created words. 357a

The outline below in 358–371 focuses on the **rules of** Ancient Greek **lexical word-formation** that seem most relevant when dealing with the Greek NT.[1] Based on BR §296–308, it is primarily intended as a help for learners and exegetes. Standard lexicons, of course, contain detailed information on the meaning or function of each word used in the NT. However, they usually have little to offer to those trying to find out how exactly the forms and meanings of the various members of a word family relate to one another e.g. δοῦλος, δουλόω, δουλεύω and δουλεία (*slave, to enslave, to serve* and *service/slavery*), or to those interested in studying the lexical meaning of a particular word on the basis of its word-formation such as ἀχειροποίητος *not made by human hands*. So, some of the more important insights of Ancient Greek linguistics relevant to such concerns will be outlined below.

2. When **interpreting texts**, the following points need to be kept in mind regarding the outline below: 357b

a) The statements of meaning accompanying the various types and examples of word-formation are not precise definitions, but simply brief descriptions of typical meanings; and these allow for all sorts of variations when it comes to dealing with concrete cases. One factor involved in this is the fact that the base words concerned may belong to different semantic categories. Take e.g. the English verbs in *-ize*: these are best explained in terms of one type of word-formation; but depending on the base word (e.g. an adjective or noun) different types of "actions"/"situations" may be referred to, such as "to make something have more of a particular quality"[2] (e.g. *to modernize*) or "to put into a particular place"[2] (e.g. *to hospitalize*). So, interpreters of texts should not apply typical meanings mechanically.

b) In any case, a typical meaning must never be given priority over the actual meaning of a word (as attested in relevant texts). As a word is used frequently, the meaning it initially had may change in the course of time, and even disappear from the minds of native speakers. Thus, the English verb *to ship* initially meant "to transport on a ship" (↑COED s.v.); in the course of time, however, its meaning was extended to "to send goods somewhere by ship, plane, truck etc" (↑COED s.v.; Longman s.v. 1). The more frequently a word is used in the course of the history of a language or in a particular period, semantic domain, frame (↑313) or genre, the more likely the initial or typical meaning is to

---

1 A few examples are from texts outside the NT (mainly from the LXX, Josephus and Philo).

2 Longman sub *-ize*.

change. In short: to make adequate use of what is said about the meanings of the types of lexical word-formation given below interpreters of texts will have to give top priority to the actual meaning of a word as it is attested in the relevant corpus of texts. In addition to the standard lexicons BDAG, LSJ and Montanari, etymological dictionaries may prove helpful, as these contain specialized information on the history of Ancient Greek words; the standard ones are Beekes, Frisk, and Chantraine.[3] Especially for problem cases ↑also MH §96–174, BDF §108–125, or Robertson: 143–176.

358 Means of lexical word-formation (↑BR §296–298; MB: W400f)

358a 1. New words may be created from existing ones by means of **derivation** (root or stem modification) or by means of **compounding** (linking together two existing words), e.g.:

"new" word:		derived from:	
σωτήρ	*saviour, deliverer*	σῴζω/ἔσωσα	*to save, to deliver*
εἰρηνικός	*peaceable*	εἰρήνη	*peace*
"new" word:		compounded of:	
οἰκοδεσπότης	*master of the house*	οἶκος + δεσπότης	*house + master*

Both types may also involve **ablaut** grade changes (↑8), e.g.:

σπ**ό**ρος	*seed*	σπείρω/σπ**ε**ρῶ	*to sow*
σώφρ**ω**ν	*of sound mind, sensible*	σῶς + φρ**ή**ν/φρ**έ**νες	*sound +mind*

The bases of word-formation may themselves have been created by derivation or compounding, e.g.:

"new" word:		derived from:	
σωτηρία	*salvation, deliverance*	σωτήρ (↑above)	*saviour, deliverer*
οἰκοδεσποτέω	*to manage one's house*	οἰκοδεσπότης (↑above)	*master of the house*

358b 2. The base of word-formation, strictly speaking, is not so much a word as its **stem** (↑21c), in the above cases e.g. σω-, εἰρην- and οἰκο-. In the case of multi-stem verbs, it is the stem of the aor. pass. or of the pf. pass. that usually serves as the base of word-formation, e.g.:

κρίσις	*judgment*	ἐ**κρί**θην/κέ**κρι**μαι: aor./pf. pass. κρίνω *to judge*
ῥῆμα	*word*	ἐρ**ρή**θην/εἴ**ρη**μαι: aor./pf. pass. λέγω *to say*

Derivation involves the modification of the stem or root of the base word (↑21a). This is done mainly by suffixation, i.e. by derivational **suffixes** being attached (↑21b), e.g. (↑also examples in 21):

κρίσις	*judgment*	stem/root: κρι-	suffix: -σις
ῥῆμα	*word*	stem/root: ῥη-	suffix: -μα(τ)

Noteworthy points:

a) In the case of words that appear to have no suffixes the stem and root are identical, e.g.:

θήρ/θηρός (CG/LXX) *wild animal* stem = root: θηρ-

3 "Etymology" (that Beekes, Frisk, and Chantraine are concerned with) is a branch of linguistic research that inter alia seeks to trace back the development of the forms and meanings of words or word families to their origin (and thus recover their "true" meaning [ἔτυμος *true*], as formerly believed, a view rightly discarded today). "In most cases our knowledge does not, however, lead us back to the origin. The best we may hope to do is to trace back the history of a word over a more or less extended stretch of time." (↑MB: W303). As Beekes, Frisk, and Chantraine inform us about the history of individual words within the word family they belong to, these titles may help us understand how the typical meaning of a word-formation type is related to the actual meaning of a word and thus help us deal more easily with semantic discomfort that may arise when faced with seeming discrepancies.

b) Suffixes, stems and roots are entities that do not exist by themselves or occur independently; rather they are abstractions that help linguists to unravel the complexities of morphology. Word forms whose root and stem are identical occur very rarely in Ancient Greek texts, and when they do, only in forms without an ending as in the above example θήρ whose nom. sg. stem corresponds to the root.

3. When new words are formed, the pattern of existing words is typically followed, i.e. "**analogy** is 358c
the driving force" (↑MB: W400.2) of word-formation, e.g.:

ποιμήν/ποιμένος *shepherd* → ποιμενικός *connected with shepherds*
which is formed in analogy to:
πατήρ/πατρός *father* → πατρικός *connected with fathers*

In such formation processes words may change in a great variety of ways, fairly frequently going against the expected patterns. The following variations occur particularly frequently:

a) **Nominalization of adjectives** (frequently via ellipsis; ↑137c, p.199), e.g.: 358d
ἡ ἔρημος γῆ/χώρα *the desolate region* → ἡ ἔρημος *the desert/wilderness*

b) **Pattern changes based on analogy** ("Umgliederung"): the derivation follows the pattern of a 358e
word other than the expected one. Thus, it happened e.g. that from a word such as βασιλεύς *king* both (1) a verb and (2) an abstract noun were derived resulting in two derivational patterns:

(1) βασιλ**εύς** *king* → βασιλ**εύω** *to be king*
(2) βασιλ**εύς** *king* → βασιλ**εία** *kingdom*

Initially there was no direct connection between the verb βασιλεύω *to be king* and the abstract noun βασιλεία *kingdom*. Such a connection was, however, created by linguistic usage: in cases where there was no noun normally required by pattern 2, but a verb in -εύω/-εύομαι, this verb was taken as the base for the formation of an abstract noun in -εία, which resulted in a new pattern (3), e.g.:

(3) παιδ**εύω** *to train* → παιδ**εία** *training*
πορ**εύομαι** *to travel/go* → πορ**εία** *journey*

c) **Suffix conglomerates**: two suffixes could merge into one, e.g. the noun suffix -τηρ (occurring 358f
with agent nouns; ↑362a) and the adjective suffix -ιος ("connected with such and such"; ↑359a) in the ntr. sg. into a noun suffix -τήριον (denoting the means or place of an "action"; ↑362d), resulting in patterns such as δικάζω *to judge* → δικασ-**τήρ** (≈ δικάστης) *a judge* → *δικαστήρ-**ιος** *connected with judges* → δικασ-**τήριον** *court of justice*, e.g.:

(1) θυσιάζω *to sacrifice* → θυσιασ-**τήριον** *altar*
(2) ψάλλω *to pluck/play* (a musical instrument) → ψαλ-**τήριον** *stringed instrument* (lyre, harp)
(3) κατοικέω *to dwell* → κατοικη-**τήριον** *dwelling place*

d) **"Incorrect" suffix analysis**: e.g. at first there was a "correct" feminine counterpart of the mas- 358g
culine Φοῖνιξ (gen. sg. Φοίνικ-ος) *Phoenician*: Φοίνισσα (< *Φοινικ-i̯α; ↑12c); from about 400 B.C. -ισσα was "incorrectly" analysed as a suffix and then used to form feminine counterparts of masculine nouns in -εύς:

Φοῖνιξ/Φοίνι**κ**ος *Phoenician* (male) → *Φοινι**κi̯α** > Φοίνι**σσα** *Phoenician* (female)
βασιλ-**εύς** *king* → βασίλ-**ισσα** *queen*

e) **Interference from other languages**: contacts with other languages may have an impact inter alia 358h
on lexical word-formation. Thus, in the NT the following suffixes have a Latin origin:

-ῖνος Ἀλεξανδρ**ῖνος** *Alexandrian* (↑Lat. *Tarentīnus* "connected with Tarentum")
-ιᾱνός χριστι**ανός** *connected with Christ* (↑Lat. *Drūsiānus* "connected with one Drusus")
-ηνός Ναζαρ**ηνός** *connected with Nazareth* (↑Lat. *Antiochēnus* "connected with Antioch")

Note that unlike Ναζαρ**ηνός** (from Ναζαρά, also Ναζαρέτ/θ) its synonym Ναζωρ**αῖος** (probably derived from *Ναζωρά [↑Aram. vowel change ā > ō; Beyer: 147) has a genuinely Greek suffix (↑359a).

2 Important derivational suffixes

(i) Derived adjectives

359 Adjectives derived from nouns (↑BR §299; MB: W402ff; BDF §113; MH §132ff)

359a 1. **Adjectives of belonging** ("belonging to/connected with such and such"):

	base:		derived word:	
a) **-ιος**:	οὐρανός	*heaven*	οὐράν**ιος**	*belonging to heaven, heavenly*
	πλοῦτος	*wealth*	πλούσ**ιος**	*wealthy* (-σι < -τι; BR §16.2)
	Ἔφεσος	*Ephesus*	Ἐφέσ**ιος**	*Ephesian*
-αιος (the base mostly has a stem in -ᾱ; ↑25):				
	δίκη	inter alia *justice*	δίκ**αιος**	*just*
	Ῥώμη	*Rome*	Ῥωμ**αῖος**	*Roman*
	βία	*force*	βί**αιος**	*forcible*
-ειος (the base has various stem types, e.g. the following):				
	θεός	*divinity (god/God)*	θ**εῖος** (< θέ-ϊος)	*divine*
	τέλος (-εσ-)	*end, outcome*	τέλ**ειος**	*complete, perfect*
	βασιλεύς (-ευ-)	*king*	βασίλ**ειος**	*kingly, royal*
	(joining these also:)			
	οἶκος	*house*	οἰκ**εῖος**	*connected with the house*
b) **-ικός** (occurring frequently from the end of the 5th century B.C.):				
	νόμος	*law*	νομ**ικός**	*connected with the law*
	κόσμος	*world*	κοσμ**ικός**	*wordly, earthly*
	πνεῦμα (-ματ-)	*spirit/Spirit*	πνευματ**ικός**	*spiritual/belonging to the Spirit*
	Γαλατία	*Galatia*	Γαλατ**ικός**	*Galatian*
-ιακός (this replaces the phonologically difficult *-ιϊκός):				
	κύριος	*lord/Lord*	κυρ**ιακός**	*connected with the lord/Lord*

359b 2. **Adjectives denoting materials** ("consisting of such and such a material")

	base		derived word	
a) **-οῦς** (< -εος; ↑44c; the base usually denotes some metal):				
	χρυσός	*gold*	χρυσ**οῦς**	*golden*
	σίδηρος	*iron*	σιδηρ**οῦς**	*(made of) iron*
b) **-ειος** (the base usually denotes an animal):				
	αἶξ/αἰγός	*goat*	αἴγ**ειος**	*of a goat/of goats*
c) **-ινος** (the base usually denotes some material/substance):				
	δέρμα (-ματ-)	*skin, hide*	δερμάτ**ινος**	*(made of) leather*
	ξύλον	*wood*	ξύλ**ινος**	*wooden*
	(but also:)			
	ἄνθρωπος	*human being*	ἀνθρώπ**ινος**	*human*

359c 3. **Adjectives denoting fullness** ("fully equipped with such and such")

	base		derived word	
-εις (st. -εντ- < -ϝεντ-, ↑46c; mainly in poetry; unattested in the NT):				
	χάρις	e.g. *outward beauty*	χαρί**εις**	*attractive* (4Macc 8:3)

4. **Adjectives referring to a period of time** (the base is a noun or an adverb; suffix also -[ερ]-ινός) 359d

-ινός:	νύξ (νυκτ-)	*night*	νυκτερ**ινός**	*nocturnal* (LXX)
	θέρος	*summer*	θερ**ινός**	*of summer* (LXX)
	πέρυσι (adv.)	*last year*	περυσ**ινός**	*of last year* (Hermas Vis. 3.10.3)

5. **Adjectives derived from verbal abstract nouns** (↑362b) 359e

-ιμος:	βρῶσις (↑113.4)	*eating, food*	βρώσ**ιμος**	*eatable*
	χρῆσις (↑86.2)	*use, usage*	χρήσ**ιμος**	*useful*

Adjectives derived from verbs 360

(↑BR §300; MB: W406; BDF §112; MH §135:2; 154)

1. The "verbal adjectives" in -τός and -τέος (↑64e) are the first ones to be mentioned here. These largely belong to the CG system of conjugation. However, many of those in -τός (in the NT all of them) were already "lexicalized", i. e. they had become part of the established vocabulary (in the lexicons they appear as separate head words). And those in -τέος occur only rarely in non-CG. E.g.: 360a

a) **-τός** (denotes the effect of an "action" [≈ ptc. pf. pass.] or the possibility of it taking place; ↑368c):

ἀγαπάω	*to love*	ἀγαπη**τός**	*beloved*
γράφω	*to write*	γραπ**τός**	*written*
ἀνέχομαι	*to endure, to bear*	ἀνεκ**τός**	*endurable, bearable*

b) **-τέος** (denotes a passive necessity: an "action" must or [when negated] must not be done [↑217c]; always used as a predicative element; only 1× in the NT [↑64e; 137c])

βάλλω	*to throw, to put*	… βλη**τέον**	*… must be put …* (Lk 5:38)
ποιέω	*to do*	… οὐ ποιη**τέον**	*… must not be done* (Philo)

2. In addition to these the following types are particularly important:

a) **-τικός** (occurring fairly frequently, they denote the ability to do sth.; ↑359a): 360b

διδάσκω (διδαχ-)	*to teach*	διδακ**τικός**	*able to teach*
κρίνω (κρι-)	*to judge, to discern*	κρι**τικός**	*able to judge/discern*

b) Types that occur less frequently: 360c

-ρός (with active or middle force):

λάμπω	*to shine*	λαμπ**ρός**	*bright*
φαίνομαι (φαν-)	*to become visible*	φανε**ρός**	*visible, clear*

-λός (mostly with active force):

δέδοικα (δοι-/δει-)	*to fear* (↑109b)	δει**λός**	*fearful, timid*

-νός (mostly with passive force):

σέβομαι	*to revere, to honour*	σεμ**νός**	*revered, honourable*
στυγέω (στυγ-)	*to abhor*	στυγ**νός**	*abhorred; gloomy* (LXX)

-μων (with active force):

ἐπίσταμαι	*to understand*	ἐπιστή**μων**	*understanding, intelligent*
οἰκτίρω	*to have compassion*	οἰκτίρ**μων**	*compassionate*

(ii) Derived nouns

361 Nouns derived from nouns or adjectives

(↑BR §301; MB: W407–412; BDF §110f; MH §134f)

361a 1. **Nouns denoting female beings** (feminine formations, "Motionsfeminina")

a) **-ια and -ι̯α** (↑12c; depending on the suffix of the masculine further elements may precede):

-τρια:	μαθητής	*disciple (male)*	μαθή**τρια**	*female disciple* (↑362a)
-αινα(<-ανι̯α):	θεράπων	*attendant (male)*	θεράπ**αινα**	*female attendant* (LXX)
-ισσα:	βασιλεύς	*king*	βασίλ**ισσα**	*queen* (↑358g)

b) **-ις, gen. -ίδος**:

Ἕλλην	*Greek*	Ἑλλην**ίς**	*Greek woman*
προφήτης	*prophet*	προφῆ**τις**	*prophetess*
πρεσβύτης	*elderly/old man*	πρεσβῦ**τις**	*elderly/old woman*

Note that the suffix -ᾱ/-η (↑25) is used somewhat rarely to form nouns denoting female beings, e.g.:

ἀδελφός	*brother*	ἀδελφ**ή**	*sister*
δοῦλος	*male slave*	δούλ**η**	*female slave*
θεός	*god*	θε**ᾱ́**	*goddess* (but also ↑below)

From early times, however, there had been "nomina communia" (sg.: "nomen commune"), i.e. nouns that without changing their form could refer either to male or female beings, the intended gender being indicated solely by noun concomitants such as the article, e.g.:

ὁ θεός	*the god*	**ἡ** θεός	*the goddess* (also ↑above)
ὁ παῖς	*the boy*	**ἡ** παῖς	*the girl*
ὁ βοῦς	*the bull*	**ἡ** βοῦς	*the cow* (LXX)

Note that ὁ θεός – ἡ θεός/θεᾱ́ belongs to the nouns termed "nomina mobilia" (sg. "nomen mobile"), which allow for both uses (↑23a).

361b 2. **Diminutives**, i.e. nouns that imply smallness, used either literally or as terms of affection or scorn (COED s.v.; Carter §539; ↑English *book* → *booklet*); in the NT these do not occur very frequently, and if they do, mostly without diminutive force; BDF §111.3; MH §138f; 156.7; Z §485):

a) **-ις, gen. -ίδος** (occurring only occasionally):

θύρα	*door*	θυρ**ίς** fem.	*window* (lit. "small door")

b) **-ίσκος, -ίσκη**:

βασιλεύς	*king*	βασιλ**ίσκος**	*kinglet* (Jn 4:46.49 Var.)
(ἡ) παῖς (παιδ-)	*girl*	παιδ**ίσκη**	*maid* (lit. "small girl")

c) **-ιον** (always ntr.; ↑30; KG legal terminology has many compounds with non-diminutive -ιον)

	θυγάτηρ (↑38)	*daughter*	θυγάτρ**ιον**	*little daughter*
	σύμβουλος	*advisor*	συμβούλ**ιον**	*advisory body*
	formations involving suffix conglomerates (↑358f):			
-ίδιον:	πίναξ (πινακ-)	*table; plank; dish*	πινακ**ίδιον**	*small writing tablet*
-άριον:	κλίνη	*bed*	κλιν**άριον**	*(small) bed, mat*
	οὖς (ὠτ-)	*ear*	ὠτ**άριον**	*(outer) ear* (lit. "small ear")

361c 3. **Nouns denoting occupations or status**

a) **-της, gen. -ου** (for fem. ↑361a):

	ναῦς	*ship*	ναύ**της**	*seaman, sailor*
-ί̄της:	πόλις	*city*	πολ**ίτης**/πολῖτις	*citizen* (e.g. in Josephus)
-ιώτης:	στρατός	*army*	στρατ**ιώτης**	*solidier* (also ↑361f)

b) **-εύς**:	τὰ ἅλια	*sea*	ἁλι**εύς**	*fisherman*
	ἵππος	*horse*	ἱππ**εύς**	*horseman, rider*
	φόνος	*murder*	φον**εύς**	*murderer*

4. **Abstract nouns** 361d

a) **-της, gen. -τητος** (Doric -τᾱς, ↑Lat. *liber-tās* "freedom"; the base is an adjective):

ἱλαρός	*cheerful*	ἱλαρό**της**	*cheerfulness*
νέος	*young*	νεό**της**	*youth*
ὅσιος	*holy, devout*	ὁσιό**της**	*holiness, devoutness*

b) **-σύνη** (the base is an adjective):

ἀγαθός	*good*	ἀγαθω**σύνη**	*being good, goodness*
δίκαιος	*righteous*	δικαιο**σύνη**	*being righteous, righteousness*
σώφρων	*of sound mind*	σωφρο**σύνη**	*soundness of mind*

c) **-ίᾱ** (the base is either a noun or an adjective):

παρθένος	*virgin*	παρθεν**ία**	*virginity*
ξένος	inter alia *stranger*	ξεν**ία**	*hospitality, guest room*
φιλάργυρος	*fond of money*	φιλαργυρ**ία**	*love of money*

-είᾱ (at first the base was a noun in -εύς; later further possibilities were added; ↑358e)

βασιλεύς	*king*	βασιλ**εία**	*kingship, kingdom*
προφήτης	*prophet*	προφητ**εία**	*prophecy*
πολίτης	*citizen*	πολιτ**εία**	*citizenship*

d) **-ειᾰ** (the base is an adjective in -εσ-; ↑45b):

ἀληθής	*true*	ἀλήθ**εια**	*truth*
ἀσθενής	*weak, ill*	ἀσθέν**εια**	*weakness, illness*

e) **-ος** ntr. (the base is mostly an adjective in -ύς; ↑46a):

βαθύς	*deep*	βάθ**ος**	*depth*
βαρύς	*heavy, weighty*	βάρ**ος**	*heavy weight, burden*

f) **-ική** (↑359a; supply in thought τέχνη *skill* or ἐπιστήμη *knowledge/scientific knowledge*):

γράμμα (-ματ-)	*letter of alphabet*	γραμματ**ική**	*grammar* (e.g. Philo)
Μοῦσα	*Muse*	μουσ**ική**	*music* (e.g. Philo)

5. **Nouns denoting places** 361e

a) **-ών, gen. -ῶνος m.**:

ἄμπελος	*vine*	ἀμπελ**ών**	*vineyard*

b) **-ειον** ntr. (really ntr. of adjectives in -ειος; ↑359a; at first the base was a noun in -εύς; later further possibilities were added; ↑358e):

πανδοχεύς	*innkeeper*	πανδοχ**εῖον**	*inn*
εἴδωλον	*idol*	εἰδωλ**εῖον**	*idol's temple*

6. **Nouns denoting inhabitants of a place** ("ethnics", <ἐθνικός ή όν *indicating nationality*; ↑LSJ s.v. III) 361f

a) **-ιος** (going back to adjectives of belonging; ↑359a):

	Αἴγυπτος	*Egypt*	Αἰγύπτ**ιος**	*an Egyptian*
	Κόρινθος	*Corinth*	Κορίνθ**ιος**	*a Corinthian*
b) **-εύς**:	Ἀντιόχεια	*Antioch*	Ἀντιοχ**εύς**	*an Antiochene*
	Ταρσός	*Tarsus*	Ταρσ**εύς**	*an inhabitant of Tarsus*

c) **-ῑ́της** (↑361c; fem. -ῖτις) in thought τέχνη *skill* or ἐπιστήμη *knowledge/scientific knowledge*):

	Σαμάρεια	*Samaria*	Σαμαρ**ίτης**	*a Samaritan*
			Σαμαρ**ῖτις**	*a Samaritan woman*
	Ἱεροσόλυμα	*Jerusalem*	Ἱεροσολυμ**ίτης**	*an inhabitant of Jerusalem*
-ιᾱ́της:	Σπάρτη	*Sparta*	Σπαρτ**ιάτης**	*a Spartan* (e.g. Josephus)

Noteworthy points:

(1) Related to ethnics, but usually distinguished from them, are the "ctetics" (<κτητικός ή όν *possessive*; ↑LSJ s. v. II): adjectives indicating that sth. or s.o. belongs (↑359a) to the inhabitants of a place:

Αἰγύπτιος	*an Egyptian*	Αἰγυπτιακός	*belonging to the Egyptians Egyptian* adj. (Josephus)
Ἕλλην	*a Greek*	Ἑλληνικός	*Greek* adj.

(2) The feminine form of ethnics or ctetics may also denote a corresponding region or language (ellipsis of χώρα/γῆ *region/land* or γλῶσσα/φωνή *language*; ↑260c; 358d):

Ἰουδαία	*Jewess*	ἡ Ἰουδαία	(sc. χώρα/γῆ) *Judea*
Ἑλληνική	*Greek* adj. fem.	ἡ Ἑλληνική	(sc. γλῶσσα/φωνή) *Greek* (language)

Note that something like "in Greek" could be expressed by the phrase ἐν τῇ Ἑλληνικῇ (Re 9:11), but more frequently by adverbs in -ιστί (↑366), e. g. Ἑβραϊστί, Ῥωμαϊστί, Ἑλληνιστί in *Hebrew/Aramaic, in Latin [and] in Greek* (Jn 19:20).

362 Nouns derived from verbs (↑BR §302; MB: W413–415; BDF §109; MH §155; 157:4)

362a 1. **Agent nouns** ("nomina agentis"; nouns denoting the one doing/causing the "action")

a) **-τήρ, gen. -τῆρος** (in CG and post-CG almost exclusively denoting instruments; ↑362d):

σῴζω (σω-)	*to save, to deliver*	σω**τήρ**	*saviour, deliverer*
δίδωμι (δω-/δο-)	*to give*	δο**τήρ**	*giver* (Josephus)

b) **-τωρ, gen. -τορος** (in CG widely-used especially in poetry):

κτάομαι	*to acquire*	κτή**τωρ**	*owner*
ἐρρήθην of	λέγω *to say*	ῥή**τωρ**	*public speaker, advocate*
κρατέω	*to hold fast*	παντοκρά**τωρ**	*the ruler of all, the Almighty*

c) **-της, gen. -του** (fem. -τρια and -τρίς, gen. -τρίδος; ↑361a):

αὐλέω	*to play the flute*	αὐλη-**τής**/-τρίς	*flautist*
κρίνω (κρι-)	*to judge*	κρι**τής**	*a judge*
ὑβρίζω (↑16b)	*to act arrogantly*	ὑβρισ**τής**	*an arrogant/violent person*
		ὑβρίστρια	*an arrogant woman* (LXX)

Note that such feminine nouns did not originally belong here, but to the masculine types in -τηρ/-τωρ. When these types were replaced by the type in -της, the feminine did not change. The combination of the types πολῖτης *citizen* (male) and πολῖτις *citizen* (female), however, is original (↑361c).

d) **-ός with o-grade ablaut** (↑8; 362b/362c; this is an ancient type):

τρέφω	*to feed, to nourish*	τροφ**ός** fem.	*nurse*
τρέχω	*to run*	τροχ**ός**	*wheel* (originally *runner*)

362b 2. **Action nouns** ("nomina actionis"; verbal abstract nouns denoting an "action"; note that there are no clearly defined boundaries between action and result nouns [↑362c])

a) **-σις, gen. -σεως**:

κρίνω (κρι-)	*to judge*	κρίσις	*act of judging, judgment*
δίδωμι (δω-/δο-)	*to give*	δόσις	*act of giving, gift*
λύω	*to loose*	λύσις	*act of loosing, release*

b) **-μός, mostly -σμός** (also ↑16b):

θερίζω	*to reap, to harvest*	θερι**σμός**	*act of harvesting* (also *crop*!)
ἀσπάζομαι	*to greet*	ἀσπα**σμός**	*a greeting*
σείω	*to shake*	σει**σμός**	*a violent shaking, earthquake*

c) **-μη**:

γινώσκω (γνω-)	*to know*	γνώ**μη**	*mind-set, opinion*
ὄζω (< ὀδ[i̯]ω)	*to smell, to stink*	ὀσ**μή** (↑13a)	*smell* (good or bad)

d) **-ᾱ/-η** (mostly with o-grade ablaut and accent on the final syllable; ↑8; 362a/362c)

προσφέρω	*to bring, to offer*	προσφ**ο**ρ**ά**	*act of offering* (also *gift offered!*)
τρέφω	*to nourish*	τρ**ο**φ**ή**	*nourishment*
ᾄδω (< ἀείδω)	*to sing*	**ᾠ**δ**ή** (< ἀοιδή)	*singing*, (mostly:) *song*
ἔφυγον of	φεύγω *to flee*	φυγ**ή**	*flight*

e) **-ίᾱ/-είᾱ** (the base is a verb in -έω or in -εύω; ↑358e)

ἀγρυπνέω	*to be awake*	ἀγρυπν**ία**	*being awake, sleeplessness*
ἑρμηνεύω	*to translate*	ἑρμην**εία**	*translation* (act or product)

3. **Result nouns** ("nomina rei actae"; nouns denoting the result of an "action"; note that there are no clearly defined boundaries between result and action nouns [↑362b]) 362c

a) **-μα, gen. -ματος, ntr.**:

κτάομαι	*to acquire*	κτῆ**μα**	*possession, property*
σχίζω (σχιδ-)	*to split, to tear*	σχίσ**μα**	*a split/tear, division*
θέλω (θελ[η]-)	*to wish, to want*	θέλη**μα**	*will* (what s.o. wants to happen)

b) **-ος with o-grade ablaut** (↑8; 362a/362b):

ἔδραμον of	τρέχω *to run*	δρ**ό**μ**ος**	*race, racecourse*
λέγω	*to say*	λ**ό**γ**ος**	*word*

c) **-ος ntr.** (normal grade ablaut; ↑8):

ψεύδομαι	*to lie*	ψεῦδ**ος**	*a lie*
βάλλω (βαλ-)	*to throw*	βέλ**ος**	*missile, arrow*

4. **Instrument and place nouns** ("nomina instrumenti et loci"; nouns that instruments, means or places of an "action") 362d

a) **-τρον** (also -θρον):

ἀρόω	*to plough*	ἄρο**τρον**	*a plough*
λύω	*to loose*	λύ**τρον**	*a ransom*
θεάομαι	*to see*	θέα**τρον**	*place of seeing, theatre; a play*

b) **-τήρ,, gen. -τῆρος** (originally agent nouns; ↑362a):

νίπτω	*to wash*	νιπ**τήρ**	*wash basin*
ἐκράθην of	κεράννυμι *to mix*	κρα**τήρ**	*mixing vessel, bowl* (LXX)

c) **-τήριον** (really a nominalized adjective in -ιος derived from nouns in -τήρ; ↑358f; also ↑16b):

ἀκροάομαι	*to listen (to)*	ἀκροα**τήριον**	*audience room*
ἐργάζομαι	*to work*	ἐργασ**τήριον**	*workshop* (Josephus)
ἐπόθην of	πίνω *to drink*	πο**τήριον**	*cup*

(iii) Derived verbs

Verbs derived from nouns or adjectives (↑BR §303; BDF §108; MH §159ff) 363

1. **Verbs in -i̯ω** 363a

a) Sound changes in the history of Ancient Greek have obscured this formation type (↑12c):

φύλαξ (φυλακ-)	*guard*	φυλά**σσω** (-**κi̯ω**)	*to be a guard, to guard*
ἄγγελος	*messenger*	ἀγγέ**λλω** (-**λi̯ω**)	*to be a messenger, to announce*
παῖς (παιδ-)	*child*	παί**ζω** (-**δi̯ω**)	*to be a child, to play*

ἐλπίς (ἐλπιδ-)	*hope*	ἐλπί**ζω** (-**δι̯**ω)	*to have hope, to hope*
εὔφρων	*cheerful*	εὐφρα**ίνω** (-**νι̯**ω)	*to make glad, to cheer*
τέλος (τελεσ-)	*end, outcome*	τελ**έω** (-ε**σι̯**ω)	*to bring an end to, to complete*

Quite early -ίζω, -άζω, -αίνω et al. started being treated as suffixes ("incorrectly"; ↑358g):

b) **-ίζω** (signifying "to make s.o./sth. sth." or "to act as though"/"to behave as"):

ἁγνός	*pure*	ἁγν**ίζω**	*to purify*
ὅρος	*boundary*	ὁρ**ίζω**	*to set a boundary, to determine*
Ἰουδαῖος	*Jew*	ἰουδα**ΐζω**	*to live like Jews*

c) **-άζω** (the base is mostly a noun in -μα [↑362c] or in -ᾱ/-η):

ὄνομα	*name*	ὀνομ**άζω**	*to name*
ἀγορά	*market*	ἀγορ**άζω**	*to buy*
αὐγή	*sunlight/dawn*	αὐγ**άζω**	*to see clearly*

-ιάζω (this replaces the phonologically difficult *-ιίζω)

ἅγιος	*holy*	ἁγ**ιάζω**	*to make holy, to sanctify*
νήπιος	*infant*	νηπ**ιάζω**	*to be like an infant*

d) **-αίνω** (the base is mostly an adjective; it denotes an activity ["to make s.o./sth. sth."] or a state)

λευκός	*white*	λευκ**αίνω**	*to make white, whiten*
ὑγιής	*in good health*	ὑγι**αίνω**	*to be in good health*

e) **-ύνω** (the base is mostly an adjective in -ύς; ↑46a)

βαθύς	*deep*	βαθ**ύνω**	*to make deep*
εὐθύς	*straight*	εὐθ**ύνω**	*to make straight, to straighten*

363b 2. **Derived vowel verbs** (they, too, largely go back to verbs in -ι̯ω)

a) **-έω** (the base is a noun or a compound adjective):

βοηθός	*helper*	βοηθ**έω**	*to help*
ὕμνος	*hymn*	ὑμν**έω**	*to sing a hymn*
ἄδικος	*unjust, unfair*	ἀδικ**έω**	*to do wrong*

b) **-άω** (the base is mostly a noun in -ᾱ/-η):

βοή	*(a) cry, shout*	βο**άω**	*to shout, to cry out*
νίκη	*victory*	νικ**άω**	*to prevail, to conquer*

c) **-όω** (signifying "to make s.o./sth. sth."):

ἄξιος	*worthy*	ἀξι**όω**	*to make worthy*
δῆλος	*clear*	δηλ**όω**	*to make clear*
χρυσός	*gold*	χρυσ**όω**	*to make golden*

d) **-εύω** (at first the base was a noun in -εύς; later further possibilities were added; ↑358e)

ἁλιεύς	*fisherman*	ἁλι**εύω**	*to fish*
βασιλεύς	*king*	βασιλ**εύω**	*to be king*
δοῦλος	*slave*	δουλ**εύω**	*to be a slave, to serve*
παῖς	*child*	παιδ**εύω**	*to train*
φυτόν	*(a) plant*	φυτ**εύω**	*to plant*

Note that variously derived verbs of the same word family may differ significantly in meaning, e.g.:

δουλ**εύω**	*to be a slave*	δουλ**όω**	*to enslave*
σωφρον**έω**	*to be prudent*	σωφρον**ίζω**	*to instruct in prudence*

In the NT, however, only few contrasting pairs of this kind occur.

Verbs derived from other verbs (↑BR §304) 364

Verbs that are derived from other verbs are very rare in Ancient Greek. Occasionally the following types occur:

1. **-έω with o-grade ablaut** (↑8; with frequentative-intensive meaning):

φέρω	*to carry*	**φορέω**	*to carry (habitually)*

2. **-σείω** ("desideratives", denoting a desire):

ὠνέομαι	*to buy*	ὠνη**σείω**	*to desire to buy* (Dio Cassius)

(iv) Formation of adverbs

Adverbs derived from case forms (↑BR §63.1; BDF §102–106; MH §66) 365

The major part of adverbs end in -ως (except for the final ς agreeing with the gen. pl. masc. of the corresponding adjective; ↑53b), e.g.:

πλούσιος *rich* → πλουσίων → πλουσί**ως** *richly*

-ως may well be an ancient case ending (with an instrumental function). Alongside these there are many adverbs, that undoubtedly go back to case forms of adjectives, nouns or pronouns (more or less clearly "fossilized" or "lexicalized"):

1. **Nominative expressions**:

masc. sg.:	εὐθύς	*straight* (adj.)	εὐθ**ύς**	*at once*

2. **Genitive expressions**:

fem. sg.:	ἐκεῖνος -ή -ό	*that (one)*	ἐκείν**ης**	*that way* (↑171; 259d)
ntr. sg.:	αὐτός -ή -ό	*(him/her/it)self*	αὐ**τοῦ**	*there/here* (↑61c)
	ὅς ἥ ὅ	*who/which*	**οὗ**	*where/where to* (↑61c)

3. **Dative expressions**:

fem. sg.:	ἴδιος	*(one's) own*	ἰδί**ᾳ**	*by oneself, privately* (↑180a)
ntr. sg.:	κύκλος	*round*	κύκλ**ῳ**	*in a circle, around* (↑181)

4. **Accusative expressions** (fairly well-attested; ↑157):

fem. sg.:	δωρεά	*gift*	δωρε**άν**	*as a gift, without payment*
ntr. sg.:	λοιπός	*remaining*	λοιπ**όν**	*henceforth*
ntr. pl.:	πολύς	*much* (adj.)	πολλ**ά**	*greatly, often*

5. **Ancient case expressions** (↑146a):

locative:	οἶκος	*house*	οἴκ**οι**	*at home* (Josephus)
		probably also:	χαμ**αί**	*on/to the ground*
instrumental:			οὔπ**ω**	*not yet*
			ἄν**ω**	*above, upwards*
			κάτ**ω**	*down, downwards*

Further types of adverb derivation (↑BR §63.2–3; 305; BDF §122; MH §66) 366

There a few further types of adverb derivation to be mentioned here:

1. **Combinations involving prepositional elements**:

παρὰ τὸ χρῆμα	*to the matter*	**παρα**χρῆμα	*instantly, at once, "on the spot"*
ἐξ + αἴφνης	*"from suddenly"*	**ἐξ**αίφνης	*suddenly, unexpectedly*

2. **With special suffixes**: **-θεν** ("From where?"), **-σε** ("To where?"; CG), **-θι** ("Where?"; CG):

οὐρανός	*heaven*	οὐρανό**θεν**	*from heaven*
ἐκεῖ	*there*	ἐκεῖ**θεν**	*from there*
		ἐκεῖ**σε**	*to there* (Josephus)
		ἐκεῖ**θι** (≈ ἐκεῖ)	*there* (Josephus)

3. **Adverbs in -α** (mainly occurring in older varieties, less frequently in later ones):

ταχύς (adj.)	*quick*	τάχ**α**	at first *quickly*, later *perhaps*

4. **Adverbs in -εί/-ί and in -τεί/-τί** (the change between ει and ι is without semantic relevance):

πάνδημος	*belonging to all the people*	πανδημ**εί**	*with the whole people* (Josephus)
ἀμάχητος	*not to be fought with*	ἀμαχη**τί**	*without fighting*

-αστί/-ιστί (connected with verbs in -άζω/-ίζω):

ὀνομάζω	*to name*	ὀνομ**αστί**	*by name* (Josephus)
ἑβραΐζω	*to speak Hebrew*	Ἑβρα**ϊστί**	*in Hebrew*

5. **Adverbs in -δην, -δόν** (mainly connected with verbs) **and in -ίνδην, -ίνδα**:

αἴρω (ἀρ-)	*to lift*	ἄρ**δην**	*on high* (Josephus)
ἔσχον of	ἔχω *to have/hold*	σχε**δόν**	*nearly* ("holding o.s. close")
πλοῦτος	*wealth*	πλουτ**ίνδην**	*according to wealth* (Plutarch)
βασιλεύς	*king*	βασιλ**ίνδα**	*playing the royal game* (Pollux)

3 Compounding

(i) Compound nouns and adjectives

367 Compound nouns and adjectives classified by form

(↑BR §306; MB: W417ff; BDF §115ff; MH §99ff)

367a 1. **Preliminaries**

a) Compound nouns and adjectives are typically made up of two elements called "**left member**" (or "first member") and "**right member**" (or "second member"), e.g.:

		left member:	right member:
σώ-φρων	*of sound mind*	σω-	-φρων
ψευδο-λόγος	*liar*	ψευδο-	-λογος

b) Compound adjectives are mostly **two-termination adjectives** (↑44d): the same forms are used for both masc. and fem.; this does not usually apply to compound adjectives in -ιος (↑367c), e.g.:

		masc.:	fem.:	ntr.:
σώφρων	*of sound mind*	σώφρων	=	σῶφρον
ἄδικος	*unjust, unfair*	ἄδικος	=	ἄδικον
ἐντόπιος	*local*	ἐντόπιος	ἐντοπία	ἐντόπιον

2. The **left member** may be: 367b

a) The **stem of a noun or an adjective**, e.g.:

μακρο-	(μακρός *long*):	**μακρο**-χρόνιος	*long-time, long-lived*
πολυ-	(πολύς *much/large*):	**πολύ**-σπλαγχνος	*full of compassion*
ναυ-	(ναῦς *ship*):	**ναύ**-κληρος	*ship-owner*

Stems in -ᾱ or consonant stems may be changed or expanded to stems in -ο, e.g.:

μητρο-	(μήτηρ [μητερ-] *mother*; ↑38b):	**μητρό**-πολις	*capital city*
αἱμο-	(αἷμα [αἱματ-] *blood*; ↑35c):	**αἱμο**-βόρος	*bloodthirsty* (4Macc 10:17)

Note that apart from "genuine" compounds there are also "pseudo" ones, so-called "**fusions**":[4] two originally independent words gradually became (were "fused" into) one word, with the left member being not a stem, but a case form, e.g.:

Διόσ-	(gen. of Ζεύς, st. Δι[ϝ]-, *Zeus*):	**Διόσ**-κουροι	*Dioscuri* ("Zeus's sons")
νεά-	(nom. sg. fem. of νεό-ς *new*):	**Νεά**-πολις	*Neapolis* ("new city")

b) The **verb stem** that is expanded by an affix such as -ε-, -σι- or -ο-, e.g. (↑368c):

δει-σι-	(δέδοικα [δοι-/δει-] *to fear*):	**δεισι**-δαίμων	*fearing the gods, devout*

c) A **numeral** (its stem if the numeral is inflected), e.g.:

δωδεκά-	(δώδεκα *twelve*):	**δωδεκά**-φυλος	*of twelve tribes*
τρί-	(τρεῖς/τρία [τρι-] *three*):	**τρί**-μηνος	*of three months*

d) A **prefixed compounding particle**:

ἀ- before consonants, **ἀν-** before vowels, the alpha "**privative**" (occurs frequently): indicating a lack or absence (like English *un-* in ***un**kind* etc., but also *a-/an-* in ***a**typical* or ***an**archy*), e.g.:

ἄ-δικος *unjust, unfair* **ἀν**-όσιος *unholy*

ἁ-, ἀ-, the alpha "**copulative**" (occurs infrequently): indicating oneness or likeness, e.g.:

ἅ-παντες (intensive) *all* **ἀ**-δελφός *brother* (lit. "from one and the same womb [δελφύς]")

δυσ- "bad/difficult/hard" (↑Lat. *di[s]-*; English *dys-* in ***dys**functional* etc.; but the significance of δυσ- is typically stronger than that of English *dys-*), e.g.:

δυσ-ερμήνευτος *hard to explain* **δυσ**-βάστακτος *difficult/hard to carry*

εὐ- "good/well" (↑English *eu-* in ***eu**logy*, ***eu**thanasia* etc.), e.g.:

εὐ-αγγέλιον *good news* **εὔ**-καιρος *timely*

e) A **preposition** or an **adverb**, e.g.:

σύν-δουλος *fellow slave* **παλιγ**-γενεσία (παλιγ-γ... < παλιν-γ...; ↑15b) *renewal*

3. The **right member** may be a noun (in some cases going back to a verb): 367c

a) with an unchanged stem-final sound, sometimes with an o-grade ablaut (↑8), e.g.:

-πους	(πούς, ποδός *foot*):	τετρά-**πους** (-ποδος)	*four-footed*
-πάτωρ	(πατήρ *father*):	προ-**πάτωρ** (-πάτορος)	*forefather, ancestor*

b) with a stem that is changed to a stem in -ο, e.g.:

-τιμος	(τιμή *value, price*):	ἔν-**τιμος**	*valued, honoured*
-ψυχος	(ψυχή *"soul"*):	ἰσό-**ψυχος**	*of like soul/mind*

Derived from such compounds there are also masculine nouns in -ης/-ᾱς, ου, e.g.:

-απάτης, ου	(ἀπάτη *deception/deceitfulness*):	φρεν-**απάτης** (-απάτου)	*deceiver*

c) with a consonant stem that is changed or expanded to a stem in -ο, e.g.:

-υδρος	(ὕδωρ [ὕδατ-] *water*):	ἄν-**υδρος**	*waterless*
-σώματος	(σῶμα [-ματ-] *body*):	φιλο-**σώματος**	*loving the body* (Philo)

---

4 On this term ↑Lieber-Stekauer: 399.

d) with a stem expanded by -ιος (frequently with a prepositional or similar left member; ↑367a), e.g.:
-θαλάσσιος (θάλασσα *sea/lake*): παρα-**θαλάσσιος** *by the sea/lake*
-χρόνιος (χρόνος *time*): ὀλιγο-**χρόνιος** *of short duration* (LXX)

367d 4. **Elision** of the short final vowel of the left member (↑19):

a) The short final vowel of the left member (except for υ) is mostly deleted before a right member with an initial vowel, e.g.:
μέτ- (μετά also *between*, ὤψ *eye*): **μέτ-ω**πον *forehead*
μετα- (μετά *between*, κόσμος *world*): **μετα-κ**όσμιος *between worlds* (Philo)

b) The vowel mostly remains undeleted before a right member with an initial vowel that originally was preceded by a ϝ (↑12a/12b) or a σ (↑13d) that is changed to a stem in -ο, e.g.:
-εργος (ἔργον < ϝεργον *work/deed*): **κακο-ε**ργός (or κακοῦργος) *criminal*

367e 5. **Vowel lengthening** between the members of the compound:

The initial ε- or α- of the right member is often lengthened to η-, the initial ο- to ω-, e.g.:
-ώνυμος (**ὄ**νομα [dialectal: ὄνυμα] *name*): ἀν-**ώ**νυμος *without name* (LXX)

367f 6. **Accentuation** of compounds:

The accent of compounds is mostly **retracted** as far as the accentuation rules allow (↑5b–5d), e.g.:
ἀγαθός *good* φιλ-**ά**γαθος *loving what is good*
φθαρτός *perishable* **ἄ**-φθαρτος *imperishable*

Exceptions:

a) Compounds in -ής (stem -εσ-), e.g.: προσ-φιλής, ές *pleasing, lovely*

b) The following types of verbal rectional compounds (↑368c)
-ποιός active/one but last syllable long εἰρηνο-ποι**ό**ς *peacemaker*
-βόλος active/one but last syllable short χιονο-β**ό**λος *snow-bringing* (Plutarch)
-βολος passive/"normal" tone/stress χιον**ό**-βολος *covered with snow* (Strabo)

368 Compound nouns and adjectives classified by meaning

(↑BR §307; MB: W417–419; BDF §115–123; MH §105–109)

The members of a compound may contribute variously to the meaning of the compound as a whole. The semantic relationship between the two members allows us to distinguish the following meaning-related types of compound nouns and adjectives (on terms used ↑Lieber-Stekauer: 332; 351):

368a 1. **Determinative compounds**

The right member denotes an entity or (if an adjective) a property or the like; the scope of what is denoted is limited by means of the left member which modifies or determines it in various ways, e.g.:

a) **Nouns**:
ἀρχ-**ιερεύς** (≈ μέγας ἱερεύς) *a high/chief priest* = "a priest, i.e. a hight/the highest one"
ψευδό-**χριστος** *a false messiah* = "a 'messiah', but a false one"
σύν-**δουλος** *a fellow slave* = "a slave, who is a slave alongside another/others"

b) **Adjectives**:
ἀν-**άξιος** *unworthy* = "not worthy"
παν-**άγιος** *all-holy* = "most holy" (4Macc 7:4; 14:7)

Note that while in English determinative compounds abound, in Ancient Greek they occur only rarely.

2. **Possessive compounds** 368b

This is really a subtype of the type just mentioned, its peculiarity being as follows: the compound as a whole denotes something that another entity "possesses" so to speak, i.e. characterizes it, e.g. (mostly adjectives, but these may be nominalized):

τετρά-**πους** (↑367c)	*four-footed* = (of an animal) "having four feet"
χρυσο-**δακτύλιος** (↑367c)	*with a gold ring* = "having/wearing a gold ring"
ἰσό-**ψυχος** (↑367c)	*like-minded* = "having the same mind"
εὐ-**ειδής** (↑367b)	*well-formed* = "having good appearance"
πρό-**θυμος** (↑367c)	*willing* = (of a person) "having the necessary determination"

Note that this subtype is widely used in Ancient Greek.

3. **Verbal rectional compounds** 368c

Here either of the two members is connected with a verb or "verbal" (↑367b/367c), having a function similar to that of a participle. The other member indicates the entity that is targeted by the "action" (or experiences it: the patient; ↑Od), the entity performing it (the agent; ↑S) or certain of its circumstances (↑adverbial; ↑254):

a) The left member is verbal (↑367b), e.g.:

δεισι-δαίμων (δέδοικα; ↑367b)	*religious, devout* = "fearing the gods (Od)"
φιλ-άργυρος (φιλέω)	*fond of money* = "loving money (Od)"
φιλό-τεκνος	*with love for [one's] child/children* = "loving child/children (Od)"

b) The right member is verbal (↑367c), e.g.:

(1) right member in -ος with o-grade ablaut – left member: a noun (on relevance of accent ↑367f), e.g.:

ψευδο-**λόγος** (λέγω)	*liar* = "one telling a lie (ψεῦδος Od)"
οἰκο-**δόμος** (δέμω *to build*)	*builder* = "one building a house (οἶκον Od)"
καρπο-**φόρος** (φέρω)	*fruitful* = "one bearing fruit (καρπόν Od)"
πρωτό-**τοκος** (τίκτω/ἔτεκον)	*firstborn* = "one who was born first (πρῶτος TempA)"

(2) right member in -ος with o-grade ablaut – left member: an adverb or preposition, e.g.:

ἐπί-**σκοπος** (σκέπτομαι [σκεπ-])	*overseer/guardian* = "one examining/looking after sth./s.o."
πρό-**δρομος** (τρέχω/ἔδραμον)	*forerunner* = "one going/running before/ahead"

(3) right member in -ος without ablaut, otherwise like types 1 and 2, e.g.:

σκηνο-**ποιός** (ποιέω)	*tentmaker* = "one making tents (σκηνάς)"
χλοη-**φάγος** (ἐσθίω/ἔφαγον)	*herbivorous* = "(animal) eating [only] plants (χλοήν)" (Philo)

(4) right member in -ης (-ᾱς); active force; the accent is retracted; mostly with verbs -άω/-έω, e.g.:

τελ-**ών**ης -ου (ὠνέομαι)	*tax collector* = "one purchasing/leasing tolls/taxes (τέλος)"

(5) right member has an -εσ-stem (↑45b), mostly middle or passive force; last syllable accented; e.g.:

ἀ-**κλιν**ής -ές (κλίνω)	*unswerving* = "without bending/not allowing o.s. to move away"
ἐκ-**τεν**ής -ές (τείνω [τεν-])	*eager/earnest* = "stretching (o.s.) out"

(6) right member is an agent noun in -της (↑362a); the accent is retracted, e.g.:

ἐπ-**όπ**της (ὁράω/ὄψομαι)	*eyewitness* = "one who keeps/kept an eye on it"
πλεον-**έκ**της (ἔχω)	*greedy* = "one who claims more (πλέον) than his due"
πρωτο-**στά**της (ἵσταμαι)	*ringleader* = "one who stands first (πρῶτος)"

(7) right member is a verbal adjective in -τος (↑360a), e.g.:

σητό-**βρωτος** (ἐσθίω/βέβρωκα)	*moth-eaten* (≈ ὑπὸ σητῶν [σής σητός] βεβρωμένος)
θεο-**δίδακτος** (διδάσκω)	*taught by God* (≈ ὑπὸ θεοῦ δεδιδαγμένος)
χειρο-**ποίητος** (ποιέω)	*made by human hand* (≈ χειρὶ [ἀνθρώπου] πεποιημένος)
ἀ-**όρατος** (ὁράω)	*invisible*

368d 4. **Prepositional rectional compounds**

Adjectives or nouns in -ος/ον (often -ιος, then mostly three-termination adjectives; (↑367a/367c). Background to each of these is a preposition phrase: the preposition serves as left member, while the noun governed by it (↑22i) leads to the right member of the compound:

πρόσ-καιρος	*short-lived* = "lasting for a (limited) time (πρὸς καιρόν)"
ὕπ-ανδρος	(of a woman) *married* = "being under a husband (ὑπὸ ἄνδρα)"
παρα-θαλάσσιος	*by the sea/lake* = "being by the sea/lake (παρὰ τῇ θαλάσσῃ)"

Note that compounds with a prepositional left member and a noun as a right member may belong to different types, e.g.:

ἔν-υδρος	*living in the water* (ἐν τοῖς ὕδασιν) (LXX) → prepositional rectional compound (↑above)
ἔν-θεος	*full of god/God* = "having god/God (θεόν) in o.s. (ἐν ἑαυτῷ)" → possessive compound (↑368b)

(ii) Compound verbs

369 Compound verbs with prepositional prefixes (↑BR §308.1; BDF §116.4; MH §109–129)

This is the only type of direct formation of compound verbs; it, however, occurs very frequently: one or more prepositional prefixes ("preverbs"; ↑183; 186) function as left member(s); e.g.:

κατ-αγγέλλω	*to announce*	**προ-κατ**-αγγέλλω	*to announce beforehand*

370 Other types of compound verbs (↑BR §308.2; BDF §119; MH §161)

When a new verb was to be created by means of an existing verb plus a noun (or particle), as first step a compound noun or adjective would be formed, more precisely a verbal rectional compound (↑368c). This then served as the base from which the desired verb would be derived (↑363), e.g.:

οἶκος *house*	+ δέμω *to build*	→ οἰκο-δόμος *builder*	→ οἰκοδομέω *to build (up)*
εὖ *well*	+ λέγω *to speak*	→ εὔ-λογος *sounding well*	→ εὐλογέω *to praise/bless*
λίθος *stone*	+ βάλλω *to throw*	→ λιθο-βόλος *stone throwing*	→ λιθοβολέω *to stone*
θεός *God*	+ μάχομαι *to fight*	→ θεό-μαχος *fighting against God*	→ θεομαχέω *to fight against God*

Alphabetic list of word-formation elements 371

Selective bibliography

Note that this is a selective bibliography, not in any way meant to provide an exhaustive list of scholarly contributions relevant to the study of Ancient Greek grammar. Its main objective is to inform about the titles used in producing the present grammar and (particularly in the systematic guide) to indicate a selection of titles that are considered especially useful.

1 A systematic bibliographical guide

For bibliographical details ↑alphabetical list p. 680ff.

1.1 Texts

1.1.1 Editions

a) Greek New Testament

- Nestle-Aland ("NA"; 28th ed.): standard concise edition.
- Greek New Testament ("UBSGNT"; 5th ed.): the text corresponds to NA; restricted to variants that are translationally relevant; textual apparatus more accessible; English subheadings.
- SBL-edition: independent of NA; very simple apparatus (referring to secondary sources only).
- Greek New Testament produced at Tyndale House Cambridge ("THGNT"): most recent edition (thorough revision of the 19th century edition of S.R. Tregelles); short, but adequate apparatus.
- Editio Critica Maior: standard major edition for detailed work with a freshly established text and a comprehensive apparatus (so far available: Letters of James, Peter, John, and Jude as well as Acts).
- Robinson-Pierpont: edition of the Byzantine Majority text.

b) Septuagint

- Rahlfs-Hanhart: standard concise edition.
- Göttingen Septuagint: standard major edition for detailed work (so far most the LXX books are covered, but not as yet those corresponding to Joshua, Judges, 1/2Samuel, 1/2Kings).

c) Extra-biblical texts

- Thesaurus Linguae Graecae: most comprehensive digital library of Greek texts.
- Perseus Project: fairly large digital library of Ancient Greek texts (linked with reference works and translations).
- Accordance, Logos, and BibleWorks: inter alia for "Apostolic Fathers", Josephus and Philo.

Also ↑BNP (or Kleiner Pauly and LAW) under authors' names for further information on available editions. For Church Fathers also ↑Lampe.

1.1.2 Textual research

a) Greek New Testament

- Aland-Aland 1995: one leading introduction.
- Metzger 2005: international standard introduction.
- Wegner: useful recent introduction for students.
- Black 2002: leading approaches to textual criticisms are compared.
- Metzger 1994: commentary on the most important decisions by the editors of the UBSGNT.

b) Septuagint

- Fernández Marcos: comprehensive introduction.

- Kenyon-Adams: on the of the Greek Bible including the Septuagint.
- Tov: standard on the Hebrew Bible with a useful treatment of the Septuagint.
- Jobes-Silva: introduction to Septuagint studies including textual criticism.

c) EXTRA-BIBLICAL TEXTS

- Pöhlmann (also BNP sub "Textual history"): important introduction.

Also ↑OCD sub "scholarship, classical, history of".

1.1.3 Concordances and comparable tools

a) GREEK NEW TESTAMENT

- Bachmann-Slaby: standard printed concordance to NA 26th ed. and UBSGNT 3rd ed.
- Moulton-Geden 2002: most useful printed concordance (to NA 27th ed. and UBSGNT 4th ed.).
- Schmoller: useful pocket concordance (9th edition based on NA 28th ed. and UBSGNT 5th ed.).
- Aland 1978/1983: most detailed concordance based on various editions; a companion volume contains statistics and other compilations.

b) SEPTUAGINT

- Hatch-Redpath: standard printed Septuagint concordance.

Also ↑Accordance, Logos, and BibleWorks, which have largely replaced printed concordances, also permitting linguistic searches in extra-biblical texts such as the "Apostolic Fathers", Josephus and Philo.

c) EXTRA-BIBLICAL TEXTS

- Thesaurus Linguae Graecae: its powerful search machine permits extensive searches.

For printed concordances also ↑BNP bibliographies under authors' names".

1.2 Linguistics

1.2.1 Ancient Greek

a) COMPREHENSIVE GRAMMARS

(1) *New Testament*

- Blass-Debrunner-Rehkopf ("BDR"): standard scholarly grammar for detailed work (but parts of it are in need of revision, especially regarding the syntax of the verb).
- Blass-Debrunner-Funk ("BDF"): translation of the 1959 edition of Blass-Debrunner.
- Zerwick: useful treatment of many parts of special relevance to text interpretation.
- Moulton-Howard ("MH") and Turner 1963/1976: most comprehensive scholarly NT grammar (note that MH is the more important part).
- Robertson: comprehensive historical grammar with many useful hints for solid exegesis.
- Siebenthal 2013: concise grammar for learners and exegetes in German.

(2) *Septuagint*

- Thackeray: thorough grammar (though incomplete; the syntax volume never appeared).
- Conybeare-Stock: useful concise grammar.

(3) *Ancient Greek in general*

- Bornemann-Risch ("BR"): standard grammar of Classical Greek for Classics students in German; contains a brief grammar of the Homeric language.
- Boas-Rijksbaron: new comprehensive grammar of Classical Greek (it appeared too late to be taken into account in the present grammar).
- Meier-Brügger 1992 ("MB"): standard introduction to the study of Ancient Greek in German.

• Bakker ("CAGL"): recent introduction to the most important areas of study of the Greek language by an international team of thirty-nine specialists.
• Schwyzer: standard historical grammar of Greek in German (parts of it are in need of revision).
• Kühner-Blass/Kühner-Gerth: comprehensive (descriptive) grammar of Ancient Greek in German.
• Smyth: useful comprehensive school grammar with many examples translated into English.
• Mayser: grammar of Early Koine Greek in German.
• Gignac: grammar of Late Koine Greek.

b) PHONOLOGY

• Lejeune: important treatment of Ancient Greek phonology in French.
• Allen: standard treatment of the sound system of Classical Greek.
• Horrocks: comprehensive treatment inter alia of sound changes from Early Ancient to Modern Greek (of great relevance to dealing with the sounds of New Testament Greek).

Also ↑titles mentioned above under a), especially
• Bornemann-Risch and Meier-Brügger 1992, supplemented by BDR/BDF and Horrocks.

c) MORPHOLOGY

• Chantraine 1961: important historical treatment of Ancient Greek morphology in French.
• Duhoux: comprehensive treatment of the Ancient Greek verb morphology in French.

Also ↑titles mentioned above under a), especially
• Bornemann-Risch and Meier-Brügger 1992, supplemented by BDR/BDF.

d) WORD-FORMATION

↑titles mentioned above under a), especially
• Bornemann-Risch and Meier-Brügger 1992, supplemented by MH and BDR/BDF, also by
• Greenlee: the words attested in the NT and other early Christian literature (↑BDAG) are broken down into their grammatical components and listed alphabetically, in part 1 according to word-initial sounds, in part 2 according to the initial sound of components.
• Jacques: Septuagint words arranged in word families.
• Chantraine 1999: comprehensive etymological dictionary of Greek in French.
• Frisk: slightly less comprehensive etymological dictionary of Greek in German.
• Beekes: most recent etymological dictionary of Greek.

e) SYNTAX

• Humbert: important syntax of Ancient Greek in French.
• Adrados 1992: detailed modern syntax of Classical Greek in Spanish.
• Duhoux: comprehensive treatment of Ancient Greek verb syntax (including aspects) in French.

Also ↑titles mentioned above under a), on NT syntax especially
• BDR/BDF and Zerwick (all partly in need of revision, especially regarding aspects); also:
• Wallace 1996: comprehensive treatment with a special focus on typical problems of exegesis.
• Porter 1992: informative treatment of many important areas of syntax (but with a partly problematic aspect theory; ↑193a).

On the syntax of aspects, tenses, moods, and non-finite verb forms in the NT ↑also
• Campbell 2007/2008a/b: thorough treatment with many examples (useful also for its information on the history of research and its bibliographies; but ↑193a and 202[50] on partly problematic views).
• Runge/Fresch 2016: groundbreaking contributions by leading specialists.
• Burton: rather dated, but still worth consulting for its useful comments on many NT passages.

On the interpretation of prepositions in NT exegesis ↑also
• Harris: very competent treatment of theologically relevant prepositions used in the NT.

Furthermore ↑especially

• Bornemann-Risch and Meier-Brügger 1992, also
• Langslow-Wackernagel: English version of a highly influential treatment of Greek, Latin, and Germanic syntax by a leading Indo-European scholar of the late 19th and early 20th century, still worth paying close attention.
• Sommer: concise comparative treatment of German, English, French, Greek and Latin syntax in German by a prominent Indo-European scholar of the first half of the 20th century.

f) STYLISTIC DEVICES OR "FIGURES OF SPEECH" (↑291a)
• Bullinger: a comprehensive classic on the "figures of speech".
• Bühlmann-Scherer: concise reference work in German on the "figures of speech" in the Bible (OT/NT) with a wealth of bibliographical information and many references to extra-biblical Greek.
On the "figures of speech" used in the NT ↑inter alia also
• BDR/BDF and the references found in 291–296.
On questions of the NT style of language (↑p.5) apart from Turner 1976 ↑especially Reiser 2001.

g) LEXICAL SEMANTICS
• Murphy: one of today's standard treatment of general lexical semantics.
• Leisi 1975 and Leisi 1985: very useful treatments in German of general relevance.
• Barr: pioneering application of findings of general lexical semantics to Biblical studies.
• Cotterell-Turner: useful introduction to semantics for exegetes.
• Louw-Nida: in the introduction to the lexicon we are told in a straightforward way how word meanings are used in linguistic communication and how this should impact text interpretation.
• Silva 1994/2014: excellent introductions to lexical semantics for exegetes.
• Siebenthal 2000: presentation in German of important principles for dealing with word meanings.

h) TEXTGRAMMAR (↑p.569ff)
• Duden Grammatik 9th ed. ("DuG9"): contains a detailed textgrammar in German by T. A. Fritz (textlinguistics specialist), methodologically relevant to Ancient Greek texts, too.
• Gansel-Jürgens: important introduction in German to textlinguistics/textgrammar.
• Porter 2015: deals competently with many issues of textlinguistics/textgrammar relevant to exegesis.
• Cotterell-Turner: contains also a useful treatment of textgrammatical matters relevant to exegesis.
• Callow: introduction to a recommendable approach to textsemantic analysis.
• Runge: competent introduction to the practice of text/discourse analysis for exegetes (only marginally taken into account as yet in the present grammar).

i) PECULIARITIES AND CLASSIFICATION OF NEW TESTAMENT GREEK
(1) *Deviations from Classical Greek*
• BDR/BDF §1–7.
• Debrunner-Scherer: a brief overview in German of the characteristics of post-classical Greek.
↑also references on p.637.

(2) *On Semitisms (or Septuagintisms)*
In addition to the titles mentioned above under (1) also ↑inter alia:
• Moulton-Howard Vol. II: 411–485: detailed treatment of the "Semitisms" in the NT.
• Moule: has a useful chapter on "Semitisms".
• Black 1967: an influential work on the Aramaic background to the Gospels and Acts; however, in many respects its claims are in need of revision in the light of findings such as those of
• Reiser 1984/2001: demonstrates (in German) that most "Semitisms" are probably Septuagintisms (mainly affecting a number of religious and theological expressions and certain idioms).

(3) *Classification of New Testaments Greek*
In addition to the titles mentioned above under (1) also ↑inter alia:

• Horrocks: his detailed history of the Greek language also deals with the classification of NT (and LXX) Greek.
• Reiser 2001: a particularly competent treatment of this subject in German.
• Kittel: an appendix included in Vol. 10 deals with this subject as part of a historical overview of New Testament lexicography accompanied by important bibliographical references.

j) LEXICONS

(1) *New Testament*
• Bauer-Danker-Arndt-Gingrich ("BDAG"): international standard lexicon.
• Louw-Nida: based on modern lexicographical insights, word meanings are stated in terms of explicit definitions (rather than mere translational equivalents), those with related meanings being contrasted within semantic domains; although it largely lacks bibliographical references, it is a very useful supplement to BDAG.
• Abbott-Smith: moderately sized dictionary competently written (in the early 20th century, but still being mostly up-to-date), informing about etymological connections, LXX usage (with Hebrew "equivalents"), and differences between NT and extra-biblical usage; useful supplement to BDAG.
• Danker: probably best concise lexicon written by the final editor of BDAG.
• Moulton-Milligan: important collection of examples drawn from Hellenistic papyri and other non-literary sources relevant to NT word usage.

Especially when dealing with details of theological exegesis also ↑the following titles:
• Kittel: classic treatment of NT words considered theologically relevant in ten volumes (on linguistic flaws found especially in volumes 1–7 ↑Barr and introduction to Silva 2014).
• Balz-Schneider: three volumes in the tradition of Kittel (but attempting to avoid its flaws).
• Brown: smaller useful alternative to "Kittel" in four volumes (↑Verbrugge for an abridgement).
• Silva 2014: now largely replaces Brown due to a thorough revision by a leading semanticist (his introduction to the work deserves to be studied carefully by anyone involved in text interpretation).

(2) *Septuagint*
• Lust-Eynikel-Hauspie: one of today's standard lexicons.
• Muraoka: the standard lexicon (produced by a leading specialist whose approach differs somewhat from the one adopted by Lust-Eynikel-Hauspie).
• Schleusner: a substantial five-volume Greek-Latin lexicon produced in the early 19th century.

(3) *Ancient Greek in general*
• Liddell-Scott-Jones: still international standard lexicon of Ancient Greek.
• Montanari: excellent new lexicon of Ancient Greek likely to become a standard tool.
• Adrados Diccionario: a massive lexical project of Ancient Greek in Spanish with seven regular volumes published so far (reaching ἔξαυος *very dry*); may be consulted online.
• Lampe: supplement to Liddell-Scott-Jones on the special vocabulary of the Greek Church Fathers.
• Sophocles: an older specialized lexicon covering the time from 146 B.C. to A.D. 1100.

For further specialized lexicons ↑BNP bibliographies under authors' names".

1.2.2 *Ancient Hebrew and Aramaic*

a) GRAMMARS

• Gesenius-Kautzsch-Cowley ("GKC"): formerly standard grammar of Biblical Hebrew (parts of it are now in need of revision).
• Joüon-Muraoka: today's international standard grammar of Biblical Hebrew.
• Rosenthal: standard grammar of Biblical Aramaic.
• Bauer-Leander: detailed historical grammar of Biblical Aramaic in German.
• Segert: comprehensive grammar of Ancient Aramaic in German.
• Dalman 1905: older standard grammar of Jewish Palestinian Aramaic.

b) LEXICONS

- Koehler-Baumgartner ("HALOT"): today's standard lexicon of Biblical Hebrew and Aramaic.
- Brown-Driver-Briggs: older standard lexicon of Biblical Hebrew and Aramaic, still worth consulting.
- Clines: a very informative modern lexicon of Classical Hebrew.
- Jastrow: important lexicon of post-Biblical Hebrew and Aramaic used in Judaic literature.

1.3 Tools for learners

1.3.1 Textbooks and other learning aids

- Whittaker: excellent textbook for learning NT Greek.
- Mounce: one of the most popular textbooks for learning NT Greek.
- Metzger 1998: valued "Lexical Aids for Students of New Testament Greek".
- Mastronade: comprehensive textbook for learning Classical Greek.

1.3.2 Aids for reading and basic text interpretation

- Zerwick-Grosvenor: high-quality linguistic companion for readers of the Greek NT.
- Haubeck-von Siebenthal: a comparable tool in German with a more extended focus on syntax.
- Greek New Testament. A Reader's Edition (UBSGNT): contains an excellent running Greek-English dictionary (parsing of verb forms included).
- Septuaginta. A Reader's Edition: offers the same for the Rahlfs-Hanhart edition.

For the NT ↑also lexicons mentioned further above, especially Danker.

For other Ancient Greek texts ↑Perseus Project, for Josephus, Philo, and the "Apostolic Fathers" also Accordance, Logos, and BibleWorks (including the NETS for the Septuagint).

1.4 Bibliographical aids

- New Testament Abstracts: abstracts and book notices regarding NT Greek are included in this standard resource regularly informing about new publications on NT and related research.
- L'Année philologique: regularly informs about new publications on Classical philology.

1.5 Digital resources

Many of the older publications referred to above are freely accessible in digital form via internet. Most of the more recent ones are accessible as well, but in many cases only against payment of a fee (e.g. to have unlimited access to the Thesaurus Linguae Graecae). Using one of the standard Bible programs seems to be indispensable as modules of many (though by all means not all) of the resources for studying Ancient Greek are included or may be added: Accordance, Logos, or BibleWorks.

A great variety of useful links are accessible inter alia at the following websites:

- http://www.tyndale.cam.ac.uk/ (focus on Bible-related matters).
- http://stephanus.tlg.uci.edu/ (focus on extra-biblical Greek).

2 An alphabetical list of titles

Aarts, Bas (2011) *Oxford Modern English Grammar*. Oxford: Oxford University Press.

Abbott-Smith, George (1937) *A Manual Greek Lexicon of the New Testament*. 3rd ed. Edinburgh: Clark.

Accordance 12 (2018) *Bible Study Software*. Altamonte Springs/Florida: Oaktree Software.

Adrados, Francisco R. (1992) *Nueva sintaxis del griego antiguo*. Madrid: Gredos.

Adrados, Francisco R. (2005) *A history of the Greek language: from its origins to the present*. Leiden: Brill.
Adrados, Francisco R. et al. (1980–2009) *Diccionario Griego-Español (DGE)*. Vol. 1–7 (α–ἔξαυος). Madrid: CSIC.
Akmajian, Adrian et al. (2001) *Linguistics. An Introduction to Language and Communication*. 5th ed. Cambridge/Mass.: MIT.
Aland, Kurt and Barbara Aland (1995) *The Text of the New Testament: An Introduction to the Critical Editions and to the Theory and Practice of Modern Textual Criticism*. 2nd rev. ed. Grand Rapids: Eerdmans.
Aland, Kurt et al. (1978/1983) *Vollständige Konkordanz zum griechischen Neuen Testament unter Zugrundelegung aller modernen kritischen Textausgaben und des Textus Receptus,* in 2 vols., plus *Begleitband mit Spezialübersichten*. Berlin: de Gruyter.
Allen, W. Sidney (1987) *Vox Graeca. A Guide to the Pronunciation of Classical Greek*. 3rd ed. Cambridge: University Press.
Allen, Joseph Henry and James Bradstreet Greenough (1903) *New Latin Grammar*. Boston/London: Athenæum Press.
Altmann, Hans and Suzan Hahnemann (2007) *Syntax fürs Examen. Studien- und Arbeitsbuch*. 3rd ed. Göttingen: Vandenhoeck & Ruprecht.
Anderson, John R. (1980) *Cognitive Psychology and Its Implication*. 1st ed. San Francisco: Freeman.
L'Année philologique, published by SIBC (Société internationale de bibliographie classique).
Bachmann, Horst, Wolfgang A. Slaby et al. (1987) *Concordance to the Novum Testamentum Graece of Nestle-Aland, 26th edition, and to the Greek New Testament, 3rd edition*. Berlin: de Gruyter.
Bakker, Egbert J. et al. (2010) ["CAGL"] *A Companion to the Ancient Greek Language*. Oxford: Wiley-Blackwell.
Baldick, Chris (2015) *The Oxford Dictionary of Literary Terms*. 4th ed. Oxford: University Press.
Balz, Horst and Gerhard Schneider (eds.) (2011) *Exegetical Dictionary of the New Testament*. 3 vols. Grand Rapids: Eerdmans.
Banker, John (1996) *A Semantic and Structural Analysis of Philippians*. Dallas: SIL.
Barr, James (1961) *The Semantics of Biblical Language*. Oxford: University Press.
Bauer, Walter, William F. Arndt, Wilbur Gingrich, and Frederick W. Danker (2000) ["BDAG"] *A Greek-English Lexicon of the New Testament and Other Early Christian Literature*. 3rd ed. Chicago: University Press.
Bauer, Hans and Pontus Leander (1927) *Grammatik des Biblisch-Aramäischen*. Halle: Niemeyer.
Baum, Armin D. (2017) *Einleitung in das Neue Testament: Evangelien und Apostelgeschichte*. Giessen: Brunnen.
Beekes, Robert (2010) *Etymological Dictionary of Greek*. 2 vols., Leiden: Brill.
Beyer, Klaus (1997/2004) *Die aramäischen Texte vom Toten Meer*. 2 vols. (Vol. 1: 2nd ed.) Göttingen: Vandenhoeck & Ruprecht.
BibleWorks 10 (2015) *Software for Biblical Exegesis and Research*. Norfolk: BibleWorks LLC.
Biblia Hebraica Stuttgartensia (1967/1977) Karl Elliger, Wilhelm Rudolph et al. Stuttgart: Deutsche Bibelgesellschaft.
Black, David A. et al. (2002) *Rethinking New Testament Textual Criticism*. Grand Rapids: Baker.
Black, Matthew (1967) *An Aramaic Approach to the Gospels and Acts*. 3rd ed. Oxford: University Press.
Blass, Friedrich, Albert Debrunner and Friedrich Rehkopf (2001) ["BDR"] *Grammatik des neutestamentlichen Griechisch*. 18th ed. Göttingen: Vandenhoeck & Ruprecht.
Blass, Friedrich and Albert Debrunner, translated by Robert E. Funk (1961) ["BDF"] *A Greek Grammar of the New Testament and Other Early Christian Literature*. Chicago: University Press.
Boas, Evert van Emde, Albert Rijksbaron et al. (2019) *The Cambridge Grammar of Classical Greek*. Cambridge: University Press.

Bornemann, Eduard and Ernst Risch (1978) ["BR"] *Griechische Grammatik.* 2nd ed. Frankfurt a. M.: Diesterweg.

Brill's New Pauly (2011) ["BNP"] Cancik, Hubert et al. (1996–2007). English edition: Salazar, Christine F. et al. *Encyclopedia of the Ancient World.* Leiden: Brill.

Brinker, Klaus (2001) *Linguistische Textanalyse. Eine Einführung in Grundbegriffe und Methoden.* 5th ed. Berlin: Schmidt.

Brooks, James A. and Carlton L. Winbery (1979) *Syntax of New Testament Greek.* Boston: Lanham.

Brown, Colin et al. (1986) *The New International Dictionary of New Testament Theology.* 4 vols. Grand Rapids: Zondervan.

Brown, Francis, Samuel R. Driver, and Charles A. Briggs (1906) *Hebrew and English Lexicon. With an appendix containing the Biblical Aramaic.* Oxford: University Press.

Brugmann, Karl and Albert Thumb (1913) *Griechische Grammatik.* 4th ed. Munich: Beck.

Bühlmann, Walter and Karl Scherer (1994) *Sprachliche Stilfiguren der Bibel. Von Assonanz bis Zahlenspruch. Ein Nachschlagewerk.* 2nd ed. Giessen: Brunnen.

Bullinger, Ethelbert W. (1898) *Figures of Speech used in the Bible.* London: Eyre & Spottiswoode.

Burton, Ernest D. W. (1898) *Syntax of the Moods and Tenses in New Testament Greek.* 3rd ed. Edinburgh: Clark.

Bussmann, Hadumod et al. (1996) *Routledge Dictionary of Language and Linguistics.* London: Routledge.

Callow, Kathleen (1998) *Man and Message. A Guide to Meaning-Based Text Analysis.* Lanham: University Press of America.

Campbell, Constantine R. (2007) *Verbal Aspect, the Indicative Mood, and Narrative.* New York: Lang.

Campbell, Constantine R. (2008a) *Verbal Aspect and Non-Indicative Verbs.* New York: Lang.

Campbell, Constantine R. (2008b) *Basics of Verbal Aspect in Biblical Greek.* Grand Rapids: Zondervan.

Carter, Ronald and Michael McCarthy (2006) *Cambridge Grammar of English.* Cambridge: University Press.

Chantraine, Pierre (1961) *Morphologie historique du grec.* 2nd ed. Paris: Klincksieck.

Chantraine, Pierre (1999) *Dictionnaire étymologique de la langue grecque.* 2nd ed. Paris: Klincksieck.

Clines, David J. A. (2009) *Concise Dictionary of Classical Hebrew.* Sheffield: Phoenix Press.

Comrie, Bernard (1985) *Tense.* Cambridge: University Press.

Concise Oxford English Dictionary (2011) 12th ed. Oxford: University Press.

Conybeare, Frederick. C. and St. George W. J. Stock (1905) A Grammar of Septuagint Greek. In: *Selections from the Septuagint.* Boston/Mass.: Ginn.

Cotterell, Peter and Max Turner (1989) *Linguistics and Biblical Interpretation.* London: SPCK.

Crystal, David (2008) *A Dictionary of Linguistics and Phonetics.* 6th ed. Oxford: Blackwell.

Dalman, Gustaf (1905) *Grammatik des jüdisch-palästinischen Aramäisch.* 2nd ed. Leipzig: Hinrichs.

Danker, Frederick W. (2009) *The Concise Greek-English Lexicon of the New Testament.* Chicago: University Press.

Debrunner, Albert and Anton Scherer (1969) *Geschichte der griechischen Sprache. Band II: Grundfragen und Grundzüge des nachklassischen Griechisch.* 2nd ed. Berlin: de Gruyter.

Delitzsch, Franz (1888) הברית החדשה *Delitzsch's Hebrew New Testament.* London: British and Foreign Bible Society.

Denniston, John D. (1954) *The Greek Particles.* 2nd ed. Oxford: University Press.

Dover, K. J. (1960) *Greek Word Order.* Cambridge: University Press.

Duden. Grammatik der deutschen Gegenwartssprache (1973) ["DuG3"] Paul Grebe et al. (eds.) 3rd ed. Mannheim: Bibliographisches Institut.

Duden. Grammatik der deutschen Gegenwartssprache (1984) ["DuG4"] Günther Drosdowski et al. (eds.) 4th ed. Mannheim: Bibliographisches Institut.

Duden. Grammatik (2009) ["DuG8"] Dudenredaktion (eds.). 8th ed. Mannheim: Dudenverlag.

Duden. Grammatik (2016) ["DuG9"] Dudenredaktion (eds.). 9th ed. Berlin: Dudenverlag.

Duhoux, Yves (2000) *Le verbe grec ancien. Éléments de morphologie et de syntaxe historiques.* 2nd ed. Louvain-La-Neuve: Peeters.

Editio Critica Maior ["ECM"], Institut für Neutestamentliche Textforschung (1997–2017) *Novum Testamentum Graecum. Editio Critica Maior.* Vol. III (Acts). Vol. IV. (Catholic Letters). Stuttgart: Deutsche Bibelgesellschaft.

English Standard Version (2016) ["ESV"] *The Holy Bible. English Standard Version.* Wheaton: Crossway.

Esser, Jürgen (2009) *Introduction to English Text-linguistics.* Frankfurt a. M.: Lang.

Fanning, Buist M. (1991) *Verbal Aspect in New Testament Greek.* Oxford: University Press.

Fernández Marcos, Natalio (2009) *The Septuagint in Context: Introduction to the Greek Version of the Bible.* Atlanta: Society of Biblical Literature.

Frisk, Hjalmar (1960–1970) *Griechisches etymologisches Wörterbuch.* 2 vols. Heidelberg: Winter.

Fortson, Benjamin W. (2010) *Indo-European Language and Culture.* 2nd ed. Oxford: Wiley-Blackwell.

Funk, Robert W. (1977) *A Beginning-Intermediate Grammar of Hellenistic Greek.* 3 vols. 2nd ed. Missoula: SP.

Gansel, Christina and Frank Jürgens (2009) ["GaJü"] *Textlinguistik und Textgrammatik.* 3rd ed. Göttingen: Vandenhoeck & Ruprecht.

Gesenius, Wilhelm, Emil Kautzsch, and Arthur E. Cowley (1910) ["GKC"] *Gesenius' Hebrew Grammar.* 2nd ed. rev. (in accordance with the 28th German ed.). Oxford: University Press.

Gignac, Francis T. (1976/1981) *A Grammar of the Greek Papyri of the Roman and Byzantine Periods.* Vol. I: *Phonology*/Vol. II: *Morphology.* Milano: Editoriale Cisalpino – La Goliardica.

Giannakis, Georgios K. et al. (2013) ["EAGLL"] *Encyclopedia of Ancient Greek Language and Linguistics.* 3 vols. Leiden: Brill.

Givón, Talmy (1993) *English Grammar.* Vol. I/II. Amsterdam: Benjamins.

Givón, Talmy (2001) ["Givón"] *Syntax.* Vol. I/II. Amsterdam: Benjamins.

Goodrich, Richard J. and Albert L. Lukaszewiski (2015) *A Reader's Greek New Testament: Third edition.* Grand Rapids: Zondervan.

Göttingen Septuagint (1931–) *Septuaginta Vetus Testamentum Graecum: Auctoritate Academiae Scientiarum Gottingensis editum* (so far 24 vols.). Göttingen: Vandenhoeck & Ruprecht.

Greek New Testament ["UBSGNT"], Institute for New Testament Textual Research (2015) *The Greek New Testament.* 5th ed. [UBS 5] Stuttgart: Deutsche Bibelgesellschaft.

The Greek New Testament. A Reader's Edition (2014) The Text of UBS 5. Plus a Running Greek-English Dictionary and Textual Notes. Stuttgart: Deutsche Bibelgesellschaft.

Greek New Testament produced at Tyndale House Cambridge ["THGNT"]: Jongkind, Dirk et al. (2017) *The Greek New Testament.* Wheaton: Crossway/Cambridge: University Press.

Greenlee, J. Harold (1983) *A New Testament Greek Morpheme Lexicon.* Grand Rapids: Zondervan.

Grice, Paul (1989) Logic and Conversation, In: Paul Grice: *Studies in the Way of Words.* Cambridge, Mass.: Harvard University Press: 22–40.

Haarmann, Harald (1991) *Universalgeschichte der Schrift.* 2nd ed. Frankfurt a. M.: Campus.

Harris, Murray J. (2012) *Prepositions and Theology in the Greek New Testament.* Grand Rapids: Zondervan.

Hatch, Edwin and Henry A. Redpath (1897) *A Concordance to the Septuagint and the Other Greek Versions of the Old Testament (Including the Apocryphal Books).* 2 vols. Oxford: University Press.

Hatzidakis, George N. (1892) *Einleitung in die neugriechische Grammatik.* Leipzig: Breitkopf & Härtel.

Haubeck, Wilfrid and Heinrich von Siebenthal (2011) *Neuer sprachlicher Schlüssel zum griechischen Neuen Testament. Matthäus – Offenbarung.* 3rd ed. Giessen: Brunnen.

Helbing, Robert (1907) *Grammatik der Septuaginta. Laut- und Wortlehre.* Göttingen: Vandenhoeck & Ruprecht.

Hoffmann, Otto and Anton Scherer (1969) *Geschichte der griechischen Sprache. Band 1: Bis zum Ausgang der klassischen Zeit.* Berlin: de Gruyter.

Hornblower, Simon et al. (2012) ["OCD"] *The Oxford Classical Dictionary.* 4th ed. Oxford: University Press.

Horrocks, Geoffrey (2010) *Greek. A History of the Language and its Speakers.* 2nd ed. Oxford: Wiley-Blackwell.

Huddleston, Rodney, Geoffrey K. Pullum, et al. (2002) *The Cambridge Grammar of the English Language.* Cambridge: University Press.

Humbert, Jean (1960) *Syntaxe grecque.* 3rd ed. Paris: Klincksieck.

Hummel, Pascale (2007) *De lingua Graeca. Histoire de l'histoire de la langue grecque.* Berne: Lang.

Hunger, Herbert et al. (1961) *Textüberlieferung der antiken Literatur und der Bibel.* Zürich: Atlantis.

Jacques, Xavier (1972) *List of Septuagint Words Sharing Common Elements.* Rome: Biblical Institute Press.

Jastrow, Marcus (1903) *A Dictionary of the Targumim, the Talmud Babli and Yerushalmi, and the Midrashic Literature.* London: Luzac.

Jobes, Karen H. and Moisés Silva (2005) *Invitation to the Septuagint.* Grand Rapids: Baker.

Joüon, Paul and Takamitsu Muraoka (2006) *A Grammar of Biblical Hebrew.* Rome: Editrice Pontificio Istituto Biblico.

Kenyon, Frederic G. and Arthur W. Adams (1975) *The Text of the Greek Bible.* 3rd ed. London: Duckworth.

Kittel, Gerhard (ed.), translated by Geoffrey W. Bromiley (original 1933–1979; translation 1964–1976) *Theological Dictionary of the New Testament.* 10 vols. Grand Rapids: Eerdmans.

Kleiner Pauly: Ziegler, Konrat, Walther Sontheimer, et al. (1975) *Der Kleine Pauly. Lexikon der Antike.* 5 vols. Munich: Artemis.

Koehler, Ludwig, Walter Baumgartner et al. (1994–2000) ["HALOT"] *The Hebrew and Aramaic Lexicon of the Old Testament.* Leiden: Brill.

Kühner, Raphael and Friedrich Blass (1890/92) *Ausführliche Grammatik der griechischen Sprache.* Part 1: *Elementar- und Formenlehre.* 2 vols. 3rd ed. Hannover: Hahnsche Buchhandlung.

Kühner, Raphael / Gerth, Bernhard (1898/1904) *Ausführliche Grammatik der griechischen Sprache.* Part 2: *Satzlehre.* 2 vols. 3rd ed. Hannover: Hahnsche Buchhandlung.

Lampe, Geoffrey, W. H. et al. (2010) *A Patristic Greek Lexicon.* 23rd impr. Oxford: University Press.

Langslow, David. Ed. (2009) *Jacob Wackernagel. Lectures on Syntax: With Special Reference to Greek, Latin, and Germanic.* Oxford: University Press.

Lee, John A. L. (2003) *A History of New Testament Lexicography.* New York: Lang.

Leisi, Ernst (1975) *Der Wortinhalt, Seine Struktur im Deutschen und Englischen.* 5th ed. Heidelberg: Quelle & Meyer.

Leisi, Ernst (1985) *Praxis der englischen Semantik.* 2nd ed. Heidelberg: Winter.

Lejeune, Michel (1972) *Phonétique historique du mycénien et du grec ancien.* Paris: Klincksieck.

Levinsohn, Stephen H. (2000) *Discourse Features of New Testament Greek. A Coursebook on the Information Structure of New Testament Greek.* 2nd ed. Dallas: SIL.

Lewis, Charlton T. and Charles Short (1879) *A Latin Dictionary.* Oxford: University Press.

Lexikon der Alten Welt ["LAW"]: Andresen, Carl et al. (1965) *Lexikon der Alten Welt.* Zürich: Artemis.

Liddell, Henry G., Robert Scott, and Henry S. Jones (1996) ["LSJ"] *A Greek-English Lexicon.* 9th ed. with Supplement. Oxford: University Press.

Lieber, Rochelle (2016) *Introducing Morphology.* 2nd ed. Cambridge: University Press.

Lieber, Rochelle and Pavol Stekauer (2009) *The Oxford Handbook of Compounding*. Oxford: University Press.

Logos Bible Software 8 (2018) Bellingham: Faithlife.

Longman Dictionary of Contemporary English (2009) 5th ed. Harlow: Pearson.

Louw, Jan P. (1982) *Semantics of New Testament Greek*. Philadelphia: Fortress.

Louw, Jan P. and Eugene A. Nida (1988) ["LN"] *Greek-English Lexicon of the New Testament Based on Semantic Domains*. 2 vols. 2nd ed. New York: United Bible Societies.

Lowth, Robert (1753) *De sacra poesi Hebraeorum …* Oxford (English version: George Gregory [1835]: *Lectures in the Sacred Poetry of the Hebrews*).

Lust, Johan, Erik Eynikel, and Katrin Hauspie (2015) *A Greek-English Lexicon of the Septuagint*. 3rd ed. Stuttgart: Deutsche Bibelgesellschaft.

Maier, Friedrich (1967) *Stilübungen und Interpretation im Griechischen*. Munich: Hueber.

Maier, Friedrich (1969) *Version aus dem Griechischen*. Munich: Hueber.

Mastronade, Donald J. (2013) *Introduction to Attic Greek*. 2nd ed. Berkeley: University of California Press.

Mayser, Edwin (1906–1938/1970) *Grammatik der griechischen Papyri aus der Ptolemäerzeit mit Einschluss der gleichzeitigen Ostraka und der in Ägypten verfassten Inschriften*. 7 parts. Leipzig: Teubner/Berlin: de Gruyter.

Meier-Brügger, Michael (1992) ["MB"] *Griechische Sprachwissenschaft*. 2 vols. Berlin: de Gruyter.

Meier-Brügger, Michael (2000) *Indogermanische Sprachwissenschaft*. 7th ed. Berlin: de Gruyter.

Meier-Brügger, Michael (2003) *Indo-European Linguistics*. Berlin: de Gruyter.

Menge, Hermann, Andreas Thierfelder, and Jürgen Wiesner (1999) *Repetitorium der griechischen Syntax*. 10th ed. Darmstadt: Wissenschaftliche Buchgesellschaft.

Metzger, Bruce M. (1994) *A Textual Commentary on the Greek New Testament*. 2nd ed. Stuttgart: Deutsche Bibelgesellschaft.

Metzger, Bruce M. (1998) *Lexical Aids for Students of New Testament Greek*. 3rd ed. Grand Rapids: Baker.

Metzger, Bruce M. (2005) *The Text of the New Testament, Its Transmission, Corruption, and Restoration*. 4th ed. Oxford: Oxford University Press.

Montanari, Franco (2015) *The Brill Dictionary of Ancient Greek*. Leiden: Brill.

Moule, Charles F. D. (1959) *An Idiom Book of New Testament Greek*. 2nd ed. Cambridge: University Press.

Moulton, William F. and Alfred S. Geden et al. (2002) *A Concordance to the Greek Testament*. 6th ed. Edinburgh: Clark.

Moulton, James H. and Wilbert F. Howard (1908/1920) *A Grammar of New Testament Greek*. Vol. I: *Prolegomena* (3rd ed.). Vol. II: *Accidence and Word-Formation*. Edinburgh: Clark.

Moulton, James H. and George Milligan (1930) *The Vocabulary of the Greek Testament*. London: Hodder & Stoughton.

Mounce, William D. (2019) *Basics of Biblical Greek*. 4th ed. Grand Rapids: Zondervan.

Muraoka, Takamitsu (2009) *A Greek-English Lexicon of the Septuagint*. Louvain: Peeters.

Murphy, M. Lynne (2010) *Lexical Meaning*. Cambridge: University Press.

Nesselrath, Heinz-Günther (1997) *Einleitung in die griechische Philologie*. Stuttgart: Teubner.

Nestle, Eberhard (1909) *Einführung in das Griechische Neue Testament*. Göttingen: Vandenhoeck & Ruprecht.

Nestle-Aland ["NA"]: Aland, Barbara et al. (1993/2012) *Novum Testamentum Graece*. 27th/28th ed. Stuttgart: Deutsche Bibelgesellschaft.

A New English Translation of the Septuagint ["NETS"] (2007). Oxford: University Press.

New International Version (2011) ["NIV"] *The Holy Bible. New International Version*. Colorado Springs: Biblica.

New Revised Standard Version (1989) *Holy Bible. New Revised Standard Version.* Oxford: University Press.

New Testament Abstracts: Chestnut Hill/Mass.: Boston College.

Perseus Project (2007) *Perseus Digital Library.* Gregory R. Crane, Editor-in-Chief. Tufts University. Medford, MA (http://www.perseus.tufts.edu/).

Pfeiffer, Rudolf (1968) *History of Classical Scholarship. From the Beginnings to the End of the Hellenistic Age.* Oxford: University Press.

Pinkster, Harm (2015) *The Oxford Latin Syntax.* Vol. I. Oxford: University Press.

Pöhlmann, Egert (2003) *Einführung in Überlieferungsgeschichte und in Textkritik der antiken Literatur.* Vol. 1: *Altertum.* 2nd ed. Darmstadt: Wissenschaftliche Buchgesellschaft.

Porter, Stanley E. (1992) *Idioms of the Greek New Testament.* Sheffield: Academic Press.

Porter, Stanley E. (2015) *Linguistic Analysis of the Greek New Testament. Studies in Tools, Methods, and Practice.* Grand Rapids: Baker.

Porter, Stanley E. and Andrew W. Pitts (2012) *Christian Origins and Greco-Roman Culture: Social and Literary Contexts for the New Testament.* Leiden: Brill.

Quirk, Randolph et al. (1985) *A Comprehensive Grammar of the English Language.* London: Longman.

Rahlfs, Alfred and Robert Hanhart (2006) *Septuaginta.* 2nd ed. Stuttgart: Deutsche Bibelgesellschaft.

Reiser, Marius (1984) *Syntax und Stil des Markusevangeliums.* Tübingen: Mohr.

Reiser, Marius (2001) *Sprache und literarische Formen des Neuen Testaments.* Paderborn: Schöningh.

Rijksbaron, Albert (2002) *The Syntax and Semantics of the Verb in Classical Greek. An Introduction.* 3rd ed. Chicago: University Press.

Risch, Ernst (1970/1971) Griechische Lautlehre. Zürcher Vorlesungsskript.

Robertson, Archibald T. (1923) *A Grammar of the Greek New Testament in the Light of Historical Research.* 4th ed. London: Hodder & Stoughton.

Robinson, Maurice / Pierpont, William (2005) *The New Testament in the Original Greek. Byzantine Textform.* Southborough/Mass.: Chilton.

Rosenthal, Franz (2006) *A Grammar of Biblical Aramaic.* 7th ed. Wiesbaden: Harrassowitz.

Runge, Steven E. (2010) *Discourse Grammar of the Greek New Testament. A Practical Introduction for Teaching and Exegesis.* Peabody: Hendrickson.

Runge, Steven E. and Christopher J. Fresch et al. (2016) *The Greek Verb Revisited: A Fresh Approach for Biblical Exegesis,* Bellingham: Lexham.

SBL-Edition: Holmes, Michael (2010) *The Greek New Testament. SBL Edition.* Atlanta: Society of Biblical Literature.

Schleusner, Johann F. (1822) *Novus thesaurus philologico-criticus sive Lexicon in Septuaginta et reliquos interpretes Graecos ac scriptores apocryphos Veteris Testamenti.* 5 vols. 2nd ed. London: Duncan.

Schmoller, Alfred (2014) *Pocket Concordance to the Greek New Testament.* 9th ed. Stuttgart: Deutsche Bibelgesellschaft.

Schwyzer, Eduard (1939/1950) *Griechische Grammatik.* 2 vols. Munich: Beck.

Segert, Stanislav (1975) *Altaramäische Grammatik.* Leipzig: Enzyklopädie.

Septuaginta deutsch: Kraus, Wolfgang, et al. (2009) *Das griechische Alte Testament in deutscher Übersetzung.* Stuttgart: Deutsche Bibelgesellschaft.

Septuaginta. A Reader's Edition (2018). 2 vols. Stuttgart: Deutsche Bibelgesellschaft.

Siebenthal, Heinrich von (1984) Mehrdeutigkeit sprachlicher Ausdrücke und Textinterpretation. In: *Fundamentum,* Heft 1, 204–227.

Siebenthal, Heinrich von (2000) Sprachwissenschaftliche Aspekte. In: Heinz-Werner Neudorfer and Eckhard J. Schnabel (ed.) (2000) *Das Studium des Neuen Testaments.* Vol. 1. 2nd ed. Wuppertal: Brockhaus, 69–154.

Siebenthal, Heinrich von (2008) *Grundkurs neutestamentliches Griechisch (basierend auf einem Lehrgang von Otto Wittstock).* Giessen: Brunnen.

Siebenthal, Heinrich von (2013) *Kurzgrammatik zum griechischen Neuen Testament.* 3rd ed. Giessen: Brunnen.

Sihler, Andrew L. (1995) *New Comparative Grammar of Greek and Latin.* Oxford: University Press.

Silva, Moisés (1990) *God Language and Scripture.* Grand Rapids: Zondervan.

Silva, Moisés (1994) *Biblical Words and Their Meaning.* 2nd ed. Grand Rapids: Zondervan.

Silva, Moisés (ed.) (2014) *New International dictionary of New Testament Theology and Exegesis.* 5 vols. Grand Rapids: Zondervan.

Smyth, Herbert W. and Gordon M. Messing (1956) *Greek Grammar.* Cambridge (Mass.): Harvard.

Sommer, Ferdinand (1931) *Vergleichende Syntax der Schulsprachen.* 3rd ed. Leipzig: Teubner.

Sophocles, Evangelenos A. (1887) *Greek Lexicon of the Roman and Byzantine Periods* (146 B.C. – A.D. 1100). New York: Scribner's.

Thackeray, Henry St. John (1909) *A Grammar of the Old Testament in Greek.* Vol. I: *Introduction, Orthography and Accidence.* Cambridge: University Press.

Thesaurus Linguae Graecae (2014) *A Digital Library of Greek Literature.* Project at the University of California. Irvine (http://www.tlg.uci.edu/).

Thrall, Margaret E. (1964) *Greek Particles in the New Testament.* Leiden: Brill.

Traduction Œcuménique de la Bible (1988) ["TOB"]. Paris: Société biblique française & Éditions du Cerf.

Tov, Emanuel (2012) *Textual Criticism of the Hebrew Bible.* Minneapolis: Fortress Press.

Trobisch, David (2013) *A User's Guide to the Nestle-Aland 28 Greek New Testament.* Atlanta: Society of Biblical Literature.

Turner, Nigel (1963) *A Grammar of New Testament Greek.* Vol. III: *Syntax.* Edinburgh: Clark.

Turner, Nigel (1965) *Grammatical Insights into the New Testament.* Edinburgh: Clark.

Turner, Nigel (1976) *A Grammar of New Testament Greek.* Vol. IV: *Style.* Edinburgh: Clark.

Vázquez, Rafael M. et al. (1999) *Gramática funcional-cognitiva del griego antiguo I.* Sevilla: Universidad.

Verbrugge, Verlyn D. (2003) *New International Dictionary of New Testament Theology: Abridged Edition.* Grand Rapids: Zondervan.

Wackernagel, Jacob (1950/1957) *Vorlesungen über Syntax.* 2 vols. 2nd ed. Basel: Birkhäuser [↑also Langslow for a recent English language edition].

Wallace, Daniel B. (1996) *Greek Grammar Beyond the Basics. An Exegetical Syntax of the New Testament.* Grand Rapids: Zondervan.

Wallace, Daniel B. (2009) *Granville Sharp's Canon and Its Kin: Semantics and Significance.* New York: Lang.

Wegner, Paul D. (2006) *A Student's Guide to Textual Criticism of the Bible. Its History, Methods, and Results.* Downers Grove: InterVarsity Press.

Whittaker, Molly (1980) *New Testament Greek Grammar. An Introduction.* 2nd ed. London: SCM.

Wilson, Deirdre and Dan Sperber (2012) *Meaning and Relevance.* Cambridge: University Press.

Zerwick, Maximilian (1963) ["Z"] *Biblical Greek. Illustrated by Examples.* Rome: Editrice Pontificio Istituto Biblico.

Zerwick, Maximilian and Mary Grosvenor (1996) *Grammatical Analysis of the Greek New Testament.* 5th ed. Rome: Biblical Institute Press.

Zinsmeister, Hans (1990) *Griechische Laut- und Formenlehre.* 2nd ed. Heidelberg: Winter.

Zuntz, Günther (1994) *Greek: A Course in Classical and Post-Classical Greek from Original Texts.* 2 vols. Sheffield: Academic Press.

Indexes

1 References

1.1 New Testament

Mark

1 Corinthians

2 Corinthians

Galatians

2 Thessalonians

1 Timothy

2 Timothy

Titus

Philemon

Hebrews

1.2 Old Testament

1.3 Apocrypha

1.4 Apostolic Fathers

1.5 Further Ancient Greek sources

2 Subject Index

A

B

C

H

I

Q

R

T

3 Greek Index

Note that prehistoric Greek i̯ is found under the letter iota (after the list of Greek expressions). Also ↑#252 (important uninflected words), 354 (connectives), and 371 (word-formation elements).

B

E

Ϝ

Z

H

Θ

Ι

Λ

M

N

Ρ

Σ

4 Hebrew and Aramaic Index

Note that “H” stands for Hebrew, “A” for Aramaic.